Can

a travel su

Mark Lightbody
Tom Smallman

Canada – a travel survival kit

4th edition

Published by
Lonely Planet Publications
Head Office: PO Box 617, Hawthorn, Vic 3122, Australia
Branches: PO Box 2001A, Berkeley, CA 94702, USA and London, UK

Printed by
Singapore National Printers Ltd, Singapore

Photographs by
Canadian Government (CG)
Robin Bjorksten (RB)
Richard Everist (RE)
Mark Lightbody (ML)
James Lyon (JL)
Tom Smallman (TS)
Front cover: Niagara Falls, GV Faint (courtesy: The Image Bank)

First Published
March 1983

This Edition
March 1992

Although the authors and publisher have tried to make the information as accurate as possible, they accept no responsibility for any loss, injury or inconvenience sustained by any person using this book.

National Library of Australia Cataloguing in Publication Data

Lightbody, Mark
    Canada – a travel survival kit.

    4th ed.
    Includes index.
    ISBN 0 86442 124 9.

    1. Canada – Description and travel – Guide-books.
    I. Smallman, Tom II. Title.

917.104647

Mark Lightbody

Mark was born and grew up in Montreal. Educated there and in London, Ontario, he holds an honours degree in journalism. Among a variety of occupations, he has worked for a while in radio news. Mark has travelled in nearly 50 countries, visiting every continent but Antarctica. He made his first foray across Canada at the age of four. Since then he has repeated the trip numerous times using plane, train, car and thumb.

Besides writing the Lonely Planet guide to Canada, Mark has worked for LP on former editions of *Papua New Guinea – a travel survival kit, Australia – a travel survival kit, Malaysia, Singapore & Brunei* and *South-East Asia on a shoestring*. He now lives in Toronto.

Tom Smallman

Tom was born, grew up and was educated in the UK and now lives in Melbourne, Australia. He has had a number of jobs including dishwasher, labourer, hospital theatre technician and high school teacher. Tom has travelled in Europe, North America, the Middle East and Asia. He joined Lonely Planet as an editor in 1988.

From the Authors

From Mark Lightbody For this edition special thanks go to Colleen Kennedy for research assistance and Diane Carpentier for much help with the Montreal section. Particular thanks to Adam Kerr whose detailed and humourous letters of his continuing adventure walking across Canada are a treat.

Again warm thanks to those who sent letters, many of whom will see that their information was not only interesting but helpful and useful.

From Tom Smallman Tom wishes to thank the following people for the information and/or hospitality they provided: Bert Noble, Heather Noble, Denise Andersen, Heather Gowan-McKenna, John McKenna, Denise & Gordon Webb, Jude Denson, Fred Bell and Deanna Swaney.

Thanks also go to Julie Maston at the Canadian Consulate in Sydney for her help and to Sue Graefe for her patience.

Both Mark Lightbody and Tom Smallman wish to thank the production staff at the Lonely Planet office in Melbourne for their hard work.

From the Publisher

At Lonely Planet in Melbourne, Australia, this edition was coordinated and edited by Frith Pike. Thanks also go to Lyn McGaurr, Debbie Rossdale, Greg Alford, Jenny Missen and Tom Smallman for additional copy editing; to Tom Smallman and Sharan Kaur for proofing; and to Sharon Wertheim for helping with the index.

Tracey O'Mara was responsible for cover design, illustrations and layout. She produced the maps for this edition.

This Edition

From Mark Lightbody I'm now convinced. The more you travel around Canada, the bigger it gets. This time around Tom Smallman covered the western and northern part of the country adding considerable detail to these sections of the book. I spent the bulk of two summers driving all around the east coast hopping ferries and gobbling seafood. Spring and fall were perfect for tooling in and around central Canada and a dare-devil mid-winter trip across the prairies turned up not frostbite but shirt sleeves and slush as well as new sights.

All the major and most of the not so major towns were visited including many rural and more isolated regions and communities. The latter, lesser known parts of the country, very often are at least as memorable as Canada's known attractions. Let us know what you find – a new downtown restaurant, a tranquil trout stream. (A list of thanks to readers is on page 730.)

Warning & Request

Things change – prices go up, schedules change, good places go bad and bad places go bankrupt – nothing stays the same. So if you find things better or worse, recently opened or long since closed, please write and tell us and help make the next edition better!

Your letters will be used to help update future editions and, where possible, important changes will also be included as a Stop Press section in reprints.

All information is greatly appreciated and the best letters will receive a free copy of the next edition, or any other Lonely Planet book of your choice.

Contents

Map Legend

BOUNDARIES

━ · ━ · ━ · ━	........International Boundary
━ · · ━ · · ━	................Internal Boundary
━+━+━+━+━	....National Park or Reserve
- - - - - - - -	.... The Equator
· · · · · · · · · · · · · · · ·	.... The Tropics

SYMBOLS

◉ NEW DELHI	........................National Capital
● BOMBAY	.........Provincial or State Capital
● Pune	...........................Major Town
● Borsi	...........................Minor Town
■	..........................Places to Stay
▼	............................Places to Eat
⬒	....................................Post Office
✈	....Airport
i	......................Tourist Information
◖	.............Bus Station or Terminal
66	............Highway Route Number
⚑ ✝ ⛪	......Mosque, Church, Cathedral
∴	...........................Temple or Ruin
✚	....Hospital
☀	.....................................Lookout
⚑	.............................Camping Area
⬠	...............................Picnic Area
⌂	...............................Hut or Chalet
▲	.... Mountain or Hill
⊢	.... Railway Station
≡	.... Road Bridge
⊬	.... Railway Bridge
⇒ ⇐	...............................Road Tunnel
→) (←	.......................Railway Tunnel
⌒⌒⌒	....................Escarpment or Cliff
⌣	....Pass
⌢⌢⌢	............Ancient or Historic Wall

ROUTES

━━━━━━━	.......Major Road or Highway
- - - - - - - -	.... Unsealed Major Road
━━━━━━━	...........................Sealed Road
- - - - - - -	..... Unsealed Road or Track
═══════	.... City Street
━+━+━+━+	....................................Railway
━━━◉━━━	.....................................Subway
· · · · · · · · · · · ·	......................Walking Track
- - - - - - - -	.... Ferry Route
━+━+━+━+	.... Cable Car or Chair Lift

HYDROGRAPHIC FEATURES

	.........................River or Creek
	...............Intermittent Stream
	........Lake, Intermittent Lake
	..............................Coast Line
	....Spring
	.....................................Waterfall
	....Swamp
	................Salt Lake or Reef
	...................................Glacier

OTHER FEATURES

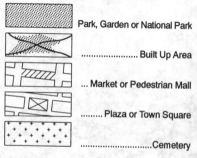

Park, Garden or National Park

.... Built Up Area

... Market or Pedestrian Mall

.... Plaza or Town Square

...............................Cemetery

Note: not all symbols displayed above appear in this book

Introduction

Canada is big, spacious, rugged, uncluttered and tremendously varied. You can stand in places where perhaps nobody else has ever stood, yet the cities are large and modern, offering art and culture as a balance.

From the Atlantic Ocean it's over 7000 km to the Pacific Coast. In between you can have a coffee and a croissant at a sidewalk café or canoe on a silent northern lake. You can peer down from the world's tallest building or over the walls of a centuries-old fort. You can hike amid snow-capped peaks or watch the sunset where it's an unobstructed 30 km to the horizon.

The four very different seasons can bring the winters Canada is known for, but also sweltering hot summer days.

It's said that the national personality was shaped by life in a northern frontier; people constantly came from the wild to the settled areas and back again. Because the country is so young, a modern identity is still forming. But it's there, distinctly different from Canada's neighbours to the south.

The cultural mosaic is made up of British, French and many other peoples, ranging from Europeans to those from the Far East.

Inflation has dropped to 5% or below in the past few years, so prices haven't been rising dramatically. The Canadian dollar remains low compared with the US greenback, making exchange rates excellent for Americans while holding steady for many other currencies. For Canadians, this is another good reason to see the homeland.

With its history, people, land and nature, Canada has a lot to offer the traveller.

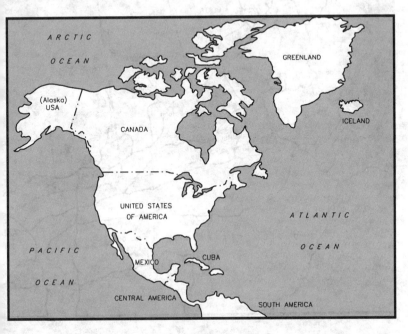

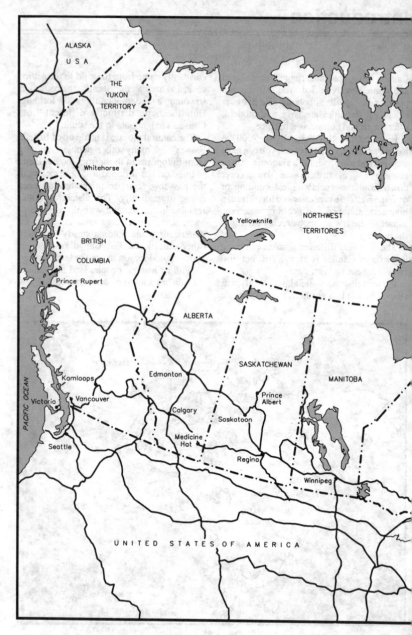

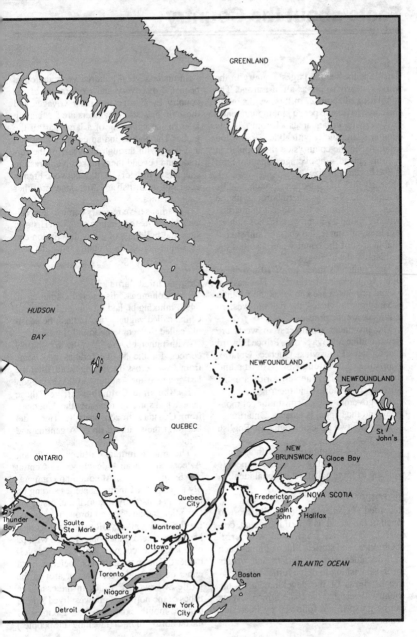

Facts about the Country

Canada is the second largest country in the world – nearly as big as all of Europe. The population of about 27 million works out to close to two people per sq km, though really 76% live in urban areas. Toronto is the country's largest city with about 2½ million residents. In the countryside the population is thinly spread – the average Canadian farm is 200 hectares in size.

Nearly 90% of Canadians, though, huddle along the 6379-km southern border with the USA. It's said to be the longest unguarded national boundary in the world. The southern region is, of course, the warmest, most hospitable area of the country and also has the best land and waterways.

The country is made up of 10 provinces and two northern territories. The eastern coastal provinces are known as the Atlantic or Maritime Provinces; the flat mid-western provinces are the prairies.

The provinces (from east to west) are Newfoundland, Nova Scotia, Prince Edward Island, New Brunswick, Quebec, Ontario, Manitoba, Saskatchewan, Alberta and British Columbia. The territories are the Northwest Territories and the Yukon.

The government is a constitutional monarchy and the capital is Ottawa, Ontario.

There are two official languages, English and French.

Canada is a young country with as much potential as anything else and a people working to forge a distinct national identity.

HISTORY

Recorded Canadian history, while short to much of the world, is full of intriguing, colourful, dramatic, tragic and wonderful occurrences and stories. Much of it has been well documented by historians and writers for those wishing to delve further. The relative briefness of the development of the country means that the basic flow of events can be grasped and followed by interested visitors.

In under several hundred years there has been the discovery and exploration of the country by Europeans. Their voyages and those of the settling pioneers are fascinating tales of the unveiling of a large part of the globe. The Native Indian cultures they met and dealt with through the years of the fur-trade and beyond them make up contrasting chapters of the story. Battles between French and English, British and Americans are other major themes.

Canadians have recently come to appreciate and admire their nation's history. Historic sites and buildings of every description can be found across the country and are well worth discovering.

Original Inhabitants

When Columbus 'discovered' America in 1492, thinking he had hit the lands south of China called vaguely 'the Indies', he sensibly called the people he found 'Indians'.

With rather bizarre irony he was nearly correct, for the Native Indians had come from Asia, across the Bering Strait, after the last great ice age – about 15,000 years ago.

By the time Columbus arrived these people had spread throughout the Americas, from Canada's frozen north to Tierra del Fuego at the southern tip of Argentina and Chile.

The major Indian cultures – Mayan, Aztecan and Incan – developed in Central and South America. Although no comparably sophisticated Indian societies sprang up in Canada, partially due to the climate, the Canadian Indian changed through the years. By the early 1500s various distinct groups had formed across the country, each with its own language, customs and level of development. The more complex societies lived either on the mild west coast or around the fertile St Lawrence Valley in the east. The tribes of the north and midwest lived a more hand-to-mouth existence. The Eskimos of the far north – or *Inuit* (meaning 'the people') as they are more normally called these days – eked out an existence in a world virtually unchanged until the past 35 to 40 years.

European Exploration

The first visitors to Canada were the Vikings from Iceland and Greenland. There is evidence that they settled in northern Newfoundland at the eastern edge of Canada around 1000 AD. How long they stayed, how much they explored and what happened to them is unknown.

It was around 1500 that all the action around the Americas started to heat up. The Spanish, French, British and Italians all wanted in.

In Canada, it was the French who got first licks. After a few earlier exploratory visits by the Europeans Jacques Cartier of France, a subject of Francis I, reached the gulf of the St Lawrence River and claimed all the surrounding area for France. The year was 1534. It was probably from Cartier that Canada got its name. Originally *Kanata*, a Huron-Iroquois word for 'village' or 'small community', its derivative showed up in Cartier's journal. The name was used for the St Lawrence area and eventually became the official name of the new country.

The French didn't bother much with this new colony throughout the 1500s, but the pattern of economic development which began then has continued through to the present. This is, put bluntly and simply, the selling of its resources to whoever is buying, thus enabling the country to pay for everything else it needs. The first commodities prized by the French were the fish of the east coast and furs for the fashion-conscious of France.

Samuel de Champlain, another Frenchman, began further explorations in the early 1600s. He settled Quebec City, and Montreal was founded soon after in 1642 as a missionary outpost. Throughout the 17th century fur-trading companies dominated this new world. In 1663 Canada became a province of France. There were about 60,000 French settlers by then – they are the ancestors of a good percentage of today's French Canadians.

Throughout the 1600s the French fought the Native Indians, who soon realised that they were getting a raw deal in land development and the fur trade. The French kept busy, too, with further explorations. They built a long chain of forts down to Louisiana – another major settlement – in what is now the southern USA. In the 1730s another of the major explorers, Pierre Gaultier de Varennes, Sieur de la Vérendrye, was responsible for another series of forts. This one stretched across the south of what are now the provinces of Ontario, Manitoba and Saskatchewan.

The Struggle for Power

Of course, the British weren't just sipping pints through all this. Though concentrating on the lands of America's east coast, the Hudson's Bay Company (still one of Canada's main department-store chains) had moved into the Hudson Bay area in northern Ontario around 1670.

The British soon muscled into settlements on the Canadian east coast. By 1713 they had control over much of Nova Scotia and Newfoundland. And then, for a while, there was peace.

In 1745 a British army from New England, America, moved north and captured a French fort in Nova Scotia. The struggle for control of the new land was on. What is known as the Seven Years' War began in 1754. The French held the upper hand for the first four years. In one of Canada's most famous battles, the British defeated the French at Quebec City in 1759. Both General Wolfe, leader of the British, and the Marquis de Montcalm, who led the French, were killed in battle. After this major victory, the British turned the tide. At the Treaty of Paris in 1763, France handed Canada over to Britain.

The British, however, didn't quite know how to manage the newly acquired territory. The population was nearly exclusively French and at that time in Britain, Roman Catholics had very few rights – they couldn't vote or hold office. In 1774 the Quebec Act gave the French Canadians the right to their religion, the use of French civil law in court and the possibility of assuming political office. The British, however, maintained positions of power and influence in politics and business. It was during this period that the seeds of the Quebec separatist movement were sown.

During the American Revolution (1775-83) against Britain, about 50,000 settlers – termed 'Loyalists' due to their loyalty to Britain – shifted north to Canada. They settled mainly in the Atlantic Provinces and Ontario.

This migration helped to balance the number of French and British in Canada. Soon after, Quebec and Ontario were formed with their own governors. Throughout the late 1700s and into the 1800s Canada's frontiers were pushed further and further afield. Sir Arthur Mackenzie explored the north (Mackenzie River) and much of British Columbia. Simon Fraser followed the river which was named after him to the Pacific Ocean. David Thompson travelled the Columbia River, also in British Columbia. In 1812, Lord Selkirk formed a settlement of Scottish immigrants around the Red River Valley near Winnipeg, Manitoba.

Also in 1812, the last war between Canada and the USA, the War of 1812, began. Its causes were numerous, but the US attempt to take over its northern neighbour was only part of the campaign against Britain. Each side won a few battles, and in 1814 a draw was declared.

The Dominion Period

With the US threat ended and the resulting confidence in themselves, many of the colonists became fed up with some aspects of British rule. Others spoke out for independence. In both Upper (Ontario) and Lower (Quebec) Canada, brief rebellions broke out. In 1840 both areas became united with one government, but by now the population in Upper (British, mainly) outnumbered that in Lower Canada (French) and wanted more than a half-say. The government bogged

down, with Britain attempting to work out something new. Again you can see the historical disputes between the British and French.

Britain, of course, didn't want to lose Canada completely as it had the USA, so it stepped lightly and decided on a confederation giving a central government some powers and the individual colonies others.

In 1867 the British North America Act (BNA Act) was passed by the British government. This established the Dominion of Canada and included Ontario, Quebec, Nova Scotia and New Brunswick. The BNA Act became Canada's equivalent to a constitution, though far less detailed and all-inclusive. John Alexander Macdonald became Canada's first prime minister. The total population was 3½ million, nearly all living in the east and mostly on farms. It had been decided at the Act's signing in 1867 that other parts of the country should be included in the Dominion whenever possible.

The completion of the Canadian Pacific Railway – one of Canada's great historical sagas – joined the west coast with the east, literally linking those areas with the Dominion. By 1912 all provinces had become part of the central government except Newfoundland, which finally joined in 1949.

In the last few years of the 19th century Canada received large numbers of immigrants, mainly from Europe.

The government continued to grapple with French and British differences. These reached a peak during WW I, which Canada had entered immediately on Britain's behalf. In 1917, despite bitter French opposition in Quebec, the Canadian government began a military draft.

The Modern Era

After WW 1 Canada slowly grew in stature and prosperity, and in 1931 became a voluntary member of the Commonwealth.

With the onset of WW II, Canada again supported Britain, but this time also began defence agreements with the USA, and after the attack on Pearl Harbor, declared war on Japan.

After WW II Canada experienced another huge wave of European immigration. The post-war period saw economic expansion and prosperity right across North America.

The 1960s brought social upheaval and social welfare programmes with their ideals and liberalism. Canada's first Bill of Rights was signed in 1960. Nuclear-power generators and US nuclear warheads in Canada became major issues.

The Quebec separatist movement attracted more attention. A small group used terrorism to press its point for an independent Quebec. In 1976 the Parti Québecois, advocating separatism, won the provincial election. Since that time, though, sentiments on the issue have risen and fallen. In 1980, a Quebec referendum found most Quebeckers were against independence and the topic was more or less dropped. In the early 1990s separation is once again a hotly debated possibility and another referendum may be in the offing. It seems at the moment that most Canadians would prefer Quebec to stay, while about half the Quebeckers feel the formation of a separate, distinct political entity is preferable and even inevitable.

In 1967 the country celebrated its 100th anniversary with the World's Fair in Montreal – Expo – as one of the highlights.

Well known Pierre Elliot Trudeau, a Liberal, became Canada's prime minister in 1968 and, except for a brief period in 1979, held power until his retirement in 1984. Despite great initial support and international recognition, Trudeau was, to be kind, not a popular man at the end of his stay. During his leadership, however, he was largely responsible for the formation of a Canadian Constitution, the last step in full independence from Britain. It came into being in 1982.

The 1984 election saw the Progressive Conservatives, led by Brian Mulroney, sweep into power with a tremendous nationwide majority, slamming the door on the Trudeau era. The government was re-elected to another four-year term in 1988.

Following the customary pattern, this government too, has now fallen from grace with a large thump. Major issues of late have been Mulroney's very controversial freetrade accord with the USA and the attempt to reach a consensus, known as the Meech Lake Accord, on overhauling the distinctions between provincial and federal powers, rights and jurisdictions. Another live wire has been the introduction of a Goods & Services Tax (GST). The colossal national debt is another concern as is dealing with the native peoples of the country, their land claims and search for more power.

As far as I can tell there is no political saviour waiting in the wings to sweep the country off its feet and sort out these heavyduty problems.

The 1988 World Economic Summit of the seven major industrial nations was held in Toronto and the winter Olympics were hosted in Calgary, each bringing increased prestige and favourable attention to Canada's somewhat fragile international self-image.

Other than the question of the future of Quebec, ongoing money matters make up the major headlines of the day. Canadian Forces participated with little homegrown controversy in the allied coalition against Saddam Hussein and his invasion of Kuwait.

GEOGRAPHY

Canada is about 7730 km from east to west yet still its only neighbour is the USA, which includes Alaska in the north-west. With such size the country can boast a tremendous variety of topography.

Though much of the land is lake and riverfilled forest, there are mountains, plains and even a small desert. Canada has (or shares with the USA) seven of the world's largest lakes and also contains three of the globe's longest 20 rivers. The country is blessed with the most freshwater of any country. About 25% of the country is covered in forest. Canada's highest mountain, Mt Logan at 5950 metres, is found in the south-west Yukon.

There are five main regions, plus the vast Arctic region. Despite being bordered on three sides by oceans Canada is not generally viewed as a maritime country. This is in part due to the large, central regions which contain the bulk of the population and dominate in so many ways. Also the Rocky Mountains and Niagara Falls, the country's two best known and most visited geographic features, are found inland. The lack of attention the coasts get, particularly in the east, is a personal sore point.

These are vast regions of outstanding topography, wildlife, history and possibilities. From eastern Quebec to the eastern edge of the country the oceans play a major part in day-to-day life and offer the visitor much to discover and explore. The same can be said of British Columbia, although parts of Vancouver Island do get the regard they deserve.

The far eastern area includes Newfoundland, Prince Edward Island, New Brunswick, Nova Scotia and part of Quebec. The land is mainly hilly and wooded.

The St Lawrence-Great Lakes Lowland is the area between Quebec City and Windsor, Ontario, and includes most of the large towns, cities and industry. In all, about half of Canada's people live here. The land, once all used for farming, is generally flat.

Most of the north is taken up by the Canadian Shield, also known as the Precambrian Shield, formed 2.5 billion years ago. This geographic area covers all of northern Manitoba, Ontario and Quebec and stretches further east and west from there. It's an enormous ancient, rocky, glacially sanded region of typically Canadian river and lake-filled timberland. It is rugged, cool and little-developed, with mining and logging the two primary ingredients in human settlement.

Through Manitoba, Saskatchewan and parts of Alberta are the plains – a huge, flat region responsible for Canada's abundant wheat crop.

The fifth area is the Mountain Region covering most of British Columbia, parts of Alberta and the Yukon. The Rocky Mountains form the eastern edge of the region. They rise from 2000 to 4000 metres. Along the western coast is another range of mountains. In between lies a long, narrow valley

called the Rocky Mountain Trench. The interior of British Columbia consists of valleys, plateaus, hills and basins. The province is by far the most scenically varied and spectacular in the country.

CLIMATE
Seasons

Summer	June-August
Fall	September-October
Winter	November-March
Spring	April-May

As you can see, the winters are long. In more than two-thirds of the country the average January temperature is -18°C. The overall warmest areas of the country are British Columbia's coast and southern Ontario particularly the Niagara Peninsula, with the longest summers and shortest winters. Manitoba through to central British Columbia get the hottest summer temperatures as well as the most sunshine.

The west and east coasts are very wet with 2500 mm of precipitation a year but much of that is through the winter months. The prairies are fairly dry all year but south-eastern Canada can be quite humid in summer, damp in winter. Ontario and Quebec have warm, fairly dry summers. The east coast is generally cooler than the rest of the country and can have more summer rain as well. The Yukon's summers can be quite pleasantly warm and of course have the added benefit of extremely long sunlit hours. Outside the main cities anywhere in Canada, nights are cool all year round.

Along the US border, summer temperatures are usually in the mid and upper 20°Cs. Each year there are a few days in the 30°Cs.

FAUNA
Canada, with so much land and much of it relatively remote, is abundant in wildlife yet conservation is an ongoing necessity. Campers and hikers, with any luck at all, can see a number of different animals in the wild. The following are some of the most interesting and/or most common.

Bears

These are Canada's largest and most dangerous animals. They are widely distributed, and as there are four types, most of the country is populated with at least one kind. For detailed information on the hazards of bears, see the Dangers & Annoyances section in the Facts for the Visitor chapter.

Grizzly Bear This is the most notorious bear and is found on the higher slopes of the Rocky and Selkirk mountains of British Columbia, Alberta and the Yukon. The grizzly is big – standing up to 275 cm high. It can be recognised by the white ends of its brownish hair and the hump on the back behind its neck. It can't see well but makes up for that with its excellent senses of smell and hearing. To make matters worse, it's a very fast animal. The best thing about a grizzly is that it can't climb trees. Like other bears, it is normally afraid of people but can be unpredictable and is easily provoked.

Black Bear This bear is found all across Canada and is the one you'll most likely spot. The black bear often mooches around campgrounds, cottages and garbage dumps. It is usually less than 150 cm long and 90 kg in weight. It's active during the day and unfortunately can climb trees.

Brown Bear Actually a black bear but brown in colour, the nocturnal brown bear is found mainly in British Columbia, Alberta and the Yukon.

Polar Bear The polar bear is very large – up to 680 kg – with thick, whitish fur. It is found only in the extreme north but can be viewed in zoos. A majestic animal, it is graceful in the water despite its size and apparent awkwardness. Due to hunting, it is now a protected animal.

Beaver

One of Canada's symbols, the beaver is an animal known for its industriousness, hence the expression 'busy as a beaver'. Found all across Canada, it is usually seen in the early morning or early evening paddling across a stream or lake with its head just above water. It chews down trees for food and for material with which to build its home. This home, a lodge, looks like a rounded pile of mud and sticks and is located in streams and ponds dammed off by the beaver.

Buffalo

The buffalo now exists only in government parks. It is a huge, mean-looking animal but is really little more than a cow. Its near-extinction has become symbolic of the Europeans' effect on North American Indians and their environment. Technically, Canadian buffalo are bison, not buffalo. There has recently been some sporadic attempts to raise buffalo for their meat and indeed it can very occasionally show up on a menu.

Wolf

The wolf looks like a large, silver-grey dog. Its ferocious reputation is more myth than fact. Hunting has pretty well banished this animal to the north land, but you may hear the wolf's howl late at night if you're in the bush. It usually hunts in packs and rarely harms humans.

Coyote

More widespread than the wolf, the coyote is smaller and more timid, with an eerie howl or series of yaps used for communicating. It is often now more scavenger than hunter and is often the victim of massive poison-bait campaigns by western ranchers and farmers.

Deer

Various types of deer are plentiful in the woodlands of Canada, ranging across the entire width of the country. They are very quiet and timid and the object of much hunting.

Moose

This is one of the largest animals and again, a popular target for hunters. The moose is found in woods and forests all across Canada, particularly around swamps. Moose are for the most part a more northerly ranging animal than deer. They have large, thick antlers and are brown.

The moose is very reclusive, generally solitary, and may be seen swimming to escape biting bugs. The male bellows in October and November in its search for a mate. At that time, their behaviour can be erratic and the normally timid moose can become aggressive. (They are also found in Europe and Asia where they are known as elk.)

Rocky Mountain Goat

This goat is as close as you can get to an all-Canadian animal. Found in British Columbia and the Yukon, it is white and hairy, has horns and looks like an old man. Around populated areas it is quite tame. Generally though, it prefers the higher, more remote mountain regions. One of its food staples is clay, and you may see one pawing at the ground and gobbling up clumps of earth – strange but true.

Lynx

Another nearly exclusively Canadian animal, the lynx is a grey cat about 90 cm long and is found all across the undeveloped Canadian woodlands. It has furry trim around its face and sharp pointed ears. The mainly nocturnal cat eats small animals. Although rarely seen, humans are its main enemy, largely by destroying its habitat. Larger and even less often seen is the majestic cougar, a full-sized cat.

Skunk

The skunk resembles a large black cat but has a white stripe down its back and a big, bushy tail. It is seen everywhere – in woods, around garbage, in larger city parks, even in residential suburbs. It's dangerous only in that its defence mechanism is the spraying-out of the foulest, longest lasting, clothes-clingingest smell you can imagine. The cure is a bath in tomato juice. Watch out!

Porcupine

A very curious animal about 90 cm long, the porcupine weighs 18 kg. It is grey, lives in the woods across Canada and feeds mainly on bark and tree buds. Its protection from abuse are its hollow, barbed quills which project from its body like long hair. They are very easily dislodged, as many a dog will remember.

Caribou

These animals live in herds in the far north and are still used by some Inuit for food and for their hides. Their numbers are now carefully monitored, as over-hunting and radioactive fallout have affected them. A full herd on its seasonal migration is said to be a wondrous sight. There are some small groups in more southern areas such as the Gaspé Peninsula of Quebec and the Lake Superior region of Ontario. (They are also found in Europe and Asia where they are known as reindeer.)

Birds

Five hundred species have been spotted in Canada but many of them are quite rare. Some of the more notable among our feathered residents are the loon, a water bird with a mournful yet beautiful call which is often heard on the quieter lakes across the country in early morning or evening. It is most abundant in northern Ontario.

Canada geese are seen across the country, especially during spring and their fall migration when their large V-shaped formations are not an unusual sight in the sky. Big, black and grey, these so-called honkers can be aggressive.

There are many varieties of duck, the mallard being the most common. The whisky jack, found mainly in the Rockies, is a fluffy, friendly and very commonly seen bird that will eat out of your hand. Bald eagles and ospreys are impressive birds of prey. Owls may be seen or heard in wooded areas across the country. Sparrows of countless, but practically indistinguishable, species are the most common garden songbirds.

Around the coasts there is a very interesting array of marine birdlife including puffins and razorbills.

Whales & Seals

Whale-watching has become so popular it is now a successful commercial enterprise (a point for the conservationists). A number of different species can be seen off the coast in British Columbia, in the St Lawrence River in Quebec, and in the Atlantic Ocean off the country's east coast.

In the Atlantic Provinces the bloody, annual seal hunt (for pelts, boots, coats, etc) diminished following the European Community's ban on imports (another point for animal welfare). Indeed, tourists with the money can now fly out to the east-coast ice floes to see, touch and photograph the newly calved icebergs.

Fish

Northern pike, bass and various trout varieties are the most common freshwater fish. Salmon in large numbers and a range of species is found on the west coast. The Atlantic salmon of Quebec and the Atlantic Provinces is a highly sought after freshwater version. Arctic char, found only in the far north (and on some southern menus), is also very fine eating. Fishing is a very popular Canadian pastime and also attracts Americans in large numbers.

National Parks

Canada has 34 national parks, ranging from coast to coast and from the US border to the

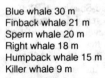
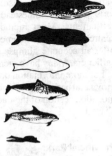

Blue whale 30 m
Finback whale 21 m
Sperm whale 20 m
Right whale 18 m
Humpback whale 15 m
Killer whale 9 m

Minke whale 8 m
Northern bottlenose whale 8 m
Beluga whale 4.5 m
White sided dolphin 2.4 m
Harbour porpoise 2 m
Human 1.8 m

far north. Each has been developed to protect, preserve and make accessible a unique, special or otherwise interesting and significant environment. The network continues to expand with a few new ones currently in the works. All of them are well worth visiting. Parks Canada, Ottawa, Ontario K1A 1G2, produces a good, free, little booklet, *National Parks of Canada*, which outlines the features and facilities of the parks.

Most have camping. Several are close to major population centres and are heavily used, others are more remote and offer good wilderness opportunities. Many manage to combine both characteristics. Among the most popular are Fundy National Park in Nova Scotia and all of the ones in the western Rocky Mountains.

Some parks rent canoes and/or rowing boats. In parks with numerous lakes and rivers, a canoe is ideal; you can portage to different lakes. Doing this a few times may be hard work but you'll be rewarded with peace and solitude.

Entrance fees to national parks cost $4 for a day visit or $9 for four days, while a $25 ticket is good in any national park for a year.

In addition to national parks, the system contains over 70 national historic parks and sites. These are for 'day use only' and present various aspects of Canadian history, from forts to pioneer homesteads to early Viking settlements. Most include interpretation centres, some with costumed workers, which offer an accurate glimpse of life during an earlier era. Many have picnic areas.

For more information on the national and provincial parks, see Camping in the Accommodation section of the Facts for the Visitor chapter.

Provincial Parks
Each province runs its own system of parks and reserves. These can vary dramatically in size, accessibility and main purpose. Some are developed for recreation, others to preserve something of historical interest, still others to protect wildlife or natural geographic features of particular beauty or uniqueness.

Some of these provide camping and other conveniences, some do not. In many provinces day use is free and admission is charged only for overnighters. Most parks have staff knowledgeable in the characteristics of that park to answer questions and offer lectures, walks and other presentations. Some parks have a biologist or a naturalist on duty.

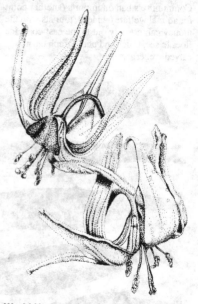

World Heritage Sites
Canada has nine sites designated by the World Heritage Convention of the United Nations. Six of these are natural and all are either national or provincial parks. They are: Nahanni National Park, Kluane National Park, the Rocky Mountain national parks, Wood Buffalo National Park, Dinosaur Provincial Park and Head-Smashed-In Buffalo Jump, Alberta. The remaining three sites involve human endeavour: Anthony Island Provincial Park in the Queen Charlotte Islands in British Columbia, an old Haida Indian settlement; L'Anse aux Meadows in

Newfoundland, a 1000-year-old Viking camp; and Quebec City, a European-style gem. All are definitely worth visiting.

GOVERNMENT

Canada is ruled by a parliamentary system with the head of state officially remaining the Queen of England. Within Canada the appointed governor general is the queen's representative. The upper house, or Senate, also made up of appointees, is deemed to be the house of review regarding potential legislation. Mostly it acts as a rubber stamp for the wishes of the elected lower house, generally known as the House of Commons. Senate reform or its abolition is an ongoing debate within the country.

The head of the political party with the most elected representatives in the House of Commons becomes the prime minister, the leader of the country. From the members of parliament within his own party he or she then selects a cabinet, which in effect runs the country and initiates any legislation. Federal elections occur every four years and, unlike in the USA, leaders can run for as long as the people let them. Governments are elected for five years, but elections can be called earlier.

The 10 provinces are largely self-governing and are presided over by premiers, elected provincially. A lieutenant-governor appointed by the federal government represents the monarchy, but takes instructions from Ottawa. The lieutenant-governor calls the leader of the party which has won an election to form the government. That leader becomes premier and forms a ministry from other elected members of the party. The two northern territories are for the most part the domain of the federal government although more independence is being sought.

Political Parties

Federally, the three principal political parties are the Liberals (who for much of the country's history have virtually owned the reins of power), the Progressive Conservatives (not a lot unlike the Liberals but without the success) and the New Democratic Party (known as the NDP or socialist menace). The Conservatives are voted in every once in a while, apparently as an effort to keep the Liberals somewhat humble and honest. The NDP has never formed a federal government and always comes up third. They have, however, ruled provincially in several provinces and seem poised to grab a larger share of the federal vote. More recently, other upstart opposition parties have become more serious. The Bloc Québecois of Quebec and the Reform Party of Alberta leading strong regional voices are threatening to steal a considerable number of votes from the three traditional choices. Canadian voters are 'cranky' entering the 90s as one recently losing politician lamented, and this general widespread dissatisfaction could mean a change from standard voting patterns in the elections to come.

Flag & Anthem

Canada's current flag was proclaimed in 1965 after 2000 public design entries were hotly debated in parliament. The side bars represent the ocean boundaries and are not blue because an important reason for the entire procedure was to fly independence from Britain and France. Both of their flags are red, white and blue. Before the new flag, the Red Ensign, which included a Union Jack, rippled over the country between 1924 and 1965.

Each province also has its own flag most of which I dare say would not be recognised by many Canadians. The white and blue 'fleur de lys' of Quebec is probably an exception.

The national anthem, 'O Canada', was composed by Calixa Lavalée in 1880.

PEOPLE

About 45 of every 100 Canadians are of British stock. French descendants of the original pioneers make up about 30% of the population. Most people of French descent live in Quebec but there are large numbers in New Brunswick, Ontario and Manitoba.

The English-speaking population has grown mainly by immigration from the old country and the USA. Over 3½ million Canadians are of Scottish or Irish ancestry.

Generally speaking, the French are Catholic, the British Protestant, but religion does not play a large part in Canadian life.

Early Central and Eastern European settlers went to the prairies but can now be found everywhere, particularly in the large cities. Canada's third-largest ethnic group is German. Other major groups are Italian, Ukrainian, Dutch, Greek, Polish and Scandinavian. More recently, Asians, particularly Chinese from Hong Kong and to lesser degrees, Latin Americans and Blacks from the Caribbean have been immigrating in larger numbers. Canada receives refugees from around the world.

Aboriginal Peoples

These now number about 330,000 Native Indians and 27,000 Inuit, roughly a third more than when White people first arrived. There are also approximately 400,000 Métis, the name used to denote those of mixed aboriginal and European blood. All together the three groups make up about 4% of Canada's total population today. The majority are found in the Yukon, Northwest Territories and Ontario but every province has some aboriginal communities.

Inuit is the general name for the Eskimo peoples in Canada. This is their preferred name, as it distinguishes them from the Eskimo of Asia or the Aleuts.

Collectively the three groups are also called Native Canadians. Another term gaining currency is 'First Nations' which recognises the one-time independent status of individual aboriginal groups.

Since the early pioneering days the Native Indians' lot has led to sadness, even tragedy. At first their numbers dropped dramatically with the influx of European diseases. Then, they lost not only their power and traditions but also their land and eventually, in many cases, their self-respect.

About 72% of Native Indians now live on government reservations, most in poverty and on some form of government assistance. In the cities, with little education and few modern skills, many end up on skid row. Infant mortality, life expectancy, literacy, income and incarceration rates all compare unfavourably with those of other Canadians.

Native Indian leaders have recently become more political, making stands on constitutional matters, land claims and mineral rights. It is through these channels, however slow-moving, that the Native Canadian voice will be heard in the future. Most Canadians now feel the aboriginal peoples have had a raw deal and sympathise with many of their complaints.

This, however, has not resulted in the introduction of concrete attempts to improve the situation. Both provincial and federal governments are finding it less and less possible to ignore the state of affairs, and many issues regarding Native Canadian rights and claims are currently before the courts. Among the many issues to be dealt with is some form of self-government for aboriginal peoples.

Note In North America, Indians from the Asian subcontinent are often called East Indians to distinguish them from the indigenous peoples.

ARTS & CULTURE
Literature

Canada has and is producing an impressive body of writing. Most of it has appeared since the 1940s.

Among the best known, most-read poets are Newfoundlander E J Pratt, Earle Birney, Al Purdy, Gwendolyn McEwen, Irving Layton, Leonard Cohen (who also wrote the less known novel, *Beautiful Losers* which I highly regard), bp nichol for concrete poetry, Michael Ondaatje, Milton Acorn and Al Purdy.

Perhaps more familiar internationally are short story and novel writers such as Margaret Atwood, Mordecai Richler, Margaret Laurence, Marion Engel, Timothy Findley, Robertson Davis, Alice Munro, W O Mitchell and Morley Callaghan.

Canada seems to produce writers who excel in the short story so an anthology of these would make a good introduction to Canadian fiction.

English writer Malcolm Lowry spent most of his productive writing years in British Columbia, many of them in a basic shack on the beach near Vancouver.

French Quebec writers who are widely read in English include Anne Hebert, Marie-Claire Blais, Roch Carrier, Gabrielle Roy and Mavis Gallant.

Two Native Canadian writers are George Clutesi and Markoosie.

Pierre Berton is Canada's best known chronicler of the country's history. He has written on a wide range of subjects in an entertaining and informative way. Peter C Newman writes on Canadian business but also has produced an intriguing book on the history of the Hudson's Bay Company beginning with the early fur-trading days. Farley Mowat writes about the north, wildlife and nature and speaks for their conservation. Among academic writers two who stand out are Northrop Frye for literary criticism and Marshall McLuhan for media observations.

Most good bookstores have a Canadiana section with both fiction and nonfiction works. Two publishers specialising in Canadian fiction are Oberon and House of Anansi. McClelland and Stewart is a very important large Canadian publishing house. Jan Morris, a Welsh travel writer who has written about many cities around the world, published *City to City* in 1990. Written after travelling coast to coast, it's a highly readable collection of essays of fact and opinion about 10 Canadian cities and their people.

Music

Canadian musicians have become increasingly well known in the past few decades with several achieving international stature. Many of the most established names have found it necessary to temporarily or permanently establish residency in the USA.

Canadians have perhaps been best known in the field of folk and folk rock. Among the top names are Gordon Lightfoot, Joni Mitchell, Neil Young, Bruce Cockburn, Leonard

Cohen and Buffy Ste Marie. In more of a country vein there is kd lang, Rita McNeil, Ian and/or Sylvia Tyson, Prairie Oyster, George Fox and Anne Murray. Sort of between the two categories are the Cowboy Junkies, Blue Rodeo, the Roches and Kate and Anna McGarrigle. Jeff Healy and Collin James both play scintillating blues guitar.

The country has always tended to produce individualistic musicians who emphasise lyrics and personal sentiments. In rock, Luba stands out in this mould. Brian Adams, Allanah Miles, Heart and Kim Mitchell have all deservedly come by their popularity as have newcomers the Tragically Hip. More corporate music successes include Loverboy and Glass Tiger.

Among Quebec singers who are rarely heard outside that province, except perhaps in France, Gilles Vigneault could be the biggest name. Others are Michel Rivard and Daniel Lavois but there are many more. The province has its own successful pop, rock and semitraditional folk bands and artists.

In the classical field three of Canada's best known artists are guitarist Liona Boyd, the late pianist Glen Gould and composer R Murray Schafer.

Pianist Oscar Peterson is the country's highest-profile jazz musician.

Painting

Artists began painting Canada as early as the 1700s and their work has grown to encompass a wide variety of styles and international influences. One of the earliest distinctive Canadian painters was Cornelius Krieghoff who used the St Lawrence River area of Quebec as his subject matter. Out west Paul Kane was equally captivated by the Native Indians and their way of life. Landscape painters travelled and explored the country often following the laying of railway lines.

Tom Thompson and the Group of Seven beginning just before WW I established the style and landscape subject matter which was to dominate Canadian art for about 30 years. Their work, drawn from the geography of the eastern Canadian lakelands, is still the country's best known both inside and outside Canada. Emily Carr in a similar tradition painted the west coast, its forests and Native Indian villages and totems.

In the 1950s, the Group of Eleven which included Jack Bush, Tom Hodgson and Harold Town helped bring new abstract influences into Canadian painting. Joyce Wieland and Michael Snow two of the best known among more contemporary visual artists grew out of this period. Well known realists include Ken Danby, Alex Colville and, for nature studies, Robert Bateman.

As with the previous music and literature sections, this is but a very brief overview of some of the country's artists the visitor may wish to be aware of.

Film

Canadian film is well respected abroad primarily through the work of the National Film Board whose productions are, perhaps surprisingly, little-viewed and scarcely known at home. Each year the film board, now over 50 years old releases a combination of animation, documentary and dramatic films. The National Film Board offices can be found in many of the country's large cities. Films are often screened at the centres and, increasingly, videos of the vast collection can be rented.

Canada also has a commercial feature-length film industry. Its output is relatively small and the quality varies in the same way as Hollywood productions. In the past few years Quebec has been the most prolific and artistically successful in film. The better known movies are subtitled and sometimes dubbed into English.

Native Art

Among the country's most distinctive art is that of the Inuit of the north, particularly their stone and bone sculptures and carvings. These also represent some of the more affordable pieces, although their prices too can range into the stratosphere for larger works by well established artists.

Materials used for Inuit carvings include bone, ivory, antler and occasionally horn or wood. By far the most common, though, is a group of rock types known generically as soapstone. They include the soft steatite and harder serpentine, argillite, dolomite and others. Quarried across the far north, the stone material can vary from black to grey to green and may be dull or highly polished.

Carving styles vary from one isolated community to the other across the far north with some better known than others. Almost all work is done completely by hand with low-tech tools. Northern Quebec tends to produce realistic, naturalistic work such as birds or hunting scenes. Baffin Island sculpture is more detailed and finer often with varying depictions of people. The central

Native Indian Mask

Arctic area art embraces spiritual themes, and whalebone is often employed.

As a result of interest and appreciation in Inuit carvings there are now mass-produced imitations which are widely seen and sold. Genuine works are always marked with a tag or sticker with an igloo symbol on it. Many are also signed by the artist. The type of retail outlet is also an indicator. A reputable store and not a souvenir kiosk will likely be stocking the real thing. Aside from the maker and the quality, imitations are not often even made of the true raw material and really are of no value or interest.

Inuit artists also produce prints which are highly regarded. Subject matter often is taken from mythology but other works depict traditional day-to-day activities, events and chores.

The best of Native Indian art is also in printmaking although there is some fine carving and basketry. Across the country much of what is sold as Native Indian art and craft is pretty cheap and tacky and a poor likeness to the work which was done at one time.

Some of the most interesting and best quality items from either Inuit or Native Indian artisans are the clothes: moccasins *(mukluks)*, knitted sweaters (from Vancouver Island, known as Cowichan sweaters) and parkas (warm winter coats). Some interesting jewellery and beadwork can also be found.

Sports

Canada's official national sport is lacrosse, an old Native Indian game similar to soccer but played with a small ball and sticks. Each stick has a woven leather basket in which the ball is caught and carried.

The sport that really creates passion, however, is ice hockey. To play professionally is the Canadian little boy's dream. This is especially true in Quebec, home of the Montreal Canadiens, a hockey legend and one of the most consistently successful professional sports teams anywhere. If you're in Canada in winter, a National Hockey League game between good teams is recommended. There are teams in seven Canadian cities and twice that many in US cities although most of the players are from Canada.

US-style football, though with some modifications in the Canadian Football League, is also very popular, and US baseball has gained a good following now that there are teams in Montreal and Toronto. Soccer and basketball have never been able to catch on and are strictly small-time in Canada. Both the summer and winter Olympics are participated in and watched with much interest.

Canadian Inventions & Discoveries

Canadians can lay claim to quite an assortment of the products of human ingenuity. The Native Indians have given the world snowshoes and the birch-bark canoe; the Inuit developed the winter parka and accompanying boots known as mukluks and the kayak. More recent Canadian inventions include the electron microscope and the clothes zipper (a mixed blessing!).

Canadians have been active in the food arena, too. Important research developed strains of wheat suitable to a variety of world climates. Pablum, a baby cereal, was created in Canada and, perhaps even more significant, was the development of instant mashed potatoes.

Other firsts include the paint roller (a simple yet great little device), the telephone, the wireless photograph transmitter, the friction match, the chainsaw and the snowmobile. The use of calcium carbide-acetylene gas for light was discovered by Canadian Thomas Wilson. It replaced kerosene, another Canadian invention, and led to the formation of the giant Union Carbide Company. Standard Time adopted around the world was devised in Canada.

For trains, the observation car known as the dome car, was designed in Canada. Canada also developed the manipulable space arm used on the US space shuttle craft. Insulin was discovered by Banting and Best in 1921.

And, perhaps to the chagrin of the country's US friends, it should be noted that the game of basketball was created in Canada. ■

Skating on frozen rivers and outdoor ice rinks is a common, pleasant way to exercise. Joggers are now a familiar sight, too. The popularity of cycling increases each year.

LANGUAGE

English and French are the two official languages of Canada. You will notice both on highway signs, maps, tourist brochures and cereal boxes.

The French spoken in Canada is not the language of France. At times it can be nearly unintelligible to a Parisian. It also varies from region to region. The local tongue of Quebec is known as Québecois or *joual*, but variations occur around the province. The preservation of French in Quebec is a primary concern and fuels the Quebec separatist movement. New Brunswick is, perhaps surprisingly, the only officially bilingual province. French is widely spoken there, particularly in the north and east. Again, it is somewhat different from the French of Quebec. Nova Scotia and Manitoba also have significant French populations but there are pockets in most provinces.

Many immigrants use their mother tongues, as do some groups of Native Indians and Inuit. In other communities it is now only the older members who know the original language. Few White Canadians speak any Native Indian or Inuit language but some words such as igloo, parka, muskeg and kayak are commonly used. The Inuit language is interesting for its specialisation and use of many words for what appears to be the same thing; eg the word for 'seal' depends on whether it's old or young, in or out of the water. There are up to 20 or so words for 'snow' depending on its consistency and texture.

Canadian English

Canada inherited English from Britain, but Canadian English has also been strongly influenced by the USA, particularly via the mass media and the use of US textbooks and dictionaries in schools. Most spellings follow British English such as centre, harbour, cheque, etc but there are some exceptions like tire (tyre) and aluminum (aluminium).

Canadian English has also developed its own distinctive idioms and expression. The most recognisable is the interrogative 'eh?' which seems to appear at the end of almost every spoken sentence. Although to many non-North Americans, Canadians and Americans may sound the same, there are real differences. Canadian pronunciation of 'ou' is the most notable of these: words like 'out' and 'bout' sound more like 'oat' and 'boat' when spoken by Canadians.

Within Canada there are regional variations in idiom and pronunciation. In Newfoundland, for example, some people speak with an accent reminiscent of the west country of England (Devon and Cornwall) and some use words such as 'screech' (rum) and 'shooneen' (coward). In British Columbia some expressions reflect that province's history: a word like 'leaverite' meaning a worthless mineral is a prospecting word derived from the phrase 'Leave 'er right there'. Canadians have added to the richness of the global English language too with words like kerosene (paraffin) and puck (from ice hockey).

French Phrases

The following is a short guide to some French words and phrases which may be useful for the traveller. The combination 'ohn' should sound very nasal. The 'n' shouldn't be pronounced. Quebec French employs a lot of English words although with unique pronunciations, so this may make understanding and speaking easier. The following is a guide.

yes
  oui
    wee
no
  non
    nohn
please
  s'il vous plaît
    seel voo pleh

thank you
merci
mehr-see

you're welcome
je vous en prie
zhe vooz ohn pri

hello (day)
bonjour
bohn joor

hello (evening)
bonsoir
bohn swar

hello, how are you?
comment ça va?
common sa vah?

I'm fine
ça va bien
sa vah bee-ahn

excuse me
pardon
par-dohn

big
grand
grond

small
petit
peh-tee

cheap
bon marché
bohn mar-shay

expensive
cher
share

here
ici
ee-see

there
là
lah

much, many
beaucoup
boh-coo

before
avant
ah-vonh

after
après
ah-preh

tomorrow
demain
de-mahn

yesterday
hier
yeah

welcome
bienvenu
bee-ahn ven-oo

toilet
toilet
twah-leh

bank
banque
bohnk

travellers' cheque
cheque voyage
shek vwoy-yazh

the bill
l'addition
la-dis-yohn

store
magasin
mag-a-zahn

a match
un feu
un feuh

museum
musée
mew-zay

gas
gaz
gaz

lead-free (gas)
sans plomb
sohn plom

self-serve
service libre
sairvees lee-br'

Questions

where/where is ...?
où/où est ...?
oo/oo ehh...?

what?
comment?
commonh?

huh? (slang)
quoi?
kwah?

how much?
 combien?
   kom-bee-ahn?

Signs
entrance
 entrée
   on-tray
exit
 sorti
   sor-tee
platform
 quai
   kay
information
 renseignments
   ron-sayn-mohn
no camping
 interdiction de camper
   an-ter-dic-shion de campay
no parking
 stationnement interdit
   stas-iohn-mohn ahn-ter-dee
tourist office
 bureau du tourisme
   bew-ro dew too-rism

Accommodation
hotel
 hôtel
   o-tell
youth hostel
 auberge de jeunesse
   o-bairzh de zheuness
room
 chambre
   shombr

Travel
bus
 autobus
   auto-boos
train
 train
   trahn
ticket
 billet
   bee-yay

plane
 avion
   a-vee-ohn
return (ticket)
 aller et retour
   alay eh reh-tour
railway station
 la gare
   lah gahr
bus station
 la station d'autobus
   leh-stas-ion d'auto-boos
left
 à gauche
   a go-shh
right
 à droit
   a drwat
straight ahead
 tout droit
   too drwat

Food
restaurant
 restaurant
   rest-a-ronh
snack bar
 casse croûte
   kass krewt
eggs
 oeufs
   er
French fries (chips)
 patates frites
   pa-tat frit
bread
 pain
   pahn
cheese
 fromage
   fro-majh
vegetable
 légume
   lay-goom
fruit
 fruit
   frwee

Drinks

water
l'eau
  low
milk
lait
  leh
beer
bière
  bee air
wine
vin
  vahn
red
rouge
  roozh
white
blanc
  blohnk

Simple Sentences

I am a tourist.
Je suis touriste.
  zhe swee toureest.
Do you speak English?
Parlez-vouz anglais?
  parlay vooz anglay?
I don't speak French.
Je ne parle pas francais.
  zhe neh parl pah fronh-say.

I understand.
Je comprends.
  zhe com-prohn
I don't understand.
Je ne comprends pas.
  zhe ne com-prohn pah.

Numbers

1	*un*	uhn
2	*deux*	der
3	*trois*	twah
4	*quatre*	cat
5	*cinq*	sank
6	*six*	cease
7	*sept*	set
8	*huit*	weet
9	*neuf*	neuf
10	*dix*	dees
20	*vingt*	vahn
21	*vingt et un*	vahnt-eh-un
22	*vingt-deux*	vahn der
25	*vingt-cinq*	vahn sank
30	*trente*	tronht
40	*quarante*	car-ohnt
50	*cinquante*	sank-ohnt
60	*soixante*	swa-sohnt
70	*soixante-dix*	swa-sohnt dees
80	*quatre-vingt*	cat-tr' vahn
90	*quatre-vingt-dix*	cat-tr'vahn dees
100	*cent*	sohn
500	*cinq cents*	sank sohn
1000	*mille*	meel

Facts for the Visitor

VISAS

Visitors from all countries except the USA need a passport, though Americans do need to take good identification. Formerly a driver's licence was all that was required (going in the other direction, too, for Canadians) but often this is no longer sufficient. A birth certificate or a certificate of citizenship or naturalisation if not a passport is highly recommended and may indeed be required before admission is granted.

Visitors from most Western countries don't need a visa nor do many people from Asia and developing countries. Communist nations definitely need one. Visa requirements change frequently and you must obtain one before arrival in Canada, so check before you leave – Europeans included. Visas are issued free by Canadian consulates in these and other cities:

Australia
    Canadian High Commission, Commonwealth Ave, Canberra, ACT 2600 (☎ 733-844)
    Consulate General of Canada, 8th Floor, AMP Centre, 50 Bridge St, Sydney, New South Wales 2000 (☎ 231-6522)
    Consulate of Canada, 6th Floor, 1 Collins St, Melbourne, Victoria 3000 (☎ 654-1433)
    Consulate of Canada, 11th Floor, National Mutual Centre, 111 St George's Terrace, Perth, Western Australia 6000 (☎ 321-1151)
Ireland
    Canadian Embassy, 65 St Stephen's Green, Dublin 2 (☎ 781-988)
New Zealand
    Canadian High Commission, ICI Building, Molesworth St, Wellington (☎ 739-577)
    Consulate of Canada, Princes Court, 2 Princes St, Auckland (☎ 393-516/7/8, 393-689/90)
UK
    Passport & Consular Services, 1 Grosvenor Square, London W1X 0AB (☎ 071-629-9492)
    Consulate of Canada, 151 St Vincent St, Glasgow G2 5NJ (☎ 221-4415)
USA
    Canadian Embassy, 501 Pennsylvania Ave, NW, Washington DC 2001
    Canada also has diplomatic representation in Atlanta, Boston, Buffalo, Chicago, Cleveland,

Dallas, Detroit, Los Angeles, Minneapolis, New York City and San Francisco, Seattle

A visa does not guarantee entry. Admission is at the discretion of the immigration officer at the border. This depends on a number of factors, some of which you control. An exit ticket is not officially required, nor a show of money, but you may be asked to present either. It's mostly common sense. If you turn up looking shabby with $20 for a six-month stay, forget it. Have a reasonable amount of money and an estimation of your daily expenses ready. If you have friends or relatives where you can stay, mention it. If you have a Hostel Card, show it. Visitors from Western countries should have little difficulty.

The normal stay granted is three months. This is renewable, though a quick trip out of the country, to the USA, may be required.

If you are refused entry but have a visa you have the right of appeal at the Immigration Appeal Board at the port of entry. Those under 18 years of age should have a letter from a parent or guardian.

Side Trips to USA

Visitors to Canada who are planning some time in the USA should be aware of a couple of things. First, admission requirements to the USA when arriving by land can be significantly different to when arriving by air or from one's country of origin. For example, residents of the UK do not need a visa when flying into the USA but do need them if entering overland from Canada. Also check that your entry permit to Canada, whatever it may be, includes multiple entry. If not, you may find your afternoon side trip across the border involuntarily extended when Canadian officials won't let you back in!

Studying & Working

Student and work authorisations must be obtained outside Canada and may take six months. A work permit is valid for one specific job and one specific time, for one specific employer. If you want to study here, get the information and apply in your own country.

It is difficult to get a work permit: opportunities go first to Canadians. However, employers hiring casual, temporary, construction, farm or forestry workers often don't ask for the permit. Visitors working here legally have Social Insurance numbers beginning with '9'. If you don't have this, and get caught, you'll probably be told to leave the country.

Many young European women come to Canada as nannies. Many countries have agencies where details on these arrangements can be found.

SWAP Of particular interest to Australian students may be the Student Work Abroad Programme (SWAP). Organised by Student Services Australia (SSA) and the Canadian Federation of Students (CFS), the programme allows Australians between the ages of 18 and 26 to spend a year in Canada on a working holiday.

After an orientation programme in Vancouver you find your own job with help from CFS. Most jobs are in the service area – as waiters, bar attendants, cleaners and maids, particularly in the snowfields over winter – although SWAP participants have worked in other kinds of jobs ranging from farmhands to bell-hops. You are issued with a one-year, nonextendable visa which allows you to work anywhere in the country. 'Swappers' must be Australian citizens and pass a medical check-up.

SSA, in conjunction with STA Travel, arranges group departures at reduced fares leaving from Sydney, Melbourne and Brisbane in November and December. Participants are given orientation information and a copy of this Lonely Planet book prior to departure.

For full details contact Student Services Australia (☎ (03) 348 1777), PO Box 399, Carlton South, Victoria, 3053.

CUSTOMS

How thoroughly customs will check you out upon arrival at a Canadian entry point depends on a number of things. First among them are point of departure, nationality and appearance. Arriving from countries known as drug sources or with a history of illegal immigration or refugees will add to the scrutiny. Always make sure the necessary papers are in order.

Don't get caught bringing drugs into Canada: this includes marijuana and hashish, as they are termed narcotics in Canada. The sentence is seven years minimum and it doesn't matter if you're a nice person – the judge has no choice by law.

If you're 19 years old or over you can bring in 1.1 litres of liquor or a case of 24 beers (it's cheaper in the USA) as well as 200 cigarettes, 50 cigars and one kg of tobacco (all also cheaper in the USA). You can bring in gifts up to $40 in value. Sporting goods, including 200 rounds of ammunition, cameras and film and two days' worth of food can also be brought in without trouble. Registering excessive or expensive sporting goods, cameras, etc might save you some hassle when you leave, especially if you'll be crossing the Canadian-US border a number of times.

If you've rented a car, trailer or any other vehicle in the USA and are driving it into Canada, bring a copy of the rental agreement to save any possible aggravation by border officials. It should stipulate that taking the vehicle to Canada is permitted.

Americans travelling in Canada may want to investigate the Canadian Nonresident Interprovince Motor Vehicle Liability Insurance Card which is only available in the USA.

If you have a dog or cat you will need proof that it's had a rabies shot in the past 36 months. For Americans, this is usually easy enough; for residents of other countries there may well be more involved procedures. If you must bring a pet from abroad, to save a lot of potential headaches check with the Canadian government or a representative before arriving at the border.

For boaters, pleasure craft may enter Canada either on the trailer or in the water and stay for up to one year. An entry permit is required and is obtainable from the customs office at or near the point of entry. All boats powered by motors over 10 horse power must be licensed.

Pistols, fully automatic weapons and any firearms less than 65 cm (26 inches) in length are not permitted into the country. Most rifles and shotguns will be admitted without a permit.

Warning

Do not make any comments, jokes or movements indicating the existence of anything illegal, particularly a weapon and especially at an airport inspection point. Customs agents do not abide this and you will be whisked off, possibly in handcuffs, faster than you'd like. Recently a Canadian politician was charged and lost his post over a gun quip at the airport. Be patient and dump your pockets quietly.

MONEY
Currency

Canadian currency is much like that of the USA with some noteworthy variations. Coins come in one-cent (penny), five-cent (nickel), 10-cent (dime) and 25-cent (quarter) pieces. There is also a 50-cent coin but this is not regularly seen. Westerners seem to use it somewhat more frequently, it is rare in the East. The new dollar, replacing the bill, is an 11-sided, gold-coloured coin known familiarly as the 'loonie' because the common loon (a species of waterbird) is featured swimming on it.

Everyday working bills come in $2 (there is no US two-dollar bill), $5, $10 and $20 denominations. The $50, $100 and larger bills are less common and could prove difficult to cash in smaller places or at night. Gas stations, for example, are sometimes reluctant to deal with larger bills. Canadian bills are all the same size but vary in their colours and images. Some denominations have two styles as older versions in good condition continue to circulate.

All prices quoted in this book are in Canadian dollars, unless stated otherwise.

Exchange Rates

US$1	=	C$1.14
UK£1	=	C$2.04
A$1	=	C$0.89
NZ$1	=	C$0.64
DM1	=	C$0.72
Y1	=	C$0.009

Changing money is best done at companies such as Deak International which specialises in international transactions. In some of the larger cities, such companies operate small exchange offices and booths along main streets. Second choice for changing money is the banks or trust companies. Lastly there are hotels (always open at least), stores, attractions and gas stations. The rates at the latter group are likely to be in your favour.

American Express and Thomas Cook are the best travellers' cheques to use in either US or Canadian dollars. Some smaller places don't know exchange rates, so you'll have to pay for a call to find the rate as well as the

mailing charges. Some banks now charge a couple of bucks to cash travellers' cheques, so ask first; if a charge is levied, cash several, as generally the charge remains the same whether it's one cheque or five. Despite this service charge, banks usually offer better rates than hotels, restaurants and visitor attractions, etc. The difference can be a few percentage points.

Chargex, Visa, MasterCard and American Express credit cards are honoured in many places in most larger centres. In smaller communities, the use of travellers' cheques or cash is advisable.

Costs

Finding a place to sleep and eat is not a lot different here than in Europe or other Western countries. The Canadian lifestyle, like the Canadian personality, is a little bit British, a little bit American and somehow different from both. There are no formal social classes, but there are widely different incomes, and therefore a range in housing, eating and entertainment prices.

For most visitors, the biggest expense will be accommodation. There are, however, alternatives to the standard hotels which can make paying for a bed nothing to lose sleep over. The larger cities generally have the more expensive lodging prices, while those in country towns can be quite reasonable. In the far north, accommodation rates are a little more than in the south, but not outlandishly so. The heavily touristed areas such as Banff, Niagara Falls and Quebec City tend not to have really inflated prices because the volume of places to stay means plenty of competition, particularly when it's not peak season. As a rule, through the summer months prices are a little higher everywhere for accommodation. After this period asking about a discount if one is not forthcoming is well worthwhile.

Food prices are lower than those in much of western Europe but are higher than those in the USA and about parallel to those in Australia.

Gasoline prices vary from province to province but are always more than US rates,

sometimes shockingly so. Fill up before crossing the border. Canada's gasoline prices are, however, lower than those in most of Europe. Within Canada the eastern provinces and the far north have the highest prices. Also, as a rule the more isolated the service station, the higher the prices will be. Alberta has traditionally had the lowest prices. Of course, these prices reflect on all transportation costs.

Buses are almost always the least expensive form of public transport. Train fares, except when using one of the various special price rates, are moderate. Again, they are more expensive than US fares, less than European ones and comparable to those in Australia.

Inter-provincial airfares are high. Distances are great and the competition minimal. Again always inquire about specials, excursion fares, etc.

Most prices that you see posted do not include taxes, which can add significantly to your costs (see the following Consumer Taxes section). It's a good idea to ask if the price of something includes tax.

Tipping

Normal tipping is 10% to 20% of the bill. Tips are usually given to cabbies, waiting staff, hairdressers, hotel attendants and bellhops. Tipping helps for service in a bar too, especially if a fat tip is given on the first order. After that you won't go thirsty all night.

A few restaurants have the gall to include a service charge on the bill. No tip should be added on top in these cases.

Canadians, it might be noted, have an international reputation as being lousy tippers.

Consumer Taxes

Provincial Tax Alberta has a sales tax on accommodation in hotels and motels, but the other provinces also have taxes on most items bought in shops and on food bought at restaurants and cafés. The Yukon and Northwest Territories have no consumer tax.

Some provinces – Quebec, Ontario, Nova

Scotia and Newfoundland – allow rebates on goods being taken out of Canada. Call a provincial government office to obtain the forms for reimbursement – it's worth the trouble on a tent, camera or similar purchase. Some conditions apply and the form must be posted to the provincial tax office after you return home.

Goods & Services Tax As of 1 January 1991 Canada's controversial Goods & Services Tax (GST) came into law despite massive repugnance by the citizenry and predictable outrage by the opposition parties of government. Known as the Gouge & Screw Tax, it replaces a largely hidden 13.5% federal sales tax on manufactured goods only, with a 7% tax to be applied to more or less every product, service and transaction. Even the government admits this will increase inflation, though by how much is debated.

Unfortunately for tourists, it hits the travel industry hard. Air, train and inter-city bus fares are all subject to the 7% increase. Ditto for taxi fares, gasoline, parking lot costs, tow truck charges, even bicycle repairs.

Perhaps worse, all hotel bills, campsite rentals, car, boat and equipment rentals (eg of skis) have all gone up by 7%.

Also fully taxed are all restaurant meals, all snack foods and drinks, alcohol, newspapers, pay phones, stationery and stamps, toiletries, golf fees, caddies and film and photo processing.

For visitors or travellers who prepare their own food, there is no tax applied to groceries.

A rebate is available for visitors on non-consumable goods bought for use outside Canada, provided the goods are removed from the country within 60 days. Some tourist homes don't charge GST for rooms, and foreign visitors should ask for an exemption from the GST on their hotel bill when making payment. The GST added to all other accommodation is refundable.

Most 'tourist' or duty-free shops have a GST rebate form or you can contact Revenue Canada, Custom & Excise, Visitors' Rebate Program, Ottawa, Ontario K1A 1J5.

WHEN TO GO
Spring, summer and fall are all ideal for touring. If you're skiing or only visiting the cities then winter's OK too.

TOURIST OFFICES
Local Tourist Offices
In Canada each province has a governmental ministry responsible for tourism and the major cities generally have an office for distributing provincial information. In addition, most cities and towns have at least a seasonal local information office. Many of these are mentioned in the text. Tourism Canada, 235 Queen St, Ottawa, Ontario K1A 0H6, can supply basic information booklets for visitors and within these are the addresses of all the provincial and territorial head offices.

Overseas Reps
There are Canadian tourist information offices, called Tourism Canada, in many countries, usually in the major city or cities. If you want information beforehand and can't find an office, try calling the Canadian embassy, consulate or high commission. Addresses follow:

Australia
    Canadian Government, Department of Tourism, 8th Floor, AMP Centre, 50 Bridge St, Sydney New South Wales 2000
France
    Office du Tourism du Canada, 35 Avenue Montagne, 75008 Paris
Germany
    Taunusstrasse 52-60, 6000 Frankfurt 1
Japan
    73-38 Akasaka, Minato-ku, Tokyo 107
UK
    Canada House, Trafalgar Square, London SW1 5BJ
USA
    Most states have an office in the major city

USEFUL ORGANISATIONS
CUTS For budget, young or student travellers, the Canadian University Travel Service (CUTS) offers a wealth of information. This is Canada's student travel bureau with offices in Halifax, Ottawa, Toronto, Saska-

toon, Edmonton and Vancouver. These offices are usually on university campuses.

For student discounts you must have an International Student Identity Card (ISIC) available at these outlets. You must have proper ID though – this isn't Athens or Bangkok.

CUTS deal mostly in ways to get you out of Canada cheaply. They also sell European train passes, arrange working holidays and set up language courses.

Within Canada, CUTS can arrange tours and canoe trips and help with domestic flights. They have a *Discount Handbook* which lists over 1000 stores and service establishments offering bargains to ISIC card holders.

IYHF Canada is a member of the International Youth Hostelling Federation (IYHF) and besides offering beds, some of the hostels run field trips, operate travel agencies or have stores selling outdoor supplies and guide books. The hostels are also great sources of information through the guests, staff and bulletin boards. For more information on them see under the accommodation section in this chapter.

BUSINESS HOURS & HOLIDAYS
Business Hours
Banks Banks have slowly been extending their often inconvenient opening hours which vary. As a rough guide, most banks are open Monday to Thursday from 10 am to 4.30 pm, and from 10 am to 5 or 6 pm on Friday. Trust companies tend to have longer hours, perhaps to 6 pm daily and are often open at least in the morning on Saturday. Some banks now also open for shorter hours on Saturday. No bank is open on Sunday and the whole lot are always closed on holidays. Many banks now have banking machines which are accessible for those with cards 24 hours a day every day.

Stores Store hours have become a confusing array in Canada with really no standard at all.

The issue of Sunday opening has been a raging debate for several years and no overall consensus has been reached.

In general, cities and their suburbs have the longest store hours. Opening time ranges from 9 am to 10 am with closing time around 6 pm. Longer hours, until 9 pm, are usually kept on Friday and sometimes Thursday. Shopping malls, plazas, large department stores and downtown stores may remain open until 9 pm every day. The western provinces tend to have unlimited Sunday shopping while central and eastern Canada are usually closed up tight.

Smaller centres and towns and country villages generally have considerably shorter hours with little evening shopping and nothing much available on Sunday but milk, bread and a movie.

Bars Hours vary according to the province. Most open at noon and close around 2 am. In Ontario last call is just before 1 am. In Quebec laws are more liberal; bars stay open until 3 or 4 am. The larger cities usually have after hours bars which remain open for music or dancing but stop serving alcohol.

National Holidays
New Year's Day
    1 January
Easter (including Good Friday, Easter Monday)
Victoria Day
    mid-May
Canada Day
    1 July
Labour Day
    first Monday in September
Thanksgiving
    second Monday in October
Remembrance Day
    11 November (banks & government)
Christmas Day
    25 December

Provincial Holidays
Newfoundland
    St Patrick's Day, mid-March
    St George's Day, end of April
    Discovery Day, end of June
    Memorial Day, beginning of July
    Orangeman's Day, mid-July

Quebec

Fête Nationale (formerly known as Saint Jean Baptiste Day), 24 June

Yukon

Discovery Day, second week in August

All other provinces 1 August (or close to it)

CULTURAL EVENTS

Major events are listed under the city or town where they occur. There are many others.

Tourism Canada publishes a small booklet each year called *Events & Attractions*, but it doesn't cover all events and offers little description.

Provincial tourist departments print up more detailed and extensive lists of their own, which include cultural and sporting exhibitions and happenings of all kinds. Military and historic celebrations, ethnic festivals and music shows are all included. Some provinces produce separate booklets for summer and winter events.

Major provincial and national holidays are usually cause for some celebration, especially in summer when events often wrap up with a fireworks display.

POST & TELECOMMUNICATIONS
Post

Mail service is neither quick nor cheap but it's basically reliable. Some useful information follows:

1st-class mail is limited up to 500 grams.

1st-class letter or postcard in Canada: 43 cents (up to 30 grams; includes GST)

1st-class letter or postcard to USA: 49 cents (up to 30 grams)

1st-class letter or postcard to other: 80 cents (up to 30 grams)

Aerogrammes are the same price

Mail weighing over 500 grams goes parcel post, which can be air, surface or a combination of these. Mail over 10 kg goes surface only – this is slow.

For added security, speed or other requirements there is registered mail, special delivery and both surface and air mail for packages. Check at the post office for details.

Some countries require a customs declaration on incoming parcels. Check at the post office.

Aside from the post offices themselves, stamps and postal services are often available at other outlets such as drug stores and some small variety stores. Finding them is a matter of asking around. Hotel concessions also often stock stamps.

Telephone

Canada has an excellent, inexpensive telephone system. Public telephones are generally quite readily available and can be found in hotel lobbies, bars, restaurants, large department stores and many public buildings. Blue or red telephone booths can be found on street corners in cities and towns. The basic rate varies but is generally 25 cents. If you use the operator you do not even need any money. There is also no charge from a public phone for dialling 411, the telephone information number.

Long-distance calls to anywhere in the world can be made from any phone but the rate varies depending on how it is done and when. A call made without the assistance of an operator is not only cheapest but quickest. This can be done if you know the area code as well as the number of the party attempting to be reached. With operator assistance, calls in increasing order of cost are, station to station (no particular person to speak to required), collect (reverse charge) and person to person.

In Canada, long-distance rates drop 35% after 6 pm and 60% from 11 pm to 8 am Monday to Friday. Anytime on Saturday or Sunday the cost is 60% off the regular weekday rate.

Reductions can also apply to calls into the USA or overseas. All international rates and codes are listed in the front pages of the telephone book.

The 800 numbers (1-800 from outside North America) which many businesses, ferries, hotels and tourist offices operate are toll free.

All Canadian business and residential phones are paid for on a flat monthly rate system, the number of calls made is immaterial.

TIME

Canada spans six of the world's 24 time zones. As shown on the map, the eastern zone in Newfoundland is unusual in that it's only a half-hour different from the adjacent zone. The time difference from coast to coast is 5½ hours.

Canada uses Daylight Saving Time during summer. It begins on the last Sunday in April and ends on the last Sunday in October. It is one hour later than Standard Time, meaning a seemingly longer summer day.

Eastern Saskatchewan uses Standard Time all year round. Why, I don't know.

MEDIA

The *Globe & Mail* newspaper, out of Toronto but available across the country daily, provides a well written record of national affairs from politics to arts. *Maclean's* is Canada's weekly news magazine.

The Canadian Broadcasting Corporation (CBC) with both national and regional broadcasts in both radio (on AM and FM bands) and TV can be seen or heard almost anywhere in the country including some of the more remote areas. It carries more Canadian content in music and information than any of the private broadcast companies. CBC Radio, in particular, is a fine service which unites listeners across the country with some of its programmes. Highly recommended is

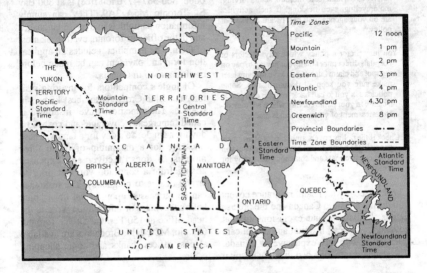

the Morningside show heard between 9 am and 12 noon weekdays hosted by Peter Gzowski. It's entertaining, educational and offers listeners a well-rounded view of what's on and in the minds of Canadians.

HEALTH

Canada is a pretty safe place to visit and little is necessary in the way of preparation. Normally no vaccinations are required and there's nothing to recommend for protection here. You need shots for smallpox, cholera and yellow fever if you're coming from an endemic area or have been in contact with these diseases.

Health Insurance

A travel insurance policy to cover theft, loss and medical problems is a wise idea. There is a wide variety of policies and your travel agent will have recommendations. Some policies offer lower and higher medical expenses options but the higher one is chiefly for countries like the USA which have extremely high medical costs. Check the small print:

1. Some policies specifically exclude 'dangerous activities' which can include scuba diving, motorcycling, even trekking. If such activities are on your agenda, you don't want that sort of policy.

2. You may prefer a policy which pays doctors or hospitals direct rather than your having to pay on the spot and claim later. If you have to claim later make sure you keep all documentation. Some policies ask you to call back (reverse charges) to a centre in your home country where an immediate assessment of your problem is made.

3. Check if the policy covers ambulances or an emergency flight home. If you have to stretch out you will need two seats and somebody has to pay for them!

Check to see if your health insurance covers you during a visit to Canada and the precise details, limitations and exclusions of that coverage. Medical, hospital and dental care is excellent but very expensive in Canada. The standard rate for a bed in a city hospital is at least $500 a day and up to $1500 a day in the major centres.

The largest seller of hospital and medical insurance to visitors to Canada is John Ingle Travel Insurance. They offer policies from a minimum of seven days to a maximum of one year with a possible renewal of one additional year. The 30-day coverage costs $84 for an adult under the age of 65. Family rates are available. Coverage includes the hospital rate, doctors' fees, extended health care and other features.

Be sure to inquire about coverage details if you intend to make side trips to the USA, Mexico, the Caribbean countries or others.

They also offer insurance policies for foreign students (at reduced rates) and to those visiting Canada on working visas. Their policies may be very beneficial in filling in coverage gaps before either a government policy kicks in, in the case of students, or the employers' paid benefits begin, in the case of foreign workers. Again, the policies may vary depending where in the country you settle.

Ingle has offices in major cities across the country and representatives in the northern territories. The head office (☎ (416) 961-0666; 800-387-4770 toll free) is at 800 Bay St, Toronto M5A 3A9. They can supply information pamphlets in over 15 languages and in the office in Toronto, even speak most of them. The pamphlet includes an application form and payment can be made before or after arrival in Canada.

Of Ingle's competitors for insuring visitors, the Blue Cross is the best known in Canada. Their medical travel insurance is called 'emergency coverage' and costs $3 a day for a single, $6 a day for a family. These rates are for a maximum of up to three months. It doesn't cover any expenses arising from a condition you had prior to arrival or due to pregnancy. The insurance can be purchased upon arrival or at home before leaving. For information write to the head office at 150 Ferrand Drive, Toronto, Ontario, M3C 1H6. Brochures are available at post offices, banks and some shopping centres.

Medical Kit

When doing a lot of driving, visiting less-populated areas or camping, hiking, canoeing, etc a good first aid kit is recommended. A possible kit list includes:

1. Aspirin or Panadol – for pain or fever
2. Antihistamine (such as Benadryl) – useful as a decongestant for colds, allergies, to ease the itch from insect bites or stings or to help prevent motion sickness
3. Antibiotics – useful if you're travelling well off the beaten track, but they must be prescribed and you should carry the prescription with you
4. Kaolin preparation (Pepto-Bismol), Imodium or Lomotil – for stomach upsets
5. Rehydration mixture – for treatment of severe diarrhoea, this is particularly important if travelling with children
6. Antiseptic, mercurochrome and antibiotic powder or similar 'dry' spray – for cuts and grazes
7. Calamine lotion – to ease irritation from bites or stings
8 Bandages and Band-aids – for minor injuries
9. Scissors, tweezers and a thermometer (note that mercury thermometers are prohibited by airlines)
10. Insect repellent, sunscreen, suntan lotion, chap stick and water purification tablets

Ideally antibiotics should be administered only under medical supervision and should never be taken indiscriminately. Overuse of antibiotics can weaken your body's ability to deal with infections naturally and can reduce the drug's efficacy on a future occasion. Take only the recommended dose at the prescribed intervals and continue using the antibiotic for the prescribed period, even if the illness seems to be cured earlier. Antibiotics are quite specific to the infections they can treat, stop immediately if there are any serious reactions and don't use them at all if you are unsure if you have the correct one.

Health Preparations

Make sure you're healthy before you start travelling. The basic rule of thumb is that if you look like your passport photo, you're too sick to travel.

If you are embarking on a long trip make sure your teeth are OK. If you wear glasses take a spare pair and your prescription. Losing your glasses can be a real problem, although in many places you can get new spectacles made up quickly, cheaply and competently.

If you require a particular medication take an adequate supply, as it may not be available locally. Take the prescription, with the generic rather than the brand name (which may not be locally available), as it will make getting replacements easier. It's a wise idea to have the prescription with you to show that you legally use the medication.

Water Purification

The simplest way of purifying water is to boil it thoroughly. Technically this means boiling for 10 minutes, something which happens very rarely! Remember that at high altitude water boils at lower temperature, so germs are less likely to be killed.

Simple filtering will not remove all dangerous organisms, so if you cannot boil water it should be treated chemically. Chlorine tablets (Puritabs, Steritabs or other brand names) will kill many but not all pathogens. Iodine is very effective in purifying water and is available in tablet form (such as Potable Aqua), but follow the directions carefully and remember that too much iodine can be harmful.

If you can't find tablets, tincture of iodine (2%) or iodine crystals can be used. Two drops of tincture of iodine per litre or quart of clear water is the recommended dosage; the treated water should be left to stand for 30 minutes before drinking. Iodine crystals can also be used to purify water but this is a more complicated process, as you have to first prepare a saturated iodine solution. Iodine loses its effectiveness if exposed to air or damp so keep it in a tightly sealed container. Flavoured powder will disguise the taste of treated water and is a good idea if you are travelling with children.

Nutrition

If your food is poor or limited in availability, if you're travelling hard and fast and therefore missing meals, or if you simply lose your appetite, you can soon start to lose weight and place your health at risk.

Make sure your diet is well balanced. If it isn't or if your food intake is insufficient, it's a good idea to take vitamin and iron pills.

Cold

Despite the perception by some that Canada is a perpetually ice-bound wasteland, health problems due to extreme cold are not likely to be suffered by many people. On winter days when frost bite is a possibility (due almost always to a combination of low temperature and high wind, the result of which is a reading known as the wind-chill factor) you will be aware of it. Everybody will be discussing it, the radio will broadcast warnings about how many minutes of exposed skin is acceptable and...it will be bloody cold.

If you are trekking at high altitudes or simply taking a long bus trip over mountains, particularly at night, be prepared. You should always be prepared for cold, wet or windy conditions even if you're just out walking or hitching.

Hypothermia occurs when the body loses heat faster than it can produce it and the core temperature of the body falls. It is surprisingly easy to progress from very cold to dangerously cold due to a combination of wind, wet clothing, fatigue and hunger, even if the air temperature is above freezing. It is best to dress in layers; silk, wool and some of the new artificial fibres are all good insulating materials. A hat is important, as a lot of heat is lost through the head. A strong, waterproof outer layer is essential, as keeping dry is vital. Carry basic supplies, including food containing simple sugars to generate heat quickly and take lots of fluid to drink.

Symptoms of hypothermia are exhaustion, numb skin (particularly toes and fingers), shivering, slurred speech, irrational or violent behaviour, lethargy, stumbling, dizzy spells, muscle cramps and violent bursts of energy. Irrationality may take the form of sufferers claiming they are warm and trying to take off their clothes.

To treat hypothermia, first get the patient out of the wind and/or rain, remove their clothing if its wet and replace it with dry, warm clothing. Give them hot liquids – not alcohol – and some high-kilojoule, easily digestible food. This should be enough for the early stages of hypothermia, but if it has gone further it may be necessary to place victims in warm sleeping bags and get in with them. Do not rub patients, place them near a fire or remove their wet clothes in the wind. If possible, place a sufferer in a warm (not hot) bath.

Sunburn & Windburn

Sunburn and windburn should be primary concerns for anyone planning to spend time trekking or travelling over snow and ice. The sun will burn you even if you feel cold and the wind will cause dehydration and chafing of skin. Use a good sunscreen and a moisture cream on exposed skin, even on cloudy days. A hat provides added protection and zinc oxide or some other barrier cream for your nose and lips is recommended if you're spending any time on ice or snow.

Reflection and glare from ice and snow can cause snow blindness so high-protection sunglasses should be considered essential for any sort of glacier visit or ski trip.

Altitude Sickness

Acute Mountain Sickness or AMS occurs at high altitude and can be fatal. The lack of oxygen at high altitudes affects most people to some extent. Take it easy at first, increase your liquid intake and eat well. Even with acclimatisation you may still have trouble adjusting – headaches, nausea, dizziness, a dry cough, insomnia, breathlessness and loss of appetite are all signs to heed. If you reach a high altitude by trekking, acclimatisation takes place gradually and you are less likely to be affected than if you fly straight there.

Mild altitude problems will generally abate after a day or so but if the symptoms persist or become worse the only treatment is to descend – even 500 metres can help. Breathlessness, a dry, irritative cough (which may progress to the production of pink, frothy sputum), severe headache, loss of appetite, nausea, and sometimes vomiting are all danger signs. Increasing tiredness, confusion, and lack of coordination and balance are real danger signs. Any of these symptoms individually, even just a persistent headache, can be a warning.

There is no hard and fast rule as to how high is too high: AMS has been fatal at altitudes of 3000 metres, although from 3500 to 4500 metres is the usual range. It is always wise to sleep at a lower altitude than the greatest height reached during the day.

Motion Sickness

Eating lightly before and during a trip will reduce the chances of motion sickness. If you are prone to motion sickness try to find a place that minimises disturbance – near the wing on aircraft, close to midships on boats (including ocean-going coastal ferries particularly the ones to/from or around Newfoundland), near the centre on buses.

Fresh air usually helps, but reading or inhaling cigarette smoke doesn't. Commercial antimotion-sickness preparations, which can cause drowsiness, have to be taken before the trip commences; when you're feeling sick it's too late. Ginger is a natural preventative and is available in capsule form. Gravol is a common over-the-counter tablet in Canada which is quite effective.

Giardia

If you're going to do a lot of camping, particularly in the backcountry and woods of Alberta or British Columbia, you should take precautions against an intestinal parasite (Giardia lamblia) which causes giardiasis, known colloquially as 'beaver fever'. Just 10 years ago the condition was considered rare and nobody had ever heard of it, but in the past few years it has been causing more and more hikers a lot of discomfort.

The organism inhabits streams, lakes and rivers, and is spread through human and animal faeces. Symptoms include diarrhoea, gasiness, cramps and vomiting. They may be mild or severe and may not hit for a week after contact. If they persist for more than 24 hours you should see a doctor.

Preventive measures include boiling water for about 10 minutes or using a water filter available at camping stores. Chemical treatment is not reliable.

Personally, I've got away without treating water at all, but the odds on this are worsening.

Sexually Transmitted Diseases

In common with other Western countries, Canada has its share of sexually transmitted diseases. As might be expected, the rates for such conditions are highest in the large cities. Sexual contact with an infected sexual partner spreads these diseases. While abstinence is the only 100% preventative, using condoms is also effective.

Gonorrhoea and syphilis are the most common of these diseases; sores, blisters or rashes around the genitals, discharges or pain when urinating are common symptoms. Symptoms may be less marked or not observed at all in women. Syphilis symptoms eventually disappear completely but the disease continues and can cause severe problems in later years. The treatment of gonorrhoea and syphilis is by antibiotics.

There are numerous other sexually transmitted diseases, for most of which effective treatment is available. However, there is no cure for herpes and there is also currently no cure for AIDS. Using condoms is the most effective preventative.

AIDS can be spread through infected blood transfusions and by dirty needles – vaccinations, acupuncture and tattooing can potentially be as dangerous as intravenous drug use if the equipment is not clean. If you do need an injection it may be a good idea to buy a new syringe from a pharmacy and ask the doctor to use it.

The homosexual community has the highest proportion of HIV-postive people in Canada but currently the disease is spreading more quickly through straight society.

Rabies

This isn't a major problem, but rabies is something to be aware of when spending any time in the woods or undeveloped areas. Animals most likely affected are the squirrel, skunk, racoon and particularly, the fox. Paradoxically, all of the above animals have learned to adapt quite well to populated regions, and may be seen in city parks and recreation areas, wooded areas around rivers and streams and even along residential streets after dark. Especially on garbage nights!

Rabies is caused by a bite or scratch by an infected animal. Any bite, scratch or even lick from a mammal should be cleaned immediately and thoroughly. Scrub with soap and running water, and then clean with an alcohol solution. If there is any possibility that the animal is infected, medical help should be sought immediately. Even if the animal is not rabid, all bites should be treated seriously as they can become infected or can result in tetanus. A rabies vaccination is now available and should be considered if you are in a high-risk category – eg, if you intend to explore caves (bat bites could be dangerous) or work with animals.

Lyme Disease

Less of a threat but still something to be aware of is the recently publicised Lyme disease (doesn't it seem as though there's always something new out there to get you?).

In the past five years or so each summer sees more of this disease although the vast majority of North American cases have occurred in the USA. The disease is really more of a condition transmitted by a certain species of deer tick, similar to a tick found on a dog but smaller. The tick infects the skin with the spirochete bacterium which causes the disease.

The disease was first identified on the continent in 1975 in Lyme, Connecticut, hence the name. Most cases still go undetected, misdiagnosed or unreported. It is a difficult disease to diagnose because symptoms vary widely. Consult a doctor if you experience the following:

Sometime within 30 days after being bitten a small red bump appears surrounded by a rash often but not always accompanied by flu-like symptoms.

Treatment with antibiotics is simple and effective, if the disease is caught at this early stage. Later symptoms can be quite severe and include a form of arthritis which affects the knees.

The best way to avoid the whole business is to take precautions in areas where it has been reported. So far the few Canadian cases seem to be in the far west or in the far east. California, Washington, Minnesota and New England have had most of the US cases. If you hear anything about it in an area where you are hiking or walking in the woods, cover the body as much as possible, use an insect repellent containing diethyl-metatoluamide (DEET) and at the end of the day check yourself, children or pets for the ticks. Chances are that you will not feel it if bitten. Of course, most ticks are not the right sort to pass on the disease and even most of the nasties do not carry the harmful bacteria.

All this horror just mentioned really isn't so bad but it's better to hear the worst than be innocently caught. Millions spend time in the bush each year and actually live to tell about it. And besides, this is the only kind of terrorism you have to concern yourself with in Canada – bugs are better than bombs.

Blackflies & Mosquitoes

In the woods of Canada, particularly in the north, the blackflies and mosquitoes can be murder – they seems to get worse the further north you get. There are tales of lost hikers going insane from the bugs. This is no joke – they can make you miserable. As a rule, darker clothes are said to attract biting insects more than lighter ones. Perfume, too, evidently attracts the wrong kind of attention. Take bug juice or spray. Two recommended names are Muskol and Off; the latter also has an extra strength version known as Deep Woods Off. It's also a good idea to minimise the amount of skin exposed by wearing a long-sleeved shirt, long pants and a close-fitting hat or cap.

June is the worst month, and as the summer wears on or if things are dry the bugs disappear. Some years they are not much of a problem but during other years it's very bad, depending on weather and other conditions.

The bugs are at their worst deep in the woods. In clearings, along shorelines or anywhere there's a breeze you'll be safe, except for the buzzing horseflies, which are basically teeth with wings.

Mosquitoes come out around sunset, building a fire will help keep them away. Try to have a tent with a zippered screen.

If you do get lost and are being eaten, submerge your body if there's water around. This will enable you to think clearly about where you are and what to do. Lemon or orange peel rubbed on your skin will help if you're out of repellent.

Other Stings & Bites

Canada is relatively problem-free regarding stings and bites. There are no poisonous spiders or insects. Rattlesnakes do live in parts of Ontario and British Columbia but are rarely seen – even by serious hikers – and actually are generally timid. Still the bite is a matter of concern and immediate medical attention is essential. The normal run of bees, wasps and hornets is found across the country. Those with allergies should carry kits outside of urban areas.

WOMEN TRAVELLERS

The smell of perfumes and fragrant cosmetics attracts bears so, if you're likely to be in an area where they're around, it's best not to wear any. Women who are menstruating should also be cautious.

Care should be taken when hitchhiking, especially if you're travelling alone – use common sense and don't be afraid to say no to lifts.

Some parts of the downtown areas of major cities should be avoided at night especially on a Friday or Saturday.

DANGERS & ANNOYANCES

Check the Health section earlier for some of the health risks you should be aware of. See also Road Rules & Safety in the Getting Around chapter for tips about driving.

Fire

When bedding down outside legitimate campgrounds do not start a fire. This is extremely dangerous and could cause untold amounts of devastation during the dry summer months.

One couple did so and when nailed by the local authorities pointed to this book and said 'He said we could set up camp anywhere!' So please give both yourself and me a break.

Mark Lightbody

In designated campgrounds make sure that anything that was burning is put out completely when you've finished with it, including cigarettes.

Bears

A serious problem encountered when you're camping in the woods is the animals – most importantly bears – who are always looking for an easy snack. Keep your food in nylon bags; a sleeping-bag sack is good. Tie the sack to a rope and sling it over a branch away from your tent. Hoist it up high enough so a standing bear can't reach it. Don't leave food scraps around the site and never, ever keep food in the tent.

Don't try to get close-up photographs of bears and never come between a bear and its cubs. If you see any cubs, quietly and quickly disappear. If you do see a bear, try to get upwind so it can smell you and you won't startle it. While hiking through woods or in the mountains in bear country, some people wear a noise-maker, like a bell. Talking or singing is just as good. Whatever you do, don't feed bears – they lose their fear of people and eventually their lives to park wardens.

ACTIVITIES

Canada's greatest attribute is its natural environment. This, for the most part, is what it has to offer visitors, what makes it unique. Much of Canada's appeal lies in the range of physical activities possible. Camping, hiking, canoeing, fishing, skiing and observing flora & fauna quickly come to mind.

There are wilderness trips of all types,

organised or self-directed. Long-distance cycling has become more popular recently. There is downhill skiing in many parts of the country – slopes in the Rockies are excellent and higher than any in the European Alps. Hang-gliding is always gaining converts. People even surf off the west coast. And if you want to try your luck, you can pan for gold. Although the season is short, boating is very popular across the country. It has been said there are more boats per capita in Canada than anywhere except Sweden.

Provincial tourist offices have information on activities in their region and also details on private businesses offering adventure tours and trips. Many provinces have booklets and maps on canoeing and hiking. All have information on national and provincial parks, many of which can be highlights of a trip to Canada.

But also enticing are the clean, safe and vital cities where you can find arts and cultural activities if the outdoors starts to wear you down.

Entering the various lotteries is a favourite Canadian pastime.

ACCOMMODATION
Camping
There are campgrounds all over Canada – federal, provincial and privately owned. Government sites are always better and cheaper and, not surprisingly, fill up the quickest. Government parks are well laid out, green and well treed. They are usually quiet, situated to take advantage of the local landscape and offer a programme of events and talks. The private campgrounds are generally less geared to tenters, more to those with trailers or recreational vehicles (RVs) of one sort or another and often have more mod cons and services available as well as swimming pools and other entertainment facilities.

RVs are mobile homes which range from moderate campers, basically a small apartment on a pick-up truck, to full-sized motor homes. The majority you'll see are from the USA, but many RVs are also rented in Canada – at rental outlets in places like Whitehorse, Vancouver and Edmonton – by non-Canadians to use as their mobile vacation hotels. If you're surprised by the size and features of some of these suckers you should be: they come with price tags of up to half a million dollars.

In national parks, camping fees range from $9 to $12 for an unserviced site, and to as high as $16 for sites with services like electricity.

The Canadian Government Office of Tourism, 150 Kent St, Ottawa, Ontario, publishes three guides on camping across Canada.

Provincial park camping rates vary with each province but range from $7.50 to $16. Interior camping in the wilderness parks is always less, about $4. Commercial campgrounds are generally several dollars more expensive than either provincial or national parks.

Government parks start closing in early September for the winter. Dates vary according to the location. Some remain open for maintenance even when camping is finished. Sometimes they let you in at a reduced rate; maybe the showers or something are turned off. Other places, late in fall or early in spring, are free. The gate is open and there is not a soul around. Still others block the road and you just can't enter the grounds. So, out of the main summer season you have to investigate. It can save you a fair bit of money.

There are also campgrounds every 150 km or so along the Trans Canada Highway.

Lastly, many people travel around the country camping and never pay a dime. For those with cars or vans, using roadside rest areas and picnic spots is recommended. I've done this many times. If there are signs indicating no overnight camping, don't do something like set up a tent. If you're asleep in the car and a cop happens to wake you, just say you were driving, got tired, pulled over for a quick rest and fell asleep: 'What time is it, anyway?'. For less chance of interruption, little side roads and logging roads off the highway are quiet and private.

For cyclists and hitchhikers, just walking

off into the woods or fields from the roadside and rolling out the sleeping bag is good enough. It's done all over the country. This is a bit of a hassle on the prairies where there's not much to disappear behind, but it can be done.

Youth Hostels

Youth Hostels, operated by the Canadian Hostelling Association in conjunction with the IYHF, are the cheapest places to stay and are where you'll probably meet the most travellers. There are about 60 hostels in Canada costing from $7 to $16.

Most of the main cities have a hostel and some provinces have quite a few scattered around more or less randomly. There are fortunately quite a few places in and around the Rocky Mountain national parks. The province of British Columbia also has an informal network of privately run hostels which charge about the same rates as the official ones. Quebec, too, has some of the unofficial variety.

In July and August space may be a problem at some Canadian hostels particularly in the large cities and in some of the small mountain places. In Montreal, Quebec and Toronto calling ahead is not a bad idea. Ottawa and Vancouver are also busy.

Hostel members are entitled to lower overnight costs but nonmembers are welcomed at all hostels. In addition, members can often take advantage of discounts offered by various businesses, including outdoor equipment sold at one of half a dozen hostel shops. Local hostels should have a list of where the various bargains can be had. Hostel stores also sell guide books, sleeping sheets and other travel accessories. At some of the regional offices outdoor activities such as canoeing, climbing or skiing are organised.

Membership costs $25 and is good around the world for a year. Family and senior memberships are also available. This is the American Express Card of budget travel: don't leave home without it. It's usually cheaper and more convenient to get a membership in your own country. The handbook will give you the hostels' addresses, dates and rules. Many Canadian hostels are closed in winter. Don't rely solely on the information in the handbook; it's often incorrect.

The national office is in a suburb of Ottawa. One-year memberships are available through this office or at the various provincial offices. The address is: Canadian Hostelling Association (☎ (613) 748-5638; fax (613) 748-5750), Suite 608, 1600 James Naismith Drive, Gloucester, Ontario K1B 5N4.

Salvation Army

Male travellers who are desperate or looking for some 'edge', can likely find a place at Salvation Army hostels for a couple of nights. They're often free and they throw in meals, but remember that they're not operated to cater for travelling youth: the Salvation Army (Sally Ann) is mainly populated by unemployed men – often alcoholics – and the environment isn't particularly pleasant.

YM-YWCA

The familiar YM-YWCAs still offer good accommodation in a style between that of a hostel and a hotel, but prices have been creeping up. In YM-YWCAs where complete renovations have occurred, costs can now be as high as those of a cheap hotel, especially if there are two of you. However, some places permit couples and doubles are pretty fair value.

YM-YWCAs are very clean and quiet and often have swimming pools and cheap cafeterias. The average price for men is from $24 to $28 a single, and usually a bit more for women. Some of the big city Ys are now concentrating more on fitness and recreation and are getting out of offering accommodation. For a complete list and information write to: YMCA National Council, 2160 Yonge St, Toronto, Ontario M4S 2A1.

Universities

Many universities rent out beds in their residence dormitories during the summer months. The 'season' runs roughly from May to some time in August with possible closures for large academic conferences, etc. Prices average $25 a day and, at many places, students are offered a further reduction. Campus residences are open to all including families and seniors.

Reservations are accepted but aren't necessary. Breakfasts are sometimes included in the price but if not, there is generally a cafeteria which cooks up low-priced meals. The other campus facilities such as swimming pools are available to guests.

Sometimes annual directories of the various residences are published and may be available on the campus through the residence manager, the alumni association or general information.

Efficiency Units
This form of accommodation includes a small kitchen and basic cooking supplies.

Guesthouses & Tourist Homes
Another alternative is the simple guesthouse or tourist home. These may be an extra room in someone's home but are more commonly commercial lodging houses. They are found mainly in places with a large tourist trade such as Niagara, Banff, Victoria and Quebec. In Quebec's principal centres they are popular and plentiful, and usually the best places to stay.

Rooms range in size and have varying amenities. Some include private bathrooms, many do not. The standard cost is about $35 to $50 a double, but could be a bit lower or a lot higher.

Some so-called tourist homes are really rooming houses rented more often by the week or longer and usually have shared kitchens. These places are normally used by local people but can be good for long stays. Rates are lower for long-term rentals.

B&Bs
B&Bs have caught on in Canada only in the past decade or so, but they are springing up quickly, offering a decent alternative to the top and bottom-end hotels. Many cities have associations which manage local member houses; other places are listed directly with tourist offices and are run independently. Some operate as businesses, others just provide part-time income for a few months in the summer. Several guidebooks dealing exclusively with this type of lodging can be found in all provinces both in towns and the countryside, and now appear regularly on bookstore shelves.

Prices of B&Bs vary quite a bit, ranging roughly from $20 for a single to $80 a double with the average being from $40 to $55 for two people. Rooms are almost always in the owner's home and are clean and well kept. Note that smoking is almost always prohibited. Some places will take children and the odd one will allow a pet.

Hotels
Good, inexpensive hotels are not a Canadian strong point. Though there is a wide range of hotel types, the word usually means one of two things to a Canadian – a rather expensive place to stay or a cheap place to drink. Most new hotels are part of international chains and are designed for either the luxury market or for business people.

Canadian liquor laws have been historically linked to renting beds, so the older, cheap hotels are often principally bars, and quite often low-class bars at that. This type of place is found all over the country. For the impecunious who don't mind some noise and a somewhat worn room they can come in handy. Prices are usually from $15 to $25 a single, but rooms are often taken by more permanent guests on a monthly basis. There are some places in this category which are quite alright and which are mentioned through the text. Perhaps they are not suitable for families in the main or females travelling alone, couples and single males may find these basic hotels more than adequate.

Between the very new and the very old hotels, there are places to be found in the smallish band in between. In the larger cities in particular, you can still find good older, small hotels which mainly rent rooms. Prices vary with the amenities and location and range from about $30 to $75 for singles or doubles.

Overall in Canada, Quebec excepted, there are few of the quaint, charming old hotels you come across in European cities. An encouraging sign is that there are a few more now than when the first edition of this guide appeared. The alternatives to the hotels are motels, B&Bs, tourist homes, and various types of hostels. It is these places which are stressed in this book.

Motels

In Canada, like the USA (both lands of the automobile), motels are ubiquitous, and until the early 1980s represented the only form of moderately priced accommodation. Mostly they are simple and clean, if somewhat nondescript. Many can be found dotting the highways and clustered on the main highway on either side of larger towns and cities. They usually range from $25 to $70 for singles or doubles with an average being about $50.

Outside the cities, prices drop so motels can be a bargain, especially if there are two or more of you. Before entering a big city it's a good idea to get off the main route and onto one of the smaller, older roads. This is where you'll find motels as cheaply as they come.

Prices tend to go up in summer or when a special event is on. Off-season bargaining is definitely worthwhile. This needn't be haggling as in a Moroccan market; just a simple counter-offer will sometimes work. Unlike many hotels, motels are still pretty much 'mom and pop' operations and so retain more flexibility and often reflect more of the character of the owners.

Farm Vacations

Each province has a farm vacation programme enabling visitors to stay on working farms for a day, a week or longer. The size and type of farm vary considerably, as do the activities you can take part in. There are usually chores you can help out with and animals to tend. In the west there are ranches to stay at. Rates range from roughly $25 to $30 for singles, $35 to $65 for doubles

depending on meals taken. There are also family rates and reductions for children.

FOOD

Canadian gastronomy was long based on the British 'bland is beautiful' tradition (although it never quite reached the unimaginative depths of British food). While there are still no distinctive national dishes or unique culinary delights, good food is certainly plentiful. The large numbers of varying ethnic groups spread across the country continue to have a large hand in epicurean improvements. In addition, speciality shops, increased sophistication and knowledge (often through travel) and the natural and health-food movements have all cut into the mainstream and taken business from the ever present and internationally familiar giant fast-food outlets.

In most cities it's not difficult to find a Greek, Italian, Indian or Chinese meal. Small bistro-type places, often with lots of plants, occur across the country with menus emphasising freshness, spices and the latest trends. They tend to fill the gap between the greasy spoons and the priciest restaurants. The former are found throughout Canada with names like 'George's' or 'Linda's Place'. Little changed since the 1930s, these small, basic places are the blue-collar workers' restaurants. Some are excellent, some bad news, but they're always cheap. There's usually a breakfast special until 11 am for about $3, followed by a couple of lunch specials. A fairly balanced, if functional, meal costs around $5.

Canadian bread, as a rule, is pathetic. For some improvement from the packaged stuff go to a baker, delicatessen or health-food store.

Fruit, in summer, is a good Canadian bargain and the apples, peaches, cherries, etc are superb. In June watch for strawberries; in August, blueberries. Farmers' stands are often seen along highways and secondary roads.

Canada produces some very good cheeses, in particular, cheddars – mild, medium and old. Oka from Quebec is a more expensive, subtler and very tasty cheese developed by monks.

On both coasts, seafood is plentiful, delicious and affordable. On the west coast the salmon in several varieties is a real treat, fresh or smoked. The east coast has the less known but highly esteemed freshwater Atlantic salmon which some consider the finest of them all. The Atlantic region is also famous for lobster and scallops. In the far north Arctic char is a speciality. The king of inland fish gastronomically is the walleye, often called pickerel.

Canadians favourite chocolate bar is the Crispy Crunch which in early 1991 was first introduced to the US market in the hope that they will feel the same way about it.

Lastly, one truly Canadian creation must be mentioned: the butter tart. This delectable little sweet can best be described as...well, just get on the outside of one and you'll see.

French Food

Most of the country's few semi-original repasts come from the French of Quebec. French pea soup is thick, filling and delicious. The *tourtières* (meat pies) are worth sampling. Quebec is also the world's largest producer of maple syrup, made in the spring when the sap is running, and it's great on pancakes or ice cream. French fries (chips) in Quebec, especially those bought at the small roadside chip wagons are unbeatable – the world's best. Further east into the Atlantic Provinces the Acadian French carry on some of their centuries-old culinary traditions in such dishes as rapie pie (*paté à la rapure*) – a type of meat pie (maybe beef, chicken or clam) topped with grated paste-like potato from which all the starch has been drawn.

Native Indian Food

Native Indian foods based on wild game such as deer (venison) and pheasant are something to sample if the opportunity presents itself. Buffalo meat, just beginning to be sold commercially in a few places, turns up on menus occasionally. It's lean and has more protein and less cholesterol than beef.

The fiddlehead is a distinctive green only edible in springtime. It's primarily picked from the woodlands of the Maritime Provinces.

Wild rice, with its black husks and almost nutty flavour is very tasty and often accompanies Native Indian-style meals. Most of it is picked by hand around the Ontario and Manitoba borders but it's widely available in natural food shops.

Markets

Many cities have farmers' markets one or more days a week where fresh produce can be bought at good prices. Roadside stands offering the crops of the season can be found in all rural areas. The corn is something to look for and is easy to prepare. On the coasts, seafood can often be purchased at the docks.

Prices

The variety and quality of meals available across the country has risen appreciably since the first edition of this book (1983). Of course prices have gone up, too, but are not out of line compared with what you'd pay elsewhere. As with most things, food here is costlier than in the USA. If you're from Europe, though, or are travelling with a strong currency, you'll find prices reasonable.

Generally for dinner under $8 is cheap, from $8 to $15 is moderate, and from $15 to $25 getting up there, and anything higher than that is expensive. Lunches are a lot less. Most of the places mentioned in this book fit into the first two categories but costlier places are listed for treats and splurges.

DRINKS
Alcohol

Getting a drink can be a little difficult or at least inconvenient due to a range of laws and regulations concerning alcohol. Alcoholic beverages as a rule must be bought at government stores which are usually closed at night and always on Sundays and holidays. In Quebec, beer and wine can be bought in grocery stores.

Closing time for bars and nightclubs is

generally 1 or 2 am. In Quebec it's 3 or 4 am. Some bars in the large cities remain open later but cannot serve booze past the 'closing hour'.

Restaurants with applicable licences, and this includes all the better ones and those in hotels, serve liquor but must conform to the same hours as drinking establishments.

Beer Canadian beer, in general, is good, not great. It's tastier and stronger than US brands and is always served cold. Lagers are by far the most popular beers but ales, light beers, porters and stouts are all available. The two big companies are Molson and Labatts, with the most popular beers being Molson Export Ale and Canadian Lager, or Labatts 50 Ale and Blue Lager.

A very welcome new trend is the advent of small breweries producing real or natural beers and pubs brewing their own for consumption on the premises. Both these new breaks from tradition are developing rapidly across the country but are most evident in the large cities.

In a bar, a pint (340 ml) ranges from $1.75 to $4.50. Draught beer, sold only in bars, is the cheapest way to drink; a 170-ml glass can cost as low as 90 cents. Prices usually go up after the night's entertainment arrives. Retail, beer in cases (bottles or cans) costs about $1 a bottle.

Wine Canadian wine has long had a deservedly poor reputation. Recently the product has improved, in some cases considerably, but the stigma continues undiminished. True, the lowest cost wines are the domestics and they taste as cheap as the price. But each of the Canadian wineries now also takes great care with at least some of their brands.

The country has two main wine-producing regions, Ontario's Niagara Peninsula with by far the largest share and British Columbia's Okanagan Valley. Wineries can also be found in southern Quebec, elsewhere in Ontario and in Nova Scotia. The best known ones are the ones of the Niagara district.

In southern Ontario there are three viticul-

tural areas, the Niagara Peninsula, the Lake Erie Shoreline and Pelee Island which is out in Lake Erie. These areas now have their own Vintners Quality Alliance (VQA) grading and classification system meant to establish and maintain standards for the better wines in much the same way as is done in Europe. Wines sporting the VQA label are among the ones recommended to sample.

Red, white, dry and sweet are all produced as are some sparkling wines, but the dry whites are Canada's best.

Import duties keep foreign wine prices up to protect the Canadian wine industry but you can still get a pretty low-priced bottle of French wine.

Spirits Canada produces its own gins, vodkas, rums, liqueurs, brandies and coolers. But Canadian whisky, generally known in the country as rye, is the best known liquor and the one with the biggest reputation. Canadian Club and VO rye whisky are Canada's most famous drinks – good stuff. Rye is generally taken with ginger ale or soda but some like it straight with ice. Canadian whisky has been distilled since the mid-1800s and has been popular in the USA as well as Canada from the early days of production. Most of the high price of spirits in Canada is attributable to tax.

Other Drinks
The fruit-growing areas of Quebec, Ontario and British Columbia produce excellent apple and cherry ciders, some with alcohol, some without. In Quebec and the Atlantic or Maritime Provinces, visitors may want to sample a local nonalcoholic brew called spruce beer. It's produced in small batches by individuals and doesn't have a large commercial base but is sold in some local stores. It varies quite a bit and you can never be too sure what will happen when the cap comes off, but some people love the stuff.

Canadian mineral and spring waters have recently become quite popular and are now readily available.

Getting There & Away

AIR

Probably the most common way to enter Canada is via its well known neighbour to the south, the good ol' USA. Apart from American visitors reaching Canada overland, most cheap overseas flights to North America go to the USA, with New York, San Francisco and Los Angeles as the major destinations. You can then either fly to a major Canadian city, such as Montreal or Vancouver, or catch a bus or train.

Shopping for airfares is another story. The airline business in and out of Canada is the same as in most places – largely a mystery. Trying to track down prices and deals is like trying to pin jello to the wall. Things change and prices go up and down by the day, even by the phone call. Nothing is consistent; deals come and go; international routes and prices change continually. The best advice is to ask a lot of questions: as always, persistence, ingenuity and luck will get you everywhere.

If it's possible, shop in a city that has a high number of budget travellers passing through; you'll find the best bargains in such cities. The most famous of these are London, Athens and Bangkok. Sydney, Hong Kong, Kuala Lumpur and Manila are others. If these departure points are not feasible, shop around the travel agents at home. There are often travel agencies which specialise in trips to North America and which will know of organised charters or good deals.

One of the difficulties in air travel is that most airlines, particularly the larger ones (including the Canadian companies flying internationally), provide the greatest discount on return tickets rather than on one-way fares. Some travellers have gotten around this by buying a return ticket, using it to get to Canada, then selling the unused portion – naturally, this is highly improper. However, tickets are still rarely checked for names.

To/From UK & Europe

The British Airways direct flight to Montreal is UK£354, C$731. There are no standby or youth fares available, but there are a number of budget and charter deals available from large travel agencies and bucket shops.

Budget Airlines Every couple of years a small upstart airline arrives on the scene and creates a sensation with fares that undercut everybody else's on the cross-Atlantic route. Unfortunately they don't seem to have any staying power. They usually fly into and out of New York from a Western European city. Laker lasted quite a while and was followed briefly by Highland Express; more recently, Virgin Atlantic, and the classic People Express have flown into history. If you're lucky, a new one will spring up just before you leave.

More stable and worth looking into is Sabena Belgian International Airlines, which may have a deal between Brussels and Montreal.

Charters If you are travelling between Europe and Canada you might investigate these. Most charter trips with a Canadian connection are between Canada and Europe. Others connect to US destinations, mostly Florida or Hawaii, or the Caribbean.

Air Canada runs charters from London, Paris and Frankfurt to Toronto. The cheapest are from London with a maximum stay of six months. Fares vary a lot depending on the time of year, with the summer months and Christmas being the most expensive season. In any case an advance booking of 21 days is required. One-way fares are expensive and generally there are not any deals to be had on them. Return fares are around UK£675 from London. These are all to Toronto. Quite often the cost of a one-way fare is not a lot different to a return. In such cases, many people sell the other half of their return ticket when they get to Canada. Canadian Airlines also runs charters from London and Amsterdam for about the same price. It is always worthwhile to check on one-way fares, though.

Private Canadian charter companies are also active but the names change relatively quickly. Some of the bigger, better established ones work in conjunction with one of the two principal Canadian airline companies.

There are probably good charters from France to the province of Quebec. Travel agencies or student offices there could help you out.

To/From USA British Airways offers some one-way fares to the new world. From the UK to John F Kennedy Airport, New York, the one-way, mid-week fare is UK£350 or C$723.

A good alternative is Icelandic Air. They fly between Luxemburg and New York via Reykjavik. These flights have always been among the cheapest across the Atlantic.

From New York, it's about an eight-hour bus ride or a 10-hour train ride to Montreal. For fares see the Getting There & Away section for Montreal.

Flights between US and Canadian cities are abundant and frequent. Between larger cities there are generally direct flights. Montreal, Toronto and Vancouver are the busiest Canadian destinations but all major cities are plugged into the extensive north American system.

Canadian Airlines flies from Los Angeles, California, to Vancouver for US$288 plus taxes, one way.

Air Canada flies in and out of New York City to Montreal and Toronto. A one-way New York City to Toronto ticket costs US$152. American Airlines also serves this route.

To/From Australia & NZ

Continental Airlines, Canadian Airlines, United Airlines, Qantas and Air New Zealand offer regular flights to Vancouver from Australia and New Zealand.

Qantas offers standard economy fares

from Australia to Canada: a one-way ticket to Vancouver is A$1337 all year. A return ticket varies through high, mid and low seasons with fluctuations even within each time period category. Prices vary from a low of $1690 to a high of $2448. As a rule, the shorter the length of stay, the lower the fare.

From Auckland the regular return economy fare is from around NZ$1800 to NZ$2000. Discount fares are available with varying conditions attached from around NZ$1600.

Coming from Australia, New Zealand or Asia, landing in the USA is often cheaper than flying directly to Canada. After arriving in Los Angeles, San Francisco, or possibly Seattle (Washington state) on the west coast, a train (as far as Seattle) or bus will take you to Vancouver.

Qantas and Air New Zealand flights from Australia to US cities (in California), are lower by up to A$150 or so. In addition, they often include many stopovers in the Pacific – in Fiji, Raratonga, Honolulu and even Tahiti.

The fares given are only the airlines' official fares. You will find the best deals by shopping around the travel agencies.

To/From Asia

From Asia it's often cheaper to fly first to the USA rather than directly to Canada. Singapore Airlines and Korean Airlines run cheap flights around the Pacific, ending on the USA's west coast.

Check in Singapore and in travel agencies in Bangkok and Kuala Lumpur. You can probably find one-way fares from these centres to the USA's west coast, with up to five stops, for under US$750, and for around US$900 return.

From Hong Kong, one-way fares to Los Angeles, San Francisco – or, for a few dollars more, Vancouver – are also decent and much cheaper than going the other way. The regular one-way fare to San Francisco is around HK$2500, to Vancouver HK$3150.

Round-the-World Tickets

If you are covering a lot of distance, a

Round-the-World (RTW) ticket could be worthwhile. A good ticket can include a lot of stops in places all over the world, with a maximum ticket validity of 12 months. Check out the huge variety of RTW tickets available.

Out of Canada, Air Canada in conjunction with other airlines offers such tickets. Air Canada uses just one other airline per ticket, but which airline that is varies. Depending on which you select the price of the fare will change. Two that are regularly part of such a deal are Singapore Airlines and Cathay Pacific.

Air Canada and Singapore Airlines offer a RTW fare of C$3131 for unlimited stopovers (their destinations only), going in one direction over a period of not more than 12 months. Side trips can be arranged in Europe at reasonable cost. Similar fares are offered out of many countries but you should investigate in the country of first departure.

LAND
Bus
The Greyhound bus network connects the major continental US cities with most major destinations in Canada. Note, however, that the multi-day passes available in the USA cannot be used in Canada. If you're using a US pass, enquire as to how close you can get to your Canadian destination before having to buy a separate ticket. Gray Line of Alaska buses connect Fairbanks, Anchorage, Skagway and Haines in Alaska with Whitehorse in the Yukon.

Train
Amtrak has three main routes between the USA and Canada: these are New York City to Montreal (10 hours), New York City to Toronto (12 hours) and Chicago to Toronto (11 hours; via Detroit 14 hours). For information about fares and schedules contact Amtrak (☎ 800-872-7245 toll free), 400 N Capitol St NW, Washington, DC 20001, USA.

Car
The highway system of the continental USA connects directly with the Canadian highway system along the border at numerous points, which then meet up with the Trans Canada Highway a little further north. Between Canada and Alaska the main routes are the Alaska, Klondike and Taylor highways. Visitors with US or British passports are allowed to bring their vehicles in for six months.

SEA
Yacht
Many flights from Australasia stop off in Hawaii. With a bit of persistence and luck it might be possible to find someone with a yacht who needs a hand. Hawaii is a favourite vacation spot with Western Canadians, but don't count on hitting the jackpot.

If you're coming from the Caribbean you might also find a yacht there (it's been done). Most head for Florida and from there, some edge up the east coast. Experienced sailors and females have the best chance at getting a place on board.

Freighter
This type of cheap, adventurous, romantic travel is pretty well extinct. What with government regulations and Seafarers Unions, etc most ships' captains won't even want to bother telling you to forget it. Regular passenger-carrying cruises and the freighters which make a point of taking passengers are now usually more expensive than flying. Most people will tell you it's boring anyway.

If you're really interested, Norwegian Shipping Lines is said to be more flexible about hiring and taking travellers on board. Check around northern Europe for a ship on its way to Montreal or New York.

Ford's International Cruise Guide is a quarterly guide listing all freighters with dates and ports of call. Single issues or annual subscriptions are available at reasonable prices. Write to Box 505, 22151 Clarendon St, Woodland Hills, California 91365. Travel agents may also be of help.

Ferry
On the west coast there are ferries between Washington state and Victoria on Vancouver

Island. From Port Hardy on northern Vancouver Island ferries also head north along the Inside Passage to Alaska. See Port Hardy and the Getting There & Away section for Victoria in the British Columbia chapter.

On the east coast, Canada is connected with the USA by several ferries. Yarmouth, Nova Scotia, is linked to Bar Harbour, Maine, and to Portland, Maine in the USA. From Deer Island, another ferry links the New Brunswick mainland.

LEAVING CANADA
Departure Tax

There is a departure/airport tax of $40 levied on all international flights out of Canada, other than those to US destinations.

Most tickets purchased in Canada for international flights out of Canada include this tax; but tickets out of Canada, purchased in another country, usually don't include it. If you did buy your ticket in another country and it didn't include departure tax, you will be asked for this tax after you pass through customs and immigration. When you're changing money, consider saving enough to cover it.

Also, sales taxes and the GST may or may not be included in any quoted airline ticket in Canada so ask.

Getting Around

Within Canada, land travel is much cheaper and, of course, much more interesting than flying. The bus network is the most expensive public transportation system and is generally less expensive than the now limited train service. VIA Rail, the national passenger train service does, however, offer some multi-day passes as well as discount prices for travelling on specific days, for example during mid-week. Driving costs are reasonable, with gasoline prices considerably lower than those in Europe although quite a bit higher than in the USA.

Still, it's a big country and if you really want to get around quickly, your wallet will be thinned. Air fares are expensive, but for those with a little extra money and not much time, the odd flight may be useful. Flying in Canada actually works out a few cents cheaper per km than owning and operating a car. And an open eye and ear can often turn up one of the ever-changing specials or 'seat sales' (last-minute ticket price reductions).

AIR

Unlike the US market, the airline business in Canada has been very regulated and this keeps prices high. There has been and continues to be talk of opening things up but when or how or by how much, nobody knows. Recently more flights by US carriers have been permitted in. An 'open skies' policy – a sort of a free trade of the air system – would mean even more US airlines in Canada and maybe lower fares. On the other hand, critics say, it would spell the end of Canadian airline companies which would be unable viably to match the lower prices.

Canadian airlines have been struggling for the past few years and this has meant the end of many and the amalgamation of others. The country now has just two major airlines: the government-owned Air Canada (although the Conservative government has talked of dumping it), and in second place, Canadian

Airlines (formerly CP Air, Pacific Western, Eastern Provincial and several secondary carriers), usually referred to simply as Canadian.

There are also numerous regional and local airlines, ranging from the fairly extensive Quebecair to tiny northern charter companies. Companies serving specific areas include Air Gaspé in eastern Quebec, Great Lakes in the central region and Norcanair in the north. Altogether, these airlines cover most small cities and towns across the country. Many of them now work in conjunction with one of the two main carriers.

The prices and schedules of flights change and fluctuate incredibly often. Phone an airline one week, and the next week they'll tell you something quite different. This is especially true of the main airlines, and often works to the buyer's advantage. The best thing to do is shop around – directly with the airline or through a travel agent – and be as flexible as you can. Waiting a day or two or avoiding a weekend flight could save you a lot.

Air Canada may be cheap for one flight, Canadian Airlines for another, although each keeps pretty well abreast of what the other is up to. Each offers some discounts through excursion rates.

Both airlines offer youth fares to passengers between 12 and 21 years of age. On Air Canada, these are valid all year. On Canadian the youth fare is valid from mid-June to mid-September, excluding weekends. Both of these youth fares are standby and can mean reductions of about 30% or more. Standby policies come and go so ask around.

The best bargains are excursion fares – a return flight with minimum and maximum stays. These normally need to be booked two weeks or a month in advance.

Occasionally, there are short-term specials for promotion of a certain flight; these can be very cheap but are irregular. Canadian Airlines occasionally offers 'seat sales'.

Economical charters between various Canadian cities as well as US destinations turn up throughout the year but highest prices are in July and August and around Christmas. There's a varying minimum stay and a maximum of one year. No student or youth fares are offered on these types of tickets.

For students under the age of 26 with an International Student Identity Card (ISIC), Quebecair and possibly still Nordair (now part of Canadian) have reductions of between 35% and 45%.

Another thing to consider is getting a ticket for points A to B and stopping off in the middle. This can often be done for little more than the straight-through fare.

Canadian Airlines and Air Canada sometimes offer fly-drive packages which cover the air fare and car rental. The packages, only available on return flights, sometimes include accommodation. Other possibilities include reductions on cars, hotels and bus tours. The hotels used, however, are expensive. Air Canada has had – and may still have – a plan with reduced rates at university dorms as well. You just have to ask about the latest gimmicks and offers. Canada's package-tour companies sometimes organise charter trips across or around the country using such exclusively charter airlines as Nationair. These trips can be very inexpensive. For information on these possibilities inquire at a travel agency; they handle all such packages.

Many economy one-way and youth fares are listed in the various Getting There & Away sections through the book. Excursion and charter fares are lower than these, but advance notice is needed and there may be other restrictions. Prices also vary depending on the season; they are high in summer and around Christmas.

One way that travellers get cheap tickets to cities around the country, is by checking the classified ads in newspapers and city entertainment papers under 'Travel' or 'Business Personals'. These often involve the sale of the unneeded half of a two-way (return) ticket, as return tickets are often the same price or even cheaper than one-ways. These offers are also advertised on university and hostel noticeboards. It isn't strictly legal as tickets are nontransferable, but it's done a lot and rarely checked. The purchaser of the return half, however, should be the same sex as the original owner of the ticket or questions may be asked!

Airfares in Canada are generally quoted as the base fare only. All taxes including the GST are added on top. Ticket agents will quickly total these for you, but you do need to ask. This is worth doing as taxes can add quite a bit to the bill, perhaps resulting in a rather nasty surprise.

The airfares listed in this book should be used as a rough guide as prices fluctuate regularly and taxes change with new governments – both provincial and federal.

BUS

Buses supply the most extensive transportation routes across the country. They go nearly everywhere and are normally cheaper than trains. They are usually clean, safe and comfortable. The two biggies are Voyageur Colonial Ltd in Quebec and Ontario and Greyhound all over the west. There are also Gray Coach Lines in Ontario, SMT in New Brunswick, Acadia lines in Nova Scotia, as well as other provincial, regional and local lines.

Reservations are not normally needed, although buses between adjacent major cities and towns are very busy on weekends and holidays – a reservation may be useful.

On long trips the journey can be broken any number of times. A one-way ticket is usually good for 30 days, a return for 60.

The bus companies in larger towns offer sight-seeing tours ranging from one day to several weeks. Some include accommodation, meals and admission fees to attractions. These can be good value: carefully check prices and exactly what you're getting. You need to make reservations for these types of trips.

Bus Passes

Canadian bus lines offer passes much like the Eurail pass. Unfortunately, the number and variety of these available has declined drastically since the last edition of this book with Canadian bus lines cancelling many of the passes. There are seven, 15 and 30-day passes available but now none of them can be bought in Canada.

Visitors from outside Canada can buy the International Canadian Pass, which is not available in Canada or to Canadian citizens, at travel agencies in their own country. These passes are primarily for Europeans and other overseas visitors and are for seven, 15 and 30 days.

The Across Canada Ticket can only be used from coast to coast in Canada. Any number of stops is allowed. Passes can be bought for seven, 15 or 30-day use and come in two types: high season, from 15 June to 17 September and around Christmas and New Year; and low season, for the rest of the year.

Prices (in Canadian dollars) are: high season $179, $270, and $299; low season $139, $210, and $299. The price for the 30-day pass stays the same all year. There is also a pass offered by Voyageur lines called Tourpass Voyageur which is good for 10 days' unlimited travel in Quebec and Ontario only. The cost for this one is $115 with extra days possible at $11.50 per day. Free connections can be made to many other bus lines covering points all over the two provinces.

Most lines offer various specials. One is a vastly reduced return fare if you go and come within five days and don't depart on a Friday. There are other return excursion fares with varying time requirements.

Student fares exist on some routes, so ask. Some routes offer reduced return fares although most do not. There's a deal on some routes where two free tickets are given with every eight purchased. There is no student age limit.

Tips

In summer, the air-conditioners on buses can be far too effective. Take a sweater on board.

Take your own picnic whenever possible. Long-distance buses stop at highway gas station restaurants where you pay an awful lot for plastic food.

All buses use the same central bus stations in Canadian cities so you can change bus lines or make connections at the same place. Buses are also convenient because reservations are often unnecessary. When one bus fills up, another is added so waiting hours for the next one is not required. Always check this, however, as it may not be the case for all routes all the time.

Most of the larger bus stations have left-luggage lockers.

TRAIN

As a result of government cost-cutting measures train travel in Canada has decreased markedly since the beginning of the 1990s. There are fewer lines, and on those lines remaining the trains are less frequent.

Generally, train travel is more expensive than taking the bus and reservations are much more important especially on weekends and holidays.

From my experience, the trains are not as reliable as the buses and are often late, but this has been an area of both management concern and improvement. On some routes there is food and bar service to your seat – this food is quite good but not cheap. The snack-bar food is usually lousy but the bar car, when there is one, can be fun. And of course, you can always get up and walk around the train.

Canada has two main rail companies: the government-run Canadian National (CN) and the privately owned Canadian Pacific (CP) rail. Yes, this is the same CP that used to have the airline and still is into trucking, shipping, hotels, mining, etc. It is one of Canada's biggest, most pervasive companies.

VIA Rail

Except for some commuter lines, the passenger services of these rail companies are now operated by VIA Rail, a federal government agency. VIA Rail uses CP and CN trains and lines but is responsible for the service independently. CP and CN were the ones who had their budget slashed.

You can pick up the *National Timetable* booklet, giving all the schedules and routes, at any VIA Rail station.

The pricing policy at VIA Rail is essentially that every trip is considered to be a one-way fare. A return trip between points A and B is billed as a one-way fare A to B, and a one-way fare B to A. There are no return or excursion fares. There is, however, one way to reduce your costs considerably. Full fare is paid on Friday, Sunday and holidays. Travel on any other day is discounted 40% if the trip is booked five or more days in advance; more than five days' notice (there hasn't been such a policy for some time now) is recommended. Children, seniors and students are also entitled to discounts.

Long-Distance Travel For long-distance travel VIA Rail offers several types of cars and different sleeping-room arrangements ranging from the basic seat to private rooms. The price of any sleeping arrangement above the basic coach seat is in addition to the travel fare or the pass. If you're going long distances you may want to take some of your own food. Train meals can be expensive and, as mentioned, the snack food is not particularly good.

The best known trains in Canada are those that travel across country, formerly the Canadian (CP) and the Continental (CN). This service, too, has been greatly cut back, but a rail ride right across much of Canada is still possible. The trip, taking approximately five days, takes in nearly all of Canada's provinces and vastly different scenery, some of it spectacular. It can be a very pleasant, relaxing way to go, particularly if you have your own room. During the summer months this trip should be booked well in advance. There are a variety of sleeping arrangements from simply staying put in your seat, to upper and lower pull-out berths to roomettes of varying sizes.

The longest continuous route in the country is from Toronto to Vancouver. The route it takes passes through Sudbury, Sioux Lookout, Winnipeg, Saskatoon, Edmonton and Jasper. The coach fare for this is $381 and it remains constant throughout the year. If you want to begin further east and go all across the country, the train can be boarded in Halifax but changes will have to be made in Montreal and Toronto. The fare from Halifax to Vancouver is $497.

Canrailpass For those who intend to travel a lot, or far, or both, VIA Rail offers the Canrailpass. It's available to non-Canadians or, in low season only, to Canadians over the age of 60. The pass is good for 30 consecutive days beginning on the day of the first trip. The *National Timetable* booklet will help you plan your travel.

The pass is good for any number of trips and stopovers. You can buy the Canrailpass in Canada or in Europe (ask a travel agent for a VIA Rail outlet) but there's no difference in cost.

The Canrailpass comes in two versions. The Systemwide Pass covers the entire country, while the Eastern Pass covers the region from Halifax, Nova Scotia to Windsor, Ontario. Within each pass there are adult fares and youth fares for passengers from 12 to 24 years of age.

From 1 November to 30 April the Systemwide Pass costs $339; during the high season, from 1 May to 31 October, the cost rises to $499. The youth fares are $295 and $449 respectively.

If the Eastern Pass is sufficient for your needs, the prices drop considerably. From 10 September to 14 June, the price is $199; here the high season runs from 15 June to 9 September and the fare is $299. The youth fares are $179 and $269 respectively.

Luxury Trains

A private tour company, Blyth & Company (☎ 800-387-1387 toll free) of Toronto, runs deluxe trips across the country and through the Rockies but has suspended operations from Toronto to Vancouver until late 1992.

The 'Royal Canadian' train used to run between

Toronto and Vancouver, taking 70 hours. Each room contained its own bathroom and a TV with VCR. The prices included food and drink and the meals were presided over by a French chef.

There were four price categories, each determined by the location of your room. The cheap spots on the Toronto to Vancouver run went for $2300. The others were considerably more.

The other route, operated by the Great Railtour Company (☎ 800-665-7245 toll free), Suite 345, 625 Howe St, Vancouver, British Columbia V6C 2T6, runs between Calgary and Vancouver via Banff (with a connection to Jasper) taking in some of the best mountain scenery. The train is called the 'Rocky Mountaineer' and the fare from Calgary to Vancouver is $425. See the Getting There & Away section of Vancouver in the British Columbia chapter for more information.

Amtrak

Amtrak is the US equivalent of VIA Rail. Good-value passes and information on Amtrak's services are available at many Canadian railway stations. See the Train section in the Getting There & Away chapter for more details.

CAR

In many ways, driving is the best way to travel. You can go where and when you want, use secondary highways and roads and get off the beaten track. It's particularly good in summer when you can camp or even sleep in the car. The cars with reclining seats are great for this – surprisingly comfortable with a sleeping bag.

Canada's roads are good and well marked. There aren't many tolls to pay. The Trans Canada Highway runs from St John's, Newfoundland across 7000-plus km to Victoria, British Columbia. There are campgrounds and picnic stops all along the route, often within 100 km to 150 km of each other. Rural routes are among the smallest road categories: they're found in rural Canada and are marked RR1, RR7, etc. Provincial tourist offices have both provincial and, often, national road maps – usually free. Service stations and variety stores sell similar maps.

City rush hours – especially around 5 pm and on Fridays – can be bad, particularly in Montreal, Toronto and Vancouver. In fact I recommend avoiding city driving as much as possible, regardless of the time. Taking the bus or walking can be cheaper with today's hefty parking fees and it's a lot less wearing on your nerves.

Road Rules & Safety

Canadians drive on the right, as in the USA, but they now use the metric system: 100 km/h = 60 miles/h, 50 km/h = 30 miles/h. The speed limit on highways is usually 100 km/h; in towns, it's 50 km/h or less.

The use of seat belts is compulsory except in Prince Edward Island, Alberta, the Yukon and the Northwest Territories. In provinces with a seat belt law, like Quebec and Ontario, fines for not wearing them are heavy. All traffic violations in money-short Quebec will cost you plenty, so take it easy there. Most provinces require motorcyclists and passengers to wear helmets and to drive with the lights on.

Traffic in both directions must stop when stationary school buses have their red lights flashing: this means kids are getting off and on. In cities with pedestrian crosswalks like Toronto, cars must stop to allow walkers across. Provided it is safe to do so, turning right at red lights (after first coming to a complete stop) is permitted in some provinces. Just watch what everybody else is doing or listen for the impatient blast of the horn behind you to figure things out.

Sleeping at roadside parks, picnic spots or other areas on the highways is OK, just don't set up a tent.

A valid driver's licence from any country is good in Canada for three months while an International Driving Permit, available in your home country, is cheap and good for one year almost anywhere in the world.

You can't drive in Canada without insurance and your home insurance may not cover you in a foreign land – investigate this beforehand.

Driving in Quebec and other areas with heavy snow can be a thrill you're best off without and it means having to buy snow tyres. If you get stuck, don't stay in the car with the engine going: every year people die of carbon monoxide suffocation during big storms.

When driving in the north of the provinces, the Yukon and Northwest Territories there can be long distances between service stations – try not to let your tank get much below half full and always carry extra gasoline. Make sure the vehicle you're driving is in good condition and take along some tools, spare parts, water and food. On the gravel roads the biggest problems are dust and flying stones from other vehicles: keep a good distance from the vehicle in front of you and when you see an oncoming vehicle, slow down and keep well to the right (this also applies to ones overtaking you). If you have to overtake wait until you reach a signposted dust-free zone to do it. A bug and gravel screen is recommended, as are covers for your tank and lights, a spare tyre, fan belt and hose.

Rental

You can save a lot of hassle when renting a car by having a credit card. Last time I tried to rent a car, cash was no good. They didn't want it! If you don't have a credit card, let the company have a few days (at least) to check you out. If you're not working, things can be sticky: bring a letter from an employer or banker if you can, and lots of good identification. You may also need to leave a deposit, sometimes as much as $250 per day. Some companies require you to be over 21 years of age, others over 26. You may be asked to buy extra insurance depending on your age, but the required premiums are not very high.

The main companies are Hertz, Avis, Budget and Tilden and Rent-A-Wreck is a well-known used-car rental place. It's best to shop around: rates vary but really haven't changed much in the past few years. Most companies have a daily rate of about $25 to $30 plus a km fee. Others offer a flat rate which is nearly always better if you're travelling far. It costs quite a bit extra to drop a car off in a place other than where you got it, but this can be readily done. Weekly rates are generally 10% less than daily rates, and many companies offer quite special weekend rates. Book early for weekend use and to get a small, more economical car. Some companies now offer vans and, with a number of people sharing, this can work out quite economically.

Campers, RVs and various trailers are other options in which some companies specialise.

Purchase

Older cars can be bought quite cheaply in North America. Look in the local newspaper or in larger centres, the weekly *Buy & Sell Bargain Hunter Press*, *Auto Trader* or an equivalent. In some cities there is also a weekly paper devoted to nothing but used car sales. It's available at corner variety stores. Private deals are nearly always best. Used-car businesses are no more reliable and must mark up the prices. Most of the cheaper cars now are the big gas-guzzlers people are trying to get rid of but there are always bargains out there.

For a few months' driving, this can be an excellent investment, especially if there are two of you. You can usually sell the car for nearly what you paid for it. An old bomb can probably be had for around $1000. West coast cars last longer because salt doesn't have to be used on the roads in winter and the cars rust less quickly.

I once bought a clunky old 1958 station wagon for $50 and got 19,000 km out of it in one summer before the transmission gave up, the wiring burnt out and the floor fell out.

Mark Lightbody

The potential problem for visitors is getting insurance at a reasonable rate. Most companies will offer a six-month term but costs vary widely and can change dramatically from province to province.

In 1990 an English couple reported they were told rates in Quebec were much less than in Ontario for such an arrangement. Checking into it they did indeed find the rate out of Montreal a little over a tenth the cost of their Toronto quotes! Quite a saving! And odd, because for residents Ontario is much cheaper.

Mark Lightbody

Regardless of where you buy, it is useful to have proof of insurance from your homeland. In addition to making a transaction easier, this might well entitle you to some discount as it makes you a more credible risk. As a rule, the rates for women are noticeably less than for a man of comparable age and driving record. If you're planning a side trip to the USA, make sure the insurance you negotiate is valid over the border, too. Also remember that rates are linked to the age and type of car. A newer car may cost more to insure but may also be easier to sell.

Drive-Aways

One of the best driving deals is the uniquely North American Drive-Away system. Basically you're driving someone's car for them to a specific destination. Usually the car belongs to someone who has been transferred and had to fly, or doesn't have the time, patience or ability to drive a long distance. You put down a deposit and are given a certain number of days to deliver the car. If you don't show up, the law is called in. Most outlets suggest a route to take and may give you a very rough km guideline.

Your services as a chauffeur are usually not paid (but may be if you really hit the jackpot and someone's in a rush) and generally you pay for gas. Sometimes a portion of the gas costs are paid and if you're lucky, again perhaps on a rush job, all the gas might be paid. With two or more people, this can be a great deal. The company will want to know how many drivers there will be.

You'll require good identification, the deposit and a couple of photos. Look for Drive-Away companies under transportation or business personal ads in the newspaper classifieds or in the yellow pages of the phone book under Drive-Away Automobiles. Most big cities have at least one outlet. They exist all through the USA too. Some trips will take you across the border: from

Montreal to Florida is a common route. About eight days is normal for a trip from the east to west coast. Try to get a smaller, newer car: they're less comfortable but cheaper on gas.

In summer when demand is highest, cars may not be as numerous and you could be asked for a payment. Occasionally you hear of a Jaguar or something similar available – class on a shoestring.

Car Sharing

In Montreal, Quebec City, some of the smaller towns around Quebec and Toronto a company called Allo Stop acts as an agency for car sharing. It unites people looking for rides with people who have cars and are looking for company and someone to share gas expenses. Prices are very good and destinations vary all over Ontario, Quebec, further afield in Canada and even down to New York City.

Gasoline

The price of gas varies quite a bit around the country, with the highest prices in the far north and on the east coast. Alberta's prices, with less tax, are relatively low. Fill up there before hitting British Columbia; fill up in the USA before crossing the border; and fill up in Ontario before rolling into Quebec. Generally, city prices are lower than country prices, and gas stations along major highways always charge more to their semi-captive customers than do the off-highway stations. On average a litre of gas costs about 60 cents, or about $2.70 per imperial gallon. The Canadian (imperial) gallon is one-fifth larger than the US gallon.

Credit cards are usually accepted at gas stations, many of which are now self-service and will not accept large bills at night. The large cities have some stations that are open 24 hours but you may have to search around. On the highways, truck stops stay open the longest hours and some have showers you can use.

BICYCLE

This method of getting around long distances

is becoming more and more popular in Canada. Obviously you'd need a lot of time to cover much of Canada. You can't really consider traversing vast regions: it's best to concentrate on one area. Some of the most popular are the areas around the Gaspé Peninsula in Quebec and all around the Atlantic Provinces, excluding Newfoundland. The Gaspé Peninsula is very hilly, Prince Edward Island is flat, and New Brunswick and Nova Scotia offer a fair bit of variety and are small, with towns pretty close together. You get a good mix of country and city. All these areas have good scenery.

The other major cycling area is around the Rocky Mountains and through British Columbia. The weather here in summer is pretty reliable and again there's grand and varied scenery.

Between these eastern and western sections of the country, cycling would be more of a chore than anything else and the landscape is similar for long stretches.

VIA Rail allows passengers to take bicycles for free on trains that have baggage cars. This would mean pretty well any train going a fair way. Local and commuter trains wouldn't be included. You don't have to pack the bike up or disassemble it, but then it may not be covered by insurance. For full protection bicycles must be boxed.

The provincial highway maps have more detail and secondary roads than the usual gas-station maps. You can pick them up at tourist offices. Bookshops may also have cycling guides, and cycling magazines might contain useful information.

Some cities, such as Vancouver and Ottawa, have routes marked around town for bikes only.

Cycling Associations

Members of the Canadian Cycling Association receive national and provincial newsletters, a million dollars' worth of liability insurance and information and discounts on events and activities. You join through an associated provincial organisation and the cost is $15 a year. Various local associations link up through the provincial associations for tours and races. They also often have group tours combining cycling and camping.

In Ontario, the Cycling Ontario Association (☎ 495-4141), 1220 Sheppard Ave East, Toronto, M2K 2X1, has maps of cycle routes around the province. Associations in other provinces have similar guides. Check the yellow pages phone books in other cities for cycling associations.

HITCHING

I've always found hitching good in Canada. It's not the UK, which is a hitchhiker's dream, but thumbing a ride is still very worthwhile. Two people, one of each gender, is ideal. Three or more I'd forget it and ditto for single women.

If you feel you've waited a long time to be picked up, remember that the ride you get may take you over 1500 km.

Out of the big cities, stay on the main highways. Traffic can be very light on the smaller roads. Always get off where there's a gas station or restaurant and not at a side road or farmer's gate.

Around towns and cities, pick your spots carefully. Stand where you can be seen and where a car can easily stop. A foreign T-shirt, like one with 'University of Stockholm' on it, might be useful.

If you're going into a large city, make sure the ride is going all the way. If it's not, get dropped where you can catch a city bus, especially after dark. When leaving a city, it's best to take a bus out a little way.

You must stay off inter-city expressways, though the feeder ramps are OK. In Toronto and Vancouver particularly, the police will stop you on the expressway.

It's illegal to hitch in downtown Calgary; fines can be steep. Generally, the scruffier you look, the more ID and documents you should have.

Around the large cities, there will be heavy traffic leaving on Friday and returning on Sunday. Despite the volume I find hitching difficult then because most cars are full with families. Weekdays are best, when you get salespeople and truckers on the road.

Many companies forbid truck drivers to pick up people, though some do anyway.

If you're in a hurry, from Toronto to Vancouver shouldn't take longer than five days; I've done it in three.

One last tip: if you don't want to spend time in Northern Ontario, get a ride straight through from Sault Ste Marie to Thunder Bay. The same in reverse.

Wawa, a small town between the two, is a notorious waiting spot. Its reputation as a tough, anti-hitchhiker, mining and drinking town is pretty outdated, but it's still a small, cold, nothing-to-do place to try to hitch from. I once heard of a guy who waited so long he finally got a job then married and settled in Wawa.

Mark Lightbody

BOAT

On Canada's west coast, ferries connect mainland British Columbia with Vancouver Island, the Gulf Islands and the Queen Charlotte Islands. For schedules and fares contact BC Ferries (☎ (604) 386-3431, 24 hours; (604) 669-1211 in Vancouver), 1112 Fort St, Victoria, British Columbia V8V 4V2.

There are numerous ferries on the east coast and details are found under the Getting There & Away sections of the port towns.

New Brunswick is connected to Prince Edward Island and to Maine, USA. From Prince Edward Island, ferries connect with the Magdalen Islands in Quebec and with Nova Scotia. Nova Scotia is connected to Maine, USA, and to Newfoundland island and Labrador.

TOURS

Organised group tours are best arranged through bus companies, travel agencies or tour companies themselves. Many of the private specialised tour companies are listed in the tourist brochures available from provincial and territorial governments. The larger transportation companies are reliable and they're your best bet if you want a general type of organised tour.

Always make sure you know exactly what sort of tour you're getting and how much it will cost. If you have any doubts about the agency or the company it may be dealing with, pay your money into what is called the 'tour operators escrow account'. The law requires that this account number appear on tourist brochures (you may have to look for a while). Doing this protects you and your money should the trip fall through for any reason. It's a good idea to pay by cheque because cash is always harder to get back; write the details of the tour, with destination and dates, on the front of the cheque. On the back write 'for deposit only'.

Many of the larger regional bus companies offer trips of varying lengths, including transportation and accommodation. Some offer sight-seeing as well.

Goway Travel is a private company which runs tours throughout the Americas for 18 to 35-year-olds. These are expedition and camping-type trips. It offers tours which cross Canada one way and return through the USA. Most of the trips are two to five weeks long and are 'city & sights' oriented. Others are more slanted towards outdoor activities, with everything included but sleeping bags. Participants must help with the chores and cooking. An example is an eight-day canoe trip in Ontario's Algonquin Park. For information contact Goway Travel (☎ 322-1034), 2300 Yonge St, Toronto, Ontario.

The Canadian Outward Bound Wilderness School, with offices in Vancouver and Toronto, runs good, rigorous outdoor adventure trips which are more like courses than holidays. Ranging from seven to 24 days, they take place in various rugged parts of the country; many programmes include a solo portion. In Toronto they can be contacted through PO Box 116, Station S, Toronto.

The Canadian Universities Travel Service Ltd (known as Travel CUTS), mentioned in the Facts for the Visitor chapter, runs various trips and outings that include activities like hiking, cycling and canoeing.

The Association of Students' Councils offers six summer canoe trips varying from eight to 17 days, everything included, sometimes even a flight. Most of these are backpacking wilderness trips, portaging canoes or something similar. For information contact CUTS (☎ 979-2406), 187 College St, Toronto.

The Canadian Hostelling Association also runs some tours and special-event trips featuring hiking, cross-country skiing, etc. Check at hostels for organised activities.

There are many small companies across the country offering a variety of adventure trips of different lengths and difficulty. Good camping stores often carry pamphlets put out by such companies. You can also pick them up at hostels and tourist offices.

Newfoundland

Entered Confederation: 31 March 1949
Area: 404,520 sq km
Population: 568,000 (2nd smallest province)

Newfoundland (pronounced 'new fen LAND') has a unique character, and even a brief encounter with it is gratifying. It's a rugged, weather-beaten land at the edge of Canada, heavily influenced by the sea and the conditions of the not-too-distant far north.

The people, of mainly English and Irish descent, have developed a culture that, if not entirely their own, is considerably different to that of other Canadians. This is apparent in various ways but perhaps the most noticeable feature is the language with its strong lilting inflections, distinctive accent, unique slang and colourful idiom. A look at the map reveals descriptive and light-hearted names such as Nick's Nose Cove, Come-by-Chance, Main Tickle and Cow Head; names that reveal something of the history and the people that made it. To people in the rest of the country the residents here are known humorously as Newfies, and though they are often the butt of Canadian humour there is no real malice felt: it's generally accepted that they are among the friendliest of Canadians.

Other peoples have played prominent roles in the development of this land. The Vikings landed and established a settlement in 1000 AD which can still be visited. Inuit and Native Indian bands were calling the area home long before that and historic sites mark some of these settlements. Today, Labrador, the larger northern mainland portion of the province, is still inhabited mainly by these 'First Nations' people.

All of Labrador and the northern portions of the island are part of the Laurentian Shield, one of the earliest geological formations on earth – possibly the only area unchanged from times predating the appearance of animals on the planet.

Across the province, the interior is mostly forested wilderness with many peat bogs, countless lakes and rivers. Almost all the people live along the coast, with its many isolating fjords, bays and coves.

From the often foggy shore, fishing folk head to waters legendary for cod and dozens of other kinds of fish. On the Grand Banks lying south-east off the most populated region (the Avalon Peninsula), fishing boats gather from around the world as they have done since before Columbus even saw the new land. In spring, what's left of the controversial seal hunt begins to supply the

66

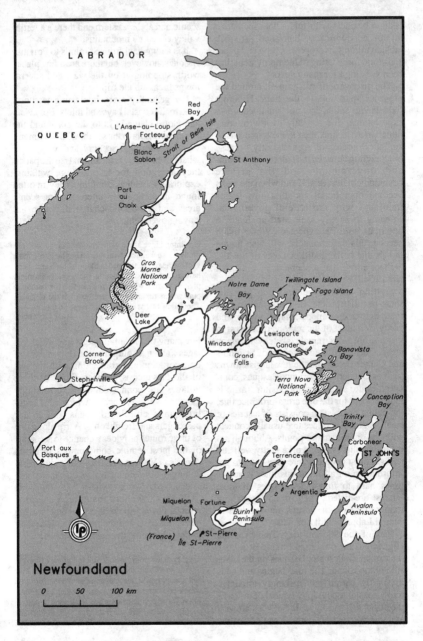

LABRADOR

QUEBEC

Red Bay

L'Anse-au-Loup
Forteau

Blanc Sablon

Strait of Belle Isle

St Anthony

Port au Choix

Gros Morne National Park

Notre Dame Bay

Twillingate Island

Fogo Island

Deer Lake

Lewisporte

Windsor

Gander

Bonavista Bay

Grand Falls

Corner Brook

Terra Nova National Park

Stephenville

Conception Bay

Clarenville

Trinity Bay

Carbonear

Port aux Basques

Terrenceville

ST JOHN'S

Argentia

Miquelon

Fortune

Miquelon

Burin Peninsula

Avalon Peninsula

(France)

St-Pierre

Île St-Pierre

Newfoundland

0   50   100 km

fashion business with furs. Other industries in this economically depressed province include mining, hydropower, pulp and paper and food processing. Unemployment has been very high for many years.

The discovery of offshore oil around the province, particularly the huge Hibernia field in the south, has not yet lived up to expectations, due partially to low international prices at first, then to the tragic loss of an 'indestructible' oil rig and, lastly, because of wrangling between the federal and provincial governments and the private development interests. If and when the wells become operational and this now seems imminent with the federal government agreeing to supply some start-up funds, a boom of sorts is expected. While much needed, this unfortunately, will also hasten the change in the traditional way of life and perhaps mean that a segment of a distinct culture will be absorbed.

Getting around the province presents some peculiar problems. The ever growing road network connects major towns and pretty well most of the regions of interest to visitors but does remain sketchy in many areas. Outside of the two cities of St John's and Corner Brook and the few largish towns such as Gander and Port aux Basques, communities are small and the visitor traffic is light. Except for the one cross-province line, the public bus system consists of a series of small, regional services that usually connect with one or more major points. Although not extensive, this system works pretty well and will get most people where they want to go. Information on all these bus lines is sometimes hard to find but the ones of most interest are listed. There is no longer any train service on the island but one line in central Labrador still operates.

Part of the 905-km-long Trans Canada Highway is the only road linking St John's, the capital, to Port aux Basques on the other side of the island. The road begins and ends in starkly barren but strikingly attractive rocky coastal topography typical of much of the provincial shoreline. In between are vast areas of wooded lakeland, some of it quite

scenic, and at the western end there's a fertile valley edged by mountains.

It is a long haul from St John's to Port aux Basques, however, but there are a few places worth stopping at on the way, and several towns break up the trip.

For generally more interesting territory, head to the coastal bays and inlets. Bonavista and Notre Dame bays to the north and the Burin Peninsula to the south, with their many villages, shoreline scenery and views, are what this province is all about. Use the parks: they are good for information, walking, exploring as well as camping. They're often found in particularly interesting or scenic areas and there's no charge if you're not staying overnight.

One thing I love about Newfoundland is that you can pretty much wander about wherever you like. Find a spot by the side of the road or along a beach and spend half a day walking, taking pictures, swimming, picking berries, whatever. You can fish for salmon in pure waters running a few metres from the highway. There aren't signs everywhere saying no this, no that.
Mark Lightbody

For many of the small, isolated coastal villages known as outports, the only means of transportation and connection with the rest of the province is by boat. Some of these villages are connected by a surprisingly inexpensive ferry service which runs regularly in a couple of areas and is for passengers and freight only. A trip along one of these routes provides a chance to see some of the most remote communities in North America. Visitors are few, but mainstream culture is still seeping in at an ever increasing rate.

Budget travellers may forgo, perhaps reluctantly, a trip to the province fearing travelling costs and the need to retrace their tracks. One route to consider follows.

Take the ferry from Nova Scotia to Port aux Basques – with no vehicle the cost is reasonable. From Port aux Basques take the inexpensive coastal ferry, on which you can sleep, along the southern shoreline. From Terrenceville catch a bus to St John's. After a couple of days there catch the bus back to Port aux Basques and the return ferry to Nova Scotia. This offers a good overall view of the province without transport of your own. Alternatively consider a visit up to Gros Morne from Port aux Basques and back.

Accommodation prices are much like those in the rest of Canada but there is less variety of places to stay. Scattered about the province are small, family-run guesthouses known here as 'Hospitality Homes'. These are often the best choice for both price and fun. Not uncommonly they are the only choice. Some are like small rooming houses, some are pretty much like small hotels and still others, probably the majority, are just an extra room in a family's home. Of course these places vary a bit but are usually friendly, informative and economical and many offer meals of the kind not available in restaurants, featuring maybe homemade bread and jam or a traditional fish dish. The tourist office publishes lists but they are never complete so other places can be found. In some of the small, out-of-the-way spots the pub manager will likely be able to suggest a couple of names.

The main alternatives to the types of places already mentioned are motel units. These are generally fairly new and reliable but more expensive and fairly uniform. The larger towns offer hotels as well.

Many visitors camp, in one form or another, and the system of provincial parks is good, inexpensive and spread evenly around with parks within a day's trip of each other. Note that facilities at many of them are minimal. There are also some privately run campgrounds but nowhere as many as you'll find in many other provinces.

Newfoundland weather is cool throughout the year, especially in Labrador, with the Arctic currents and north winds. There's a lot of precipitation all year too, mainly around the coasts where fog is not at all rare. Summer is short but July and August are generally quite warm. The sunniest and driest places are central, inland areas.

Sometime between April and June each year are the province-wide St George's Day celebrations. But throughout the year there are numerous festivals, celebrations and community events. Traditional Celtic-style music remains very popular and numerous folk festivals are held around the province during the summer months.

In closing, here are a few odd bits of information. The province was the last to join Canada, doing so as recently as 1949. The island portion of the province is located in its own Newfoundland time zone, a half an hour ahead of Atlantic time. There are no skunks, snakes or ragweed pollen. The province has a rich aviation history hosting 40 pioneering transatlantic flights between 1919 and 1937 including the Lindbergh's and Amelia Earhart's.

St John's

St John's, the province's capital and largest town, is a city that manages to feel like a town: invigorating yet warm, busy yet homey. Both a modern high-rise city and a fishing village, the feel of St John's derives partly from its splendid geographical location and partly from the aura of its tumultuous, romantic history. The land is inhospitable, the weather not much better and the economy still pretty much dependent on the whims of the sea. This will alter with the oil field's exploitation, and already the past few years have seen a quickening of controversial downtown development.

As the oldest city in North America and England's first overseas colony, the establishment of St John's has been said to mark the birth of the British Empire. The city must now make some hard decisions on its future and, in fact, the future of the entire province.

John Cabot in 1497 was the first to find the excellent and beautiful protective harbour that led to the city's development. As it's the closest point to Europe in the New World and as the famous Grand Banks teem with fish offshore, a European settlement sprang up in 1528. Unfortunately, this brought to an end not only the lifestyle but the very existence of the Beothuk Indians.

From its inception the settlement was the

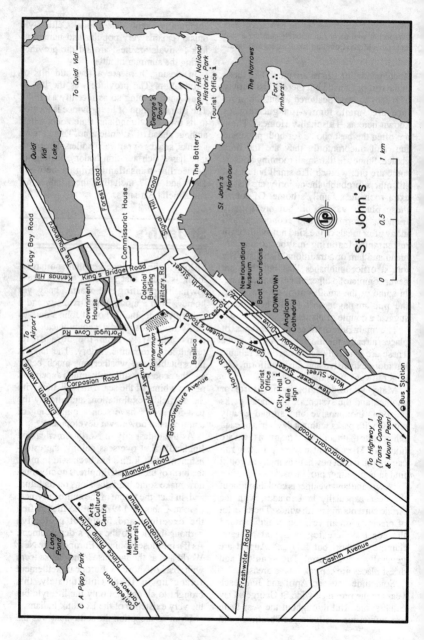

scene of battles, raids, fires, pirates, deprivations and celebrations.

The Dutch attacked in 1665. The French ruled on three occasions, but each time the English regained the settlement from them. In the 1880s it became a centre for shipbuilding and for drying and smoking fish. Its location has inspired more than trade, warfare and greed, however. The first transatlantic wireless cable was received here; 40 pioneering aeroplane crossings – including Earhart's and Lindbergh's – used the site, and even Pan Am's inaugural transatlantic flight touched here.

The wharves have been lined with ships for hundreds of years and still are, acting as service stations to fishing vessels from around the world. As befits a port of adventurers and turbulent events, the tradition of raising a glass is well established. Eighty taverns were well in use as long ago as 1775, and in the early 1800s rum was imported to the tune of 220,000 gallons annually. Today the city might well lay claim to the most watering holes per capita.

St John's rises in a series of steps, sloping up from the waterfront. Everywhere there are stairs, narrow alleys and winding streets. Several of the downtown roads are lined with colourful, pastel clapboard town houses – the kind found all over the province. The more modern sections are mostly in the suburbs sprawling out in all directions.

There's lots of rain and fog, so pray for good weather.

Orientation

On the approach to St John's, the highway passes the newer subdivisions, the suburb of Mount Pearl and then some of the older rectangular pastel houses which in sections look somewhat like stacked-up prefabs.

The road winds around slowly and then suddenly you end up in the centre of town, surprised at the beautiful setting and picturesque streets.

The main streets are Harbour Drive which runs right along the bay; Water St, one street up; and Duckworth St, still further up from the waterfront. The rest of the city continues to rise, rather steeply, up the hill away from the sea. It's said that everyone in town has strong legs.

Water St is lined with shops, restaurants and bars. Much of the recent redevelopment has been happening and continues to happen here, modernising this central area but making it less unique. Nearly all the tall buildings are new and controversial – after all, they don't do much for the view.

In town, New Gower St is noted for its many multicoloured Victorian terrace houses. These attractive old English and Irish style houses are now protected for their historic character.

Towards the west end of town are the Murray Premises, a restored market building from 1846, now with stores and a museum. Further west is City Hall with the 'Mile 0' sign marking the start of the Trans Canada Highway out the front (see map). Continuing to the south-west edge of the downtown area the bus station is underneath the overpass.

At the other end of Water St is the small Harbour Side Park, with a monument to Sir Humphrey Gilbert whose landing near here on 5 August 1583 marked the founding of Newfoundland and Britain's overseas empire. Lord Nelson and Captain Bligh also landed here. Across the street in a sharply rising park there's a War Memorial and benches with views. Prescott St acts as the division between Water St East and Water St West.

Further east is the unmistakable Signal Hill, looming over both the harbour and the downtown area. At its base is a small group of houses known as the Battery, one of the oldest sections of the city. Many fishing boats tie up here and, if you ask around, a skipper might take you out for the day.

Ships from many countries moor along the waterfront by Harbour Drive. Among the most commonly seen flags are the Russian, Spanish and Japanese. For a view over the area, drive or walk to the top of the brown car-park building across the street.

The airport is about six km from town near Torbay.

Information

The Tourist Commission's main office (☎ 722-7080) is in City Hall, in town on New Gower St, open every day. If you start to chat you'll find the staff very friendly, helpful and knowledgeable. Here, you can get a booklet describing a self-guided walk of the downtown area taking in many of the older buildings, and supplying some historical background. Halfway up Signal Hill by road, east of town, there is another information office in the parks building.

There is also an information chalet 16 km west of the city on the main highway.

The book department in Bowring's Department Store, Water St has a large and excellent selection of titles on the city and Newfoundland.

Newfoundland Museum

Though small, the displays here are good and interesting. There are a few relics and a skeleton – the only remains anywhere of the extinct Beothuk Indian tribe that once lived here. Also on display are exhibits about the Vikings and the history of St John's. The museum, at 285 Duckworth St, is open every day and Thursday evenings; admission is free.

Incidentally, a fine attraction nearby is the now nearly extinct Canadian traffic cop, gesticulating his commands on the corner of Prescott and Duckworth Sts.

Murray Premises Museum

Within this restored market building on Water St West are some shops, a pub and the second branch of the Newfoundland Museum. It's larger than the original on Duckworth St and has exhibits stretched over four floors. Topics covered include the marine, military and naval history of the province. There's some interesting information on the Basques who came to the area in the early 1500s to whale. The museum entrance is marked by a fine example of the huge Newfoundland dog. The hours are the same here as at the Duckworth St location and it is also free.

Courthouse

By the Duckworth St museum, the courthouse dates from 1904 and in the late 1980s had a major facelift.

City Hall

Five blocks west of the courthouse is the new City Hall and 'Mile 0' sign, from where the Trans Canada Highway starts westwards on its 7775-km journey across Canada to Victoria, British Columbia.

Masonic Temple

Up the hill from the museum you'll see the striking, renovated temple – a private men's club.

Anglican Cathedral

Across the street is the Anglican Cathedral of St John the Baptist, dating from 1816. Inside, note the stone walls, wooden ceilings and long, thin stained-glass windows. To enter, go to the side facing the harbour and into the doorway by the toilet. Ring the bell and someone will probably come to let you in.

Basilica of St John the Baptist

Further north up Church St to Garrison Hill, and then right on Military Rd you'll find this Roman Catholic church. Built in 1855, it's considerably more impressive from the outside than the cathedral and, in fact, the Gothic facade dominates the cityscape. Inside, however, it's rather plain although the ceiling is interesting and the pipe organ is a 'beaut'.

There are good views out over the bay from the front steps. Within walking distance are about half a dozen other churches.

Signal Hill National Historic Park

The view alone makes this site a must. East of town along Duckworth St, this park rises up the hill forming the cliff edge along the channel into St John's Harbour. The view of the town and out to sea is superb night and day; you can watch for the many types of fishing vessels moving in and out of the port.

Halfway up the road from the end of Duckworth St is the Visitors' Centre, with a small museum where you can get information about the park or the city in general. During the Battle of Signal Hill in 1762 the English took St John's and pretty much ended French control of North America. Queen's Battery further up has some cannons and the remains of the British battery of the late 1700s. Cabot Tower at the top of the hill honours John Cabot's arrival in 1497. Built in 1900, this tower was where Marconi received the first transatlantic message in 1901 – the wireless broadcast was sent from Cornwall, England. There are guides and displays in the tower.

Admission is free and the park is open daily in summer until 5 pm. Near the tower is Ladies Lookout, which at an elevation of 175 metres is the highest point in the park and offers views over what seems like half the province.

Highly recommended in either direction is the 1.7-km walking trail connecting Cabot Tower with the Battery section of town down in the harbour. Going up, the trip takes about 90 minutes. The tourist office has a map of the park.

Fort Amherst

Across the Narrows you can see the remains of this fort. With the Battery and the fort to face, enemy ships wouldn't have had an easy time getting into the bay. On the point, on the fort side, the lighthouse dates from 1813. Here you're about as close to Europe as you can be without getting wet.

Other Historic Sites

Commissariat House On King's Bridge Rd near New Gower St, Commissariat House is one of the most complete historic sites. Built in 1818, the late-Georgian mansion was used by the supplies officer of the British military. When British forces left in 1870, the building was used as a church rectory, nursing home and children's hospital. It is now restored to reflect the style of the 1850s with many period pieces inside. The house is open daily in summer and by appointment at other times, admission is free. There's an interpretive centre.

Colonial Building This building, nearby on Military Rd, was the seat of the provincial legislature from 1850 to 1960. It's built of stone from Ireland which was formerly used as ships' ballast and contains many of the province's old records. The building is open in summer Monday to Friday from 9 am to 5 pm, free.

Government House This residence is beside Bannerman Park close to the two sites previously mentioned. Built in 1830, it was the official residence of the governor of Newfoundland until it became part of Canada and since then the lieutenant-governors have called it home.

Arts & Cultural Centre

At the Arts & Cultural Centre you'll find the art gallery – with displays of Canadian painting and sculpture and open from Tuesday to Sunday, free – and a theatre. The complex is about two km north-west from the downtown area on the corner of Allandale Rd and Prince Phillip Drive, near the Memorial University. For theatre information call ☎ 726-5978.

Confederation Building

Nearby, just off Confederation Parkway, east of the arts centre, is the new home of the provincial government. You can visit the building and the small military museum inside for free. It's closed on weekends.

C A Pippy Park

Aside from the Arts & Cultural Centre and Confederation Building, this huge park on the city's northern edge also contains **Memorial University**. Much of the park is natural with walking trails, picnic areas and a botanical section. There's also a campground.

Bowring Park

West of the downtown area off Pitts Memorial Drive, this is another popular city park and it's big too. A couple of streams and walkways meander through the park.

Ocean Sciences Centre

Tours can be taken at this research unit, part of Memorial University's science department. Ongoing research examines the life cycle of salmon, seal navigation, ocean currents and many other aspects of life in the colder ocean regions. There is a visitor interpretive centre and guided tours of the facility which take about an hour. Seals can be seen and there is a hands-on tank where various creatures can be touched. It's open everyday in July and August and from Monday to Friday for the rest of the year. Admission is $2.50. The centre is about eight km north of town just before Logy Bay. From town take Route 30, Logy Bay Rd and follow Marine Drive.

Quidi Vidi

Over Signal Hill, away from town, is the tiny, picturesque village of Quidi Vidi. This little fishing port has one of the oldest houses in North America, dating from the early 1700s. You can walk to the village from Signal Hill in about 20 minutes or go around by road from St John's. Take Forest Rd, which runs along the lake and then turns into Quidi Vidi Village Rd.

French Battery Built in 1762, the battery is up the hill from the village, guarding the bay. It's free to look around.

Quidi Vidi Lake Inland from the village is this lake, site of the St John's Regatta, which is held on the first Wednesday in August. Records show that the event started in 1818 and it's probably the oldest competition in North America. Pleasantville, now a suburb at the end of the lake, was a US military base until the 1950s or '60s when they packed up and gave it to Newfoundland.

The Rennies River flowing out of the lake is an excellent trout stream. A conservation group is developing the area and a walking trail from the lake along the river to Long Pond has been set up, with others planned.

Trout can be seen leaping in the autumn as they get ready for spawning. The tourist office has a pamphlet with a map of the river system.

Organised Tours

For a relatively small city, the number and variety of tours available is noteworthy. The Newfoundland Historic Trust offers walking tours of the old city twice daily in summer leaving from the Murray Premises. In addition, some years the city does much the same tour from mid-June to mid-September, leaving from City Hall, free. Call the tourist office for times.

McCarthy's Party (☎ 834-5705) offers four different excursions. The three-hour tour of the city costing $12 is good, but really doesn't provide too much that you can't do yourself for free. The other ones are more worthwhile and include a trip along Marine Drive, one to Cape Spear and another day-long spin around Conception Bay. Lots of interesting historical tidbits and humour is woven into the commentary.

Fleetline (☎ 722-2608) offers trips ranging from half a day around town to a full 10 days around the province which includes Saint Pierre and Miquelon islands. Another trip covers the Northern Peninsula. The company has an office on George St. There are other places with a range of bus tours to various points around the province.

Other tours are done by boat. Harbour Charters, for example, runs a trip from the waterfront out to sea in search of whales and icebergs using a classic old Grand Bank schooner. The 2½-hour trip costs $20. Try to pick a calm day as it allows the boat to travel further and also permits a little cod jigging. There are great views along the coastline, but it can get rough (this is the North Atlantic, after all – no reason to mention how I lost my breakfast overboard!) and cold, so take warm clothes – it may be balmy in the protected harbour but it's quite a different story once outside the Narrows.

Bird Island Charters (☎ 753-4850) is similar but visits the Sea Bird Sanctuary Islands which include the largest puffin

Puffins

colony on the east coast of America. They offer daily departures from Bay Bulls, south of town. There's a shuttle service to get you to the dock.

The tourist office will have information on other tour possibilities.

Festivals

The Newfoundland & Labrador Festival is held annually around 27, 28, 29 June in C A Pippy Park, from 1 to 10 pm daily. There's camping and the music is great. The festival is held indoors if the weather is bad.

For other festivals – there are several during summer – ask at the tourist office.

The Quidi Vidi Regatta is held on the first Wednesday in August.

The Signal Hill Tattoo takes place from 17 July to 17 August on Tuesday and Thursday evenings; it's very colourful.

Places to Stay

As might be expected, there are more accommodation possibilities here than anywhere else in the province and the price range is wide. Overall, prices are higher here than elsewhere but many of those that follow are close to average.

Camping Conveniently located right in the city by the university there is camping in *C A Pippy Park*. They charge $5 for tenting, $10 for unserviced sites and $14 for serviced ones.

Hostels The hostel situation in Newfoundland is very changeable and usually minimal.

In town here, however, a *Youth Hostel* (☎ 737-7590) is set up on the university campus in Hatcher House from May to mid-August. There are buses to town but you can walk there in less than half an hour, even if the roads are not direct. From the campus Newtown Rd leads downtown.

Other than the hostel, the university offers no rooms and the YM-YWCA has no accommodation either.

Tourist Homes Aside from the established places listed here, the tourist office takes calls from local people throughout the day who call in to offer a room for the night – sort of a part-time hotel system. So, if things are busy and you're having trouble getting a room, call in more than once as the situation can quickly change. That said, there is usually not a major problem finding something anyway.

The *Sea Flow Tourist Home* (☎ 753-2425, 781-2448) is at 53-55 William St. Mrs Hutchens has four rooms at singles/doubles for $30/35 and up. The cheapest room has no bath and one room, the most costly, has kitchen facilities.

A second choice is the *Bird Island Guest Home* (☎ 722-1675) at 150 Topsail Rd, away from the centre a bit west on Cornwall Ave which turns in to Topsail Rd. Rates for singles/doubles are $35/45 with a continental breakfast included.

Also out of the town centre there's the *Fireside Guesthouse* (☎ 726-4869) at 28 Wicklow St near the Avalon Mall Shopping Centre. Call for directions. Including a full breakfast, singles/doubles cost $35/40, making it one of the better buys, and you can use the indoor swimming pool – a short walk from the house.

Back in town, *Prescott Inn* (☎ 753-6036) is a very good B&B at 19 Military Rd, centrally situated on the eastern side of the downtown area. It's a well-kept old house with balconies looking out over the harbour. Singles/doubles cost $46/56 with a full breakfast included, for an extra person add $10.

Less expensive, with no heritage designation but fine and quite central, is the *Red Beech Manor* (☎ 579-5281) at 94 Freshwater Rd with two double rooms at $40 including a light breakfast.

There are a couple of places on New Gower St, the *Fort William* (☎ 726-3161) at No 5 and the *Gables Hospitality Home* (☎ 754-2318), at No 115, which has just one room priced slightly lower at singles/doubles $42/52. The latter place has laundry facilities. Both places include breakfast in the price.

If you find these places full, try the tourist office. They should have an up-to-date list, the places available in people's homes change frequently. There are usually other places not mentioned in the printed provincial accommodation guides and pamphlets.

Hotels Hotels have been getting fairly pricey but there are still some good, inexpensive places around town among the more costly ones.

For a plain, very central but clean and inexpensive place, try the *Catherine Booth House* (☎ 738-2804), at 18 Springdale St, which is a short walk from the bus station. Singles/doubles cost $30/35, and a family of four pays $40. Four adults can get a room for $48 and rates include breakfast and a snack at night. It's run by the Salvation Army. PS – there's no smoking, not even in the TV lounge.

The very central *Parkview Inn* (☎ 753-2671) is the big green, barn-like house with white trim at 118 Military Rd, corner of King's Rd. Singles range from $40 to $45, doubles from $45 to $50 and triples aren't bad value at $60. Weekly rates are less 10% and rates are lower out of high season. If you're trying to cut corners make sure you ask for the simplest room. They have a small breakfast room.

Old Inn (☎ 772-1171, 576-9409), run by Amon Rosato, is a lodge of 14 rooms with singles/doubles from $30/40 and good weekly rates. It's at 157 Lemarchant Rd, the black and white place built in 1892. It's a long walk but the bus goes along Lemarchant Rd.

Bonaventure House (☎ 753-3359) at 34 Bonaventure Ave, not far from the Basilica, is similar but smaller. There are five rooms at singles/doubles $34/46 including breakfast. Free parking is available too.

Moving up-market a bit, the *Victoria Station Inn* (☎ 722-1290), at 290 Duckworth St, is not bad value for its 10 rooms at singles/doubles $55/65. The rooms are nicely furnished and many have a fireplace. Away from the town centre about six km, at 102 Kenmount Rd is *Hotel St John's* (☎ 722-9330). About a third of its 85 rooms come with kitchen facilities. Singles/doubles go for $58/64. Also on Kenmount Rd is the *Best Western Travellers Inn*, one of a chain seen in many places across the country. They're fairly standard, reliable mid-range hotels. This one costs about $5 more than the St John.

The *Hotel Newfoundland* on Cavendish Square at the end of Duckworth St is the top-end classic in town; there's some history behind its stone façade.

Motels Motels are priced in the middle range or higher. *1st City Motel* (☎ 772-5400) is at 479 Kenmount Rd, about six km from the city centre. Prices are $50 for a single and $5 more for the double and additional people.

The *Kenmount Motel* (☎ 726-0092) at 389 Elizabeth Ave is the same price.

Maybe a few dollars less is *Greenwood Lodge & Motel* (☎ 364-5300) towards Mount Pearl, off Route 60, close to town. They've got colour TV and a games room, and housekeeping units are available.

The *Crossroads Motel* is at the junction of routes 1 and 60. Rates for singles/doubles are $45/50 and this place has all the facilities.

Places to Eat

At 183 Duckworth St is the *Duckworth Lunch*, a small café popular with the artsy and student crowds. They serve good health food at reasonable prices and there are lots of newspapers to read.

In Bowring's Department Store on Water St, the *Captain's Cabin* cafeteria has a good selection of inexpensive meals from breakfast to dinner, and has fine views of the harbour as well. It's recommended.

Also cheap and busy is the *Ports of Food*, a food-booth assortment in the Atlantic Place Mall on Water St. It only has fast food – Chinese, soup and salads, doughnuts, etc, but it's open every day. *Woolworth's* cafeteria is also very low-priced.

Up on George St around the corner from Water St, the *Continental Café* is a small, dark place specialising in very good salads. They also serve burritos, felafels, desserts and coffees.

The *Fishing Admiral Pub* is a good place for a drink at night but also serves up a good-value lunch. There's a selection of seafood platters, chowders and fish & chips. Most meals are about $5 to $6 at lunch but it's more expensive at dinner.

St John's has the best fish & chips in the world, and quite a few places to prove it to yourself. Locals tend to have their favourites and competitions are held to determine popularity, but to me they were all top-rate. Try *King Cod* at 122 Duckworth St, *Caram's* in the middle of Water St near McBrides Hill or the ever popular *Ches's* at both Nos 5 and 9 Freshwater Rd, a short walk from the centre. Unless you're very hungry don't order the large serves, because you *really* get a piece of fish. There are other places to try, just ask around.

The *Cavendish Café*, at 73 Duckworth St, is good for a soup and sandwich and has a view of the harbour area.

Upstairs at the King Cod, the *Upper Flat*, a less casual dining room, offers other seafood like salmon, scallops and a local dish called brewis. The latter is a blend of fish, onion and a bread-like mix that's soaked overnight. Another local speciality is cod tongues which are really closer to cheeks. They're often served deep-fried with very unimpressive results but, if you can, try them pan-fried.

Casa Grande is a nicely decorated Mexican restaurant at 108 Duckworth St. It holds about 10 small wooden tables encircled by wicker chairs and has dishes from around $6. It's open daily, but does not offer lunch on Sunday.

At 223 Duckworth St is the St John's version of the *Spaghetti Factory* chain, with good-value Italian dishes. And at 106 Water St (the door is around the side), the *Curry House* serves Indian food.

Lastly, you may want to check out the *Fish Market* at the end of Harbour Drive at the western end of town.

Entertainment

St John's at night is a lot of fun. You won't have to search too long in this town if you're thirsty because, per capita, there must be more watering holes here than anywhere.

George St is pretty crazy with crowds and queues at a variety of bars. The *Corner Stone* has videos and live rock, *Weekenders* has new wave music and others cater to different age groups and musical preferences. All are cheap or free to get in.

The *Graduate House*, known as the Grad, at 112 Military Rd has a free movie night on Wednesday or Thursday and often has very popular weekend parties.

The *Ship Inn* down the steps beside the Arts Council, 267 Duckworth St, is good with live music. *Kibbitzer's*, down one of the narrow alleys off Water St, is like being in someone's living room and offers various games like chess to play. It's friendly and open very late. *Bridgett's Pub* at 29 Cookstown Rd, but with the door on Freshwater Rd has meals and a variety of music – folk on Wednesday and anything from blues to traditional the rest of the time.

There are several pubs along Water St and one in the Murray Premises. The *LSPU Hall*, up the stairs from Duckworth St near the Arts Council, often has plays, concerts, comedy nights, etc. This place is worth checking out as it's the centre for the very active arts community.

Try to seek out some live Newfie music – excellent folk music with Celtic origins, usually based on the fiddle. You may also want to sample Screech – a particularly strong rum once available only here, but now widely available across Canada and still tasty.

Apart from these suggestions, you can drink in the quiet lounges of the better hotels or attend a theatre or dance performance at the Arts & Cultural Centre on Confederation Parkway.

Getting There & Away

Air Air Canada to Halifax costs $270, to Montreal $385. Canadian Airlines flies to Charlottetown for $301.

Bus The bus system is a little confusing but if you can track things down it can work pretty well for you. The system, unlike that in other provinces, isn't monopolised by one or two operators but consists of a lot of small local and regional services. Finding out who they all are and where they go can take some digging. I've now got many of them listed but there are others, I'm sure.

The main bus station (☎ 737-5911) is at the far west end of town on Water St, underneath the overpass. It's about a 20-minute walk from town. Terra Nova, the main provincial line, operates the Road Cruiser buses from here. It operates on only one route across the province along the Trans Canada Highway to Port aux Basques stopping at many places along the way. So many places, in fact, that it becomes somewhat of a marathon. There was at one time a direct bus too. Ask about it if you're going right through. To Port aux Basques there's one bus daily at 8 am which costs $67.50 one way. To Grand Falls buses leave at 8 am and 5.30 pm daily and cost $42. Note that across the province the Road Cruiser bus is often referred to as the CN bus.

For Argentia, Placentia and Freshwater there is Newhook's Transportation which runs buses down to the south-west Avalon Peninsula. There is an office at 13 Queen St. Share taxis also run between St John's and the ferry terminal. In Argentia you can make dockside arrangements.

Cheeseman's Transportation runs a share taxi service to points around the Burin Peninsula and has a depot in the town of Burin and in St John's.

Fleetline Bus Service, with an office on George St, goes to Carbonear and the lower Conception Bay area daily.

There are others in St John's, for example, one runs to the Old Pelican area beyond Carbonear to the end of the north arm of the Avalon Peninsula. People at the main bus station or the tourist office will be able to help with information but you may find it necessary to ask more than one person.

Train The last passenger trains in the province died in late 1984. It was the end of an era when the narrow-gauge trains, each car heated with its own oil stove, finally succumbed to economics. Now the final freight train has hauled its last load as well and even the tracks have been pulled up. Now the buses have become the sole means of transportation.

Ferry The Marine Atlantic ferry for North Sydney, Nova Scotia, docks at Argentia on the south-west coast of the Avalon Peninsula. Newhook's runs a minibus between Argentia and St John's. The fare is about $10 one way and they have an office in downtown St John's.

The new MV *Joseph & Clara Smallwood* goes in each direction twice a week and runs from 15 June to 15 September only. It departs Argentia on Wednesday and Saturday, and North Sydney on Tuesday and Friday all at 9 am. With the new ship, crossing time has been decreased markedly from 18 to 13 hours but the price has not gone up dramatically. Still, a ticket is $38.50, a car $93.25. Rooms and beds are extra. Many people, your humble writer included, find this fare a bit steep and prefer instead to land in Port aux Basques and drive across the province twice to avoid it.

As on the sister ship to Port aux Basques, however, passengers don't face hardship: there is a movie theatre, bar with live band, tourist booth, children's play area, outdoor decks – the works. In July or August reser-

vations are a good idea: call toll free ☎ 800-565-9470 in Nova Scotia and New Brunswick or ☎ 800-563-7701 in Newfoundland. Usually one or two days' notice is all that is necessary.

If you're in a car, you'll get a free car wash as you board the ferry back to the Canadian mainland. This is to get rid of two bugs harmful to potatoes and found only in Newfoundland.

Car & Motorbike There are several agencies in town. Among the chains there is Budget (☎ 726-1707) at 51 Lemarchant Rd. For a local outfit try Hickman Motors (☎ 726-6990) on Kenmount Rd. Gas (petrol) is expensive in Newfoundland – the costliest in Canada. Also, if you drive a car one-way between St John's and Port aux Basques, you'll have to pay a return charge of at least $100. Basically though, the rates are about the same here as anywhere else.

Getting Around

To/From the Airport There is no city bus to the airport, about six km north of town out along Route 40 towards Torbay, going by taxi is the only way.

Bus For information phone ☎ 722-9400. There are a few bus routes in and around town and together they cover most areas – No 1 does the central area. By transferring from this one to an adjoining loop, say the No 12 going west, you can get a pretty good tour for a couple of bucks.

AROUND ST JOHN'S

Marine Drive, north of St John's up towards Torbay, goes past nice coastal scenery. There are rocky beaches at both **Middle Cove** and **Outer Cove** – good for a walk or picnic.

Offshore around **Torbay** is a good whale-watching area. Puffins live and feed here also. Marine Drive ends at **Pouch Cove** but a gravel road continues to **Cape St Francis** for good views. West of town, head to

Topsail for a great view of Conception Bay and some of its islands.

Ten km south of St John's towards **Petty Harbour** don't miss Bidgood's, a supermarket with a twist. It's become known far and wide for its Newfoundland specialities. Popular with local residents, this is also the place where those back on a visit stock up on their favourite items before returning to jobs on the mainland. Recently more tourists have been showing up. Where else can you buy caribou steak, moose in a jar or seal meat pie? Depending on the time of year the selection may also include cod tongues, saltfish or lobster. There are jars of the province's distinctive jams – try partridge berry or the elite of the island's berries, bakeapple. You may also want to take a gander at the bakery section which regularly sells out.

Further south, along the coast, about 13 km from town is **Cape Spear** where there is a national historic park centred around the lighthouse which dates from 1835. A guide will show you around and offer all sorts of information, like how many coats of wallpaper layer the inside walls (you won't believe it). Cape Spear is the most easterly point in North America: next stop, Ireland.

Continuing south, the area around **Goulds** has some unusual things to see – cows and fields of vegetables. This is one of the very few good farming districts in the province.

Bay Bulls and **Witless Bay** are excellent places from which to observe sea birds. Three islands off Witless Bay and southward are bird sanctuaries collectively known as an ecological reserve. Together they represent one of the top sea-bird breeding areas in eastern North America. Every summer thousands of puffins, kittiwakes, murres, cormorants, storm petrels and several other species make these rocky islands home and hatch their young there. Several operators run highly recommended trips out to the colonies. No one is permitted on the islands but the boats do get close enough for you to consider taking ear plugs as well as camera and binoculars! The din overhead is incredible. The best months for visiting are June and July which is also good for whale-watch-

ing – humpback and minke are fairly common here. If you really hit the jackpot, an iceberg might be thrown in too.

Out of Bay Bulls, Bird Island Charters (☎ 753-4850) has 2½-hour trips and passes by two of the islands. A good feature is that they also run a shuttle bus to the dock from the major hotels in St John's, 30 km away.

Gatherall's (☎ 334-2887) runs a similar boat tour and also has a guesthouse in Bay Bulls. The town was the site of a repair station for Allied ships in WW II and a German submarine actually surrendered here.

In **Tors Cove**, the *Seal Meadows B&B* (☎ 334-3345) is run by a well-travelled woman, Victoria Walsh.

Cape Broyle further down the coast also has a bird-sanctuary trip run by Great Island Tours. Their trip includes a seaside view of an abandoned coastal village wedged into the cliffs. They also offer shuttle buses to and from the city.

Regardless of the weather take a jacket or sweater and, call me a wimp, a Gravol pill is not a bad idea either. I know.

AROUND THE AVALON PENINSULA

The peninsula, more like an island hanging onto the rest of the province by a thin strip of land, is the most densely populated area of Newfoundland: nearly half its population lives here.

Apart from St John's, **Conception Bay** is lined with scores of small communities but all around the coast you'll find fishing villages. In the southern central section is a large wilderness area with a growing herd of caribou.

At **Argentia** in the south-west is the ferry depot connecting with Nova Scotia. The tourist office can suggest driving and camping tours around the peninsula.

Southern Avalon

Despite its proximity to St John's this section of the province is very good for viewing wildlife and has several good parks. The coast has a long history having been visited and settled by various Europeans from the 1600s onward.

Down the coast at **La Manche Provincial Park** are two excellent, scenic walking trails: one to a waterfall, one to the remains of a coastal village.

In the interior is the huge **Avalon Wilderness Reserve** with an increasingly large herd of woodland caribou. Permits, available in St John's at the government Parks Department, are required to visit the area for hiking or canoeing. Caribou, however, can sometimes be seen right at the edge of the road between **Biscay Bay** and **Trepassey** at the bottom of the peninsula.

Trepassey has played some part in the history of aviation including being the launching place of Amelia Earhart's first-woman-across-the-Atlantic flight in 1928.

Going back up the coast, the area from St Vincent's to St Mary's provides an excellent chance of seeing whales, particularly the humpback which feeds close to shore. The best times are between mid-June and mid-July. A fishing boat may take you for a closer look at other whales including the fin, blue, sperm and minke.

On Highway 90, **Salmonier Nature Park** is in the centre of the Avalon Peninsula, 12 km south of the junction with Highway 1. Here you can see many animals found in the province, enclosed in the park's natural settings. A marked trail through the woods takes you past the animals – moose, caribou, beaver, etc – as well as indigenous flora. The park is open daily from June to September from noon; there's a small admission fee.

Conception Bay Area

Like the rest of eastern Newfoundland, Conception Bay is rich in history and coastal scenery. The winding road of the indented, densely populated coastline runs by dozens of nearly adjacent but distinct towns and villages. Much of the early history of Canada was played out here. The arm reaching out into Conception Bay to **Bay de Verde** in the north can be seen in a day driving to and from St John's but, if time permits, there are places to stay. Fleetline Bus Service connects St

John's with Carbonear and makes stops along the way.

Brigus

Despite its small size, Brigus, 80 km from St John's, has quite a reputation for its pleasing old European atmosphere. Its distinctive character draws many visitors. A former resident, one Captain Bartlett, accompanied Peary on part of his 1909 voyage to the North Pole. Now his house is an historic site. Another thing to see is the tunnel, cut through rock in 1860, to make berths for Bartlett's ships. There are also a couple of craft shops in town.

With four places to stay there is more accommodation here than anywhere else on Conception Bay. The *Brittoner Guest Home* (☎ 528-3412), on Water St, is right in the middle of things and, with singles/doubles for $35/40 including full breakfast, is the best priced.

Harbour Grace

Up past Cupid's where the first official English settlement of Newfoundland was attempted in 1610, is Harbour Grace where the Spanish and French had been since the early 1500s. In the 1700s it was used by pirates. The old Customs House is a museum.

Many of the first attempts to fly across the Atlantic began in Harbour Grace beginning in 1919. In 1932, four years after her flight from Trepassey on the Avalon Peninsula to Europe, Amelia Earhart took off from here and became the first woman to cross the Atlantic solo too. The airstrip is designated an historic site. Fish processing is the main economic activity.

Carbonear Island

Carbonear Island has had a tumultuous history with international battles, pirate intrigues, shipwrecks and more recently, seal-hunt controversy. Carbonear Island is designated an historic site and there are many examples of old architecture in town. The annual summer folk music festival here is not to be missed.

Other

EJ Pratt (1883-1964), one of Canada's best known poets, was born in Western Bay and a national historic plaque here commemorates him. The following lines are from the poem *The Titanic* and describe the destructiveness mixed with beauty of the iceberg which sank the unsinkable ship.

But when the months of voyaging it came
To where both streams – the Gulf and Polar – met
The sun which left its crystal peaks aflame
In the sub-Arctic noons, began to fret
The arches, flute the spires and deform
The features, till the batteries of storm
Playing above the slow-eroding base,
Demolished the last temple touch of grace.

Further north up the coast, **Northern Sands Provincial Park** has beautiful beaches. On the inland side is a good spot for freshwater swimming, the ocean is too cold.

From **Lower Island Cove** there is some fine coastal scenery. At **Bears Cove** near **Bay de Verde** a short walk leads to dramatic views.

At the very tip, at **Grates Cove**, there is a rock on the shore; it is said, that John Cabot scratched his name into and became, I suppose, the first to mark the continent with graffiti.

Along Trinity Bay

On the other side of the peninsula are several towns which well exemplify the wonderful place names so often seen and enjoyed around the province. How about the absolutely lovely **Heart's Delight** or **Heart's Content**?

In Heart's Content an historic site tells the story of the cable station here, where the first transatlantic cable was laid.

Both towns mentioned have a place to stay (appropriately, nearby Heart's Desire doesn't!) In Heart's Delight is *Legge's Hospitality Home*, at 2 Farm Rd, near the Irving Station. It's run by Mrs Gertie Legge (☎ 588-2577) who charges singles/doubles $30/35 and a little more for breakfast.

Heart's Content has a small, more costly motel.

At the bottom of Trinity Bay, **Dildo** (when you stop sniggering) is a good spot for whale-watching. Pothead whales come in by the school; humpbacks, a larger species, can also be seen in summer. Both can be viewed even from the shore.

Argentia

The south-west portion of the Avalon Peninsula is known primarily for Argentia with the large ferry terminal for boats to Nova Scotia. For ferry information see St John's. Newhook's Transportation connects both Argentia and Placentia with St John's by road.

Since WW II the USA has operated a naval and air base here but it is being phased out. There isn't much to see in Argentia and, surprisingly, given the presence of the ferry dock, there's nowhere to stay.

Placentia

Nearby in Placentia, settled in 1662, you'll find the remains of a French fort at historic Castle Hill, with a visitors' centre and fine views. In the early 1800s Placentia was the French capital of Newfoundland and French attacks on the English at St John's were based from here. The old graveyard by the Anglican church offers more history as does the O'Reilly House Museum at 48 Riverside Drive. In a home built in 1902 the museum offers details of both the house and the area. The courthouse and the Roman Catholic church are other notable historic buildings. Plaques and cannons mark the sites of other former local fortifications. A boardwalk runs along the waterfront and there is a beach.

Placentia has one hotel, the *Harold Hotel* (☎ 227-2107), five km from the ferry, and it has a restaurant.

Cape St Mary's

At the southern tip of the peninsula is the **St Mary's Ecological Reserve**, an excellent place for seeing sea birds. An unpaved road leads into the sanctuary where there is an interpretive centre and a lighthouse. A walk in from there offers views of Bird Rock, the second largest gannet nesting site in North America. Throughout the summer the shoreline and cliffs are home to thousands of birds including kittiwakes, murres and razorbills. There is no admission charge.

Eastern Newfoundland

This is the smallest region of the province and consists of the area just west of the Avalon Peninsula on the edge of the main body of the island. Geographically it is also distinguished from the central portion of the province by the jutting peninsulas at each end: the Bonavista to the north and the Burin to the south. Like the Avalon Peninsula area, Eastern Newfoundland was settled early and the convoluted coastlines are lined with historic old fishing villages.

The ferry for the islands of Saint Pierre and Miqueleon departs from Fortune in the south. To this day, the islands are French possessions and certainly not in name only. Spending a couple of days here is like a mini trip to Europe.

Terrenceville is at one end of the south coastal ferry line which services outports all the way to Port aux Basques at the southwestern tip of the province.

Leaving the Eastern region the principal road travels through Terra Nova National Park providing a microcosm of the area's varied topography and plant and animal life.

BONAVISTA PENINSULA
The Bonavista Peninsula has some superb coastal scenery with many small, traditional fishing communities including some of the oldest in the province. Some people claim that historic Trinity is the oldest town in North America. Several companies around the peninsula offer boat tours and Terra Nova National Park preserves a section of the peninsula in its natural state.

Clarenville
This is the access point to the peninsula and

it's best to pass right through. In 1955, Clarenville became the North American terminal for undersea telephone cables connecting with Oban, Scotland. To the west are many small communities lining the three long arms to the sea. North of town along Highway 230 is a bird sanctuary protecting large numbers of Canada geese which nest here.

Up the Coast
Highway 235 along the edge of **Southern Bay** has some fine coastal scenery and a picnic spot with a view at Jiggin' Head Park. At the 300-year-old fishing village of **Keels** boat tours of the rugged coastline are available.

Along the beaches here and around the Avalon Peninsula in late June and early July, millions of capelin – a small silver fish – get washed up on shore by the tides. I think this is partially due to spawning and to being chased by hungry cod. Anyway, the shore is alive with the fish, and people go down with buckets and bags to scoop up a free meal.

Bonavista
This largish town with 5000 residents is at the end of the peninsula where John Cabot landed on 24 June 1497 and first saw the 'new found land'. Later he drifted down to the St John's harbour and stopped there. For his troubles the King of England rewarded him with the royal sum of £10. It wasn't until the 1600s that Bonavista became a permanent village and from then through the 1700s, the English and French battled over it like they did for other settlements along the coast.

There is a museum in town on Church St and, in the garden at the old courthouse, is a whipping post where instant justice could be meted out. The lighthouse dating from 1843 has been restored and is now a provincial historic site with guides in period costume. The scenery of Cape Bonavista is dramatic. The Dungeon is an unusual rock formation at the shoreline. In early summer whales may be seen off the coast.

For accommodation, there is *Whiffen's*

Hospitality Home (☎ 468-7361) with singles/doubles at $35/40 including breakfast. It's the white two-storey house opposite the Royal Canadian Legion Hall.

Newhook's Transportation runs a daily bus service between St John's and Bonavista.

Outside of town at the village of **Maberly** is a park with views over some islands where thousands of birds roost. Principal species are puffins, kittiwakes and murres.

Port Union

The Fisherman's Protective Union was formed here in 1910 and a monument and a museum honour its founder. The province's largest fish-processing plant is here and one of Newfoundland's largest trawler fleets operates out of this ice-free port.

Trinity

First visited by the Portuguese explorer Corte-Real in 1500 and established as a town in 1580, Trinity is one of the oldest settlements in the province and might be the oldest town on the entire continent. The village has a fascinating history which includes the first court in North America – convened in 1615. Many buildings along the town's narrow streets have been restored or renovated. An interpretive centre has much information on the history, houses and buildings in town. Also see the museum and fort remains.

Also in town is **Ocean Contact**, a whale-watching and research organisation. They offer day expeditions, short holidays and all-inclusive, expensive week-long trips that take in other wildlife and local geographic and historic attractions. Aside from whales, other marine life includes porpoises and dolphins.

Places to Stay Ocean Contact operates from the *Village Inn* (☎ 464-3269), a good place to stay with rooms from $40 to $45. Films and slides on whales and other sea life can be seen.

Alternately, there is *Trinity Cabins* (☎ 464-3657), with housekeeping cabins in the $29 to $39 range. There's a beach nearby but they have a pool as well.

Thirdly, in the village of Trinity East is the *Peace Cove Inn* (☎ 781-2255) in a restored turn-of-the-century house.

Terra Nova National Park

This east coast park split by the Trans Canada Highway typifies the regional geography. The rocky, jagged coastline on beautiful Bonavista Bay gives way to long bays, inland lakes, ponds, bogs and hilly woods. There's canoeing, fishing, hiking, camping, sandy beaches, even swimming in Sandy Pond. You can rent bicycles in the park – a good way to get around. You'll see lots of wildlife – moose, bear, beaver, otter and bald eagles – and, from May to August, icebergs are commonly seen off the coast.

At the visitor centre staff will recommend activities depending on the length of your stay.

Within the park is Ocean Watch Tours, recommended for their good-value boat tours. One trip explores the fjords and islands and sometimes stops in at old abandoned outports. Another trip specialises more in wildlife and seeks out whales, seals, birds etc. On either one, icebergs from as far away as Greenland may be sighted.

The tour boat also offers a fantastic ferry service to backcountry campers which means dropping you off at an otherwise inaccessible cove and picking you up at a predetermined time later. Hiking trails lead into the park from the two drop-off points. You do have to take one of the boat tours for the service but they are no burden. Backcountry camping is free!

Aside from the two campgrounds in the park, there are 24 housekeeping chalets available by the Newman Sound campground. There is a grocery store at the chalets as well as canoe and kayak rentals. From Malady Head campground there are good views.

BURIN PENINSULA

Jutting south into the Atlantic Ocean, the peninsula has been the base for European fishing boats since the 1500s. The Grand

Moose

Though the moose is a fairly common animal across the country it is mainly found in the less populated, heavily forested northern regions. Nowhere in Canada are you as likely to see one as in Newfoundland. There are some 40,000 of them here and many of them live close to towns and roads including the Trans Canada Highway. This, of course, increases the chances of getting a good look at one but also presents some hazards. There is more than one moose/vehicle collision a day across the province and smacking into a beast the height of a horse weighing 400 kg with antlers nearly two metres across is more wildlife than most people care for.

Moose tend to like the highways for a number of reasons. The open space makes walking easy, there is usually more breeze and fewer insects and, in spring, the salt from winter de-icing makes a nice treat. For these reasons they also enjoy the train tracks, a habit which decreased their population at the rate of some 2000 per year until the train service was discontinued.

The areas of heaviest concentration are well marked and should be heeded particularly when travelling after dark when most accidents occur. Ninety per cent of the run-ins take place between 11 pm and 4 am. If you do see a moose on or beside the road, slow down and if it doesn't want to move approach slowly with the lights off as they seem to get mesmerised by the beams.

I've seen them during the day on the Trans Canada Highway on each of my trips. Get out and take pictures if you like, moose are generally not aggressive and are very impressive, if unusual-looking animals. They can be unpredictable, however, and anything of this size should not be approached too closely or startled. During rutting (mating) season in October and November the males (bulls) can become very belligerent and downright ornery; it's a good time to stay in the car and well out of their way.

Calves are born in the spring, and throughout the summer it is not uncommon to see a cow moose with her young. Females and the young do not have antlers. Adult males grow a 'rack' each year in summer, only to have it fall off each fall. ∎

Banks off the peninsula (part of the continental shelf) teem with fish. The hilly, wooded northern area supplied timber for building and ships; the southern end is mostly barren, glacier-stripped rock interspersed with bogs and marshes.

Cheeseman's Transportation with depots in St John's and Burin, connects points around the peninsula and the big city by share taxi. There was a similar service called Slaney's Taxi, also with an office in St John's, but this may have stopped running.

Terrenceville

Terrenceville is the eastern port for the southern coast Marine Atlantic ferry which skips along the south of the province from Port aux Basques. This trip is one of the province's unique adventures and, with new roads always being built, is likely to be history within a decade. The ferry serves about 10 mostly otherwise isolated communities. It carries the sick to the doctor and later brings the bill in the mailbag. Each trip is somewhat different as the stops made vary. The trip is generally scheduled as taking 19 hours but it can be longer. It's possible to break the journey and although none of the stops have official hotels, it's not uncommon to find someone to take you in for the night. The ferry fare is very low, for full details call Marine Atlantic (☎ 695-2124).

In Terrenceville there is, unfortunately, no place to stay but the ferry arrives the night before the morning departure, so you can sleep on board.

Marystown

Although the largest town on the peninsula, there is not much here for the visitor but Marystown does have a tourist office and the most shops and services in the area. There is camping and freshwater swimming at **Frenchman's Cove Provincial Park**.

Burin

Settled by fishing folk from Europe in the 1700s, Burin is one of the oldest towns on the south coast. It is a pretty town or rather a series of villages sparsely scattered around coves and the lumpy, treeless hills.

Unlike some of the region's towns, Burin has maintained its important role in the Grand Banks and now has a major trawler repair facility as well as a processing plant.

Captain Cook's Lookout provides good views of the harbour and area. The English built fortifications here in 1812. The French were based across the bay in Placentia. Along the coast northward at **Tides Point** is a lighthouse.

The Golden Sands is a popular beach and there is camping at the provincial park.

St Lawrence

A little further down the coast, St Lawrence is a mining town with the only deposits of fluorospar in Canada. It was once the world's largest producer and although this is no longer the case, the mine still operates and a small museum outlines its history.

Grand Bank

Its role now diminished, this was one of the main centres of the early Grand Banks fishery and some of that history remains. The Burin Peninsula long served as the base for the famous Banks fishing grounds. A walk through town shows the varied architecture of the 1880s in the homes, churches and Water St storefronts.

The Southern Newfoundland Seaman's Museum depicts both the era of the banking schooner and the changes in the fishery over the years. It's free and, in summer, open every day. You can't miss it – it's like a large white boat on Marine Drive.

If you're spending the night in Grand Bank the big, old *Thorndyke* (☎ 832-0820), a designated historic home, makes a fine place to stay. It's at 33 Water St, just 6.5 km from the Fortune ferry; the rooms are offered at very good prices. From the roof there are views over the town and bay. It's busy, so call for reservations. There is also a motel in town.

Fortune

Fortune is the jumping-off point for trips to

The Grand Banks

The fabulous portion of the Atlantic Ocean known as the Grand Banks, lying just south-east off Cape Race at the southern part of the Avalon Peninsula, is one of the prime reasons anybody ever bothered with the New World. After 500 years of serious plundering it remains one of the world's best fishing grounds.

The banks are a series of submarine plateaus stretching from north-west to south-east about 80 km out to sea from Cape Race. They extend to cover an area about 500 km long by 300 km wide with a depth ranging from just five up to 350 metres.

Though mostly in the Labrador Current, the waters are met by the Gulf Stream and this blending of the warm and cold gives rise to the legendary fogs. It also helps plankton, a surface plant, to thrive and it is this that results in the millions of fish. The main catch is cod but there is also halibut, flounder and herring among others. Boats come from around the world, notably from Norway, Japan, Portugal, Spain and the Soviet Union, to fill their hulls. Canada has imposed restrictions and regulations but has an impossible task in trying to enforce its limits and authority.

It was John Cabot, an Italian working for England, who first put down a net and found his eyes bulging as much as the net did. From that time, 1497, Europeans began to arrive and set up fishing communities. As well as the fog, nasty storms and marauding icebergs are hazards that fisherfolk have had to contend with through the centuries. ■

Saint Pierre and Miquelon and 20,000 people a year pass through on their way to the islands. Aside from looking after them, many of the town's people are employed at the large fish-processing plant. There is also a shipbuilding and repair depot.

The *Eldon House* (☎ 364-9274) guesthouse at 56 Eldon St is open from the middle of June to early September. There are just three rooms which go for $35, including breakfast. The *Fair Isle Motel* (☎ 832-1010) with 10 rooms at $55 single or double is the alternative.

There is also a fairly large campground with sites for tents and trailers on the edge of town.

Saint Pierre & Miquelon

This is probably the oddest side-trip in Canada. Once called the 'Islands of 11,000 Virgins', these two dabs of land, lying 16 km west off Newfoundland's Burin Peninsula, belong to France. The tiny islands represent the only French holdings left in North America. The 6000 residents drink French wine, eat baguettes and pay for it in francs.

First claimed by France in the 1500s, the islands were turned over to the English along with Cape Breton after the Seven Years' War. They were then ceded to the French by the British in 1783 under the Treaty of Paris. Battles over fishing rights continued with Newfoundland and the islands changed hands a couple of times until 1815. Since then they have remained under French control. The disputes persist, however, and in 1989 there was a fairly serious flare-up with France getting involved in the bickering over territorial fishing limits.

An interesting aside is Saint Pierre's role during the Prohibition period. Canada would legally export what amounted to oceans of booze to the French island where American rum runners would pick it up to take home.

A few days make a good visit – exploring, relaxing, enjoying a different culture. Like much of the Newfoundland coast, the islands are very barren and rocky (although there are some relatively wild areas as well as cliffs and sandy beaches). As always, the main livelihoods are fishing and supplying fishing boats, but today tourism brings in quite a bit of extra money.

The archipelago consists of numerous islands. Saint Pierre, although not the largest, is the principal one, the most populated and its town of the same name is the largest on the islands.

Miquelon is actually two islands separated by a narrow isthmus of sand. The northern section, Miquelon, has pretty well all the rest of the people and a small town. The southern island called Langlade is quite wild. The remaining islands are all very small.

In Saint Pierre you can see the museum which outlines the island's history and the cathedral. Also visit the interesting French cemetery. From mid-July to the end of August folk dances are often held in the town square.

Outside town there is a lighthouse at **Gallantry Head** and good views from **Cap aux Basques**. Out in the harbour, a 10-minute boat ride away is **Île aux Marins** with a small museum. You can take a bilingual guided tour around the island which had its own fishing village at the turn of the century.

Miquelon, 45 km away, is less visited and less developed. The people here are largely of Acadian background while Saint Pierre's inhabitants are French (mainly from Brittany and Normandy), and Basque.

The village of **Miquelon**, centred around the church, is at the northern tip of the island.

From nearby **l'Étang de Mirande**, a walking trail leads to a lookout and waterfall. From the bridge in town a scenic 25-km road leads to **Langlade**.

The island of Langlade remains pretty much the same as it has always been. There are some summer cottages but no year-round inhabitants – human ones, that is. There are some wildish horses and smaller animals such as rabbits and, around the rocky edges and lagoons, you'll see seals and birds. Walks or horseback rides can be taken through the area, in the woods, along the beaches or through the sandy grasslands.

Several annual holidays and festivals occur in July and August. On 14 July is Bastille Day. On 4 August Jacques Cartier's arrival in the islands in 1536 is celebrated. The following week, a two-day festival on Miquelon recalls the Acadians' heritage and, later in the month around 25 August, another two-day event on Saint Pierre celebrates the Basques' heritage. These, of course, are busy as well as interesting times to visit.

Places to Stay & Eat

For lodging, Saint Pierre has about half a dozen hotels and the same number of guesthouses or pensions which are more reasonably priced. *Hotel Robert* (☎ 722-3892), on the waterfront with 54 rooms, is the largest place. The *Hotel Paris-Madrid* (☎ 412933) at 14 Quai de la République is much smaller, simpler and cheaper. *Motel Roger Rode* (☎ 413747) has five rooms with kitchens. For the pensions ask the tourist office for listings. At a couple of these places meals are available. Accommodation can be tight in high season so you may want to check before you go. A guide with the latest lodgings should be available at one of the Newfoundland tourist offices.

Miquelon has one hotel, one pension and a small campground at l'Étang de Mirande near town.

As might be expected on French islands, restaurants are numerous relative to the size of the population and the food is good. In both Saint Pierre and Miquelon there are several places serving traditional French food. *Chez Dutin* on Saint Pierre has been recommended. Saint Pierre has more choice and a number of less expensive places for sandwiches, pizza and the like. *Le Maringoiun'fre* has crêpes for a compromise between the two.

Getting There & Away

Canadian and US visitors need neither passports nor visas for a visit, but good ID such as a birth certificate or driver's licence with photograph is recommended. For citizens of the European Community countries, Switzerland and Japan, passports are required. All other nationals need both a passport and a visa.

Note that the time on the islands is half an hour ahead of Newfoundland time. Also keep in mind that there is a duty-free shop for alcohol, cigarettes, etc.

Air Air Saint Pierre flies from Montreal,

Halifax and Sydney, Nova Scotia during the summer.

Ferry There are two ferries, neither taking vehicles, running between Fortune and Saint Pierre. The MV *St Eugene 5* with a capacity of 200 passengers, does the trip in 50 minutes and costs $27 one way, $44 return, less for children. From mid-June to late September (with some exceptions in June and September) there is one trip a day in each direction departing in the early afternoon. If you're pressed for time, ask about the cheaper same-day return trip. For tickets and information call Lloyd Lake Ltd (☎ 832-2006) in Fortune.

The MV *Arethusa* also makes daily trips during the same period but also travels in May and the first half of June on a reduced schedule. The one-way fare costs the same but the return on this one is slightly cheaper. Although new and comfortable this boat is considerably slower, taking about 1¾ hours. This isn't necessarily a bad thing as there is an open upper deck and, besides the coastal views, you might be lucky enough to see a whale. For tickets and information, there is an office at the terminal (☎ 832-0429). There is also an office (☎ 738-1357) in St John's at 38 Gear St. This office is open all year, the other one is seasonal.

To catch either boat, arrive at the dock close to an hour ahead of departure. The Fortune ferry terminal has a parking lot for those who have driven to the ferry. Check the arrival and departure times of both ferries as one may suit your plans better.

Several companies offer various package tours which may include the bus trip to the ferry, ferry crossings, hotel and sight-seeing or some combination of the above. Two companies to try are the same outfits which run the ferries, Lloyd Lake Ltd in Fortune and SPM Tours in Fortune and St John's.

Getting Around
Between the Islands The MV *St Eugene 5* travels to Miquelon and returns later the same day three times a week. The fare is $16

return, less for kids and the trip takes just under an hour.

Around the Islands In Saint Pierre rent a 'rosalie', a four-wheeled bicycle that comes in two sizes, two and four-person models are available. There are regular bicycles as well or small motorbikes. In both Saint Pierre and Miquelon, tours on horseback are offered.

Also on Saint Pierre there are tours by bus and mini-train and on Miquelon a bus trip takes visitors around the island and across the isthmus to Langlade. In a couple of days much can be seen on foot.

Central Newfoundland

The vast, little-populated central area is the largest geographic region of the island portion of the province. For the visitor it is the area of least interest and most travel although there are still some very fine places to see, particularly the Notre Dame Bay coast and its intriguing, small islands. From Lewisporte ferries depart for northern Newfoundland and Labrador. The southern area is mostly inaccessible lake-filled woodland. One road leads down to the coast linking many small remote villages to the rest of the province.

GANDER
Gander, with a population of 13,000, is at the crossroads of the east-west Trans Canada Highway and Highway 330 which leads to Notre Dame Bay. Though there isn't a lot to do, it is a convenient stopping point whichever way you're going. On the long, stretched-out Gander Lake in a fairly wild and rugged region it is best known for its airport. There is also a Canadian Forces base.

Gander served the first regular transatlantic flights and then, during WW II, was a major link for planes on their way to Europe. The first formation of bombers made in the USA for the UK left here in February 1940. The location was chosen because it is close to Europe and yet far enough inland to be free of the coastal fog which often plagues St John's. Numerous US and Canadian airlines also used it for transatlantic flights beginning in the 1930s. The airport, a major Aeroflot refuelling stop, is known for being the site of thousands of defections from Russia, Cuba and former Eastern Bloc countries: the plane touched down and passengers ask for political asylum. The airport lies 3744 km from London, 2782 km from Chicago and 12,536 km from Tokyo.

There is a tourist chalet on the Trans Canada Highway at the central exit into town. Keen plane buffs will notice that almost all the street names are related to aviation and its history.

Aviation Attractions

There are three planes mounted and on display around town. On the west side of town is a Beech 18 from the Canadian navy. In the downtown area near the City Hall is a McDonnell CF100 Voodoo and out at the airport is the third, a Hudson Bomber.

Also at the airport is a small aviation display pertaining mainly to Gander's history and, of more interest, there's a huge tapestry depicting the history of flight. It's in the passengers waiting lounge but, if you don't have a ticket, ask the security officials and they'll let you in for a look.

Just east of town, south off the Trans Canada Highway, the Silent Witness Monument unveiled in June 1990 tenderly marks the site of an horrendous early morning crash in December 1985 in which 248 US soldiers returning home from the Middle East for Christmas were killed along with eight crew members. The possible causes are still debated. The size of the swath of forest taken out by the crash is astounding.

Places to Stay

There is a campground 16 km north of town at Jonathan's Pond and at Square Pond 34 km, east of Gander. The *Cape Cod Inn* (☎ 651-2269) at 66 Bennet Drive is in a newish residential area very close to the centre of town. Rates from $40 to $55, breakfast

included. Other Newfoundland-style meals are available at extra cost.

There are numerous motels on the highway but they're decidedly pricey. The basic *Fox Moth* (☎ 256-3535) with some efficiency units is the cheapest with singles from $50. Also try *Skipper's Inn* (☎ 256-2534) where there is a dining room. Consider heading to Notre Dame Bay for the night where prices are lower.

Places to Eat

On Airport Drive in town are the usual fast-food outlets. Better is the *Highlight* in the little mall strip on the corner of Elizabeth St and Airport Blvd, the two main streets of Gander. It's very popular and, though the food is good, I suspect some people come just for the remarkably lavish decor. Standard Canadian fare is also available.

Continuing east on Airport Blvd towards the airport turn south (left) at Bennet St. At 136 Bennet St, beside the Gander mall, is the *Bread Shoppe*, a good bakery with a wide selection of breads and pastries.

NOTRE DAME BAY & AREA

This coastal area north of Gander is the highlight of Central Newfoundland. Though relatively heavily populated it has typically rugged but especially scenic Newfoundland coast. About 80 little villages are found around the bay nestled in small coves or clinging to the rocky shoreline. From Gander there are two road loops – one through Lewisporte, the other eastward to Wesleyville – that make good circular tours. A few of the towns have small museums dealing with various aspects of local history.

Offshore is a large cluster of islands, including New World, Fogo and Twillingate which should not be missed and where whales and icebergs may be seen.

If you go north along Highway 330 (watch for moose), you'll reach the coast at Gander Bay which has a good place to stay: *Doorman's Cove Lodge* (☎ 676-22554) in a century-old house across the street from the sea in the village of Doorman's Cove. Singles/doubles cost $30/40 and there is a triple room as well. Breakfast is included and the jams are terrific. The owners also run trips along the Gander River for nature watching, fishing or hunting.

Change Islands

These two islands, reached by ferry from Farewell at the end of a what seems a long road from the main highway, don't change much, name notwithstanding. There are five (four on Sunday) 20-minute trips in each direction daily costing $3 per car and $1 per person. From Farewell the first ferry leaves at 8.30 am, the last at 9 pm with the others scattered evenly through the day. Check schedules as the times vary. There is no real town at Farewell but there is a restaurant at the ferry landing.

The two main Change Islands with a population of just 500 or so are connected by a short causeway at the northern end where the largest village is. The islands are very quiet with many traditional wooden houses and some old fishing-related buildings painted in a red ochre colour common to the area. At the northern end is a small store and one place to stay: the *Seven Oakes Tourist Home* (☎ 621-3246). Singles/doubles cost $50 – nonsmokers only; meals are available.

Fogo

Fogo is the largest of the islands in Notre Dame Bay but is still just 25 km long. Tread carefully because the Canadian Flat Earth Society has stated that Fogo is at the edge of the world! Indeed, say they, Brimstone Head is one of the four corners of the earth. Standing here looking out to sea it's not difficult to agree with them.

Like the Change Islands, Fogo is reached by ferry from Farewell. Again, there are five services daily (four on Sunday) leaving from early morning to evening. The fare is $7 for car and driver, $2 for adult passengers. This trip takes about 45 minutes.

The island is very pleasant for just exploring slowly and enjoying the coastal scenery. It has an interesting history being first settled by Europeans in the 1680s. There are about 10 villages on the island, together making up

a population of about 4500. There is a provincial park for picnicking and maybe a quick dip, a couple of fine walking trails, a sandy beach at **Sandy Cove** and a small herd of caribou and some free roaming ponies on the island. At **Burnt Point** is a lighthouse. There are several fish plants on the island and visitors can have a look around them.

Icebergs can often be seen and in July there's a folk festival. Lastly, a heritage house once the residence of a merchant has been converted into the small **Bleak House Museum** in Fogo and, of course, you can pick berries.

Places to Stay For those wishing to stay, *Payne's Hospitality Home* (☎ 266-2359) in the town of Fogo, is one of the best bargains in the province. Singles range from $28 to $35, doubles from $48 to $56 depending on facilities; rates include all three meals. Alternatively, there is the *Quiet Canyon Hotel* (☎ 266-2556) not far from the ferry terminal at Stag Harbour. They offer 11 rooms and have a restaurant. Singles/doubles cost $50/56. *Fogo Island Motel* (☎ 266-2556) rounds out the accommodation situation. It's a good idea to book ahead before arriving in July and early August.

New World Island

From the mainland, causeways almost imperceptibly connect **Chapel Island**, tiny **Strong's Island**, New World and Twillingate islands.

At **Newville** is a tourist office with maps of the area, advice on what to see and a sheet describing some of the trails and walks on Twillingate which are well worth taking advantage of.

There is a good, central provincial park, **Dildo Run**, with camping and picnicking, set in a wooded area by a bay. Due to currents, swimming is not recommended.

The western section of New World Island is far less visited and has some of the older houses in the area in the small fishing villages clinging to the rough, rocky edges of the sea. At **Moreton's Harbour** is a small museum in an old-style house furnished in much the manner it would have been when the town was a more prosperous fishing centre than it is today. There is one small, basic store in town but not much is stocked.

There are several very small parks around where picnicking and even camping are possible although facilities are minimal. One of them is **Wild Cove Park**, not far north of Moreton's Harbour; look for the clearing surrounded by rocky hills right by the water on the left-hand side of the road.

TWILLINGATE ISLAND

Actually consisting of two islands, north and south Twillingate, this is the area in all of Notre Dame Bay that gets the most attention and very deservedly so. It's a stunningly beautiful area, with every turn of the head let alone turn of the road revealing new ocean vistas, colourful fishing wharves or tidy groups of pastel houses perched on cliffs and outcrops.

Long Point Lighthouse

The lighthouse is a spectacular place with dramatic views of the coastal cliffs. Tell me if this isn't the cleanest, clearest air you've ever had the privilege of looking through.

This is an ideal place to watch for icebergs which are fairly common in May and June and not unusual in July. Seeing one in August is possible too, but fairly rare. (I missed out by a week in mid-August once.) They tend to drift southward from Labrador then eastward towards Bonavista Bay slowly melting in these warmer waters. Icebergs of some size have been seen just outside of St John's.

In June and July whale-watching is very good here and all around the islands. If you miss both of these attractions, memorable sunsets occur all year round!

You can visit the 114-year-old lighthouse itself and take the winding stairs to the top. Note how all the buildings are connected by enclosed walkways, a clue to just how foggy and/or nasty the weather can be.

Twillingate Museum

In Twillingate town, the museum in what was formerly the Anglican rectory provides an overview of the local history. Twillingate, one of the oldest towns in this part of the province, was settled by English merchants in the mid-1700s. One room displays articles brought back from around the world by local sea captains and includes a cabinet from India, a hurdy-gurdy from Germany and an Australian boomerang. Another room details the seal hunt and its controversy. There is also a craft shop at the museum. Next door is St Peter's Church dating from 1844, one of the oldest wooden churches in Newfoundland. Many other attractive churches are found around the island and, on the south side. The United church is a heritage site.

Durrell

Don't neglect touring around unbelievably scenic Durrell. What some people see out their window when they get up in the morning!

Many of the two-storey box-like wooden houses are over 100 years old. The **Iceberg Shop**, for crafts, is here in a 130-year-old house. They also run a very good recommended boat tour out to see whales, 'bergs and along the jagged local shores.

Also here is the **Durrell Museum** perched way up on a hill with great views. It has displays on what the fishing community of the early 1900s was like. It's open daily and, as in all local museums, the admission fee is just a token.

Numerous walks are possible, see the tourist office map for ones to French Beach and the natural arch. Smith's Lookout provides a panoramic view of the island.

Fish, Fun & Folk Festival

Held each year during the last week of July this four-day event is 'a don't miss' one if you're anywhere near the region. It features traditional music and dance some of which goes back to the 16th century. There are fishing exhibits, lots of great food and crafts as well. This is a very busy time of year what with the possibility of whales and icebergs lurking offshore so book early if possible.

Places to Stay

The *Sleepy Cove Inn* (☎ 629-3287), at Crow Head within walking distance of the lighthouse, can't be missed and is a good place to start. They have four rooms: singles cost from $30 to $35, doubles from $35 to 40 and that includes a light breakfast and evening snack.

The *Anchor Inn* (☎ 884-2776) with views from on top of a hill has some rooms in the lodge, some more motel-style rooms and some with cooking facilities. There is also a dining room featuring fish. Motel rooms aren't badly priced at singles/doubles $42/50. For campers, there are sites other than Dildo Run: *Sea Breeze Park* beside the Long Point Lighthouse is a glorious, very inexpensive place to bed down. It's also a good place for a picnic. Contact the tourist office for locations of some of the other small parks around the area.

Apart from staying at these few places, spending the night means going back to New World Island or beyond. For example, there is the *High Tide Summer Cottage* (☎ 629-3261) in Virgin Arm on New World. It can be rented by the week as well as nightly and, if there are a few of you, it can be an excellent bargain as it has lots of space and a kitchen.

Places to Eat

The *R&J* has fish & chips and a great view of one of the many harbours. The *Anchor Inn* has a dining room and bar.

In Durrell, the *Bayside Restaurant* serves chicken or pizza, but again the fish is recommended.

LEWISPORTE

From Twillingate the road leads through Birchy Bay past a mainly lumbering but also farming district once roamed by the Beothuk Indians. Near Campbellton watch for Indian Cove Neck, a small park with a beach and fine views of the shoreline. Anglers may want to try a cast into the Campbellton River for the chance of a salmon dinner.

Lewisporte with a population of 4500 is the largest town along the coast and is known primarily for its Marine Atlantic ferry termi-nal. Other than the boats, there really isn't much reason to visit – though as a distribution centre it does have all the goods and services. West of Lewisporte, the bay becomes less populated and, as the road network declines, less accessible. The **museum** by the Bay & Craft Shop in the large wooden building displays locally collected articles pertaining to the area's history. A pair of sunglasses from 1895 struck my fancy but the showpiece is a long, colourful handmade rug depicting various facets in the life and times of Lewisporte.

Several people offer boat trips for some cod jigging or a visit to the quiet, rocky **Exploits Islands** where local people have summer cottages.

Places to Stay & Eat

There are a few places where you can put up for the night including three guesthouses right on Main St. At No 92, a short walk from the ferry terminal *Northgate B&B* (☎ 535-2258) offers singles/doubles at $35/45 including a breakfast of bread, muffins and homemade jams. It's in an old house with views of the harbour. At No 313 is *Chaulk's Tourist Home* (☎ 535-6305) with five rooms from singles/doubles $30/35 and a balcony overlooking the street. Out the front the sign says 'Seaside Lodge'.

On the way into town from Highway 341 is *Brittany Inns* (☎ 535-2533) with 34 hotel, motel and housekeeping rooms from $48. There is a dining room.

You can camp in town at the *Municipal Park* or at *Notre Dame Provincial Park* about 14 km from town.

For other places to eat try the mall near the junction of highways 340 and 341. There is a bakery here and a Sobey's grocery store which could be useful if you're getting on board one of the ferries. Main St also has a Chinese restaurant.

Getting There & Away

Bus The CN Roadcruiser bus running between Port aux Basques and St John's makes a stop at Notre Dame Junction at the Irving Gas Station south of town where Highway 340 meets the Trans Canada Highway.

Ferry Two ferries (☎ 800-563-7381) depart here for points north. One, a car ferry goes to Cartwright on the Labrador coast and then on through Hamilton Inlet to large Lake Melville, which the Vikings may have visited, and on to Goose Bay in the heart of Labrador where there is an important military base. With a vehicle you can go from here across central Labrador to Churchill Falls and beyond to Labrador City with a train connection (which takes cars). Soon, if it doesn't already, the new road will go all the way through to Quebec. The ferry to Goose Bay is a serious ride taking about 34 hours and only making the two stops. Needless to say, it is not cheap but many people travelling are having the fare paid for them. A one-way ticket is $65, add $104 for a car. Cabins are available at additional charge. There are two ferries a week in each direction from mid-June to mid-September.

The other boat, opening up a different part of Labrador, provides the coastal service which runs up the northern peninsula making stops to St Anthony and then heading over to the coast of Labrador for a series of outport stops. This is strictly a passenger and freight service – no cars. Of course, except in a couple of places, there are no roads at any of these destinations anyway, that is their appeal. This is approximately a 14 to 16-day return trip with Nain the northernmost point, about 2100 km from Lewisporte. The ferries run on this route from sometime in July until around mid-December when the coastal ice meets the Arctic pack ice and everything is sealed up until the summer thaw. Towards the end of the season, throughout November and into December, the weather plays havoc with the schedule and the one-way trip can take weeks. With high winds and waves close to 15 metres high, the ship is often harbour-bound for days at a time.

Normally, it's a very comfortable ship with four meals a day (you didn't forget 'night lunch' did you?) and a choice not unlike that found in any mainland restaurant but with prices slightly higher. Fares are low and determined by the number of nautical miles travelled. The rate is 14.1 cents per nautical mile and an additional 13.2 cents per nautical mile for a regular two-berth cabin. To St Anthony it's 130 nautical miles, to Red Bay it's 194 and to Goose Bay it's 700. There are 46 possible ports of call along the entire return route and the number of stops partially determines the length of the trip. You can get off at the village of your choice. Some of these places have accommodation but check to see when the ferry returns. You can always sleep on the boat – in or out of port.

The low prices make the trip a real bargain. Because of that, the chance to visit some of the country's most remote settlements and see the fine scenery with granite cliffs and long fjords the trip has become somewhat popular with visitors. Space is limited and, as most of it is required for local residents and their gear (everything from food to music cassettes to snowmobiles), reservations for the trip must be made from within Newfoundland.

If you have driven, the car can be left at the ferry terminal in Lewisporte. There is a security guard but a waiver must be signed discounting responsibility.

There are four trips a month in July, August and September and three during October.

For either of the two ferries, arrive 90 minutes before departure and have reservations. For these and all information call ☎ 800-563-7381.

On either trip huge icebergs are not uncommon.

The federal government which has developed air links to these northern communities is talking about trying to phase the runs out – in 10 years the boat voyage may not be possible.

GRAND FALLS & WINDSOR
These two small towns sit in pulp and paper country. Actually Windsor seems more like a suburb of Grand Falls and it is the latter

which is of more interest to the visitor. The huge Abitibi-Price pulp mill sits in the centre of Grand Falls and offers tours in summer.

There is a tourist chalet on the highway a couple of km west of town. The **Mary March Museum** on the corner of Cromer Ave and St Catherine St is very well done and among other things outlines the life of the extinct Beothuk Indians. They lived in much of this, the central portion of the province, before the Europeans arrived but the clash of cultures spelled the end for this tribe. The last two surviving women, who supplied much of the information used in the museum, died in the early 1800s. Mary March was the name given to one of them by the English, her Beothuk Indian name was Deasduit. The museum is open daily and is free.

Adjacent to the museum set in the woods is a re-creation of a **Beothuk Indian village.** It's also free but donations are accepted.

Not far west of town, **Beothuk Provincial Park** has an exhibit simulating a turn-of-the-century logging camp.

There are a couple of expensive motels in town or the *Poplar Inn* (☎ 489-2546), a B&B at about half the rate. It's at 22 Poplar Rd which runs off Lincoln Rd behind the Mt Peyton Hotel which is visible from the Trans Canada Highway.

In Grand Falls there's the obligatory Chinese restaurant on Church Rd (the main street) and a pizza place. There are other places on the highway.

The CN Roadcruiser bus stops in town.

The Bay d'Espoir Bus Service links Grand Falls to St Alban's way down Highway 360 south. There are also other small services based here so ask around if you have a particular destination in mind.

SOUTH OF GRAND FALLS

One fairly recent road runs down 130 km through the centre of the province to the south coast. It's a long way down to the first settlements at the end of **Bay d'Espoir**, a huge fjord. The cliffs at **Morrisville** offer the best views. **St Alban's** is the main town and is connected with Grand Falls by bus. **Conne River** is a Micmac Indian town. The region supports itself with a large hydroelectric plant, forestry and salmon farming. There is one motel and a campground around the end of the bay.

Going further south you'll find a concentration of small, remote fishing villages, some connected with still less accessible ones by the south coast ferry. The scenery along Highway 364 is particularly impressive. Harbour Breton has a motel but a better choice is the cheaper *Olde Oven Inn* (☎ 888-3461) in little English Harbour West which is noted for its knitted sweaters.

RED INDIAN LAKE

Set in a huge wilderness area west of Grand Falls, the lake is the centre of a prime fishing and wildlife region with large concentrations of moose and caribou. Mining and lumbering support the local towns.

Beothuk Indians

Scattered around much of north central Newfoundland the Beothuks, a distinct cultural group, lived from about 500 years ago until 1829 when the last woman died. It was they, their faces painted red with ochre, who were first dubbed 'redmen' by the arriving Europeans, a name that was soon to be applied to all the Native peoples of North America. Semi-nomadic, they travelled the rivers, notably the Exploits, in birch bark canoes between the inland lakes and the sea at Notre Dame Bay. They were not a violent people and there weren't large numbers of them. With White hostility, firepower, and diseases the ultimate tragedy unfolded. Before anybody had enough gumption or time it was realised there were just a handful of Beothuk Indians left. By the early 1800s there were only two women alive to leave what knowledge they could.

There is a museum dedicated to them in Grand Falls and also a re-created village. The museum in St John's also has a display, including a skeleton – the only known remains anywhere. The Beothuk Trail, Highway 380, leads through some of their former lands but otherwise is just a name. ∎

BAIE VERTE PENINSULA

Little-visited Baie Verte (Green Bay) is a traditional region of small fishing and mining villages with a long history of human habitation. The Maritime Archaic Indians originally settled the edges of the peninsula and were followed by the Dorset Inuit who had a camp at and around **Fleur de Lys** from 1000 BC for several hundred years. There is a soapstone outcrop here from which the Inuit gouged the material for household goods such as lamps and for carvings. Within the stone carvings, holes and other evidence of digging can be seen.

Around Baie Verte and the islands archaeologists have turned up Beothuk Indian artefacts. And as you'll notice by the town names, the French also were here in some number.

The Baie Verte area is very pretty with green rounded hills edging the shore. Short ferry trips connect several of the islands. Springdale has some accommodation.

At Baie Verte, the area's largest town, see the **Miners' Museum** and **tunnel**. There is a tourist office in town. Just out of town, open-pit asbestos mining can be seen from an observation point off the main highway. The peninsula also has deposits of copper, gold, silver and zinc though much of it has been mined out. You can also visit some of the many abandoned mines nearby. In the past at little **Tilt Cove**, on the coast, 5% of the world's nickel was mined.

La Scie is another good place to see an iceberg; boat trips are available.

Western Newfoundland

DEER LAKE

There is very little here for the visitor but it is the centre of a small farming area which appears so noticeable because it's so uncommon across the province. It also is convenient as the jumping-off point for trips up the northern peninsula.

In town the *Driftwood Inn* (☎ 635-5115), a large white, green-trimmed wooden build-

ing at 3 Nicholas Rd – an easy walk from Main St – is a good place to stay, although it's not cheap with rooms from $50 a single. It has a popular bar and restaurant. Also for eating, the *Tai Lee Garden* is a simple, cheap Chinese place in the middle of Main St; it serves up surprisingly good meals.

Between Deer Lake and Corner Brook the road passes through scenic landscape alongside Deer Lake where many locals have summer cottages or trailers. Around Pasadena Beach there are some motels and cabins available for visitors.

NORTHERN PENINSULA

From Deer Lake the immense northern peninsula extends 430 km northward to Labrador along one of the most extraordinary, beautiful, rugged, historic roads in eastern North America. Called the Viking Trail, the little-known Highway 430, extends between the coast and the Long Range Mountains to two UNESCO world heritage sites (there are 10 in Canada), another national historic site, two provincial parks, wonderfully barren far north topography and views over the history-filled Strait of Belle Isle to the coast of remote Labrador. There's lots of wildlife, ranging from large mammals to specialised fauna, unbelievably various and abundant edible berries, spectacular fjords, excellent salmon fishing, small coastal fishing villages and very friendly people – some with accents so distinct an outsider can barely catch much of the conversation.

Even for those without a lot of time a trip from Port aux Basques to the northern peninsula if only as far as Gros Morne makes a memorable visit to Newfoundland. Many people make this region the focus of their trip to the Rock and never go further east than Deer Lake. L'Anse aux Meadows, a 1000-year-old Viking settlement (by far the oldest European landing site in North America, centuries ahead of Chris Columbus) has become somewhat of a pilgrimage site drawing a small but determined group from all over the USA and, to a lesser extent, Europe.

Top: Husky Puppy (TS)
Middle left: Mountain Goat, (TS) Middle Right: Duck in Stanley Park (TS)
Bottom Left: Hedgehog Bottom Right: Elk

Top: The Battery, an old section of St John's, Newfoundland (ML)
Bottom: Typical small fishing village near St John's, Newfoundland (ML)

Despite my enthusiasm a few cautionary words are in order. Public transportation is minimal although a bus does do the entire route. There is only one road; it's long with some uninteresting stretches so the return trip is somewhat redundant. In addition gas prices are outrageous and increase at each successive station as you head north until they reach exorbitant peaks at St Anthony. Services, while certainly adequate, are not overly abundant. There are not a lot of places to stay and food supplies are pretty basic. Probably most of the people who make the entire trip are campers but they mainly have vans or trailers of one sort or another. I tented like many others but it can be windy, wet, foggy and rather cool even in summer. There can be lots of bugs as well, so be prepared for maybe the odd night in a motel. If camping, it's a good idea to stock up on supplies in Corner Brook.

Towards Gros Morne

There are many berry farms just north of Deer Lake and if you're passing by in August (a late season compared to most of the country) take advantage of one of the pick-your-own farms offering raspberries, strawberries or blueberries. Roadside stands are common and a jar or two of homemade jam is worth stopping for.

At **Wiltondale** there is a small pioneer village, a reconstruction of an early 20th-century country community. There's also a tea room at the site.

Gros Morne National Park

Gros Morne is a must for its spectacular, varied geography which has earned it status as a world heritage site. Special features include fjords that rival Scandinavia's, the majestic barren Tablelands, excellent mountain hiking trails, sandy beaches and historic little fishing communities. There are rivers, lakes and highland tundra as well as plenty of wildlife including caribou and moose. Offshore there are seals and, occasionally, whales. Part of the UNESCO designation is due to the park's Precambrian, Cambrian and Ordovician rock and the evidence this rock supplies researchers with for the theory of plate tectonics. Another factor was the site's 4500 years of human occupation.

There are five campgrounds, several more primitive camping areas, scattered picnic sites and a smattering of villages, towns and other areas that, while within the park boundaries, technically lie outside the park's jurisdiction. At these areas commercial establishments offer lodging, restaurants and other services. The park information centre is about 25 km in from the entrance on Highway 430 but maps are available at the entrance to the park and at campgrounds. Actually there isn't that much at the centre but the attendants and rangers can answer questions about trails, wildlife, etc. There is also a booklet available describing and listing the various trails which range from easy and short (from one to two km) all the way up to strenuous three to four-day trips.

Things to See & Do The day hike up the James Callahan Trail to the peak of the park's namesake, Gros Morne, at 806 metres provides spectacular views. It takes a full day (16 km return) and is one of the park's most rigorous trails so be prepared for exertion as well as exhilaration. Caribou sometimes wander about the summit area.

More accessible, by the road's edge, but equally compelling are the **Tablelands**. This is a barren 80-km ledge of rock 700 metres high shoved up from beneath the ocean floor – a glimpse of the earth's insides. It often retains snow all year round. Trails lead out to it and there are viewpoints along the road.

Western Brook Pond is the park's feature fjord with dwarfing cliffs nearly 700 metres high running vertically from the cool waters. The boat tour from one end to the other and back is definitely recommended.

The gentle, safe sand-duned beach at **Shallow Bay** at the other end of the geographic spectrum seems almost out of place – as if transported from the Caribbean by some bizarre current. The water, though, provides a chilling dose of reality, rarely getting above 15°C.

Woody & Norris Points

In the southern portion of the park, Highway 431 leads to Woody Point and beyond to the Tablelands. The village of Woody Point with its large old houses makes a good centre for seeing some of the park. Martin's Bus Service connects Woody Point with Corner Brook. The Viking Express bus from Corner Brook via Deer Lake to St Anthony running three times a week makes a stop at Rocky Harbour.

Another Viking Express bus runs from Deer Lake to Norris Point and Rocky Harbour daily except Sunday. Also from Woody Point a ferry runs across Bonne Bay to Norris Point allowing circular trips around the southern area of the park. The ferry runs every two hours from each side between early morning and dinner time daily. The price is $10 per car and driver, $3 for passengers, and half-price for a return ticket.

Places to Stay & Eat There are a couple of places to stay in Woody Point including a *Youth Hostel* (☎ 453-2442), a rare find in Newfoundland. At any rate this makes a great place for one. It's open from the end of June to the beginning of September. It's a small hostel with 10 beds at $8 for members, a little more for nonmembers.

There is also the *Victorian Manor* (☎ 453-2485), a hospitality home with rooms in the nice old house or new two-bedroom efficiency cabins where you can cook your own meals. In the main house the four rooms go for singles/doubles $36/40 with a light breakfast included. Laundry facilities and bike and canoe rentals are also offered. Across the bay in Norris Point are two more choices. *Shear's* (☎ 458-2275) has two rooms available from June to September for singles/doubles $30/35 including a light breakfast. A little more expensive is *Terry's B&B* (☎ 458-2373).

There are restaurants and grocery stores in both villages and a drug store in Norris Point.

Around Woody & Norris Points

From the government wharf in Norris Point two-hour boat trips of scenic **Bonne Bay** depart daily stopping over in **Woody Point** for more people to board before cruising the Arms. Sunday trips are longer and include some live traditional music.

Not far from Woody Point are the Tablelands. Going west, Green Gardens is a beach hike with camping a possibility. In **Trout River**, a small fishing community, the *Seaside Restaurant* is very good for fresh seafood.

Back at Highway 430 going north there are good views along the East Arm fjord. The James Callahan Trail up Gros Morne Mountain begins in this area.

Near Rocky Harbour is a recreation complex with a swimming pool and whirlpool. It's open everyday for a small fee and lockers are available.

The main community in the park is **Rocky Harbour**, where there are all the amenities including a laundrette and grocery stores. You could stay at *Gros Morne Cabins* (☎ 458-2020) in individual log cabins with kitchens and views over the ocean. Inquire at Endicott's variety store. The price is $50 for a one-bedroom place for up to two adults and two kids.

For a munch *Jackie's* has good homemade french fries and fruit pies. More substantial meals are available elsewhere.

Further up the coast past Sally's Cove, parts of the wreck of the SS *Ethie* which ran aground in 1919 can be seen on the beach. The storm and subsequent rescue sparked the writing of a song about the incident.

At **Western Brook Pond** is the 15-km long fjord where boat tours are offered. I know, big deal – a little boat trip on a narrow lake. Many people say that but not once they've done it. This trip is like 2½ hours of the best Norway has to offer, with sheer cliffs towering at the water's edge. These trips are very popular. Make reservations at the park's interpretive centre and the Ocean View Motel in Rocky Harbour.

The tours run from 1 June to the end of September with three trips daily in the high season each taking up to 40 passengers. A ticket costs $20, less for kids. The dock is reached after an easy 30-minute walk from the road and is worth doing even if the boat is not being boarded.

At **Broom Point** restored fishing premises depicting the inshore fishery of the 1960s can be visited. The premises are open daily from June to September. Paleo Inuit used the site as a base for seal hunting from 300 BC to 600 AD.

St Paul's is a small fishing village now without a lot of work. Boat tours take passengers to Seal Island where seals and views of the Long Range Mountains can be seen. Several trips are run daily.

The most northerly community, **Cow Head**, has a small museum, hospitality home, the *Shallow Bay Motel & Cabins* with a restaurant and walks along the shoreline and beach. The Viking Express bus makes a stop here.

The Arches

Out of the park back northward on Highway 430, The Arches is worth stopping at for a stroll down to the beach which is littered with beautiful, smooth, coloured rocks about the size of footballs. The main attractions, though, are the three limestone arches and the remains of maybe three or four more formed some 400 million years ago. There are picnic tables overlooking the beach.

Daniel's Harbour

Just outside town the world's highest grade of zinc concentrate is mined, supplementing the fishing industry. There is a new motel and restaurant.

Table Point Ecological Reserve

North of Bellburns along the shore there are protected sections of limestone 470 million years old containing abundant fossils.

River of Ponds Provincial Park

On the Pond River which is good for salmon, this is the only provincial government campground on the Northern Peninsula other than the one way up at the northern extremity. Swimming and canoeing are possible although, for canoeists, some parts of the river call for white-water experience.

Hawke's Bay

Halfway to St Anthony from Deer Lake Hawke's Bay was a whaling station at the turn of the century. There are some excellent salmon waters here and at the salmon ladder, a device to aid the fish in getting upstream, they can be observed jumping on their difficult journey inland to spawn. For anglers with a different angle, trout are also plentiful.

Just behind the tourist office there is a small campground from where the Hogan Trail along the Torrent River begins. Most of the six-km walking trail is on a boardwalk and leads over marsh and through the woods to the salmon ladder. There's a swimming area near the beginning and three lookout stations along the way where birds may be observed.

Hawke's Bay is one of the few places with any roads leading east towards the Long Range Mountains. If you have a good vehicle capable of handling some smaller, less maintained roads there are 150 km of routes leading to small lakes and rivers. There is a tourist office here which may have advice on places to visit, which roads are easily passable and which are rougher.

Maynard's Motel (☎ 248-5225) has 20 units and another half-dozen with housekeeping facilities. The regular rooms are not cheap, but average for the area, at singles/doubles $48/55. There is a restaurant (watch for the steak specials on weekends), lounge, gasoline bar and laundrette. Also they can arrange salmon fishing trips.

Port au Choix

Busy and interesting Port au Choix is one of the biggest towns between Gros Morne and St Anthony and a main stop for travellers on the Viking Trail. It is a major fishing port with boats down at the docks from all along the coast and across the strait in Labrador. Tours of the fish plant can be taken.

The principal attraction is the national historic park with its helpful staff. Admission to this two-part park is free. Each section deals with different peoples who lived thousands of years apart. In the centre of town beside the museum and visitors' centre is the main site, a **Maritime Archaic Indian cemetery** dating from 3200 to 4300 years ago. The remains of about 100 individuals as well as tools, weapons and ornaments were discovered here accidentally in 1967. Some of these artefacts are on view in the museum. Not a lot is known about these people who lived in the region for many centuries but they did no farming and instead relied on the sea and on gathering for survival.

The other section of the park is a short distance away through town by road followed by a 20-minute walk along a trail. It deals with the Dorset Inuit people who settled on the Cape Riche Peninsula between 1500 and 2200 years ago. Excavation of this site, known as **Philip's Garden**, was done in the 1960s and revealed the remains of several ancient houses. Archaeologists are still working in this area and hope to unearth more articles and perhaps some clues to the Dorset's disappearance. Beyond the site, continue on to the **Point Riche lighthouse** which you can also reach by car going around the other way.

Later the same day I was there, a visitor saw a very large shark washed up on the beach not far past the historic site.

Mark Lightbody

For a little more recent history, just out of town is a plaque outlining some of the tussles (between the French and British for the fishing rights in the area) which continued from the 1600s until the 1900s. In 1904 yet another treaty was signed in which the French relinquished their rights here in exchange for the privilege in Morocco – ah, the days when all the world was a monopoly game. There is also a French cemetery from the 1700s in the area.

It's not difficult at all to spend a full day or two in and around town.

Places to Stay & Eat
There isn't a lot of accommodation but there are two guesthouses in nearby Port Saunders. Try *Marie's B&B* (☎ 861-3921) with singles/doubles $35/45 including a full

breakfast and evening snack too. Boat trips on Ingornachoix Bay can be arranged and, from the house, there are trails to the beach. In the centre of town is *Biggin's Hospitality Home* (☎ 861-3523) with singles the same price and doubles a little cheaper with a continental breakfast included.

In Port au Choix, is the more expensive but well kept *Sea Echo Motel* (☎ 861-3777) with 19 rooms. The dining room is quite good, friendly and has good-value lunch specials that sometimes are based around fresh Atlantic salmon.

About 50 km north of town right beside the provincial picnic park is a private campground, *Three Mile Lake Campground*, which is modelled so much after a government park it might as well be one. It's very quiet, wooded and has a beach on the lake. Take all necessary supplies as there is nothing at all available at the campground. There are 30 sites.

North from Port au Choix
Close to town the long, treeless mountain range to the east is quite close to the road although it's not as high as the peaks averaging 650 metres or so south to Gros Morne. After this close encounter, the mountains veer off easterly and don't have as much a presence all the way up to the tip of the Northern Peninsula. The landscape becomes more and more barren until it appears pretty much like that found in the far Canadian north – an essentially flat, pond-filled primeval expanse. There is probably no other place in the country where this type of rugged terrain is as accessible. There's a majestic simplicity and awe to it that, despite the harshness, makes it appear somehow less daunting than it should.

At **Plum Point** there is a gas station and a motel but after this point there is very little until you reach St Anthony.

From Plum Point a gravel road connects with the eastern shore. At **Main Brook** there is *Tuckamore Lodge* (☎ 865-6361), a new A-frame B&B cottage with four guest rooms, a dining room and fireplace. Meals are available as is a sauna. Singles/doubles are priced at $40/50 with a light breakfast. It's often used by hunters or anglers.

The main town over on this side is **Roddickton** and here, as in Main Brook, there are outfitters for hunting and fishing. It also has an expensive motel. There is also some hiking and a trip up **Cloud Hill** affords good views of the islands offshore.

Back on Highway 430, Saint Barbe is the site of a ferry to Labrador, see the Labrador section for details. From here on up the coast Labrador is visible on clear days.

Just beyond Eddie's Cove at **Watt's Point**, off the main road is another ecological reserve. This one protects limestone barrens where rare flowers persevere.

North from Eddie's Cove watch for the little vegetable plots etched into the terrain beside the road where the soil is drained and deep enough for garden vegetables such as potatoes. Many are marked by whimsical scarecrows, others simply by a name painted on a board, Christopher's or Matthew's. About halfway between Eddie's Cove and the other side of the peninsula is the first St Anthony airport. The one used now is at Hare Bay.

Pistolet Bay Provincial Park
With about 30 sites in a wild but wooded area about 20 km from the main road and about 40 km from the Viking site, this is the place to stay if you're camping.

My first morning there, awakening at 6 am, I stepped out of the tent and stared right into the eyes of a fox four metres away.

Mark Lightbody

The park is not on the water but it's probably preferable to have the scrubby, stunted trees around to provide some windbreak. Be prepared for the mosquitoes and blackflies, they seem to have a real mean streak. There is a comfort station at the park with hot showers and laundry facilities and it's heated! What luxury!

Also on Pistolet Bay is the privately run *Viking Trailer Park* for camper vehicles.

Raleigh
The closest little town for milk and bread (and beer) is Raleigh a fishing village where everybody runs to the dock to greet the incoming fishing folk and a couple of cows stroll freely around the streets like their Hindu brethren. It's a treat to walk around and have a chat in the isolated villages at the end of the peninsula here with their traditional uncomplicated ways.

Saint Lunaire to Straitsview
There are five very small old fishing villages on the way to the historic site of L'Anse aux Meadows. You may see kids by the road's edge selling berries collected out on the barrens. In mid-August this will include the queen of all Newfoundland berries, the golden bakeapple sold here for $30 per gallon (4.5 litres – the people here still use imperial measurements, unlike those in much of the country) and fetching as much as $50 further south. No wonder free samples are not offered! Bakeapples are very often used for jam and chances aren't bad that it may be offered for your morning toast at one of the B&Bs somewhere.

People living in these picturesque little communities have quite strong, almost British accents and you may catch some of the unique expressions for which the Newfoundlanders are renowned.

St Anthony has a reputation for the warm parkas sold there but they are also available in one shop in each of Saint Lunaire and Straitsview where they may be a little cheaper. In Griquet there is a restaurant which is open everyday from 11 am. Note that you can't get anything to eat or drink at the historic park.

Anse aux Meadows National Historic Park
This is a fascinating place made all the more special by the unobtrusive, low-key approach of the park developers. In an unspoiled, waterside setting – looking pretty much like it did in 1000 AD when the Vikings from Scandinavia and Greenland became the first Europeans to land in North

Wild Berries

Delicious berries proliferate all over the province and should be picked and eaten with great gusto as much as possible. Compared with much of the country, the fruit season here is late with most types of berries ripening in August, some even later.

The variety seems almost infinite with many kinds which I, for one, had never heard of: crackerberries, dewberries, dogberries, marshberries, partridgeberries, red currants, squashberries as well as the more common blueberries, blackberries and raspberries. Strawberries are grown commercially and many farms have a pick-your-own deal.

The unofficial queen of all the berries seems to be the bakeapple which can sell for as much as $50 a gallon (4.5 litres)! It's a small, golden berry which grows close to the ground out on the barrens and is usually eaten in a parfait or as jam.

Seeing people bent over bushes or strolling through the landscape in rubber boots, pail in hand is very common. At picnic sites and campgrounds, fresh desserts and fruit on the breakfast cereal is the order of the day. Just ask what's what. Along the main roads berries are offered for sale and, in some areas, homemade jams too. Many craft stores and the shops at tourist offices also sell the jams. The red partridgeberry jam is a favourite. Lastly, many of the hospitality homes offer some form of a berry or two with their meals and restaurants often have pies on the dessert menus. ■

America – are the remains of their settlement. Replicas of the sod buildings complete with smoky smell almost transport you back in time.

These guys, led by Leif Eriksson, son of Eric the Red, built their own boats, sailed all over the North Atlantic, landed here, constructed houses which still remain, fed themselves and they were practically all 20-something years old. Oops, let's not forget they smelted iron out of the bog and forged nails with it – 1000 years ago! And as far as I can tell, they did it for the hell of it. They weren't out to save souls or bring back gold riches for the monarch or lay claim to half the planet – not too shabby.

Allow from two to three hours to browse through the interpretive centre with its artefacts, see the film and walk around the eight unearthed original wood and sod buildings and the three reconstructions. Guided tours are offered and everything is free.

Also captivating is the story of Norwegian explorer Helge Ingstad who discovered the site in 1960 ending years of searching. His tale and that of his archaeologist wife is told in the interpretive centre. A short walk behind the replica buildings leads to a small graveyard where lies the body of local inhabitant George Decker who made Ingstad's day and this site by pointing out the mounds in the terrain.

St Anthony

You made it! Unfortunately it's a little anti-climatic. With a population of 3500, and as the largest town in the north of the Northern Peninsula, it's very functional and an important supply centre and fish-processing depot but it's not what you'd call pretty. There are a couple of things to see though.

This is the final stop for the Viking Express bus and the ferry from Lewisporte en route to communities along the Labrador coast can be picked up here. At the Viking Mall in the centre of town there is a Sobey's grocery store for stocking up if you're taking the boat north or heading back down to Deer Lake. The bus departs St Anthony for Corner Brook three days a week.

Grenfell Museum Have a look around the former home of Sir Wilfred Grenfell, somewhat of a local legend and hero and, by all accounts, quite a man. Born in England and educated as a doctor, he first came to Newfoundland in 1892 and for the next 40 years he built hospitals, nursing stations and organised much needed fishing cooperatives along the coast of Labrador and around St Anthony. The fine old house with large wrap-around porch outlines his life and work and displays mementoes and artefacts collected over the years. One thing that struck me was the wooden coachbox used to transport patients to hospital by dogsled in 1930.

The museum is open daily from mid-June to the beginning of September and for a few days a week in May and late September. The display is well done and there is a small admission charge. The Grenfell Mission and the Curtis Memorial Hospital are still two of the largest employers in town. Near the museum is Teahouse Hill where Mr and Mrs Grenfell are buried. The site is marked with several plaques.

Activities In August, watch for the annual cod filleting contest held in town. Admission is free. These guys can clean fish!

In the rotunda at the hospital is a series of ceramic murals done by Montreal artist Jordi Bonet in 1967 depicting life in the area and Labrador.

There are a few walking trails around the edges of town: they're marked on the map available at the museum.

Places to Stay & Eat There are three places to put the head, one guesthouse and two motels. *Howell's Tourist Home* (☎ 454-3402), at 76B East St, has been here for a while and has four rooms at a good rate of singles/doubles $25/30. Meals are available and it's open all year.

Alternatively *St Anthony Motel*, on Goose Cove Rd, has 22 rooms but is a little pricey at $60 a double. The new *Vinland Motel* costs less and also offers some housekeeping units as well as a few serviced trailer sites.

Other than the motels there aren't a heck of a lot of places. *Pizza Delight* has an outlet and there is the ubiquitous fried chicken takeout (I guess they all get enough fish at home).

Things to Buy There are three craft outlets in town including Grenfell Handicrafts with parkas embroidered by hand, whalebone and ivory carvings, and other articles. The Mukluk Factory has sealskin leather goods and some carvings and jewellery. A mukluk is a traditional Inuit soft winter boot made of

sealskin or caribou and sometimes fur lined. Northern Crafts has a bit of everything.

CORNER BROOK

With 30,000 people, this is Newfoundland's second largest town. There are a few things to see and do in and around this city. Up high beside the water, it is fairly attractive despite the often all-pervading smell – a reminder that the focus of the town is the huge pulp and paper mill. The Corner Brook area is likely the sunniest region of the province and the warm, clear skies of summer can be a real treat. There is some good walking in the area and freshwater swimming south of town at a couple of parks.

There are very good views on the road through town and beyond along the Humber Arm leading to the sea. Big log booms can be seen out in the bay. Also, from Corner Brook there are boat and fishing trips, ask at the tourist office.

Part of the Memorial University of St John's including the Fine Arts Department is in Corner Brook. The centre of town is Main St by Remembrance Square and up along maple tree-lined Park St towards the heritage district. There are a few restaurants here, the post office and, further along, City Hall.

Information

The large tourist office and craft shop can't be missed out on the Trans Canada Highway near the turn-offs into town. They have lots of local information and are very helpful.

The More or Less store at 35 Broadway at the west end of town near the Valley Shopping Mall is good for hiking and camping foods.

Captain James Cook Monument

North-west of the centre of town up on some cliffs overlooking the Humber Arm is a national historic site commemorating Captain Cook and affording excellent views of the city and area. A map from the tourist office is necessary as the road access is pretty convoluted. Mr Cook certainly got around. He surveyed this entire region in the mid-1760s and his names for many of the islands,

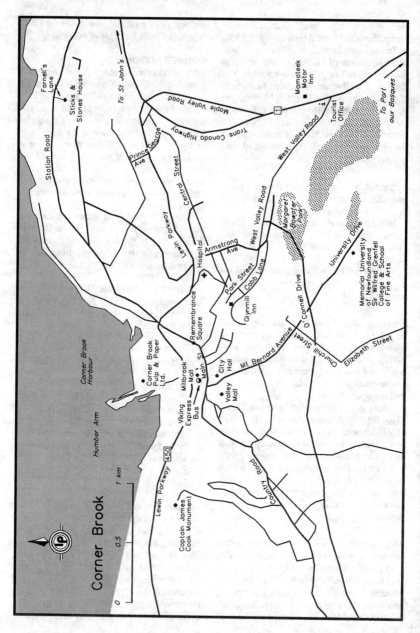

Corner Brook

ports and waterways such as the Humber Arm and Hawke's Bay remain. His work here was so successful it led to the voyages to New Zealand and Australia. Replicas of some of Cook's charts are displayed.

Sticks & Stones House

On the opposite side of town, in a residential area (see the map), sits this folk art masterpiece/one man's life obsession that must be seen to be believed. I don't know where to start. It seems that for 30 years the owner, Mr Clyde Farnell, spent every spare moment elaborately decorating the walls and ceilings of the house with found and discarded objects. When he died and others entered the house, his secret floored the neighbours. The university was notified and soon the house became protected as a folk art museum. The primary material used in the densely packed visual feast is the popsicle stick – some 53,000 of them! Students of psychology might find it intriguing (or downright creepy) to learn that Farnell was blinded in one eye as a child by a popsicle stick. Other materials include wittily used pebbles, ashtrays, glasses, buttons and a flashcube as the light in a lighthouse.

It's open from 1 to 5 pm daily at 12 Farnell's Lane and is well worth the very small admission fee.

Heritage District

The older section of town dating from 1925 to 1940 surrounds Central St. It's primarily a residential area though there are some shops and a few restaurants. There are also restaurants out along the Trans Canada Highway and still others out along the Humber Arm towards Lark Harbour.

Old Railway Display

Even when the trains were in service in Newfoundland they operated on a different, narrower gauge than those in the rest of the country. On display is a train from before Confederation consisting of a steam locomotive and five various cars. It can be seen near Station Rd not far from the large gypsum plant in the eastern part of town during the

summer. If you're lucky there'll be someone around to let you have a look inside too.

Curling Kennels

This is not really a tourist attraction but a private kennel whose owner, Gord Grant, breeds the well known but now rarely seen Newfoundland dog. Visitors who just have to see these big beautiful, black beasts (or buy one to take home) can go to the kennels at 6 Clifton Ave.

Places to Stay

For camping, *Blow Me Down Park* is at the end of Route 450 which leads from town along the Humber Arm. Out here at the tip of the peninsula there some good views of the Bay of Islands.

Corner Brook has half a dozen small tourist homes with prices lower than those in much of the province at around singles/doubles $25/30 sometimes including breakfast.

The central *Townsite Tourist Home* (☎ 639-1960) is in the older section of town at 21 Armstrong Ave.

Another place to try is *Brake's Hospitality Home* (☎ 785-2077) away from the centre west along the Humber Arm at Bartlett's Point. A city bus takes you almost to the door. The address is 25 Cooper's Rd. They have three rooms and include breakfast. A good park with walking trails by the water is just up the road.

For more gracious accommodation the *Glynmill Inn* (☎ 634-5181), on Cobb Lane in the centre of town, is recommended. It's a large Tudor-style inn set off by surrounding lawns and gardens and offers a good dining room as well.

There are also a couple of motels in town not far from the main highway.

Getting There & Away

The CN Roadcruiser depot, for points east and west along the Trans Canada Highway, is in the north-east section of town on the corner of the Lewin Parkway and Prince George Ave. The Viking Express (☎ 634-47100) bus which goes up the northern peninsula arrives and departs from the Millbrook Mall shopping centre not far from Main St in the centre of Corner Brook. Eddy's Bus Service runs to Stephenville. Martin's Bus Service goes to Woody Point in Gros Morne. Devin's Bus Line heads to Burgeo on the south coast.

Around Corner Brook

Bay of Islands Boat Tours goes around the scenic **Bay of Islands**; call Byron Moore (☎ 783-2576).

The **Humber River** which flows into the Arm from Deer Lake is renowned for its salmon. The area from the beginning of the Humber Arm, a long narrow bay, back to **Little Rapids** is both pretty and rich in little fishing pools. *Log Cabin Lodge* in Spruce Brook caters for fishing and can arrange guides, etc.

Marble Mountain, in the Humber Valley eight km east of town, is becoming an established downhill ski centre; the area is also very nice in the fall (autumn) with the colourful foliage. A trail less than 500 metres long leads from the rear parking lot of Marble Mountain to **Steady Brook Falls**. Another trail, 3.5 km one way, leads to the mountain summit, about 500 metres.

For more serious walkers, including overnighters, there are numerous hikes in the **Blomidon Mountains** (also spelt 'Blow Me Down'), south of the Bay of Islands along Highway 450 to Lark Harbour. These mountains were formed about 500 million years ago from brownish peridotite rock pushed up from the earth's mantle when the geographic plates of North America and Europe bumped together. What makes this special is that Newfoundland is one of the few places in the world where this type of rock is exposed and can be walked over.

Other features are the great views over the bay and islands and a small caribou population. Some of the trails especially ones up on the barrens are not well marked at all so bringing topo maps and proper equipment is recommended. Ask at the tourist office for the small booklet on the local trails which shows the various access points. One of the easiest as well as most popular trails begins at a parking lot on the left side of Highway 450 (500 metres from the bridge which crosses Blow Me Down Brook). The trail can be taken for an hour or so or, for more avid hikers, it continues well into the mountains where you're on your own. At Blow Me Down Park near the end of Highway 450 there are also well-used marked trails which still provide fine views of the coastline.

South of town there is very good freshwater swimming at **Stag Lake** and also fairly warm waters at the **Blue Ponds Provincial Park** a little further out.

STEPHENVILLE

Formerly a large military base town with the decaying evidence visible from the road in, Stephenville with a population of 10,000, now relies mainly on the Abitibi-Price pulp mill which you can tour. The town sits on St George's Bay between Corner Brook and Port aux Basques and acts as entrance to French Port au Port. There is not much here for the visitor.

The Stephenville Festival is a two-week English theatre event, usually held in late July with local and internationally known participants. The festival offers theatre ranging from Shakespeare to modern Newfoundlanders' plays. Good student reductions on tickets are offered.

Main St offers a couple of places to eat, *Ildi's* for a coffee and two hotels for overnighters. Less expensive is the *Harmon House* (☎ 643-4673), a B&B, at 144 New Mexico Drive not far from the hospital.

During lobster season (from April to July), the tasty devils are sold in the streets from trucks and trailers at good prices.

PORT AU PORT PENINSULA

The large peninsula west from Stephenville is the only French area of the province and has been since the early 1700s when it became known as the **French Shore**. It was used by the French for fishing in the **Strait of Belle Isle** right up until the the early 1900s. **Red Island** was at one time France's most important fishing base in the New World.

Today, the further west you go the stronger the French culture is. At the south-west tip of the Port au Port Peninsula in **Cape St George** the children still go to French school preserving their dialect which is now distinct from the language spoken in either France or Quebec. Mainland, Lourdes and Black Duck Brook are also very French. In late July or early August each year there is a major French folk festival held in Cape St George with lots of music and other events.

In **Port au Port West**, a small community not far from Stephenville the Our Lady of Mercy Church is worth a look. Begun in 1914, it is the largest wooden building in Newfoundland. During the summer, a guide is on hand to show you around and provide some details and stories about the church. On the way there from Stephenville after going across the small bridge continue straight on the small road, don't follow the road around to the left or you'll miss the church like everybody else does.

South-Western Newfoundland

Within the small south-western corner of the province the visitor is offered a remarkable variety of geography and history. It is well worthwhile spending some time exploring it rather than just doing the usual mad dash to or from the ferry. Hilly Port aux Basques built up and around a jutting, jagged peninsula and offering all the services including a major tourist office is the centre of the region. To the east a good glimpse of the coastal barrens and small fishing villages which surround much of the province is accessible by road before it ends at Rose Blanche. North from town, the treeless landscape gives way to one of the few farming areas in the province, the gorgeous Codroy Valley with some very fine walking trails.

CODROY VALLEY

North of Port aux Basques beyond Cape Ray the broad green, fertile Codroy Valley runs from the coast north-east alongside the Long Range Mountains for about 50 km. This is one of the prime farming regions of the province and compared with the generally rugged, rocky landscape looks lush.

The Grand Codroy River and its many offshoots running through the valley make it especially pretty and there are some fine walks to enjoy. Probably the best of these start at the *Starlight Inn*, a small lodge with eight rooms, in Doyles at the southern end of the valley.

You needn't be staying at the lodge to hike on these trails though. There is a campground nearby just off the Trans Canada Highway. A good spot for a view of the valley (accessible by car) is down near the sea by the town of **Searston**.

Further along, the road goes up a mountain at **Cape Anguille**; there are views as far as the mainland on a clear day. Back at the inlet, the estuary of the Grand Codroy River is an important wetland area for birds which is impressive at migration times when thousands of geese, black ducks and other species can be viewed. At Grand Codroy Park there is a beach and picnic areas.

Despite its long period of settlement and the many quiet farms, the valley does have a nasty side to it. It can be the windiest place in Newfoundland and that's saying something. Along the highway breezes can reach 200 km/h. They used to have to stop the trains at times to prevent them from blowing off the tracks – and you wanted to bring your bicycle!

Though now a blend of English, French, Irish and Scottish the population was at one time primarily Scottish. They developed a community tight enough that Gaelic was spoken until the 1950s. Now just a few of the older people know it but much of the song and dance of the area retains its Scottish roots.

PORT AUX BASQUES

For many visitors this is the first glimpse of

Newfoundland. Approaching by ferry from Nova Scotia, the rocky, barren treeless landscape can look a little forbidding but also appealing in a rough, undeveloped way. For the many people heading to the province to enjoy its ruggedness, this uncommercialised port is a welcome sight.

The town itself, at least the older section built on and around the hills to the left of the ferry as it approaches, is very attractive with narrow, winding roads edged with the traditional wooden houses offering different views and angles at every turn.

Port aux Basques was named by Basque fishermen and whalers in the early 16th century who came to work the waters of the Strait of Belle Isle which separates the province from Quebec. The French and Portuguese also used the port as a fishing station centuries ago.

Today, Port aux Basques with a population of 6100, is the principal terminal for the Marine Atlantic ferry which links the island with the Canadian mainland.

The ferry company is now the largest employer in town, though there are also freight-handling and fish-packing industries.

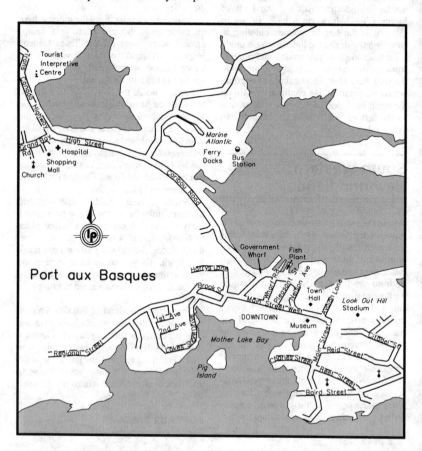

Orientation

The ferry pulls into a small but well-protected bay. The town centre is to the west of the landing and back the way you came in. It consists of narrow, hilly streets overlooking the sea. They're lined with the brightly coloured wooden houses so common in the province.

To get to the old section of town, cross the bridge after leaving the ferry and turn left.

For the new part of town, turn right along the Trans Canada Highway. Go past a number of gas stations and turn left at the Motel Port aux Basques at the corner of Grand Bay Rd and High St. This will take you to the shopping mall, the centre of the new district. If you have time to kill before the ferry, there's a movie theatre in the mall.

Information

The tourist office with information on all parts of the province is on the Trans Canada Highway a few km out of town on the way to St John's. It's on the eastern side.

Gulf Museum

In the old town, on Main St near the corner of Avalon Lane, the two-storey museum is very well done and for the price of $1 you can't really go wrong. The bulk of the collection is Maritime artefacts of one sort or another – many from shipwrecks.

The showpiece of the museum is a navigational instrument from the 17th century known as an astrolabe. I know this doesn't sound fascinating, it didn't to me either, but it's actually quite interesting. The thing itself is a striking brass contraption about 17.5 cm in diameter made in Portugal in 1628. The design is based on a principal discovered by the ancient Greeks to allow for charting of the heavenly bodies.

Variations on it have been used for nautical navigation since 1470. This one is in remarkable condition and is one of only about three dozen in the world. It was found by a diver off Isle aux Morts, along the south coast from town, in 1982 and is the only one in Canada although another one, Samuel de Champlain's, was found in Ontario. The one

in Port aux Basques is believed to have been on board either a Portuguese or Basque fishing boat.

Among some of the other items are some old photographs of the Codroy Valley taken at the turn of the century and some soapstone relics taken from the Cape Ray Dorset Inuit site dating from around 100 to 500 AD.

Places to Stay

Luckily, for campers, there is a good place close to town, in fact, close enough to be convenient when arriving late or leaving early. It's the *JT Cheeseman Provincial Park* north of town about 12 km along the Trans Canada Highway.

At the *Heritage Home* (☎ 695-3240) guesthouse you can practically stay in bed until the ferry blows the whistle before getting up and walking down the hill and onto the boat. It's at 11 Caribou Rd beside the dock, and each of the three rooms costs singles/doubles $35/40.

Further out is *Caribou House* (☎ 695-3408), a B&B, at 30 Grand Bay Rd about three km from the ferry terminal. Prices range from $35/$40 to $45 for singles/doubles.

St Christopher's Hotel (☎ 695-7034) with a fine view from its hilltop location on Caribou Rd is a larger, commercial hotel offering more amenities and a dining room. A double room costs $55.

There are also several motels in about the same price range as the above hotel. The *Grand Bay* (☎ 695-2105) is very close to the centre of town and the ferry near the shopping mall, and has a bar and restaurant.

The *Motel Port aux Basques* is even more expensive. The *Gulfside Inn* with 20 rooms is about four km from the ferry on the Trans Canada Highway.

For more reasonable prices you'll have to hit the highway. *Tompkins Motel & Tourist Home* in Doyles, 34 km away, is a start.

There are numerous places in the Codroy Valley. *Muise's Tourist Home* (☎ 955-2471) is in South Branch, 57 km from Port aux Basques and has rooms from $20.

Places to Eat

The *Blue Rose Cafe*, at 77 Main St beside Radio Shack in the old town, is a good little place for casual, inexpensive meals. They serve homemade bread, soups and desserts. In summer, to cater for visitors, they also offer fish platters and a distinctive Newfoundland offering, brewis, which involves bread being soaked in a broth overnight. The café is closed on Sunday.

The *Harbour Restaurant*, on Main St closer to the ferry terminal, is open later. It is convenient and has good views of the waterfront if you're waiting for the midnight boat. The menu is mainly fried chicken or fish & chips.

At 116 Main St is the *San Yuan* for Chinese and not far away is a *Pizza Delight*.

In the shopping mall in the new part of town is an *A&W Restaurant* specialising in hamburgers and root beer.

Getting There & Away

Bus The Roadcruiser bus service (known as the CN bus but operated by Terra Nova – a little confusing) leaves once a day at 7 am from the ferry dock terminal for the 904-km trip to St John's. The trip takes about 14 hours and costs $67.50 one way. You can stop at any of the towns along the way. Connections can be made in other towns with other, more local, bus companies which service destinations other than those on the main route to St John's covered by Roadcruiser. For example in Deer Lake, the Viking Express bus goes north up the peninsula.

Train There are no passenger trains in Newfoundland and even the freight service has ended.

Ferry Marine Atlantic operates both the ferry routes from Nova Scotia to Newfoundland: one going to Argentia and this one to Port aux Basques. There is a minimum of one trip daily and from mid-June to mid-September, it's more often two or three a day. During midsummer reservations are a good idea and can be made by calling ☎ 800-565-9470 toll

free from New Brunswick, Prince Edward Island or Nova Scotia. Generally one or two days' notice is sufficient. Early morning or late night trips are usually less busy and, if you're walking or just taking a bicycle, there shouldn't be any trouble.

The fare is $14.25, less for children and seniors, $43.50 per car, more with a trailer or camper. The night ferry saves you the cost of a night's bed because you can sleep anywhere and everywhere on board, and people do just that. Upon boarding there is a rush to the decks to secure a comfortable, quiet location away from hallways and most traffic. Sort of wedged between aisles of seats in the TV rooms is popular, fairly dark and quiet. Bring a sleeping bag or blanket – whatever you want – everybody does. When you get up in the morning, the bodies lying everywhere make you wonder if the food was poisoned!

If it's a warm night the outside decks can be pleasant and there are a few benches that you can stretch out on. For those with extra cash, berths and cabins are also available. Whichever way you choose you miss nothing by going at night – there's nothing to see.

There are now two ferries plying this route. The new, large MV *Caribou* with a 350-car capacity is very deluxe; it's like a cruise ship complete with bar and live entertainment, movies, nursery and cafeteria – the works. Much smaller is the MV *John Hamilton Gray* which is used only during the summer peak season. It's considerably smaller taking just 165 cars and, while not quite as comfortable, is quite alright. Both ships take from five to six hours for the crossing, longer in winter.

Ferries also go along the south coast to Terrenceville from Port aux Basques (see the Outports and Terrenceville sections).

SOUTH COAST

The often ignored Highway 470, which heads east out of Port aux Basques for about 50 km, is a fine short excursion. If you've got an afternoon or a day waiting for a ferry this is an ideal little side trip. Edging along the shoreline the road rises and falls over the rounded, eroded windswept terrain looking as though it's following a glacier that ploughed through yesterday. There's not a tree in sight, just the cool pools and ponds left in the many dents in the rock and muskeg. Visible along the other side of the road are half a dozen evenly spaced fishing towns.

Isle aux Morts (Island of the Dead) came by its name through the many shipwrecks just offshore which have occurred over some 400 years. The astrolabe, a navigational device and prize of the museum in Port aux Basques was found here. There's a restaurant in town offering the standards at reasonable prices.

Further east is **Otter Bay Provincial Park** with picnicking and some trails leading over the surrounding hills. It's a very scenic and quiet spot; camping is possible but there are no facilities – I got my drinking water from a stream running through the park.

The highlight of the trip is the last village along the road, **Rose Blanche**, a very pretty, traditional looking village nestled in a little cove with a fine natural harbour – a perfect example of the classic Newfoundland fishing community. Follow the signs for the lighthouse which lead to some houses on a hill overlooking a small bay. From here there's a 20-minute walk along a path that cuts right in front of someone's front door and winds its way up the rocky slopes to a lighthouse. There are nice views along the way and, late in the afternoon and evening, it's surprising how many local people are out strolling. The original stone lighthouse dating from 1873 has been partially restored but a new one does the duty now. Along the way is a small restaurant/café, the *Hook, Line & Sinker*, accessible only by foot and a friendly, casual place recommended for a light meal or just a tea.

For those who long to go that one step further, a trip can be taken by boat (ask around the docks) across the bay to the smaller village of **Petites** with about 30 families. Here, and visible from the Rose Blanche lighthouse, is probably the oldest wooden United church in North America

(although now the Anglicans have taken over) dating from about 1860. It's a plain and simple church kept in excellent condition and has registers of births, deaths, marriages etc to pore over for details of local history.

NORTH OF PORT AUX BASQUES

If you travel early in the morning, the odds are better that you'll see some of the abundant provincial wildlife. Coming off the ferry at 6 am within an hour of Port aux Basques, I saw half a dozen long-haired horses on the road and a cow moose with her calf.

Near Cape Ray there is an excellent walk up Table Mountain which is a little over 518 metres high. Look for the sign across the street from the Cape Ray Rd turn-off. Cape Ray has a sandy beach and campground and was the site of a Dorset Inuit camp around 400 BC to 400 AD. A little further north is more camping at **Mummichog Park.**

Outports

'Outport' is the name given to any of the tiny coastal fishing villages accessible only by boat. Some are on one of the three intra-provincial ferry lines, others are not. These little communities represent some of the most remote settlements left in North America. Change is coming at an ever quickening pace, but for the moment these outports harbour the rough Newfoundland life at its most traditional. Many of these places don't have TV or any outside contact, and some have adult residents who have never seen a car. These villages clinging to the rocky coastlines are perhaps the best place to see the unique culture of the Newfoundland people of European blood born in Canada.

If you want to visit – now is the time, as this way of life inevitably erodes under the modern wave. More and more roads are being built to these out-of-the-way places. Other areas remain isolated but very difficult to reach as only private vessels supply them from other more accessible points.

There are really only two coastal services to choose from, both run by Marine Atlantic. One runs from Lewisporte on Notre Dame Bay up the coast of Labrador. For details see the Labrador and Lewisporte sections. Another trip also departs from Lewisporte but goes more or less directly to Goose Bay which is hardly an outport, with soldiers from a handful of countries stationed there.

The other major outport service runs along the southern coast from Port aux Basques to Terrenceville with about a dozen villages in between as possible stops. The trip takes about 19 hours and leaves Port aux Basques on Sunday, Tuesday and Friday. It goes in the reverse direction on Monday, Thursday and Saturday. Fares are low at about 8.5 cents per km, more for a cabin the price of which is also calculated on a per km basis.

Other trips only run part of the way, for example between Terrenceville and Burgeo or between Port aux Basques and Hermitage.

There is food service on board but you may want to bring some of your own too.

For places to stay on either the south or north coastal trip, ask around beforehand or just take a chance on arrival. You can always stay on the ferry if you're continuing on without a stopover. This can be tiring if you're doing it on the cheap: sleeping on the floor or in a chair can be pretty uncomfortable after a few days, especially if the sea is rough. On a longer trip consider a cabin, the prices actually are quite fair. Ask about stopovers and how long the ticket is good for.

An excellent and inexpensive circular trip around the province, including outports, can be done without the expense of a car. Take the ferry to Port aux Basques, then the coastal service to Terrenceville. Go on by public road transport to St John's or wherever and then catch the main cross-province bus back to Port aux Basques.

Labrador

Labrador is that part of Newfoundland – three times the size of the island – that is adjacent to the Quebec mainland. The Strait of Belle Isle separates Labrador from the Newfoundland island. This vast, rugged land is one of the last incompletely explored areas in the country and one of the largest, cleanest, natural areas anywhere. For this reason it is beginning to attract more and more visitors to its varied regions.

The geological base of Labrador is the ancient Laurentian Shield – possibly the oldest unchanged region on earth. It's thought the land looks much the same as it did before life on the planet began. Four great caribou herds, including the world's largest with some 750,000 head, migrate across Labrador to their calving grounds each year.

Until very recently, small numbers of Inuit, Native Indians and longtime European descendants known as 'liveyers' were the only human residents. They lived in little villages dotted along the rocky coasts as they had done for centuries, eking out an existence fishing and hunting. The interior was virgin wilderness.

Today a new people, with a completely different outlook and lifestyle, has arrived. White southerners have been lured by the overwhelming and nearly untouched natural resources and potential they see.

And so, not far away from the traditional way of life of the original inhabitants, lie some of the world's most modern, sophisticated industrial complexes. Most of the development has been far inland, near the border of Quebec. Labrador City and Wabush, with the latest technology, are two towns that produce half of Canada's iron ore. Churchill Falls is the site of an enormous hydroelectric plant that supplies power for the north-eastern USA.

Happy Valley-Goose Bay is an older settlement first established as an Air Force base in WW II. It's now mainly a supply centre, you can get there from Lewisporte, Newfoundland by ferry.

The east coast, accessible by boat from Newfoundland, is in its own way at least as interesting. Tiny villages dot the coast all the way to the far north. As in western New-

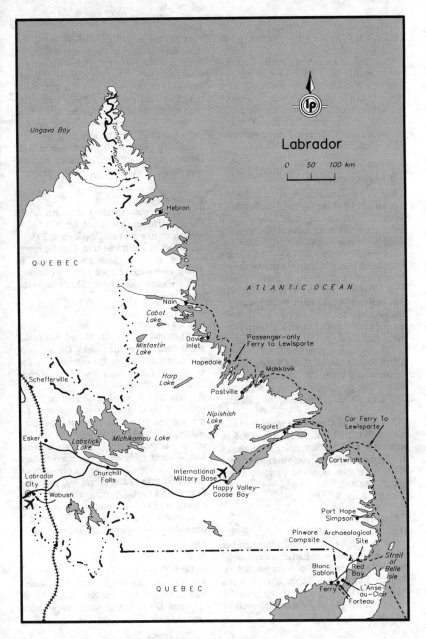

Labrador

0   50   100 km

Ungava Bay

Torngat Mountains

QUEBEC

Hebron

ATLANTIC OCEAN

Nain

Cabot Lake

Davis Inlet

Passenger-only Ferry to Lewisporte

Mistastin Lake

Hopedale

Makkovik

Harp Lake

Postville

Schefferville

Nipishish Lake

Rigolet

Car Ferry To Lewisporte

Esker

Lobstick Lake

Michikamau Lake

Cartwright

Labrador City

Churchill Falls

International Military Base

Wabush

Happy Valley–Goose Bay

Port Hope Simpson

Pinware Campsite

Archaeological Site

Blanc Sablon

Red Bay

Strait of Belle Isle

Ferry

L'Anse-au-Clair

Forteau

QUEBEC

foundland, with some planning, you can take a unique trip on the supply ferries which could be excellent.

Camping is an option all across Labrador but is mostly done in a van or camper. Tenting is possible but be prepared: although summers can be pleasantly warm, even hot, this is often a cold, wet and windy place. The amount of accommodation is steadily increasing in all regions and the larger places all have hotels of one sort or another.

LABRADOR STRAITS

Lying 18 km across the Strait of Belle Isle and visible from the northern peninsula of Newfoundland, this region of Labrador is in some ways the most accessible. There are about half a dozen small, permanent communities connected by road along the historic coast here. Many of the inhabitants are the descendants of the fishermen who crossed from Newfoundland to fish in the rich strait centuries ago. Attractions include the simple but awesome far north landscape, icebergs, sea birds and whales and the historic Basque site at Red Bay.

The ferry from Newfoundland docks at **Blanc Sabon**, which is in Quebec right at the provincial border. There are a couple of fairly priced guesthouses. From here the only road runs 80 km north along the Labrador coast.

At **L'Anse-au-Clair** is the *Northern Light Inn* (☎ 931-2332), a middle-sized modern motel with a few housekeeping rooms and a dining room. Rates are singles/doubles $50/55. Nearby is some fine trout and salmon fishing.

L'Anse-Amour

The remains of a Maritime Achaic Indian burial site dating from 7500 years ago has been uncovered here. Earlier people lived here as long ago as 9000 years just behind the retreating glaciers. Later, other Inuit and Native Indian people used the area for summer fishing and they were followed by the Europeans.

Forteau

Forteau, the largest community along the coast here, is home of the annual Bakeapple Festival, a three-day event of music, dance, food and crafts. There is one small hotel, *Seaview Housekeeping Units* (☎ 931-2840) with four double rooms at $50 a piece. The high lighthouse at **Point Amour** with views of the strait and maybe whales or seals is eight km away. On the way to L'Anse-au-Loup is the **Labrador Straits Museum** with exhibits on the early local residents and their way of life. It's open daily in summer.

L'Anse-au-Loup

The best accommodation deal around is *Barney's Hospitality Home* (☎ 927-5634) with three rooms at singles/doubles $25/33 and meals at additional cost. Call for reservations. Between here and Red Bay is *Pinware Provincial Park* with 15 camping sites and some picnic tables. Don't forget the insect repellent.

Red Bay

The national historic site at Red Bay is the prime attraction of the region. The interpretive centre chronicles the discovery in the late 1970s of three Basque whaling galleons from the 1500s on the sea bed just off Red Bay. The ice cold waters have kept them well preserved and they are to stay where they are, making the area an underwater museum. Subsequent research has found that this was the largest whaling port in the world in the late 16th century. Some of the excavated land sites can be visited including a cemetery on nearby **Saddle Island** where 140 skeletons have been found. Ongoing work areas can also be seen and the centre has a collection of artefacts unearthed thus far. The park is open daily throughout the summer and is free.

Getting There & Away

Air Air Nova has flights from Deer Lake, Newfoundland, to Blanc Sabon, and IntAir connects Blanc Sabon with many points around Quebec.

Ferry From 1 May to the end of the season in November a vehicle and passenger ferry runs from Saint Barbe, Newfoundland, to Blanc Sabon, Quebec. During the 80-minute crossing you may see ice floes drifting southward to the melting warmer waters. Whales may also be seen. Shrimps grow like crazy in these waters. The ferry runs from 1 May to the end of November. From the beginning of July to the end of August when things are at their busiest the boat runs two or three times a day, at other times service drops to once or twice daily. Every day though a ferry leaves at 8 am, other times vary. The cost is $7.35 per person, $14.50 for a car and more for trailers, vans etc.

A coastal freight service, the *Nordic Express*, runs up the Quebec coast from Sept-Îles on the Gulf of St Lawrence to Blanc Sabon with stops along the way.

The coastal service from Lewisporte on Notre Dame Bay, Newfoundland, up the Labrador coast makes a call at Red Bay as well but it's a passenger-only service. For details see the Lewisporte section.

NORTHERN COAST

Beyond Red Bay all the way up to **Ungava Bay** are dozens of small pretty traditional communities and settlements accessible only by sea or air along the rugged, jagged and in some parts mountainous unspoiled coast. This area of Labrador doesn't get a lot of visitors but offers the persistent a look at some of the most remote regions of North America.

The original people were Inuit and they still make up a large part of the population. About 200 years ago Europeans began to settle and fish, which remains the principal way of making a living. Moravian missionaries established missions from as early as 1765 along this coast and their schools, churches and influence continue to play a part in the local culture.

The Marine Atlantic Ferry from Lewisporte, calls in at St Anthony on Newfoundland's northern tip and then 'bounces' along the Labrador coast into Goose Bay and as far north as the town of Nain. Private vessels can be hired to reach still further north. See Lewisporte in the Central Newfoundland section for details. This trip is really the only way to see something of isolated coastal Labrador and its changing older settlements.

The accommodation situation is a bit of an unknown as most people use the ferry as a floating hotel. For those wishing to get off and hang around somewhere until the next boat, it means winging it and asking around town for a spare bed. Although not often listed in tourist information, there are guesthouses in some places but, of course, they come and go.

At **Makkovik**, an early fur-trading post, is a traditional fishing and hunting community. Both new and old-style crafts and materials can be bought.

In **Hopedale** a national historic site preserves the old wooden Moravian mission from 1782. **Davis Inlet** is home to a different group of Native Canadians, the Naskapi, who tend to inhabit the interior rather than the coast. Crafts can be purchased here too, including some interesting work with grass.

Nain

This is the last stop on the Marine Atlantic ferry and with a population of 1000 is the last town of any size as you go northward. Fishing is the main industry and the processing plant is an important employer. As in the other smaller settlements, after the fishing season hunting and trapping continue as they have for centuries. The **Piulimatsivik-Nain Museum** in one of the old mission houses, outlines both Inuit and Moravian history with artefacts relating to both traditions.

Again, there is a craft outlet and Nain has a hotel and a couple of guesthouses.

North, beyond here is another Moravian historic site in **Hebron**. Close to the northern tip of Labrador the wild **Torngat Mountains** are popular with climbers because of their altitude (some of the highest peaks west of the Rockies) and their isolation.

CENTRAL LABRADOR

Making up the territorial bulk of Labrador,

the central portion is an immense, very sparsely populated ancient wilderness. Paradoxically, it also has the largest town in Labrador, Happy Valley-Goose Bay in the south with a population of 7000.

Goose Bay was established during WW II as a staging point for planes on the way to Europe and has remained an aviation centre. Today there is a Canadian military base and a lot of testing goes on, particularly of controversial low-flying jets which the Inuit say disturb their way of life.

The town has all the services including hotels but for the outsider there is not a lot to see or do and it is very isolated. The remote, forested landscape however attracts many anglers and hunters and there are numerous fly-in possibilities for camping.

The **Labrador Heritage Museum** outlines some of the history of the area and includes a trapper's traditional shelter, samples of animal furs and some of the minerals found in Labrador. At the **Northern Lights Museum** some of the military history of the city is displayed. At the Northern Lights Building a lifelike exhibit shows many of the animals and birds found in the region.

There are at least three fair-sized hotels, none of them cheap. The *Royal Inn* (☎ 896-2456) at singles/doubles $55/65 is the most economical. It's at 5 Royal Ave and it also has some housekeeping units at a higher rate. There are also some hospitality homes but these seem to change quickly so try the tourist-office lists and ask around.

Getting There & Away
Air Goose Bay is well served by air.

Road A road runs westward through the heart of Labrador through Churchill Falls to Esker which is nothing more than a dropping-off point, no one lives there. From there a train (which will take your car) goes south to Labrador City/Wabush and down to Sept-Îles in Quebec. Arrangements for this train link must be made in advance by calling the Quebec North Shore & Labrador Railway (☎ (709) 944-8205).

By the time this book hits the stores the road connecting Goose Bay all the way to Labrador City will be complete and much of inland Labrador will be accessible by vehicle. A driving circuit all the way through Labrador from Quebec will be possible with the car ferry taking you from Goose Bay to Newfoundland.

Ferry The slow coastal service from Lewisporte ties in here but there is also a more direct car ferry from Lewisporte which makes the trip to Goose Bay with just a stop at Cartwright on the way. See Lewisporte in the Central Newfoundland section for details on this marathon 33-hour ferry ride.

WESTERN LABRADOR
Accessible from Quebec this is the area of Labrador where everything is oversized in the extreme: mega-developments in a mega-landscape which the visitor can explore relatively easily.

Labrador City/Wabush
These twin mining cities with a collective population of 12,000 just 15 km from Quebec represent modern, industrial Labrador. The largest open-pit iron ore mine in the world is in Labrador City. Since 1958 a very modern town has developed around this mine. Another open-pit mine operates in Wabush. You can tour both facilities. All the resource development in this part of the world is colossal in scale as the tours will reveal. Eighteen-metre-long dumptrucks with three-metre-high tyres are almost like absurd works of art.

There is a regional tourist office in Wabush which will help with reservations and information on Churchill Falls and other local spots as well as answering questions about the cities here.

The **Height of Land Heritage Centre** in a former bank is a museum. See the Tom Thompson paintings in the Labrador City Town Hall.

Most people want to see the land away from town and you don't have to go far to do that. The landscape, a vast expanse of low rolling forested mountains interspersed with areas of flat northern tundra, was scraped down by glaciers.

The **Wapusakatto Mountains** are just five km from town and parts have been developed for skiing. About 10 km from town is **Duley Lake Provincial Park** which even has a wide, long sandy beach and good swimming. There are 100 camping sites here too. Another park, 33 km from the city, is **Grand Hermine** also with a beach, camping and some fine scenery.

The 15-km-long Menihek hiking trail goes through wooded areas with waterfalls as well as open tundra. Outfitters can take anglers to excellent fishing waters.

Bus tours of the towns or surroundings are available. A real treat is the free lightshow – the Aurora Borealis, also called the northern lights – about two nights out of every three. Evidently these otherworldly coloured, waving beams are charged particles from the sun which are trapped in the earth's magnetic field. Personally, I vote for the spirit theory of the Inuit.

Places to Stay & Eat

There are several somewhat pricey hotels and motels some with dining rooms. Ask around for guesthouses. The *Hotel Wabush* (☎ 282-3221) is the cheapest commercial place at $76 a double so you get the idea. Advance booking is recommended. Most of the eight or so restaurants are in Labrador City and include a couple of pizza places and *Ted's Pub*. Fish and sometimes caribou show up on menus.

Getting There & Away

Transportation here, while improving in giant strides, is still an adventure in itself.

Several airlines connect with Labrador City including Canadian from Newfoundland and Air Alliance from Quebec City.

From Baie Comeau, Quebec, itself a rather isolated town on the north shore of the St Lawrence River, a 576-km partially paved roads runs up through little-developed northern Quebec, past Manic Cinq with its huge dam to Labrador City. A little surprisingly, Voyageur bus lines of Quebec does the trip.

A second method is to get to Sept-Îles, Quebec (even further east than Baie Comeau) and from there catch the Quebec North Shore & Labrador Railway to Labrador City or beyond to Schefferville back in Quebec. Vehicles can be taken and the train connects with the road for Goose Bay at Esker. This car-dropping service at Esker may end as a result of the opening of the road from Goose Bay to Wabush. See Sept-Îles in the Quebec chapter for more details of trips around the Labrador City area.

Churchill Falls

Not quite halfway to Goose Bay, modern Churchill Falls developed in the early 1970s is built around one of the largest hydroelectric generating stations in the world. The diverted Churchill River falling over a 300-metre ledge powers the underground turbines and kicks out 550 megawatts, enough to supply almost the entire needs of the New England states. It's quite a piece of engineering, tours are offered.

The town is connected by road with Goose Bay and to Wabush by train via Esker. There's a new road link to Wabush. The *Lobstick Motel* (☎ 925-3235) offers rooms and meals at no more than the usual prices. Another is the *Churchill Falls Inn*; booking ahead is recommended.

Nova Scotia

Entered Confederation: 1 July 1867
Area: 55,491 sq km
Population: 847,442

You're never more than 56 km from the sea in Nova Scotia, a feature which has greatly influenced the history and character of the province. For generations the rugged coastline, with countless bays and inlets, has provided shelter for small fishing villages, especially along the southern shores.

It was here the first settlers and pirates came followed by Loyalists and immigrants from across Europe. Fishing remains important with Lunenberg maintaining a significant east coast fleet and where fabulous fresh fish is served. The boat, the *Bluenose*, seen on the Canadian 10-cent coin (dime) was built here.

The typical Maritime scenes and towns along the coast give way to Halifax-Dartmouth, one of the country's most attractive major metropolitan areas – a modern, cosmopolitan urban centre that retains an historic air.

Inland, much of the province is covered with forest, while low hills roll across in the north. The Annapolis Valley, famous for its apples, is gentle, scenic farm country – beautiful in springtime with pink and white blossoms. The area contains some reminders of Canada's oldest and most captivating history.

The Bay of Fundy region is dominated by the world's highest tides. As a consequence, the rivers carry brackish waters far inland to connect with the 400 or so lakes. Due to the vast number of waterways, canoeing in the province is excellent. Diving all around the coast is also good.

Along the Northumberland Strait, wide sandy beaches washed by the warmest waters around the province offer a place to relax for a day or two.

Visiting rugged, mountainous Cape Breton Island which provides another side to the varied topography is the highlight of a trip to Nova Scotia.

The province's people are of English, Scottish, Irish and French ancestry. The Highland Scots landed in familiar looking Cape Breton in 1773 and thousands more Scots followed to settle Nova Scotia, which means 'New Scotland'. In some areas you can still hear Gaelic spoken, in other areas French culture and language lives on.

A visitor wouldn't notice it, but manufacturing is the most important industry – there are shipbuilding, dairy and paper industries. Fishing, of course, is also a major business – the catch includes cod, lobster and scallops.

The sea generally keeps the weather moderate. Summer and autumn are usually sunny, though the eastern areas and Cape Breton are often windy. Rain is heaviest on the east coast. The entire southern coast from Shelburne to Canso is very often wrapped in a morning fog which frequently may take until noon or later to burn off. Winters can be very snowy.

The Nova Scotia tourist office has designated 10 different road routes through the province which best show the scenery and sights.

The tourist routes are generally on the older, smaller roads, not the main highways. Each route is marked with roadside symbols. A booklet detailing all the routes is available free and is worth having, although at times it's prone to hyperbole.

Tourists who spend three or more days in the province may become members of the Order of the Good Time. This social organisation was founded at Port Royal (now called Annapolis Royal) in 1606 by the French explorer Samuel de Champlain. Ask about it at information offices. They can also

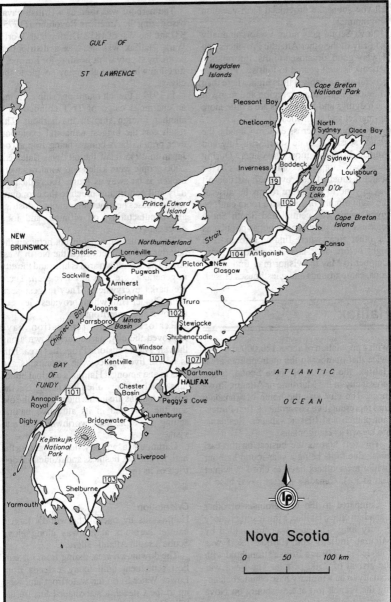

Nova Scotia

0   50   100 km

tell you about the provincial farm vacation programmes.

Nova Scotia gets more visitors annually than any of the other Atlantic Provinces and its very good, organised tourist information network is well geared to tourists. Prices in general are probably a little higher here than in much of the Atlantic region and many of the lodgings and restaurants are a little more up-market and sophisticated.

As is the case across eastern Canada, the visitor season is quite short with July and August bringing most travellers. During these two months accommodation can be scarce in much of the province. It just doesn't pay anyone to add more rooms because of the eight months or so when a room can't be given away. The central and South Shore regions of the province are not as popular as the other areas where finding a room each night before dark is recommended. From October to May the visitor may find attractions, campgrounds and guesthouses closed.

Halifax

With a population of about 120,000 and over twice that number in the metropolitan area, Halifax, the capital of Nova Scotia, is the largest city in the Maritime or Atlantic Provinces. The city was the home of Canada's first representative government, first Protestant church and first newspaper. Residents are known as Haligonians.

The port here is the busiest on the east coast, due to its being a year-round harbour (while most others have to close in winter due to ice). Canada's largest naval base is here.

Compared to the backgrounds of other Canadian cities, Halifax's interesting history is very long. The area was first settled by Micmac Indians and Halifax itself was founded in 1749 as a British stronghold with the arrival of 2500 people. The town was actually to be a military base counterbalancing the French fort at Louisbourg on Nova Scotia's south-east tip.

The harbour was used as a British naval base during the American Revolution (1775-83) and the War of 1812. During both World Wars, Halifax was used as a distribution centre by supply ships heading for Europe, a function which brought many people to the city.

In 1917 a French munitions ship carrying an enormous cargo of TNT collided with another foreign ship in the harbour. The result was the biggest unnatural explosion ever, prior to the A-bombs' being dropped on Japan in 1945. Half the city was flattened, 2000 people were killed and windows were broken as far away as Truro. Today the military still contributes much to the economy, with six bases nearby. Other major industries are manufacturing, oil refining, and food processing.

The city lies on a peninsula between the harbour and an inlet called the North West Arm. The downtown area is hilly and the city in general as green as any I've seen. There are parks everywhere. They're best seen from Citadel Hill, which provides views of the town and waterfront.

Restoration and renovation have improved the city, particularly down along the water in the Historic Properties area. This is now a lively place with restaurants and bars in and amongst Halifax's original buildings which are very often lost in fog. But the city's strengths are in this blending of the old and the new and in its attractive natural setting. It's a pleasant, worthwhile place to visit.

Dartmouth, a twin city, lies west across the harbour and has business and residential districts of its own.

Orientation

Halifax sits by one of the world's largest natural harbours at midway along Nova Scotia's south Atlantic shore.

The downtown area, dating from the earliest settlement until today, extends from Lower Water St on the waterfront and west up to the Citadel, a star-shaped fort on the hill. Cogswell St to the north and Spring

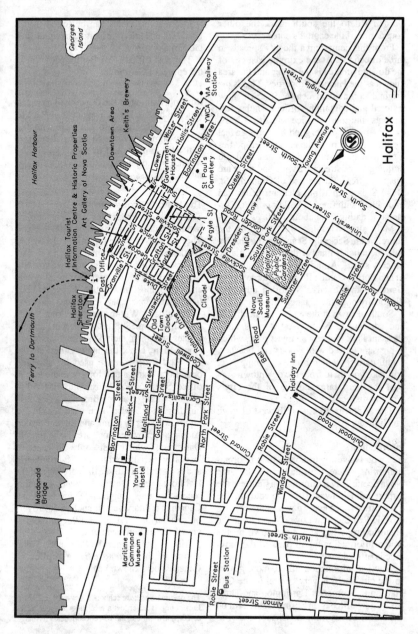

Garden Rd to the south mark the other boundaries of the capital's core.

From this central area the city spreads in three directions. At the extreme east end of the downtown area is the water and the area known as the Historic Properties. This is the original commercial centre of town, now restored and containing offices, shops, restaurants, the tourist office, etc. It's a busy, visitor-oriented place, good for getting a feel for the city. Up from the Historic Properties there's an interesting mix of new and old buildings. The streets are wide and there are plenty of trees. At the end of Granville St, Duke St is a small but pleasant pedestrian mall, lined with fine old buildings in Italianate-style dating from about 1860.

Main streets leading west up from the shoreline are Sackville St and Spring Garden Rd. The latter is lined with shops, including grocery stores. At the corner of South Park St and Spring Garden Rd are the large Public Gardens, an attractive Victorian city park diagonally opposite Citadel Hill.

South of town at the end of the peninsula and adjacent to North West Arm is Point Pleasant Park, the city's largest park, which is pleasant indeed with woods and beaches. South Park St, which becomes Young Ave, will take you there from the downtown area past the very large houses of the city's wealthy district.

The airport is 40 km north-west of town on Highway 102.

Information

You won't have any trouble getting information or maps here. Outside town is the large Nova Scotia Travel Information Centre at the airport on Highway 102. Downtown, the main office (open every day in summer) is in the Old Red Store on Lower Water St, in the Historic Properties area right down by the water. Information on all parts of the province is offered here.

Another information office, more geared to the city itself, is very central in the City Hall on the corner of Barrington and Duke Sts. A new office is on Spring Garden Rd on the corner across from the Citadel.

Information booths can be found in the Lord Nelson Hotel, the Delta Barrington and the Holiday Inn.

The post office is on Bedford Row near the corner of George St.

Parking Parking in the downtown area can be a real hassle. For a cheap, central place to stash the wheels go to Citipark with the yellow signs on Water St near Salter St. It will take campers and has a cheap all-day ticket. From 6 pm through the night the flat rate is even less.

The Historic Properties

The Historic Properties are a group of restored buildings dating from 1800 to 1905. They were used in the original settlement of Halifax and now represent the town's seafaring past. Many of the buildings here are long two-storey places for easy storing of goods and cargo, most now house shops and boutiques but there are also restaurants and bars.

Privateer's Warehouse, the long building dating from 1800, is the oldest in the area. Pirates brought in their booty for dealing and storage here, hence the name. Others are the **Old Red Store** – once used for shipping operations – and a **sail loft**, now the tourist office. Simon's Warehouse, built in 1850 of granite, was used as an office and warehouse building. It was also once used for storing liquor, and later by a junk and salvage dealer. Along the renovated dock area is the ferry to Dartmouth, which costs only 50 cents. It leaves every half hour for the 10-minute trip and is a good way to see the harbour and the Halifax skyline. Out in the water you may see yachts, tugs, freighters, cargo boats and Canadian military vessels such as destroyers or submarines. About 3500 commercial vessels tie up here each year.

Moored at the wharf by Privateer's Warehouse is the *Bluenose II*, a replica of Canada's best known boat.

The original *Bluenose* schooner was built in 1921 in Lunenburg. It never lost a race in its 20-year racing career, and in tribute, the 10-cent coin bears its image.

The *Bluenose* has become as familiar a Canadian symbol as the maple leaf.

The *Bluenose II* was launched in 1963 and now has a permanent berth at the Historic Properties when not on display at another Canadian port. Two-hour harbour tours are given on her, but when she's docked you can walk on board, free, to look at this beautiful piece of work.

Cable Wharf The blue cable wharf building along the pier by the ferry terminal is a centre for handicrafts and souvenirs. There are a couple of offices for boat tours including the McNabs Island ferry. Small, typical Maritime fishing boats often moor alongside.

Brewery Market
Also part of the restored waterfront, this complex is in the Keith's Brewery building dating from 1820, at 1489 Hollis St. It now contains boutiques, restaurants and a pub or two. It's all very new-looking, and seems a bit contrived and lacking in atmosphere, compared to what else is around. A farmers' market is held on the lower level on Friday and Saturday from 7 am to 2 pm.

Historic Downtown Area
The tourist office has maps for a self-guided walking tour of the Historic Properties, the waterfront boardwalk and the old buildings west up the hill from the water. Most of the buildings which made up the early commercial area are marked with plaques giving a brief history.

The brochure adds a few details and makes them easier to find. Using the map, you'll take about an hour to do the circuit. Descriptions of some of the best spots follow.

Province House On Hollis St near Prince St, this fine example of Georgian architecture has been the home of Canada's oldest provincial legislature since 1819. There are free guided tours Monday to Friday from 9 am to 5 pm.

Government House This is between Hollis and Barrington Sts, near the corner of Bishop St. Since 1807 (again it's Canada's oldest) Government House has been the residence of the provincial lieutenant-governor. It was built by Governor John Wentworth.

St Paul's Cemetery Across the street from Government House on Barrington St, this cemetery first used in 1749 has graves of people from all faiths, many of whom died young. Numerous soldiers, sailors and stories lie buried here.

St Paul's Church This is on Barrington St near Prince St. It was the first Protestant church in Canada (dating from 1749) and the first church of British origin in the new land. It's open to visitors Monday to Friday from 9 am to 5 pm, with guided tours after 1 pm. The tour includes some interesting tidbits about the church; you'll hear about the silhouette cast by a certain hole in the stained glass.

City Hall This is at the opposite end of the sunken courtyard from St Paul's Church. Built in 1890, it's a gem of Victorian architecture.

Citadel National Historic Site

The Citadel – a huge, oddly angled fort on top of Halifax's big hill – has always been the city's towering landmark. In 1749, with the founding of Halifax, construction of a citadel began.

In the mid-1750s, the English realised that the crunch was coming with France over possession of the new land. Halifax was a good location for English purposes: it could be used as a centre for ruling over Nova Scotia and, more importantly, as a military base from which to deal with the French who had forts of their own in Louisbourg and Quebec City.

The fort visible today, built between 1828 and 1861, is actually the fourth one on the site. It is open daily from 9 am to 8 pm in summer, and 9 am to 5 pm from early September to 14 June. Admission is $2 in summer, free the rest of the year. I recommend the guided tours, which include theatrical presentations; the movie is also worthwhile. The guide will explain the fort's shape and how, despite appearances, it was not very well designed or constructed. There are excellent views in all directions – of the city, Dartmouth and waterfront areas.

Citadel Hill is a good park in itself and a popular sun-bathing spot. Halfway down towards the Historic Properties, or up from George St, is the old town clock, built in London but erected here in 1803. It was designed by the Duke of Kent while he was Commander of the Citadel.

Also in the compound is the Army Museum with exhibits relating to Atlantic Canada's military history.

Nova Scotia Museum

The main part of the Nova Scotia Museum (☎ 429-4610) is at 1747 Summer St, near the corner of Sackville St, south-west of the Citadel. History, wildlife, geology, people and industry are all covered. The three-dimensional animal exhibits are excellent – you feel you can reach out and touch the display; the fish of Nova Scotia are also presented well. There's a good history section, with an old stagecoach and a working model of a late-1800s sawmill. Also worth noting is the excellent mushroom display. It's free and open from 9.30 am to 5.30 pm, Wednesday to 8 pm but on Sunday only from 1 to 5 pm.

Maritime Museum of the Atlantic

This large museum is a must for boat buffs but also has enough interesting displays to warrant a peek from anyone. It's very spacious and contains full-scale examples of many regional vessels, with plenty of models, photographs and historical data as well. The lens from a Halifax lighthouse is impressive but I particularly liked the painted figureheads taken from various ships, many of them wrecks. Also very good is the portion of a boat you can enter which sways realistically as though out on the sea. There is also a display on the ever interesting *Titanic*.

Outside at the dock you can explore the CSS *Acadia*, a retired survey vessel from England. The museum is open from 9.30 am to 5.30 pm daily, but on Sunday from 1 to 5.30 pm only. It's at 1675 Lower Water St and is free.

Also docked here is the HMCS *Sackville*, the last of 122 warships of its kind. It can be boarded daily, donations go to its much needed restoration work.

Maritime Command Museum

This is on the Canadian Forces Base, off Gottingen St between North and Russell Sts near Macdonald Bridge. It's in the fine-looking stone building on large grounds protected by numerous cannons. You'll see mementoes like uniforms, medals, etc from the military past of the Maritimes. It' s open Monday to Friday from 9.30 am to 3.30 pm, Saturday and Sunday from 1 to 5 pm.

Art Gallery of Nova Scotia

The Art Gallery, housed in the old post office, is a heritage building dating from the mid-1800s which has very recently had a lot of exterior restoration work. It's very central at 6152 Coburg Rd near the harbour. Provincial and other Canadian works make up much of the large collection. There are both permanent and changing exhibits. Admission is $2 and it's closed on Monday.

Nova Scotia Sport Heritage Centre

In the Halifax Trade & Convention Centre between George and Prince Sts is the sports hall of fame dealing with provincial heroes and teams through displays of trophies and photographs. Some of the old equipment is fun to look at. Admission is free. It's open daily but on Sunday during the afternoon only.

Halifax Public Gardens

The public gardens are a small but well kept and pleasant formal Victorian city park on the corner of South Park St and Spring Garden Rd. Bands give concerts in the gazebo on Sunday throughout the summer.

Point Pleasant Park

Point Pleasant Park is highly recommended. This is a 75-hectare wooded park with walking trails, picnic spots, a restaurant, a beach, and an old Martello tower – a round defence structure. There are lots of joggers and sun-bathers, good views all the way around the perimeter. No cars are allowed.

The park is at the far south end of town at the tip of the peninsula. The No 9 bus goes to and from it from the downtown Scotia Centre or you can drive to the park's edge. Whichever way you come, check out the size of the houses along Young St. At the city edge of the park is the Port of Halifax, a very busy terminal with containers piled high and ships from everywhere steadily coming and going. Walk out to the lighthouse by the port for great views and a peek at the shipping activity; kids'll be tossing in lines hoping for the big catch.

York Redoubt

The remains of a 200-year-old fort make up this national historic site which overlooks the harbour from a bluff just south of the North West Arm (south of the centre). It was designed to protect the city from an attack by sea and is built at the narrowest point of the

outer harbour. The site was used in various capacities by the military as late as 1956.

Aside from the view, there are mounted guns, a Martello tower and historical information and displays. The grounds are open all year but the buildings from 15 June to Labour Day, 10 am to 6 pm.

McNabs Island

Out in the harbour and easily seen from York Redoubt, visiting this small island makes a good break from the busy and/or hot city. The island offers guided walks, beaches, picnic tables and hiking. There's also a teahouse for basic snacks or seafood. Ferries depart for the island through the day from the dock area, and tickets costing $7.50 can be bought at the little office by Cable Wharf Market.

Hemlock Ravine

A system of linked walking trails winds through this large wooded estate once called home by Edward Duke of Kent, Queen Victoria's dad. It includes a view of Bedford Basin and amidst the gardens some very impressive 30-metre-tall trees. To get there, drive along the Bedford Highway (Highway 2) past Birch Cove and then look for the signs. It's not far and, once there, feels a long way from a city.

Beaches

If you're looking for a beach, try **Black Rock Beach** in Point Pleasant Park; **Crystal Beach**, 20 km west of town, with some areas for nude sun bathing; or **Queensland Beach**, 35 km west of town.

Ask at the tourist office for activities on the lakes within the Dartmouth city borders.

Canoeing

To rent a canoe in Halifax for exploring nearby waterways, try the Trail Shop (☎ 423-8736). They can also give you some tips on good spots to go to. The tourist office has information on canoeing too. The city's Recreation Department offers rentals on the North West Arm, along which you can paddle.

Diving

There are about 50 wrecks at the mouth of Halifax Harbour and good diving along the coast. For info and equipment rentals, try Northern Shore Diving Centre (☎ 429-8265) at 1549 Lower Water St or the Aqua Dive Shop (☎ 469-6948) at 77 Prince Albert Rd in Dartmouth.

Organised Tours

A wide selection of tours by bus, boat or foot is available. For a complete list see the tourist office, but some of the more established and interesting ones follow.

Gray Line (☎ 454-9321), a tour bus company represented across Canada, also has tours in and around town and they will pick you up from your hotel. Gray Line always has competitive fares and is reliable. The 2½-hour town tour is $12 and takes in many of the essential sites. There is also a double-decker bus tour (☎ 420-1155), which leaves from the Historic Properties several times a day and also costs $12.

Cabana Tours (☎ 423-6066) can supply guides, and has city bus trips but also offers longer day trips to various points around the province such as Peggy's Cove, Lunenberg and the Annapolis Valley for relatively small groups. The Peggy's Cove trip, for example, takes four hours and costs $20. Full-day trips are about $40.

Halifax Water Tours (☎ 423-1271), from Privateer's Wharf at the Historic Properties, has boat tours of the Halifax Harbour. The two-hour, narrated trip goes past both new and old city landmarks and at $10 is pretty good value. From 15 June to 25 August there are four runs daily. Out of peak season there are two trips daily and in winter they close down completely. The boat carries 200 people and has both open and closed decks, a snack counter and a bar.

The *Bluenose II*, perhaps the country's best known boat, also goes out on two-hour harbour cruises but is slightly more expensive at $12. Usually the sails are not unfurled until the boat is at the outer reaches of the harbour; it only leaves on clear days.

The *Mar II* does tours around the harbour as well including some evening party trips.

A number of private entrepreneurs offer tours of the harbour or charters on their yachts, especially on weekends and holidays (in summer). Shop around the boats tied along the wharf area. There's likely to be one with moonlight sailings and the *Harbour Queen* trip includes an historical commentary.

Helicopter trips to Devil's Island (reputed to have ghosts) and over the city are also offered.

Some summers the Waterfront Development Corp (☎ 422-6591) plans free guided-walking tours of the historic water's edge.

Festivals

The Nova Scotia Tattoo is held in Halifax from 6 to 9 July or around that time every year. It's called the province's 'greatest entertainment extravaganza'. The city also hosts schooner races in July.

The now annual Buskers Fest draws street entertainers from far and wide who perform at a number of places around town, mainly along the waterfront, and is a lot of fun. These guys are no slouches! The festival runs for 10 days in August. Also in mid-August is the International Town Criers Festival.

Places to Stay

Camping *Smith's Camping Ground* (☎ 835-3713) is 11 km west from Halifax. It's on Route 2 which runs off Highway 102. Take the Bedford exit and it's about two km along, at the traffic lights. There are only 15 places at $9 each, open from 1 June.

Haverstock's Campgrounds are 15 km from town on the Highway 213, six km from Bedford exit 3, five km west of Highway 102.

Along highways 103 and 333 are three campgrounds within 25 km of town: *Seaside Camping, Safari Camps Wayside Park* and *King Neptune Campground*.

There are also a couple of campgrounds on Highway 102, south and west of town. *Woodhaven Park* is in Hammond Plains, a small town near Bedford just off Highway 213, north of town about a 15-minute drive.

Hostels The *Youth Hostel* (☎ 422-3863) is in a big, old building at 2445 Brunswick St. There's room for 50, and cooking facilities as well. Prices are $12 for members, $14 for nonmembers and the rates go down if you stay more than one night. The hostel is closed through the day and open from 6 pm to midnight. It's one block from Macdonald Bridge, west of the Historic Properties, and a 10 to 15-minute walk from downtown. This is not the best area of town; take care late at night. The Hostel Association office for the province is at 5516 Spring Garden Rd for any information on hostelling in the region.

The *YMCA* (☎ 422-6437) is in an excellent location at 1565 South Park St, across from the public gardens and very near Citadel Hill. Single rooms for men and women are $26 and a room for couples goes for $35. The weekly rate is cheaper. The Y was renovated during the summer of 1984 and there's a small, cheap cafeteria and you can use facilities like the gym and swimming pool. It's open all year.

The *YWCA* (☎ 423-6162), for women only, is at 1239 Barrington St between the city centre and the VIA Rail station. There are 30 rooms; singles/doubles cost $22/34 or you can take half a double for $17 and they'll pair you up. Good weekly rates are available.

Halifax has the highest ratio of educational facilities per capita on the continent; this is good for the traveller, as rooms are offered in dorms during the summer months.

At *Dalhousie University*, rooms are available from mid-May to mid-August in the Howe and Sherref Hall residences. Contact Room 210 in the Dalhousie Student Union Building (☎ 424-8840) at 6136 University Ave. Both are on the campus: Howe residence is on the corner of Coburg Rd and LeMarchant St; Sherref Hall is on the corner of South and Oxford Sts. Reservations are required. Singles cost from $26 to $28, doubles from $34 to $40, with breakfast. For students with ID singles/doubles cost $17/22, no breakfast. All three meals are available very inexpensively.

Rooms are also available from mid-May to mid-August at *Fenwick Place*, an off-campus high-rise residence at 5599 Fenwick St. For information call the Accommodation Office (☎ 424-2075) in the building. It's central and close to the university. Rooms cost $10, around $5 more if you need sheets and a blanket.

The *Technical University of Nova Scotia* (☎ 429-8300) also has rooms from mid-May to the end of August for singles/doubles $20/30; students pay $14/22. It's off Barrington St on Bishop St, a 10-minute walk east from the central core. *Mount St Vincent University* rents rooms from 15 May to 15 August; contact the Conference Officer (☎ 443-4450) at 166 Bedford Highway (Highway 2) on the campus. Student rates are singles/doubles $15/20, others pay singles/doubles $24/32. They offer excellent weekly and monthly rates, especially for students. Meals are available and there is a coin laundry. The university is a 15-minute drive west of town on the Bedford Highway and overlooks the Bedford Basin.

Yet another university with accommodation is *St Mary's University* (☎ 420-5486), which is also cheap and not far from the centre.

B&Bs, Tourist Homes & Hotels Halifax is very well blessed with plentiful, moderately priced, central, good-value accommodation. In fact, for quality and selection downtown it's one of the country's best cities. There are many B&Bs in town and over in Dartmouth as well. Some fine ones, though more costly, are found in heritage houses and mansions.

The Metropolitan Area Tourism Association (☎ 835-0677) promotes over 30 commercial B&Bs in and around town and publishes a listing of them.

The *Halifax B&B Organisation* (☎ 429-7685) helps connect visitors with residents who have a room or two in their own home. They'll help out if you're stuck or have some special preferences.

Note that some of the less expensive, more casual places (often named after the owner) are not as predictable as the others, so calling a couple of this type of place may be necessary.

The *Fountain View Guesthouse* (☎ 422-4169) is the bright blue place with white trim at 2138 Robie St, between Compton Ave and Williams St, across from the park and west of Citadel Hill. It's open all year. The seven rooms, all with TV, go for $24 to $28 for singles, $24 to $30 doubles plus tax. Each extra person costs $5 more. It's popular, so try in the morning. There are also rooms to rent next door (though there is no sign); ask at the Fountain View.

The *Waken 'n' Eggs B&B* (☎ 422-4737) is within walking distance of the downtown area at 2114 Windsor St. It's in a restored house. Singles/doubles cost $25/35 with shared bath, or $5 more for private facilities. All prices include breakfast.

Hartley House (☎ 422-5859), at 2177 Windsor St, is another nearby possibility.

Mrs Daisy Andrews (☎ 455-6591), at 3614 Robie St, has one double room and charges singles/doubles $22/30. Also on Robie St, at No 1520, is the *Illusions Tourist Home* (☎ 425-6733) which is reasonably priced with singles from $25 to $30 and doubles for just $30 too. It's open only from April to October.

Also open for the summer only is the *Birdland B&B* (☎ 443-1055), at 14 Bluejay St, which is close to Mt Allison University. It costs $30 a single and from $40 to $45 a double or triple including breakfast and afternoon tea. It's open from June to October. Cyclists, children and pets are all welcome. The host, Diana, also knows the area's attractions.

There are also a couple of informal places to check on MacAra St, running off Gottingen St a few blocks north of North St. *Jean Walsh* (☎ 455-2215), at No 5671, has one housekeeping room at $35 a night but just $100 a week. A couple of blocks away at No 5685 is *Mrs Blakeney's* (☎ 454-8914), with one room at $30 a single or double.

Better is the very central *Running Lights Inn* (☎ 423-9873) at 2060 Oxford St, with

rooms furnished with antiques and nautical bric-a-brac. Singles/doubles are $28/35.

Winnie's Lodge (☎ 423-8974), at 5492 Inglis St near the park, has rooms at $28/35 for singles/doubles and very good weekly rates, but only for the singles. There's a kitchen for guests. Definitely call ahead for this one as it may have closed.

The following places are in the next bracket up and tend to be larger, more expensive and often in heritage or historical houses or buildings.

Heritage House (☎ 423-4435) is a B&B at 1253 Barrington St, next to the YWCA. Rooms cost from $30 to $40 for singles, $40 to $58 doubles or triples. Free afternoon tea is included. This place is in an excellent location and there is a quiet courtyard and rooftop deck to enjoy.

For hotels try the *Gerrard* (☎ 423-8614) at 1234 Barrington St. It's a small place in a good location, and the building is an historic residence built in 1860. There are nine rooms at singles/doubles $30/45 and free coffee and parking are offered.

The *Queen St Inn* (☎ 422-9828) is at 1266 Queen St near Morris St. It's also an old house dating from about 1860, with six tastefully decorated rooms, all different. Singles/doubles cost $35/45.

Within walking distance of the centre is the cheaper, plainer *Welcome Inn* (☎ 423-6470) at 1254 Hollis St. Singles/doubles here cost $27/30.

Immaculately kept and finished is the *Halliburton House Inn* (☎ 420-0658) at 5184 Morris St, built in 1820 and recently renovated. It has antiques, a library, a garden and a very good licensed dining room. Rates have taken quite a jump here to singles/doubles $90/100. Each of the 40 rooms has a private bath and a continental breakfast is included.

A number of the more traditional, large hotels are also conveniently located in the central core. The *Prince George*, for example, is ideally situated on the corner of George and Price Sts, close to the Citadel and the waterfront. A double here will set you back $150 a night.

Top: Traditional Magdalen Islands Haybarn, Quebec (ML)
Bottom: Nova Scotian boat sheds (RE)

Top: Market in Saint John, New Brunswick (ML)
Bottom: New Brunswick's longest covered bridge, Hartland (ML)

Motels Motels here tend to be a little expensive and are clustered along the No 2, Bedford Highway, north-west of town along the bay called Bedford Basin. They offer good views of the bay and cool breezes; bus Nos 80 or 81 go into town – a 15-minute drive away.

The *Travellers Motel* (☎ 835-3394), open year-round, is right at the city limits. The small cottages (rather than the motel units) are the best buy at $43 for two people with shower, TV and pool.

The *Sea King* (☎ 443-0303) is the big brown place at 560 Bedford Highway and has 33 fully equipped rooms at $45/59 for singles/doubles. Breakfast is available, and there's a pool.

A third choice is the *Bluenose* (☎ 835-3388) at No 636 on the highway. Rooms cost singles/doubles $48/55. Breakfasts are served from 7 to 11 am. Off-season rates are available from 1 October to 15 May. It's away from the road and quiet.

Further out is *Stardust Motel* (☎ 835-3316), 1067 Bedford Highway, which is bigger with 51 rooms, 31 with kitchenette. Singles/doubles cost from $50 to $55.

Places to Eat
Halifax has a good selection of restaurants offering a variety of foods in all price ranges, and generally the quality is high.

For breakfast, the *Athens*, on the corner of Barrington and Blowers Sts, offers the works for $2.49; or try *Smitty's* across from the Public Gardens, on the corner of Spring Garden Rd and Summer St, for inexpensive pancake breakfasts and limitless coffee refills.

Also very good for breakfasts or lunches is *Mrs Murphy's Kitchen*, a small place tucked away in the basement of the Citadel Assurance Building at 5670 Spring Garden Rd. Go around the side on Brenton St and you'll see the door around the back. They serve very cheap, very tasty fresh food including some vegetarian and macrobiotic dishes. It's open from 6.30 am to 4.30 pm Monday to Friday only.

Down Spring Garden Rd, an area of recent regentrification, the food market in the Spring Garden Place Mall on the corner of Dresden Place is a cut above the usual mall fare with soups, salads and sandwiches.

At *Juicy Jane's*, 1576 Argyle St, they sell good sandwiches to take out.

The *Midtown Tavern*, on the corner of Prince and Grafton Sts, is highly recommended – a good example of the Canadian workers' tavern. It's packed with locals at lunch and is noisy, friendly and cheap. An excellent sirloin steak with vegetables, French fries and coleslaw all washed down with draught by the glass won't even dent the wallet.

Not far away, *Christopher's*, at 5218 Prince St, has changed from a casual café to more of a real restaurant but still has bargain lunches of chowder and a sandwich. Now more expensive evening meals in the $10 to $16 bracket are also offered.

Halifax is well blessed with pubs and many are good for a meal. The *Thirsty Duck* is at 5470 Spring Garden Rd; go through the store and up the stairs. They've got burgers, fish & chips, etc, and draught beer at low prices. There's an outdoor patio too.

The *Granite Brewery*, at 1222 Barrington St, is more up-market and brews its own beer which is very good.

Several other pubs can be found in the mall area of Granville St on the corner with Duke St. Both the *Split Crow* and the *Peddlar's Pub* have outdoor sections and the latter has live music on Saturday afternoons.

Also for lunch or dinner, *Satisfaction Feast* is a well established vegetarian restaurant. It's at 1581 Grafton St in the pale blue building, open from 11 am to 9 pm. It's recommended and a meal is always under $10.

Lawrence of Oregano has a spaghetti special that's hard to beat if you're economising: from 4 to 8 pm, dinner with garlic bread is just $3. Other Italian dishes cost about $6. It's at 1712 Argyle St opposite the park. The *Bluenose*, on the corner of Duke and Hollis Sts, is another place packed with locals at lunch. It's cheap, casual, good for kids and has all the basics.

Travellers will appreciate small, unpretentious *Ludy's Kitchen* on the corner of Grafton and Blower Sts for its inexpensive Filipino cooking. There are rice and noodle dishes with native country drinks and desserts.

There are two places for Indian food. The *Guru* at 1580 Argyle St is good and charges about $7 for main dishes. It's closed on Sunday. Cheaper is the *Chicken Tandoor*, open for dinners only with dishes for $6. It's downstairs at 1264 Barrington St, and is closed on Tuesday.

There are two good Vietnamese places in town. The *Tu-do* (meaning 'freedom') at 2085 Gottingen St, two blocks from Cogswell St is recommended. They serve very reasonably priced curry dishes, some with vermicelli noodles and some with my favourite South-East Asian ingredient, lemon grass. It's open every day until quite late, especially Friday and Saturday nights. The alternative is the slightly more casual *King Spring Roll* on Barrington St out towards the railway station. Also busy and good with a more extensive and cheaper menu, it's good value.

Continuing with the inexpensive, ethnic places there is the *Czech Inn* also near the station at 5163 South St with schnitzels, borsch and the like or the *Hungary Hungarian* (run by the same man) for goulashes at 5215 Blowers St, downtown.

And there is seafood here, of course. The *Silver Spoon*, at 1865 Hollis St, primarily a seafood house, is more pricey but prepares meals with interesting sauces and spices. *McKelvie's*, on the corner of Prince St and Bedford Row, and the *Five Fishermen*, 1740 Argyle St, are also established seafood places with meals from $14 up. McKelvie's has a cheaper dinner from 4 to 6 pm.

The *Sheraton* beside the Historic Properties has a lobster buffet outside on Wednesday and Saturday through the summer with entertainment that you might want to consider. The *Halifax Lobster Feast* is at the foot of George St on the waterfront in the old Dartmouth ferry. It's an all the lobster, fish, and vegetables you can eat deal but it's a little pricey at $27 per person.

Cogswell St and its continuation, Quinpool Rd, are commercial streets with plenty of eating spots. The *Anchor Restaurant* is one of the most noteworthy. It's a simple inexpensive and popular place that does what it does very well. The menu has about half a dozen Greek main courses and the remainder is mostly seafood.

For do-it-yourself ocean fare, go to *Fisherman's Market* in the white building beside the ferry terminal. Boiled lobster is $6.99 a pound (500 grams) – a one-pounder being the usual meal and as small as they can legally catch them (they're also available live). All over town you'll see chip wagons which are always good for a quick snack of decent French fries.

Lastly, the *Cave* at 5244 Blowers St, tucked in the little doorway, is open to 4.30 am on weekends. Down in the basement, this small bistro offers good desserts and is particularly well known for its cheesecake.

Entertainment

Halifax is lively at night and there is a very active pub and music scene.

Privateer's Warehouse in the Historic Properties (near the *Bluenose II's* docking area on the waterfront) has two bars and a restaurant. The *Middle Deck* presents rock and blues bands for a cover charge of $3. The *Lower Deck* has lesser names and is cheaper. It often presents Maritime folk music – good stuff. The long wooden tables are like those in an old-style beer house.

Scoundrels at 1786 Granville St is a very popular pub-style spot with no cover charge.

Secretary's on Sackville St near Granville St is definitely not highbrow, with lots of contests and hijinks for young drinkers.

The *Misty Moon* (☎ 422-5871) on the corner of Barrington and Sackville Sts is one of the best known rock bars. Sometimes it stages well-known bands from across Canada, and they're nearly always good ones. The Moon is open seven days a week until 3 am. Admission varies, but can be high.

The *Palace* (☎ 423-7154) at 1721 Brunswick St, across from the Citadel, brings in name acts of every type. Performances are jazz or rock – usually just one-night stands. There are several pubs with no admission fees in the downtown Historic Properties section – along and around Hollis and Granville Sts.

Cinema For repertory films there's *Wormwood's Cinema* (☎ 422-3700) at 2015 Gottingen St. The National Film Board of Canada at 1572 Argyle St also has frequently changing films drawn largely from their own stock.

Getting There & Away
Air Air Canada (☎ 429-7111) has services to Montreal ($258) and Toronto ($336). Canadian Airlines (☎ 427-5500) flies to St John's, Newfoundland.

Bus The principal Nova Scotian bus line is the Acadian line which connects with the New Brunswick SMT lines. There are also a couple of smaller, regional lines which service specific regions only. They all use the Acadian bus station (☎ 454-9321) at 6040 Almon St, which runs south off Robie St, west of the Citadel. The No 3 city bus on Robie St goes from the station into town and back.

One Acadian line runs through the Annapolis Valley and down to Yarmouth. Others cover the central region, the Northumberland Shore and parts of Cape Breton. Following are the one-way fares to several destinations. To North Sydney (one express service daily and other milk runs) it's $35, to Yarmouth $31, Amherst $20.25, Saint John in New Brunswick $45.50, and Fredericton $49.

The MacKenzie bus line serves Nova Scotia's South Shore between Halifax, Lunenberg, Bridgewater and Yarmouth.

Zinck's bus company runs services along the Eastern Shore from Halifax to Sherbrooke stopping at all the small villages along the way. It runs once a day except Sunday eastbound and every day but Sunday and Monday westbound.

Train The railway station (☎ 429-8421) is a bit of a walk from the downtown area out along Hollis St. It's on Terminal Rd by the big old Hilton hotel and is a beautiful example of Canadian railway station architecture. Here as elsewhere, however, services have been cut down considerably and the train is more for out-of-province destinations than getting around Nova Scotia. Services to Saint John, New Brunswick depart on Monday, Thursday and Saturday 1 pm ($44). Trains to Montreal depart 1 pm ($113) on Tuesday, Friday and Saturday passing through Maine, USA arriving the next morning, about 20 hours later.

To avoid unnecessary complications, make sure your visas and documents are in order if you're not North American.

Car & Motorbike Byways (☎ 429-0092), at 2156 Barrington St, charges $43 per day with 150 free km, or $230 a week with no km charge at all.

Rent-A-Wreck (☎ 454-6401) is less expensive and has a lower rate again if the driving is to be done outside the city.

Other car rentals in town are Budget (☎ 454-8501) at 6194 Young St, and Avis (☎ 423-6303) on Scotia Square. Both have offices at the airport.

There are several other choices of car rental places at the airport.

Getting Around
To/From the Airport There are no city buses to the airport. It's a long way out on Highway 102, north towards Truro.

An airport bus leaves frequently from the major hotels like the Lord Nelson. The trip takes about 45 minutes for the 33-km ride and is no bargain at $10. Allow 90 minutes before flight time.

An alternative is Share-A-Cab (☎ 429-7777). Call at least three hours before flight time and they'll find other passengers and pick you up. The price works out about the same as the bus.

Bus City bus fares here are quite reasonable.

For information on bus routes call ☎ 426-6600.

The No 1 bus goes from Halifax Shopping Centre, through town and along the Bedford Highway where the motels are. Bus Nos 7 and 80 leave from town for the bus station.

Ferry A ferry runs continuously from near the Historic Properties dock across the bay to the city of Dartmouth. A ticket is 50 cents one way and the ride makes a nice, short mini-tour of the harbour. Ferries run every 15 minutes until 6 pm, then every 30 minutes. The last one is at 11.30 pm. On Sunday they run from noon to 5.30 pm.

Bicycle Bicycles can be rented at the Trail Shop (☎ 423-8736) at 6260 Quinpool Rd. They have hourly or daily rentals.

For any bike information or to join a bicycle tour of the city or Halifax region call the Velo Bicycle Club (☎ 443-5199).

Rickshaw Powered by muscular young men real old-style Asian rickshaws can be hired around the downtown area.

DARTMOUTH
Dartmouth is Halifax's twin city, a short distance north-west across the Halifax Harbour. It's a city of 70,000 people spread over a large area and, compared with Halifax, is more residential and the city centre is less commercial. For visitors the waterfront and older section near the Halifax-Dartmouth ferry terminal are most interesting – and the fact the city has 23 lakes within its boundaries. Many of these lakes are good for swimming, seven have supervised beaches, some are stocked with fish and there's in-town boating and canoeing. Most popular of the beaches are Birch Cove and Graham's Grove both on Lake Bannock.

The city was founded in 1750, one year after Halifax, when Governor Cornwallis sent troops over to get wood for construction and fuel. Sort of makes you wonder how congenial a guy he was, doesn't it?

Today the two are connected by passenger ferry and two bridges – the 'old' Macdonald Bridge and, further inland, the 'new' MacKay Bridge.

The ferry from Halifax lands you at the centre of things in Dartmouth.

Information
There is a tourist booth for Dartmouth in the ferry terminal on the Halifax side near where the tickets are bought. The main Dartmouth information office is on the corner of Wyse Rd and Alderney Drive to the west of the downtown area in Dartmouth.

Orientation
Portland St is the main street. It's been completely overhauled and is quite attractive with the planted trees and wide sidewalks. Unfortunately there isn't much along it and the stores and businesses seem to be having a tough time. What's there includes several inexpensive restaurants, a couple of antique/junk shops and a bar or two.

There are, though, a number of historic sites near the waterfront and the neighbouring downtown area. You can pick up a walking-tour guide at a tourist office in either city. Buildings in old Dartmouth are primarily made of wood rather than of brick or stone as in Halifax.

Beside the large ferry terminal is a small park with good views. A walking path leads along the water from either side of the terminal but extends further on the park side. From the park Halifax-Dartmouth Industries, a shipyard, can be seen.

Beside the docks shipyard in Dartmouth Cove is the home of Canada's largest coastguard base. The distinct red and white ships are used for search and rescue, icebreaking, maintaining coastal navigational aids and responding to any ocean emergency. There is also a fleet of helicopters based at the site which has been in Dartmouth for about 90 years.

Shubenacadie Canal
A little further around the corner from the shipyards is the Shubenacadie Canal Interpretive Centre at 140 Alderney Drive. The canal connects Dartmouth (through a series

of waterways, lakes, and locks) with the Bay of Fundy on the other side of the province. Built in the mid-1800s along an old Micmac portage route, much of the canal has now been restored. It's used by canoeists but parks and various historic sites along it can be reached by road.

The centre here has some information on the whole system but mainly deals with the historic marine 'railway' which moved vessels from the harbour inland a couple of hundred metres to where the interconnecting water system really began. It's open every day and is free.

For more details on the entire canal, its history and a look at two of the restored locks visit the **Fairbanks Centre** on 54 Locks Rd at Lake Charles in north Dartmouth. It's open daily through the summer but note during the afternoon only on weekends.

Dartmouth Heritage Museum

The museum is at the junction of Alderney Drive and Wyse Rd, about a 15-minute walk left off the Halifax ferry. It houses an eclectic collection pertaining to the city's natural and human history and includes some Native Indian artefacts and crafts, various tools and fashions and industrial bric-a-brac. The museum is free and is open every day in summer but afternoons only on Sunday. Next door is the tourist office.

Evergreen House

Built for a judge in 1862 Evergreen House, part of the Heritage Museum, is a fine example of a 19th-century house for the well-to-do. Many of the 20 rooms are open to the public and have been furnished in the style of the 1880s. Admission is free and it's open daily in summer, afternoons only on weekends. The address is 26 Newcastle St which is in the vicinity of the Shubenacadie Interpretive Centre.

Other Historic Places

At 59 Ochterloney St near the museum and tourist office, within walking distance from the ferry is the **Quaker Whaler House**, the oldest house in the Halifax area having been built in 1786. The Quakers came to the region as whalers from New England. Guides in costume lead visitors around the house.

There is a **farm museum** at 471 Poplar Drive out of the centre.

Moosehead Brewery

Free tours of the plant at 656 Windmill Rd are offered through the summer months.

Bedford Institute of Oceanography

Just outside of Dartmouth is this large government marine research centre which has set up a free self-guided tour for visitors. A walk around the exhibits concerning the fishery and various ocean studies takes a little less than an hour. There is a video and some aquarium specimens to see. The centre is open Monday to Friday only, from 9.30 am to 4.00 pm. To get there from Dartmouth by car take Windmill Rd to the Shannon Park exit which is near the MacKay Bridge or you can get a bus from the Dartmouth ferry terminal.

Activities

The city's lakes are used for fishing, swimming and boating.

The Shubenacadie Canal connects Dartmouth with the Minas Basin in the Bay of Fundy. The Micmacs once used it as a route across the province; it's now interrupted in places but is a fine canoe route with some portages needed.

Festivals

Festivals include the Pipe & Drum Festival from mid to late July; an old-time fiddlers' contest in early July; the Dartmouth Natal Day Celebration in early August; and the Winter Carnival, 10 days in early February. A three-day multicultural festival is held in June along the waterfront and features ethnic foods and arts. The Olands Grand Prix Hydroplane Regatta in early August down at the waterfront has become a major event with some of the world's fastest boats – 260 km/h!

Places to Stay

There are places to stay on this side of the bay as well. They tend to be scattered around and less central than in Halifax. Close to the harbour is the *Martin House B&B* (☎ 469-1896) at 62 Pleasant St with rooms from $45 to $58. Less expensive is *Caroline's* (☎ 469-4665) with three rooms with singles/doubles at $25/30 including a continental breakfast. It's at 134 Victoria Rd not far from the Macdonald Bridge.

There is camping in the Shubie Beach Park.

Places to Eat

Aside from the fast places with a view in the ferry terminal complex there are a couple of places in the old section near the dock. *Tea and Temptions*, at 44½ Ochterloney St east of the ferry landing, is good for an afternoon break. *Healthy Habits*, at 86 Portland St, has good soup and sandwich lunches at about $5.

There are a couple of takeout places up Portland St, and the park next to the ferry terminal is not a bad spot for a picnic lunch.

Central Nova Scotia

The central part of Nova Scotia, in geographic terms, essentially takes in the corridor of land from the New Brunswick border down to Halifax. With a few exceptions it's an area to be passed through on the way to somewhere else. For many coming by road from elsewhere in Canada this is the introduction to Nova Scotia. But don't turn against the province because of what you see from the Trans Canada Highway here as it passes through flat, uninteresting terrain on the way to the province's main highway at Truro which makes a beeline to Halifax. Springhill is an interesting stop south of Amherst and there is some good scenery to the west along the shores of the Bay of Fundy.

AMHERST

Amherst is the geographical centre of the Maritimes and a travel junction. For anyone heading into Nova Scotia passing by is a necessity and Route 104 leads south towards Halifax and then cuts east for Cape Breton Island. Also from Amherst it's not far to the Northumberland Shore and the north coastal route across the province. Route 16 to the ferry for Prince Edward Island is just across the border in New Brunswick.

There's not much to do or see, but it's a pleasant town with some fine buildings and many from the 19th century have been restored. You'll find many of these along Victoria St, the main street whose intersection with Church St is the main one in town. In the 1800s and into the early part of the 1900s Amherst was a very busy manufacturing centre.

The Acadian bus lines terminal is a couple of blocks from Church St, on the corner of Prince Arthur and Havelock Sts. There are three buses a day for Halifax; points east and west are served as well.

The Amherst Point Migratory Bird Sanctuary is not far from town along the marshy coast of Cumberland Basin, part of the Bay of Fundy. Much of the area is a national wildlife area but it's really only of interest to serious bird-watchers. The sanctuary is difficult to find: look for the small blue signs along the edge of Highway 6. There are various trails through the woods and around the ponds. The tourist office has a pamphlet detailing it.

On the east coast there is a good beach at Lorneville on Northumberland Strait.

Places to Stay

There are a few tourist homes in town and motels on the outskirts. There are also several campgrounds nearby, three of them south off the Trans Canada Highway.

Brown's Guest Home (☎ 667-9769) is at 158 East Victoria St and reasonably priced with singles/doubles for $23/26. There are three rooms for one to three people. For a motel, since my former choice the *Tantramar* seems to have lost it, try *Victoria Motel* (☎ 667-7211) at 150 East Victoria St.

Places to Eat

The classic *Hampton Diner* is recommended for good, cheap food and quick, courteous service. They've been open every day from 7 am to 9 pm since 1956. You can't miss it as you come into town from the highway off exit 2.

Right in the middle of town at 125 Victoria St, the *Country Rose Tea Room* is very good for salads and sandwiches. It's a small quiet place with pine furniture and lace curtains well suited to the afternoon teas it serves.

CHIGNECTO

For lack of a better name to call the region south and west of Amherst I've named it after the bay, the cape at the western tip and the large game sanctuary in the middle of it. This is one of the least visited, least populated areas of the province. The road network is minimal, although the Glooscap Trail tourist route goes through the eastern portion. It's an area with some very interesting geology and ancient history which attracts dinosaur detectives, fossil followers and rock hounds. The Minas Basin shore has some good scenery.

Joggins

A short distance from Amherst on Chignecto Bay is the village of Joggins known for its seaside cliff full of fossils. It exposes one of the world's best Carboniferous-period fossil collections consisting of trees, insects, reptiles and others 300 million years old. There is a footpath down to the beach and along the cliffs but you're better off first visiting the new Fossil Centre open daily to 6.30 pm from 1 June to 30 September. Here you'll see samples of what there is and learn more about the site. There are guided tours which aren't cheap at $6.60 but they do last two hours and mean almost certain success in finding something of interest. One tour is offered daily but the times vary and are tied to the tides. The tourist office in Amherst might have a schedule for the tours, if not, they will know the times of low tide so you'll be able to have a look around on your own.

Parrsboro

Parrsboro is the largest of the small towns along the Minas Basin shore in this relatively little-visited region of Nova Scotia. The area is interesting geologically and is known for its semiprecious stones, fossils and dinosaur prints.

Rock hounds scour the many local beaches and rock faces for agates and amethyst and attend the annual Rock Hound Roundup, a get-together for rock, mineral and fossil collectors, with displays, demonstrations, guided walks, boat tours, concerts, etc. The August event is now over 25 years old.

A museum has a collection of the various stones of the region and fossils. The largest batch of fossilised bones ever discovered in North America was found nearby at **Wassons Bluff** in 1986 and along the shoreline thousands of prehistoric footprints have been seen.

There are a few places to stay in town including the *White House* (☎ 254-2387), on Upper Main St, with singles for $25, double or triples $40 with a continental breakfast.

Partridge Island on the coast with exposed rock 200 million years old is good for rock collecting.

Islands Provincial Park

East of Parrsboro the park here offers camping, a beach and picnicking possibilities. Walking trails show the terrain's variety, some leading to the 90-metre-high cliffs at the edge of the Minas Basin and views of the islands. Nearby tidal flats are good for clam digging.

The town has a few simple restaurants and not much else.

SPRINGHILL

Springhill is a small, modest working-class town known to many Canadians for two things: horrendous coal mining disasters and as the birthplace of one of the country's most popular singers, Anne Murray.

The stories of both are told in museums. Springhill is also said to be the world's first town to be thermally heated using flooded coal mines.

Anne Murray Centre

More or less right in the centre of town on Main St is the centre honouring Springhill's best known local. It's pretty well just for real buffs though with a rather high (relative to most provincial attractions) entrance fee, at $4. For that you learn details of Anne Murray's very successful career through pictures, videos, gold records, and awards. There's a gift shop.

The centre's open from May to October every day, 10 am to 7 pm.

Miners' Museum

On the other hand, three km from the centre (follow the signs), this site is a story of bravery, toil, guts and tragedy – life and death.

A visit is very worthwhile: interesting, educational and perhaps emotional. The displays brought tears to the eyes of a couple of visitors on my tour.

Springhill became a centre of the dirty coal mining business beginning as early as 1834. From 1872 when large-scale operations began, the black stuff was dug out and shipped out in large amounts. Major accidents in 1891 and again in 1956 claimed a total of 164 lives.

Two years later North America's deepest mine (4.3 km!) had a 'bump', a cave-in – disaster had struck again. Seventy-five miners were killed in this, one of the continent's worst mining accidents. Newspaper headlines far and wide told the story of the dead and the search for survivors until, 6½ days later, 12 men buried underground were found alive.

That, finally, was the end of that section of the mine and in 1970 all the other mining operations here ceased.

Today, the Miners' Museum allows visitors a first-hand look down a mine as well as displaying equipment, tools, photographs, etc. The guides are all retired miners, they lead the tour with a beautifully warm, human grace.

Admission is just $1.50 for seeing all the above ground displays and $3 for the complete tour which includes the guided talk and a trip down a shaft. Go for the latter, although when you feel the cold, damp air at the opening you'll be glad you're not going to work there.

The museum's open from the beginning of June to 15 October.

Miners' Monument

In the centre of town by the Miners' Hall is a monument to all those who have died. Many die still, from bad lungs and other coal-related illnesses.

TRURO

Truro with its very central position in the province is known as the hub of Nova Scotia. The Trans Canada Highway passes through the north and east of town; Highway 102 goes south to Halifax. The VIA Rail line goes by and Truro is also a bus transfer point.

The main part of this town with its population of 13,000 is around the corner of Prince and Inglis Sts, where some redevelopment has gentrified the streets.

There is a tourist office in Victoria Square at the eastern end of the downtown area by the corner of Prince and Commercial Sts.

Victoria Park

If you're making a stop in Truro or just passing through, a trip to large Victoria Park is worthwhile. There are hundreds of wooded hectares with walking trails, two small waterfalls, a stream and a swimming pool.

It's a good place to break up a day of cycling or driving. Getting there is a little complicated but from Bible Hill, the city landmark, anyone will be able to direct you. The park closes at 10 pm.

Colchester Museum

At 29 Young St in the centre of town this small museum in the large building has exhibits on the region's and town's natural and human history.

Tidal Bore

The Bay of Fundy is known for having the highest tides in the world, and an offshoot of these is a tidal wave or bore which flows up the feeding rivers when high tide comes in. The advancing tide is often pretty small but with the right moon, can be a metre or so in height and runs upstream giving the impression of flowing backwards. You can have a look for free at a few spots in and around town. The closest place is at the Salmon River which runs through the north part of town. Another is not far from town on the Shubenacadie River at Tidal Bore Day Park off Highway 215. Tide schedules are available at the tourist office.

Millbrook Indian Reserve
This reserve is just south of town on Highway 102. The Micmac Indians here sell handicrafts, notably baskets.

Festivals
Nova Scotia's largest provincial exhibition and agricultural and amusement fair is held here in August.

Places to Stay
There are several B&Bs in Truro and a number of motels on the outskirts. The YMCA in town has no rooms to rent and the nearest hostel is near Wentworth, on the way to Amherst. As you come into Truro via Bible Hill you'll find *Foothill Motel & Cabins* (☎ 895-4143), seven km east of town. It's a cheap place to stay, offering cabins with cooking facilities at $30 for two people. It's open from 1 May to 31 October. Nearby is a bakery with homemade treats.

Better is the *Blue House* (☎ 895-4150), at 43 Dominion St, one of several B&Bs which have opened in the past few years to fill a gap in the low-priced end of the market. It's central, has three rooms and offers good value at singles/doubles $30/35, including a full breakfast and tea in the evening.

The best deal amongst the more expensive motels is *Berry's Motel* (☎ 895-2823) at 73 Robie St. They have 31 units at $38 a single or $48 a double/triple.

The *Youth Hostel* (☎ 548-2379) is not quite halfway to Amherst near Wentworth on Valley Rd. It's open all year and costs $8.50

for members, $10.50 for nonmembers. The bus stop is three km away. There's good hiking nearby.

Places to Eat
At 517 Prince St in town, the *Iron Kettle* is a friendly, inexpensive restaurant in a building dating from 1875. Also on Prince St but heading out of town, the *Rainbow Motel* has an all-you-can-eat lobster buffet during the summer. Further out on Robie St towards the Trans Canada Highway, there are numerous eating places.

For light meals, *Paul & Darlene's* is beside the railway station.

Just off exit 14 into Truro along Highway 2 which becomes Robie St are a number of the standard chain restaurants. *Smitty's* for pancakes and *Ponderosa* for cheap steak and an excellent all-you-can-eat salad bar are good choices.

Getting There & Away
Bus The bus station (☎ 895-3833) is at 280 Willow St. It's near the hospital along the motel strip – you'll see the blue and white Acadian bus terminal sign. To Halifax there are three buses a day for $8.25 and to Sydney, four a day with different stops for $30. To Saint John, New Brunswick there's one morning and one afternoon bus daily with a stop in Amherst for $38.

Train The railway station (☎ 800-561-3952) is in town on Esplanade St, near the corner of Inglis St. All trains into and out of Nova Scotia pass through Truro so connections can be made for Halifax, various points in New Brunswick and to Montreal via one of two different routes. Trains to Halifax depart once daily for $12 except on Tuesday and to Saint John, New Brunswick, on Monday, Thursday and Saturday for $35.

MAITLAND & SHUBENACADIE CANAL
To the west of Truro on the Bay of Fundy is the little town of Maitland at the mouth of the Shubenacadie River. Extending south along the river then through various locks and lakes the continuous water system even-

tually leads to the city of Dartmouth and the ocean.

Opened in 1861, the canal is now a national historic site and has a variety of sites and parks that can be visited along its course including the Tidal Bore Day Park mentioned under Truro. It is also used by boaters and canoeists. Maps are available at tourist offices which list all the points of interest, walking trails, etc.

The main interpretive centre is in Dartmouth on the harbour.

STEWIACKE

At this little town south of Truro, you're halfway between the north pole and the equator.

SHUBENACADIE WILDLIFE PARK

This provincial park contains examples of Nova Scotia's wildlife including birds, waterfowl, foxes and deer in large enclosures. It's off Highway 102 at exit 10, 38 km south of Truro, just north of the town of Shubenacadie. It is open every day during daylight hours from mid-May to mid-October and is free.

South Shore

The South Shore refers to the area south and west of Halifax stretching along the coast to Yarmouth. It contains many fishing villages and several small historic towns. Some of the coastal scenery is good – typically rocky, jagged and foggy. The latter qualities have made the coast here and along the Eastern Shore as much a favourite with modern day smugglers transporting illegal drugs, as it once was to rum runners.

The first third of the area, closest to Halifax, is the city's cottage country and is quite busy. The tourist route through here, on the older and smaller roads, is called the Lighthouse Route and is probably the most visited region of Nova Scotia other than Cape Breton. Various museums and points of interest are found along the route, which was

named for the many lighthouses along the shore. Accommodation is not plentiful considering the traffic in high season so plan to find a place before dark each night. For eating, as might be expected, fresh seafood is abundant and excellent.

MacKenzie bus line services the region from Halifax to Yarmouth with at least one and usually two departures in each direction daily. Yarmouth can also be reached via a northern route through the Annapolis Valley from Halifax on Acadian bus line.

PROSPECT

South-west of the city is quiet and little-visited Prospect, a very small but attractive old coastal village. The view from the cemetery at the top of the hill on the approach to town is very impressive especially if the fog bank is obscuring some of the islands and shoreline. There is a wharf, rocks to clamber over along the shore and a lighthouse.

PEGGY'S COVE

Canada's best known fishing village lies 43 km west of Halifax on Highway 333. It's a very pretty place with fishing boats, nets, lobster traps, docks and old pastel houses that all seem perfectly placed to please the eye. Although not unlike many other such communities, Peggy's Cove does have a quintessential postcard quality about it.

The 415-million-year-old granite boulders, known to geologists as erratics, littered all over the surroundings add an odd touch.

The smooth shoreline rock all around the lighthouse just begs to be explored (although do not get too close, every year visitors are swept into the cold waters by unexpected swells) and the ambience-creating fog completes the enticing effect. Count on the fog too: it enshrouds the area at least once every three days and is present most mornings.

Peggy's Cove is a very popular destination – probably one of the most visited in the Atlantic or Maritimes Provinces – and it's close to the capital too, so crowds detract. The best time for a visit is before 10 am or, second best, later in the afternoon. Many full tour buses arrive in the middle of the day.

Surprisingly, the village which dates from 1811, has just 50 residents and most of them are fishermen.

See the pictorial in-the-rock monument done by local artist DeGarthe near the provincial parking lot at the entrance to Peggy's Cove.

Down near the lighthouse is a restaurant and coffee counter with a variety of souvenirs.

ST MARGARET'S BAY

A little beyond Peggy's Cove, large St Margaret's Bay is an area of small towns, craft shops, and small sandy beaches with a number of motels, campgrounds and cottages which some visitors prefer to use as a base for exploring the Halifax/Peggy's Cove region. It's a developed area where many people who work in the city live or have summer places.

Near the head of St Margaret's Bay is the start of the Bowaters Hiking Trail. At the top of the bay are the beaches. Queensland Beach, the one furthest west, is the largest and busiest and has a snack bar.

One of the most attractive places to spend a night or two is the *Bayview Motel & Cottages* (☎ 8226-7462) nicely laid out by the water in Boutilier's Point. The cottages tend to be rented by the week but the motel units go from $34 to $48 a double.

MAHONE BAY

Mahone Bay with its islands and history has become a sort of city escape with the town of the same name being the centre for that. It's a popular destination for a Sunday drive or an afternoon tea. The town has antique and craft shops and a decided tourist orientation. There's often a flea market set up on summer weekends. The approach from Halifax about 100 km away is noteworthy for the view of the three church spires by the roadside. You can see fine examples of Victorian gingerbread-house architecture around town and the cemetery is interesting with many gravestones inscribed in German.

At 578 Main St is the **Settlers' Museum**

& Cultural Centre which deals mainly with the first German settlers to the area. Displays in two rooms cover the 1850s period. Admission is by donation.

Places to Stay & Eat

There are a dozen B&Bs an indication of the trendiness and popularity of the Mahone Bay area. They are very reasonably priced however. The *Book Barn* (☎ 624-9843) is at 255 West Main St and has three rooms with shared bath with a single for $25, a double or triple for $35 including breakfast. In the centre of town is the *Heart's Desire B&B* at 686 Main St.

Among the shops are two pubs, a cafe and at 662 Main St, *Zwicker's Inn* – a very busy but not inexpensive restaurant with a range of seafood and pasta dishes which are highly regarded.

CHESTER

Chester, an old village with 1000 residents overlooks Mahone Bay. Established in 1759 it has had a colourful history as the haunt of pirates and Prohibition bathtub gin smugglers. It's now a small summer resort and, although there isn't a lot to do in town, a lot of visitors pass through each summer.

The centre of town is along Pleasant St between King and Queen Sts. The Chester Playhouse which runs inexpensive comedies, musicals and dramas through July and August is on Pleasant St.

Tancook Island

Offshore is Tancook Island which can be reached by a 45-minute very inexpensive passenger-only ferry ride departing from the Chester wharf several times a day. Chester also has a back harbour which is used mainly for pleasure craft. The islands, there is a **Big and Little Tancook**, are primarily residential but visitors are welcome to stroll around. Big Tancook has a tourist office, a B&B and a simple food outlet. A walking-tour brochure is available at the Chester tourist office and paths lead over much of the island.

The island is known for its plentiful cabbage and sauerkraut. Distinctive little cabbage storage houses can be seen around the island. There are also some old homes on the island including a Cape Cod cottage dating from 1790.

Places to Stay & Eat

At 78 Queen St *MacNeill Manor B&B* (☎ 275-4638) is a nice looking place set in an old house which has private balconies adjacent to some rooms. Prices are from $45/55 for singles/doubles and include breakfast. Another place to stay is the cheaper *Casa Blanca* (☎ 275-3385) with eight cabins at 463 Duke St, close to the centre.

There is a provincial park with camping just east of town. For a casual bite, there's the *Fo'c's'le Tavern* and *Rosie Grady's* restaurant on the corner of Pleasant and Queen Sts.

At 69 Queen St is the *Thirsty Thinker's Tearoom* affiliated with a charity group and, along the waterfront, is the *Rope Loft* with a varied menu – if you want to save a bit of money, they'll supply the food and you can cook it yourself.

NEW ROSS

At this small lumbering town 26 km northwest of Chester in the interior of the province, is a **living agriculture museum** set up like a working 19th-century farm. Also in New Ross which is about halfway to Kentville in the Annapolis Valley is a youth hostel.

GOLD RIVER

Not far west of Chester, the salmon fishing is said to be very good here.

OAK ISLAND

What a story! This is treasure island with no treasure – so far. Said to be the burying place of the treasure of the infamous Captain Kidd or Blackbeard or Captain Morgan – maybe of Inca gold taken by the Spanish or...the list goes on.

Despite nearly 200 years of digging, it's still up for grabs and has become one of the country's biggest ongoing mysteries.

Three farmboys stumbled upon a deep shaft in 1795, and since then six lives and millions of dollars have been lost on the world's longest running and most costly treasure hunt.

Before you grab your shovel and rush over, you need a permit you can't get. The search – now using a lot of sophisticated equipment – is carried on by an international consortium determined to solve the mystery of the money pit once and for all.

The exploration company runs tours of the site which explain some of the history and the incredible shafts, tunnels and chambers with their flooding systems which have been investigated as well as some of the articles found thus far. To get there, turn off Highway 3 at Oak Island Rd.

LUNENBURG

This very attractive town with 3000 residents is best known for building the *Bluenose* sailing schooner in 1921 which can be seen on the Canadian dime. Always a shipbuilding and fishing town, it is now the centre of the provincial fishing industry and has one of the major fleets of the north Atlantic seaboard. The largest fish-processing plant in North America, employing 1000 people is here. From it come the Highliner supermarket seafood products.

Lunenberg is an old town where Acadians lived until the mid-1700s. It was officially founded in 1753 when the British encouraged Protestants to emigrate from Europe. It soon became the first largely German settlement in the country. This now diminished German heritage is reflected in some of the local foods.

Orientation & Information

Montague St, running parallel to the harbour, is the main street. Along it are many of the town's commercial enterprises including a few places to eat and a couple of places to stay. There are some interesting stores with gifts, crafts, antiques and prints for sale.

Many of the restaurants along Montague St have patios out the back facing Bluenose

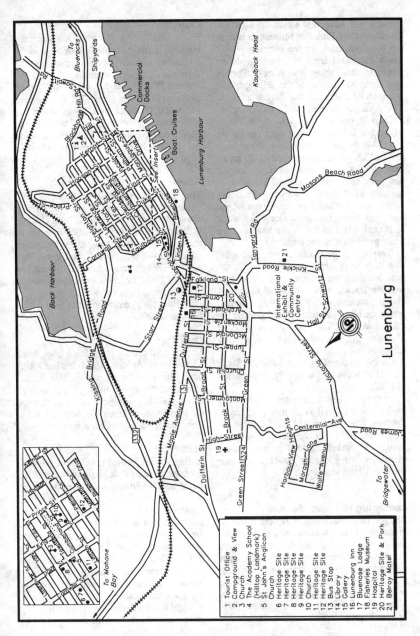

Lunenburg

1 Tourist Office
2 Campground & View
3 Church
4 The Academy School (Hilltop Landmark)
5 St John's Anglican Church
6 Heritage Site
7 Heritage Site
8 Heritage Site
9 Heritage Site
10 Church
11 Heritage Site
12 Heritage Site
13 Bus Stop
14 Library
15 Gallery
16 Lunenburg Inn
17 Bluenose Lodge
18 Fisheries Museum
19 Hospital
20 Heritage Site & Park
21 Belroy Motel

Drive which runs right along the wharves. The Lunenburg Fisheries Museum is here as are the boat tours. In the evening people catch mackerel from the various docks where smaller fishing vessels moor. Further east along Montague are the shipyards and commercial docks for the bigger trawlers. The principal intersection is with King St. Pelham St, one street back up the hill from Montague St also has a number of shops. At No 134 is the house where Earl Birney lived and had his studio. He was one of the area's best known seascape painters despite having had polio and having to wield his brush in his teeth. His brother now lives in the house which can be visited to view some of the paintings. Going up the hill along Lincoln St to Blockhouse Hill Rd, is the tourist office and a great view of the area.

Despite its popularity, the residential streets are surprisingly quiet and free of tourists. Strolling around turns up many fine wooden houses: some are made in the old shingle style, some are brightly painted, others are raw – the wood turned grey by the coastal weather. There are also some huge Victorian gingerbread places which really can only be termed mansions.

On the corner of Duke and Pelham Sts is the oldest house in Lunenberg, constructed in 1760.

The town is built on a peninsula and has a back harbour as well as the main one across the bay from which the golf course on Kaulback Head can be seen. The back harbour, in a mainly residential area, is used primarily for pleasure boats and some inshore fishing vessels.

Lunenburg Fisheries Museum

The good and interesting provincial museum is down on the waterfront on Bluenose Drive. It has one building and three ships in the water for inspection: a dragger, a rum runner and a fishing schooner. In the building are exhibits on fishing and fish processing, and a 25-minute film on marine life. There's also an aquarium. It's open daily from mid-May to September and admission is $2.

Churches

For a small town the churches are very impressive and there are five of them in the downtown area. St John's Anglican on the corner of Duke and Cumberland Sts is a real stunner. The beautiful black and white wooden place dates from 1753 and is one of the oldest churches in Canada. Tours are given through the summer. The Lutheran church on the corner of Cornwallis and Fox Sts isn't much younger having been built in 1772.

Academy

The Academy, a school, is the huge black and white turreted structure on a hill seen rising above the town on your way in from Halifax. Built entirely of wood in 1895, it is one of the rare survivors of the academy system of education – a private and prestigious high school. Though now a national historic site it is still a working school and therefore can not be entered.

Beside it is a cemetery with many graves from the 1800s.

Organised Tours

Several boat cruises are offered from down by the docks. Anchor Boat Tours has a 2½-hour trip around the point to Blue Rocks. Others offer deep-sea fishing or sailing on a traditional-style schooner. At times through the summer, the *Bluenose II*, built in 1963 in Lunenberg, docks here for a few days.

Festivals

In July, a craft festival is held and, a month later, the popular Folk Harbour Festival is a weekend of traditional music and dance.

Places to Stay

Lunenberg is a popular destination and during midsummer making reservations early in the day is not a bad idea. During the folk festival, in particular, accommodation will be scarce. There is a good variety of places here, though, from camping to classic old Maritime inns.

Right in town beside the tourist office with great views there is a little campground for trailers or tenters. It's an ideal, incredibly convenient place which charges $9. It does get full so arrive early. Too bad more towns don't have something similar. There are three or four other privately run campgrounds near town.

The *Margaret Murray B&B* (☎ 634-3974), a short distance west of the centre off Dufferin St, is good value at singles/doubles $30/35 with a full breakfast.

Right in the middle of town the *Compass Rose Inn* (☎ 634-8509) is at 15 King St. It's a very attractive old place with a good restaurant where the rooms are priced below what might be expected with singles at $35 and doubles/triples from $45 to $55.

Bluenose Lodge (☎ 634-8851), at 10 Falkland St, is a big place about 125 years old on the corner of Lincoln St with singles/doubles for $50/55, meals are available. *Mrs C's* nearby on Lincoln St is a more modest, cheaper B&B.

The *Lunenberg Inn* (☎ 634-3963) is another large, historic, comfortable hostelry with antique furnishings and a good dining room.

In the motel category, the *Bel Roy* (☎ 634-8867) is quite central, at 39 Knickle Rd south-west of the centre around the harbour, and charges singles/triples $44/54. The public pool across the street can be used and there is a little restaurant, good for breakfast.

Places to Eat

Sampling the fish here is an absolute must. Most of the restaurants along the waterfront, many offering views of the harbour, specialise in seafood. Three of us tried the *Dockside* at 90 Montague St, one of the cheaper places, and had the daily fish special which was a full halibut dinner, from bread to dessert for $9.95. When the food arrived we all burst out laughing – it was the biggest piece of fish any of us had ever seen, thick and literally hanging off both ends of the plate – and it was superb. They have an outdoor patio as well as the dining room.

There are a number of places side by side here, many with menus posted, some offering pizza and the like.

Again for the fish or lobster, there is the *Capt'n Angus* overlooking the water from the Fisheries Museum building. Good fresh seafood at moderate prices in a casual but nice setting where you can take the kids and still feel you're having a night out.

Away from the waterfront try *Magnolia's Grill*, at 128 Montague St, the eclectic inside of which is like a cross between an artist's café/bistro and someone's small, comfortable country cottage. They have an inexpensive menu. There's some emphasis on seafood with a Cajun angle. It's open for lunch and dinner daily.

The more elegant dining room in the *Compass Rose*, which also has accommodation, is very good but considerably more expensive. It's in a beautiful building dating from 1830 on the corner of King and Pelham Sts. More topnotch food is available at the *Lunenberg Inn*, another fine old building, at 26 Dufferin St.

BRIDGEWATER

Bridgewater is an industrial town on the LaHave River and is the largest centre on the South Shore with a population of close to 7000. Visitors will find all essential services and a couple of museums.

The **Desbrisay Museum** on 10 hectares of parkland has a small collection of goods relating to the early, mainly German, settlers of Lunenberg County. It's free.

The **Wile Carding Mill** (carding is the straightening and untangling of wool fibres in preparation for spinning), on Victoria Rd, is an authentic water mill dating from 1860, admission is free here too.

The South Shore Exhibition held each July is a major five-day fair with traditional competitions between Canadian and US teams in such events as the ox pull.

Around **New Germany** further up the river are many Christmas tree farms. The trees are shipped from the Bridgewater docks to expectant households along the US seaboard.

THE OVENS

Route 332 south from Bridgewater edges

along the LaHave River to the sea. It's a very pleasant country road with the huge old trees and mammoth old riverside houses fondly associated with the history and good life of the Maritimes.

At the end of the road is The Ovens, a sort of nature park and campground which is highly recommended for its scenery and general easy-going atmosphere.

Gold was found here in 1861 and still can be found on Cunard Beach. Rent a dish at the office and try panning. There's plenty there, I saw several people pocketing small nuggets. In a different area a trail leads along the shore past (and into) numerous caves. The camping is very good with many sites right by the shore with fine views over the ocean and a rocky ledge to explore at low tide.

There are also a couple of cottages which can be rented, a swimming pool and a comfortable little restaurant which serves up inexpensive and delicious fish & chips.

LAHAVE

From Riverport a 50-cent, five-minute cable ferry ride takes you across the river to the town of LaHave where a stop at one of the best bakeries (physically and gastronomically) in the country is a must. You can't miss it – it's just to the south of the ferry landing, on the main street.

Upstairs is a hostel for cyclists, backpackers or any like-minded soul looking for a good cheap place to spend the night. Also based at the bakery is LaHave Outfitters who run coastal boat excursions.

On the outskirts west of the village is the **Fort Point Museum**, a national historic site. It was here in 1632 the first batch of French settlers soon to be known as Acadians landed from France. A fort, Sainte-Marie-de-Grâce was built later the same year but very little of it remains today. The site was supplanted by Port Royal on the north coast and never became a major centre. A museum in the former lighthouse keeper's house at the site tells more of this early settlement and its leader, de Raizilly. It's open daily through the summer months.

From LaHave the gentle, green landscape continues towards Liverpool, the slow coastal road passing through a series of villages. At **Petite Rivière** is a pioneer cemetery on the west side of town on top of the hill.

Rissers Provincial Park has a very busy campground and an excellent long, sandy beach although the water is none too warm. There is also a saltwater marsh with a boardwalk trail.

At **Broad Cove** there is an inn with a tea room.

MILL VILLAGE

In the midst of all the South Shore history this town offers an odd attraction, the **Mill Village Satellite Earth Station**, an international telecommunications centre. Free 45-minute guided tours are offered which include a look at the control room, three large dishes or antennas and a film. It's open from mid-June to the beginning of September.

LIVERPOOL

Situated where the Mersey River meets the ocean, Liverpool is another historic English-style town with an economy based on forests and fishing. The tourist office on Henry Hensey Drive, just off Main St, has a walking-tour pamphlet which leads past many of the notable houses and buildings in the downtown area and waterfront.

Perkins House built in 1766 is now a museum with articles and furniture from the colonial period. Next door, the **Queen's County Museum** has some Native Indian artefacts and more materials relating to town history as well as some writings by early citizens.

At **Fort Point**, marked with a cairn, is the site where Samuel de Champlain landed from France in 1604. There is also a memorial to the British privateers who were active in the local waters at the beginning of the 1800s and protected the British trade routes from American incursions.

There are four sandy **beaches** nearby: Beach Meadows, White Point, Hunt's Point and Summerville. All are within 11 km of town and there are others further west.

Places to Stay & Eat

You'll find motels in the area too, as you will all along the coast. There is a low-priced summer *Youth Hostel* (☎ 354-3533) here on Main St in Trinity Parish Hall, by the Kinsmen Service Centre. Moving up-market is *Lane's Privateer Inn* (☎ 354-7220). It's the white wooden building with balconies built in 1798 on Highway 3 by the bridge over the Mersey River just east of the centre. A bed with breakfast is $45 a double and there is a good restaurant which specialises in seafood.

On the corner of Bristol Ave and Main St is the *Lunch Kettle* which offers inexpensive homemade food.

SEASIDE ADJUNCT KEJIMKUJIK NATIONAL PARK

The main body of this large national park is in the interior north-west of Liverpool, south-east of Digby, but in 1985 this undeveloped region of the south coast between Port Joli Bay and Port Mouton Bay was made part of the same park. It protects a beautiful and wild stretch of shoreline and the animals, most particularly, the endangered piping plover bird, within it.

Services are nonexistent – no campground (although there are some tent sites), no toilets, no drinking water and no fires allowed. What there is is pristine coastline with two great beaches, coves, vistas, rock formations and lots of birdlife.

Two trails, one leading in from each end provide the only access. Both tend to be a little wet. From **South West Port Mouton** an eight-km track leads to Black Point and the shore. From **St Catherine's River**, a little village, a three-km walk leads to the sea on the western side.

LOCKEPORT

At the end of a jutting arm is the little town of Lockeport with what is known as an historic streetscape. The town was founded by New Englanders in the 1700s but became prosperous in the mid-1800s as a fishing and, more importantly, a trading centre with the West Indies. It was during this time that the wealthy built the large, ostentatious homes seen at the waterfront. One street has five such homes, all impressive in their own way and all built by members of the Locke family between 1836 and 1876 using different architectural styles. The short street has been designated an historic site, although none of the houses are open to visitors.

Coming into town over the causeway there is a tourist office and next door in a former one-room schoolhouse, a small museum with local relics including a replica of a 19th-century classroom. Just behind is a large crescent-shaped sandy beach. A short visit will suffice as there is little else in town and nowhere to stay or eat.

SHELBURNE

For my money this is one of the most attractive and most interesting of towns anywhere on the South Shore. The whole place is pretty much like a museum with fine buildings and historic sites at every turn. It sits on a hill overlooking a good harbour, has a nice waterfront area, some good places to eat and stay and you can walk to everything along tree-lined streets.

This shipbuilding town with a population of 2500 is known as the birthplace of yachts. As well as the prize-winning yachts, though, it also produces several other types of boats. Shelburne also boasts a towncrier, Perry Wamback, who has won national and international competitions.

Shelburne, like many towns in the Fundy region, was founded by Loyalists and in 1783 had a population of 10,000, making it the largest community in British North America. Many of its inhabitants were former members of the New York aristocracy. Some of the Loyalist houses still stand.

Water St, the main street, has many houses from 100 to 200 years old and quite a few of the two-storey wooden homes are marked with dates.

Dock St along the harbour has several historic buildings and museums to visit and the tourist office.

The commercial fishing wharf is interesting in the mornings when the cod are unloaded from the ships into ice-filled bins and reloaded onto trucks. This is a major port and boats from Quebec's Gaspé and the Magdalen Islands, from New Brunswick and Prince Edward Island may be moored. People cast for mackerel right off the dock too. A little further out the shipyards can be seen where repairs to the Marine Atlantic ferries and others vessels are carried out.

Ross-Thompson House

Built in 1784, this house (which has an adjacent store) belonged to well-to-do merchants who arrived from England via Cape Cod and now acts as a small museum. Furniture, paintings, artefacts and original goods from the store may be viewed. The house is surrounded by gardens as it would have been formerly. It's open daily from May to October and is free, as are all the places on Dock St.

Shelburne County Museum

Nearby is this Loyalist house dating from 1787 with a collection of Loyalist furnishings, displays on the history of the local fishery and other articles from the town's past. The oldest fire engine in Canada, a wooden cart from 1740, is quite something. There is also a small collection of Micmac artefacts including their fine, typical porcupine-quill decorative work. The museum is on the corner of Dock St and Maiden Lane.

Dory Shop

Shelburne has long had a reputation for its dories, small boats first used for fishing from a mother schooner and in later years for inshore fishing and as lifeboats. Many were built here from the 1880s until the 1970s. At the museum you can learn about them and their history and see examples still being made in the workshop upstairs.

The very large building across the street was once used as a warehouse and also, at one time, was one of the country's largest department stores.

Places to Stay

Out of town west just a few km is a good provincial park, the *Town Islands*. The campsites are in mature forest and there is swimming too. It's quiet during the week but unfortunately has a bit of a problem with area rowdies on weekends who prefer loud drinking parties to sleeping. Ask if the situation has been cleared up or be prepared to join in.

The *Bear's Den* (☎ 875-3234) is a small, attractive and economical B&B on the corner of Water and Glasgow Sts. You'll pass it on the way into the centre of town. Singles/doubles cost $25/35 and that includes a complete breakfast.

The *Toddle In* (☎ 875-3229) B&B is very central on the corner of Water and King Sts. Singles/doubles go for $25/35 with breakfast in the pleasant dining room downstairs where lunch is available too.

The *Cooper's Inn* and the *Loyalist Inn* both in larger, fine historic buildings are more expensive choices, but not by much.

There are also a few motels at the edge of town including the attractive *Cape Cod Colony Motel*.

Places to Eat

The *Toddle In* has a small, cosy and friendly dining room for inexpensive, fresh breakfasts and lunches.

Claudia's Diner on Water St, open every day, is a low-priced restaurant with style and standard fare. The cinnamon rolls are good.

For a bit of a splurge the dining room in the *Coopers Inn* from 1785 is very good. They offer just four dishes and four desserts nightly and do them well. Of course, there is seafood but there's always an alternative. *Hamilton House* is also said to be a cut above the others.

Bruce's Wharf is a pub on the water along Dock St.

BARRINGTON

The small village of Barrington has four

museums all within walking distance of one another. The tourist office in the middle of things has an example of the Cape Island boat, the classic small fishing boat of the North Atlantic originating on Cape Sable Island and now seen all around eastern Canada.

The **Barrington Meetinghouse** reflects the town's early Quaker influence and was used as both church and city hall. The Woollen Mill is representative of a small manufacturing mill of the late 1800s. It was the last woollen mill of its age to cease operating; it ran until 1962.

The **Seal Island Light Museum** is a replica of the lighthouse found on Seal Island 30 km out to sea and is a record of the original and its keepers.

Aside from the museums, there are many heritage buildings in town, get details of them from the walking-tour guide published by the local tourist office.

The tourist office should also have information on some of the local walking trails including the one which runs along the old railway line from Yarmouth to Halifax.

In Barrington Passage is the *Old School House Restaurant* with a natural food store and bakery too. Good sandwiches and salads with more substantial meals are also available. It might be possible here to exchange some work for a night's lodging.

From Barrington there is not much of interest until Yarmouth. **Cape Sable** and **West Pubnico** were both once Acadian settlements and each has a small general museum. Pubnico remains French and is considered the oldest village in Canada still lived in by the descendants of its founders. Fishing remains important in the many traditional local villages.

Yarmouth to Windsor

This region of Nova Scotia stretches from Yarmouth northward and along the south shore of the Bay of Fundy to Windsor and the Minas Basin. It consists, primarily, of two distinct geographical and cultural regions.

The area between Yarmouth and Digby was one of the first European-settled areas in Canada. This municipality of Clare, formed part of Acadia, the French region of the New World colonies. The 'French Shore' and its history are still very much in evidence today.

The best known area, however, is the scenic valley of the Annapolis River which runs more or less from Digby to Wolfville. It's famous for apples and in springtime the blossoming valley is at its best.

The Evangeline Trail tourist route passes through the entire region taking in both these disparate districts.

YARMOUTH

With its population of nearly 10,000, Yarmouth is the largest town in western Nova Scotia. It's also a transportation centre of sorts where aside from the main highway and the district airport, ferries from Portland and Bar Harbour, Maine, dock. It's an old city and recent town improvements have stressed this heritage and historical side. A number of souvenir shops and other businesses have also recently opened to cater for visitors. Whichever way you're going, chances are you'll be passing through this good place to stop.

There's a huge tourist office down at the ferry docks with both local and provincial information available. They have a walking-tour guide of the city with a map and some historical information.

Every Saturday through the summer a farmers' market and flea market is held at the Centretown Square on the corner of Main and Central Sts.

On the corner of Main and Brown Sts is Toots, a shop you won't want to miss if you're getting on the ferry. It has a large selection of candy and an absolutely mammoth magazine selection.

Yarmouth County Museum

Open every day in summer (on Sunday from noon only) the museum, at 22 Collins St, in the grey stone building formerly a church, is

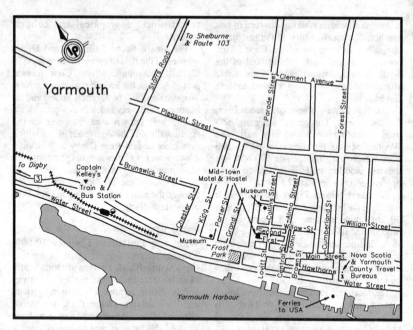

quite good and worth a look. Admission is very cheap and the staff friendly and helpful.

Most of the exhibits are to do with the sea – ship models, a large painting collection, etc. Many articles were brought back by sea captains from their travels in the Far East and include things such as ebony elephant carvings from Ceylon and fine ivory work from Japan. There are also some rooms done in various period styles.

One of the highlights is a runic stone found near town in 1812 and believed to have been carved by Viking Leif Erikson some 1000 years ago. Other evidence has been discovered which suggests that the Vikings were indeed in this area. Ask for the pamphlet on all the theories connected with the stone.

Another interesting item is the 'pleasure vehicle', which, perhaps disappointingly, is only an electric car from 1915.

It's open from 9 am to 5 pm daily in summer, Sunday from 1 to 5 pm; shorter hours in the off-season and closed on Monday. Admission is $1.

Firefighters' Museum

This museum on Main St has a collection of beautiful fire engines dating from the 1930s. They look like the kind in children's stories that have personalities and abused emotions. Admission costs $1; it's open from 9 am to 9 pm, and until 5 pm on Sunday.

Places to Stay

For a fairly small town there is no shortage of accommodation with a choice of some pretty good places. There are half a dozen B&Bs or guesthouses, a couple of hotels and plenty of motels.

A *Youth Hostel* (☎ 742-5333) can be found at the very central Mid-town Motel, at 13 Parade St and a 10-minute walk from either the ferry or the bus station. There are also standard motel rooms for nonmembers.

Collins St B&B (☎ 742-3713) at 11 Collins

St charges singles/doubles $25/40 but call, it may have recently closed. *Sophie's Guesthouse* (☎ 742-7447) is at 504 Main St. It has just three rooms which cost singles/doubles $20/25 including a continental breakfast.

Another guesthouse is the *Oceanside* (☎ 743-4343) at 12 Vancouver St with more expensive rooms each with private bath facilities.

The *Rodd Colony Harbour Inn*, right across from the ferry terminal, is a large and modern hotel/motel. It has all the amenities including a restaurant and bar.

The most economical of the motels is the *Lakelawn* (☎ 742-8427) at 641 Main St where breakfast is available.

Places to Eat

Racine's, a basic all-purpose place at 353 Main St is good for breakfast and also serves pizza. The *Lobster Trap* has dinner specials which aren't bad value at $7 to $9, even cheaper between 4 and 6 pm. The cafeteria in the *Met*, a Woolworth's-style store on Main St near Lovitt St, is extremely inexpensive with everything under $6.

Not far away in the big gabled place at 577 Main St, is *Captain Kelley's*, a pub-style place which specialises in fish and beef. Best of all is *Harris' Quick 'n' Tasty*, four km from town on Route 3 (Main St) towards Digby. It's a very busy, good and reasonably priced seafood spot. There are both more expensive and cheaper places in town. At 3 Jenkins St, in the downtown area is a natural foods outlet with a good bakery.

Getting There & Away

Bus The bus station is now in the old railway station which wasn't needed when the train service to the area was cancelled in the late 1980s.

Acadian bus lines (☎ 742-5131), Nova Scotia's biggy, has two trips daily to Halifax taking five hours via Digby and the Annapolis Valley. The morning trip is called 'the limited' and makes about a dozen stops along the way. The other trip, 'the regular', leaves around noon and stops everywhere – at any

little junction someone asks for. To Digby the fare is $9.75, to Halifax it's $30.75.

MacKenzie line also runs to Halifax but uses the South Shore route through Shelburne, etc. These buses arrive and depart from the Texaco gas station on the corner of Main and Beacon Sts, opposite the railway station.

Train There is no longer any train service to this part of the province.

Ferry There are two major ferry routes in and out of Yarmouth, both to the state of Maine in the USA; one connects with Bar Harbour, and the other with Portland.

The Marine Atlantic (☎ 742-3515) ferry to Bar Harbour, Maine, takes about six hours to travel the 160 km. It leaves Yarmouth at 4.30 pm daily during the summer months and less frequently the rest of the year. The fare is $36.25 per adult, $67 per car and $8 per bicycle. The prices go down a bit from October to May. There is also a bargain on a one-day return trip which is offered at half price and really amounts to a 12-hour cruise. Private cabins are available at additional cost.

The other ferry is operated by Prince of Fundy Cruises (☎ 742-5164 Yarmouth) and it sails back and forth to Portland. The trip to Portland, Maine is 320 km – double the distance and therefore about twice the duration and more expensive – but you could win back the fare in the casino! This is a popular trip and for many it's as much a holiday cruise as simply ferry transportation. Quite a few people just go and come back not even bothering to leave ship in port. Like the Bar Harbour boat this is well appointed and comfortable but the casino adds a touch of glamour. A cruise ticket is available for walk-ons and includes cabin, breakfast and a good dinner buffet.

Sailing time is about 11 hours one way. Through the summer the ferry leaves Yarmouth at 10 am and Portland at 9 pm. The fare is US$68, less in the off-season. A vehicle is $93. If you sail on a Tuesday or Wednesday the car can be taken for half-price and there is 10% discount for return trips on full-fare days.

For either trip call ahead as reservations will probably be required.

In Portland there is a Nova Scotia Tourist Office in the Portland Pier area, across from the old Thomas Block Building.

Getting Around

For car rentals there is a Budget office (☎ 742-9500) at 150 Starrs Rd. The Texaco gas station at the far south end of town rents cars.

FRENCH SHORE

From roughly Salmon River for 50 km up the coast along St Mary's Bay towards Digby, Old Acadia is where the province's largest, mainly French-speaking Acadian population lives. It's an interesting region where traditional foods and crafts are available, a few historic sites can be seen and, in summer, festivals are held in some of the small villages. The history and sights of the area are detailed in a booklet titled the *Acadian Shore*, available from the tourist office. Among the crafts offered out of people's houses along the way the best two are the quilts and the woodcarvings both of which have earned good reputations.

For campers, there are several campgrounds between Yarmouth and Digby.

Cape St Mary's

Mavilette Beach is marvellous: a long wide arch of fine sand. The marsh behind the beach is good for bird-watching. From the *Cape View Restaurant* the beach looks great at sunset and the food is good too. The menu is mainly seafood, clams are a local speciality, but also available is rapie pie, an old Acadian dish. For details see Church Point. Main dishes at dinner range from $8 to $10.

Across the street the *Cape View Motel* (☎ 645-2258) has some individual cabins. Prices are singles/doubles $38/45 in the units; the cabins are more costly.

Meteghan

On the main street is **La Vieille Maison**, one of the oldest houses in the region and now

set up as a museum depicting Acadian life here during the 18th century. This is a busy fishing port and there is a large commercial wharf where the boats moor.

The Wood Studio has carvings and quilts to see or buy. For a light meal there is the *Meteghan Tea House* or *Café Terrasse du Vieux Marin*.

For accommodation there are the *Anchor Inn*, a B&B in a big old house, which is very low priced at singles/doubles $20/30 and the *Blue Fin Motel* (☎ 645-2251). The motel charges about twice as much as the B&B.

Comeauville

This is one of Canada's major mink-ranch areas; arrange a visit to one through the local tourist offices. There are a couple of B&Bs. The *Gulf Course View* (☎ 769-2065) is a bargain at just $20/24 for singles/doubles.

Church Point (Pointe de l'Église)

Église Sainte Marie towers over the town and most other churches too. Built between 1903 and 1905, it is the tallest and biggest wooden church in Canada and perhaps the USA as well. It has an impressive multi-spired steeple and a very bright, airy interior.

In the corner by the altar is a small museum which contains articles from the church's history including various vestments and chalices. A guide will show you around and answer any questions.

Nearby is the **Université de Sainte Anne**, the only French university in the province and a centre for Acadian culture.

The oldest of the annual Acadian cultural festivals is held here during the second week of July.

There is an inexpensive B&B here or, for camping, *Belle Baie Park* just out of town where the best spots along the shore are saved for overnight tenters.

Just beyond the church towards Yarmouth on the coast side of the road with the Acadian flag outside is *Rapure Acadienne*, the place where all the local establishments get their rapie pie (*paté à la rapure*). Inside several women are busy preparing the three varieties: beef, chicken or clam. The result is difficult to describe but it's a type of meat pie topped with grated paste-like potato from which all the starch has been drawn. They are very bland, filling and inexpensive and can be bought piping hot. In fact, they are all you can get here; you can't even get a coffee. Many of the French Shore restaurants offer this pie, often as an appetiser, but it's less than half the price right here.

Belliveau Cove

There is a wharf on the attractive little harbour here where the tides are particularly high. Stop at the pleasantly old-fashioned *Roadside Grill*, a comfortable local restaurant/diner with low prices for sandwiches and light foods but also lots of seafood – try the steamed clams, a local speciality and rapie pie is offered. The walls are adorned with stuffed animals and various memorabilia.

There are a few wood-carving outlets here but if you have any interest in these do not miss Clement Belliveau's shack, as he calls it, across the street from the Roadside. Despite constantly whittling the blocks of pine that have made him a big reputation he enjoys a conversation.

St Bernard

Here the grandest of the coast's churches stands – a mammoth granite Gothic-style monument which took 32 years to complete beginning in 1910. Again, a guide is on hand to show visitors around.

DIGBY

An old, attractive town with 2500 residents, Digby was built around a hill in the Annapolis Basin, an inlet of the Bay of Fundy. It's famous for its scallop fleet and busy with its terminal for the *Princess of Acadia* ferry which plies the waters between Digby and Saint John, New Brunswick. The town is also well known for its 'Digby chicks' a type of smoked herring. In summer historic Water St has a bit of a resort flavour with many visitors spending a day or so having a look around and feeding on scallops.

The town was founded by United Empire Loyalists in 1783 and since then its life has been based on fishing. The central area is small enough for walking to be the best way of getting around. At Loyalist Park on Water St is the town tourist office. Up Mount St from here is Trinity Anglican Church and its graveyard. A couple of blocks away at the south edge of the downtown section is the old Loyalist cemetery on Warwick St.

From the top of the hill by the high school on King St between Church and Mount Sts, five blocks back from Water St, there is a good view of the area.

From the ferry landing, it is about five km into Water St in downtown Digby.

Admiral Digby Museum

At 95 Montague Row in town, this small museum displays articles and photographs pertaining to the town's marine history and early settlement. It's open daily in July and August, but closed on Sunday during other months. Admission is free.

Places to Stay

For a place to sleep, the *Admiral's Landing* (☎ 245-2247), a B&B, is perfectly located at 115 Montague Row opposite the Digby Bandstand with views of the waterfront. Singles/doubles cost from $36/43. Most rooms are equipped with at least a sink and some have TV. It's open all year and a continental breakfast is included.

Westway House (☎ 245-5071) is a B&B at 6 Carlton St, a quieter street but still within walking distance of things to see. Singles/doubles are $28/34 including full breakfast and outside there is a barbecue and picnic table to use.

The *Thistle Down Inn*, another B&B, is the big old white house at 98 Montague Row. There are chairs out the back on the lawn from where you can watch the harbour. It's a little more expensive than the others.

Lovett Lodge (☎ 467-3917) is another B&B and also good value. Singles/doubles cost $26/33, with full breakfast. It's eight km east on Highway 101 in Bear River.

Wingberry House (☎ 834-2516) at Sandy

Cove is $30 a double, with breakfast and dinner available and swimming nearby. To get there, take Highway 217 west from Digby. Turn left at the bottom of the first long hill in Sandy Cove, and go to the end of the road. Turn right and it's at the end of the street. There are also a few private campgrounds around Digby.

Places to Eat

There are a few seafood places where you can take advantage of the scallops and other local sea creatures. *Le Grand Marnier* in the centre of Water St is reasonably priced, the food is very good and the dining room provides views over the harbour area. If it's not too sunny there is also an outdoor patio to enjoy.

The *Captain's Cabin*, on the corner of Water and Birch Sts, is casual but nice and offers similar seafood; it's more expensive with meals ranging from $10 to $15. Steak is offered as an alternative to fish.

The *Chowder House* for chowders and pies at 139 First St between Church and Sydney Sts is good and very economical.

Lastly, consider buying some seafood fresh at the *Royal Fundy Seafood Market* by the docks on Prince William St. The selection is wide, the prices low. If you're camping or have cooking facilities at the motel, even a bag of scallops can make a remarkably cheap and delicious dinner. Boil them until they turn white and then sautée them in butter. And that's it, pig out. Of course there is also shrimp available and lots of fish including different types of smoked fish which keeps for a few days without refrigeration. The Digby chicks, the heavily smoked herring for which the town is well known, will last up to two weeks.

Getting There & Away

Bus The bus depot is at the Irving gas station on the corner of Montague Row (an extension of the main street, Water St) and Warwick St, a short walk from the centre of town. There are two buses a day to Yarmouth ($9.75), and two the other way to Halifax.

Ferry In summer Marine Atlantic (☎ 800-565-9470) runs three ferry trips from Digby to Saint John, New Brunswick, daily. The crossing takes about 2½ hours. Prices are a bit steep at $16.75 per passenger and $52.50 per car, with bicycles $6. Reservations are a very good idea for this trip; call Marine Atlantic toll free from any of the Maritime Provinces. A one-day return ticket saves a few dollars off the full fare and makes a five-hour Bay of Fundy mini-cruise.

You can drive around in a small car for less in gas money than the cost of the ferry ticket but it takes longer as you must go right around the bay and up through Moncton, New Brunswick.

DIGBY NECK

The long, thin strip of land which protrudes into the Bay of Fundy from just north of town is known as Digby Neck and is visible from much of the French Shore. Two short ferry rides connect the two sections that have become split from the main arm so a road links Westport at the far end. The many small villages are primarily fishing ports and there is some good scenery. Brier Island has three lighthouses with picnic tables and shoreline views and numerous walking trails. Agates can be found along the beaches.

What draws many people though is the sea life off **Long and Brier islands**. From June to October whale and bird-watching boat cruises run from Westport. Conditions make it a very good location for seeing whales; the season is relatively long beginning in May, building up through June and remaining steady with a good population of three species – finback, minke, humpback – dolphins and porpoises too, through August.

There is a lot of other sea life to be seen and over a dozen bird species in the area. The tour company Bios (☎ 839-2995) is part of a research organisation. Reservations are a good idea and can be made by phone.

Westport is about 90 minutes from Digby so leave with plenty of time if you've a boat to catch and remember there are two ferries. They are timed so that if you drive directly there is no wait for the second one.

To make things a little less hectic, there are two places to stay in Westport, both reasonably priced. The *Brier House* (☎ 839-2300) has three rooms on top of a 40-metre bluff; singles/doubles cost $30/40 with a full breakfast. The alternative is *Westport Inn* (☎ 839-2675), it's slightly more expensive and lunch and dinner are available.

ANNAPOLIS VALLEY

The Evangeline Trail through the valley is really not as scenic as might be expected although it does pass through or by all the major towns and the historic sites. To really see the valley though, and get into the countryside, it is necessary to take the still smaller roads parallel and either north or south of Route 1. From here the farms and orchards, generally hidden from the main roads, come into view.

There are a number of quiet, pretty towns through the valley as well as some fascinat-

ing history in such places as Port Royal and Grand Pré.

For those seeking a little work in late summer, there should be some jobs available picking apples. Check in any of the valley towns – Bridgetown, Lawrencetown, Middleton, etc. Line things up a couple of weeks before picking time, if possible. MacIntosh apples arrive first at the end of August but the real season begins around the first week of September.

ANNAPOLIS ROYAL

This little town is near the site of Canada's first permanent European settlement and was founded by Samuel de Champlain in 1604. As the English and French battled over the years for the valley and land at the mouth of the Annapolis River, the settlement often changed hands. In 1710, the English had a decisive victory and changed the town's name from Port Royal to Annapolis Royal in honour of Queen Anne.

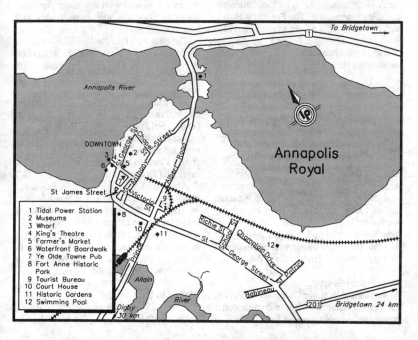

1 Tidal Power Station
2 Museums
3 Wharf
4 King's Theatre
5 Farmer's Market
6 Waterfront Boardwalk
7 Ye Olde Towne Pub
8 Fort Anne Historic Park
9 Tourist Bureau
10 Court House
11 Historic Gardens
12 Swimming Pool

It's a busy town with most things on the long, curving St George St or close to it. There is a waterfront boardwalk behind King's Theatre on St George St with views over to the village of Granville Ferry.

A farmers' market is held every Saturday morning in summer.

Anne National Historic Park
Right in the centre of town, this park preserves the memory of the early Acadian settlement plus the remains of the 1635 French fort. Two gunpowder magazines can be entered and the ground fortifications of mounds and moats can be observed. A museum has replicas of various period rooms, artefacts, uniforms and weapons; the Acadian room was transferred from an old homestead. The museum's open daily and there is no charge.

Lower St George St
This street in town along the water contains many historic buildings with three different centuries represented. The **Farmer's Hotel**, which possibly dates from as early as 1730, is the oldest building in English Canada. The **O'Dell Inn Museum** and **Robertson-McNamara House** both provide historic displays, the former of the Victorian era, the latter of local history. Admission to both is free.

Runciman House, dating from 1817 and furnished in Regency style, is run by Heritage Canada and also offers glimpses of former years.

Historic Gardens
Around the large, green grounds numerous distinct types of garden, including Acadian and Victorian, are set out. There is an interpretive building, a restaurant and gift shop. Admission is charged. The gardens are not far from the centre of town on St George St near the corner of Prince Albert Rd.

Tidal Power Project
At the Annapolis River Causeway this offers visitors the chance to see a hydroelectric prototype harnessing power from the Bay of Fundy tides. There's also an interpretive centre that explains how it works. The site is free and open every day in summer.

Places to Stay
All budget categories of places to stay are well represented here from inns to motels to cabins by the sea. There are a good half-dozen B&Bs in or near town and a couple of motels along the primary routes.

Right in town, at 372 St George St, is the *Turret B&B* (☎ 532-5770), an historic property with three rooms at just singles/doubles $26/38 with a full breakfast. Not far away is the *Annapolonian* (☎ 532-7891), at 808 St George St, with rooms at about $10 more. Half of the eight rooms have their own baths.

At 82 Victoria St is the *Bread & Roses B&B* (☎ 532-5727) in a restored house built in 1882. Singles/doubles are $44/48.

About one km east of town on Highway 201, Rural Route 1, are *Helen's Cabins* (☎ 532-5207) which cost singles/doubles and triples for $24/30 with hot plates for quick cooking. They are open from 1 May to 1 October.

The *Shining Tides* (☎ 532-2770) is a few km from the Habitation National Park in Port Royal. There are three rooms, with singles/doubles for $27/32, including a light breakfast.

At Victoria Beach, 26 km from Annapolis Royal, are the *Fundy View House & Cabins* (☎ 532-5015) with rooms in the house or in cabins with kitchens. Singles range from $22 to $25, doubles $27 to $33. This place is open from 15 June to 15 September; there's swimming and fishing here.

About 25 km from Annapolis Royal is a *Youth Hostel* (☎ 532-2497), in South Milford on Highway 8. It's open from mid-May to mid-October and there are nine beds, which cost $8/10 for members/nonmembers. The hostel is in the Beachside Park Campground; to get there, turn west in South Milford onto Clementvale-Virginia Rd.

Places to Eat
The *Ye Old Town Pub*, on Church St just off St George St by the wharf, is a busy place for

lunch and a brew. Otherwise, there's the cheap and basic *Fort Anne Café*, on St George St opposite the historic site, or expensive and decorative *Newman's*.

AROUND ANNAPOLIS ROYAL
Port Royal Habitat
National Historic Park
Fifteen km from Annapolis Royal, this is the actual site of the first European settlement north of Florida. It has a replica, constructed in the original manner, of de Champlain's early 1600s fur-trading habitation. It was destroyed by the English a few years after it was begun. Costumed workers help tell the story of this early settlement. It's free and open daily.

Delap Cove
On the coast north of town is a series of typical small fishing villages from Delap Cove at the west all the way to the Minas Basin.

At Delap Cove is a 12.1 km hiking trail which runs through woods, along the shoreline and across the beach while providing a cross section of the provincial coastal scenery. There are streams and waterfalls at various places and an assortment of birds and animals. There is an interpretive office where you can get a map just west of Delap Cove and a couple of toilets where the trails are but that's it.

KEJIMKUJIK NATIONAL PARK
This park contains some of the province's least touched wilderness. It's an area of glacial lakes, good for canoeing, and evergreen forests, where the hiking is easy on the gentle, rolling hills. Some portage routes are marked; many were used by the Micmac Indians. Lots of frogs and reptiles inhabit the many bogs. Deer also abound in the park.

There are primitive campsites along the trails and a main campground at Jeremy's Bay. Access north or south is by Highway 8. Canoes are available for rent.

The *Whitman Inn* (☎ 682-2266) in Caledonia is a comfortable place to stay for non-campers. It's a restored turn-of-the-

century house that now has an indoor swimming pool, saunas – the works. Yet the simplest of the range of rooms are moderately priced at $45 a double. All meals are available.

BRIDGETOWN
Back along the Annapolis Valley, Bridgetown has many trees and some fine examples of large Maritime houses. There's also the small **James House Museum** among the shops along Queen St. In the museum is a tea room for an afternoon break.

MIDDLETON & KINGSTON
Middleton and Kingston, two of the larger valley towns, aren't as attractive as Annapolis Royal or Bridgetown. They are more or less just commercial and shopping centres for the numerous very small local farming communities. There really isn't much reason to stop until reaching the end of the valley. For scenery try getting off Route 1 through the central region. This is the area where soil and climate combine to create one of the best orchard districts in the country. Aside from apples and other fruits, grains, vegetables and dairy cows are raised. Roadside stands offer the fresh crops at good prices.

COLDBROOK
This village is home to Scotian Gold, a large apple-processing facility where juice and apple sauce are produced. The plant offers visitors a look around in late summer and fall when things are really getting cranked up.

KENTVILLE
Kentville, with a sizeable population of 5000, marks the east end of the Annapolis Valley and acts as a focal point to a couple of nearby places of interest.

The town, itself, is functional and is not of particular note but there are a few places to stay or eat. There is a miltary base outside town and its vehicles are often encountered on the roads.

At the eastern end of town is the **Agriculture Research Station** with a museum related to the area's farming history and particularly its apples. There is a pleasant walking trail through the woods – woods that contain old growth – one of the few areas in the province with original forest.

Neighbouring **New Minas** is strictly a shopping town with a couple of malls and a branch of every chain restaurant you care to name.

Places to Stay & Eat
Highly recommended is the *Camelot Campground* which feels miles from anywhere with its peaceful woods and bubbling brook but is just 1.6 km from the main intersection in town – the junction of Main and Cornwallis Sts. There is a warm swimming pool surrounded by trees that is perfect at the end of a day.

There are some very conveniently central places to choose from. The *Wildrose Inn* (☎ 678-7368), at 160 Main St just out of the downtown area towards New Minas, is the very attractive old grey and pink house. Rates are singles/doubles $35/40 and include a full breakfast as well as use of the swimming pool.

There are also two motels in town. Not far away, in Port William, the *Country Squire* (☎ 542-9125) on Main St is similar to the Wildrose.

The *King's Arms Pub* is on Main St and *Paddy's*, a similar place, is over on Aberdeen St. Both provide inexpensive lunches.

NORTH OF KENTVILLE
The area up to Cape Blomidon on the Bay of Fundy makes for a fine trip for half a day or longer with good scenery, a memorable view of much of the valley and a couple of beaches.

Canning
There is a guesthouse and a small, simple restaurant in Canning where the main street through the tiny town is dark on a sunny day because there are so many large overhanging trees.

The Lookoff
From the road's edge at nearly 200 metres

high this could well be the best view of the soft, rural Annapolis Valley, its rows of fruit trees and farmhouses appearing like miniatures.

Across the street is a campground and snack bar.

Blomidon
At the provincial park here there is a beach and camping. As at Kingsport's sandy beach further south, the water can get quite warm.

Scots Bay
The road continues north to Scots Bay with a large pebbled beach. From the end of the road, a spectacular 13-km-long hiking trail leads to the cliffs at Cape Split.

Halls Harbour
On the often foggy coast Halls Harbour to the west is a classic, scenic little lobster village with a pier and lobster pound where they cook live lobsters from 1 to 6 pm and sell them at the best prices you'll ever find. All that's sold is the lobster, rolls and butter. There are picnic tables around the dock area.

There are some very nicely kept and decorated houses in town and a small variety store opposite the wharf for drinks, etc. The tides are very high, leaving the entire wharf area high and dry when the water's out.

Along Highway 359 to Halls Harbour you may see some of the small local tobacco crop growing.

WOLFVILLE
Wolfville is a quiet, green university town best known as the home of artist Alex Colville. With its art gallery, comfortable inns and impressive historic homes there is a wisp of culture in the air.

The tourist office is in Willow Park at the east end of Main St. The bus stop for Acadian bus lines is in a place called Nowlan's Canteen at the far west end of town on Main St on the corner of Hillcrest Ave. It's a bit of a walk into town.

St Andrew's United Church on Main St strikes me as being a particularly attractive structure.

The farms in the Wolfville area regularly produce some of the world's largest pumpkins. These are serious pumpkins – I mean you could use a chain saw to carve a Halloween face in these guys.

Acadia University Art Gallery
The gallery in the Beveridge Arts Centre building, on the corner of Main St and Highland Ave, exhibits mainly the work of other Maritime artists. It also has a collection of the work (mainly serigraphs) of Alex Colville some of which is always on display. Admission is by donation.

Carriage House Gallery
In the middle of Main St this commercial gallery has the works of local artists for sale as well as some Colville prints.

Randall House Museum
Set in a house, dating from the early 1800s, the museum deals with the early New England planters or colonists who replaced the expelled Acadians and the Loyalists who followed later. It is at 171 Main St and is free and open every day through the summer.

Places to Stay
The residences at the central university are open to visitors through the summer and are not expensive.

Victoria's Inn (☎ 542-5744) is a very ornate place with rooms in the lodge or in a motel section. The best deal is in the shared bathrooms of the main lodge where singles are $40 and doubles or triples cost $50. They also have a dining room.

Birchcliff B&B (☎ 542-3391), at 84 Main St, has just two rooms offered through the summer at about $10 less than the above.

There are also three up-market inns in town.

Places to Eat
Main St has both cheap places and more expensive ones offering seafood. The *Colonial Inn*, with historic decor and waitresses in period costume, has a good varied menu of standards and does them well. It's open for all three meals and isn't too badly priced either.

For a real splurge *Chez La Vigne* on Central Ave is said to be good.

GRAND PRÉ
Now a very small English-speaking town, Grand Pré was the site of one of the most dramatic stories in eastern Canada's history. The details of this sorry but fascinating tale can be learned at the national historic site north of the main highway and town, itself, five km east of Wolfville.

Grand Pré National Historic Park
Grand Pré means 'great meadow' and refers to the farmland created when the Acadians built dykes along the shoreline as they had done in north-west France for generations. There are 1200 hectares below sea level. It's a beautiful area and one you wouldn't want to leave involuntarily especially after the work that made it home. The park is a memorial to the Acadians, who had a settlement here from 1675 to 1755 and then were given the boot by the British.

It consists of an information centre, church, gardens, space and views.

Free tours of the site are offered and if all the guides are as humorous as the young woman I had then the tours are a good laugh as well as being informative.

There is a worthwhile gift shop with a selection of books on the Acadians among other things.

A new stone church, built in the Acadian style, sits in the middle of the site as a monument to the original inhabitants. Inside, the history of those people is depicted in a series of colourful paintings done in 1987 by New Brunswick painter, Claude Picard.

Walk down through the gardens to the old blacksmith's shed where there are views of gorgeous, fertile farmlands and pastures with green hills in the background. Smell the air: a mix of sea breeze and worked fields.

In the gardens are a bust of Longfellow, honoured for his poem which chronicles the Acadian's saga and a statue of Evangeline, now a romantic symbol of her people.

The Acadians

The story of the Acadians is one of the most interesting, dramatic and tragic in Canada's history. It was played out in what are now five of the country's provinces, the USA, the West Indies and Europe. And although it began in the 1600s it is not over.

When the French first settled the area around the south Minas Basin shore of the Bay of Fundy in 1604 they named the land Acadia. By the next century these settlers thought of themselves as Acadians. To the English, however, they were always to be 'the French'. The rivalry and suspicion between these two powers of the New World began with the first landings and was only to increase in hostility and bitterness.

The population of Acadia continued to grow through the 17th and 18th centuries and, with various battles and treaties, changed ruling hands from French to English and back again. Finally, in 1713 with the Treaty of Utrecht, Acadia became English Nova Scotia. The Acadians refused to take an oath of allegiance although for the most part they weren't much interested in France's point of view either and evidently wanted most of all to be left alone. Things sort of drifted along in this state for a while and the area around Grand Pré became the largest Acadian community. By this time the total regional population was not far off 10,000 with 3500 more people in Louisbourg and still others in Prince Edward Island.

Unfortunately for them tensions once again heated up between England and France with squabbles and trade-offs taking place all over the east coast. When a new hardline lieutenant-governor Charles Lawrence was appointed in 1754 he quickly became fed up with the Acadians and their supposed neutrality. He didn't trust them and decided to do something about it. He demanded an oath of allegiance and, as the game had always been played, the Acadians said forget it. This time, though, the rules had changed.

In late August 1755 with the crowns of France and England still locked in battle and paranoia increasing, what was to become known as the Deportation or the Expulsion began. All told, about 14,000 Acadians were forced out of this area. Villages were burned, the people boarded onto boats.

The sad, bitter departure was the theme for Longfellow's well known lengthy narrative poem, *Evangeline*, titled after its fictional heroine. Many Acadians headed for Louisiana and New Orleans, where their name became Anglicised to 'Cajun' (often heard in songs and seen on restaurant menus). The Cajuns, some of whom still speak French, have maintained aspects of their culture to this day. Others went to various Maritime points and north-eastern America, others to Martinique, Santo Dominigo, back to Europe, some even to the Falkland Islands. Nowhere were they greeted warmly with open arms. Some hid out and remained in Acadia. In later years many of those people deported returned.

Today, most of the French people in Canada's Atlantic Provinces are the descendants of the expelled Acadians and they're still holding tight to their heritage.

In Nova Scotia the Cheticamp area in Cape Breton and the French Shore north of Yarmouth are small strongholds. A pocket in western Prince Edward Island and the Port au Port peninsula in Newfoundland are others. New Brunswick has a large French population stretching up the east coast past the Acadian Peninsula at Caraquet and all around the border with Quebec.

There has recently been an upsurge in Acadian pride and awareness and in most of these areas you'll see the Acadian flag flying and museums dealing with the past and the continuing Acadian culture. There is another major national historic site dealing with the Acadians and their expulsion near St Joseph, New Brunswick, not far from the Nova Scotia border – a visit is recommended. Festivals held in some of these areas provide an opportunity to see traditional dress, sample foods and hear some of the wonderful fiddle-based music. ■

The park is open daily from June to September, admission is free. Acadian Days is an annual festival held sometime towards the end of July consisting of music, storytelling, arts & crafts. Many of the events are held at the historic park.

Grand Pré Winery

The winery is one of only two in the province, the other being at Jost, near Malagash on the Northumberland Shore. It sits adjacent to the main road through town and can be visited.

A self-guided tour around the grounds and to the edge of the vineyards explains the history and wine-making procedures. In the cellar a variety of wines may be sampled free of charge and favourites purchased upstairs.

WINDSOR

Windsor is a small town on the Avon River, at one time the only British stronghold in this district of French power and Acadian farmers.

Highway 1 becomes Water St in town and the main intersection is with Gerrish St. Nearby, off King St there's an **old blockhouse** still intact amid portions of the British Fort Edward dating from 1750.

Another site is **Haliburton House**, once the home of Judge Thomas Chandler Haliburton, one of the founders of written American humour. He created the Sam Slick character in Mark Twain-style stories. Although these aren't read much now, many Haliburton expressions are often used today, like 'quick as a wink' and 'city slicker'. Haliburton's large estate is open to visitors, free, from mid-July to mid-September. It's on Clifton Ave which runs off Grey St, itself leading from Gerrish St just north of Lake Pesaquid, in the eastern section of town.

Shand House is a small museum on Water St.

There's an internationally performing puppet theatre, the **Mermaid Theatre**, and the window of the theatre on Gerrish St is worth a look whether you're seeing a show or not.

Tides

The tides in the bay and Avon River near Windsor are impressive – falling and rising up to 12 metres. At Poplar Grove, off Highway 14 East, you can view a tidal bore. Ask at the tourist office for good times and locations for observing this phenomenon because it varies a lot. Port Williams near Wolfville is also a good place to see the difference between high and low tides.

Places to Stay

The *Meander Inn* (☎ 798-2325) at 153 Albert

St is a place for overnighters with singles/doubles from $30/45.

Getting There & Away

Acadian bus lines from Halifax to Windsor continues on to Yarmouth via numerous stops through the Annapolis Valley.

Northumberland Shore

This is the north coastal district of the province from the New Brunswick border to Cape Breton Island. The Northumberland Strait is between this shore and Prince Edward Island and has some of the warmest waters north of the US Carolinas. Highway 6, also called the Sunrise Trail, tourist route, runs along this strip of small towns, beaches and Scottish history.

On Highway 104 right at the New Brunswick border is a large tourist office with maps and overviews of the driving trails around Nova Scotia.

Although there are no major attractions along this shore it is busy and, as accommodation is not plentiful, places to stay easily get filled up. It's strongly recommended to find a place around lunch time in July and August.

PUGWASH

On the coast along the Sunrise Trail from Amherst is this small port with good beaches nearby. On average, the water temperature along this coast is slightly over 20°C in summer. Pugwash's two claims to fame are the large saltmine which produces boatloads shipped from the town docks and the colourful Gathering of the Clans festival which takes place each year on 1 July. Street names in town are written in Gaelic as well as English.

Pugwash once hosted the International Thinkers' Conferences, organised by Cyrus Eaton, a Nova Scotian and one of America's top financiers.

There are several craftspeople in town and their wares are sold along the main street.

WALLACE

There is no reason to stop here really but there is an interesting town tidbit. The sandstone from the quarry just out of town has been used to build many fine buildings including the Parliament Buildings in Ottawa and Province House in Nova Scotia.

MALAGASH

The Jost Winery here is one of only two vineyards in Nova Scotia, the other being at Grand Pré in the Annapolis Valley. Run by a German family, the winery began operation in 1970 and now with 13 hectares produces several varieties with the Reisling-style perhaps the best known. Free tours are offered at 3 pm through the summer and there is a store on the premises. Jost products can also be bought at the government liquor outlets with the best selection being in the local ones.

TATAMAGOUCHE

Despite having a population of just 550, Tatamagouche is somewhat of visitor's centre with a lot of people passing through and a few things to see. Pretty well everything is along Main St which is really the highway going east and west.

Not to be missed is the quirky **Fraser Culture Centre**, a sort of museum-cum-art gallery. The showpiece is the room dedicated to Anna Swan, who at 2.4 metres tall and weighing 187 kg, was known as the giantess of Nova Scotia and who went on to achieve some celebrity. Born in one of the surrounding villages in 1896 she parlayed her size into a lucrative career with Barnam & Bailey's circus and even ended up meeting the Queen in London where she was married. Clothes, newspaper clippings and photographs tell the big story.

Next door a room houses two stuffed calves – each with two heads. (I told you it was quirky.) But actually there is more to it including some historical artefacts and paintings in the gallery section.

There is a very inexpensive pleasant little tea room with home baking in one of the rooms too. The tourist office is also here in another of the many rooms.

A few doors down is the less idiosyncratic **Sunrise Trail Museum** of local history with emphasis on the shipbuilding industry, once of major importance here. Other items pertain to household and farmyard tools and articles including a dog-powered churn. The Acadian French settled this area in the 1700s and a display tells of them and their expulsion.

In Tatamagouche an Octoberfest is held annually at the end of September or beginning of October.

Places to Stay & Eat

For a place to sleep in town the *Victorian Charm Inn* (☎ 657-3222) at 354 Main St is good, central and not badly priced either at singles/doubles $32/40. Another, a bit more expensive, is in the old railway station. Ten km away at Brule Beach are the *Brule Shore Cabins* (☎ 474-7240) which are small, basic, and have seen better days. They fill up most nights, however, and have a certain funky charm – and they're cheap at $34 a double or triple.

Aside from the café in the museum if you're looking for a bite, the *Villager Inn & Restaurant* has inexpensive specials, some seafood and the chowders are quite good.

German food is available at the *Balmoral Motel* dining room. Also in town is a pizza place and a submarine-sandwich shop. There is a farmer's market through the summer in the old railway station.

AROUND TATAMAGOUCHE

There are a couple of other small museums in the region. South down Route 311 at **Balmoral Mills** is one of the oldest grist mills in the province. It opened in 1874. You can't miss the bright red building down by the stream. Demonstrations show the flour- (oatmeal, barley, wheat) milling process from start to finish and the finished products are even offered for sale. It's open daily from 15 May to 15 October and is free; there are some picnic tables by the creek.

Nearby, outside the village of **Denmark** is

the Sutherland Steam Mill. Built in 1894 the sawmill was run continuously by family members until 1953 but the machinery and steam engine still run.

This part of the province has a bit of a German colony and at the *Bavarian Garden Restaurant* in Denmark various made-on-the-premises German foods are offered. It's open every day in July and August but only on weekends in May, June and September. The Pork Shop next door sells a wide variety of German sausage, kassler, hams, etc.

At **River John** look for the community lobster dinners held from May to July and the chicken barbecues in August. The lobster boats operate out of the small pier with its nearby storage shanties at **Cape John**.

CAPE SKINNER
Back at the coast, Cape Skinner has a small wharf with boats that are engaged in the collection of Irish moss. This is a type of seaweed from which a gelatin is extracted for use in making ice cream and other products that require gel.

PICTOU
Pictou (pronounced 'pik toe'), one of the most attractive and interesting towns along the North Shore, was where the Highland Scots first landed in 1773 to be followed by thousands in the settling of 'New Scotland'. They spread from the Northumberland Shore through Cape Breton, reminded of home by the landscape and weather. In town, among the many older structures are several buildings and historic sites relating to the early Scottish pioneers. Pick up a walking-tour brochure at the tourist office at the rotary (traffic circle, roundabout) north-west of the town centre.

Water St, with most of the commercial enterprises, is the main street and reflects the architectural style of the early Scottish builders. Above it Church, High and Faulkland Sts are lined with some of the old, very large houses the town is also noted for.

There's a farmers' market, where you'll find baked goods and farm produce, every Saturday from April to December in the Community Centre on Front St.

The ferry to Prince Edward Island leaves from just north of here at Caribou. For details see the Charlottetown Getting There & Away section, in the Prince Edward Island chapter.

Part of the waterfront is being redeveloped to preserve both history and access.

Hector National Exhibit Centre
Away from the town centre but within walking distance on Haliburton Rd, a continuation westward of High St, this centre presents a variety of ever changing shows. On my last visit it featured the tartans of Scotland and their histories. It's open daily and is free. The pond, just to one side of the museum, is home to a seemingly limitless number of frogs.

McCullogh House
Open every day from May to October the house built in 1806 for Tom McCullogh, a minister and important educator, now displays articles pertaining to his career and life but also those of other early Scottish settlers as well. The house is the one just up the hill from the Hector National Exhibit Centre.

Grohmann Knives Ltd
The small family-run business at 88 Water St has a well-deserved reputation for the very fine outdoor and kitchen knives it produces. One of them, a classic belt knife available in many countries, is in the Museum of Modern Art in New York.

Many of the production stages are done by hand as they were when the operation began in the mid-1950s and can be seen on the free tours around the plant offered three times a day Monday to Friday from May to September. You'll observe an interesting procedure which in one stage employs thick walrus-hide belts for polishing. The tour highlight though is watching the guide's hands as he sharpens a knife to a razor's edge.

There is a wide and very tempting selection of knives for sale. (Yes, I did...a Russell.)

Northumberland Fisheries Museum

On Front St in the old railway station, the museum tells the story of the area's fishing, both past and present. Shipbuilding remains important – the yards are nearby – and is also depicted in the museum. It's open seven days a week in July and August.

Festivals

The Lobster Carnival is a three-day event at the beginning of July marking the end of lobster season with music, parades and the like.

The Hector Festival in the mid-August is four days of Scottish heritage including concerts.

Places to Stay

Fraser's Tourist Home (☎ 485-4294), 12 High St, is recommended. There are three rooms in the century-old house, with singles/doubles $20/35 including a continental breakfast.

The *Willow House Inn* (☎ 485-5740) is a grander B&B developed in a large historic house dating from 1840 and once belonging to the mayor. It too, is very central at 3 Willow St. There are 10 rooms, the more expensive of which have private bath facilities. Singles/doubles cost $32/36 and up.

Away from the downtown area near the tourist office by the rotary is *Johnston's Motel* (☎ 485-4157). It has some newish motel units and a number of older individual cabins with their own kitchens, some with two bedrooms which can make for a pretty good bargain. Singles are $40 but doubles and triples are just $5 extra. If this place is full, there is another just down and across the road towards town.

Bear in mind that Pictou, while not crowded, has a steady stream of people passing through and most accommodation is full or close to it through the summer.

Places to Eat

For breakfast go to *Smith's* on Church St which is one block back from and parallel to Water St. It's open from 6 am every day but Sunday.

Right in the centre at 11 Water St, is the *Stone House Café & Pizzeria* where the food isn't great but the selection is wide. There is a nice outside patio and local entertainment is often on tap in the evenings. A meal costs about $6.

The *Golden Boat* Chinese place at 93 Water St is open until midnight all week.

For a splurge amidst the surroundings of a very tasteful, warm, country lodge step into the *Braeside Inn* up the hill at 80 Front St overlooking the water. The food is very good, the menu is varied with a slant towards seafood. Built in 1938, the inn has recently been redone and has 20 overnight guest rooms.

Though out of the way and virtually impossible to reach without a car, one of the best known restaurants in the area is the *Lobster Bar* across the bay from Pictou in Pictou Landing where there is a Native Indian reserve and not a lot more. Driving involves a rather circuitous route over one of the bridges towards New Glasgow – get the map distributed at the Pictou tourist office. It's a pleasantly casual (take the kids), busy and not badly priced seafood house specialising in lobster. A full lobster meal costs about $15. There is no help-your-self-buffet as at some lobster-supper places but portions will satisfy most people. They've been serving up fish, clams and all the rest for over 35 years and have fed former US president Jimmy Carter as well as Brian and Mila Mulroney although some may view the latter two as an appetite suppressant.

AROUND PICTOU
Beaches

There are a couple of very good beaches outside Pictou. The most popular and sort of 'the in place' is **Melmerby Beach** ('the Merb') which is actually north of New Glasgow but draws 'em from far and wide. It's a long, wide sandy beach; there is a basic hamburger stand but no shade.

My choice is **Caribou Beach** which is equally sandy with gradually deepening water but is more scenic with picnic tables along a small ridge above the beach and trees for when the sun gets too intense. It is much closer to town, north of Pictou near the Prince Edward Island ferry terminal. Both beaches are free and the water along this strip of ocean is as warm as any in Nova Scotia, heated by the Gulf Stream to around 19°C in midsummer – not bad at all if you keep moving.

NEW GLASGOW

With a population of 10,000, New Glasgow is the largest town along the Northumberland Shore. It originally was and remains a small industrial centre. There is little to see in town but it can be useful as a stopping point as it's close if you're coming or going to the ferry for Prince Edward Island.

Provost St is the main retail and shopping avenue and it has a couple of restaurants. Temperance St, parallel to Provost St and up the hill from the river, is attractive with lots of trees, some large older houses, a couple of churches and Stewart House. The latter, at 86 Provost St, is an historic building housing a small museum illustrating the town's history in shipbuilding and coal mining.

For railway buffs, see the **Samson**, the first steam locomotive in North America. It operated nearby in 1837 and has been restored to its odd-looking glory. It sits encased in glass beside the library on Archimedes St.

Fraser's Mountain not far from town offers excellent views of the entire region. Drive east through town on Archimedes St and turn right on George St. Continue up the hill, veering left around the church and keep going straight to the summit.

Out of town at nearby Abercrombie St towards Pictou is the **Sobey Collection of Canadian Art** featuring some of the country's best known 19th and 20th-century painters. There is no admission charge.

Places to Stay

For spending the night, the *Wynwood Inn* (☎ 752-4527), a B&B since 1930, makes a fine choice. Actually an attractive old house, it's very central with a nice balcony. It's at 71 Stellarton Rd. Rates for singles range from

$30 to $34, doubles are $35 with a light breakfast.

Mackay's B&B (☎ 752-5889) at 44 High St is also central but more modest and cheaper with singles/doubles for $25/30.

There are motels on the highway on the way in and out of town.

ANTIGONISH

If you're coming from New Brunswick or Prince Edward Island, this is the place to spend the night or even a couple of days. Antigonish is also a good stop between Sydney and Halifax. A pleasant, small town with a few things to see, it has some good places to stay and the beach is nearby. It's a university and residential town with no industry. The name is pronounced with the accent on 'nish'.

Information

The tourist office is just off the highway at the west entrance to Antigonish, coming from New Glasgow at exit 32.

St Ninian's Cathedral

This is the seat of the Catholic diocese for the adjoining three counties and all of Cape Breton. It was begun in 1868 and is built of blue limestone and granite from local quarries. Work in the interior comes from a variety of sources including Quebec, New Hampshire and Europe. St Ninian was an obscure priest from Ireland who travelled and taught in the Scottish Highlands in the 4th century.

St Francis Xavier University

The attractive campus of this 125-year-old university is behind the cathedral near the centre of town. It's a nice place to walk around just for a look-see.

County Courthouse

In 1984 this 129-year-old building was designated a national historic site. Restored in 1970 although it was in good repair, it still serves as the county's judicial centre. The design by Alexander Macdonald is typical of many of the province's courthouses from the mid-19th century.

Festivals

Antigonish is known for its annual Highland Games held in mid-July. These Scottish games have been going on for 120 years. You'll see pipe bands, drum regiments, dancers and athletes from far and wide; there are competitions, performances, singing, dancing, fiddling and a pipe band tattoo. The events last a week. The international Gathering of the Clans took place here in the summer of 1983. There is also a theatre programme through the summer.

Places to Stay

West of town near Addington Forks just off the Trans Canada Highway is a good, very quiet provincial park, *Beaver Mountain*, for camping. It's up on a hill in the woods and there is hardly anyone ever there.

Whidden's Campground & Trailer Court (☎ 836-3736) right in town on the corner of Main and Hawthorne Sts is an unusual

accommodation complex. It's a very large place and offers a real blend of choices. There is straight camping which is $13 for a tent but just half that for hikers, cyclists or, basically, for anybody else without a car. Serviced sites cost more. Then there are motel apartments from $50 with kitchens and mobile homes with complete facilities at $65 a double and $5 for each additional person. The grounds have a swimming pool and a laundrette for all guests to use.

For rooms at the central *University* from mid-May to mid-August, call the Residence Manager (☎ 867-3970, 867-2258). It has a dining room, laundrette and pool. Singles/doubles are $22/30 and good weekly rates are available. There are also numerous inns, motels, cottages and a couple of B&Bs. *Green Haven* (☎ 863-2884) is a central B&B at 27 Greening St. It's close to the bus station and has singles at $25.

Another is the *Old Manse* (☎ 863-5696) in a house dating from 1874, at 5 Tigo Park a couple of blocks from the corner of Main and West Sts.

Girls in traditional Scottish dress

Hillside Housekeeping Cottages (☎ 232-2888), 19 km east of town at Tracadie, are a better bargain than motels in the area. Basic cottages cost singles/doubles $28/34 or, with cooking facilities, $34/40. The cottages are 10 minutes from the beach.

Places to Eat

A stroll down Main St and around the town will turn up several places for a bite. At *Adam's Bakery* there's decent food and prices. The *Sunshine Café* at 194 Main St is good for soups, salads and sandwiches under $5.

Farmer Brown's, in the big red and white barn by the old railway station, is the place for breakfast and offers quick meals of burgers and the like through the day. *Wong's* is friendly and provides the local Chinese option with the standard moderate prices of dishes under $7 or so. The *Venice* has a few Greek dishes among the mainly Italian fare.

West out of town along the Trans Canada Highway, the more costly *Lobster Treat* restaurant is good for seafood.

Getting There & Away

Bus The bus station (☎ 863-6900) is on the Trans Canada Highway at the turn-off for James St into town, on the west side of the city and is within walking distance of the downtown area. Buses include those to Halifax once a day for $20, to Sydney (one morning and one afternoon trip costing $18), and to Charlottetown at 1.15 pm daily for $26 including the ferry.

Train The train service has been discontinued here.

AROUND ANTIGONISH
Monastery

East of town in the small village of Monastery the old monastery is now home to the Augustine Order of monks. It was originally a Trappist monastery established by French monks in 1825. Visitors are welcome; you get a tour of the buildings and grounds.

Beaches

There are some good sandy beaches on the coast east or north from town. For the eastern ones take Bay St out of town.

Organised Tours

Drives Several driving tours of the area, no more than 80 km a piece, can be done with a descriptive pamphlet available from the tourist office. They try to take in some good scenery and points of historical note. One recommended sort of off-the-track route goes north along the coast to Cape George on Highway 337 with some fine shoreline views. At Crystal Cliffs, along the way, are huge cormorant roosts.

Eastern Shore

The 'Eastern Shore' designation refers to the area east from Dartmouth to Cape Canso at the extreme eastern tip of the mainland. It's one of the least visited regions of the province; there are no large towns; there's little industry and a slow, narrow road almost as convoluted as the rugged shoreline it follows. As in much of the province, the population is clustered in many small coastal villages. Marine Drive, the designated tourist route, is pretty much the only route through the area and despite its descriptions and alleged beauty spots is neither very scenic nor particularly interesting. There are a few good things, nonetheless, and these are emphasised here. There are some campgrounds and good beaches along the coast but the water on this edge of the province is prohibitively cold.

MUSQUODOBOIT VALLEY

A side trip away from the coast follows the course of the Musquodoboit River into the forested interior and along the valley's farming regions to the village of Upper Musquodoboit. Despite its light population, this was an area settled by Europeans as early as 1692. The following century saw people arriving from Ireland and New England.

There isn't a lot to do, although there are some walking trails. Consider it as an alternative route to the north coast as it leads quite directly to New Glasgow.

MARTINIQUE BEACH PROVINCIAL PARK

Martinique, 4.8 km south of the village of Musquodoboit Harbour, is the longest beach in the province and a good place for a break.

JEDORE OYSTER POND

Quite the name for a town, I'd say. See the small museum here – it's a model of a typical 1900s fishing family's house. Also here on the water is the *Golden Coast Restaurant* for seafood.

CLAM HARBOUR

There is a good beach with a small, basic restaurant and a picnic area. In mid-August each year a sand-sculpting contest is held.

SHIP HARBOUR

Off the shore here you'll see the buoys and nets of the local aquaculture industry. This is North America's largest mussel-farming centre.

TANGIER

A visit to **Willy Krauch's smokehouse**, a short distance from the main road in Tangier is worthwhile. Begun by Willy, a Dane, and now run by his sons, it's a small operation that has rightly earned a big reputation. They smoke Atlantic salmon, mackerel and eel. But to my tastebuds, the ultimate is the Cape Breton smoked trout; easily the best smoked fish I've ever had. It's great stuff for travelling too, because you can keep it without refrigeration. It can also be mailed, as it has been to Queen Elizabeth at Buckingham Palace in England.

The shed is open everyday until 6 pm. Ask the person at the counter if you can see the fish being smoked out the back.

TAYLOR HEAD PROVINCIAL PARK

Just east of the village of Spry Harbour at this day-use park is a very fine, sandy beach

fronting a shallow protected bay. The water, though, doesn't seem to warm up much. A walking trail (about a two-hour walk) runs along the shore and through the woods. At some points are good examples of Krummholz vegetation – trees and plants stunted and twisted from the poor, seaside conditions. Near the parking lot are a few picnic tables under the trees. The park is free.

LISCOMB PARK GAME SANCTUARY

North of Sheet Harbour lies this large preserve 518 sq km in area. There's lots of wildlife and some good canoeing. In Sheet Harbour is a decently priced motel of the same name. Between Sheet Harbour and the sanctuary is the *Sunset Wilderness Resort* on Marshall Flowage Lake with 10 housekeeping cottages and a campground. Call Eve or Rolf Villmann on ☎ 885-2534. It's a good area for swimming, fishing, canoeing and hiking. All equipment, even tents, can be rented.

LISCOMB MILLS

In a green wooded area where the Liscomb River meets the sea is one of the provincial government's resort lodges. It has all the amenities and prices to match but you may want to have a look or a tea or splurge on one of the seafood meals.

SHERBROOKE

Inland towards Antigonish the pleasant little town of Sherbrooke is overshadowed by its historic site which is about the same size.

Sherbrooke Village excellently recreates life around 125 years ago through buildings, demonstrations and costumed workers. It's called a living museum which means that almost all of the houses, stores, various workshops and buildings are the original ones standing in their original locations. The green, quiet setting helps to arouse a genuine feeling of stepping back in time.

The site is open daily from 15 May to 15 October and a real bargain at the amazingly cheap price of $2. The hotel on the site serves snacks and simple lunches.

About half a km away is the **Sherbrooke Village Sawmill**, the former town mill which is in working order and has a guide to answer questions, free. Across the street and a nice walk through the woods along a stream is a cabin the workers at the mill would have lived in.

Sherbrooke, itself, although not the major centre it was at the turn of the century, is one of the biggest towns in the area so stop here for tourist information, groceries and gasoline. There are a few picnic tables by the tourist office and a couple of craft shops to have a look at.

Places to Stay & Eat

If you're spending the night, consider the central *St Mary's River Lodge* (☎ 522-2177) with rooms from singles/doubles $22/26 with shared bath facilities. Breakfast is available.

Something else to look for is the *Bright House* restaurant in town. In an inn dating from 1850, it specialises in roast beef and fresh seafood and does them well. It's open daily for lunch, maybe a chowder, and dinner. It's not cheap but not expensive either with meals around $8 at lunch time.

There is camping nearby with one place north of town and one place south to choose from.

CANSO

With a population of just 1200, this town at the edge of the mainland is probably the largest on the whole eastern shoreline. Since the first attempted settlement in 1518, Canso has seen it all: Native Indian battles, English and French landings and captures, pirates, fishing fleets and the ever present difficulties of life ruled by the sea.

A museum, **Whitman House**, on the corner of Main and Union Sts has reminders of parts of this history and a good view from the roof.

An interpretive centre on the waterfront tells the story of the **Grassy Island National Historic Site** which lies just offshore and can be visited by boat. In 1720 the English built a small fort here to offer some protec-

tion from the French who had their headquarters in Louisbourg. Despite all the turmoil and events which took place here or, perhaps because of them, there isn't much of anything now on the barren island and the fort ruins are minimal.

Cape Breton Island

Cape Breton, the large island adjunct at the north-east end of Nova Scotia is justly renowned for its rugged splendour. It's the roughest, highest, coolest, most remote area of the province and is the one area a visitor should not miss. The coast is rocky and ragged; the interior a blend of mountains, valleys, rivers and lakes. The nearly 300-km-long highway, the Cabot Trail, around the Cape Breton Highlands National Park is one of Canada's grandest and best known roads. It winds and climbs to 500 metres between mountain and sea providing access to a variety of physical, historical and cultural attractions.

The island offers more than natural beauty – it has a long and captivating human history encompassing the original Native Canadians, the English, French and especially the Scottish. It was this part of the province, with its strong resemblance to the old country's Highlands, that drew numerous immigrants from Scotland.

Though not so true now, Cape Breton has long conjured up notions of remote isolation. Except for the industrial centres of Sydney and Glace Bay, most towns do remain small enough to be considered villages. People in some areas still speak French, in others, even Gaelic can be heard. Life is hard here and unemployment is very high. Fishing and mining are the main industries.

For the visitor it is a very appealing, relatively undeveloped area with the excellent national park in the highlands and a top historic site in Louisbourg.

Seafood is plentiful, the salmon fishing memorable, the beaches have water warm enough for swimming in, the walking trails

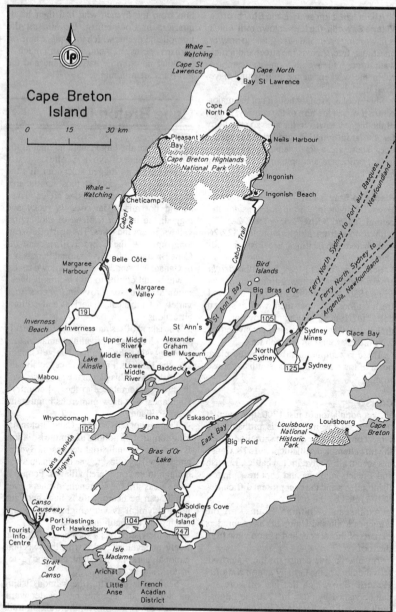

Cape Breton
Island

0   15   30 km

Whale – Watching

Cape St Lawrence

Cape North

Bay St Lawrence

Cape North

Pleasant Bay

Neils Harbour

Cape Breton Highlands National Park

Ingonish

Whale – Watching

Cheticamp

Ingonish Beach

Cabot Trail

Cabot Trail

Ferry North Sydney to Port aux Basques, Newfoundland

Ferry North Sydney to Argentia, Newfoundland

Belle Côte

Bird Islands

Margaree Harbour

Big Bras d'Or

Margaree Valley

St Ann's Bay

19

105

Inverness Beach

Inverness

St Ann's

Sydney Mines

Glace Bay

Upper Middle River

Alexander Graham Bell Museum

North Sydney

Middle River

125

Sydney

Lake Ainslie

Lower Middle River

Baddeck

Mabou

Whycocomagh

Iona

Eskasoni

Louisbourg National Historic Park

Louisbourg

Cape Breton

105

East Bay

Big Pond

Bras d'Or Lake

Trans Canada Highway

104

Canso Causeway

1

Soldiers Cove

Chapel Island

Tourist Info Centre

Port Hastings
Port Hawkesbury

247

Isle Madame

Strait of Canso

Arichat

Little Anse

French Acadian District

are fine, the music irresistible. And remember if you want to call home, the telephone was invented by Alexander Bell who lived in Baddeck on Bras d'Or Lake.

North Sydney is the terminal for ferries to Newfoundland.

The Cabot Trail, understandably the most popular area, can be busy, even a little crowded in July and August but it isn't difficult to get away if solitude is what you seek. The words most often used to describe the weather are windy, wet, foggy and cool. Summer days, however, can be warm and sunny.

Information

As you cross the Strait of Canso onto the island you'll be hit for $1.50 for using the causeway. (It's free on the way back – they say that's why the locals who leave never return.) A big and busy tourist office sits on the east side of the causeway and from here you can pick up information on all parts of Cape Breton. Smaller offices are found in many towns and the national park has its own information centres. If you need to make ferry reservations, call toll free from anywhere.

There is a B&B programme in Cape Breton, the tourist office should have a complete list. There are many private and some government campgrounds besides those in the national park. In addition, there is sometimes a youth hostel or two around the island but nothing seems to last more than a couple of years.

NORTH COAST

From the Canso Causeway Highway 19, known as the Ceilidh (pronounced 'kay lee') Trail, goes up the northern side of the island to the highlands. The first part of the route is not very interesting but it still beats the Trans Canada Highway (No 105) which goes straight up the middle.

At **Mabou**, things pick up. It's a green, hilly region with valleys following numerous rivers, and sheltering traditional towns. This is one of the areas on Cape Breton where Gaelic is still spoken and actually

taught in the schools. Right in the centre of little Mabou is the Gaelic & Historical Society Centre in a storefront. Aside from information they have books, tapes and various items relating to their Scottish heritage. On 1 July a Scottish picnic is held with music, dancing, etc. There is a restaurant in town.

At the coast, off the main road, around Mabou Harbour and Mabou Mines are the **Mabou Highlands** with some good walking trails.

Between Mabou and Inverness on Highway 19 the thirsty may wish to stop at **Glenora Falls** where North America's only single malt Scotch whisky is made. You can have something to eat or drink and tour the distillery. It's very new and actually the local brew is still ageing and won't be ready for a few years, but in the meantime, there is a pretty good substitute from the old country available.

INVERNESS

This is the first town of any size on the northern shore. There are miles of sandy beach with some nice secluded spots and very few people and, surprisingly, the water temperature is not too bad reaching temperatures of 19°C to 21°C which is about as warm as it gets anywhere around the Atlantic Provinces – cool, but definitely swimmable. Pilot whales can sometimes be seen off the coast.

In town there's not a lot to see but notice, on the north side of the street under the trees, the old houses which were originally built by the mining company for its workers. The mine is now closed but there is a small museum depicting those days.

Places to Stay & Eat

The *Inverness Lodge* (☎ 258-2193), in the centre, is a hotel and motel offering accommodation and a dining room. A double room costs $50. The *Gables Motel* (☎ 258-2314) is less expensive and at the north end of town try the comfortable *Cayly Café* for a munch.

LAKE AINSLIE
Inland from Inverness, large Lake Ainslie provides opportunities for freshwater swimming at a couple of parks and there is camping.

MARGAREE VALLEY
North-east of Lake Ainslie in a series of river valleys is a pretty and relatively gentle region known collectively as the Margaree Valley. With a half dozen different towns named Margaree this or Margaree that, it's an oasis of sorts in the midst of the more rugged, wild and unpopulated highlands.

The local waters, particularly the Margaree River, have long been renowned for the excellent salmon (and trout) fishing. Numerous hiking trails lead through the scenic countryside.

In North East Margaree is the **Salmon Museum** with information on the river, its fish (and what human artifices they must avoid) and also the **Museum of Cape Breton Heritage** with displays about the Scottish and French settlers emphasising their various textiles. There is also a gift shop. Both museums are open daily.

Places to Stay
As a small resort area, although thankfully a low-key one, there is a fair bit of accommodation as well as some places to eat scattered around the valley. Best known of all of them is the *Normaway Inn*, a three-star luxury country inn begun in 1928. No doubt, it is a fine place to stay and the food is said to be excellent. In high season expect to pay $90 a double. Complete meal plans are available or meals can be bought separately by guests or visitors.

Getting back to reality there's *Brown's Brunaich na H'Aibhne B&B* (☎ 2488-2935) in Margaree Centre. I didn't say you had to pronounce it, I just said you could stay there. Rates are from $25 single and double or triple $30. Call for details and reservations. It's open all year. In Margaree Forks there is a motel and a lodge, both of which are moderately priced. There is also a campground.

Places to Eat
In Margaree Forks *Van's* is primarily a pizza place but other things are offered. In Margaree Harbour, out of the valley on the coast, the *Schooner Restaurant*, in a converted boat, has inexpensive fish, chowders and non-seafood items, and is licensed.

BELLE CÔTE
From Belle Côte, where the Cabot Trail meets the coastline, northward to the Cape Breton Highlands National Park another strong culture adds a different interest to the island. The people here are predominantly French, the descendants of the Acadians who settled the area in the 1750s after being expelled from the mainland by the British during the Seven Years' War. This region and one north around the coast from Yarmouth on the mainland are the two largest remaining French districts in the province.

The strength of this culture in Cape Breton is remarkable because of its small size and isolation from other French-speaking people. Almost everyone, it seems, speaks very good English at the least although an accent is sometimes detectable. Amongst themselves, they switch to French keeping the language very much alive. Evidently there are differences in vocabulary and accent between this and the French of Quebec with the former retaining some older characteristics. Aside from the language there are French foods, music and dance worth sampling.

At Belle Côte look for the **Theatre of Scarecrow** by the highway beside Ethel's Takeout restaurant. It's a humorous quasi-macabre outdoor collection of life-sized stuffed figures. Watch out after midnight.

Further up the coast, the bakery near Grand Étang is good with huge loaves of bread as well as other things.

CHETICAMP
Just before the Cape Breton Highlands National Park, Cheticamp with a population of 3000, is the centre of the local Acadian community. It's a busy little town with many visitors passing through on their way to the

park. From Cheticamp the Cabot Trail becomes more scenic with great views and lots of hills and turns as you climb to the highest point just before Pleasant Bay.

The church, St Pierre, that dominates the town as is so often the case in French centres, dates from 1883 and has the characteristic silver spire. Feel free to have a look inside.

From the Government Wharf, across and down from the church, whale-watching cruises are run. The most common species in the area is the pilot whale, also called the pothead, but fin whales and minkes are sometimes seen as are a couple of species of sea birds, and there's always the mountainous shoreline.

Two days before my last visit about half a dozen whales had washed up on the beach here and many tourists were down with the locals helping to push them back out to sea. I'd call the three-hour boat excursions pretty good value.

Mark Lightbody

Over on Île de Cheticamp, Plage Saint Pierre is a good sandy beach with picnic tables and camping. The island is connected by road to the mainland at the south end of town.

The Country Music Store is an excellent place for records and tapes of traditional and contemporary Maritime music – French, English, Scottish, Cape Breton fiddle. They'll mail things home for you.

The Acadians have a tradition of handicrafts but in this area one product, hooked rugs, has long been viewed as of particular beauty and value. Many of the local women continue this craft; their wares are displayed and are for sale in numerous outlets in and around town. A good rug costs from $200 to $300 and up so they aren't cheap but they are distinctive and attractive. Each is made of wool, and to complete the intricate work takes about 12 hours per 30 sq cm.

Les Trois Pignons
At the north end of town this cultural centre and museum, among other things, shows the rugs and tapestries of many local people including those of Elizabeth Lefort who has achieved an international reputation. Her detailed representational rugs and portraits in wool hang in the White House, the Vatican and Buckingham Palace. Admission is a couple of bucks.

Also here is a library, shop and information and genealogical centre to promote the Acadian heritage.

Musée Acadienne
In the middle of town don't miss the Acadian museum which has a small but interesting display of artefacts, furniture and some older rugs. It's interesting to see how the old motifs and designs are incorporated into the rugs made today.

Upstairs from the museum is a craft shop where I thought the nicest rugs for sale were the ones with the traditional geometric patterns. Flora's, south of town, is the largest and most promoted craft store in the area. It has a good large assortment of textiles including some small, less expensive pieces. Besides the textiles, though, most of the stuff is not of much interest.

Perhaps the highlight of the Acadian museum is its restaurant with a large menu of mainly standard items but with low prices and freshness separating them from what's offered in run-of-the-mill places. The best dishes however are the three or four traditional Acadian ones all of which are excellent. The soup and meat pie make a great lunch. Fishcakes may be sampled (here, as in Newfoundland fish means cod; other types are called by name). The desserts which are all freshly made include gingerbread and a variety of fruit pies. Everything is good and cheap (under $6); the women who run the place and do the cooking and baking, wear traditional dress.

Places to Stay
Throughout July and August accommodation is very tight and calling ahead or arriving early in the afternoon is advisable. This is particularly true if the weather is poor and campers are being forced out of the woods or if there is an event of some sort on. Almost all the lodging is in motels.

Cheapest of the lot and good is *Albert's*

Motel (☎ 224-2077), on Main St, with doubles at $32 but there are very few rooms. Just before the park are *Cabines Leblanc* (☎ 224-2822) with six cabins, singles or doubles from $30 to $35, the higher price for ones with cooking facilities. The *Cheticamp Motel*, on Main St on the south side of town, is more expensive but friendly and it has a dining room for breakfast. Doubles here are $40.

As mentioned, there is camping at Île de Cheticamp.

Places to Eat

Aside from the museum restaurant, there are quite a few other places for a small town. One of the main catches from the sea here is crab which turns up on several menus. *Wilf's Restaurant*, at 838 Main St, is reasonably priced for seafood or chicken with dishes around $8. For more of a night out, try the *Harbour Restaurant* which has a view to complement the food. Very highly rated but more expensive again is the dining room at *Laurie's Motel*.

Getting There & Away

There is, unfortunately, no bus service although connections can be made from Canso to Inverness and from Ingonish, on the other side of the national park, to Baddeck.

CAPE BRETON HIGHLANDS NATIONAL PARK

In the middle of the highlands, this park not only has some of the most impressive terrain in the area, but it is also one of the most scenic places in Canada.

Park entry is $4. Conditions can be a rather rainy, foggy and windy even while remaining fairly warm. The driest month is generally July with June and September the runners up. Maximum temperatures in midsummer don't usually reach over 25°C and minimums are around 15°C.

At either of the entrances, Cheticamp or Ingonish, there are information centres for maps (including topographical ones), hiking brochures and advice. Both have a wide selection of nature books for sale too. Mountain bikes can be rented.

The Cabot Trail, one of the best known roads in the country, gets its reputation from the 106-km-park segment of its Cape Breton loop. It's at its very best along the northern shore and then down to Pleasant Bay. The road winds right along the shoreline between mountains, across barren plains and valleys up to **French Mountain**, the highest point at 459 metres. Along the way are lookout points, the best of which is at the summit. If possible save the trip for a sunny day when you can see down the coastline.

From French Mountain the road zigzags through switchbacks and descends to Pleasant Bay, just outside the park. If you're driving, make sure your brakes are good and can afford to burn off a little lining. Despite the effort required, the park is a popular cycling destination. I wouldn't make it my inaugural trip though.

Hiking trails abound and are, of course, the best way to see the park and maybe glimpse some of the wildlife. Black bears, lynx, fox, otter and moose are some of the animals you might see, along with 185 species of birds. Most of the trails are short and near the road. For longer, overnight camping hikes, ask for advice at the information office.

There are eight campgrounds in the park, some for tenters only. These tend to be small, with space for 10 to 20 people. Camping is $9 for a tent with any number of people. In the campgrounds, pick a site and set up. A warden will come around, probably in the evening, to collect the money.

Coming from Cheticamp there are a few highlights to watch for. The top of **Mackenzie Mountain** affords great views of the interior. The **Grande Anse Valley** contains virgin forest.

In the very small town of **Pleasant Bay** the *Black Whale* restaurant is recommended for very good, fresh seafood at reasonable prices in a casual, pleasant setting. The menu has everything from lobster to fish & chips; you can sit on the patio and watch for the very regularly seen pilot whales just offshore. A lunch of fresh fish costs about $8 depending on the species. There are other places to eat, also specialising in seafood, and a couple of motels which are both considerably more expensive than what's available in Cheticamp.

Towards Ingonish, the short **Lone Sheiling Trail** leads through 300-year-old maple trees to a replica of a Scottish Highland crofter's hut, a reminder of the area's first settlers. Other short trails lead to waterfalls at a couple of points along the road.

From the village of **Cape North** out of the park, the extreme northern portion (also called Cape North) of Cape Breton can be visited. At Bay St Lawrence whale-watching boat tours are run several times daily. Not far from here is where John Cabot is believed to have landed in 1497. A re-enactment is held annually every 24 June on the beach at Sugarloaf Mountain. In Cape North village there is a gas station and food store.

A side trip to **Neils Harbour** is recommended, a very attractive little fishing village. In fact, I'd say it's one of the nicest you're likely to see in Nova Scotia. Down at the wharf, you can buy fish and lobster. Or try something at the inexpensive *Chowder House* by the water at the lighthouse.

At the eastern entrance to the park are **Igonish** and **Igonish Beach**, two small towns with accommodation and basic supplies. There are several campgrounds, both government and private ones, motels and a park information office.

The beach at Ingonish Beach is a wonderful place with a long, wide strip of sand tucked in a bay surrounded with green hills. The water can get pleasantly warm here after a few sunny days and the beach really catches the late afternoon light in a special way.

Places to Stay & Eat
Eight km north of the park entrance near Igonish is *Driftwood Lodge* (☎ 285-2558), run by Mrs Kulig. Rooms in the older building are cheapest and start at $35 for doubles without bath, if you want the view you'll pay more. Off-season rates apply in early June

and from September to October. Breakfast is served, and a German-Polish lunch and dinner are available.

Also in Ingonish, *Stella's Housekeeping Cottages* (☎ 285-2316) are a good deal with the two-bed room at $45 and the three-bed room at $50. There are only three cottages, so calling early is a good idea.

Ingonish Centre also has a few places as does Ingonish Beach (where up on the hillside is the very expensive deluxe government hotel, the *Keltic Lodge*). Overall the prices aren't too bad.

For a place to eat, the coffee shop downstairs at *Doucette's Variety Store* near Ingonish Beach has good soups, sandwiches and pies.

CAPE SMOKEY
From Ingonish south and up to Cape Smokey there is some fine scenery. At the peak on Cape Smokey at a small park with picnic tables there are very good sea and coastal views. Walking trails lead both north and south offering even better viewing points.

The road descends sharply from here (smell those brakes!) leading out of the highlands.

ST ANN'S
The interesting preserver and promoter of Scottish heritage, the Gaelic College of Celtic Arts & Crafts, is at the end of St Ann's Bay. Founded in 1938 and the only one of its kind in North America, the college offers programmes in the Gaelic language, bagpipe playing, Highland dancing, weaving and kilt-making and other things Scottish to students of all ages from across the land. Drop in anytime during summer, chances are you'll hear a student sing a traditional ballad in Gaelic or another play a Highland violin piece; mini-concerts and recitals are performed throughout the day. You can stroll around the grounds, see the museum with its historical notes and tartans or browse the giftshop for books, music tapes or kilts. There is also a cafeteria serving light meals or tea.

During the first week of August each year a Scottish festival, the Gaelic Mod, is held with events daily.

The campus is pretty much the town – there really isn't any thing else here.

BIG BRAS D'OR

After crossing the long bridge over an inlet to Bras d'Or Lake on the way towards Sydney a secondary road branches off and leads to the coast and the village of Big Bras d'Or. Offshore are the **Bird Islands** with large colonies of razorbills, puffins, terns and others. Boat tours run from town from May to September. Nesting time is June and July so these are the prime months for a visit.

NORTH SYDNEY

Small and nondescript, North Sydney is important as the Marine Atlantic terminal for ferries to either Port aux Basques or Argentia, Newfoundland. For details see under those destinations.

There isn't much in town but it makes a convenient place to put up if you're using the ferry. Tourist information is available at the ferry landing or you can also call the Board of Trade (☎ 564-6543).

The main street in town where you'll find the stores and places to eat is Commercial St.

Places to Stay

North of town off the Trans Canada Highway there are a few privately owned campgrounds. The *Arm of Gold Campground* mainly for trailers, is closest to the ferry, just 3.2 km away.

With a view over the water, the *Kawaja Tourist Lodge* (☎ 794-4876) is two km west of the ferry terminal. It's at 88 Queen St, which is called Commercial St in town. This is a nice place, open year-round and reasonably priced at singles from $20 to $24 and doubles $28.

Other than this there are several motels in the vicinity at about twice the above rate. One to try is the *Clansman Motel*, on Peppett St, off exit 2 on Highway 125.

Places to Eat

You'll find a few basic restaurants in town such as *Papa J's* which is not bad for submarine sandwiches and Italian fare. Order spaghetti for $5.50 and the portion will feed half the restaurant. *Rollie's Wharf* restaurant and lounge is on the water near the ferry dock. Nearby at the ferry landing on Commercial St is *Robert's Home-style Bakery* where you can pick up a few things for the ferry trip.

Out of town beside the highway towards Baddeck is the notoriously named *Lick-a-Chick*, a chicken takeout place.

Getting There & Away

Bus There is no real bus station in North Sydney; the station proper is in Sydney. But the bus between Sydney and Halifax can be picked up at the North Star Inn beside the ferry terminal. It's the Acadian line which runs three trips a day. There is also a local bus which runs back and forth between Sydney and North Sydney for $2. It too, can be caught at the ferry dock or at some points along Queen St.

Train The train service in Cape Breton has been cut entirely.

Ferry For detailed information on ferry crossings, see the St John's and Port aux Basques sections in the Newfoundland chapter. Reservations may be required, call Marine Atlantic in North Sydney on ☎ 794-7203.

SYDNEY MINES

Long known simply as the Mines, this small town north-east of North Sydney on the coast was a depressed and dirty mining centre from as early as the 1700s. The mines were operating until recently and working in them was no picnic. Most of the shafts were out under the sea – one ran 6.4 km from shore below the ocean floor. Imagine working here every day? After closing, a portion of the mine functioned as a museum but this too, has now closed and there really isn't much reason to visit. Glace Bay has a mining museum as does Springhill near the New Brunswick border.

SYDNEY

Sydney is the third largest town in the province, the only real city on Cape Breton and the centre of the island's industrial sector. It's a very old town and, as the heart of a coal-mining district has seen its share of grief and hardship. Until quite recently it was a drab rather grim town with a hard-drinking, if warm and friendly, population. The people haven't changed but the appearance of the place has – there is more pride in the past and hope for the future. Though still somewhat at the whim of economic vagaries, it has the largest self-contained steel plant in North America and numerous other industries including machine works, foundries and pulp and paper manufacturing. Heritage buildings have been preserved and there is a variety of hotels and restaurants for visitors.

The main street downtown is Charlotte St, with or close to, many of the stores and things of interest (or necessity) for the traveller. There isn't a lot to do but, with the ferry to the north and Louisbourg to the south, many people do pass by.

There is a tourist office on King's Rd, the motel strip, also known as Highway 4.

Northend

Just north of the city centre on Charlotte St, the Esplanade which runs parallel to the river and the adjoining streets is the old historic part of town with half a dozen buildings from the 1700s and many built during the 19th century. The tree-lined streets make for pleasant walking and, if you're keen on history, a few places can be seen from the inside too. On the Esplanade across from the Government Wharf, you can visit the oldest Roman Catholic Church in Cape Breton: **St Patrick's** dating from 1828.

Cossit House on Charlotte St dating from 1787 is the oldest house in Sydney and is a museum with period furnishings. Nearby is **St George's** an Anglican church and the oldest of all the churches on Cape Breton. There are three more heritage churches in

Whitney Pier, an old residential part of town near the steel plant where early immigrants from Poland, the Ukraine and the West Indies found homes and work then built their houses of worship.

At the Lyceum, the former cultural centre, 225 George St, is the **Centre for Heritage & Science**, a museum on the human and natural history of this part of the province. There is also an art gallery. The centre is open daily through the summer and with reduced hours the rest of the year.

Places to Stay

Right in town is *Paul's Hotel* (☎ 562-5747) at 10 Pitt St with 24 rooms, some with shared facilities and the more expensive ones with private bath. Rates range from $20 to $33. Also central is *Cliefdon House* (☎ 564-6311) at 106 Bentinck St which is near the park at the southern edge of the downtown area. Singles/doubles are $28/33.

Another small homey place is *Macleod's Lodge & Cottage* (☎ 564-8304) at 620 George St within walking distance of everything downtown. Also quite central at 169 Park St is the *Park Place* (☎ 562-3518) a turn-of-the-century B&B with low rates at singles/doubles $25/30.

The larger, more modern choices are mostly along King's Rd which runs south of the centre along the Sydney River towards Highway 125. Here you'll find numerous motels, most with restaurants attached.

Places to Eat

Jasper's with several locations around town, including a central one on the corner of George and Dorchester Sts, is an inexpensive family restaurant good for any meal of the day. Even at dinner there is nothing over $13 on the large menu.

Joe's Warehouse at 424 Charlotte St in the centre has a varied menu featuring steak or beef and a large salad bar. There's also an outdoor patio with views of the water.

Getting There & Away

Bus The new Acadian bus line's station (☎ 564-5533) is away from the centre a bit (walkable if necessary) across the street from the big Sydney Shopping Centre Mall on Terminal Drive. There are five buses a day to Halifax: the first at 8 am, the last at 6 pm. The charge is $35.50. One bus in the morning is direct, three others go to the ferry terminal in North Sydney and make many other stops along the way.

For Charlottetown, Prince Edward Island, the fare is $40 and the bus leaves at 8 am.

Train There is no longer any train service due to government cutbacks.

GLACE BAY

As part of the Sydney area's industrial region, the difficulties of Cape Bretoners have been and are reflected here. The district has a long, bitter history of hard work – when there is any – with low pay and poor conditions and, regularly, one of the highest unemployment rates in the country; there's a high degree of work-related illness. The hardships, however, have resulted in a people able to smile at misfortune and be generally friendly and hospitable to strangers.

Glace Bay is one of the places where the coal-mining tradition lives on and its livelihood really depends on the luck of the miners.

The **Miners' Museum**, less than two km east from the town centre on Birkley St, provides a look at the history of local coal mining with equipment displays and a re-created village depicting a miner's life at the beginning of the century. The highlight, though, is a 20-minute underground tour led by a retired miner. It's $5 for the complete tour, less if you forgo (but don't) the mine visit. There is a restaurant at the site.

A national historic site marks the place where, in 1902, Italian Gugliemo Marconi sent the first wireless message across the Atlantic. It was received in Cornwall, England. There is a model of the original transmitting station and other information on the developments in communications that followed.

MARCONI TRAIL

The coastal road south of Glace Bay leads past small fishing villages and rocky beaches to the town of Louisbourg and its top-rate historic site. The main, more direct route, running south of Sydney has half a dozen campgrounds along it.

LOUISBOURG

At the edge of the ocean with an excellent harbour sits Louisbourg, the largest of the region's fishing towns, now famous for its adjacent historic fort. There is no transportation down this way but hitching is pretty easy.

There's still a fair-sized fishing fleet and the processing plant is an important employer. Aside from the park there are a couple of other things to see in the old town.

The **Sydney & Louisbourg Railway Museum** and the tourist office are at the entrance to the town. The museum has displays pertaining to the railway which ran up to Sydney from 1895 until as late as 1968, shuffling fish one way and coal the other. Entry is free.

In an historic building on Main St is the **Atlantic Statiquarium Marine Museum** with exhibits on the fishery, artefacts recovered from wrecks, and marine life including some live specimens. There is a small admission fee. Both museums are open daily through the summer.

The local heritage society has an exhibit in the impressive **Victorian rectory** beside the Anglican church.

Along the waterfront examples, of crafts can be seen and bought. At the **House of Dolls** is a collection of nearly 2000 miniature people. Lastly, south of town are the ruins of Canada's oldest lighthouse and an interpretive display.

Places to Stay & Eat

For those wishing to do more than a day trip, Louisbourg with four B&Bs is good for inexpensive accommodation.

On Main St is *Ashley Manor* (☎ 733-3268) with three rooms at just $25/35 a single/double or triple. At 17 Strathcona St is the *Manse* (☎ 733-3155) with singles at the same price but doubles costing only $30 with breakfast included. Back on Main St a fifth option is the large *Louisbourg Motel*.

There are a couple of places with varied, reasonably priced menus, which include numerous things from the sea. Beside the tourist office is *Anchor's Aweigh* – good for breakfast as well as the other meals. The chowders are pretty good. A stroll down Main St will turn up the alternatives. The *Grubstake* is the place for a good seafood dinner but it is not in the low-budget category.

LOUISBOURG HISTORIC NATIONAL PARK

This excellent, historic fort site about 50 km south of Sydney on the south-east tip of Cape Breton Island, is worth the out-of-the-way trek. The park is open daily in summer and admission is $5.

After the Treaty of Utrecht in 1713, the French lost their bases in Newfoundland. This left them Prince Edward Island, Saint Pierre and Miquelon islands, and Cape Breton Island which became the centre for exporting cod to France. It was also chosen as the spot to build a new military base. Louisbourg, a massive walled fort and village complex, was worked on continually from 1719 to about 1745. It looked daunting but was poorly designed, and the British took it in 46 days during 1745 when it was barely finished. It was returned to the French under the terms of another treaty, only to fall with the British siege of 1758. In 1760, after Wolfe (who had led the Louisbourg onslaught) took Quebec City, the walls of Louisbourg were all destroyed. It was abandoned and having no commercial use, began to decay.

In 1961, with the closing of many Cape Breton coal mines, the federal government formed a make-work project: the largest historical reconstruction in Canada. Today the site depicts what French life was like here in the 1700s in remarkable detail. All the workers, in period dress, have taken on the lives of typical fort inhabitants. Ask them

anything – what the winters were like, what they ate, what that tool is for, how this was made, who they had an affair with – and they'll tell you. There are many interesting buildings with appropriate contents. The restaurant serves food typical of the time. Definitely go to the bakery and buy a one-kg loaf of soldiers' bread. It's delicious; one piece with cheese makes a full meal. (But take a plastic bag – they won't give you one as they didn't have plastic in 1750!)

You'll need a lot of time to see the park properly: plan on spending about half a day at the site. The best times to visit are in the morning – when there's more going on and fewer tourists – and during June or September. It's a popular site so early in the day or outside the peak months of July and August are best because the workers are not as harried and have more time to talk. Regardless of this, a visit is most interesting. Take in the movie in the interpretive centre first.

The weather here is very changeable and usually bad. Take a sweater and raincoat even if it's sunny when you start out and be prepared for lots of walking.

AROUND BRAS D'OR LAKE
Baddeck

An old resort town in a pastoral setting, Baddeck is on the north shore of the lake, halfway between Sydney and the Canso Causeway.

It's small but is a bit of a visitors' centre and seems to receive everybody travelling in Cape Breton for at least a couple of hours. This is making it a little too touristy but it remains attractive; you can't detract from the interesting and extensive **Graham Bell Museum**.

Chebucto St, the main thoroughfare with more or less everything on it makes for a pleasant walk. On Water St, along the waterfront, the Government Wharf is lined with pleasure craft, tour sailing boats and, occasionally, the *Bluenose* which will take passengers out for a spin around Bras d'Or Lake. Worse ways of spending a sunny afternoon could be found. In midsummer there is a free shuttle-boat service across the bay to

Kidston Island just offshore where there is good swimming.

Alexander Graham Bell Museum

Alexander Graham Bell, the inventor of the telephone, had a summer place in Baddeck. This large museum is dedicated to him and his work. It's a national historic park that covers all aspects of this incredible man's inventions and innovations: written explanations, models, photographs and objects detail his varied works. On display are medical and electrical devices, telegraphs, telephones, kites and seaplanes. You'll need a few hours if you want to see it all. Admission is free, it's open daily until 9 pm in summer.

The museum is set on a hillside amidst gardens and picnic tables and there is a good view of the bay and part of the saltwater Bras d'Or Lake from the roof.

Places to Stay

There are a few B&Bs in and around town and half a dozen or so rather costly motels.

The *Duffus House Inn* (☎ 295-2172) on

Alexander Graham Bell

Water St has nine rooms furnished with antiques starting at $35 a double with shared bath. Nearby is the *Point B&B* (☎ 295-3368) with similar rates which include a full breakfast – no smoking permitted. Lowest priced is the *Restawhyle Tourist Home* (☎ 295-3368) on Shore Rd with singles from $20. Call for directions and information.

For a motel, the *Telegraph House* right in the centre of town is very attractive in grey with white shutters but a double is in the $90 range. Others are closer to a measly $75.

Places to Eat

Baddeck has a wide selection of good quality eating places which tend to be a bit pricey. The best and one that offers some cheaper possibilities while maintaining high standards is the *Highwheeler Café/Deli/Bakery* with a mouth-watering selection of things to eat there or to take out for picnics. It has the simple basics or smoked salmon and brie to go with the bagels.

The *Old Chowder & Dessert Bar* off the main street, one block back and parallel to Chebucto St has good soups at good prices. Moving up-market, the *Bell Buoy* by the wharf is good for seafood but is not cheap. Lobster suppers, with a one pounder and everything else you can eat from the buffet, are available in the centre of town in the old Legion Hall. At $25, they don't compare with the value of the real Prince Edward Island lobster suppers but the food is good. They're open daily from June to October.

A surprise is the Indian restaurant the *Taj* in the grounds of the Bell Museum with dishes from $6 to $8.

Don't bother with the fish & chips from the dock takeout place, it's all appearance and potential: they're greasy and have been frozen.

Iona

This is a small village south of Baddeck, on the south side of the peninsula by Barra Strait in Bras d'Or Lake (on Highway 223). Iona is a bit out of the way, but may appeal for that reason. The **Highland Village Museum** shows examples of Scottish homes, the first pioneer houses in the new land, and later ones in which new skills and materials were employed. A Highland festival is held on the first Saturday in August.

In this area as well as in other rural parts of Victoria County, you may still hear Gaelic spoken.

A short ferry ride connects with roads for the south side of Bras d'Or Lake.

SOUTH OF BRAS D'OR LAKE

This is a little-visited, sparsely inhabited area of small villages, lakes and hills. It's a farming and forestry region where many of the roads have not been paved.

Eskasoni

Not far from the ferry on the edge of East Bay, Eskasoni is the largest Micmac Indian reserve in the province. The Micmacs were the largest Native Indian group in the Atlantic area when the Europeans arrived and they are still found in all of the four eastern provinces. Their language is still spoken by some people in Nova Scotia and their basketry is available at roadside shops on some reserves, for example, the one near Whycocomagh on the busy Trans Canada Highway.

Big Pond

On the south shore of East Bay, Big Pond has *Rita's Tea Room* run by the hometown Cape Breton singer Rita MacNeil and helpers. If she is not away touring or recording you'll likely get a chat while you're sipping. Every July, the Big Pond Concert, a sizeable annual Cape Breton music event is held.

Soldiers Cove

Further east along Route 4, at Soldiers Cove and Chapel Island, is another Micmac reserve, in an area they have long occupied. Each year on the last weekend of July a major cultural festival takes place.

The French Corner

The extreme south-west corner of Cape Breton, like the Cheticamp area, is largely French. The region all around Île Madame was settled by Acadians who had first tried to make Martinique in the West Indies home after the Expulsion but later returned to Nova Scotia. Arichat, on the ocean, is the largest town and has a restaurant and a traditional style wooden Acadian inn called L'Auberge Acadienne whose dining room offers some Acadian dishes.

Just down the road Petit-de-Grat holds an annual Acadian festival in August with music, food, etc. This small town is the oldest on Île Madame and was a busy trading port during Prohibition. Now it is a fishing centre.

There is a campground near Arichat and several parks with shoreline to explore. From Little Anse a trail leads to a lighthouse.

Port Hawkesbury

Though a fairly large town there is little here for the visitor; it's essentially a modern shopping and industrial centre for the district.

Sable Island

Lying south of Cape Breton about 150 km from the mainland is the 'graveyard of the Atlantic'. Countless ships from the 1500s to the present have gone down around the island with its rough seas and hidden sandbars. The island, 32 km long by 1½ km wide, is little more than a sandbar itself with no trees, or even shrubs. There are about a dozen inhabitants, a small herd of tough, wild ponies and lots of cranberries. The people maintain the two lighthouses, a meteorological station and a few other installations. The ponies are believed to be descendants from some which survived a shipwreck in the 1500s.

Prince Edward Island

Entered Confederation: 1 July 1873
Area: 5657 sq km
Population: 123,000 (the smallest province)

The Micmac Indians say Glooscap, a god, painted all the beautiful places on earth. Then he dipped the brush in all the colours and created this, Abegweit, his favourite island.

Visitors may find it a favourite as well. If you're suffering big city burn-out or any kind of modern malaise and want to put a few years back on your life, this is the place to spend some time. If you can't unwind here, I'm sorry, you're a terminal case.

Now known as the Island, or PEI (pronounced as the three letters separately), Prince Edward Island is a very pastoral, peaceful, wonderfully Irish-green expanse of quiet beauty. Mainlanders are seen all over the island on the roadsides trying to capture the landscape on film: a few black and white cows there, some purple lupins, perhaps a wave of sea in the distance. The pace of life here is very slow. Laws against billboards further add to the old-country flavour of the island.

This is not an exciting place; there is not a lot to do, particularly after dark when the province basically closes and, if you get a week of rain, you'll be more than a little restless. But for a really lazy holiday take the chance. The island is popular with cyclists, families and anybody else looking for an inexpensive change of scenery – prices here are among the lowest in the country.

Prince Edward Island is the smallest and, surprisingly, the most densely populated province. You'd never guess this though, as it's very rural and the towns aren't big at all. Countless little-used roads, do however crisscross every segment of land. PEI is mainly a farming community with the main crop, potatoes, being sold all over the country. The rich, distinctively red soil is the secret the locals say. Fishing, of course, is also important, particularly for lobsters,

oysters and herring. The tasty, reasonably priced lobster suppers held throughout the province, have become synonymous with the island.

There is little manufacturing, as transportation costs are prohibitive. Industry hasn't been helped either by the lack of energy sources.

Once again there has been recent political talk of connecting the province to the mainland via some sort of causeway or bridge, but also once again the notion appears to be going nowhere – thankfully, to my mind.

The quiet, gently rolling hills edged with good beaches have made tourism a reliable moneymaker. Because of warm ocean currents the province has a milder climate than most of Canada and the sea gets warm enough for swimming.

Conveniently, July and August are the driest months of a fairly damp year. As in all of the Atlantic or Maritime Provinces the visiting season is short. This is perhaps noticed here more than anywhere with many attractions, guesthouses and even bus services shutting up tight.

One last note – the quality of drinking water is dubious due to the effects of overuse of fertilisers and pesticides on the groundwater. Many visitors and residents alike prefer to buy bottled water which is widely available.

Charlottetown

Charlottetown is an old, quiet country town that also happens to be the historic provincial capital. Its slow-paced and tree-lined colonial and Victorian streets make it the perfect

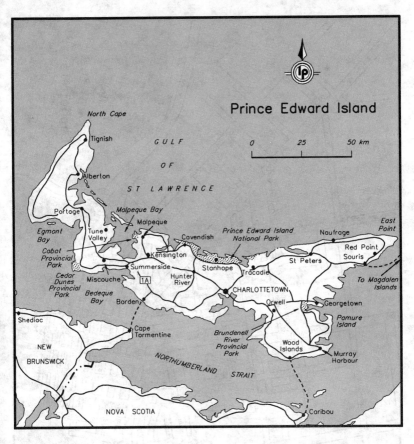

urban centre for this gentle and bucolic island.

The population is 45,000 in this, Canada's smallest capital, with a downtown area so compact that everything is within walking distance.

When the first Europeans arrived in the early 1700s, they found the area had already been settled by the Micmac Indians. But they established Charlottetown as a district capital of their own in 1763. It was named after Charlotte, Queen of Great Britain & Ireland (1744-1818).

In 1864 discussions to unite Canada were first held here. An agreement was finally reached in 1867, when the Dominion of Canada was born. Though times are much less heady these days, many of the town's people are employed by the various levels of government. Indeed, one out of four people across the island works directly for the government.

Today, the city is the focal point of the large tourist trade as well as being the business and shopping centre for the province. In July and August the streets are busy with visitors but out of season things are rather quiet.

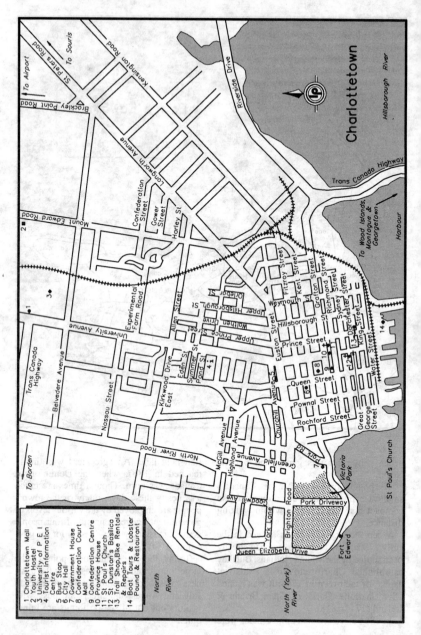

Charlottetown

KEY:
1 Charlottetown Mall
2 Youth Hostel
3 University of P E I
4 Tourist Information Centre
5 Bus Stop
6 City Hall
7 Government House
8 Confederation Court Mall
9 Confederation Centre
10 Province House
11 St Paul's Church
12 St Dunstan's Basilica
13 Trail Shop, Bike Rentals & Repairs
14 Boat Tours & Lobster Pound & Restaurant

Orientation

Highway 1 from Borden (never mind the approach into town – it's the only ugly stretch of road on the island) becomes University Ave, the city's main street. On the corner of University Ave and Grafton St is the large, modern art centre complex. A few blocks south is the city harbour.

On Water St, at the harbour, are the new law courts and the yacht club.

Another main street is Queen St, parallel and one street to the west of University Ave. From the harbour, up a few blocks on and around Queen St, is old Charlottetown. A number of buildings have been renovated and are now often used as government offices, restaurants and shops. Many of the buildings have plaques giving a bit of the history and the date; some are over 100 years old. The farmers' market is held in this area on Saturday mornings.

West of town is the large Victoria Park, with a road running along its edge and the bay.

The streets just out of town are pleasant to stroll along, and look almost as though they belong in a different era. Lots of trees and flowers line the front of the large old, well-kept wooden houses.

Information

The tourist office (☎ 368-4444) for Charlottetown and the main office for the whole island is on the corner of University Ave and Summer St. Coming into town from Borden, you'll find it on the right in a shopping centre, about two km from the downtown area. It's open all year and conveniently until midnight in summer, Sunday included.

Confederation Centre of the Arts

This is the large modern structure at the foot of University Ave. Its architectural style, at odds with the rest of town, has made it controversial since construction began in 1960. Inside you'll find a museum, an art gallery, a library and a theatre. The art gallery and museum charge $1 admission fees in July and August but are free for the rest of the year

and are always free on Sunday. Free tours of the centre are given all year.

Province House

Next door to the previously mentioned arts centre this neoclassical three-storey sandstone building is both a national historic site and the base of the current Provincial Legislature. The 2nd floor Confederation Room is known as the 'Birthplace of Canada' for it was here in 1864 that the 23 representatives of the New World British colonies began working out the details for forming the Dominion of Canada.

This room and a couple of others have been restored to what they looked like in 1864. Inside or perhaps out at the entrance you may also see costumed workers, each representing one of the original founders.

The current Legislative Chamber is also on this floor and the summer breeze wafting in through wide open windows to this small, comfortable room lends an intimate informal atmosphere quite unlike that of the legislatures in Canada's larger provinces. Various rooms can also be seen on the 1st floor. Province House is open daily and is free.

St Dunstan's Basilica

South of Province House, on the corner of Great George and Richmond Sts, is the large basilica built in 1898. The town's Catholic church is surprisingly ornate inside. It's painted in an unusual style, with a lot of green trim which blends well with the green and blue tints in the marble.

St Paul's Church

On Church St east of Province House, this red sandstone building dating from 1747, is the oldest Protestant church on the island.

Beaconsfield House

This beautiful yellow Victorian mansion at 2 Kent St, was built in 1877. It is now the headquarters of the PEI Heritage Foundation. The rooms on the 1st floor are used for local history exhibits. There is also a bookstore specialising in books about PEI. The house is open during the week and is free.

Government House

Across Kent St is Victoria Park and Government House, another beautiful old mansion. This one has been used as the official residence of the province's lieutenant-governor since 1835. No visitors are allowed here, but you can walk around the grounds.

UPEI Planetarium

At the university, the Planetarium (☎ 892-4121, ext 383) shows a variety of interesting, educational astronomy programmes from 1 June to Labour Day. Admission is $3.50, students $2.50

Lord Selkirk Pioneer Settlement

Just over the bridge from the capital is this collection of hand-hewn log buildings dating from 1803, when Selkirk brought a small group of Scottish people to the island. The buildings contain artefacts. Admission is $2.50.

Sailing Charters

A 12-metre yacht moored at the foot of Pownal St in the yacht club runs charter tours for a maximum of 10 people. You may find others down around the fish market.

Organised Tours

Abegweit Sightseeing Tours (☎ 894-9966) at 157 Nassau St, Charlottetown, offers double-decker bus trips around the island. They have three trips: to the north shore, the south shore and Charlottetown itself.

Each takes in some of the commercial attractions of the area. The north shore trip takes about six hours and costs $20 – all inclusive. The city tour takes just an hour and costs $4.25. There's a south shore trip with a stop at Fort Amherst National Historic Park.

If you just want to go to the beach for the day, you can take the North Shore Tour bus. They'll pick you up on the way back. The cost is $5 one way, $7.50 return.

Festivals

The Charlottetown Festival is held each year from mid-June to mid-September. This is a theatrical event with drama and musicals; each year, *Anne of Green Gables* is performed. It's called 'Canada's favourite musical' and is a family show. Tickets to any of the plays are available at the Arts Centre and range from $8 to $15 for most plays, but $15 to $25 for 'Anne'.

Recently, some less conservative contemporary plays have been added to the programme, including one about Elvis Presley a couple of years ago which stirred up some controversy due to its colourful language. There are also summer theatre and dance programmes both in town and around the province.

A new tradition seems to be developing: the annual Blue Grass Music Festival held in July. It's a two-day, camping event held at a park or campground. Tickets are not costly.

All across the province watch out for the local ceilidhs: mini-festivals at which there is always some music (usually of the traditional Celtic-based variety) and dancing. There is almost one a week.

Places to Stay

Camping The island is covered with campgrounds – private, provincial and one national. Provincial parks are $10 or so for an unserviced site depending on facilities. Privately owned places charge more but accept reservations. Government parks which operate on a first-come, first-served basis, are usually better and often full. The tourist office can give you vacancy reports. Near Charlottetown there's the *Southport Trailer Park*, at 20 Stratford Rd overlooking the Hillsborough River. The nightly rate is $12, less if you're tenting or staying a week or longer. This is the only one near town.

Hostels The *Canadian Youth Hostel* (☎ 894-9696) at 153 Mount Edward Rd is good, close to town and friendly. There's room for about 65 people in this barn-like building very close to the university. There's a kitchen available and the rates are $9, or $12 for nonmembers. It's about three km from the downtown area. To get there, follow University Ave west from town towards Borden. Turn right at Belvedere Ave. The hostel is near Mt St Mary's Convent. The hostel is open from the beginning of June to the beginning of September. Some years there is maybe an additional hostel somewhere around the island, they seem to come and go – mostly go.

The *university* itself has rooms from mid-May to the end of August. Reservations are a good idea. Singles or doubles cost $40.

Charlottetown has a YM-YWCA and a Salvation Army but neither of them rent rooms.

Tourist Homes Across the province there are very few hotels but fortunately, the city, like the entire island, has an abundance of guesthouses. The quality is high and the prices excellent. PEI guesthouses and tourist homes offer some of the best accommodation deals in Canada. A double room can cost as little as $18, averages about $25 or $30 and rarely goes above $40 and sometimes that includes breakfast. Much accommodation is in beautiful old east-coast-style wooden homes. The tourist office has a complete list of these places and will make reservations for you. In town, there are quite a few. Here are several to try.

Gateway House (☎ 894-9761), at 206 Fitzroy St, has three rooms, two with double beds. It's open from mid-May to mid-September and singles or doubles cost $18.

Very central at 234 Sydney St is the *Aloah Tourist Home* (☎ 892-9944) in a large old house with a variety of room sizes and features. A simple double costs $30 and there is a kitchen visitors can use.

Also right downtown is the *Blanchard* (☎ 894-9756) at 163 Dorchester St. Here singles/doubles cost just $20/30.

In behind the tourist office at 18 Pond St is the spotless and friendly *Cairn's Tourist Home* (☎ 892-1547) in a modern house on a residential street. The rate is $24 for a double and an extra $5 per person.

The *Orlebar Tourist Home* (☎ 892-0044)

is at 64 Orlebar St, again close to the centre. Orlebar St is five blocks east of University Ave and runs parallel to it. This tourist home is open during summer only and costs $25 for two people.

Some of the least expensive choices are a little beyond the one above still further east, close to the race track. You might check along Edward St or York Lane. Houses here are smaller and older than many but it's still not a long walk to the city centre.

At the opposite end of the scale, the *Dundee Arms Inn* (☎ 892-2496), at 200 Pownal St, is an impressive, restored turn-of-the-century mansion complete with antiques, dining room and pub. A double here will cost $95 with a continental breakfast included.

Motels There are motels along Highway 1 west of Charlottetown towards Borden. Also on this commercial strip are drive-in movies, restaurants and gas stations. Motels here usually cost at least $50 a double. The ones further from town tend to be more modest in appearance, amenities and price. Those in town provide more comforts and the price goes up accordingly.

Close to town on the south side is the *Garden Province Motel* (☎ 892-3411). It's small and well off the highway but, like many of the motels, expensive. The rate is singles or doubles $58.

Three km from town on the Trans Canada Highway is the *Queen's Arms Motel* (☎ 368-1110), with a heated pool. Rooms cost about $55 and up for two people. Also housekeeping units are available.

Further out, near the Highway 2 junction, is the brown *Zenith Motel* (☎ 892-2981). Doubles are $50 and rooms for up to four people $60. There is a laundrette.

Places to Eat

For a small city there are a surprising number of quality restaurants but mostly they fall into the higher price bracket. Still, with the ocean minutes away, a fresh seafood dinner is not too outrageous and the low prices elsewhere around the island make up for costs here.

Cedar's Eatery, open every day and right in the middle of town on University Ave, is a fine little place. At the chunky wooden tables the speciality is Lebanese food, ranging from felafels to more expensive kebabs. But there is also standard Canadian fare: soups, salads, sandwiches, steaks and Old Abbey, a local beer. Cedar's stays open late, one of the few places which does.

For a simple meal or snack, the cheap and unpretentious *Lunch Bar* at 34 University Ave fills the bill. It's been here forever. Also small and cheap but with a certain charm is *Linda's Old Town Coffee Shop* at 32 Queen St.

The *Old Dublin Pub* is at 131 Sydney St, with pub meals for around $6 and live entertainment at night.

There are a couple of inexpensive Chinese places around town; my choice would be the *King's Palace*, on Queen St near Grafton St, with its good-value lunches.

In Confederation Court Mall on the corner of Kent and Queen Sts, the 2nd floor has a collection of cheap fast-food outlets offering pizza, chicken, burgers, etc.

Pat's Rose & Grey Room, on Richmond St behind the Confederation Arts Building with the great front window, is highly regarded and they have a nice bar section as well. The tasty lunch specials change daily. At night features include pastas and steaks but note, this is decidedly not for those on a low budget.

Also in this higher price bracket and serving good food is the *Queen St Café* with choice of pasta, lamb or seafood. It offers main courses for around $16. Again in the splurge category, the dining room of the *Dundee Arms Inn*, at 200 Pownal St, offers fine eating in a traditional setting with top-notch service.

Among the seafood spots in town are *Samuel's* in the Inn on the Hill, and the *Claddagh* in the old historic area at 129 Sydney St. Down at Charlottetown's waterfront on the Prince St wharf is *Mackinnon's*

where you can buy fresh mussels, clams, and oysters, as well as live or cooked lobster.

Out at the *university*, you can get an inexpensive feed in the *cafeteria* on the ground floor of the Steele's Building. It's open Monday to Friday from 7.30 am to 6 pm, Saturday and Sunday from 10 am to 6 pm. Full meals are served. It's near the youth hostel across the field off University Ave.

Back in town, along Sydney St or around the big Arts Building you'll always be able to find a café for a cappuccino.

Cows on Queen St near Grafton St is very small but they turn out good homemade ice cream.

Entertainment

Charlottetown may be the capital city, but it's really a country town and therefore doesn't have much action at night.

The *Avenue Bar*, on Kent St off University Ave, is the most popular spot and serves up loud rock music.

Further down Kent St is the *Tradewinds*, a much spiffier dancing spot which is open until 1 am.

A third spot is *Silverados*, at 36 Grafton St, for country music and a huge sunken dance floor for kicking up your heels.

Getting There & Away

Air Charlottetown has a small airport, north of the city. Air Canada and Canadian Airlines connect PEI with the major Canadian cities and some New England US points like Boston. Air Canada flies one way to Toronto for $373 and Canadian Airlines flies to St John's, Newfoundland, for $301; to Montreal for $284 and Halifax, $144.

Bus There are once-daily buses to and from PEI using each of the two ferries. One connects with Pictou, New Glasgow, or Antigonish, Nova Scotia, and from there connections can be made for points around Nova Scotia although transferring in Amherst may be necessary. The other uses the Borden ferry and connects with Moncton, New Brunswick. Tickets include the price of the ferry. For Moncton, a ticket is $23.75.

The station, in the VIA Rail building, is on the corner of Queen and Euston Sts. This is also the home of Island Transit, the provincial bus service.

Train There is no passenger train service to, from or on the island, but you can still buy a train ticket to Charlottetown. The VIA Rail system will get you to Amherst, Nova Scotia. From here you use the ferry and bus, all included in the same ticket.

Ferry Most people get to PEI by ferry, either from New Brunswick or Nova Scotia. There are two ferries linking the island with the mainland. They take cars, buses, bicycles and pedestrians.

One ferry links Cape Tormentine, New Brunswick, with Borden in south-west Prince Edward Island. This 14-km trip, takes 45 minutes and is run by Marine Atlantic, a government ferry system. The fare is $2.75 per person, $7.25 per car and $1.10 per bicycle. There are nearly 20 crossings a day between June and September, slightly fewer the rest of the year.

In peak season, arrive before 10 am or after 6 pm to help avoid long delays. Still, this is one of Canada's busiest ferry routes and having to wait for two or even three ferries is not so uncommon. Reservations are not taken for this route but calling in will give you an idea of the situation. In Borden, call ☎ (902) 855-2030. In Cape Tormentine call ☎ (506) 538-7654. There's also a toll-free long-distance number (☎ 800-565-9470) that can be used anywhere in New Brunswick, Nova Scotia or Prince Edward Island. Sometimes there are mini-concerts staged by the waiting queues which help the time to pass. The ferry has a cafeteria.

Charlottetown is about 60 km from Borden and the drive takes about 40 minutes.

The other route, run by Northumberland Ferries, joins Wood Islands in the eastern section of PEI province to Caribou, Nova Scotia. This 22-km trip takes 1½ hours. Fares are $3.50 per person, $11.25 per car, and $1.75 per bicycle. In summer there are 20 runs in each direction daily. This route too, is very busy: during peak season you may have a one or two-ferry wait. There's a cafeteria on board. The head office is in Charlottetown at 54 Queen St, or for telephone reservations call ☎ 800-565-0201 toll free.

Car & Motorbike A car, for better or worse, is the best and sometimes only means of seeing much of the island. There are several outlets in the capital.

Avis Rent-A-Car is on University Ave. Their cars cost from $34 to $40 per day depending on the size, with unlimited km. Without a credit card, you'll have to pay in advance and put a deposit on top of that.

Getting Around
To/From the Airport A bus leaves the airport for the downtown area after each flight arrival, and also to meet departures. The airport limo is $6. Otherwise take a taxi, it's only a few km to the airport so a cab isn't costly.

See also Bus, Bicycle and Hitching in the following Around the Island section.

AROUND CHARLOTTETOWN
Amherst National Historic Park
There is one point of interest south out of town which needs mentioning and that is the site of the old French capital and more recently Fort Amherst, built by the British in 1758 after they had taken over the island. There isn't really anything left to see other than foundations but in the interpretive centre there are exhibits and an audiovisual show. And there are views of the city and three lighthouses and a beach within the park area. While not far at all by boat south from the city across the Charlottetown Harbour, it ends up being a long and circuitous route by road. Admission to the park is free.

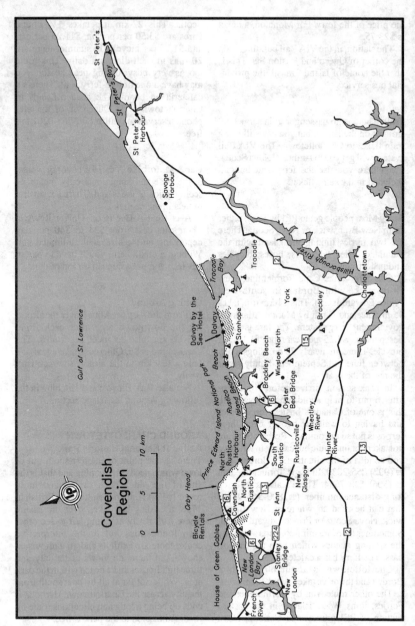

Around the Island

The island is small and easy to get around. In one day it's possible to drive from Charlottetown up to the beaches for a swim, along the north coast all the way up to North Cape, then back along the western shoreline, over to Summerside and down to Borden to catch the evening ferry. And you're not even rushing!

There are about 12 tourist offices around the island, including one at each of the ferry terminals. Any one of them can arrange accommodation anywhere on the island within an hour.

Prince Edward Island offers a wide variety of attractions: oddities, local museums, historical sites and many child-oriented activities. You can get a list at the information offices or just check these things out as you come across them.

Three equal-sized counties make up the island: Prince, in the west, Queen's, in the middle and King's to the east. Each county has a scenic road network mapped out by the tourist bureau. Though far from the only routes, these ones do take in the better known attractions, and the historical and geographical points of note.

Accommodation & Food

Tourist homes are found in towns and on farms all over the province and are generally very reasonably priced. Get details at the tourist offices.

Around the north coast by the national park are scores of cabins and cottages for rent with varying features and prices but many are rented by the week.

There are 15 provincial parks with campgrounds and these charge $8 for unserviced sites, $10 to $11 for trailers. There are plenty of privately owned campgrounds too.

These often offer more commercial extras. Prices are up to $11 unserviced (but usually less), and from $7 to $14 for hook-ups.

There are nearly 40 outlets around the island for buying fresh seafood – good if you're

Lobster

Unfortunately for this mottled green or bluish or blackish prehistoric wonder somebody realised it tasted bloody good. This has meant that we've learned a lot about it. But the facts on this 100-million-year-old crustacean read like a joke book. It tastes with its feet, listens with its legs (of which there are 10), and has teeth in its stomach (which is found just behind the head). The kidney is in the head, the brain in the neck and the bones (shell) are on the outside.

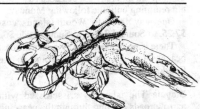

Lobster is widely associated with the east coast of Canada but perhaps Prince Edward Island, with its famous lobster suppers, is most closely linked with this symbol of gourmet dining. It's now hard to believe but there wasn't much interest in the delicate meat until a good way into this century. In fact, they used to use lobster as fertiliser for the island's farms!

There are two fishing seasons, one in the spring ending in late June and one in the winter. Traps of wood, or now sometimes of metal mesh, baited with herring bits are dropped overboard to rest on the bottom and are checked soon after. The ingenious cage design allows the lobster's claws to narrow on the way in, but once inside they spread apart again and there is no way crawling back out is possible. The older wooden traps are available for purchase around the island at about $5 each and will one day be museum pieces. Huge holding tanks allow fresh, live lobster to be offered pretty well all year round.

The standard restaurant lobster in Canada weighs a pound or a little less than half a kg. Two and three pounders are often available but bigger ones are not often seen. Along the Quebec coast of the St Lawrence around Rivière-du-Loup I've seen five and six pounders (2.5 kg) for sale but tell me who's gonna pick one of those suckers up and put it in a pot of hot water? ∎

camping and can cook your own food. Some guesthouses offer cooking facilities or use of barbecues.

Also look for the famous lobster suppers held in church basements or community halls or restaurants – these are usually buffet style and good value. Perhaps not as much fun, the restaurants offering lobster suppers at least do so on a regular basis whereas the others are sometimes hit and miss.

Getting Around

Bus Island Transit in the VIA bus station (☎ 892-6167), 308 Queen St, runs the limited bus service around the province. There are two summer routes and one year-round run.

In summer, Route 1 goes between Charlottetown, Wood Islands and New Glasgow, Nova Scotia. Route 2 runs between Charlottetown, Souris and the ferry terminal for the Magdalen Islands. Each run has many daily trips.

The year-round run goes from Charlottetown to Tignish and back, and stops everywhere along the way. There are no buses on national holidays, Wednesday or Sunday. On Saturday the bus goes east only, not returning until the following Monday.

One-way fares to Wood Islands cost $7.25, to Souris $8, and to Summerside $6.

There is no real bus line to the north coast beaches but see Organised Tours in the Charlottetown section on how to get there.

Bicycle The island is crisscrossed with narrow roads running through the peaceful, unhurried countryside. The gently rolling landscape offers no major hardship for cyclists. It's here you see the island at its most natural with few or no tourists.

At the Bike Shop in Charlottetown they rent bikes and have touring supplies. Rentals are also available in Stanhope at the Stanhope Beach Lodge.

Rent-A-Bike is at the junction of routes 6 and 13, at Cavendish village, near the beach and has hourly and daily rates. It's open every day in summer. There's some good riding in the area, like along the Gulf Shore Parkway.

Hitching Thumbing around the island is common, accepted and is often done by residents. The island is almost free of violence; you can hitch without expecting trouble.

NORTH OF CHARLOTTETOWN

The area north of the capital in Queen's County is where all the action is on Prince Edward Island (refer to the Cavendish Region map). The national park is here with its camping and beaches; most of the island's main attractions are in this area; and to feed and house the vacationers, many of the province's lodging and dining establishments are found not far from the north coast. After York, my description covers areas from east to west *outside* the park and then, again in the same direction, areas within the park boundaries.

York

Not far out of Charlottetown in York the *Potato Blossom Tea Room* makes a pleasant afternoon stop for a sip and snack. It's at the **Jewell's Country Gardens** which has a small pioneer village and glass museum.

Tracadie

Little more than a crossroads at the south-eastern edge of the national park and not far from the entrance to it, this is a 'must stop' for *Beulah's Bake Shop*, a tiny shed beside the house and kitchen where all the cooking is done. The strawberry and raspberry pies are unbelievable (I confess to having eaten a whole raspberry one at a sitting) and are cheap, to boot. There are other things too, including bread and a variety of buns. Campers at Stanhope, stock up here.

Stanhope

There is really nothing in this town but near the park entrance are a couple of restaurants. There is one basic place and another, more up-market one, in the old-time *Stanhope by the Sea* hotel dating from 1817 and refurbished in 1988. You can also get a bite at the golf course or at *Dick's Pub* next door to the hotel.

Stanhope is one of the major accommodation centres with dozens of places renting cottages, often by the week or longer. Weekly rates vary but most are between $300 and $450. The daily rate for most of the housekeeping units is around $50.

Campbell's Tourist Home (☎ 672-2421) in Stanhope is a B&B with a double for $35.

From Stanhope to Cavendish there are about 10 privately operated campgrounds. (See also information on places to stay *within* Prince Edward Island National Park in that section.)

Winsloe North

South of Brackley there is a dairy farm where gouda cheese is produced. It sounds interesting but there is nothing at all to see and the various cheeses which can be purchased on the premises are expensive.

North Rustico

There is a post office and a government liquor store here. Across the province these liquor stores are the outlets for beer, wine and all alcoholic beverages.

PEI is the home of *Fisherman's Wharf Lobster Suppers* probably the best known, busiest restaurant in the province. It's huge but in peak season it still gets crowded with queues from 6 to 8 pm. It's a fun casual holiday-style restaurant offering very good-value dinners. For $20 you get served a half-kg lobster and can help yourself to an impressive salad bar as well as unlimited amounts of chowder, very good local mussels, rolls and a variety of desserts. If you get really lucky, along the back wall there are tables with a view of the ocean.

Less commercial is the *Barn*, south along Route 6 out of town for a few km, with all-you-can-eat chicken dinners at $11. Everything is homemade – you can see the local women carrying in their designated dishes at opening time. It's just like going home for a Sunday meal.

Just east of town on Route 6 is one of the more popular family attractions: **Ocean Park**, a recreational water complex which includes a variety of slides and boats. There are also some animals and picnic areas and fast-food outlets.

At **Rusticoville** fishing charters can be arranged down at the quay and you can buy fresh lobster and fish.

Outside South Rustico on the small Route 242 is, for me, the quirkiest of island attractions, **Jumpin' Jack's Old Country Store Museum**. It's in the middle of nowhere and doesn't charge admission – on our visit there was nobody but one old man waiting patiently to show someone around. The museum is a junk collector's dream – an old two-storey house jammed with dust-covered articles of every description and function collected from far and wide for who knows how many years. There are all kinds of household and farm tools and toys to pick up and prompt 'What the heck is this?'.

North Rustico also has a lot of accommodation including many tourist homes where it's possible to get something for less than a week fairly easily. A double room in someone's home can be had for $25 to $35.

North Rustico Harbour is a tiny fishing community with a lighthouse which you can drive to from North Rustico or walk to from the beach once you're in the national park.

The Rustico area is the base for one of the largest of the province's fishing fleets. Prince Edward Island's fishing industry is inshore (as opposed to offshore) meaning that the boats head out and return home the same day.

Cavendish

More or less just a crossroads at the junction of routes 6 and 13 south of the park, this little town is the area's commercial centre. You're in the centre of town when you see the gas station, Cavendish Arms Pub and the church and cemetery.

Just east of town is a restaurant complex all done in cedar shakes. It contains a few fast-food places including one for breakfasts. *Thirsty's*, across the street, is a bar. Nearby is a bicycle rental outfit.

The Cavendish Tourist Mart is a grocery store open from 8 am to 10 pm daily and is good for all essential supplies and there is a bakery a few doors away.

East of Cavendish is a large **amusement park** and close by are a **wax museum, go-kart tracks**, and other newish diversions including, for some reason, a life-size replica of the space shuttle. At Stanley Bridge the **Marine Aquarium** is not worth the $5 admission.

To the west of town, near the park entrance, is **Cavendish Boardwalk** with some stores and a few places to feed at including pizza, chicken and 'sub' outlets.

Fiddles 'n' Vittles, three km west of town on Route 6, has been described as a fun place to eat; the food is good and they have a half-price kids' menu. The menu includes a variety of seafood but also steak, chicken and burgers all at low or moderate prices.

More tourist homes, motels and cottages, some even within the national park, and close to the beach can be found around Cavendish. Remember this is the busiest and most expensive area for accommodation. See also the following Cavendish Beach & Campground sections in the description of Prince Edward Island National Park.

Around Cavendish
More Lobster Suppers Three lobster-supper houses are nearby, one in New London eight km west, one in the village of New Glasgow and one in St Ann about the same distance from Cavendish on Route 224. All offer a lobster plus all you can eat – chowder, mussels, salads, breads and desserts. And you may get some live music to help the food go down too. None is quite the operation of the one in North Rustico, the selection is not as large and the price a few dollars less.

The one in St Ann is an original and still operates in the church basement as it has done for the past few decades. It's very busy, casual and friendly and full of people from all over Canada, the USA and Europe.

New London
Aside from the *Lion's Club Lobster Supper* which runs from 4 to 8.30 pm daily, New

London is also known for being the birth place of Lucy Maud Montgomery. The house where she was born in 1874 is now a museum and contains some personal belongings.

In New London you can also visit several pottery studio/shops and there is a seafood restaurant down near the water, open from 9 am to 9 pm through the summer.

Not far away in the village of **Park Corner** is a house which was owned by Lucy's uncle when she was a girl. This was one of her favourite places and now is also open to the public. It's called the Green Gables Museum at Silver Birch and is open from June to October.

Prince Edward Island National Park
Just 24 km north of Charlottetown, this is one of Canada's smallest national parks, but it has 40 km of varied coastline including some of the country's best sand beaches.

Sand dunes and red sandstone cliffs give way to wide beaches (widest at Cavendish) and the warmest waters around the province. The Gulf Stream does a little loop around the island, causing water temperatures to be higher than those found even further south along the east coast. This is not quite tepid bathwater, however, but temperatures do get up to around a comfortable 20° C.

There are several long stretches of beach in the park and they are all good. **Cavendish Beach** at the west end of the park is the most popular and gets relatively busy in peak season. **Brackley Beach** in the middle of the park is also well attended, the others less so. There is virtually no shade to be had at any of the beaches so consider using an umbrella or lots of lotion.

All the north coast beaches tend to have red jellyfish. They are known locally as bloodsuckers but they aren't. Most are much smaller than a closed fist and, while unpleasant, are not really dangerous although brushing against one can irritate the skin. The beaches of the southern coast don't have these jellyfish but they don't have the sand either, some tend to be rather rocky with debris and logs scattered around.

A day pass to the park is $3, a three-day

pass is $6 and camping is about $10, depending on where you camp and what services you require.

Some of the many local rental cottages are in or back onto park. Many visitors do rent a cottage for a week or two but the places just a short walk from the beach tend to be pricier. There are also many tourist homes out of the park but nearby. However, without a car or bicycle, it's difficult to get around.

Outside the park and occasionally adjacent to it are many private campgrounds supplementing the ones inside the park. *Forest Hill* and *Marco Polo* are popular with young people.

For munchies there is not much within the park, just a couple of snack bars.

Dalvay Beach This is the easternmost beach and a couple of short hiking trails begin in the area. One called Long Pond is quite good with a small graveyard, some remnants of old stone dykes and a spring for a cool drink.

A very appealing landmark is the *Dalvay by the Sea Hotel* built in 1895 and looking like something out of F Scott Fitzgerald. For a splurge this Victorian seaside lodge offers a varied menu – lobster bisqué to coq au vin. Reservations are required.

If you're thinking of spending the night, the price of a double room (from $150 and up) includes dinner and breakfast.

Stanhope Campground This campground within the park is recommended for good sites with lots of trees and a fine sandy beach opposite. An unserviced site is $10.50 and there is a well-stocked store.

There are no cliffs or dunes here, the landscape is flat and the beach is wide. At the entrance to the beach is a snack bar and change rooms with showers. A boardwalk leads to the beach which has lifeguards on duty through the day.

Brackley Beach Long, very wide Brackley Beach backed by sand dunes is popular with locals, young people and visitors. There is a snack bar and change rooms by the board-

walk to the beach. Lifeguards are on hand but watch out for riptides.

Rustico Campground The relatively isolated Rustico campground on an island has good camping, again with lots of trees but the beach was entirely washed away in a storm in the summer of 1987. A walk along the shoreline with its debris and upturned trees shows how nasty the sea can get. There is literally no sand left. The campground has no showers and the fee is also reduced at $8.50 a site.

Orby Head Between Rustico and Cavendish is some of the park's most impressive terrain. At Cape Turner there is a good look-out area but don't miss Orby Head with its trails leading along the high red cliffs with great seaside views. There are other stopping-off points along this stretch of coastal road.

Cavendish Beach & Campground The beach at Cavendish, despite being the widest of them all and edged by large sand dunes, is not really physically superior to the others but it is easily the most popular. Still, on the hottest day of summer this busiest of the island's destinations could not be termed crowded.

The Cavendish campground at the centre of things with nearby attractions and restaurants as well as the beach is usually full. If this is where you want to stay, check the office early in the morning for available spaces which are $10.50 unserviced.

House of Green Gables In the park near Cavendish town, this is, apart from the national park itself, the most popular attraction in the province.

The house is known as the place where Anne, the heroine of many of Lucy Montgomery's books, lived. The surrounding property was the setting of the 1908-novel *Anne of Green Gables* – a perennial favourite not only in Canada but around the world having been translated into close to 20 languages. The warm-hearted book tells the story of young orphan Anne and her childhood tribulations in turn-of-the-century

Prince Edward Island in a way that makes it a universal tale.

Lucy Maud Montgomery was born down the road in New London. In *Anne of Green Gables* and many subsequent novels she developed a world based on the land, life and times of this quiet, staid region.

Everything relating to either the story or the author anywhere on the island has now pretty well become part of the Green Gables industry but despite that, the original charm of place and character do remain.

At House of Green Gables, actually a rather attractive and comfortable place, the over popularisation reaches its zenith with tremendous crowds arriving daily all through the summer. Bus loads arrive at the door continuously. Visiting first thing in the morning is highly recommended. It's free and worth a visit for the period furniture and the feeling it gives of life here in the late 19th and early 20th centuries. The house is open from 9 am to 8 pm in high season, till 5 pm otherwise.

Also worthwhile are the quieter trails from the house through the green, gentle creek-crossed woods. 'Lover's Lane', particularly, has maintained its idealistic childhood ambience.

Not far away near the United Church in the town of **Cavendish**, you can visit the site of Lucy Montgomery's house where she lived with her grandparents. **Anne of Green Gables** was written here. The farmhouse no longer stands, just the stone foundations and surrounding gardens.

Windsurfing Rentals and lessons are available within the park at the Stanhope Beach Lodge. The rate is $10 an hour for a board, less by the day. Canoes and sailboats are also for rent. On Thursday nights surfboard races offering prizes are held.

WEST OF CHARLOTTETOWN
Lady Slipper Drive
The western third of the island is made up of Prince County. Lady Slipper Drive is 288 km long and the marked tourist route around this

portion of the island. It pretty much circumnavigates the entire region.

The northern section of Prince County is, like so much of the province, pretty farm country but the southern portion is rather flat, less scenic and possibly the least visited part of the island. The southernmost area along Egmont and Bedeque bays retains some evidence of its Acadian French history.

Summerside
The second largest city in the province, Summerside, has a population of 10,000. At one time residents of the capital would move to this side of the island in the hot months. Now it's more a town in its own right, although the closure of the large military base here has caused a major economic setback.

The approach along Highway 1A is much like that to Charlottetown, lined with motels and hamburger joints, but also a few campgrounds.

There isn't much in town; everything is on the one main street, Water St. It's a quiet village with nice old homes on streets trimmed with big trees.

For a week each year in mid-July there's the Lobster Festival with nightly feasts, contests, and games.

South of Summerside, **Borden** is the terminal for ferries to Cape Tormentine, New Brunswick.

Places to Stay Accommodation is sufficient if not abundant in Summerside, but there are many places to stay in the surrounding area during the busy periods should the need arise. The villages of Wilmot, St Eleanors and Miscouche all have tourist homes.

In town, *Faye & Eric's* (☎ 436-6847) is a B&B at 380 MacEwan Rd. They have three rooms with one double bed in each plus a deluxe suite with all the extras, including a whirlpool bath. The price of $35 to $45 depends on the features of the room and includes a light continental breakfast. The suite is $75 a day and there is a reasonably priced housekeeping unit.

Also in a modern house is *Morrison's*

B&B (☎ 436-3031) with somewhat lower rates beginning at singles/doubles $27/32. This one is at 253 Maple Ave and a full breakfast is included.

The *Summerside Inn* (☎ 436-5208), at 98 Summer St, is in an 1800s house three blocks from the centre of town. Six rooms are available, ranging from $35 to $50 a double, a continental breakfast is included.

Motels can be found as well. The *Cairns* (☎ 436-5841), on the east side of town on the north side of Water St, charges $35 and up for a double.

Places to Eat Of the several restaurants, *Ann's Place* is recommended. It offers a good selection at reasonable prices. Chicken and lobster plates from $5 to $8 are good value. You can also try *rapure*, an old island dish. It looks like green cake but is a tasty pork and spice concoction. On the east side of town, *Seafoods Delight* is reasonably priced.

Around Summerside
Miscouche As you head west of Summerside along Route 2, the **Acadian Museum** in Miscouche has a small collection of early Acadian memorabilia. Most of the descendants of these early French settlers live in this section of the province. Six thousand of them still speak French as a first language. Admission to the museum is $2 and it's open every day in summer.

Mont Carmel A little further west from Miscouche and then south down to the coast, is the little village of Mont Carmel home to the **Pioneer Acadian Village**. This is a replica of a settlement of the early 1800s. The village has a school, store and church among other things. A highlight is the restaurant in the grounds which offers a couple of traditional Acadian dishes such as chicken fricot and paté à la rapure. Admission is $2.50 and it's open daily. There is also a small **religious museum** nearby.

Malpeque Bay
North of Summerside, this bay produces the world-famous oysters of the same name. About 10 million of them are harvested each year from the controlled 'farms' of the bay.

Cabot Provincial Park, north of Malpeque village, is one of the larger parks on the island and a popular place with the island residents. There is camping, a beach and lots of picnic areas.

South of Malpeque towards Kensington are the **gardens**, landscaped beds of roses, begonias and mostly dahlias. It's open daily through the summer and admission costs $2.50.

Continuing Around Prince County
If you're in the vicinity **Tyne Valley** is worth a visit. Stop at the *Crafts & Tea Shop* for some home-baked goodies out on the little sun porch. There are a few craft places here including a pottery.

A band of about 40 Micmac families live on **Lennox Island** in Malpeque Bay. The scenery is good and there's a museum dealing with the history of the tribe, along with an Indian craft shop. It is connected by road from the west side of the bay near the village of East Bideford north of Tyne Valley.

The inland town of **O'Leary** right in the middle of Prince County is a small commercial centre which sees few tourists. Despite that there are several craft outlets with the primary article being knitted goods. The **Macausland's Woollen Mill**, an old town business, remains in operation and can be toured. Pure woollen goods can be bought at the mill. A small museum outlines the history of the PEI potato. There is also another church lobster supper here.

If you're near **Tignish** at mealtime, drop in at the Royal Canadian Legion. It's cheap, and you're bound to find conversation.

Up at the northern tip, **North Cape** is a wind-blown promontory with a lighthouse. There's a weather station here and along the east side in particular are some pretty high cliffs.

Cedar Dunes Provincial Park at the south-east tip of Prince County has a lighthouse, restaurant and beach. The lighthouse dating from 1875 has been restored and there is now a museum outlining its history. Overnight guests can stay in the inn part of the former lightkeeper's premises. Alternatively there is camping or a less expensive B&B called *Red Capes* (☎ 859-3150) three km away on Route 14.

EAST OF CHARLOTTETOWN
The King's Byway

The 374-km-long, circular sight-seeing route around King's County (the eastern third of the province) is called the King's Byway. It's a lightly populated, rural region of farms and fishing communities. Much of this section of the province is peopled by ancestors of Scottish settlers, rather than by the French of the western side or Irish of the central district. The ferry to Nova Scotia is on the south coast, the ferry to the Magdalen Islands at Souris on the east coast.

The shoreline is a mixture of parks with beaches, fishing ports and a few larger but quiet towns. The interior is crisscrossed with roads between farms.

Orwell

Just out of town is the **Orwell Corner Historic Site**, a 19th-century community recreation consisting of a farm, blacksmith's, post office and store. It's open every day in summer and costs $2.50. Concerts are held on Wednesday evenings.

Wood Island

Down on the south coast, 'Woods' is where you'll find the PEI-Nova Scotia ferry terminal and as such it's a busy visitor centre even though there isn't much in town itself. The mainland is 22 km or 75 minutes across the Northumberland Strait.

The *Cozy Nest* (☎ 962-2030) is a B&B one km from the ferry landing on the Trans Canada Highway towards Charlottetown. A double room costs $22 and breakfast is a few dollars more. There is also a motel which is two km west of the ferry. In town there are about half a dozen places to eat.

Murray Harbour

Little-visited and tucked out of the way,

Murray Harbour is a fishing town with its own canning plant. There is also a small museum on the outskirts.

Brudenell River Provincial Park & Around

The campground in the park is just a bare field but there's a lodge and a golf course for those not roughing it. At **Panmure Island Provincial Park**, just south down the coast, there is a good beach, swimming and picnicking.

Georgetown is a shipbuilding and repair depot. **Cardigan**, an old shipbuilding centre north of the park, has a lobster-supper house right down by the harbour; it's open daily from June to October. The hours are early: from 4.30 to 8.30 pm.

Fortune River

The Fortune River flowing near Highway 2 which cuts across the island is another place good for canoeing.

Souris

With a population of 1500, Souris feels like a real town after you've passed through so many small villages. It's actually one of the larger towns of the province and is the shopping and supply centre for the eastern region. First settled by the Acadian French in the early 1700s it was named Souris, meaning 'mouse', due to several plagues of the little creatures. Today the name has been anglicised and the last 's' is pronounced. The town is an important fishing and processing port and is also important for having the ferry which departs for the Magdalen Islands of Quebec five hours and 134 km north in the Gulf of St Lawrence.

Main St, a strip with buildings from the 1920s and '30s and some older distinctive architecture, is pleasantly slow with cars stopping to let pedestrians cross. The shops, the newspaper office and a few simple restaurants are found here.

St Mary's Roman Catholic Church built of island sandstone in 1901, off Main St on Pacquet St, is the dominant structure in town. However, the **Town Hall** on Main St, the

Georgian-style **Beacon House** and several other buildings are worth a look on the way by.

There is a tourist office down at the beach on the south-west corner of town. Across the small bay at the breakwater on the other side of town is the large fish-processing plant and the dock for the red and white coastguard ship.

Places to Stay For a small town Souris gets quite busy due to the ferry traffic. On Main St are a couple of convenient B&Bs, the Abbie Isle (☎ 687-3307) at No 153 and the Baycliffe (☎ 687-3096) at No 40. The latter charges just $25 for two but breakfast is extra.

The good *Hilltop Motel* (☎ 687-3315), although not cheap, gets full with ferry traffic even when the ferry arrives from Quebec at four or five in the morning. It's one of the few places where checking in at any hour is alright. Call from the Magdalen Islands for a reservation before leaving. The motel has a restaurant good for breakfast. It's on the east side of town. If calling from Quebec add 1-902 before dialling the telephone number. Rates are $50 for a double.

The *Sundunes Inn* (☎ 687-2324), at 16 Washington St overlooking the harbour, in a Victorian mansion is good value at $40 a double with the morning meal included.

Red Point Provincial Park
Red Point is a small park with a sandy beach and some nice shaded tent sites. The beaches around here are known for the squeaking sound they make when you walk on them.

Basin Head
Not even really a village, Basin Head at the ocean's edge, has a fisheries museum displaying equipment, a beach, a few old fishing buildings, a snack bar and a canoe-rental outlet. There is a fair bit of inland water here to paddle around and explore.

East Point
At East Point, the north-east tip of the island, cliffs are topped by a lighthouse which can

be climbed with a little tour for $1.50. Until the late 1980s it was run by a keeper but is now automated like almost every other lighthouse in Canada. The old assistant's house nearby with the radio room has been restored and there is a gift shop. It's expected that in a few years the whole thing will have to be moved (as the lighthouse has been previously) because of the creeping erosion of the shoreline. The lighthouse is open from 9 am to 9 pm daily mid-May to mid-October.

The north shore area of King's County all the way along towards Cavendish is more heavily wooded than much of the island but that doesn't mean the end of farms and potatoes altogether. Notice that many of the beautiful old cedar shake farmhouses are now being supplanted by modern, more energy-efficient bungalows not unlike those you can see in suburban Toronto. The older places often sit empty, quietly decaying or being suffocated by the now chaperone-free lilac bushes.

There is a lot of fishing done along the coast here – you could try a charter in search of tuna. Inland there are a couple of trout streams worth investigating.

The people of the north-eastern area have a fairly strong intriguing accent not unlike that heard in Newfoundland.

North Lake
This is one of the four fishing centres found along the north coast of King's County. Although small, the dock area with its lobster traps, storage sheds and boats is always good for a poke around. There is some irresistible potential for picture taking. Anglers may take passengers along for a little deep-sea fishing. With autumn comes tuna season and quite a busy sport-fishing period drawing anglers from abroad.

Some of the world's largest bluefin tuna have been caught in these waters. Indeed the world record catch, a 680-kg behemoth, was reeled in off North Lake in 1979.

Campbell's Cove Provincial Park
Very quiet and relaxing through the day this

small park, the best one in the county, fills up by evening in July and August. As always shade is at a premium with about half the campsites offering some sun relief. Most campers are tenters and there are no electric hook-ups. Facilities are minimal so bring all necessary supplies.

The beach is very good with cliffs at each end.

St Margaret's

At the big church in St Margaret's, lobster suppers are held from Thursday to Sunday only and cost a few bucks less than the ones

around the Cavendish area. Aside from the deep-sea fishing there are some good trout streams along the road and one of them, the **Naufrage River**, is just west of town. At the village of **Naufrage** on the coast is another lighthouse and some colourful fishing boats around the wharf area.

St Peter's

The nets for commercial mussel farming can be seen stretched around St Peter's Bay. In town don't miss *Wilma's Bake Shop* for bread, muffins and cinnamon buns.

New Brunswick

Entered Confederation: 1 July 1867
Area: 73,437 sq km
Population: 696,403

New Brunswick, which in 1984 celebrated its 200th birthday, is one of Canada's three Maritime Provinces. It was also one of the four original members of the Dominion of Canada established in 1867. Despite its long history, the province's essential characteristic is that it remains largely forested. Yet, for most visitors, it is the areas apart from the vast woodlands that have the most appeal.

From the Quebec border the gentle, pastoral farming region of the Saint John River Valley leads to the Bay of Fundy with its cliffs, coves and tidal flats caused by the world's highest tides. Saint John, the largest city, and Fredericton, the capital, both have intriguing Loyalist histories. The eastern shore offers warm, sandy beaches and, flowing out of the forested interior, some of the finest salmon fishing rivers anywhere.

The wooded highlands of the north contain one of the highest mountains in eastern Canada and provide opportunities for a variety of outdoor activities.

New Brunswick has never had a very strong image and, although many people pass through, it is nowhere near as popular a vacation destination as Nova Scotia or Prince Edward Island, having neither the tourist orientation nor the volume of visitors of these two neighbours.

Lumber and pulp and paper operations are two of the main industries. Manufacturing and minerals are also important as are mixed farming and fishing.

Roughly 60% of the residents live in urban areas. You may be surprised at how much French you hear spoken in the province. Around 37% of the population have French ancestors and, even today, 16% speak French only. New Brunswick is Canada's only officially bilingual province.

Summers are usually not blisteringly hot and winters are very snowy and cold. The driest month of the year is August; generally, there is more rain in the south.

Fredericton

Fredericton is the queen of New Brunswick's towns. Unlike most, it is non-industrial and a very pretty, genteel quiet place. The central area has some visible history to explore.

Three hundred years ago, the Maliseet and Micmac Indians lived and fished in the area. In 1762 the British founded a town over the abandoned French settlement. They named it in honour of Prince Frederick, the second son of King George III. When the American Revolutionary War ended in 1783, about 6000 people arrived in town which became the capital of the newly formed province separated from Nova Scotia in 1785.

Long ago the town produced Canada's first English-speaking poet, Loyalist Jonathan Odell. Later, Lord Beaverbrook, who was to rise to international prominence, was born here. Today, Fredericton still presides over high society as home of the province's lieutenant-governor, the Legislature and the university dons.

About a fifth of the 45,000 residents work for the government because this is the capital of New Brunswick. Of the light industry here food processing, woodworking and the manufacturing of leather goods are the most important.

Some remarkable old buildings and beautiful houses remain, the river runs gently by and the streets are tree-lined, prompting the title 'City of Stately Elms'. There's not a lot

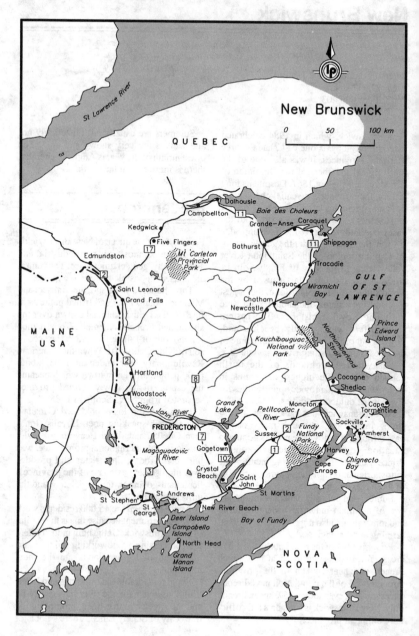

New Brunswick

0   50   100 km

QUEBEC

St Lawrence River

Dalhousie
Campbellton
Baie des Chaleurs
Grande-Anse
Caraquet
Kedgwick
Five Fingers
Mt Carleton Provincial Park
Bathurst
Shippagan
Edmundston
Tracadie
Saint Leonard
Grand Falls
Neguac
Miramichi Bay
GULF OF ST LAWRENCE
MAINE USA
Chatham
Newcastle
Prince Edward Island
Kouchibouguac National Park
Northumberland Strait
Hartland
Cocagne
Shediac
Woodstock
Saint John River
Grand Lake
Petitcodiac River
Moncton
Cape Tormentine
FREDERICTON
Gagetown
Sussex
Fundy National Park
Sackville
Amherst
Magaguadavic River
Crystal Beach
Saint John
Harvey
Chignecto Bay
St Stephen
St Andrews
St Martins
Cape Enrage
St George
New River Beach
Deer Island
Campobello Island
Bay of Fundy
NOVA SCOTIA
North Head
Grand Manan Island

to do, but Fredericton makes a nice spot to relax for a day or two.

Orientation

The city is on a small, rounded peninsula that resembles a slight hump of land jutting into the Saint John River.

There are three bridges: two for cars and the middle one for trains only.

The Westmorland St Bridge connects the downtown area with the north shore. Further east, the Princess Margaret Bridge links the Trans Canada Highway segments across the river. Not far over the river are the green woods and farmlands typical of the river valley. From the Westmorland St Bridge you can see some fine big houses and a couple of church spires on the north side, away from town.

Coming into town from the Trans Canada Highway, take exit 292B (Regent St). Regent St will take you straight down to the centre of town.

In town, King St and the parallel Queen St are the main streets, just a block up from the river. Northumberland and Saint John Sts are the west and east edges of the small downtown area. The park on the corner of Queen and Regent Sts, called Officers' Square, is pretty much the centre of things.

As you head east from Queen St, out of the downtown area, there's a small strip of park known as The Green between the road and the river. This park extends eastwards for several blocks. Near the Art Gallery is a statue of Scottish poet Robbie Burns. There are good views along the river here and big shade trees to relax under. Several points of interest lie in The Green.

As you go further east, Queen St becomes Waterloo Row. Here it's the houses on the other side of the street that deserve your attention. Each is different from its neighbour and all are large and well maintained, some with grand balconies, turrets and bizarre shapes. Nos 50, 82 and 146 particularly impressed me. The residence of the lieutenant-governor is around here; look for the coat of arms. There aren't too many streets in the country like this one.

Back on The Green you'll pass the Loyalist Memorial beside Waterloo Row, commemorating the British founders. Not far away is the old Loyalist Cemetery, similar to the one in Saint John. The tombstones show that many of these people were born in England, Ireland or other countries, and died young. Strangely, the inscriptions make the pioneers and their hardships come alive.

Church and Brunswick Sts, branching out from near Christ Church Cathedral, also have numerous large brick or wooden houses. The grey one at 767 Brunswick St was 200 years old in 1984.

Information

The Visitors' Centre (☎ 455-9500) is in City Hall on Queen St. It's open Monday to Friday year-round from 8.30 am to 5 pm but keeps later hours during the summer.

You can also get information at the Legislative Assembly (☎ 453-2527) on Queen St. This office is open weekdays all year, with longer hours in summer. From 15 June to 15 September it is also open Saturday, Sunday and holidays from 10 am to 9 pm.

There's a tourist bureau (☎ 455-3092) on the Trans Canada Highway near Hanwell Rd, exit 289. It's open daily from early June to late September, from 9 am until the evening.

Tourism New Brunswick (☎ 800-442-4442) will also help with information about most places in the province.

Downtown, the post office is on Queen St not far from Regent St. A good thing to know if you're driving is that there is free parking behind the Legislative Assembly on Queen St. Just tell the attendant you're a visitor from out of town.

Historic Walking Tour

A walking tour around some of the following places mentioned plus other historical sites is outlined on the map of Fredericton, available at tourist offices. A booklet gives descriptions of the various sites. The walking tour includes 21 spots in the historic downtown area, starting from City Hall.

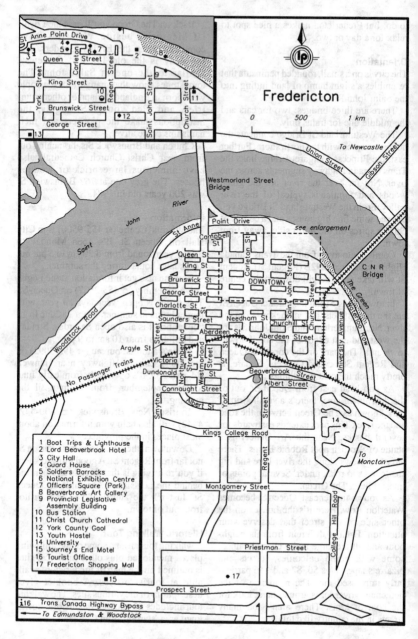

Fredericton

0   500   1 km

St Anne Point Drive

Queen Street
King Street
Brunswick Street
George Street

York Street
Carleton Street
Regent Street
Saint John Street
Church Street

To Newcastle
Union Street
Gibson Street

Westmorland Street Bridge

Saint John River

St Anne Point Drive

see enlargement

Campbell St
Queen St
King St
Brunswick St
George Street
Charlotte St
Saunders Street
Needham St
Aberdeen St

DOWNTOWN

C N R Bridge

Woodstock Road

No Passenger Trains

Argyle St
Victoria Street
Dundonald
Connaught Street
Albert St
York Street

Smythe Street
Northumberland Street
Westmorland Street

Aberdeen Street
Churchill St
Beaverbrook Street
Albert Street

Carleton St
Saint John Street
Church Street

University Avenue
Waterloo Row
The Green

Kings College Road

Regent Street

To Moncton

Montgomery Street

1 Boat Trips & Lighthouse
2 Lord Beaverbrook Hotel
3 City Hall
4 Guard House
5 Soldiers Barracks
6 National Exhibition Centre
7 Officers' Square (Park)
8 Beaverbrook Art Gallery
9 Provincial Legislative
   Assembly Building
10 Bus Station
11 Christ Church Cathedral
12 York County Gaol
13 Youth Hostel
14 University
15 Journey's End Motel
16 Tourist Office
17 Fredericton Shopping Mall

Priestman Street

College Hill Road

Prospect Street

Trans Canada Highway Bypass
To Edmundston & Woodstock

Officers' Square

This is the city's central park – on Queen St between Carleton and Regent Sts. The square was once the military parade ground and still sits amongst several military buildings.

At 10 am Monday to Friday, from mid-July to the third week in August, you can see the full-uniform Changing of the Guard ceremony. At 2 pm the troops go through a brief tattoo with a rifle salute.

Also in the park, on summer Tuesday evenings at 7.30 pm, free band concerts are given, attracting crowds. It might be a marching, military or pipe band and sometimes classical music is played too. If it rains, the performance is switched to Thursday night.

In the park is a statue of Lord Beaverbrook, the press baron and the province's most illustrious son.

On the west side of the square are the former Officers' Barracks built between 1839 and 1851. The older section, closest to the water, has thicker walls of masonry and hand-hewn timbers. The other, newer end is made of sawn timber.

York-Sunbury Historical Museum

This museum is in the old officers' quarters off the park, a building typical of those designed by the Royal Architects during the colonial period. The museum has a collection of items from the city's past: military pieces used by local regiments and by British and German armies from the Boer and both World Wars; furniture from a Loyalist sitting room and Victorian bedroom; Native Indian and Acadian artefacts and archaeological finds.

The highlight of the museum is a stuffed 19-kg frog. It was the pet of a local innkeeper. Nineteen kg! Perhaps he fed it the patrons who were incapable of walking home. Hours in summer are Monday, Friday, Saturday from 10 am to 6 pm; Tuesday, Wednesday, Thursday from 10 am to 8 pm; Sunday from 12 to 6 pm. During other seasons it's open Monday, Wednesday and Friday afternoons. The fee is $2.50.

Soldiers' Barracks

On the corner of Carleton and Queen Sts in the Military Compound you can see where the common soldier lived in the 1820s and also the Guard House (dating from 1828) where the naughty ones were sent. The Guard House now contains military memorabilia. A well-written, interesting history of it is available at no charge. Likewise, visits to this national historic site are free.

New Brunswick Legislative Assembly Building

Built in 1882, this government building stands on Queen St near Saint John St, east of Officers' Square.

Guides will show you around pointing out things of particular merit, like the wooden Speaker's Chair and the spiral staircase. When the Legislative Assembly is in session, visitors are welcome to listen to the proceedings. It's open to visitors daily and is free.

Regent Street Wharf

Down at the river with an entrance off Queen St beside the Beaverbrook Hotel is the small wharf with a lighthouse and pier from which the boat cruises depart. The lighthouse contains a museum and the open top level affords views down the river. At ground level, with no admission charge, there is a snack bar and gift shop. The lighthouse is open daily in summer but out of the peak season, it's only open on weekends from noon.

Beaverbrook Art Gallery

Another of Lord Beaverbrook's gifts to the town is this gallery, right opposite the Legislative Assembly on Queen St. There's a collection of British paintings including works by Gainsborough, Turner and Constable. They also have a Dali as well as Canadian and provincial works. The gallery is open Tuesday to Saturday from 10 am to 5 pm, Sunday and Monday from 12 to 5 pm. Admission is $2.

Christ Church Cathedral

Built in 1853, this is a fine early example of

the 19th-century revival of decorated Gothic architecture. The cathedral is interesting because it's very compact – short for the height yet with balance and proportion that make the interior seem both normal and spacious.

You'll see good stained glass, especially around the altar, where the walls are painted above the choir. Free tours are offered. The church is just off Queen St at Church St, by the river, east of town.

There are other fine houses of worship about town including the Wilmot United on the corner of King and Carleton Sts. It's a huge wooden black and white place with a plain, simple wooden interior open to visitors through the week. Use the side door.

Old Burial Ground

An easy walk from downtown is the Loyalist cemetery (dating from 1784) on Brunswick St on the corner of Carleton St. The Loyalists came from the 13 colonies after the American Revolution and were instrumental in settling this area. Many of the earliest Loyalists to arrive are buried here and it's interesting to browse around the grounds, open from 8 am to 9 pm daily.

National Exhibition Centre

On the corner of Queen and Carleton Sts in town, this building dates from 1881 and has been used as a post office, customs house and library. The exhibition centre on the first floor displays travelling exhibits which vary dramatically. Newfoundland folk art, hooked mats, art photographs from the National Gallery and Japanese kites are some examples. The displays are usually good and always free.

Upstairs is the Provincial Sports Hall of Fame with tidbits about achievements of local sportspeople.

Boyce Farmers' Market

This market is on George St between Regent and Saint John Sts. It's open Saturday only, from 7 am to noon. There are nearly 150 stalls selling fresh fruit, vegetables, meat and cheese, and also handicrafts, homemade desserts and flowers. Goofy Roofy's Restaurant is here too.

Conserver House

On the corner of Brunswick and Saint John Sts is this house dating from 1890, now used as a model of and information centre for energy conservation. Tours and advice are free. The house is closed on Saturday afternoons and Sunday.

Parks

In addition to the riverfront park and several smaller city parks, you can visit the following two. Odell Park, south-west of the downtown centre off Smythe St, covers 156 hectares that contain some primeval provincial forest. There are picnic tables, a kids' zoo and walking paths. Killarney Lake Park is about five km from town over the Westmorland St Bridge. A spring-fed lake is used for swimming and fishing.

Activities

Rent a canoe for drifting along the river. One place they're available is at Woolastock campground, 29 km west of Fredericton. Another is McGivney Boat & Canoe (☎ 472-1655), Lower St Mary's, five km east of Howard Johnson's on the Trans Canada Highway.

You can rent a sailboard from Atlantic Boardsailing (☎ 455-2220), on Queen St, for $8 an hour or $35 a day. Windsport Fredericton (☎ 472-2503), 71 Riverside Drive, offers kayak instruction and white-water trips.

There are free swimming pools at Henry Park and Queen Square. At the YM-YWCA, 28 Saunders St, there is a small admission fee.

Organised Tours Throughout July and August, an actors' group leads a free walking tour around town. Ask at the tourist office for details.

Trius Tours (☎ 459-3366) offer inexpensive car tours around town; for larger groups a van is used. (Trius is primarily a taxi company.) Some years, bus tours are offered on summer afternoons from the tourist office. A replica of an old paddle-wheeler, the *Pioneer Princess* (☎ 458-5558), which docks at the Regent St wharf provides river cruises, some with dinner. The basic cruises with employees wearing period costume last either one or 1½ hours and cost $8.50 or $10.50. The more costly 2½-hour version includes dinner and entertainment. There are also pricier one-day trips to Saint John with meals included. Reservations are required for the longer trips.

Festivals

The annual New Brunswick Day Canoe Race is held in early August in the Mactaquac Headpond.

A free provincial handicraft show is held at Mactaquac Park on the weekend before Labour Day. All types of handicrafts are exhibited and sold. Fredericton is a centre of the old craft of pewtersmithing. Examples can be seen anytime of year at Aikens Pewter downtown at 81 Regent St or you can arrange tours of the main plant there. Other craftspeople in the town do pottery and woodcarving.

The Fredericton Exhibition is an annual six-day affair starting on Labour Day (the first Monday in September). It's held at the exhibition grounds, on the corner of Smythe and Saunders Sts. The exhibition includes a farm show, a carnival, harness racing and stage shows.

From May to September each Saturday night at the Playhouse Theatre, various country music artists from Atlantic Canada perform.

South of town, Oromocto holds a two-day Scottish Highland Games festival each summer with music, dancing, and contests.

Places to Stay

Camping The best place nearby is *Mactaquac Provincial Park* (☎ 363-3011), 20 km west off the Trans Canada Highway on Highway 105, on the north side of the river. A tent is $7. There's swimming and a grocery store. Another provincial park is just south of King's Landing on Lake George.

There are several camping places closer to Fredericton though not as nice as the parks. They're OK for stopping overnight or short stays. There are three privately owned sites on the Trans Canada Highway before you reach Hanwell Rd.

Another place that's a little quieter is towards town from the Trans Canada highway, *Kelly's Camping & Trailer Court* (☎ 455-6827). Head for the downtown area on Hanwell Rd from the Trans Canada Highway. Turn left at Colonial Heights and then left again at Golf Club Rd. The campground is on your left.

South-east 30 km from town is the *Sunbury Oromocto* campground at French Lake, off Highway 7.

Hostels Fredericton has a member *Youth Hostel* (☎ 454-1233) and it's a good one. It's central in a big, old schoolhouse at 193 York St on the corner of George St, by the church. It's easy to walk there from the bus station. Rates are $8.50 members, $10 nonmembers for the 30 beds. Breakfasts cost $2 and dinners are available. The hostel opens at 4.30 pm and the people there are friendly. It's open early June to the beginning of September. And it has the strangest toilets I've yet seen.

There's no accommodation in the YM-YWCA building here.

The *University of New Brunswick* rents single and double rooms in the dorms, available from mid-May to mid-August. For tourists singles/doubles are $24/30, and for students the price drops to $14/20. Contact the Director of Housing on ☎ 453-4891. Facilities include a pool. The campus is within walking distance of the downtown area in a south-east direction. It runs south of Beaverbrook St about five blocks from Regent St.

Hotels & Tourist Homes There isn't a vast selection of budget places in town but the ones that exist are good.

The *Manger Inn* (☎ 454-3410) is the nice yellow-and-black house at 269 Saunders St. This is a tree-lined residential street two blocks south of Brunswick St. Rates are $25 singles, one bed (two people) $30, two beds (two people) $35; kitchen facilities are available.

The central *Back Porch B&B* (☎ 454-6875), at 266 Northumberland St, has two rooms priced the same as at the Manger Inn and good breakfasts on the back porch. It's open all year.

The *Carriage House B&B* (☎ 454-6090) is over at 230 University Ave, also central but more expensive at singles/doubles $40/45 and up with breakfast included. There's a shared TV room.

Moving up-market, the venerable *Lord Beaverbrook* (☎ 455-3371), at 659 Queen St, is relatively moderate at singles/doubles $80/90 for a place of its class. They have 165 rooms with all the amenities used mainly by business and government people.

Motels The bulk of the city's accommodation is in motels around the edges of town. On the west side of town on Rural Route 6, which is the Trans Canada Highway West, there are a couple of places.

Country Host Motel (☎ 459-3464) has rooms for singles/doubles $35/42.

The *Roadside Motel* (☎ 455-8593 is much bigger but the prices are about the same at singles/doubles $38/40.

On the east side of town on Rural Route 8 (also known as Highway 2 or Trans Canada Highway for Moncton) is the *Norfolk Motel* (☎ 472-3278). Singles/doubles here are only $27/30.

Just off the highway before Princess Margaret Bridge, east of the university, is Forest Hill Rd. At No 502 is the *Fredericton Skyline Motel* (☎ 455-6683), with singles/doubles $35/45. To get there, head for the highway over the bridge toward Moncton; Forest Hill Rd runs east of the highway. A taxi fare here from the centre of town costs $5.

The *Journey's End Motel* (☎ 453-0800) has large, clean rooms for singles/doubles $46/53. Part of a Canadian chain, it's at 255 Prospect St, one block north of the Trans Canada Highway towards town off Regent

St within walking distance of a few places to eat.

Places to Eat

The *JM&T Deli*, a small but comfortable and casual delicatessen with an interesting noticeboard, sits at the bottom of Regent St at No 62. It serves all the standards, including smoked meat from Montreal's Ben's. Various sandwiches, bagels and cheeses are served at the stools for about $3.50 and up. It's not open on Sunday.

At 596 Queen St is *Dimitri's*, good for an inexpensive Greek lunch or dinner of souvlakia, pitta, brochettes, moussaka and the like.

McGinnis, on King St at Westmorland St, has beer and outside tables to help a feeding along.

Opposite the Justice Building on Queen St is *Zellers*, a Woolworth's-type store with the least expensive meals in town. Lunch is about $4. They serve all the usual basic stuff but also shrimps, seafood and even lobster sandwiches.

On Queen St is a place for Chinese food: the *Capital Garden*, by the post office. From 11.30 am to 2.30 pm, Monday to Friday there is an all-you-can-eat buffet for $7.50. It includes ribs, chicken balls, egg rolls and rice. On Saturday and Sunday nights dinner is $9.50.

Mei's, at 74 Regent St, is better and offers some Sichuan-style dishes. Dinner for two is in the $25 range.

Goofy Roofy's is a small place set up in the Saturday market, open only Saturday mornings for breakfast and lunch. Prices range from $3.50 to $5.50. The 'goofy' is the boisterous, brash, notorious celebrity who runs the place. Get your quips ready. The *Subway*, a small place not bad for sandwiches, is mentioned because it's one of the few places in the centre open on a Sunday. It's on King St near Westmorland St.

In the enclosed King's Place shopping mall for shopping on the corner of Brunswick and York Sts is *California Dreaming* with a range of inexpensive meals, sandwiches and salads. Later at night it's more of a bar. Also in the mall is *Krispins* with cheap cafeteria-style lunches.

At 536 Queen St, *Benoit's* for seafood or game is the place for those with no financial worries.

Nearby, at 594 Queen St on the corner of Regent St, is *La Vie en Rose Café*, a snazzy little place for desserts and coffee.

For a tea try *Keay's*, at 72 York St, a sort of old-style counter eatery in a fruit market.

Away from the centre near the Trans Canada Highway have a look along Prospect St West off Regent St South. The Fredericton Mall is here with a grocery store, Sobey's, and there is a liquor outlet. Further along is *O'Tooles*, a pub, and on the corner of Smythe St the *Ponderosa* has good-value steak or shrimp and all you can eat from the variety of salads for $8.

Entertainment
At 625 King St is the *Lunar Rogue*, a pub. Also on King St, but between Regent and Carleton Sts, is the *Club Cosmopolitan* with a fairly expensive restaurant, a lounge and the local singles disco.

The University of New Brunswick often has concerts and folk performers. Cheap films are also shown at the university in the Tilley Hall Auditorium.

Getting There & Away
Air Fredericton is a small city but as the provincial capital it does get a fair bit of air traffic. Many flights in and out are stopovers between various other points. Air Canada serves the city and has one nonstop flight daily from Toronto.

Bus The SMT bus station (☎ 455-3303) is on the corner of Regent and Brunswick Sts. Schedules and fares to some destinations include to:

Moncton – noon, 5.30 pm daily ($21)
Quebec City via Campbellton – 12.30, 6 pm ($58)
Halifax – noon ($49)
Amherst, Nova Scotia – noon ($30)

Train There is no longer any passenger

service into or from Fredericton. But there is a bus service which connects with trains at Fredericton Junction about 40 km south of town. For information and tickets, there are several agents in town including Blaine Thomas, at 99 York St, and Maritime Travel, at 498 Queen St. Buses leave from the Beaverbrook Hotel and from the Student Union Building at the university, so you could inquire at these points as well.

Car & Motorbike For car rentals Budget (☎ 452-1107) is at 407 Regent St. Their rate is $36 a day with 150 free km. By the week it's less with 1050 free km, then 12 cents per km.

Delta, at 304 King St, is more reasonable at $25 a day with 150 free km, then 12 cents per km. There is also a good weekend package available. Tilden on Prospect St is a third possibility.

Distances in the Atlantic region are small; a few hours of driving will take you across any of the provinces. Cape Tormentine is 300 km away via the Trans Canada Highway, and highways 16 and 2. To Halifax (415 km) take highways 102, 104 and then the Trans Canada Highway. To Quebec City (576 km) take the Trans Canada Highway, known here as Highway 2.

Getting Around
To/From the Airport The airport is 16 km south-east of town. There's an airport bus from the Lord Beaverbrook Hotel before and after flights. It leaves from 45 to 60 minutes before flight time and costs $5. Generally there is no service on Sunday and holidays though. A taxi to the airport costs around $15.

Bus The city has a good system and the fare includes free transfers. For information, ring ☎ 474-0212.

The university is a 15-minute walk from the downtown area; if you want to take the bus, take No 9 south on Regent St. It runs about every 20 minutes.

For hitching on the Trans Canada Highway you want the Fredericton Mall bus, the No 10 from town. If you get off up near the mall, off the Trans Canada Highway, take the No 2 for downtown.

Car Free tourist parking passes are available from the Visitors' Centre, City Hall; these enable you to park in lots and at meters free.

SOUTH-EAST OF FREDERICTON
Gagetown
Gagetown refers to both a small town and the largest military base in the Commonwealth of Nations. This is the source of all the military vehicles you've probably seen on the highways. Both are down the Saint John River a short distance from Fredericton. At Camp Gagetown, the base, you can visit the military museum with articles from both World Wars, the South African War and the Korean War. Admission is free. Along the way from Fredericton are farmers' markets and roadside stalls offering fresh produce.

Gagetown itself, on the river, has numerous craft outlets and good examples of earlier architecture, some dating from the 1700s.

Grand Lake
From Highway 2, along the river east of town, there's beautiful farmland and eventually you reach the dairy centre of Sussex. Other than the views though, there is very little along the way.

Grand Lake, the province's largest lake, is a busy summer resort area with lots of cottages and a couple of provincial campgrounds. At Cambridge Narrows on nearby Washademoak Lake is the *Lake Resort*, a well-known R&R spot with European-style saunas and spas. *Café Mozart* here is a very good restaurant and the German tortes have quite a reputation.

Sussex
Sussex is a small country town in the middle of some pastoral and productive dairy lands. Fortunately all the local cows aren't the size of the one seen on the outskirts of town.

On Highway 2 at the exit into the centre is a tourist office. In town one of the streets, Queen St, has been somewhat remodelled and is reminiscent of earlier decades. It's off

Main St opposite the VIA Rail station. Here you'll find the licensed *Broadway Cafe*, a little sanctuary from the standard small-town greasy spoons offering good, inexpensive lunch specials in a comfortable and casual atmosphere complete with 'tasty' recorded music. It's also open for breakfasts and until 9 pm Friday and Saturday.

The surrounding King's County has 17 of the appealing old wooden covered bridges often situated so prettily they look like pictures peeled from a calendar.

On towards Moncton also look for the old potato storage houses and barns half-buried in the ground.

SOUTH-WEST OF FREDERICTON
Mactaquac Provincial Park
Twenty-two km west of Fredericton is New Brunswick's biggest provincial park. It runs along the 100-km-long pond formed by the Mactaquac Power Dam. The park offers swimming, fishing, picnic sites, camping and boat rentals. There's also a golf course where you can rent all equipment. It's a busy campground through the summer and is often full but there are a couple of others not too far away: the attendants will have some suggestions.

Mactaquac Power Dam
The Mactaquac Dam across the park is responsible for creating the small lake and therefore the park's location. The 400,000 kilowatt output makes it the largest in the Maritime Provinces. Free tours, lasting about 45 minutes, include a look at the turbines and an explanation of how they work. The site is open seven days a week from 9 am to 4.30 pm.

Woolastock Wildlife Park
Just a few km west of the Mactaquac Park, Woolastock Wildlife Park (☎ 363-2352) is open daily from 9 am to sunset. The park has a collection of Canadian animals, many typical of this region. You'll see moose, bear, wolves, coyotes, foxes, caribou, hawks, owls and more. There are also some water slides,

Bald eagle

picnic areas and camping. If you camp, the wildlife section is free. Up the river around here are several campgrounds and many touristy attractions. For example, there's horse riding, craft shops and small museums.

King's Landing Historical Settlement
The settlement is 37 km west of Fredericton, on the way to Woodstock. Take exit 259 off the Trans Canada Highway. Here you can get a glimpse of (and taste) pioneer life in the Maritimes. A community of 100 costumed staff inhabits 11 houses, a school, church, store and sawmill typical of those used a century ago. The staff will answer questions about their chores, the tools, or life in general in such a village. The *King's Head Inn* serves traditional foods and beverages.

The settlement is open from 6 June to 26 June and from 8 September to 12 October from 10 am to 5 pm, and from 27 June to 7 September between 10 am and 6 pm. Admission is $6. On weekends in July and August and on Sunday only in June, there's a bus from the SMT terminal in Fredericton. It leaves for King's Landing at 10 am and 1 pm and costs $6.50 return. With the bus ticket, admission to the site is only $4.

Saint Croix Waterway Recreation Area
This area of 336 sq km is south-west of Fredericton near the Maine USA border. The town of McAdam is pretty much the commercial centre of this little-developed territory of woods and lakes. In McAdam itself, check out the Canadian Pacific railway station dating from 1900: it's one of the finest in Canada and was made a national historic site in 1983.

Sixteen km from McAdam is **Spednic Provincial Park**, with rustic camping and access to some of the Chiputneticook chain of lakes. The Saint Croix River is good for white-water canoeing. Other canoe routes connect lakes, and about 100 km of hiking trails wind through the area. There's another campground at Wauklehegan.

Fundy Shore

Almost the entire southern edge of the province is presided over by the ever present, constantly rising and falling, always impressive waters of the Bay of Fundy.

The fascinating shoreline, the English-style resort town of St Andrew's, the wonderful quiet Fundy Isles, the city of Saint John and the Fundy National Park make this easily one of the most appealing and varied regions of New Brunswick. Despite the features which make it the best known and one of the most visited areas of the province it usually isn't even very busy.

ST STEPHEN

Right at the US border across the river from Calais, Maine, St Stephen is a busy entry point for US visitors coming east. It's a small, old town that forms the northern link of what is known as the Quoddy Loop – a circular tour around south-eastern New Brunswick and north-western Maine around Passamaquoddy Bay. From St Stephen the loop route goes to St Andrew's, St George and then on to Deer Island and lastly to Campobello Island which is connected by bridge to Maine. It's a popular trip taking anywhere from a day or two to a week and includes some fine seaside scenery, interesting history and a number of pleasant, easy going resort-style towns. In St Stephen the Festival of International Cooperation is held in August with concerts, parades and street fairs. Note that there is a duty-free shop for alcohol and cigarette bargains opposite the Canadian Customs building.

St Stephen also has quite a reputation as a chocolate Mecca as the home of **Ganong's**, a family chocolate business since 1910, whose products are known all around eastern Canada. Some say the chocolate bar was invented by the Ganong brothers. You can visit the old factory on the main street of town, Milltown Blvd. It's just a store now with not much to see but plenty to buy ranging from boxed chocolates to bars such as Pal O' Mine, a very sweet little number. The modern factory is away from the centre toward St Andrew's on Chocolate Drive near the Charlotte Mall. In typical low-key Canadian style it is not open to visitors and there are no tours except during the annual Chocolate Fest which occurs in August.

Around the bay a little north and west of St Stephen on the border, is **Milltown** with one of the continent's oldest hydroelectric plants operated by Power NB of New Brunswick. Free tours are given from 1 June to 31 August, 9 am to 4.30 pm daily.

Nearby at 443 Milltown Blvd, 2.8 km from the border-crossing is the **Charlotte County Museum** with exhibits concerning the history of 200 years of settlement including the Loyalists and other ties with the USA. There are displays on shipbuilding and lumbering as well as other local industries. The museum is closed on Sunday and is in a substantial house built in 1864.

For a place to eat, there is the straightforward *Carman's Diner* in town on Main St or outside town on the way to St Andrew's, the *Lobster House*.

Also out of town in this direction are a number of motels and, by the corner of Milltown Blvd and King St near the turn-off for Fredericton or St Andrew's, there is a large tourist office.

ST ANDREW'S-BY-THE-SEA

As its name suggests, this is a summer resort of some tradition and gentility. Together with the fine climate and picturesque beauty, St Andrew's has a long, charming and often visible history – it's one of the oldest towns in the province and for a long period was on equal terms with Saint John. Today the wealthy and the less fortunate provincial residents and visitors alike have made a St Andrew's summer both popular and well known.

The aboriginal Indians were the Passamaquoddies, a very few of whom still live in the area.

White settlement began in 1783 after the American Revolution. Many British pioneers wanting to remain loyal, deserted their new towns and set up home in the British territory around the fort in Castine, Maine – a very pretty area.

The British-American border was changed with the war's end and these people once again found themselves on American soil. The tip of the bay across the water was scouted around and agreed upon as being a place of equal beauty. So the pioneers loaded

Native Indian family

up ships and headed out, some even dragging their houses on rafts behind them, and St Andrew's was founded in 1784.

Prosperity came first with shipbuilding and, when that was dying, continued with tourism. Oceanic research is now also an important industry. In the early part of the century, the Canadian Pacific railway owned and ran the Algonquin Hotel, which more or less started St Andrew's as a retreat. Soon moneyed Canadians and Americans were building luxurious summer cottages alongside the 19th-century mansions of the lumber trade and shipbuilding barons. Nearly a hundred of the beautiful houses first built or brought here from Maine are still used and maintained in excellent condition. Though many well-known families keep houses here, the casual visitor is now also important to the town's affairs.

Water St, the main street, is lined with restaurants, souvenir and craft shops and some places to stay. King St is the main cross-street; one block from Water St, Queen St is also important. There are information offices in town and near the junction of highways 1 and 127.

Walking Tour

There are over 200 houses more than a century-old in town, many marked with plaques. A lot of them are real gems. Pick up the walking guide from the tourist office – it gives a map and brief description of 35 particularly interesting places.

Even without the guide, walking around the residential streets with their well-looked after, colourful wooden houses and flower gardens is worthwhile.

Algonquin Hotel

Also worth a look is the classic 1899 resort hotel with its veranda, gardens, tennis courts and pool. Inside, off the lobby, are a couple of places for a drink, be it tea or gin.

Opposite the hotel you may want to take a peek at the English-style thatched-roof cottage called Pansy Patch with its surrounding garden.

Blockhouse Historic Site

The restored wooden guardhouse is the only one left of several that were built here for protection in the War of 1812. As it turned out, they weren't needed. Made of hand-

Whales
The great mammals of the depths, seemingly first became attractive to non-hunters in California then later up the coast in British Columbia, have now become major attractions around Atlantic Canada. Tours out to sea to photograph the awesome creatures depart from ports in places ranging from Quebec's Gulf of St Lawrence to Newfoundland's east coast. From most accounts, the trips are generally successful and well worth the uniformly reasonable cost, averaging $25 for a couple of hours.

Some of the best areas for such a trip are around the Bay of Fundy islands in New Brunswick or from the tip of Digby Neck in Nova Scotia. Also in Nova Scotia the north shore of Cape Breton up around the national park is good. Over in Newfoundland the region of Notre Dame Bay is a 'fruitful' one, with some tours based out of Twillingate. Whales can even be seen up and down the coast out of St John's from where more tours originate.

In the St Lawrence River, Quebec, boat tours operate in the Saguenay River area. Although the huge blue, finback and minke whales are seen here, probably the principal species is the beluga, whose numbers are declining alarmingly due to horrendous pollution levels. Regulations now suggest that no boat approach belugas too closely as they have enough problems to deal with.

So you're much better off in the Bay of Fundy or the open ocean in one of the Atlantic Provinces. Around the Grand Manan region the most commonly seen whales are the fin (or finback), one of the world's largest at 20 metres; the humpback (12 metres); the right (12 metres and less commonly seen); and the minke (8 metres). In addition porpoises and dolphins are plentiful. In this area the best whale-watching begins in early August and lasts through September.

From Westport at the tip of Digby Neck the season seems to begin a little earlier with good sightings reported in late June although by mid-July there are good numbers of all species. ■

---

hewn timber, structures like this were easy to make, practical to live in, and strong enough to withstand most attacks. Down toward the shore is a battery of three cannons. The blockhouse is open daily in summer. Admission is free, and there are some good views through the gun holes on the 2nd floor. The park is at the north-west end of Water St.

Huntsman Marine Science Centre
Out past the Blockhouse and then the Fisheries & Oceans Biological Station is the Huntsman Centre with research facilities and labs. It's part of the Federal Fisheries Research Centre – St Andrew's most important business. Some of Canada's leading marine biologists work here supplying knowledge to international markets.

At the Huntsman Lab there's an aquarium open to the public as well as a small museum. The aquarium displays most specimens found in the local waters including seals. There is a good seaweed display and one pool where the various creatures can be touched, even picked up. It's quite interesting and great for kids too. The centre, west of town on Brandy Cove Rd, is open daily from May to October and admission costs $3.25.

Ross Memorial Museum
The museum is in a neoclassical house of some size on the corner of King and Montague Sts, downtown. It features the furniture, metal objects and decorative arts collections of two of its former owners, Mr & Mrs Ross, who lived in the house until 1945. It's open daily through the summer but afternoons only on Sunday.

Sheriff Andrew House
On the corner of King and Queen Sts is this restored middle-class home dating from 1820 and now redecorated in period style (even the paint colours) and attended by costumed guides. The back garden is also typical of this past era.

Sunbury Shores Arts & Nature Centre
This is a non-profit educational and cultural centre offering instruction in painting, weaving, pottery and other crafts in summer, as well as natural science courses. Various changing exhibits run through the summer.

It is based in Centennial House, an old general store at 139 Water St.

The centre has a nearby conservation area through which there is a walking trail.

Katy's Cove

Just north of town, this sheltered bay is good for swimming.

Whale-Watching

Cline Marine runs very good whale-watching trips from the town wharf. The same outfit also runs out of both Deer and Campobello islands. Because the waters best for whale-watching are further out in the bay, the trip from St Andrew's is longer and therefore more expensive. A six-hour trip costs $36 and goes in search of humpback, right, fin and minke whales – sightings are generally assured. There's also a shorter tour around the shoreline in more sheltered waters and a sunset cruise. Whichever trip you chose, take plenty of warm clothes and make reservations a day ahead.

Minister's Island

Minister's Island is accessible at low tide, even by car, when you can drive on the hard-packed sea floor. A few hours later this route is under three metres of water.

Atlantic Salmon Centre

North of town about six km, in the village of Chamccook, the Salmon Centre tells the story of Atlantic salmon, prized by anglers and gourmets. Displays, including live fish, show the fish's history and life cycle. It's open from May to September daily, 10 am to 6 pm and is designed to encourage knowledge and preservation of this fine creature.

Dochet's Island

In the Saint Croix River, eight km from town on Highway 127, is Dochet's Island with a national historic site marking the place where in 1604 French explorer Samuel de Champlain spent his first winter in North America. The island itself is inaccessible without a boat but looking at it from the shore makes a good, quick sunset drive. There is

also a plaque on the Maine shoreline across from the island.

Places to Stay

As a small but busy resort town St Andrew's has plentiful accommodation and there is quite a range in the type and price of places to stay including many guesthouses and B&Bs.

Camping There are several places to choose from. At the far east end of town on Indian Point is *Kiwanis Passamaquoddy Park* for tents and trailers.

Near St Andrew's are two provincial parks with beaches. *Oak Bay* is eight km east of St Stephen, north of St Andrew's. There is a protected bay where the water warms up nicely for ocean swimming and there's shoreline to explore at low tide. Further afield is *New River Beach*, a little more than halfway to Saint John. They have 115 camping spots.

B&Bs & Hotels The central *Heritage Guesthouse* (☎ 529-3875) is a modest but very appealing place at 100 Queen St that has the added benefit of having been around for years. It is also one of the least expensive places with singles/doubles $25/30; breakfasts are offered.

With three rooms at 159 Water St is the *McNabb House* (☎ 529-4368) which charges the same rates. A few doors down at the water's edge is *Snore by the Shore* (☎ 529-4255) which would deserve mention for its name even if it wasn't the decent place it is. Rates are a little higher with singles/doubles from $30/40 with breakfast included.

Also along the main street near the town wharf is *Smuggler's Village* with waterfront efficiencies (some with balconies overlooking the bay) rented by the day, week or month.

Best Western now runs the *Shiretown Inn* (☎ 529-8877) which has been a hotel since 1881 and now is a blend of the old with modern conveniences and a dining room. It's right in the middle of town and is a little pricier at singles/doubles $60/70.

The classic Canadian-Pacific-run *Algonquin Hotel* has rooms that start at $110 so you pay for the charm of a former era and the amenities.

Places to Eat

For decent, plain and cheap food there is the *Copper Grill* on Water St. It's closed on Sunday, and is otherwise open from 7 am to 7 pm daily.

Right in the middle of town with a pleasant patio on the water, the *Smuggler's Wharf* has a bit of everything. Also with outdoor tables, the *Brass Bull* has pub meals at around $6. The *Shiretown Inn* dating from 1881 is a very well-kept place and has more expensive seafood meals. Perhaps the best meals are at the cosy *L'Europe*, a German-style white stucco place on King St which is open for dinner only. Lobster is the main dish at the *Lighthouse Restaurant*. Lastly, through the summer, the *Algonquin Hotel* has a deluxe Sunday brunch for $16.

Getting There & Around

SMT bus line connects St Andrew's and the surrounding area with Saint John with one bus trip daily which takes 1½ hours.

The Algonquin Hotel runs a more expensive service which they call the airport shuttle to downtown Saint John and its airport for $30 one-way, less if you're a guest at the hotel.

HMS Transportation at 260 Water St rents cars and runs tours. The Carriage House store at 153 Water St has bicycles for rent.

ST GEORGE

St George, 40 km east of St Stephen on the Magaguadavic River, is a small town with 1500 residents. The river gorge and falls near the tourist office between the highway and the centre of town are a local beauty spot. A salmon ladder has been built to facilitate the fish's upstream struggle over the gorge and dam and they can be seen jumping its stages in summer.

In town the Presbyterian kirk from 1790 is one of the oldest churches in Canada. The Protestant cemetery at St Mark's Anglican Church is of similar vintage. O'Neill House at 7 Main St was built in 1835 and is now an antique shop and café. The restaurant is a good little place for breakfast or lunch and for sampling the town water – said to be the best in the country. It comes from deep artesian wells and is indeed absolutely delicious.

Across the street is the *Town House* B&B (☎ 755-3476), an attractive large home dating from the 1840s with rooms at singles/doubles $35/45.

Another good place to stay is the *Fundy Lodge Motel* (☎ 755-2963) about 15 minutes' driving west of town. It has a pretty location on the water; the rooms are entirely lined with pine, inside and out. It's not really cheap at $55 a double but that's about par for the area. It's better than most places and includes a help-yourself continental breakfast with fresh muffins.

There is freshwater swimming north of town on sandy beaches at Lake Utopia.

FUNDY ISLES
Deer Island

From Letete on the mainland south of St George a free 25-minute government ferry runs to Deer Island, the closest of the three main Fundy Isles. Ferries run every half hour. Deer Island has, as it has been for centuries, a modest fishing community with lobster as the main catch. Around the island are half a dozen wharves and the net systems used in aquaculture or fish farming. There is not a lot to see on the island as it is primarily wooded and residential. Roads run down each side toward Campobello Island.

There is a tourist booth at the ferry landing. At **Northern Harbour** is a huge, it could well be the world's largest, lobster pound which sometimes during the year contains 400 kg of live lobster. In **Lambertville** is the *Darby Hill B&B* (☎ 747-2069) 800 metres from the ferry landing. A double costs $30.

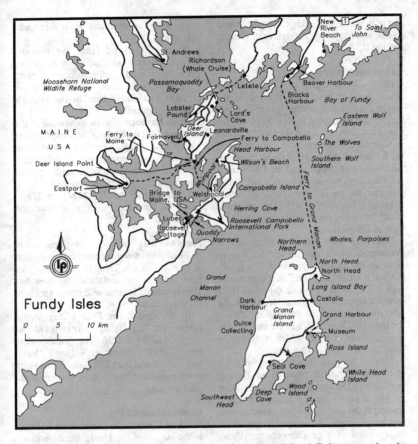

Fundy Isles

0   5   10 km

Cline Marine Charters (☎ 747-2023) in Richardson on Deer Island offers whale-watching tours for $10 an hour. There's a minimum of three hours, which is standard.

At **Leonardville**, halfway down the island is *Camick's* (☎ 747-2929) where you can rent a camper van for $20 a night with crockery and bedding included.

At the other end of the island is 16-hectare **Deer Island Point Park** where whales and **Old Sow** (the world's second largest natural tidal whirlpool) can be seen offshore. Nearby in **Fairhaven** is the *49th Parallel Restaurant & Motel*, the only sit-down place to eat on Deer Island.

From **Deer Island Point** two privately operated ferries leave, one for Campobello Island which is connected by bridge to the US mainland and one to Eastport, Maine. The ferry to Campobello costs $2 per person, from $10 to a maximum of $15 per car. It's basically a floating dock strapped to an old fishing boat. It's a very scenic 45-minute trip past numerous islands and Eastport, an attractive seaside town where you may see freighters moored. During the summer there are six trips a day between 9 am and 6.15 pm.

For Eastport the ferry leaves every hour on the hour and is a bit cheaper than the one for Campobello. Either ferry can be used as part of the circular Quoddy Loop tour around Passamaquoddy Bay through both Canada and the USA.

Campobello Island

Campobello is a gently scenic, tranquil island that has long been enjoyed by the wealthy as a summer retreat. Due to its accessibility and proximity to New England, the island has always been at least as American as Canadian. Like many moneyed families, the Roosevelts bought property in this peaceful coastal area at the end of the 1800s and it is for this that the island is best known. Today you can see the 34-room 'cottage' where Franklin D Roosevelt (1905-21) grew up and which he visited periodically throughout his time as US president.

The ferry from Deer Island arrives at **Welshpool** which is pretty well halfway up or down the 16-km-long island. The southern half is almost all park. The southernmost region is taken up by the 1200-hectare **Roosevelt Campobello International Park**, the principal island tourist destination. This is the site of the Roosevelt's house and a reception-information centre which is open daily from late May to mid-October.

Most of the park, however, has been left in its natural state to preserve the flora & fauna which Delano appreciated so much. A couple of gravel roads meander through it leading to the shoreline, beaches and numerous nature trails. It's a surprisingly wild, little-visited area of Campobello Island. Deer and coyote are among the mammals in the park and seals can sometimes be seen offshore on the ledges near **Lower Duck Pond**. Among the many birds along the shoreline are eagles, ospreys and loons.

Below the park at the southern tip of the island a bridge connects with Lubec, Maine. On the Campobello side is a tourist office with a moneychanging desk.

Along the international park's northern boundary is New Brunswick's **Herring Cove Provincial Park**. Here too, are several seaside walking trails and paths as well as a campground and a picnic area on an arching 1.6-km-long beach. It makes a fine, picturesque place for lunch and again is remarkably quiet.

Going up island from Welshpool, **Wilson's Beach** has a large pier where fish can be bought and a sardine-processing plant with an adjacent store. There are various services and shops here in the island's biggest community.

Head Harbour with its lighthouse at the northern tip of the island is the second busiest visitor spot. Whales can often be seen from here and many people put in some time sitting on the rocky shoreline with a pair of binoculars enjoying the sea breezes.

Cline Marine (☎ 752-2424) on Lighthouse Rd has a three-hour whale-watching boat cruise.

Places to Stay There are a few places to stay in Welshpool as well as some cabins for rent at Wilson's Beach. Things tend to be pricier here than on the mainland: the area has always catered to those who needn't account for every shekel.

In Welshpool the *Friar's Bay Motor Lodge* (☎ 752-2056) is reasonable at singles/doubles $30/36. The *Quoddy View* (☎ 752-2981) cabins at Wilson's Beach aren't a bad deal from $38 a double and some more expensive ones where you could do your cooking.

Grand Manan Island

South of Campobello Island, Grand Manan is the largest of the Fundy Isles – a quiet, peaceful lovely relaxed and interesting island I can't say enough about. It's a marvellous place to spend a couple of days or a week away from the rest of the world observing nature on the land, at sea, and where the two meet. As the woman at the campground office told me, 'people like Grand Manan because you can park anywhere you want and you can walk anywhere you want'. And that, perfectly accurately sums it up.

There is some spectacular coastal topography, excellent bird-watching, fine hiking trails, sandy beaches and a series of small fishing villages along the island which is approximately 30 km long.

On one side are ancient rock formations estimated to be billions of years old. On the other side, due to an underwater volcano, are volcanic deposits *only* 16 million years old, a phenomenon which draws many geologists.

In 1831, James Audubon first documented the many birds which frequented the island. About 312 species live or pass by each year, including puffins and Arctic terns so birdwatchers come in number as well. If possible try to catch the puffins' fishing act.

Offshore it's not uncommon to see whales feeding on the abundant herring and mackerel. Whale species include the humpback, finback (rorqual), minke and pothead. Tours are offered in several places.

Despite all this, the relative isolation and low-key development mean there are no crowds and little obvious commercialisation. It's a good place for cyclists and it's not uncommon to see riders along the roads.

One thing of possible interest to sample on the island is the dulce, an edible seaweed, for which Grand Manan is renowned. It's a very popular snack food around the Maritime or Atlantic Provinces and most of it, and the best, say connoisseurs, comes from this island. It's sold around the island mostly from people's homes, watch for signs.

North Head The ferry terminal is at North Head. There are more business establishments in this village than elsewhere on the island but it is still small enough to walk through.

There are a few craft and tourist-oriented stores along the main drag but of most interest is the Whale & Sea Bird Research Station with a lot of good information on the marine life of the surrounding waters. Exhibits include skeletons and photographs and there are some books on whales and the island in general.

Ocean Search offers a different sort of whale-watching tour. Firstly they use a sailing schooner, secondly a marine biologist is on board to answer questions and, thirdly at least some of the trips include an evening lecture. These up-market, more in-depth

tours are, naturally, more expensive than others but will be of interest to keen whale-watchers.

North End Some of the most popular of the numerous short walking trails around the island are in this area, particularly the one to 'Hole in the Wall', an unusual rock formation. It begins north of North Head at the site of the old airport and leads through the woods to a natural arch at the cliff's edge. There are also great views of the coast from this vantage point.

Highly recommended is the somewhat pulse-quickening (especially in the fog) trail and suspension bridge out to the lighthouse at Swallow Tail on a narrow cliff-edged promontory. Further up-island, the rock formations (reaching 80 metres high at Seven Days' Work) and the lighthouse at Northern Head are also fine walks with seaside vistas. From either of the lighthouses whales may be seen most easily on calm days.

Grand Harbour At Grand Harbour is the Grand Manan Museum open from mid-June to 30 September daily but only during the afternoon on Sunday.

It has a marine section, displays on the island's geology, antiques and reminders of the Loyalist days but the highlight is the stuffed-bird collection with examples of species seen on the island.

US writer Willa Cather worked here for many years and some of her personal belongings, including a typewriter are still here. There is also a good book selection, one on trails around the island, and bird checklists are available too. Admission is $2.

Dark Harbour This, the only village on the west side of the island, is the centre of the dulce industry. The seaweed is hand-picked at low tide along the shores of the island. It is then dried in the sun and is ready to eat.

A trail to Little Dark Harbour provides fabulous coastal views.

Ross Island Uninhabited Ross Island can be visited at low tide. Or rather you can walk there at low tide, spend about four hours exploring the place, and then return before the tide gets too high. The island was the site of the first settlement on Grand Manan established when Loyalists arrived from America in 1784.

Seal Cove

In this small community is Sea Watch Tours, one of the island's principal whale and bird-watching boat-tour companies. They've been around for 25 years and know the waters. Most of the trips are long (around six hours) so take a lunch, a gravol antimotion sickness pill and a warm sweater. Apart from whales there are seals and porpoises to see, a variety of sea birds and the coastal landscapes. Whale-watching begins in early August and continues through September.

Down at the docks the tasty island-smoked herring can be bought at Helshiron Sundries, a small all-purpose store. Smoked fish is also available at a couple of other places around the island. You could try MG Fisheries in Grand Harbour.

Southwest Head

The walk to the lighthouse and beyond along the edge of the 180-metre cliffs here should not be missed. With the sun out and ocean air drifting in bending the flowers in high summer – thistles, butter-cups, daisies – time can be made to stand still for part of an afternoon.

Places to Stay

The good news just doesn't stop here. There are over two dozen places to stay and the prices tend to be low. They're not slick and glitzy but homey and comfortable places; many of the cabins have a really unpretentious country feel to them.

The *Cross Tree Guesthouse* (☎ 662-8263) in Seal Cove has just three rooms and charges from $25/35 for singles/doubles. Also in Seal Cove are the *Spray Kist Cottages* (☎ 662-8640), run by Mrs M Laffoley. Her four units cost from $45 per day for a double or $225 per week. Nearby are the *Cliff Side Cabins* (☎ 662-3133), five unique places scattered amongst the trees in a superb setting.

There are several places at North Head. The *Fundy Folly Guesthouse* (☎ 662-3731) is a good-value B&B at singles/doubles $25/36 with a full breakfast. The beach is within walking distance of the century-old house.

Lastly, at Grand Harbour Mr & Mrs Hobbs run the *Grand Harbour Inn* (☎ 662-8681) where singles/doubles cost $32/38, including a continental breakfast.

There are many other places to stay on the island, most are very reasonably priced. Weekly rates for the various cabins and cottages are around $250.

For camping the only place is the good *Anchorage Provincial Park* where, even though it's not large, they never turn anyone

Seal pup

away. Most people are tenters and, if you arrive early, there are some nice sites with trees edged into the woods, otherwise, you'll be out in the field where it can be very breezy. You should guy-wire out the tent. There is a kitchen shelter for rainy days, a playground and a very long sandy beach.

Places to Eat Restaurants are not overly numerous on the island but there are enough casual, friendly and reasonably priced places.

North Head village has the widest selection with a couple of takeout places, two or three regular restaurants and a finer dining room in the *Marathon Inn*. The *Griff-Inn*, good for breakfasts and light lunches, is the kind of place where the island's cop comes in for a coffee.

There are two more places in Grand Harbour halfway up the island, one serves lobster.

In Seal Cove is the small, plain *Water's Edge* which is not on the water but does have good food. There are burgers and pizza and other basic Italian dishes such as lasagna for $9 which are all homemade or there are more costly full-course fish dinners. A speciality is the lobster trap, a puff-pastry shell stuffed with chunks of lobster and covered in a creamy garlic sauce.

Getting There & Away The ferry is from Blacks Harbour, south of St George on the mainland. Actually, there are two ferries, one old and one new. The *Grand Manan V* which began sailing in July 1990 is larger and quicker, knocking half an hour off the two-hour trip. Both ferries have snack bars, outdoor decks, inside chairs, and are operated by the government. The trip is a very agreeable little cruise with good scenery particularly near Blacks Harbour; you'll drift by various islands and bays. Seeing a whale is not uncommon and on my recent trip I saw several groups of porpoises.

In summer, there are six trips on weekdays and four on Sunday, but there are still usually queues if you have a car and there is no reservation system. For walk-ons, bicycles,

etc there is no problem. Trips are more frequent from June to early September. There are advance-ticket sales for the trip back but only for the first trip of the day and tickets must be bought at North Head on Grand Manan Island.

For either boat the return fare is $6 per adult, less for children and $18 for a car. For camper vans and trailers you pay according to their length.

Getting Around Three operators run boat tours for viewing whales, birds and the dramatic coastlines. For details see the previous text.

In Grand Harbour, Avis Green Taxi Service offers sight-seeing tours of the island or you can arrange to be taken anywhere for hiking, etc.

White Head Island

White Head Island, connected by car ferry from Ingalls Head, is the only other inhabited island in the archipelago. A few families make a living fishing. There are six of the 20-minute ferry services daily. The island has a good long sandy beach, another lighthouse to visit and some plant and animal life not found on Grand Manan. Note that the last ferry back leaves at 4.30 pm.

Machias Seal Island

Sixteen km south-west of Grand Manan is this small island bird sanctuary. Unlike at many other sanctuaries visitors are permitted on shore here accompanied by a wildlife officer and the number is limited to 25 people per day. The feathered residents include terns, puffins, razorback and several others in lesser numbers. Sea Watch offers these trips too, if the seas aren't rough.

BEAVER HARBOUR

If the islands cannot be visited but you still want a chance to see some whales, check out Rawja Tours in the village of Beaver Harbour back on the mainland. There are two two-hour trips daily out to The Wolves, five small islands, around which whales feed.

NEW RIVER BEACH

Between St Stephen and Saint John, about 35 km from the latter, New River is one of the best beaches along the Fundy Shore and there is camping.

SAINT JOHN

Historic Saint John (whose name is always spelt out in full, never abbreviated, to avoid confusion with St John's, Newfoundland) is the province's largest city and leading industrial centre. Sitting at the mouth of the Saint John River, on the bay, it is also a major port able to remain open all year.

In the past 10 years the city has undergone considerable refurbishing (a process still continuing) and the downtown area is much improved.

As well as the restorations, Saint John has a proud past. Known as 'the Loyalist City', it is the oldest incorporated city in the country. You'll see evidence of this Loyalist background everywhere. The town museum dating from 1842 is Canada's oldest.

The Maliseet Indians were here when the British and French began squabbling about furs. Samuel de Champlain had landed in 1604, soon a fort was built and was changing hands between these two old world enemies. However, the area remained pretty much a wilderness until 1755, when about 4000 British people loyal to the homeland and fleeing the revolutionary USA arrived.

They built up and incorporated the city in 1785. It soon became a prosperous shipbuilding centre. Though now using iron and steel rather than wood, shipbuilding is still a major industry in town. The dry dock is one of the world's largest. Fishing is also important.

Fog very often blankets the city, particularly in the mornings. This helps to keep the area cool, even when the rest of the province is sweating it out in midsummer.

Orientation

Saint John sits on the waterfront at the mouth of the Saint John River. The downtown area lies on a square peninsula jutting into the bay east of the river.

King Square, a small, pleasant park, marks the centre of town. Its pathways are placed to duplicate the pattern of the Union Jack flag. To the east of the square, across the street, is the Loyalist burial ground with graves dating from 1784.

Going west from the square are the principal downtown streets – Charlotte, Germain, Canterbury and Prince William – running south off King St. One block further west to Water St takes you to the Saint John Harbour. Here is the newly developed waterfront area and market square with shops, restaurants and the Trade & Convention Centre.

Across the street from the King Square is City Hall and across the inlet there are container terminals and the ferry landing for Digby, Nova Scotia.

South from King Square a few blocks is Queen Square, laid out in the same fashion. On Courtenay Bay, to the east, you'll find the dry dock and the shipbuilding yards.

North of town is large Rockwood Park, a sports and recreation area with a campground.

The famous Reversing Falls are west of town where the river flows into the harbour, under the bridge on Highway 100.

Further west going out of town is a mostly residential and industrial district built on rolling hills overlooking the river and the Bay of Fundy.

Information

The Visitor & Convention Bureau (☎ 658-2990), on the 11th floor of City Hall at the foot of King St, has an information desk and is open all year.

Down at the waterfront in summer there's the more convenient tourist office in an old one-room schoolhouse which still has a couple of the original desks.

There is another information office at the Reversing Falls Visitor Centre (☎ 658-2937) at the falls. It's in Saint John West on Highway 100, and is open from mid-May to

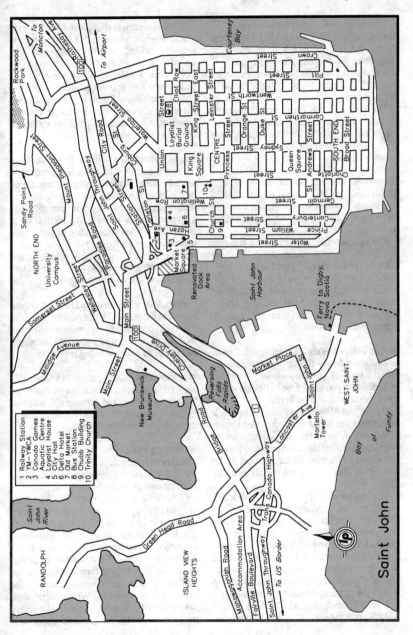

1 Railway Station
2 YM-YWCA
3 Canada Games Aquatic Centre
4 Loyalist House
5 City Hall
6 Delta Hotel
7 Old Market
8 Bus Station
9 Chubb Building
10 Trinity Church

Saint John

mid-October. A fourth alternative for information (☎ 658-2940) is on Highway 1 (the Saint John Throughway) at Island View Heights in Saint John West. It's handy if you're coming from St Stephen or Fredericton and is open from 1 June to early September.

The post office is on Prince William St between Princess and Duke Sts. At any of the tourist booths ask for the free parking pass with a list of where it can be used in the downtown area.

Downtown Historic Walks

The central city and surrounding residential side streets have some very fine architecture and a stroll along the impressive façades is well worthwhile.

The tourist office produces three separate self-guided walking tours: Prince William Walk of the commercial buildings, the Loyalist Trail which points out places of Loyalist origin and a Victorian Stroll highlighting many of the houses from the late 1800s. Some of the churches are particularly impressive.

Prince William Walk This self-guided walk around town details the heritage commercial architecture of the downtown area and includes many of those fine buildings you'll stroll by on the Loyalist Trail.

By the mid-19th century Saint John was a prosperous industrial town, the third largest in the world, important particularly for its wooden shipbuilding enterprises. In 1877 two-thirds of the city, including most of the mercantile district, was reduced to ashes by fire.

The replacements, primarily of brick and stone, are now considered some of the country's best examples of 19th-century commercial architecture. This walk takes in much of a preserved 20-block area.

Tree-lined Germain St with its rows of three-storey brick houses and, at No 164, the United Church of St Andrew and St David strikes me as being particularly attractive.

Trinity Church built on Charlotte St near King Square between King and Princess Sts

in 1880 is a remarkable piece of work with much stained glass and a fine detailed wooden ceiling. A very congenial and knowledgeable guide is on hand to lead visitors around offering interesting bits of history and pointing out details.

Historic Trinity Royal is the area around the corner of Prince William and Princess Sts where many businesses have set up in the restored old buildings.

Loyalist Trail The British Loyalists were really the founders of Saint John, turning a fort site into Canada's first legal city. Some of the early landmarks are still visible and interesting. The walking-tour pamphlet has a map and details of the best historical spots in the downtown area. Many of the places mentioned are no longer there; you just see the site of such and such – which is not exactly helpful unless you have a very active imagination – but some things do remain to see or visit.

Also, following the route is a good excuse to look at the many fine old buildings around the city, contrasting effectively with the modern ones. A good many old buildings have been or are now being restored.

Victorian Stroll Taking about 1½ hours, this walk takes in the area south and west of King Square away from the commercial area and includes primarily Victorian houses, many of them very substantial dwellings.

Reversing Falls

The Bay of Fundy tides and their effects (see the Tides section following Moncton) are unquestionably an interesting and predominant regional characteristic. The falls here are part of that phenomenon and are not only the biggest attraction in the city but one of the best known sites in the province. However, 'reversing falls' has to be called a misnomer at best and at worst a bit of a joke. When the high Bay of Fundy tides rise, the current in the river reverses, causing the water to flow upstream. When the tides go down, the water flows in the normal way. By no stretch of the imagination could this trickle be termed falls and it always strikes me, at least, as somewhat incredible to see so many people crowding to look at this non-attraction. Since you'll probably go anyway, at least it's free and the tourist office here is worthwhile and helpful. At various points around the bay, you can see the tides to better advantage.

Loyalist House
On the corner of Union and Germain Sts, the Loyalist House dating from 1810 is the city's oldest unchanged building. The Georgian-style place is now a museum depicting the Loyalist period and contains some fine carpentry. This attraction is open every day in midsummer, weekdays only in June and September. Hours are from 10 am to 5 pm and admission is $2.

Loyalist Burial Ground
This interesting site is just off King Square, in a park-style setting. Here you can see tombstones, dating from as early as 1784, slowly eroding and falling to the earth.

Chubb Building
Back in town on the corner of Prince William and Princess Sts is the Chubb Building erected in the late 1800s. Chubb, the owner, had likenesses of all his children and half the town's politicians placed on the façade in little rosettes. Chubb himself is immortalised as a grinning gargoyle.

Old Courthouse
The County Court of 1829 is noted for its spiralling stone staircase, rising three storeys without any support.

Old Market
On Market St between Germain and Charlotte Sts is the colourful, interesting market that's been held in the same building since 1876. Inside the door is a guest book to sign, a pamphlet with historical information and a tape-recorded commentary. Check out the heavy old roof beams with the shipbuilding design influences. Unfortunately, for more than a century time has taken its toll, and

major work is now required on the roof to keep the market going. The weight of winter's snow is the main problem.

Inside, the atmosphere is friendly but busy. Apart from fresh produce stalls, most active on Friday and Saturday when local farmers come in, there are several good eating spots, a deli and some antiques for sale. Good bread is sold; dulce and cheap cooked lobster are available.

Market Square
At the foot of King St is the redeveloped waterfront area known as Market Square. It offers views over the working dockyards and container terminals along the river. In summer there is an information booth here.

In the adjacent complex is a major hotel, a convention centre and a new shopping and restaurant centre. The indoor mall is one of the best designed I've seen and is actually pleasant to be in. Someone told me there are 35 restaurants in here, and that count must be close. There is also a library, art gallery, craft shop and benches for just sitting. An enclosed walkway connects with City Hall across the street.

Many of the restaurants are along the outside wall and have patios under umbrellas in summer.

Barbour's General Store
This is a renovated old general store near Market Square. Inside it's packed with the kind of merchandise sold 100 years ago, including old stoves, drugs, hardware and candy. Most items are not for sale. Beside it the Old School is now a tourist information kiosk.

City Hall
On King St near Prince William St in the modern section of town is the new City Hall. On the top floor is an observation deck with a good view (on fog-free days) of the city and harbour. Go to the 15th floor and you'll find the 'deck', it's an unused office.

New Brunswick Museum
West of town at 277 Douglas Ave, near the

Reversing Falls, this is an eclectic place with an odd collection of things – some good, some not. There's a very good section on marine wildlife, with some aquariums and information on lobsters (you may as well know about what you'll probably be eating). There's a collection of stuffed animals and birds, mostly from New Brunswick. The displays on the marine history of Saint John are good, with many excellent models of old sailing ships.

In the other half of the museum is an art gallery which includes local contemporary work. Museum hours are from 10 am to 5 pm daily from May to September. It's closed on Monday for the rest of the year. Admission is $2, students 50 cents.

Carleton Martello Tower

This national historic site is just off Lancaster Ave, which leads to the Digby ferry terminal. Look for the signs at street intersections. A Martello tower is a circular two-storey stone coastal fortification. They were built in England and Ireland at the beginning of the 19th century. In North America the British built 16 of these during the early 1800s. You can see others in Halifax and Quebec City. There are guides to show you around, answer questions, and give you some background information. Go when there's no fog because the view from the high promontory is good. The tower is open daily from 1 June to 31 September, free.

Partridge Island

Out in the bay, Partridge Island was once a quarantine station for the Irish who were arriving after fleeing the homeland's potato famine. There are the remnants of some houses and a few old gun placements on the island. An effort is being made to turn the island into either a national or provincial historic site but little has been done so far. In summer, 2½-hour boat tours are offered out to the island leaving from the Market Square wharf but service seems sporadic. The boat doesn't go (a situation that appears to arise fairly frequently) unless enough people

show up. Ask about the boat trip at the tourist office down by the wharf.

Telephone Pioneers' Museum

This museum, in the lobby of 1 Brunswick Square, is small but good with an extensive collection of telephone equipment from the earliest models to the latest technology. It's open Monday to Friday from 10 am to 4 pm and is free. To find it, enter the mall off Germain St opposite Reggie's Restaurant.

Jewish Historical Museum

Now a diminishing ethnic group in the city, the Jewish community was a sizeable and vital one from the 1920s until the 1960s; the museum is designed to preserve this heritage. There is a collection of articles used in the faith at home and in the synagogue and an outline of local Jewish history. The museum, at 29 Wellington Row, is open every day except Saturday in summer but is closed on weekends during the rest of the year.

Aitken Bicentennial Exhibition Centre

The centre is at 20 Hazen Ave near the YM-YWCA in an attractive rounded sandstone building dating from 1904. It was built as a library and has five galleries which offer changing displays on art, science and technology. Many of the building's original features remain. Exhibits range from satellite images to wood sculptures to superconductivity to endangered species. In summer the centre is open daily, otherwise it's closed on Monday.

Rockwood Park

On the north-east edge of the city centre, the park consists of 800 hectares of recreational facilities, picnic spots, paths through the woods and small lakes and swimming. There's also the recently remodelled zoo.

Cherry Brook Zoo

The zoo has about 25 species of animals, including many endangered species. It's at the far northern edge of Rockwood Park in the north of the city and opens every day from 10 am to dusk. Admission costs $3, students $2.

Lakewood Reservoir Park
On Route 111 south-east of town (15 minutes by car) there is swimming and a sandy beach at Lakewood Reservoir Park.

Organised Tours
The Saint John Transit Commission offers three-hour bus tours around the city during the summer months. Go to Barbour's General Store at Market Square for departures and tickets; there's one tour daily early in the afternoon. In September and October there are fall (autumn) foliage tours up the valley, lunch is included. This part of New Brunswick is one of the best places in Canada for appreciating the leaves changing colour.

There are no longer any harbour boat tours but a pleasant day's outing is to take the boat over to Partridge Island (see the previous Partridge Island section).

Festivals
Loyalist Days, a five-day event held annually during the third week of July, celebrates the city's Loyalist background. Featured are a re-creation of the first arrival, period costumes, parades, arts and crafts, music recitals, lots of food and performances. It all ends with fireworks, as do many Canadian events, on the last night of the festival.

In 1985 the city marked its 200th birthday as Canada's first incorporated city and also hosted the Canada Games – a sort of mini-Olympics involving young Canadian athletes. A swimming pool complex – the Aquatic Centre – was completed near City Hall for the Games.

Places to Stay
Camping Just north of Rothesay Ave, north of the downtown area, is huge *Rockwood Park* with its small lakes, picnic area, golf course and part of the University of New Brunswick's campus. It's an excellent place to camp with pleasant sites, a view of the city. It could not be more convenient, close to the

downtown area and the main roads out of the city. If only more cities had something similar!

The rate for tenters is $9, less for longer stays and the ticket office is also a mini tourist centre.

Hostels The *Youth Hostel* (☎ 634-7720) in Saint John is in the now amalgamated YM-YWCA at 19-25 Hazen Ave. It actually isn't a hostel at all, rather hostel members can get a small discount off the regular rates which fortunately are quite low. The bad news is the place is only for men. It is central and clean with private single rooms regularly priced at $21 or $69 per week. You can use facilities like the pool, common room and snack bar with its cheap food. There are 30 rooms; you get your own room key and the lobby is always open.

For women, there's the *Salvation Army Evangeline Home* (☎ 634-1950) at 260 Prince William St. They charge $12 a night, $6 for students.

Tourist Homes & Inns Manawagonish Rd seems to be accommodation street in Saint John. Along this road are guesthouses, B&Bs, cabins and motels charging varying but mostly reasonable prices. It's west of the downtown area, parallel to and north of highways 1 and 100. City buses go into town from Manawagonish Rd.

One place to try is the *Tartan B&B* (☎ 672-2592) with singles/doubles $25/35. The address is at 968 Manawagonish Rd.

Not too far away, at 238 Charlotte St, is the *Five Chimneys B&B* (☎ 635-1888) which charges singles/doubles $40/45. Right in town at 96 Leinster St, a short walk from King Square in a turn-of-the-century three-storey building, the *Earl of Leinster Inn* (☎ 693-3462) is definitely worth checking out. There are only three rooms, all very comfortable and a good breakfast is included for $40 a single or double. The evening meal is also offered at extra cost and there are laundry facilities. Although it's a bit out of the centre at 280 Douglas Ave opposite the New Brunswick Museum near Reversing Falls, the

Travis House (☎ 693-0475) is good value. It's a huge old Victorian-looking place dating from 1904. Rooms cost from singles/doubles $30/40, including a full continental breakfast.

Hotels There are actually few hotels in Saint John and they tend to be in the upper-price brackets. The *Hilton* is right in the centre of things in Market Square. The *Holiday Inn* is also central at 350 Haymarket Square and is about $30 cheaper at $70 a single. *Keddy's Fort Howe* (☎ 657-7320) is more reasonably priced and really quite good. It's on the corner of Main and Portland Sts.

Motels There are also many motels along Manawagonish Rd; they tend to be less expensive than average.

Fundy Ayre Motel (☎ 672-1125), at No 1711, is quite small with only 11 units at just $40 a single or double with one bed. As with other motels, it's more if two people use two beds.

Further out is the *Anchor Light Motel* (☎ 672-9972). Singles/doubles are $25/28. Further along, still going westward, the road becomes Ocean West Way. Here at No 2121 you'll find the *Regent Motel* (☎ 672-8273). They have 10 rooms for $35 a single or double.

Other places in the area range up to $45 with many charging around $35. These offer more extras and may be newer and/or larger.

On the other side of town is a strip of motels along Rothesay Ave on Highway 100, which leads out to Moncton. It's north-east of the city centre but a little closer to it than Manawagonish Rd. Most of the places here are more expensive.

The small *Bonanza Motel* (☎ 633-1710), 594 Rothesay Ave, is OK at singles/doubles $23/25.

Places to Eat

The eating situation in this town has changed tremendously since my initial visit (perhaps it was my comments in the first edition that did it, ha! ha!). Taking most of the credit is Market Square, which single-handedly has added more than two dozen places to munch at. So we'll start there.

Grannan's, not strictly budget but not expensive either, has a good selection of seafood with steaks too. They have a bar downstairs. *Keystone Kelly's* is less expensive and more casual with various finger foods at $8 to $12 for a meal. On the lower level with tables and chairs outside are a couple of other places which stay open for drinks later in the evening.

Upstairs on the second level, is *Pizza Delight* a popular inexpensive Atlantic Canada chain which offers some other Italian fare too.

In the *Food Hall* at one corner of the main floor are many fast-food places with shared tables. They offer cheap food including chicken, donner kebabs, submarine sandwiches and doughnuts. A plate of rice with vegetables and chicken from the Chinese place is $4.50, including green tea. Also look for the place offering blueberries presented in every imaginable way.

Reggie's Restaurant, at 69 Germain St near the Loyalist House, is a classic downtown no-nonsense diner which specialises in smoked meat from Ben's, a famous Montreal deli. Also on the menu are lobster rolls – a local favourite – and chowders at $3. It's a good, casual place open at 6 am for breakfast specials. *Reggie's II* is a smaller outlet at the YMCA.

Marco Polo's, formerly the old time Partown Tavern has set up at 74 Prince William St near the corner of Church St. Though new, it still attracts the working crowd and offers cheap steaks, tavern meals and draught beer – good value.

Woolworth's, beside the market, offers cheap, basic meals from $4. *Diana*, across from the park between Union and King Sts, is the standard basic with cheap breakfasts and lunch specials.

The market is a good place to be when hunger strikes. Aside from the produce there are a few small restaurants or takeout counters. *Jeremiah's* is a deli and sandwich bar. On the east side is a salad-to-go booth with lots of cheeses too.

Incredible Edibles, at 42 Princess St in the Brodie Building, is a nice spot for a bit of a splurge. It offers pastas, curries, omelettes and local desserts such as blueberry cobbler – a fruit-based dessert with a crispy cake crust, usually topped with milk or cream. Yummy!

Nearby at 48 Princess St, the *Earl of Sandwich* is an inexpensive and quick lunch place.

For Italian food there's *Vito's* on Hazen Ave on the corner of Union St. It's a bit pricey at around $11, but on Monday nights there's as much spaghetti as you can eat for $4.50.

Lastly, the *Bamboo East* at 136 Princess St offers Chinese food. The weekday buffet is $7.95, weekend dinner buffet $9.95 and there's *dim sum* at noon on Sunday. Food is available à la carte, but it's not cheap.

La Belle Vie on Lancaster Ave by the Reversing Falls is a more elegant choice with a fairly expensive continental menu.

Entertainment

Market Square also has a number of nightspots some with live music and dancing; several places here have outdoor sections.

The *Harbour View Lounge* in the same complex, but near the Hilton Hotel in the Trade & Convention Building, is a place for a quiet drink.

Club 74, on the corner of Price William and Church Sts, has live blues and rock.

Getting There & Away

Air Air Canada (☎ 693-1231) to Montreal costs $223. Canadian (☎ 657-3860) flies to St John's, Newfoundland for $303.

Bus SMT lines is the provincial carrier. It connects with Voyageur lines in Edmundston for Quebec destinations and Acadia lines in Nova Scotia. The station (☎ 693-6500) is at 300 Union St on the corner of Carmarthen St, a five-minute walk from the town centre.

Buses to Quebec City depart at 10.30 am and 3.45 pm for $56, to Fredericton there's a service twice daily which costs $12.25. The bus to Moncton leaves at 5 pm and the fare is $16. For Cape Tormentine (to Prince Edward Island), go to Moncton and transfer from there.

Train The VIA Rail station (☎ 642-2916 or 800-561-3952 after 5 pm), on Station St, is a 10-minute walk from the downtown area, north-west of King Square near the Loyalist House and the YM-YWCA. Fares listed are one way. To Quebec City, the train goes to Lévis, across the river from Quebec City, three times a week for $86. To Fredericton $11, it's the same schedule as above. Trains to Truro, Nova Scotia, cost $35 and leave on Tuesday, Friday and Sunday. To Montreal (via Maine) there are services on Monday, Thursday and Saturday costing $82.

Ferry The Marine Atlantic ferry, the *Princess of Acadia*, sails between Saint John and Digby, Nova Scotia, across the bay. To make reservations in New Brunswick, Nova Scotia or Prince Edward Island call ☎ 800-565-9470 toll free. Depending on where you're going, this can save a lot of driving around through Moncton and then Amherst, Nova Scotia, but the ferry is not cheap. In comparison with the other Marine Atlantic routes around the region and for the distance covered, the price is inexplicably high. This route is heavily used by tourists which could be one explanation. Fares are $15.25 per person one way and $46.75 per car. Bicycles are $5.30. There is a very slightly reduced return passenger-only fare if you want to make a day cruise out of a trip there and back.

Crossing time is about 2½ hours. In summer there are three services daily: one in the morning, one in the afternoon and one at night. Arrive early or call ahead for reservations, as the ferry is very busy in July and August. Walk-ons should be OK. There's a restaurant and a bar on board.

Driving around the bay with a small car will save money but take more time.

Car & Motorbike There are several choices for rentals. Delta (☎ 634-1125), at 378 Rothesay Ave, is open seven days a week.

They charge $34.95 with 100 free km, then 12 cents per km. There is also a weekly price of $199 with 1000 free km.

Avis (☎ 634-7750) is conveniently located right behind the market building at 17 North Market St. For a middle-sized car, the rates are pretty much the same as the above. Ask about the weekend special which is quite good value. A third option is Rent-A-Wreck (☎ 632-8889) at 390 Rothesay Ave where the daily rate can be quite low.

Here's some useful road information. West of the town centre, the Trans Canada Highway (Highway 1) crosses over the Saint John River. There's a toll bridge where you pay 25 cents. Further out, connections can be made with Highway 7 for Fredericton.

Getting Around

To/From the Airport The airport is east of town out along Highway 111. There is an airport bus costing $5.50 that leaves approximately 1½ hours before all flights, from top hotels like the Hilton on Market Square and the Delta Brunswick on Brunswick Square. For a share taxi call Vets (☎ 634-1554).

Bus For information on local routes and times call ☎ 635-1986 or ask at the tourist office.

NORTH OF SAINT JOHN

This is a green rural area interspersed with deeply indented bays, rivers and islands, eventually leading to Grand Lake and Fredericton. It's prime New Brunswick cottage country. The Saint John River flows south through here to its mouth at the Bay of Fundy and the ferries connecting roads in the area are all free. The **Kingston Peninsula**, not far from Saint John, has scenery typical of the river valley landscapes. It's beautiful in the fall with the leaves changing colour; **Crystal Beach** is a popular spot for camping and swimming. If you're driving to Fredericton, don't take dull Highway 7. Go along Highway 102, which winds along by the river through small communities. At **Gagetown** there is a huge Canadian Forces base.

ST MARTINS

A 2½-hour rather uninteresting drive east of Saint John will take you to the worthy destination of St Martins, one of the province's historic towns, situated on the Bay of Fundy. It's a small, pretty out-of-the-way place that was once the centre of the wooden shipbuilding trade. On entering the town you'll see a quintessentially Maritime, picturesque scene: **Old Pejepscot Wharf** edged with beached fishing boats waiting for the tide, two wooden covered bridges and a lighthouse. The **Quaco Museum** depicts the shipbuilding period. But keep going over one of the bridges and around the corner where a vast expanse of beach opens up; there are a couple of caves cut into the shoreline cliffs to explore at the far end. At the parking lot is a snack bar, right by the beach.

Back in town there is the *Fundy Breeze Lodge* (☎ 833-4723) for spending the night or having a meal in the restaurant. There is also a B&B or camping just out of town at the *Seaside Park*.

Hiking

The cliff-edged coastal region between St Martins and Fundy National Park and inland toward Sussex is a rugged undeveloped section of the province which has spectacular, wild beauty. The experienced may wish to investigate the trail which runs mainly along the shoreline and extends some 40 km to the park. The hike takes three to five days.

From the park, another long-distance trail leads to the town of Riverview near Moncton.

FUNDY NATIONAL PARK

You can reach the park, 129 km east of Saint John and about halfway to Moncton, by following Highway 114. Next to Banff's, this is Canada's most popular national park. On the Bay of Fundy with the world's highest tides, the park has five campgrounds, about 80 km of hiking trails and some dirt roads for touring around in your car. There's also an arts and crafts school amongst the more developed attractions. Irregularly eroded sandstone cliffs and the wide beach at low tide make a walk along the shore interesting. There's lots of small marine life to observe and debris to pick over. There's also a fair bit of wildlife in the park – on one visit I nearly drove into a deer, and it was high noon! The ocean is pretty cool here, so there is a salt-water swimming pool (not far from the eastern entrance to the park) where you can have a dip, but you must pay for the privilege.

Camping with a tent is $9. Aside from the campgrounds, there are sites along the back-packing trails. In addition, there are motel-style rooms and chalets at the *Caledonia Highlands Inn* (☎ 887-2930) within the park. The chalets have cooking facilities and are very comfortable. The *Fundy Park Chalets* (☎ 887-2808) cost about $10 less at $50 for doubles.

At the small town of **Alma**, just east of the park on Highway 114, you absolutely *must* stop at the *Home of the Sticky Bun* and buy heaps.

CAPE ENRAGE
Heading east to Moncton take the smaller road, Highway 915, as it detours closer to the coast and offers some fine views. At Cape Enrage out on the cliffs at the end of the peninsula, the power of the elements is often strong and stimulating.

SHEPODY NATIONAL WILDLIFE AREA
South of the town of Riverside-Albert and the village of Harvey at Mary's Point on the Bay of Fundy is this gathering place for literally hundreds of thousands of shore birds. From mid-July to mid-August the beach is almost obliterated by huge numbers of birds, primarily semi-palmated sandpipers. Along the dykes and marsh there is a nature trail.

South-East New Brunswick

The corner of New Brunswick leading to Nova Scotia and Prince Edward Island is most interesting for its various geographic or topographic attributes. Here you'll find the regional centre of Moncton whose two principal attractions where things appear to defy gravity. Outside the city are some fine, sandy beaches and, on the Petitcodiac River, the Rocks are the impressive result of seaside erosion.

MONCTON
Moncton, with a population of 60,000, is the third city of the province and a major transportation and distribution centre for the Atlantic Provinces. It's near the ferry for Prince Edward Island and the train to Nova Scotia passes through it. Moncton is small and nondescript, but a much needed face-lift has improved the downtown area. And due to a couple of odd attractions – Magnetic Hill and a tidal bore – it's worth a brief stop on your way by.

The area was first settled by the Germans from Pennsylvania. Initially the town was called 'The Bend' after the turn in the Petitcodiac River, and specialised in ship-building. There's a fairly large French population and many people are bilingual: the Université de Moncton is the only French university outside Quebec province.

Orientation
The small downtown area extends north and south off Main St. The river lies just to the south and the Trans Canada Highway goes past north of town. Between Duke and Foundry Sts, the sidewalks have been gentrified and many of the old buildings now contain restaurants and nightspots.

Lengthy Mountain Rd leading in and out of town from the Trans Canada Highway is the main street for gas stations, chain restaurants and the same franchises seen in most Canadian cities. There are also some motels along here.

Information
There are several tourist offices. The central bureau is on the corner of Main and Bendview Sts near Tidal Bore Park. The

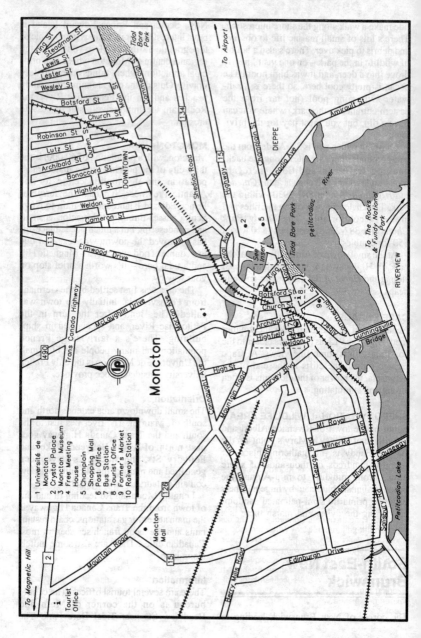

King St
Steadman St
Lewis St
Lester St
Wesley St
Botsford St
Church St
Robinson St
Lutz St
Archibald St
Bonaccord St
Highfield St
Weldon St
Cameron St

Main St
Queen St
Commercial St
DOWNTOWN

Tidal Bore Park

To Airport

134

Shediac Road

Highway 115

Champlain St

DIEPPE

Amirault St

Acadia Ave

Petitcodiac River

To The Rocks
& Fundy National
Park

RIVERVIEW

115

Elmwood Drive

Mill

Assumption

Mountain Rd

490

McLaughlin Drive

Trans Canada Highway

Moncton

2

5

Main St

King St

See
Insert

Tidal Bore Park

Botsford St

Church St

Archibald St

Highfield St

Weldon St

Gunningsville
Bridge

Gordon St

9

Fundy

1

High St

Norton Ave

Connaught Ave

V Harvey Blvd

Mountain Road

Lewisville Rd

Killam

Pacific Ave

Killam Drive

St George Blvd

MT Royal

Milner Rd

Wheeler Blvd

Causeway

Petitcodiac Lake

126

Moncton
Mall

Mountain Road

Berry Mills Road

15

Edinburgh Drive

Salisbury Rd

To Magnetic Hill

2

Tourist Office

1 Université de
   Moncton
2 Crystal Palace
3 Moncton Museum
4 Free Meeting
   House
5 Champlain
   Shopping Mall
6 Post Office
7 Bus Station
8 Tourist Office
9 Farmer's Market
10 Railway Station

year-round office is in City Hall on Main St but is closed on weekends. There's another office south across the Gunningsville Bridge in Riverview. A third one, and the largest, is right beside Magnetic Hill where Mountain Rd meets the Trans Canada Highway, north-west of the downtown area.

Magnetic Hill

This is the best known attraction in the area and is worth a visit. Gravity here seems to work in reverse: start at the bottom of the hill in a car or bike and you'll drift upward. Go as many times as you like, maybe you'll figure it out. The hill is on the corner of Mountain Rd (Highway 126) and the Trans Canada Highway; it's free and the kids will like it. In recent years the hill has become the centre of a variety of attractions which now include a small zoo next door, a water park with slides of various sorts, restaurants and stores. A mini-train links the different diversions.

Tidal Bore Park

The tidal bore is a twice-daily incoming wave caused by the tides of the Petitcodiac River, which are in turn related to the tides in the Bay of Fundy – known as the world's highest tides. The bore rushes upstream and sometimes raises the water level in the river by six metres in a few minutes. The wave itself varies in height from a few cm to over 30 cm.

A good place to watch for it is in Tidal Bore Park at the east end of Main St where there is a large, bright bore timetable display. The pleasant park is filled with old men sitting on the benches until close to bore time when the water's edge gets really crowded with expectant visitors. Don't anticipate anything spectacular though – mostly the wave is not at all impressive. This is so frequently the case that often street performers are now on hand to entertain the watchers – the performers that I've seen have been quite good and invariably steal the show from mother

Tides

The tides of the Bay of Fundy are the highest in the world. This constant ebb and flow is a prime factor in the life of the bay, the appearance of the shoreline and even how residents set shipping and fishing schedules.

The explanation for these record tides is in the length, depths and gradual funnel shape of the bay. As the high tide builds up, the water flowing into the narrowing bay has to rise on the edges. It is pushed still higher by the shallowing sea bed. A compounding factor is called resonance. This refers to the sloshing or rocking back and forth from one end to the other of all the water in the bay like in a giant bath tub. When this mass swell is on the way out of the bay and meets a more powerful incoming tide head on, the volume of water increases substantially.

The eastern end of the Bay of Fundy and around the Minas Basin is where the contrasts between the high and ebb tide are most pronounced with tides of 10 to 15 metres twice daily about 12½ hours apart. The highest tide ever recorded anywhere was 16.6 metres (54 ft), the height of a four-storey building, at Burncoat Head near the village of Noel, Nova Scotia. Other places around the world with noteworthy (that is, over 10 metres high) tides are Bristol in England, the Bay of St Malo in southern France, and Turnagain Arm in Alaska.

All tides, large and small, are caused by the rise and fall of the oceans due to the gravitational pull of the sun and the moon. Consequently, the distance of the moon and its position to earth relative to the sun determine tidal size. When the moon is full or new the gravitational forces of the sun and moon are working in concert, not at cross purposes, and the tides at these two times of the month are higher than average. When one of these periods coincides with the time (perigee, once every 27½ days) when the moon is at its closest to earth the tides are at their most dramatic.

Throughout the centuries various methods have been used around the bay to tap the tides as an energy source. Simple but successful grist mills spurned dreams of grandiose generating stations feeding the eastern seaboard. There is still no commercial electricity production but there is an experimental and working tidal power plant which can be visited at Annapolis Royal, Nova Scotia. ■

Tidal Bore

A feature related to the tides is the tidal bore, a daily occurrence in some of the rivers flowing into the Bay of Fundy, most notably the Saint John River running through Saint John, the Petitcodiac River in Moncton and the Salmon River in Truro, Nova Scotia.

As the tide advances up a narrowing bay it starts to build up on itself forming a wave. The height of this oncoming rush can vary from just a few cm to about a metre. The power behind it forces the water up what is normally a river draining to the sea. This wave flowing upstream is called a tidal bore.

The size and height of the bore is determined by the tide, itself regulated by the moon. In the areas where the bore can be most interesting it is not difficult to get hold of a bore schedule. Like with the tides, there are two bores a day, roughly 12 hours apart. While this is an interesting occurrence, especially in theory, the bores are not often overwhelming experiences to observe. Notice I resisted the term 'boring'. ■

nature. The bore is best in spring and fall, if it's raining or if the moon is right.

Moncton Museum

At 20 Mountain Rd near Belleview St, the museum has a collection of memorabilia covering the town's history, from the time of the Micmac Indians and early settlers to the present. Displays show the influence of ship-building and the railway on the area and an old-style street has been re-created. The museum's free and open daily in summer, but is closed on Monday for the rest of the year. Next door is the oldest building in town, the **Free Meeting House** dating from 1821, used by numerous religious congregations over the years.

Acadian Museum

On the university campus, this museum has a collection of artefacts belonging to the Acadian people, the first French settlers of the Atlantic region. The displays offer a brief history and chronicle aspects of the day-to-day life of these people who were driven out of Nova Scotia to New Brunswick and abroad by British troops. The museum's free and open daily but on weekends it's open only during the afternoons.

Thomas Williams's House

Built in 1883, this 12-room Victorian Gothic-style house remained in the family as a home until 1983 when it was bequeathed to the city as a heritage house. Much of the fine original work remains intact both inside

and out and the furnishings add to the overall effect. The tea room on the veranda is fun. The house is open from June to September except for Monday, it's at 103 Park St in the downtown area.

Crystal Palace

Just north-east out of the downtown core, at 499 Paul St near Highway 15 to Shediac, is Crystal Palace, an indoor amusement park complex with adjacent hotel and shopping centre. Featured are rides, including a roller coaster, and games.

Festivals

In mid-August is the Acadian Handicraft Festival at the College Notre Dame d'Acadie on Archibald St. In early May there's the Acadian Art Festival, and in July a bluegrass and old-time fiddle music festival is held.

Places to Stay

Hostels There was once an official hostel here but it met its demise due to hefty heating expenses. There hasn't been another one since.

However, the *YWCA* (☎ 855-4349), near the railway station in a nice old stone place on the corner of Highfield and Campbell Sts, runs a summer hostel programme. There are very inexpensive dorm rooms or, for a few more dollars, a bed in a double room. The regular room rates are not bad at all either at $21. It's for women only and the cafeteria serves low-priced, good-value meals.

The *Université de Moncton* (contact Housing Services, ☎ 858-4008) rents rooms during summer in two of the residences. They have shared washrooms and there is a cafeteria. Singles/doubles cost $23/28 and for students and seniors singles/doubles are $15/18. Very good weekly rates are available.

Tourist Homes The lack of hotels is partially offset by quite a few guesthouses and B&Bs. *Mountain View Tourist Home* (☎ 384-0290) is at 2166 Mountain Rd. They have three rooms with very reasonable prices: singles/doubles $20/25. It's a simple place but is good.

Within walking distance (but a fair jaunt of seven or so blocks) is the *Bonaccord B&B* (☎ 388-1535) at 250 Bonaccord St. There are four rooms at singles/doubles $32/42.

Wilbur B&B (☎ 382-0406), at 613 McLaughlin Drive, is cheaper but not so central. It costs singles/doubles $22/28.

Out of town off Highway 2 on Rural Route 1 is *Lutes B&B* (☎ 384-7974) with singles/doubles for $25/35. Call them up and they'll give you directions.

Hotels The *Sunset Hotel* (☎ 382-1163) at 162 Queen St is central, well kept and the least expensive spot. Rooms cost singles/doubles $25/30. There's a TV in the lobby and free parking.

At 46 Archibald St in a central location near Main St, is the yellow, wooden *Hotel Canadiana* (☎ 382-1054). It's a beautiful place – as if you've stepped back in time, with wood everywhere and hanging lamps; it's now over 100 years old. Prices have been really creeping up here and now are singles or doubles from $50 to $55.

The *Hotel Beauséjour* on Main St is the largest and most expensive place in town and is primarily for business clientele.

Motels There's no shortage of motels, and a fair range of prices.

Not far from town is the *Beacon Light Motel* (☎ 384-1734), at 1062 Mountain Rd, reached by taking Highway 126. It's decent and costs $45 for doubles. Mountain Rd has a couple of other places as well.

On Highway 2 near Magnetic Hill are numerous motels. The *Atlantic* (☎ 384-2509) charges singles/doubles $42/47. The *Restwell* (☎ 384-6400) in the other direction (east) is from $40 to $45 a single or double.

There are several others strung out along Rural Route 1, towards and in River Glade.

Right in the centre of town is the *Midtown* which is at 61 Weldon St. It's pricier with singles/doubles for $54/59.

Places to Eat
At 700 Main St, *Crackers* is a nice place for sandwiches, salads, ribs or Italian food. At night it becomes a sort of club and is open very late on weekends. Across the street is *Spanky's*, a cleaned-up tavern with inexpensive food and beer, and late afternoon happy hours. *Len's* at 840 Main St is a classic workers' restaurant, open every day and packed for lunch and with everything under $6 or so.

In summer, a couple of takeout booths pop up in the little mall area on the corner of Main and Robinson Sts in the centre of town, where there are benches to sit at. The *Metropolitan* store has the lowest prices in town with meals at or under $5.

Probably the best known restaurant is *Cy's*, a very well established seafood place at 170 Main St. It is not cheap and may be a little over-rated, but it's certainly alright.

Mountain Rd has quite a number of eating spots, including *Ming Garden* for Chinese food at No 797; the inexpensive and recommended *Ponderosa* for good-value steak dinners for $7; and an all-you-can-eat salad bar with or without a meal at No 956 and *Kelsey's* at No 938, a loud, casual something-for-everyone establishment. For things like pizza and spaghetti try *Vito's* at 726 Mountain Rd.

Deluxe French Fries is a local fresh-cut fries institution with fish, burgers and other seafood too. They've been around for 40 years and have several locations about town including one on the corner of St George Blvd and Church St and also one on the corner of Mountain Rd and Connaught Ave.

Entertainment

The *Urban Corral*, 333 St George Blvd, has live country and western music from 9 pm to 1 am, except on Sunday. *Ziggy's* on Main St attracts the young with a different diversion each night. The *Coliseum* is home to major shows, concerts and sporting events.

Getting There & Away

Bus The station for SMT lines (☎ 857-2980) is at 961 Main St between town and the railway station on the corner of Bonaccord St. Some schedules follow with one-way ticket prices:

Fredericton – 8 am, 1.15 and 5.50 pm daily ($21)
Saint John – 8 am, 1.15 and 6 pm daily ($16.75)
Halifax – 10.30 am, 3 pm daily ($28.75)
Prince Edward Island – 1 and 5.45 pm ($23.75)

Train The railway station (☎ 382-7892) is south-west of the downtown area near Cameron St off Main St. Look for it behind the building at 1234 Main St. It's only open from 10 am to 6.30 pm. (The following prices are for one-way fares.) Trains to Halifax cost $30 and to Saint John it's $18. There's a service to Montreal every day except Wednesday for $93. There is one run daily to Campbellton and Edmundston.

To Montreal, there are two different trains using different routes. One train, the Atlantic, goes through Maine three times a week; the other, the Ocean goes through northern New Brunswick and Quebec, also three times a week.

If you take the US route, note that you must have proper ID and comply with US immigration requirements although the situation now seems less stringent and, actually passing through customs is unnecessary if you don't get off the train.

AROUND MONCTON

Covered Bridges

Within 100 km of Moncton, 27 of the province's historic covered bridges can be seen. They were known as 'kissing bridges', because you and yours could tuck the old horse and buggy in there away from curious eyes. Two driving trips south of Moncton, called the Scenic Trail and the Covered Bridge Trail, take in many of these bridges.

Dobson Trail

Just south of Moncton in Riverview, this 60-km hiking trail leads you through the Albert County hills and maple forests down to Fundy National Park.

Hillsborough

Hillsborough, about 20 km south-east of Moncton, is a small town overlooking the Petitcodiac River. From here a restored steam engine pulls antique coaches along the river to Salem, about eight km away. It takes an hour for the return trip. The fare is $6, less for kids, and half-price on rainy days. Through July and August there are four trips daily. There is also a longer trip with dinner served on board.

The Rocks Provincial Park

Continuing south-east from Hillsborough, you'll encounter the park at Hopewell Cape, the point at which the river meets the Fundy waters in Shepody Bay. The 'rocks' are unusual erosion formations known as 'flowerpots'. The shore is lined with these irregular geological forms, caves and tunnels created by erosion from the great tides. An exploratory walk along the beach at low tide is well worthwhile – check the tide tables at any tourist office. You can't hit the beach at high tide but the rock towers are visible from the trails above. Camping is not allowed but there are picnic areas and a restaurant.

Saint Joseph

Here, 24 km south of Moncton, the Survival of the Acadians National Historic Site opened in the summer of 1990. It had been housed in what was one of the buildings of College Saint Joseph where many Acadians were educated until its recent closure. The museum-style displays tell the enthralling but difficult history of the Acadians, the early French settlers of the Bay of Fundy region most of whom were expelled by the British in 1755. The exhibits, including paintings, crafts, and life-sized models are well done and, unlike those at many such history-based sites, also devote some attention to the subjects' lives through the years to the present.

Saint Joseph is in the Memramcook Valley, the only area near the Bay of Fundy where some Acadians live on what was the land of their forebears before the mass banishments.

The site is open from 15 June to 15 September, from 9 am to 5 pm daily and is free. It's between Moncton and Dorchester off Route 106 and, if you're interested in the Acadians or will be seeing some of the other sites relating to them, it's worth the slight detour.

SACKVILLE

Sackville is a small, staid university town. While there isn't a heck of a lot here it seems to be in the right place for a pit stop on the way through. The park in the university grounds right in the centre of town is good for stretching the legs. The art gallery on campus displays the work of students.

Along some of the side streets a number of huge homes from the 1800s can be seen; a couple have been restored and converted to an inn and a B&B.

On the way into town off the Trans Canada Highway along East Main St look for the booster pump by the edge of the road. All the locals stop here for a drink or to fill a jug with the ever flowing, excellent pure water.

Around Sackville are the **Tantramar Marshes**, an expanse of a couple of thousand hectares of wetlands, home to great numbers of waterfowl which have made the area of some interest to bird-watchers. Twenty-four species of ducks and other marsh birds live in or visit the area.

On the edge of town, off East Main St, is the **Sackville Waterfowl Park** on a major bird migration route. Boardwalks have been built over portions of it and there is another trail and some interpretive signs. Also in the Sackville area is the **Tintamarre National Wildlife Reserve**. Biologists at the Wildlife Service in Sackville will offer information for those wishing to know or see more.

Mt Allison University (☎ 364-2251), right in the centre of town, opens rooms to overnight guests from May to August. They cost singles/doubles $25/35, a few dollars less for students. They also serve inexpensive meals.

There's a good B&B at 146 West Main St called the *Different Drummer* (☎ 536-1291). It's a fine old Victorian house; each of the four rooms is furnished with antiques and comes with a bath. Breakfasts include homemade muffins and bread. Prices could be a little lower though: singles/doubles cost $36/44. *Borden's Motel* is less.

At the *Marshland's Inn* on Bridge St, you can get a very good dinner whether you're spending the night there or not. Ask about the chef's special. Meals are not cheap but are good value. *Borden's Motel*, which you can see from the highway, offers good cheap meals and the lobster rolls have been recommended. On York St, across from the university, the little *Vienna Coffee House* is the place for a coffee and snack.

On the road south from town all the antennae are part of the CBC's international short-wave broadcasting equipment.

FORT BEAUSÉJOUR NATIONAL HISTORIC PARK

Right by the Nova Scotia border at the shoreline, the park preserves the remains of a French fort built in 1751 to hold the British back. It didn't work. Led by Colonel Monckton, the fort was taken over before it was even finished. Later it was used as a stronghold during the American Revolution and the War of 1812. There are some pretty good displays within the fort and some evocative pictures set in the surroundings. A museum provides more details and guides will answer questions. The park is free and open daily. The views over the marshy end of the Bay of Fundy alone make a trip out here worthwhile. Picnic tables are provided.

SHEDIAC

Just 22 km north-east of Moncton on the coast, Shediac is a popular summer resort town with a population descended mainly from the Acadian French. The beaches along the Northumberland Strait are blessed with warm waters but especially so here because of sand bars and shallow water. Most popular are **Parlee Beach** (east of Shediac) and **Pointe du Chêne**, with water temperatures of 20°C all summer. The waters of the Northumberland Strait are possibly the warmest north of the US Carolinas and if you've ever put a toe in around Maine or even the Cape Cod area the difference will be appreciated.

There are other beaches on the small coastal roads and north and south of Shediac, and lots of camping places.

The area also is a lobster centre of some repute and Shediac is home to the annual lobster festival in July. And watch out for the 10-metre-long clawed beast which may be seen around town. Many restaurants offer seafood all through the summer.

There is little to see in town itself, but at night the many lights and the decorative seagulls add a festive touch. Pascal Poier House, built in 1835 is the oldest house in town and is now open as a small museum. The big white *Hotel Shediac* dating from 1853 is prominent and the dining room offers both seafood and steaks.

East of town is a strip of eateries and takeout joints. You'll find clams and lobsters, cooked or fresh, dead or alive. *Fisherman's Paradise* packs 'em in with fair prices, but that doesn't mean cheap. The *House of Lobster* with a large smorgasbord of seafoods is an all-you-can-eat buffet. *Shediac Pizza* is good and inexpensive, try the pizza burger. Also along the strip are a couple of motels, a bar or two and a new water-slide complex.

Lobsters can be bought at various outlets and at the wharves. Boil them in ocean water and, with a bottle of wine and some French bread, you've got a cheap deluxe meal. Dig for clams and mussels too.

For camping there is a lot of choice in the area but best is probably *Parlee Beach Park* (☎ 532-1500), beside the provincial beach where it's $8 for one person with tent. Res-

ervations should be made for holiday weekends, for any weekend arrive as early as possible on Friday.

Aside from camping, the aforementioned *Hotel Shediac* (☎ 532-4405) is a central, middle-range place to spend a night or two. Doubles cost $50. Accommodation is not plentiful, but one less expensive option is the *Neptune Motel* (☎ 532-4299) with singles/doubles $35/45. There are also a couple of places with cabins rented by the week.

CAP-PELÉ

East of Shediac there are a series of less used beaches such as the one at Cap-Pelé where there is also a water slide. Further south at Murray Corner, is a provincial park with more sandy beach.

CAPE TORMENTINE

Further east of Shediac and also on the coast is Cape Tormentine with the terminal for the ferry to Borden, Prince Edward Island.

Just north of Bayfield is a very long, almost empty beach with the remains of an old wreck at one end.

North & East New Brunswick

North of Fredericton and Moncton lie the province's vast forests. Nearly all the towns are along the east coast or in the west, by the Saint John River along the US border. The interior of northern New Brunswick is nearly inaccessible rocky, river-filled timberland.

Inland, highways in this area can be quite monotonous with thick forest lining both sides of the very straight roads. It's like driving down unending corridors, most particularly on the routes south from Campbellton to Saint Léonard, from Bathurst to Chatham and from Chatham to Moncton.

Fortunately these routes need not often be used. In the eastern section of the province the coastal roads are where pretty well everything of interest lies. Kouchibouguac National Park protects a variety of littoral environments and their natural flora & fauna. Most of the larger towns of the east coast, are pulp and paper centres with not a lot to hold the visitors attention. Newcastle sticks out as a place to break up the trip.

The Acadian Peninsula with its little-touristed islands and French population based around Caraquet is one of the most geographically appealing regions with the Baie des Chaleurs shoreline. The peninsula has a major historic attraction.

Campbellton and Dalhousie at the edge of the northern uplands are access points to the province of Quebec.

The Miramichi and Restigouche rivers are both widely known, highly respected and very fetching salmon-fishing nuclei.

COCAGNE

North up the coast from Shediac, Cocagne hosts a hydroplane regatta around the second week of August.

KOUCHIBOUGUAC NATIONAL PARK

The highlights of this park (pronounced 'koo she boo gwak') are the beaches, lagoons and offshore sand dunes stretching for 25 km. The sands are good for beach-combing, bird-watching and digging clams. Seals are often seen offshore. For swimming, the water is warm but much of it is too shallow for adults. There are, though, a number of designated swimming areas with deeper waters.

Inland there is canoeing (with rentals), hiking trails both short and long, and quiet roads for cycling. Bikes can also be rented and make a fine way to get around the very flat landscape. Telescopes along the bike route by the sea offer close-ups of the many great blue herons.

There's freshwater fishing for a variety of fish, and the park also has moose, deer, black bears and smaller mammals. Other features are the salt marsh and a bog with an observation platform.

The camping season is from May to October, primarily at a large campground with firewood supplied. There are also less expensive campsites for backpackers and canoeists.

At Ryan's there is a modest restaurant and the bicycle rental booth. At Kelly's with the main beach is a takeout food counter with the usual beach fare.

The park is very popular and busy throughout July and August, particularly on weekends. Get there early in the day to obtain a campsite for about $8. The park is 100 km north of Moncton.

MIRAMICHI BAY

North of the national park in and around Miramichi Bay are more beaches. Folks here, like those further south and in north Prince Edward Island and Nova Scotia, claim the waters are the warmest north of either Virginia or the US Carolinas depending on who you hear it from. In any case, the water at all these places is quite suitable for swimming in, having been warmed by spin-off currents of the Gulf Stream.

CHATHAM

This was a prosperous town when it was the centre of the wooden shipbuilding industry, but the development of steel ships put an end to that. Since WW II there has been a Canadian Forces base here. For visitors there is little to recommend but the revamped downtown area along Water St by the Miramichi River is pleasant enough in a quiet way.

Two blocks away from the waterfront the **WS Logge Cultural Centre** in a restored Victorian house at 222 Wellington St, is primarily a locally oriented art gallery.

On the corner of Wellington St and University Ave, the **Natural History Museum** has a small idiosyncratic collection which is open from mid-June to the end of August.

There is quite an Irish history here and, to commemorate this, a sizeable Irish festival is held annually usually in July with music, dance, food, film, crafts, a parade and even genealogy experts to help trace your Irish roots. There are a few B&Bs in and around town.

In **Douglastown**, halfway between the

Chatham bridge and Newcastle is a tourist office and the **Rankin House Museum.**

NEWCASTLE

Though the site of another huge paper mill, Newcastle is a pleasant little town – a good place to break up the trip north or south. Around the attractive town square are some fine old wooden buildings and shops, some unpainted and ancient-looking, others well tended.

In the central square park bounded by Castle and Henry Sts is a statue to Lord Beaverbrook, one of the most powerful press barons in British history and a statesman and philanthropist of no small reputation. Beaverbrook was born Max Aitken in 1879 and spent most of his growing years in Newcastle. Among the many gifts he lavished on the province are the 17th-century English benches and the Italian gazebo in the square here. His ashes lie under the statue presented as a memorial to him by the town. Around the square and along Water St are most of the shops.

South of town off Highway 8 is another of Lord Beaverbrook's gifts – a forest park called **The Enclosure,** now part of a provincial park. If you just want to look around The Enclosure, tell them at the gate and you won't have to pay the park fee. From 19 June to 15 September there is camping and swimming in the park. Archaeologists have been working at the park which has been occupied on and off by a number of different peoples for about 2000 years. There is an historic cemetery.

Each summer the Miramichi Folksong Festival, now over 30 years old and the oldest one in North America, is held. Through traditional song, the local history and culture are preserved. It's good fun, and worth catching.

Just off the park on the corner of Castle and Pleasant Sts is an odd-looking but excellent place to stay. It's called *Castle Lodge* (☎ 622-2442). Inside the old vine-covered, red-and-green wooden house are five rooms rented out by – yes – an old lady. Singles/doubles cost $14/17 and you share

the one bathroom. An alternative is *Governor's Mansion* (☎ 622-3036), across the river in Nelson-Miramichi. Also good value, they have five rooms at singles/doubles $20/26.

For a bite there is a quick little coffee shop in Barett's Store by the town square.

MIRAMICHI RIVER

South-west of Newcastle, the Southwest Miramichi River extends beyond Doaktown, about halfway to Fredericton. The area, in particular the main river, is renowned for Atlantic salmon fishing. Together with the Restigouche and Saint John rivers it has gained the province an international reputation amongst serious anglers. Even Prince Charles has fished the Miramichi! Both residents and visitors need licences and there are special regulations for nonresidents. Check at the tourist office or the Forest Service of the Department of Natural Resources.

Doaktown has become more or less the unofficial fishing centre for the region. There are numerous fishing lodges and outfitters in and around town as well as motels and B&Bs.

Also in town is the **Salmon Museum,** which is actually pretty interesting and includes pools of live salmon ('king of the freshwater game fish') on the 1½-hectare grounds.

Other points of interest include the **Glendella Mansion** (a rather unexpected sight) and **Doak Historic Park,** concerning local history and with a preserved house from the 19th century and costumed interpreters for the farm section. Near town is a 1870s **covered bridge,** one of the province's oldest. And, oh yeah, don't miss the moose on the east side of town.

ACADIAN PENINSULA

The large peninsula, extending from Chatham and Bathurst out to two islands at the edge of the Baie des Chaleurs, is a predominantly French area which was first settled by the Acadians who were the unhappy victims of the colonial battles between Britain and France in the 1700s. The descendants of Canada's earliest French settlers proudly fly the Acadian flag around the region and many of the traditions live on in music, food and the language which is different to that spoken in Quebec.

For visitors, by far the most interesting section is around Caraquet and the scenery is better there too.

Tracadie

From Neguac, north of Chatham, the road passes by a mixture of old houses and modern bungalows. It's not a wealthy area and there isn't much to see as the road is too far inland for coastal views. In the little town of Tabusintac is a small museum and, down a few doors, a B&B which is open in the summer months only.

In Tracadie notice the Quebec-style Saint Jean Baptiste double silver spired church and the *La Boîte à Pain* bakery.

Shippagan

At the tip of the mainland, Shippagan has a **Marine Centre**, the highlight of which is the aquarium. Examples of many of the species found in the Gulf of St Lawrence region are displayed including seals. There is also a freshwater exhibit. Other displays show all the electronic equipment used by today's fishing folk and other information related to the fishery.

The centre is also used for ongoing research. It's open everyday from 10 am to 6 pm during the summer, the admission price is low.

Adjacent to the centre is a **marina** with a restaurant and gift shop.

A causeway connects **Île Lamèque**, a boggy island where the collection and shipping of peat competes in importance with fishing. Île Miscou, reached by a short free ferry ride, is less populated with quiet stretches of sandy beach. At the far tip is a lighthouse.

Caraquet

The oldest of the Acadian villages, Caraquet was founded in 1757 and is now the main centre of the peninsula's French community. Stretched out more or less along one street, it has one of the oldest churches in the province, Sainte Anne du Bocage. Down at the dock area on Boulevard Saint Pierre Est is a big fish market with fresh, salted, and frozen seafood for sale. Also there is a seafood restaurant.

Acadian Museum In the middle of town, with views over the bay from the balcony, is the museum with a neatly laid out collection of artefacts donated by local residents. Articles include household objects tools, photographs and a fine wood stove in the corner. What most impressed me was the desk/bed at which you can work all day and then fold down into a bed when exhaustion strikes. Is there a workaholic in your life? It belonged to a superior at the Caraquet Convent in 1880.

The museum is open daily in summer, closed Sunday in the off-season and has a modest entry fee.

Other Behind the museum is the **Théâtre Populaire d'Acadie** which puts on shows in midsummer.

In August there is an Acadian Festival with a variety of events.

A few km east out of town near Caraquet Park is the **Sainte Anne du Bocage** religious shrine.

Places to Stay Back a bit from the street at 143 Boulevard Saint Pierre Ouest is the *Hotel Paulin*, (☎ 727-9981), an old red house with a green roof, by the water. Open in summer only, a double is $28 and there is a restaurant for lunches and dinners.

Out close to the shrine is *Maison Touristique Dugas* (☎ 727-3195) with rooms at $34 a double or much less costly campsites. It's at 683 Boulevard Saint Pierre Ouest also called Rural Route 2. Also for camping there is a provincial park close to the shrine.

Getting There & Away At the Irving gas station on Boulevard Saint Pierre Ouest the

Gloucester bus for Bathurst arrives and departs. SMT line buses which cover pretty well the entire province are not seen in this region at all. The Tracadie line covers the route from Newcastle to Tracadie where a connection with the Gloucester line can be made to Caraquet.

Acadian Historic Village

Fourteen km west of Caraquet is this major historic museum (Village Historique Acadien) set up like a village of old, with 17 buildings and workers in period costumes reflecting life from 1780 to 1880. The museum depicts daily life in such a typically simple post-expulsion Acadian village and makes for an intriguing comparison to the obviously prosperous English King's Landing historic village outside of Fredericton.

A good two hours is required to see the site and you'll want to eat. For that there are two choices: a cafeteria or restaurant, the latter serves Acadian dishes.

The museum is open from 10 am to 6 pm daily in summer. It's on Highway 11 towards Grande-Anse. The bus from Bathurst goes right by the door. An adult ticket is $6 and there is a reduced family or senior rate.

Grande-Anse

This small town boasts the popular **Pope's Museum**, which houses images of 264 popes from St Peter to the present one, as well as various religious articles. There is also a detailed model of the Basilica and St Peter's Square in Rome.

The *Auberge de l'Anse* (☎ 732-5204) is a B&B on the main route, eight km from the Acadian Historic Village site or there are a couple of inexpensive motels and a restaurant.

GRANDE-ANSE TO BATHURST

All along the route from Grande-Anse to Bathurst the scenery is good with cliffs, views of the bay and across it to the mountains of the Gaspé Peninsula. There are some

beaches (the one at **Maisonnette** is good), picnic sites and, at **Pokeshaw Provincial Park**, coastal erosion features to see. If you're making a return trip to Bathurst, follow this same route both ways as going around the rest of the peninsula is not worthwhile. Note that many of the small towns may not have either a gas station or a grocery store.

Near **Janeville** there is a restored grindstone mill which can be visited.

For an overnight camping place *Chapman's Tent & Trailer Park*, 14 km east of Bathurst on Highway 11, is highly recommended for its open sites overlooking the beach and ocean.

BATHURST

Bathurst, yet another industrial town, but based on extremely rich zinc mines as well as lumber and pulp and paper, has little to recommend to the casual visitor. Really quite small with about 15,000 people, the town is split into three sections: South, East and West Bathurst by the Nepisiguit River and the Bathurst Basin. The principal street is Main St in South Bathurst and where there are a couple of restaurants.

You can walk to this old downtown section at the end of Nepisiguit Bay from the railway station which is at 690 Thornton Ave on the corner of Queen St. The station is open only when there is a train – just once a day except on Wednesday when there aren't any trains. Three times a week the VIA Rail train goes north and south.

St Peter Ave has the range of food-chain places, gas stations and grocery stores.

On the coast north-east of the harbour at the edge of the city is the **Daly Point Reserve**, a good place for observing birds. There are several trails through the woods or by the salt marsh. An observation tower provides views to the Gaspé Peninsula and along the Acadian Peninsula shoreline.

North of town towards Dalhousie in **Petit-Rocher** on the coast is the **New Brunswick Mining & Mineral Interpretation Centre**, a mining museum with various exhibits, including a deep shaft to descend, features the local zinc-mining industry. The site is open every day during summer and a tour takes about 45 minutes.

DALHOUSIE

Dalhousie is a small, sort-of-stretched-out but agreeable town on the north-east coast of New Brunswick on the Baie des Chaleurs opposite Quebec. The town's main industry is newsprint, but Dalhousie 'wears it well' and there are a few things to do.

Boat tours leave from the town wharf at the foot of Renfrew St and there is a car ferry across the bay to Miguasha, Quebec. The ferry, which leaves every hour on the hour from 9 am to 9 pm cuts about 70 km off the driving trip around the bay. The trip takes about 15 minutes and costs $12 with a car – good if you're heading for the Gaspé Peninsula. It runs from the end of June to sometime in September.

The cruise boat *Chaleur Phantom* departs from here on scenic cruises of either the bay or along the Restigouche River. Various coastal rock formations can be seen as well as sea birds and some historic sites. Other trips offer fishing opportunities at reasonable rates.

Two km east from the ferry dock at the end of Victoria St is **Inch Arran Park** right on the water with camping sites, a swimming pool, the tourist office, the beach and fine views across the bay.

William St and the parallel Adelaide St near the dock are the two main streets with most of the commercial enterprises. On the corner of Adelaide and George Sts is a **local history museum**.

Between Dalhousie and Campbellton, Highway 134 offers good views of the bay and the very green, lumpy hills of the Gaspé Peninsula's south shore. All along the Baie des Chaleurs there are lots of camping spots and motels.

CAMPBELLTON

Campbellton, on the Quebec border, is in the midst of a scenic area at the edge of the Restigouche Highlands. The Baie des Chaleurs is on one side and it seems like green, rolling irregularly shaped hills encase the town on the remaining sides.

Across the border is Matapédia and Highway 132 leading to Mont Joli, 148 km into Quebec.

The last naval battle of the Seven Years' War was fought in the waters just off the coast here in 1760.

Main streets in this town with about 10,000 residents are Water St and Roseberry St around which the commercial centre is clustered. It is truly a bilingual town with store cashiers saying everything in both French and English.

Nearby, **Sugarloaf Mountain** rising nearly 400 metres above sea level and dominating the skyline, is the principal attraction and provides excellent views of the town and part of the Restigouche River. It looks remarkably like its namesake in Rio. From the base, it's a half-hour walk to the top; another trail leads around the bottom. From the tourist office a chairlift runs up another, lower mountain. There's camping in **Sugarloaf Park** and skiing in winter. The tourist office also has a small museum with interesting exhibits on the Atlantic salmon.

About 10 km west of town toward Matapédia is **Morrisey Rock**, another place for a good view of the scenic river area.

The **Restigouche River**, named by the Micmacs, is excellent for salmon fishing. It runs south-west from Campbellton. All along the river there are fishing camps, clubs, supply stores and some pools open to the public.

Places to Stay

There is little to see or do in town and no reason to stay. But if you need accommodation there are a few places to choose from. There is a *Youth Hostel* (☎ 759-7044), at 1 Ritchie St, open from early June only until mid-August.

Idlewilde Cabins (☎ 753-4665), at 417 Mountain Rd, are simple but reasonable at $30 a double. The central *Caspian Motor Inn* (☎ 753-7606), on Duke St, is a good choice if you'd like a better place. There are several others, check along Roseberry St. Between here and Dalhousie on Highway 134 are numerous motels and campgrounds, many with attractive seaside locations. Others are found on Highway 134 West.

Places to Eat

In the centre is *Dixie Lee*, a fried chicken outlet commonly seen around the province. An alternative is *Pizza Delight*. Better restaurants will offer salmon and, in spring, another local delicacy, fiddleheads – a wild and very tasty green.

Getting There & Away

The bus station or rather the bus stop is at the Pik-Quik variety store on Water St near Prince William St. The railway station is conveniently central on Roseberry St. There are three trains a week going south to Moncton and Halifax and three heading the other way to Montreal.

MT CARLETON PROVINCIAL PARK

Access to Mt Carleton Provincial Park, the largest and wildest in the province, is from **Five Fingers**, a town south-west of Campbellton along the Restigouche River. The park is roughly 130 km south of Campbellton.

The central northern section of the province known as the **Restigouche Highlands** is a mountainous, river-crossed largely uninhabited region. From the town of **Kedgwick** a superb 85-km canoe trip for a couple of days can be taken along the Restigouche River to Campbellton. The Mt Carleton Provincial Park, surrounded by a large tract of unspoiled land used only by loggers, encloses Mt Carleton (820 metres), one of Atlantic Canada's highest mountains. There is little development in the park and gas and groceries are not available, but there are maintained hiking trails and camping areas. Canoe rentals are available at **Riley Brook** and **Nictau**.

Saint John River Valley

The Saint John River which has been likened to the Rhine begins in Maine, USA, at the north-western corner of New Brunswick and flows south for over 700 km before entering the Bay of Fundy at Saint John.

It winds along the western border of the province past forests and beautiful lush farmland, through Fredericton between tree-lined banks, and then around rolling hills to the bay. The valley that protects it is one of the most scenic places in the province. It's particularly picturesque and gentle scenery from just north of Saint John to near Woodstock.

There are bridges and ferries across the river at various points. The Trans Canada, Highway 2, follows the river up to Edmundston and then crosses into Quebec. In earlier days the river was the highway for the local Native Indians.

Because of its soft, eye-pleasing landscape and because the main highway connecting the Atlantic Provinces with central Canada runs along the river, not surprisingly, it is a busy route in summer. So much so that accommodation, which is limited at the best of times, can be difficult to find in July and August. It is advisable to stop early or use the tourist office toll free reservation service to book ahead. In the off-peak season there is no problem at all.

On one trip south I started looking at dusk in the Edmundston area and was told everything was booked down the road as far as Woodstock. Eventually I and a group of weary travellers of every description were found overpriced rooms in the basement of an old folk's home in Grand Falls.

Mark Lightbody

Aside from the bigger centres, some small towns along the route have a B&B or two. There are also campgrounds along the way. There is a choice of two routes, the quicker Trans Canada Highway mostly on the west side of the river or Highway 105 on the east. The slower route is not any more scenic but does go right through many of the smaller villages.

WOODSTOCK

A small town set in a rich farming area, Woodstock acts as a tourist crossroad: the Trans Canada Highway goes through here, as does the road to Maine, USA. Highway 95 to Bangor, Maine, and then Highway 2 is an alternative and shorter route to Montreal.

Main St through Woodstock has some fine, old large Maritime houses. On the north side of town is the *Hometown* (you can't miss it), a good spot for a meal.

There is a bluegrass music festival held in town in summer. For spending the night there is a bit of choice here and prices aren't bad. At 133 Chapel St is the *Queen Victoria B&B* (☎ 328-8382) at singles/doubles $35/40. Among the motels there's the *Mount Haven* on Route 2 at singles/doubles $28/30.

HARTLAND

Hartland is an attractive little town with a nice setting and, though there is not much else to see, it does have the grand-daddy of New Brunswick's many wooden covered bridges, now things of the past. This bridge, 400 metres long, is the longest in the world. There are 74 of these bridges dotted around the province; the tourist office has a complete listing if you're interested. The bridges were covered to protect the timber beams used in the construction. With such protection from rain and sun, a bridge lasts about 80 years. They are generally high and wide because cartloads of hay pulled by horses had to pass through. Nearly all of the bridges that remain are on secondary or smaller roads.

The *Ja-Se-Le Motel* (☎ 375-4419) (named with letters from the names of the original owner's daughters) north of town is the only local motel, average priced and has a pretty good restaurant with German food.

Halfway between here and Grand Falls is a provincial park at Kilburn.

GRAND FALLS

A town of 7000, Grand Falls consists essentially of one main street and the falls which make it an interesting short stop.

In a park in town, the falls drop about 25 metres and have carved out a gorge 1.5 km long with walls as high as 70 metres. At the site is an interpretive building and trails, with lookout points, which lead along the gorge. Entrance to the park is $1 and there are picnic tables, a restaurant and a place to swim.

The town celebrates its primary resource, the potato, in a festival each year around 1 July.

At 142 Main St is the *Maple Tourist Home* (☎ 473-1763) an inexpensive B&B. Along the highway on both sides of town are several motels and camping is possible near the falls.

For something to munch there are a couple of quick places down the main street, Broadway. *Bob's Deli* has salads and baked goods. The *Patricus* south of town on the highway is good for breakfast. Definitely avoid the *Chinese Village* restaurant in town.

Around Grand Falls

East of Grand Falls around the farming community of New Denmark is the largest Danish population in North America. In the middle of July is a festival celebrating all things Danish. In New Denmark is a restaurant which serves Danish foods all year.

Highway 108, the Plaster Rock Highway, cuts across the province to the east coast. The highway sluices through forest. Animals such as deer and moose are commonly seen on or beside the road – take care at night. There are some camping spots along the way.

SAINT LÉONARD

As the name suggests, Saint Léonard is primarily a French town, like many in this region – some are old Acadian settlements.

In Saint Léonard is the Madawaska Weavers group, which uses hand looms to make material for ponchos and scarves.

From here, Highway 17 runs north-east through the dense forests of northern New Brunswick. Near Saint Quentin, Highway 180 branches off eastwards and leads to Mt Carleton Provincial Park.

EDMUNDSTON

If you're coming from Quebec there's a good chance this'll be the first town in the Maritimes you get a look at, as the border is only about 20 km away. At the border is a large, helpful tourist office. From here it is three hours' driving to Fredericton. Maine is just across the river and there is an international bridge on Dupont St at the south end of town not far from City Hall.

Edmundston is an industrial pulp and paper centre with numerous mills in and around town. It's split pretty well in half by the Madawaska River and the old central district on the west side of the river is built around some low hills which give it a little character.

The population of about 13,000 is 85% French-speaking. Nearly all of them, like most of New Brunswick's French, speak English.

Where there are French people there are impressive churches and cathedrals, and Edmundston is no exception. Their cathedral here is the Roman Catholic Cathedral of the Immaculate Conception, quite an impressive sight up on a hill at the end of Church St near the centre of town.

The main intersection downtown is that of Church and Canada Sts. Within a couple of blocks of this corner are many of the shops, a couple of restaurants, City Hall plus an indoor shopping mall. Victoria St, between the highway and this central section is also a busy commercial street.

There is no inner-city bus service so you'll have to do some walking here, but the distances are not great.

The local citizens have a somewhat whimsical notion of Edmundston as the capital of a fictitious country known as Madawaska whose inhabitants are known as Brayons. Evidently this traditional community-uniting concept has historical origins in a period during the late 1700s when the region existed in a sort of political vacuum between the border-bickering of the American and British governments.

Information

The local tourist office is in the museum building on the corner of the Trans Canada Highway and Boulevard Herbert, the street which leads into the centre.

Madawaska Museum

At 195 Boulevard Herbert on the corner of the Trans Canada Highway across from a shopping centre, is the Madawaska Museum which outlines the human history of the area from the time of the original Malecite Indians through colonial times to the present. The museum also has displays on local industries such as the timber trade. It's open daily in summer, but closed on Monday during the rest of the year. There's a nominal admission fee.

Festivals

Each year on the nine days preceding the first Monday in August is the 'Foires' Festival, which celebrates the physically nonexistent republic of Madawaska. The local people with various national ancestries term themselves 'Brayons', the inhabitants of Madawaska. There are cultural, social and sporting activities as well as some good traditional Brayon cooking to sample.

Places to Stay

On Power St, in the north-west section of the city just off Highway 2, are a couple of cheap tourist homes.

The *Modern Tourist Home* (☎ 739-7438), 224 Rue du Pouvoir, charges just singles/doubles $20/22. The *City View* (☎ 739-9058), at No 226 next door, has five rooms for singles/doubles $20/22.

There are also plenty of motels around town. *La Roma* (☎ 735-3305), about 1.5 km south of town, is reasonable as is the *Motel Guy* (☎ 735-4253). There are several other more expensive places including a *Journey's End* in this busy border stopover town.

There are also a couple of provincial parks within 15 km of town.

Places to Eat

The centre of town actually has very few

restaurants although there are a couple of pizza places around the corner of Canada and Church Sts.

The *Bel Air*, with the sign that can't be missed, is on the corner of Victoria St and Boulevard Herbert on the way into the centre from the highway. It's open 24 hours and has Italian, Chinese, seafood or basic Canadian fare to choose from and has been here for many years. For barbecue chicken there is *May's* at 325 Victoria St with some competition just down the street. There are also a couple of Chinese places along Victoria St.

Getting There & Away

Bus The SMT terminal is across the street from Restaurant Bel Air on Victoria St near the corner of Boulevard Herbert at the bridge. It's a little hard to find and not clearly visible from the restaurant but it is there around the back.

You can catch buses here for Quebec City, Halifax, Moncton, and also for Maine and Boston, USA.

There are buses daily to Quebec City for $35 on Voyageur lines. To Halifax and Moncton there are two services daily on SMT lines which serves New Brunswick: Halifax for $78 and Moncton for $51.

Train Train service to and from Edmundston has been discontinued.

Car

Heading to Quebec there is an alternative to the main route, the Trans Canada Highway toward Cabano, Quebec, and on to Rivière-du-Loup. Route 120 leads west out of town and then heads north through Lac Baker before reaching the Quebec border and going on to the St Lawrence River. In the interests of thoroughness and diversity I used this route on a recent trip and unreservedly class it as a lousy choice – it's slow, boring and without redeeming features along its entirety.

Quebec

Entered Confederation: 1 July 1867
Area: 1,540,687 sq km
Population: 6,438,403

'Kebec', an Algonkian Indian word meaning 'where the river narrows' is the heart of French Canada. Explorer Samuel de Champlain of France first heard and recorded the word when he founded Quebec City in 1608. Jacques Cartier, another explorer, had landed here in 1534 (the 450th anniversary of the landing was celebrated in 1984) when the settlement was known as Stadacone.

The province is Canada's biggest, and the largely French population makes it quite different from other parts of North America. This is reflected in various aspects of life here including architecture, music, food and religion. About 90% of the population is Roman Catholic, though the Church's influence has declined sharply in recent decades.

Quebec is often at odds with the rest of English-speaking Canada, particularly in its politics. Most people are familiar with the movement for Quebec to separate from the rest of Canada. This desire was formally

Quebec's Population Crunch or Who's Making Babies?

The dominant issue in Quebec and the one that fuels all the talk of independence is the threat, real or perceived, of cultural assimilation with and submersion into English North America. In this context the primary concern is the preservation, promotion and continuation of the all-critical component of any groups' cultural identity – their language. Hence we have the controversial provincial language laws meant to ensure the use of French in various aspects of life such as economic activity, education, etc.

Perhaps the most significant factor advancing the possibility of cultural decline (or extinction say some panicky demographers) is the little-discussed but inescapable fact of Quebec's disastrously low birth rates. With a fertility rate of 1.5 among women of childbearing age, it is the lowest in the Western world except for former West Germany's. A rate of 2.1 is considered necessary for replacing the existing population.

For generations, starting with colonisation in the 1500 and 1600s, Roman Catholic Quebec was synonymous with huge families. Couples with 10, 12, and even more children were by no means rare. Right up until the 1950s, French families of five and six kids were more or less the norm.

The changes occurring since then throughout the Western world have had a great impact on the women of Quebec. Those of child-rearing age in Quebec have been more inclined to want to shed the past with its dominance by the Church in things moral and by the English in things political and economic. Economic changes, the move to a less rural society, and the general loosening of traditional lifestyle constraints have also had their effect. Marriage rates dropped and births declined dramatically with the swing towards the search for independence and freedom, power and control, and personal satisfaction.

The provincial government has reacted in a number of ways to the alarming numbers. Quebec now has some generous financial packages including tax incentives and cash payments for couples considering children. The more children, the better the dollars become. There is large-scale luring of emigrants from French-speaking countries. It is quickly being discovered that French-speaking or not, people from nations as diverse as Senegal in West Africa, Vietnam in Asia and Haiti in the Caribbean instant Québecoises do not make.

With a population of some five and a half million, French Quebec is not going to disappear overnight in any case. With a combination of schemes and plans and, most importantly, another societal attitudinal shift, the situation will probably resolve itself. It's just that it had best hurry up. ■

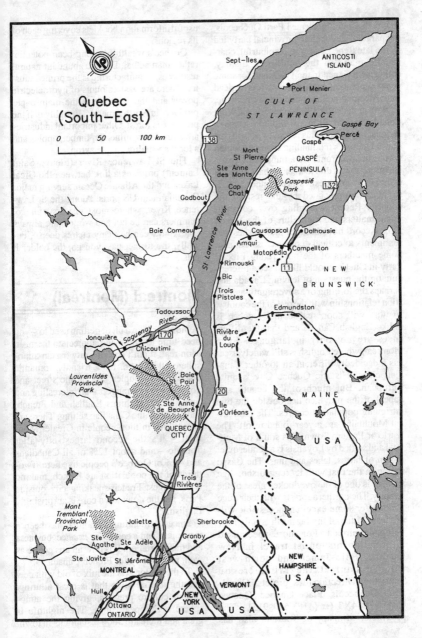

Quebec
(South–East)

0   50   100 km

ANTICOSTI ISLAND

Sept-Îles

Port Menier

GULF OF ST LAWRENCE

Gaspé Bay

138

Percé

Gaspé

Mont St Pierre

GASPÉ PENINSULA

Ste Anne des Monts

Cap Chat

Gaspésié Park

132

Godbout

Matane

Causapscal

Dalhousie

St Lawrence River

Baie Comeau

Amqui

Campbellton

Matapédia

Rimouski

11

Bic

NEW BRUNSWICK

Trois Pistoles

Edmundston

Tadoussac

Saguenay River

170

Jonquière

Rivière du Loup

Chicoutimi

MAINE USA

Laurentides Provincial Park

Baie St Paul

20

Ste Anne de Beaupré

Île d'Orléans

QUEBEC CITY

Trois Rivières

Mont Tremblant Provincial Park

Joliette

Sherbrooke

Ste Agathe

Granby

Ste Adèle

NEW HAMPSHIRE USA

Ste Jovite

St Jérôme

MONTREAL

Hull

VERMONT

Ottawa

 ONTARIO

NEW YORK

USA

USA

channelled into the elected Parti Québecois, a separation-advocating provincial party led by the late René Lévesque, a colourful, charismatic man. To the hardliners' dismay, enthusiasm waned in the 1980s and for some years separation was more or less a dead issue, deemed neither practical nor realistic.

Now in the early 1990s, Quebec's leaving Canada in one form or another seems a serious possibility. This recent twist is in part due to Quebec's rebounding economy which was in the doldrums for a number of years. But more so it is due to a sense that Quebec's differences and desires are neither understood nor appreciated by the rest of the country. Recent wrangling over constitutional matters and the failure of the Meech Lake Accord have brought these issues and sentiments to critical debate across Canada. Some members of the now ruling Liberal Party in Quebec would like to see a referendum on the question of leaving Canada and perhaps the forming of a sovereignty-association relationship with the rest of the country. Visitors will soon realise that Quebec is unlike English Canada and that the differences are not only in language. Even Montreal, where English is still widely used, has a decidedly different air to other Canadian cities. Historic Quebec City is quite European. But much of the beauty and appeal of the province lies outside the two intriguing population centres. The Laurentian Mountains are a year-round resort. The Estrie or Eastern Townships south of Montreal and settled by Loyalists is a gentle, quiet region of farms, lakes and inns. The Gaspé region in the east with its rugged shoreline scenery is one of the overlooked areas of the country. The northern forests with their huge parks offer some excellent accessible wilderness. Much of the far north is only now being developed. For more specialised information on tourist travel in New Quebec, Baie James and north-west Quebec contact the Ministère du Tourisme, Direction des projets, Grand-Nord Québecois, Place Québec, Quebec City G1R 4X3 (☎ (418) 643-9131). The provincial Ministry of Tourism also has useful information booklets covering each of its regions.

Quebec's wealth has long been potential rather than actual. Despite abundant natural resources, manufacturing is the prime industry. There are vast amounts of hydroelectric power and the province is the main paper producer in North America. Roughly half the province is forest. Other important industries are aluminium, minerals, timber, apples and a local speciality, maple syrup.

The St Lawrence River (Fleuve Saint Laurent) provides a link between the Great Lakes and the Atlantic Ocean, serving major Canadian and US ports. Along the St Lawrence River, where most visitors will go, summers can be hot and winters are always cold. Snow can be many metres deep. Generally, the further east you go, the colder it gets.

Montreal (Montréal)

Some cities take a bit of getting used to – you need time to know and appreciate them. In Montreal, it ain't so. This city has an atmosphere all its own. It's a friendly, romantic place where couples kiss on the street and you can talk to strangers – an interesting and lively blend of things English and French, flavoured by the Canadian setting. There are about three million people in Greater Montreal – it's the second largest city after Toronto – and about 12% of all Canadians and 40% of Quebec's people live here. Two-thirds of the population are French, making it the largest French-speaking city outside Paris, but the downtown core is surprisingly English.

Since its founding, Montreal has been a major port and a centre for finance, business and transportation. It is now an arts centre as well, particularly for French Canada.

To the visitor, it is the mix of old with new and the *joie de vivre* that is most alluring. French culture prevails, giving the atmosphere a European tinge. The nightlife is great and there are 5000 restaurants in town.

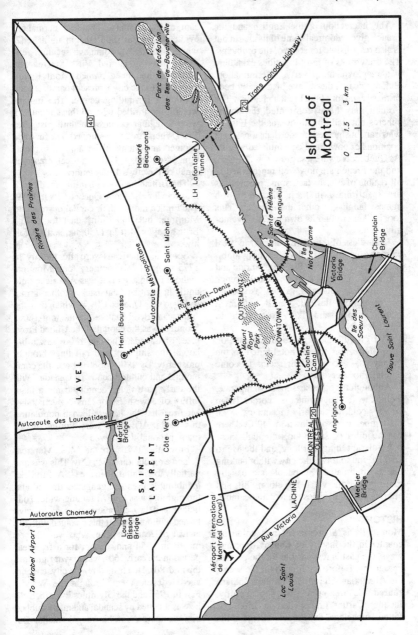

Island of Montreal

0   1.5   3 km

The interaction of the English and the French gives Montreal some of its charm but is also responsible for some of the problems. The drawbacks of most big cities exist here – unemployment, poverty, discrimination. But, atypically, these have historically been primarily the lot of the French majority. The French may have dominated the social spheres but traditionally it was the English who ran businesses, made decisions, held positions of power and accumulated wealth. As Québecois awareness grew, this changed, and the French are now well represented in all realms of life. In fact, some recent laws are reactionary in their discrimination against languages other than French. This too, is likely to find its own balance eventually.

Regardless of these difficulties, Montreal exudes a warm, relaxed yet exciting ambience. It is as if the city itself has a pride and confidence in its own worth. Speak French if you can. If you can't, as long as you are not arrogantly defiant, you'll find most people helpful and likely to respond to English.

The city has a reputation for fashion savoir-faire, but this is not limited to the moneyed – a certain flair seems to come naturally to everyone.

Although the other seasons are temperate, a quick word about winter is in order. It can be very cold, particularly in January, when the temperatures get down to -40°C. There can be piles of snow too, although these don't disrupt things for long, and the Métro enables you to travel the city without taking one crisp breath. The people are usually more gregarious when big storms hit, and afterwards, sunny skies make it all bearable.

HISTORY

Montreal's is a prominent and colourful chapter in the history of Canada. In many ways, the past is responsible for the politics here today. Before the French hit the scene, the Algonkian, Huron and Iroquois Indians shared the area, not always peacefully. Jacques Cartier first visited in 1535 and found Hochelaga, an Iroquois village at the

foot of a mountain. The first permanent White settlement didn't begin until 1642, when Sieur de Maisonneuve set up a religious mission named Ville Marie. The mountain had been named Mont Royal, which led to the city's present name. It soon became a fur-trading centre. The Indians weren't too thrilled with all this and attacks were a regular occurrence until just after 1700, when a treaty was signed. The fur trade boomed and Montreal became an exploration base. Today, Old Montreal preserves much of the city's 17th-century past.

The British had been battling the French for some time and took Quebec City in 1759. The French moved their capital upstream to Montreal but that didn't last long. The British captured it in 1760 and settlers followed.

Soon the Americans were after the city. In 1775 General Montgomery took Montreal without firing a shot. It was American only until the British beat back another group trying to take Quebec City, at which time the Americans fled Montreal. In the mid-1800s Montreal was the capital of the United Provinces of Canada. The late 1800s saw a big boom; the shipping and rail lines brought prosperity. By 1900 Montreal was the commercial and cultural centre of Canada. With the early part of the century came a huge influx of Jewish Europeans – even today Montreal has the largest Jewish population in Canada. After both wars, immigrants of many nationalities arrived.

From the 1920s to the '40s, Montreal gained a reputation as Sin City. This was due partially to Prohibition in the USA. Brothels, gambling houses and gangsters thrived and the nightlife was known far and wide. Politicians and law-enforcers are said to have turned a blind eye. All this changed with the arrival of Jean Drapeau, who was elected mayor in 1954 and, except for a five-year period in the early '60s, was mayor right into the mid-80s. He cleaned up the city, encouraged redevelopment, brought the World's Fair in 1967 and the Olympics in 1976. Still, he was touched by scandal and many dubbed him 'Emperor' for his megalomania. But

Drapeau was popular and he certainly helped develop Montreal's international reputation.

For years, decades even, Montreal has been a very stable city with very little change in the downtown area. Returning after a long absence was always comforting, as though you hadn't really been away. The last few years, however, have seen the end of that equanimity as redevelopment and modernisation have struck markedly at points all over the downtown area. The changing and stylish look, a sort of blend of European and North American forms, has sparked plenty of debate the results of which will soon be determining future projects and streetscapes.

ORIENTATION

The city sits on an island roughly 40 km long by 15 km wide where the Ottawa River flows into the St Lawrence River. There are bridges connecting all sides with the mainland; this reinforces the impression of really not being on an island at all. Despite the size of the city and the island, it's both easy to orient yourself and to get around Montreal. In the middle of the island is Mont Royal, a 233-metre-high extinct volcano. The core of the city, which is actually quite small, is below this, in the south central section of the island.

Street Names

Montreal is a bilingual rather than a French-speaking city. The bulk of visitors are English-speaking, English is widely used in the central area, and in addition, many of the streets were named by the British who dominated the city until recently. However, in this book, the Montreal street names are given in French. Many squares, parks and other sites are known by their French names. It may seem a little strange to read 'Rue Peel' instead of 'Peel St', but this has been done for the sake of consistency.

A street with east and west sections is referred to by its French name too. *Est* means East and *Ouest* means West. Hence, the east part of Rue Sainte Cathérine is known as Rue Sainte Cathérine Est and the west part, Rue Sainte Cathérine Ouest.

A street which was recently renamed is Dorchester Boulevard. It is now known officially as Boulevard René Lévesque, in honour of the late Québecois leader and premier. The two names will probably be in use for the next few years.

The downtown area is bounded by Rue Sherbrooke to the north, Avenue Atwater to the west, Rue Saint Antoine to the south and Boulevard Saint Laurent to the east. This is the busy area of skyscrapers, shops, restaurants, offices and luxury hotels.

The small park, Square Dorchester (formerly Dominion Square), marks the centre of downtown. It's a peaceful spot surrounded by some new and many old buildings some with green oxidised copper roofs.

The tourist office is on the north side along with the horse-drawn carriages known as *calèches* which can be taken around parts of town or up the mountain. On the south-west corner is Windsor Station, the venerable CP railway terminal. To the south is the top-end CP hotel, Château Champlain, where you probably won't be staying. On the east side is the stone Sun Life Insurance building.

The Cathedral of Montreal (Marie-Reine-du-Monde Catédrale, or Mary Queen of the World Cathedral) with its pastel, gilt-trimmed interior is to the south-east.

Just to the east is the Queen Elizabeth Hotel below which is the CN-VIA Rail Central Station from where most passenger trains now depart. South, down the hill from the park on Rue Peel, is the main post office.

North, a block up Rue Peel from the park, is Rue Sainte Cathérine, the main east-west artery. This is the main shopping street where the department stores and many cinemas are. It's one way only, for eastbound cars.

North of Rue Sainte Cathérine is Boulevard de Maisonneuve and then Rue Sherbrooke, the two other main east-west streets. All three run a long way in each direction.

At 2025 Rue Peel is the Canadian Guild of Crafts which has interesting Native Indian, Inuit and Québecois crafts.

If you keep walking uphill on Rue Peel for a number of blocks you'll finally come to Avenue des Pins, across which is the edge of

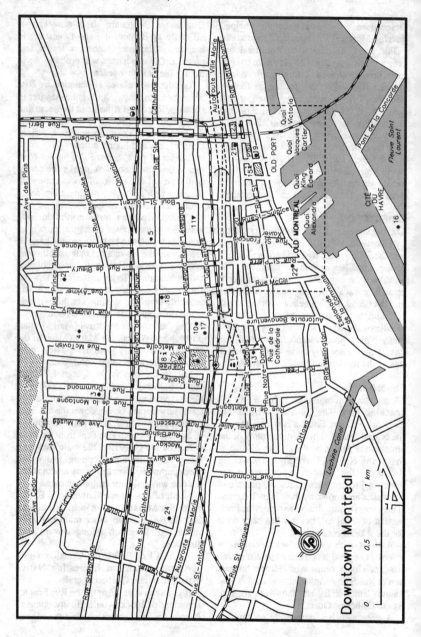

Downtown Montreal

1	Lookout
2	Montreal Youth Hostel
3	Museum of Fine Arts
4	McGill University
5	Place des Artes
6	Bus Terminal
7	Square Dorchester
8	Tourist Office
9	Cathedral of Montreal
10	Central Station
11	Chinatown
12	Windsor Station
13	Dow Planetarium
14	Main Post Office
15	Tourist Office
16	Contemporary Art Gallery
17	Place Ville Marie
18	Place Phillips
19	Place Jacques Cartier
20	Place d'Armes
21	Hôtel de Ville
22	Marc Aurèle Fortin Museum
23	Sir George-Étienne Cartier Museum
24	Canadian Centre for Architecture

Mont Royal Park. You'll see some steps. At the top is an excellent view of the city, the river and the surroundings to the south – great day or night. This is the city's largest park and is pleasant to stroll in on a warm day. The cross, on top and lit at night, is a city symbol.

Other good vantage points for views over the city are the Olympic Stadium Tower (charging an admission fee), the bar at the top of the Château Champlain hotel and the restaurant on top of the Grand Hotel, 777 Rue University. There are also pretty good views from St Joseph's Oratory and from various points along the road around Mont Royal.

At 705 Rue Sainte Cathérine Ouest by the corner of Rue University, is one of the city's largest shopping complexes, the new and modern showpiece, the Eaton Centre – almost (I hate to say it) an attraction in its own right. The Promenade de la Cathédrale is an underground portion of the complex which runs beneath a church! The old and new houses of worship?

Avenue McGill College, a street north of

Rue Sainte Cathérine was once a narrow student ghetto but has recently (and controversially) been opened up and now presents an imposing boulevard edged with some of the city's newest corporate architecture. Structures aside, the channel of space leading from the city's main street to the campus of McGill University and beyond to the mountain is certainly impressive. A number of statues and sculptures including the eye-catching 'Illuminated Crowd' are found along the avenue. Inside the Place Montreal Trust building are five levels of shopping lit by windows running along Avenue McGill College.

The area downtown and west to Loyola Campus on Rue Sherbrooke is pretty much English and residential. Westmount at the foot of the mountain is one of the city's wealthiest and most prestigious districts.

Running north and south of Rue Sainte Cathérine west of Rue Peel are Rue Bishop, Rue Crescent and Rue de la Montagne – the centre of one of the nightlife areas. There are many restaurants, cafés and discos here. The two big cafés on Boulevard de Maisonneuve between Rue de la Montagne and Rue Crescent are a good place to get a feel for the area.

Below and parallel to Rue Sainte Cathérine is Boulevard René Lévesque (formerly Dorchester), a wide street known for its high buildings. Place Ville Marie (sometimes referred to as the PVM) on the corner of Rue University across from the Queen Elizabeth Hotel, is one of the city's best known buildings. It's in the shape of a cross and is another landmark.

East along Rue Sainte Cathérine you'll see Phillips Square, a meeting place where guitarists and bums busk and bask. Further east, just past de Bleury, is Place des Arts, a complex for the performing arts. A few more blocks east is Boulevard Saint Laurent (St Lawrence Blvd) known as The Main. This is one of the city's best known streets, with an interesting history and ethnic make-up, and lots of inexpensive restaurants.

To the east of The Main, Rue Sainte Cathérine Ouest becomes Rue Sainte Cathérine Est and arbitrarily separates east from west Montreal; east of here is predominantly French. About 10 blocks east (you can get a bus) is Saint Denis, which has been transformed into a Paris-style café district. Saint Denis was originally an all-student area, but more expensive establishments are moving in. However, there is still something for everyone. Little bars, some with jazz, abound. French is the tongue spoken here but don't let that deter you – it's a good chance to practise.

Two blocks further east is Rue Berri. Terminus Voyageur, the bus station with US and Canadian destinations is a block north on Rue Berri at Boulevard de Maisonneuve.

Old Montreal is south-east of the downtown area; both Boulevard Saint Laurent and Rue Saint Denis lead into it.

There is a small but determined Chinese community clustered along Rue de la Gauchetière between Rue Saint Urbain and Rue Clark. Rue de la Gauchetière runs east-west past the railway stations. The area along Rue Sainte Cathérine Est between Rue Saint Denis and Avenue Papineau, long neglected, is now seeing some new life as a gay district. The streets of east-end Montreal and some parts of the northern section are lined with distinctive two or three-storey apartments with outside staircases. Such housing, peculiar to Montreal, was built in the '20s and '30s. The stairs were put outside to save space inside.

Many of the wealthy French people, a fairly new and growing segment of Montreal's population, live in the neighbourhood around Rue Laurier just to the east of Mont Royal. There are a number of pricey boutiques and restaurants along a small portion of Rue Laurier but there really isn't anything to see in the area. A number of politicians live in the district.

INFORMATION

The main Montreal tourist office (☎ 871-1595) is now very central at 1001 Rue Square Dorchester on Square Dorchester (formerly known as Dominion Square). Square Dorchester is bounded by Boulevard René Lévesque and Rue Metcalfe and Rue

Peel. Both railway stations are nearby and Rue Sainte Cathérine is just a short walk away. This new, large centre is efficient and helpful and can supply information on all areas of Quebec. It's open daily through the year from 9 am to 6 pm but from June to September remains open until 7.30 pm.

The other main information centre is also well located at 174 Rue Notre Dame Est in Old Montreal (☎ 871-1595), not far from Place Jacques Cartier. It's busy but helpful, open from 9 am to 7 pm daily in season, 9 am to 5 pm with an hour and a quarter for lunch at 1 pm the rest of the year. This one mainly deals only with Montreal.

The airport also has an information kiosk which is open all year round. The Convention & Tourist Bureau (☎ 871-1129) is at 1555 Rue Peel in Suite 600.

Additional numbers to call are ☎ 800-363-7777 for Montreal information and ☎ 873-2015 for other provincial destinations.

Note that all Montreal's museums are closed on Monday.

Warning

Pedestrians, beware in Montreal. Might is right and drivers take full advantage of this. The careless may not get a second chance.

OLD MONTREAL (VIEUX MONTRÉAL)

This is the oldest section of the city, dating mainly from the 1700s. The square **Place Royale**, is where Ville Marie, Maisonneuve's first small fort-town, was built, when fighting with the Iroquois was both lengthy and fierce.

The narrow, cobblestoned streets divide old stone houses and buildings, many of which now house intimate little restaurants and clubs. Throughout the area are squares and churches and the waterfront is never far away. Old Montreal is a must for romantics, though it's unfortunately a bit crowded in peak season. With all the activity and history, it's a perfect area for just wandering where your feet take you. Do yourself a favour and don't bring your car down here – it's too busy and you won't find a parking spot.

The main streets are Rue Notre Dame and

Rue Saint Paul. The area is bounded by Rue McGill on the west, Rue Berri on the east, Rue Saint Antoine on the north and the river on the south, with Boulevard Saint Laurent dividing the area east from west. The Métro stops in Old Montreal are Place d'Armes or Champs de Mars.

Near **Hôtel de Ville** (City Hall) and the Rue Notre Dame tourist office is the square **Place Jacques Cartier**, the centre of the area which in summer is filled with visitors, vendors, horse-drawn carriages and musicians. At the tourist office nearby, there's an *Old Montreal Walking Tour* booklet available, which is free and has all sorts of interesting historical tidbits, and points out the most noteworthy spots.

Many buildings are themselves marked with informative plaques. Some descriptions of the highlights follow.

Place d'Armes
The other major square in the area is Place d'Armes. A monument to Maisonneuve stands in the middle. On the square is Notre Dame Cathédrale, which you shouldn't miss. Built in 1829 and big enough to hold 5000 people, the church has a magnificently rich interior. There's a small museum at the back.

Église de Notre Dame de Bonsecours
This church is on Rue Saint Paul. It's also known as the Sailors' Church and has several models of wooden ships hanging from the ceiling. From the tower in the church there's a good view. The vignettes in the small museum are also quite good.

Calvet House
Across from the church, Calvet House which dates from 1725 has been restored and is now a museum showing the furnishings of that time. It's closed on Monday and is free.

Château de Ramezay
On Rue Notre Dame, across from the Hôtel de Ville, is the Château de Ramezay which was the home of the city's French governors for about 40 years in the early 1700s. The building has housed a great variety of things

since, but is now a museum with a collection of artefacts, tools and miscellanea from early in Quebec's history. The house is closed on Sunday mornings and all day on Monday. Admission is $2, students $1.

Montreal History Centre
Also in Old Montreal is the Montreal History Centre in the old fire hall on Place d'Youville. Audiovisuals and displays depict some of the city's history, with tours running every 20 minutes. It's closed Monday and holidays and is inexpensive.

Musée Marc Aurèle Fortin
Not far away is the Musée Marc Aurèle Fortin, at 118 Rue Saint Pierre, which is less of a museum than a gallery dedicated to this Quebec landscape painter who lived from 1888 to 1970. Other painters are also represented in the changing exhibitions. Again, this one is closed on Monday. Admission costs $2.

Sir George-Étienne Cartier National Historic Park
The Sir George-Étienne Cartier National Historic Park consists of two historic houses owned by the Cartier family. One details the life of the prominent 19th-century lawyer and politician and the changes in society in his lifetime, and the other offers a glimpse of a middle-class home during the Victorian era. It's at 458 Rue Notre Dame Est. The park is free and open every day in summer, and from Wednesday to Sunday for the rest of the year.

Quai Jacques Cartier
Quai Jacques Cartier and the waterfront is a district of riverfront redevelopment south of Place Jacques Cartier which is still evolving and changing as construction and ideas continue. Quai Jacques Cartier includes an art gallery, restaurants, a large open flea market (*marché aux puces*) and a handicraft centre.

At the eastern edge is the old port of Montreal with its **Sailors' Memorial Clock Tower** now used as an observation tower open to the public. Boat tours of the river depart nearby. Music, dance and mime performances take place here through the summer. The Esplanade de la Commune is a wide promenade along the river from Rue Berri west to Rue McGill.

On Quai King Edward at the foot of Boulevard Saint Laurent is **Images du Future**, a centre for holography, computer-generated films, satellite images and various other high-tech novelties, games and art forms. At the time of writing it was uncertain if this display would be permanent and, if so, whether this would be the location.

From Quai Alexandra, a block east of Rue McGill, a ferry goes over to **Parc de la Cité du Havre**, where there's a restaurant and some picnic tables. A hovercraft did run from here to Île Sainte Hélène but this service may now be discontinued.

The huge present-day port and container terminal is found at the foot of Rue McGill. Also there is the Iberville Passenger Terminal, the dock for cruise ships which ply the St Lawrence River as far as the Magdalen Islands out in the Gulf of St Lawrence.

RUE SAINT DENIS
This street, east of Boulevard Saint Laurent between Boulevard de Maisonneuve and Rue Sherbrooke, is the centre of a café, bistro and bar district with lots of open-air places and music. Snoop round on the side streets too. Some places are cheap, so many students still frequent the area which is very lively at night. There are also some good small hotels in the area.

Going south along Rue Saint Denis will lead you into Old Montreal. North up Rue Saint Denis towards Rue Sherbrooke, you'll see Place Saint Louis, a small park surrounded by old houses. East of the square is Rue Prince Arthur – with good, varied ethnic eating places.

BOULEVARD SAINT LAURENT
Still called St Lawrence by some and known by many as The Main, Boulevard Saint Laurent has always been an interesting, busy commercial street. Stores are topped by apartments in the two to four-storey rows

that line both sides of the street. Boulevard Saint Laurent running north-south divides the city into east and west, historically French and English, and has long had a multi-ethnic make-up. Around Rue Sainte Cathérine it's a little sleazy (but interesting) and from here the boulevard runs north for countless blocks.

Small businesses, cheap restaurants, cafés, and shops with all manner of goods can be found. The area around Rue Prince Arthur is good for strolling and eating as is the section further north around Rue Duluth.

The Upper Main running between Avenue Laurier and Rue Saint Viateur is in the midst of an energetic change from decay to hip. One of the early trendsetters was Lux at 5220 Boulevard Saint Laurent, a café magazine store unlike any other; it remains open 24 hours a day.

Mont Royal
Known as 'the mountain', this is the city's best and biggest park. It was designed by the same man who did New York's Central Park. The **Chalet Lookout** has great views of the city: you can walk up to it from downtown (see the Orientation section), or drive most of the way through the park and walk the rest. East of the lookout is the huge steel cross, lit up at night and visible from all over the city. Within the park is **Beaver Lake**, a depression-era 'make work' project. The park has lots of trees and is used in summer for walking, picnicking, horse riding and frisbee throwing. In winter there is skating and skiing. There are some nice trails with views.

In the middle of the park is the **Mont Royal Art Centre**, with paintings on display and a sculpture garden surrounding the building.

If you're driving here, take Rue Guy from the downtown area to Chemin de la Côte des Neiges and then look for signs. To the left is another small park called **Parc Summit**. There is another good lookout here; this one has a view of the western residential districts.

UNDERGROUND CITY
To alleviate congestion and to escape the

harsh winter, Montreal created a huge underground city in the city centre. Though much of it is actually underground, the term really covers anything connected by underground passageways. Thus you can go to the railway stations, find a hotel, see a movie, eat out, go dancing or shopping, all without taking a step outside.

The notion is very functional and innovative, but there's really not much to see. The shops are all modern and most of the system looks no different from a contemporary shopping mall, the differences being this is bigger and has the Métro going through it.

Major building complexes like Place Ville Marie, Place Bonaventure and Place du Canada are all connected and within easy walking distance. Others, like Place des Arts and Complèxe Desjardins, are a Métro ride away. The new Eaton Centre is part of the network. The tourist office has a good map of the entire system; it's a good place to go on rainy or snowy days.

MUSÉE DES BEAUX ARTS (FINE ARTS MUSEUM)

This is the city's main art gallery (☎ 285-1600), with both modern and pre-Columbian works. Europe, Africa, the Middle East and other areas are covered. There's also a display of Inuit art and special shows from time to time. Like all Montreal's museums, this one is closed on Monday and open from 10 am to 5 pm other days. It's at 1379 Rue Sherbrooke Ouest on the corner of Rue Crescent. Admission is $4, students $2; it's more if there's a major travelling exhibition.

CONTEMPORARY ART GALLERY

The Contemporary Art Gallery (☎ 873-2878) is out of the way on Cité du Havre, which is south of the downtown area on the waterfront near Victoria Bridge. The times I've been there, at least half of it has been closed off, everything was disorganised and the shows were nothing to write home about. It's free but not worth it. Plans are afoot to move into a much larger and central location in a couple of years at the Place des Arts complex – perhaps this will improve things.

To get to the gallery take bus No 168 from either the McGill, Bonaventure or Victoria Métro stations.

CANADIAN CENTRE FOR ARCHITECTURE

Opened in 1990 the centre is both a museum and working organisation promoting the understanding of architecture, its history and future. The numerous exhibition rooms feature permanent and changing shows of local and international architecture, urban planning and landscape design. It may sound dry but most people will find at least some of the displays (incorporating models, drawings or photographs) of interest.

A portion of the centre has been created in and around Shaughnessay House, built as home for a wealthy businessman in 1874 of the characteristic grey limestone seen so often around the city. A wander around its 1st floor is interesting for the details and architectural features. A highlight is the solarium garden and the wonderfully ornate tea room with intricate woodwork and fireplace (sorry no refreshments served).

There is a very busy bookstore in the centre with books on famous architects and topics ranging from international styles to photography.

Across Boulevard René Lévesque (opposite the back of the centre) don't miss the sculpture garden and lookout. About 15 sculptures of varying styles and sizes are scattered about a terrace overlooking parts of south Montreal. Directional markers set in the border wall point out various buildings of note below. The old banks, mills etc provide intriguing evidence of the centre's conviction that the study of architecture is the study of history and civilisation.

The centre's open from 11 am to 5 pm daily, until 8 pm on Thursday and closed on Monday and Tuesday. Admission is $3, $2 for students and seniors. On Thursday it's free all day for students and for everybody else from 6 to 8 pm.

McCORD MUSEUM

The city's main history museum, the

McCord Museum, is closed for major expansion and renovation until at least 1992. At 690 Rue Sherbrooke Ouest, the museum deals with Canada's early history, mostly before the arrival of Europeans. The collection includes Native Indian and Inuit works, early Canadian costume and textiles, folk art and 700,000 photographs!

SAIDYE BRONFMAN MUSEUM

This museum, at 5170 Rue Sainte Cathérine, on the west side of Mont Royal, has a collection of contemporary art. It's free and open from Sunday to Thursday.

ST JOSEPH'S ORATORY

The impressive modern-style basilica, completed in 1960 and based on and around a 1916 church, honours St Joseph, patron of healers, and Brother André, a monk said to have the power to cure illness. Piles of crutches testify to the strength of this belief. Brother André's heart, which is on view here – a display ranking with the weirdest – was stolen a few years ago but was finally returned intact.

You can see the dome of the oratory from anywhere in the south-west of Montreal. From the dome, the view of that part of the city is good. The site is open daily and is free. There is a small museum dedicated to Brother André. On Sunday there are free organ concerts at 3.30 pm.

The oratory is at 3800 Chemin Queen Mary, off the western slope of Mont Royal. From downtown, take the Métro to Guy, then transfer to bus No 65.

CANADIAN HISTORICAL MUSEUM

Really a wax museum , the Canadian Historical Museum (☎ 738-5959) sits across the street from St Joseph's Oratory. It contains about 200 international historic figures, many in period or geographical settings. It's nothing too special and is open daily in summer until 9.30 pm, in winter until 5.30 pm.

GEORGE STEPHEN HOUSE

This Renaissance-style mansion dating from 1880 was built for the man who gave it his name, the first president of the Canadian

Pacific Railway. The 15 rooms inside are rich with quality materials and have been skilfully crafted: the woodwork is tremendous. Long the home of the private Mount Stephens Club, it is now open to the public for a small fee from Thursday to Sunday, noon to 4 pm during July and the first week of August only. It's at 1440 Rue Drummond.

CHÂTEAU DUFRESNE
MUSEUM OF DECORATIVE ARTS

Château Dufresne displays decorative art and handicrafts. It's a fine building dating from 1916-18. Each room is furnished with objéts d'art and finery and is open from Wednesday to Sunday only, 11 am to 5 pm. Admission is $2. The museum's in front of the Botanical Gardens on the corner of Boulevard Pie IX (pronounced 'pee neuf').

INSECTARIUM

Whether you love or hate the creepy crawlies, this collection of bugs from around the world will fascinate you. The Insectarium is a new museum in the east end of the city at 4101 Rue Sherbrooke Est, take the Métro to Pie IX. It's open daily from 9 am to 6 pm and is $4.

DOW PLANETARIUM

The planetarium (☎ 872-4530) is at 1000 Rue Saint Jacques Ouest near Windsor Station. It offers laser shows as well as regular star and solar system programmes; the shows are usually good and interesting. Admission costs $3, laser shows $5.

CATHEDRAL OF MONTREAL

The Cathedral of Montreal or Marie-Reine-du-Monde (Mary, Queen of the World), is a smaller version of, and is modelled on, St Peter's Basilica in the Vatican. The cathedral was built in 1870. You'll find it just off Dominion Square near the Queen Elizabeth Hotel. Note the unusual canopy over the altar.

ST JAMES UNITED CHURCH

This church, at 463 Rue Sainte Cathérine Ouest, is unusual in that the portals open onto the street but have stores and offices built in beside them. The church is actually behind the street.

McGILL UNIVERSITY

On the corner of Rue University and Rue Sherbrooke, this is one of Canada's most prestigious universities. The campus is rather nice to stroll around, since it sits at the foot of the mountain. The **Redpath Museum** houses McGill's natural history collection, which includes animals and birds.

PLACE DES ARTS

Place des Arts is Montreal's modern centre for the performing arts. There are three main theatres in the complex on Rue Sainte Cathérine on the corner with Rue Jeanne Mance and a new contemporary art gallery is under construction. Free tours lasting about 45 minutes are given on Tuesday and Thursday at 1, 2, 3 and 4 pm. There's not that much to see on a tour but it's a good place to catch a show or concert.

COMPLEX DESJARDINS

Complex Desjardins is one of the city's modern, multi-use structures with offices, plenty of stores and a hotel (the Méridien) all connected to the vast underground building network. It's several storeys high with a large open space in the centre for walking, watching and putting on shows. You can keep an eye on things from the Hôtel Méridien's café on the top floor.

The mall is open 24 hours a day and has lots of benches and places to sit. It is linked with Place des Arts across the street and the subway system. Alexis Nihon Plaza on the corner of Rue Sainte Cathérine and Avenue Atwater is much the same as Place Bonaventure on the corner of Rue de la Gauchetière Ouest and Rue Mansfield.

OLYMPIC SPORTS COMPLEX

Ask any Montrealer and you'll find that the scandal, indignation and tales of corruption and government incompetence surrounding these buildings are as great as the structures themselves. Nevertheless, the complex, created at enormous cost for the 1976 Olympic Games, is magnificent.

The showpiece is the multi-purpose **Olympic Stadium** able to hold 80,000 spectators. It certainly is a grand structure, even if it did take until 1990 to get it finished. The infamous retractable roof eventually arrived from Paris, France in late 1981 (five years after the games) and then sat for several years before the money was found to hoist it into place. It then took yet more time to get it operating. In summer, professional football and baseball were played in the stadium and it was also used for concerts until the summer of 1991 when a huge chunk of concrete fell from the stadium forcing its indefinite closure and once again raising the ire of the Montreal taxpayers.

Also in the grounds is the **Velodrome**, another boldly designed stadium, built for cycling and now used for roller-skating and skating as well. A museum on the environment is now planned for the velodrome as it has not been popular as a sporting facility.

The **swimming complex**, also impressive, has six full-sized pools including a 20-metre-deep scuba pool. Public swimming costs $1.50.

Also in the complex is **Olympic Village**, the housing sector with apartments and restaurants.

Guided tours of the site in French and English (☎ 252-4737) leave from the lobby of the swimming complex every day but call to check what the tour includes – the stadium will be off-limits until it is safe for visitors again. The fee of $4.40 (students $3.30) chisels away at the local citizens' debt. It's worth it for those with a special interest in either architecture or sport but otherwise I'd say give it a miss at that price.

A cable car runs up the arching tower which overhangs the stadium to a glassed-in observation deck which provides outstanding views of the city and beyond for a distance of 80 km. A ticket to the top is $5. Combination tickets which include the tour and a shuttle service to the nearby Botanical Gardens make a less expensive package than buying the components separately.

There is an information centre by the Velodrome which includes a souvenir shop.

The entire site is in Parc Maisonneuve on the extreme eastern side of the city, off Rue Sherbrooke on the corner of Boulevard Pie IX. The Métro stop is Viau.

BOTANICAL GARDENS

These 81-hectare gardens are the third largest in the world after those in London and Berlin. You'll see 26,000 types of plants in 30 garden settings and various climate-controlled greenhouses. The collection of 700 orchid species is particularly impressive, as are the new Japanese Garden and bonsai and Chinese *penjing* with plants up to 100 years old. Displays change with the seasons.

The gardens are open every day and free but to view the greenhouses costs $3. The gardens are next to the Olympic Buildings in Parc Maisonneuve. The Métro stop is Pie IX. A shuttle bus runs to the Olympic Park.

HABITAT 67

At Cité du Havre, a jutting piece of land between Old Montreal and Île Sainte Hélène connected with the island by the Pont de la Concorde, is a residential complex known as Habitat 67. It was constructed for the World's Fair as an example of a futuristic, more liveable apartment. It has aged well, is still appealing with its block modular look, and has become a popular, but not cheap, place to live.

THE ISLANDS

South of the city in the St Lawrence River largely in the area between the Jacques Cartier and the Victoria bridges are Sainte Hélène and Notre Dame islands. They were the site of the immensely successful 1967 World's Fair, Man & His World. For the event Île Sainte Hélène was considerably enlarged and Île Notre Dame was completely created with landfill. They are now primarily parkland though a couple of vestiges remain of the fair and there are a number of other attractions of note.

Île Sainte Hélène

At the extreme northern end of Île Sainte Hélène is **La Ronde**, the largest amusement park in the province with restaurants and bars as well as an assortment of games and rides. 'The Monster', a roller coaster, is ranked as one of the world's best – hold on to your stomach. A variety of concerts and shows are held through the summer often including circus performances and excellent firework displays. A schedule is available.

Adjacent to the amusement park is **Aqua Parc** with 21 water slides and a very large heated swimming pool. There are also restaurants and bars.

Also at the La Ronde site is the **Montreal Aquarium** with 300 species of marine life including penguins and trained dolphins. There is also a good beer garden.

Full admission to La Ronde including all the rides, Aqua Parc and the aquarium, is $22. Without Aqua Parc the ticket is $16.95. Admission to Aqua Parc only is $14 and the aquarium separately is $3.

In May La Ronde is open only on weekends, from 11 am to 11 pm. Through the summer it's open daily from 11 am to midnight but stays open an hour later on the weekends. Aqua Parc stays open only until 6 pm.

There are also some portions of an old fort near La Ronde. Inside the remaining stone ramparts is the **David M Stewart Museum** (☎ 861-6701) with artefacts and tools from Canada's past. There are demonstrations by uniformed soldiers and others in period dress, and military parades are held daily in summer by the museum. Admission is $2.50.

There are a couple of different ways to get to the islands but all access is through Île Sainte Hélène. Two bridges lead to the island if you're driving: the Pont Jacques Cartier and Pont de la Concorde. Definitely consider taking the Métro to the Île Sainte Hélène stop rather than driving, as they hit you pretty hard for parking. From the Métro stop, where there is an information desk, there are bus trips around to the island's various attractions.

Île Notre Dame

Île Notre Dame, largely parkland, has some attractions of its own. First among them is the new – and very popular – artificial sandy beach with room for 5000 people. There are picnic facilities and snack bars at the site. It's open every day from 24 June to Labour Day (at the beginning of September) from 10 am to 7 pm. A ticket is $5, less for children. To get there take the Métro to Île Sainte Hélène and from there a bus runs to the beach.

Also on Île Notre Dame is the Outdoor & Nautical Centre based around the former Olympic rowing basin. In summer you can rent windsurfers and paddle boats but perhaps it's more fun in winter when the area becomes a huge skating rink. There are lockers and a snack bar and you can rent skates – a lot of fun. There is also some cross-country skiing; equipment can also be rented. The centre's open until 9 pm daily.

Major exhibitions of various kinds are held in the **Palais de la Civilisation** during the summer months and they are worth inquiring about. Much of the surrounding grounds are parkland which you can stroll around for free. At the **Gilles Villeneuve race track** (named after a Quebec racing-car driver) the occasional Formula 1 Grand Prix race is held.

Buses run from Île Sainte Hélène to the various attractions around Île Notre Dame.

PARC LA FONTAINE

This is a large city park which also has a children's zoo. It's off Rue Sherbrooke Est between Avenue du Parc La Fontaine and Avenue Papineau, a few blocks east of Rue Saint Denis.

MARKETS

Two fairly central markets are the **Atwater Market**, south on Avenue Atwater, below Rue Sainte Cathérine at the Lachine Canal, and the **Marché de Maisonneuve** at the corner of Rue Ontario and Avenue Létourneaux in the east end of the city. These markets are open daily except Sunday; Saturday is best.

At Atwater Market, aside from all the

usual stuff, maple syrup is available, often from farmers who produce it. They can answer any questions about this traditional Quebec treat.

MONTREAL EXCHANGE

Another market to visit is the stock exchange (☎ 871-2424), where tours are given for a nominal fee, daily during July and August. For details and times, ring the above number. The exchange is on the 4th floor at 800 Place Victoria.

LACHINE

Out in Lachine, a suburban town south of Montreal, is a national historic park called the Fur Trade in Lachine (☎ 283-6054). It's at 1255 Boulevard Saint Joseph on the corner of 12th Avenue. The museum tells the story of the fur trade in Canada, which was so critical to the development of the country. Take the Métro to Lionel Groulx and then bus No 191. Admission is free. It's not well known and is about 10 km from the downtown area and has been recommended by a reader.

Nearby, on Boulevard Saint Joseph but down near 7th Avenue, free walking tours are given along the Lachine Canal which was built for trade purposes. The tours run from Wednesday to Sunday only.

KAHNAWAKE INDIAN RESERVE

South of Lachine where the Mercier Bridge meets the south shore is the Kahnawake (pronounced 'con-a-wok-ee') Indian Reserve where some 5000 Mohawks live. This reserve, about 18 km from central Montreal, was the location of a major confrontation which lasted for months between the Mohawks and the Quebec and federal governments through the summer of 1990 which made headlines internationally. The residents' support of the Mohawks in Oka over their land dispute exploded into a symbolic stand against the continuing treatment of Native Indians across the country on any number of problems.

There's a museum (☎ 632-1098) as well as mission buildings from the early 1700s.

Visits are free and can be made daily from 10 am to noon and from 1 to 5 pm. Sunday mass at 11 am is sung in Mohawk. Also on the site is a cultural centre with an extensive library relating to the Six Nations of the Iroquois Confederacy as well as exhibits dealing principally with this reserve and its history. Some crafts are sold and shows with traditional dancing were held before the events of summer 1990. Call the museum for information.

ST LAWRENCE SEAWAY

The seaway system of locks, canals and dams opened in 1959 along the St Lawrence River and enables ocean-going vessels to sail 3200 km inland via the Great Lakes. Across Victoria Bridge from the city is an observation tower over the first locks of the system, the Saint Lambert Locks, where ships are raised five metres. There are explanatory displays. The observation area is open from April to December between 9 am and 9.30 pm, free. In January, February and March the locks are closed – they're frozen like the river itself, until the spring thaw.

CANADIAN RAILWAY MUSEUM

This museum (☎ 632-2410) is at 122A Rue Saint Pierre in Saint Constant, a district on the south shore near Châteauguay. The museum, with Canada's largest collection, has examples of early locomotives, steam engines and passenger cars. Admission is $3 and it's open from May to early September. To get there, take Champlain Bridge from town to Highway 15, then Highway 137 at the Châteauguay cut-off to Highway 209.

JET-BOATING

A couple of companies offer boat trips through the nearby Lachine Rapids. Lachine Rapids Tours (☎ 284-9607), at 105 Esplanade de la Commune Ouest, have 90-minute trips leaving from Old Montreal, costing $30. They also have trips using rubber rafts, which cost about $20. Another company running rubber-raft trips is Voyageur Lachine (☎ 637-3566).

LANGUAGE PROGRAMMES

The Association Québecois des Écoles de Français (☎ 343-7386) administers and organises intensive French courses for non-French speaking students in conjunction with five universities and five colleges. Each year some 10,000 students from around the world come to Quebec to learn French and something about Quebec. Most linguistic and cultural programmes are co-ordinated through this association. Some of these courses are in Montreal, others in smaller centres in various regions of the province.

For information contact them at 3333 Chemin Queen Mary, No 528, Montreal, Quebec H3V 1A2, or telephone the above number.

ORGANISED TOURS

Gray Line (☎ 934-1222), at the tourist office on Square Dorchester, operates eight sightseeing tours. The basic city orientation tour takes 2½ hours and costs $15. You'll take in some of the sights and residential districts. The full-day trip is 7½ hours for $30.50. Other bus trips are to the Laurentian Mountains north of Montreal and a sunset tour.

The other major tour company is Murray Hill (☎ 937-5311) now also at 1001 Rue du Square Dorchester in the tourist office. Tours leave from here and all major downtown hotels. They have six tours: some in town, others around the outskirts and as far as the Laurentians. Like Gray Line, Murray Hill is a reputable company charging more or less the same prices.

Montréalistes Walking Tours (☎ 744-3009) offers walking tours in the popular areas of town such as Chinatown and Old Montreal, and also some in other less visited, interesting areas of town. Historic sites, galleries, museums and cafés may be included. The cost is very reasonable, it's more if a meal is included.

A couple of companies offer boat trips. Montreal Harbour Cruises Ltd (☎ 842-3871) has boat tours from Quai Victoria, the pier at the foot of Rue Berri in Old Montreal. The 1½-hour trips around the port are $12. Longer sunset trips and later night cruises

with disco-dancing and drinks are other options. *Le Maxim* (☎ 849-4804), a more deluxe vessel departs Quai Alexandra (Alexandra Boarding Pier) at the Iberville Maritime Harbour west of Jacques Cartier Bridge, or easier, they'll pick up at most of the major downtown hotels. Call for details.

FESTIVALS

Towards the end of May and into June on weekends the International Benson & Hedges fireworks competition lights the skies.

The Montreal Jazz Festival held at the end of June and the beginning of July is now a major event with both internationally known and local players. Indoors and out, concerts are held at various places around town, and many shows are free. There's usually quite a few performances around the Saint Denis area.

The Montreal World Film Festival is held in mid to late August and early September with screenings at cinemas around town.

Several big cycling races are held through the summer including one around the island and one through the streets.

PLACES TO STAY

Montreal, like Quebec City, is very popular with tourists in summer, so rooms can be hard to find and cost slightly more than during the rest of the year.

Camping

There's not too much camping close to town. It's best to check on Highway 134, on the south shore on the mainland (Boulevard Tashereau). The highway leads east-west from town and has some small lots for spending the night. They're mainly designed for RVs; further out it's a bit better for tents. There are also some places including a *KOA* (Kampground of America) as you come from the west, before you actually get on the island of Montreal. They're just off the highway around Dorion. The same goes for the Quebec City side.

A half-hour drive south-west of Montreal will get you to *Camping D'Aoust* on Highway

342 in Hudson-Vaudreuil. Take exit 26 from Highway 40 (the Trans Canada Highway) then it's three km down the road.

Hostels

Montreal has one permanent hostel, the central *CHA Hostel* (☎ 843-3317), at 3541 Rue Aylmer, with 104 beds. Members pay $12 and nonmembers, $14. It's open all year from 8 am to 2 am. Rue Aylmer runs off Rue Sherbrooke, just to the east of McGill University; get off at the McGill Métro stop. The 19 rooms take from four people each. Some places have mixed 'dorms'. There is a maximum stay of seven nights and making reservations three weeks in advance is a good idea in summer. The hostel has shared kitchen facilities.

A new youth hostel, evidently unofficial, was reported to be the process of opening at the time of writing. It's very central, at 267 Rue Rachel near Rue Saint Denis and the Mont Royal Métro stop. It's in a fine old building which needs a lot of work; a bed costs $10. There's no breakfast and no kitchen but there is a fridge, microwave and a pleasant back yard.

The *YMCA* (☎ 849-5331) is at 1450 Rue Stanley. It's central too, and huge, with 350 beds. Singles/doubles are $32/40 and they take both sexes although couples are supposed to be married. The cheap cafeteria is open from 7 am to 3 pm.

The *YWCA* (☎ 866-9941), for women only, is at 1355 Boulevard René Lévesque Ouest. Singles/doubles cost from $32/46. There's a cafeteria and a pool.

McGill University, on the corner of Rue Sherbrooke and Rue University, opens its residences from 15 May to 15 August. The accommodation office (☎ 398-6367) is at 3935 Rue University. Singles cost $30, for students $22. There are cafeterias, laundry rooms, etc and some residences include breakfast but are more expensive.

The very central *Concordia University* (☎ 848-4756), at 7141 Rue Sherbrooke Ouest, is even cheaper. The student rate here is $16 per person, single or double. Non-students pay $22/34 for singles/doubles.

Open all year and very good value is the *Collège Français* (☎ 495-2581) at 5155 Rue de Gaspé with a range of cheap beds. Dorms go for as little as $8.50. There are good-value rooms with four beds and a shower and sink at $10.50 per person. A double room goes for $14.50 per person and there are good rates for a single room. You can buy an inexpensive breakfast or there is a full-board programme at bargain prices.

After 5 pm or on holidays ring ☎ 270-9260 for details or information. Facilities include the cafeteria and a gym. Although there are 120 beds it's very busy in the summer months so call ahead to check availability. To reach the college take bus No 51 west from the Laurier Métro stop.

The college also has two residences out of the centre in Longueuil (pronounced 'long guy').

Lastly, the French *Universitaire de Montréal* (☎ 343-5431), 2350 Rue Édouard-Monpetit west of the downtown area, offers rooms at $18/28 for students/non-students.

Pretty inexpensive rooms are also available at St Joseph's Oratory.

Tourist Homes & Small Hotels

Most standard hotels in the city are costly. Tourist homes are the alternative and there is a good, central assortment. Nearly all are in older houses and buildings with 10 to 20 rooms. Quality ranges from the plain and functional to old-world-charm comfortable. Price is the best indicator of quality but sometimes just a few dollars can make quite a difference. All these places are OK, though. Practically all the smaller ones have a variety of rooms with price differences depending on what facilities the room has – whether it has a sink or toilet or a full bathroom. Air-con adds a few dollars too. Prices are highest from June to October.

My first choice of location would be the convenient Saint Denis bus station area. There are quite a few places here. *À l'Américain* (☎ 849-0616), a small hotel at 1042 Rue Saint Denis, between the café district and Old Montreal, is good and European in style. It has 20 rooms at singles from $30 to $40 and doubles from $40 to $55. The rooms on the top floor are like those in tryst scenes in French movies but, as the manager has mentioned, there is nothing wrong with the other rooms!

You'll find plainer, cheaper rooms nearby at such places as the *Hôtel de la Couronne* (☎ 845-0901) at No 1029. A little nicer place, with a wider range of rooms and prices, is *Hôtel Saint Denis* (☎ 849-4526) at No 1254.

Further north up Rue Saint Denis there's the *Castel Saint Denis* (☎ 842-9719) at No 2099, up the hill just south of Rue Sherbrooke. It's close to the bus station, has been renovated and redecorated a couple of times, and is good value. It's not fancy but it's clean and convenient. Singles range from $35 to $45, doubles from $40 to $50.

East of Rue Saint Denis is *Le Breton* (☎ 524-7273), in an excellent location on a pleasant street. It's at 1609 Rue Saint Hubert, beside the bus station. Singles go from $30 to $45, doubles from $40 to $60; some rooms come with shower or bath, TV, etc. Further south, at 1001 Rue Saint Hubert on the corner of Avenue Viger, is the cheaper but good *Hôtel Viger Centre Ville* (☎ 845-6058). They have a wide variety of rooms from singles/doubles $30/35. The least expensive of the 22 rooms come with sink, colour TV and fan. Near Rue Sainte Cathérine at 1216 Rue Saint Hubert is *Maison Kent*, (☎ 845-9835) with singles from $29 to $48, doubles from $35 to $55. If you don't need your own bathroom, you'll save quite a bit.

West of Rue Saint Denis there are a couple of places to stay on Rue Ontario. At No 307, *Maison de Tourist Villard* (☎ 845-9730) has good rooms with good prices for singles at $28 but the doubles aren't such a bargain at $44. Next door is the *Karukera Hotel* (☎ 845-7932) with prices about the same for a single but less for the doubles and with more of a range of rooms in both categories.

On Rue Sherbrooke Est at Hôtel de Ville, between Boulevard Saint Laurent and Rue Saint Denis, are three tourist homes next door to each other, all in old houses. *Hôtel Pierre* (☎ 288-8519) is at No 169. The *Hôtel Manoir Sherbrooke* at No 157 is now run by

the same people as the *Armor Tourist Lodge* (☎ 285-0410) on the corner. The latter is a large place, lined with natural wood inside. Both are busy places with prices from $29/35 for singles/doubles with no room costing over $55.

At 258 Rue Sherbrooke Ouest, west of Rue Jeanne Mance, is the yellow and green *Maison Casa Bella* (☎ 849-2777). The price range at this central hotel is quite wide with singles from $35 to $60, doubles from $40 to $68.

There are also places scattered about the downtown area. Several can be found along Rue Sainte Cathérine near Boulevard Saint Laurent, where the men, painted ladies and some in-betweens appear at about 6 pm. They're *not* selling insurance but the area is not really tough. *Villa de France* (☎ 849-5043) at 57 Rue Sainte Cathérine Est, is a well-kept, friendly place with a pair of antlers on the lobby wall. Without a bath, singles/doubles cost $30/35; with bath, add $5 or $10. There is another fairly well-kept place at 17 Rue Sainte Cathérine Ouest, with prices about the same.

At 9 Rue Sainte Cathérine Ouest is the *Hebergement l'Abri du Voyageur*, which is nothing fancy. The rooms are simple but clean and, if you're really on a budget, they're quite OK. Rates are $25/35 singles/doubles. Other places nearby tend to be a little dubious.

Going west, the *Ambrose* (☎ 844-0342), at 3422 Rue Stanley, is nicer and in a better location but it costs more, of course, with singles from $30 all the way up to $75, and doubles from $55 to $75. Compared to the sterile international hotels, it's still a bargain and has 22 rooms. One street over, at 1208 Rue Drummond, is the very central *Vines* (☎ 861-8745), which has nine simple rooms costing singles/doubles $27/36.

Lastly, on Rue Mackay south of Boulevard Dorchester, the *Aux Berges* (☎ 878-9393) at 1070 Rue Mackay has an unusual approach limiting itself to serving male homosexual visitors. It's central but on a quiet street and has rooms in the $35 to $40 range.

B&Bs

Another alternative to the high-priced hotels are the B&Bs. Though a relatively new phenomenon in the province, these have caught on so much in Montreal that it's hard to keep up with all the various associations which organise rental rooms in people's homes. There are some individually operated places and some commercial establishments offering this style of accommodation but the majority, by far, are listed by agencies. If you're staying a while, it's worth asking about a weekly rate.

Downtown B&B Network (☎ 289-9749) is an agency run by Bob Finkelstein which has been operating successfully for a number of years now. He has checked over 50 private homes for quality, hospitality and uniqueness beyond minimum requirements. Hosts range from students to lawyers, the places range from mansions with fireplaces in the bedrooms, to Victorian homes, to apartments filled with antiques. Rates are quite reasonable at $25 to $40 for singles, $35 to $55 for doubles and triples are available too. For info and reservations, call or write to 3458 Laval Avenue, Montreal, H2X 3C8.

Montreal B&B (☎ 738-9410) now 10 years old, is a similar organisation with some higher priced homes as well which offer something special.

A newer organisation is *Montreal Oasis* (☎ 935-2312) run by Swedish Lena Blondel out of her own B&B place 3000 Chemin de Breslay (off Avenue Atwater just north of Rue Sherbrooke). Almost all of her participant homes are in older houses in the central core and they pride themselves on the quality of their breakfasts. Ask about the places on quiet and particularly attractive Rue Souvenir which is perfectly located near Rue Sainte Cathérine. Prices range from $45 to $60 a single, $50 to $85 a double and, again, triples are available. Most of the places welcome children.

Welcome B&B (☎ 844-5897) is a smaller outfit that specialises in turn-of-the-century places around the interesting French area of Rue Saint Denis and Carré Saint Louis. Call or write to 3950 Laval Avenue, Montreal

H2W 2J2. Laval Avenue is one block west of Rue Saint Denis and the office is a couple of blocks north of Rue Sherbrooke, a short walk from the Sherbrooke Métro stop.

There are several other organisations, the tourist office will have a complete list. Prices are generally quite moderate.

Hotels & Efficiencies

If you really like a more conventional, modern hotel but not the prices accompanying the usual downtown luxury choices try the newly renovated *Hôtel Europa* (☎ 866-6492) now part of the Best Western chain. It will fill the bill with prices as reasonable as you're likely to find: from singles/doubles $60/80. The Red Lobster restaurant in the hotel is not too bad for reasonably priced seafood either. The very central hotel is at 1240 Rue Drummond near Rue Sainte Cathérine.

Comfort Suites (☎ 878-2711), at 1214 Rue Crescent, has rooms with complete cooking facilities for $80 a night for two people. If you stay for six nights, you get the seventh night free. All kitchen supplies are included, as are air-con and TV. There are several other similar apartment-style places downtown: the tourist office can help you find one.

Other middle-priced hotels include the *Hôtel Montréal Crescent* (☎ 878-9797), at 1366 Boulevard Dorchester, with prices from $75 to $90 and the *Auberge Ramada* (☎ 256-9011), at 5500 Rue Sherbrooke Est by the Olympic Park, from $130 to $160.

Motels

There are two main motel districts in Montreal; other motels are scattered. All charge less in the off-season (ie not in summer): the rates here are summer ones. The area closest to town is conveniently situated along Rue Saint Jacques. It's west of the downtown area, south and parallel to Boulevard de Maisonneuve. Look around where Rue Cavendish runs into Rue Saint Jacques from Rue Sherbrooke. This area is about a 10-minute drive from the centre. Coming from the west (from places like Dorval Airport), highways 2 and 20 flow into Rue Saint Jacques.

Motels – bottom end & middle The *Colibri* (☎ 486-1167), at 6960 Rue Saint Jacques, charges singles/doubles $24/28. It's behind Harvey's hamburger place and is white with purple polka dots.

The smallish *Aubin* (☎ 484-5198) with 20 rooms, at 6125 Rue Saint Jacques, has singles/doubles for $48/53.

The *Cavalier* at No 6951 charges from $35 to $45 for singles, from $45 to $50 for doubles. Nearby at No 7455, *Motel Raphaël* (☎ 485-3344), is good value at $44.50 for doubles, with swimming pool and restaurant.

The second district for motels is on Boulevard Tashereau on the south shore, across the river on the mainland. The street is also known as Highway 134 and stretches out of the city in both directions. Many of the motels are at the bridges – check at the Jacques Cartier (in Old Montreal) and Champlain in the west end. Victoria Bridge is between these two.

At 1277 Boulevard Tashereau is *La Parisienne* (☎ 674-6291). Singles/doubles cost $55.

The *Falcon Motel* (☎ 676-0215) is at 6225 Boulevard Tashereau, with singles from $40 to $49, doubles from $42 to $52. Ask for the rooms with no extras.

The *Florence* (☎ 676-7938) at 5791 Boulevard Tashereau has 32 rooms from $37 to $55. There are several other places in the blocks around No 7000.

A couple of places on Rue Sherbrooke are *Le Paysan* (☎ 640-1415), at 12400 Rue Sherbrooke Est, from $45 to $85 and *Le Marquis*, at No 6720, similarly priced. Others in the area are more costly.

The *Hôtel Métro* (☎ 381-2577), at 9925 Rue Lajeunesse, is a good bargain with singles/doubles for $30/50, TVs and city maps included. From the Metropolitan East Highway take exit 73 (Rue Saint Hubert), go to Sauvé and then you'll see Rue Lajeunesse. Or get off at the Sauvé Métro station.

Lastly, you may want to try *Chomedy Inn* (☎ 681-9251) at 590 Boulevard Labelle – it has adult movies, water beds and mirrors on the ceiling. There are reduced prices on – oh my God – Sunday.

Motels – top end The following hotels are in the 'expensive' category. Despite the rather hefty prices, geared mainly to the business traveller, what irks the most in these places is being nickled and dimed outrageously for parking, telephone calls, drinks in the room fridge, and every other time you turn around. Some of the major hotels do have pretty good lower-priced weekend specials which may appeal to some for a splurge; prices are generally lower in summer when there is less commercial traffic.

Le Château Champlain (☎ 878-9000), Place du Canada, has rooms from $190 to $240. This hotel is right across the street from the Windsor railway station. Ask for a room facing Square Dorchester and the view will be quite good. The top-floor bar also has windows overlooking the city. There's a restaurant and Vegas-style revues are often presented.

Nearby is the *Bonaventure Hilton* (☎ 878-2332), Place Bonaventure, with rooms from $155 to $375.

The *Ritz Carlton* (☎ 842-4212), 1228 Rue Sherbrooke Ouest, with rooms from $235 to $340, has long been a hotel of distinction and reputation. The penthouse suite here is the most expensive place to stay in Canada (and it's probably not too shabby either). This seems to be the hotel of choice for business, entertainment and, if it's not an oxymoron, political superstars.

PLACES TO EAT

The French have long been responsible for Montreal's excellent restaurant reputation, which various immigrant groups have only added to over the years. There is no shortage of restaurants here, some 5000 at last count, and you'll find good food in all price ranges. Many places have lunch specials – always the best bargains – and at dinner, a table d'hôte fixed-price complete dinner.

Many Montreal restaurants, generally in the lower and middle-price brackets, have a 'bring your own' wine policy. If you want to take advantage of this great idea and bring your own wine for a meal, you can get it in a *dépanneur* (convenience store) if there is no government outlet around or it's past closing time. In Quebec you can pick up a bottle of French wine, bottled in the province, for $6 to $8 at the liquor outlets, or from grocery stores where the price goes up from 50 cents to $1.

In Montreal, women aren't allowed in the very few remaining taverns but even these places haven't been barring females. Tavern-style places more geared to both sexes are called brasseries and, aside from being good places for buying cheap draught, are usually sources of decent low-priced meals which you can eat in a casual atmosphere.

Many restaurants, particularly the better ones, don't start to get busy until around 8 pm and will stay that way for a couple of hours. If you're an early eater in this city, you may have the place to yourself.

Central Area

At the corner of Boulevard de Maisonneuve and Rue Metcalfe, *Ben's* is an institution. Montreal is known far and wide for its smoked meat and the Ben's name is familiar across the country. It's a very informal deli, full of office workers at lunch time. Sandwiches are served lean or fatty – you can ask for your preference – and they're $3 something or an extra buck or two with French fries, pickle and coffee.

The *Bar B Barn*, at 1201 Rue Guy, is too small – it's usually packed, with a queue out the front to boot – but they serve the best and biggest spareribs you've ever had. It's a comfortable, attractive place as well. The only other thing on the menu is chicken. This place is good value with meals costing from $11 to $16 and there's parking around the back.

Rue de la Montagne and Rue Crescent offer a range of places. *Aida's*, 2020 Rue Crescent on the corner of Boulevard de Maisonneuve, has felafels and other cheap light meals. At 2170 Rue de la Montagne *Katsura* is a popular Japanese place which is quite reasonably priced at lunch but more pricey for the evening meal. *O Blitz* at 1189 Rue de la Montagne is one of several good brasseries in the area. They're busy at noon

because of the cheap beer and meals for $4.50. On weekends they open at 4 pm.

Further east along Rue Sainte Cathérine on the 3rd floor of the Eaton Centre is the *Magic Pan Crêperie*, with crêpes from $5.50 to $7.25. The address is actually 1500 Avenue McGill College.

The busy *Tramway* is in the centre of town at 1122 Rue Sainte Cathérine Ouest. It's basically a brasserie, although spiffier, with standard meals and steaks. The *International Pub*, formerly the males-only Rymark Tavern, around the corner and south of Rue Peel towards Windsor Station, is an old gem that's been around for a long time. They serve cheap beer with inexpensive, standard tavern fare; the speciality is ham boiled in beer with baked beans, and it makes a decent lunch. Check out the wood panelling. Another similar but older style tavern, with women clientele though, is the lively *Taverne Carré Dominion*, at 1243 Rue Metcalfe, just south of Rue Sainte Cathérine.

Out of the beer parlours, for a splurge there is *Chez Pauze*, another old-time place (it began in 1862) with a good name. It's on the north side of Rue Sainte Cathérine Ouest at No 1657, towards the Forum on the corner of Avenue Atwater. Seafood is their speciality. Meal prices range from $12 to $25.

On Rue Metcalfe up from Rue Sainte Cathérine are two well-known, long-established steak houses – *Joe's* and *Curly Joe's*, with similar menus and prices. At *Curly Joe's*, good steak dinners range from $8 to $17; the meal includes a baked potato or French fries and an excellent all-you-can-eat salad bar. You can have just the salad bar to catch up on some greens for just $6. All meals though are good value.

Dunn's, at 892 Rue Sainte Cathérine Ouest near Rue Peel, is a deli open (and usually pretty busy) 24 hours a day. It's good for a late night snack or early morning breakfast.

There are several Indian restaurants in this central area. At 1241 Rue Guy is the *Woodlands New Indian Restaurant* with a very extensive vegetarian menu. Next door the *Pattaya* is a fancier place offering Thai food, and next to that, the *Curry House* has dinner for three for a little over $40 and some very interesting dishes available. There is also *Pique Assiette*, at 2051 Rue Sainte Cathérine Ouest, one of the city's oldest Indian restaurants. Dinner for two costs about $25. This was the first of the international Bombay Palace chain of Indian restaurants.

For lingering over a coffee, there are numerous cafés in the Rue Crescent and Rue de la Montagne area. There are a couple of Parisian-style ones on Boulevard de Maisonneuve here. Less ostentatious is *Café Drummond* at 2005 Rue Drummond.

For making up your own meal, try shopping around *Le Fauberg* at 1616 Rue Sainte Cathérine Ouest. The basement of this new Parisian-style mall is devoted to food and is a sort of market, which includes a bakery and liquor store. Also see Markets at the end of the Things to See section earlier.

Old Montreal

Old Montreal is a fine place to splurge. Menus with prices are posted outside. For good French seafood, try *Le Fripon*, at 436 Place Jaques Cartier in front of the Hôtel de Ville, with dishes from $14 to $17. The Dover sole is good with lobster soup and *escargot* from the 'prix fixe' menu. If you need help with the French menu, the waiters will explain. The only drawback is the price of the wine. Another place worth investigating is on the corner of Rue Saint Paul and Rue Saint Sulpice. The renovated *La Belle Poule* will re-open with a new chef. It has long been a reliable place for lingering over a meal. Their former chef is now employed at the new Le Fripon mentioned above. Also good is *La Sauvagine* at 115 Rue Saint Paul on the corner of Rue Saint Vincent. Lunch prices range from $5 to $8, dinners from $13 to $18. Both restaurants are comfortable and friendly.

Another fine but more expensive place is *Les Filles du Roy* at 415 Rue Bonsecours. The dining room here is softly lit by a skylight until it's dark. They serve French food and offer a bountiful lunch buffet for $13.95 on Sunday and a more modest one at $8.95 from Monday to Friday.

There are inexpensive places in this busy part of town too. *À la Bonne Bouffe*, at 250 Rue Saint Paul on the corner of Place Jacques Cartier, is a real bargain. Lunches cost from $4.25, everything included. The food is good and this is a dining room, not a greasy spoon. At 273 Rue Saint Paul Est is *L'Usine de Spaghetti Parisienne* with meals from $6 to $12, including all the bread and salad you can eat.

On the east side of Rue Saint François Xavier at No 447 is a small student-type Tunisian place specialising in North African meals, including various couscous and lamb dishes. Prices range from $4.50 to $7.50. This is a pleasant café mostly frequented by young people. Bring your own wine.

The very informal *Brasserie Lambert Closse*, at 435 B Rue Saint Vincent near Rue Thérèse, is also cheap. It's not far from Rue Notre Dame and the tourist office – around the back, down the alley. Tables are available outside in summer. They serve various lunch specials costing from $3.75 to $5.50 and cheap mugs of beer. Dinner, much the same, is served until 7 pm. Another brasserie is on the corner of Rue Saint Paul and Boulevard Saint Laurent. They offer very cheap breakfasts and lunches.

Chez Delmo, 211 Rue Notre Dame Ouest, is slightly away from the heavily touristed area and relies on locals for business. It's very busy at lunch time serving its inexpensive seafood specialities; the daily specials are cheapest. It's open for lunch until 3 pm, then later for dinner. Lunches cost around $8 and are served at the long counters on both walls – a strange set-up. Dinners are more expensive at $16 for a main dish but the food is good. It's closed on Sunday but open Saturday evening from 6 to 11 pm.

There are lots of cafés set up around Place Jacques Cartier. In summer, it's great for sipping a coffee, resting the feet or contemplating life's mysteries at the outside tables. The *Restaurant des Gouverneurs* is cheapest although they all charge more for the outdoor tables. The small café, at 143 Rue Saint Paul Ouest away from the crowds, is reasonable with light lunches for $4. They serve croissants and espresso too.

Rue Prince Arthur

Rue Prince Arthur is a small street which was converted into a very pleasant eating area about 10 years ago. The restaurant segment runs west from Place Saint Louis on Rue Saint Denis (just north of Rue Sherbrooke) to a block west of Boulevard Saint Laurent. Many small, mostly ethnic restaurants line the 'pedestrians only' street. Greek and Vietnamese restaurants are most prominent but there are also French and Polish places among others. Most of the restaurants here have a 'bring your own' wine policy. The Greek places specialise in a Montreal favourite, brochettes, known to many as kebabs. Generally the more traditional dishes such as moussaka are absent but vine leaves or spanokopita show up as appetisers and there is always Greek salad.

For Vietnamese food, try *Xuan* at 26 Rue Prince Arthur Ouest. Meals range from $6 to $12 and they serve very good food.

An excellent Greek dinner can be had at *La Casa Grèque*, at 200 Rue Prince Arthur Est, for about $20 for two – very good value. I've also had a good lunch at *Cabane Grèque Restaurant*, another Greek place. For a bit of a splurge the *Akito*, a Japanese place on Rue Prince Arthur, does everything well. Before 7.30 pm the set meal is good value.

The *Croissanterie* on the east side of Rue Saint Denis, downstairs just south of Rue Ontario, is a great place for breakfasts. *Café au lait* and one or two of the fresh sweet buns or croissants will hold you for a few hours.

On Rue Ontario just west of Rue Saint Denis, in the 300 block, there are several cheap cafés, mostly patronised by students and arty types, offering light meals. One of them, *Le Petit Peu*, serves health foods. At 2115 Rue Saint Denis, *Le Commensal*, open everyday from 11 am to midnight, offers self-serve vegetarian meals priced by weight. You can really heap it up and the cost won't be high.

Le Calife, at 1633 Rue Saint Hubert, is a small, unpretentious place with offerings like vegetables with couscous and mint tea or coffee for $4.25. You can select other Tunisian meals as well.

A well-established, very popular low-cost restaurant is *Da Giovanni* at 572 Rue Sainte Cathérine Est. You can have a good, complete meal (from soup to dessert) featuring spaghetti for under $5. Other dishes such as fish or meat are available at not much higher prices. Arrive before 5.30 pm to avoid waiting in line. It closes at 8 pm.

The Main & Avenue Duluth

Boulevard Saint Laurent, the major north-south street which divides the city streets east from west has long had a reputation for its characters, varied ethnic groups, their businesses and restaurants. As I've said before, it's affectionately known as The Main.

Just south of Rue Sainte Cathérine are several of the city's best known French fries/hot dog places – memorably good. The dogs are known as 'steamies' because of the way they're cooked. If you ask for 'all dress', everyone will understand and you'll get the full Quebec treatment, complete with chopped cabbage.

Much further north is a must: *Schwartz's* at No 3895. It's a small, very casual, friendly deli that's practically never closed. It is always packed and has absolutely the best smoked meat in town. They make it right on the premises and age it naturally without chemicals.

The section of Boulevard Saint Laurent around Rue Prince Arthur has numerous places in either direction, many of them very reasonably priced. But anywhere along the street you could discover a new Indian or African restaurant.

Avenue Duluth runs east-west off Boulevard Saint Laurent at about the No 4000 block. Much like Rue Prince Arthur it's a narrow old street, once a red-light district, that has been redone as a restaurant centre although it is not quite as busy as Rue Prince Arthur. From just east of Boulevard Saint Laurent, running east to Rue Saint Denis and beyond, there are numerous Greek, Italian and Vietnamese eateries. Near Boulevard

Saint Laurent at 65 Avenue Duluth Est, *Le Camelia* is a moderately priced Vietnamese place. At No 450 try *La Maison Grèque*, which is very busy but large, with an outdoor area for good-value brochette dinners. There's a dépanneur nearby for grabbing a bottle of wine. Further east near Rue Saint Hubert, there are a couple of more expensive French restaurants.

Chinatown

Montreal's Chinatown is a small but well-entrenched part of the city. Though its restaurants can't compare to those in Toronto's or Vancouver's Chinatowns, there are quite a few of them. As always, it's best to eat with three or more people so you can sample more dishes. The district is centred on Rue de la Gauchetière Ouest between Rue Saint Urbain and Boulevard Saint Laurent, east of Dominion Square, north of Old Montreal. The food is mainly Cantonese although some spicier Sichuan dishes show up on more menus these days. Many places offer lunch specials from as low as $5 or $6.

Places both cheap and not so cheap can be found along Rue de la Gauchetière. The *Restaurant Hunan*, at 1092 Boulevard Saint Laurent, is not very low-budget but has some hot dishes.

Also on Boulevard Saint Laurent, the *Cristal de Saigon* at No 1068 has very cheap but plain Vietnamese food, and the *Fung Lam* across the street at No 1071 is the same but has Cantonese food. *Maison Kam Fung* is a huge, moderately priced place at 1008 Rue Clark which stays open until midnight daily.

Avenue du Parc

Avenue du Parc, running north up beyond the mountain, has numerous more traditional Greek restaurants (no kebabs or brochettes), many specialising in fish. There are also a few Portuguese places along here too.

ENTERTAINMENT

Montreal nightlife is good, varied, and comes in two languages. Clubs serve alcohol until 3 am – that's civilisation. Many places don't get going until around 10 pm or later. Films, plays and shows are not censored here as in more puritan places, eg Ontario.

The *Mirror* is a free weekly entertainment newspaper which can be picked up around town. The Saturday *Montreal Gazette* also has club and entertainment listings.

Live Music & Disco

The *Rising Sun*, (☎ 278-5200), at 5380 Boulevard Saint Laurent, brings in established blues, jazz and reggae acts – good but admission can be hefty.

Rue Crescent and Rue de la Montagne are lively at night, with mostly disco-type places (no jeans allowed). *L'Esprit*, at 1234 Rue de la Montagne below Rue Sainte Cathérine, is in a former funeral parlour. It's sort of dressy and admission costs $7 on weekends. *Thursdays* on Rue Crescent is a singles-style spot. Nearby, over on Rue Bishop, there are several pubs. It's fun just to wander around this area at night, maybe have a beer and people-watch.

The *Limelight* is on Rue Stanley in the busy nightclub area just off Rue Sainte Cathérine. It's a giant disco with a light-and-sound extravaganza. The busy Limelight is constantly changing, but seems to draw people of all sexual persuasions. Admission is charged.

The *Metropolis*, at 59 Rue Sainte Cathérine Est, is the largest dance club in town, with bars spread over three floors and impressive sound and lighting systems. It's only open from Thursday to Sunday. For the business and professional crowd, the *Pacha* at 1207 Boulevard de Maisonneuve on the corner of Rue Drummond is popular.

The *Old Munich* is in the large, square building on Rue Saint Denis on the corner of Boulevard Dorchester. Inside it's a vast, cavernous, pub-style place that's often full with people of all types and ages. The place has a real party atmosphere. In the centre, amidst the smoke and noise, a band encourages a break from drinking with a dance to German oompah Oktoberfest-type music – no cover charge.

The *Yellow Door Coffee House* (☎ 392-

6743), at 3625 Rue Aylmer, is a survivor
from the '60s – US draft dodgers found
refuge here – where folk music in a casual
ambience is still presented.

In Old Montreal at 104 Rue Saint Paul, *Les
Deux Pierrots* is a huge, two-storey spot with
local French singers and a casual atmosphere
– it's free.

New wave music can be heard cheaply at
Les Foufounes, 87 Rue Sainte Cathérine Est.

There are several good spots for jazz in
town. *L'Air du Temps* (☎ 842-2002) is in Old
Montreal at 191 Rue Saint Paul Ouest on the
corner of Rue Saint François Xavier. Solo
music starts at 5 pm, groups after 9.30 pm;
performers are mostly local musicians.
There's no cover charge and the atmosphere
and decor are pleasant.

At *Biddles* (☎ 842-8656), at 2060 Rue
Aylmer, you might get a standard trio, a
swing band or a vocalist. You can eat here
too; there's no cover charge. The *Grand
Café*, at 1720 Rue Saint Denis, presents live
jazz and blues at a modest price. Not far away
on Rue Ontario, local musicians play at *Café
Thélème* also with no cover charge.

Other

For a view of the city, try the rooftop bar in
the luxury *Château Champlain* on Dominion
Square. Drinks are costly but the view is fine.

The *Comedyworks* upstairs at 1234 Rue
Bishop presents stand-up comics, usually
several in a night. Admission is charged. For
theatre, the *Centaur Theatre* (☎ 288-3161) at
453 Rue Saint François Xavier, generally has
the best in English presentations. *Les Ballet
Jazz*, a Montreal modern dance troupe, has a
very good reputation and often performs in
town. *Place des Arts* presents an array of
concerts, the symphony, and dance.

Cinema

There are several English-language repertory film theatres around town, usually
offering double bills and midnight movies on
weekends. These theatres are always cheaper
than the chains showing first runs.

The *Rialto* (☎ 274-3550), at 5723 Avenue
du Parc, presents two different showings a
night. Most are US releases but there are also
some European films shown.

More central, but with a similar policy, is
the *Paris Cinema* (☎ 875-7284) at 896 Rue
Sainte Cathérine Ouest.

The McGill and Loyola campuses often
run film series. There is an IMAX (☎ 469-
4629) large-format theatre in the Vieux Port
(Old Port) area of Montreal.

THINGS TO BUY

The Canadian Guild of Crafts, at 2025 Rue
Peel, has a small and rather expensive collection of the work of Quebec artisans and
other Canadiana, as well as Inuit prints and
carvings. It's free to look around.

Although inconveniently located in west
suburban Kirkland, the Baffin Inuit Art
Gallery (☎ 694-1587), at 28 Piper's Crescent, has a fine varied collection of stone
carvings. Call ahead for an appointment to
have a look. You can buy as well, but the
pieces here are real collectables and are not
cheap.

GETTING THERE & AWAY
Air

There are two airports. Dorval, 20 km west
of the centre of town, is used for domestic
and North American flights. Mirabel Airport
is just over 50 km north-west of the town's
centre and handles all other international
flights.

Many airlines serve Montreal, including
the major Canadian ones. Quebecair also
serves the province of Quebec. A selection
of fares includes Air Canada (☎ 393-3333),
to Halifax $258, Toronto $118, and Winnipeg $426. Canadian Airlines (☎ 931-2233)
has the same prices as Air Canada.

A good place to start looking for cheap
fares is Voyages CUTS which has an office
on Rue Saint Denis and another at the McGill
University campus. (Montreal can also offer
very low fares to Florida, Mexico and parts
of the Caribbean.)

Czechoslovak Airlines is worth checking
for cheap flights to New York.

Bus

The terminal is very central on the corner of Boulevard de Maisonneuve and Rue Berri, near Rue Saint Denis. It's right beside the Berri-UQAM Métro stop. The station serves Voyageur lines (☎ 842-2281) and Greyhound from the USA, and also Vermont Transit, which runs between Montreal and Boston, about seven hours away. When dealing with Greyhound for US destinations make sure you know which currency is being discussed.

Voyageur destinations and services include to Ottawa every hour for $21.50; to Toronto about five services daily, more on weekends for $48; and to Quebec for $29.50.

Murray Hill (☎ 937-5311), at 1380 Rue Barre, runs ski bus expresses in season. They make two runs into the Laurentians and two to Vermont destinations. Most runs start at a major downtown hotel.

Train

There are two railway stations right near each other in the central area. You can walk underground from one to the other in 10 minutes.

The CN-VIA Rail station, also called Central Station, below the Queen Elizabeth Hotel on the corner of Boulevard René Lévesque and Rue Mansfield, gets most VIA Rail (☎ 871-1331) passengers. Use the Bonaventure Métro station.

Windsor Station, the CP terminal, is on the corner of Rue Peel and Rue de la Gauchetière, a few blocks from the CN station. Use the same Métro stop. It's mainly local commuter trains which use this venerable old station now.

There are three trains a day to Ottawa most days and five trains a day to Toronto, starting at 7.30 am. Fares are: Ottawa $27, Toronto $67, and Quebec City $33.

For information about US destinations call Amtrakon ☎ 800-426-8725 toll free. Amtrak to New York costs $US72 one way, with very cheap returns available. Fares vary depending on the month in which you travel. Remember when inquiring about fares to US destinations to check whether prices are being given in US dollars. They probably are.

Car & Motorbike

The Trans Canada Highway runs right through the city and Highway 15 leads south to US 87 heading for New York. Highway 401 joins Montreal to Toronto and beyond. For car rentals Budget (☎ 866-7675) with offices around town has one in Central Station downtown charges $40 per day with 100 free km, 14 cents per km over that for their economy cars. Tax is extra. Tilden (☎ 878-2771), at 1200 Rue Stanley, has exactly the same rates as Budget.

For cheaper rates try Via Route (☎ 871-1166), at 1444 Boulevard René Lévesque Ouest, or Mini-Prix, at 2000 Rue Sainte Cathérine Est. The latter has vans as well as cars. Getting a small group together could be quite economical.

There are many other companies and outlets all over town including at both airports. Prices tend not to vary a heck of a lot but differences can be found among the weekend specials and other multiple-day offers.

Car Sharing Allo Stop (☎ 282-0121), at 4317 Rue Saint Denis, is an agency that gets drivers and passengers together. Call a day ahead and tell them where you want to go. Prices are good; it's $12 to Quebec City, for example. Allo Stop also goes to Toronto, New York and other cities. You must pay a $2 membership fee. They have offices in Toronto, Quebec City and other points around Quebec.

GETTING AROUND
To/From the Airport

The cheapest way to Dorval Airport is to take the Métro to Crémazie, then catch bus No 100 west towards the airport and ask the driver to let you off to catch bus No 209, which will take you right in. The total cost is $1.50.

There is also the Aérocar bus (☎ 379-9999) to Dorval Airport for $7, leaving every 20 minutes from the Queen Elizabeth Hotel.

The ride takes a little under half an hour. The Aérocar bus to Mirabel taking about 45 minutes costs $9 and runs every 30 to 60 minutes. A taxi to or from Dorval is about $20, to Mirabel over double that.

Murray Hill (☎ 937-5311) runs a limo service to either airport; they'll pick you up anywhere but the cost is high, more than a cab.

Bus & Métro

The city has a fairly widespread, convenient Métro-bus system. The Métro runs until 1.30 am and some buses run even later. One ticket can get you anywhere in the city as it entitles you to a transfer to any connecting bus or train. On the buses, get a transfer from the driver and on the Métro from the machines past the turnstiles. A strip of six tickets is $7 for six or single tickets cost $1.50 each. Buses take tickets, transfers, or correct cash only.

Métro routes are shown on the tourist map

and stops are indicated above ground by large blue signs with a white arrow pointing down. The system runs basically east-west with a north-south line intersecting at Berri-UQAM. It runs on rubber tyres and is safe, clean, fast and quiet. For information on how to get to any particular spot, call ☎ 288-6287.

Car

In town, most streets are one way and the drivers are very aggressive. Watch the action at yellow lights. Pedestrians are fair game; pedestrian crossings mean little.

Bicycle

Montreal is continuing to improve as a biking city. The city publishes a map of routes and trails which should be available at tourist offices. If not, try one of the libraries or police stations.

One route leads from the edge of Old Montreal, south-west all the way to Lachine along the old canal. Parks Canada (☎ 283-

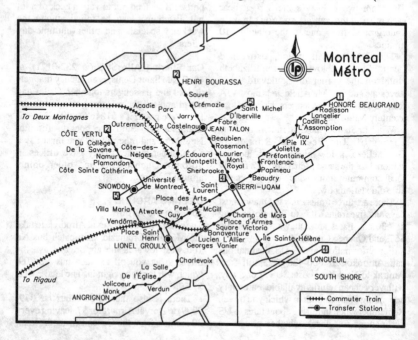

6054) runs guided historical trips along this bike path.

At Parc des Îles-de-Boucherville there are 22 km of trails connected with the islands by bridges and ferries. The main entrance on Île Sainte Marguerite is served by city buses. Bikes can be rented at the park. A ferry connects Quai de Boucherville with Île Grosbois Thursday to Sunday, from 10 am to 4 pm for $1.50. Most of the trails offer good views of the city.

Le Monde à Bicyclette (☎ 844-2713) is a cycling association which runs free trips through various parts of the city. They meet downtown on Sunday mornings and start from there. Their office is at 20 Rue Guilbault Est.

For rentals, try Cycle Peel (☎ 486-1148) at 6665 Rue Saint Jacques Ouest. Another rental place can be found at the Old Port and there is one in the tourist office on Square Dorchester.

Bicycles can be taken on the Métro in the last two carriages of the train.

Calèche

These horse-drawn carriages seen mainly around Square Dorchester, Old Montreal or up on the mountain, charge from $30 to $40 an hour. Four or five people can ride at a time. In winter, sleighs are used for trips up and around Mont Royal.

Around Montreal

OKA

This is a small town about 60 km west of Montreal, where the Ottawa River meets the St Lawrence River. It's on the north mainland shore, north of Dorion on the edge of Lac des Deux Montagnes, a bulge in the river. The place is well known for the Trappist monastery, now 100 years old, and the cheeses it produces. The cheese-producing was taken over by business people, and the monastery of 70 monks has been opened to visitors. There are religious artworks, a

mountain with the Stages of the Cross and several old stone buildings.

Oka became internationally known late in 1990 as the site of a major confrontation between Mohawk people and the federal and provincial governments. At first a local land squabble, this issue soon came to represent all the continuing problems such as land claims and self-government which Native Indians across the country would like to see properly resolved.

ROUGE RIVER

Not far north-west of Montreal near the Ontario border, the Rouge River is well known for white-water rafting. Several companies offer day or weekend trips which most people reckon are a lot of fun. One to try is New World River Expeditions with an office in Montreal. They have an office in Calumet, Quebec on the river or you can call toll free (☎ 800-567-6881). They have a lodge with pool and bar, so you're not roughing it in the bush the whole time. Another is Eau Vive which has operated for 10 years.

THE LAURENTIANS (LAURENTIDES)

Between 80 km and 150 km north of Montreal, this section of the ancient Laurentian Shield is a mountainous, rolling lake-sprinkled playground. The land proved a dismal failure for lumber and mining, but when skiing caught on, so did this area as a resortland. The district today is used not only for the best in eastern skiing but for camping, fishing and swimming in summer. The many picturesque French towns dominated by their church spires and the good scenery make it popular for just lazing and relaxing as well. Plentiful accommodation and restaurants provide a wide range of services, from elegant inns with fine dining rooms to modest motels.

The Laurentian Autoroute (Autoroute Laurentienne), also known as Highway 15 (with tolls), is the fastest route north from Montreal and is the way the buses go. The old Highway 117 north is slower but more pleasant. A second major route goes north-east of Montreal to Joliette and then smaller roads continue further north.

The better known towns and resorts are all clustered near the highways. Cottage country spreads out a little further east and west. In general terms the busy area ends at Mont Tremblant Provincial Park. The smaller villages on the upper areas of Highway 117 are quiet and typically 'Laurentian'.

To find less developed areas or to camp, you pretty much have to head for the big parks, as most of the region is privately owned. Many of the towns have tourist offices so you can ask about things as you go. Outside the parks, campgrounds are generally privately owned too, and tend to be small and busy. Motels are next up the economic scale; the lodges are generally (but not always) quite pricey. There is usually a hostel somewhere in the area, but locations change often, so ask in Montreal.

The busiest times in the Laurentians are July, August, around Christmas, February and March. At other times, prices tend to be reduced, like the crowds. Fall is a good season to visit, the hills are very colourful and the cooler air is ideal for walking. The whole area (in all seasons) has a festive, relaxed atmosphere.

In ski season, special buses operate between Dorval Airport and various hills. They're a little more expensive than the usual bus fares; return tickets are cheapest.

Saint Saveur

Saint Saveur, the first stop-off on the way north, is a small pleasant resort town with four nearby ski hills. Summer or winter, day or night, the main street with its restaurants, cafés, bars and shops is busy.

Mont Rolland

Mont Rolland is a summer-winter recreation centre based at Mont Gabriel. There's excellent skiing in winter and in summer the mountain turns into a huge slide complex, a trend which many of the area's resorts have embraced. This one differs in that it is not a

water slide, as such, but instead uses bob-sleds sliding on ball bearings. Hang on tight!

The Rolland Paper Company one of the oldest and most important paper makers in the country is based here.

The *Auberge Mont Gabriel* on top of the mountain is one of the larger, more expensive lodges in the Laurentians.

Sainte Adèle

Sainte Adèle is one of the nicer-looking highway towns, with a popular recreation area, Lac Rond.

A museum recreates a story by one of the towns most illustrious sons, popular Quebec author Claude-Henri Grignon.

At 151 Rue Lesage, there's a place to stay called *Pension Sainte Adèle en Haut*. It's in an old house and has five rooms for rent (with breakfast included) at moderate rates; dinner is available.

Sainte Agathe des Monts

With about 7000 people, this is the largest town in the Laurentians and a busy resort centre. With numerous bars, cafés and restaurants, as well as shops for replenishing supplies, there is always plenty of activity. The local bakery, on Rue Sainte Agathe, is known far and wide.

At the edge of Lac des Sables, more or less in town, there is room for a picnic, and cruises of the lake depart from the wharf. Around the lake are beaches and places to camp.

B&Bs, inns (auberges) and motels all tend to be quite busy, especially on weekends, so planning ahead is advisable. Try the B&B *Auberge la Caravelle* (☎ 326-4272) at 92 Rue Major. At the end of July, watch for the annual music and dance festival.

Val David

Close to Sainte Agathe but to the east off Highway 15, Val David is a considerably smaller town that's become a sort of arts and crafts centre. Studios and workshops can be visited, and stores sell a variety of handicrafts.

There is a *Youth Hostel* (☎ 322-1972), at

1451 Rue Beaumont, in a rustic log chalet perched on a hill with great views. If you call from Montreal a shuttle bus will meet the bus from Montreal and take you to the hostel. This is the only hostel in the region but it's in a good location typifying what the Laurentians are all about.

Saint Faustin

Saint Faustin has a population of about 1200 and a large nature interpretive centre on grounds containing 15 km of walking and hiking trails. It's free and maps are available at the centre where there is information on the flora & fauna of the area.

Also here in a nice setting is a trout hatchery which can be visited. The fish raised here are used to restock the rivers and lakes of the Laurentians.

Saint Jovite

Heading further north, this smaller town is south of but near **Mont Tremblant** which lies just outside the provincial park of the same name. The mountain, with its 650-metre vertical drop, is the highest peak in the Laurentians. With over 20 runs, it's the most popular skiing spot, and marks the northernmost point of the easily accessible Laurentian destinations. Saint Jovite is a supply centre for the Mont Tremblant area with its many lakes.

At the foot of the mountain, 146 km from Montreal, is Mont Tremblant Village, an accommodation centre which has a chair lift to the peak in summer and winter.

In Weir, not far south of Saint Jovite, is the **Laurentides Satellite Earth Station**, an international telecommunications installation. There are free guided tours of the facilities and 10-storey-high antennae, as well as slide presentations. It's open daily from mid-June to Labour Day. Follow the signs from Weir.

Saint Donat

North-east of Sainte Agathe, this little lakeside town is a supply centre for the main entrance to Mont Tremblant Provincial Park which lies just to the north.

There are beaches on **Lac Archambault** and, in summer, 90-minute cruises around the lake.

Accommodation of all types can be found in and around town. Bars and cafés along the main streets are lively at night.

Mont Tremblant Provincial Park

Opened as early as 1894, this is a huge area – over 1500 sq km – of lakes, rivers, hills and woods. There are many campsites in the park – some with amenities but most are basic. The most developed area is north of Saint Donat. Roads are paved, canoes can be rented, and the campgrounds have showers, etc. Not too far from the entrance there are a couple of good walking paths with views and, a little further in, a fair-sized waterfall with nearby picnic tables.

Towards the interior, some campsites are accessible only by foot, canoe or unsurfaced roads some of which are rough old logging routes. The more off-the-track areas abound in wildlife.

In the far eastern section one September, we had whole lakes to ourselves, saw moose and heard nearby wolves howling as we sat around the fire. Nights were very cold so be prepared.

Mark Lightbody

LANAUDIÈRE

Lanaudière refers to the region north-east of Montreal and, though it is essentially still 'up north' or 'the Laurentians', it has cultivated its own identity. Without the quality ski hills and far fewer large towns it is, though still popular, a less visited region. There are plenty of parks with walking trails over mountains and along rivers to enjoy. The southern area has its own cowboys. And food and lodging is noticeably cheaper than in the places further west along the autoroute. For any specific area information call the Lanaudière tourist office toll free on ☎ 800-363-2788.

Terrebonne

Believe it or not the Moulins region of southwest Lanaudière around the towns of

Terrebonne and Mascouche and along the north shore of Rivière des Milles Îles is cowboy country. Here, about a 45-minute drive from downtown Montreal, there are about 30 ranches, thousands of horses and plenty of events for their fully Western-style riders to compete in. Through the summer various horse shows, rodeos and gymkhanas are an almost weekly occurrence.

Pretty well every Saturday night at Tico-Smokey Ranch outside Terrebonne there is a competition of one sort or another. On Friday and Saturday nights, fans and riders meet for country music and dancing at the Chalet de la Vallée at 1231 Chemin Pincourt in Mascouche, but don't arrive too early – these cowboys don't have to get up before the sun.

Frequently throughout the summer there are major two-day rodeos with calf roping, steer wrestling, bronco busting, the whole bit. For a schedule of events and locations call the Lanaudière tourist office. Many stables in the area offer horses and trail rides, some not ending until midnight.

When your legs have had enough, the Wild West can be left far behind with a visit to the village of Vieux Terrebonne along the Rivière des Milles Îles, opposite Île des Moulins. Here along the waterfront are numerous restaurants and cafés.

Joliette

Joliette is a principal town and centre for the local tobacco-growing industry. You may notice that in some areas, the farmland is divided into long strips. These are known as *rangs* and were a traditional way of divvying up the land not seen outside the province.

There is also a lot of maple syrup production in the area. In spring, many farmers allow visitors to the 'sugar shacks' for a look-see and a taste. Or you can see how it's done all year at Chez Madeleine in Mascouche, where they provide information and sell various maple goodies. I don't want to rush you, but it's said that acid rain could well wipe out this traditional industry.

Joliette is the site of the annual Festival International de Lanaudière, a major interna-

tional classical music festival, which draws crowds of thousands to the 50 or so concerts which take place through the summer. Many events are held at the new outdoor amphitheatre which has a capacity of 10,000. Free half-hour tours of the facility are offered.

Rawdon

Rawdon, the other main town, has **Moore Canadiana Village**, a re-created 1800s town, complete with workers in costume. Most of the buildings are authentic. (The schoolhouse is from 1835.) Other attractions include a museum and art gallery.

Lakeside Rawdon has long been a local beauty spot. Trails and observation points wind along the Ouareau River with the **Dorwin Falls**. Nearby there are other hilly, wooded areas good for walking. Ask at the tourist office.

There are numerous lakes in the region, many with inns, resorts or campgrounds.

Berthierville

To the east of Joliette on the St Lawrence River is Berthierville, the birthplace of the late Gilles Villeneuve, the Formula 1 racing car driver. A museum details his exciting career on the Grand Prix circuit.

Eastern Townships (Estrie)

The Eastern Townships area (Les Cantons de l'Est), the 'Garden of Quebec', generally known as Estrie by the French, extends from Granby to the New Hampshire border. The area is appreciated for its rolling hills, green farmland, woods and lakes – an extension of the US Appalachian region.

It's a very popular resort area, with fishing and swimming in the numerous lakes in summer and excellent skiing in winter. Estrie abounds in cottages and chalets both private and commercial, and inns. The region also has a reputation for its many fine but expensive dining rooms.

In spring, 'sugaring off' – the tapping of trees for maple syrup, and then boiling and preparing it – takes place throughout the region. In the fall, a good time to visit, colours are beautiful as the leaves change, and apple harvesting takes place with the attendant cider production.

The Eastern Townships have a long history and, as evidenced by the place names, were until quite recently predominantly English. Though originally occupied by the Abenakis Indians much of the region was first developed by Loyalists fleeing the USA after the revolution of 1776. Later in the next century many Irish people arrived. Soon after, French settlers arrived to help with the expanding economy and that made up the mix of people which has continued to today.

Many of the towns and villages are popular with antique hunters; small craftshops and galleries line many a main street. Another lure is the area's growing reputation for its spas and health centres where the stressed-out can be treated like Hollywood actors for a couple of days. Around the countryside on the smaller roads keep an eye out for the remaining wooden covered bridges and the round barns.

There is a B&B programme in the region (the tourist office will have the latest guide) and dozens of campgrounds. Estrie is one of the good cycling regions of the province and rentals are available in Magog, Orford, North Hatley and other places. Both cycling and B&B maps are for sale at the regional tourist offices.

Granby

This town is known far and wide for its zoo, even though it was never particularly good. I swear everybody in Quebec knows of it, if in fact they haven't seen it at one time or another. It seems it has been there forever.

Newer exhibits such as the insectarium containing 100,000 little creatures, the reptile displays and a dinosaur exhibit with moving beasts have improved the zoo in recent years.

Granby is also well endowed with highly respected restaurants and hosts a gastronomical festival every autumn.

Knowlton (Lac Brome)

Nearby, south of Highway 10 on Highway 243, is Knowlton on Lac Brome. In fact nowadays the town is often called Lac Brome. Many of the main street's Victorian buildings have been restored and it's become a bit of a tourist town with craft and gift shops, etc. The good local history museum includes a tea room. A favourite meal in this area is Lac Brome duck and it shows up frequently on the better menus.

Sutton Junction

Near this village on Rural Route (RR) 4 sits the farm of Madame Benoît, Canada's best known cook. For many years she has appeared on national TV and she's written a couple of dozen cookbooks. Well, this is her home – a 125-year-old farmhouse. You can't get a meal but a shop sells the books and various local sheepskin products. The property is indicated simply with a mailbox marked 'Bernard Benoît'.

Sutton

Further south, Sutton is synonymous with its important ski hill, one of the area's highest. In summer, there are hiking trails in Sutton Park. The area around Sutton and south of Cowansville near the village of Dunham supports Quebec's wine industry and some of the wineries can be visited. This is also an important apple-growing region where you can get casual work in the fall.

Lac Champlain

Although essentially a US lake which divides Vermont from New York state, it does protrude into Quebec as well. Steeped in history, the area is now very popular with Canadians and Americans as a summer vacation and cottage spot.

The lake is good for swimming and fishing and, in places, is very scenic. At Plattsburgh, New York state, there is a very good and very busy beach, where any weekend you'll find plenty of Quebeckers. The short ferry trip across part of the lake is quite pleasant and worth doing if you're travelling through the area.

Magog

Magog, sitting right at the northern tip of large Lac Memphrémagog, is an attractive town with 15,000 residents. The main street, Rue Principale, has a resort flavour with its numerous cafés, bars, bistros and restaurants.

On this same street, but just west of town, the tourist office can help provide information about the area. Daily boat cruises lasting a little over two hours are offered around the lake in summer.

There are numerous places to stay in and around town, mostly motels in the singles/doubles $40/50 range. Right in the centre of things is *Hotel Union* with very low rates; other places are rather pricey.

Lac Memphrémagog

This is the largest and best known lake in the Estrie area. Most of the lakefront properties are privately owned. Halfway down the lake at Saint Benoît-du-Lac is a **Benedictine monastery** where monks continue the tradition of the ancient Gregorian chant. Visitors can attend services and there's a hostel for men and another for women if you want to stay. One of Quebec's cheeses – L'Ermite, a blue – is made and sold here. Also try to taste the cider the monks make.

Rock Island, the busy border crossing to the USA, is at the southern end of the lake and contains four of the Eastern Townships' best French restaurants.

Mont Orford Provincial Park

Just out of Magog, this is a good but relatively small park (though the largest in the Eastern Townships). Dominated by Mont Orford (792 metres), the park is a skiing centre in winter but fills up quickly with campers in summer as well. You can swim here, use the walking trails, and the chair lift operates through the summer.

Each summer, the Orford Art Centre presents the Jeunesses Musicales du Canada music and art festival.

North Hatley

Just east of Magog, North Hatley sits at the north end of Lac Massawippi.

I nearly drowned here during a storm in my adolescence. I guess what they said about its long thin shape and surrounding hills contributing to waters which quickly turn rough is true.

Mark Lightbody

North Hatley was a popular second home for wealthy Americans who enjoyed the scenery but even more the lack of Prohibition during the 1920s. Many of these huge old places are now inns and B&Bs. Try the Massawippi dark beer at the Le Pilsen pub.

Sherbrooke

Sherbrooke is the principal commercial centre of the region and a fair-sized city in its own right. It's a bilingual town with several small museums, a wide selection of restaurants and is a pleasant centre lying between the Magog and Saint François rivers. The tourist office (☎ 564-8331) is at 48 Rue Depôt.

The **Musée des Beaux Arts** in the centre on Rue du Palais is a sizeable art gallery open every afternoon except Monday. The annual fall fair is a big local event held each August.

On the outskirts is the **Shrine of Beauvoir**, dating from 1920, a site of religious pilgrimages with good views over the city and the surrounding area. In **Lennoxville**, there's Bishop's, an English university. Also in Lennoxville are a couple of cottage breweries and some antique and craft shops to browse through.

Places to Stay & Eat The *Youth Hostel* (☎ 567-9717) is at 154 Boulevard Queen North; they charge $10. In summer, rooms are also available at low rates at the university.

Here as elsewhere around the Eastern Townships, the motels, hotels and inns are not at all cheap. Alternatives can be found through the *Sherbrooke B&B Association* (☎ 565-7780) at 1464 Rue Vermont, with rooms from $25/35 for singles/doubles.

Two well-established four-star eateries are *Au Petit Sabot* and *l'Élite*.

Getting There & Away There's a VIA Rail station in Sherbrooke and frequent bus services to Montreal. The train goes through town three times a week in each direction between Montreal and Saint John, New Brunswick. It passes through Maine, USA en route.

South-west of town, join Highway 55 leading south to Rock Island, a small town which is the major entry point into the USA, close to the states of New York, Vermont, and New Hampshire.

MONTREAL TO QUEBEC CITY

Along the St Lawrence River, on Highway 138 east of Montreal, you begin to get a sense of what small-town Quebec is like. Stone houses with light blue trim and tin roofs, silver-spired churches, ubiquitous chip wagons called *cantines* and main streets with shops built right to the road, are some characteristics. The best section is from Trois Rivières onwards to the north-east.

A much quicker route is Highway 40, a four-lane expressway that can get you from Montreal to Quebec City in 2½ to three hours. There are not too many services along this route, so watch your fuel levels.

From Montreal there is also one fast and one slow route along the south shore to Quebec City and beyond. The old Highway 132 edges along the river but isn't as nice as its north shore counterpart (Highway 138), and the No 20 (the Trans Canada Highway) is fast but boring until at least Quebec City, where it runs a little closer to the water. At Trois Rivières, you can cross the river.

Saint Antoine de Padoue Church

This is on the north side of the St Lawrence River in Louiseville. It would be hard to miss, but take a peek inside too; it's one of Canada's grandest churches – very impressive. Next door, the tourist booth is helpful.

La Domaine Joly de Lotbinière

This is a stately museum on the south shore of the St Lawrence River, between Lotbinière and Sainte Croix. It was built for Henri Gustave Joly de Lotbinière (1849-1908), once the prime minister of Quebec. Not only is this one of the most impressive manors built during the seigneurial period of Quebec, it remains nearly as it was in the mid-1800s. It's now a government-operated museum containing period furniture and furnishings, and the grounds and outbuildings are a treat in themselves. Lunch and teas are served.

Trois Rivières

Trois Rivières, over 350 years old and the largest town between Quebec's two main cities, is a major pulp and paper centre.

The **old section** around Rue des Ursulines, with its reminders of a long history, is small but good for a stroll. There is a tourist office in the Manoir Boucher-de-Niverville, an historic house on Rue Bonaventure near the corner of Rue Hart. The bus station is at 1075 Rue Champflour.

On Rue des Ursulines are several **old houses** now open to the public as small free museums and examples of various architectural styles. The **Ursuline Museum** at No 734 displays materials relating to the Ursuline Order of nuns who were prominent in the town's development.

The **cathedral** at 362 Rue Bonaventure is nearly 150 years old and is open daily.

Two-hour **cruises** along the river aboard the MS *Jacques Cartier* depart from the dock in **Parc Champlain** at the foot of Boulevard des Forges in the centre of the old town.

Also in the park is an exhibit with models and videos on the local paper industry but there are no tours of the plant itself.

Just north of town is the **Saint Maurice Ironworks National Park** which was the first major iron-ore operation in North America. Built in 1730, the forge ran sporadically with a number of owners until 1883. An information centre details the historic significance and also explains how the iron was produced and used.

Also out of the town centre at 2750 Boulevard des Forges is the **Archaeological**

Museum with displays on fossils, early pottery discoveries and North American Indians. It is free and closed on Monday.

Back in town along with several motels, there is a youth hostel, *La Flotille* (☎ 378-8010) at 497 Rue Radisson. Rooms cost members/nonmembers $11/13; an inexpensive breakfast is available. There is also a communal kitchen and laundry facilities. It's about a 10-minute walk from the bus and railway station.

Beyond the city, the road becomes very hilly with gradients of up to 17%. There are lots of camping places along the way as well as stands offering fruit, cider and wood sculpture – an old Quebec folk art. The old-style double wooden swings on many a front lawn are popular in Quebec but rarely seen in the rest of Canada.

Grand Mère & Shawinigan

These medium-sized towns north up the Saint Maurice River are rather grim, with little to hold the visitor. Both are industrial: pulp and paper has long been the backbone of the area. At Shawinigan, you can visit a large hydroelectric power station. If you're heading for any of the northerly parks, stock up here because the food and supply selection doesn't get any better further north.

Between here and La Mauricie National Park, there isn't much in the way of accommodation, so you're pretty much stuck with one of the few ordinary motels in Grand Mère or Shawinigan. But the small town of Sainte Flore, between Shawinigan North and the entrance to the national park, has four restaurants of note, all on its main street. One has crêpes, two have seafood and steak, and the most expensive place serves French cuisine.

La Mauricie National Park

North from Trois Rivières, up past Shawinigan and Grand Mère, La Mauricie National Park is the only national park among the many very large provincial wilderness parks north of the St Lawrence River.

The park covers 550 sq km, straddling northern evergreen forests and the more southerly hardwoods of the St Lawrence River Valley. The low, rounded Laurentian Mountains, probably the world's oldest, are part of the Canadian Shield that covers much of the province. Between these hills are many small lakes and valleys. Within the park, mammals include moose, fox, bear and beaver.

The park is excellent for canoeing. There are maps of five canoe routes, ranging in length from 14 km to 84 km, for beginners to experts. Canoes can be rented for about $12 a day at Lake Wapizagonke, itself very scenic with sandy beaches, steep rocky cliffs and waterfalls. There's also fishing for trout and bass.

Hiking trails, guided nature walks and an interpretive centre are offered. Some of the trails go along or offer views of the Saint Maurice River, which is one of the last rivers in the province where logging companies still float down their timber to the mills. Along the edges of the river you can see the strays that get collected periodically.

There are serviced campgrounds available, at $7.50 a night, with free firewood.

Interior camping is free but you do need to pre-plan your route and register. On holiday weekends in summer, calling ahead to check on availability is a good idea; phone ☎ (819) 532-2414. No fires are permitted so take a stove. Supplies are available in Grand Mère, but the selection is minimal; it's better to bring most stuff with you.

The park is 220 km north-east of Montreal. There is no longer a bus from Montreal up here nor even to Shawinigan, so driving is the only method of transport.

Two adjacent provincial parks also offer wilderness camping: one is to the north, one to the west, but road access is more difficult.

English is at a premium up here, so be prepared to communicate in French.

Quebec City (Québec)

Quebec City, rich in history, culture and

beauty, is the heart of French Canada. If you're anywhere in the eastern part of the country, make the effort to visit.

The town is unique in several ways, most noticeably in its European appearance and atmosphere. It has the charm of an old world city. Montreal has this feel to some degree, as does the French Quarter in New Orleans, but nowhere in North America is the picture as complete. The entire old section of town, essentially a living museum, has been designated by UNESCO as a World Heritage Site.

As the seat of the provincial parliament and Laval Université, this is the centre of Québecois consciousness, in both its moderate and extreme manifestations. Quebec City has been the Canadian centre of French nationalist thought for hundreds of years and many of today's intellectuals and politicians speaking for independence are based here.

Although many people are bilingual and there is a small English minority, the overwhelming majority are French-speaking and 94% have French ancestors. But this is a tourist town, ranking with Banff and Victoria among the country's most visited destinations, so English is spoken around the attractions and in shops. However, if you can, speak French, this will make you more

friends and enable you to feel more comfortable away from the busiest areas. Quebec City is a year-round tourist centre, though in July and August it gets very crowded.

Quebec City is also an important port, lying where the St Charles River (Rivière Saint Charles) meets the St Lawrence River. It sits on top of and around a cliff, an excellent setting with views over the St Lawrence River and the town of Lévis (pronounced not as in jeans but 'lev-ee') across the river.

Much of Quebec City's past is still visible: the many churches, old stone houses and narrow streets make it an architectural gem, and the old port of Quebec remains the only walled city in North America.

The climate in Quebec City must be mentioned as this is a city with both summer and winter attractions. Summers are much like those of Montreal or southern Ontario, though generally not as hot and always a bit shorter. The real difference is in winter: it gets cold then, and I mean *cold*. There can also be mountains of snow; if you're visiting in winter, especially during January and February, you can't take enough sweaters. Life does go on, however – the locals don't hibernate. If you come prepared, this time of the year has its benefits.

HISTORY

One of the continent's earliest settlements, the site of Quebec City was an Iroquois Indian village called 'Stadacone' when the French explorer Jacques Cartier landed here in 1534. The name 'Quebec' is derived from an Algonkian Indian word meaning 'the river narrows here'. Explorer Samuel de Champlain founded the city for the French in 1608 and built a fort in 1620.

The English successfully attacked in 1629, but Quebec was returned to the French under a treaty and became the centre of New France. Repeated English attacks followed. In 1759, General Wolfe led the English to victory over Montcalm on the Plains of Abraham. This is one of North America's most famous historical battles and virtually ended the conflict. In 1763 the Treaty of Paris gave Canada to Britain. Despite

Jacques Cartier

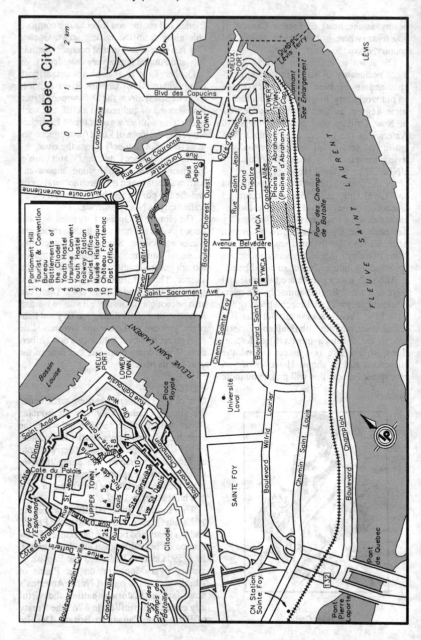

this, in 1775, the Americans had a go at capturing Quebec. They were promptly turned back.

In 1791, the divisions of Upper Canada (Ontario) and Lower Canada (Quebec and the Maritime Provinces) were created, with Quebec City as capital. In the 1800s Lower Canada became known as Quebec and Quebec City was chosen as provincial capital.

ORIENTATION

Because part of the city sits on top of the cliffs on Cap Diamant (Cape Diamond), it is divided into Upper Town and Lower Town. The Citadel, a famous landmark, stands on the highest point of Cap Diamant overlooking the city. Upper Town lies north of the Citadel on top of the plain. Lower Town lies mainly between the rivers and Cap Diamant by the Quebec Harbour.

The best and maybe only way to orient yourself in Quebec City is to walk around. The city is surprisingly small covering 93 sq km, with nearly all things of interest to a visitor packed into one area. The southwestern end of the upper city is still surrounded by a wall and is called the Old City. You'll find just about everything to do and see here.

Outside the wall are some things of note, including the Parliament Buildings and some restaurants. The two main streets heading west are Boulevard Saint Cyrille and, to the south, Grande Allée, which further west becomes Chemin Saint Louis and eventually Boulevard Wilfrid Laurier. The Old City area is just 10 sq km, and it's very appealing. Lower Town is mainly the business and industrial area, lying mostly to the north-east of Upper Town.

There is a small part of Lower Town in the Old City, between the river, harbour and the cliffs of Cap Diamant. There are some very old streets here such as Rue Sous le Cap and Rue Champlain, which are only 2½ metres across. The focal point of this small area, at the south-eastern edge of Old Quebec, is Place Royale around which you'll find the most interesting things to see in Lower

Town. From here, you can walk (it's not hard, nor far) or take the funicular railway (elevator) for 75 cents one way to the top of the cliff or Upper Town. The funicular in Place Royale is on Rue Petit Champlain. The ferry, which plies across the river to Lévis, docks in Lower Town.

To the extreme west of the city you'll see signs for either Pont de Québec or Pont Pierre Laporte. Both these bridges lead to the south shore.

The area north of Boulevard Saint Cyrille is mainly residential. Then you'll encounter the cliff again – this time its northern edge. Beneath it, the section of Lower Town is of little interest and is residential or industrial. This is also true of the eastern parts of Lower Town.

Much further north in Lower Town are the highways leading east and west. In this section of the city you'll find some of the motels.

Back in the old, walled section of Upper Town, the streets run pretty haphazardly. Rue Saint Jean is a main street with many bars and restaurants. Running south from it, Côte de la Fabrique is another main street. Further south, running into Côte de la Fabrique, is Rue Buade, another of the central streets. At the bottom of Rue Buade and a little to the east is the post office, in a huge old stone building. Across from it, towards the water, is nice little Parc Montmorency with good views

A well-known landmark in Old Quebec is the copper-topped, castle-style Château Frontenac hotel dating from 1892 which lends an old-world air. Behind the château, a large boardwalk edges along the cliff providing good views over the river. The boardwalk leads to the Promenade des Gouverneurs, a path which runs between the cliff's edge and the citadel. Beyond the citadel, outside the walls, is the huge park called Parc des Champs de Bataille. This is where the battles over Quebec took place. The park has several historical monuments and some sites within its boundaries.

The views are good from the boardwalk behind the Château Frontenac, called the

Terrasse Dufferin. There are always people strolling and often musicians and other street entertainers doing their numbers there. At one end is the wooden slide used during the winter carnival.

For a look from higher up, go to the government building called Edifice 'G' at 675 Boulevard Saint Cyrille Est. The observation deck on the 31st floor is open from 9 am to 4 pm Monday to Friday, from March to October. Alternatives are the top floor of the Hilton where the disco is, or the restaurant at the top of Loews Le Concorde Hôtel, 1225 Place Montcalm off Chemin Saint Louis, outside the wall.

INFORMATION

There are several tourist offices where the staff are bilingual and well supplied with maps and other information.

The main office is at 60 Rue d'Auteuil, just north of Grande Allée. It's in the Parc de l'Esplanade, near the Porte Saint Louis. Usually they will help out with off-beat questions and will even make telephone calls for you and help with booking accommodation. Most of the workers are friendly, considering the crowds they get at peak times. Through the summer it is open from 8.30 am to 8 pm daily otherwise it closes at 5.30 pm.

A second tourist office (☎ 643-2280) is on Place d'Armes, to the east side of the Château Frontenac hotel. This one deals primarily with destinations elsewhere around the province.

Another tourist office is at 215 Rue de Marché-Finlay on the corner of Rue de l'Union in Lower Town. It's on a large square near the water, south of Place Royale and deals mainly with the Place Royale area.

There is a post office in the walled section of Upper Town, at the bottom of Rue Buade, opposite Parc Montgomery; another one is in Saint-Paul near the corner of Ruelle des Bains.

THINGS TO SEE

Nearly every second building in Old Quebec is of some interest; a list of all the sites in this area would fill a book. For a more complete guide, ask at the tourist office for the walking-tour booklet. Following are some of the most significant sites in the old section as well as some outside the walls.

Watch for a symbol in the shape of a key on buildings and businesses around town. It indicates something of historical note is on display. The tourist office has a guide to the 'key' locations as well.

Citadel

The French started to build here in 1750 when bastions were constructed for storing gunpowder. The fort itself was built by the British as the eastern flank of the city's defence system. It was begun in 1820 and not completed for 30 years. The irregularly sided structure sits on the plain over 100 metres up from the river with an appropriate vantage point.

Today the citadel is the home base of Canada's Royal 22s (known in bastardised French as the Van Doos), a French regiment that developed quite a reputation through WW I and II and the Korean War. There is a museum outlining their history and a more general military museum containing documents, uniforms and models situated in a few different buildings including the old prison at the south-east end.

The entrance fee of $3.25 includes admission to these museums and a guided tour, as well as the Changing of the Guard ceremony which takes place at 10 am daily in summer, and the Beating of the Retreat at 7 pm on Tuesday, Thursday, Saturday and Sunday during July and August. There are also cannon firings at noon and 9.30 pm from the Prince of Wales Bastion. The citadel is still considered a working military site so wandering around on your own is not permitted.

Parc des Champs de Bataille

This is the huge park running west from the citadel. Its hills, gardens, monuments and trees make it very pleasant now; however, the park was once a bloody battleground, the site of a conflict that may have determined the course of history in Canada. The part closest to the cliff is known as the Plains of

Abraham and it was here that the English finally defeated the French in 1759 with both generals dying in the process. In the park is a Martello tower and a fountain with a lookout.

Musée du Québec

Towards the south-western end of the park is this museum, with changing exhibits mainly on Quebec's art: modern and more traditional, with ceramics and decorations as well. It's small and not memorable, but is free and open daily until 9.30 pm through the summer, until 5.45 pm during the rest of the year when it is also closed on Monday. Nearby is the old prison, now boarded up.

Old Wall

Now a national park, the largely restored old wall can be visited for free. In fact, you can walk a complete circuit on top of the walls 4.6 km all around the Old City. In the old Powder Building beside Porte Saint Louis, an interpretive centre has been set up, which provides a little information on the wall's history. Along the circuit are two other information booths, one on Terrasse Dufferin and one on the Promenade des Gouverneurs.

Parc d'Artillerie

Beside the wall at Porte Saint Jean, Parc d'Artillerie has been used militarily for centuries. A munitions factory built cartridges for the Canadian Forces here until 1964. It's now an interpretive centre with a scale model of Quebec City the way it was in the early 1800s. In the Dauphine Redoubt, there are costumes and displays about the soldiers for whom it was built during the French regime, and in the officers' quarters there's a history lesson for children.

Musée du Fort

This is a small museum, at 10 Rue Sainte Anne near Place d'Armes, dealing with more provincial military history. With the aid of a large model of 18th-century Quebec City, six sieges and battles are retold using sound and light (son et lumière). The half-hour show isn't bad and costs $3.50.

Musée Historique

Also facing Place d'Armes, this is actually a wax museum with scenes depicting historical events like Columbus's landing in America. Admission is $3.50, for students $2.50.

AROUND OLD UPPER TOWN

In the 1700s Upper Town began to grow after Lower Town was destroyed once too often in battle.

Place d'Armes is the small square to the north of the Château Frontenac. It was once a military parade ground and is now a handy city orientation point.

Rue du Tresor is up, away from the water, off Place d'Armes. This very narrow street, linking Rue Sainte Anne with Rue Buade, is jammed with painters and their wares – mostly kitsch stuff done for the tourists but some pretty good work too. At the end of Buade is the **Hôtel de Ville** (City Hall) dating from 1833. Next to the Hôtel de Ville, the park is used for shows and performances throughout the summer, especially during festival time.

On the corner of Rue Buade and Rue Sainte Famille is the **Basilica of Notre Dame**, dating from 1647. The interior is very ornate and contains paintings and treasures from the early French regime.

URSULINE CONVENT & MUSEUM

This convent is on Rue des Jardins; it's the oldest girls' school on the continent. There are several buildings on the estate, many undergoing restoration. The Ursuline Museum, which you enter at 12 Rue Donnacona, deals with the Ursulines and their lives in the 1600s and 1700s, and also displays paintings, crafts, furniture and other belongings of the early French settlers. Admission is $1.50, students $1. The convent, chapel and museum are open daily from 9.30 am to noon and 1.30 to 5 pm but closed Sunday mornings.

Nearby, on the same street, is the Anglican **Cathedral of the Holy Trinity**, built in 1804, which is open from noon to 5 pm.

LATIN QUARTER

This refers to a section of Old Upper Town surrounding the large Quebec seminary complex. The seminary was originally Université Laval but it outgrew the space here and was moved in the 1960s to Sainte Foy, west of here. Many students still live along the old, narrow streets which look particularly Parisian. To enter the seminary grounds, go to 7 Rue de l'Université. In the grounds are many stone and wooden buildings, a toy museum, the university's museum and several grassy, quiet quadrangles.

PARC DE L'ESPLANADE

Just inside the Old City by Porte Saint Louis and Rue Saint Louis is this city park where many of the Quebec Winter Carnival's events are held. Calèches, the horse-drawn carts for sight-seeing, line up for business.

OLD LOWER TOWN

The oldest section of Quebec City, like the Upper Town, is well worth exploring. Get down to it by walking down Côte de la Montagne by the post office. About halfway down on the right there is a shortcut – the break-neck steps – that leads down to Rue Petit Champlain. Alternately, you can take the funicular down; it also goes to Rue Petit Champlain, to Louis Jolliet House. The house dates from 1683 and Jolliet lived in it when he wasn't off exploring the northern Mississippi. Rue Petit Champlain, a very busy, attractive street, is said to be the narrowest in North America and is also one of the oldest.

Place Royale

This is the central and principal square of the area with 400 years of history behind it. The name is now often used to refer to the district in general. When de Champlain founded Quebec, it was this bit of shoreline which was first settled. For the past few years the entire area has been under renovation and restoration, and the good work is now nearly complete.

There are many houses and small museums to visit, some with period furniture

and implements. The streets are full of visitors: people going to restaurants and cafés, and school children from around the province getting history lessons. It's not uncommon to see a bride coming down the church steps either. Other places are now galleries, craft shops and the like.

Also on the square are many buildings from the 1600s and 1700s, tourist shops (don't buy film here, it's too expensive!) and in the middle a statue of Monsieur de Champlain who started it all.

At 25 Rue Saint Pierre near the square is an interpretive centre which gives a free outline of the history of Lower Town and Quebec City. Right on the square at No 3A is another interpretive centre, the Centre of Trade in New France, with some exhibits and an audio-video show dealing with early French settlement. Again, this is free. See the Quebec City Information section earlier for details of the tourist office which specialises in this part of town. They can tell you of the many free events, concerts and shows which frequently take place in and around the Lower Town streets.

Right by the interpretive centre on the square, the house of wines is a mouth-watering vintage wine store in a restored 1689 dwelling. It's free to visit and includes a drink. It's closed on Sunday and Monday.

Church of Notre Dame des Victoires

This church (dating from 1688) on the square is the oldest stone church in the province. It's built on the spot where 80 years earlier de Champlain set up his 'Habitation', a small stockade. Hanging from the ceiling is a replica of a wooden ship, thought to be a good luck charm for the ocean crossing and early battles with the Iroquois.

Royal Battery

This is at the foot of Rue Sous le Fort, where a dozen cannons were set up in 1691 to protect the growing town. The Lower Town information office is just off the park here.

The Canadian government gives free tours of the coastguard base near the ferry terminal, Monday to Friday from 9 am to 4 pm.

Top & Bottom: High & low tides near Fundy National Park, New Brunswick (RE)

Top: Québecois Cowboy (RE)
Left: Quebec City's historic Lower Town, towered over by the Château Frontenac (ML)
Right: Modern Montreal architecture (JL)

Here you'll find equipment, information and boats.

VIEUX PORT (OLD PORT)

Built around the old harbour in Lower Town east of Place Royale, Vieux Port is a recently redeveloped multi-purpose waterfront area. It's a large, spacious assortment of government buildings, shops, condominiums and recreational facilities with no real focal point but a few things of interest to the visitor.

Near Place Royale at the river's edge you'll see the MV *Louis Jolliet*, offering cruises downriver to the waterfalls Chute Montmorency and Île d'Orléans. You'll get good views of the city, but you can also get them from the cheap ferry plying the river between town and Lévis. Near the wharf is the Musée de la Civilisation.

Strolling along the waterfront leads to the Agora, a large outdoor concert bowl and site of many summer shows and presentations. A little further along is a warehouse-style building housing numerous boutiques.

Musée de la Civilisation

Opened in 1988 this large, striking waterfront museum deals with both Quebec and broader historical and communication topics through permanent and changing exhibits. Human history and culture is explored through new and old artefacts and the creations of humankind.

It's very spacious and well laid out. Aside from the static exhibits, it includes dance, music and other live performances.

It's definitely worth seeing and unlike many museums around the province there are English-speaking guides on hand. The museum admission costs $4 and it's open from 10 am to 7 pm daily from 24 June to 6 September. Note that on Tuesday it's free. The rest of the year it closes at 5 pm and is not open at all on Monday.

Port of Quebec in the 19th Century

South towards the city a short distance is the Port of Quebec in the 19th Century National Historic Park, housed in a building on Rue Saint André. It's a large, four-storey museum depicting shipbuilding and the timber industry, with good exhibits and often live demonstrations as well. Admission is free.

Antique Shop District

The district is on Rue Saint Paul, north-west around the corner from Place Royale in Lower Town very near the Port of Quebec in the 19th Century Museum. From Place Royale, take Rue Saint Pierre towards the harbour and then turn left at Rue Saint Paul. About a dozen shops here sell antiques, curiosities and old Québecois relics. There are also some good little cafés along this relatively quiet street. Right against the cliff on Côte de la Canoterie, you can walk up to Upper Town. Further along is the farmers' market on the right-hand side, and a little further, the Gare du Palais railway station.

OUTSIDE THE WALLS

National Assembly

Back in Upper Town, the home of the Provincial Legislature is just off Grande Allée, not far from Parc de l'Esplanade, in this castle-style structure dating from 1886.

There are free tours of the sumptuous interior all day, with commentaries in English and French. The Assembly sits in the Blue Room. The Red Room, equally impressive, is no longer used as the Upper House has been discontinued.

Grand Theatre

On the corner of Boulevard Saint Cyrille and Rue Claire Fontaine is this grand, three-storey home to the performing arts. People also visit to see the building's design and the gigantic epic mural by Spaniard Jordi Bonet. Free one-hour tours are given of the painting which is in three parts: Death, Space and Liberty.

Le Bois de Coulonge Park

Not far west of the Plains of Abraham is this large area dedicated to the plant world. Long the private property of a succession of Quebec's religious and political elite, the area of woods and extensive horticultural displays is open to the public. It's wedged between Boulevard Champlain and Chemin Saint Louis.

Archaeological Site

North of the upper walled section of Quebec City on the corner of Rue Saint Nicholas and Rue Vaillier, just a block south of Rue Saint Paul a major street which runs into Boulevard Charest Est, is this interesting idea for an historic site. It's set up as a working dig of the first city intendant's house, actually a palace. Platforms lead over foundations, firepits and outlines of several buildings which local university students uncovered and explored. There's an interpretive centre to supply background information. From the beginning of May to the beginning of September it is open in the afternoons each day except Monday.

Cartier-Brebeuf National Historic Park

On the River Saint Charles north of the central walled section of the city, this park marks where Cartier and his men were nursed through the winter of 1535 by the local Native Indians. Later the Jesuits established a settlement here. Displays provide more information on Cartier, his trips and the Jesuit missionaries.

There is a full-scale replica of Cartier's ship and one of a Native Indian longhouse in the park's green riverside setting. Through the summer it is open every day, but on Monday only in the afternoon. It is free. From the downtown area take Boulevard Dorchester north by car or go by bus to Rue Julien from where you can walk to the park.

Aquarium

This is in Sainte Foy at 1675 Avenue du Parc. They have about 300 species of fresh and saltwater fish. There's a cafeteria and, out on the grounds, picnic tables. It's open daily and costs $3.50 for adults, $2 for children.

ORGANISED TOURS

There is no shortage of tour possibilities here. Some companies use minibuses for rather private tours, others offer a driver and you use your own car. Several companies offer bus tours of the city or full-day regional trips.

Gray Line (☎ 622-7420) runs numerous narrated tours from Place d'Armes. A 1½-hour trip around town costs $15, and a 4½-hour one to Beaufort and the falls Chute Montmorency with a short visit to Île d'Orléans, is $22. Several other companies offer similar tours which may offer more time around Île d'Orléans or some other variation. Gray Line seems to have the lowest prices. The tourist office has promotional pamphlets on the various tours available; there is also a ticket booth on Terrasse Dufferin representing many of the tour companies.

Maple Leaf (☎ 649-9226), with an office at 240 3rd Avenue, has six different tours in and around Quebec City costing from $15 to $49. One of their trips is done partially by bus and partially by boat. Free pick-up from your (or any) hotel is available so you needn't ever go to the out-of-the-way office. This company also runs the airport shuttle service.

The less established operators tend to charge a few dollars less or provide longer tours for the same money.

A worthwhile alternative is Quebec by Foot (☎ 658-4799), which provides a walking tour lasting around 2½ hours guided by history or architecture students. It's educational but not dry. Reservations may be made at the Musée du Fort on Place d'Armes. There are two walks a day. They cost $12.

Sonores (☎ 692-1223) rents spoken tape cassettes which you can use for your own walking or driving tours. Rental costs $7.95. The cassettes are available at tourist booths.

A new service which may last is a shuttle bus called Carrousel Touristique, which goes around Old Quebec. For one fare of $3 you can hop on and off at will for the day. Pick up a copy of their schedule.

River Cruises

A variety of boat tours is given on the big open decked MV *Louis Jolliet*, which has an 800-passenger capacity. Tickets (☎ 692-

1159) may be purchased in the Kiosque, on the boardwalk behind the Château or at the booth along the waterfront near Place Royale.

The basic one-hour trip costs $14, but there is a longer one further downriver to Île d'Orléans and Chute Montmorency and a three-hour evening trip with music and dancing for $18. All these cruises are very popular so getting a ticket early is a good idea.

Another company with a smaller vessel, the *Saint André*, does similar day cruises around Quebec City and down the river at slightly cheaper rates. For information call ☎ 659-4804 or see them at quay No 22 along the Old Port dock opposite the Agora.

Excursions
Plein Air Quebec (☎ 843-3750) organises canoe, bicycle and other trips around the area.

FESTIVALS
Summer Festival
This festival held at the beginning of July, consists basically of free shows and concerts throughout the town, including drama and dance. Ask about it at the tourist office: they should have a list of things going on indicating what, where and when. Most squares and parks in the Old City are the sites of some activity daily, especially the park beside Hôtel de Ville at noon and in the evening.

Winter Carnival
This is the big, famous annual event in Quebec City. While the Carnival sambas in Rio and the Mardi Gras takes place in New Orléans, Quebec indulges itself in its unique way. The festival lasts for about 10 days, always including two weekends, around the end of February. If you want to go, organise the trip early as the city gets packed out (and bring lots of warm clothes). Featured are parades, ice sculptures, a snow slide, boat races, dances, music and lots of drinking. The town goes berserk. If you take the train into Quebec City during Carnival, be prepared for a trip like no other.

Many activities take place in Parc de l'Esplanade. The slide is on the Terrasse Dufferin behind the Château. Other events take place above the Gare Saint Rôche, between Pont Dorchester and the bridge of the Autoroute Dufferin.

Quebec City Provincial Exhibition
This summer event is held around the end of August each year and features individual and commercial displays, handicrafts, a Black Jack parlour, horse racing and midway a large carnival with 65 rides. The entrance fee is $7 which includes everything, even rides. Nearly three-quarters of a million people visit each year. Parc de l'Exposition (Exhibition Park) is north of the downtown area, off Route 175, Laurentienne.

PLACES TO STAY
There are many, many places to stay in Quebec City and generally the competition keeps the prices down to a reasonable level. There are relatively few standard hotels – by far the bulk of the accommodation is in small guesthouses, and family-run European-style hotels. As you'd expect in such a popular centre, the best cheap places are very often full. Midsummer and Carnival time are the busiest times. If you can't find a place in the Old City, consider one of the motels slightly out of the centre or be prepared to stretch your budget.

Outside the peak periods, prices do drop. For accommodation assistance call ☎ 643-2306 or better still, go to the tourist office on Rue d'Auteuil where they have lists of places and a phone you can use. Do not take their occupancy information as gospel, however. They may have a place down as 'full' when in fact a call will turn up a room, after everybody else has ignored it. The tourist accommodation guide also doesn't list all the places – a wander around will turn up others. Lastly, remember that morning is the best time to find a place and Friday is often the worst.

Camping
There are two provincial campgrounds fairly

close to town. One is north of Quebec City. To get there, take Highway 40 towards Montmorency and turn north on Highway 369; the park is not too far, on the left. It costs $8.50.

The other provincial campground is on the south shore, east of Lévis near the small town of Beaumont. It offers views out to Île d'Orléans.

There are many private campgrounds on this south shore road particularly west of Quebec City. There is a *KOA* (Kampground of America) (☎ 831-1813), about 10 minutes west of the city, five km west of the Pierre Laporte bridge on the south shore. They offer tours into Quebec City.

Hostels

There are two well established and very busy hostels here. I like the one called *La Paix Hôtel* (☎ 694-0735) at 31 Rue Couillard. It's open all year and has 40 beds. The hostel is marked with a peace sign on the white, European-style building. The cost is $12 with breakfast, and $1.50 extra if you need a sleeping sheet and blanket. The doors close at 2 am. The location is perfect; there is a grocery store, a drugstore, bar and restaurant all minutes away. It's best to arrive early in the morning to assure yourself of a bed. It's walkable from the bus station (about 30 minutes), or the closer railway station, but it's uphill all the way.

The other hostel, *Auberge International* (☎ 694-0775) affiliated with the international organisation, is also well located at 19 Rue Sainte Ursule. Despite its great size, it's usually full in summer. It costs $13 with breakfast and there are some cheaper double and some family rooms.

There are no rooms at the YMCA but the *YWCA* (☎ 683-2155) at 855 Avenue Holland takes couples and also single women. Singles/doubles cost $28/40 and they have a cafeteria and pool. The Y is often full, so reservations may be useful. Avenue Holland runs off Chemin Sainte Foy, which becomes Saint Jean in the old section. Bus No 7 along Chemin Sainte Foy goes past Avenue Holland. Walk south on Avenue Holland – it's not far.

The *Université Laval* (☎ 656-2921), between Chemin Sainte Foy and Boulevard Wilfrid Laurier to the east of Autoroute du Vallon, rents rooms in the summer from May to 21 August. Rates are $25 for singles and a few dollars less in a twin room. Student price is $14.50 or, again, less if sharing a room. Bus No 8 from the Old City will get you there; it's about halfway between the bridges and the walled area.

Tourist Homes

Other than the hostels, the cheapest and best places to stay are these small, sometimes family-run hotels, often created out of old houses. There are literally dozens of them within the walls, which lets you stay in the centre of things and experience their individual characters.

Most of the cheaper ones are in one specific area, which makes looking easy. This area is roughly bounded by Rue d'Auteuil on the west, Rue Sainte Anne to the north, the Château Frontenac to the east and Avenue Saint Denis to the south. The two most fruitful streets as far as places to stay are concerned are Rue Sainte Ursule and Rue Saint Louis. Rue Sainte Anne and Rue Laporte are also good.

Again, many places are nearly always full in summer. Prices at these places can be flexible, depending on the time of year and other factors but, like the restaurants, are not the real bargain they were just a few years ago. On one visit, we got a single bed and a foam mattress on the floor for the price of a single, but generally the approach is more formal. Consider bargaining if you're staying for more than a couple of days. Compared to the motels or larger downtown hotels here or in most cities, the places in this category still aren't bad value.

Long one of the best of the cheapies, *Auberge Saint Louis* (☎ 647-9350), at 48 Rue Saint Louis, has now been completely renovated. The 23 rooms now start at a reasonable $35 a single or double but go up to twice this. Parking is available but costs extra.

Next door at No 50 *Le Gîte Saint Louis* (☎ 692-2233) was undergoing some changes on last visit. I don't imagine prices have gone down at what was a small, modest place above a store.

Further down at 72 Rue Saint Louis is *Maison du Général* (☎ 694-1905). There are 11 rooms which range in price from singles/doubles $28/33, without bath. As in many of these places, it's cheaper without TV, showers, the view or the biggest room. The cheaper rooms are sometimes noisier as they're often on the street but despite these drawbacks they always seem to be the ones to go first.

Also on Rue Saint Louis at No 71 is *Hôtel Le Clos Saint Louis* (☎ 647-9305) with 15 rooms at $40 to $80 for singles or doubles when things are busy, and dropping to $35 to $65 at other times. You may notice signs in some store windows along here offering rooms: it's worth going in and asking.

On one visit for me this turned up a small but fine low-priced room, yet on another visit, not even a 'maybe' – I think it just depends on the whim of the proprietor and whether he or she likes your face.
Mark Lightbody

Running off Rue Saint Louis is Rue Sainte Ursule, a pleasant, much quieter street. There are several places worth checking here. *Le Manoir La Salle* (☎ 647-9361) is at 18 Rue Sainte Ursule and has become one of the best buys because it has held its prices while those at so many other places have jumped. They have nine rooms at $23 to $40 for singles, $40 to $55 for doubles and there's free parking.

La Maison Sainte Ursule (☎ 694-9797) at No 40, looks more expensive and is, at $39 to $59 for singles and $48 to $69 for doubles, but the rooms have a kitchenette. They also have some rooms on the adjacent side street.

Across the street at No 43 is *Maison Acadienne* (☎ 694-0280). Rooms cost from $22 to $45 depending on the number of people, size and facilities. I've stayed here –

it's good, and if you're lucky you may get one of the parking spots around the back.

La Maison Demers (☎ 692-2487), at No 68, charges about the same rates for its eight rooms although the better doubles cost more and include a TV.

Further north-west off Rue Sainte Ursule is Rue Sainte Anne. *Maison Doyon* (☎ 694-1720), at No 9, has 20 rooms some of which have been spruced up. The plain, simple ones go for singles/doubles $35/45 and the prices go way up from there. Taking a washbasin rather than a shower saves at least $10.

There are numerous places on and just off the Jardin des Gouverneurs to the south of the Château Frontenac. *Manoir Sur le Cap* (☎ 694-1987), situated at 9 Avenue Sainte Geneviève, has 14 rooms carved out of the old house, some of them have views of the park. Singles/doubles cost from $30 to $70.

The *Manoir de la Terrace* (☎ 694-1592) is at 4 Rue Laporte. Singles or doubles are the same price here and range from $34 to $60.

At the corner of Rue Saint Louis and Rue d'Auteuil is *Manoir de L'Esplanade* (☎ 694-0834), a large old place recently renovated and now a little steep in price. The 36 rooms cost between $60 and $90 and the corner rooms here can be noisy.

B&Bs

While certainly not a tradition in Quebec, a few places providing the morning meal are now showing up. An agency to try is *Bonjour Québec* (☎ 527-1465) at 3765 Boulevard Monaco. The nine places they list are all quite central and priced at singles/doubles $40/55, give or take a few dollars.

Motels

I don't think I've ever seen a city with more motels than Quebec City. Whether you have a car or not, they may be the answer if you find everything booked up downtown.

There are three major areas to look in for motels, each a good distance from the Old City, but not really far and not difficult to reach.

Beauport One area is Beauport, a section of
Quebec City to the north of the downtown
area. You pass by on the way to Sainte Anne
de Beaupré or on a trip along the northern
coast. The easiest way to reach it if driving
from the downtown area is to head north up
Boulevard Dorchester to Boulevard Hamel.
Turn right (east); Boulevard Hamel becomes
Rue 18 and then, further east, Boulevard
Sainte Anne. This is Beauport. Look when
the numbers are in the 1000s. Most of these
motels are off the road with the river running
behind them.

At 1062 Boulevard Sainte Anne is *Motel
Chevalier* (☎ 661-3876). Rooms cost from
$45 to $60 for singles/doubles.

Motel de la Capitale (☎ 663-0587) is at
1082 Boulevard Sainte Anne. The rate is
singles/doubles $60/65.

Nearby, there's the *Motel Olympic* (☎ 667-
8716), at 1078 Boulevard Sainte Anne,
where prices range from $45 to the outra-
geous $90. They have just 16 rooms here.

Motel du Cosmos (☎ 661-2463), at 1154
Boulevard Saint Anne, is the cheapest of the
lot with singles/doubles from as low as $35.

North-west of the centre at the intersection
of Boulevard Henri IV and Highway 138 up
towards the airport is *Journey's End Motel*
(☎ 872-5900). It is quite good value at
singles/doubles $47/54. This Canada-wide
budget chain is always reliable.

Boulevard Wilfrid Laurier The second
major area for motels is along Boulevard
Wilfrid Laurier, west of the city. The motel
section runs just east of Boulevard Henri IV,
which runs into the bridges from the south
shore. Check around the 3000 numbers.
Prices are generally quite a bit higher here,
but it is closer to town.

The *Motel Fleur de Lys* (☎ 653-9321), at
No 3145, has good prices with doubles from
$60 all the way up to $75.

Further east after Boulevard Wilfrid
Laurier turns into Grande Allée, there are a
few smallish, reasonably priced places
around the 600s addresses. The places closer
to town are generally more deluxe and more
expensive.

Boulevard Wilfrid Hamel The third area for
motels is on Boulevard Wilfrid Hamel,
marked only as 'Hamel' on street signs. To
get to this area, head north up Boulevard
Henri IV from the river or south from
Highway 40. It's about seven km from town.
Start looking around the 5000 block,
although the road is lined with motels.

Motel Delisle (☎ 872-7476), at 5957 Boulevard Hamel, has just seven rooms but they
only cost from $25 to $38 without extras.
This motel is open only from 15 June to 15
September.

Motel Plaza (☎ 877-1552), at 5155 Boulevard Hamel, has singles/doubles from
$40/50.

Motel Rourke (☎ 688-5667), at 2177 Boulevard Hamel, offers singles/doubles from
$30/38.

Other reasonable places are *Motel Pierre*
and *Hotel First Canada*.

PLACES TO EAT

There are dozens of restaurants here and the
food is quite good, but recently prices have
become fairly standardised at rather a high
rate. Still, there are some reasonably priced
exceptions, and the costlier restaurants do
generally provide good service in an attractive setting.

Most restaurants post their menus outside
at the door, which is helpful when you are
shopping around. If you're here for any
length of time you're likely to find a favourite.

At dinner the set menus include soup, a
roll, dessert and coffee. Many of these same
dining rooms offer midday specials which
aren't bad value, but more modest places
have the usual cheap lunches of pizza, sandwiches and the like.

The ethnic restaurants, which aren't
numerous in Quebec City, provide an alternative. The restaurants of Upper Town,
within the walls as a rule, offer the least price
range and tend to be costly.

Outside the wall or down in the quieter
sections of Lower Town less expensive and
more casual places are easier to find.

Upper Old Town

If you're anything like me you can tolerate a bit of a pricey lunch and don't mind spending a little extra on dinner. But paying a lot for breakfast really grates. The morning meal has always been a bit of a problem here and now the one good, cheap bacon and eggs place has gone trendy and up-market and doesn't offer the morning meal.

So now, for eggs, a moderately priced (not cheap) restaurant which is always busy for any meal of the day is *l'Omelette*, at 66 Rue Saint Louis, specialising in – what else – omelettes.

They have about a dozen varieties which are served with home-fried potatoes. Three breakfast specials are also offered which include juice, toast and coffee with a choice of cereal, eggs or croissants.

For a more French-style breakfast there is *Le Petit Coin Latin* at 81/2 Rue Sainte Ursule near Rue Saint Jean. Open every day, this small café has croissants, muffins, eggs, *café au lait*, etc, with low-priced lunch specials which include a glass of wine. At 25 Rue Couillard, one block east of Rue Buade, *Chez Temporal* is a little café which serves coffee, croissants, salads, etc. It's perfect for snacks, breakfasts and light meals. The café feels very French – a good place to sit in the morning and plan the day.

Now fairly pricey at lunch and dinner times, the re-done *Café Buade* right in the middle of everything on Rue Buade beside Holt Renfrew, just south of Rue des Jardins, has simple, light breakfasts in the downstairs section from $2.50 to $3.25.

There are a few places worth checking on Rue Garneau opposite the Hôtel de Ville. At No 36, *La Siesta* is a pleasant little place with a vast selection of moderately priced crêpes. At No 48, *Croissant Plus* is busy day and night with snacks and light meals. Also on Rue Garneau is the *Fleur du Lotus* which offers complete dinner specials at $16 from its Thai, Cambodian and Vietnamese menu.

Along Rue du Tresor from Rue Buade you'll find the Place d'Armes. In the *Hôtel du Tresor* is a dining room – very pleasant, done in wood with ceiling fans and white tablecloths. The evening meal will set you back around $20, which is about the norm.

One of the main streets for restaurants is Rue Saint Jean. There are many places to eat as well as night spots scattered along here, both inside the wall and further out. Some places act as both. At 1136 Rue Saint Jean, near Côte du Palais, is *Casse Crêpe Breton*, a small restaurant specialising in crêpes of many kinds, starting as low as $1.80. I like it because it hasn't been dressed up for the tourists at all. You sit right up at the counter. The restaurant looks as though it's been there for a good, long while.

La Terrasse du Roy, on the corner of Rue Sainte Ursule, is completely modern in concept and design. The small tables, some inside just off the pavement, are pleasant. It looks more like a café, and true enough the menu is small, but it's a cheap and popular place with good salads.

For excellent South-East Asian fare, try *Apsara* at 71 Rue d'Auteuil. Dishes are about $9 or a complete dinner for two will cost around $34. A few doors down at No 23, there's a cheap Lebanese spot.

Not far from Rue Saint Jean, at 48A Rue Sainte Ursule, is *Le Sainte Amour* with a $25 table d'hôte and a very good reputation. The menu offers about six meat and six fish dishes daily. For a splurge you're probably better off in a place like this, on one of the quieter streets.

There are plenty of other places for a night out, many specialising in seafood. A modest one to try is *Le Biarritz*, at 136 Rue Sainte Anne, which has fish dishes for $12 and beef from $14 to $16. It's been recommended by local people.

Café de la Paix, at 44 Rue des Jardins, is very French in decor and atmosphere and offers a varied menu of seafood, fowl and meats. It's very well established and is recommended and, while not cheap, is not exorbitant either. *Restaurant au Parmesan*, nearby on Rue Saint Louis, is always busy and festive. They have a large menu with most dishes from $13 to $16. They also have a huge collection of about 2000 bottles and live music.

In one of the oldest houses in the city and interesting for its reliance on traditional dishes and typically Quebécois specialities, is *Aux Anciens Canadiens* at 34 Rue Saint Louis. It's not cheap, but costs no more than many of the upper-middle places and is one of the few with a distinctly different menu. Here one can sample such provincial fare as apple wine, pea soup, duck or trout followed by dessert of maple syrup pie.

Place Royale (Old Lower Town)
At the bottom of the funicular is Rue Petit Champlain. If you're coming from Lévis, walk north off the dock and veer to the left. A few doors along on Rue Petit Champlain you'll see *Le Couchon Dingue* (with a pig for a symbol). They serve meals but it's a good place for breakfast, with *café au lait* in a bowl (as it's served in parts of France) and croissants. At dinner French-style steak frîte is a speciality.

Along Rue Saint Paul, an old quiet street away from the main tourist haunts, there are several inexpensive places although this area too, has recently been seeing some redevelopment. *La Bouille Café* at No 71 is good for light meals or a coffee. And at No 95 there is a small simple place for things like sandwiches or hamburgers at non-tourist prices. They even have a few tables out on the pavement. Further along on the corner of Côte Dambourges is *Café Bazaar* another modest cheapie. On Rue Sault au Matelot which runs perpendicular to Rue Saint Paul look for the *Le Lotus Plus* for inexpensive Asian meals.

Moving up-market, *Le Vendome*, at 36 Côte de la Montagne, is an expensive French restaurant which has had a European-style menu for close to 40 years.

Le Pape-Georges a wine bar on Cul de Sac near the corner of Rue Notre Dame sells grape juice by the glass.

Outside the Wall
Outside the city centre, things are a little quieter and not so densely packed. Rue Saint Jean, west beyond the gate, has numerous bars, cafés, taverns and restaurants. For eating there is Vietnamese, Lebanese and Mexican food. Keep walking and looking.

At 778 Rue Saint Jean is *Le Kisma*, an Indian place. On Rue Scott at No 821 south just around the corner from Rue Saint Jean is *La Pailotte*, a small good, casual Vietnamese place.

Along Boulevard Saint Cyrille Est is Avenue Cartier. There are a few Chinese restaurants here if you feel like a change. There are also a few standard French ones. At the corner on Boulevard Saint Cyrille is *Restaurant La Reserve*, below which is a small delicatessen. I'm told they have the best croissants anywhere outside France.

Along Grande Allée, past the Quebec National Assembly and other government buildings, and just past Rue d'Artigny, is a bustling, popular and lively strip of about 10 alfresco restaurants. They make a good spot for a beer or lunch if you're out near the Plains of Abraham. All have complete lunch specials for $6 to $9 (from soup to coffee) and at most places, dinners range from $10 to $20. *Restaurant Patrimoine* is one of the cheapest. At No 625, *La Veille Maison du Spaghetti* offers a variety of pasta dishes at below average cost.

Market
The Farmers' Market is on Rue Saint André in Old Lower Town near Bassin Louise, not too far from Vieux Port (Old Port) or the railway station. It's a covered open-air building where you'll find fresh bread, cheeses, fruit and vegetables. The best time to visit is busy Saturday morning.

ENTERTAINMENT
Though Quebec City is quite a small city, it's active after dark and there are plenty of nightspots although they change faster than editions of this book. Many of the cafés and restaurants – some mentioned under the eating section – have live music at night. Others are clubs open only at night. Most of the nightlife is in the Old City or just outside the walls. Brasseries – taverns for men and women – close at midnight while bars stay open until around 3 or 4 am.

Rue Saint Jean is alive at night – this is where people strut. There are good places for just sitting and watching, and places with music.

Folk clubs known as *boîtes à chanson* come and go along and around Rue Saint Jean and are generally cheap with a casual, relaxed atmosphere.

The upper portion of Rue Saint Jean near the gate is blocked off to traffic in summer and becomes a pedestrian mall. (I've always felt cities with such promenades are a little more civilised than those without them.)

At *Bar Le d'Auteuil*, at 35 Rue d'Auteuil, there is often live blues.

Lastly, there are a couple of spots on Rue Saint Pierre in Place Royale. There are also lots of dancing venues around town but they change quickly, so ask.

Just Sitting

The restaurant with a bar at the top of the Lowes Hôtel on Grande Allée on the corner of Rue Bethelot, is good for views. Away from the clubs, if you just want to sit, Terrasse Dufferin behind the Château is perfect. It's cool, with views over the river.

Cinema

Cinema Le Clap (☎ 650-2527), at 2360 Chemin Sainte Foy in Sainte Foy, is a repertory theatre showing both English, French and other international films, many with subtitles. There are two films nightly. *La Boîte à Films* (☎ 524-3144), at 1044 3rd Ave, is similar but it may have closed by the time you read this. One other cinema in town shows English movies. It's near Place Québec, the convention centre on Avenue Dufferin.

GETTING THERE & AWAY

Transportation can be a bit of a hang-up in Quebec City. Driving in the old section (and worse, trying to park) is a headache. The airport is a fair distance out and the bus station is none too convenient either. But the situation is better than it used to be: the new railway station is central and there is an airport bus.

Air

The airport is west of town, off Highway 40, near where Highway 73 intersects it on its way north. The number for Quebecair information is ☎ 872-3736. For reservations call ☎ 692-1031. For Nordair information, ring ☎ 681-7381. For Air Canada information phone ☎ 925-2311. The Air Canada fares to Montreal are $98 and for students, $55. To Ottawa, it's $120 and for students, $66.

Bus

Voyageur Colonial Ltd (commonly referred to simply as Voyageur) serves Quebec City. The station is Gare Centrale d'Autobus (☎ 524-4692) at 225 Boulevard Charest Est. This is quite a way west of the downtown area. Buses to Montreal run nearly every hour; the fare is $24. There are also regular services to Rivière-du-Loup and to Edmundston, New Brunswick. The fare to Edmundston is $35. This town is the connecting point with SMT bus lines for Atlantic Canadian destinations.

In summer, Autobus Fortin Poulin and Greyhound link up for a Boston-Quebec City trip, which takes 11 hours. If you're going to or from New York, change buses in Boston.

To get to town from the Voyageur bus station, take a No 3 or a No 8 city bus. Going to the station from downtown, take the bus to the corner of Avenue de la Canonne and Boulevard Charest. From there walk two blocks west along Boulevard Charest to the station.

Train

Until recently there were only two railway stations, neither of them in downtown Quebec City. One of these is in Sainte Foy (☎ 692-3940), south-west of town by the bridges over to the south shore. There's one station (☎ 833-8056) on the south shore in Lévis, right opposite Quebec City, closer to the downtown area.

But there is now also the newly renovated and absolutely beautiful old station complete with bar and café on Rue Saint Paul in Lower Town. The only trains going in and out of it are for Montreal though. To call, use the same number as above for the Sainte Foy station.

Trains to and from the east (the Maritimes and the Gaspé Peninsula) use the Lévis station. Some Montreal trains do still go to Lévis. But in general, trains going west, to and from Montreal and beyond, now use the new station and Sainte Foy. Train schedules include to Montreal (three services daily for $32) and to Moncton, New Brunswick, from Lévis on Monday, Thursday and Saturday for $70.

Car & Motorbike

For car rentals Budget (☎ 692-3660) is at 29 Côte du Palais or there's an office at the airport. For sub-compact vehicles the rate is $43 a day with 100 free km.

Car Sharing

Allo Stop (☎ 522-0056), at 467 Rue Saint Jean, is an agency that gets drivers and passengers together. Membership for passengers is $2, then you pay a portion to the agency three hours before the trip, and the rest goes to the driver. They offer good deals, such as to Montreal $11, Ottawa $21, Toronto $32, New York $46, and Gaspé $25.

Ferry

The ferry between Quebec City and Lévis runs constantly – all day and for most of the night. Fares are $1.05, less for kids and seniors; it's $2.55 extra for a car. You'll get good views of the river, cliffs, Quebec skyline and Château Frontenac even if the cruise only lasts a few minutes. The terminal in Quebec City is in Place Royale, Lower Town. In Lévis, the ferry terminal is right beside the VIA Rail station.

GETTING AROUND

To/From the Airport

A bus service operated by Maple Leaf Sight-seeing Tours (☎ 687-9226) saves you from paying the $30 taxi fare. This bus makes four trips a day during the week with a reduced service on weekends. It leaves from major hotels, but will make pick-ups around town if you call at least one hour before flight time.

Bus

There is a good city bus system (☎627-2511) which costs $1.40 with transfer privileges. The buses even go out as far as Sainte Anne de Beaupré on the north shore. The terminal, Gare Centrale d'Autobus, is at 225 Boulevard Charest Est in Lower Town and will supply you with route maps and information or you can call the above telephone number. City bus No 15 goes from the downtown area to the railway station in Sainte Foy and back regularly – all day until about midnight. You can catch it on Avenue Dufferin or in Place d'Youville near the National Assembly.

To the Beauport motels, take bus No 53 north from Boulevard Dorchester. Bus No 8 goes from downtown to Laval Université.

Autobus Mont Sainte Anne runs buses between Quebec City and the Basilica at Sainte Anne de Beaupré allowing stops anywhere along the way and letting you hop on a future bus in either direction. One-way for the full trip is $3.50. There are four or five services a day. In town, you can catch the bus at the Hilton Hotel, Place d'Armes or the railway station.

Car

In Quebec City, driving isn't worth the trouble. You can walk just about everywhere; the streets are narrow and crowded, and parking is an exercise in frustration. Don't bother.

Bicycle

Vélo Didacte (☎ 648-6022) is at 249 Rue Saint Jean. Also central and within the Old City is Location Mobylettes & Vélos (☎ 692-4178), at 92 Rue Petit Champlain in Lower Town, which rents scooters and bikes. You may see bikes for rent along Rue Saint Louis near the Château too. Ten-speed and mountain bikes are available. The Auberge de la Paix at 31 Rue Couillard also has bikes for rent.

Calèche

Horse-drawn carriages (calèches) cost $30 an hour.

Around Quebec City

NORTH SHORE
Chute Montmorency
Just out of Quebec City are the pleasant Montmorency waterfalls, higher than those at Niagara but not nearly as impressive. They're set in a park with picnic grounds.

Île d'Orléans
The 30-km-long, very green island gives a picture of traditional rural Quebec life. It offers great scenery and views, and you'll see old wooden or stone houses and cottages, some in Normandy style. Some of the villages are over 300 years old. Then, as now, the prime activity was farming for the Quebec City market. Recently, city folks have been building homes here, at least at the western end. There's lots of fruit, especially apples and strawberries. A view tower stands at the eastern tip. There's a campsite in the middle of the south side at Saint Jean.

Sainte Anne de Beaupré
This gaudy little tourist town is justly renowned for its immaculate, mammoth church. From the mid-1600s this has been the site of Québecois pilgrimages. The beautiful basilica now standing replaced earlier chapels and was begun in the late 1920s. Note the many crutches inside the door. There's good tile-work on the floor, and stained glass and ceiling mosaics.

Check the hotel across the street. It's designed like a chapel, stained glass included – yuk!

Also in town are a museum, a monastery with a seminary and a few other churches. There's a 360° painting of Jerusalem on the day Jesus died. Admission to see it costs $3.

An annual gipsy pilgrimage takes place here in late July, attracting thousands of people. The grounds become a huge camp.

About three km north of town towards Mont Sainte Anne is *La Camarine*, a fine place for a splurge on a good French meal. It's run by a woman in an old Quebec-style house and offers complete dinners from $21 and up – not cheap but very nice.

Chute Sainte Anne
Six km east of town, in a deep chasm, are the Sainte Anne waterfalls which are 74 metres high. You can walk around and across them on a series of steps and a suspension bridge for about $3. Though busy this is quite a nice spot and more dramatic than the falls at Montmorency.

Mont Sainte Anne Park
A little further east Mont Sainte Anne Park is best known as a ski area – it's the best near Quebec City and one of the best in the province. There are about a dozen lifts. You can also camp here in summer. There's a gondola to the mountain's summit. Buses depart from downtown Quebec City.

A few km east are more waterfalls at **Les Sept Chutes** with a hydroelectric station no longer operating and a dam. Trails wind along the river past the various falls and through the woods and there is information about the old power-production facilities. There's a restaurant and picnic tables as well. Admission will set you back a few bucks.

The Laurentians
As in Montreal, the Laurentians north of town are a summer/winter playground. **Lac Beauport** is one of the most accessible resort lakes.

Laurentides Provincial Park
Considerably further north is this huge wilderness park with its wooded hills and mountains, and lots of lakes and streams. You can hike and fish here and there are campgrounds along the road through the park.

In the southern portion, **Jacques Cartier Park** (☎ 848-3169) has camping, hiking trails and canoeing along the Jacques Cartier River.

SOUTH SHORE
Lévis
There's not much here for the visitor. It's a

cross between a smallish town and a suburb of Quebec City. The ferry ride over makes a mini-cruise and the views of Quebec are good. Near the terminal is a railway station (☎ 833-8056) for trips east and to Montreal. For more information about trains, see the Getting There & Away section of Quebec City.

Part of the way up the hill into town are the remains of a fort from where there are excellent views.

Between 1865 and 1872 the British built three forts on the south shore cliffs to protect Quebec. One, known as Pointe-Lévis Fort No 1 has been restored and operates as a national historic park, which has free guided tours. It's on the east side of Lévis in Lauzon.

The *Hôtel Saint Louis* (☎ 837-0071), opposite the railway station, is run by a friendly French woman and has small, clean rooms from singles/doubles $32/38. The dining room is inexpensive and neat.

Eastward

Leaving Quebec City, the landscape is pretty flat but looking across the river you can see the mountains and hills; the large one with the ski runs is Mont Sainte Anne. Going along Highway 132 through the little towns, Île d'Orléans lies just offshore. Without offering anything of particular note, **Saint Michel** strikes me as very attractive and a quintessential example of small-town Quebec. About 60 km east of Lévis is the first main point of interest, the Gross Île National Historic Site.

Gross Île National Historic Site

The new park here commemorates the significant role this small island has played in Canada's history. It lies just offshore from the town of Montmagny along Highway 132. For 105 years, from 1832 until as late as 1937, Gross Île was the major Canadian quarantine station for immigrants coming to the new land from Europe.

Through the last century and into the middle of this one, four million people passed through Quebec City en route to points across North America. Isolated Gross

Île was meant to screen out those amongst the thousands of people of varying nationalities with typhus, cholera and the like. In attempting to perform this service it became, in a sense, a city of woe.

There are over 100 buildings or remains of buildings still on the historic site including churches, a school, the 'hotel' residences and hospital. And, of course, the cemeteries.

There are half or full-day excursions but, in either case, reservations are required and can be made by calling ☎ 648-4168 in Quebec City or ☎ 248-9196 in Montmagny. Bilingual guides are available to lead visitors around the site which is open from early June to early September.

From Montmagny there are several different operators who run boats the short distance over to the park but these trips, some including a meal, can be very pricey. For information on the various choices call the above numbers.

Other day trips are run to Île-aux-Grues where there are a couple of inns and a restaurant but they are even more expensive and are geared to those in need of a quick splurge escape.

In and around Montmagny there are numerous places to stay including lodges, motels and campgrounds. About a dozen places to eat can be found in town including a pub at 186 Boulevard Taché Ouest.

Saint Jean-Port-Joli

This small but spread-out town, with the big two-spired church right in the middle, is a centre for the Quebec art of woodcarving. Good examples can be seen in the **Musée des Anciens Canadiens** where admission costs $2.50. The museum has work done by some of the best known local sculptors. There is a gift shop and snack bar here too.

More recent carvings in the same style and in a variety of other styles can be seen in the many workshops and stores in and around town. Some carvers specialise in figures, others in religious themes, and still others in boats and ornate murals. Courses in carving can be taken as well. Other crafts produced and sold here are ceramics and textiles but they are distant seconds to the number of works in wood.

On the east side of town, with the 1953 Constellation aircraft out the front, is the **Musée Les Rétrouvailles** with an assortment of farm and household articles from the past decades. There is an admission fee. There is also a **maritime** museum in town for those with a special interest.

The impressive **church** dates from 1890 and the priest's house next door was built even earlier in 1872.

Pretty well everything can be found along one street, Rue de Gaspé. In town you'll find a restaurant or two, including the *Dorian Casse Croûte* for topnotch fries and burgers. There are a few motels, a B&B, a campground, and a youth hostel. Right in the middle of town is a tourist office.

On the west side of town is a good picnic area with views over the river. Voyageur bus lines stop right in the town centre.

East along the St Lawrence River

East along the St Lawrence River from Quebec City are some of the most scenic landscapes in the province – the shoreline becomes more typical of that found in Eastern Canada. With neat small farms and little villages dominated by the church – usually topped by a silver spire – this is rural Quebec. With few changes, life has been pretty much the same here for well over a century. You won't hear English spoken in this part of the province, but you won't find any hostility either.

From Quebec City you can take either the north or south shore up towards the Gaspé. Just don't take the super Highway 20 from which you'll see nothing. The north shore is hillier and more dramatic as the northern mountains come down close to the river. It also has more physical points of interest.

There are ferries across the river at various points. The further east you go, the wider the river becomes and the more costly the ferry.

NORTH SHORE

Beyond Sainte Anne de Beaupré is the scenic coastal district known as Charlevoix. For 200 years this pastoral strip of hilly, flowery farmland counterbalanced with steep cliffs and woods wedged between northern wilderness and the river has been a summer retreat of the wealthy and privileged. Though vestiges of this remain and prices are on the high side it is now a more democratic destination. UNESCO has classed it as a biosphere or heritage cultural and environmental region and this has meant worthwhile restrictions on the types of permitted developments.

It's long been a popular district with artists, and numerous galleries and craft shops in the towns and villages. Inns and less expensive B&Bs abound and there is no shortage of quality restaurants. Aside from the summer visitors, people from Quebec City enjoy Charlevoix as a place for a weekend break or a short holiday destination. Due to its popularity as well as upper-class tradition (and quality), prices for food and lodging are higher here than elsewhere up the St Lawrence but the terrain and parks make a short visit worthwhile even for those on tight budgets.

Voyageur buses serve the area stopping at many of the small as well as the larger towns.

Cap Tourmente

At Cap Tourmente is a **bird sanctuary and wildlife preserve.** Flocks of snow geese come here in spring and autumn. There are walking paths through the swampy land. The area is open every day from 9 am to 5 pm.

Baie Saint Paul

Heading east along the St Lawrence River the first urban stop after Quebec City is Baie Saint Paul, with its old streets and big church. There are good views from the tourist chalet and a picnic area on the west side of town. The main street of this attractive town is lined with historic houses some of which have been converted into galleries and restaurants. Artists' studios and craft shops are scattered around the side streets.

A *Youth Hostel* (☎ 435-5587) overlooks the bay and town, one km uphill from the highway at the eastern edge of town. Rates are from $10 to $11. The bad news is it may have closed by the time you read this. An option is the inexpensive *Maison Chez Laurent* (☎ 435-3895) with motel units and chalets starting at singles/doubles $30. The simple *Hôtel Château Morin* (☎ 435-6512), at 160 Rue Saint Jean Baptiste, is also priced about the same again with some costlier rooms as well. There is also good camping on Île aux Coudres down towards Saint Louis.

Highway 381, north from Baie Saint Paul, runs along the edge of Laurentide Park and offers good scenery and steep hills. Going east don't even consider taking Highway 138 but take the coastal Highway 362 which goes up and down hills along the river. In the villages along the coast here, such as Saint Joseph de-la-Rive and Pointe-au-Pic, there are several small hotels with good food.

La Malbaie

The old-fashioned *Hôtel Lapointe* in front of the church is a fine, very cheap place to spend the night. See if you can get a peek at the mahogany cupboard in the old dining room.

In Cap-à-l'Aigle, the recommended *Auberge des Peupliers* has lunches at $10 and dinners costing $24.

Saint Siméon

The ferry to Rivière-du-Loup on the south shore departs from Saint Siméon.

Pointe-au-Pic

There is a new museum here with a good view and exhibits on the life and times of Charlevoix. A major part of the museum is the art gallery which has both a permanent display as well as changing shows which promote the works of local artists. The museum is open daily from 10 am to 5 pm and admission is $3.50, less for students.

Also in this small town outside of La Malbaie is the *Manoir Richelieu* dating from 1928 – a huge, elegant, romantic hotel worth a look. They offer one, two and three-day packages including some meals and entertainment but we're talking serious dollars. One exception is that the cafeteria in the basement has a low-cost breakfast – a good excuse for going to peek around.

North of La Malbaie and Pointe-au-Pic is the impressive **Parc Hautes-Gorges** a geographically and scenically intriguing area of mountains cut through by the Malbaie River and its valley. The sheer cliffs along the river reach 700 metres high at places. Very fine hiking trails crisscross much of the park. In Pointe-au-Pic cruises along the northern section of the river can be organised. The three-hour cruises cost $18. Organised hiking and bus excursions through the park with naturalist guides are offered out of Baie Saint Paul at the Natural History Centre, 152 Rue Saint Jean Baptiste.

Excellent hiking and rugged topography can also be found in the new **Grands Jardins Provincial Park** which encompasses an area of mountains and taiga (northern evergreen forest) which includes caribou amongst the wildlife.

Baie Sainte Catherine

Back on the road the scenery is superb around Les Éboulements, with farms running from the town's edge to the river. You may have to stop while a farmer leads cattle across the highway. Note the piles of wood used for the long winters and the many carving outlets.

At Baie Sainte Catherine, you can stay at *Hôtel Saguenay et Cabines* (☎ 237-4271), on Highway 294, for singles/doubles $20/40 or check out the *Maison aux Berges du Saguenay* on the main street and eat across the street. During the first week in August is the Cod Festival.

Baie Sainte Anne

At the end of Charlevoix at the Saguenay River whale-watching has become a major activity. There are several operators working out of this small port, the biggest of which is

Navimex Cruises which offers four trips daily. A ticket costs $30.

Beluga whales which are suffering most from the regional pollution, live in and around the Saguenay River all year round. In June, minkes and finbacks arrive from up the river and, later in the summer, the huge blue whale shows up to feed on the krill which is produced in copious amounts where the two rivers meet.

Tadoussac & Saguenay River

The Saguenay is the largest of Eastern Canada's few fjords – a spectacular saltwater inlet, edged in part by steep cliffs and running to a depth of 500 metres along a crack in the earth's crust. Ocean-going ships can ply the deep black waters as far as Chicoutimi.

From 15 June to 15 September, a ferry runs across the river to Tadoussac every 20 minutes from 8 am to 8 pm, then every 40 minutes. The 10-minute trip is free.

In Tadoussac, at the seemingly out-of-place huge old resort Tadoussac Hôtel cruises on a 1922 Nova Scotia schooner up the Saguenay River or out into the St Lawrence for whale-watching can be arranged. Trips upstream past the cliffs are interesting, as you lose your ability to judge size and distance against the rock walls.

The river can become very stormy very quickly. Where it meets the St Lawrence, shrimp and capelin abound, attracting beluga, finback, humpback, rorqual and even blue whales. Some boat trips head out to whale-watching territory.

For a splurge, dinner prices are relatively reasonable at the hotel and a walk through the lobby and around the grounds is certainly an experience. The hotel was built in 1941 but was renovated in the mid-1980s under new ownership.

Also in town is the red and white *Auberge du Lac* (☎ 235-4403), at 187 Rue de Pionniers, with very reasonable rates at $30 a double. There is a *Youth Hostel* at 158 Rue de Bateau-Passeur. Another low-priced place is *Manoir Audet*, at 16 Rue Principale, which is about $25 for singles/doubles.

There's camping two km from the ferry on Highway 138.

Pointe Noire Coastal Station This whale-study post (☎ 237-4383) on the Saguenay River has an exhibit, a slide show and films, and an observation tower with a telescope for views over the mouth of the river. Once numbering 6000, only 500 beluga whales still remain and the area around Pointe Noire has become their refuge.

Other types frequent the area; in fact, I saw a minke very close to shore. Entrance to the centre is $3 and recommended. Three-hour boat cruises run through the summer season for $30 and go where whales are most likely to be. It is not uncommon to see a few whales from the ferry across the river. The station also has a B&B at $18 per person. Twenty-two km east of Tadoussac is a nature interpretive centre with a whale-viewing deck, displays and also whale-watching trips out into the river.

Up the Saguenay River

Just north of Tadoussac the Saguenay Park, which protects the river's edges almost all the way to Chicoutimi, begins. Visit the interpretive centre at 120 Rue de Pionniers in town. They can recommend walks and have information on some of the boat trips available. There is camping in the park or guesthouses in the nearby villages.

One cruise departs from Rivière d'Éternité in the middle of the park region. Two trips run daily through the summer for $12. Another trip leaves from La Baie just south of Chicoutimi. There are several other trips to choose from, leaving from various places along the fjord.

Chicoutimi

The roads along the Saguenay River up to Chicoutimi offer good views of the river. Chicoutimi lies not far from Lac Saint Jean, the source of the Saguenay. There are a couple of wilderness parks in the vicinity and boat trips south down the river and fjord from town.

Despite being one of the province's largest

northern towns, Chicoutimi is quite small with a population of 60,000. It's set attractively between mountains with the Saguenay flowing through. Partially due to the number of students in town, what with a university as well as a CEGEP (community college), this is quite a lively place with a lot of nightlife. Rue Racine is the city's main street.

See the **house of Arthur Villeneuve** at 669 Rue Taché Ouest. In the late 1950s when Monsieur Villeneuve retired as a local barber, he began painting. His depictions of the town and landscape along the river attracted a lot of attention and are now sold and collected around the world. The house, he and his wife's former home, is now a museum known not so much for the paintings it contains but for the painting it is. The entire house has been painted inside and out like a series of canvases in Villeneuve's bright, naive folk style. It's open weekdays from mid-May to mid-October, admission costs a couple of bucks.

At 534 Rue Jaques Cartier Est is the **Musée du Saguenay-Lac Saint Jean** with displays on the history of the area including some Native Indian and Inuit artefacts. It's open every day but only in the afternoons on weekends. Admission is charged.

You can visit the large pulp mill, once the world's biggest. If you want a tour in English, call ahead for reservations on ☎ 543-2729. The mill is at 300 Rue Dubuc.

From the old harbour area tour boats depart for trips down the Saguenay River.

North of Chicoutimi the highway continues on to Lac Saint Jean and then through northern timberland and a huge nature reserve to the town of Chibougamou. From there the roads start to peter out.

Places to Stay Chicoutimi has a *Youth Hostel* (☎ 543-5103) at 27 Rue Bossé Ouest. There is also low-budget accommodation in the CEGEP college from May to mid-August. There are very low weekly rates if you're staying awhile.

Hôtel Chez Gérard, at 104 Rue Jacques Cartier, has been recommended as a good, cheap central place. There is a choice of basic rooms or more costly ones which have their own bathrooms. Either way a TV is included.

Also good value is *Motel au Parasol* (☎ 543-7771), at 1287 Boulevard Saguenay Est, with moderately priced rooms and a great view.

There are many other hotels, motels and some fine auberges (inns) around the region.

Places to Eat Rue Saint Jacques has numerous places to eat. *La Forchette* near the Chez Gérard Hôtel is said to be good value.

At night the *Guiness Pub* on Rue Racine is good and has a wide selection of beers. Along Rue Racine are several other places for raising a glass or kicking up the heels.

Jonquière

West from Chicoutimi along Highway 170, Jonquière is about the same size but not as interesting as Chicoutimi but it's worth a look if you've come this far. It has an enormous aluminium smelter and two paper mills.

The lookout at the **Shipshaw Dam** is a good stop. Turn right after crossing the Aluminum Bridge which is before downtown if you're arriving from Chicoutimi.

There are a number of cheap hotels and very inexpensive summer accommodation at the CEGEP at 2505 Rue Saint Hubert.

Rue Saint Dominque, the main street, has a number of bars and cafés which are very busy at night.

A puppet festival is held during the first week of July.

Baie Comeau

Beyond Tadoussac on the north shore of the Saint Lawrence, the road continues northeast through hilly and less populated areas to the newsprint town of Baie Comeau with a population of 26,000.

There isn't much to see here but in a small part of town known as the **Quartier Saint Amélie** there is another of the grand north shore hotels, Hôtel le Manoir. It's surrounded by a heritage district with much more modest houses dating from the 1930s.

Baie Comeau is one of the regional semi-remote industrial centres which seem to proliferate in this part of the country. Aside from the pulp mill, there is a huge aluminium smelter, **Reynold's**, which runs free guided tours through the summer twice on weekday afternoons.

But most associated with the town is hydropower because of the absolute mega-projects along the Manicouagan River. Each of three 'ginormous' **dams** operated by Hydro-Quebec – Manic Deux, Trois and Cinq – can be visited free. The first dam is 50 km north of town and the last one 200 km north. The scope and scale of these projects will really boggle the eyes and mind.

From Baie Comeau, Highway 389 runs north past the Manicouagan projects and then beyond to Wabush and Labrador City on the border of Quebec and Labrador, Newfoundland. For details of these similarly awesome towns and Labrador see the Labrador section of the Newfoundland chapter. About 120 km north-west of Manic Cinq are the **Groulx Mountains** which reach as high as 1000 metres. This is a fascinating far-north landscape with lake-filled barrens and tundra.

Sept-Îles

Sept-Îles is the last town of any size along the north shore and from here a train provides access to part of Quebec's north and the western portions of Newfoundland's Labrador. See also the Labrador section of the Newfoundland chapter.

From Sept-Îles, you can go to Île Grand Basque for camping and hiking, the beaches, and a few other things to see. Camping costs $7. There are frequent ferries to Île Grand Basque which cost $5.

You can also take cod-fishing trips from Sept-Îles out among the many islands for $15.

Getting There & Away

The twice weekly train from Sept-Îles offers a fascinating trip through northern spruce forest and open tundra which runs over a

900-metre-long bridge 50 metres over the Moisie River and past the 60-metre-high Tonkas Falls. The dome car is from the famous Wabush Cannonball train.

The route through the remote, rugged terrain was begun in 1950 and took 7000 workers four years to finish – a dirty job. These people had to be flown in, making the largest civilian airlift ever. For information in Sept-Îles call ☎ (418) 968-7539.

Around Sept-Îles

A side trip from Sept-Îles or Labrador City in Newfoundland can be made to Fermont a mining town 27 km west. Built in 1974 it has a unique design consisting of a 1.5-km-long five-storey arched building which contains most of the town's commercial establishments. The housing is all built inside the windbreaking curve. The train continues to Schefferville, another mining town.

Mingan Archipelago National Park

From Sept-Îles the road continues as far as Havre-Saint Pierre which has become the jumping-off point for this recently formed island national park just offshore. The park features some interesting 'flowerpots' and other odd erosion-shaped limestone formations. A variety of sea birds can be seen around the islands and, in the water, there are seals and whales. Many visitors bring their own boats – kayaks are good, but commercial boat trips run from the mainland too.

There is also a ferry from here to Île d'Anticosti.

SOUTH SHORE
Rivière-du-Loup

Rivière-du-Loup, on the south shore of the St Lawrence River, is really a pleasant surprise for many people. Although a small, second-level city sort of in the middle of nowhere, it's a lively and attractive town with an appealing and distinctively Quebécois atmosphere.

Much of it is built along winding, hilly

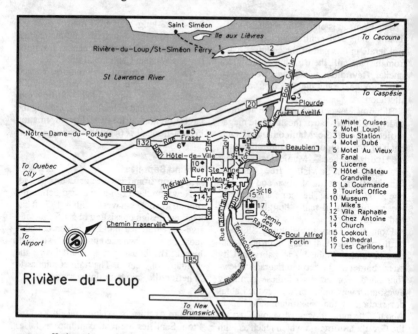

Rivière–du–Loup

1 Whale Cruises
2 Motel Loupi
3 Bus Station
4 Motel Dubé
5 Motel Au Vieux Fanal
6 Lucerne
7 Hôtel Château Grandville
8 La Gourmande
9 Tourist Office
10 Museum
11 Mike's
12 Villa Raphaële
13 Chez Antoine
14 Church
15 Lookout
16 Cathedral
17 Les Carillons

streets offering views of and across the river to the mountains beyond. The location also makes it quite a busy stopping-off point for those going either through the Maritimes or further east into the Gaspé region of Quebec.

The tourist office is in the Hôtel de Ville (City Hall) on the corner of Rue Lafontaine and Boulevard Hôtel de Ville. You can't miss it coming into town. There is another office on Highway 20 just west of the city.

Rue Lafontaine is the main street and leads up towards the cathedral which dominates the skyline.

Across the street from the tourist office is the **Musée du Bas Saint Laurent** (Museum of the Lower St Lawrence) at 300 Rue Saint Pierre on the corner of Boulevard Hôtel de Ville which runs across town. The museum deals with local history and all descriptions are in French; there's also a small art gallery.

The main street, Rue Lafontaine, leads up the hill from Highway 132 and Boulevard Hôtel de Ville. Many of the restaurants are here.

Following Rue Frontenac east off Rue Lafontaine for a few blocks you'll reach some waterfalls and a picnic table or two.

The illuminated cross, another landmark from which there are good views of the river, is easily seen but difficult to reach. You'd better get a map and directions but Chemin des Raymond will get you close.

At 393 Rue Témiscouata are **Les Carillons**, a large collection of over 200 new and historic bells, some of which are enormous. All are oddly mounted and displayed on Hydro-Quebec pylons. This collection is open daily in summer until 8 pm for a small fee which entitles you to ring the bells, from the smallest at 35 kg to the the two-tonne monster.

Le Château de Rêve is a small amusement park with children's rides, a swimming pool, farm animals among other things. It's off Highway 20, east of the centre.

There is free parking all around the central

area, look for the signs with the letter 'P' on them.

Ask at the tourist office about boat tours and whale-watching.

The ferry to Saint Siméon runs from early morning to early evening and the trip takes 1¼ hours. About seven services a day run in summer costing $17.20 per car and $7.20 per person. There is a restaurant and bar on board. Same-day return passenger-only fares, in other words a three-hour cruise, are very reasonable. Boarding is on a first-come-first-served basis and hopeful passengers should be at the dock an hour before departure.

I've heard of hitchhikers asking to have their ride requests broadcast over the PA system before docking and being surprised by having their announcement meet with success.

Mark Lightbody

Just west of town the river holds a smattering of islands; going eastward, it really begins to widen.

Places to Stay Most accommodation is in motels, the majority of which are just north of Boulevard Hôtel de Ville on Rue Fraser. They are scattered along here in both directions from the centre of town and while quite pricey, are large and comfortable; some offer heated pools and good views of the river. They are all well kept and some are exceptional in appearance, the ultimate being the *Motel Loupi* (☎ 862-6898), at 50 Rue de l'Ancrage, which is the only motel I've ever seen that could be termed eccentrically spectacular. It's surrounded by immaculate terraced gardens complete with aviaries, pool, swings and lawn chairs. A double goes for $65 and up.

Also good is the *Dubé Motel* (☎ 862-6354) at 182 Rue Fraser. Across the street is a campground which has a pool. *Au Vieux Fanal Motel*, at 170 Rue Fraser, has views of the river and a heated swimming pool which is good for the typically cool evenings. A double costs $60. *Journey's End* is somewhat (but not much) cheaper and seems pedestrian

in relation to the settings offered by the others.

Less expensive is the interesting looking *Hôtel Château Grandville* (☎ 862-3551), at 94 Rue Lafontaine on the corner of Rue Iberville, with rooms from $30 a single or double. This is north of the centre nearer the motel district.

There is a farm B&B about 48 km southeast of town, inland at Saint Clement. Yvette and Georges Veilleux run the *Fermes des Peupliers* (☎ 963-6120); singles/doubles cost $24/28. They don't speak a lot of English, but if you don't care, they don't either.

Places to Eat There is good eating in this town. Many restaurants can be found along Rue Lafontaine along with a smattering of drinking places. *Gino's*, at No 362 near Rue Sainte Anne, is very good value with a good table d'hôte for under $10 and a varied menu.

Mike's is a very classy submarine-sandwich shop across the street which actually makes a pretty tasty inexpensive meal. At No 433 *Chez Antoine* and, next door, the busier *Villa Raphaële* are both very attractive, enticing places with more expensive complete dinners. For breakfast head to *La Gourmande* at 170 Lafontaine. It's a café and bakery. *Le Pantagruel*, at No 274, bills itself as a natural-foods restaurant and features, salads, pittas, and pastas. The other major eating area is along Rue Fraser and serves the motel crowd. The *Lucerne* is a moderately priced place good for families as well as those without children.

Towards New Brunswick
Highway 185 with its forests and pulp and paper mills broken occasionally by farms provides a foretaste of New Brunswick. A highlight is the privilege of passing through and being able to say you've been to Saint Louis du Ha! Ha! Also pleasant is the beautiful, green rolling landscape around Lac Temiscouta. There is some camping and, most notably around Canso, a number of motels where, as is so typical of Quebec, the amenities include a bar. In summer a ferry

runs across the lake but this remains a largely undeveloped area.

SOUTH-EAST ALONG THE ST LAWRENCE RIVER

Trois Pistoles

The coast becomes more hilly and less populated as you head for the Gaspé Peninsula – it looks somewhat like the Scottish Highlands. People in the area cut and sell peat for garden fertiliser. The town of Trois Pistoles is dominated by a massive church. There's a ferry (☎ 851-3099) here, going to Les Escoumins. The trip takes 1¼ hours and costs $13.50 per car, $6 per person. It runs from May to November, with three services a day in July and August.

Between Saint Simon and Saint Fabien there is a lot of peat-moss production. The coast between Saint Fabien sur Mer and Bic is particularly scenic.

Bic

Bic was a little village in a beautiful setting a few km from Rimouski but is now a sort of suburb. There are some good coastal views in the area and a visit to **Parc Bic** is recommended. The village has a good picnic spot and the park offers camping.

Parc Bic protects an unusual landscape of conical but irregular and lumpy mountains that edge the rough, rocky shoreline here. Numerous bays, coves and islands link land and sea. The park is a vegetation transition zone which makes for an interesting mix of southern deciduous and northern Boreal forest. The diverse flora reflects these two influences. The park is also rich in wildlife. Of most interest are the varied sea birds and most of all, the colony of grey and harbour seals offshore.

Roads and walking trails (with a free map available in English) lead to mountain tops and beaches and cut through portions of forest. There is good camping in the park as well as picnic sites. Guided walks are offered. On my visit the guest book listed visitors from Holland, London, Paris, California – and none from English Canada. A visit is recommended, bring binoculars if

you have them. The park is easily big enough to spend a couple of days exploring. Note that it is officially closed from September to May but people do set up camp nearby.

Rimouski

Rimouski is a fairly large, growing industrial and oil-distributing town. The main streets are Rue Saint Germain which runs east and west from the square, Place des Veterans, where the tourist office is and Avenue Cathédrale. There is a helpful tourist office by the highway near the **regional museum**, and a neo-Gothic **cathedral** from the 1850s in the centre of town. The museum, closed on Monday, presents varied changing exhibits including the works of Canadian artists.

Out of the centre right along Highway 132 about five km east of the tourist office is **Maison Lamontagne**, an 18th-century house which is now an historic site, with some period furniture and other displays set in a park. It's open daily through the summer and represents a now almost extinct style of construction. Ten km east of town in **Pointe au Père** past the ferry terminal is a maritime museum and lighthouse with displays on a shipwreck and other marine matters. Admission is $2.75.

Places to Stay There are plenty of motels especially on Rue Saint Germain Ouest where there are also a couple of places with small, simple individual cabins for rent. There is a *Youth Hostel* (☎ 724-9595), at 186 Rue Rouleau, which is open all year. Patricia Calcaneo has a *B&B* (☎ 772-0399) at 220 Rue Lepage.

Places to Eat For eating there is a pretty good selection. *La Nature*, at 208 Rue Saint Germain Est, is an inexpensive vegetarian place where you can take your own wine. *Le Riverain*, at 38 Saint Germain Est, has recently upgraded and is now specialising in seafood. There has been a corresponding jump in prices but it's still good. Le Saint Germain restaurant complex east of Avenue Cathédrale on Rue Saint Germain has three or four popular restaurants and bars with outdoor tables and live music. Avenue Cathédrale also has a number of eateries and some more nightspots.

Restaurant Marie Antoinette on the highway is always reasonable with a selection of Canadian standards. Just east of town you'll see quite a few fish shops (*poissoneries*) where bargains can be had on sole, cod, Atlantic salmon, shrimps and the biggest lobsters I've seen outside a museum. Some 2½-kg brutes! Aside from fresh fish, many shops offer dried or smoked fish. Also in this area are some seafood restaurants.

Getting There & Away A ferry departs here for the 11-hour crossing to Sept-Îles on the north shore. The Voyageur bus station is at 186 Rue des Gouverneurs.

After leaving Rimouski the land becomes noticeably more wooded as you enter the Gaspé region.

Gaspé Peninsula (Gaspésie)

This is the rounded chunk of land that juts out north of New Brunswick into the Gulf of St Lawrence. To the people of Quebec it's 'the Gaspésie'. From west of Matane the characteristic features of the region really become evident: the trees and woods become forests, the towns become smaller and further apart, the weather becomes windier and cooler. The landscape is very hilly and rocky with excellent views along the rough coastline.

To my mind the area is at least as impressive as the much better known Cape Breton Island of Nova Scotia, and it's much less crowded. There is less development and less organised tourism, which compensates for the fewer attractions and possible communication difficulties. The numerous parks are excellent for getting out into the rugged terrain or exploring the shoreline.

The Gaspé Peninsula is popular with cyclists, despite the hard climbs, and there

are plenty of hostels, campgrounds and unoccupied woods to sleep in. All towns of any size have motels and there is a good number of guesthouses as well. Lots of seafood is available and the little trucks and chip wagons throughout the area make superb French fries and real meat hamburgers. You should expect cool evenings even in midsummer.

You may see some of these French signs so here's a quick run-down:

pain de ménage – homemade bread
gîte du passant – B&B
à vendre – for sale
des vers – worms (not a tasty snack)
bière froide – cold beer (available at most stores)
crêtons – a local pork paté

Prices in the region are relatively low (except for gasoline) and a trip around this part of the country is highly recommended.

SAINTE-FLAVIE/MONT JOLI
In Sainte-Flavie on Highway 132 is a large information centre for the Gaspé Peninsula. From Mont Joli, Highway 132 south goes through the Matapédia Valley directly to New Brunswick, useful for those wishing to bypass the Gaspé Peninsula. See the end of the Gaspé Peninsula section for a description of this route.

In Sainte-Flavie the **Centre d'Art Marcel Gagnon** is worth a visit. It's an inn, restaurant and art school based around an exhibit of some 70 life-sized stone statues by sculptor and painter M Gagnon. It's open daily from May to September and admission is free. There is other artwork on display. Aside from having a meal, you can just sit with a coffee.

Also in town is the **Salmon Interpretative Centre** with various displays on this queen of fish, an aquarium, videos, a restaurant and walking trails. There is a rather high admission charge, though.

There are four motels in town with *Motel Rita* (☎ 775-7269) the most modestly priced.

GRAND MÉTIS

On the west side of Grand Métis, the **Jardins de Métis** are an oddity worth looking at. It's an immaculately tended, Japanese-style garden with streams, flowers, bushes and trees – all labelled. There's a fantastic view over the coast by the old wooden mansion. The garden was started by a Mrs Reford, who inherited the land from her uncle, the first president of the Canadian Pacific railway. Begun in 1910, it is now looked after by the government. Admission is $3.50 per car. In the house at the centre of the park is a restaurant with lunches from $6 to $9.

At **Pedore**, inland about seven km from Grand Métis, is a farm B&B (☎ 775-5467) run by the Hartons, who speak only French. Singles/doubles here cost $25/30. It's a working farm and very quiet.

MATANE

A small, typical French town, Matane makes a good stopover. There's an information office by the lighthouse off the highway and it's open daily. The small museum is also here. Avenue Saint Jérôme and Boulevard Saint Pierre are the main streets. Matane is a fishing town with salmon and shrimp among the catch. In mid-June is the shrimp (crevette) festival: a time when you can feast on them.

Salmon go up the river here, beginning in June. The government has set up a monitoring system where you can see the fish heading upstream and listen to taped explanations. It's in the little building by the dam, adjacent to the park and near the Hôtel de Ville.

You can buy salmon and other fish at the packing plant on Rue Saint Pierre, on the corner of Avenue Fraser.

Behind the Hôtel de Ville is a large park with an open-air theatre for summer shows.

Matane Wildlife Preserve

The preserve (☎ 562-3700) can be reached south of Matane off Highway 195. It's a huge area with camping, canoeing, hiking, fishing, and boat rentals. You'll see lots of moose. The road continues on to New Brunswick but don't follow it. Go around the rest of the Gaspé Peninsula.

Places to Stay

The best places to stay are the motels strung out along the highway. Some are expensive. Les Mouettes (☎ 562-3345), at 298 Rue McKinnon, is one of the cheapest from $38 to $42. Priced similarly is the Motel Le Beach (☎ 562-1350). As alternatives there are the Hôtel de Roy at 74 Rue Saint Pierre, or Hôtel L'Ancre at No 292. Both are primarily drinking establishments; they both offer basic accommodation for $18.

The very modern-looking Collège de Matane, on the outskirts of town, offers its rooms to visitors at very low rates through the summer months.

Places to Eat

For the stomach, the Café des Îles at 50 Avenue d'Amours is recommended. They offer three complete dinner choices from between $7.50 and $10. Prices are lower at lunch time.

The Café aux Delices on Rue Saint Jean near Avenue Saint Jérôme is a standard, bit-of-everything restaurant. A block away, on the corner of Rue Bon Pasteur and Avenue Saint Jérôme near the river, is a health-food store with a few snacks and sandwiches.

Getting There & Away

Bus The terminus (☎ 562-1177) is at 701 Avenue du Phare Ouest. There are two buses a day for Gaspé and four a day for Quebec City.

Ferry The ferry to Baie Comeau on the north shore of the St Lawrence River does the run furthest east from the south shore. There are two services a day on Sunday, Monday and Friday and one a day for the rest of the week. The trip takes two hours and 20 minutes and costs $20.40 per car and $7.85 per person. Bicycles are free and there is a cheaper same-day return fare. For information call ☎ 562-2500. The ferry's a large vessel capable of handling 600 passengers and 125 cars.

Another boat goes to Godbout, a small town a little further west from Baie Comeau.

CAP CHAT

At Cap Chat the St Lawrence River meets the Gulf of St Lawrence. Locals will take you out cod fishing for about $8 to $10 an hour. It's best to spend a couple of hours early in the morning – the waters tend to be calmer then. Try Olivier Boucher (☎ 786-5802), Jean Lepage (☎ 786-2143), or Raymond Amiot (☎ 786-2229).

Basic roads lead south inland to two different wildlife regions with camping.

Lac Joffre, Lac Simoneau and Lac Paul are good for trout fishing and there's salmon fishing in the river, Rivière Cap Chat.

Rocher Cap Chat (the rock) is a well-known landmark. It sits by the shore on the west side of town and you can walk there along the beach.

Three km west of the bridge is the odd looking hi-tech vertical axis windtower, the world's highest and most powerful one.

Places to Stay & Eat

A good place to spend the night is the *Cabines Goémons sur Mer* (☎ 786-5715), right on the beach. The cabins have kitchens and go for $30 and up. Further east, the smaller, simpler *Cabines Sky Line* (☎ 786-2626) cost only singles/doubles $20/22. They are perfectly fine, though the location is not as good.

Le Cabillaud Restaurant on the east side of town is surrounded by flowers and is a good eating spot. It's not really cheap, however, at $8 to $22. They specialise in seafood.

SAINTE ANNE DES MONTS

Sainte Anne is another fishing town, with smoked fish for sale down by the dock opposite the church. From 25 June to 3 August, tours (☎ 763-3366) offering insights into the past and present are given by local people. There's one tour to Cap Chat for $6 and one to Gaspésie Park for $8. They leave from the Motel à la Brunante (☎ 763 3366) at 94 Boulevard Sainte Anne Ouest.

For a cheap and decent meal go to *Le Patriote* in Les Galéries Gaspésiennes near the junction of highways 132 and 299. It's good for breakfast or lunch.

GASPÉSIE PARK

From Sainte Anne des Monts, Highway 299 runs south to the excellent Gaspésie Park (☎ 763-3039). It is a huge rugged, undeveloped area of lakes, woods and mountains. There's lots of wildlife like deer and moose. The fishing is good; hiring a boat for three people costs $30.

At Gite du Mont Albert there is camping and a lodge (☎ 763-2288) with a highly praised restaurant. Rooms can be reasonable; the range is great but they start at singles/doubles $30.

The roads leading through the park are very rough and will take you to various hiking trails – some overnighters – and look-outs over the lumpy Chic Choc Mountains (Monts Chic Choc).

You can enter the park at Sainte Anne des Monts and return to the coast highway at Mont Saint Pierre.

Mont Jacques Cartier, at 1270 metres, is the highest peak in this part of the country. It rises above the tree line and epitomises the conditions of the Gaspé Peninsula: cold, windy and often wet at the peak too.

Hiking up, it takes about 3¾ hours for the return trip, but it's well worthwhile – the alpine scenery and views are fantastic and it is fairly common to see some of the herd of woodland caribou near the top. These are the last of the caribou found this far south; they seem to find the barren lands quite fine and happily munch on lichen all day. You can also climb **Mont Albert**, a longer but easier hike.

MONT SAINT PIERRE

Not far from Sainte Anne des Monts on Highway 132 is this little white village nestled in a short bay. The setting is spectacular with a nearby crescent-shaped beach and this small community, far from any big city, is famous for hang-gliding. The spot is

considered one of the best in North America.
Each year around the end of June is the
two-week hang-gliding festival (La Fête du
Vol Libre). A rough road goes to the summit
of Mont Saint Pierre where there are three
take-off stations and excellent views from
the summit. A 4WD vehicle is recommended
if you're not hoofing it up.

There is a youth hostel, *Des Voiles*, with
meals available, a campsite and several
motel-hotels in town. The grocery store has
hot chicken to takeout.

The cliffs east of town are etched with
interesting rock patterns. They continue like
this for some km out of town. In and around
town you'll see lots of signs here for *pain
frais* or *pain chaud* (fresh or hot bread).
Tours from the hostel to local sites cost from
$5 to $7.

East of Mont Saint Pierre there are lots of
good picnic areas with coastal views and
great sunsets. There are also plenty of campgrounds, motels or cabins with cuisinettes
(kitchenettes).

Other Attractions

At Anse Pleureuse, turn off to Murdochville
for tours of its **copper mine**. Madeline
Centre, a particularly beautiful village, has
lots of baked goods for sale. At Pointe à la
Frégate, the *Auberge*, in the old white house,
has good food for $25 to $35.

FORILLON NATIONAL PARK

The park lies at the extreme north-eastern tip
of the peninsula and is well worth a stop. The
northern coast consists of steep limestone
cliffs – some as high as 200 metres – and long
pebble beaches. See Cap Bon Ami for the
best of this topography. There is a telescope
for whale-watching – good from May to
October. Sometimes you can hear the whales
surface.

There are good trails through the park,
some with overnight camping. Two trails are
16 km long and take about six hours each to
walk but there are others that take from 30
minutes to three hours to travel.

The Parks Service naturalists offer information programmes and free guided tours.
You can also use the information chalet. Boat
trips to bird sanctuaries and seal colonies are
possible. In the woods there are moose, deer,
and an increasing population of black bears.
The shoreline cliffs attract numbers of sea
birds.

The south coast has more beaches – some
sandy – and small coves. **Penouille Beach**
is said to have the warmest waters. Petit
Gaspé is the most popular organised campground as it is protected from sea breezes and
it has hot showers too.

The hike along the southern shore to **Cap
Gaspé** is easy and pleasant, with scenery
that's good though not spectacular. The

Snow goose

headlands, with a lighthouse, have viewing stations.

At **Grand Grave** the Haymen & Sons store is an interesting place for a snoop around.

CAP DES ROSIERS

This is a small, old and interesting little village on the north shore. The **graveyard**, right on the cliff, tells the town's history – how the English came from Guernsey and Jersey, how the Irish settlers were Kavanaghs, O'Connors, etc; and how both groups mingled with the French. Generations later, the same names live on.

The **lighthouse**, built in 1858, is one of the highest in the country at 37 metres and is now classed as an historic site. It can be visited for a small admission fee.

Saltwater sport-fishing trips depart from the wharf on the *Anna-Lucie* for $16.

There are a couple of places to stay. The *Chalets Cap Cabins*, (☎ 892-5641) costing about $25, are pleasantly rustic with views over the bay. There's also a restaurant in town.

CAP AUX OS

On the south side of Forillon National Park, this small village has a good youth hostel overlooking the bay (☎ 892-5153). The address is 2095 Boulevard Forillon. It's a fairly large three-storey place which can accommodate 56 people. (There are some rooms for families.) It's open 24 hours and breakfast and dinner are available.

SAINT MARJORIQUE

Past this village towards Gaspé look for *Marguerite's Mini Restaurant-Casse Croûte*, a little café that has been highly recommended for its inexpensive French food with an emphasis on fish.

GASPÉ

After all the good scenery and attractive little villages, the town after which the entire peninsula takes its name seems pretty ordinary. It does, however, have all the amenities and services, petrol stations and grocery stores,

etc. A fair bit of English is spoken too. Perhaps surprisingly, from here around the head of the peninsula and down along the Baie des Chaleurs, there are quite a few historically English towns which have stuck it out.

The **Jacques Cartier monument** at the north side of town, is worth a look. It's different and well done. It was here that the explorer landed in 1534, met the Iroquois and claimed the area for the king of France. He took two sons of Chief Donnacona back to see Paris and later returned them. (I'd guess they had a few stories to tell.) Beside the sculpture is a museum showing maritime exhibits, some crafts and a bit on traditional foods. Admission costs $2.50. It's open daily but afternoons only on weekends.

Also interesting is the **Cathédrale de Gaspé**, the only wooden cathedral in North America.

Continuing in a religious vein, the **Sanctuaire Notre Dame des Douleurs** is a church which has been a pilgrimage site since 1942. It's open daily from 7 am to 9 pm from early June to late October.

South of town there are beaches at Sandy Beach and Haldimand but the water is cool. There's camping by the Fort Ramsay Motel near the water.

For eating or sleeping most people will prefer to be in nearby Percé. A place worth checking for a cheap bed is the very central CEGEP de Gaspé, a regional college which rents its many residents' rooms through the summer at very reasonable cost. A cheap breakfast can be had at one of the motel dining rooms.

DOUGLASTOWN

Like some other small English towns, Douglastown was established by Loyalists. Their ancestors continue to fish and farm.

PERCÉ

Named after the large offshore rock formation with the hole pierced through it (one of Canada's best-known landmarks), this town is the main tourist attraction of the Gaspé Peninsula. Despite this, it's a pleasant, pretty place and the **Rocher Percé** (Pierced Rock) is truly an impressive sight. Percé is the only place on the peninsula that gets busy and, because of this, June or September make good visiting times. The weather is usually good then too. The tourist office is in the centre of town beside the dock for boats to Île Bonaventure.

Just north of town is the Pic de l'Aurore (Peak of Dawn), which dominates the north end of town. From the next hill you'll see Rocher Percé below and, further out, Île Bonaventure, an island bird sanctuary. Other good views of Rocher Percé are seen from the road, south of town.

You can also walk out to the rock at any time and it's even possible to walk around much of it at low tide.

For $8, a boat will take you to the green **le Bonaventure** beyond Rocher Percé. There are Wildlife Service-sponsored walks on the island and a gannet colony of 50,000 among other birds and some intriguing hardy plant life. The service also runs a **Wildlife Interpretive Centre** south of town on the Route d'Irlande road, which is open from 10 am to 5.30 pm. There's a walking trail, film, slide show. Naturalists are on hand to answer questions on the geology, flora & fauna of the area.

In town there are lots of souvenir shops selling glasswork, pottery and some good quilts. At the south end is a well laid-out museum.

Behind the town are some interesting walks, which you can use a tourist office map for. Hike up to **Mont Sainte Anne** for a great view and to see the deep crevice between two sections of mountain and the grotto near Mont Blanc.

At nearby beaches, rock hounds can look for agate, which is abundant. There is also some diving in the area and an underwater park; check the dive shop by the tourist office.

At night there is often folk music or jazz at *Les Fous de Basson Café*.

Places to Stay

The seasonal youth hostel has closed. Look for another to take its place. Regardless, the tourist office will help with cheap lodging. They will even call places for you including some very inexpensive farmhouses away (say eight km) from the centre.

There are a number of guesthouses around which are good value. *Maison Avenue House* (☎ 782-2954) is on Rue d'Église, which runs off the main street in the middle of town. Before the church, you'll see this fine house with five rooms of varnished wood at just $16 a single, and from $20 to $24 a double. There are sinks in the very clean rooms. The guesthouse is in an excellent location and both English and French are spoken. The place next door also rents rooms.

A little more expensive is *Maison the Haven* (☎ 782-2374), on the main street, with rooms from $15 to $25.

South of town are a few bargains. The *Étoile Chalets*, little cabins with good views, are just singles/doubles $14/18. Further along on the other side of the road is *Hillside Farm Guesthouse*. And a few doors further along is *Mahan's Guesthouse* (☎ 782-2294) – a deal at $15/18 for singles/doubles. Triples cost $20. It's an old wooden house set back from the road, six km from town. The rooms are comfortable, with some antique furniture.

In town, *Horseshoe Cabins (Cabines Fer à Cheval)* (☎ 782-2802) are central, on the sea side. There are 10 units, each with a balcony and a great view of the rock and island. A small boardwalk runs along the shoreline by a restaurant, with indoor and outdoor sections, attached to one of the cabins. Singles/doubles $25/35 and up are recommended.

Across the street, the green and white *Fleur de Lys* (☎ 782-2772) charges from $35 to $55. The *Sea Gull* costs $26, or $30 with TV.

There are many other places to stay, mostly motels. The lower priced ones are out of the centre a bit. There are also campgrounds with views on both sides of town.

Places to Eat

Les Fous de Basson is the café in the centre

of town, beside the art gallery. They serve breakfasts of yoghurt, granola, croissants and other foods. Lunches cost from $3.50 to $5. Dinners are from $8 to $15. There's seafood on the menu too.

Biard's is on the highway in town, just slightly north of the centre. It's a standard sort of place with OK prices for such a town. It serves cheap breakfasts and the daily special costs $6; lobster is $14.

There is a *brasserie* on Rue d'Église. It's always good for a cheap feed and a couple of cold ones.

The *Pantagruel*, five km east out of town, has complete dinners for $8.95. They have fresh cod. Back in town, *La Table à Roland* and *Au Pigalle* are cheap, the latter has Chinese food.

For a good splurge, the *Auberge le Coin du Banc* is recommended. They have an extensive menu with table d'hôtes in three price ranges – $9.95, $14.95 and $19.95. There's good seafood, and you help yourself from six homemade desserts. The dining room is comfortably casual with a hotch potch of antiques, odds and ends and farm tools. No credit cards are accepted. It's about seven km west of Percé; you won't miss it – the yard is scattered with junk.

There's also a *bakery* north of town, on the left-hand side.

Getting There & Away

Bus Voyageur buses link Percé to Matane, Rimouski, Quebec City and Montreal. They also go to Edmundston and Campbellton, New Brunswick.

Train From Montreal VIA Rail serves the south side of the St Lawrence River with main stops at Lévis, Rivière-du-Loup, Rimouski and as far as Matane. The train then goes south through the Matapédia Valley and along the Baie des Chaleurs and up and around past Percé to the town of Gaspé. Many of the smaller places (along the entire route) are serviced. The train runs three times a week from Montreal: on Monday, Thursday, Saturday. The one-way fare from Lévis to Percé is $120.

THE BAY SIDE

The south shore of the Gaspé Peninsula along the Baie des Chaleurs is quite different from the north coast. The land is flatter and less rocky, the weather warmer, and so, farming in addition to various small industries is more important. Also unlike on the north side there are quite a few English towns on this southern shore. Much of the French population is descended from the original Acadian settlers.

Chandler

For a long time a pulp and paper town, Chandler is still based on the huge Abitibi-Price newsprint mill which can be toured for free. Freighters carry the finished product to South America and Europe from the town's own port facilities.

Port Daniel

Halfway between Chandler and New Carlisle Port Daniel is mentioned for the attractive blue and white *Maison Enright B&B* (☎ 396-2254).

Paspébiac

Descendants of Normans, Bretons and Basques live in this town. An historic site, open daily throughout summer, depicts the early life of the village as a fishing port. There are tours around the site which has a restaurant and craft shop.

New Carlisle

One of the area's English towns, New Carlisle was founded by Loyalists and has some grand colonial homes. Hamilton House, on the north side of the road at the east end of town, is open for tours.

Bonaventure

A small, pleasant Acadian town by the water, Bonaventure is the focal point for the area's farming community. There is an Acadian museum here, a wide sandy beach and a shop which sells various items made of fish-skin leather. It's soft, supple and attractive and, no, it doesn't smell.

Outside town in **Saint Elzéar** some of the

oldest caves in the province were discovered in 1976. There is an information centre with displays but unfortunately the public is not permitted in the caves.

New Richmond

Nestled in the bay near the mouths of two rivers New Richmond with a population of 4000 is another Loyalist centre. Just east at Duthie's Point in the **British Heritage Centre** there's a re-created Loyalist village of the late 1700s period which is open daily from July to September. It consists of 14 buildings including an interpretive centre, houses, a general store and a lighthouse and also covers the influence of later Irish and Scottish immigrants.

Carleton

About half the size of Richmond, Carleton has a pretty location on the water backed by rounded hills. Walking paths and a road lead to the top of Mont Saint Joseph which provides fine views over the bay and over to New Brunswick.

From the docks there are boat excursions (☎ 364-3926) for fishing or sight-seeing. Daily bus tours also leave from Motel Baie Bleue.

Good food is available at *Café l'Independant*, specialising in fish. There is both a picnic site and campground near the centre of town.

At **Miguasha** west of town, a free park and information centre has been set up around a 365-million-year-old fossil site.

The ferry to Dalhousie, New Brunswick, from Miguasha is a short cut across the Baie de Chaleurs. See Dalhousie for details.

There is both a picnic and campground near the centre of town.

Restigouche National Historic Park

A few km west of the bridge from Pointe à la Croix, the park (Parc Historique National La Bataille de la Ristigouche) details the 1760 naval battle of Restigouche which pretty well put the kibosh on France's New World ambitions. An interpretive centre explains the battle's significance and has

articles salvaged from a sunken French frigate. It's open from the end of June until early September.

There's a youth hostel at Pointe à la Garde.

Restigouche

Restigouche has always been and remains a Micmac Indian community. These east coast Native Canadians have always produced very fine basket work. The best pieces are now seen in museums but modern versions can be viewed or purchased on the reserve here.

MATAPÉDIA VALLEY

From the village of Matapédia, Quebec, across the Ristigouche River from the province of New Brunswick near Campbellton, the Matapédia Valley runs northward to Mont Joli on the St Lawrence River. This very pretty valley is unlike any other portion of the Gaspé Peninsula. Alongside the Matapédia River and the railway line, traffic-free Highway 132 passes through fertile farmland with a backdrop of green mountains for about 70 km. Aside from the good farming areas, the valley differs from much of the rocky, more sparsely vegetated peninsula by supporting broad-leafed maple and elm trees. The river is renowned for its salmon fishing. There are several smallish towns along the way, a few sites to see and, around Lac Matapédia, a couple of picnic sites as well as a campground.

Routhierville

The first of many wooden bridges seen through the valley is in this very small village. Some of them, known as settler's bridges, are covered, like the ones seen in greater abundance across New Brunswick. The picnic site here is about all there is. Anglers, out in the river with waders and fly rods, are the main attraction.

Sainte Florence

This larger town with a good sized lumber mill is situated where the valley is broadening out and the landscape is more gentle.

There's a place for gas and one cantine for burgers and fries.

Causapscal

Say this name three times quickly. Causapscal is the best place for a stop on the trip through the valley. It's a pretty town with a traditional look, a beautiful stone church and many older houses with the typically Québecois silver roofs.

The Causapscal and Matapédia rivers meet here. There are a couple of covered bridges south of town and, in the centre, a pedestrian-only suspension bridge across the Matapédia. Again, sawmills are the main economic focus and the smell or smoke from the processing chimneys is ever present.

There is a tourist office near the interesting **Domaine Matamajaw** or Salmon Lodge Museum. The museum, in what was the lodge, the outbuildings and much of the riverfront property were all part of a private fishing estate built by Lord Mount Stephen of Canadian Pacific railway fame in 1870. In the early part of the century a group of moneyed Canadian and US businessmen bought the place and ran it as a private club for 60 years. Take a look in the lodge some of which remains much the way it was – some people knew how to live. Other rooms are devoted to the Atlantic salmon, the impetus for all this. The site is open from 10 June to 10 September from 9.30 am to 8.30 pm daily and costs $2.50.

Across the street from the museum is a craft shop with some unique items – wallets, jewellery and more made of salmon and cod 'leather'. Other articles include tablecloths and rugs woven by local women and some homemade jams.

Fifteen km north are some waterfalls with riverside walking trails.

Places to Stay & Eat For spending the night or having dinner, there is the *Auberge La Coulée Douce* (☎ 756-5270) on the hill opposite the historic site. *Les Pignons Verts* (☎ 756-3754), at 100 Rue Morin, is a B&B with slightly less expensive rooms at singles/doubles $25/38. There are also a few cheaper rooms to let where the Voyageur bus linking New Brunswick to the St Lawrence shore stops at 122 Rue Saint Jacques Sud.

North of town is a motel and a campground. Also in town there are a couple of restaurants and the ubiquitous takeout cantines or chip wagons.

Amqui

The largest town in the valley doesn't have much to recommend it. All the basic needs can be met, and north of town beyond the bridge is a campground. Towards the end of summer you may see people standing by the side of the road waving jars. They're selling locally picked wild hazelnuts *(noisettes)* which are not expensive. Around **Lac Matapédia** there are some viewpoints over the lake and picnic spots.

The Gulf Islands

MAGDALEN ISLANDS (ÎLES DE LA MADELEINE)

Out in the Gulf of St Lawrence, closer to the Maritime Provinces than to Quebec, lies this lovely 100-km-long string of islands. There are about a dozen islands, 120 km north-east of Prince Edward Island, and most of them are linked by long sand spits. In fact, the islands are little more than spits themselves, so excellent sand beaches line the shores.

Because of their remoteness, the quiet life, the superb seashore scenery of carved red and grey cliffs and the great beaches, the islands have appeal and are becoming more popular with visitors. Other Quebeckers have been the first group to discover the islands and they make up at least 90% of the tourists. Most people stay two to four days and this enables them to look around most of the islands. More time can easily be spent walking the trails and beaches and exploring in depth.

The local people make their living mainly from fishing as they have always done but now the two months of busy tourism, July and August, are supplementing many an

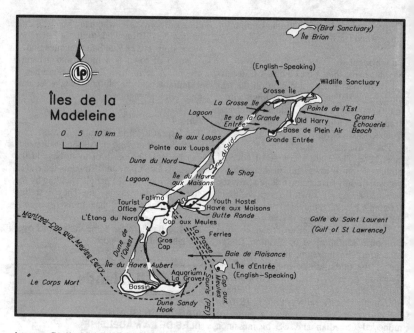

Îles de la Madeleine

0   5   10 km

(Bird Sanctuary)
Île Brion

(English–Speaking)
Grosse Île
Wildlife Sanctuary
La Grosse Île
Lagoon
Île de la Grande
Entrée
Old Harry
Grand
Échouerie
Beach
Base de Plein Air
Grande Entrée
Île aux Loups
Pointe aux Loups
Dune du Nord
Dune du Sud
Île Shag
Lagoon
Île du Havre
aux Maisons
Fatima
Youth Hostel
Tourist
Office
Havre aux Maisons
Butte Ronde
L'Étang du Nord
Cap aux Meules
Golfe du Saint Laurent
(Gulf of St Lawrence)
Ferries
Montreal-Cap aux Meules Ferry
Gros
Cap
Dune de
l'Ouest
Baie de Plaisance
Île du Havre Aubert
L'Île d'Entrée
(English–Speaking)
Le Corps Mort
Aquarium
La Grave
Bassin
La Passe
Cap aux Meules
Souris (PEI)
Dune Sandy
Hook

income. Sealing used to be important, but the commercial hunt is disappearing under international pressure from those opposed to it. Some former hunters are now taking tourists out on the ice in early spring to see and photograph the baby seals.

Over 90% of the population of 14,000 speak various French dialects, but many Scottish and Irish descendants live on L'Île d'Entrée and La Grosse Île. The towns and the people too, are sophisticated despite the remote, isolated nature of the islands. Restaurants and living rooms could be transplanted from downtown Montreal. Unlike many fishing or farming regions, the islands seem quite prosperous and don't really have the old-time feel of, say, Prince Edward Island. Food and accommodation prices can, but need not, reflect these characteristics.

The main islands are Havre aux Maisons, which has an airport, and Cap aux Meules. At the town of Cap aux Meules, the ferry from Souris, Prince Edward Island, ties in

and there is an information office (☎ 986-2245).

Things to See & Do

Most of the islands' activities and sights revolve around the sea. Beach-strolling, and exploring lagoons, tidal pools and the cliff formations can take up days. More time can be spent searching out the best vistas, skirting around the secondary roads and poking around the fishing villages. The waters aren't tropical by any stretch of the imagination but are warmed (slightly) by the Gulf Stream. Swimming is possible in the open sea or, preferably, in some of the protected, shallow lagoons. Currents are strong and venturing far from shore is not advisable. With nearly constant breezes, windsurfing is very good and several places offer boards and lessons.

There are also some historic points of interest such as the **old churches** and unusual **traditional buildings** such as the now-disappearing hay barns. Also around the countryside look for the old smoke houses (marked on the islands' map) now disused but once part of the important herring industry. Keep an eye out for the many fine and distinctive houses dotting the largely barren terrain.

In the evenings during the summer, you may find a concert, a play, or an exhibition of some sort.

Festivals

At Grande Entrée, a lobster festival is held during the first week in July. Fishing expeditions can be arranged and diving on the reefs is possible.

Also in July watch for the annual sandcastle-building contests along a two-km stretch of beach on Havre Aubert.

Accommodation

From June to September the islands are very busy and accommodation gets seriously scarce. If, upon arrival, you do not have a place booked (as most people appear to) go directly to the tourist office and have them find you something. Once there and settled a bit, you can always look around for something else. You could call the tourist office from Prince Edward Island and ask them to book a place in an area that appeals to you.

A good portion of the Magdalen Islands' accommodation is in people's homes or in cottages and trailers they rent out. These represent by far the most interesting and best-value lodgings averaging $20 a single, from $25 to $30 a double. The tourist office has a sheet listing many of these places but it is far from complete. The tourist office will call and book the ones they know (including ones not on the list) for you, still others can be found by following roadside signs or just asking people. The residents are a very friendly and enjoy even a broken French-English conversation.

More commercial accommodation is increasing all the time but remains mostly in motel form at often more than double the guesthouse rate. Cottages go for about $300 a week. The bulk of the places to stay are on either Cap aux Meules or Havre aux Maisons.

There is a *Youth Hostel* (☎ 969-4286) on Havre aux Maisons and there are about half a dozen campgrounds scattered around the islands. The campgrounds never seem full but remember this can be a wet and very windy place. If you've got a cheap Canadian Tire tent, you're pushing your luck.

Food

Another of the islands' lures is the fresh seafood. One of the main catches is lobster; the lobster season runs from mid-May to mid-July. Snow crabs, scallops, mussels, perch and cod are other significant species. A local speciality available at many of the better restaurants is *pot-en-pot*, a dish of mixed fish and seafoods in a sauce baked in its own pie crust. The adventurous eater may want to try seal meat which is served a couple of ways.

All the major villages have some sort of a restaurant but out of Cap aux Meules choices are limited. Cantines with burgers, hot dogs and fries are seen here and there.

Cap aux Meules

With the ferry depot and Cap aux Meules, the largest town of the islands, this is the commercial centre of the archipelago. It's quite busy and very modern which can be a little disconcerting for those looking for something else. This first glimpse is, however, atypical of the rest of the towns, villages and landscapes around the islands. Supplies, banking and any necessary reservations should all be taken care of here.

The islands' tourist office is a short distance from the ferry landing on the left-hand side.

There really isn't anything of note to see in Cap aux Meules but the town has more hotels and restaurants than any other one place in the Magdalen Islands. The rest of this island is also fairly densely populated.

Places to Stay & Eat The half dozen hotels and motels are all rather pricey and, as Cap aux Meules isn't particularly interesting, you'd be better off finding something away from town in the spacious, scenic countryside. Of course if you're arriving late this may not be feasible but the tourist office has a list of local tourist homes which make a stay more pleasant and easier on the wallet.

A number of guesthouses can be found on the other side of the island in the Fatima or Étang du Nord areas. One place very near the beach is *Cummings* (☎ 986-2978). Of course nobody lives too far from the sea here.

Probably the least expensive place for dinner in town is the *Belle-Vue* with a choice of Chinese, Italian and some Canadian standards. More expensive and very popular is the dressier *Pizza Patio* on the main street, Chemin Principal, a few blocks south from the ferry terminal. *Casse Croûte Raymond* is good for breakfasts and fries and burgers. The *Alexandre* has seafood.

La Belle Anse

The coast around La Belle Anse on the northwestern side has some dramatic red cliffs and interesting coastal erosion features. There are some paths right along the cliffs offering excellent views. For a very good and inexpensive meal go to the *Cooperative de Gros-Cap*, a lobster *(homard)* processing plant with a cafeteria-restaurant known as *La Factrie* upstairs with a large window overlooking the plant below. Just follow the road, Chemin de Gros Cap, north of the town of L'Étang du Nord. You needn't eat lobster, there is a selection of other seafoods with soups and salad all very reasonably priced. It's open from noon to 9 pm daily except for Sunday when it's closed. In Fatima, the small plain looking *Decker Boy Restaurant* is cheap and very good. Try one of the chowders.

North of La Belle Anse at the good sandy beach at Anse de l'Hôpital is a small complex of tourist-oriented shops and a snack bar.

One afternoon, on a trip to the beach here for a quick picnic, strains of irresistible traditional fiddle were heard coming from the building complex. Showing no shame we edged through the drinking and laughing crowd on the porch and invited ourselves in to what was some kind of a reception with people clapping and jigging to the music of one guitar and the distinctive violin.

An old man I'd noticed outside because of his thick, pure white hair and bright red shirt with cheeks to match began slowly making his way across the dance floor to the lavatory. After gingerly hobbling halfway across he was mercilessly grabbed by a woman about half his age and forced to dance. For a moment he stood still and unsure and then his feet took on a life of their own. For a good five minutes using every trick in the book he brought whoops of approval and amazement as he mopped the floor with the rest of the dancers and egged on the musicians to quickening reels. And all the while he was slowly edging towards the bathroom into which on the appropriate beat he quickly slipped followed by his partner half a step behind.

The door shut to the applause of the spectators but before the uproar had a chance to diminish the door once again flew wide open framing the old man peeing in the toilet. The woman, hands on hips, was still beating hell out of the floorboards. Well, you can imagine the frenzied crescendo the crowd attained when confronted by this spectacle.

Mark Lightbody

Île du Aubert

South of Cap aux Meules, connected by long strings of sand at points barely wider than the road, is the archipelago's largest island.

The section of the most lively town **Havre Aubert** is known as La Grave, an old section by the water at the south-eastern tip of the island. The main street is lined with small craft shops and gift shops, some restaurants and many old houses. There is a theatre here for summer productions in French only.

On any rainy day the interesting aquarium is packed with visitors disturbed from their seaside activities. A pool with various creatures which can be handled is a major attraction. The **Musée de la Mer** has displays on shipwrecks and various aspects of the islands' transportation and fishing history. Both are open daily in summer and have low admission fees.

Near town is the **Centre Nautique de l'Istorlet** with sail boat and windsurfer courses and rentals. There is also a simple campground at the coastal property.

Places to Stay & Eat The *Auberge Chez Denis à François* (☎ 937-2371) is somewhere you could stay over night. There are

Top: Rainbow over Niagara Falls (JL)
Bottom: Niagara Falls from the top (RE)

Top: Downtown Toronto from the observation level, CN Tower (RB)
Bottom: Roadside novelty, Highway 132, Quebec (ML)

six rooms at singles/doubles $25/30 and meals are available in its restaurant which is open to non-guests.

In La Grave, the *Café de la Grave* is a good place for simple, inexpensive meals or a coffee and cake. *La Saline* open at lunch and dinner time only is a pricier seafood restaurant where the local speciality, pot-en-pot can be sampled.

Havre aux Maisons

All-told, probably the most scenic of the Magdalen Islands, Havre aux Maisons has a bit of everything. Definitely take the south shore road (Chemin des Montants) from Pointe Basse up around Butte Ronde and into a beautiful little valley. Excellent views, some traditional-style houses, smoke houses and a lighthouse are all seen along this route. There are several restaurants along the main road across the island.

For a place to stay on Havre aux Maisons, the *Auberge Les Sillons* (☎ 969-2134) is friendly, has a good location, and is reasonably priced at $40 a double and meals are available. A guesthouse, on the main road across the island, is *Rina Arseneau's* (☎ 969-2579). It charges $25 a double and is a five-minute walk to the beach. There is a *Youth Hostel* (☎ 969-4286) on Havre aux Maisons too.

The coastal area around Dune du Sud is also very attractive and there are some fine places to stay in the area including some little cottages right on the water by a beach with huge sandstone arches.

Pointe aux Loups

On either side of this small community in the middle of the long sand spits connecting the north and south islands are stretches of sand beaches and dunes. For a quick dip, the water is warmer on the lagoon side.

La Grosse Île

This, the principal English section of the Magdalen Islands, was settled by Scottish pioneers. As soon as you arrive, you'll notice all the signs are in English. Despite generations of isolation, many of the local people

barely speak a word of French. La Grosse Île, East Cape and Old Harry are the main communities.

Trinity Church, known for its stained glass depicting Jesus the fisherman, is worth a look. Out through the windows the eye captures the graves, the piles of lobster traps, some solitary houses and then the sea: the island's world in microcosm.

There is a commercial **saltmine** just off the main road en route to Old Harry. No tours are given but there is an information office open in the afternoon. Begun in 1983 the mine is 223 metres deep.

For eating, the *Country Kitchen* is recommended for its wide selection, modest prices and simple, casual atmosphere. The house Bordeaux is a pleasant treat at lunch. Many of the people around La Grosse Île rent a room or two during the summer but are not listed in the guides.

About 16 km off La Grosse Île is **Île Brion**, an ecological reserve, once but no longer inhabited by humans. It remains home to 140 species of birds and much interesting vegetation. On days that are not too windy it can be visited. Even camping is possible, but for details, call the office of the Corporation for the Access to and Protection of Brion Island in Cap aux Meules (☎ 986-6622).

Île de l'Est

Linking La Grosse Île and Grande Entrée is this wild region which boasts the islands' most impressive beach: from Pointe Old Harry, **La Grande Échouerie Beach** extends, a curving sweep of pale sand, about five km down Île de l'Est. A short road with parking areas and trails stretching down to the beach begins near the Old Harry harbour. From Highway 199 (through Île de l'Est which, other than the beach is entirely a national wildlife refuge area) a few turn-offs lead to hiking paths.

Île de la Grande Entreé

On this island is Old Harry, a fishing wharf with about 10 boats and some spectacular shoreline cliffs, portions of which have caves embedded into them. At one time walruses inhabited the area but they were slaughtered with little concern. Sea Cow Lane is the site of the walrus landing.

In the other direction from Old Harry don't miss **St Peter's by the Sea**, a beautiful, peaceful little church overlooking the sea and bounded by graves, belonging almost exclusively to members of the Clark and Clarke families. It's open to visitors and well worth a visit. On a breezy day the inside offers a quiet stillness broken only by the creaking rafters. It's all wood, including a richly carved door done in honour of some drowned fishermen.

Across the street is a fine area for watching the sea explode into sparkling bits up onto the rugged, rocky shoreline.

Base de Plein Air (☎ 985-2833) is a resort built around the island's nature and the activities it affords such as walking, windsurfing, boat tours, bird-watching etc. Package deals include rooms at $55 and all meals and organised activities. The same package is offered to tenters for $35 per person per day. Very little English seems to be spoken. If you just want to tent, the fee is $8 a night and you can use the cafeteria-style restaurant.

At the far tip of the island are more colourful fishing boats to check out along the docks and a couple of places to eat. Best is the blue place with no name where lobster is cheap and other seafood is offered. The nearby *Café Spello* is also an attractive little place.

Île d'Entrée

This is the one inhabited island not interconnected by land with the others. A ferry links it to the port at Cap aux Meules. The boat runs twice a day from Monday to Saturday: once early in the morning and once in mid-afternoon. Board in front of the coastguard building. The ferry crossing takes between 30 and 60 minutes. The virtually treeless island has an English-speaking population of around 175 and is primarily a fishing community. It's about four km long and less than one km wide with walking trails leading over much of it. The gentler western section sup-

ports some farms before ending in high red cliffs. The eastern section is mountainous with the highest point, Big Hill, at 174 metres above sea level. A trail from Post Office Road leads up to the views from the top.

There is one guesthouse (☎ 986-5744) on the island but call before arriving if you wish to stay. Also on the island are a couple of grocery stores and one basic snack bar.

Getting There & Away

Air Canadian Airlines flies in daily from Halifax; Quebecair has two flights a day from Montreal, Quebec City, Sept-Îles, Gaspé and other points.

Ferry The cheapest and most common way to get to the Magdalen Islands is by ferry from Souris on Prince Edward Island. The boat leaves once daily at 2 pm except Tuesday. On Tuesday the ship leaves at 2 am. In midsummer arrive at least two hours ahead of time. I mean it, at least two hours. The boat, the MV *Lucy Maud Montgomery*, with a capacity of 90 vehicles and 300 passengers is always completely full and no reservations are taken. If, after waiting in line for hours, you do not get aboard they will give you a reservation for the very next ferry only. Sometimes at peak season there is another boat put into service but it leaves Prince Edward Island at 2 am. Nonetheless, it too, will be packed.

For the return trip, reservations can be made. It's advisable to do this on arrival or not soon after. You can book up to seven days in advance. In peak season there will be at least several days worth of returns choc a bloc as soon as you arrive. The return to Prince Edward Island departs at 8 am except on Tuesday when it leaves at 8 am. Again, the supplementary trip is at night.

This is not a cheap trip. The cost is about $25 per person for the five-hour, 223-km cruise. It's the car fee that really kills you though. That's another $48. And these are both one-way fares only. Campers, trailers etc are still more costly. Bicycles can be taken for $6. Credit cards are accepted for payment.

The ship is very well appointed, however, with a surprisingly inexpensive cafeteria. For those with a little extra money there is also a white-tablecloth dining room with meals in the $16 to $20 range and a full course (from soup to dessert) table d'hôte daily which is not bad value. The ship has some outdoor decks, various inner lounges and a bar with live entertainment.

Passenger boats cruise to the islands down the St Lawrence River from Montreal, but are expensive. There is also a passenger and cargo ship once a week from Montreal, which is less costly but still over $300 one way. The MV CTMA *Voyageur* taking cargo and 12 passengers departs Montreal once a week for Cap aux Meules and returns four days later. In Montreal call ☎ 257-0323. Meals are included in the price of the ticket. In the off-peak tourist season the price drops by about one third.

Getting Around

Five of the main islands are linked by road but distances are small and cycling is not uncommon. Bicycles can be rented at Le Pedallier in Cap aux Meules. The office is closed on Sunday.

There is a guided bus tour of the islands available out of Cap aux Meules and taxis will take you to specific parts of the island.

A ferry connects Île d'Entrée with the two principal islands.

One boat tour operator, Excursion de Pêche Îles, offers day trips to Île d'Entrée, fishing excursions and trips around the coast to see the cliffs.

ÎLE D'ANTICOSTI

A large island at the mouth of the St Lawrence, halfway between the Gaspé Peninsula and the north shore, Anticosti was privately owned by different companies and individuals from 1680 to 1974. One of these was Henri Menier, a French chocolate whiz. The island is now a natural wildlife reserve. There are about 300 residents, living mainly around Port Menier on the western tip, from where the island's lone road ventures to the interior. It's a remote heavily wooded, cliff-edged island with waterfalls and good salmon rivers. The one basic road leads along the north coast where there are a couple of simple camping areas.

There is also campground not far from Port Menier towards West Point at the end of the island. A ferry runs between the town here and Havre Saint Pierre on the north coast of the Gulf of St Lawrence where the road eastward ends. A longer ferry runs from Sept-Îles further upstream from which there are also flights into Port Menier. Due to the dense population of some 100,000 white-tailed deer the island has become somewhat of an attraction to hunters. Ones who don't like to have to look too hard, I presume.

Ontario

Entered Confederation: 1 July 1867
Area: 1,068,587 sq km
Population: 8,625,107

The name 'Ontario' is derived from an Iroquois Indian word meaning 'rocks standing high near the water', probably referring to Niagara Falls.

Ontario, smack in the middle of the country, is the centre of Canadian politics and economics, and much of the arts as well. It is by far the richest, most populous province, with about a third of all Canadians living here. Over 80% of Ontarians are urban dwellers, most living between Kingston and Windsor along the great waterways that make up the southern boundary. The country's largest city, Toronto, is here, as are Niagara Falls and Ottawa, Canada's capital. These three places alone make this region one of the most heavily visited in the country. Historic Kingston, in between Ottawa and Toronto, and some of the middle-sized towns to the west of Toronto with their country flavour and varying attractions such as the Shakespeare Theatre of Stratford and the German Oktoberfest of Kitchener are also busy tourist centres.

Less travelled but equally representative of the province are areas such as the beaches of Lake Huron and Georgian Bay with its shoreline made archetypally Canadian by the country's best known painters. Further north again are accessible wilderness parks offering respite from the densely populated southern regions and opportunities to see the northern transitional and Boreal forests. The resource-based cities, Sudbury, Sault Ste Marie and Thunder Bay, each with their own attractions also provide starting points for trips around the more rugged areas of Ontario from the Lake Superior shoreline to as far north as James Bay with one of the province's oldest settlements.

Economically, the area around the western shore of Lake Ontario generates much of the provincial wealth. There is as much manufacturing in Ontario as in all the other provinces combined. Hamilton is Canada's iron and steel centre and nearby cities make Ontario the national leader in car production.

Odd as it may seem, Ontario is also tops in farm income, although the area of excellent farmland (around the Great Lakes) shrinks each year as fields are lost to asphalt. Fruit is a major market crop and to an ever decreasing extent, tobacco. The Niagara Peninsula is also a significant wine-producing region. Further north are tremendous resources. Sudbury produces a quarter of the world's nickel; Elliot Lake sits on the largest uranium deposits known – and, of course, there are the forests.

Despite all this, there remains much uncluttered wooded lakeland and large areas of quiet country towns surrounded by small market gardens. And, within the northern regions, vast areas of wilderness still exist.

I guess you can see why Ontario is called one of the 'have' provinces. It is also very conservative – politically and socially. Recently the provincial social democratic party was elected for the first time so it'll be interesting to see what changes this produces or heralds.

Within Ontario is the country's most southerly region, important when considering climatic factors. Around Niagara the summers are long, the winters mild. Lake Ontario keeps the bulk of the population from being too cold in winter. Summers can be hot and muggy. Temperatures drop progressively (and considerably) the further north you go.

Ontario has many excellent government parks for outdoor activities.

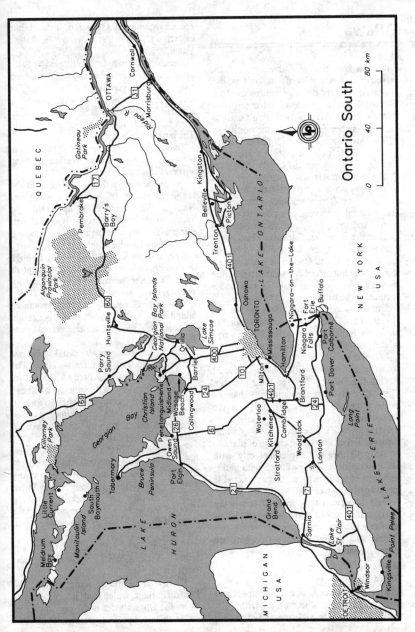

Ontario South

Ottawa

Ottawa is known to all Canadians with the mixed emotions worthy of a nation's capital. It sits attractively on the south bank of the Ottawa River at its confluence with the Rideau River. The gently rolling Gatineau Hills of Quebec are visible to the north.

The government is the largest employer, and the stately Gothic-style Parliament Buildings act as landmarks.

The city attracts four million tourists a year, many to see just what the heck the capital's like. The abundance of museums and cultural activities are another enticement. And then, of course, in summer you can see the numerous Canadian Mounties.

A surprise may be the amount of French heard around town. Quebec is just a stone's throw away but probably as important is that most Federal Government workers are now required to be bilingual.

Ottawa is not an exciting city but the streets, if not lively, are wide and clean; the air is not fouled by heavy industry. Everywhere people are jogging and cycling.

In 1826 British troops founded the first settlement in order to build the Rideau Canal linking the Ottawa River to Lake Ontario. First called Bytown, the name was changed in 1855 and Queen Victoria made it the capital in 1857.

After WW II, the Paris city planner Jacques Greber was put in charge of plans to beautify Ottawa. This pleasant city with 300,000 residents is now dotted with parks, and most of the land along the waterways is for recreational use.

Hull, Quebec, easily reached across the river, is smaller but noted for good restaurants and late-hour nightlife.

Note that many of Ottawa's sights are closed on Monday.

Orientation

Ottawa's central core is quite compact and many of the places of interest are within it – walking is a very feasible method of getting about. Downtown Ottawa is divided into eastern and western sections by the Rideau Canal.

On the western side, Wellington St is the principal east-west street and has Parliament Hill and many government buildings. The Ottawa River lies just to the north. One block south of Wellington St is Sparks St, a pedestrian mall with shops and fast-food outlets. The post office is at No 59.

Bank St runs south and is the main shopping street, with many restaurants and several theatres.

Just to the west of the canal is Elgin St and large Confederation Square with the National War Memorial in its centre. The tourist office is here, in the National Arts Centre. The large, French-looking palace is the Château Laurier hotel.

The Rideau Canal goes south through town with walking and cycling paths at its edge. In winter the frozen canal is used for skating.

Gladstone St roughly marks the southern boundary of the downtown area. About eight km from the Château Laurier, the canal joins Dows Lake.

On the other side of the canal is Ottawa East, with Rideau St as the main street. The new Rideau Centre is here, a three-level enclosed shopping mall with an overhead walkway across the street. North, at York St, is Bytown Market, an interesting renovated area with lots of activity which peaks on Saturday, market day.

Crafts are sold in the market building, and there are many restaurants. Along Wellington St and up Sussex Drive are many 19th-century buildings. Along Sussex Drive between George and Patrick Sts walking through the archways or alleys leads to a series of old connected courtyards where you may find an outdoor café.

North up Sussex Drive and to the left (east) is Nepean Point, well worth the short walk for the view.

There are four bridges across to Hull. The Pont du Portage, which leads into Wellington St on the Ottawa side, is the one to take in order to end up in downtown Hull. The

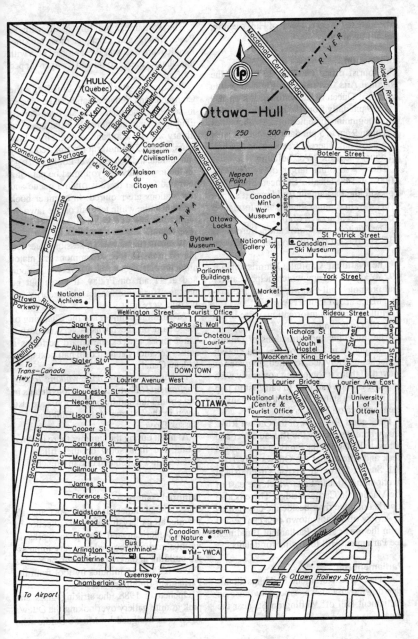

Ottawa–Hull

0   250   500 m

HULL (Quebec)

Rue Laval
Rue Kent
Boulevard Maisonneuve
Rue Colombia
Rue Notre-Dame
Rue Laurier

Promenade du Portage

Rue Hôtel de Ville

Canadian Museum Civilisation

Maison du Citoyen

Pont du Portage

OTTAWA RIVER

Nepean Point

Alexandra Bridge

Macdonald Cartier Bridge

RIVER

Rideau River

Boteler Street

Ottawa Locks

Bytown Museum

Canadian Mint War Museum

National Gallery

Sussex Drive

St Patrick Street

Canadian Ski Museum

York Street

Parliament Buildings

Mackenzie St

Market

King Edward Street

Rideau Street

Ottawa Parkway

National Archives

Wellington Street

Tourist Office

Sparks St Mall

Chateau Laurier

Nicholas St

Jail Youth Hostel

Walter St

Wellington St

To Trans-Canada Hwy

Sparks St
Queen St
Albert St
Slater St

DOWNTOWN

MacKenzie King Bridge

Laurier Avenue West

Gloucester St
Nepean St
Lisgar St
Cooper St
Somerset St
Maclaren St
Gilmour St
James St
Florence St
Gladstone St
McLeod St
Flora St
Arlington St
Catherine St

OTTAWA

Gladstone St

Kent Street
Bank Street
O'Connor St
Metcalfe St

National Arts Centre & Tourist Office

Elgin Street

Laurier Bridge

Laurier Ave East

University of Ottawa

Queen Elizabeth Driveway

Colonel By Street

Cartier St

Macdonald

Nicholas Street

Rideau Canal

Canadian Museum of Nature

Bus Terminal

YM-YWCA

Bronson Street
Percy St
Gay St

Queensway

Chamberlain St

To Ottawa Railway Station

To Airport

others are to the east or west of Hull's centre, but not by much.

Information

The tourist office (☎ 237-5158) is in the National Arts Centre, at 65 Elgin St on the corner of Queen St, downtown. It's open 9 am to 9 pm daily from the beginning of May to the beginning of September. At other times it is open 9 am to 5 pm daily but Sunday just 10 am to 4 pm. There is free parking (for half an hour) under the NAC building.

There is another larger office (☎ 239-5000) at 14 Metcalfe St, near Sparks St, opposite the Parliament Buildings. It's open every day. In summer there is an information booth in the Sparks St Mall.

The Visitors and Convention Bureau (☎ 237-5150) is on the 7th floor at 222 Queen St.

The National Capital Commission (☎ 992-4231), an agency which helps beautify and promote Hull-Ottawa, has an information office at 161 Laurier Ave West.

Hull has its own information office in the City Hall in downtown Hull.

The museums and attractions of Ottawa are frequently in a state of flux and closed, either being renovated, repaired, upgraded or moved. If there is something you really wish to see it is not a bad idea to call first to find out its current status. Also note that many of them are free on Thursday.

For a good, free view of the Ottawa River area where it's met by the Rideau River and across to Hull go to the 8th floor observation deck and cafeteria at the Ottawa City Hall, 111 Sussex Drive. It sits on Green Island overlooking Rideau Falls which are east of the Macdonald Cartier Bridge. There is also a park along the river beside the city hall.

A view of the downtown area can be had from the tower at the Parliament Buildings, see Parliament Hill following for details.

Parliament Hill

The Federal Government buildings dominate downtown Ottawa, especially those on Parliament Hill off Wellington St, near the canal.

The Parliament building itself, with its Peace Tower and clock, is most striking. Beside it are East and West blocks, also with the sharp, green, oxidised copper-topped roofing.

Inside the Parliament building, the Commons and Senate sit and can be viewed in session. The interior is all hand-carved limestone and sandstone. See the beautiful library with its wood and wrought iron. Free tours, about 20 minutes long, run frequently and include the Peace Tower Lookout. To go up the tower elevator you must be part of a tour and for that there is often a queue and reservations are required. In summer book the tour in the white tent out on the lawn. In winter there is a desk inside for making the reservation.

When Parliament is in session Question Period in the House of Commons is a major attraction. It occurs early every afternoon and at 11 am on Friday. It's free but be prepared for some hassle. The security has become very tight.

At 10 am in summer see the Changing of the Guard on the lawns – very colourful. Three times a week the Guard performs a sunset ceremony at their drill hall next to the Rideau Canal.

Pick up a free copy of the *Walking Tour of Parliament Hill* which lists various details in and around the buildings. Free tours are also given in the External Affairs Building, 125 Sussex Drive.

At night during the summer there is a free sound and light show on the Hill – one version's in English and one in French.

National Gallery

The National Gallery is a must. As Canada's premier art gallery, it has a vast collection of North American and European works in various media all housed in a very impressive building in the centre of town, on Sussex Drive. It's just 15 minutes by foot from the Parliament Buildings.

Opened in 1988, the striking glass and pink granite gallery overlooking the Ottawa River was designed by Moshe Safdie who

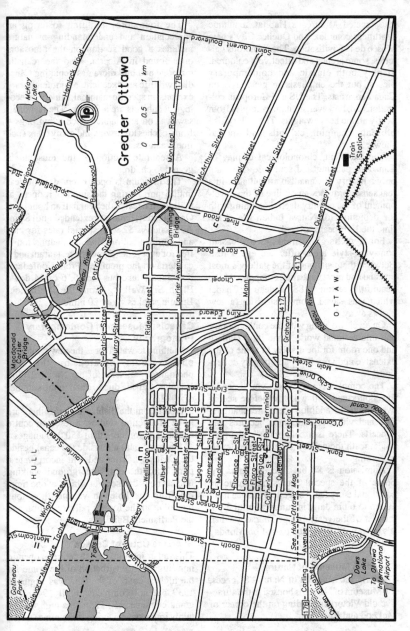

also created Montreal's Habitat, a unique apartment complex, and Quebec City's new Musée de la Civilisation. The numerous galleries, some arched and effectively coloured, display both classic and contemporary pieces, but the emphasis in general is on Canadian artists. The US and European collections do, however, contain examples from nearly all the heavyweights. The gallery also presents changing exhibits and special shows.

The excellent, chronological display of Canadian painting and sculpture gives not only a history of Canadian art but also, in a real sense, provides an outline of the development of the country itself, beginning with the depictions of Native Indian life at the time the Europeans arrived.

For a recharging break, two pleasant courtyard-style areas offer the eye a rest. Between them sits one of the gallery's most unusual and most appealing components, the beautifully restored 1888 Rideau St Chapel which was saved from destruction a few blocks away.

On level two along with the contemporary and international work, is the Inuit Gallery and one room for the display of some of the extensive and very fine photography collection.

The complex is very large; you'll need a few hours and still will tire before seeing everything. In addition there are changing film and video presentations, lectures and concerts. There is a café and a restaurant. Underneath the gallery, there are two levels of parking.

Admission is $4 but free on Thursday. Some of the special shows may have an additional entry fee. The gallery is open from 10 am to 6 pm daily in summer (until 5 pm the rest of the year) except Thursday when it's open until 8 pm. It's closed on Monday and holidays.

Canadian Museum of Nature

Formerly the Museum of Natural Sciences, the Museum of Nature is housed in the attractive old Victorian building on the corner of McLeod and Elgin Sts.

The four-storey building fostering an appreciation and understanding of nature includes a good section on the dinosaurs once found in Alberta. Also the realistic mammal and bird dioramas depicting Canadian wildlife are excellent. Major temporary exhibits on specific mammal, mineral or ecological subjects are a feature. The last one I saw was on all manner of crawling bugs – from roaches to earwigs and many other such fine creatures.

A separate section of the museum is geared to children.

The museum is open every day all year until 5 pm. During the summer it opens at 9.30 am, the rest of the year half an hour later. On Thursday, hours are extended until 8 pm. Admission is $2 with special rates for kids and families but on Thursday, admission is free for everyone. There is a restaurant and a cafeteria on the premises. From Confederation Square take bus Nos 5, 6 or 14 down Elgin St. Walking from the Parliament Buildings takes about 20 minutes.

Canadian Museum of Contemporary Photography

Something to watch for is the new photography museum, created by the still photography division of the National Film Board of Canada due to open in the summer of 1992.

Apart from the display galleries there are to be production studios, a research centre and storage for more than 150,000 images.

It is to be built alongside the canal beside the Château Laurier and will incorporate a portion of the old, underground walking tunnels now disused but which, at one time, ran from the hotel in various directions including to the former railway station and the Parliament Buildings.

Supreme Court of Canada

This rather intimidating structure is open to non-litigants. Construction of the home for the highest court of the land was begun in 1939 but not completed until 1946. The grand entrance hall, 12 metres high, is certainly impressive. During the summer a visit will include a free tour given by a law student. The court's on the corner of Wellington and Kent Sts.

Bytown Museum & the Ottawa Locks

Focusing on city history, Bytown Museum is in the oldest stone building in Ottawa. It's east of Parliament Hill beside the canal – go down the stairs from Wellington St and back to the locks at the river. Used during construction of the canal for storing military equipment and money, it now contains artefacts and documents pertaining to local history.

On the ground floor, Parks Canada runs an exhibit about the building of the canal, open from mid-May to mid-October, 10 am to 4 pm and Sunday 2 to 5 pm. It's closed on Tuesday. In spring and fall, it's open from Monday to Friday and there's a small admission fee.

The series of locks at the edge of the Ottawa River in the Colonel By Valley between the Château Laurier and the Parliament Buildings marks the north end of the 198-km-long Rideau Canal which runs to Kingston and the St Lawrence River. Colonel By who was put in charge of constructing the canal set up his headquarters right here in 1826. Though never used for any military purpose, the canal was used commercially for a while and then fell into disuse. The locks are now maintained as heritage parks by the government.

Canadian War Museum

At 330 Sussex Drive, this museum with the country's largest war related collection, contains all manner of things military and traces Canadian military history. There's a life-sized replica of a WW I trench that's good. You'll also see large displays with sound, showing the American invasion of 1775 and the Normandy D-Day landing. The museum also contains the country's largest collection of war art.

The museum is open from 9.30 am to 5 pm daily. Admission is $2 or $1 for students and seniors but is free on Thursday.

Royal Canadian Mint

Next door to the War Museum is the mint (☎ 992-2348). No longer producing day-to-day coinage, it is now used for striking special-edition coins, commemorative pieces, bullion investment coins and the like. Founded in 1908 and renovated in the mid-1980s, this imposing stone building has always been Canada's major refiner of gold. Tours are given by appointment, call to arrange one, and see the process – from sheets of metal to bags of coins. Hours are from 8.30 to 11 am and 12.30 to 2.30 pm Monday to Friday and it's free.

The main circulation-coin mint is now in Winnipeg, Manitoba.

Currency Museum

For those who like to look at money without possessing it, you can see more money at the Currency Museum in the Bank of Canada at 245 Sparks St. It's open daily in summer, closed on Monday in winter. Various displays tell the story of money through the ages, from whales' teeth to collectors' bank notes. The emphasis is on Canadian monies. And despite all the focus on money the museum is free and tours are offered too.

National Aviation Museum

This collection of over 100 aircraft is housed in a huge triangular building (about the size of four football fields) at the Rockcliffe Airport, not too far from the centre of town. See planes ranging from the Silver Dart of 1909 to the first turbo-powered Viscount passenger carrier, to more recent jets. Peace and wartime planes are equally represented; included is the renowned Spitfire. The Cessna Crane is the very one my father trained in for the RCAF.

Other exhibits include aviation-related video games and audiovisual presentations.

Admission is $4, less for seniors and kids and, again, it's free on Thursday. From May to September the museum is open from Wednesday to Friday 9 am to 8 pm, Saturday to Tuesday 9 am to 6 pm. In winter it's open until 8 pm on Thursday only. On Monday it's closed unless it is a holiday when it remains open. Call ☎ 993-2010 to check on opening hours as they tend to vary according to attendance levels and the time of year.

The airport is off Saint Laurent Boulevard north-east of the downtown area near the river and the Canadian Forces base.

National Museum of Science & Technology

At 1867 Saint Laurent Boulevard at Russell Rd (☎ 998-4566), this museum has all kinds of participatory scientific learning exhibits. Try things out, test yourself, watch physical laws in action, see optical illusions. It's great for kids; those without children could avoid weekends. Also on display are farm machines, trains, model ships and stagecoaches. The bicycle and motorcycle collections and the computers are good; don't miss the incubator where you can see live chicks in various stages of hatching.

An astronomy section has films and slides about the universe; on clear nights take a peep through the large refracting telescope.

Admission is $4, free on Thursday. In summer, opening hours are from 9 am to 6 pm daily but until 8 pm from Wednesday to Friday; it's closed on Monday. In winter it closes earlier in the day.

National Postal Museum

In Ottawa you'll find many museums and attractions are either being renovated, repaired, upgraded or moved. The postal museum is one such place. While the new permanent location will be in Hull, some of the displays can be seen at 365 Laurier Ave on the corner of Kent St (☎ 995-99048). For now it's open from Tuesday to Saturday 9 am to 5 pm but afternoons only on Wednesday. You'll also find the philatelic library and a sales counter for various collectables here.

Canadian Ski Museum

The ski museum has a small, specialised exhibit at 457A Sussex Drive near the market with a collection of equipment and memorabilia outlining the 5,000-year-old history of skiing. The museum is open from 11 am to 4

pm Tuesday to Saturday in summer, from noon throughout the winter. Entry fee is $1.

Canadian Centre for Caricature

At 136 St Patrick St by the corner of Sussex Drive at the edge of the market is this very unusual collection from the National Archives. It consists of 20,000 drawn cartoons and caricatures concerning Canadian history and people culled from periodicals from the past two centuries. The vast majority of the collection is from the past 30 years though. If you like political cartoons and social satire this is the place. It's free and open every day except Monday. As far as I know it's one of a kind.

Cathedral Basilica of Notre Dame

Built in 1839, this is one of the city's most impressive houses of worship. A pamphlet available at the door outlines the many features including carvings, windows, the organ and Gothic-style ceiling.

Central Experimental Farm

This farm on the corner of Queen Elizabeth Driveway and Carling Ave (☎ 995-5222) are about 500 hectares of flowers, trees, shrubs and gardens. The site is still used for research on all aspects of farming and horticulture. A big flower show is held here in November, and both Canadian and foreign species are shown. There are tours, or you can go on your own walking tour. You'll also see livestock and show-case herds of cattle, an observatory, and the arboretum which is good for walking through. The farm is linked to the rest of Ottawa's cycling routes. Admission is free.

Laurier House

This Victorian home at 335 Laurier Ave was built in 1878, and was the residence of two prime ministers – Laurier and the eccentric Mackenzie King. It's beautifully furnished throughout – don't miss the study on the top floor. Each of the two prime ministers is represented by mementos and various possessions. It's free and open daily but only during the afternoon on Sunday; it's closed on Monday.

An early morning visit is suggested, that is before the tour buses arrive, when you'll have the knowledgeable guides all to yourself.

Prime Minister's & Governor General's Houses

You can view the outside of the present prime minister's house at 24 Sussex Drive as well as Rideau Hall, the governor general's pad, around the corner up from the river. New, tighter security has meant the end of strolling around the grounds at the latter residence but 45-minute walking tours are still given with stories of some of the goings-on through the years.

The house was built in the early 1900s. At the main gate there's the Changing of the Guard ceremony which happens every hour on the hour from the end of June to the end of August. Both houses are north-east of the market area. Rideau Hall is off Princess Drive, the eastern extension of Sussex Drive.

Rockcliffe Village

East along Sussex Drive, this is one of the poshest, most prestigious areas in the country. Behind the mansion doors live some very prominent Canadian citizens and many foreign diplomats.

Prince of Wales Falls

Where the Rideau River meets the canal south of town (at the junction of Colonel By St and Hog's Back Rd) there are falls, walking and cycling paths and some historical plaques.

RCMP Stables & Practice Ground

Even the Mounties have to practice and the RCMP Stables & Practice Ground is where the musical ride pageant is perfected. The public is welcome to watch the practice sessions and the other equestrian displays held from time to time. Call ☎ 993-2723 for details. The grounds are out of the centre. If travelling by car, take Sussex Drive east to the Rockcliffe Parkway. At Birch St turn

right to the grounds. No admission fee is charged.

Log Farm

A re-creation of a 19th-century farm, complete with costumed workers, the site is 20 km west of Parliament Hill. Both here and at Jacques Cartier Park there are historical exhibits and activities, some of which you can participate in. The farm is open Sunday to Wednesday from the end of May to the beginning of September. Admission is charged.

Activities

In summer you can rent a boat for trips along the canal. Canoe and rowing boat rentals are at Dows Lake or at the marina on Hog's Back Rd (☎ 733-5065). The rates are hourly or weekly at the marina.

Surrounding the city on the east, south and west and connecting with the Ottawa River on each side is a broad strip of connected parkland known as the Greenbelt. Within this area of woodlands, marsh and fields are nature trails, bicycle paths, boardwalks and picnic areas. In the western Greenbelt, 20 minutes by vehicle from the downtown area off Richmond Rd, is the Stony Swamp Interpretation Centre with displays about the area, a staff naturalist and trails. It's open from Friday to Sunday. On the eastern side of the Greenbelt is another conservation area, Mer Bleue. The Greenbelt is not entirely a reserve: the airport lies within it, for example.

There are several outfits not far from Ottawa which run white-water rafting trips for one or two days. No experience is needed, and the locations are less than two hours from town. Two organisations to call, both situated in Foresters Falls, are Wilderness Tours (☎ 648-2241) in Quebec or toll free (☎ 800-267-9166),and OWL Rafting (☎ 800-267-8506). The Ottawa and the Magnetawan are two rivers that are used.

In winter there's skiing as close as 20 km from town in the Gatineau Hills. Two resorts with variously graded hills are Camp Fortune and Mont Cascades. Tow passes are more expensive on weekends. Gatineau Park has excellent cross-country ski trails with lodges along the way for warming up in. In warm weather, the park is good for walking and picnicking.

Again in winter, the Rideau Canal is famous for the skating along five km of maintained ice. Rest spots on the way serve great doughnuts to go with the hot chocolate. Ask at the tourist office about skate rentals.

The city has an excellent parks system with a lot of inner-city green space. There are many walking, jogging and cycling trails as well as picnic areas. You'll even find some fishing. The tourist office has a sheet, with map, of all the parks and a description of each. Bicycle paths wind all over town; get a map of them. For rentals see the Getting Around section.

Organised Tours The government offers several free tours. From 9 June to 31 August there are three downtown Ottawa walking tours lasting 1½ hours. They depart every 15 minutes from the visitor centre at 14 Metcalfe St.

Visibus is a system of green and blue buses which travel a circular route around and between Ottawa and Hull past 20 central attractions any one of which you may stop at. A day pass allowing any number of rides is $3 or $7 for a family. On board, guides offer some information. The buses run from 9 am to 6 pm daily from 15 June to the beginning of September. For more information call ☎ 239-5000. Passes can be bought on the bus or at the tourist office on Metcalfe St. The entire route takes 20 minutes and the buses are very frequent.

The tourist office in Hull offers two free walking tours in the central area, see under Hull for details.

Gray Coach Line (☎ 748-4426) offers a 50-km two-hour tour of the city. They operate daily from April to October. Tickets are available from the departure point on Wellington St near the Château Laurier on the north side of Confederation Square. They also do longer tours of the region.

A double-decker bus makes a similar, though shorter, trip. It operates only during summer and is run by Piccadilly Tours.

Paul's Boat Lines (☎ 235-8409) runs cruises on the Ottawa River and the Rideau Canal. Each takes about 1½ hours and costs $7, less for kids. There is a dock at the Rideau Canal across from the National Arts Centre for tickets and information. The Ottawa Riverboat Company (☎ 232-4888), at 173 Dalhousie St, does much the same thing. Some trips include dinner and/or dancing.

The National Museum of Science and Technology runs a two-hour trip by steam engine up the Gatineau River area to Wakefield periodically through the summer. The Gatineau is a major north-south tributary of the Ottawa River. The lunches in the Railway Station Restaurant in Wakefield are very good.

Voyageur bus lines (☎ 725-3045) runs several day trips to attractions in Eastern Ontario, for example the Thousand Islands, Upper Canada Village and Kingston. Phone or ask at the bus terminal for details.

Festivals

The big annual event is the Festival of Spring in May when the city is decorated with 200 types of tulips, mainly from Holland. Festivities include parades, regattas, car rallies, dances, concerts and fireworks.

In July and August the outdoor stage in Major's Hill Park, known as Astrolabe, is used for concerts, dance, mime and other performances. It's open nightly and is free.

The Central Canada Exhibition is an annual event held towards the end of August. There are 10 days of displays, a carnival and entertainment. The exhibition is held at Lansdowne Park.

The Canada Canoe Festival celebrates Native Canadians and the first pioneers, fur traders and voyageurs.

In late January and early February is the good and popular Winterlude, a week of festivities mainly on or around frozen Dows

Lake and the canal. The ice sculptures are really worth seeing.

Places to Stay

Camping There is an excellent camping site practically right in the centre of town for $6 a night, with a stay limited to five nights. You'll find room for 200 tents on the corner of Fleet and Booth Sts. The site is called *Camp Le Breton*, west along Wellington St past the government buildings. The camp, designed primarily for cyclists and hikers, has no electric or water hook ups, and is for tents only. It's open from mid-May to Labour Day, early in September. The city bus from the downtown area goes right to the campground which is near the Ottawa River. Close to the campground are some rapids in the river known as Chaudière Falls.

Camp Hither Hills is 10 km south of the city limits on Highway 31 and charges $10. There are places both east and west of town on Highway 17. You'll also find some in Gatineau Park.

The tourist office has lists of other places in the Ottawa area and there is camping in Gatineau Park across the river in Quebec province.

Hostels The *CHA Hostel* (☎ 235-2595), at 75 Nicholas St, is in the old Ottawa jail – see the gallows at the back. It has a very good, central location near the Parliament Buildings. Nicholas St is just east of the Rideau Canal off Rideau St. There are 160 beds in the restored building, some of them in old cells – wake up behind bars. Prices are $12 for members and $16 for nonmembers, but they have a sauna and cheap breakfasts are available. There are kitchen and laundry facilities and an information board as well. This is another busy hostel but fortunately it's quite large and is open all year.

The *YMCA* and *YWCA* (☎ 237-1320) are in the same building at 180 Argyle St, in the southern downtown area under the Queensway. They're on the corner of O'Connor St. Singles for either sex are $36 with a shared bathroom; better value doubles go for $45. More expensive rooms with

private bath are available. There's a cafeteria and a pool which guests can use.

The *University of Ottawa* (☎ 564-5400) downtown has some of the cheapest dormitory space in Canada. The dorms are open for visitors from May to August. The rates for students are singles/doubles $15/28 and for non-students singles/doubles $28/37. They have laundry facilities, a swimming pool, parking and a cafeteria with cheap meals. Reception is at 100 Hastey St. The university is an easy walk south-east of the Parliament Buildings. They also offer accommodation at Little White Fish Camp in Gracefield, Quebec, where there are extensive sports facilities.

Carleton University (☎ 788-5609), pretty central but south of the downtown core, has a residence offering summer rooms at 1233 Colonel By St. Singles/doubles go for $25/38, which used to include a breakfast but now apparently does not. Athletic facilities and full meal service are available. Check at the Tour & Conference Centre in the Commons Building at the university. Families are welcome.

Tourist Homes & B&Bs While not necessarily the cheapest form of accommodation in Ottawa (motels and some hotels are now about the same price) this category generally has the advantage of central location, a bit of personality and breakfast. There are quite a few places under this classification; the prices and facilities vary quite a bit. Some are simply an extra room in a resident's house, others are commercial enterprises in the small European hotel tradition. Many fall somewhere in between the two.

Ottawa B&B (☎ 563-0161) is an organisation listing, promoting and booking such places. There are city, suburban and country locations and prices begin at singles/doubles $35/45.

Another such service is Capital B&B Reservation Service (☎ 737-4129) again with a variety of places and locations and they can find places all year round. Prices vary, some locations offer perks such as fireplaces or swimming pools but nearly all have free parking at least.

The tourist office also should have some information about tourist homes.

Generally, whether independent or under an agency, the places closer to the centre of town are more expensive than ones further out. I've included mostly the central ones because of their added convenience to the city's sites and because they do not require a car for easy access. Many of them offer free parking, however. Almost all places include breakfast in the price but it may vary from continental to full.

In the downtown area, just east over the canal and south of Rideau St, is a small pocket where many of the central guesthouses are found. Convenient Daly St has some good places but they are not among the cheapest.

The old-country-style *Gasthaus Switzerland Inn* (☎ 237-0335) has one of the best locations in town at 89 Daly St two blocks south of Rideau St and the market. Go south along Cumberland St to Daly St and it's near the north-east corner. The No 4 bus runs along Rideau St from the downtown area. The guesthouse has been created out of a large, old stone house and now has 17 rooms with varying amenities. Cheapest are the rooms with shared bathroom which go for singles/doubles $38/50 with a breakfast of muesli, bread, cheese and coffee. Prices go down a few dollars through the winter. The managers, from Switzerland, speak an impressive array of languages including German and French. Another plus is the laundry.

At 201 Daly St is the heritage *Maison-McFarlane House* (☎ 236-0095) with singles/doubles at $45/55. There are only three rooms but they include amenities such as full bathroom, air-con and there is parking.

Also on Daly St, at No 185 is *McGee's Inn* (☎ 237-6089) with 14 rooms in a restored Victorian mansion. Prices have jumped here and now begin at singles/doubles $62/68 and increase with the number of facilities. Some rooms here have private bathrooms, which is

not the norm in tourist homes, and a full breakfast is included.

Guesthouses of varying size and price seem to constantly open and close along Stewart St, one block south of Daly St. A stroll along the street may also turn up someone who has just opened a few rooms for the summer. There are certainly some fine Edwardian-style houses in the neighbourhood. *Ottawa B&B* (☎ 233-4433) is at 264 Stewart St with singles/doubles at $40/50 including a full breakfast.

Another good street to check is Marlborough St, south-east of Daly and Stewart Sts, south from Laurier Ave, west of the Rideau River. It is still quite central but a bit of a walk to the downtown area – it takes around half an hour to the Parliament Buildings. Prices here are quite a bit lower.

Australis Guesthouse (☎ 235-8461) with three rooms is at 35 Marlborough St and quite good value. Singles/doubles cost $32/40 including breakfast and there are lower weekly rates. The *Appletreewick Guesthouse* (☎ 237-2753) is down the street at No 58 and has singles/doubles starting at $35/45.

Not far away at 329 Laurier Ave East is the *Laurier Guesthouse* (☎ 238-5525) with three rooms from as low as singles/doubles $25/35. There is also a more deluxe suite with a fireplace but in any case a breakfast is included.

There are a couple of places to check in the Bytown Market area north of Rideau St. The *Foisy House* (☎ 562-1287), at 188 St Andrew St with three rooms, charges $34 for a single but is especially good for doubles at $36. St Andrew St runs east-west through the market area a couple of blocks north of most of the action. Lastly, a very central place to try is in the Bytown Market area – *L'Auberge du Marché* (☎) at Guigues Ave. It's a recently renovated older house with three rooms costing singles/doubles $38/48 and there is parking.

Closer to the downtown area, but on the other side of the canal, *Beatrice Lyon* (☎ 236-3904) takes in guests all year long at her home at 479 Slater St. The three rooms are good, simple and some of the cheapest in town with singles/doubles at $30/35 including breakfast. Slater St runs east-west from Bank St and No 479 is about four blocks west of Bank St near the corner of Percy St. The owner will not only take in children but will even look after them.

There is also *Albert House* (☎ 236-4479), at 478 Albert St in this section of town but this is more a real inn with 17 rooms. It is considerably more expensive with rooms from $65 to $85, has a good location, and is a heritage home with all the comforts.

If Ottawa seems pretty booked up or you want to try staying across the river in Quebec there are some guesthouses listed under Hull.

Hotels – bottom end There are few older or budget hotels in Ottawa. Most moderate accommodation is in motels away from the town centre or in tourist homes.

One of the very few older no-star hotels left in town is the *Somerset House Hotel* (☎ 233-7762) at 352 Somerset St West, with 35 rooms starting at $34 a single with shared bath, $51 with private facilities. Doubles are $45 and $62. Somerset St runs perpendicular to Bank St about 10 blocks from the Parliament Buildings.

The next two choices cost much more but have little character. The *Townhouse Motor Hotel* (☎ 236-0151), at 319 Rideau St, charges singles/doubles $59/67. The *Parkway Motor Hotel* (☎ 232-3781), at 475 Rideau St, is also close to the downtown area. Singles/doubles are $55/62 and breakfast is included in the inexpensive coffee shop.

The *Butler Motor Hotel* (☎ 746-4641) is comparable but rooms are a little cheaper at singles/doubles $50/58. The 95 rooms are large and it's a five-minute drive downtown. The hotel is at 112 Montreal Rd.

Hotels – middle & top end The central *Doral Inn* (☎ 230-8055), at 486 Albert St, is good value with 35 rooms at $59 a single or double. There are also a few housekeeping units although there is a coffee shop as well. There's a swimming pool too. The renovated

Beacon Arms Hotel (☎ 235-1413) at 88 Albert St is much larger and has kitchen facilities, but prices reflect this at $75/85 for singles/doubles. Still, relative to the high-priced downtown hotels it's good value. Also in the middle-range but slightly cheaper is the *Journey's End Hotel* (☎ 563-7511) at 290 Rideau St.

The *Hotel Roxborough* (☎ 237-5171), 123 Metcalfe St, is one of the city's top hotels and is expensive, with rooms starting from just under $100 but they have some good weekend specials.

The classic *Château Laurier* is the one that looks like a castle at 1 Rideau St by the canal and is the city's best known hotel and a landmark in its own right. Rates are from $100 to $150.

During the summer when Parliament is in recess and business traffic is light, many of the good downtown hotels offer very good daily and weekend specials. For example, the *Aristocrat Hotel* (☎ 232-9471) at 131 Cooper St rents its rooms for $59 for up to four people. The old stately *Lord Elgin* (☎ 235-3333) at 100 Elgin St (with free parking) has summer prices starting at $60. Even the *Château Laurier* gets in on it and has a large indoor swimming pool to take advantage of.

Motels There are two main motel strips, one on each side of the downtown area. On the east side look along Montreal Rd, an extension of Rideau St, which leads east out of town. The motels are about six km from the downtown area.

The *Miss Ottawa* (☎ 745-1531), 2098 Montreal Rd, charges singles/doubles $45/52 and has a pool.

Le Normandie (☎ 824-1350), at 6825 Highway 17, charges singles/doubles $40/48. They too have a pool.

Closest to town the *Eastview* (☎ 746-8115), at 200 Montreal Rd, charges singles/doubles $40/45.

On the west side of town check along Carling Ave where there are numerous to choose from. These places are about 10 km from downtown. The *Stardust* (☎ 828-2748) at 2965 Carling Ave charges singles/doubles

$37/49 for its 25 rooms. The *Bayshore* (☎ 829-9411) at 2980 Carling Ave charges singles/doubles $48/59. There are others closer to the centre but they tend to be more costly.

Places to Eat

Hull has the very best restaurants but Ottawa has a pretty good range of places in the lower and mid-price brackets. I've grouped them by area.

Market We'll start with the market – it's central, just about everybody goes there, and there is a good selection of places to eat. During the warm months many of the eateries in the area have outdoor tables.

For breakfast try *Zak's Diner*, a '50s-style eatery at 16 Byward St which opens early and stays open late. It's usually busy and is cheap.

The *Café Bohemian*, at 89 Clarence St, is good for lunch or dinner. It's a busy European-style place with meals like quiche, fish and the latest trendy foods for $5 to $8. Sunday brunch is good value, with desserts and coffee. *Café au lait* is good here, especially the large size served in a bowl.

Across the street, *Bagel Bagel* has all sorts of bagel toppings and sandwiches as well as salads and other light meals and deli items. It's inexpensive, open daily and is also a good spot for breakfast.

The *William St Café*, at 47 William St, is pleasant with one side for eating, one for drinking. The place is good for snacks or a meal costing from $4 to $9. Try the carrot cake. There is another café, the *Heritage Café*, across the street in the market building itself.

La Crêpe de France, 76 Murray St, specialises in crêpes and has a patio bar and glassed-in terrace. Similar, but a bit less casual and a little more expensive, is the *Crêperie* on the corner of York and Byward Sts with salads and crêpes from $4.50 to $8.95.

The *Khyber Pass* is recommended for a slight splurge on its Afghani food – kebabs, pilau, rice and meat dishes that are less hot than Indian ones. Lunches are cheap; at dinner time prices double but portions are larger too. The ownership has recently changed here after quite a few years so we'll have to see if the same good standards continue.

For very inexpensive pasta dishes there is *Oregano's* on the corner of William and George Sts. There is a good-value all-you-can-eat lunch for $5.95 or for another dollar, an early-bird dinner (from 4.30 to 7 pm) of pasta, salad and soup. On Sunday the menu changes slightly and there is a brunch.

Le Jardin Grec Brochetterie, at 53 York St, is a place for a bit of a splurge for good Greek-style food, particularly kebabs, ranging in price from $9 to $20.

For another international choice, *Las Palmas* at 111 Parent Ave has been recommended for its Mexican food. The *fajitas* are especially not to be missed.

Also in the market building at the York St end look for the stand selling 'beavertails'. Hot, fresh flat doughnuts which first became popular when sold to skaters along the canal in winter. There is a food fair in the Rideau Centre.

Nearly all day and night the market is a very busy place. Very late at night, however, it does get a bit of an edge to it with some drug and prostitution traffic. Walking in the quieter areas alone in the wee hours should probably be avoided.

Downtown Along Bank St and its side streets are numerous restaurants.

At 202 Bank St, hidden in the back of a video arcade, is the *Silver Ball Café* for cheap vegetarian fare.

Further south at No 294 is the *Bank Café* in an old bank beautifully decorated in '30s style. There's also an outdoor section. Fixed-price dinners cost $17 and include a ticket to the movie at a theatre up the street. For lighter fare, the hamburgers sound good but aren't.

Suisha Gardens, on Slater St near the corner of Bank St, is a highly recommended Japanese place. The food is excellent though somewhat Westernised, the environment is authentic, and the service perfect. The best room is downstairs and to the left. It's very inexpensive at lunch; prices are higher after 6 pm.

There are several British-style pubs around; try the *Royal Oak* at 360 Bank St for British beer and food. They're friendly and you can play darts. The *Duke of Somerset* at 352 Somerset St West is similar.

Kamal, at 683 Bank St, has good Lebanese food from $3 to $9 and is licensed.

Flippers, upstairs on the corner of Bank St and 4th Ave, is a reliable fish restaurant with main courses (entrées) from $10 to $16.

Further south, the *Glebe Café* at 840 Bank St is good. They offer a few Middle Eastern dishes, some vegetarian food, and burgers. Prices are from $4 to $9. It's a casual place where there are newspapers to read, local information and an entertainment noticeboard.

At 895 Bank St *Mexicali Rosa's* is pleasantly decorated and has tasty moderately priced Mexican food. There are three other locations around town too.

All through the downtown area and around the market, look for and try one of the numerous chip wagons with names like *Chipsy Rose*. They're excellent for French fries and hamburgers.

Chinatown Ottawa also has a small Chinatown within walking distance west of the centre. It's based around the corner of Bronson St and Somerset St West. There are quite a few restaurants; for Cantonese food the *Yeng Shang*, right on the corner, is cheap and not bad.

Ben Ben's, at 699 Somerset St, has been recommended for Sichuan and Cantonese food as has the *Mekong* at 637 Somerset St for Vietnamese as well as Chinese.

There are also a few Chinese places on Rideau St.

For a splurge, *Chez Jean Pierre* at 210 Somerset St West is said to be good for French food.

If you're out this way why not go a little further to 200 Preston St which runs north-south, a few blocks west of Bronson St and try the *Paticceria-Gelateria Italiana* for a dessert and coffee.

Rideau St Across the canal from Wellington St, this area also has a number of eateries. The difficult to find *Sitar*, not far east from the canal at No 417A in the bottom of a high-rise building, is not cheap but the food is good. Prices range from $22 to $34 for two.

Nate's, at No 316, is somewhat of a local institution. This Jewish delicatessen is known far and wide for its low prices on good food. The very popular breakfast special is the cheapest in the country – $1.75 for the works. Ask for the Rideau Rye, good bread for toast. The service is incredibly fast. They also serve things like blintzes and creamcheese bagels. It's open and busy on Sunday.

Elgin St A stroll along Elgin St always turns up a couple of places to eat; it's popular for night spots too. The *Ritz*, at 274 Elgin St, is very good for Italian food, in fact, there's usually a line of people waiting to get in. Prices range from $5 to $12. *Charlie's Party Palace*, at 252 Elgin St with the neon sign jutting out over the sidewalk, is a locally famous place which has been around forever. It serves the usual low-cost Canadian standards well and quickly and is another place that's good for breakfast.

Entertainment
Check Friday's *Ottawa Citizen* for complete club and entertainment listings. *Barrymores* on Bank St has live rock and blues and is a busy spot. The *New Live Penguin Café*, at 292 Elgin St, brings in a very good assortment of jazz, blues and folk acts. There is a cover charge which varies.

Patty's Place is a cosy Irish pub with music from Thursday to Saturday and an outdoor patio in summer. It's on the corner of Bank and Euclid Sts.

Yuk Yuk's in the Beacon Arms Hotel, at 88 Albert St, has live stand-up comedy from Thursday to Saturday – admission is not cheap, however.

The *National Arts Centre*, known as the NAC, has theatres for drama and opera and is home to the symphony orchestra. It also presents a range of concerts and films. It's on the banks of the canal in Confederation Square.

The *Hotel Lafayette* in Bytown Market on York St is good for its cheap draught beer day or night. It's your basic dive, but its character and characters attract a wide cross-section of people.

For jazz, *Friends & Company*, at 221 Rideau St, has a live band on Saturday afternoons and Tuesday nights. There's folk music upstairs at night. For details of more local entertainment, see the Hull section.

Cinema There are several repertory theatres around Ottawa, showing two films a night. The *Mayfair* (☎ 234-3403), at 1074 Bank St, charges $7 for nonmembers but there are less expensive matinees. The *Bytown Cinema* (☎ 230-3456), at 325 Rideau St between King Edward and Nelson Sts, is about the same price. Another place is the *Phoenix* (☎ 232-0456) which is at 413 Bank St.

The Phoenix has a deal with the Bank Café down the street at No 294: a three-course dinner and a movie for $17. *Cinémètheque Canada*, the Canadian Film Institute, also presents non-commercial films on a regular basis.

For what's happening in the National Arts Centre, check the box office or newspaper.

Getting There & Away

Air The airport is 20 minutes south of the city and is surprisingly small. The main airlines serving the city are Canadian Airlines (☎ 237-1380) and Air Canada (☎ 237-5000). Canadian Airlines destinations (and fares) include Toronto ($185), Halifax ($290), Winnipeg ($420). Excursion fares (return) are much cheaper. Air Canada fares, promotional sales aside, are much the same.

Bus The bus station is at 265 Catherine St near Bank St, about a dozen blocks south of the downtown area. The main bus line is Voyageur Colonial (☎ 238-5900). One-way fares include to Toronto $43, Kingston $21, Montreal $21.50 and Sudbury $54. Students can get a third off the price for a book of tickets, ask about it. Return tickets on a seven-day excursion, to Montreal for example, are considerably cheaper.

There are about 10 buses daily to Montreal and Toronto, some are express. There are frequent departures for Kingston, Belleville, Sudbury and other towns.

Train The railway station (☎ 238-8289) has been moved from town to a big, new centre a long way south-east of the downtown area. It's at 200 Tremblay Rd near the junction of Alta Vista Rd and Highway 417 just east of the Rideau Canal.

There are three trains a day to Toronto, six to Montreal.

One-way fares include to Toronto $57, Kingston $24, and Montreal $26. For trips west, say to Sudbury, there is no longer a direct line. Connections must be made in Toronto so it's now a long trip.

Car & Motorbike Tilden (☎ 232-3536) is at 199 Slater St and also at the airport. Their rate is $50 per day with 200 free km, and 11 cents per km after that or, not bad value at $200 a week with 1400 free km.

Budget and Hertz also have outlets which aren't as central as the Tilden office.

Ride Sharing Allo Stop, a popular service in Montreal, Quebec City and Toronto which gets drivers together with passengers may now have an office in Ottawa. They do run to Ottawa; consider asking in one of their offices elsewhere.

Hitching Hitching is easy between Montreal and Ottawa, but is convoluted if you're heading for Toronto. Going to Montreal take the eastbound Montreal-Ogilvy bus on Rideau St which leads to Highway 17 East where you can begin. For Toronto take Highway 31 south to Highway 401 near the town of Morrisburg. The busy Highway 401 (probably the most travelled route in

Canada) connects Toronto with Montreal and hitching is fairly common along the way.

For a more rural trip take Highway 7 to Tweed and Highway 37 to Belleville, then Highway 401 from there.

Getting Around
To/From the Airport The cheapest way to get to the airport is by city bus. Take bus No 5 on Elgin St going south (away from the river) to Billings Bridge and then transfer to the No 83 to the airport.

There is also an airport bus leaving every half hour on the half hour from in front of the Château Laurier hotel from 6.30 am to midnight. It costs $7 and takes about 25 minutes. The bus is not as frequent on weekends so ask about scheduling.

Bus Both Ottawa and Hull operate bus systems. A transfer apparently is no longer good from one system to the other but ask about it anyway. Things may have changed again. The city bus system here is very volatile and there are frequent changes. The fares are run on a two-tier system. During peak hours, until 8.30 am and from 3 to 5.30 pm Monday to Friday a ticket is $1.90. Any other time the fare drops to 95 cents.

For Ottawa information phone ☎ 741-4390 – they're very helpful. All Ottawa buses quit by 1.30 am, most earlier. Drop in at the office of OC Transport which runs the city buses and get a Tourpass good for unlimited use for one day but beginning after 9.30 am. The office is central at 294 Albert St. You can take the following buses from downtown to:

Bus station – No 4 south on Bank St or, more frequently, either the No 1 or No 7 stop within a block of the terminal
Railway station – Transitway No 95 east on Slater St
Museum of Nature – No 5 or 6 on Elgin St
Aeronautical Museum – Transitway Nos 95 or 99 to Saint Laurent Boulevard and transfer to No 198 to the museum
Hull – No 41 west on Wellington St

Car & Motorbike Visitors to the city can park free at many locations: get the details at any tourist information office.

Bicycle Ottawa is the best city in Canada for cyclists. There is an extensive system of paths in and around town and through the parks. Get a bicycle route map from a tourist office.

For rentals try Cycle Tour Rent-A-Bike (☎ 233-0268) at the Château Laurier. They're open every day from May to September and rent three, five and 10-speed bikes. ID is required. They run tours, with discounts for hostel members, and have a repair shop as well.

HULL
Across the river in Quebec, Hull is as much the other half of Ottawa as it is a separate city (that's why it's included in the Ontario chapter of this book). It warrants a visit for more than the new Canadian Museum of Civilisation. Hull now has its share of government offices and workers cross the river in both directions each day, but the Hull side remains home to most of the area's French population. On the street you'll feel the difference. The architecture is different (at least the older stuff), you'll find the top restaurants here and livelier later nightlife.

Promenade du Portage, easily found from either Pont du Portage or Alexandra Bridge, is the main downtown street. Between the two bridges are numerous and varied eating spots, bars and discos, Place Aubry (a square), as well as a few places where people have to work.

The City Hall known as Maison du Citoyen is an attention-getting, dominating modern building with the 20-metre-high glass tower in the centre of town at 25 Rue Laurier. It also contains an art gallery and a medititation centre and the tourist office is here. A free two-hour walking tour of Hull begins at the tourist office at 10 am during July and August, from Monday to Friday and takes in much of the history and green areas of central Hull.

In July Hull hosts both a jazz festival and a folklore festival. In August there is a five-

342 Ontario – Ottawa

day bicycle event with races, competitions and more.

Hull is also the main city of the region of Quebec known as Outaouais which is pronounced basically as though you were saying Ottawa with a French accent. The Quebec government has a booklet outlining the attractions and activities, mostly of the outdoor variety, of the region. Within a few hours drive there are some huge parks and reserves.

Canadian Museum of Civilisation

This museum is now in the large, modern complex with the copper domes at 100 Rue Laurier, Hull, on the river bank opposite the Parliament Buildings. The museum is principally concerned with the history of

Canadians. The permanent upper-level History Hall presents displays and realistic re-creations tracing the story of the European founding, voyages of the country's explorers, settlement and historical developments through to the 1880s. The Basque ship section, complete with the sound of creaking wood in the living quarters, brings to life the voyages undertaken to reach the New World. Also particularly good are the Acadian farm model and the replica of the early Quebec town square.

The main level consists of three halls containing temporary exhibits on varying aspects of human history, culture and art.

The Native Indian & Inuit Art Gallery usually, but not always, offers various shows by Native Canadian artists – painting, dance, crafts and more. Don't miss the chance to see the art of British Columbian Indians, especially that of the Haida, if there is any on current display.

You'll need roughly three hours for a reasonably thorough look at the above two levels: they're not laid out especially well and you'll need some time to get oriented.

The Grand Hall of the lower level with its simulated forest and seashore offers explanations of the huge totems and other coastal Native Indian structures.

In the entertaining and educational Children's Museum section, exhibits permit hands-on interaction.

Cineplus is a film theatre for IMAX and OMNIMAX, realistic large-format presentations. The always changing shows are extremely popular with waits of two to three shows not uncommon, so arrive early for a ticket.

There is a good cafeteria offering, among other things, sandwiches and a salad bar or economical full meals all served within view of the river and Parliament Hill.

There is also a bookstore and gift shop which are worth a look.

From April to September the museum is open every day, for the rest of the year it is closed on Monday. On Thursday it stays open until 8 pm, otherwise it closes at 6 pm during the summer and an hour earlier during the rest of the year. Admission is $4.50, less for seniors and kids. A cineplus ticket is $6.50 and the combination $10. Again, it's less for kids and seniors. Parking can be found under the museum.

Places to Stay

If you want to stay on this side of the river there are a number of accommodation choices.

The *Couette & Croissant* (☎ 771-2200), at 330 Champlain St, a short drive north-east is a B&B in central Hull. Although a bit of a walk from Promenade du Portage, it's quite close to the Canadian Museum of Civilisation.

There are others as well as a B&B agency, called *Les Châtelaines* (☎ 561-7575), which is based in Hull. Prices tend to be a bit lower than the Ottawa average. The tourist office also has information on B&Bs in the surrounding area with places around Gatineau Park and Aylmer, Quebec, just up the Ottawa River. Prices are about the same as in Ottawa or a few dollars less.

Motels can be found along Boulevard Taché which runs beside the river to the west of downtown Hull after coming across the bridge from Ottawa.

There are also some large, typical business oriented hotels in the central area.

Places to Eat

For a bite, head for *Café Le Coquetier* at 147 Promenade du Portage, an unpretentious, casual bistro with very good yet cheap food. *Le Bistro*, on Rue Aubry just off Promenade du Portage, is a bar/café serving light lunches for no more than $6 or $7, usually less. There's an outdoor patio in summer. A similar place is found at 44 Rue Laval.

The central *Brasserie Le Vieux Hull*, at 50 Rue Victoria on Place du Portage, is a very inexpensive tavern for a beer or two or a cheap meal.

Rue Papineau and Rue Montcalm have several restaurants including some of the expensive French ones for which the city has a reputation.

Entertainment

Boulevard Saint Joseph has several popular, up-market discos. Also a bit out of the centre but with live music in a large, friendly, typically Québecois brasserie is *Les Raftsmen* at 60 Rue Saint Raymond which runs east of Boulevard Saint Joseph. They also have a menu of standard beer-hall fare at very good prices which is served until 9 pm.

After 1 am, when the Ontario bars close, the partygoers head across the river from Ottawa to Hull where things are open until 3 am and later. Promenade du Portage in the middle of the downtown area: has numerous nightspots, some with live music, some dressy, some quiet and dark – there's a good range. *Chez Henri* on Promenade du Portage is an up-market disco. *Le Bistro* attracts a more casual and younger crowd for loud dance music. It's on Rue Aubry at the top of the hill on the brick pedestrian mall off the Promenade. There are plenty of other places in the area. Local jazz groups play at the *Saint Jacques*, Rue Saint Jacques, every Friday and Saturday night in Hull.

Getting There & Away

From downtown Ottawa bus No 41 goes from Rideau St or Wellington St to Promenade du Portage. Within Hull, the No 19 connects with the other line and covers the area up and around Boulevard Saint Joseph.

A bicycle route over the Alexandra Bridge from Ottawa connects with a trail system which goes around much of the Hull centre and to Ruisseau de la Brasserie (Brewery Creek) a park area east of downtown Hull.

AROUND OTTAWA-HULL – GATINEAU PARK

Gatineau Park is a deservedly popular 36,000-hectare area of woods and lakes in the Gatineau Hills of Quebec lying across the river from Ottawa, north-west of downtown Hull.

It's only a 20-minute drive from the Parliament Buildings in Ottawa. On weekends some roads may be closed to cars.

There is plenty of wildlife in the park, including about 100 species of birds. Around the park are 150 km of hiking trails. Lac Meech, **Lac Phillipe** and **Lac Lapêche** have beaches for swimming and so are most popular. Many of the camping facilities are around Lac Phillipe. You can fish in the lakes and streams. The hiking trails are good for cross-country skiing in winter. **Pink Lake** is recommended for swimming, on one side are some cliffs from which you can jump or dive in. They're a short walk through the woods from the parking lot. The lake is best during the week when there are fewer people around. There is a nude beach at Lac Meech but don't say I told you.

Also in the park is Kingsmere, the summer estate of William Lyon Mackenzie King, prime minister in the 1920s, late 1930s and early 1940s. Here he indulged his hobby of collecting ruins, both genuine and fake. In 1941, King had bits of London's House of Commons brought over after the German blitz. His home, **Moorside**, is now a museum. An astute politician, King was much interested in the occult and apparently talked to both his dog and his deceased mother. There's a tea room at Moorside.

Festivals
Fall Rhapsody Occuring in September or October, the event celebrates the brief but colourful season when the leaves change colour: a time when the maples and birches of the Gatineau Hills are having their last fling before winter. An arts festival is part of the affair, as are hot-air ballooning and various concerts and competitions. Events are held in the park with a few around town as well. During Fall Rhapsody, there are cheap buses from Ottawa-Hull.

Eastern Ontario

West from Ottawa there are two main routes through Ontario. The northern one goes towards Pembroke, then either north or south past Algonquin Park on to North Bay and Sudbury. This is the route the Trans Canada Highway follows so it is the quickest way to western Canada.

The southern route goes to the more populated southern region of Ontario, the St Lawrence River, the Great Lakes and Toronto.

EGANVILLE
North-west of Ottawa, this small town is worth a stop for the nearby **Bonnechere Caves**, eight km south-east. The caves and passages were the bottom of a tropical sea about 500 million years ago and contain fossils of animals from long before the dinosaur age. You'll see some stalactites. Tours are offered through the summer months.

MERRICKVILLE
South-west of Ottawa, Merrickville is a small, pleasant historic town dating from the 1790s situated along the Rideau River/Canal route from Ottawa to Kingston. There are a couple of B&Bs in town and some places to eat and a bakery along St Lawrence St. A couple of craft and antique shops can also be found in the central area.

Historic sites include the **locks** dating from 1830 and the **blockhouse** with walls a metre thick built by the British in 1832 to protect the canal in case of attack. The blockhouse is now a small museum.

SMITH FALLS
Smith Falls is midway along the Rideau Canal system. It's a small centre for recreational boats using the system. Unfortunately, there are no commercial ventures here or anywhere else for trips along the canal.

Smith Falls has become known as much for its Hershey Chocolate Factory as for its history or canal location. A tour of the plant of this US chocolate company based in Hershey, Pennsylvania, is possible and recommended. Find out all about how chocolate bars are created and then start eating. It's open from Monday to Friday only and is on Hershey Drive off Highway 43 East – just follow your nose.

CORNWALL

Cornwall is the first city of any size in Ontario along the St Lawrence Valley and has the Seaway International Bridge to the USA.

The Pitt St Mall in the centre of town is a pedestrian-only two-block section of stores and gardens.

There are a couple of **museums** in town and the **Energy Information Centre** which has displays on the big, important hydroelectric facility here. It's open daily in July and August and on weekdays only in June. Tours of the power facilities at the dam are available.

Just out of town on the Native Indian reserve on Cornwall Island at the college there is a **log cabin museum** focused on the Cree, Iroquois and Ojibwa Indians. It's not open on weekends. The big Native Indian powwow held at the reserve in July or August is worth catching as it's one of the biggest in the province. Traditional crafts and souvenirs can be purchased.

Cornwall is another busy port of entry for US visitors with the bridge over to Massena, New York.

Despite this corner of Ontario's having Scottish and Loyalist ancestry, there is a good-sized French population in Cornwall.

In **Maxville** to the north, the Scottish Highland Games are held at the beginning of August and commemorate the region's Scottish heritage. **St Raphael** has some interesting church ruins dating from 1815.

West of Cornwall the **Long Sault Parkway** connects a series of parks and beaches along the river.

MORRISBURG & UPPER CANADA VILLAGE

This small town lies west of Cornwall on the St Lawrence River and despite its small size is known far and wide for its good historic site – Upper Canada Village, a detailed historic site fashioned to re-create a country town a century ago. About 40 buildings and costumed workers bring that past period to life. There's a blacksmith's shop, inn and sawmill and the setting is a nice one on the river.

You'll need at least several hours to fully explore the site, which is open from 15 May to 15 October. Admission is $5.50, less for kids. Nearby **Crysler Battlefield Park** is a memorial to those who died fighting the Americans in 1812.

Highway 2 along the river is slower to travel on but provides a more scenic trip than Highway 401. It's used by cyclists including long-distance riders between Montreal and Toronto. There are numerous provincial parks along the way, especially east of town along the Long Sault Parkway. Going west there is a seaway-viewing platform at **Iroquois** and a good campground for cyclists.

BROCKVILLE

A small community along the river, Brockville is a particularly attractive town, with its many old stone buildings and the classic-looking main street. The courthouse and jail in the centre of town date from 1842. During the summer many of the finest buildings are lit up giving the town more of the slight resort flavour it already has as a casual river port by the Thousand Islands.

The historic museum in **Beecher House** provides a look at the area's history.

For the Thousand Island Parkway area west of Brockville see the Around Kingston section at the end of the following Kingston description.

KINGSTON

Kingston, with a population of 60,000, is a handsome town that retains much of its past through preservation of many historic buildings and defence structures. Built strategically where Lake Ontario flows into the St Lawrence River, it is a convenient stopping-off point almost exactly halfway between Montreal and Toronto.

Once a fur-trading depot, Kingston later became the principal British military post west of Quebec and was the national capital for a while. The many 19th-century buildings of local grey limestone and streets of

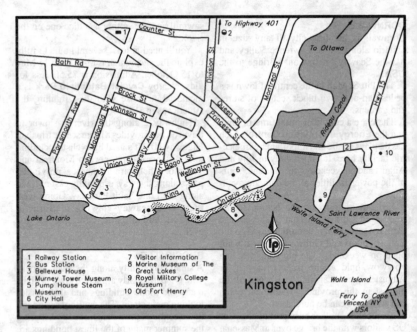

1 Railway Station
2 Bus Station
3 Bellevue House
4 Murney Tower Museum
5 Pump House Steam
  Museum
6 City Hall
7 Visitor Information
8 Marine Museum of The
  Great Lakes
9 Royal Military College
  Museum
10 Old Fort Henry

Kingston

Victorian brick houses give the downtown area a certain distinctive charm. The attractive waterfront is pleasant too.

There is a major university here, Queen's, and the city is also known across the country for its several prisons.

On Tuesday, Thursday and Saturday, a small open-air market takes place right downtown behind City Hall on King St. It's not difficult to spend an interesting and enjoyable day or three in and around town.

Orientation

The town lies a few km south of Highway 401. Princess St, the main street, runs right down to the St Lawrence River which has many fine old buildings along it: some limestone, others red brick. The whole city is low-rise, few buildings are higher than two or three storeys and there aren't many modern ones either.

At the bottom of Princess St, Ontario St runs along the harbour by the start of the

Rideau Canal to Ottawa. This is the old, much-restored area with a tourist office, old military battery and Martello tower. There are views across the mouth of the canal to the military college. The market is on the corner of Brock St and King St East.

King St leads out along the lake's shore towards the university. Here you'll see many fine 19th-century houses and parkland. The impressive limestone County Courthouse is near the campus facing a small park. Further out is Lake Ontario Park, with camping and a small beach.

Information

The main downtown tourist office is the Kingston Tourist & Visitors' Bureau (☎ 548-4415) at 209 Ontario St in Confederation Park, across from City Hall.

Away from the city core, the Old Fort Henry Information Centre (☎ 542-7388) is at the fort, at the junction of highways 2 and 15. It's open only from May to September.

Old Fort Henry

The restored British fortification dating from 1832 dominates the town from its hilltop perch and is the city's prime attraction. It's a bit of a disappointment though, as there is more space inside than anything else. But the beautiful structure is brought to life by colourfully uniformed guards trained in military drills, artillery exercises, and fife and drum music of the 1860s. Entrance is $5, less for children, and includes a 20-minute film and guided tour. If you just want to walk around on your own, it's free. The soldiers put on their displays periodically throughout the day. They're best at 7.30 pm on Monday, Wednesday and Saturday when there is a rifle-firing, cannon-blasting ceremonial military retreat. Note this is held mid-season only. Inside the fort's rooms are artefacts, uniforms, weapons and more. The location provides good views. The fort is open daily through its season but is closed from 15 October to 15 May.

Without a car, the fort is a little difficult to reach as there is no city bus. You can walk, it's not that far, over the causeway from town but the last half km or so is all uphill. Other than hoofing it try to share a cab and maybe talk yourself a ride back with a fellow visitor. Or if you have a few things to do around town consider renting a bike for the day.

City Hall

The grand City Hall which can't be missed in the downtown area, is one of the country's finest classical buildings. Built of limestone, it dates from 1843 when Kingston was capital of the then United Provinces of Canada. Free tours are given daily in summer.

Waterfront

Kingston was once a waterfront defence town; evidence of this is found in Confederation Park, which runs from City Hall down to the river where yachts tie up. Shoal Tower is here.

Marine Museum of the Great Lakes

Further east is the Marine Museum at 55 Ontario St. Kingston was long a centre for shipbuilding, and the museum is on the site of the shipyard. In 1678 the first vessel built on the Great Lakes was constructed here. Amongst its list of credits are ships which were built during the War of 1812. The museum details these and other aspects of the Great Lakes' history. The 3,000-tonne ice-breaker *Alexander Henry* can be boarded. In fact, you can sleep on board – it's operated as a B&B and is inexpensive too (see the Places to Stay section later for more information). Admission to the museum costs $3 and there is a family rate.

Macdonald Park

On the corner of Barrie St and King St East is Macdonald Park, right along the river. Just offshore, in 1812, the British ship *Royal George* battled with the USA's USS *Oneida*. At the western end of the park is the **Murney Martello tower**, dating from 1846. This round defence structure was part of the early riverside fortifications and is now a museum housing local military and historical tidbits. There's a small admission fee. The museum's open daily from the end of May to the beginning of September. There are walking and bicycle paths along here and further west by the water's edge.

On the corner of King St East and West St is a big city park with a statue of Sir John Alexander Macdonald.

Bellevue House

This national historic site (☎ 542-3858) is an immaculately maintained Tuscan-style mansion, which apparently means a very odd-shaped, balconied, brightly painted architect's field day. It works, though, and in the garden setting this is an impressive and interesting house. It was once the home of Canada's first prime minister, Sir John A Macdonald. The mansion at 35 Centre St houses many good antiques. It's open daily all year from 9 am to 5 pm and admission is free.

Brock St

Brock St was the middle of town in the

1800s, and many of the original shops still stand along it. It's worth a walk around. Take a look in Cooke's Fine Foods at 61 Brock St. It's a gourmet shop with old wooden counters and a century-old pressed-tin ceiling. There are great smells and a curious assortment of goods and shoppers, including local professors drinking the fresh coffee at the back of the store.

Pump House Steam Museum

Here we have a one-of-a-kind, completely restored, steam-run pump station. First used in 1849, it now contains several engines and some scale models, all run on steam. The address is 23 Ontario St. It's open from the start of May to Labour Day but is closed on Monday.

Also here train buffs will want to see the 20 model trains from around the world displayed in a special exhibit room.

Fort Frederick Museum

In the Fort Frederick Martello tower on the grounds of the college is the Royal Military College Museum. This is the largest of the city's towers and has a collection on the history of the century-old military college. You have to wonder how or why, but also here lies the small arms collection of General Porfirio Diaz, the President of Mexico from 1886 to 1912. The college's history is also outlined. The museum is just east of town, off Highway 2 and is open daily in summer.

Hockey Hall of Fame & Museum

On the corner of Alfred and York Sts, this collection honours the history and stars of Canada's most loved sport. The displays include lots of photos and mementos and some equipment. The museum is open from mid-June to mid-September daily and for the rest of the year on weekend afternoons only. There's a small admission fee.

Kingston Archaeological Centre

If you've been out along Highway 401 you probably noticed the sedimentary rock outcrops, one of the few bits of interest along that highway's entire length from Montreal to Toronto. The Kingston Archaeological Centre, at 370 King St West in the Tett Centre, has displays on the 8,000-year-old human history of the area dug from the surrounding landscape and found along the shoreline. It's open weekdays only and there is no charge to have a look around at the artefacts, photographs, etc.

Kingston Mills Blockhouse

Away from the centre, up Kingston Mills Rd just north of Highway 401, is a restored blockhouse dating from 1839. The purpose of the lock station and what it was like to run it are part of the explanatory exhibits. The blockhouse is open daily through the summer and is free.

Antique Doll & Toy Museum

In a turn-of-the-century mansion, Polliwog Castle, the museum has a collection of toys and other children's mementos. This museum is also north of the city, above Highway 401 but on Division St. It's open daily in July and August and on weekends in May and September. Admission is charged.

Other Museums

There are several more specialised museums in or near Kingston (see the around Kingston section), including one on county schools, one at the military base detailing the history of military communications and electronics and others on such things as geology and mineralology and art. Ask for details about all these small museums at the tourist office.

Wolfe Island

It is possible to have a free mini-cruise by taking the car ferry from Kingston to Wolfe Island. The 20-minute trip affords views of the city, the fort and a few of the Thousand Islands. Wolfe Island, the largest in the chain, lies halfway to the USA and is basically flat farmland, although many of its inhabitants now work in town.

There is not a lot to see on the island, but there is the *General Wolfe Hotel*, a short walk from the dock, with its three busy and highly regarded dining rooms. Prices are moderate to slightly expensive. There are also some moderately priced cabins on the island and a campground. On the Kingston side, the ferry terminal is at the intersection of Ontario and Barrack Sts. The ferry runs continuously about every hour from very early to very late each day taking about 50 vehicles at a time.

From Wolfe Island another ferry links Cape Vincent, New York, but on this segment a toll is charged, at least if you have a car.

Activities

The Kingston Boardsailing Academy, a windsurfing school, with rentals, has an office in Macdonald Park, at the foot of Emily St.

For local swimming head to Macdonald Park on King St west of Princess St.

Organised Tours

The tourist office has a pamphlet which outlines a detailed self-guided walking tour, or you can rent a cassette which leads you through the historic section of town.

A train on wheels departs from the tourist office area for a tour of the central Kingston area regularly on summer days.

St Lawrence Cruise Lines, 253 Ontario St, runs cruise ships out of Kingston to Quebec City, to the Saguenay River for whale-watching and other trips up the Ottawa River to Ottawa aboard either the MV *Canadian Empress* or the replica steamship the *Colonial Explorer*. Trips last from two to five days and include all meals, entertainment and activities.

There are also several more local boat tours out of Kingston going around the Thousand Islands; see the Around Kingston section for details of these.

Places to Stay

Camping There are quite a few places to camp in the area. *Hi-Lo Hickory* on Wolfe Island is reached by ferry from Kingston. There's a beach. A bridge on the other side connects the island with New York state. The campground is east of the Kingston ferry about 12 km.

In town, only four km from the centre, there is camping at *Lake Ontario Park* (☎ 542-6574) which is operated by the city's Parks Department. It's west out along King St and there is a beach too. A city bus runs from downtown right to the campground from Monday to Saturday until 7.30 pm and on Fridays until 10.30 pm. The park almost always will be able to fit in another tenter.

KOA (Kampgrounds of America, seen all over North America) has a branch 1.6 km north of Highway 401 off Highway 38. These places can be very plastic, having as little to do with camping as possible. They're also expensive, but big and generally pretty busy. They cater mainly for trailers but there are some tent sites here too.

Hostels The *International Youth Hostel* (☎ 546-7203), at 320 William St, is within easy walking distance of most places and has 23 beds. Rates are members\nonmembers $10\14. Continental breakfasts are available. The hostel is open from early May to early September only. During the rest of the year there is a home hostels programme; phone for details or ask at the tourist office.

Rooms are available in residences at *Queen's University* (☎ 547-2775) from mid-May to mid-August. Rooms cost $30, and $18 for students. Meals are available. The campus is on the corner of University and Union Sts.

Waldron Tower (☎ 544-6100) is a residential complex of the Kingston General Hospital. It's great if you can get in, but it's usually full so call ahead. The rate is $24 a day with a good weekly rate. There are only single rooms. They have a cafeteria, kitchens, all manner of facilities and a view over the river to boot. The tower is on 17 King St West near Macdonald Park.

The *YM-YWCA* (☎ 546-2647) is at 100 Wright Crescent. It has beds for women only. There are kitchen facilities and a pool.

The *Salvation Army* (☎ 548-4411) here is for men who are broke or close to it.

B&Bs Mrs Ruth MacLachlan (☎ 542-0214) runs a B&B agency in Kingston, at 10 Westview Rd. There are about 25 participating homes in and around town. Tell her where you want to be and what your interests are, and you'll be matched up suitably. Rates are from singles/doubles $37/48 with full breakfast included; and from $10 to $15 extra for children. Cheaper rates are available for extended stays.

A unique B&B is on a moored, retired 64-metre icebreaker, the *Alexander Henry* (☎ 542-2261), which is part of the downtown Marine Museum of the Great Lakes. Beds are in the former crew's quarters and a continental breakfast is served from the galley. It hasn't been gentrified at all – it's plain, simple and functional. Rooms are pretty much like those on a working ship. This partially explains the good prices which begin at $32 for a double and go up to $52 if you want the captain's cabin. Rooms are available only in the summer and you can wander all over the ship.

O'Brien House (☎ 542-8660), at 39 Glenaire Mews up near the railway station, north-west of the downtown area, is a little less costly than the city norm. It's a B&B where the owner seems to particularly like overseas visitors. Singles/doubles cost $35/45 including a full breakfast and coffee or tea at any time. There are reduced rates for children too.

Hotels Kingston doesn't have a lot of hotels, most accommodation is in motels and now more and more in B&Bs. A couple of the older, central hotels have been overhauled and make pleasant, if a bit pricey, central places to stay.

Among the old cheapies only the *Plaza Hotel*, 46 Montreal St on the corner of Queen St remains. It's basically for the downstairs bar but it's not badly kept – not a family place but cheap at singles/doubles $26/32, with own bathroom.

There's another new place, the *Donald Gordon Centre* (☎ 545-2221) at 421 Union St very near Queen's University. Rooms go for singles/doubles $35/40 and are quiet and

air-conditioned. Breakfast is available too. I'm not sure what it's like but it sounds worth calling.

Moving up and offering more services are the *Princess* (☎ 542-7395) and the *Shamrock* (☎ 546-2266), at Nos 720 and 671 Princess St respectively. They charge singles/doubles $50/58; it's less after September.

The *Queen's Inn* (☎ 546-0429), dating from 1839, was completely renovated in 1987 and now offers modern facilities in 17 rooms in an old central setting. It's one of the oldest continually running hotels in the country. Rooms vary from $55 to $95 in high season, from April to November, and are from $40 to $75 for the rest of the year.

The *Prince George Hotel* (☎ 549-5440) dates from 1809 and is now restored with national heritage recognition. It has comfortable rooms, with balconies overlooking the lake, at splurge prices ranging from $75 to $130.

Motels There are plenty of these. In town at 1454 Princess St is *Journey's End* (☎ 549-5550), a two-storey place. Rooms are a couple of dollars cheaper upstairs and range between $50 and $55 for singles or doubles.

A little cheaper is the *Hilltop* (☎ 542-3846), at 2287 Princess St, with singles/doubles $37/43. There are many other motels on Princess St and some along Highway 2 on each side of town.

Places to Eat
Kingston has pretty good eating, especially considering its relatively small size.

The *Sunflower Restaurant*, serving good vegetarian food, is a bright spot with sturdy wooden tables and batiks on the walls. Meals cost from not much over $5 and there are lots of desserts and snacks. It's at 20 Montreal St and is open until 9 pm daily except Sunday.

The *Delightfully Different Café*, at 118 Sydenham St, is an unlikely looking place which turns out excellent fresh sandwiches, salads, bagels, etc for lunch and muffins and the like for breakfast. It's only open from 7 am to 4 pm Monday to Friday but is worth getting to for a light meal and is very inexpensive. It's between Brock and Johnson Sts.

At 34 Clarence St, the *Kingston Brewing Co*, is a pub which brews its own ales and lagers and has a good selection of non-house brands as well. There is also a good selection of inexpensive tavern-style things to munch on and, interestingly, a daily curry.

Cultures, at 335 King St, is recommended for its sandwiches and excellent yoghurt smoothies. Try the chicken salad item – it's a meal.

Kresge's Store, at the back of 124 Princess St, has probably the cheapest food counter in town. You can get a meal for under $4.

E P Murphey & Sons & Daughters at 70 Brock St has been around for ages and, though the restaurant upstairs is closed, fish & chips are still offered in the store front. Back over on Princess St at No 479 you can get a good Indian meal at the *Durbar* which serves the usual northern dishes including tandooris. It's open every day for lunch or dinner.

For a more up-market place try the *Canoe Club* in the Prince George Hotel near the waterfront. It's across from Confederation Park and is a nice place, but moderate in price. Seafood is the speciality.

For a real splurge there's *Chez Piggy*, probably the city's best known restaurant, in a renovated early 19th-century building at 68 Princess St but really down a small alley off King St between Brock and Princess Sts. At lunch, from 11.30 am to 2 pm, soup and a sandwich or the good salads are not expensive. Dinners starting at 6 pm range from $9 to $17 for the main course so the final bill can be quite high. The selection includes lamb, steaks and omelettes with some interesting appetisers to start with.

There is also a Sunday brunch with some items you don't see on a standard brunch menu, but again it is not for the budget conscious.

The restaurant is owned by a member of a successful (and tuneful) 1960s American pop band. No clues, he likes it that way. It's closed on Monday.

Lino's, on the corner of Division and Ontario Sts, is open 24 hours.

Away from the centre a bit, the *Bonanza* at No 2455 offers very good value for steak and chicken with an all-you-can-eat salad bar.

Division St towards Highway 401 has a good cross section of places representing the standard restaurant chains.

Entertainment

The *Cocama*, at 178 Ontario St, is a huge dance bar down near the water. It's styled after the Limelight in New York City. *Dollar Bills* in the Prince George Hotel, one of several student drinking spots, has videos and dancing.

The *Manor*, at 28 Yonge St, never has a cover charge for rock, new wave bands or contests.

Kingston has quite a few British-style pubs. The *Toucan*, at 76 Princess St near King St, often has live music.

On the corner of King St East and Brock St near City Hall, the *Duke of Kingston Pub* serves British beers amidst British-style decor.

Cinema The *National Film Theatre* (☎ 547-3059) is in the Ellis Hall Auditorium on University Ave. Admission costs $4.50 for US or foreign films, and shows start at 8 pm.

Things to Buy

The Canadian Shop, at 219 Princess St, near Montreal St sells handicrafts, including Cowichan sweaters from Vancouver Island for about the same price they are there. The shop also sells Inuit carvings and all kinds of books about Canada.

The Book Bin, at 225 Princess St, sells used books.

Getting There & Away

Bus The Voyageur station (☎ 548-7738) is at 959 Division St, a couple of km south of Highway 401. Services going to Toronto, are very frequent throughout the day (at least eight trips), to Montreal buses are slightly less frequent, but there are still plenty of them. To Ottawa there are fewer buses but still some each morning, afternoon and evening. Services also go to some of the smaller centres such as Pembroke and Cornwall. Good return or excursion fares are available on the major inter-city routes: to Montreal $37 one-way, Ottawa $29 one-way, and to Toronto it's $31.

Train The railway station (☎ 544-5600) is very inconvenient, a long way from the downtown area. It's on Counter St near the corner of Princess St, north-west of town. There are no city buses; you can try hitching or take a taxi. There are six to eight train services to Montreal daily (morning, noon and night) costing $37. To Ottawa, there are three trains a day (morning, afternoon and evening) for $24. To Toronto there are eight services daily for $39.

Car & Motorbike For car rentals there's Tilden at 2212 Princess St with daily, weekly and longer rentals.

Getting Around

For information on Kingston Transit call ☎ 544-5289. The city bus office is on the corner of Barrack and King Sts.

For getting into town, there is a city bus stop across the street from the bus station. It departs at a quarter to and a quarter past the hour.

Bicycle rentals are available at Alford's Sports Shop, on Princess St, or at Rent-A-Bike, at 35 Johnson St (near City Hall), by the hour, day or week. A bike may provide a way of easily getting to the fort and getting around a bit.

AROUND KINGSTON
Thousand Islands Parkway

East of Kingston between Gananoque (which is pronounced 'gan-an-ok-way') and Mallorytown Landing, a small road – the Thousand Islands Parkway – dips south of Highway 401 and runs along the river. The route is recommended and offers picnic areas and good views out to many of the islands from the pastoral strip of shoreline. There is

also a bicycle path along the route over the fibre-optic telephone lines.

Boat cruises around the islands depart from Rockport and Gananoque.

Sixteen km east of Kingston, in Grass Creek Park in a log house, you'll find the **MacLachlan Woodworking Museum.** The museum outlines the development of working in wood through an extensive collection of tools. Other displays are on trees themselves, some common wooden objects for varying purposes and a changing exhibit area which had a show of decoys when I was there.

Close to the town of **Lansdowne** between Gananoque and Rockport is the busy bridge to New York state. The **Skydeck**, a 125-metre high observation tower is here with three decks and binoculars to provide great views over the river area. From May to October it is open every day. Admission is charged but it's reasonable and there is a restaurant on the premises.

At **Mallorytown Landing** is the headquarters for the **Thousand Islands National Park**, Canada's smallest national park consisting of 17 islands together with the mainland location.

Along the parkway are privately run campgrounds and numerous motels as well as cottages to rent for longer stays.

There is a bit of an art colony in the area and in the fall many of the local studios are open to the public. Ask the tourist office for a list of the painters, sculptors, woodworkers, glass workers, weavers, etc.

The Thousand Islands This very scenic area just east of Kingston has more than 1000 islands which dot the river between the two national mainlands. In spring the islands are an undulating white with the blooming trillium, the provincial flower.

Boat tours from Kingston trip around some of the islands. A couple of companies run daily trips in summer. The short and straightforward one is aboard the *Island Princess* (☎ 549-5544), a 1½-hour trip around the interesting Kingston shoreline. There is a commentary on some of the noteworthy sites. Departing from the same place is the *Island Queen* showboat providing live family entertainment or a three-hour evening cruise with a buffet dinner. Through the summer they offer two or three trips a day leaving from the *Island Queen* dock at the foot of Brock St on Ontario St.

Others leave from Rockport and Gananoque, two small towns east down the river a bit. Most tours last about 3½ hours, cost around $11, and include glimpses of some of the island curiosities like **Boldt Castle**. The Rockport Boat Line has two-hour trips out among the international islands for $8. The dock is three km east of the Thousand Islands International Bridge. Trips depart hourly in peak season, less frequently in spring and fall.

The Gananoque Boat Line does much the same thing but the trip is 90 minutes long going through the Admiralty and Fleet group of islands. They also have sunset cruises. At impressive looking Boldt Castle you can get off for a closer look and get back on a later boat.

A new angle is to do it all yourself on a rented houseboat. This can be a lot of fun and is gaining in popularity all over Ontario, but you've got to get a few people together or it can be a little pricey. If you want to look into it check out Thousand Islands Houseboats in Kingston. They rent by the day, week or for part of a week. Prices depend on when you go: at weekends it costs considerably more than midweek. The boats come with all the kitchen necessities and sleep eight people.

St Lawrence Islands National Park Within the gentle, green archipelago, the park covers 17 islands scattered along 80 km of the river. At Mallorytown, aside from the park interpretive and information centre, there is a 60-site campground. There are no camper or trailer hook-ups. There are some trails and a beach.

Many of the islands have picnicking and camping although facilities are at a minimum. Thirteen islands offer primitive campsites accessible only by boat. Water taxis and boat rentals are available from many of the small towns along the parkway and from the headquarters. Tourist offices or park headquarters will have information on what's available. Park islands stretch from just off Mallorytown all the way down to Gananoque.

West of Kingston

West of town along the coast, Highway 33 has been designated the Loyalist Parkway. It retraces the steps of the Loyalists who settled this area some 200 years ago after fleeing the American Revolution. The parkway runs for 94 km from Kingston to Trenton passing over Quinte's Isle.

Just west of Kingston in Amherstview is **Fairfield Historical Park** along the shoreline. It includes **Fairfield House,** one of the province's oldest, built by Loyalists from New England in 1793. North about 10 km, in Odessa, is the historic **Babcock Mill,** a working water-powered mill which now again produces the baskets originally made here in the mid-1800s.

At **Adulphustown** catch the continuously running short, free ferry ride over to Glenora on Quinte's Isle and continue on to Picton.

North of Kingston

North of Kingston is the **Rideau Lakes** region, an area of small towns, cottages, lodges, marinas and opportunities for fishing and camping.

From the city in a day's or just an afternoon's drive you can explore some of the smaller, rural Ontario villages.

Wilton has one of the many southern Ontario regional cheese factories with a retail outlet. In the little town of **Yarker,** straight up Highway 6 from Highway 401, the *Waterfall Tea Room* right on the river by a waterfall has been highly recommended.

Camden East, home of Harrowsmith Magazine, has an excellent bookstore on outdoor, nature, gardening, country living and related matters as well as a range of how-to books.

The region has attracted back-to-the-landers and countercultural people. Their influences show up in the number of health-food stores, craft outlets and bakeries. In **Tamsworth**, where there is a big art & craft outlet, try the *Devon Tea House*. In nearby **Marlbank** there is *Phioloxia's Zoo, Bakery, B&B and Vegetarian Restaurant*. What, no discotheque?

New Frontenac Provincial Park straddles both the lowlands of southern Ontario and the more northern Canadian Shield so the flora, fauna and geology of the park are an admixture. There is one campground, at the main gate, but the park is really designed for overnight hikers and canoeists. Trails have been mapped out and campsites are located through the park. Though the park is large, there aren't many designated camping sites; this has not yet been a problem as the park remains relatively unknown.

The entrance and information centre are at **Otter Lake**, off Highway 5A north of Sydenham. The swimming is excellent and I drink the water straight from the lakes although it's probably not recommended to do so without boiling it. There are no bears to worry about and pretty good bass fishing.

North-west from Kingston, up Highway 41, is **Bon Echo Provincial Park**, also good for canoeing. Some of the lakes are quite shallow and get very warm. There is walk-in hiking or roadside campgrounds with facilities. At **Mazinaw Lake** there are Native Indian rock paintings on granite cliffs. This is one of the largest parks in eastern Ontario and, generally speaking, the larger the park the better because you can lose your fellow humans for a spell and wildlife viewing is more likely.

Rideau Canal The 150-year-old, 200-km-long canal/river/lake system connects Kingston with Ottawa. The historical route is good for boating or canoeing trips, with many places to stop en route. When travelling from one end to the other, boats must pass through 47 old lock systems. There are parks, small towns and lakes. The old defence buildings along the way have been restored.

Roads run parallel to much of the canal, so walking or cycling is also possible.

Currently there are no commercial trips offered along the river but rumour has it that this may soon change. There may be businesses along the canal which rent houseboats so you can meander about at your own speed, but so far this area hasn't been developed like that along the Trent Canal System running from Georgian Bay to Lake Ontario. The tourist office has information on history, times, lock fees which are minimal, and boat rentals.

Rideau Trail The Rideau Trail is a 400-km-long hiking-trail system which links Kingston with Ottawa. It passes through Westport, Smith Falls and many conservation areas on the way. Forests, fields and marshes as well as some stretches of road are used. There are some historic sites on the route and you'll see the Rideau Canal. There are also 64 km of side loops. Most people use the route only for day trips, but longer trips and overnighting are possible. The main trail is marked by orange triangles, side trails by blue triangles. The Rideau Trail Association which has an office in Kingston prints a map kit for the entire route.

Camping Between Kingston and Smith Falls are numerous camping spots. The rest of the way there is not as much provision for camping, but there is commercial accommodation. Camping on private land is possible, but get the owner's permission.

Belleville & Around
There's not much for the visitor in this town with 35,000 residents – it's more a departure point for Quinte's Isle to the south. In July the Waterfront & Folklorama Festival is three days of events, music and shows.

North of Belleville up Highway 37, roughly 10 km north of Highway 401, is Mapledale Cheese, worth a visit to buy some of the excellent cheddar.

Highway 37 continues north through old Tweed to Highway 7 which is the main route to Toronto from Ottawa. It's a bit slow with only two lanes, but the scenery is good and there are a couple of parks along the way and several places to eat.

QUINTE'S ISLE

Irregularly shaped Quinte's Isle is a quiet rural, scenic, historic retreat from the bustle of much of southern Ontario. The rolling farmland is reminiscent of Prince Edward Island and, in fact, Quinte's Isle is also known as Prince Edward County. Many of the little towns were settled in the 18th and 19th centuries. The cemeteries adjacent to the village churches reveal clues to these earlier times.

It's only been in the past few years that the island has been somewhat discovered and developed for visitors, but it still hasn't changed very much.

Things to See

Traffic is light on most of the island's roads which lead past large old farmhouses and cultivated fields. The **St Lawrence River** is never far away and many routes offer good views. Fishing is quite good in the **Bay of Quinte** and the locals use the waters for sailing. The island is popular with cyclists: it's generally flat and some of the smaller roads are well shaded.

The excellent strawberry-picking in late June draws many outsiders.

There are two provincial parks, **North Beach** and the fine **Sandbanks**. Sandbanks, the only one offering camping, is one of the most popular parks in the province. Book ahead, reservations are definitely required for weekends when a fair bit of partying goes on. The park is divided into two sections: the Outlet with an excellent strip of sandy beach and Sandbanks, itself, containing most of the area's sand dunes, some over three storeys high. There's a large undeveloped section at the end of the beach – good for walking and exploring the dunes and backwaters.

Picton This small town is the only town of any size on the island and has one of the six district museums. There is a tourist office here with detailed maps of the island and some information on current accommoda-

tion. Pick up the walking-tour guide of Picton. The tour leads you past some of the fine historical buildings in town. Another guide lists various island attractions including **Bird House City** with dozens of painted birdhouses including a fire station and court-house.

Lake on the Mountain Park On the other side of the island, this is really nothing more than a picnic site but is worth a visit to see the unusual lake. It sits on one side of the road at a level actually higher than that of the road, while just across the street is a terrific view over Lake Ontario and some islands hundreds of feet below. Geologists are still speculating as to the lake's origins. The local Mohawk Indians have their own legends about the lake which appears to have no source.

Tyendinaga Indian Reserve This is just off Quinte's Isle and is also mainly farmland. In mid-May the original coming of the Mohawks is re-enacted in full tribal dress.

Places to Stay

There are numerous resorts, cottages, motels and B&Bs covering a range of prices. For a day or two you're best off at a B&B but for longer stays check into one of the simpler cabins or cottages. Some of the less costly places seem to be in the Cherry Valley area.

Isiah Tubbs Resort (☎ 393-2090) is one of the more expensive places on the island but relative to Toronto or Muskoka prices is not bad for its luxury facilities and very fine design.

The area, however, is best known for its camping. There are several commercial campgrounds nearby which, if you can't get in to Sandbanks, aren't quite as busy. There's a large one opposite the Outlet, geared mainly for RVs and quite a nice one, good for tenting as well, out at the tip of Salmon Arm. It offers minimal facilities but great sunsets.

TRENTON

Small Trenton is known as the starting point

of the **Trent Canal**, which goes 386 km through 44 locks to Georgian Bay in Lake Huron. Yachties and sailors of every description follow this old Native Indian route each summer.

Presqu'île Provincial Park is west of town and has a long, sandy beach. There's camping and bird-watching in spring and fall. At Beach 3, you can rent boats of various types, sailboarding equipment and bicycles.

The Loyalist Parkway road route leads down onto Quinte's Isle and heads east.

Trent-Severn Waterway

The Trent-Severn Waterway cuts diagonally across southern Ontario cottage country following rivers and lakes for 386 km from Trenton on Lake Ontario to Georgian Bay at the mouth of the Severn River near Port Severn and Honey Harbour. It travels past, through or near many of the region's best known resort towns and areas including the **Kawartha Lakes, Bobcaygeon, Fenelon Falls** and **Lake Simcoe.**

Used a 100 years ago for commerce, the system is now strictly recreational and is operated by Parks Canada. They regulate the waterflow by a series of 125 dams along the route and open the canal for use in mid-May and close it in mid-October.

There is a cruise ship which plies the route, taking seven days. Shorter, four-day trips are also available. These are not cheap, but for details inquire in Peterborough. Perhaps of more interest is the idea of renting your own houseboat to explore the canal. This has become amazingly popular in the past few years. Several companies at varying points along the route now rent boats by the weekend, week or longer.

The houseboats come more or less fully equipped, some even throwing in the barbecue and can accommodate up to eight people (six adults) which not only makes for a good party, but also a reasonably priced one. The trips are also good for families, with separate sleeping rooms for the kids.

One organisation to try for a houseboat is Sunburst Houseboat Rentals (☎ (705) 799-5745) at Egan Marine, RR4 in the village of Omemee west of Peterborough on Route 7. They've been in business for 20 years and the location, right by the Kawartha Lakes, is good giving the option of hanging around the lakes or going all the way to Lake Simcoe. You get some brief training – anyone can operate the boats with little difficulty. Rates vary quite a bit depending on timing but they start at about $400 a weekend or midweek for the basic boat. They range to about $1500 for a full week on the larger deluxe model during the peak season in July. On average, you will use about $80 worth of gas in a week.

Even if you're not on the water there are things to see along the route including all the locks.

KAWARTHA LAKES
Peterborough & Around

Peterborough is a middle-sized Ontario town, more or less at the centre of the Kawartha Lakes vacation region. The older downtown area has some fine buildings; it's all very green although the city seems in some danger of becoming a Toronto suburb. You'll find Trent University here.

The Trent-Severn Waterway passes through the large hydraulic-lift lock, a major landmark in town. A visitor centre shows how the locks along the system operate and there is a working model. You can go on a trip through the locks into the Otonabee River or, if you're hooked, there are three and five-day cruises through the locks and along part of the system.

In late July or early August is the Summer Festival, with various events and shows.

Century Village

South-east of Peterborough is Century Village, a pioneer village with costumed workers, demonstrations, and 20 buildings dating from 1820 to 1899.

Lakefield

A few km north is Lakefield, a very small town with a boys' school that Queen Elizabeth II saw fit to send Prince Andrew to.

Other Attractions

Many of the pretty towns in the region have a good restaurant or two and, usually, a couple of antique dealers. **Bobcaygeon** and **Fenelon Falls** are two that are worth dropping into if you're up this way. (The former also hosts a big fiddle contest annually in July.)

Nearby, **Balsam Lake** is popular for swimming and fishing. In **Lindsay**, a more ordinary small town, don't miss the *Dutch Treat* on Kent St for excellent, very cheap food – good homemade muffins and various treats. This town has a summer theatre programme.

At **Burleigh Falls** who could resist a place called the *Lovesick Café*? It's a typical country shop with food, souvenirs, fishing tackle, etc. The date squares are recommended.

Canoeing

There are several possibilities for canoeing.

From Peterborough you can get to Serpent's Mound Provincial Park. Possibilities are easy trips on the canal or tougher white-water trips in spring on rivers in the area. Ask at the tourist office in town. The Ministry of Natural Resources publishes a map called *North Kawartha Canoe Routes* which shows some possible trips and their portage distances.

Parks

The district has some interesting parks as well. **Petroglyphs Provincial Park** has probably the best collection of prehistoric rock carvings in the country. Rediscovered in 1954, there are reportedly 900 figures and shapes carved into the park's limestone ridges. The portions of the collection which are easy to view are much smaller than is suggested by the figure 900 and, though interesting, it is not an overwhelming site. Recently, this relatively small, exposed section has had to be enclosed in order to

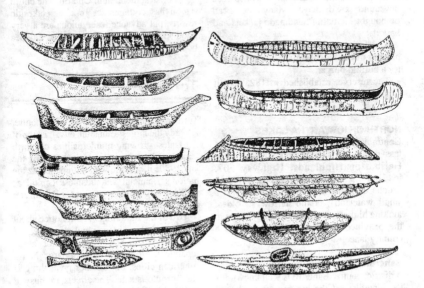

protect the rock from acid rain, a serious problem over much of Ontario. The people in positions to do something about the situation continue to sit on their butts. The area and small lake within the park remain important spiritual sites for the local Native Indians.

Serpent's Mound Provincial Park is the site of an ancient Native Indian burial ground. The **Warsaw Caves Conservation Area** contains tunnels eroded into limestone; there are walking trails here.

Curve Lake Indian Reserve About 900 Ojibwa people live on this 400-hectare reserve roughly 34 km north of Peterborough. A trip to the reserve's Whetung Ojibwa Arts & Crafts Gallery is well worth while. The log building contains both new and old examples of Native Indian art. There is a museum section with traditional pieces and valuable works from such artists as Norval Morrisseau, perhaps Canada's best known.

In the gallery area newer articles drawn from Native Indian craftspeople from across the country are displayed. Many articles can be bought including handmade jackets and baskets.

Lunch is available: you can sample a number of traditional Native Indian foods or try a buffalo burger.

The reserve, established in 1825, is off Curve Lake Rd which runs out of Highway 507.

NORTH OF KAWARTHA LAKES

Continuing north you come to a less busy, less populated hilly region known as the Haliburton Highlands. Highway 507, leading up from Bobcaygeon through Catchacoma and Gooderham (which has a small waterfall), is the narrowest, oldest looking highway I've driven on anywhere in the province. It often looks more like a country lane.

Bancroft

A district centre, Bancroft is well known for its minerals and the big gem festival held each August. Examples of 80% of the minerals found in Canada can be dug up in this area.

Combermere

The **Combermere Catholic Commune** (☎ 756-5031) is a religious, cooperative farm, run by J Scanlon primarily as a learning experience and as a place to practise the group's ideas (which originated in Russia). The farm will take in travellers for a few days in exchange for work around the farm. Also in Combermere is the **Madonna House Pioneer Museum**.

Barry's Bay

The old lumber town is now a supply centre for the cottagers in the area on and around **Lake Kaminiskeg**. It's also pretty close to **Algonquin Park** and is on the main highway to Ottawa. Odd as it may seem, this is the centre for a sizeable Polish population attracted to the hilly, green topography which is much like that along the Baltic Sea in northern Poland. Nearby **Wilno** was the first Polish settlement in Ontario. The entire region has cottages for rent and lakeside resorts, but advance reservations are a very good idea. **Pembroke**, east at the Quebec border, is the nearest town of any size.

Toronto

Toronto is the country's major urban centre. Already the largest Canadian city, it is one of the fastest growing municipalities of North America. With the economic boom of the late 1980s it became well entrenched as the nation's financial and business capital as well as being a primary focus for British arts and culture.

Two of the first things you'll notice about Toronto are the vibrancy and cleanliness of the downtown area. These two factors alone separate it from the bulk of large North American cities, but another great thing is that Toronto is safe. The streets are busy at night with all the restaurant and entertainment places staying open and the downtown streetcars and subway are generally used without hesitation. Of course some prudence is always wise and women alone should take care after dark. There are some rougher parts of town but these tend, as a rule, to be away from the centre and not where visitors are likely to be.

There is a lot of central housing in the city, part of urban planning which has kept a balance in the city and made it a more liveable place. Despite high costs, there are no areas of concentrated poverty. Toronto is one of the most expensive cities in North America to live in, but fortunately this is not overly evident to visitors for much of the cost is in real estate. Throughout the city, various ethnic and immigrant groups have collected in fairly tight communities to form bustling, prosperous districts. These various neighbourhoods are one of the best and most distinctive aspects of the city and have helped to warm up what has been the rather stand-offish character of Toronto.

Toronto celebrated its 150th birthday in 1984 but has only recently attained its prominent stature and international attention. About 25 years ago, the city scored points in its traditional rivalry with Montreal by surpassing it in size. Since this largely symbolic achievement, Toronto has grown in every way. It is the busiest Canadian port on the Great Lakes and is a major centre for banking, manufacturing and publishing. The Toronto Stock Exchange is one of North America's most important and the city is the provincial capital.

As you will notice, Toronto is new and shiny. Much of the downtown area has been rebuilt during the past 15 to 20 years. I swear every time I turn around there's still a new building going up. This rapid modernisation and embracing of progress and change was not always so, however.

The Seneca Indians first lived here in the 1600s. Étienne Brule, on a trip with Samuel de Champlain in 1615, was the first European person to see the site. The Native Indians did not particularly relish the visit and it wasn't until around 1720 that the French established a fur-trading post and mission in what's now the west end of the city.

After years of hostility with the French, the British took over. John Simcoe, lieutenant-governor of the new Upper Canada, chose Toronto as the capital in 1793 and it became known as York. Previously, Niagara-on-the-Lake had served as capital.

During the War of 1812, the Americans held York and burnt the Legislature. In retaliation, British forces headed towards Washington and burnt the Americans' political headquarters. Apparently the burn marks were painted over in white, leading to the name the 'White House'.

When the war ended in 1814, York began to expand. Stagecoach service began on Yonge St in 1828. In 1834, with William Lyon Mackenzie as first mayor, York was renamed Toronto, a Native Indian name meaning 'meeting place'. During this time under conservative politicians, the city became known as 'Toronto the Good', a tag which only began to fade in the 1970s. Religious restraints and strong anti-vice laws (it was illegal to hire a horse on Sunday) were largely responsible for this. Not all that long ago curtains were drawn in department-store windows on Sunday because window shopping was considered sinful, and movie theatres were also closed on the holy day.

Like many big cities, Toronto has had its great fire. In 1904, about five hectares of the inner city burned, levelling 122 buildings. Amazingly, no one was killed. The 1920s saw the first population boom, but in 1941 80% of the population was still Anglo-Saxon.

It was after WW II that the city began to change. Well over half a million immigrants have arrived since then, mainly Europeans from all corners. Italians make up the largest non-British ethnic group. The influx of new tongues, customs and food has livened up a place which was once thought to be a hopeless case.

With its staid background and some excellent urban planning, Toronto has developed cautiously. Construction, at least until the current mayor's arrival, was regulated, and

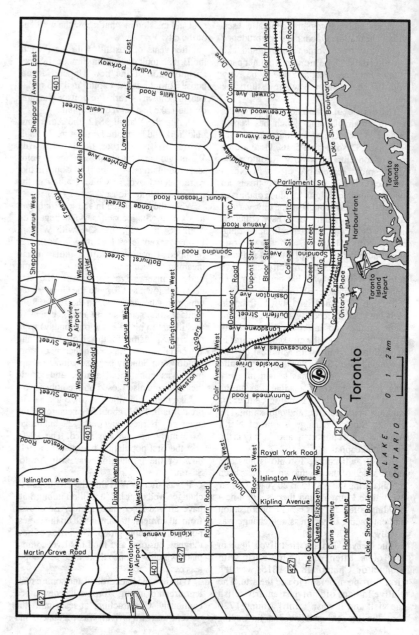

parks, housing and retail places are built alongside offices. Progressive and reactionary forces continue to do battle, the pendulum swinging first to one side and then the other. In general, for a city of its size and importance, Toronto remains conservative, particularly on moral issues, but perhaps this is the price to be paid for the benefits.

Orientation

The land around Toronto is very flat and the city tends to sprawl over a large area. Despite the size, it's easy to get oriented, as the city is laid out in grid style with nearly all the streets running north-south and east-west.

Yonge St (pronounced 'Young'), called the longest street in the world, is the main north-south artery. It runs from Lake Ontario north to the city boundary, Steeles Ave, and beyond. The central downtown area is bounded by Front St to the south, Bloor St to the north, Spadina Ave to the west and Jarvis St to the east. Yonge St runs between Spadina Ave and Jarvis St, a few blocks from each of these. Street names change from 'East' to 'West' at Yonge St, and the street numbers begin there.

Bloor St and College St (called Carlton St east of Yonge St which is about halfway between Bloor St and the lake) are the two main east-west streets.

At the foot of Yonge St or nearby York St is the lake and the re-developed waterfront area called Harbourfront. The old docks have given way to restaurants, galleries, artists' workshops, stores, condos and some parkland. The ferry for the Toronto Islands also moors here as do many private vessels.

North a few blocks is Front St, where you'll find Union Station, the VIA Rail terminal, the classic old Royal York Hotel, the post office and the O'Keefe Centre, a theatre for the performing arts. West two blocks is the CN Tower and, next door, Skydome, the large sports stadium.

Continuing up Bay St, at Queen St you'll hit Nathan Phillips Square, site of rallies and concerts and the unique City Hall buildings. To the east, the Victorian building dating from 1899 is the old City Hall, now used mainly for law courts. Check out the gargoyles. On the west side is Osgood Hall, home of the Law Society.

One block east is Yonge St lined with stores, bars, restaurants and theatres catering mainly to the young. On the corner of Dundas and Yonge Sts is the enormous modern shopping complex known as the Eaton Centre. It's worth a look and the tourist office is here too. Further east is an area known as 'Cabbagetown', a formerly run-down neighbourhood now renovated and trendy in sections but still retaining some of its earlier character.

West along Dundas St, from Bay St and continuing to Spadina Ave, is Chinatown. Spadina Ave, an interesting old street, was once a strictly Jewish area which now shares its remaining delis and textile shops with the burgeoning Oriental businesses.

University Ave, lined with offices and trees is Toronto's widest street and the location of most major parades. The lit beacon atop the stately Canada Life Building on the corner of University Ave and Queen St is a guide to the weather. The light at the top is colour coded this way: green – clear, red – cloudy, flashing red – rain, flashing white – snow. If the tower lights are ascending the temperature will rise, if descending it will cool. Temperatures are stable if the lights are on and static.

University Ave leads north to Queen's Park at College St. Here are the provincial Parliament Buildings. To the west is the University of Toronto.

North of the park the street is called Queen's Park Ave, which leads to Bloor St where the city's principal museum, the Royal Ontario Museum is situated. Just north of Bloor St, between Avenue Rd (Queen's Park Ave) and Yonge St is Yorkville St, once the scene of the 1960s folk music and drug vanguard. Now it's been done over with expensive shops and restaurants.

Back southwards, Queen St West between Spadina Ave and University Ave and beyond to Bathurst St has seen a rebirth and is now busy with many restaurants (some cheap) and book, record and distinctive clothing shops. A lot of young people involved in the arts and on its fringes live in the area.

Dundas St and College St West are mainly Italian.

The city is served by expressways on all four sides. Along the lake, the Gardiner Expressway runs west into the Queen Elizabeth Way (the QEW). The QEW goes to Niagara Falls. Just at the city's western border is Highway 427, which runs north to the airport and Highway 401. Highway 401 runs east-west above the downtown area east to Montreal and west to Windsor, Ontario, which is opposite Detroit, USA. On the eastern side of the city the Don Valley Parkway runs south from Highway 401 to the Gardiner Expressway.

Information

The Tourist & Convention Centre (☎ 368-9821) has an office in the Queen's Quay terminal down at the lake at Harbourfront between Yonge and York Sts. It's on the 5th floor and is only open from 9 am to 5 pm Monday to Friday, but you can phone on weekends and holidays and someone will answer questions. To get to the office, take the elevator (midway down the mall) up to the Galleria offices on level 4.

There is also a year-round city information booth outside the Eaton Centre on the south-west corner of Yonge and Dundas Sts.

Two additional such booths operate through the summer months. One is at Nathan Phillips Square in front of City Hall, off Queen St, west of Yonge St. The other can be found on the corner of Yonge and Bloor Sts, on the south-west side in front of the Bay department store in the Hudson Bay Centre. These are open every day.

For information on other areas of Ontario there is the Ontario Travel Centre (☎ 965-4008) conveniently located on the lower level of the Eaton Centre which is at 220 Yonge St on the corner of Dundas St. It's open the same hours as the shopping centre, currently from 10 am to 9 pm weekdays, Saturday 9.30 am to 6 pm and closed on Sunday. They can also help out with information on Toronto.

The main post office with general delivery is on Front St between Yonge and Bay Sts.

The Canadian Hostelling Association's regional office is just a few doors from the hostel itself at 217 Church St.

Travel-Related Stores For travel books, guides, maps and a range of books on nature, camping and outdoor activities see Open Air at 25 Toronto St near the corner of Adelaide St East and Yonge St. It's on the corner of Adelaide St, the door is downstairs off Toronto St.

Also selling maps, including a wide selection including topos, is Canada Map at 211 Yonge St on the lower level.

CN Tower

The highest free-standing structure in the world, the CN Tower (☎ 360-8500) has become a symbol and landmark of Toronto. The tower is in the southern end of the city near the lake, south of Front St West at Walkway. The top antenna was put in place in 1975 by helicopter, making the tower 533 metres high. Its primary function is communications – radio and TV signals – but up at the top there is a restaurant, disco and two observation decks. The one outside is windy. On a good, clear day you can see for about 160 km, which easily includes US cities across the lake.

A glass elevator travels up the outside of the tower. The cost for a trip up and entry to the observation deck is $10.75 for adults. If you're eating either lunch or dinner at the restaurant at the top, the elevator ticket price is waived. The catch is that there is a minimum food bill which is quite high. Call for the latest menu prices.

The tower is open every day and night until 10 pm, an hour later on Saturday. The time and weather display at ground level is worth a look.

At the base of the tower is an attraction known as the Space Port. Entry includes a walking tour of a simulated space port, a laser show, and a special-effect film which suggests a shuttle ride through space. Most people find it all quite good. Admission costs

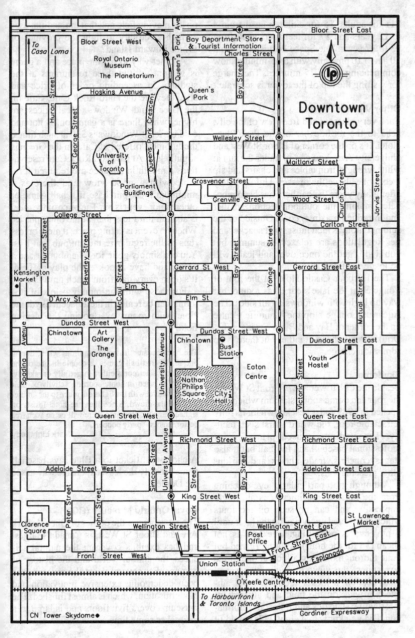

Downtown Toronto

$11 for adults, $5 for children aged from 4 to 12 years and $7 for teenagers aged from 13 to 17 years. The Space Port is open from 10 am to 10 pm daily with a 45-minute show commencing every 15 minutes. The charge for visiting the top of the tower is separate.

Other Views

For a very pleasant and free view of the city, head to the rooftop bar of the Park Plaza Hotel. It's on the corner of Bloor St West and University Ave. You can sit under the sun at white wrought-iron tables and chairs and sip a cool one above the masses. Unfortunately after many years the bar here has been renovated making the outdoor section smaller and introducing a dress code. Outside of the summer months men must sport a jacket and tie. Regulations are relaxed in summer but you'll still get the once over and jeans will no longer be tolerated.

The Harbour Castle Hotel at the foot of Yonge St at the lake's edge has a quiet bar way up high with windows on all sides. The Aquarius Lounge atop the Manulife Centre on the corner of Bay and Bloor Sts is similar. Drinks aren't cheap at either but there is no admission charge.

Skydome

Beside the CN Tower at 277 Front St West is the rounded dome sports stadium which was opened in 1989 and is best known for its fully retractable roof, the world's first such facility. The stadium is used primarily for professional baseball and football but it also stages concerts, trade shows and various other presentations.

Although not particularly eye-catching from the outside, the interior is strikingly impressive and can be seen on the tours which are offered every day on the hour until 5 pm, events permitting. The tour is not cheap ($8 for the hour). It's a bit rushed but quite thorough offering a look at one of the box suites, the view from the stands and press section, a locker room (without athletes), a walk on the field and all sorts of informative statistics and tidbits of information. Did you know that eight 747s would fit

on the playing field and that the stadium uses enough electricity to light the province of Prince Edward Island?

Another way to see the place and a game is via one of the three restaurants at the stadium. In ascending order of price and style they are the Hard Rock Café, Café on the Green and Windows. Meal prices are higher when there is a game on. A hot and cold buffet at Windows is $30 at such times, the full meal offered at Café on the Green is slightly less. At the Hard Rock Café reservations a month in advance are required for a table with a good view and there is a minimum meal purchase if a ball game or other major event is on. The price of the meal is about a third less than at the other places. When no event is taking place, it more or less runs as the regular restaurant/pub that it is. You can simply go in for a hamburger and a coffee and have a look at the playing field. It's open every day from lunch until late.

For those with the money – lots of it – rooms can be rented in the adjacent Skydome Hotel with rooms overlooking the playing field.

The hotel became instantly notorious when, during one of the first ball games, a couple in one of the upper-field side rooms either forgetfully or rakishly, became engaged in some sporting activity of their own au naturel with the lights on, much to the amusement of the crowd. Since then the hotel insists on signed waivers stipulating there will be no such free performances – party poopers.
Mark Lightbody

A cheap-seat ticket to a Blue Jays baseball game is easily the least expensive way to see the Dome.

Royal Ontario Museum (ROM)

The museum, on the corner of Queen's Park Ave and Bloor St West, is Canada's largest and has exhibits covering the natural sciences, the animal world and the history of humans. For several years the museum has been undergoing extensive renovation and modernisation, which is almost finished. The museum covers five floors and is large so a visit takes some time.

The collection of Chinese crafts, textiles and assorted arts is considered one of the best anywhere. The Egyptian, Greek, Roman and Etruscan civilisations are also represented. The newly designed dinosaur and mammalogy rooms are very good with the latter containing a replica of part of an immense bat cave found in Jamaica. Another section outlines the history of trade between the East and West from the ancient caravan routes through to more modern times. There are often in-depth touring exhibits – these are generally excellent but a surcharge is added to the admission fee.

The museum is open daily from 10 am to 6 pm and until 8 pm on Tuesday and Thursday. Admission is $6, less for seniors and students and is free on Tuesday from 4.30 pm until closing time. If you go to the planetarium the same day, you'll get a discount.

The subway is very close by (Museum stop) but, if you're driving, there is parking on Bedford St, west of Avenue Rd north of Bloor St.

An annexe to the museum is the Canadian Decorative Arts Department, down the street in the Sigmund Samuel Building at 14 Queen's Park Crescent West. The focus is on Canada's early artists and craftspeople. It's free and open daily from 10 am to 5 pm and on Sunday from 1 to 5 pm.

George R Gardiner Museum of Ceramic Art

At 111 Queen's Park Ave, this museum is also part of the ROM just across the street. The collection is divided into four periods of ceramic history: pre-Columbian, Italian majolica from the 15th and 16th centuries, English delftware of the 17th century and English porcelain of the 18th century. (I particularly admire the pottery from Mexico through to Peru done before the arrival of Europeans.) It's quite an extensive collection spread over two floors. Admission costs $3 and the opening hours are Tuesday to Sunday from 10 am to 5 pm.

Art Gallery of Ontario (AGO)

This is one of the top three art galleries in the country, the others being in Ottawa and Montreal. Though not the Louvre, it is excellent and, unless you have a lot more stamina than I do, you'll need more than one trip to see it all. It houses works – mainly paintings – from the 14th century to the present. There is also a Canadian section and rooms for changing exhibitions, which can sometimes be the highlight of a visit. The gallery is best known for its vast Henry Moore sculpture collection. One room holds about 20 of his major sculptures of the human form.

The gallery is on Dundas St West, two blocks west of University Ave. There is a cafeteria if you need a break, and a good gift/book store. At the door, pick up a schedule of the films and lectures that go on in the gallery.

Hours are Tuesday to Sunday from 11 am to 5.30 pm, Wednesday 11 am to 9 pm, closed Monday. Admission is $3, students and seniors $1 and free to all on Wednesday evenings. The Ontario Art College is next door.

The Grange The Grange is a restored Georgian house adjoining the AGO. The door is down in the basement beside the cafeteria. Admission is included with the gallery ticket. Authentic 19th-century furniture and workers in period dress represent life in a 'gentleman's residence' of the time. The Grange is also closed on Monday.

Casa Loma

This is a 98-room medieval-style castle-cum-mansion built between 1911 and 1914 by Sir Henry Pellat, a very wealthy and evidently eccentric man. The interior is sumptuous, built with the finest materials imported from around the world. Note especially the conservatory. Pellat even brought in stonemasons from Scotland to build the walls around the estate.

Despite all this it's not a great attraction, but there is a good view as the house is on the top of a hill. Bring your camera. A ticket is $7.50 and it's open every day but only until 4 pm. The mansion (☎ 923-1171) has been a tourist site since 1937, when the cost of upkeep became too much for its owner. With the view and relative seclusion, it's a classic spot for couples to go 'parking' at night. The address is 1 Austin Terrace off Spadina Ave. From the corner of Dupont and Bathurst Sts, it can clearly be seen, perched impressively above the surroundings.

Provincial Parliament Buildings

The attractive pinkish sandstone Legislature sits in Queen's Park just north of College St on University Ave. The stately building was completed in 1892 and is kept in superb condition. Free tours are given frequently throughout the day. For a flashback to your 1st grade class, head for the visitors' gallery when Parliament is in session, roughly from October to December and February to June.

City Hall

In Nathan Phillips Square on the corner of Queen and Bay Sts, this distinctive three-part building represented the beginning of Toronto's becoming an important and modern city. It was completed in 1965 to Finnish architect Viljo Revell's award-winning design. The twin clamshell towers, with a flying saucer-style structure between them at the bottom, are unmistakeable. Free tours are given throughout the day. The square out the front is a meeting place and location for concerts, demonstrations and office-worker lunches.

In winter the fountain pool is a very attractive, popular artificial skating rink. Rental skates are available until 10 pm daily for this recommended activity. It's a lot of fun, don't feel intimidated if you are a novice, you won't be alone. Immigrants from around the world are out there gingerly making strides towards assimilation.

Ontario Science Centre

The science centre (☎ 429-0193) has an interesting assortment of scientific and technological exhibits and demonstrations, most of which you can take part in. It's a museum where you can touch everything. You might even learn something, although it's best for children and on weekends, when there are

hundreds of them visiting. The fitness-testing machines are worth challenging. You'll find good changing exhibits here too. The design of the centre and its location in a small ravine are assets.

It's on the corner of Eglinton Ave East and Don Mills Rd. To get there, take the subway to Eglinton, transfer to the Eglinton East bus, and get off at Don Mills Rd. The centre is open from 10 am to 6 pm daily, admission is $5.50 and parking is $2. On Friday nights it remains open to 9 pm and is free from 5 pm until closing time, parking is included.

Fort York

Fort York (☎ 392-6907) was established in 1793 by the British to protect the town, then called York. It was largely destroyed at the end of the War of 1812 against the Americans, but was quickly rebuilt. Now restored, it has eight original log, stone and brick buildings. In summer, men decked out in 19th-century British military uniforms carry out marches and drills, and fire musket volleys. The fort is open every day, all year, from 9.30 am to 5 pm. Admission is $4.25 for adults, less for kids and seniors. It's on Garrison Rd which runs off Fleet St West which in turn is near Bathurst St near the corner with Front St. Take the streetcar south on Bathurst St.

McLaughlin Planetarium

McLaughlin Planetarium (☎ 586-5750), next door to the ROM, at 100 Queen's Park Ave, has entertaining and informative shows about the solar system and universe. The realistic and interesting programmes last 45 minutes. On the 2nd floor, the Astrocentre includes hands-on exhibits, slide shows, astronomy equipment and a solar telescope enabling viewers to watch sun flares as they actually occur. Admission is $5 and less for students, kids, families, etc. The fee entitles you to $1 off the admission to the museum on the same day.

Laserium or laser rock shows are given a few nights a week for $7. For any of the shows, arrive early – once the programme begins you cannot get in. Phone for programme details and times. By subway, get off at the Museum stop.

City Neighbourhoods

Toronto has a very wide variety of ethnic groups, some in large, concentrated numbers. Throughout the city, these neighbourhoods maintain the homeland cultures, and offer outsiders glimpses of foreign countries. These areas are good for restaurants and several are mentioned in the Places to Eat section. All these neighbourhoods have changed considerably through the years and continue to do so as other groups such as West Indians and Latin Americans arrive in Canada. Descriptions of a few of the most prominent districts follow.

Chinatown Toronto easily has the largest (and growing) Chinese population in the country and the principal Chinatown area is right in the centre of town. The original old area runs along Dundas St from Bay St, by the bus station west to University Ave. There are many restaurants here, but this area has become rather touristy and isn't really where the local Chinese shop.

The bigger and more interesting segment of Chinatown is further west. Also on Dundas St West it runs from Beverley St, near the Art Gallery, to Spadina Ave and a little beyond. Most of Spadina Ave, from south of Dundas St all the way north to College St and then east and west for a bit along College St, is now primarily Chinese.

The narrow residential side streets of the area are home to many Chinese people. Again there are lots of restaurants but also variety and grocery stores, jobbers, herbalists, bakeries and places selling many things known only to the customers.

In addition to all the businesses, vendors often set up along the sidewalks. The area gets packed on weekends, it's sharp with sounds and smells, and restaurants do good business. There are also a few Japanese and more and more Vietnamese places in the neighbourhood.

There is also a small group of Chinese merchants and restaurants around Gerrard St and Broadview Ave in the city's east end and many in the north-eastern suburb of Scarborough. Neither of these areas is of particular interest to visitors but it does indicate the size of Toronto's Chinese community.

Elm Ave One of the city's wealthiest areas is just north-east of the corner of Yonge and Bloor Sts. Driving or walking up Park Rd north of Bloor St leads to Elm Ave where nearly every house on the north side is listed by the Historical Board as being architecturally or historically of note. All the streets branching from Elm Ave contain some impressive domains, however. East along Elm Ave, Craigleigh Gardens is a fine, old park.

Cabbagetown Cabbagetown, east of Yonge St, is both a residential district ranging from poor to very comfortable, and a commercial district. Aside from the differences between its denizens, the area is distinguished primarily by its 19th-century Victorian terrace houses. It's bounded roughly by Gerrard St East to the south, Wellesley St to the north, Parliament St to the west (which is the main business centre) and Sumach St to the east. The last couple of decades have seen considerable gentrification of the once very run-down area and there are some very attractive and interesting-looking houses, no doubt about it. The new money has brought a certain uniformity to the neighbourhood but the remaining unrenovated places add a little conflict.

The necropolis off Sumach St at Winchester St is one of the city's oldest and most interesting cemeteries. Across the street is the Riverdale Farm, a popular place for families and kids, run as a real working farm. There are two barns to wander through and a selection of waterfowl and animals some of which may permit a pat or two. Also at the site, which is free, there may be an art or craft display or some other activity.

Danforth Ave In the east end of town along Danforth Ave, roughly between Pape and Woodbine Aves, is a large Greek community.

There are many restaurants, smoky men's cafés, and also a few big, busy, colourful fruit and vegetable and flower stores which stay open into the night.

Little India Also out this way is Little India, where you'll see numerous speciality stores and women in saris. It's along Gerrard St East, one block west of Coxwell Ave.

St Clair Ave West Italians, in number, are found in many parts of the city but if there is one centre of the community it's probably on St Clair Ave West, east and west of the Dufferin St intersection. Here you'll find Italian movies, clothing stores, espresso cafés and pool halls for the young men. The area went nuts when Italy won the World Cup Soccer Championship in 1982. I've heard that the crowd that gathered was the largest ever recorded in Toronto. Another significant Italian area is on College St between Manning and Ossington Sts.

Nearby is a Portuguese neighbourhood based along Dundas St West between Ossington and Dufferin Sts.

Yorkville
Once Toronto's small version of Greenwich Village or Haight-Ashbury, this old counter-cultural bastion has become the city's trendy boutique area. Along the narrow, busy streets are many art galleries, cafés, restaurants, nightspots and expensive shops. The whole area has been renovated and in summer can be pleasant with its outdoor cafés and people-watching. It's worth a stroll but the pretension and snobbery can grate. I mean, a boutique that sells only men's underwear?

Still, there are some intriguing shops. The galleries present a range of work, several offer Inuit work for viewing or purchasing (for very big dollars). The Inuit Gallery on Prince Arthur St specialises in Inuit art. The Bellair Café has long maintained its position as the place to go but is not too costly for either a drink or a coffee.

The district is very central, just above Bloor St between Yonge St and Avenue Rd. It's centred around Cumberland Ave, York-ville Ave and Hazelton Lane. The shops of the enclosed Hazelton Lane are some of the most expensive and exclusive in the country.

Markham Village
As you approach the corner of Bloor and Markham Sts (one block west of Bathurst St) you'll see Toronto's most colourful, gaudy store, the zany Honest Ed's. Giant signs say things like 'Don't just stand there, buy something'. Hardly subtle but you won't believe the queues outside the door before opening time. Most patrons are from the nearby Italian and Portuguese districts. There are some good buys – cheap running shoes, T-shirts and various household necessities. With the money Eddie has made, he has established quite a reputation and become a major patron of the arts. Markham St, south from Bloor St with its galleries, boutiques and bookshops, is mostly his doing.

There are some interesting little specialised import shops to browse in. The Mirvish bookshop has good sales on Sunday. Bloor St around this area is fun to stroll along and has numerous restaurants and bars, patronised mostly by a mix of students and immigrants.

Harbourfront
Harbourfront is a strip of lakefront land running from the foot of Bay St westward to roughly Bathurst St. Until the past few years, redevelopment had usurped old warehouses and factories and converted them to good, park-style places with community-oriented exhibitions, displays, artists' workshops, craft shows and concerts. Since then, it's now generally acknowledged, construction has been let run amok and too much of the waterfront has been blighted by ugly condos. My blood boils to think of what might have been.

For visitors the centre of activity remains the attractive York Quay at 235 Queen's Quay, where there is an information office. Something goes on nearly every night: it might be a dance or a concert or who knows what. There are a couple of nearby restaurants and a place or two for a drink. Some presentations are free. They may be held outdoors or inside in the various theatres and galleries.

Just to the east is the impressive-looking Queen's Quay terminal with the green glass top. It's a refurbished 1927-warehouse now containing some interesting speciality and gift shops, restaurants and, up above, offices and apartments.

Contemporary art is displayed in the Power Plant, an old power station, near Queen's Quay and admission is free.

On weekends the area is popular for a walk along the pier or a browse in the antique and junk market. Try the French fries from one of the many chip wagons. The Canoe School rents canoes which can be used for an enjoyable paddle out to the harbour or by the shore either east or west. Various boats offer trips out on the water.

To get to Harbourfront, first get to Union Station, the railway station on Front St, a few blocks north of the lake. The subway will take you this far south. From here either walk south on Yonge St or take the LRT streetcar which goes south, running along the harbourfront area on Queen's Quay to Spadina Ave and then returns the same way. Service is continuous through the day and evening. Parking in the area can be a headache and/or costly so seriously consider public transit.

Toronto Islands

From the foot of Bay St near the Harbour Castle Hotel, you can take a 10-minute ferry ride out to the three Toronto Islands: Ward, Centre and Hanlan's Point. Once mainly residential, the islands are largely park now, and very pleasant. Centre Island has the most facilities, many summer events and the most people. Boats can be rented and there is a small animal farm and an amusement area for kids. Beaches line the southern and western shores.

Hanlan's, to the west, is the best beach. You may see some nude sun-bathing at Hanlan's southern end – it's popular with homosexuals – but it is illegal, even though

the law is only sporadically enforced. Inland from the beach are picnic tables and some barbecue pits. Towards the city on Hanlan's Point is a small private-craft airport.

Ward Island, the one on the east side, still has quite a few houses that are lived in all year. There is a small restaurant here for snacks and light lunches out on the lawn.

Ferries run frequently especially in summer and cost just $2.25 return, less for children and seniors. A ferry ride is as good as a harbour tour, with views of the city. You can walk around the islands in under two hours. The cool breezes are great on a hot, sticky day, and it's pretty quiet during the week. Cycling along the islands' boardwalk on the southern shores is nice. You can take bicycles on some of the ferries or rent them on Centre Island.

Ontario Place

This is a 40-hectare recreation complex (☎ 965-7711) built on three artificial islands offshore from the CNE grounds, 955 Lake Shore Blvd West. The futuristic-style buildings and parkland contain about a dozen restaurants, beer gardens, an outdoor concert stage called the Forum and a Cinesphere for 70-mm films with a six-storey-high curved screen. Check what film is showing; the effects can be amazing. There is also a large, well-stocked, supervised playground with wading pool and slide for kids where you can just let them go nuts.

In summer there are concerts every night, with everything from ballet to rock. Even on a hot day bring a sweater; it gets cold at night down by the water. At the western end is another stage with a waterfall as a curtain where amateurs or lesser names perform concerts, shows, etc. Also here is the new 700-metre-long flume water slide with simulated rapids and tunnels. A ticket is $2.50. A new attraction is the Baseball Hall of Fame & Museum.

The park is open from mid-May to October, from 10 am to 1 am, and entry is free. If there is a concert you really want to see or, if the act is a big name, arrive early or even better, very early with a picnic dinner.

The price of the concerts varies from $4 to $12. The cinesphere prices are from $3 to $4. If you are driving, parking is another $5. Take a subway or streetcar to Bathurst St and then the streetcar south down Bathurst St to the CNE exhibition grounds. There may also be a new shuttle bus running from downtown to the site, but you'll have to inquire.

Moored off one of the islands is the *Haida*, a destroyer, open to visitors.

High Park

The city's biggest park is another people-place used for picnics, walking, cycling and jogging. There is a small children's zoo, a lake where people fish and a pool for swimming which is free. Some parts of the park are well-maintained garden; others are left as natural woods. No cars are allowed on summer weekends.

Also in the park is Colbourne Lodge, built by one of Toronto's first architects and now run as an historical site with costumed workers. It's open daily. Not far from the swimming pool on the main road through the park is a restaurant which serves a vast selection of quite good homemade meals at low prices. The park is off Bloor St West at Parkside Drive and runs south down to Lake Shore Blvd, west of the CNE. The subway stop is either Dundas West or High Park.

Tommy Thompson Park & the Port

Formerly called and often still known as the Leslie St Spit, this artificial landfill site extends out into the lake and has become an unexpected, phenomenal wildlife success. It was designed to improve and develop shipping facilities but within a few years became the second largest ring-billed seagull nesting place in the world. Terns and other bird species nest here too, and you may spot many more types which drop by.

The spit is now a sanctuary for ducks, geese, swans and sandpipers as well as plantlife. Nearly 300 kinds of plants, some found nowhere else in Toronto, have also taken root here. Even mammals such as foxes, rabbits and mink are arriving – from where?

The area, a narrow five-km-long strip, is open to the public on weekends and holidays only. It's still under construction and arguments over development continue. Marinas are being built on portions of it. During the week, heavy trucks continue the dumping of excavation waste. The park is south of the corner of Queen St East and Leslie St, actually on the corner of Unwin Ave and Leslie St.

In summer, from June to Labour Day, there may be a shuttle bus that runs the length of the spit. And maybe a bus from the corner of Leslie and Queen Sts down to the beginning of the spit. If it is important for you to know, call the Metro Toronto Conservation Authority on weekdays. At the far end (named Vicki Keith Point after a local long-distance swimmer) out by the eastern edges of the Toronto Islands, there is a lighthouse and a bathroom (toilet block). The park closes at 6 pm. No vehicles are permitted but many people use bicycles as the Martin Goodman Recreational Trail runs by in both directions. At the gate there is a map, a bird checklist and that's it.

At the foot of industrial Cherry St, connected to Leslie St by Unwin St is a sandy beach popular with windsurfers. There's a snack bar and some walking paths along the shoreline.

The Port of Toronto is along Cherry St further north towards Lake Shore Blvd. Freighters can be seen moored along the docks but you can't get very close and there is no public access or viewing station. Off Cherry St, there is a small park at the end of Poulson St from where there is a very fine view of the harbour, the islands and the city skyline.

The Beaches & The Bluffs

The Beaches is a rather wealthy, mainly professional neighbourhood along Queen St East at Woodbine Ave down by the lakeshore. For non-local residents, The Beaches means the beach itself and the parkland along the lake – very popular in summer even if the water has been condemned and is off-limits. The sandy beaches are good for sun bathing and picnicking and a long board-walk edges along the sand.

You can rent sailboards, with or without lessons. Beach Park is the centre of things, although there are other adjacent parks. At the west end, in Woodbine Park, there is a public swimming pool.

About five km further east are the Scar-borough Bluffs, 90-metre-high limestone cliffs set in parkland. Erosion has created some odd shapes and revealed layers of sed-iment indicating five different glacial periods. There are paths here with views. Below, in the lake itself, landfill has been used to form parkland and boat-mooring space. Access to the bluffs is from several points but one main way of getting there is from Brimley Rd, which runs south from Kingston Rd. Look for Cathedral Bluffs Park.

Not far (by vehicle) east of the park is the Guild Inn with its large lakefront grounds. From behind the inn there are good views along the shoreline to some bluffs. In the garden is a collection of statues and sculp-tures as well as many columns and gargoyles that were taken from old buildings being demolished.

There is one nearly complete façade that looks like something from the Parthenon. Tea is served on the patio in the afternoon. The Guild Inn (which does rent rooms) is on Guildwood Parkway, south from Kingston Rd at Livingstone Rd.

Other Parks

Allan Gardens is an often-mentioned, much-publicised park that's rather over-rated. Most of the park is nothing more than a city block of grass interspersed with a few trees and benches. The highlight, the large old round-domed greenhouse with its three arms is a worthwhile site, however, particularly in winter or any day the weather is depressing. It's open daily from 10 am to 5 pm and is free. Plants include many tropical specimens among them huge palm and flowering trees from around the world. One room is devoted to cactuses. The greenhouses are at the western edge of the park which is a few

blocks east of Yonge St. It's bounded by Carlton, Jarvis and Gerrard Sts. After dark the entire place is unsavoury enough for me not to recommend visiting or even taking a shortcut through it.

Toronto does have some very fine largely natural parks in numerous ravines formed by rivers and streams running down to the lake. Start in Edwards Gardens, on the corner of Lawrence Ave West and Leslie St. It's a big, cultivated park with flower gardens, a pond and picnic sites. You can take a ravine walk from the gardens via Wilket Creek Park. The Science Centre backs onto the park here. Along Wilket Creek you can walk for hours all the way down to Victoria Park Ave, just north of Danforth Ave. Much of the way is through woodland.

From the corner of Yonge St and St Clair Ave, walk east to the bridge and the sign for the nature trail. This leads down into the Don River Valley, another good walk.

Markets

Kensington Market is the city's prime one; it's a colourful and lively multi-ethnic old-style market squeezed along Baldwin St and Augusta Ave off Spadina Ave, just south of College St and east of Bathurst St. It's open every day but is wild on Saturday morning. The cheese shops are good, and there's all manner of fresh fruit and vegetables. You can bargain over prices. This was the heart of the city's Jewish area, but as you'll see, people from many countries have changed that. There are a few small restaurants in the area too. On Saturday don't even think of driving down here.

The St Lawrence Market is at 92 Front St East at Jarvis St in what was Toronto's first City Hall, dating from 1844. Here nearly everyone is British and the atmosphere is closer to sedate – there are even classical musicians playing – but it is also very lively on Saturday. Although it's best on Saturday, it is open every day but Monday. The range and quality of produce – from fish to more rice varieties than you knew existed – is excellent.

On Sunday there is an antique and flea

market here. Just north of this building is St Lawrence Hall, topped with its clock tower. It is one of the city's finest old buildings; used as a public meeting hall in the last century, it is now – among other things – used by the National Ballet for rehearsals.

The Market Gallery on the 2nd floor of the market building is the city's exhibition hall and displays good, rotating shows (paintings, photographs, documents, artefacts) on Toronto's history. It's free but is closed Monday, Tuesday and holidays.

Historic Sites

There isn't a lot for history buffs as the city is so new, but the few small sites are well presented and the tourist office has a guide to the historic homes and sites. Many of these remaining old buildings stand where the old town of York was situated – in the southern portion of the city. Descriptions of some of the best sites follow.

Mackenzie House Owned by William Lyon Mackenzie, the city's first mayor and leader of a failed rebellion against the government, this mid-Victorian home is furnished with antiques dating from the 1800s. In the basement is an old print-shop, where it's said the machines can be heard mysteriously working some nights. The house is at 82 Bond St, a couple of blocks east of Yonge St. Afternoon tea is served.

Churches On the corner of King and Church Sts, the town's first church was built in 1807. St James's Cathedral now stands here and is the city's tallest church. Nearby on the corner of Queen and Parliament Sts, the first Catholic church was constructed in 1822. On this site a second St Paul's Anglican Church now stands, one of Toronto's most impressive Renaissance-style buildings.

Spadina House This was the gracious mansion of local businessman James Austin. Built in 1866, the impressive interior contains fine furnishings and art collected over three generations. About 10 of its 35 rooms are open to the public. The family gave the house to the historical board in 1982. The address is 285 Spadina Ave, just east of Casa Loma, and it's open daily but only in the afternoon on Sunday and holidays. Admission is $3.50.

Campbell House Downtown on the corner of Queen St and University Ave, this house was once the residence of the chief justice of Upper Canada. It is a colonial-style brick mansion furnished in early 1800s fashion. The house is open daily in summer, Monday to Friday only from October to late June. There is a small admission charge.

Colbourne Lodge This place in High Park, built in 1836, is a Regency-style cottage and contains many original furnishings, including possibly the first indoor flush toilet in the province. Informative tours are offered by the costumed staff and may include baking or craft demonstrations. Admission is inexpensive and the site is quite popular.

Gibson House This Georgian-style house which belonged to a successful surveyor and politician offers a glimpse of daily life in the 1850s. Costumed workers demonstrate crafts and cooking and offer a tour around the house daily except Monday. Special activities are planned regularly through the year. On weekends it's only open in the afternoons. In the far northern part of the city, at 5172 Yonge St north of Sheppard Ave, it's not far from the Sheppard subway stop. A small admission fee is charged.

Montgomery's Inn Built in 1832 by an Irish military captain of the same name, Montgomery's Inn is a fine example of Loyalist architecture. It has been restored to the period from 1830 to 1855. Costumed staff answer questions, bake bread and demonstrate crafts. Open daily but afternoons only on weekends and holidays, it's at 4709 Dundas St West near Islington Ave, in the city's far western end. Afternoon tea is served.

Enoch Turner Schoolhouse The school (☎ 863-0010) dates from 1848. It's a restored, simple, one-room schoolhouse where, quite often during the week, classes show kids what the good old days were like. It's also open free to the public when classes or other special events are not being held. If you want to see it call ahead and check the schedule. Through the summer months there shouldn't be much problem arranging a visit. The address is 106 Trinity St which is near the corner of King and Parliament Sts.

Post Office Toronto's first post office, dating from the 1830s, is at 260 Adelaide St East. This is one of only two original city buildings still in its original location and has been designated a national historic site. The other is the Bank of Upper Canada. Letters can still be sealed with wax by costumed employees and sent from here. It's open seven days a week.

University of Toronto The principal campus of the large, prestigious university is just west of the Queen's Park Parliament Buildings off College St at University Ave. The attractive grounds feature a range of architectural styles from the University College building of 1859 to the present. Free walking tours of the campus are given on weekdays through the summer months departing from Hart House three times daily, weather permitting.

Other The northern part of the city also has a few historical attractions. Gibson House, at 5172 Yonge St, shows the 1850 farmhouse of a prosperous surveyor and politician.

Todmorden Mills Historic Site, near the location of an important 1794 sawmill and gristmill on the Don River, preserves two houses, complete with period furnishings and a brewery dating from around 1825. Also on the site is a railway station moved from nearby, now a small railway museum, and a former paper mill now used as a playhouse. The park is at 67 Pottery Rd and is open from May to December daily except Monday. A small admission fee is charged.

The large, red-brick houses found all over downtown Toronto were built around the 1920s. The taller, narrower ones often with more ornately decorative features are Victorian and mostly date from 1890 to 1900 – a few are older.

Black Creek Pioneer Village

A replica of an Ontario village a century ago, Black Creek Pioneer Village (☎ 661-6610) is the city's top historic attraction. It's about a 30-minute drive from the downtown area, on the corner of Steeles Ave and Jane St in the north-west section of town and is accessible by public transportation.

Restored buildings and workers in authentic dress give a feeling of what rural life was like in the 19th century. Crafts and skills of the times using the old tools and methods are demonstrated. One reader raved about the herb garden. You can buy the results of the cooking and baking. In one of the barns is a large toy museum and woodcarving collection. It's open daily from April to December. Usual adult admission is $6.25. Special events are offered regularly through the season.

Toronto Zoo

Opened in 1974, this huge zoo (☎ 392-5200) has quickly gained an excellent reputation and, although still expanding, is one of the country's best. There are over 4000 animals on the 283 hectares, some in natural-setting pens the size of football fields. Of course, with enclosures so large, it takes a lot of walking around. In fact, there's a small train that goes around the site, but walking is best. You need a full day to see it all.

The animals are in five areas, each covering a major world geographical zone. Each area has outdoor areas and there are simulated climates in indoor pavilions. A good idea is the black-light area that enables you to observe nocturnal animals. Through the use of lights, the animals' days have been turned upside down so we can see them at their active time. Other good exhibits include the ones which allow for underwater viewing of such animals as beavers, polar bears and seals. There's also a children's area with displays especially geared to them with some animals to touch and ponies to ride.

The zoo is on Meadowvale Rd, north of Highway 401, at the eastern edge of the city. To get there using public transit, take the subway on the Bloor St line east to Kennedy, the last stop. From there get the No 86A Scarborough bus to the zoo. It's quite a trip – about 20 minutes on the subway from the centre of town and then about 40 minutes on the bus, plus waiting time.

Admission is $8.50, less for kids. Openinghours are from 9 am to 6.30 pm daily with an extension of an hour or so during the summer months. Call for the current schedule if in doubt.

You may want to take your lunch as McDonald's has an exclusive food contract for the grounds.

Wonderland

Away from the centre of town, Wonderland (☎ 832-2205) – a sort of Canadian Disneyland – opened in May 1981. The large-scale $120-million theme park has exhibits, games, animals, shows and, of course, rides, including some killer roller coasters, one going 80 km/h. There is a huge artificial mountain with a waterfall and areas made to look like scenes from fairy tales.

Covering 150 hectares, the park can't be seen all in one day. Get a guidebook at the entrance and decide what you want to see the most. Prices vary but are not low. A one-day pass, good for all attractions and rides is $23. A ticket which includes some rides and attractions is $20 and straight admission to the grounds is $15. Children's passes cost less. Parking is another $4. Top-name entertainers appear in summer at the Kingswood Theatre but tickets for these shows are extra. Wonderland is open from approximately early June to early September, and weekends a month before and after these dates. Opening hours are from 10 am to 10 pm in peak season, 10 am to 8 pm on summer weekends.

Wonderland is on Highway 400, 10 minutes north of Highway 401. Exit at Rutherford Rd if you're travelling north, at Major

Mackenzie Drive if you're going south. There are buses from Yorkdale and York Mills subway stations.

Sunshine Beach Water Park

Open daily from June to September, this huge water park offers about half a dozen twisting water slides and a couple of steep, high straight speed slides, along with a wave pool and huge whirlpools. There are picnic grounds and food concessions. An all-day ticket is $15, less for kids. The park is 1.6 km west of Highway 427 on Finch Ave northwest of the centre of Toronto.

Museum for Textiles

Obscurely situated with no walk-in traffic at all, this excellent museum is highly recommended for anyone with the slightest interest in textiles. It's the only museum in the country to exclusively collect and display handmade textiles and tapestries from around the world – what a collection it is. There are pieces from Latin America, Africa, Europe, South-East Asia and India. The Tibetan collection is particularly fine as is the one from Indonesia. Some pieces are on permanent display, others are incorporated into in-depth temporary exhibits.

In addition to the international and historic displays there are also changing shows of contemporary fibre works, weavings, rugs and all manner of cloth art.

The museum can be found (look hard, the door is sort of tucked back from the street) at 55 Centre St running south off Dundas St West in Chinatown between Bay St and University Ave. It's behind the Toronto City Hall. It's open Tuesday to Friday from 11 am to 5 pm and from noon on weekends. Admission is $2.50.

Marine Museum of Upper Canada

In the officers' quarters of an 1841 army barracks at Exhibition Place, this museum shows the history of the city as a port. On exhibit are models, old ship relics and, in summer, there's a restored steam tugboat moored outside. Admission is $2.75, less for children. It's open Monday to Saturday from

9.30 am to 5 pm, Sunday from noon. In the basement of the museum is a restaurant.

Sports & Hockey Halls of Fame
Also at Exhibition Place are these two museums, one the National Sports Hall of Fame and the other dedicated to the passion of Canadian sports fans – hockey. The famed Stanley Cup, hockey's grand prize, is housed in the hockey museum. Both places are open daily.

Police Museum
A new police museum is being developed in the impressive new headquarters building at 40 College St. It's due to open in 1992 or 1993 and will have a collection of equipment, details of some cases and more.

Museum of the History of Medicine
Another speciality museum, this one outlines healing practices and health care from before recorded history. On display are 5000 years of torture, I mean medical, instruments. It's central at 288 Bloor St West and is free. It's open Monday to Friday all year.

Redpath Sugar Museum
Along the waterfront at 95 Queen's Quay West a free museum is part of the large sugar mill. There is a film on the production of the sweet stuff as well as exhibits of equipment. The museum is open weekdays only.

Toronto Dominion Gallery of Inuit Art
Housed on the mezzanine floor of the IBM Tower of the Toronto Dominion Centre, on the corner of King and Bay Sts, this gallery (☎ 869-2604) displays a top-rate collection of far northern art mainly dating from WW II to the present. It consists primarily of sculpture in stone and bone which is the foremost form of Inuit art.

The gallery is free and open daily but hours seem to vary on weekends so calling ahead is recommended. Free tours are given once a day on Tuesday and Thursday but can be arranged for any day by calling and asking. For this service, there's a different phone number (☎ 982-8473).

Toronto Stock Exchange
The city's exchange is Canada's largest and one of the most modern anywhere. Stock worth $100 million is bought and sold each day so it's a fairly hectic place. There is a visitors' centre and tours are given from Monday to Friday. The stock exchange is in the Exchange Tower, Canadian Place, on the corners of King or Front and Bay Sts, right in the centre of the city's financial district.

Ecology House
Ecology House (☎ 967-0577) offers a free tour on Sunday at 2 pm. Otherwise, wander around by yourself reading the explanations that show how houses can be made more energy conscious and conservation-efficient. You can pick up some good ideas, especially if you want to buy or build a house. The Ecology House is at 12 Madison Ave on the corner of Bloor St West and is open Wednesday to Sunday, from noon to 5 pm. Admission is free.

Activities
Cycling For cyclists, the Martin Goodman Trail is a bicycle route along the waterfront which stretches from The Beaches in the east end, past Harbourfront and the downtown area, to the Humber River in the west end. From here, it connects with paths in parkland running along the Humber northwards. This section is a really fine ride and you can go as far as Eglinton, at least – that's quite a few km. Visit the tourist office for a free pamphlet detailing sights along the path.

The Toronto Bicycling Network runs short, medium and long weekend trips (some overnight) throughout the summer.

Other Free swimming in public pools can be found in High Park, the Sunnyside Natatorium south of the park at the lake off Lake Shore Drive, and in Woodbine Park at The Beaches in east-end Toronto at the foot of Woodbine Ave.

Sandy beaches, a boardwalk and, on any hot summer day especially on weekends, lots of people can also be found around The Beaches. Kew Beach is the most popular section and the boardwalk goes through here. The same thing on a smaller, more low-key scale can be enjoyed at Sunnyside Beach in the west end, south of High Park. Both are fun, relaxed and relaxing with everybody in bathing suits but you can't go in the water. It's too polluted.

There is windsurfing at The Beaches too, rentals are available in the Ashbridges Bay area at the western end of the beach.

In winter, three good free places to skate are at City Hall and Harbourfront, both with artificial ice; and, if it's been quite cold, large Grenadier Pond in High Park. Skates can be rented at the City Hall rink.

For out-of-town outdoor activities two of cities best known camping stores, Trail Head at 40 Wellington St East and Mountain Equipment Co-op nearby at 35 Front St East, have information on adventure trips such as white-water canoeing and wilderness hiking.

There are several places to go hot-air ballooning near Toronto, but it's big bucks at about $135 an hour or more. One place to try is the Balloonery at the Millcroft Inn, just outside Acton near Caledonia. Flights go on summer weekends and champagne is included in the price.

For indoor stimulation the excellent Toronto Public Library is on Yonge St about a block north of Bloor St.

Organised Tours The reliable Gray Line (☎ 393-7911) runs a basic two-hour inner-city tour for $15. Various other more specialised tours lasting from 2½ hours and up are offered, with stops at sites included. Two others are 'Toronto by Night' and one to Niagara Falls. They pick up passengers at downtown hotels and the office is at 180 Dundas St West by the main bus terminal at 610 Bay St.

A unique tour takes visitors around the inner city on a restored 1920s trolley car. The very popular 90-minute tour departs four times daily from the west side of the Sheraton Centre on York St south of Queen St. The trip costs $16, less for children and tickets should be obtained in advance. They can be purchased at Ontario Travel desks which are found in the larger downtown hotels, including the Sheraton or from Gray Line. There has been talk of discontinuing the tours due to the costs of maintaining the old clangers. But they've been saying that for years.

Another company, Gray Coach, offers numerous one-day trips around Toronto ranging from $30 to $45. Examples are to Elora and to Georgian Bay. You'll find them in the bus station.

At the tourist office pick up a free copy of *A Walking Tour of Old Toronto* for a self-guided tour starting at Union Station. It covers about four blocks and 25 buildings of the early city's downtown area. A similar map/information sheet is available for the Canadian National Exhibition (CNE) grounds in west Toronto. Twenty historic buildings and monuments are highlighted.

The University of Toronto (☎ 978-5000) runs free guided tours of the campus through the summer, three times daily. This is the country's largest university and the campus has some fine buildings.

Several companies run boat tours in and around the harbour and the islands. Most depart from Harbourfront around Queen's Quay, York Quay or John Quay. The *Island Queen* has a one-hour cruise for $10.

C O Charter & Tours (☎ 599-5666) also runs harbour tours around the islands using four different boats. Their hour-long trip with a narration about history and other facts is the same price.

Almost hourly departures take place from May to October from 145 Queen's Quay West, at the foot of York St. Tickets can be bought at the dock at Queen's Quay.

A second ship does much the same but also provides night cruises for views of the lit skyline. There are also more costly lunch, dinner and moonlight dance cruises aboard a different ship which moors further west at the western side of Maple Leaf Quay. Lastly, there are cruises aboard a three-masted schooner.

Some privately owned sailing ships and schooners offer trips which are of varying duration as far as Niagara-on-the-Lake. Some boats are geared for fishing. Look around the dock area; you'll see some signs advertising these.

The island ferry has good views of the city and it is cheap. If you're visiting the islands, remember to check the time of the last return trip. In summer the ferries run about every half an hour but not very late at night.

Festivals
Canadian National Exhibition (CNE) The
CNE claims to be the oldest (about 100 years old), and the largest annual exhibition in the world. It includes agricultural and technical exhibits, concerts, displays, crafts, parades, a good air show, horse show, and all manner of games and rides and fireworks. The exhibition is held during the last two weeks of August at Exhibition Place, which is by the CNE football stadium on Lake Shore Blvd West, at the lake.

Mariposa Begun in the early 1960s, Mariposa is a festival of mainly folk but also bluegrass and American Indian music. Having grown from just a three-day event, the festival now schedules concerts throughout the year at various venues around town. The main annual event is often held in Molson Park just out of Barrie, north of Toronto. At last word the festival was going to be moved back into Toronto, perhaps to the original site on the Toronto Islands. Anywhere in town would certainly be beneficial for visitors. The three-day affair is usually held in July. Workshops, jam sessions and ethnic folk dancing are featured as well. For information on all the events call ☎ 769-3655 or the tourist office.

Caribana An ever growing annual West Indian Festival, Caribana hit its 25th year in 1991. It takes place around the beginning of August and is a weekend of reggae, steel drum, and calypso music and dance held on Centre Island.

The main attraction, however, is the very lengthy and colourful parade featuring fantastic and outrageous costumes a la carnival in Rio. This parade can have perhaps 6000 people in it and can take five hours or longer

to pass by! Other events and concerts are spread over the two weeks leading up to the island weekend.

Caravan This is a nine-day event of cultural exchange where ethnic groups offer music, dance and food native to their homelands. There are about 50 different ethnic pavilions set up around the city. A passport entitles you to go into all the pavilions.

The event takes place during the last days of June. A passport costs about $12 and buses travel between the pavilions. Ask the tourist office for a complete list of events and things to see and do. The Japanese pavilion is always rated highly and has taken first prize in recent years.

International Picnic At the beginning of June each year to welcome summer, the huge International Picnic is held on Centre Island. Admission is free and there's music, dancing, contests and lots of food. The picnic is to welcome the summer.

Queen's Plate The year's major horse race and one of North America's oldest (held since 1859), the Queen's Plate is held at the Woodbine Track on the last Saturday in June. Get lucky and your trip will be paid for.

Toronto Star Great Salmon Hunt This annual fishing Derby attracts anglers to Lake Ontario from far and wide, hoping to catch some of the hundreds of thousands of dollars in prizes for landing the big one.

Film Festival The annual film Festival of Festivals is now a prestigious and major international cinematic event. Usually held in September, it lasts about a week and a half and features films of all lengths and styles, includes gala events and well-known stars.

You can get more information from the tourist office. All the papers have special guides and reviews as well. You can obtain tickets for individual screenings or buy expensive, all-inclusive packages.

Jazz Festival The annual Molson Jazz Festival is held at Harbourfront in July or August. It has three days and evenings of generally traditional, swing and Dixieland jazz with local and US players and is free.

International Festival of Authors Held in the fall at Harbourfront this very engaging event presents well-known fiction writers from around the world. Readings are also held through the year on a weekly basis and generally feature less prominent authors.

Places to Stay

Camping There are several camping/trailer grounds within 40 km of the city. The tourist office has a complete list.

Two of the closest are: *Clairville Conservation Area* (☎ 678-1233), north up Indian Line Rd in Downsview, beside the airport. It's near Steeles Ave. This is probably the best one for tenters.

The second is *Glen Rouge Park* (☎ 947-8092), on Kingston Rd (Highway 2) at Altona Rd, near Sheppard Ave East. It's at the border of Scarborough – part of Metropolitan Toronto – and the town of Pickering at the eastern edge of the city and is on the lakefront. There are about 120 sites.

Moodies (☎ 683-1995) is at 248 Kingston Rd, west of Pickering. It's east of town. There are 40 sites costing from $10.

KOA is on RR1 Bradford on the corner of Highway 400 and Highway 88. It costs a little more than others at $15 to $18.

Hostels Toronto has a year-round *CHA Youth Hostel* (☎ 368-0207) right downtown. It opened in a three-storey renovated brick building during 1982 and has expanded into several nearby places. The location, three blocks east of the Eaton Centre on Yonge St, is excellent and central. The address is 223 Church St, just south of Dundas St East; the subway stop is Dundas.

The hostel is open all year and there are about 200 beds. Facilities include a kitchen in the main building and a laundry. Also good are the hours: the hostel is open from 7 am to 2 am every day. It may seem a little expensive at $15 for members and $20 for nonmembers, but this is in the heart of one of the priciest cities on the continent. Semi-private rooms for four are also available at a slightly higher cost. If you don't have a sleeping sheet one will be supplied. During July and August the hostel does get full and reservations are a good idea.

The *Ontario Hostelling Association* (☎ 368-1848) where memberships may be purchased has an office a few doors down. Beside that is a very casual, cheap little café with walls covered in maps. This is the *Armchair Traveller* where you can get a meal, a coffee or a beer. During warm weather there is a pleasant outdoor patio.

The *YWCA* (☎ 923-8454), for women only, is central at 80 Woodlawn Ave near Yonge St. There's a cheap cafeteria and pool. The price for a single room is $38, less if you share a double. There is a dormitory where a bed goes for $17, but either way a continental breakfast is included. In the dorms there is a maximum stay of seven nights. The YMCA in town doesn't rent rooms.

Colleges

The *University of Toronto* (☎ 978-8735) rents rooms in various college residences. The campus is by the corner of University Ave and College St. Rooms are available from the middle of May until late August. Singles/doubles are $32/40, and there are very good weekly rates. Rooms are also available at another campus which is smaller and more suburban, and there are still more beds in other downtown residences such as Trinity College.

York University (☎ 667-3098) has a similar deal. They rent rooms from May to the end of August. They have good recreational facilities, but the trouble with accommodation here is that it's a long way from the downtown area, at the northern boundary of the city. The address is 4700 Keele St near Steeles Ave. Reservations are required; singles/doubles are $30/42 with breakfast included.

Neil Wycik College Hotel (☎ 977-2320), an apartment-style student residence and hotel, is at 96 Gerrard St East, right downtown by Ryerson Polytechnical Institute. During the summer the residence's rooms are rented out, but long-term only, for four months. The hotel rooms, though, are available by the day at the good-value rate of singles/doubles $39/44. The location is excellent. There is a student-run cafeteria for breakfasts.

Tartu College (☎ 925-4747), at 310 Bloor St West, not far from Yonge St, rents rooms in the summer. A single is $150 (per week) and must be rented at least by the week.

Tourist Homes There aren't a lot of commercial guesthouses in town but the ones that do exist are generally very central, pretty well established, fairly priced and good. For the most part, unlike the hotels, the guesthouses charge a constant price throughout the year. *Karabanow Guesthouse* (☎ 923-4004) has a good location at 9 Spadina Ave, just north of Bloor St West. The tariff includes parking, daily cleaning and cable TV. Singles are $35 and up, and doubles range from $45 to $55, less with a Youth Hostel card. Except during peak summer months, a weekly rate saves the cost of a night or two.

Another recommended guesthouse is the *Beverley Place* (☎ 977-0077), at 235 Beverley St, a small north-south street running between Queen and College Sts between University and Spadina Aves. The guesthouse is excellently situated near the corner of College St, very near the university. Chinatown, Queen St West and even the CN Tower are all within walking distance. The house is a well-restored three-storey Victorian place dating from 1877 with lots of original features and wonderfully high ceilings. The entire place, rooms included, is furnished and decorated with interesting antiques and collectables.

One of the most appealing attributes is the small, comfortable courtyard with a huge tree off the kitchen. A full breakfast is included in the room prices, and guests are encouraged to enjoy eating it on the patio.

The prices are quite reasonable and vary depending on the room. Singles/doubles

begin at $40/50. The 'Queen Room' with an impressive bed costs more as does the 3rd-floor self-contained apartment with its own balcony and city view.

The busy season lasts from June to November and during this period reservations of a week or more if possible are not a bad idea. This would be true of all the places listed in this section.

The owner, Bill Ricciuto, also runs another similar house across the street. Guests staying here come over to No 235 for breakfast.

Very convenient, just north of College St at 322 Palmerston Blvd, a quiet tree-lined avenue, is the *Burkin Guesthouse* (☎ 920-7842). It's a well-kept large older house with eight guest rooms and a pleasant 2nd-storey balcony. Prices are a little higher than at the others, from $45 to $55 for singles and $60 to $65 for doubles depending on the size of the room. and a continental breakfast is included. Smoking is not permitted.

On King St West at No 1233 is the simpler *Candy Haven Tourist Home* (☎ 532-0651). It's right on the King St streetcar line; look for the bright paint job and sign. It's central and there are sinks in the rooms. Singles/doubles are $40/45.

Still further west, at 1546 King St near Roncesvalles Ave, is the *Grayona Tourist Home* (☎ 535-5443). It's a renovated old house run by Marie Taylor, a friendly, enthusiastic Australian. Singles range from $35 to $45 and doubles are from $45 to $55. Every room but the small single has a fridge and a TV.

Marginally more expensive rooms which are good for families (there is even a cot) have cooking facilities. It's about seven km from the centre of town and, although some of the European visitors walk, there is a streetcar along King St which stops practically at the door. There are two other guesthouses within a few doors to the west towards Roncesvalles Ave.

In the east end, steps from the Greenwood subway stop and just around the corner from the Greek restaurant district, is the *Allenby* (☎ 461-7095) at 223 Strathmore Blvd. The top floors of this three-storey house contain very comfortable guest rooms and there is a basic kitchen with a microwave for visitors to share. It's only open through the summer, from 1 May to 30 October. The room rates vary, mainly depending on size, with singles from $35 to $50 and doubles from $40 to $60.

B&Bs There are now several B&B associations in town which check, list and book rooms in the participating homes. Indicate where you'd like to be and any other preferences, and attempts will be made to find a particularly agreeable host. Prices are fairly standardised at singles/doubles $45/55 with some variation, mostly upward. Places in suburban areas rather than downtown cost $5 or so less.

There is generally no need to go to the agency, a telephone call should get things organised. This has become an increasingly popular form of accommodation and most participating homes seem to be quite busy, particularly in summer although frequently guests are not vacationing but are on courses or maybe a week's business trip.

Metropolitan B&B Registry (☎ 964-2566), is the largest outfit with members in and out of town. The office is at 615 Mount Pleasant Rd, Suite 269, Toronto M4S 3C5. They seem to have the lowest rates for singles with rooms at $40. Doubles are $55. Foreign languages are spoken at some places and, as is the norm generally, smokers will be told to butt out their cigarettes.

Toronto B&B (☎ 961-3676), at 253 College St, Toronto M5T 1R3 has about 30 members with singles averaging $45, and doubles $55.

Thirdly, there is the B&B Association of Downtown Toronto Guesthouses (☎ 977-6841) at 153 Huron St or PO Box 190, Station B, Toronto, M5T 2W1. Their rooms are all downtown, mainly in renovated Victorian houses, and cost from $40 to $60 for singles and from $50 to $75 for doubles. The association's founder, Susan Oppenheim, rents rooms in her own house and

serves breakfast in a kitchen that you won't forget.

Each of these associations produces a booklet listing the participating hosts and the type of places and features they offer. Send a stamped self-addressed envelope to receive one of the listing guides.

A new agency is B&B Accommodators: contact them at the Allenby Guesthouse (☎ 461-7095).

Hotels – bottom end & middle Toronto has an abundance of large new, modern hotels and more are being added continually. There are many downtown places, plenty around the city's edges and a good number out around the airport. Of course, they tend to be rather pricey and sterile to boot. The city, unfortunately, lacks smaller older hotels with character. There are a few exceptions, but most of these places fall into the middle-price ranges rather than being low-budget. Many hotels offer weekend packages at lower than usual rates and practically all have higher rates during summer.

The inner city still does have some older, cheaper hotels and a good number of these are found in the Church, Jarvis and Sherbourne Sts area east of Yonge St. Sections of this part of town can be a little rough and some hotels' rooms are used for more than sleeping. Single women may not like walking in the area alone at night and may well be asked their price. This is particularly the case around Church and Jarvis Sts near Isabella St and again down around Dundas St. The southern section of Jarvis St, say between Carlton and Queen Sts, and the streets nearby, should probably be avoided late at night.

Despite these considerations this is not a battle zone and there are perfectly safe places to stay. Best in the low-budget category and good value is the *Selby* (☎ 921-3142) at 592 Sherbourne St north of Wellesley St. The turreted Victorian mansion, dating from 1882, and designated as a heritage site, has an interesting history. At one time it was a girls' school. Later Ernest Hemingway lived here when he worked for the *Toronto Star* in his younger days, before heading to Paris.

Much of the hotel has recently been upgraded. Rooms cost from $50 to $80 for either singles or doubles depending on size, upgrades, features and whether there is an ensuite bathroom. This makes the less expensive rooms quite a bargain for two people sharing. There is a slight discount through the slower winter months and a weekly rate is always in effect. A continental breakfast is included in the price. Reservations are recommended from May to October. A wide variety of people use the hotel while the separate in-house bar and grill are popular with men from the local gay community.

Further south the *St Leonard* (☎ 924-4902) at 418 Sherbourne St is worn, perhaps a little less judicious in screening guests, but clean and friendly. They have 22 simple rooms, some with private bath and TV. Prices start at $42 for singles and rise to $50 for a room with all the extras. Doubles range from $49 to $59.

The *Whitehouse Hotel* (☎ 362-7491) at 76 Church St is a narrow, unobtrusive place that takes up nine floors with its 35 rooms. It has been popular with out-of-towners, mostly Americans, but in the past few years maintenance and service has slipped quite a bit. A single is $65; the same room with one double bed is $75 for two people in high season. Ask to see the room before checking in. Nearly everything downtown is within walking distance.

For connoisseurs of classic dives, there's the *Gladstone* at 1214 Queen St West. It's a beautiful old building long past its day (although recently sandblasted) with plenty of 'rubbies' throwing 'em back in the bar downstairs. Rates are cheap, under $30.

The middle-range *Strathcona* (☎ 363-3321) is also an older place that has been overhauled and upgraded and now has all the usual amenities and yet is, for the downtown area, moderately priced at $75 for singles up to $90 for the top doubles.

The Strathcona is in an excellent location at 60 York St, very near the railway station.

There's a dining room, a coffee shop and a bar.

One of the best of the small, old downtown hotels is the *Victoria* (☎ 363-1666) at 56 Yonge St, near its southern end. The hotel has changed ownership and has been completely refurbished. Some of the features (like the fine lobby) remain and the place has a lot of history, but it's no longer the real bargain it was. Prices are now between $80 and $100. Also in the more European mode is the *Brownstone Hotel* (☎ 924-7381) at 15 Charles St which is slightly more expensive.

The more standard high-rise *Bond Place* (☎ 362-6061) is busy with vacationers – there are often tour buses out the front. It has a great location near the Eaton Centre at 65 Dundas St East. Prices range from $75 to $100 for singles and doubles.

More like a motel but perfectly good and far cheaper is the *Executive Inn* (☎ 362-7441) at 621 King St West. The 75 rooms are priced from $50 to $70. It's central and the streetcar goes right by.

Hotels – top end The costliest rooms in town are found at the *Four Seasons* (☎ 964-0411) in Yorkville at 21 Avenue Rd where prices are around $225 a night and up. Also very well appointed with a good reputation and a fine lobby area, is the *Hilton International* (☎ 869-3456), right in the centre at 145 Richmond St West. Singles/doubles cost from $185/200.

The *Harbour Castle Westin* (☎ 869-1600) has a fine location right at the edge of the lake opposite the Toronto Islands. The address is 1 Harbour Square, very near the bottom of Yonge St. They offer a revolving restaurant and bar with good views over the city and lake. Prices start at about $20, less than at the Hilton. Others in this category are the comfortable *King Edward* and the *Skydome Hotel* at the downtown stadium.

Lastly the venerable *Royal York* (☎ 368-2511), at 100 Front St opposite the railway station, deserves mention. Among the top-class hotels it's the oldest and has served people from rock stars to royalty. There are several bars and places to get a bite to eat on the premises. You can grab a single here from just under $150.

Apartment Hotels Numerous fully furnished rooms with kitchen facilities have sprung up in apartment buildings, private homes and hotels in recent years. Although they can provide reasonable value, they are mosty in the luxury category with all mod cons and are geared to the corporate client and business executive. Many have a minimum stay which ranges from three days, to a week to a month.

The *Andrews Apartments* (☎ 267-1118) require a three-week stay in their private home units with from one to five bedrooms. They also have some housekeeping motel units on their premises at 2245 Kingston Rd between Midland Ave and Danforth Ave. One of these costs about $375 a week.

Executive Travel Suites (☎ 273-9641) has four such properties in the downtown area with prices starting at about $90 a day with a three-day minimum. Each unit has a separate bedroom and living room and each building offers one or more extras, such as a pool, balconies, roof deck or restaurant. A lot of contract signing is required including for damage liability. Make sure the contents are in good shape before moving in. Complaints have been received concerning some of the stipulations, the quality of the furnishings and especially the service. Despite this, Executive has been around for quite a few years. It is primarily geared to the business traveller and perhaps those visiting for pleasure are not as well cared for.

Another place is the *Cromwell* at 55 Isabella St but the minimum rental here is for one month.

The tourist office will know of other apartments for short-term rent.

Motels For such a large city, Toronto is rather short on motels and, consequently, in summer they are often full. There are two main districts for motels in the city and others scattered throughout and around the perimeter.

On the west side of town, a strip of motels (now threatened with redevelopment) can be found along the lake on Lake Shore Blvd West, formerly Highway 2. Many are between the Humber River and Park Lawn Ave, just west of High Park. The area has become widely known for its prostitution and the problems that it can bring. Several of the motels are now short-time places but many perfectly legitimate motels are suffering from a lack of business unnecessarily.

This district isn't too far from the downtown area, about 12 km from Yonge St, and the streetcar lines run the whole way. To get there, take the Queen St or King St streetcar from downtown to Roncesvalles Ave, and continue on the Queen St streetcar to the Humber River. Switch (for no charge) to the Humber streetcar, which goes along the lakeshore. The motels edge right along the shoreline and there are several parks nearby on the waterfront for cool breezes in summer and good views of the city and islands. About a dozen motels run more or less side by side. The better ones are often full in summer.

The one furthest west with the yellow sign, the *Beach Motel* at 2183 Lake Shore Blvd West (☎ 259-3296) is good with 40 rooms from $55 and it's right beside the entrance to a park.

A little cheaper is the *Silver Moon* (☎ 252-5051) at 2157 Lake Shore Blvd with rooms from $40 and up to $60.

The *Hillcrest* (☎ 255-7711), a little closer to town at 2143 Lake Shore Blvd, is also good at about the same prices.

Another one to check is the *North American* (☎ 255-1127). It's the bigger greenish two-storey place at 2147 Lake Shore Blvd West.

The large modern, well-maintained *Seahorse* (☎ 255-4433), probably the most prosperous of the lot, features rooms for the amorous with waterbeds, lots of mirrors, etc. And there is a swimming pool. Of course, it is more expensive but some of the simpler rooms aren't too badly priced.

Back closer to town, the *Inn on the Lake* (☎ 766-4392) at 1926 Lake Shore Blvd West is very popular with US visitors; a look in the parking lot reveals cars from all over the

USA. Room prices are often posted on the motel's sign and start at around $50. The adjacent *Golden Griddle* pancake house is a good place for a buffet breakfast and packs them in at weekends for brunch.

Not too far away, but west on the Queensway, try the *Queensway Motel* (☎ 252-5281), at No 638 the Queensway. It's sort of away from the traffic, and may have rooms when others are booked out and its prices are lower. Another place, still further west, in the block around No 1500 is the *Deluxe* (☎ 252-5205). Motels dot the road all the way to Hamilton but there is no real concentration like the one by the Humber River. Further out vacancies may not be a problem.

More motels, although not in great numbers, can be found along Dundas St West, west of Highway 427 which is in the suburb of Mississauga rather than Toronto proper. From the Lake Shore go north up Highway 427 and turn left (west).

The other main motel district is on the east side of town, on Kingston Rd which is an extension of Queen St East and later turns into the old Highway 2 to Montreal. Motels start just east of where Danforth Ave begins, branching off from Kingston Rd. This district is further from the centre and from much of Toronto's in-coming traffic (particularly that from the USA) and so tends to be less busy and less costly. Again there are good places and ones best avoided.

The *Avon* (☎ 267-0339), at 2800 Kingston Rd just past Bluffers Park, gets top billing and is quite an attractive looking place. Rooms here cost from $35 to $50 with TV and radio and there is a heated pool.

Next door the *Royal Motel* (☎ 264-4381), at 2746 Kingston Rd, is also good and has rooms from $38 to $55.

At 3126 Kingston Rd is the *Park* (☎ 261-7241) with prices about the same or slightly lower.

More basic and further east at 3370 Kingston Rd is the *White Swan* (☎ 261-7168), a brick place with the blue and white sign. The rates are from $36 to $48. They have weekly rates too.

Lastly and still further out, east of Eglinton, is the *Idlewood Inn* (☎ 286-6861) a large, modern motel often used by business people. Rates here are higher ranging from $50 to $70.

There are quite a few other places along this strip between the ones listed here.

Places to Eat

Toronto has a good selection of restaurants in all price categories and a very wide variety to choose from, thanks to the many nationalities represented in the city. The following places are mostly central and accessible by public transport. I've listed places according to area and cuisine categories.

Yonge St & Around Yonge St, itself, although very busy night and day, is not one of the prime restaurant districts of the city. In the downtown centre Yonge St has, in general, become swamped with fast-food franchises and cheap takeout counters. But there are exceptions on and near Toronto's main street although some places tend to be geared more to lunch than dinner.

South of the Eaton Centre on Yonge St has always been a bit of a backwater so we'll start with the centre itself and work north to Bloor St. Among the many places to eat in the huge mall are a couple of busy pubs and the *Magic Pan* for crêpes. On the lower level, *Michel's Baguette* stands out amid an inexpensive and otherwise undistinguished food fair, a collection of takeout places which share central tables. This little spot offers a tasty array of fresh goods baked on the premises, salads, sandwiches, and good coffee.

At 362 Yonge St, *Swiss Chalet* is an outlet of the very popular Canadian roast chicken and chips chain. The economical meals are tasty and good value.

The large crowded, noisy cafeteria at *Ryerson Polytechnic Institute* serves up reasonable meals at student prices. Food is served at meal times only in the cafeteria in Jorgenson Hall, which is on the corner of Gerrard St East and Victoria St.

Most of the better places to munch at are between College and Bloor Sts. Between the

Eaton Centre area and College St there isn't much, but north of there things pick up again and it's very busy all the way to Bloor St and beyond. At the hole-in-the-wall *Papaya Hut* at 515 Yonge St, the homemade vegetable soup, one of the sandwiches such as avocado with tomato and a papaya drink or smoothie provide an alternative to the nearby junk food. Another bargain can be had at *Aida's*, which at 597 Yonge St north of Wellesley St, is even smaller but cranks out quite decent and cheap felafels, tabouli and a very limited number of other Lebanese basics.

British-style pub grub can be had with a brew at one of the city's four *Nag's Head Taverns*.

The Eaton Centre has the slickest and most expensive one of these; the corner of King and Yonge Sts has the working-class version. More British and offering a variety of beers and an outdoor patio is the *Artful Dodger* on Isabella St, a few doors east from Yonge St.

The *Vegetarian Restaurant*, situated at 4 Dundonald St just a few doors from Yonge St, is one of the few of its kind in the city and is recommended. The tasty and inexpensive fare includes daily specials, soups, salads and create-your-own-sandwiches, all offered cafeteria-style. They have good desserts. It's a very quiet, low-key place open every day, but on Sunday it's closed until late in the afternoon.

There are several places with outdoor patios nearby, especially around St Joseph St. The *Fair Exchange* at 4 Irwin St is good for lunch or dinner with well-prepared meals with an understated nod to nouveau cuisine but it is no longer cheap. Further north the Hungarian *Goulash Pot*, at 15 Hayden St east off Yonge St, has low-priced (under $7) full meals with an Eastern European slant. Every day but Sunday there is a cheap daily special.

All along Yonge St, usually on corners, are *Mr Submarine* outlets where they make good submarine sandwiches for $4 and up. A simple cheese sub, microwaved, is good. Also with a couple of outlets is *La Maison du Croissant* which is a fine place for a quick breakfast or an afternoon pick-me-up. The

place on the corner of Yonge and Maitland Sts. is especially good

Church St, around Wellesley St, has quite a few cafés and restaurants as well as a range of nightspots. This area is Toronto's gaytown: a lively, busy, and somewhat more up-market district principally centred along Church St.

For a splurge on a good steak, try *Le Baron* further south at 425 Church St, an established place in an area with many new restaurants. They've been doing it for over 30 years and steaks are the only main-course item on the menu. The restaurant offers soft lights and attentive service but dress is casual.

Over at 131 Jarvis St, the *Groaning Board* is a casual semi-self-serve place offering some vegetarian dishes but meat as well. The soup is good, as are the sandwiches and there is a large salad bar, but the hamburgers are not recommended. Folk music is presented on weekends. The rest of the week they show a two-hour reel of the year's best commercial films chosen at Cannes.

Bloor St Bloor St offers all sorts of eating along its considerable length. Around Yonge St, an area of expensive shops and fashion boutiques, there is a very good never-advertised spot: the *Fresh Market* on the 3rd floor of Holt Renfrew, a department store for the well heeled at 50 Bloor St West. It used to be a real bargain but at last visit the increases were a bit of a surprise. However, the afternoon tea with scones and Devon cream is still a little pleasure. It's open from 10 am to 5 pm on retail sales days.

A very cheap place, worth going to if you're in the area, is the *Masters' Restaurant* at 10 Bloor St West in the University Faculty of Education Building, just east of Spadina Ave. Mostly for students, it's open from 9 am to 7 pm Monday to Friday. Cafeteria-style meals like lamb, sole and shepherd's pie are served at rock-bottom prices. Complete breakfasts are also available. Bloor St West around Bathurst St is a lively student area with many good and generally cheap restaurants, a few cafés, the *Brunswick Tavern* – an institution – and the popular Bloor St Cinema.

The *Continental*, a Hungarian place at 521 Bloor St West, is cosy with the usual red and white checked tablecloths. About five meal choices are offered each day, including rice dishes and schnitzels for an average of $10.

By the Way Café, with the former 'Lickin' Chicken' sign still in place, is a popular sitting and meeting place which also serves pretty decent food – Middle Eastern or vegetarian food. The desserts are excellent. There are some outdoor tables. The café is on the north-western corner of Bloor and Brunswick Sts.

Queen St West Queen St West between Spadina and University Aves has been the site of a mini-boom in restaurants in the midst of a general local revival. First claimed by the arts community and their followers, numerous shops and eateries sprang up – many to be replaced as the money moved in. Some of the places cater more to trend than quality but it's a very interesting and varied area with some good and reasonably priced restaurants.

One of the better and more stable of the eateries is the comfortable *Queen Mother* at 208 Queen St West. They offer a good, varied menu for full meals and serve coffee and snacks all day.

Barney's at 385 Queen St West is definitely not a newcomer. Over 35 years old, this has become one of the small elite of classic local institutions that North American inner cities seem to produce. The few mini-tables and 13 stools are usually full at lunch and you'll be reminded that dawdling is *verboten*. The chilli, corned beef and breakfasts are highlights. The *Black Bull* is a licensed place with a busy outdoor patio on the corner of Queen and Soho Sts, right in the middle of the Queen St action.

Many of the area's younger residents and more impecunious artists have now moved further west to between Spadina Ave and Bathurst St or beyond. Along here you'll find various new, small restaurants and speciality stores including quite a few bookshops.

Natalie's is a funky café/restaurant/bookshop at 752 Queen St West with wholesome cheap food in the soup, salad and sandwich category. Breakfasts are also served. The cakes which Natalie makes with natural, fresh ingredients are memorable, particularly the heavy chocolate ones. It's closed all day on Monday and every day after 6 pm.

Theatre District Down on the corner of King and Simcoe Sts is Ed Mirvish's one-man development complex. Across from Roy Thompson Hall and centred around the Royal Alexander Theatre are his unmistakeable restaurants which are famous for the garish exteriors, the sumptuous interiors and the straight, simple food served at low prices. The meats are good, the instant potato and frozen vegetables are just filler.

Old Ed's is a fairly casual place with dinners costing from $10 to $15 and lunches a few dollars less. Selections include lasagna, chicken, fish, ribs and veal. As in all Ed's restaurants, which run in a line linked by the white signs and lightbulbs, the main course comes with potato, salad and rolls. *Ed's Warehouse* (☎ 593-6676) is a bit more up-market. No jeans are allowed and jackets are required. At the door they usually have some jackets and ties to hand out to those without them. Call ahead to make sure, if you don't have one. Here prices are from $13 to $17 at dinner, and again a few dollars less at lunch. The menu offers a couple of selections of roast beef and steak only.

The main attraction of both these places is the decor – a wild, sense-stunning compilation of antiques and oddities lit by dozens of Tiffany lamps. Wedged in and around these two places now are others specialising in either Italian, seafood or Chinese foods. I'm telling you, this guy leaves no stone unturned. The restaurants are one block north of the CN Tower.

Around the corner on John St and up two blocks is the *Amsterdam* which is Toronto's first brew pub and a good place for a quaff after a show or trip up the tower. I prefer the similar *Rotterdam* nearby at 600 King St West at Portland St which also brews its own fine beer but can sell you beer from around the world.

Further east by the O'Keefe Theatre and St Lawrence Market is another busy eating, entertainment and nightclub area popular with both visitors and residents. Toronto, like many Canadian cities of any size, has its *Spaghetti Factory*. This one is at 54 The Esplanade behind the O'Keefe Theatre on Front St near the corner of Yonge St. The restaurant offers good value with meals ranging from salad through to dessert starting at $7.50 served in an interesting eclectic, colourful atmosphere popular with everybody including families and teenagers. The lunch menu is even cheaper. They make numerous spaghettis and other Italian dishes like lasagna and chicken cacciatore.

Nearby are several other places to eat, many with large outdoor sections. Church St has a number of places for dinner. At 6 Market St across from the market building, the *Old Fish Market* with lots of nautical adornments offers a variety of seafood from $15 to $22 at dinner, or standard English fare like shepherd's pie for $7 at lunch.

Chinatown The city's large Chinatown is based around the corner of Spadina Ave and Dundas St West and it is home to scores of restaurants. As the area developed, so did the tastes of restaurant patrons. As well as the standard Cantonese fare, the city now has Sichuan, Hunan, Mandarin places and more. Browse around reading menus. The district extends along Dundas St West, especially to the east of Spadina Ave and north up Spadina Ave to College St. For tasty inexpensive Chinese food in a variety of styles, including some fine spicy dishes, *Peter's Chungking Restaurant* at 281 College St is recommended. As well as the superior food, the decor is a cut above the usual fluorescent and plastic, yet prices are no higher at around $25 to $35 for two. Longstanding *Lee Garden* at 358 Spadina Ave offers a consistently good and unusually varied Cantonese menu and is also not expensive at all.

Until the 1970s the Jewish community dominated Spadina Ave. Despite the Oriental influx, a few restaurants, textile shops and jobbers remain. *Switzers* at No 322 seems to have been there forever. It's a popular deli with dishes such as smoked meat and pickles with prices from $7 or $8 for a meal.

Once again, the area seems to be changing with more and more Vietnamese restaurants opening as some Chinese people leave the central core for more suburban areas. A very good, quick little noodle shop is the *Swatow* at 309 Spadina Ave. Excellent meals of soups and noodles cost from $5 to $15. It's open for lunch and until very late daily except Wednesday when it's closed.

Also for Vietnamese, the simple *Pho Hung* at 374 Spadina Ave is recommended. Despite the emergence of the Vietnamese restaurants on Spadina Ave and Dundas St, one of the best and oldest places is not in the neighbourhood but on a small street a few steps from Yonge St, north of Bloor St. The *Saigon Star* is at 4 Collier St, right behind the massive Toronto Public Library. The menu includes soups, salads, seafood, curries and brochettes (kebabs) with main dishes ranging from $8 to $11, less at lunch.

An interesting street on the edge of Chinatown, which not too many out-of-towners get to, is Baldwin St running east off Spadina Ave about two blocks north of Dundas St. About three blocks from Spadina Ave towards the east end of Baldwin St on the corner of McCaul St is a small, low-key commercial and restaurant enclave. Long a blend of Chinese and Western counterculture, it's especially pleasant on summer evenings when many of the very varied restaurants have outdoor patios.

On the other side of Spadina Ave, the market area on Kensington Ave and particularly on Augusta Ave, is busy during the day and has some small cheap cafés. Formerly here but now a little further north, the *Kensington Kitchen* at 124 Harbord St is a very fine and comfortable Middle Eastern restaurant.

They serve generous portions; try the soup with a felafel or grilled cheese. Afterwards I'll bet you'll have a favourite little lunch spot in Toronto. Also the appetisers are definitely worth sampling at around $6 at lunch, $10 or a bit more at dinner.

Little India Little India, based on Gerrard St East just west of Coxwell St, has numerous inexpensive restaurants. The *Moti Mahal* at No 1442 is very plain (and bright!) but the food is good and ridiculously cheap. The *Bar-Be-Que Hut* (peculiarly named) at No 1457 is plusher than most; again the food is good but the portions are pretty small.

The *Madras Durbar*, a tiny, exclusively vegetarian place serves South Indian dishes. The thali plate is good and makes a complete meal for only $5.50. The address is 1435 Gerrard St East. Best of the lot and not expensive is *Haandi* at 1423 Gerrard St East. The menu offers a varied selection from the numerous breads through to desserts and the ambience is pleasantly more subtle than that offered by many of the competitors. After dinner, take a walk around the area and pop into one of the shops to ask for a paan made to order. With or without tobacco, this is a cheap, exotic taste experience.

A smaller, less visible Indian community has developed on Bloor St West around the Lansdowne and Dufferin Sts area. There are a number of small, modest Indian restaurants here but the overall atmosphere is not as interesting.

All on its own, but closer to the central core and good is the *Indian Rice Factory* at 414 Dupont St between Spadina Ave and Bathurst St. Quite unlike many of the Gerrard St choices, this is a sedate, tastefully decorated dining room. The food is top-rate and offers a little more finesse than many places. It is more expensive but the only real drawback is the interminably slow service. It's open every day.

Danforth Ave The Greek community along Danforth Ave is also a good place to get a meal. Restaurants are mostly noisy and informal and suitable for children. Some are old-style places where you can check out the kitchen and tell the chef what you'd like but these are disappearing. *Ellas* at 702 Pape Ave carries on the tradition of presenting most of the Greek standards. To find others means walking out of the busiest sections. *Zorba's* at 713 Danforth Ave is smaller and cheaper.

Kebab houses have become popular in the past few years and there are now quite a few in the neighbourhood. One that's good and cheap – just look for the queue – is *Omonia* at 426 Danforth Ave. The outside tables are a little less hectic. Similar, and as busy, is the *Astoria* at 400 Danforth Ave with several barbecue-style dishes to try.

Moving up-market, the new, popular *Ouzeri* at 500A Danforth Ave presents a range of more sophisticated main courses amid colourfully trendy surroundings and fellow diners. A full meal for two with appetisers and wine is roughly $50. I've had the rabbit pie and thought it was very tasty but the calimari salad was a bit leathery.

Most of the restaurants along here get very busy on weekend nights and there's quite a festive air to the street. Eating early or after 8.30 or 9 pm is recommended if you want to avoid the crowds.

Other Also out in this Greek area is a good seafood restaurant, the *Round Window* (☎ 465-3892) at 729 Danforth Ave. Phone for reservations – it gets full. A meal with a glass or two of wine costs from $35 to $55 for two. The food is always fresh and cooked simply without much in the way of sauces or spices. The meals are always good value.

For as authentic a Mexican meal as you'll find, *La Mexican* at 229 Carlton St a few doors east of Parliament St is recommended. Aside from enchiladas and the like there are tamales, moles and a sort of Mexican lasagna. It's open for dinner every day and on weekends begins filling up before 6 pm. Dinner for two with a couple of beers ranges from $30 to $40. After dinner a stroll along Parliament St is interesting with its varied shops and will turn up a small place for coffee and/or dessert.

An excellent and very cheap meal of Thai food can be had at the *Thai Shan Inn*, 2039 Eglinton Ave West. It's open every day. The trip to this part of town is well worth it. Meals average $25 for two. Don't miss the *kang ped*, a hot, spicy beef dish with lemon grass. It's a very small place which fills up easily and quickly. Arrive early or late or be prepared to queue.

Another good Asian place is the *Ole Malacca*, a Malaysian restaurant at 886 St Clair Ave West. Satays (kebabs), which you cook at your table over a small barbecue grill, are good to start with. Meals cost from $30 to $45 for two.

If you're down at Harbourfront, the *Water's Edge Café* at York Quay isn't bad with a selection of fairly simple cafeteria-style food. When the weather is fine and the windows are all open, lunch with a beer can be pretty nice. There are several more substantial restaurants nearby in the Queen's Quay terminal too.

Entertainment

Toronto is busy after dark with countless nightspots, concerts, films, lectures and the country's largest theatre scene.

Bar hours are from 11 am to 1 am, as they are all over Ontario. Numerous clubs stay open after-hours until 3 or 4 am without serving any more alcohol, but who knows how many unofficial boozecans there are where pricey drinks can be had at all hours.

Beer can be bought retail at Brewers Retail Stores, now often marked as the Beer Store, and liquor and wine at Liquor Control Board of Ontario (LCBO) outlets. Addresses for both outlets can be found in the yellow pages of the phone book. There are plenty of shops around town but hours vary and they are all closed on Sunday and holidays. The drinking age in the province is 19 years and drunken driving is a very serious offence.

All three daily newspapers provide weekly entertainment listings. Check in either the *Thursday Star* or the *Friday Sun* for full listings or the *Saturday Globe* for film and theatre. The most complete entertainment guide is provided by *Now Magazine*, a good weekly tabloid-style paper available free around town. Find it at cinemas, restaurants, cafés, record stores and some street-corner newsboxes. It offers detailed information on the arts including concerts, theatre and general events as well as local news and comes out every Thursday.

Sipping Alfresco During good weather, Ontario Place or Yorkville are good spots to sit outside for a drink. Ontario Place usually has nightly concerts. There are several bars here and it's cool and festive on a summer night. Yorkville is one area where there is some concentration of outdoor cafés and restaurants which, until a few years ago, the city had sorely lacked. It's a place to be seen and a bit pricey but it's still OK if you're in the right mood.

Queen St West east of Spadina Ave, and Bloor St near Bathurst St now have several places for a glass with tables outside.

Live Music The small, crowded *El Mocambo* on Spadina Ave, just south of College St, is one of the local institutions and the city's best known, if no longer so popular, bar. It has a long, celebrated history, and the Rolling Stones once played here. Shows feature live rock and blues. Admission varies with the band upstairs and can be a bit high, but downstairs admission is free and there's cheaper drinking with a local band.

Just down the street at 379 Spadina Ave is *Grossman's*, which is bright and grubby but one of the cheapest places in town. They sometimes have very good bands and there's usually an interesting, mixed crowd. Both Sunday afternoons and nights are reserved for blues jams. Admission is free. Some of Toronto's best known musicians played the place in their very early days.

Further down Spadina Ave at King St is the *Cabana Room* in the Spadina Hotel (☎ 368-2864). Entertainment includes live rock, art-school bands and new wavish groups. Admission costs about $5 and the drinks are fairly cheap.

The *Bamboo* at 334 Queen St is very popular with excellent music in the ska, reggae, African and similar genres. Great dancing music and it's always busy. In summer they have a rooftop patio to catch a breath and in addition the kitchen serves tasty, spicy meals. Admission costs from $5 to $10. Nearby the *Horseshoe* at 370 Queen St West presents good live folk, blues, rock and blends of all three.

The *Legendary Blue Note* attracts a 30-ish crowd with its live rhythm & blues and dancing. The address is 138 Pears Ave.

Yonge St has numerous places. The *Gasworks* is a long-time popular heavy metal and hard rock bar. The *Brunswick* at 481 Bloor St West is a funky place, a bit like a pub and a bit like a frat house and often a lot of fun. It has good, well-known jazz or blues players upstairs and downstairs, where there is never a cover, all kinds of entertainment from contests to bizarre amateur nights. The downstairs area is cheap, upstairs less so but it varies.

There's live folk music at the *Free Times Café* at 320 College St.

For jazz, there's the *Bermuda Onion* at 131 Bloor St West, sometimes with very big names and the *Café des Copains* at 48 Wellington St. For more experimental music , the *Music Gallery* is at 1087 Queen St West. *Meyer's Deli* at 69 Yorkville St has more conventional jazz.

Disco For dancing to recorded music try the *Copa* on the corner of Yorkville and Yonge Sts, a huge sort of New York-style disco-dancing bar with videos. Garb ranges from jeans to dressy. Admission costs vary and, although never very low, go up if there is a live band. It's open after hours, which means dancing but no drinking after 1am. *RPM* at 132 Queen's Quay has DJ-dancing every night.

Cinema There are several repertory film houses around town.

The *Bloor Cinema* (☎ 532-6677) at 506 Bloor St West is popular with the many students of the area. A wide variety of films is shown – American, European, old and new. The *Revue* (☎ 531-9959) is at 400 Roncesvalles Ave, in the west end. They also feature different films nearly every night.

Prices are a couple of dollars less than those at first-run theatres and much less for those with an inexpensive annual membership card. There are three or four similar theatres around town and also the *Art Gallery of Ontario*, smaller independent galleries and *Cinémathèque Ontario* screen non-commercial films. IMAX large-format movies can be seen at *Ontario Place*.

Theatre There is more theatre in Toronto than in any other Canadian city and productions range from Broadway-type spectacles and musicals to Canadian contemporary dramas. Also big is dinner theatre with topical entertaining presentations. Check newspapers or the guides to Toronto available at hotels for current listings. Theatre costs vary widely. A dinner show costs from $40 to $60 per person for a meal and show.

The city's longest running play is *The Mousetrap*, an Agatha Christie, which has played at the Toronto Truck Theatre for 13 years. A ticket is about $12. One of the more physically impressive theatres is the traditional Royal Alex on King St West which presents established plays and performers.

The *Dream* in High Park is a great summer theatre presentation in which one Shakespearean play is put on each night through July and August, free. The Toronto Free Theatre's production and acting is top-rate. For details, call their downtown theatre. Shows begin at 8 pm, but go very early with a blanket and picnic or you'll require binoculars.

Five Star Tickets (☎ 596-8211) sells theatre and dance tickets at half-price for shows the same day with leftover seats. They have a booth at the Eaton Centre, on the corner of Dundas and Yonge Sts. You can't place telephone orders. The booth is open from noon to 7.30 pm daily, Sunday 11 am to 3 pm.

Spectator Sports The Toronto Blue Jays play major-league baseball against American teams of the National League at the Skydome. Sipping a beer and watching the game on a warm night is pleasant and the cheap seats are very low-priced. Take a jacket – things cool off down here at night, it's fairly close to the water.

The Toronto Argonauts of the professional Canadian Football League (CFL) also play in the 'Dome'.

For horse racing, Greenwood track is quite central on the corner of Queen St and Woodbine Ave on the streetcar line. Last time I went I could do no wrong and won $144. It's just $2 to get in and a bet need only cost another deuce.

In winter, National League Hockey is played at Maple Leaf Gardens on the corner of Carlton and Church Sts, downtown a couple of blocks from Yonge St. Despite years with a poor team, tickets are still hard to get as a rule but can be bought without difficulty from scalpers outside the door just before the game.

Other Toronto has a place for comics called *Yuk Yuks* (☎ 967-6425) at 1280 Bay St. Presentations are sometimes funny, sometimes gross, sometimes a joke. Admission ranges from a low of $4 on some weekdays to $8 and then up to $15 on weekend nights when there are two of the two-hour shows. Dinner packages are also available.

The Toronto Symphony plays at the new *Roy Thompson Hall*, 60 Simcoe St, not far from the CN Tower. A range of other, mainly classical, concerts are presented here. The Canadian Opera Company performs at the *O'Keefe Centre* on Front St in early fall. The National Ballet of Canada is based in town and also performs at the O'Keefe.

Pantages, a beautiful restored 1920s cinema, now presents Broadway-style shows such as *The Phantom of the Opera*. For dance, look into what's happening at Harbourfront's *Premiere Dance Theatre*.

Things to Buy

ABC at 552 Yonge St, north of Wellesley St, is a very good place for camping gear, tents, sleeping bags, packs and footwear. It's not a trendy place at all, doesn't have any fashion wear but does have good quality stuff at good prices and the staff is straightforward.

Europe Bound, at 2 McCaul St off Queen St West near the Art Gallery of Ontario, has a selection of camping and hiking clothing,

gear, and books. They will even rent you a tent or take a passport photo.

For the very best in outdoor clothing visit Tilley Endurables, a small Canadian company begun in 1980 which turns out some of the finest, toughest, low-maintenance threads imaginable. All their stuff looks good, needs no ironing and comes with the washing instruction 'Give 'em Hell'. Their clothes (pants, shirts, skirts and the well-known hats) have been used on various expeditions, from mountaineering to sailing. The shorts at $70 are guaranteed for life. Hats cost around $40. The main store is at 900 Don Mills Rd and there is an outlet at the Queen's Quay terminal at Harbourfront.

For cyclists, quite a few bicycle shops can be found along a strip of Bloor St around Dufferin St, but there are others all over town.

Getting There & Away

Air The airport, Pearson International, is about 24 km north-west of the downtown area in a part of the city known as Malton. This is actually a separate city but you wouldn't know it with the continuous urban landscape. The major Canadian airlines fly in and out of Toronto, as do many international companies. Pearson is by far and away the busiest airport in the country.

It has long been a congested and confusing place but the new third terminal, known as Trillium Terminal, added in early 1991 has alleviated much of the crowding and annoyance. This is the first airport terminal in Canada to be developed, owned and operated by private interests rather than by the government. Aside from the main hall with the 15-metre-high vaulted glass ceiling offering natural lighting, the most distinguishing feature is the number of shops, including a Harrod's outlet, and restaurants. But the main benefit is simply the speeding up of getting in and out.

When departing from the airport or picking someone up at arrivals be sure to ask the terminal number. Signs on the roads into the airport direct you to each terminal and indicate airlines they serve. Trillium is the main terminal for Canadian Airlines, American, British Airways, KLM, Lufthansa and Air France. Within the Trillium Terminal, Pier A handles domestic flights and Pier B, international ones.

Some one-way fares on Air Canada (☎ 925-2311) are: to Montreal $215, Halifax $350, and to Calgary $585. Canadian Airlines (☎ 675-2211) has virtually the same prices but they do vary during the numerous special promotions. Intair runs very cheap flights to Ottawa.

The many large immigrant and ethnic parts of the city are good places to seek out travel agencies for charters and cheap flights to a particular homeland, be it Hong Kong, the Philippines or Poland. Also check the Youth Hostel Travel Agency and CUTS, a travel agency specialising in flights for students. The newspapers also are sources of tickets for sale.

Small independent airlines which fly in and out of Toronto to either Montreal, Ottawa, London, or even Buffalo at very low cost come and go but none ever seems able to survive. Some of these upstart companies tend to use the small Toronto Islands Airport on the lake at the foot of Bathurst St. The airport is used by these commuter airlines as well as being busy with private planes. It's worth inquiring about.

At the moment Air Ontario is the only regularly scheduled company using the Toronto Islands Airport. The short take-off and landing aircraft get you to where you're going a lot quicker than the major carriers because you don't have to drag yourself all the way out to the airport. When things are going well for one of these airlines there could be a shuttle bus running from the Royal York Hotel down to the two-minute ferry across to the airport. Otherwise there is TTC service (see Getting Around later) from downtown.

It is not uncommon for Canadians (and visitors) to skip over to Buffalo to take advantage of the generally much cheaper US airfares. For example, a flight from Buffalo to Seattle could cost hundreds of dollars less than the fare say from Toronto to Vancouver.

At either end, a short bus ride links the Canadian city.

The real heyday for gutbucket US fares seems to have ended with the demise of People Express. When it was in full swing, a shuttle bus ran from downtown Toronto to the Buffalo airport from where $19 would fly you into New York City. For longer trips it's still worth calling some US carriers such as Continental or American.

Bus The revamped bus station for out-of-town destinations (☎ 979-3511) is central on the corner of Bay and Dundas Sts at the edge of Chinatown, a few blocks west of Yonge St. It's the depot for the Gray Coach, Voyageur and Greyhound lines which collectively pretty well cover Quebec, Ontario and beyond to western Canadian and US cities. Destinations and one-way fares include to Ottawa at 8, 9.30 and 11.30 am and frequently throughout the afternoon and evening for $43.

To Thunder Bay, services depart at 8 am, 12.45 and 5.30 pm and 1 am for $103. (This journey takes about 20 hours.)

To Montreal, buses run regularly all day for $48. To Niagara (about two hours) services depart at 8.15 and 10 am and every hour until 7 pm for $20.

There are regular buses for New York, Buffalo and Detroit. Return tickets used within 10 days provide substantial savings. Lockers can be found on the lower level and the upper floor has a restaurant although there is a bakery and café across the other side of Bay St.

Adjacent to the terminal on the western side is the bus depot for GO buses, a government line which services many of the nearby surrounding towns stopping frequently along the way. It's mainly used by commuters but goes a relatively long way (to Hamilton for example) to the west of Toronto.

Train Grand old Union Station (☎ 366-8411) is also conveniently situated. It's on Front St (which runs east-west) at the extreme south end of the city at the bottom of University

Ave, York and Bay Sts. The subway goes right into the station; the stop is called Union.

Trains leave for Ottawa at 9 am, 1 and 5 pm ($60, about six hours); others go to Kingston with bus connections for Ottawa. To Montreal there are six trains daily for $70.

To Sudbury, the train departs at 11.59 pm ($52, 7½ hours). Note that for Sudbury the train actually goes to Sudbury Junction, a station about 10 km from the centre of town.

Reservations are needed for all trains. Return trips, providing you don't travel on a Friday, are better value.

Amtrak runs trains to and from Toronto out of New York City and Chicago.

The station has several restaurants, some fast-food outlets and a bar. Sometimes on the arrival level, just as you come out the gate from the train, a travellers' aid booth helps with basic directions. and questions.

GO trains also use the station; see the Getting Around section. The introductory Getting Around chapter has information on luxury excursion trips from Toronto through the Rocky Mountains.

Car & Motorbike If you're renting a car, be aware that many places require that you be 21 years old or more, for some places the minimum age is 23. There are countless rental agencies in the city. Surprisingly, it can be difficult to get a car on holiday weekends so plan ahead.

The cheapest place to try is Rent-A-Wreck (☎ 961-7500), at 374 Dupont St between Spadina Ave and Bathurst St, with used cars at $35 a day for a middle-sized vehicle, less for compacts. The charge is 12 cents per km with 200 free km. There are weekly and monthly rates too. Insurance is extra, as it is at all places, and goes up as the driver's age decreases. If you're going for a used car, check it out before proceeding too far: I haven't had much luck with them.

A place with a choice of new or used cars and with a good central location is Downtown Car & Truck Rental (☎ 597-3837) at 77 Nassau St in Kensington Market off Spadina Ave. The used ones, best for using in the city (or near it), start at $10 a day plus km trav-

elled and the new vehicles for trips further afield are priced competitively.

Tilden (☎ 364-4191), with an office in Union Station as well as several other downtown locations and one at the airport, is a more standard rental company and offers new cars. Their rate is $40 per day with 200 free km and 15 cents per km over that for the smallest economy cars. They offer weekend specials; book early. Also available and a good idea, are child seats and ski racks.

Avis (☎ 964-2051) is in the Hudson Bay Centre with the Bay department store on the corner of Yonge and Bloor Sts. Rates here are comparable to those at Tilden and elsewhere. Again reservations are often required. Another major company is Budget.

Car Sharing & Drive-Aways Allo-Stop is a service based on a great idea – getting drivers and cars together with passengers. Their Toronto office (☎ 323-0874) is central at 663 Yonge St. They mainly deal with trips to Montreal and Ottawa but other things come up too, including rides to New York City and even Florida. Give them a call a couple of days before you want to go and they may be able to line up a ride. Rates are very good.

For long-distance trips there are driveaway cars. There are about half a dozen places listed in the *Yellow Pages* phone book. One company is Toronto Drive-Away Service (☎ 225-7754), with cars for Canadian and US destinations. Also check the business personal columns in either the *Toronto Sun* or the *Star*.

Hitching Thumbing is illegal on the expressways in the city. On city streets there's no problem but it's not commonly done. You can hitch on Highway 401 out of town or on the lead-in ramps in town. If you're heading east for Montreal, the best bet is the city transit to roughly the corner of Port Union Rd and Highway 401 in Scarborough, near the Metro Zoo. To get there from downtown is a bit complicated and the fastest way takes about 1½ hours. Take the subway east to Kennedy stop. From there catch the No 86A Scarborough bus to the corner of Sheppard

Ave and Meadowvale Rd. Transfer (free) to the Rouge Hill bus down to Highway 401.

If you're going west, take the subway to Kipling. Transfer to the West Mall bus, Nos 112 or 112B, and go to the corner of Car-lingview Drive and Highway 401. This is just at the city limits so you are OK on the highway, but it could be very busy and diffi-cult for cars to stop at rush hour. The bus takes about one hour from downtown.

If you're northbound go back up to the Trans Canada Highway at Sudbury; it's a bit tricky. I think the best bet is to take the bus to Barrie and then hitch the rest of the way on Highway 400.

Getting Around

To/From the Airport In Toronto, there are several ways to get to the airports. The cheapest is to take the subway to Kipling on the east-west line. From there, take the Kipling or Martingrove bus (Nos 45 or 46) north up to Dixon Rd. Transfer to the Malton No 58A bus which goes west to the airport. Keep your transfer from the subway, but the second bus will cost $1.40 extra. Take the same route to get downtown from the airport.

Alternatively take the subway to the Law-rence stop on the north-south Yonge St line and from there catch the Malton No 58A bus. Again, the bus costs an additional $1.40.

The next method is a little easier, a little quicker and a little more costly. Between the Islington subway stop (one before Kipling), at the far western end of the Bloor Line, and the airport there is a direct bus run by Gray Coach (☎ 393-7911). It leaves about every 40 minutes, every day, takes 25 minutes and costs $5.50. The bus also runs between the airport and the Yorkdale and York Mills subway stations. Each of these stops costs a bit more.

There are also buses every 20 minutes to and from half a dozen major hotels such as the Royal York, Sheraton, Harbour Castle and the Holiday Inn, which is very near the bus terminal. The fare one-way is $10 and the trip takes about 40 minutes.

Of course, there are taxis and, for a couple more bucks, limousines.

TTC The city has a good subway, bus and streetcar system (see the following Toronto Subway map), called the TTC. Fares are $1.30 cash or seven tickets or tokens for $7.50. Tickets or tokens (small dime-like coins) are available in the subway or at some convenience and corner variety stores. Once one fare is paid, you can transfer to any other bus, subway or streetcar within one hour. One ticket can get you anywhere the system goes. Get a transfer from the driver, or in the subway from the machine inside the turn-stiles where you pay the fare.

A day pass can be purchased for $5 which allows for unlimited travel after 9.30 am. On Sunday and holidays the day pass is good for two adults and up to four children.

The subway system is clean, safe and fast. There is one east-west line which goes along Bloor St and Danforth Ave and two north-south lines, one up Yonge St and one along Spadina Ave where some of the stops are decorated with the work of Canadian artists. The above-ground Scarborough RT train line connects the subway with the north-east part of the city, from the Victoria Park stop to the Scarborough Town Centre. The Harbour-front LRT (light rail transit) car runs above and below ground from Union Station on Front St to Harbourfront along Queens's Quay West to Bathurst St and back again.

The subway runs until about 1.30 am and begins at 6 am except on Sunday when it starts at 9 am. Bus hours vary; some run late but are infrequent. Some of the buses are electric, running on above-the-street cables. These are known as trolley buses.

For transit and route information call ☎ 393-4636 daily from 7 am to 11.30 pm.

The Toronto system connects with bus routes in surrounding suburban cities such as Mississauga, Markham and Vaughan.

GO Train The GO train system (☎ 665-0022) leaving from Union Station from 7 am to 11.30 pm daily, services the suburbs of Toronto east to Whitby and west to Hamil-ton. Deposit half the ticket as you enter and save the other half for when you get off. Service is fast and steady through the day and

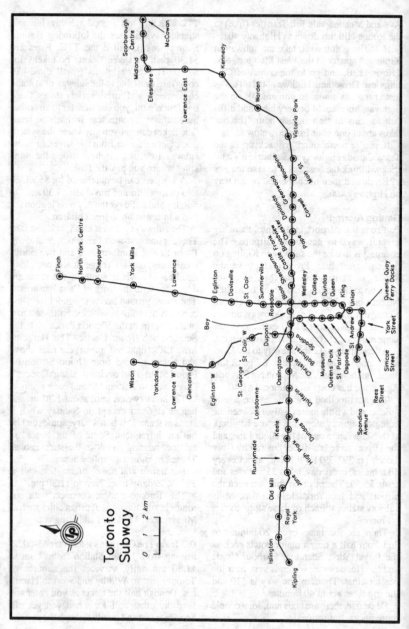

frequent during weekday rush hours. There is now also a run north to Barrie.

Streetcar You may want to try the streetcars. Toronto is one of the few North American cities still using them and, in fact, has added some new models to the old yellow and red fleet. Find them on St Clair Ave and College, Dundas, Queen and King Sts all of which run east-west.

Car All over Ontario you can turn right on a red light, after stopping. Parking is expensive, usually about $1.50 to $2.50 for the first half hour, then slightly less. Most places have a flat rate after 6 pm. Look for the city of Toronto municipal lots which are scattered around the downtown area and are marked by green signs. These are cheaper than the privately run lots.

Rush hours are impossible so avoid them. Watch where you park during rush hours because the tow trucks show no mercy and to get your vehicle back will cost a bundle in cash and aggravation. Pedestrians use the painted crosswalks across the street and traffic must stop for them. If you're driving keep an eye out for these. Hitting someone on a crosswalk in Toronto is a big no-no. When driving, always stop when streetcar doors are open.

Bicycle The most central place to rent bicycles is McBride Cycle (☎ 367-5651) found at 180 Queen's Quay West in Harbourfront. There are also rentals on Centre Island at Toronto Island Bicycle Rental (☎ 365-7901) on the south shore more or less straight back from the ferry landing.

Further out but cheaper is Brown's Sports & Cycle (☎ 763-4176) at 2447 Bloor St West, near Jane and on the subway route. They rent 10-speed bikes for the day or offer good weekly rates. It's not really that far from High Park, the Lake Shore and the Martin Goodman Trail.

Lastly, High Park Cycle (☎ 532-7300) at 1168 Bloor St West will rent you wheels.

When cycling, be careful on the streetcar rails – cross at right angles or you'll land on your ear.

Pedicab A fairly recent appearance on Toronto streets are pedicabs – deluxe bicycle rickshaws peddled by sweating students. You see them during summer along Yonge St and in Yorkville. Prices are around $7.50 for 15 minutes.

AROUND TORONTO

Within approximately 1½ hour's drive or less from the city are a large number of small, old towns that were until fairly recently centres for the local farming communities. Some of the country's best land is here, but working farms are giving way to urban sprawl and many of the old downtown areas are now surrounded by modern housing developments. Day trips around the district, especially on a Sunday, are popular. There is still some nice rolling landscape and a few conservation areas, which are basically parks used for walking or picnicking and incorporate a river or other geographical feature. Quite a few of the towns attract antique hunters and craft and gift shops are plentiful.

Caledon is one of the larger and closer examples and is set in the Caledon Hills. Not far south-west in **Terra Cotta** is an inn of the same name, which makes a good place to stop later in the day for afternoon tea served with scones, cream and jam. Terra Cotta is also one of the closest points to Toronto for access to an afternoon's walk along part of the **Bruce Trail** which runs for 700 km north-south.

The **Hockley Valley** area near Orangeville provides more of the same. The **Credit River** has trout fishing and in winter the area is not bad for cross-country skiing, but the hills aren't high enough for downhill skiing.

Kleinburg

The **McMichael Collection** is an excellent art gallery, just north of the city in the village of Kleinburg. The gallery – handmade wooden buildings in a pleasant rural setting – displays an extensive and impressive collection of Canadian paintings. Very well

represented are Canada's best known painters, known collectively as the Group of
Seven. If you're going to see northern
Ontario, where much of the group's work
was done, a visit to the McMichael Collection is all the more worthwhile. The work of
other Canadian painters is also on view.
Other exhibits include Inuit and West Coast
Native Indian art. On display are sculptures,
prints and paintings. Special changing exhibitions may feature photography or one
particular artist or school of work. The surrounding wooded property is crossed with
walking trails where deer may be seen. The
gallery has a book/gift shop and restaurant.

Admission is $4.25, less for children,
seniors and families. Schoolchildren often
visit on weekday mornings. The gallery is
open daily in summer, but is closed on
Monday from November to April. The hours
are from 10 am to 5 pm in the summer
season, an hour shorter at each end during
the rest of the year.

In Kleinburg itself, a rather pricey retreat
from Toronto, there are numerous antique
shops, small galleries, craft shops and places
for a nosh.

Getting There & Away Kleinburg is 18 km
north from the corner of Islington Ave and
Highway 401 in Toronto. To get there by car,
go north up Highway 427 to Highway 27 and
continue north. Turn right at Nashville Rd.

By public transportation it's a little
awkward but can be done. First, take the
Toronto subway west to Islington on the
east-west line. From there, catch the No 37
bus north for around 35 minutes to Steeles
Ave. At this point transfer to the No 3A
Vaughan bus. The only one of these early in
the day is at 11.45 am so you must make this
connection. The bus will take you to the
gallery gate in about 20 minutes, from where
it is a 10-minute walk in. On the way back,
the No 3A bus goes at 5.30, 6 and 7.30 pm.
The No 37 is much more frequent.

Dunlap Observatory
Just north of the Toronto limits, the Dunlap
Observatory (☎ 884-2112) has what was

once the world's second-largest telescope; it
remains the biggest in Canada. From April
to October it is open to the public on Saturday evenings. A brief introductory talk is
given to accompany a slide show which is
then followed by a bit of stargazing through
the scope.

The programmes are free but it is essential
that you call ahead on a weekday for reservations. On Tuesday at 10 am throughout the
year, tours of the grounds and buildings are
offered. To reach the observatory, drive up
Highway 11 (the continuation of Yonge St)
towards Richmond Hill and you'll see the
white dome on the right. For public transportation, check with the TTC and their
Vaughan Transit connections.

Pickering Nuclear Plant
About 40 km east of Toronto on the Lake
Ontario shoreline is this nuclear power
station, which has portions open to the
public. Whether you're pro or con nuclear
plants, you could find out something you
didn't know. Free films, displays and a drive
around the site explain the operation. It's
open from 9 am to 4 pm daily. Look for the
signs on Highway 401 – the plant is at the
foot of Liverpool Rd. If your kids are born
glowing in the dark, don't blame me.

Local Conservation Areas
South-western Ontario is urban. To offset
this somewhat, the government has designated many conservation areas – small
nature parks for walking, picnicking and
sometimes fishing, swimming and cross-
country skiing. These are not wild areas by
any means and some are not even pretty, but
they are close to major centres and do offer
some relief from concrete. The tourist office
has a list of those around Toronto and within
a 160-km radius of town.

One place which makes a good, quick
escape on a nice summer day is the large
Albion Hills Conservation Area. This one
also allows for decent cross-country skiing.
On the west side of town, take Indian Line
(by the airport) north. It becomes Highway
50 which leads to the park. In this region also

is the Kortright Centre for Conservation, near Kleinburg. There are trails here, too, but it's more of a museum with displays and demonstrations on resources, wildlife, ecology, etc. It's open daily to 4 pm.

On the east side of town, one not too far away is Milne Lake. To get to this conservation area, go north on Markham Rd, which later becomes Highway 48.

Cullen Gardens & Miniature Village

About a 45-minute drive from Toronto, east on the Highway 401 in the town of Whitby is a 10-hectare site of carefully tended gardens interspersed with miniature models. A path, which will take two or three hours to walk if you're looking at all the impressive detail, winds through the gardens. On the way are miniaturisations of a village, a modern suburban subdivision, a farm and a scene from cottage country. The buildings, people and activities portrayed offer, in a sense, a glimpse of life in southern Ontario. It's quite nifty the way small plants have been sculpted to represent trees and other larger, full-sized flora.

The gardens are on Taunton Rd West, off Highway 12 about five km north along Highway 401. It's open daily from the middle of April to the beginning of January. The floral aspect of the gardens, although colourful and quite extensive, should not be confused with botanical gardens but viewed rather as the setting for the various scenes. The park appeals to a variety of people but is particularly fascinating to children. Admission is $7, less for children and seniors. There is a pleasant picnic and snack bar area (bring your own food) or a fairly pricey sit-down restaurant for when hunger strikes.

Canadian Automotive Museum

Further east near Oshawa, a centre for car assembly, is this museum with a collection of over 50 cars. Included are a Redpath Runabout from 1890, a Model T, of course, and various automotive memorabilia. It's at 99 Simcoe St and is open daily all year.

Parkwood

Also in Oshawa, at 270 Simcoe St North, Parkwood is the estate of R S McLaughlin, who once ran the Canadian division of General Motors. The property consists of a 55-room mansion with antique furnishings set amidst large gardens. Admission is $3 and it's closed on Monday, unless it's a holiday when it remains open. Afternoon tea is served during summer.

Cathedral of the Transfiguration

It seems nobody builds churches anymore, especially on the grand scale of the old world. But north of Toronto, straight up Highway 404 in Markham is one heck of an exception. Opened in 1987, this Byzantine Catholic cathedral is one of the country's largest and stands 62.7 metres high at the tip of its copper-topped spire. Based on a smaller version found in Czechoslovakia, this is a 1000-seater church. One of the impressive features is the French-made main bell, ringing in at 16,650 kg, second in size only to the one in Paris' Sacré Coeur. Also, it is the first cathedral in the Western hemisphere to be blessed by a pope – John Paul II did the honours in 1984.

North & West of Toronto

BARRIE

A little over an hour north of the big city is the town of Barrie, which is more or less the unofficial gateway to Toronto's cottage country. Around Lake Simcoe, north through the Muskoka's region (named after one of the larger local lakes) and along the vast Georgian Bay shoreline, the mostly wooded hills, scores of lakes and rivers and numerous parks make for fine summer R&R. Fishing, swimming, camping, lazing – just what the doctor ordered. In winter the area is busy with winter recreation: skiing, snowmobiling and lots of ice fishing. In September and October, the region is toured for nature's annual, brilliantly coloured tree show.

Travel information centres can be found

in Barrie, in the County Administration Building, in Collingwood at 101 Hurontario St and in Orilla on Sundial Drive. Many other towns have small information booths where you can pick up local information on sights, events, festivals and places of historic interest. Despite the emphasis on outdoor activities, this is a pretty busy and developed area. For more space or wilderness, head further north or to the larger government parks.

From Toronto, Barrie is straight up Highway 400. From here buses go in all directions. For a snack on the way, stop at *Webber's*, a hamburger joint so popular that a pedestrian bridge had to be put in. It's on Highway 11, south of the Severn River. On Friday afternoons and Sunday nights, expect a lot of traffic.

WASAGA BEACH

Wasaga is the beach resort closest to Toronto. Around Wasaga Beach and the strip of beaches (about 14 km long) running up along the bay are hundreds of cottages, a provincial park and several private campgrounds. The centre of activity is the decidedly unsubtle town of Wasaga Beach and the excellent beach with fine swimming at Wasaga Beach Provincial Park.

A very popular weekend spot, Wasaga Beach is nearly empty during the week. Some areas of the beach are more for families, others (like those around the snack bars) are more for the younger crowd, although drinkers are now often fined on the spot. Water-slide complexes are one of Canada's fastest growing diversions and Wasaga Beach has not one, but two water slides, including one right on the shore in town. One slide is over 100 metres long.

Places to Stay

For accommodation assistance in the area, call ☎ 445-0748. There are many motels around the district, including several along Main St or Mosley St and they range from $35 for singles to $50 for doubles. They're slightly cheaper for a two-night stay, more so by the week. Also check on Rural Route 1.

Others places to stay are right on the beach. Lots of cottages with housekeeping facilities are available as well, but these are generally for stays of a week or longer.

Getting There & Away

Two buses run daily in both directions between Toronto and Wasaga Beach; one in the morning and one in the afternoon. It's a 2½-hour trip, with a change of buses in Barrie. In Wasaga Beach, the bus travels right down the main road.

COLLINGWOOD

In the centre of the Blue Mountain ski area and right on the water, this little resort town has a reputation for being pretty, but really isn't. The surroundings are scenic enough, with the highest sections of the Niagara Escarpment nearby. The escarpment runs south all the way to Niagara Falls. The caves along it near town are heavily and misleadingly promoted; they are not what you and I expect of that term, but are really more like overhangs. There is some good walking, however, and the hour-long trail by the caves loops over interesting terrain and the views are excellent. An admission fee is charged to the area around the caves, with an additional charge to actually see the caves.

A chairlift runs to the top of Blue Mountain, from where there is a choice of the chairlift or a water slide down in summer.

The area is known for its 'blue' pottery which is very nice but not cheap. A bluegrass music festival is held here in summer.

Places to Stay

Collingwood has an excellent youth hostel. The *Blue Mountain Hostel* (☎ 445-1497) is open all year but is often booked out. There are about 60 beds and a kitchen in a chalet-style building. The hostel also has a sauna. You'll find it on Rural Route 3, near the ski hills north of Craigleith – two hours from Toronto. Members are charged $11 in summer, $15 in winter and it's several dollars more for nonmembers.

There are plenty of motels here, too. The *Fireside* (☎ 445-1917), on Rural Route 2, is small and a good deal with rooms from as low as $35. Also offering budget accommodation is the *Glen Lake Motel* (☎ 445-4280) on the same street and the *Village Store* (☎ 445-1617), on Rural Route 3, close to the Blue Mountain Slides. Of course, there are more expensive places in the area including some resorts, lodges and inns with all the amenities.

MIDLAND

This small commercial centre in the area known as Huronia has a number of sites relating to the early Native Indian population and the arrival of White settlers. **Huron Indian Village** is a replica of what the Native Indian settlements were like until the early 1600s. Things changed not long after this date, when in 1639 some French Jesuits arrived on a soul-saving drive. **'Sainte-Marie Among the Hurons'** is an historic site which reconstructs the 17th-century Jesuit mission and tells the story of a rather dramatic chapter in the book of Native Indian/European clashes. Graphic depictions of missionaries' deaths by torture are forever etched in the brains of countless Canadians by elementary school history texts. Six of the eight martyred missionaries in North America were based at the Sainte-Marie mission. **Martyrs' Shrine** here is a monument to them and the site of pilgrimages each year. Even the pope showed up in 1984.

Also in town is a small museum but there are other attractions in the area unrelated to human history. The **Wye Marsh Wildlife Centre** provides boardwalks, trails and an observation deck over the marsh which houses abundant birdlife. Displays offer information on the flora & fauna found in the area. Canoe trips through the marsh are also possible.

From the town dock, 2½-hour boat cruises depart for **Georgian Bay** and the islands around **Honey Harbour**. Cruises run from mid-May to the first week of October, with two trips daily during the summer months.

PENETANGUISHENE

This town (pronounced 'pen-e-tang-wish-een') slightly north of Midland is smaller but similarly historic and has both a British and French population and history.

The **Historic Naval & Military Establishments** is a reconstructed naval base. It was built by the British after the War of 1812 against the Americans, but never used. The site, open daily through the summer, contains 15 buildings, costumed workers and a ship replica.

For somewhere to eat, try the place down at the docks. You can't miss it.

Between Penetanguishene and north of **Parry Sound** the waters of Georgian Bay are speckled with 30,000 islands – the highest concentration in the world. This and the nearby beaches make it somewhat of a boating and vacation centre and the dock area is always very busy in summer with locals and out-of-towners. Three-hour cruises, which are popular not only in summer but in fall as well when the leaves are all reds and yellows, depart from here and from Midland. At this end try the *Georgian Queen*, a three-decker.

CHRISTIAN ISLAND

Off the north-west edge of the peninsula and connected by toll ferry, this island, part of an Ojibwa reservation, is the site of an archaeological dig which will form the basis of a tourist draw for this Native Indian band. Two thousand years of Native Indian settlement will be surveyed and excavated and work is focusing on a very well-preserved 650-year-old fort. It was built by the Hurons in an attempt to protect themselves and some French soldiers and priests from the Iroquois. The Iroquois decided to starve them out. Inside, the Jesuits controlled the very limited rations and exchanged food for the Hurons' attendance at Mass. Within a year, 4000 Native Indians had starved to death, spelling the end of that band as a significant people in the area.

AWENDA PROVINCIAL PARK

Awenda, right at the end of the peninsula

jutting into Georgian Bay, is one of the youngest provincial government parks. Though relatively small and busy with both day visitors and overnighters, it's pretty good. The campsites are large, treed and private. There are four good beaches, all connected by walking paths. The first one can be reached by car and the second and third are the sandiest. And this is one of the few places around Georgian Bay where the water gets pleasantly warm.

There are also a couple of longer trails through the park, one supplying a good view of the bay. Awenda is north of Penetanguishene, where food and other supplies should be bought. Basic staples can be bought not too far from the park entrance.

The campsites cost $9.50 and reservations are advised for weekends, or arrive early. There are no electrical hook-ups so many people are tenters. Cooking grills are available free for use over fires. The park office has a list of commercial campgrounds in the district if it's booked out when you arrive. The roadside signs on the approach indicating that the park campground is full are not always accurate so persevering can be worthwhile. By evening on a Friday, however, it may well be choc-a-bloc until Monday morning.

SIX MILE LAKE PARK
Six Mile Lake (☎ (705) 728-2900), another provincial park in the region, is on Highway 69 north of Port Severn. There are 192 basic sites, but no showers or electricity. Boat rentals are nearby and the park has access to a canoe route. You can go swimming here too.

GEORGIAN BAY ISLANDS NATIONAL PARK
This park, consisting of some 50 islands in Georgian Bay, has two completely separate sections. The principal segment is not far from Six Mile Lake – take Highway 400 from Toronto then Highway 69 to Honey Harbour. Once there, water taxis can be taken to the islands.

Beausoleil Island is the largest island and

is the park centre, with campgrounds and an interpretive centre. Several of the other islands have primitive camping facilities at just $5 a site. The islands are home to the now quite rare, eastern Massasauga rattlesnake. You may like to know that it is rather small and timid – usually.

Recreation includes swimming, diving, snorkelling and fishing: the bay is great for bass and pike. Boating is very big in the area, what with all the islands and the Trent-Severn Canal system. Many boaters, and they range from those putting along in aluminium 14-footers (four-metre boats) to would-be kings in their floating palaces, tie up for a day or night at the park islands so they are fairly busy. The park is really centred around the boating subculture and otherwise is not particularly interesting.

For those seeking some sort of retreat, it is disappointingly busy and rather ostentatiously competitive. The water taxis are not at all cheap and provide very limited access.

For park information, there is an office (☎ 765-2415) in Honey Harbour near the grocery store. In summer a shuttle service runs over to Beausoleil relatively inexpensively. Water taxis are not cheap and, while providing some flexibility in destinations and schedules, still offer rather limited access.

Section two of the park, consisting of a number of smaller islands, is further north up the bay, about halfway to Parry Sound. This section, although quieter, is inaccessible except to those with their own vessels.

ORILLIA, GRAVENHURST, BRACEBRIDGE & HUNTSVILLE
These four towns from south to north are the principal centres of the Muskokas. They supply cottage country. None of them is especially attractive as a destination but there are a few things of interest. Orillia was the home of Canada's best known humorist, Stephen Leacock. He wrote here and built a house in 1919 which can now be visited.

In Gravenhurst is the **Bethune Memorial House**, in honour of China's favourite Canadian, Dr Norman Bethune, who travelled throughout China in the 1930s as a surgeon and educator, and died there in a small village. The house details this and other aspects of his career and life.

All of these towns have numerous places to eat and many nearby motels and resorts.

ALGONQUIN PROVINCIAL PARK

Algonquin is Ontario's largest park and one of Canada's best known. Just 200-odd km north of Toronto, it offers hundreds of lakes in approximately 7800 sq km of near wilderness. There are 1600 km of charted canoe routes to explore, many of them interconnected by portage paths. There is one road through the park, Highway 60, which runs through the southern edge. Off it are lodges and nine campgrounds as well as wilderness outfitters who rent canoes and just about everything else. Maps are available at the park.

If you want some peace and quiet and a bit of adventure, I highly recommend this park. Algonquin and the Temagami area represent the two closest wilderness regions to Toronto and southern Ontario and provide a good opportunity to experience what much of Canada is all about.

There is a lot of wildlife in the park and not bad fishing either. And, for the most part, you can drink the water right out of the lakes. The canoe route maps, available for $3, have a lot of good information on the reverse side about the park as well as camping advice. (It's handy reading material for when you're inside the tent waiting for the storm to pass.)

At two access points off Highway 60 – Canoe Lake and Opeongo Lake – there are outfitters for renting canoes. This is where most people begin an interior canoe trip. Canoes are about $18 a day. At all other access points you must bring your own canoe. Because summer weekends are busy, a system of admitting only a certain number of people at each point has been established. Arrive early, or book at Algonquin Interiors (☎ (705) 633-5538 or 633-5725), PO Box 219, Whitney, Ontario, K0J 2M0.

The further in you get by portaging, the more solitude you'll find. I've had a whole lake to myself. A good trip takes three to four days. I find the western access points – Nos 3, 4 and 5 on the Algonquin map – good, with fewer people, smaller lakes and plenty of moose.

One of my very favourite spots is the campsite on the island in Timber Lake, which is accessible either from the south or the west. This is where my mind goes when I'm stuck in city traffic.

Mark Lightbody

Rick Ward's (☎ (705) 636-5956) in Kearney, north of Huntsville, rents canoes for just $15 a day, including paddles and life jackets. Another outfitter which has been recommended is Algonquin Outfitters in the village of Oxtongue, just outside the western edge of the park on Highway 60.

Interior camping is $3 per person per night. At the campgrounds, where there are showers and real toilets, a site is $9 or more. Among the highway campgrounds I would suggest Mew Lake. It has its own warm lake for swimming, some fairly attractive sites by the far side of the lake away from the highway, some walking trails nearby, and a store within walking distance.

The park runs its own wilderness canoe trips which include all equipment – canoe, food, supplies, and even sleeping bags – for about $40 per day or less for longer trips. Phone ☎ 633-5622 or visit the outfitting stores mentioned. Commercial outfitters can be found outside the park at either end.

There are also some interesting hiking trails within the park ranging from short half-hour jaunts around a marsh to several day-long treks.

The park museum on Highway 60 has displays on the history, geology and wildlife of the area and also has a good book store.

PARRY SOUND

Parry Sound sits about midway up Georgian Bay and is the largest of the small district supply towns during the summer vacation. There is a lookout tower with views over the bay.

Boat cruises of the 30,000 islands on the

Island Queen push off from Government Wharf. The trips are about three hours long, departing in the early afternoon, and run from June to September .

The town is also known for its summer classical music festival called the Festival of Sound. Quality live theatre is also presented in July and August.

Places to Stay

The *Sound House* (☎ 746-8806), a B&B place at 67 Church St, charges $45 for doubles. There are literally dozens of motels and cottages for rent in the area, some quite reasonably priced. The Parry Sound B&B Association lists such places available in and around town.

KILLBEAR PROVINCIAL PARK

Georgian Bay of Lake Huron is huge and grand enough to dwarf most of the world's waters. It's cool, deep, windy and majestic. The deeply indented, irregular shoreline along the eastern side, with its myriad islands, is trimmed by slabs of pink granite barely supporting wind-bent pine trees. This unique setting represents for many central Canadians, in words taken from the national anthem, '...our home and native land...'. The country's best known painters, the Group of Seven, have in their work linked this landscape to the Canadian experience.

Killbear Provincial Park is one of the best places to see what it's all about. There is shoreline to explore, three short but good walking trails, numerous little hidden sandy beaches and camping. Of course it's popular; in July and August call ahead to determine camping vacancies. I was there in September, however, and it was less than half-full. Many of the visitors spent the day painting and photographing. May and June would also be less busy. It's highly recommended even if an afternoon is all you have.

From Parry Sound east to Burk's Falls is more lake and timberland with numerous cottages, both private and commercial. Out of the summer season things are pretty quiet up here.

SHELBURNE

A rather nondescript small southern Ontario country town between Toronto and Owen Sound, Shelburne comes alive once a year for the old-time fiddlers' contest. It's held for two days in August and has been for over 40 years. There's a parade and free music shows, and the contest finals are only $4. Saturday night grand finals are $8 and those tickets must be reserved. For rooms in peoples' homes for the weekend, phone ☎ (519) 925-5535. For camping contact the Kinsmen Camp, Box 891, Shelburne.

DURHAM

Slightly to the north and west of Shelburne, this little town is the location of the annual North American banjo contest.

OWEN SOUND

Owen Sound, with a population of 20,000, is the largest centre in the region and, if you're going up the Bruce Peninsula or north to Manitoulin Island, you'll pass by it. It sits at the end of a deep bay surrounded on three sides by the steepness of the Niagara Escarpment.

Although still a working port it is not the shipping centre it was from the 1880s to the first years of this century. In those early days before the railway, the town rocked with brothels and bars battled by the believers. One intersection had a bar on each corner and was known as Damnation Corner, another had four churches and was called Salvation Corner. I guess the latter won out because the churches are still there. In fact for 66 long years from 1906 to 1972 you couldn't buy alcohol. There aren't too many sailors on the waterfront now but sections of it have been restored and it's an attractive setting for the marinas and restaurants.

Orientation & Information

The Sydenham River drifts through town, dividing it between east and west; the main street is Second Ave. A folder for a two-hour, self-guided historic walking tour of the city is available at City Hall.

Old Stores

Quite a few of the original brick buildings remain and there are some pretty old stores still open for business. Check out McKay Brothers with its old floors, cabinets and a cash register system that takes your money in a little box along a pulley line to the rear of the store, where your change is made up and then sent back the same way. Apparently there are only three such systems left in the country. And don't miss the mannequin heads either, with their real hair and teeth. There are other interesting places from the turn of the century, too.

Harrison Park

This is the large, green park right in town and along the Sydenham River. It has picnic areas, trails, fishing and even camping.

Tom Thomson Memorial Art Gallery

Thomson was a contemporary of Canada's Group of Seven and is one of the country's best known painters. He grew up here and many of his works were done in this part of the country. The gallery, at 840 1st Ave West, displays the work of some other Canadian painters as well. It's open daily in July and August; closed Sunday and Monday in other months.

County of Grey & Owen Sound Museum

Here you can see exhibits on the area's geology and human history. There's a half-sized replica of an Ojibwa Indian village as well as an eight-metre-birch-bark canoe on display. The museum is at 975 6th St East.

Mill Dam & Fish Ladder

In spring and fall it's interesting to see the struggle trout must go through to reach their preferred spawning areas – this dam and ladder were set up to help them.

Billy Bishop Heritage Museum

Home-town boy Billy Bishop, who became a flying ace in WW I, is honoured here. The museum is in the Bishop home. He is buried in town at the Greenwood Cemetery.

Kelso Beach

North of downtown on Georgian Bay is Kelso Beach. Free concerts are held regularly here in summer.

Inglis Falls

Six km south of town, off Highway 6, the Sydenham River falls over the Niagara Escarpment. The falls, a 24-metre drop, are set in a conservation area which is linked to the Bruce Trail. The trail runs from Tobermory south to the Niagara River. See under Tobermory for details. The segment by Owen Sound offers good views and springs, as well as the Inglis, Jones and Indian Falls. It makes a nice half-day walk.

Market

The Saturday market is beside City Hall.

Festivals

The three-day Summerfolk music festival, held annually around the second or third weekend of August, is a major north American festival of its kind. The event is held in Kelso Park right along the water and attracts crowds of up to 10,000. Musicians come from around the continent. Tickets cost about $14 a day – and each day is a full one. There's camping nearby.

Places to Stay

Camping Very conveniently, there are campgrounds right in town. One is across the road from Kelso Beach, ideal for the music festival. Another is in Harrison Park (☎ 376-5151), which charges $10 per site without electricity, and you can use the heated pool. (Georgian Bay is known for its cold water.)

Hotels The old downtown hotels, such as the *Seldon* at 1005 2nd Ave East which was built in 1887, are being converted to other uses but new, more expensive places are springing up around town and along the waterfront. An example is the *Inn on the Bay* (☎ 371-9200) with 60 rooms at 1800 2nd Ave East.

Motels Most of the accommodation here is provided by motels. There are several on 9th

St including the low-priced *Owen Sound Travellers Motel* (☎ 376-2680). The *Key Motel* (☎ 794-2350), 11 km south of town on highways 6 and 10, is costlier but still in the moderate range with rooms from $41 to $55.

Places to Eat

The *Erie Belle* has quite a British feeling, with pub grub and British brews. *Norma Jean's*, with a Marilyn Monroe theme, serves burgers, salads and other casual inexpensive fare. There are a few places along the waterfront and most offer seafood. One, the *Jolly Rodger* is on a boat moored off the harbour.

PORT ELGIN

Port Elgin is a little resort town on Lake Huron, west of Owen Sound. There are sandy beaches, the warm waters of Lake Huron, cottages and camping. MacGregor Provincial Park, with campgrounds and some walking trails, is five km south.

Further south is the Bruce Nuclear Plant, which is controversial, of course, as are all nuclear plants in Canada. They offer free tours and a film on nuclear power.

SAUBLE BEACH

Sauble Beach is a summer resort town due to its excellent, sandy 11-km beach. The coast all along here is known for good sunsets. There are plenty of hotels, motels and cottages for rent as well as entertainment diversions.

There are also many campgrounds in the area, all busy on summer weekends. Best is the *Sauble Falls Provincial Campground*. Reservations are a good idea. Further north along the road are several commercial grounds – for example, *White Sands* (☎ 534-2781) in Oliphant. Four of us in two tents paid $20 for one night here. The sites at the back have trees and are quiet.

Brown House (☎ 422-2504), a guesthouse, is at 24 Graham Crescent about two km south of the town's main intersection. Singles/doubles cost $28/38.

Cottages tend to be cheaper than motels. *Chilwell's Cottages* (☎ 422-1692) at 31 3rd Ave North has six small cottages and is one of the cheapest at $25 to $30 for doubles. Prices generally range from $35 to $70.

DYER'S BAY

If you have a car, a good scenic drive can be made around Dyer's Bay, which is about 20 km south of Tobermory. From Highway 6 take Dyer's side road into the village and then the road north-east along the coast. It's not long, but with Georgian Bay on one side and the limestone cliffs of the escarpment on the other, it is impressive. The road ends at the Cabot Head Lighthouse. Before arriving there, you'll pass by the ruins of an old log flume where logs were sent over the edge.

The road south of Dyer's Bay is also good, leading down to another flowerpot formation, this one known as the Devil's Monument. This secondary road goes to Lion's Head, where you can connect back with the main highway.

DORCAS BAY

On Lake Huron, about 11 km south of Tobermory, there is a preserve owned by the Federation of Ontario Naturalists. This preserve is not developed but mainly it's the wildflowers which attract the many walkers and photographers Up to 50 species of orchids can be spotted. To reach the site turn west from Highway 11 towards Lake Huron. You're there when you reach the parking lot with a few picnic tables and a toilet.

TOBERMORY

This small town sits at the northern tip of the Bruce Peninsula, which juts into Lake Huron. On one side of the peninsula are the cold, clear waters of Georgian Bay, and on the other is the much warmer main body of Lake Huron. There is not much to see in town itself, but it is a busy spot in summer for several reasons. Firstly, the ferry to Manitoulin Island departs and arrives here. Many people driving across Ontario take this route as it saves time driving around Georgian Bay. Manitoulin Island has its own charms as well.

In addition, Tobermory is the centre for several government parks and marks the end of the Bruce Trail. The town is also a diving centre; the waters offshore contain 50 known sunken ships.

To reach Tobermory see under Manitoulin Island.

Bruce Trail

Tobermory marks the northern end of this 700-km footpath, which runs from Queenston on the Niagara River to this point on the tip of the Bruce Peninsula on Georgian Bay, over private and public lands. You can hike for an hour, a day or a week. The scenery is good as the trail edges along the Niagara Escarpment, and much of it is inaccessible from the road.

The most northerly bit from Dyer's Bay to Tobermory is the most rugged and most spectacular.

The Bruce Trail Association (☎ 529-6821, in Hamilton) puts out a detailed map of the entire route for about $20, less for members. The head office is at Raspberry House, PO Box 857 Hamilton, L8N 3N9. There is also an office in Toronto. The Grey-Bruce Tourist Association has a map of the top portion of the trail for $2. Other tourist offices can tell you where there are access points. Some parts of the trail are heavily used on summer weekends. Near Hamilton at the southern end is a popular day walking area at Rattlesnake Point Conservation Area. Another southern one is at Terra Cotta not far from Toronto. Yet another is at the forks of the Credit River.

There are designated areas for camping along the path, although in the gentler, busy southern sections some huts are provided where even a shower can be taken.

In another section there is accommodation in B&Bs or old inns. Country Host is a network of B&Bs which caters to hikers with homes along the trail. Prices are around $40/45 to $50 for singles/doubles. Contact Grace Conin (☎ (519) 941-7633), Rural Route 1, Palgrave, Postal Code L0N 1P0.

Don't drink the water along the trail and bring good boots: much of the trail is wet and muddy. And don't forget the insect repellent.

Fathom Five National Marine Park

Newly enlarged, Ontario's first partially underwater park was developed to protect and make more accessible this interesting area. Nineteen wrecks lie in the park's waters, scattered between the many little islands. There is a visitor's centre on Little Tub Harbour in Tobermory. They have displays and can offer information and advice on things to see and do.

Flowerpot Island, five km offshore from Tobermory is one of the park's interesting sections and is more easily enjoyed than the underwater attractions! Flowerpot Island, with its unusual, precarious-looking rock columns formed through years of erosion, can be visited by boat from town.

There are various trails on the island, taking from a little over an hour for the shortest one to 2¼ hours for the more difficult. The island has cliffs, caves, picnic spots and just a few camping sites. Reservations are needed and you should take all supplies.

Various companies offer boat trips to the island, where you can hop off if you wish and catch a later boat back. The cost is $10. The *True North* boat doesn't charge any extra to drop you at Flowerpot Island. The price also includes a cruise past some of the shipwrecks visible in the very clear waters.

The offices for boat trips are all around the harbour in Tobermory.

Bruce Peninsula National Park

This newly formed national park has several components including Cypress Lake, some of the Georgian Bay coastline and the Niagara Escarpment between Tobermory and Dyer's Bay. See under Bruce Trail for details.

Parks & Canoeing

Between Tobermory and Wasaga Beach are three provincial parks and several river canoe routes. Local tourist offices have information on them.

The **Saugeen River** has been divided up into canoeing sections ranging from 20 km to 40 km. Half-day and longer trips have been mapped out. There's camping along the

Saugeen River at several points. A shorter trip is along the **Rankin River**.

Just south of Tobermory there is camping available at **Cypress Lake** for $9. One section is for RVs, another is for tenters only. Swimming in Georgian Bay in August can be good and warm but not around here. The shallow lake in the park is definitely a more sane choice. Further south on the bay at **Wasaga Beach** and **Penetanguishene** the water is quite pleasant.

Part of the Bruce Trail – right along the bay – goes through the Bruce Peninsula National Park, and a good day's hike is possible. You may even see one of the rare Ontario rattlesnakes.

Diving

The waters here are excellent for scuba diving, with many wrecks, geological formations and very clear water. The water is also very cold, however. Programmes are available for beginners to advanced divers. Equipment is available in town. Snorkelling is possible in some areas, too. The Ontario government has a pamphlet listing dive sites with descriptions, depths and recommendations. It's available free at the tourist office.

Places to Stay

There are many places to stay in and around town but prices are a little high. The *Grandview* (☎ 596-2220) right by the harbour has a fine view and the meals are quite good. Nearby motels are less costly.

MANITOULIN ISLAND

The world's largest freshwater island, Manitoulin Island is basically a rural region of small farms. It's about 140 km long and 40 km wide. About a third of the population is Native Indian. Recently, tourism has become the island's main moneymaker and many southerners own summer cottages.

The island has a scenic coastline, some sandy beaches, 100 lakes, including some very large ones, lots of small towns and villages, plenty of hiking trails. It has remained fairly undeveloped.

From the ferry landing on the island, 3½-hour sight-seeing tours (☎ 282-2848, on the island) by bus operate during July and August daily, except Sunday. Tours depart early in the afternoon and include stops at some of the scenic spots as well as at Native Indian craft shops.

West of the ferry landing at the village of **Providence Bay** is the island's best beach. Beyond **Meldrum Bay** at the far western tip of the island at **Mississagi Point** is an old lighthouse (1873) which provides views over the strait. There is a campground here, a restaurant and a museum. Meldrum Bay has an inn with a restaurant. Along the north side of the island from Meldrum Bay to Little Current is some of the best scenery.

Gore Bay on the rocky north shore has one of the island's many small museums and displays articles relating to the early island settlers. See the prisoner's dining room table from the jail. From the eastern headland at the edge of town the lookout offers fine views. On the other side of town, the headland has a lighthouse and campground. One of the main beauty spots, **Bridal Veil Falls**, is 16 km east.

The largest community is **Little Current**, at the beginning of the causeway over to the mainland towards Espanola. The tourist office for the island is here. There are two viewpoints of note near town and one very good walk. The Cup & Saucer Trail, 19 km east of town, leads to the highest point on the island at 351 metres, which has good views over the North Channel. Closer to town is **McLeans Mountain**, four km west, and 16 km south on Highway 6 is a lookout with views towards the village of **Killarney** on the mainland.

As mentioned, Manitoulin Island has a considerable Native Indian population. At the **Wikwemikong Reserve**, the largest powwows (which are loosely translated as 'cultural festivals') in the province are held in spring and summer.

Native Indians from around the country participate. Tourist offices may know the schedule. It's an interesting event with dancing and music, food and crafts.

Wikwemikong is in the north-east part of Manitoulin Island.

Two principal attractions of the island for many visitors are the fishing and boating. There are several fishing camps around the island. For cruising, the 225-km North Channel is superb. The scenery is great: one fjord, **Baie Finn**, is 15 km long with pure white quartzite cliffs. And the water is clean enough to drink from the side of the boat.

Getting There & Away

Bus Getting to the island is a little difficult, particularly without a car. From Toronto, buses run to Tobermory only in summer and are infrequent even then. The trip takes almost the whole day. The schedule varies each year so call for the latest information, but at last check, the bus ran inconveniently in both directions only on Friday, Saturday and Sunday. This means you either get at least a week or just a day at Manitoulin Island. It's quite a long bus trip and not cheap either. Furthermore, there is no train service up this way.

Ferry From Tobermory, two ferries run over to South Baymouth on the southern edge of Manitoulin. The principal ship is the *Chi-Cheemaun* which, despite being able to handle 600 passengers and 115 cars, became so busy that a second ferry, the MS *Nindawayma*, has been added. In midsummer the *Chi-Cheemaun* makes four crossings daily, two in spring and fall. From Tobermory, departures times are 7 and 11.20 am, 3.40 and 8 pm. Tickets are $10 per adult, $22 for a car; it's slightly cheaper in spring and fall.

The *Nindawayma* runs twice daily. There's a small charge for bicycles. The ferry season is from early May to mid-October and out of the prime season the second ship does not operate. The trip of 50 km takes about 1¾ hours and there are cafeterias on board. For reservations, call ☎ 800-265-3163 toll free. It's not uncommon to have to wait in line for a crossing.

The island also makes a good short cut if you're heading to northern Ontario. Take the ferry from Tobermory, cross the island and then the bridges to the north shore of Georgian Bay. The route can save you a few hours of driving around the bay and is pleasant.

South-Western Ontario

This designation covers everything south of Toronto to lakes Huron and Erie, which border the USA. For the most part the area is flat farmland – the only area in Ontario with little forest – and population density is high. With the warm climate and long growing season, this southern tip of Canada was settled early.

Arching around Lake Ontario is a continuous strip of urbanisation. This 'Golden Horseshoe' helps make the region one of the most industrialised and wealthy in the country.

Hamilton, the largest city in the area, is a major steel town. Niagara, with its famous falls, is an important fruit-growing district.

Further west, the soil becomes sandier and the main crop is tobacco, although this is changing as the cigarette market shrinks. Around Kitchener and London the small towns are centres for the mixed farming of the region. Lake Erie and Lake Huron both have sandy beaches. In some of the older country towns crafts and antiques are available.

Windsor – like its counterpart across the river, Detroit, Michigan – is an auto-manufacturing centre.

Because the area is heavily populated and the USA is close by, attractions and parks do get busy in summer. This is an area for people-related activities and pastimes, not for nature or rugged landscapes.

HAMILTON

Hamilton, sometimes referred to as Steeltown, is a heavily industrialised city with about 310,000 residents. It's situated halfway between Toronto and Niagara Falls.

This is the centre of Canada's iron and steel industry with two major companies, Stelco and Defasco here. Because of this industry, the city has a bit of a reputation as a pollution centre.

Action has been taken to clean it up and work in this direction continues. Although the air cannot be compared to that of the far north (what can?), these days some of what one sees billowing from the many smoke-stacks is actually steam. While Hamilton is obviously not a tourist centre, there are none-theless a few good things to see in and around town. As accommodation is reasonable here, it may be worth considering spending the night if you're planning a look around Niagara-on-the-Lake with its very high prices.

Orientation

King St (one way going west) and Main St (one way going east, parallel to and one block south of King St) are the two main streets. King St has most of the downtown shops and restaurants. King and John Sts are the core of the downtown area. Jackson Square, on King St between Bay and James Sts, is a large, new shopping complex that includes restaurants, cinemas and even an indoor skating rink. The Convention Centre with an art gallery is on the corner of King and MacNab Sts. Just south across Main St is City Hall. The bus terminal is on Rebecca St, off John St, about three blocks from the centre of town.

Information

The downtown central tourist office (☎ 522-7772) is at 127 King St East and operates seven days a week, all year. Other summer-only information centres are in busy visitor centres around the city such as the Royal Botanical Gardens or at the African Lion Safari.

Royal Botanical Gardens

The Royal Botanical Gardens – nearly 1000 hectares of flowers, natural park and wildlife sanctuary – is probably the big attraction in the area. It is one of the largest of its kind in

the country and only one of five in the world to be designated 'Royal'. The grounds are split into sections with trails connecting some areas.

In July and August, the Trial Garden – the rock and herb gardens – and Hendrie Park are best. The arboretum has the world's largest lilac collection (what an olfactory treat) which is best in May. There is also an interpretive centre and two restaurants at the gardens. It is a little out of town on Plains Rd, at the junction of highways 2 and 6 and is open daily all year. It's free, but donations are invited.

Art Gallery

The art gallery, the province's third-largest, is new, very spacious and has a good selection of Canadian and international painting. They also run an interesting film series with screenings mainly on weekends.

Tours of the gallery are given if requested in advance. The gallery is open from Tuesday to Saturday from 10 am to 5 pm, except on Thursday when it's open to 9 pm and on Sunday from 1 to 5 pm. It's closed on Monday and holidays. Admission is $2, students $1.

Hamilton Place

In the same complex as the art gallery is this theatre-auditorium for the performing arts. Shows of various types are featured almost nightly, including regular performances by the Philharmonic and the Opera Company. Tours are available.

Hess Village

Two blocks west of the Convention Centre on Hess St is this renovated area of old houses now containing boutiques, restaurants and cafés. It is well promoted but small and not particularly interesting.

Dundurn Castle

One man's castle, Dundurn is actually a 36-room mansion once belonging to Sir Allan Napier McNab, the prime minister from 1854 to 1856. It's furnished in mid-1800s style. The mansion is on York Blvd just out of town, about a 15-minute walk or you can grab the York city bus. It's open daily all year but from June to September is open only during the afternoon.

Concerts and various shows are held on the grounds through the summer.

Also at the site is a miltary museum with weapons and uniforms dating from the War of 1812 to more modern times.

Canadian Warplane Heritage Museum

The museum has about 40 vintage planes, all in flying condition. A new addition is a huge, restored Lancaster bomber from WW II. Many of the planes, together with newer ones from a variety of sources, are part of an excellent two-day air show held in mid-June which attracts tens of thousands of people. The museum is at the Hamilton Airport in hangars Nos 3 and 4. There is a cafeteria and a gift shop.

Museum of Steam & Technology

The old pumphouse dating from 1860 was built to supply clean water when cholera and typhus menaced the city. Now restored, these steam engines are among the largest in North America. Trimmed with mahogany and brass, they are quite attractive objects. Also featured are photographs and engine exhibits. Admission costs $2.25 and the museum, at 900 Woodward Ave, is open daily but in the afternoon only from October to May.

Confederation Park

Not far north of town on Centennial Parkway, this park contains Wild Waterworks, with a water slide and a swimming pool with waves. There is also a beach along Lake Ontario and picnic and camping facilities.

African Lion Safari

Here you'll see about 1000 animals and birds in one vast park, where there are no cages. You drive through, sometimes getting very close to lions, tigers and other animals. Monkeys climb all over the car. Or you can take the park tour bus. African Lion Safari is open from April to October, with the longest

hours in July and August but it still closes at that time of the year at 5.30 pm. The park is between Hamilton and Cambridge on Highway 8.

Festivals

The Festival of Friends happens each August in Gage Park and features music, crafts and foods from many countries.

Each June, in the town of Stoney Creek south of Hamilton an interesting spectacle is the re-enactment of a War of 1812 battle between British and US soldiers. It's held at Stoney Creek Battlefield Park.

Places to Stay

Camping There are numerous local campgrounds including one in Confederation Park, just north of town on Centennial Parkway.

Hostels For low-budget lodgings the *YMCA* (☎ 529-7102) at 79 James St is a large place with 171 rooms, for men only, at $25 a single. The *YWCA* (☎ 522-9922) at 75 McNab St is comparable, although much smaller, with rooms at $30/44 for singles/doubles. Both have pools and inexpensive cafeterias.

Tourist Homes Try the *Cobblestone Lodge* (☎ 545-9735), a huge old place now a tourist home at 684 Main St East, on the corner of Holton Avenue. It is often busy and the owner, Aileen Harvey, prefers to see you rather than speak over the phone, but it's worth a try. Rooms run from $32 to $55 a double depending on facilities.

Hotels Though many of the downtown hotels are new and large there are some choices which are not too expensive. Accommodation is generally more reasonable here than in either Toronto or around the heavily touristed region of Niagara-on-the-Lake.

At 737 King St East is the *Budget Motor Hotel* (☎ 527-2708) with singles/doubles at $38.

The *Town Manor Motor Hotel* (☎ 528-

0611) is also central, at 175 Main St near Caroline St, near Hess Village. A single here is $33, a double $40 or so, depending on whether it's a double bed or twin beds.

The new *Visitors Inn* (☎ 529-6979), at 649 Main St West, is more expensive but also quite good value.

Further out, close to McMaster University at 1870 Main St West, the *Mountain View Motel* (☎ 528-7521) costs from $38 to $48 for two people.

On the outskirts, either east or west, motels abound and for the most part are in the low to moderate price category, much lower than those around Niagara-on-the-Lake.

Places to Eat

The downtown area around King St in St Catharine's has numerous restaurants – various ethnic places.

You can choose between Chinese, Greek and Italian food.

At Ferguson St, the *Black Forest Inn*, with a German and Austrian slant, is pleasant and reasonable with soups and sandwiches. At dinner time it has a more expensive and extensive menu featuring a variety of schnitzels.

Le Ganges at 234 King St is not really cheap but serves good Indian food.

In Hess Village the *Gown & Gavel*, a British-style pub at 24 Hess St serves light meals and beer under the umbrellas.

There are many places to eat in the Jackson Square shopping mall. Many others suiting a range of budgets can be found along King, Main and William Sts.

Don Cherry's *Grapevine* (owned by one of the country's best known hockey commentators, who is admired or vilified for his strong and vocal opinions) is a popular sports bar and watering hole at 157 Main St East.

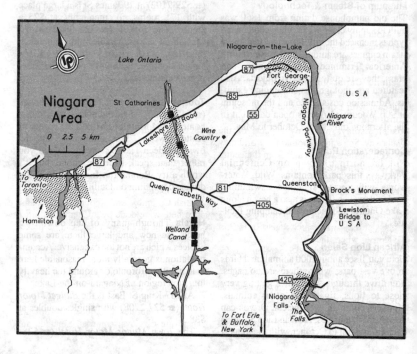

ST CATHARINE'S

Lying between Hamilton and the Niagara River on Lake Ontario, St Catharine's is the major town of the Niagara fruit and wine growing district. To each side are farms and small towns with vineyards and wineries.

In late September, the Niagara Grape & Wine Festival is held with concerts, wine and cheese parties and a parade.

WELLAND CANAL

The most noteworthy feature of the area is the historic Welland Canal, a bypass of Niagara Falls which connects Lake Ontario with Lake Erie. A series of locks along the 40-km-long canal overcome the difference of about 100 metres in the lakes' water levels.

Remnants of the first three canals built in 1829, 1845 and 1887 can be seen at various points. The forth version, still in use but with some modifications and additions, was built between 1914 and 1932.

At ⌐, in the area along the lake at the corner of Mountain and Bradley Sts, old locks, lighthouses and various structures from the last century can be viewed.

For a more up-to-date look, visit the **Welland Canal Viewing & Information Centre**. It's at Lock III and includes a museum with exhibits on the canal and its construction, a viewing platform and audiovisual displays on many aspects of the waterway. Ships from around the world may be seen on their way to and from the centre of North America and the Atlantic Ocean. Fifty million tonnes of cargo are transported through the canal annually. The centre is open daily all year.

Fortune Navigation is a company offering cruises of the canal, which depart from Port Dalhousie where the first canal began. The three-hour trip, costing $15, continues as far up the new canal at Port Wellar as possible, but passing through Lock I depends on freight traffic, so trips will vary in distance covered. There are family and kids' rates.

The cruises depart at 2 pm and run from mid-May to October. Getting to the dock area is a little tricky. It's near Lakeside Park in Port Dalhousie. If driving, take the Ontario St exit off the Queen Elizabeth Way (QEW) and continue north to Lakeport Rd, where a left turn should be made. From there just keep going over the bridges and you should see a sign.

At **Mountain View Park,** on the corner of Mountain and Bradley Sts, there are locks at the escarpment from the second canal along with some other 19th-century buildings.

For hikers, there is the Merritt Trail, a walk which stretches from St Catharine's to Port Colbourne, mainly following along the Welland Canal. It is detailed in the Bruce Trail guidebook; see under Tobermory in this chapter. Local tourist offices will also have information about this trail.

WELLAND

Despite the predominance of agriculture in the region, Welland is primarily a steel town. A portion of the canal cuts right through town while a larger, newer, busy bypass channel is two km from the downtown area; from there, international freighters can be viewed.

The city has become known for its two dozen painted murals depicting scenes from the history of the area and the canal. Begun in 1988, they can be seen around town on the sides of buildings. The heaviest concentration of murals is along East Main St and the streets connecting it to parallel Division St, one block away. There are others along King and Niagara Sts. This interesting idea has been immensely successful in Chemainus, British Columbia and a couple of the paintings here were done by a Chemainus artist. A pamphlet on the paintings can be picked up in an office upstairs at 800 Niagara St in the Seaway Mall, or at one of the local tourist offices.

The museum at 65 Hooker St offers more details on the canals.

In early June the two-week-long Rose Festival celebrates the queen of flowers. There are displays, contests, a parade and other events.

PORT COLBOURNE

At one end of the Welland Canal on Lake Erie, Port Colbourne has one of the largest water locks in the world. There are also beaches in the area and a number of cottage communities nearby along the shoreline.

NIAGARA-ON-THE-LAKE

This small, pretty village is about 20 km downstream from the falls, and with its up-market shops and restaurants, well-known George Bernard Shaw Festival, and curbs on development, acts as a sort of foil to the hype and flash of Niagara Falls. The surrounding vineyards and history-filled parkland add to its appeal. Originally a Native Indian site, it was settled by Loyalists from New York state after the American Revolution. It is considered one of the best preserved 19th-century towns in North America and in the 1790s was made the first capital of Ontario.

The main street, Queen St, has many well-preserved shops from the 1800s. With its lakeside location, tree-lined streets and old houses, it makes a nice place to see before or after the falls. The village does get very busy on good summer days, though generally only on the main street. Stroll down the side streets and you'll get a quiet taste of former times in a prosperous small Ontario town.

Information

The tourist office (☎ 468-4263), in the Chamber of Commerce on the corner of King St and Prideaux/Byron Sts, is very good, friendly and helpful. They will book accommodation for you although there is a fee for the service. From May to early September the office is open every day; later in the year, the hours are shortened and it's closed on weekends. On the eastern side of the downtown area towards Niagara Falls, King St crosses Queen St at large Simcoe Park on the east side of Queen St.

Queen Street

The town's main street, Queen St, is the prime attraction. Restored and well-maintained wooden buildings and shops now contain antiques, bakeries, various speciali-

ties, Scottish souvenirs and restaurants. Note particularly the apothecary dating from 1866, now a museum, fitted with great old cabinets, remedies and jars. Also recommended is a jam sample from the Greaves store; the people here are fourth-generation jam-makers. There are a couple of fudge shops too.

The recently renovated courthouse, also on Queen St, is another impressive building.

From the tourist office, pick up a copy of the *Historic Guide* which lists many of the historically noteworthy structures around town and indicates them on a map. Towards the falls, but still in town, Queen St becomes Picton St.

Museums

The **Historical Museum** at 43 Castlereagh St is the oldest local museum in the province. It opened in 1907 and has a collection of early 20th-century items relating to the town's past. Admission is $2. Through the summer it is open daily from 10 am to 6 pm. The remainder of the year, it is open in the afternoons only, and during January and February only on weekends.

McFarland House is a handsome Georgian-style place built around 1800 by John McFarland, a carpenter from Scotland. Restored in 1959, it is now furnished with articles dating up to 1840. During the War of 1812 it was used as a hospital. The house is on the Niagara Parkway North out of town and is open daily during summer from 11 am to 5 pm. Also in town is the **Fire Museum** with firefighting equipment that dates from 1816 to 1976.

Historic Military Sites

Just out of Niagara-on-the-Lake towards the falls, **Fort George**, dating from 1797, is one of several local historic military sites. It's open daily and admission is $2 for adults. It was the site of important battles during the War of 1812 and changed hands between the British and Americans a couple of times. Within the walls, you can see the officers' quarters, a working kitchen, the powder magazine and storage houses. There isn't a lot to see, but the various costumed demonstrators, particularly the soldiers performing different exercises, are interesting.

Tucked behind the fort at the water's edge is **Navy Hall**, where only one building remains of what was a sizeable supply depot for British forts on the Great Lakes during the 1700s. It was destroyed during the War of 1812. Fort Niagara is across the river.

In a fine location on the other side of town, at the opposite end of Ricardo St, are the minimal remains of **Fort Mississauga**. There are some plaques but no organised tours or facilities.

Also in town are **Butler's Barracks**, off John St at King St; pedestrians can reach it either from Mary St or along a trail leading from Fort George. First used by the British at the end of the War of 1812 as a storage and barracks site, the location has been used since for a variety of purposes by the Canadian military. Troops for both world wars and the Korean War trained here. Some buildings remain from the various periods of use and markers lead visitors around on a mini-Canadian military history tour.

Organised Tours

C Peter Neufeld (☎ 468-7347) runs Gardenland Tours, by appointment only, during the summer months. Where they go varies with the customer's wishes so they can be quite individual and specialised. A tour might include visits to 19th-century houses and maybe a farmer's market or a winery.

Cruises of the river down to Queenston are offered aboard *The Senator* which docks at the Olde Boatworks, off Ricardo St sort of tucked in behind Fort George. Ricardo St is a couple of blocks from Picton St. Rather ordinary from the outside, the ship's interior is quite elegant and has a very attractive dining room. Trips range from straightforward sight-seeing tours, to longer dinner or moonlit dance cruises.

Festivals

The Shaw Festival is an internationally respected theatre festival held here annually (May to September). It features the plays of G B Shaw and his contemporaries, played by top actors. There are three different theatres, and the location has a bearing on ticket prices. Cheapest are the weekday matinees.

Tickets range from $10, and up to $34 for the best seats in the house on Saturday night. Cheaper rush seats available on the day of performance go on sale at 9.30 am, but aren't available for Saturday performances. There are brief lunch time plays for $12.50. The box office (☎ 468-2172) is open from 10 am to 9 pm every day from June to mid-October.

Places to Stay

Accommodation here is expensive. For most people a few hours looking around will suffice before finding cheaper lodging elsewhere.

There are some very fine inns in town as well as several good hotels. By far the bulk of the accommodation, though, is in the many less expensive tourist homes and B&Bs. And though I said less expensive, this does not mean cheap, with rates at about $65 and up for a double. The tourist office will find you a room but then ask $5 booking fee.

At 341 Dorchester St, one of the least expensive of the tourist homes belongs to *Dietlinde Witt* (☎ 468-3989) who charges single/double $35/45. A German-style breakfast is included. No smoking is permitted.

Similarly priced is *Arnold Wiens* (☎ 468-2091) at 189 William St. Also with reasonable rates is *Amberlea Guest House* (☎ 468-5607) found at 285 John St. There are a couple of rooms from $55 to $65 which includes a full breakfast.

A fourth possibility is the central *Saltbox* (☎ 468-5423) in an old house at 223 Gate St. Again a full breakfast is provided and smoking is not permitted. It's open all year. Rates here are around $65 for doubles.

Lastly, *Mrs Lynda Kay Knapp* (☎ 468-3935) offers a separate, private unit, almost like a little apartment, with some cooking facilities and a fridge for $75 for two people. It's not open in winter. Her house is close to the centre of town at 390 Simcoe St. Couples, note that she may ask if you're married and not want to rent if you don't answer satisfactorily.

Among the pricier options is the *Angel Inn* (☎ 468-3411), dating from 1823, one block south from Queen St on Regent St. The slightly older *Old Bank House* is a B&B at 10 Front St, on the corner of King St by the lake. The *Moffat Inn* (☎ 468-4116) is a very attractive white-and-green place at 60 Picton St with all the amenities at the relatively reasonable rate of about $90.

Places to Eat

There are a number of good places to eat in town. In fact, for the money, you're better off eating here than at the falls, especially at lunch.

At 45 Queen St, the *Stagecoach* is very cheap and always very busy. You can get a good-value breakfast before 11 am.

The *Old Time Ice Cream Shoppe & Restaurant* has inexpensive breakfasts and sandwiches.

For a pub meal, try the *Buttery* at 19 Queen St with a pleasant patio. Saturday nights they put on Henry VIII-style feasts with entertainment, drink and victuals aplenty.

The *Angel*, just off Queen St on Regent St and dating from 1823, is another British pub-type place with fish & chips, sandwiches and various beers. Prices range from $4 to $8.

Fan's Court, around the back at 135 Queen St, provides some very fine ethnic diversion in this most Anglo of towns. It serves moderately priced Chinese and Asian dishes such as Singapore-style noodles with curry. Aside from the pleasant dining room there are also a few tables outside in a small courtyard.

The *English Tea Room*, at 65 Queen St, is the perfect place for a tea and scone or piece of freshly baked pie.

The *Prince of Wales Hotel* has a good dining room for finer, more costly eating. Most of the inns and hotels have their own dining rooms.

A few blocks from Queen St, Queen's Royal Park along the water makes a good place for a picnic.

Entertainment

In Simcoe Park, right in town, there are often free classical music concerts on summer Saturdays.

Getting There & Away

There are buses between here and Toronto on Tuesdays, Thursdays and Saturdays, but only during the summer. The fare is $12.05 one way.

A local bus, the Blue Bird, runs between here and Niagara Falls, leaving from the Prince of Wales Hotel and going to the main bus station in Niagara Falls. The express bus is $8, the milk run $5. It leaves Niagara-on-the-Lake at 10 am and 6 pm.

Getting Around

Bicycle Cycling is a fine way to explore the area and bicycles can be rented by the hour, half-day or full day at Old Town Sportwear, 122 Queen St.

AROUND NIAGARA-ON-THE-LAKE
Vineyards & Wine Tours

The triangle between St Catharine's, Niagara-on-the-Lake and Niagara Falls is, along with the Okanagan Valley in British Columbia, the country's most important wine-producing area.

The ever increasing number of wineries – there are around a dozen – are now producing some pretty fine grape juice and many offer visitors a taste and a look around. A full day could be enjoyed touring the countryside and emptying glasses. Some of the commercial tour operators include a winery or two on their bus excursions. Most of these are operated out of Niagara Falls.

Some of the principal wines are riesling, chardonnay and gewurztraminer. Whites tend to dominate but reds are also produced. Canada's oldest winery Bright's (☎ 357-2400) is at 4887 Dorchester Rd, Niagara Falls, north off Highway 420. Free one-hour tours with wine sampling are given at 10.30 am, 2 and 3.30 pm every day except Sundays and holidays.

There are plenty of others around this area. In St Catharine's, around the shoreline

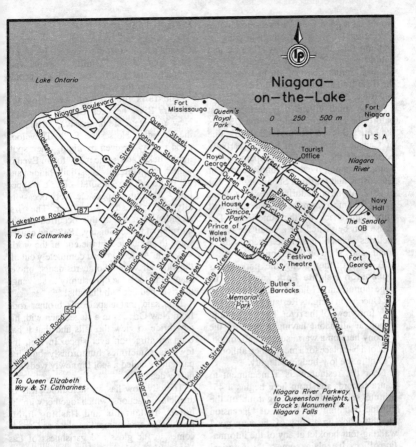

towards Hamilton, are Jordan and St Michelle wineries. The latter, at 120 Ridley Rd, has tours Monday to Friday at 10 am, 1 and 3 pm.

Also there is Barnes (☎ 682-6631), open Monday to Saturday, which offers free tours with a taste at the same times as the above. It is off Martindale Rd near the Queen Elizabeth Way. Or you could try André's free tours and samples. It's in Winona, close to Hamilton on the lake (between Hamilton and Grimsby). Inniskillin has been developing a very good reputation and winning awards. Or lastly, try Château des Charmes (☎ 262-

4219) in St David's, between the falls and Niagara-on-the-Lake. It's on Line 7 off Four Mile Creek Rd, not far from the highway, and is open all day, from Monday to Saturday.

NIAGARA PARKWAY

A slow, 20-km trip along the **Niagara Parkway** to Niagara Falls is most enjoyable. Along the way are parks, picnic areas, good views over the river and a couple of campgrounds making up part of the Niagara Parks System, which runs along the river for 55 km from Niagara-on-the-Lake, past the falls to Fort Erie. Riding a bike on the excursion would be a good idea. A three-metre-wide recreational trail for cycling, jogging or walking runs the entire way. Historic and natural points of interest are marked with plaques. Perhaps best of all, in season, are the fresh fruit stands with cold cherry ciders and juices.

In the small village of Queenston, just before the Lewiston Bridge to the USA, is the **Laura Secord Homestead**. Laura, one of Canada's best known heroes (partially because of the chocolate company which bears her name), lived here on the corner of Queenston and Partition Sts during the War of 1812. At one point during the war she went nearly 30 km to warn the British soldiers of impending attack by the Americans. The house can be visited for a small fee which includes a chocolate sample. There is also a small candy shop on the premises.

A little further along the parkway is **Queenston Heights Park** known for its large monument of Major General Brock and the Queenston Heights Restaurant which has very fine views of the river. There is nothing wrong at all about having a beer on the balcony here on a warm summer afternoon. It's not a bad place for a meal either, although it's not in the low-budget category.

Near the restaurant is a monument to Laura Secord, and from here begins a 45-minute self-guided walking tour of the hillside detailing the Battle of Queenston Heights. Pick up a copy of the very good walking-tour booklet at any of the information offices. It explains some of the historical background, outlines the War of 1812 and describes how the British battle victory here was significant in Canada's not becoming part of the USA. Interpreters are on hand at the huge Brock monument and the guidebook should be available there.

Also in Queenston is the southern end of the Bruce Trail, which extends 700 km to Tobermory on Georgian Bay. There are numerous access points in the Niagara and Hamilton area. For more details on the trail, see under the Tobermory section in this chapter.

NIAGARA FALLS

The roaring falls make this town one of Canada's top tourist destinations. It's a very busy spot, about 12 million people visit annually, and you'll hear and see people from all over the world.

The falls themselves, spanning the Niagara River between Ontario and upper New York state, are impressive, particularly the Canadian Horseshoe Falls. They look good by day, or even by night, when spotlights flicker across the misty foam. Even in winter, when the flow is partially hidden and the edges are frozen solid – like a stopped film – it's quite a spectacle. Very occasionally the falls stop altogether. The first recorded instance of this occurred on the morning of Easter Sunday, 1848, and caused some to speculate that the end of the world was nigh. An ice jam had completely cut off the flow of water. Some residents, braver than I am, took the opportunity to scavenge the river bed beneath the falls!

It is said that Napoleon's brother rode from New Orleans in a stagecoach with his new bride to view the falls and that it has been an attraction ever since. In fact, the town is sometimes humorously but disparagingly called a spot for newly weds and nearly deads.

The city now has an incredible array of artificial attractions, which together with the hotels, restaurants and flashing lights produce an environment as close as Canada comes to the gloss and garishness of Las Vegas. It's a sight in itself.

Niagara Falls is approximately a two-hour drive from Toronto by the Queen Elizabeth Way (QEW), past Hamilton and St Catharine's. Public transportation between Toronto and Niagara Falls is very frequent and quick.

Orientation

The town of Niagara Falls is split into two main sections: the older commercial area where the locals go about their business and the other part around the falls which has been developed for visitors. In the 'normal' part of town, known as downtown, Queen St and

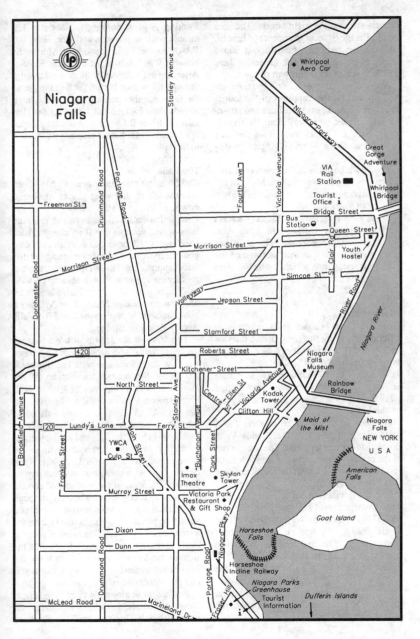

Niagara Falls

Victoria Ave are the main streets. The area around Bridge St, near the corner of Erie St, has both the train and bus stations and a couple of cheap hotels. But generally there is little to see or do in this part of town.

About three km south along the river are the falls and all the trappings of the tourist trade – restaurants, motels, shops and attractions. Going the other way along the river is scenic parkland which runs from the falls downstream about 40 km to Niagara-on-the-Lake.

The youth hostel is in the downtown area not far from the railway station. Many of the local tourist homes are also between the two sections of town.

In the vicinity of the falls, the main streets are the very busy Clifton Hill, Falls Ave, Centre St and Victoria Ave. The latter has many places to stay as well as some of the numerous restaurants which can be found on all the main streets.

Information
There are three Niagara Falls information offices, each using the same phone number (☎ 356-6061). Among other things, they can help in locating a room for the night. One of the offices is at 4673 Ontario Ave at Bridge St, just up the street from Whirlpool Bridge away from the town centre towards Niagara-on-the-Lake.

Another is closer to Horseshoe Falls, south along the river at the Rapids View People Mover bus terminal. The third is out of the centre, on the corner of Lundy's Lane and Beaverdams Rd, near the QEW to either Fort Erie or Toronto.

The provincial tourism ministry runs the large Ontario Travel Information Centre (☎ 358-3221), which can be found on Roberts St (Highway 420) leading from Rainbow Bridge to the Queen Elizabeth Way. The nearest cross street is Stanley Ave. The tourist office is about halfway between the bridge and the highway. Information on destinations across the province and Ontario maps can be picked up here. It's open until 8 pm through the summer.

Parking A good parking lot, about a 15-minute walk to the falls and free, is by the IMAX movie theatre, south of Murray St between it and Robinson St near the Skylon. After leaving your car, walk down the stairs through the woods beside the hotel to get to the falls. Another parking place is the huge Rapids View Parking Lot 3.2 km south of the falls off River Rd where the bus loop depot is situated. From here a pleasant walk leads to the falls.

The Falls
The 56-metre falls are a great sight – close up, just where the water begins to plunge down, is the best spot. Also good is the observation deck of the souvenir shop by the falls, which you can use at no charge. After checking out all the angles at all times of day, you can try several services offering yet different approaches. For overall views, there is the Skylon Tower at 5200 Robinson St, with its outside glass elevators. There is also an observation deck in Maple Leaf Village, a boutique-style shopping mall at 5705 Falls Ave by Rainbow Bridge.

The *Maid of the Mist* boat takes passengers up to the falls for a view from the bottom – a view that's loud and wet. The ride costs $7. Board the boat at the bottom of the incline railway at the foot of Clifton Hill. From Queen Victoria Park at the falls you can pay $4.50, don a poncho and walk down through rock-cut tunnels for a close-up (wet) look from behind the falls and halfway down the cliff. If I was going to bother with any of these extras, the latter, called the Table Rock Scenic Tunnels, is the one most worth paying for, with the *Maid of the Mist* second choice. It's one way to cool off on a hot day although the tunnels do get very crowded and you should be prepared to wait in line in them for a turn beside the spray. The wall of water is thick enough to pretty well block out the light of day. A million people a year see the falls from this vantage point – as close as you can get without getting in a barrel.

Further north along the river is the Great Gorge Adventure, an elevator to some rapids and whirlpools. Don't bother. They also have a collection of barrels and vessels that many of the wackos attempting to shoot the falls have used. Surprisingly, a good proportion of those who have gone over purposely, suicides aside, do live to tell about it. But only one who took the trip accidentally has had the same good fortune. He was a seven-year-old boy from Tennessee who surged over from a tipped boat upstream and did it without even breaking a bone. Mind you, I don't think he wants to do it again.

One daredevil, though, has done it twice. The 1980s was a particularly busy period with five stunt people taking the plunge, all successfully. One of them said he did it to show teenagers there were thrills available without drugs – right. The first attempt of the 1990s, witnessed and photographed by startled visitors, was original. No conventional barrel here, it was over the edge in a kayak. He's now paddling the great white water in the sky.

A little further out is the Whirlpool Aero Car, a sort of gondola stretched between two outcrops, both on the Canadian side, above a whirlpool created by the falls. It offers a pretty good angle of the falls for a picture. Tickets can be bought for each of the above three land-based views separately or there's one ticket for all three which is less than the total of the individuals.

Other Views

The Skylon Tower at 5200 Robinson St is the large, grey tower with yellow elevators running up the outside. There is an observation deck at about 250 metres with both indoor and outdoor viewing. Aside from great views of the falls, both Toronto and Buffalo can be seen on clear days.

There are also a couple of dining rooms at the top, the more expensive of which revolves once per hour. The other one offers buffet-style breakfasts, lunches and dinners at more moderate but not inexpensive prices. In the revolving restaurant the early bird dinner special from 4 to 5.30 pm saves some money.

The Minolta Tower, at 6732 Oakes Drive, very close to the falls and virtually overlook-

ing the lip, also has a restaurant with spectacular views and observation galleries. An incline railway leads from the base of the tower down the hillside close to the falls.

Bridges

Two bridges run over the river to New York state, the Whirlpool Bridge, and, closer to the falls, Rainbow Bridge which celebrated its 50th year in 1991. You can walk or drive across to explore the falls from the US side but have your papers in order.

Niagara Falls Museum

The original of the many 'daredevil collections' of objects in which people have gone over the falls, is found here. Aside from telling the stunt stories, also on display are curios and artefacts from around the world, including Egyptian mummies and a dinosaur exhibit. The address is 5651 River Rd and the museum is open all year.

Clifton Hill

This is the name given to the part of the downtown area near the falls. Here is every type of commercial attraction in Disney-like concentration. You name it – museums, galleries, displays like Ripley's Believe It or Not, Tussaud's Wax Museum, Houdini's Museum – they're all here. Looking is fun but in most cases paying the entrance fee will leave you feeling like a sucker. I know – I've done it. They don't live up to their own hype. Also in this bright, busy section are dozens of souvenir shops and restaurants.

Marineland & Game Farm

Of the dozens of commercial attractions, this is probably one of the best. Marineland (☎ 356-8250) is an aquarium with special family shows by dolphins, sea lions and killer whales. Admission includes the game farm which has buffalo, bears, lions, deer and others in an outdoor park setting. There is also a large roller coaster. It's open from 9 am to 6 pm, and admission is about $7. It's roughly two km from the falls, south on Portage Rd.

Brown bears

IMAX Theatre

The large format (the screen is six stories high) IMAX cinema, at 6170 Buchanan Ave near the Skylon Tower, presents a 45-minute show about the falls, its history and some of the stunts that have been pulled in and over them. Shows run continually and cost $6. In the same complex is a museum with artefacts from some of those who have run the falls.

Niagara Parks Greenhouse

Flowers and gardens are plentiful in and around Niagara Falls which has moderate temperatures. The greenhouse and conservatory just south of the Horseshoe Falls provide a year-round floral display and they're free. Across from the falls, Victoria Park also has varied and colourful floral displays through most of the year.

School of Horticulture Gardens

Also free for browsing around are the 40 hectares here which are open all year. The school and gardens are along the Parkway towards Queenston, about nine km from the town of Niagara Falls. A little further north is the floral clock, which is over 12 metres in diameter. Beside the floral clock don't miss the Centennial Lilac Gardens which are at their fragrant best in late May.

Dufferin Islands

Upstream from the falls, there are walking trails around the undeveloped Dufferin Islands.

Organised Tours

Double Deck (☎ 366-7633) offers bus tours on British red double-decker buses. For about $10, their bus runs between Niagara Falls and Niagara-on-the-Lake three times a day. They also have an all-encompassing tour which includes entrance to a number of attractions and stops at other free sites. You can stay on or get off at will, even taking two days to complete the tour. Another 50-km-long trip takes in Niagara-on-the-Lake and a winery.

Gray Line offers seven different bus tours. Their depot is opposite the Panasonic Tower.

The Niagara River Sightseeing Package Tour takes in most of the area's features and includes admission to a number of attractions and the *Maid of the Mist* boat trip. The tour takes about six hours, costs $30 and includes a meal. Tickets and information are available at Table Rock House (by the falls) or in the Victoria Park Restaurant.

More extravagant, helicopter tours over the falls are offered by Niagara Helicopters (☎ 357-5632) at 3731 Victoria Ave.

Festivals

The Blossom Festival is held in early or mid-May, when spring flowers bloom in the many parks. Featured are parades and ethnic dances.

The annual Niagara Grape & Wine Festival is held in late September. There are many events, including parades and tours of five major wineries. In addition, activities are planned throughout the region.

For winter visitors, the annual Festival of Lights is a season of day and night events stretching from the end of November to the middle of February. The highlight is a series of night lighting displays set up along a 36-km route.

Places to Stay

Accommodation is plentiful and, overall, prices aren't too bad what with all the competition from both sides of the border. Outside the peak summer season, costs drop and through the winter there are some good bargains. At this time many of the hotels and motels offer two or three-day packages, often including some meals, discounts on attractions and maybe even a bottle of wine thrown in. Checking weekend newspapers in the travel section in town or Toronto will turn up some deals. Since a room is a room, other enticements such as waterbeds, saunas, heart-shaped jacuzzis, FM stereos, movies, etc are offered at many places for a 'dirty weekend' escape.

Camping There are campgrounds all around town. Three are on Lundy's Lane, leading out of Niagara Falls, and two are on Montrose Ave south-west of downtown. They are decidedly not primitive.

At the government-run *Miller's Creek Park* (☎ 871-6557), each large site has some privacy and a fireplace. It's open from mid-June to early September. Sites are $9.50 with no electricity.

Hostels Best bet in town is the *Brock Hall Youth Hostel* (☎ 357-0770), 4699 Zimmerman Ave off River Rd near Queen St in the old town, near the railway station. The hostel is in a nice Tudor-style house near the Niagara River, and has good facilities. Members pay $8 and nonmembers pay $12. There is only room for 25 males and 20 females. The hostel is open all year. They offer bicycle rentals and discounts for some of the museums and the *Maid of the Mist*.

The *YWCA* (☎ 357-4555) is at 6135 Culp St. They have rooms for women only, costing $20. The YMCA has no residence.

Tourist Homes Other than the hostels, the tourist homes are the best bargains here. They are often cheaper than either motels or hotels and are usually more interesting. Many are centrally located.

There are basically two kinds of tourist homes: the cheaper kind is a family home with a spare room or two to rent. Unfortunately this type of place seems to open and close frequently so keeping track of them is difficult. Others, although small, are actually commercial establishments. While more expensive, these tend to be more permanent and reliable.

The season for many tourist homes, particularly the ones in people's houses, is from May to October, when they're all open. The tourist office might (but doesn't always) have a complete list. A look around some of the streets mentioned here will turn up something as many of the guesthouses put a sign out the front. Prices range from about $35 to $75 with the average being $45 for singles and $60 for doubles.

River Rd links the falls area with old Niagara Falls downtown, three km upriver. There are quite a few tourist homes along here, with good views of the river and a convenient location. The *White Knight Inn* (☎ 374-8767), at 4939 River Rd, is more like a small hotel complete with baths, air-con, full breakfasts and parking. There are doubles from $50 to $65, but also rooms for four people which, at $70 to $85, can be not a bad deal. The *Butterfly Manor* (☎ 357-1124), at 4917 River Rd, is $55 a double with kids under 12 free. Note that the price goes up $10 on weekends though. If they're full, they'll be likely to help you find someone else with a room. Breakfast is included in the price.

Also with four rooms and charging the same price is the nearby *Glenmhor Guesthouse* (☎ 354-2600) at 5381 River Rd. Another is the *Rose & Kangaroo* (☎ 374-6999) at 5239 River Rd; they'll pick you up at either the railway or bus station.

At 4407 John St (☎ 374-1845), opposite the Rainbow Bridge, is the appropriately named *Rainbow View* with four rooms from $40 to $65, with continental breakfast included. If you're a student or have a hostel card it's worth asking about a lower rate: they have been known to knock a good bit off the price. And, of course, the rooms with shared bathroom are less costly. They also have reductions for stays of four days or longer. John St is a quiet residential street and not far from the falls.

A look along either Robert St or Victoria Ave may turn up something. The other main area for guesthouses is along Lundy's Lane.

B&Bs From 2631 Dorchester Rd, a B&B programme (☎ 358-8988) also operates. The organisation has homes all around town; some include a little extra something like a swimming pool or air-conditioning. Note that not all of them necessarily include a breakfast. Prices range from $50 to $70 for a double.

Hotels There are few hotels in town; most accommodation is in motels or various styles of motor inn. True hotels tend to be new and expensive. A couple of budget alternative hotels can be found away from the falls, near the railway and bus stations. The better of the two is the *Europa* (☎ 374-3231), on the corner of Bridge St and Erie Ave, where a room can cost less than $30. Nearby is the slightly tattered *Empire* (☎ 357-2550) on Erie Ave.

Motels There's millions of 'em. The cheapest ones seem to be along Lundy's Lane, which leads west out from the falls and later becomes Highway 20. There are many other motels on Murray and Ferry Sts. The wide

price ranges are partially because many places have honeymoon rooms with double bathtubs, waterbeds and other price-bumping features. Rates vary dramatically by season but are most costly in July and August. Later it's a buyer's market. You may be able to strike a deal if you're staying two, three or more nights.

The *Thunderbird Motel* (☎ 356-0541), at 6019 Lundy's Lane, has rooms from $35 all the way up to $85. At 6267 Lundy's Lane is the *Bonanza* (☎ 356-5135) with 50 rooms. Prices here range from as low as $28, up to $68 depending on the room and season. There is a heated pool.

The *Caravan Motel* (☎ 354-6038), at 8511 Lundy's Lane, charges from $23 to $65. *A-1 Motel* (☎ 354-6038), at 7895 Lundy's Lane, charges from $44 to $75 and has 20 rooms and a pool.

At 7742 Lundy's Lane is the small *Alpine Motel* (☎ 356-7016). Their rates are from $40 to $58, and they also have a pool. The *Melody Motel* (☎ 227-1023), at 13065 Lundy's Lane, charges from $45 to $70 and has a pool. This street has literally dozens of other motels.

On Main St, the *USA Motel* (☎ 295-4481), at 6541 Main St near George's Parkway, is modestly priced. Ditto for the *Lennox Motel*, at 3769 Macklem St, which is only $30.

The always reliable *Travelodge* (☎ 357-1626) is at 5591 Victoria Ave, with rooms beginning at $50.

Places to Eat

Down by the falls around Clifton Hill and along Victoria Ave or Stanley Ave there are scores of restaurants. Japanese, German and Hungarian eateries can all be found. Some offer breakfast and/or lunch specials. Just look around.

Taking a leaflet from one of the hustlers on the street can lead to a good bargain. Very good value at $6 to $9 is *Ponderosa*, a budget steak house where all meals are accompanied by a huge help-yourself salad bar. Chicken and pasta are also available. It's a couple of blocks from the falls at 6519 Stanley Ave, by the corner of Main St. *Mama*

Mia's, at 5719 Victoria Ave, has been serving up Italian fare at moderate prices for many years. Good for breakfast is the *Niagara House of Pancakes* at 7241 Lundy's Lane. Inexpensive meals can also be found at the *Victoria Park Cafeteria*, opposite the American Falls in the building complex in the park of the same name, and run by the Parks Commission. On the 2nd floor is a more expensive restaurant and an outdoor beer patio.

In the northern, older section of town there's *Tony's Place*, a large, popular place at 5467 Victoria Ave which specialises in ribs and chicken. Until 6.30 pm they offer an early-bird special at $8.75. Regular à la carte dishes range from $7 to $15 and there is a lower priced children's menu. Across the street there is a little place for ice cream or a cup of cappuccino. On Queen St is *Woolworth's*, which has a cafeteria serving breakfasts and full lunches and dinners for under $5.

Lundy's Lane also has many restaurants.

Getting There & Away

Bus The new bus station is away from the falls area across the street from the railway station, in the older part of town on the corner of Bridge St and Erie Ave.

This is the depot for buses to other cities but there is also a shuttle to the falls, regular trips to Niagara-on-the-Lake and even bus tours departing from here.

For Toronto, service is very frequent with nearly a bus an hour from early (around 7.30 am) to about 10.30 pm. The one-way fare is $18 and the trip takes about two hours. On weekends there are fewer runs. Buses also depart from here for the airport in Buffalo, New York, and for Detroit, Michigan.

To Niagara-on-the-Lake there are three services a day at $16 return. The shuttle over to the falls is $4.75, less for children.

Train The station is in the older, non-tourist part of town on Bridge St, close to this area's downtown section.

There are four runs a day to Toronto and the fare is $16. Departures for the VIA Rail

trains are spaced fairly evenly through the day, beginning after 9 am. This trip also takes about two hours. There is a special reduced fare if you go and return between Toronto and Niagara on the same day, and another good special if you go and return within five days, provided you don't travel on a Friday. There is one train daily west to London, Ontario, and one daily to New York city.

Getting Around

Walking is best; most things to see are concentrated in a small area.

For getting further afield there is the Niagara Parks People Mover bus system, which operates from mid-May to mid-October. It runs in a straight line from upstream beyond the falls, past the Greenhouse and Horseshoe Falls, along River Rd past both the Rainbow and Whirlpool bridges to the Whirlpool Aero Car attraction. From there, it turns around and follows the same path nine km back. From the falls it gets you pretty close to either the bus or railway station. One ticket is good for the whole day and you can get on and off as much as you like at any of the 12 stops.

For an extra charge, transfers can be made to the regular city bus system. Such a connection will get you right to the door of the train or bus station. The People Mover ticket is good value at $3 and can be purchased at any one of the stops. Throughout the summer the bus runs daily from 9 am to 11 pm, but after 8 pm does not go further out than the Rainbow Bridge. In spring and fall the schedule is somewhat reduced and in winter the system does not run at all.

Niagara Transit runs two similar shuttle services around town. One route goes around the downtown area by the bus and railway stations and connects with the People Mover. The other runs from the Rapids View depot at the southern end of the People Mover route by the falls, along Portage Ave and up Lundy's Lane. This is a 30-minute trip and the bus runs half hourly from 8.30 am to midnight. Free transfers can be made from these shuttles to any city bus.

Bicycles can be rented at Cupulos, on

Ferry St on the corner of Stanley St. It's open from 9 am to 9 pm.

AROUND NIAGARA FALLS
See Around Niagara-on-the-Lake for details about the area between Niagara Falls and Niagara-on-the-Lake.

South from Niagara Falls, along the parkway, is a reconstruction of Fort Erie which the Americans seized in 1814 before retreating home. At the fort a museum, military drills and uniformed soldiers can be seen. Admission is $2.

Fort Erie
The town of Fort Erie, situated where the Niagara River meets Lake Erie and across from Buffalo, is connected to the USA by the Peace Bridge. This is a major border-crossing point and buses from Toronto connecting with many eastern US cities use it. On summer weekends expect queues. Some air travellers find it worthwhile to go by bus to Buffalo from Toronto and its vicinity to take advantage of cheaper US airfares. For example, a flight from Buffalo to Seattle is often much less than one from Toronto to Vancouver with only short bus trips at each end. At times, there are buses from Toronto direct to the Buffalo airport, and some connecting with specific flights, such as the ones to New York city which have very low fares. This situation varies with airlines opening and folding and fares increasing and decreasing, but is worth remembering.

Fort Erie is also well known for its old, very attractive, green, horseracing track. Races are held from May to October. The track is off the QEW at Bertie St.

Slightly south of town is **Crystal Beach**, a beach-cottage resort with a sandy beach. This is one of the warmest areas of the country and the one with the longest summer.

BRANTFORD
West of Hamilton and surrounded for the most part by farmland, Brantford is known for several things. It has long been associated with Native Indians, as Chief Joseph Brant led the Six Nation Indians who lived in an area stretching from here to parts of upper New York state. The **Brant County Museum** at 57 Charlotte St has information and artefacts on Brant and his people. **Her Majesty's Chapel of the Mohawks**, three km from the centre of town on Mohawk St is the oldest Protestant church in Ontario and the world's only Royal Indian Chapel. It's open every day in summer, and from Wednesday to Sunday the rest of the year.

Woodland Cultural Centre Museum, at 84 Mohawk St, has displays on the various aboriginal peoples of eastern Canada and offers some history of the Six Nations Confederacy. The confederacy, made up of the Mohawk, Seneca, Cayuga, Oneida, Onendaga and Tuscarora tribes, was a unifying cultural and political association which helped settle disputes between bands.

Brantford was the home of Alexander Graham Bell, the telephone's inventor. The **Bell Homestead** displays some of his other inventions and is furnished the way it was when he lived in it. It's at 94 Tutela Heights and is closed on Monday.

The town is also known for local son Wayne Gretzky, the greatest hockey player the world has yet produced.

There are some additional attractions such as **Myrtleville House**, dating from 1837, and the interesting eight-sided (what else?) **Octagon House**, now a restaurant.

SIX NATIONS INDIAN RESERVE
To the east of Brantford in Ohsweken is this Iroquois reserve, one of the best known in the country. Established in the late 1700s, it provides interested visitors with a glimpse of Native Indian culture. Through the week (and on weekends by appointment) tours are given of the reserve and its Band Council House, the seat of decision making. Various events are held through the year including the major Grand River Powwow, a summer theatre programme and a handicraft sale in November.

ONTARIO AGRICULTURAL MUSEUM
With 30 buildings on 32 hectares of land, the museum brings to life the farming history of

the area through demonstrations, displays, and costumed workers in historical settings. It's near Milton, 52 km south-west of Toronto, about a 45-minute drive. Leave Highway 401 at exit 320 and there should be signs to follow. The museum is on Townline (also called Tremaine Rd) and it's open daily from the middle of May to October.

GUELPH
Down Highway 401 from Toronto, Guelph is an old, attractive middle-sized university town that makes a nice place to live but doesn't have much of interest to a visitor. There are some fine houses along tree-lined streets, and the Speed River and downtown area is pleasantly overseen by the dominant **Church of Our Lady**.

The **Macdonald Stewart Art Centre** at 358 Gordon St often has good shows in its galleries, which specialise in Inuit and other Canadian art. It's open every afternoon but Monday, and is free.

McRae House is the birthplace of John McRae, the author of the antiwar poem 'In Flanders Fields' written during WW I, which every Canadian reads as a kid in school. At 108 Water St, the museum is open in the afternoon daily.

Through the summer, cheap accommodation can be found at the university.

Near the main intersection of town, Wyndham St and Quebec St, the *Bookshelf Café* at 41 Quebec St is a good, inexpensive place for a bite and it's licensed.

KORTRIGHT WATERFOWL PARK
This is a wildlife area and waterfowl research centre with 3000 birds and 75 species. There is an observation tower and an interpretive centre as well as some nature trails. The park is open daily, all year. Admission is $3.50. The park is near Guelph on Kortright Rd, west of Highway 6 on the Speed River.

ROCKWOOD & THE CONSERVATION AREA
About 10 km east of Rockwood along Highway 7, Rockwood Conservation Area makes a good destination for an afternoon outdoors. It's definitely one of the best conservation areas within the Toronto area. Admission is $2.50.

The park offers swimming, canoeing and picnicking; but of most interest are the wooded landscape and natural features which include cliffs, caves and glacial pot-holes, all of which can be explored on foot. Trails wind all through the park and canoes can be rented. There is also overnight camping available.

In the village of Rockwood, an hour or so can easily be spent strolling along the main street with its antique and junk shops, craft boutiques and eateries of various types. Saunders Bakery has been turning out baked goods for 75 years. Good inexpensive food can be had at the *Out-to-Lunch* restaurant, open everyday but Monday. The afternoon tea with fresh scones is good value. There is a B&B or two in town as well.

Nearby **Acton**, a larger town, is known for its leather goods warehouse with its *Tannery* restaurant.

KITCHENER-WATERLOO
These twin cities – amalgamated to form one – are about an hour west of Toronto, in the heart of rural southern Ontario. About 55% of the 210,000 inhabitants are of German origin. The city also acts as a centre for the surrounding Amish and Mennonite religious farming communities. It is these two factors that attract visitors and make the towns stand out from their neighbours. There is not a lot to see, and at a glance things here are much the same as in any other large town. However, it's worth a short visit, particularly if your timing is right and you arrive for Oktoberfest. The towns share two universities and therefore have a fair number of young people.

Orientation
Kitchener is the southern portion of the twin cities and is nearly three times the size of Waterloo, but you can't really tell where one ends and the other begins. The downtown area refers to central Kitchener. King St is the main street and runs roughly

north-south; at the northern end it runs to the two universities and beyond.

The farmers' market on the corner of King and Frederick Sts marks the centre of downtown. This area of town has the railway and bus stations, hotels and restaurants. King St runs south to Highway 8, which continues to Highway 401, west for Windsor and east for Toronto.

Highway 8 West, at the junction of King St, heads to Stratford.

Information

Maps and information are available at the Kitchener Chamber of Commerce (☎ 576-5000), 67 King St East, on the 2nd floor of

the Canada Permanent Trust Building. It's open from 9 am to 5 pm on weekdays.

Farmers' Market

One market is in a new building right downtown on the corner of King St East and Frederick St. The market began in 1839 and features the products of the Amish and Mennonites – breads, jams, many cheeses and sausages as well as handicrafts such as quilts, rugs, clothes and handmade toys.

Whether they like it or not, it is the farmers themselves who are often the main attraction. Some of these religious people, whose ancestors were originally from Germany via Pennsylvania, live much the way they did in

---

The Mennonites

The Mennonites are one of Canada's most and least known religious minorities. Everybody knows of them but few know about them. Most people will tell you they wear black, ride in horse-drawn carriages and, eschewing modern life, work farms in a traditional manner. And while basically true, these characteristics are, of course, only part of the story.

The Mennonites originated in Switzerland in the early 1500s as a Protestant sect among the Anabaptists. Forced from country to country due to their religious disagreements with the state they arrived in Holland and took their name from one of their early Dutch leaders, Menno Simons. To escape persecution in Europe and to develop communities in rural settings, they took up William Penn's promise of religious freedom and began arriving in North America around 1640, settling in south-eastern Pennsylvania where they are still a significant group. Most of North America's 250,000 Mennonites still live in that state. In the early 1800s, lured by the undeveloped and cheaper land of southern Ontario, some moved northwards.

There are about a dozen Mennonite groups or branches in Ontario, each with slightly different approaches, practices and principles. The Mennonite Church is the middle ground with the numerous other branches varying in degree to either the liberal or strict side. The majority of Mennonites are moderates. Most visible are the stricter or 'plain' groups known for their simple clothes. The women wear bonnets and a long, plain dress; the men tend to wear black and grow beards. Automobiles, much machinery and other trappings of modern life are shunned. The Old Order Mennonites are the strictest in their adherence to the traditions.

The Amish, who took their name from Jacob Ammon, a native of Switzerland, are another Mennonite branch. They split from the main body, believing Mennonites to be too worldly. Traditional Amish are the plainest of the plain and won't wear buttons on their clothes, considering them a vanity. They don't worship in a church but hold rotating services in houses in the community. Homes are very spartan with no carpets, curtains or wall pictures.

Despite their day-to-day differences, all the groups agree on a number of fundamentals, which include the freedom of conscience, separation of Church and State, adult baptism, refusal to take oaths, practical piety and education stressing the moral and practical. Science is rejected by many. The simple life is esteemed. Mennonite and Amish communities are largely self-sufficient and they do no proselytising. Less than 10% of their followers are not born into Mennonite families.

Mennonite sites can be visited in Kitchener-Waterloo, St Jacob's and Elmira. It is not uncommon to see their carriages rolling along local roads, or on Sundays, parked by their country churches.

Many local stores and farmers' markets feature Mennonite goods. Perhaps the best known, most sought after of crafts are the beautiful, but pricey, bed quilts. Their simple, well-made furniture is also highly regarded. More recently their organic produce and meat has become of interest. Their baked goods and jams are readily available, very good and inexpensive. ■

the 19th century. They use horse-drawn buggies for transportation, and don't drink alcohol, vote or use the courts. Some do not use any modern machinery. The strict Old Order members are easily recognisable, with the bearded men in black suits and hats, and the women in bonnets and ankle-length skirts. There are also many merchants, including bakers, craftspeople and farmers who aren't Mennonite. The market is held on Saturday from 5 am to 2 pm and during summer on Wednesday too, from 7 am.

On Sunday, you may see the wagons rolling down the country roads and lining up outside the old wooden churches of the district.

Across the street, on the corner of King and Benton Sts, is a 23-bell glockenspiel that rings at noon and at 5 pm.

National Historic Park

This park contains the 100-year-old mansion where former prime minister William Lyon Mackenzie King (Canada's 10th prime minister) once lived. It has been restored and refinished in upper-class 1890s style. The basement houses displays on the life of Mackenzie King. On weekends you can witness demonstrations of period crafts, music and cooking by guides in costume. The park is at 528 Wellington St North in Kitchener. It is open daily and admission is free.

Universities of Waterloo & Wilfrid Laurier

In Waterloo, west off King St, these two universities are right beside each other and have attractive, green campuses. Waterloo has an art gallery and the **Museum of Games** which depicts the history of games around the world. The museum is open weekdays.

Doon Heritage Crossroads

The Doon Heritage Crossroads is a re-creation of a pioneer settlement, just south of Kitchener. The 27 buildings include a general store, workshops and sawmill. There is also a model of an original Russian Mennonite village and a replica of an 1856

railway. The site is down King St, right on Fairway, left at Manitou St and left again at Homer Watson Blvd. It's open from spring to fall. Admission is $3.50, less for students. Special events are often held on weekends.

Joseph Schneider Haus

At 466 Queen St South, not far from the market, is this Heritage Canada site, the restored house of a prosperous German Mennonite. It's a museum depicting life in the mid-1850s, with demonstrations of day-to-day chores and skills.

Seagram Museum

Set in a section of the original Seagram distillery in Waterloo, this neatly laid out museum (☎ 885-1857) shows the history and technology of booze production. On display are 2000 artefacts from around the world and many different time periods. You'll see some beautiful tools and equipment. Explanatory films are shown. Also on the premises are an elegant restaurant, a gift shop and a speciality liquor store. The address is 57 Erb St. The museum is open Tuesday to Friday from 11 am to 8 pm, Saturday and Sunday from 11 am to 5 pm.

The Centre in the Square

On the corner of Queen and Ellen Sts is this performing arts complex, with the art gallery and a theatre.

Festivals

Oktoberfest is the event of the year and is the biggest of its kind in North America, attracting 500,000 people annually. The nine-day festival starts in early to mid-October and includes 20 beer halls, German music and foods, and dancing. A huge parade wraps up the festivities on the last day. For more information, ring K-W Oktoberfest Inc on ☎ 576-0571. Upon arrival, visit one of the reception areas for a map, tickets, information and all the details on how to tie on your stein so you don't lose it. Reservations for accommodation during the festival should be made well in advance. For getting around, there is a free bus in addition to the usual city buses.

The Mennonite Relief Sale is a large sale of homemade foods and crafts and also includes a quilt auction. It's held on the last Saturday in May in New Hamburg, 19 km west of Kitchener-Waterloo.

Worth catching is the now annual Busker Carnival, a festival of street entertainers which takes place in late August. Some of these performers are very, very good and the whole thing is free.

Places to Stay

Hostels There is no youth hostel here. The *YWCA* (☎ 744-0120) is at Frederick and Weber Sts in Kitchener. The YWCA charges $28 per night including breakfast and offers weekly rates. They take women only. The YMCA no longer has a residence. The *House of Friendship* down the street from the YWCA may have some rooms available, on or off the premises, for men only.

The *University of Waterloo* (☎ 885-1211) has rooms. Singles/doubles are $25/40, including breakfast. Other meals are available.

At *Wilfrid Laurier University* (☎ 884-1970) contact the housing officer at 75 University Avenue West. Singles/doubles are $22/35. Rooms are available from 1 May to 15 August. The dining room is open in the summer, too.

B&Bs Out of Millbank, a village to the west of Kitchener, there's a local B&B association. Give them a call on ☎ (519) 595-4604 for the latest on guesthouses in Kitchener. The rates aren't bad, starting at $20/30 for singles/doubles. During Oktoberfest many more local residents offer rooms.

Hotels For the dollar conscious, the *Mayfair*, right downtown on the corner of King and Young Sts and close to the bus station, is basic but gets the job done. Singles/doubles cost $25/30 with toilet and shower. There's a bar downstairs.

In a different league altogether is the *Walper Terrace Hotel* (☎ 745-4321), also central at 1 King St. It's an old place that has been restored and won an heritage award. They have over 100 rooms at $75, which is actually rather good value compared to the other top-end places in town. In between is the *Barons Motor Inn* (☎ 744-2215), at 901 Victoria St, with beds in the $42 to $47 range.

During Oktoberfest many people rent out rooms. For information, call K-W Oktoberfest Inc on ☎ 576-0571.

Motels Motels are numerous, good and clean. Most of them are on Victoria St, which runs east-west off King St, just north of downtown Kitchener. Two of the cheapest are the *Mayflower* (☎ 745-9493), at 1189 Victoria St, which costs $36/48 for singles/doubles, and the *Shamrock* (☎ 743-4361), situated at 1235 Victoria St, with singles/doubles at $35/45.

Places to Eat

There are many restaurants on King St. At Water St on King St is *À la Cape Breton*, which serves crêpes and breakfast specials. It has a salad bar as well. On the corner of Cedar and King Sts is *Checkerboard*, a small, quick lunch spot serving homemade soup, chilli, pies and real hamburgers. At 258 King St is *Angelo's Pizza & Spaghetti House*, with all manner of Italian food for between $5 and $10. *Harvey's*, further down, is the best of Canada's hamburger chains. The *Rathskeller*, at 151 Frederick St, offers German food. At 130 King St in Waterloo, the *Ali Baba* is a steak house which has been in business for over two decades.

Entertainment

Kitchener Waterloo has two nightspots of particular note. The *Bop the Gator* is a top-quality live blues bar. Known far and wide, *Lulu's* is an immense, very popular disco-dancing bar. Buses arrive here even from Toronto of a weekend evening.

Entertainment Parks Sportsworld is an entertainment park containing, among other diversions, a water slide, wave pool, go-kart track and snack bars and restaurants. Also here is the Canadian Country Music Hall of Fame. It's at 4370 King St East, close to Highway 401. Admission and parking are both free. You pay for what you do. Bingeman Park, at 1380 Victoria St North on the Grand River, offers much the same thing but is older and not as big.

Getting There & Away
Bus The station is on Gaukel St, west off King St and two blocks down, in central Kitchener.

Train Kitchener is still served by VIA Rail. From Toronto there are two trains a day. The station is on the corner of Victoria and Weber Sts, an easy walk north of downtown Kitchener.

AROUND KITCHENER-WATERLOO
St Jacob's
Just north of town is St Jacob's, a small historic village with the **Meeting Place**, a little museum and interpretive centre on the Mennonites and their history, and numerous arts & crafts shops housed in original buildings dating from the 1800s. The museum at 33 King St is open daily through the summer, but on Sunday in the afternoon only. Through the winter, it is closed on weekdays. Admission is by donation. The MCC Craft Shop sells Mennonite goods.

Also in town have a look at the **Maple Syrup Museum** with exhibits on the production of this Canadian speciality. The museum is at 8 Spring Rd and is open daily all year, except for Mondays in January and February.

The **Waterloo Market** is another, more authentic version of the farmers' markets, with horse and buggy sheds still in place. It's near St Jacob's. It's open the same days as the market in Kitchener-Waterloo (Saturday and Wednesday), but doesn't begin as early in the morning.

If you want to stay there is an inn, *Benjamin's*, and a guesthouse, *Jakobstetta*, in town as well as a couple of restaurants. The St Jacob's B&B Association (☎ 664-2890) can fix you up with a less costly bed in the area. Singles/doubles average $40/45.

Whether you spend the night or not, drop into the bakery. The main street also has numerous craft shops to browse through.

A Local Drive
Take Highway 401 past Kitchener (going west) to the Doon exit and go to New Dundee. From there, travel north-west to Petersburg, where you'll find the Blue Moon Pub. Then on to St Agatha with the church steeple, followed by St Clements and Lindwood – both are Mennonite towns with some interesting stores. Drive back east to Hawkersville, with its blacksmith shop, and take a gravel road with fine scenery to St Jacob's. Continue north up to Elmira and over to West Montrose, where there is a covered bridge – one of the few left in Ontario.

ELMIRA
Not far north of Kitchener-Waterloo and slightly west is Elmira, another Mennonite centre. In spring, there is a Maple Syrup Festival with street activities and pancake breakfasts. The Sap Bucket is a store specialising in local crafts, including the fine quilts, but these are not given away. Brox's Old Towne Village is a shopping centre designed to look like it belongs to an earlier era. Brubacher's Country Store in the complex is a 19th-century general store. You'll find antiques and restaurants in the centre.

You can visit the Elmira Mennonite Church at 58 Church St West and see a film. The MCC Thrift Shop sells Mennonite products.

There are quite a few B&Bs in the area, many on farms and with owners who speak Pennsylvania Dutch or German. For information on who has a room available, call the local B&B Association (☎ 669-2379) in Elmira up until 5 pm. Rates are $35/50 for singles/doubles. One farm B&B is *Washa Farms* (☎ 846-9788), seven km north of town at $55 for two with breakfast. It's on a 88-hectare working farm where the house dates from 1877.

ELORA

Not far from Kitchener-Waterloo, north-west up Highway 6 from Guelph, is this small, heavily touristed town. Named after Ellora in India with its famous cave temples, this was once a mill town using the falls on the Grand River which runs through town. The falls, the old mill, the pleasant setting and the nearby gorge and park make the town a popular day trip for visitors and Ontarians.

Things to See & Do

Not far from town, at the **Elora Gorge Conservation Area**, the river flows through a deep limestone canyon. Much of the area is park and trails lead to cliff views and caves at the water's edge. Riding the water in a rubber inner tyre tube is a fun way to spend a warm afternoon. There are also picnic areas in the park. The nearby quarry is worth a look or a swim.

The Grand River is good for canoeing and overnight trips are possible. You can actually paddle along the river all the way to Lake Erie. More information is available at the park.

Organised Tours

Elora Tours (☎ 846-5567), at 201 Smith St, offers minibus trips around town, with an historical commentary. The tours take only an hour, include the gorge and park, and cost $5, less for students.

Festivals

During the first two weeks of August is the Three Centuries Festival, a classical music event with an emphasis on choral works. Highlights are the night concerts held at the quarry. Other events include the annual summer Antique Show & Sale and, in May, the Open House Tour when many of the older local houses are open to the public.

Places to Stay

There is a large campground at the *Elora Gorge Conservation Area* which, though usually full on holiday weekends, has a number of sites that can be reserved one week in advance. The *Desert Inn* operates a very pleasant B&B, just down the street from its busy café, with rooms for $60 per couple.

There are at least 12 other B&Bs in and around town. For information, call Mrs Groves (☎ 846-0640) at 36 David St. Average price is $45 for two with breakfast.

One to try that's very central and costs a little less is *Clark House* (☎ 846-0218), at 89 Water St, with singles/doubles at $30/40 including a pullout bed for extra people or kids. A full breakfast is included.

The *Elora Mill Inn* (☎ 846-5356) is the prestige place to stay in town; it offers a convenient location, views of the river, fireplaces and dining room but you may have to look in both pockets to pay the bill.

Places to Eat

The town has several good eating spots near the mill. I've eaten several times in the *Desert Rose*, a sort of health food, home-made foods speciality place with a Mexican slant, and I've always found the food good and reasonably priced. They serve soups, salads and sandwiches. *Wellington Fare* at 163 Geddes St is a restaurant, bakery and delicatessen. *Tiffany's* is a fish & chip place at 146 Metcalfe St. Other places along Mill St and the dining room of the *Mill Inn* offer more expensive menus.

Things to Buy

For shoppers there are plenty of small stores in Elora offering crafts, jewellery, paintings and pottery, etc much of it produced by the numerous local artisans.

FERGUS

Fergus is Elora's neighbour and a quiet, farm-area town. As the name suggests, the heritage here is Scottish and this is best appreciated at the annual Highland Games, held during the second week of August. Included are Scottish dancing, pipe bands, foods and sports events such as the caber toss. It is one of the largest Scottish festivals and Highland Games held in North America.

Many of the town's attractive buildings are of limestone, again suggesting the old country. The **Templin Gardens** are in the centre of town along the Grand River. A farmers' market is held on weekends.

Between Fergus and Elora Sts is the **Wellington County Museum** with artefacts relating to the history of the county.

Canoes can be rented in town at Templin Gardens for a paddle down the gorge to Elora. An oddity in town are the painted fire hydrants.

Another event is the Old Time Fiddle & Step Dance Contest, held every year on the second weekend in July.

As in Elora, Fergus is quite busy and accommodation is not overly abundant. For B&Bs, call ☎ 843-2747 or drop around to 550 St Andrews St East. They can put you in touch with local lodgings. Prices are from $30/40 for singles/doubles, in general, a little less than in Elora.

Within walking distance of the downtown area is the *4 Eleven* (☎ 843-5107), at 411 St Andrew St East. It's closed from November to April.

For food try the *Honeycomb Café*, at 135 St David St North, which has homemade soups, breads and desserts.

STRATFORD

With a population of 25,000, this commercial centre surrounded by farmland is a fairly typical slow-paced town, though rather prettier than most places in Ontario. Many of the numerous older buildings in the attractive, architecturally interesting central area, have been restored and the layout along the river adds to the charm. But what makes Stratford notably different and special is the now world-famous Stratford Shakespearean Festival. Stratford's Avon River and its swans, the green lawns and theatres, help the town deliberately and successfully resemble Stratford-upon-Avon in England. London (Ontario) is about 60 km or 45 minutes' drive west, and Toronto is about two hours' drive east.

Ontario St is the main street and everything is close to it. At the foot of Huron St is the Perth County Courthouse, one of the town's most distinct and dominant landmarks.

Information

There is a friendly, helpful and well-informed tourist office (☎ 273-3352) on the corner of York and Erie Sts in the heart of town. You can see pictures of some of the guesthouses and peruse menus from some of the town's restaurants.

Heritage walks from the tourist office depart at 9.30 am from Monday to Saturday, on fine days from 1 July to Labour Day (early September). Or, with one of the descriptive maps available you could do your own walking tour.

Between November and May, information can be obtained from the tourist office in City Hall at 1 Wellington St.

Shakespearean Festival

Begun humbly in a tent in 1953, the theatre now attracts worldwide attention. The productions are first-rate, as are the costumes, and respected actors are featured. The season runs from June to October each year. Tickets cost from $16.50 to $39.50 and go on sale from the first week of March. By showtime, nearly every performance is sold out. A limited number of rush seats are available at good reductions and, for some performances, students and seniors are entitled to discounts. Tickets are available by mail at the Festival Theatre Box Office, PO Box 520, Stratford, Ontario, N5A 6V2, by telephone (☎ (519) 273-1600), or at the box office.

There are three theatres – all in town – that feature contemporary and modern drama and music, operas, and works by the Bard. Main productions take place at the Festival Theatre with its round, protruding stage. The Avon Theatre, seating 1100 people, is the secondary venue and the Third Stage is the smallest theatre.

Aside from the plays there are a number of other interesting programmes to consider, some of which are free; for others a small admission is charged. Among them are post-performance discussions with the actors, Sunday morning backstage tours, warehouse tours for a look at costumes, etc and workshops and readings take place.

The Gallery

This is a good art gallery in a fine old building near Confederation Park at 54 Romeo St North. Featured are changing international shows of modern painting, with the emphasis on Canadian works. Three shows are presented at any given time. The gallery is closed on Monday.

Queen's Park

Down by the river, near the Festival Theatre, this park is good for a picnic or a walk. Footpaths from the theatre follow the river past Orr Dam and a 90-year-old stone bridge to the formal English flower garden.

Shakespearean Gardens

Just north of the courthouse by the stone bridge dating from 1885, these gardens on the site of an old wool mill run along the waterfront. Near the bridge is a bust of Shakespeare and the mill's chimney. Here and there picnic tables can be found.

Shakespeareland

This is a miniature model of Stratford in England, in a park setting on Romeo St North. It's open daily from June to September and admission is $4. There's a good discount for students.

Organised Tours

Festival Tours runs trips around town several times daily through the summer, using red British double-deckers. The tour lasts one hour. Ask at the tourist information office for details.

Another outfit, Coach House Tours, has a similar trip but also runs a longer one around Mennonite country. Again get details at the tourist office, from where the bus tour departs.

Boat Trips A small tour boat runs around the lake and beyond the Festival Building from behind the tourist office. The 35-minute trip costs $4 and the boat glides by parkland, houses, gardens, and swans. Also at the dock, canoes and paddle boats can be rented.

Places to Stay

Because of the number of visitors lured to town by the theatre, lodging is, thankfully, abundant. By far the majority of rooms are in tourist homes, B&Bs and in the houses of residents with a spare room or two. In addition, in the higher price brackets, there are several well-appointed, traditional-style inns in refurbished, century-old hotels.

There is often a youth hostel here but it changes location and comes and goes. Check in Toronto or at the local tourist office.

Tourist Homes By far the most economical method of finding a cheap bed is to book a place through the Stratford Festival Accommodation Department, at 55 Queen St, or by calling them on ☎ (519) 273-1600. They will find a room in someone's home for $25/29 singles/doubles if you have a ticket to a play. Many of these places offer breakfast for a couple of dollars extra. Payment must be made in full when booking.

B&Bs Among the dozens of B&Bs around town, there are, conveniently, quite a few in the central area. Rates are around $30 to $35 for singles and $45 to $65 for doubles.

The *Burnside Guest Home* (☎ 271-7076) is at 139 William St, which runs along the bulge in the river Lake Victoria, across from the downtown core. A 15-minute walk will get you to any of the theatres and the downtown area. Singles cost from just $20 and doubles range to $55.

Fairly close to the centre, *Attard's Guesthouse* (☎ 273-5197) at 99 Centre St is the same distance from downtown as the Festival Theatre but in the opposite direction. Singles/doubles cost $30/45.

Right in the middle of things, within easy walking distance of most salient destinations, is *Joanne's Guesthouse* (☎ 273-4960) at 269 Ontario St. Such a location is worth a little more and a room is $50. Breakfast is served; the bathroom is shared, as it is in most B&Bs, and there is no smoking allowed. This place is open all year. Also very central at 220 Church St is the *Maples* (☎ 273-0810) in a large Victorian house. A double goes for $48, with a good continental breakfast included. Another place nearby is the *Windermere* (☎ 271-1093) at 20 Shrewsbury St.

Moving up in price, one to try is *Stratford Knights* (☎ 273-6089) at 66 Britannia St, away from the centre a bit on the other side of the river off Mornington St . It's a fine old house with a pool in the yard which guests can use. Doubles start at $55 including a continental breakfast.

Close to the theatre on Ontario St is the *Heinbuck Tourist Haven* at 411 Ontario St; it's open through the summer and may be slightly cheaper.

Hotels The *Queen's Inn* (☎ 271-1400), at 161 Ontario St near Waterloo St, is around 135 years old – the oldest hotel in town. Refurbished and re-opened in 1988, it's a fine place to stay though prices have recently risen sharply. A double will cost at least $85 although prices drop in the off season. The *Albert Place Hotel*, at 23 Albert St, is another updated old inn with somewhat lower prices.

Motels Motels are expensive. Try the *Noretta* (☎ 271-6110) on Highway 7 towards Kitchener. Rooms cost from $45 for a double. The *Majers* (☎ 271-2010), a little further out, is slightly more expensive. There are also other motels along here.

Places to Eat

At 9 York St near the tourist office is a small sandwich shop, which is literally a hole in the wall with takeout orders only. They make very good sandwiches and picnic plates which might include a bit of smoked salmon or corn on the cob. The park by the river right across the street makes a good eating spot.

Annie's Café at 30 Ontario St has inexpensive breakfasts and lunches with hamburgers the speciality. It's closed on Monday. *Connie's*, at 159 Ontario St near Waterloo St, covers the basics and has pizza and spaghetti. Away from the centre a little over the bridge and down Huron St is *Madelyn's Diner*, a fine little place for any meal, which has good

breakfasts served from 7 am. It's closed on Sunday evening and all day Monday.

As befits an English-style town, there are quite a few pubs about. *Stratford's Olde English Parlour* with an outdoor patio is at 101 Patrick St near Wellington St. The *Queen's Inn* at 161 Ontario St, with several different eating rooms, brews its own beer and the pub has an inexpensive and standard menu including a ploughman's lunch.

Dining rooms in some of the inns, including the good one in the *Queen's Inn*, cater to the theatre crowd, and have more expensive fare. Less costly and good value are the Queen's Sunday and Wednesday evening buffets. Expensive *Rundles* at 9 Coburg St has a good reputation.

Let Them Eat Cake is a dessert and coffee bar at 82 Wellington St. There are a few fast-food joints and a Chinese place on Ontario St heading out of town.

Getting There & Away

Train and bus services depart from the VIA Rail station, quite central at 101 Shakespeare St off Downie St about eight blocks from Ontario St. There are twice-daily trains to Toronto or you can go west to London, with connections there for Windsor. Several small bus lines operate out of the station servicing the region. Chatham bus lines connect Stratford with Kitchener from where you can go to Toronto.

SHAKESPEARE

Twelve km east of Stratford along Highway 8, this village is geared to visitors, and the main street has numerous antique, furniture and craft shops. The *Shakespeare Inn* is a large, up-market hotel. At the west end of town is a moderately priced restaurant.

ST MARY'S

To the west of Stratford, St Mary's is a small Victorian crossroads with a former opera house and some fine stone homes as reminder of its good times last century.

The *Westover Inn*, down a side street, Thomas St, and surrounded by lawns and trees is a quiet, five-star hotel with a dining room.

Several km from town, off Highway 7 back towards Stratford, is the **Wildwood Conservation Area**. It isn't particularly attractive but you can camp there or go for a quick swim. For better swimming, try the spring-fed limestone quarry just outside St Mary's. It costs a couple of dollars and there are change rooms and a snack bar. Apparently Prime Minister Trudeau took a dip here some years ago after fulfilling his official functions in Stratford.

TILLSONBURG & DELHI

These two small towns are in the centre of a flat, sandy, tobacco-growing region. The number of smokers has been declining more rapidly in Canada than in other Western countries, so various crop alternatives are being sought to keep the area productive.

On Highway 3 west of Delhi there is a **Tobacco Museum** with displays on its history and production. It's open daily through the summer, and on weekdays only the rest of the year.

Casual work picking tobacco may be found starting in mid-August. Ask at the Canada Manpower offices in these towns. Jobs last roughly a month. It's hard work but room and board are often thrown in with the wage, and you can have a good time. Watch your valuables in the bunkhouse.

TEMAGAMI

Temagami is a small town north of North Bay on Lake Temagami. More importantly, the name also refers to the fabulous wilderness of the area, renowned internationally for its 300-year-old red and white pine forest, an excellent interconnected canoe-route system, archaeological sites and Native Indian pictographs, and scenery that includes waterfalls and some of the province's highest terrain. There are few roads (one of the major assets) but within the region, north of Temagami, is **Lady Evelyn Smoothwater Provincial Park** accessed by canoe or fly-in trip. Many visitors, never make it to the park but spend time canoe

camping on the surrounding crown land. Maps are available and there's no charge for camping in the region outside the park. The local canoe routes are suitable for all levels of expertise.

The area is under some threat from logging interests which are being opposed by local conservation groups as well as the respected International Union for Conservation, based in Switzerland.

Just two km from the town of Temagami is **Finlayson Provincial Park**, which has a commemorative plaque for English author Grey Owl, who lived with the local Ojibwa Indians for several years and then convinced the world, through his writing on nature and its preservation, that he was a Native Indian himself. For more information on him see under Prince Albert in Saskatchewan.

The town of Temagami is the supply centre where canoes can be rented, trips into the park organised, and where there are motels and restaurants.

For all your canoeing, fishing or camping needs or for organising trips into the region, visit the centre run by the Wilsons, Smoothwater Outfitters. It's a short distance from the town centre off the main road. Hap Wilson literally wrote the book on the area and their place is highly recommended. They can suggest trips based on your skill and the amount of time available to you.

Ontario North

SUDBURY

For over 100 years, Sudbury, sitting on the rocky Precambrian Shield, has been supplying the world with nickel. Inco Ltd, the world's largest nickel producer, is the town's biggest employer and, until recently, its lifeblood. While still vitally important, Inco and its rival Falconbridge have seen their fortunes decline with the drop in international demand and price. But Sudbury, for the first time in its history, is trying to diversify from being a 'one-industry town'.

The city is not attractive: it's been a rugged

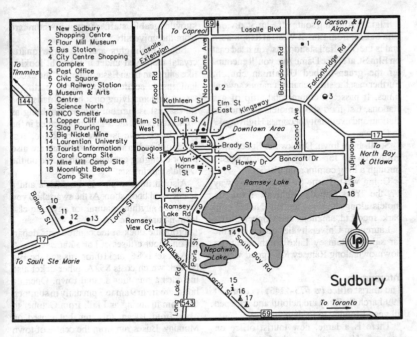

1	New Sudbury Shopping Centre
2	Flour Mill Museum
3	Bus Station
4	City Centre Shopping Complex
5	Post Office
6	Civic Square
7	Old Railway Station
8	Museum & Arts Centre
9	Science North
10	INCO Smelter
11	Copper Cliff Museum
12	Slag Pouring
13	Big Nickel Mine
14	Laurentian University
15	Tourist Information
16	Carol Camp Site
17	Mine Mill Comp Site
18	Moonlight Beach Camp Site

mining town for a long time and is best known for its treeless, moon-like landscape, which is so like what the US space team expected to find on the moon that astronauts trained here before the real lunar launch.

The bleakest area is seen along the railway tracks, though if you're driving you'll pass by the dull, brown-grey hills west of town. The complete lack of vegetation is mainly due to discharges from the mining and smelting operations, but the naturally very thin soil-covering doesn't help. Inco recently built a giant smokestack, which allowed some plants and grasses to take hold in previously barren, dead areas. As for the districts where the wind blows the effluvium...

Despite all this, much of the town and its vicinity is not strikingly like a desert at all. In fact, Sudbury is surrounded by a vast area of forests, hills and lakes, making it a centre for outdoor and sporting activities. On the east side of town, away from the mineral operations, the land is green and wild-looking. There are over a dozen lakes just outside of town, including the large Ramsey Lake at the south-east edge of the city. And Sudbury gets more hours of sunshine than any other industrial city in Ontario.

Sudbury isn't the place to make an effort to get to, but if you're heading cross country you'll probably pass through, and there are a few interesting things to see and do, mostly related to mining.

Youll find a very large French population here and a Scandinavian community.

Orientation

The main streets downtown are Elm St running east-west and Durham St going north-south. The core runs along Elm St from Notre Dame Ave to Lorne St.

On Elm St is the new shopping centre complex, City Centre, and the Holiday Inn. The post office is across the street. The local bus routes start nearby.

Elgin St, running south off Elm St, divides Elm St East from Elm St West; at its southern end is the VIA Rail station. As you head east on Elm St, at Notre Dame Ave you'll encounter the green-bulbed Ukrainian church. Further east the street changes names several times. It passes a commercial strip of gas stations, fast-food spots, motels and the bus station, and eventually becomes Highway 17 to Ottawa.

South from town, Drinkwater St becomes Highway 69 for Toronto. It also passes through a long commercial district.

Going west, Lorne St leads to Highway 17, the Trans Canada Highway. There are motels along the way, the Big Nickel coin park, Inco Ltd, smelters, and Copper Cliff.

Laurentian University lies on a hill on the far side of Ramsey Lake south-east from downtown along Ramsey Rd – good views.

Information

The tourist office (☎ 675-4346) is central at 199 Larch St. They are helpful and are open all year, Monday to Friday.

There is a large, new tourist office on Highway 69, eight km south of town. There is also a booth, open in summer only, a long way from town on Highway 17 west towards Sault Ste Marie and another on Highway 144 north-west of town. The Chamber of Commerce (☎ 673-7133) at 100 Elm St also has information.

Science North

Opened in the mid-1980s, this large participatory science centre (☎ 522-3700), at the south-western end of Lake Ramsey, has quickly become a major regional attraction. The museum complex is conspicuously housed in two snowflake-shaped buildings built into a rocky outcrop at the lake's edge.

Inside, after you enter by tunnel through the 2½-billion-year-old Canadian Shield, is a collection of exhibits and displays on subjects ranging from the universe to insects, communications to fitness, animal life to rocks. Visitors are welcome to get involved with the displays through the many computers, the hi-tech equipment and the helpful,

knowledgeable staff, many of whom are from the university.

Some highlights are the white quartz crystal displayed under a spotlight looking like a lingam in an Eastern temple, the excellent insect section (how about patting a tarantula?) and lying on a bed of nails. The fitness test is fun but can be humbling as well. And lastly, the 3-D film presented in the pitch black cave is quite remarkable. Just reach out and grab that fish. There are also major changing exhibits, such as one on the world's rainforests.

Also in the complex is a cafeteria and a science and book shop. At the swap shop you can trade anything natural for anything else from nature's wonders.

From the dock at the centre boats depart for one-hour cruises of Lake Ramsey.

A ticket is $6, or $10 for this and the Big Nickel, which costs $5. Another ticket also includes a bus tour around town. Opening hours are from 9 am to 7 pm daily in summer, till 5 pm in spring and fall; from October to May, from 10 am to 4 pm but closed on Monday. Buses run from the centre of town to Science North every day. Catch the No 18.

Big Nickel Numismatic Park

Just west of town on Highway 17 West, up on the hill, is the **Big Nickel**, the symbol of Sudbury. The huge nickel, however, is actually made of stainless steel. At the site there are four other large mounted coins including a penny and a Kennedy memorial. Also in the park is the **Big Nickel Mine**. You can go down a 20-metre mine shaft, view equipment and see an exhibit of mining science & technology and history. The mine is open every day from mid-May to mid-October and keeps the same hours as Science North. Entry is $5, and city bus No 940 will get you there. From up at the Big Nickel there's a good view of the surrounding area.

Path of Discovery

From the Big Nickel this 2½-hour bus tour takes visitors on a geological tour around the city on the rim of the Sudbury basin, a 56-

km-long, 27-km-wide depression or crater formed two billion years ago. The principal theories for the origin of the basin are volcanic activity or a crashing meteorite. The trip includes a look at the deepest open-pit mine in the country. A ticket costs $9 and may be combined with one or both of the previous two attractions at a small saving.

Inco Metals Tour
Inco Ltd (☎ 682-2001) runs a free tour of their giant surface operations just west of town, including a look at the mill, smelter and refinery. The tours operate every day in summer from 9 am to 2.30 pm; each is about 1½ hours long.

Falconbridge Nickel Mines
This other steel giant (☎ 693-2761) also offers free tours, which include surface or underground trips at either Strathcona or Falconbridge mine, which is more genuine than Big Nickel Mine. Phone for information on times and exact location. Tours are held every day from 9.30 am to 1.30 pm. Falconbridge is about 18 km north-east of town, near the Sudbury airport.

Copper Cliff Museum
On Balsam St in Copper Cliff, where Inco has its operation, this pioneering log cabin with period furnishings and tools is open June to August, from 10 am to 5 pm during the week and on Sunday afternoon.

Flour Mill Heritage Museum
This is a similar place – a pioneer house (☎ 675-7621) with period implements, artefacts and furnishings from the late 1800s. The museum is at 514 Notre Dame Ave and is named after the three flour silos on this street. It is open Monday to Friday and Sunday from 1 to 5 pm.

Slag Pouring
When wind conditions are right, there are good views at night from Highway 144. Tonnes of slag – like molten lava – are poured, lighting up the sky. Another viewing spot is from Highway 17 just west of the Big Nickel.

Organised Tours
Tours are given, free, of the Civic Square (Sudbury's government building) from Monday to Friday. The tours depart from the information desk. There are also tours of Laurentian University.

Festivals
Voyageur Days is a 10-day summer festival starting about 15 July each year.

Concerts and theatre are presented at Bell Park regularly through the summer. It's on the corner of Paris and York Sts and overlooks Ramsey Lake.

Places to Stay
Camping Sudbury is surrounded by rugged, wooded, lake-filled land. There are quite a few government parks within about 50 km of town. One, a little further out at about 90 km, is *Halfway Lake* on Highway 144 northwest of town. *Windy Lake Park* is on the way there and just 26 km from town. There is also a campground on Ramsey Lake at Moonlight Beach.

Hostels There's a new *CHA Youth Hostel* (☎ 674-0104) in town central at 302 Cedar St. They charge members $10 for one of the 25 beds. It's open from May to September.

Laurentian University (☎ 675-1151, ext 300) on Ramsey Lake Rd rents rooms from mid-May to mid-August. There is a cafeteria (which is closed on weekends), vending machines and use of physical education facilities. The only problem is that the university is away from the downtown area, south-east around the other side of Ramsey Lake. The views are good, though, and the area is nice. They charge $25/35 for singles/doubles.

The *YWCA* (☎ 674-2210) is at 111 Larch St, downtown. They have a few rooms for women only, but they are used mainly as crisis accommodation. If there are rooms left over they will rent you one for $17. They have a cafeteria. You can't stay at the YMCA

(☎ 674-8315) as it burned down a few years ago and has been rebuilt at 185 Elm St East without accommodation facilities.

There's a *Salvation Army* for men in trouble, on Elm St a few blocks from the corner of Notre Dame Ave.

B&Bs There is a B&B, the attractive *Red Geranium Guest House* (☎ 675-8000), on the corner of Paris and Van Horne Sts. Singles/doubles cost $34/40. The tourist office may know of any new ones.

Hotels For budgeters the *Elgin* is a small, almost Asian-looking Chinese place at 196 Elgin St, on a strip belonging to the street people. There are lots of gritty urban life, grubby hotels and busy lunch counters. But the Elgin is not bad, with singles/doubles for $17/20. The hotel closes at 3 am nightly, but 1 am on Sunday.

The *Ledo* (☎ 673-7123) is also on Elgin St, right opposite the old railway station. The place is reasonably clean and there are 25 rooms at $23/27 for singles/doubles, although they charge more for semi-private rooms. Ask in the bar about the rooms.

The *Hotel Coulson* (☎ 675-6436), downtown on the corner of Durham and Larch Sts, is a better and more friendly place, still in the low-budget category. Their rate is $32/35 for singles/doubles. There are two bars downstairs – one with strippers, one with live rock or country music. Both are very popular.

A good central hotel is the *President* (☎ 674-7517) at 117 Elm St West with rooms priced around $60. Similar, but not as good at about the same price, is the *Senator* (☎ 675-1273) at 390 Elgin St.

Motels The bulk of Sudbury's accommodation is in motels found around the edges of town.

Highway 17 West is called Lorne St near town and a few km from the centre there is a collection of motels along it. At 965 Lorne St is the *Canadiana* (☎ 674-7585) with a glassed porch and a black and white sign.

Single and double rooms cost $48 and up. The *Imperial* (☎ 674-6459), at 1111 Lorne St, is a colourfully painted place that serves breakfast. Singles/doubles cost from $40 to $50.

The better motels are found south of town on Highway 69. The *Cedar Motel* (☎ 522-3757) is here, 16 km south of town. They have singles/doubles for $36/44. The *Brockdan Motor Hotel* (☎ 522-5270) is five km south on Highway 69. Rooms cost from $38 to $45.

There are other motels along Highway 69, or on Kingsway leading to Highway 17 East. Along the latter both the *Sorrento* and the *Ambassador* are overpriced, but the small and simple *Medallion* is fine at $36 a double. The *Laurentian* is also a more modest place to stay.

Places to Eat
Like the accommodation and bars, many of the eating spots are not in the centre.

The *Friendly* on Elgin St is a typical Canadian working-class greasy spoon: friendly (like the sign says), cheap, open long hours and good for breakfast. *Frank's* is a deli on Durham St near Larch St. A newer place is *Delights*, at 115 Larch St, with salads, quiches and other light fare, and cheap beer too.

There is a good cafeteria, the *Richmond Room*, in Kresge's on the corner of Elm and Durham Sts. Good-value breakfasts are served from 8 to 11 am, with five choices from $2.75. There are eight daily specials: for example, roast beef dinner is $5.25. It is closed on Sunday. At 302 Notre Dame Ave, a few blocks from Elm St, is the *Continental Café* with German and European fare, most notably the wiener schnitzel. It's open every day and offers low dinner prices before 7 pm.

For good-value fresh seafood, *Seafoods North* is at 1543 Paris St in a small shopping plaza. The front of the place is a seafood store; the restaurant, tucked at the back, offers good fish & chips or chowder at lunch and more complete meals at dinner. Unless you state otherwise the fish is fried, but they will broil it and it comes accompanied by potato, a roll and coleslaw.

Regent St South (Highway 69 to Toronto) is a commercial strip which has a few restaurants. Among the many offerings are *McDonald's*, *Marconi's* specialising in steaks and Italian fare and with an extensive salad bar, and *Smitty's Pancakes* where the pancake breakfast is good value. Best is the *Ponderosa Steak House* with lunches from $4 and up and dinner from $6 to $9. Dinner includes a small steak and an all-you-can-eat salad bar. This restaurant chain often has promotional specials. The complete meals are good, filling and a bargain.

At 1893 Lasalle Blvd is *Teklenburg's*, a good seafood house. Watch for the lighthouse.

Casey's, at 1086 Kingsway, is a loud, popular restaurant with a very varied menu. It's nothing great but there's something to satisfy most people.

The Friday or Saturday newspaper lists the weekend restaurant specials and Sunday brunches.

Entertainment

Pat & Marios, away from the centre on the corner of Lasalle Blvd and Barrydowne Rd near two big shopping malls, is a fairly dressy popular drinking and carousing spot.

Downtown the lowbrow *Coulson Hotel*, on the corner of Durham and Larch Sts, draws a mixed crowd for live rock or country music. There is no admission charge, and drink prices are good.

My Place (☎ 675-3210) in the Northbury Hotel, 50 Brady St, has commercial rock music nightly. Admission is a few dollars. Women are admitted free on Wednesday.

Joe's Rock Palace (☎ 522-5270) brings in good bands. It is on Highway 69 South.

Getting There & Away

Air Companies flying here are Air Canada and Norontair.

Bus The Greyhound bus station (☎ 560-1444) is east of town at 200 Falconbridge Rd, about five km from the downtown area on the corner of Kingsway (which is Highway 17 East).

There are five eastbound buses a day for North Bay/Ottawa/Montreal, and five a day westbound: for Sault Ste Marie/Winnipeg/Vancouver. One northbound bus goes to Timmins; it leaves at 6.15 am. There are 10 buses a day southbound for Toronto, some express.

One-way fares are: to Ottawa $55, Sault Ste Marie $32, and Toronto $46.

Train The VIA Rail station (☎ 800-268-9520, 673-4771) is on the corner of Minto and Elgin Sts, about a 10-minute walk from the centre of town. It's in the low grey building that is mostly black roof.

Train services in and out of Sudbury have been severely curtailed and the remaining trains apparently are now all using a less central station known as Sudbury Junction, which is about 10 km from the old downtown station. You'll find it on Lasalle Blvd past Falconbridge Rd in the north-east section of town.

There are three trips a week to Toronto: Tuesday, Thursday and Sunday. The fare is $52 one way.

Going north the route now heads straight up through basic wilderness to Geraldton, on to Sioux Lookout and eventually across the border to Winnipeg in Manitoba.

No direct route runs to Ottawa, you must go via Toronto.

Car & Motorbike Hertz (☎ 566-8110) is at 1090 Kingsway Blvd. Their rate is about $150 per week.

Hitching Highway 17, which becomes Kingsway in town, goes east to Ottawa. Drinkwater St runs south from town into Highway 69 south to Toronto. If westbound, head out along Lorne St, which eventually becomes Highway 17 West.

Getting Around

For transit information call ☎ 560-1111. The city buses collect on Lisgar St beside the post

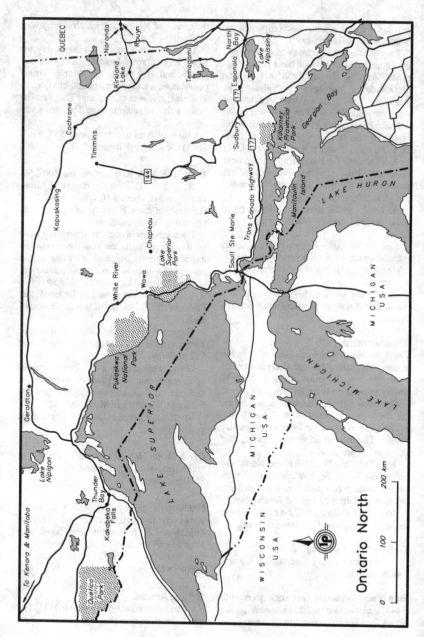

Ontario North

office between Elm and Larch Sts, and this is a major transfer point.

Outside the Eaton's store is the stop for regional buses to some of the surrounding small towns. Route 40 goes to the Copper Cliff Mine smelter site and the Big Nickel site, at a quarter to and a quarter past each hour.

AROUND SUDBURY

The area around and north of Sudbury is both one of the richest mining districts in the world and a destination for those seeking outdoor adventure and recreation. The fishing, camping and other activities attract visitors from the populated southern regions and the USA.

Many of the mines and smelters are open to the public; the tourist office has a *Mine Guide* of the area. For sportspeople there are endless lodges, camps and guide services – usually fairly costly, especially the fly-in trips.

French River

South of Sudbury, the French River is famous for its fishing. There is also white-water canoeing. One group which organises such trips here and elsewhere is the Voyageur School of Canoeing (☎ (705) 932-2131) in Millbrook, Ontario. There is also white-water rafting on the Spanish River.

Killarney Provincial Park

Killarney is one of the provinces's most impressive parks and a visit is highly recommended, even if only for a day's paddle.

Because the lakes are relatively small, the maximum number of overnight campers is low and the park's beauty is outstanding. The park is very popular and often full. Make reservations, including booking a canoe, before arriving and try to go midweek. Calling as much in advance as possible is advised. Getting in on holiday weekends is nearly impossible.

The park is a uniquely mountainous forested area about 80 km south-west of Sudbury on the shores of Georgian Bay. It's one of Ontario's three wilderness parks and has few conveniences. Access around the park is by canoeing, hiking or skiing. There is excellent scenery with birch and pine forest edged by the **La Cloche Mountains.** Some lakes are lined on one side by white quartz mountains, and on the other side by more typical reddish granite. The lakes themselves offer astoundingly clear water with remarkable visibility, but unfortunately this is in part due to acid rain. Indeed, some of the lakes are essentially dead, devoid of life. Portaging from lake to lake is relatively easy as the trails tend to be short, at least for the first few most visited lakes. Two lakes could be explored from the dock at **Lake George**, making a fine day's outing for those without camping gear.

There is a campground at the park headquarters on Lake George and another at the village of **Killarney**, but to see more of the park, venture to the interior via 75 km of portages. There are places for pitching a tent along the way and there's outfitting at Killarney village and along the road between the park entrance and Killarney.

Members of Canada's Group of Seven artists worked in the park and the Provincial Artists Association was instrumental in its establishment.

Also in Killarney village is a small, rustic but comfortable and reasonably priced lodge, the *Sportsman's Inn* (☎ 287-2411) with rooms from $35. Excellent fresh fish & chips can be had down at the dock area.

Halfway Lake Provincial Park

This is one of the many small, relatively developed parks with camping that surround Sudbury. Within this park are various hiking trails of four, 10 km and 34 km in length. There are several scenic lookouts. The park is about 90 km north-west of town on Highway 144.

Gogama

Continuing north about two-thirds of the way to Timmins up Highway 144, is the Arctic watershed, at Gogama, from where all rivers flow north to the Arctic Ocean. Did you notice it was getting a bit cool?

TIMMINS

Way up here in northern Ontario is Timmins, the largest city – in area that is – in Canada. This notwithstanding, it's small (with about 50,000 people) and particularly neat northern town. Originally the centre of the most productive gold-mining area in the western hemisphere, Timmins still acts in the same capacity but the local mines now work silver and zinc. The world's largest zinc mine is here as is Canada's second largest silver mine. One mine is the country's deepest, going down nearly 2.5 km! Together with the rest it makes up well over 2000 km of underground workings in the area. Forestry products are also important in this rough, rugged cold region of primary industry. And, oddly, there are 45 registered trap lines within city limits – not a bad idea for New York city.

Orientation

Highway 101 passes through the centre of town, where it is known as Algonquin Blvd, on its way west to Lake Superior and east to Quebec. In town the main streets are 3rd St, which runs parallel to the highway, Pine St and Cedar St. The central core is marked by the brick streets and old-style lampposts.

The railway and bus stations are in the same building on Spruce St, not far from Algonquin Blvd. The Ontario Northern Railway from here connects with Cochrane for the Polar Bear Express.

As in much of north-eastern Ontario, there is a large French population in and around town and Native Indians are a significant ethnic group.

Information

In addition to the usual local information, the Chamber of Commerce east of town on the the main road has information on numerous industrial tours of the Porcupine-Timmins area and sells the tickets for them. The information office is at 916 Algonquin Blvd East.

Gold Mine Tour

The Pamour Schumacher mine is still in operation. Visits include demonstrations of some of the procedures to get at the gold stuff. Take a sweater, other equipment is supplied. The tour is good and with an introductory video lasting 2½ hours. It's not cheap, though. In fact, it's prohibitively costly, but if you've got gold fever get tickets at the Chamber of Commerce. Tours are offered daily from the end of June to September.

Mill Tour

Tours are offered at the Pulp & Paper Path Mill in Iroquois Falls three times daily from Monday to Friday. The mill is a major newsprint producer.

Tours can also be taken of other mine and lumber operations.

Ukrainian Museum

This museum, at 98 Mountjoy St, has articles and information on the Ukrainians in general and on their life in Canada. First arriving in Canada in 1891, many Ukrainians settled across northern Ontario. Admission to the museum is free.

Timmins Museum

In South Porcupine, at 70 Legion Drive near Algonquin Blvd East, this museum is good and doubles as an art galley and exhibition centre presenting changing exhibits ranging from paintings to masks to performances, and more. In the museum section see the prospector's cabin, which gives an idea of the life these people led. The history of the area is outlined. The museum is open every day but in the afternoon only on the weekend. Admission is free.

Other

As a resident told me there is really very little to do so people drink. And she wasn't lying. Sports are also popular, but winter sports, as there isn't really much of a summer. These two characteristics are not unique to Timmins but are rather common to all northern towns.

At the Kidd Lake Metallurgical Site along the highway there is a herd of buffalo which can often be seen from the road.

Places to Stay

Accommodation is limited and includes a couple of motels on each side of town. The *Matagami Motor Hotel* on the west side is OK at $40 for doubles, and there's a restaurant. In town there are a couple of basic hotels and the good *Venture Inn* at 730 Algonquin Blvd East.

Places to Eat

Pedro's has Mexican and finger foods and is open late on weekends and on Sunday. *Casey's*, east of town, is a popular general restaurant and place to have a beer.

COCHRANE & THE POLAR BEAR EXPRESS

Little Cochrane, with under 5000 people and situated roughly 100 km north of Timmins, is the departure point for the Polar Bear Express, the best known line of the small Ontario Northland Railway service. The Polar heads north through northern wilderness to Moosonee, the oldest permanent settlement in the province, on the edge of James Bay, part of vast Hudson Bay. Three hundred years ago this was the site of an important fur-trading centre. The large polar bear statue at the entrance to Cochrane symbolises the importance of the train to the town.

In Cochrane there are several motels and a provincial park campground to service the passengers. Drury Park, for camping, is close to the railway station. Note that the motels tend to fill up in mid-summer. Arriving early in the day or calling ahead is not a bad idea. One place to try is the low-priced *Riverview* (☎ 272-4004).

There is also a museum with some early railway, Native Indian and pioneer exhibits. From Cochrane, Ontario Northland Railway also connects south with Timmins, North Bay and other regional towns. There are also buses between these points.

Those taking the train have two choices. There is a one-day return trip or a slower, cheaper two-day trip. The express runs primarily for tourists or those in a hurry and leaves early in the morning, returning late the same day, taking 4½ hours each way, and allowing for a look around Moosonee and Moose Factory.

The slower local train caters for an odd mix of tourists, Native Indians, trappers and geologists. Both are run by Ontario Northland Railway and the fare is the same ($38 return), with reservations required. There are family, child and senior discounts. Trips can be booked from Ontario Northland Railway in Toronto, North Bay, Timmins and Cochrane.

In Toronto, there is an information office in Union Station, the main railway station, found on Front St. Ontario Northland Railway also offers three, four and five-day all-inclusive tours (excluding most meals) out of North Bay and Toronto.

The train runs from 21 June to 1 September. Simple lunches and snacks can be bought on the train but you're better off taking your own food for the trip. If you've driven to Cochrane, there is free parking beside the railway station.

Moosonee

Moosonee is as far north as most people get in eastern Canada. There are no roads and it sits near the tundra line. Once there, see the historic sites and the two museums.

Moose Factory Island, the actual site of the Hudson's Bay trading post, founded in 1672, is two km and 15 minutes from town by boat out in Moose River. An inexpensive large 'freighter' canoe takes visitors to the island. There are some buildings to see at the historic site, a cemetery, an Anglican church and one of the museums. Moose Factory itself is a community of about 1500 people at the far end of the island. More costly tours are available which include the trip to the island, a bus tour around it and other optional side trips down the Moose River or out to James Bay.

On **Tidewater Island**, between the mainland and Moose Factory, is a provincial park to which trips can be arranged.

Boat trips or the freighter canoes (for $15) also take people upstream to **Fossil Island**.

Fossils over 300 million years old can be found.

The other museum, back in Moosonee, documents the Hudson's Bay Company's rival. The James Bay Educational Centre has some crafts done by local Cree Indians.

Another attraction is the sometimes visible northern lights.

If you're staying overnight in Moosonee, which is very likely if you take the overnight train, there are a couple of places to stay, but they are not cheap.

Rooms at the *Polar Bear Lodge* (☎ (705) 336-2351) and *Moosonee Lodge* (☎ (705) 336-2345) cost $56/70 for singles/doubles.

The *Lilly Pad*, (☎ 336-2353) is slightly cheaper at $55/65 with breakfast, but it may have closed. Reservations are pretty well a necessity. You may be able to camp, ask about it in Cochrane.

NORTHERN ROUTE

Highway 11 runs west from Cochrane, eventually connecting with Thunder Bay. It's the province's most northerly major road and cuts across rough forest through several mining towns. There are campgrounds along the way.

The principal town along the route is **Kapuskasing** with its circular downtown centre. In town, a river tour-boat runs upstream to **Beaver Falls** providing historical and geological commentary and allowing for glimpses of local wildlife like beaver and muskrat.

WEST OF SUDBURY
The Budd Car

This is the local nickname for a one-car VIA Rail train that three times a week makes the trip from Sudbury through northern bush past Chapleau to White River, north of Lake Superior. It's an interesting eight-hour trip through sparsely populated forest and lakeland. For many villages and settlements – some nothing more than a few buildings and the odd tourist lodge – this is the only access in and out. The train stops and starts as people along the way, often wilderness seekers with their canoes and gear, flag it

down. A moose or bear on the track also means an unscheduled stop. There's lots of birdlife, including hill cranes and great blue herons. You might even do a bit of fishing or berry picking if you're stuck waiting for a freight train to pass. The train doesn't make money – there's regular talk of cancelling it.

Espanola

Espanola is the largest centre between Sudbury and Sault Ste Marie and how it got its name is an interesting tale.

In about 1750 the Ojibwa Indians of the district went on a raid down south in what is now the USA, but at the time was under Spanish control. They brought back a captive woman who later taught her children Spanish. When the French explorers arrived on the scene I guess they were a little surprised to hear familiar Spanish being spoken. They called the settlement Espanole, which was subsequently anglicised to its present form.

It's a pulp and paper town (E B Eddy, one of Canada's biggies, has a mill here) and also acts as a gateway for the Manitoulin Island ferry. The island can be reached by road on this side but connects with southern Ontario by ferry. (See Tobermory.)

There are a couple of standard motels and a few places to grab a bite. White-water rafting is offered on the Spanish River.

SAULT STE MARIE

'The Soo', as the city is called, sits strategically where Lake Huron and Lake Superior meet. Once a fur-trading outpost, the city is now an industrial town important as a shipping centre. For here, on St Mary's River, are a series of locks which enables ships to navigate the seaway system further west into vast Lake Superior. Aside from the busy canal, the steel, pulp and paper as well as lumber mills are major employers.

The International Bridge connects the city with its twin in Michigan, USA. Going west to Winnipeg it's slightly shorter via Michigan and Duluth than going over the lake, but not as impressive.

With the bridge and the Trans Canada Highway, 'the Soo' is a convenient stopover and acts as a tourist supply centre. I find it the most appealing of the northern cities and there are some fine outdoor possibilities within range to complement it. With a population around 85,000 it's the last big town until Thunder Bay to the west. Sudbury is a few hours east.

Orientation

The approach to Sault Ste Marie from the east or west is a long row of eateries, gas stations and motels. Highway 17 North becomes the Great Northern Rd and then Pim St in town. Highway 17 East becomes Wellington St, which is the northern edge of the downtown core. If you're passing through, use the bypass to avoid traffic hassles.

The city itself is quite small with pretty much everything on the long, recently upgraded Queen St. South from Queen St is the waterfront area, which has also undergone a fair bit of renovation in the past few years. Several of the sites of interest, the bus station and the tourist office are down in this section.

A couple of interesting buildings in town are the imposing courthouse in the middle of Queen St and the Precious Blood Cathedral, constructed of local red-grey limestone in 1875 and originally a Jesuit missionary.

Queenstown refers to the renovated downtown core.

Information

There is a huge, modern tourist information centre (☎ 253-1103) in town on the corner of Huron St and Queen St West, just north of the International Bridge leading to the USA. Here you can get maps, guides and advice and can change money. The office is open daily in summer. There are also booths on the highway on each side of town.

The Chamber of Commerce, at 360 Great Northern Rd (Highway 17 North, near the large white mushroom-like water tower), also has an information desk. It is, however, closed on the weekend.

Locks & Canals

At the south-west corner of downtown, at the bottom of Huron St (by the bridge), are the locks linking Lake Superior to Lake Huron. Joining the two great lakes is the small St Mary's River with its rapids. It is here that in 1895 the locks were built, enabling lake freighters to make the journey hundreds of extra km inland.

Lake Superior is about seven metres higher than Lake Huron. The often continuous lake traffic can be watched from a viewing stand or anywhere along the locks for no charge. There are four US and one Canadian (the oldest) lock. About 80 freighters a day pass through in summer.

Walking trails from the locks lead to the islands and canals in the river under the International Bridge. The paths, winding through the woods, make a nice retreat and there are views of the shorelines and ships. The oldest canal, built in 1895, is on the Canadian side and is now used by small pleasure craft. There's a boardwalk, rapids and picnicking over on **Whitefish Island** which has been designated a national historic site. For 2000 years the Ojibwa Indians fished the plentiful waters here.

Boat tours (☎ 253-9850) of the locks depart from the dock by the Holiday Inn at the foot of Elgin St. Two boats operate several times daily from June to October. The two-hour cruise, which includes passing through the Canadian lock, costs from $8.50 to $10.50 and for my money doesn't offer anything you can't see from shore.

MS *Norgama*

Moored near the foot of Elgin St in the main waterfront area, this ship, now a museum, was the last one built for passenger use on the Great Lakes. The museum is open daily.

Steel Tours

It now seems as though the Algoma Corporation's tours of their plant, Algoma Steel, have ended permanently. It's worth inquiring at the tourist office if the tours have been reinstated as new management has differing views on opening to the public. This is one of the largest mills in Canada and the tour showing the entire process from raw material to steel was worth seeing. The mill is on Queen St West.

St Mary's Paper Mill

The large paper mill, on Huron St at the south-eastern edge of downtown, offers walking tours on Tuesday and Thursday afternoons.

Sault Ste Marie Museum

Housed in an Ontario heritage building on the corner of Queen and East Sts is a small but well-put-together museum. Various displays represent the Native Canadians, exploration, fur trading, lumbering, geology and other aspects of the area. Another section, on the Inuit, is very good. In the turn-of-the-century exhibits, the cigarettes for asthma relief are a lark. The museum is open from 10 am to 5 pm Monday to Saturday, in the afternoon only on Sunday. Admission is by donation.

Historical Museum

This museum (☎ 256-2566) has a small col-

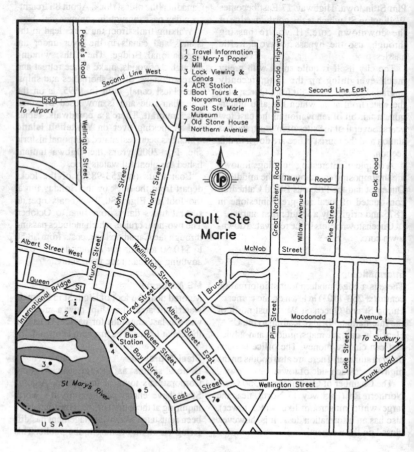

1 Travel Information
2 St Mary's Paper Mill
3 Lock Viewing & Canals
4 ACR Station
5 Boat Tours & Norgoma Museum
6 Sault Ste Marie Museum
7 Old Stone House Northern Avenue

Sault Ste Marie

lection of artefacts and curios from the city's past. It's on the 2nd floor of the Pine St Armoury on the corner of Macdonald Ave and Pine St. Admission is free and the museum is closed Sunday, Monday and holidays.

Bellvue Park

On the water two km east of town along Queen St near the university, this is the city's largest park. There is a small zoo as well as picnic areas, sports fields, and a marina.

Old Stone House

Also known as Ermatinger House (☎ 949-1488), this was built in 1814 by a British fur trader and his Ojibwa wife. It's the oldest stone house west of Toronto and was where many explorers, including Simon Fraser and Mackenzie, put up for the night. Inside, the house has been restored and contains furnishings from the 1800s. Someone there will answer questions. It's open every day in summer, from Monday to Friday during other seasons, and admission is free. The museum is on Queen St near the corner of Pine St.

Great Lakes Forestry Centre

The research centre (☎ 949-9641), at 1219 Queen St East, runs free tours from Monday to Friday at 10 am and 2 pm. The work here, and therefore the tour, is mostly about forest pests. There is also an audiovisual presentation.

Forest Ecology Trail

Also operated by the government forestry service is this 2.5 km self-guided nature trail out of the town centre off Highway 565. There is an attendant to answer questions.

Mini Aquarium

Down near the locks is a sea lamprey control and research centre where you can see lampreys and some fish. It's open Monday to Friday in summer only and is very 'mini'. At night when it's closed you can still peek into the lighted building, but there isn't much to see.

Kinsmen-Crystal Creek Conservation Area

Known locally as Hiawatha Park, this is about a 10-minute drive from Great Northern Rd, north-west of downtown Sault Ste Marie. Stop at the big Hiawatha Lodge where there is a swimming pond and waterfalls in Crystal Creek, and from where there are lots of walking trails ranging in length from two km to 10 km. Admission is free.

Gros Cap

About 20 km west on Highway 550 is this ridge about 150 metres above Lake Superior and Blue Water Park. Hike up the cliffs for excellent views of Lake Superior where there's usually a ship or two cruising by. Or take Voyageur Trail marked by white slashes which winds up along the ridge edge providing views of St Mary's River and the lake. The trail will one day run all the way from Espanola to Thunder Bay, but so far stretches from Gros Cap 260 km east to Serpent River on Highway 108 along the North Channel.

Beside the park and parking lot is the *Blue Water Inn*, a great place to eat, especially popular on weekends when the Yugoslavian owner puts on big barbecues. The inn is open in summer only.

Agawa Canyon

This is a wilderness area accessible only by the Algoma Central Railway train. The 200-km route due north from town to Hearst goes through a scenic area of mountains, waterfalls, valleys and forests. The one-day return trip gives you a two-hour stopover for a quick walk, fishing or lunch. There are also trips that allow you to stay in Hearst for as long as you wish. The one-day return is $35. There is a dining car on board. The train departs daily at 8 am from June to October, arriving 3½ hours later in Hearst.

The trip is spectacular in the fall when the leaves have changed colour and the forests are brilliant reds and yellows. Normally the colours are at their peak in the last two weeks of September and early October. During winter a snow and ice run is added on weekends only.

The station (☎ 254-4331) is on the corner of Bay and Gore Sts. The normal passenger service follows the same route, stops at many tiny communities along the way, and is much slower.

Organised Tours Hiawathaland Sightseeing Tours (☎ 253-3235) has a ticket booth next to the Algoma Central railway depot and runs six different bus tours in and around Sault Ste Marie. The double-decker bus city tour is a two-hour trip costing $6. Out-of-town trips stop at various beauty spots and sites. There is a night tour and also a trip out of town through some of the local forests.

Places to Stay

Camping There are several campgrounds, and they are close to town, if not very rustic. *Rock Shop Campground* is 12 km from town on Highway 17 North (called the Great Northern Rd in town).

KOA (☎ 256-2806) tent & RV park is eight km north of town on Highway 17. Turn west at the flashing amber light, 5th Line. The park is on a river and is equipped with laundry, store, and pool.

A little further is *Pointe des Chênes* on St Marys River, 12 km west on Highway 550 to Highway 565, then 10 km south past the airport to the community park. There are 82 sites.

All these campgrounds cost from $8 to $12 for two people tenting. There are others close to those listed here.

Hostels There is a small and very central *CHA Youth Hostel* (☎ 946-4804) at 8 Queen St East, not far from either the bus or railway station. It's open all year, and the charges are $11 for members, $15 for nonmembers.

Hotels At 2 Queen St East is the refurbished *Royal Hotel* (☎ 254-4321) with an interesting-looking entrance. The location is good and since the renovations, rooms are $40 to $50 for a double. The bus station is across the street.

Better still is the *Stel Hotel* (☎ 759-8200), at 320 Bay St opposite the Agawa railway

depot, right downtown. The hotel offers all mod cons at prices from $55 to $85 for doubles.

Motels Sault Ste Marie's location means a lot of people passing through, consequently it is one of those places with scores of motels. Most of them are on Highway 17 either east or west of town, some downtown. Prices vary but the average is $40 for singles and from $45 to $55 for doubles. Generally, the closer to town the more costly.

The *Shady Pines Motel* (☎ 949-4980), out a little way east at 1587 Highway 17, is a good bargain. It's one of the cheapest around and though ugly at the front is actually very good. Big, modern rooms open out on a treed back yard with picnic tables and barbecues. Singles/doubles cost just $25/35.

The *Evergreen Motel* (☎ 253-4241), at 1447 Highway 17 East, has singles/doubles for $28/32.

The *Travellers Motel* is the white one at 859 Trunk Rd, which is part of Highway 17 East. It has colour TV, and kitchenettes are available. Doubles cost from $36 to $50.

The *Holiday* (☎ 253-4381) is at 435 Trunk Rd. Single or double rooms cost $36.

Lastly, *Journey's End* at 333 Great Northern Rd is good at $55 a double. It's very neat and busy and part of a Canadian hotel and motel chain. You can save a few bucks by taking the 2nd-floor rooms. It's on Great Northern Rd north of Northern Ave.

Places to Eat

Most of the restaurants, many of which are the ubiquitous franchises, line the highway but I've listed mainly local establishments found in the city centre. Queen St has a real assortment of good, atmospheric old lunch-counter type beaneries.

The *Coral Coffee Shop*, at 470 Queen St near Spring St, is a basic classic. They offer good prices for homemade soups, muffins, chilli and the like, and have cheap breakfasts and various specials. It's the only place I've ever seen braille menus.

Recommended is *Country Life*, at 326 Queen St, a health-food store and vegetarian

Top: Windswept shore of Ontario's Georgian Bay (ML)
Bottom: Brillant fall display, Ontario (ML)

Top: Fish Sculpture, Kenora, Ontario (ML)
Bottom: The Caribana Festival, a major West Indian celebration, Toronto, Ontario (ML)

restaurant serving excellent, inexpensive food without meat or dairy products. Try the avocado and tomato sandwich. They only open between 9 am and 5 pm and are closed on Saturday.

Tiny *Mike's* with just half a dozen stools at 518 Queen St has been serving its very regular customers since 1932. Meals are under $5 at this friendly time warp.

At 663 Queen St East near the corner of East St is the old-fashioned *Mary's Lunch*, which serves a lot of homemade stuff, including bread. Mary is quite a character, too.

Two town specialities are lake trout and whitefish and both turn up on menus all over Sault Ste Marie. *Vavalas*, on the corner of Queen and Dennis Sts at the western end of town, offers them as well as various specials like a complete meal with cabbage rolls for $5.25. Can't beat that, and it's open on Sunday.

Moving up-market, *Aurora's* is a fancier seafood place where the lobster is said to be good. Italian food is very popular in town and *Soriano's* is well patronised.

Barsanti Small Frye, 23 Trunk Rd (Highway 17 East), is recommended for its basic good food, low prices, friendly waitresses and style. They've been in the business for 60 years and have got it right. Conveniently, it opens long hours daily from 6 am to midnight.

The *Movieola Café*, on Great Northern Rd, is open late on weekends with finger foods, burgers, Mexican food and dancing to pop music.

On Wednesday and Saturday mornings a farmer's market is held in the parking lot at Memorial Gardens Arena downtown.

Getting There & Away
Air There are regular Air Canada and Nordair flights to Sault Ste Marie.

Bus The bus station (☎ 949-4711), with Greyhound buses, is right downtown on the corner of Queen St East and Tancred St. Buses leave for Ottawa at 7.15 am and 5.50 pm, the fare is $85. There are four or five

buses a day to Toronto (one way $76) and four or five to Winnipeg ($105). There is one bus a day to Detroit and one to Chicago.

Train There is no VIA Rail service in or out of Sault Ste Marie.

Hitching 'The Soo' is a major drop-off point for those thumbing east and west. In summer there are plenty of backpackers hanging around town. If you're going west, remember that from Sault Ste Marie to Winnipeg is a long way with little to see in between. Nights are cold and rides can be scarce. Try to get a through ride to Thunder Bay (715 km) and then go on to Winnipeg from there.

Getting Around
The city bus terminal is on the corner of Queen and Dennis Sts. The Riverside bus goes from downtown east to Algoma University near Belvedere Park.

The airport is 13 km west on Highway 550, then seven km south on Highway 565. There are airport buses between the airport and the major hotels like the Holiday Inn and the Empire Hotel.

AROUND SAULT STE MARIE
Batchawana Bay
North of town along the lakeshore, Batchawana Bay offers beach, swimming (the water is cool) and numerous motels, resorts and cottages for rent. **Chippewa Falls** is called the centrepoint of Canada and it probably is close to being this. The area has a couple of waterfalls and two provincial parks; what with these and the shoreline, an enjoyable afternoon can be spent poking around. And you can visit the garbage dump at **Camp River** in the evening to watch bears waddle in for a snack. It's not a bad idea to stay in your car.

St Joseph Island
St Joseph lies in the channel between Michigan and Ontario, 50 km east of Sault Ste Marie. It's a rural island visited for swimming and fishing and for **Fort St Joseph National Park**. The fort ruins date from the

turn of the 18th century and the new museum displays Native Indian, military and fur-trade artefacts. A bird sanctuary surrounds the fort. It's reached by a toll-free bridge off Highway 17.

NORTH AROUND LAKE SUPERIOR

From Sault Ste Marie to Thunder Bay the Trans Canada Highway is one of the few roads cutting through the thinly populated northern Ontario wilds. This huge area is rough, lake-filled timberland. So far, development has been slow to penetrate, and the abundant minerals and wildlife remain undisturbed. There are areas where there's logging but these are rarely seen. You may see signs of forest fires which are common each year.

This is a quiet and beautiful part of the country presided over by awesome Lake Superior – once known as Gitche Gumee (Big Sea Water) to the Ojibwa Indians. The largest of the five Great Lakes (and one of the world's largest lakes), it's sometimes pretty, sometimes brutal, but always worthy of respect and admiration: a symbol of nature itself. Even today there are disastrous ship-wrecks here when the lake gets angry, and according to a Canadian folk song, Superior 'never gives up her dead'.

Several of the Canadian Group of Seven painters were inspired to work here, as was the poet Longfellow. Along the highway are many provincial parks, which make good places to stay to get a feel for the lake and surrounding forest.

Lake Superior Provincial Park

Highway 17 runs for 80 km through this large natural park north of Sault Ste Marie, so luckily you can't miss it. It's a beautiful park with a few things to see even if you don't stay. The rugged scenery is good, with rivers in the wooded interior and a shoreline with rocky headlands or sandy beach. Several of the aforementioned Group of Seven painters worked in the park.

There are three campgrounds, short and long hiking trails usually accessible from the highway, fishing, and seven canoe routes.

Naturalists give talks and guided walks. A variety of mammals lives in the park, including the odd bear.

At **Agawa Bay**, see the Native Indian pictographs on the shoreline rocks which are believed to commemorate a crossing of the lake. There is no charge. Note the crevices in the rocks along the path. Further along, stop at **Sand River** and walk down to the beach. Though the water is cold, the beautiful sandy beach, long and empty, looks as if it's been lifted from a Caribbean island.

For access to the eastern side of the park, inquire about the train from Frater at the southern end of the park or at Hawk Junction, east of Wawa and north of the park.

Distance hikers and canoeists should cross their fingers for good weather – this is one of the wettest areas in Ontario. Trails are often enveloped in mist or fog, which lends a primeval, spooky air to the woods. As always, interior camping is a few dollars less than the campgrounds with their facilities.

Wawa

This small mining centre has a big, bad 20-year-old reputation for hitchhiking. The story is told of one man who got stuck here waiting so long for a lift that he finally had to get a job. He ended up meeting a woman, getting married – and still lives here. As traffic has picked up over the years and the locals have mellowed, things aren't like they were, but it's still better to get a ride right through. There is nothing down at the highway and it can be a cold place at night, even in midsummer. A lot of cars have passengers by the time they get here.

During migration periods, thousands of geese stop off and are welcomed by the huge steel statue of a goose at the edge of town. Wawa is a supply centre for the surrounding parks.

Chapleau

Chapleau is a small logging and outdoors centre inland from Wawa. There are numerous provincial parks in the area, three within 80 km. **Missinaibi Lake Park** is in the middle of **Chapleau Game Reserve**, the

largest in the western hemisphere. You can go wilderness camping or fishing. The tourist offices around the area have a listing of canoe routes.

There are 12 trips ranging from one to 14 days with five to 47 portages. The longest one is a river and lake circle route going through part of the reserve; it's good for viewing moose.

White River
Back on the Trans Canada Highway, this is called the coldest place in Canada, with temperatures recorded as low as -50°C. Get your picture taken near the thermometer.

Pukaskwa National Park
Find out how tough you are. There is no road into this park (pronounced 'puk-a-saw') and

access is by hiking or boat. From Heron Bay, off the highway near Marathon, is a small road which goes to the edge of the park. The park officially opened in 1983 and now has a small (67 sites) campground. There is also the old 68-km coastal hiking trail with primitive camping spots along the way. The terrain is rough but beautiful, and the weather is very changeable, switching from sun to storm quickly. The interior offers some challenging canoe runs including runs down the Pukaskwa or White rivers. There is a visitor's information office at Hattie's Cove. The park is open from late May to the third weekend in September.

Slate Islands Provincial Park

Situated offshore from the small town of **Terrace Bay** is this cluster of islands, home to the highest density of woodland caribou anywhere. The islands, without natural predators, support hundreds of caribou. At times, there are too many for their food stocks and winters can take a heavy toll. The herd is studied by researchers looking into preserving the herds of mainland Ontario. Ask around Terrace Bay or the nearby provincial parks about trips over to the islands to see or photograph the caribou.

Ouimet Canyon

About 40 km east of Thunder Bay, north-east of the highway, is this small park with a great canyon 150 metres both wide and deep. The walls on either side of the chasm are virtually perpendicular. Fences and viewing stations have been built, preventing you from getting so close to the open edge that you hear your heart pounding. The canyon is definitely worth a quick stop. Officially, there's no camping.

THUNDER BAY

Known as 'The Lakehead', Thunder Bay on the northern shores of Lake Superior is an amalgamation of the towns of Fort William and Port Arthur. Despite being so far inland, Thunder Bay is a major port and is as far as ships using the St Lawrence Seaway get westward. The main cargo switching hands

here is prairie wheat going to market. The docks make the city the world's largest grain handler.

The city, halfway between Sault Ste Marie and Winnipeg – 720 km to either one – is a good stopping-off point. The place itself may not hold you long, but the setting is scenic and it makes a handy centre for experiencing some of the things to see and do in northern Ontario's rugged timberland.

The first Europeans here were a couple of Frenchmen who reached the area in 1662. For hundreds of years this was a fur-trading settlement. In 1869 the Dawson, the pioneer's road westward, was begun. In 1882, the Canadian Pacific railway arrived, and soon the prairie's first shipment of wheat was heading east.

Coming into town from the east on the Trans Canada Highway, you'll pass mountains and see the city at the edge of the bay. Along the shoreline are pulp mills and grain elevators. Out in the harbour ships are moored, and beyond is a long rock formation and an island or two. The unusually shaped mass of rock offshore is important in Native Indian legend and is said to be the Great Spirit, Nana-bijou, who turned to stone after a promise made to him was broken. Today the formation is known as the Sleeping Giant.

Orientation

Thunder Bay still has two distinct downtown areas which are connected principally by Fort William Rd and Memorial Ave. The area between the two is pretty much a wasteland of fast-food outlets, the large Inter City Shopping Mall and little else. Port Arthur (Thunder Bay North), closer to the lakeshore, appears more prosperous, is more modern and generally more attractive. The main streets are Red River Rd and Cumberland St. Port Arthur's Landing, off Water St, is redeveloped waterfront and includes parkland, a tourist office, the marina, fishing charters, a small art gallery and restaurant, and the old railway station. This half of Thunder Bay has a sizeable Finnish population which supports several specialised

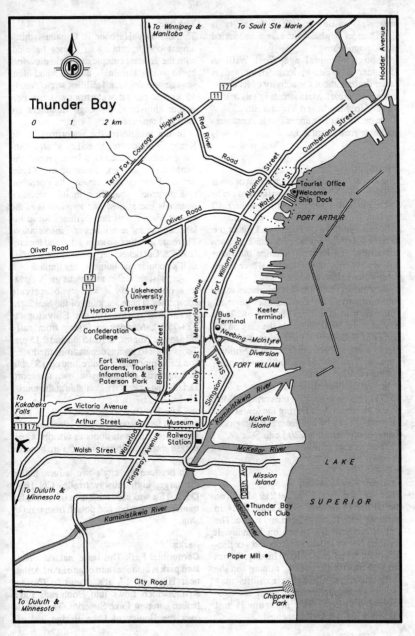

Thunder Bay

0   1   2 km

To Winnipeg &
Manitoba

To Sault Ste Marie

Hodder Avenue

Terry Fox Courage Highway

Red River Road

Algoma Street

Cumberland Street

Water St

Tourist Office
Welcome
Ship Dock

PORT ARTHUR

Oliver Road

Oliver Road

Lakehead University

Fort William Road

Keefer Terminal

Harbour Expressway

Bus Terminal

Memorial Avenue

Confederation College

Balmoral Street

Neebing–McIntyre
Diversion

FORT WILLIAM

Fort William Gardens, Tourist Information & Paterson Park

May St

Simpson Street

Kaministikwia River

To Kakabeka Falls

Victoria Avenue

Arthur Street   Waterloo St

Museum

McKellar Island

McKellar River

11 17

Walsh Street

Kingsway Avenue

Railway Station

LAKE

To Duluth & Minnesota

Kaministikwia River

108th Ave

Mission Island

Mission River

Thunder Bay Yacht Club

SUPERIOR

City Road

Paper Mill

To Duluth & Minnesota

Chippewa Park

restaurants on Bay St. Indeed, for a city its size Thunder Bay has quite a large and varied ethnic population.

Though of equal age, Fort William (Thunder Bay South) looks older and is rather drab, without the activity of its cross-town counterpart. Main streets in this half of the city are May St and Victoria St.

On each side of Thunder Bay is a commercial motel/restaurant strip.

Information

One tourist information office is east of town on Highway 11/17, just before the turn-off to Lakeshore Drive and Port Arthur – about 40 km out. It's open in summer only. Another office east of town on Highway 17 is in the parking lot of the Mackenzie Inn. These are temporary, and locations change but there will always be something somewhere along the highway close to town.

Downtown there are several places to go for information. In Port Arthur the main summer tourist office (☎ 345-6812) is central in the 1910 Pagoda in the park on the corner of Red River Rd and Water St. A few blocks away at 79 North Court St is North of Superior Tourism for any additional information required.

In Fort William there's an office (☎ 623-7577) in Paterson Park on the corner of May St and Northern Ave. During the low season information can be had from the Visitors & Convention Bureau at 520 Leith St.

There is also an information booth at Old Fort William.

Thunder Bay Museum

The small history museum, at 219 May St on the corner of Donald St, is open daily in Summer from 11 am to 5 pm and is free. The rest of the year it's closed on Monday. It contains Native Indian artefacts and a collection of odds and ends of local history. Topics covered include fur trading, mining and the early pioneers. Changing exhibits may include photography, furniture or archaeological displays. The museum is not extensive but it is well presented.

The Port

Thunder Bay Harbour is Canada's third-largest port according to tonnes handled, with the greatest complex of grain elevators in the world. Terminals, elevators and other storage and docking facilities stretch along 45 km of central waterfront. At the Port Arthur shipyards, the huge freighters are built and repaired.

In the middle of the waterfront is the Keefer Complex (☎ 345-6812), a cargo-handling facility where ships from around the world come and go. Tours of the Keefer Terminal are given, showing its operation and purpose – handling mainly resource materials and grains. The terminal is at the end of Main St off Fort William Rd at the lake. Phone for tour times and information. There are usually two tours a day and the cost is $2.25. Get tickets early at the tourist office as it's popular and numbers are limited.

Very visible are the numerous grain elevators operated by a variety of private companies. There are tours of the Saskatchewan Wheat Pool Grain Elevator (☎ 623-7577), Monday to Friday from early July to late August, at 10.15 am and 2.15 pm. Tours last 1½ hours, depart from the Paterson Park information centre, and cost $3, but note that you also need your own transport. Details and tickets are available at the tourist office.

Thunder Bay Terminals Ltd, a bulk entrepôt facility on McKellar Island just offshore, also opens its doors to visitors. Coal, potash and agricultural products are handled here.

In between the city's two halves, notice the large, high railway trestle, CN High Dock. This was used until the mid-1980s for transferring iron ore and potash from train to ship.

Parks

Centennial Park This large, natural woodland park is at the eastern edge of Port Arthur near Highway 17. It's alongside Current River, which flows into Boulevard Lake before entering Lake Superior. The park is over the Boulevard Lake Bridge just off

Arundel St. Entry is free. There are nature trails along the river and through the woods – quite nice. On the grounds is a simulated logging camp of 1910 – not much to see but the log cabins and buildings themselves are good. A small museum has a cross-cut section of a 250-year-old white pine tree on display. Various dates in history are marked at the corresponding growth rings. It's amazing to think what has gone on while this tree quietly kept growing. You'll find canoes and boats for rent here as well. Up the road from the park is the Bluffs Scenic Lookout for a view of the lake and shore.

International Friendship Gardens This good-sized city park is off Victoria Ave near Waterloo St. Various local ethnic groups such as the Finns and Hungarians have erected monuments and statues. There is a pond and some flowers but no extensive gardens. The park is west of downtown Fort William on Victoria Ave.

Waverley Park This is another city park. Free summer concerts are held in the Rotary Thundershell on Wednesday evening and Sunday afternoon in summer. It's on the corner of Red River Rd and High St in Port Arthur.

Hillcrest Park Just to the west of Waverley Park, also on High St, Hillcrest has a lookout point for views of the harbour and to the Sleeping Giant.

Chippewa Park At the edge of Lake Superior, just beyond the southern end of Fort William at the foot of City Rd, Chippewa Park has a beach, picnic and camping sites, a small amusement park and some wildlife.

Sleeping Giant Provincial Park Formerly called Sibley Park, this is a larger, more natural and scenic park further out and on the east side of the city. The scenery is pleasant – woods, hills, shoreline. There are some good walks, including one out along the top of the Sleeping Giant rock formation from where there are fine views. You can get details of the Native Indian legend about this formation at the park. Activities include swimming, fishing and camping. The park makes a good stop if you don't want to go into town to sleep. Note that it is further in off the Trans Canada Highway than it looks on the map. Last trip in, just after dark we saw three foxes at the road's edge, and there are also moose in the park.

Thunder Bay Art Gallery
The gallery at Confederation College campus collects, preserves and displays contemporary art by Canadian Native Indians. Works include paintings, prints, masks, sculptures and more. There are displays from the permanent collection as well as travelling exhibits which are usually by non-Native Indian artists. Norval Morrisseau, perhaps Canada's best known Native Indian painter, was born in Thunder Bay and some of his work is on view. Admission is free, and the gallery is open from Tuesday to Thursday, noon to 8 pm and Friday to Sunday, noon to 5 pm. Take the city bus to the campus.

Canada Games Complex
The Canada Games recreational complex, at 420 Winnipeg St, includes an Olympic-sized swimming pool, large water slide, saunas, whirlpools and a restaurant. It's open daily.

Biloski Site
This Native Indian archaeological site was discovered in 1984 when the Cherry Ridge subdivision was being developed for new houses. The site is just east of Highway 11/17 by the shoreline. Many of the tools and weapons found are on display, along with explanations, in the Thunder Bay Museum.

Old Fort William
Some of Thunder Bay's best known attractions are some distance from downtown, as is this Old Fort William (☎ 577-8461), perhaps the city's feature site.

The old fort settlement, with 42 historic buildings spread over 50 hectares west of town, not far past the airport off Broadway Ave, is worth getting to.

From 1803 to 1821 Fort William was the headquarters of the North West Fur-trading Company. Here the voyageurs and Native Indians did their trading and settlers, and explorers arrived from the east. In 1821, after much haggling and hassling, the company was absorbed into its chief rival, the Hudson's Bay Company, and Fort William declined. The fort re-creates some aspects of the early thriving fur-trading days through buildings, tools, artefacts and documents. Workers in period dress demonstrate skills and crafts, perform historical re-enactments and will answer questions. Interesting displays include the Native Indian camp and the woodwork of the canoe building. Each year, it seems, there are new expansions and ideas. A thorough but relaxed visit can take half a day or more.

Animals can be seen at the separate farm section.

Good, cheap homemade food is available in the fort's canteen.

Entry is $6.50 with family rates available; watch for the free special-event days held regularly in summer. The fort is open all year. From the end of June to the beginning of September the opening hours are from 10 am to 6 pm.

City buses go to the fort from the terminal in either Fort William or Port Arthur every hour; the last bus from the fort leaves at 5.45 pm. For any other information call the fort at the number above.

Kakabeka Falls
This waterfall is about 40 metres high, and is set in a provincial park 25 km west of Thunder Bay off Highway 17. It's most impressive in spring when the water in the river is at its highest. Sometimes the water flow is very small, as it's dammed for power. Most people go to take pictures at the falls but the park itself isn't bad. There's also camping, swimming at small beaches, and picnicking.

Mt Mackay
Mt Mackay is the tallest mountain in the area's north-western mountain chain, rising

to 350-odd metres. It offers excellent views of Thunder Bay and environs. However, the lookout is on an Ojibwa reservation and, in keeping with the Native Indians' new-found assertiveness, they charge $5 per car. It's not really worth it. The lookout is south-west of Fort William. Take Edward St to City Rd on the west side of Kaministikwia River and follow signs.

Terry Fox Courage Highway
A segment of the Trans Canada Highway north-west of town has been named after the young Canadian who in the early 1980s, while dying of cancer, attempted to run across Canada to raise money for cancer research. After having one leg amputated, he made it from Newfoundland to Thunder Bay, raising millions and becoming a national hero before finally succumbing. A monument sits at a lookout just east of town.

Activities
Canoeing Wildwaters Outfitters, at 119 North Cumberland St, offer various canoe expeditions of varied lengths and costs. They include wildlife, photography, fishing and a special trip for women only. With everything included, the cost is about $50 a day and up. Some white-water trips are offered as well.

From Thunder Bay to Kenora, near the Manitoba border, there are almost limitless fishing camps and lodges. Many people fly in to remote lakes. Tourist offices will have more information. I'm sure these are nice trips, but ask me if I can afford them! There are also places for canoe rentals.

Amethyst Searching Amethyst, a variety of quartz, is a purple semiprecious stone found in many areas around Thunder Bay. There are many superstitions surrounding amethyst, including the early Greek one that it prevents drunkenness. The ever practical Greeks therefore often fashioned wine cups from the stone. It is mined from veins which run on or near the earth's surface, so looking for the stone and digging it out are relatively easy. Within about 50 km of the city are six sites where you can go looking for your own.

Each site has some pre-found samples for sale if you should miss out on finding some. Shops in town sell jewellery and finished souvenir items made of the purple quartz.

Two of the mines are off East Loon Lake Rd east of Thunder Bay off Highway 17. East Loon Lake Rd is east of Highway 587 South. Thunder Bay Amethyst Mines is a huge property where entry is $2. Nearby is N Dzuba's, which is free. It's run by a friendly and unpredictable old man and his wife. Check out the huge chunk of amethyst in the parking area. You pay by the quality of what you find and want to keep. The road to the sites from the Trans Canada Highway is long, rough and steep in places. The tourist office will be able to direct you to other local mines and the stores around town that sell a range of stuff produced with the finished stone – mostly pretty tacky. The stone generally looks better raw.

Sauna You can get a sauna at Kanga's (☎ 344-6761), 379 Oliver Rd. Finnish saunas are popular in the region. At Kanga's there are also some Finnish eats and good desserts. See also under Canada Games Complex.

Organised Tours Forty-five-minute historical walking tours are available daily (not Sunday) through the summer from the Pagoda tourist office in Port Arthur.

In the booth pick up a folder on a self-guided architectural walking tour of Port Arthur. The firehall, some churches, various houses of note and other buildings are pointed out and described.

Bayway (☎ 345-3673) on Memorial Drive offers city and area bus tours which may include the Kakabeka Falls or a visit to an amethyst mine. One tour goes to Ouimet Canyon, which otherwise is difficult to reach without a car. Phone for information, prices and departure points.

Canadian Pacific Forest Products (☎ 475-2641), one of the city's largest employers, shows visitors the paper-making process in their mill. Tours are free and start at 9 am and 1 pm in June, July and August – times may vary according to demand. Follow Highway

61 to Broadway Ave; turn left and then right at the mill.

Tours of the Thunder Bay Thermal Generating Station (☎ 623-2701) are offered in July and August. Ontario Hydro operates this coal fired electricity-generating station on Mission Island over Jackknife Bridge. The 1½-hour tours are on Tuesday and Friday and must be booked in advance. They won't take you if you're wearing sandals or high heels. The station is on 108th Ave.

Ask at the tourist office if there is anyone now running tours of the harbour area. These were offered for several years but then were discontinued. See The Port section earlier for details of tours there.

Festivals
Jamboree This is an annual sailing event in the harbour with festivities centred around the Marina at Prince Arthur's Landing, on the waterfront in Port Arthur.

Places to Stay
Camping There are a couple of places close to town, east of Port Arthur, just off Highway 17. Between Hodder Ave and the youth hostel on Lakeshore Drive is *Wild Goose Park*, about 20 km from the city. Camping at this pleasant, quiet spot costs just $5.

Nearby, off Highway 17 at the junction of Highway 800, coming from the east on the Trans Canada Highway, is a *KOA* campground. It's about $12 for a site. Look for the road to the Mt Baldy ski area: it's nearby on the opposite side of the road. Continuing west on Highway 17 past Hodder Ave on the right is the *Trowbridge Falls* camping site.

There is also camping at *Chippewa Park* on the lake at the end of City Rd, and a good place at Kakabeka Falls.

Hostels There is a good youth hostel called *Longhouse Village Hostel* (☎ 983-2042), which is a member of the Canadian Hostelling Association. It's a fair way from town – 22 km east at 1594 Lakeshore Drive – but worth it. Most beds are in a big co-ed log house. Other rooms for women only are in the main house. The couple who run it, Lloyd and Willa Jones, spent six years as missionaries and Baptist teachers in Borneo. You'll see mementos all over the place.

The Joneses are knowledgeable about things to do around Thunder Bay and there is swimming and walking nearby. Basic food is available and you can use the kitchen. Beds cost $10 for members, $14 for non-members. Camping on the lawn is $5. From the highway head down Mackenzie Station Rd, and it's near the corner – the only hostel I've seen with an electric sign. Note that there are no city buses into town, but see the Getting Around section later for information on the Greyhound bus. The hostel is open all year.

The YM-YWCA has no beds for rent. There are places available in the *Lakehead University Residence* (☎ 345-2121) from 1 May to 20 August. Singles/doubles cost $24/34, and $20/30 for students. The university is at 855 Oliver Rd between the two downtown areas and slightly west. The cross-town city bus goes past the campus in both directions.

There's a *Salvation Army* hostel on Cumberland St at around the 500 numbers. It's free to men for a night or two if you're hard up.

B&Bs Also economical are the B&B places run from people's homes, which in Thunder Bay generally cost around $35 to $45 for doubles, with breakfast. Unfortunately, these change very fast: not being true commercial establishments they sometimes close very quickly. Listings tend not to be printed in the general information available on the city but the tourist office should know of any current places worth checking out. The Unicorn Inn (☎ 577-1034), mentioned under places to eat, may still act as co-ordinator of the local B&B association.

Hotels For a reasonable price in Port Arthur there is the *Shoreline Motor Hotel* on Cumberland St on the corner of Camelot St. It's recommended, very central and good value at $40/45 for singles/doubles.

I guess the best place in town is the nearby *Ramada Inn* on the corner of Cumberland St and Red River Rd, right by the Pagoda tourist office. It's large, has several places to eat or drink and costs about twice as much as the Shoreline.

Over in Fort William, which is more convenient for the airport, railway and bus stations, a decent cheap place is the *Intowner* (☎ 623-1565) on the corner of Arthur St East and Brodie St South. There is an adjoining restaurant and you can use the pool in the health club. Singles cost $34.50.

Best of the skid-row specials is the *Hotel Empire* (☎ 622-2912), at 140 Simpson St, with singles/doubles $18/24 plus $2 for the key. There is a snack bar and a drinking bar downstairs.

Motels Most of the moderately priced accommodation is in the newer motel strips. There are two areas of heavy motel concentration, one on each side of the city, and there are a few rather good places in between the two downtown areas along Memorial Ave. The *Circle Inn* (☎ 344-5744) and the *Sleeping Giant Motor Hotel* (☎ 345-7316) are here with 50 rooms each and prices range from $38 to $42. More up-market is the nearby *Venture Inn* (☎ 345-2343).

The motel area in Port Arthur is on and around Cumberland St. It heads out to Hodder Ave, which then leads to the Expressway or Highway 17 East. The motels are mainly found near the grain elevators along the lakefront. Cumberland St leads right into the downtown area of Port Arthur.

The *Strathcona* (☎ 683-8351), at 546 Hodder St, is a very small, well-kept blue and white place. Singles or doubles range from $30 to $45.

The *Hodder Avenue Motel* (☎ 683-8414), situated at 321 Hodder Ave, is a nice place. Singles/doubles are $28/32.

The *Lakeview* is the pale yellow place at 391 Cumberland St on the left-hand side approaching town. Singles and doubles are $42; there's cable TV. There are other lower priced places along Cumberland St.

The other motel district is along Arthur St, heading out of town from downtown Fort

William past the airport. There are a few motels side-by-side on Kingsway Ave, off Arthur St, but these are priced higher than they're worth.

The *Ritz Motel* (☎ 622-4112) is at 2600 Arthur St East. Rooms cost from $48 to $55 in this red brick building close to town. Less expensive is the *Paradise Motel* at 221 Arthur St West.

Places to Eat

Port Arthur The *Appolon Restaurant*, on Red River Rd not far from Cumberland St, has good-value daily specials. Complete standard meals are about $5 and they serve cheap breakfasts too.

At 11 South Cumberland St, *Cultures* is recommended for very good soups, salads and fresh sandwiches at tasty prices. Also in this area is the *Prospector*, a steak and roast beef house serving meat from a local cattle ranch. Steaks cost from $15 to $18. It's on the corner of Cumberland St and Park Ave.

The *Hoito*, at 314 Bay St, is a Finnish place set up about 60 years ago. It is known for its homemade food served in plain surroundings. They give large portions and offer a smorgasbord. There are a few similar places in this Finnish neighbourhood.

On the corner of Red River Rd and Junot Ave is the *Brasserie*, the city's only brew pub where, in addition to the usual meals, they have a Sunday brunch.

On the corner of Red River Rd and Court St, *Kresge's*, a Woolworth's-style variety store, has a lunch counter offering simple, very cheap meals. For something from the Far East the *Cumberland*, on Cumberland St across from the Keskus Mall, has cheap noodle lunches.

The shopping malls also have restaurants. The *Office* in the Keskus Mall, Red River Rd, is a pub with inexpensive meals and live music – top 40 and often blues – at night.

There are numerous spots offering hamburgers and similar fare on Memorial Ave, which links the two parts of the city. Best is *Bonanza*, at No 1075, where full meals are not expensive and include an all-you-can-eat salad bar. Known for their cheap steaks, they

also serve chicken and fish. Also on Memorial Ave are the Inter-City Mall, which has a cheap food fair, and the *Golden Griddle*, a good place for a pancake breakfast.

Fort William The *Pastry Pedlar*, on the corner of May and George Sts, has croissants, pastries, muffins and sandwiches. It's good and inexpensive but closed on Sunday. The *Venice Grill*, at 636 Simpson St, is a good basic place, fine for a cheap breakfast and open every day.

Trifons Pizza & Spaghetti House, on the corner of May and Mills Sts, sells pizza half-price on Wednesday. The *Polish Legion*, at 730 Simpson St, has a small coffee shop where they serve up large, filling portions at low prices.

Victoria Mall, or the Victoria Centre, right in the centre of town has a food fair. *Boston Pizza*, at 217 Arthur St West, also has pastas and ribs at moderate prices.

The pricey, dressy *Unicorn Inn*, about half an hour south of the city off Highway 61 on Unicorn Rd, is probably the best restaurant in the region.

The *Valhalla Inn*, at 1 Valhalla Inn Rd, has a very good Sunday brunch for $15 which includes free use of the swimming pool, sauna, and fitness equipment.

The *Williams Restaurant*, at 610 Arthur St West, has a menu of standard Canadian and some Mexican-style dishes. The food is good and the portions large, although not strictly low-budget with dinner costing $20.

Entertainment

Expressway, in the Landmark Inn on the corner of the Expressway and Red River Rd, brings in rock groups from around the province. They also have DJ dancing. Admission varies.

The *Innplace* is another motor hotel bar. It's in the Intowner, on the corner of Arthur and Brodie Sts. Entertainment is live commercial pop-rock; shows change frequently, as does the cover charge.

The *Elephant & Castle*, in the Intercity mall, is a pub-style place with a large dance floor. *Casey's*, at 450 Memorial Ave, is basically a restaurant but also serves as a casual place for an evening's drink accompanied by recorded pop music. *KelseyUs* at the end of Red River Rd near the highway, is a popular, dressier place.

There is a summer theatre programme, Moonlight Melodrama, in Chippewa Park.

Getting There & Away

Air Thunder Bay Airport is about 15 minutes' driving south-west of town, at the junction of Highway 11/17 (the Trans Canada Highway) and Highway 61 to Duluth, Minnesota and the USA.

Air Canada (☎ 623-3313) and Canadian Airlines (☎ 577-6461) offer flights to Winnipeg for $216 and to Toronto for $270.

Norontair (☎ 623-3313) services the region and other northern portions of the province.

Bus The Greyhound bus terminal (☎ 345-2194) is in Fort William at 815 Fort William Rd. It's not far east of the downtown area, towards the lake.

For Winnipeg and points further west there are about five buses a day, beginning very early in the morning and running until the wee hours.

For Sault Ste Marie and points east, such as Toronto, there are also about five trips daily and again the schedule is evenly spaced out through the 24 hours with some departures at rather ungodly hours.

For Sudbury there is just one trip a day, departing in the early evening.

One-way fares to Winnipeg are $63, to Sault Ste Marie $73, to Toronto $99, and to Sudbury $95.

The Mainline bus across the street goes to Fort William.

Train The VIA Rail terminal is in the Canadian Pacific railway passenger station in Fort William. It's on Syndicate St just south of Arthur St near the City Hall. At the time of writing all train services in and out of Thunder Bay had been cut. The train across Ontario now runs north of Thunder Bay. It's hard to know why.

Car & Motorbike Avis (☎ 577-5766) is at 1475 Walsh St West. They charge $31.95 a day with 200 free km. Additional km are 15 cents each.

Budget Rent-a-Car (☎ 345-2425), at 899 Copper Crescent, has weekend specials which may be useful. Tilden also has an office in Port Arthur. There are several agencies with desks at the airport.

Thunder Bay is 720 km from Sault Ste Marie, 731 km from Winnipeg and 315 km from Duluth, Michigan, USA.

A circular tour of northern Ontario can be made by car from Thunder Bay by backtracking to Lake Nipigon and following Highway 11, the most northerly provincial route, through Geraldton and Kapuskasing and returning south via Timmins, Sudbury or North Bay. Provincial parks are found at regular intervals along Highway 11. Towns are small.

Hitching Westbound travellers head out to Arthur St; the airport bus will take you to a good spot. Alternatively, if you can get to Highway 102 (Red River Rd-Dawson Rd) on the north edge of Port Arthur you save a few miles along Highway 11/17 before the turnoff to Winnipeg. If you're eastbound, anywhere on Highway 17 is OK. For $3 the eastbound Greyhound bus will take you to the edge of town.

Getting Around

To/From the Airport An airport bus departs from the local city bus terminal, beside the Paterson Park tourist office (in Fort William on the corner of May and Miles Sts) every 20 minutes until 6 pm, then every 40 minutes. The ride takes about 15 minutes.

A city bus, the Arthur Route, also goes from town to the airport. It's much slower but costs less. Catch it anywhere on Arthur St.

Bus There is a good bus system which covers all areas of the city. For information call ☎ 344-9666.

In Fort William the terminal for the local buses is across the street from the tourist office on the corner of May and Miles Sts. To get to the Port Arthur end of town take the Memorial bus on May St, or the Mainline bus along Fort William St. Same thing going the opposite way.

In Port Arthur the terminal is on the corner of Water and Camelot Sts, just down from Cumberland St by the waterfront. The Pagoda tourist office is next door.

The cross-town bus from either end of Thunder Bay goes to the university. The Neebing bus goes to Old Fort William from the Fort William terminal.

For the youth hostel there are no city buses, so take the eastbound Greyhound bus from the terminal at 815 Fort William Rd. For $3 they'll take you to Lakeshore Drive – or better, to Mackenzie Station Rd, which leads off the highway. From there it's a good walk straight to the hostel. Be sure to tell the driver beforehand that you want to get off for the hostel. There is a trip into town in the morning and one back in the evening, but ask about up-to-date scheduling. A city bus runs from the railway station to the Greyhound bus terminal.

City buses go to and from the motel and fast-food strips on both sides of town.

WEST OF THUNDER BAY
Quetico Provincial Park
A huge wilderness park linked to another border park in Minnesota, Quetico is very undeveloped for the most part but has one major organised campground. It offers excellent canoeing, primarily for those wanting peace and quiet. The park is a maze of lakes and rivers, with lots of wildlife and some Native Indian pictographs. It can be accessed from several points. There are outfitters and maps available in and around the park.

Atikokan
This is the supply town for the park and it has two small museums. Between here and Ignace lies **White Otter Lake**, site of **White Otter Castle**, a locally well-known oddity built in 1904 by a Scottish immigrant, Jimmy McOuat. He did it all by himself and nobody

knows why. He was a bachelor and it's a huge timber place with a four-storey tower. It's on the north-western arm of the lake, accessible only by canoe.

There's lots of wilderness camping in the district but you really need topographic maps.

Fort Frances
Situated on Rainy Lake opposite International Falls, Minnesota, this is a busy border-crossing point into the USA. Both sides are popular outdoor destinations with countless lakes, cottages, fishing, camping, etc. In town you can visit a paper mill. A causeway across **Rainy Lake** towards Atikokan offers great views of the lake.

The **Fort Frances Museum** examines Native Indian history and the fur trade as well as more recent developments. The museum also operates **Fort Saint Pierre**, a replica fur-trading post and lookout tower at **Pither's Point Park** on the eastern side of town.

North Highway 71 connects with Kenora and Winnipeg.

Kenora
Kenora is the closest town of any size to the Manitoba border. It is a pulp and paper town and centre for much of the local tourist activity, which is mainly fishing (the fish are all at least as big as the model by the highway on the western side of town) and hunting. The setting is a nice one on the **Lake of the Woods**. Cruises of the lake are available and last two hours.

On Main St South in Memorial Park is a **small history museum**. There's an international sailing regatta in late July, in and around the 14,000 islands in the lake. Provincial parks are nearby. A folk festival is held each year in early July.

Many Native Indians still live in the area and it is they who hand-pick the Canadian wild rice which grows locally; it's $10 for half a kilo in most places (natural food stores) across the country and is delicious.

Sioux Narrows

About 80 km south of Kenora on the eastern side of Lake of the Woods, Sioux Narrows is a local resort town.

In addition to the residents from around the region many Americans and people from Winnipeg spend time around here during the summer months. The town and its surroundings have a range of cottages, lodges, motels, campgrounds and even houseboats for rent. Lake of the Woods fishing is renowned far and wide.

Manitoba

Entered Confederation: 15 July 1870)
Area: 650,090 sq km
Population: 1,026,241

Manitoba, Canada's fifth province, probably gets its name from the Algonkian Indians. Manito means 'great spirit'; and in Lake Manitoba there is a strait where the water hits the limestone edges, making an odd echoing sound; the Indians associated this sound with the 'great spirit' and named the spot 'Manito Waba', which means Manito Strait. Manito Waba became Manitoba.

Winnipeg, the capital, has had a long and interesting history which influenced greatly the development of the west in general. The city has a variety of things to see and do and many things are within walking distance of each other along architecturally diverse streets.

Winnipeg is a major cultural centre and offers plenty of choice in accommodation and eating out. Neighbouring St Boniface is the largest western French community in Canada. Scattered across the province are large parks, ideal for exploring the terrain. Way up on Hudson Bay, Churchill with its intriguing wildlife is one of the destinations most alluring to visitors.

The province is the first of the three prairie provinces as you head westward. The southern half is low and flat, the western edge is best for farming. Much of the land is forested and dotted with lakes and rivers. The Canadian Shield, which covers about half the country, cuts across northern Manitoba, making it rocky, hilly forest.

The winters are long and cold, but the summers can be hot and are usually very sunny. Generally there is a decrease in temperature as you go from south-west to north-east. There's about 130 cm of snow a year.

Manufacturing is the main source of income. Food processing and clothing facto-ries are also important contributors to the provincial economy.

Wheat is the most important agricultural product, with various other grains and cattle following closely behind. In the northern Shield area there are good deposits of gold, copper, nickel and zinc.

Fishing and hunting attract many visitors to this province, especially those from the USA. A map indicating all the campgrounds in Manitoba is available from the tourist office in Winnipeg.

There's also an excellent guide detailing canoe routes around the province (including some wilderness trips). In addition there is a farm vacation programme.

A little novelty you'll notice if you enter the province by road is the 'put your garbage in orbit' signs, referring to the spherical containers at the highway's edge.

Winnipeg

Winnipeg sits in the geographical centre of the country but it feels very much like a western town. I'd say Winnipeg seems like the most US-style city in Canada, although Toronto actually has this reputation. Indeed, Winnipeg is often compared to Chicago – its Mid-Western, grain-handling, transportation counterpart.

Winnipeg also feels much bigger than it is, although with 650,000 residents it is the fourth largest Canadian city. About half of Manitoba's population lives here.

The city has some fascinating history which visitors can explore in museums and at various sites.

The Cree Indian people called the area

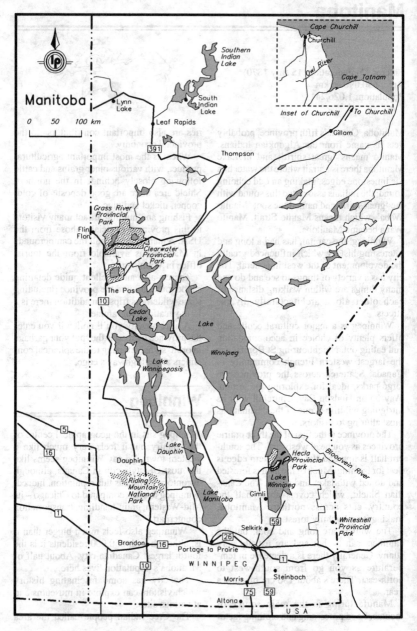

'Winnipee' meaning 'muddy water'. They shared the land Winnipeg now occupies with the Assiniboines, before de la Vérendrye, the first White trader, arrived in 1738. In the early 1800s the area was the centre of rivalry over the fur trade between the Hudson's Bay Company and the North West Company. In 1812 Lord Selkirk led Scottish and Irish immigrants to the area to create the first permanent colonial settlement. Later Fort Garry was built. Louis Riel, a native son, and one of Canada's most controversial figures, led the Métis in voicing concerns over their way of life. He is considered the father of Manitoba. The railway arrived in 1881, bringing people and industry.

The 1970s saw urban redevelopment upgrade the provincial capital. The main street, Portage Ave, has recently undergone a massive change with the building of a mega-mall complex, taking over several blocks. Today the wide downtown streets, edged with a balance of new and old build-ings, give a sense of permanence as well as development and change.

Summers are very hot and winters very cold in Winnipeg – the corner of Portage Ave and Main St is said to be the windiest corner on the continent.

If you're crossing Canada you'll have to pass through this city, which can be a pleas-ant stopover.

Orientation

As you approach Winnipeg from the east, the trees start to disappear. With about 50 km to go, the flat prairie land that stretches to the Rockies appears. Near town is a sign marking the longitudinal centre of Canada.

Main St is the main north-south street; Portage Ave (pronounced 'Port-idge') the main one running east-west, it's also the main shopping street, leading westward towards the airport and eventually to the westbound Trans Canada Highway. The downtown core spreads out evenly from

The Métis & Louis Riel

The Métis were and are people of mixed Indian and French blood, almost always the result of unions between white men and Indian women. Many Métis can trace their ancestors to the time of western exploration and fur-trading when the French voyageurs travelled the country, living like and often with the Indians.

The term is also used more loosely to include English-Indian mixed bloods in order to avoid the term half-breed.

As time passed and their numbers grew, many Métis began to use the St Boniface/Winnipeg area as a settlement base, living a life which was part European, part traditionally Native. This odd separation became an identity and they began to think of themselves as a distinct people with their own needs. The ensuing rebellions were the almost inevitable product of this consciousness.

Born in St Boniface in 1844, Louis Riel led the Métis in an anti-government uprising in 1869, partly to protest the decision to open up what they saw as their lands to new settlers, and to prevent possible assimilation. When complaints went unheeded, he and his men took Upper Fort Garry. Government troops soon reversed that and to the Canadian government, Riel became a bad guy. Land was allotted to the Métis, however, and the province of Manitoba was created. As part of the turning twists of Riel's fate, he was then elected to the House of Commons, but was forbidden to serve!

There is some question about what transpired in the next few years; he may have spent time in asylums. In any case he took refuge for several years from all the stress of personal persecution and political machinations in Montana returning once again to lead the protesting Métis. This time it was in Saskatchewan during 1885: they fled there seeking autonomy. They lost the battle, Riel surrendered and after a dramatic trial, was called a traitor and hanged. The act triggered French anger and resentment towards the English that has not yet been forgotten. Riel's body was returned to his mother's house in Winnipeg and then buried in St Boniface. Riel is now considered the father of the province.

Important sites relating to the Métis and Riel can be seen in Winnipeg, St Boniface and Saskatoon and vicinity. ■

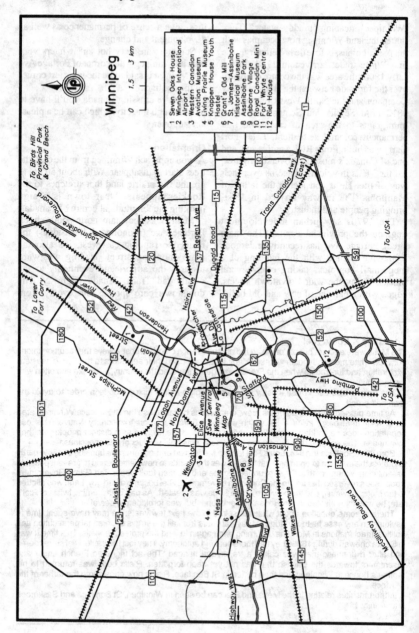

Winnipeg

0   1.5   3 km

1   Seven Oaks House
2   Winnipeg International
    Airport
3   Western Canadian
    Aviation Museum
4   Living Prairie Museum
5   Knappen House Youth
    Hostel
6   Grant's Old Mill
7   St James–Assiniboine
    Historical Museum
8   Assiniboine Park
9   Osborne Village
10 Royal Canadian Mint
11 Fort Whyte Centre
12 Riel House

To Birds Hill
Provincial Park
& Grand Beach

Lagimodière Boulevard

Trans Canada Hwy (East)

101

15

Regent Ave

37

Dugald Road

To USA

59

135

20

Nairn Ave

115

150

100

Red River Hwy

52

42

Henderson

180

5

52

12

Main Street

Provencher

Ave De La Cathédrale

62

Pembina Hwy

42

McPhillips Street

101

Logan Avenue

47

Notre Dame Ave

9

5

70

Stafford

St

To USA

80

Elice Avenue

57

See Central
Winnipeg Map

95

Inkster Boulevard

90

Wellington

3

2

Kenaston

90

Ness Avenue

Assiniboine Avenue

8

Corydon Avenue

105

11

155

4

6

Wilkes Avenue

7

Robin Blvd

145

To Lower
Fort Garry

To Birds Hill

McGillivray Boulevard

25

Highway West

101

their junction. Most of the hotels and restaurants and many of the historic sites are within a 10-block square around this point.

The railway station is central on the corner Main St and Broadway Ave. The Legislative Building and other government buildings are on Broadway Ave too.

The corner of Portage Ave and Main St has many office buildings and examples of newer architecture. Portage Place, a redevelopment project of stores and offices, runs from Carlton St all the way to Vaughan St and has transformed much of the north side of Portage Ave. Enclosed walkways, known as skywalks, over Portage Ave connect Portage Place to major department stores on the south side. Many of the downtown side streets are one-way streets which alternate in direction as a rule.

To the north-east of the city core is the old warehouse area known as the Exchange District. Nearby, north up Main St is the Centennial Centre, an art and cultural complex. Many other city sights are in this area, including Chinatown.

North of Rupert St on Main St is an area of cheap bars and dingy hotels, peopled by various down-and-outers, many of them lost or alcoholic Native Canadians.

Further north on Main St, you'll find some evidence of the many ethnic groups, primarily Jews and Ukrainians, that once lived here in greater numbers.

South of the downtown area, across the Assiniboine River on Osborne St, is Osborne Village, a newish area with boutiques, stores and restaurants. There are a couple of good bookshops here, Mary Scorer and Global Village. Back across the bridge in the downtown area, the art gallery is on the corner of Memorial Blvd and Portage Ave and the bus station is nearby.

In the southern part of the city, along Corydon Ave for a few blocks near where it meets Osborne St and the Pembina Highway, is a small Italian district. The tourist office plays this up but it really isn't of interest to a visitor. There are a couple of cappuccino bars and some pizza places but not much else.

Information

The main tourist office (☎ 945-3777) is in the Legislative Building on Broadway Ave, near Osborne St downtown. It's open from 8 am to 9 pm daily, in winter Monday to Friday only until 4.30 pm. You can also call Travel Manitoba toll free on ☎ 800-665-0040 ext 35.

Another office is the Convention & Visitors' Bureau (or Tourism Winnipeg) (☎ 943-1970), on the 2nd floor of the Convention Centre on the corner of York Ave and Edmonton St, also downtown. It's open business hours, weekdays only.

There are information booths in summer on Highway 1 East (at the bypass) at Highway 1 West, and also at the city bypass.

There is also an office in City Hall on Main St, a few blocks north of Portage Ave. Lastly, there's a good information desk with maps and helpful staff at the airport.

Travel books and maps can be found at the Global Village bookshop in Osborne Village.

The post office is at 266 Graham Ave. The general delivery window is open on Saturday mornings as well as the regular weekday hours.

For a view of the city, go to the Observation Gallery of the Richardson Building on the corner of Portage Ave and Main St. Unfortunately it's only open on Wednesday. For information on visiting, call 956-0172. Advance notice is required but phoning on Wednesday morning is fine.

Walking Tour

Free 'Historic Winnipeg' walking tours begin at the museum information booth. They take place Monday to Saturday at 11 am and 1.30 pm, Sunday at 1 and 3 pm, and Wednesday and Thursday evenings at 7 pm. The tour lasts one hour.

Centennial Arts Centre

On Main St, north of Portage Ave, the Arts Centre is a complex which houses several things to see. You can get an all-inclusive ticket for admission to all three of the following museums at a reduced rate over the individual admission fees.

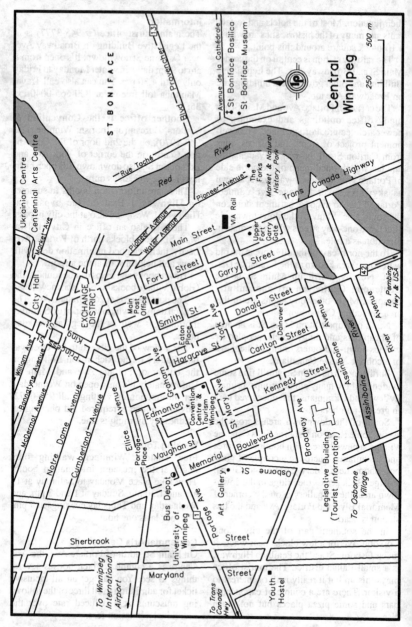

Central Winnipeg

Museum of Man & Nature This good museum has exhibits of history, culture, wildlife and geology. The dioramas of Native Indian life and animals are realistic, incorporating sights, sounds and even smells. There is an excellent recreation of a 1920s town with barber shop, drug store and old cinema. One room has a full-sized replica of the *Nonsuch*, a 17th-century ketch that took the first load of Hudson's Bay Company furs to England. The museum is worth a few hours' visit. Admission costs $3.50. It's open every day from 10 am until 8 pm in summer. From September to June it's open from noon until 5 pm weekdays, to 6 pm on the weekend and is closed on Monday.

Planetarium The Planetarium (☎ 943-3142) has good programmes on space, the solar system and different aspects of the universe. There are also laser rock shows, fashion shows and other performances held in the planetarium, which utilise its unique equipment. The usual programmes are $4, the laser rock shows are more expensive. Ring for information and programme times.

Touch the Universe In the museum basement is a 'hands-on' science gallery with participatory displays designed to help reveal how our senses perceive the world. The staff put on demonstrations on a range of scientific topics. Admission is $3, less for kids.

The Forks

A national historic site has been developed at the forks of the Red and Assiniboine rivers behind the VIA Rail station off Main St near Broadway Ave.

There isn't a lot to see but it's a great location along the water and the area has been the site in one way or another of pretty much all of Manitoba's history.

Park staff on duty every day (find them at the round office structure) can provide information on what's gone on through the years at this river junction. Indians first used the area. The early explorers and fur traders stopped here, forts were built and destroyed,

and later Métis and Scottish pioneers settled The Forks.

The site is essentially a riverside park and there are some paths with historic plaques and boat-docking facilities. Boat tours of the river depart from nearby. In winter there is skating on the river or you can walk over to the impressive-looking St Boniface Basilica.

Also part of The Forks development is the market situated in one of the several old warehouses in the area. Inside are craft shops, an art gallery, produce stalls with such things as cheeses and breads and a handful of restaurants, cafés and food outlets. It's a fine place for a coffee and cinnamon bun breakfast with a newspaper.

Two free buses run to and from the site. Monday to Friday the No 99 Dash runs from here up to Broadway Ave and around by the Art Gallery. The No 96 bus, which runs on weekends, links Portage Ave to The Forks. It's not that far to walk from downtown, either.

Legislative Building

The Legislative Building on Broadway Ave at Osborne St, is one of the world's great examples of the neoclassical style. It was built using rare limestone and is now one of the most valuable buildings in North America. 'Golden Boy', a bronze statue perched atop the building, is covered in 23½-carat gold and has become a city symbol. There are good, free tours given throughout the day and the building has a cheap cafeteria.

Behind the Legislative Building a park with a monument to Louis Riel, the Métis leader, runs beside the river. At night this is an area for commercial sex – as it has been for many, many years.

Art Gallery

This is the pie-shaped building at 300 Memorial Blvd near Portage Ave. It has a good collection of Inuit art and shows mainly Canadian works, including those by young, little-known artists. The gallery is well designed and laid out. It's open Tuesday, Friday, Saturday and Sunday from 11 am to

5 pm, and Wednesday and Thursday 11am to 9 pm. It's closed on Monday. Admission costs $2. Free tours are given at 2 pm on Sunday. There's a restaurant on the roof which you may want to investigate.

Exchange District

To my mind this is one of the city's most interesting and unusual features. It's a 20-block area of fine turn-of-the-century commercial buildings and warehouses now being restored for housing, restaurants and a variety of businesses. There's some very substantial architecture here as well as distinctive old advertising signs painted directly on to the brick walls of numerous buildings. Though rarely seen in most of Canada today, this form of billboard seems to be undergoing a mini-revival in this part of Winnipeg.

The various Edwardian and Victorian buildings here arose to fill the needs of the many stock and commodity exchanges, which boomed in the city from 1880 to the 1920s. Market Square, on the corner of King St and Bannantyne Ave, is a focal point of the area and there's often something going on here: on weekends either a flea market or some live music, for example.

The tourist office has maps to follow for an informative walk in the district, or free walking tours are offered daily in the summer, beginning in the foyer of the Museum of Man & Nature. The area also contains many of the city's theatres and some clubs, so it doesn't close up after dark.

Northern Traditions

This is a gallery specialising in new and traditional Métis, Native Indian and Inuit art, which includes works in wood, stone, hides, beads, etc. It's at 277 McDermot Ave near Market Square in the Exchange District.

Portage Place

The city's downtown redevelopment indoor shopping mall runs along the north side of Portage Ave for three blocks. It's a three-storey affair connected to large department stores on the south side of the street by enclosed overhead walkways. Aside from

being a place to shop and hang out, the mall has three first-run movie theatres, and an IMAX movie theatre on the 3rd floor for large-format film presentations. There are also some places to eat in the complex.

This development is part of a major plan to keep the inner city viable and prevent the population becoming too suburban. It seems to be busy but the nearby stores outside appear to be having a tough time.

Winnipeg Square & Eaton Place

Each of these is another large shopping complex. The first is underground beneath the corner of Portage Ave and Main St. It connects by skywalk or tunnel with many of the area's buildings including Eaton Place, which lies between Portage Place and Winnipeg Square along Hargrave St.

If you'd spent a winter in Winnipeg you'd know why these indoor, protected retail centres are so commonplace. There are food fairs in both as well as several restaurants covering a variety of price ranges.

Manitoba Children's Museum

Hold on to your head, here's a museum set up for the kids themselves, especially those between the ages of three and 11 years. Hands-on exhibits encourage play and education at the same time. In one section they can dress up in costumes and pretend they're in the circus. It's just off Main St at 109 Pacific Ave, and admission is inexpensive. It's closed on Monday and in the morning on Sunday and holidays.

Winnipeg Commodity Exchange

Canada's largest commodity futures market is here and has a visitors' gallery which overlooks the trading area. You can see grains and other crops being traded and prices fluctuating with the Chicago markets. Don't forget to find out how pork bellies are doing! Guides can explain some of this very different world to you at no charge. The exchange is open Monday to Friday from

9.30 am to 1.15 pm only. It's in the Exchange Tower at 360 Main St.

St Boniface

Primarily a residential district, St Boniface, across the Red River on Boulevard Provencher, is one of the oldest French communities in Canada. There's not much to see, but the façade of the St Boniface Basilica of 1908 is worth a look. The rest of the church was destroyed by fire in 1968. Churches were built and rebuilt on this site from as early as 1818. In front, facing the river, is a cemetery for the local French from the 1800s to the present. Louis Riel, the Métis leader who was born in St Boniface, is buried here.

The Métis people, of mixed North American Indian and French Canadian ancestry, founded a culturally and politically distinctive society in the late 19th century. In 1885 Riel led an unsuccessful rebellion against the British government of the east, and was later executed.

Next door at 494 Rue Taché is the St Boniface Museum, in what was the nunnery around 1850. This is the oldest building in Winnipeg and evidently is the largest oak-log construction on the continent. It contains artefacts and relics pertaining to Riel and other French, Métis and Indian settlers as well as to the Grey Nuns, who lived and worked here after arriving by birch bark canoe from Montreal, nearly a 3000-km trip.

There is also some information on Jean Baptiste Lagimodière, one of the best known of the voyageurs, who canoed between here and Montreal. There is a diorama of a Métis hunter's camp, with an example of the famous Red River Cart which could be floated across rivers by repositioning the wheels. Also in the museum are some articles that were saved from the destroyed basilica.

Admission is by donation. In summer, it's open Monday to Friday from 9 am to 9 pm, and from 10 am to 9 pm Sunday and holidays, and until 5 pm on Saturday. In winter it closes at 5 pm every day.

The St Boniface Historical Society offers walking tours of older parts of the area, including discussions of local history and culture. The tourist office has a booklet on St Boniface which includes a map and self-guided walking tour.

To get there from downtown, take the bus east along Portage Ave across the bridge and then walk along the river to the church and museum. Taché Promenade follows the Red River along Taché Ave past much of St Boniface's history. A couple of plaques indicate the major points of interest.

Riel House National Historic Park

At 330 River Rd in a residential area known as St Vital, quite a distance south of downtown, is Riel House (☎ 257-1783) which details Louis Riel's (an enduring figure's) life here in the 1880s. The restored and furnished traditional French Canadian-style log farmhouse, built in 1881, belonged to Louis' parents. He was brought here to lie in state after his execution in Saskatchewan in 1885.

A staff interpreter offers information on the Riels and on the Métis in general.

To get there, take the No 16 bus from Portage Ave going west; after passing through Osborne Village it'll take you nearly to the door. The site is only open during the summer and looks well-out-of-place beside the modern bungalows which surround it. Opening hours are 9.30 am to 6 pm, and it's free; but phone to be sure it is open before making the trip out here.

Royal Canadian Mint

South-east of town, on the corner of Lagimodière Blvd and the Trans Canada Highway, is where the real money is made. This ultra-modern glass pyramid building contains some of the most modern minting machinery in the world. There are free tours every half-hour, which show the procedures used in cranking out two billion coins a year. The mint produces Canada's coinage as well as coins for many other countries, especially in Asia. It's open Monday to Friday, 9 am to 3 pm. (No free samples!)

Ukrainian Centre

The Ukrainian Centre, on 184 Alexander Ave

near the museum, contains a gallery and museum. Set up to preserve and present the culture of the Ukraine, the museum has costumes, textiles, ceramics and painted Easter eggs (*pysankas*). The gallery displays both old and contemporary works. A specialised library holds 40,000 volumes relating to this important Canadian immigrant group.

It's free, and open Tuesday to Saturday from 10 am to 4 pm, Sunday from 2 to 5 pm.

Assiniboine Park
Assiniboine is the largest city park and is open from 7 am until dark. Of course, it's free. The grounds hold an English garden and a 40-hectare zoo with animals from around the world. There are also playing fields.

The conservatory has some tropical vegetation and a small art gallery.

The park is south of the Assiniboine River and just off south-west Portage Ave, about seven km west of the downtown area. Entrances are off Corydon Ave or at the west end of Wellington Crescent.

Assiniboine Forest
South of the Assiniboine Park, between Shaftsbury and Chalfont Aves, is this largely undeveloped forest area which is even larger than the park itself. In the middle there's a pond with an observation area for bird-watching, and you can see deer along the winding trails. No admission is charged.

Fort Whyte Centre
The centre is in a conservation area with walking trails, and is an environmental education centre with exhibits, demonstrations and slide shows on local wildlife. Outdoor activities are led, too. It's open daily at 1961 McCreary Rd.

Macdonald House
Near the Legislature at 61 Carlton St is this beautiful Victorian house, also called Dalnavert (☎ 943-2835). It was built in 1895 for the son of John A Macdonald, Canada's first prime minister. The house is decorated with period pieces. It's closed on Monday and Friday, admission is $2.50.

Seven Oaks House
This is the oldest habitable house in the province, a big house built (without nails) in 1851. It's about four km north of Portage Ave and Main St on Rupertsland Ave. It's open daily from July to Labour Day (early in September) and on weekends in spring.

Grant's Old Mill
Grant's is a reconstruction of an 1829 water mill, which is thought to be the first use of hydropower in the province. There's not really very much to see, although grist (grain) is ground every day and offered for sale. It's open from 10 am to 8 pm from Monday to Saturday, from 2 pm Sunday. It's on the corner of Booth Drive and Portage Ave West, near Sturgeon Creek.

Living Prairie Museum
At 2793 Ness Ave, north of Grant's Mill, the Living Prairie Museum is really a park or rather a preserve where 12 hectares of now very scarce original, unploughed tall grass prairie is protected and studied.

Within this small area 200 native plants can be found as well as a variety of animal and birdlife. There is an interpretive centre at the site which is open on weekends and naturalists are on hand. There are walking trails and guided walks are offered. The museum is free.

Upper Fort Garry Gate
In the small park on Main St, near Broadway Ave and across from the railway station, is the old stone gate and some remaining wall (restored in 1982) of Fort Garry. Since 1738, four different forts have stood on this spot, or nearby. The gate dates from 1835 and was part of the Hudson's Bay fort system. There are also some photographs and written descriptions.

North Point Douglas
This section of the city is the only area west of Montreal to be classified an historic area.

Many of the houses are over 100 years old. Plaques and monuments commemorate various historical events.

St James-Assiniboine Historical Museum

This small museum has a collection of pioneer and Indian artefacts. It's at 3180 Portage Ave and is open from 10 am to 5 pm daily, but closed on weekends after Labour Day until the following spring. Admission costs $1. Next door is a 100-year-old log house with authentic furnishings.

Western Canadian Aviation Museum

One of the country's largest aviation museums, the WCAM (☎ 786-5503) is still for plane buffs only. They have a good collection of 35 planes from over the years but only some of them are on display at any given time. There are a few particularly historic aircraft, including Canada's first helicopter. Other exhibits include uniforms, photographs, engines and various related artefacts. The museum is at the international airport in hangar T-2, 958 Ferry Rd. It's open every day, but on Sunday and holidays during the afternoon only. Admission is inexpensive, and for a small additional fee a tour is offered.

Parks

There are numerous parks in and around the city, some quite large. Aside from the ones mentioned previously, there is Little Mountain Park, which has hiking trails and examples of local forest and prairie vegetation. It's two km east of Sturgeon Rd off Oak Point Highway.

Activities

Swimming A couple of swimming pools in the city are open to the public. There's Central Outdoor Pool, administered by the City of Winnipeg Parks & Recreation Department, and the Pan-Am Pool (☎ 284-4031), which is one of the country's largest. Admission here costs $1.50 and the pool is at 25 Poseidon Bay.

Other In summer the larger city parks are good for walking. In winter there is skating on the rivers. Perhaps the best spot is on the Red River near The Forks in front of the St Boniface Basilica.

Organised Tours Gray Line (☎ 942-4500) has nine boat and bus tours ranging in length and price. The basic downtown double-decker bus tour lasting three hours is $8.

Paddlewheel boat tours depart from a wharf down by The Forks Historic Site, at the foot of the Provencher Bridge on the corner of Water Ave. The ticket office is also here.

There are straight along-the-river or more costly evening dinner-dance cruises. Another travels up to Fort Garry. The MS *Lord Selkirk* also has dinner cruises, dance cruises and Sunday afternoon cruises. The boat docks beside Redwood Bridge, north up Main St from Portage Ave. River Rouge is another company with bus and boat tours.

Festivals

The annual Winnipeg Folk Festival (☎ 453-2983) is probably the country's biggest and best known. It takes place for three days in summer with about 100 performers, shows and workshops. The festival is held at Bird's Hill Park, 20 km north of downtown.

Folklorama is the city's ethnic festival of nations. The tourist office will have up-to-date details. This festival celebrates about 50 years of the city's various ethnic groups through two weeks of music, dance, food, etc with pavilions in and around downtown Winnipeg.

Black-O-Rama is an annual summer festival of music, dance and poetry of West Indian origin.

The Red River Exhibition, held in late June at the Winnipeg Arena, is a week-long carnival, with an amusement park and lots of games, rides and exhibits.

If you happen to be out here in the dead of winter, Le Festival du Voyageur in mid-February is a week-long event commemorating the early French voyageurs or fur traders with concerts, a parade, art & craft displays and lots of outdoor activities.

Places to Stay

Camping There are a few places to camp around town but most are way out of town, off the main highways.

The *Whitehorse Campground* (☎ 284-5300), is 14 km west on Highway 1. Unserviced sites are $10. *KOA* (☎ 253-8168) has a site on the Trans Canada Highway East at Murdock Rd, with rates from $13 to $17. Both campgrounds are open from May to mid-October.

Hostels The *Youth Hostel* (☎ 772-3022) is good and central. It's in an old grey house at 210 Maryland St, near the corner of Broadway Ave and Sherbrook St not far from the bus station. The hostel has kitchen facilities. In summer it's often full, so don't arrive late. It's closed during the day, opening at 5 pm. The rates are $8 for members, $12 for non-members.

From the airport, catch the No 15 bus to the corner of Sargent and Maryland Sts. From there, then take bus No 29 to the corner of Broadway Ave and Maryland St.

Until recently both the central YMCA and the YWCA rented inexpensive rooms, but now they have amalgamated into one building and there are no longer any residences.

The *University of Manitoba* rents rooms from mid-May to mid-August. They're not cheap at singles/doubles $28/40 and they're only available with a reservation and one night's deposit. For information, contact the conference coordinator (☎ 474-9942) at 26 MacLean Crescent, Pembina Hall.

B&Bs The province has a B&B programme and fortunately many of the members are located in Winnipeg. The tourist office has a complete list. Prices aren't bad at all, with most in the range of singles/doubles $25/35. Breakfast is included although it may vary from a light continental breakfast to a complete hot meal.

In the central area near The Forks is the home of *Daisy Paully* (☎ 772-8828) at 141

Furby St. It's close to three bus routes and the price is good at singles/doubles $25/35. Nonsmokers only are requested though.

Chestnut House (☎ 772-9788) is in a pleasant old tree-lined residential area near Portage and Broadway Aves. The address is 209 Chestnut St. A double here is $40 and again, no smoking.

There are many other places although some are not as central. You can also find hosts who speak French or German.

Hotels – bottom end Winnipeg has lots of small, older hotels in the downtown area. Most of these are pretty basic and cater to locals on the skids, but they are cheap. Others are much better but still moderately priced.

A few blocks up Main St, towards Portage Ave from the railway station, is the *Winnipeg Hotel* (☎ 942-7762), which is clean and friendly and the best of the very bottom-end places. Singles/doubles cost $16/18.

Many of the cheapies are clustered around the Exchange District near the intersection of Notre Dame Ave and Albert St. The *Market Inn* and the *Wellington* are here. Neither is particularly good and the nearby *Oxford Hotel* (☎ 942-6712) is less so. The downstairs bar is the primary feature. Rooms start at about $15/18 for singles/doubles; rooms with a bath cost more.

The *Garrick*, at 287 Garry St on the other side (south) of Portage Ave, seems a little better. Singles/doubles cost $17/22. Avoid the *Windsor* (☎ 942-7528), down at 187 Garry St, which has had terrible reviews lately and has really fallen into decay.

There are other, similar hotels in this area; all these types of hotels have very low weekly rates.

One of the best of the cheapies is the well-run, looked-after and clean white stucco *Aberdeen Hotel* (☎ 942-7481) in the centre of the downtown area at 230 Carlton St. Singles are $21 without bath and toilet, $25 with, plus taxes. Doubles are from $26 to $32. There's a pub downstairs and a TV lounge for guests.

Also a cut above the shoestringers is the *Gordon Downtowner Motor Hotel* (☎ 943-

5581). It's central at 330 Kennedy St, a few blocks from Portage Ave. It has a restaurant and a couple of bars. Singles/doubles are $42/52.

Down in Osborne Village is *Osborne Village Motor Inn* (☎ 452-9824). The 32 rooms are quite reasonably priced at singles/doubles $32/34.

Hotels – middle The *Balmoral* (☎ 943-1544), on the street of the same name, is on the corner of Notre Dame Ave and has singles/doubles at $38/48.

The *St Regis* (☎ 942-0171) is a good, very central hotel with all the mod cons. It's at 285 Smith St just south of Portage Ave, and charges singles/doubles $45/48.

Two other good-value places are the always reliable *Carlton Inn-Best Western* (☎ 528-1234) at 220 Carlton St, with singles/doubles from $52/57; and the *Charterhouse* (☎ 782-0175), which is a middle-sized, middle-priced, very central place on the corner of York Ave and Hargrave St. Each room here has a balcony and the rates are singles/doubles $60/65. There's a restaurant specialising in ribs downstairs.

Hotels – top end The *Delta Winnipeg* (☎ 956-1410), at 288 Portage Ave, has singles/doubles for $120/130. The *Westin* (☎ 228-3000), at 2 Lombard Place, has doubles from $140 and up.

The attractive *Hotel Fort Garry* (☎ 942-8251), built in 1913, is the city's classic old hostelry. It's at 222 Broadway Ave, close to the railway station whose passengers it was meant to serve. The casino is here.

Motels The *Assiniboine Gorden Inn* (☎ 888-4806), at 1975 Portage Ave on the park, has singles or doubles for $46 and a dining room offering food at good prices. *Down's Motor Inn* (☎ 837-5831), at 3740 Portage Ave, charges singles/doubles $36/40. There are others along Portage Ave going away from the downtown area.

Pembina Highway going south out of town has many motels. The *El Siesta* (☎ 269-7723), at 2028 Pembina Highway, has

singles/doubles for $35/38. *Journey's End Motel* (☎ 269-7370), at 3109 Pembina Highway, is immaculate with rates at $42/49 for singles/doubles.

There are many other motels that are newer, better and more expensive. Generally, the larger ones cost more.

Places to Eat

The cheapest place to eat in town is the *cafeteria* in the Administration Building, in the cluster of government offices between Main and King Sts on William Ave. Different lunches are served each day. The cafeteria is on the 2nd floor and opens from 8.30 am to 4.30 pm Monday to Friday. I don't know if you have to be an employee to eat here, but you shouldn't have any problems getting in unless you look like you've slept in the woods for a week.

The *cafeteria* in the Legislative Building is similar and is definitely open to the public.

Downtown on a Sunday you'll find most things closed, but there are several *Salisbury House* restaurants around town which tend to be open early and close late every day. There's one at 212 Notre Dame Ave and another at 352 Portage Ave. This local chain began in 1931 and has remained successful serving cheap, plain food in a cafeteria-style setting. They're good places for breakfast but their reputation has been built on their hamburgers, which are known as 'nips'. The *Old Chocolate Shop Restaurant* at 269 Portage Ave is a likeable place whether you go for lunch, dinner, coffee and sweets or for the popular tea cup and tarot card readings. It's moderately priced.

Mr Greenjeans in Eaton Place at the corner of Hargrave St and St Mary Ave offers finger foods, chicken and ribs, all served with rock music.

The *Old Swiss Inn* at 207 Edmonton St offers steaks, veal, schnitzel and seafood. The food is good, priced at $16 to $22. *Hy's* at 216 Kennedy St is a well-established steak house.

The popular *Grapes*, at 180 Main St near the railway station, is a big bar-restaurant with lots of wood and plants. The menu offers a bit of everything at moderate prices. While certainly OK, the food's not great; it's more the place, the people and the drinks that make it work.

Down in the Exchange District are numerous eating spots. Around Market Square on Albert St, the *Old Market Café* is a small comfortable place for an expresso.

Nearby, the *King's Head Tavern* at 120 King St is a busy British-style pub. In summer, chip wagons set up all around the park. The very European *Chopin's Café*, on the corner of Albert St and McDermot Ave away from the park, is inexpensive and has delicatessen-style sandwiches, among other things.

Winnipeg has an *Old Spaghetti Factory*, which is always reliable and good value, if it doesn't have stupendous food. It's at 219 Bannantyne Ave and offers very reasonable, complete Italian meals at lunch or dinner in a well-designed space.

At 179 Bannantyne Ave is *Norm & Nates*, an inexpensive Jewish deli open for lunch and late at night for the after-theatre or show crowd. They have Reuben sandwiches (hot grilled sandwiches with cheese, meat and sauerkraut), blintzes, and plenty of dessert selections including cheesecake.

At 180 King St is the new Chinese Dynasty Building, with the Heritage Gardens out the front and the adjacent Chinese gate over the street. Slightly beyond is the city's small Chinatown on Rupert, Pacific and Alexander Aves. The restaurants are mainly on King St. *Marigold* is the biggest and poshest restaurant. The *Spring Garden* at 214 Alexander Ave is cheaper and also has some Vietnamese dishes.

The Forks Historic Site is a pleasant place for a bite, and along with the food stalls and the small café or two, there is *Branigan's* for a more substantial meal. Weekend brunches are offered. They also have a lounge which is open late.

There are several places worth getting to in the area around Sherbrook St and Broadway Ave. At 106 Sherbrook St, is the busy *Impressions Café*, which is licensed and open every day to midnight. It has a nice

European atmosphere, with paintings and photographs on display, and sells sandwiches, bagels and omelettes mostly priced at under $5. The freshly baked cinnamon buns at breakfast with tea or coffee make life worth living.

Bistro Dansk at 63 Sherbrook St is a perennial favourite with well-prepared food and good lunches at $7. It also has dinner specials. It's open from 11 am to 9.30 pm daily, closed on Sunday.

Down near the corner of Broadway Ave at 218 Sherbrook St, is the *Cork and Fork*, a pricier but congenial spot for a dinner out. The speciality is fondue; try the bouillon fondue, but there are non-fondue items on the menu as well.

Nearly next door, across from the gas station, *Champions* serves pretty decent, basic Chinese and Vietnamese food.

An off-beat place to try in this general part of town where you won't see any tourists is *Mrs Liptons* at 962 Westminster Ave on the corner of Lipton St. Westminster Ave is a tree-lined residential street running perpendicular to Sherbrook St. Lipton St is about 10 blocks from Sherbrook St. Mrs Lipton's is a vegetarian/natural foods place in a funky old store-front corner building. It's only open for lunch but there now seems to be someone else in the building serving Indonesian food in the evenings. In any case, it's closed on Monday.

Over at 595 Broadway Ave is the *Indian Curry House*, which offers vegetarian and meat dishes. Main courses are priced at $6 to $8. This place is said to be very good. It's open every day.

Nearby, but across the street at 576 Broadway Ave, the *Wheatsong Bakery and Café* has vegetarian meals at lunch and dinner. It's closed on Sunday.

Main St North, once a thriving Jewish, Ukrainian and other ethnic groups' area, now has its best days behind it. There are some remnants such as *Kelekis* at 1100 Main St, a locally famous semi-Jewish restaurant with the traditional photographs of stars and pseudo-stars on the walls. Though not especially good it is still busy, partially for its nostalgic value (it's been here since 1931 – Mom and Dad probably came in for a snack when they were dating) and partially for its hot dogs.

At 911 Main St, the *Blue Boy Café* has Ukrainian food.

In Osborne Village there are many restaurants, and they're mostly pretty good. The *Courtyard Café* at 100 Osborne St is very good for soups, salads and sandwiches or for just a coffee and a sweet. It's cheap but only open until 6 pm daily. Larger and less casual is *Basil's Café*, at 117 Osborne St, with various speciality items and European snacks and sweets, as well as sandwiches and salads. They have a selection of teas and 12 different coffees.

Restaurants offering foreign cuisines regularly open and close. At the moment *Messob* at 106 Osborne St serves very cheap Ethiopian fare daily until late.

More established is *Carlos & Murphy's* at 133 Osborne St, a Mexican place with an outdoor patio, a big menu and moderate prices. *Baked Expectations*, primarily for sweets, is open late and is not too pricey. *Pasquale's* has cheap pizza, spaghetti and other more expensive Italian dishes, and stays open until 2 am.

There are many other restaurants here, some a fair bit pricier than those just mentioned. The *Tea Cozy* is a posher place with highly rated food.

The downtown shopping centres have food fairs, and the Convention Centre has a cheap cafeteria. Also, many of the better downtown hotels have Sunday brunches at noon, which are good value.

Out of the downtown area, St Boniface has several French restaurants, and the Pembina Highway has numerous restaurants including the familiar franchises.

Entertainment

To find out what's going on in the city, the *Winnipeg Free Press* has complete bar and entertainment listings on Friday.

Winnipeg is the only city in the country where you can gamble legally. The somewhat controversial *Crystal Casino* is on the 7th floor of the Hotel Fort Garry, at 222 Broadway Ave. It's open from 6 pm to 2 am Monday to Friday and from noon on Saturday. Try your luck at blackjack, baccarat, roulette or the slots. 'Proper attire' is required, which for men means a jacket and tie.

Music *Wellington's* (☎ 942-2079), at 22 Albert St, has live rock 'n' roll and new wave music. The cover charge varies but is generally low. At 65 Rorie St, the *Rorie St Marble Club* is a dressy, trendy dance spot.

The *Blue Note* an intimate little place at 220 Main St has live blues and jazz until very late. Nearby on the corner of Main St and St Mary Ave, close to the railway station, is the good *Times Change Café*, again for jazz and blues. Live shows are on Friday, Saturday and Sunday nights. It's inexpensive.

There are several nightspots on McDermot Ave near Rorie St, such as *Act II*, for late night reggae and jam sessions. The *Palladium*, out of the centre at 2935 Pembina Highway, is a huge disco with lots of flashing lights and a band on weekends.

The boat *River Rouge* has night cruises with pop bands from Wednesday to Saturday, and jazz music on Sunday and Monday nights.

The *West End Cultural Centre*, at 586 Ellice Ave, often has cheap folk or classical concerts in a relaxed, casual atmosphere.

The *Centre Culturel Franco-Manitobain* presents all kinds of interesting shows, concerts and productions. It's in St Boniface, call ☎ 233-8972 for information.

During the summer there are often free evening outdoor concerts in parks around town. One place to ask about is the park off Preston Ave near the youth hostel.

Theatre The *Royal Winnipeg Ballet* has an excellent international reputation. Their new home is downtown on the corner of Graham Ave and Edmonton St, and they offer student rates on tickets.

Various plays and concerts are performed at the *Centennial Arts Centre*, at 555 Main St.

Cinema The *Cinema 3* on the corner of Ellice Ave and Sherbrook St is a good, low-priced repertory cinema. The *Art Gallery Cinema* in the Winnipeg Art Gallery shows frequently changing foreign and alternative films. Prices are low here, too.

Other *Yuk Yuk's* in Osborne Village, which may have recently closed presents stand-up comics.

The *Winnipeg Symphony Orchestra* is also good; their seasons usually run from November to May.

Spectator Sports The Winnipeg Jets play National League Hockey at the Winnipeg Arena about 40 times through the winter. In summer and fall the Winnipeg Blue Bombers, representing the province, play professional football. Games are played at the Winnipeg Stadium on the corner of Portage Ave and King Edward St, central but west of the downtown core. The hockey arena is here as well.

Things to Buy

Factory Outlets Shoppers should know that Winnipeg has a surprising array of straight-from-the-factory-to-you retail outlets. Canada's only Ralph Lauren factory store is here. Other such outlets include Arrow, Izod Lacoste and Woolrich.

Getting There & Away

Air The international airport is about 20 minutes north-west of the city centre. Several airlines serve Winnipeg, both for local trips and destinations in the USA.

Nordair (☎ 786-4435) flies to Sault Ste Marie twice daily. The phone number for Air Canada is ☎ 943-9361.

Canadian Airlines flies to Churchill four times a week but it ain't cheap. If you want to go, book at least two weeks in advance for the best deal. For more information about Churchill, see the relevant section at the end of this chapter.

Bus The station for both Greyhound and Grey Goose lines is the Mall Centre Bus Depot at 487 Portage Ave. It's central and open from 6.30 am to midnight. There are lockers and a restaurant in the station.

Greyhound (☎ 775-8301) covers all Ontario destinations and many western cities. They run five buses daily, both morning and evening schedules, to Thunder Bay $55, Toronto and Saskatoon $65.

The Greyhound desk also handles the small Beaver Bus Line which serves Fort Garry and other points north of town. There's at least one an hour.

Grey Goose Lines (☎ 786-8891) serves Regina, Thunder Bay and many of the small towns in the area and in northern Manitoba.

There are also buses here for Selkirk (Fort Garry).

Train The VIA Rail station is centrally located where Broadway Ave meets Main St. In summer there's a tourist information booth in the station. Like everywhere else, train service has been greatly reduced here. The western route goes to Edmonton and Jasper and then down to Vancouver. The eastern route goes north, way over Lake Superior en route to Sudbury and the major cities of Ontario. There is no train at all to Regina.

For Edmonton the fare is $128 and the train departs on Monday, Thursday and Saturday.

For Sudbury the fare is $150 and it, too, runs just three days a week.

There is also a train to Churchill, see the Churchill section of this chapter for more information.

Car & Motorbike Hertz is in the Bay department store on Portage Ave.

Budget (☎ 786-5866) is on the corner of Sherbrook St and Ellice Ave. Their rates are $36 per day with 100 free km, and 12 cents per km over that. Weekly rental is $165 with 1500 free km. They'll pick you up for no charge.

Dominion (☎ 943-4477), at 15 Marion St by the Norwood Bridge in the Dominion Centre, offers good three-day specials and a half-day rate.

Hitching For hitching west out of town, take the Express St Charles bus along Portage Ave. After 6 pm take the Portage Ave-St Charles bus.

For hitching east on Highway 1, catch the Osborne Highway 1 bus or the Southdale bus on Osborne St South, at the corner of Broadway Ave.

Getting Around

To/From the Airport Very conveniently and economically, a city bus departs for the airport every 20 minutes from Vaughan St at the corner of Portage Ave. It's called the Sargent No 15 airport bus and costs $1.15 exact change.

The airport limo runs from 9 am to nearly 1 am from the better hotels and costs about $9 if you're sharing with some fellow passengers. If there are three of you, a taxi works out about the same.

Bus All city buses cost $1.15 exact change. For transit info, you can call ☎ 284-7190, open 24 hours a day. Routes are extensive but you need a transfer if you're changing buses.

From 11 am to 3 pm the city operates Dash, a free bus service around the downtown core. Broadway Ave, Main St, the Exchange area and The Forks are covered. Another free shuttle is The Forks Shuttle, which runs from The Forks to Portage Ave.

Bicycle There are bicycle routes through town and some out of town. Ask at the tourist office about them.

The youth hostel (☎ 772-3022) rents bicycles.

AROUND WINNIPEG
The Prairie Dog Central

The Prairie Dog is a 1900s-style steam train which takes passengers on a two-hour and some 50-km trip north to Grosse Isle and back. From June to September the train makes two trips a week, on Sunday at 11 am and 3 pm, and costs $11, less for kids. The station (☎ 832-5259), which is a bit hard to find, is on Portage Ave West near Kenaston

Blvd, just behind Manitoba Hydro across from the Viscount Gort Motor Hotel.

Dugald Costume Museum

Dugald, not far from Winnipeg east along Route 15, is the home of a collection of 5000 items of dress and accessories, dating from 1765 to the present. The various garments are displayed on mannequins to give a somewhat natural sense of how they appeared when worn. The costume museum is open daily from 10 am to 5 pm during summer, closed Monday and Tuesday the rest of the year. Admission is $3 and there is a tea room.

Also here is a restored pioneer home dating from 1886 furnished as it would have been originally.

Museum of Childhood

About 25 km east of town on the Trans Canada Highway, this museum has a collection of furniture, toys, clothing and other articles which may remind visitors of their youth. Admission is $2.50.

Oak Hammock Marsh

Southern Manitoba has several very important, very large marshes. These critical wetlands are home to thousands of waterfowl and other birds and act as way stations along major migration routes for thousands more.

Oak Hammock Marsh is a swamp area just north of the city, about halfway to Lake Winnipeg and eight km east of Stonewall. It's noted as one of the best bird sanctuaries on the continent; over 260 species can be seen. You can amble about on viewing boardwalks and there is an information centre. You can also go canoeing.

Lower Fort Garry

Lower Fort Garry, 30 km north of Winnipeg on the banks of the Red River, is a restored Hudson's Bay Company fort dating from 1830. It's the only stone fort from the fur-trading days still intact.

Although the fort was a failure as a fur-trading post, it remained in use as a police training centre, a penitentiary, lunatic asylum, Hudson's Bay Company residence and later a country club.

The buildings are furnished and the grounds are busy with costumed workers who'll answer questions. Go early in the day to avoid the crowds, and see the film at the entrance for the historical background. You should allow one or two hours for a visit. Admission to the fort costs $3. It's open 10 am to 6 pm daily from mid-May to Labour Day at the beginning of September. During the rest of September it's open on weekends only. There's a restaurant and a picnic area.

To get there, take the Beaver Bus Line from the main depot and tell the driver you're going to the fort – the fare is about $6 return.

Selkirk

The Marine Museum of Manitoba is here, with five ships including a restored steamer and an icebreaker.

South of Winnipeg

South and slightly west of Winnipeg and bordered by North Dakota is an area known as the **Pembina Valley**. The Red River flows northward through this prime farming region.

Morris is the site of a major annual rodeo; in fact, second in size only to Calgary's. It takes place for five days at the beginning of August.

This is also sunflower country and there is a festival to mark this, held in **Altona** on the last weekend in July. The Mennonites of the area supply some very fine homemade foods for the occasion.

Eastern Manitoba

MENNONITE HERITAGE VILLAGE

South-east of Winnipeg, about an hour's drive down through sunflower country, is the town of Steinbach. Two km north of the town on Highway 12 is a museum featuring the Mennonites, a religious utopian group originating in Europe which reached Manitoba via Pennsylvania and Ontario. An informa-

tion centre gives some of the history of the movement.

But the bulk of the site is a re-created late 1800s Mennonite village with some century-old buildings. Various special events are held through the summer.

There's a restaurant on the grounds which serves good, fresh traditional Mennonite food. The village is open from 1 May to 30 September.

WHITESHELL PROVINCIAL PARK

Due east of Winnipeg and lying along the Ontario border is this 259-sq-km park. Though some parts are heavily commercialised (particularly around Falcon Lake), other areas especially northward, are less developed. The park contains 200 lakes and all kinds of outdoor activities are available, summer and winter. There are some good hiking trails – ranging from short ones to some as long as 60 km.

The park has 17 campgrounds and there are moderately priced lodges which are rented by the day or week. More expensive, well-equipped resorts can be found at several locations.

At Bannock Point, not far from Betula Lake, are centuries-old Indian petroforms: rock formations in the shapes of fish, snakes and birds.

ATIKAKI PROVINCIAL PARK

Heading north, the province quickly becomes pretty wild. This wilderness park is best visited by canoe. In it, along the Bloodvein River, there are remnants of Indian cliff paintings thought to date back 6000 years.

Northern Manitoba

The area around Lake Winnipeg is where Manitobans play in summer. The region between it and Lake Manitoba, also with some good beaches, is known as the Interlake Region. Beyond here the population thins considerably and the real north begins. Flin Flon, The Pas and Thompson are

Top: Beware the bears on the beach, Hudson Bay, Churchill, Manitoba (RB)
Bottom: Bear-proof shack, Churchill, Manitoba (RB)

Top: Ice-bridge, Athabasca Glacier, Jasper National Park, Alberta (RB)
Left: The town of Banff in the Rockies, Alberta (RB)
Right: Calgary cowboy tests his strength (JL)

important towns. Way up on Hudson Bay is Churchill, which is remote but of interest to visitors.

LAKE WINNIPEG

This huge lake, Canada's fifth largest, lies about 50 km north of the city. The eastern shoreline is lined with beaches, including Grand Beach, which has light coloured sand and dunes as high as eight metres. It's very popular and a good place to relax.

The other side of the lake is less accessible as much of it is privately owned; many people have cottages in the area. However, there are some good, popular public beaches, such as Winnipeg Beach – it's very good for windsurfing.

There are motels and restaurants along the strip at the resort town of Winnipeg Beach.

At the southern end of the lake is Netley Marsh with high concentrations of water-fowl. There is a viewing tower at the Netley Recreation Park.

GIMLI

Ninety km north of Winnipeg, on the western shores of Lake Winnipeg and marked by the Viking statue, this is the centre of a large Icelandic fishing and farming community. Once known as the Republic of New Iceland, the area was settled by Icelanders around 1880. There's a museum showing the history and some artefacts of the local settlement. Every summer, around the beginning of August, the Icelandic Festival is held, comprising three days of games, contests, parades and folk music.

The wide, sandy beaches of the south-western shore continue into the Gimli area.

HECLA PROVINCIAL PARK

Jutting out into the lake north of Gimli is this peninsular provincial park which includes a couple of large islands. There are lots of birds as well as other wildlife; it's good for hiking, camping and fishing. Another park adjacent to it is still under development.

SNAKE PITS

Snake lovers: you're in luck. Here in Mani-toba is the world's largest population of garter snakes, concentrated in wiggling mega-dens for up to 10,000 of the little fun-sters. Researchers, pet dealers and those with a taste for the macabre come from distant continents to view the snake pits, which are about six km north of Narcisse, off Highway 17 in the Interlake Region between Lake Winnipeg and Lake Manitoba.

In fact, the pressure of attention on them has resulted in a drastic decline in the numbers of snake dens, and harvesting reg-ulation is likely. The mating ritual, when tens of thousands emerge from their limestone sinkhole lairs to form masses of entwined tangles, takes place the last week in April and the first two weeks in May.

Bring the camera and the kids. You can really make a day of it by visiting nearby Komarno where there's a statue of the world's largest mosquito.

Other locations for snake pits are around Chatfield and Inwood.

LAKE MANITOBA SHORELINE

The area between the lakes is important for beef-cattle ranching.

Some of the farms take in overnight guests. Much less developed than Lake Win-nipeg but with a series of small towns and some cottage communities, Lake Manitoba also has some fine, sandy beaches particu-larly at Twin Lakes in the south, around the town of Lundar and at Silver Bay, west of Ashern.

NORTHERN WOODS & WATER ROUTE

This is a series of roads – now linked as one – which connects Winnipeg across northern portions of Saskatchewan and Alberta, with British Columbia. Most of the roads are sur-faced though there are stretches of gravel. There are no cities but many small commu-nities, nine provincial parks and numerous campgrounds along the way. There are lots of lakes and woods up here, as well as fishing areas and wildlife. Nights are cool.

From Winnipeg the route heads to The Pas in the north-west of the province, continues on to Prince Albert in Saskatchewan (near the Prince Albert National Park), on into Alberta, ending up at Dawson Creek, British Columbia. The road is marked on signs as 'NWWR'.

DAUPHIN

The National Ukrainian Festival is held here each year in August. It has lots of old country food, music and dance as well as colourful costumes.

THE PAS

Two-thirds of the province still lies northwards of The Pas, above the two big lakes at the 53rd parallel.

Once an important meeting site for Indians and British and French fur traders, The Pas is now a district centre and acts as a 'gateway to the north'. Although lumber is important, this is a rich agricultural area as well. During summer, days are long and sunny.

It is connected to Winnipeg by air, Grey Goose bus lines and VIA Rail. Driving takes about eight hours if you take Route 327 and Highway 6. The bus takes a longer route. VIA Rail continues on to Thompson and Churchill.

The small Northern Museum, begun by a missionary in 1911, provides some historic background on the area.

There is an annual Indian festival held each year in August. A reserve lies just out of town across the river.

Camping is possible not far from town in Clearwater Provincial Park. Within the park, you can see the deep crevices along the Caves Trail.

FLIN FLON

Further north, right on the Saskatchewan border, is Flin Flon, a copper and zinc-mining centre. The unusual name is taken, it's said, from the protagonist of a novel some prospectors found up here in 1915.

The Hudson's Bay surface mine in town can be toured in July and August. Flin Flon sits on the rugged Canadian Shield and is surrounded by rocky, wooded lakeland. There are canoe and camping outfitters in

town and the huge Grass River Provincial Park is not far east. The fishing is excellent.

There is a tourist office and campground run by the Chamber of Commerce, on Highway 10 as you come into town. At the tourist office, have a look at the examples of birch-bark biting. This is an old Cree women's craft which has almost disappeared. Using their teeth, patterns, often of animals, are etched into the bark. I've also seen examples of this art in some of the better Indian craft outlets around Saskatchewan.

There are about half a dozen places to stay in town. Buses run to The Pas and Winnipeg.

THOMPSON

The last town northwards connected by road, Thompson, with 15,000 people, is another mining centre but this time for nickel. There is virtually nothing but wilderness on the long road up here, whether you've come from The Pas or along Lake Winnipeg. And just out of town in any direction civilisation disappears pretty quickly. If driving, make sure you have the necessary supplies and fuel, as services are few to nil especially on Highway 6 north of Lake Winnipeg.

The Inco nickel mine can be visited but the tour does not descend into the earth; it shows instead all the surface operations.

There is a campground operated by the city close to town. VIA Rail, en route to Churchill, serves the city as does Grey Goose Lines.

GILLAM

Situated about halfway to Churchill on the train line, Gillam exists because of its hydropower development.

CHURCHILL

This is one of Canada's few northern outposts that is relatively accessible, with a train line running right up to it. Despite its forbidding location and extremes of weather – July and August are the only months without snow – it has always been of importance. Explorers, traders and the military have all been here and it was one of the largest grain-

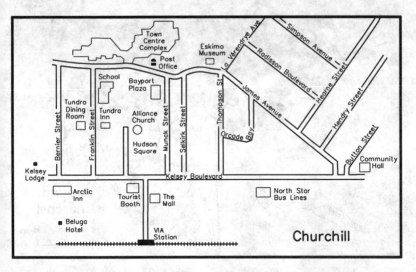

Churchill

handling ports in the world. The railway was completed in 1929, giving the prairies an ocean port. Now, due to the decline in grain-handling, it is relying more on its natural resources to draw business.

Tourism has become very important and the town bills itself as the Polar Bear Capital of the World. It sits right in the middle of a polar bear migration route, which means the great white bears are often seen in and around town. Visitors are also taken out on the frozen tundra in large motorised buggies to see the huge and very dangerous bears.

Despite the remote location, the area is one of the oldest in terms of European exploration in the country. The first Hudson's Bay Company outpost was set up here over 250 years ago and much of the exploration and settlement of the west came via this route.

Natural Attractions

Churchill is a great spot for viewing the phenomenon known as the Aurora Borealis or northern lights, and is excellent for observing wildlife, including beluga whales, seals, caribou and birds. Listed here are some of the attractions and the best times to see them.

Northern lights	September-April
Polar bears	September-October
Whales	July-August and early September
Birds	May-June and early July
Fishing	all summer
Flowers	all summer

Visitors' Centre

This is in town; it shows films on the area, its history and the polar bears. There's also a display of furs from the Hudson's Bay Company. So widespread in area and influence is the company that it's been said the initials HBC stand for 'Here Before Christ'.

Eskimo Museum

The museum has a good collection of Inuit artefacts and carvings, including kayaks from as early as 1700 BC. There are also displays about northern fauna. It's open every day, but only in the afternoon on Sunday, and is free.

National Historic Sites

Fort Prince of Wales Parks Canada administrates three national historic sites in the Churchill area. Water taxis run (tides and weather permitting) across the Churchill River from town to Fort Prince of Wales (not Whales!), now one of the three government

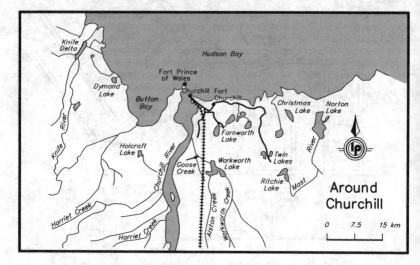

parks. This partially restored stone fort was originally built to protect the fur-trading business of the Hudson's Bay Company from possible rivals. From 1 July to 1 September, guides working for the ministry are on hand to tell the fort's story. A second battery is by the mouth of the river.

Sloop's Cove Private operators run boat trips to Sloop's Cove, three km upriver from the fort. The cove was formerly used by European boats out on whaling excursions and on trading trips with the local Inuit. Names of some of the early HBC people,

including that of Samuel Hearn, the local 18th-century governor, can be seen scratched into the seaside rocks.

Cape Merry The third site, Cape Merry, is three km from town at the end of the Cape Merry Centennial Parkway. Here, a plaque honours Sir Thomas Button, believed to be the first European to have sailed into the mouth of the Churchill River. There are the remains of a stone battery built in 1746. Guides are on duty from 15 June to 15 September.

Bird Cove
Bird Cove, about 15 km east of town and accessible by vehicle (tours are available), is known for its abundant birdlife. There is the wreck of a freighter which went down in a storm in 1961 at the western edge of the cove.

York Factory
Further afield and accessible only by air or (for the determined) by canoe, is York Factory, a fur-trading post that operated for over 250 years. Run by the HBC (who else?) it, too, is now a national historic site.

Organised Tours

Several companies offer tours for viewing whales or bears, or you can even go on dog-team trips. If you're planning ahead, arrangements can be made at travel agencies in Winnipeg. It may be worth calling to see if things are busy and reservations are required.

Sea North is one company to try, another is North Star Tours. Boat and bus tours are not exorbitantly priced but the tundra buggy trips to see the polar bears are not cheap. North Star Tours will book accommodation and transportation, too. Ask about any all-inclusive package deals.

Places to Stay & Eat

Churchill is not a cheap place to visit. However, there are about half a dozen places to stay and a few more places to eat. Accommodation costs about $55 for singles and from $65 to $75 for doubles. Reservations are suggested.

The *Beluga Motel* (☎ 675-2150) charges $45/52 for singles/doubles. It's open from June to October only. Slightly more expensive but recommended is the very friendly *Kelsey Lodge* (☎ 675-8801) run as a B&B with nine rooms. The people who operate it also run a pizza place in town so chances are you'll get a slice during your visit too. Singles/doubles are $50/60, with a good reduction on a week's stay. Many of the temporary professional workers such as bush pilots and photographers stay here. Also open all year, the *Arctic Inn* (☎ 675-8835) is the other low-priced place in town at singles/doubles $55/65. The pricier places have in-house bars and restaurants. Meals in town cost from $6 to $14.

Things to Buy

Various outlets sell contemporary Inuit arts & crafts. The Arctic Trading Company is one place amongst several places where interesting souvenirs such as carvings and Inuit-style boots called *mukluks* can be purchased. Also have a look in the Bay store.

Getting There & Away

There is no road to Churchill; you must either fly in (Canadian Airlines has four flights a week) or catch a train. There are three trains a week from Winnipeg departing at 9.55 pm on Sunday, Tuesday and Thursday. The return fare for the cheap coach seat is $282 for the 1½-day 1600-km trip.

Western Manitoba

From Winnipeg westwards towards the Saskatchewan border the flat prairie landscape is dominant. Get used to it, it lasts until halfway through Alberta.

PORTAGE LA PRAIRIE

A farm centre, Portage la Prairie has a museum on Fort La Reine which was built by explorer de la Vérendrye in 1738. There is also a Pioneer Museum which depicts life in a simple village of the 1800s.

J & J's Camping is west of Winnipeg on Highway 1 (the Trans Canada Highway) near Portage La Prairie and, at just $7 for a tent, is good value. It's grassy and quiet, with lots of trees.

BRANDON

The second largest city in the province, with a population of 40,000, Brandon has little to recommend for the visitor. It's a purely functional centre. The main street is Rossen Ave.

Commonwealth Air Training Plan Museum

At the airport is the Commonwealth Air Training Plan Museum which tells the story of the thousands of recruits from around the British Commonwealth who were trained as pilots and navigators in Canada from 1939 to 1945 before heading over to Europe. There are 13 original training planes housed in the original Brandon hangar. Small training centres such as this one literally dotted the prairies.

Other displays include photographs, aircraft engines and other artefacts and memorabilia. It's open daily and there is a small admission charge.

Places to Stay & Eat
There are plenty of motels and hotels and a YWCA at 148 11th St, if you don't want to haul into Winnipeg.

Along 18th St there's a variety of restaurants.

CANADIAN FORCES BASE SHILO
South-east of Brandon on Route 340 there is a Canadian military base in Shilo. On the base, for those with a special interest, is the Royal Regiment of Canadian Artillery Museum with a vast collection of uniforms, guns, ammunition, even vehicles, and more dating from 1796 onwards.

There are both indoor and outdoor exhibits. The museum is open daily through the summer, but only in the afternoons on weekends and holidays.

SPRUCE WOODS PROVINCIAL HERITAGE PARK
Within the park is a 25-sq-km area of desert-like sand dunes which supports a number of snakes, lizards, and even cactuses which are not found elsewhere in the province.

There are more hospitable areas in the park, too, with woods, lakes and camping areas. Rides are given from the information centre to the dunes and other attractions.

RIDING MOUNTAIN NATIONAL PARK
North of Brandon, 300 km north-west of Winnipeg, Riding Mountain is in a highland area, on a forested escarpment. Within the park are deciduous forests, lakes, rivers and meadows. Around Clear Lake is the developed area but most of the park is wilderness. On this lake, Wasagaming is a casual resort town with all the amenities.

Canoe rentals are available; here is a good place to use the list of canoe routes in the

Bison

province, which is available from the tourist office in Winnipeg. There are over 300 km of hiking trails in the park, and at Lake Audy you might see a small herd of bison.

Camping is not expensive, with both serviced campgrounds or backcountry opportunities. The park information centre is in Wasagaming.

Saskatchewan

Entered Confederation: 1 September 1905
Area: 651,903 sq km
Population: 968,313

Saskatchewan is a Cree Indian word which refers to the Saskatchewan River and means 'river that turns around when it runs'.

Saskatchewan and wheat are pretty much synonymous. The province is the greatest grower of wheat in North America and, with over a third of Canada's farmland, produces two-thirds of Canada's crop. Besides wheat, other grains such as barley and rye are important, as are sunflowers and beef cattle.

Many people find the scenery monotonous; the south of the province is mercilessly flat, often without a tree in sight. But such wide open space is a scene much of the world cannot even imagine. And the sight of golden, ripening wheat rippling in all directions to the horizon can be beautiful. The sunsets, sunrises, cloud formations and night skies are all fantastic. There's a lot of space.

You might hear people out this way say 'the Rocky Mountains are nice but they get in the way of the view'.

The far north of the state – part of the Canadian Shield – is rocky timberland and a wilderness of lakes and forests inhabited by few people. Of those who do live here, many are Métis.

Between this area and the bald, open prairie of the south is a transition zone stretching across the province covering the lower middle section of Saskatchewan in rolling hills and cultivated farmland. This range is called the parklands and contains some large government parks and both the North and South Saskatchewan rivers.

Tourism is not a major industry but many people do pass through. Each of the two major cities has some interesting things to

Wheat

Since it's all you're looking at, I suppose a word about the golden grain is in order.

Wheat, brought to the New World by European settlers, was largely responsible for the development of the Canadian prairies. It is the primary crop across Manitoba, Saskatchewan and Alberta but by far the bulk of it is grown in Saskatchewan.

So productive are the fields here that Canada is the world's sixth largest producer after the Soviet Union, China, the USA, India and France. The majority of wheat is produced for the export market. The Soviet Union, despite its own massive wheat production, is one of Canada's most important clients. Canadian wheat is sought after for its quality and high protein content.

Because of the cold climate the principal variety grown is hard red spring wheat, a bread wheat which is planted in spring and then harvested in August and September. The other main type is durum wheat whose characteristics make it especially suitable for the production of pasta.

In late summer, when the ripened wheat is golden brown it is not uncommon to see the huge self-powered combines cutting and threshing through the fields at any hour of the night or day, often in teams. At night in particular, with the bright light beams skimming across the fields from the droning machines, it's quite a memorable sight.

The Canadian Wheat Board markets the crop. This organisation represents the farmers, the consumers and the government in buying, selling, setting quotas and regulating export. Needless to say, the Board's actions are hotly debated.

Farmers are paid when they deliver their bushels to the grain elevators, where the entire crop is pooled and then sold by the Board. Once that is accomplished the wheat is carried to ports by train and loaded onto freighters for destinations far and wide. ∎

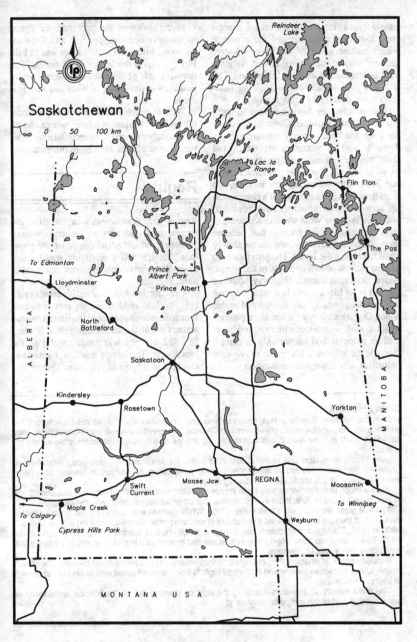

consider on a stopover, and there are several good historical parks around the province which outline some of the Native Native Indians' way of life. Prince Albert National Park is accessible Canadian timberland. The southern region has some intriguing landscapes and desert-like topography.

The weather in Saskatchewan is very changeable and extreme. Generally, winters are long and cold: the temperature can get down to -50°C. Summers are warm and short, but the maximum temperature can get to 40°C as well. I've always found August and September warm and dry months, but even then the nights are cool. It's common to see signs of fronts moving across the sky, so you usually know what weather's coming.

In the past few years, oil has become increasingly important; you'll see the slowly cranking rigs in the fields. The province also has the richest potash deposits in the world. Along the Trans Canada Highway, some of the soil is jet black – this is natural because the area was once totally submerged under water. Occasionally you'll see large patches of white stuff which looks like snow. This is sodium sulphate and occurs only in certain climatic conditions. It's used in various industries, like detergent preparation.

In the north of the province, 55 canoe routes have been mapped out, and there are canoe outfitters at Lac la Longe and in Flin Flon, just over the border in Manitoba. The northern half of Saskatchewan has literally hundreds of thousands of lakes and very few roads.

With so much farmland in this province, it's possible to stay on a farm, which can be a reasonably priced arrangement; the relevant tourist offices have more information.

Regina

Regina is Saskatchewan's capital. It is the largest city and acts as the commercial, financial and industrial centre of the province, but it's still a relatively small, quiet town that pretty much closes down after dark.

The Cree Indians lived in this area, butchering buffalo and leaving the remains along the creek, which prompted the first European settlers to dub the settlement 'Pile o' Bones'. In 1882 the city was made capital of the Northwest Territories and its name was changed to Regina in honour of Queen Vic-

Grain Elevators

The unique, striking, columnar red, green or grey grain elevators seen along rail lines across the province are the classic symbol of mid-western Canada. These vertical wheat warehouses have been called the 'castles of the New World' and to this day are the artificial structure most visible across the plains.

Very simple in design and material and built solely for function they have been described as Canada's most distinctive architectural form. Western painters, photographers and writers have taken them as objects of art, meditation and iconography.

Across much of the province they have represented the economic life of the town and district and indeed have topped in size, if not in importance, that other traditional landmark, the church.

The first grain elevators were built in the 1880s. While Canada was becoming the 'breadbasket of the world' at the turn of this century, the number of elevators mushroomed, reaching a peak of nearly 5800 in 1938. Through consolidation and changing conditions that number is now down to just under 2000. This decline has concerned many individuals and groups who hope to prevent (not just lament) any further major loss of elevators.

Formerly made all of wood, they are now built from materials such as steel and cement. The classic shape, about 10 metres square and 20 metres high, is being experimented with as well, in an attempt to improve efficiency.

The stark beauty of elevators catching the light or looming out of the horizon is certainly an unmistakable part of the prairie landscape. ■

toria. The Northwest Mounted Police used the city as a base from the 1880s, and in 1905 it became the capital of the newly formed Saskatchewan.

In 1933, the Cooperative Commonwealth Confederation (CCF), a socialist party, held its first national meeting in Regina and called for the end of capitalism. In 1944 they became the first socialist party to form a Canadian provincial government. The CCF merged with the New Democratic Party (NDP) in 1961, to form Canada's present left-wing party.

The population of Regina is approximately 180,000.

Wascana Creek and its parkland run through town, providing a change from the dry, golden wheat fields stretching in all directions.

Two interesting little city tidbits: Regina is the sunniest capital city in Canada and, oddly, every single tree you see anywhere was planted by hand. It's not known as the bald prairie for nothing.

Orientation

The city's two main streets are Victoria Ave, running east-west, and Albert St, going north-south. Both streets are lined with fast-food places and petrol stations.

Going east, Victoria Ave becomes the Trans Canada Highway to Winnipeg. Highway 1 West continues from Albert St in the far south of town. Albert St North leads into Highway 11 for Saskatoon.

The downtown core is bounded by Albert St to the west, 13th Ave to the south, Osler St to the east and the railway tracks to the north.

Victoria Park sits in the middle of the downtown area. Scarth St and 12th Ave, which edge the park, are important shopping streets. Scarth St, between 11th and 12th Aves, has been converted into a mall which, though small, is pleasant with trees and benches. On the north-east corner is the old City Hall, which houses a theatre, shops and a museum. With its pyramid shapes, the new Continental Bank building on the south corner is unusual and interesting. The large

Cornwall Centre is a major shopping mall opposite the Scarth St mall on 11th Ave.

The area on and around Osler St gets pretty tacky at night even though the police station is here. Be careful downtown after dark; the streets get very quiet and wandering around is not advisable.

Wascana Centre, a 1000-hectare park, is the dominant feature of the city and aside from its own natural appeal contains many of Regina's primary attractions. It lies four blocks south on the corner of Victoria Ave and Albert St.

The airport is south-west of downtown, about a 15-minute drive away. The bus station is on Hamilton St just south of Victoria Ave.

Information

The handiest information office is in the old streetcar (☎ 789-5099) in the Scarth St mall. It's open from Monday to Saturday, 9.30 am to 6 pm, but only during the summer.

The main, year-round office is Saskatchewan Travel Information in the Ramada Renaissance hotel, on the corner of Saskatchewan Drive and Rose Ave. It's open from 8 am to 7 pm Monday to Friday and from 10 am to 4 pm on Saturday. When you see the elk at the door you'll know why you don't want to get one of these animals mad. The office has information on the city as well as on other destinations across the province.

In summer, there are two or three temporary booths set up around town on the lead-in highways.

Interested parties should inquire about free heritage walks around town.

The post office is on Saskatchewan Drive, a few blocks west of Broad St.

Views

SGI Building From the cafeteria on the 18th floor of this building, at 2260 11th Ave near the corner of Lorne St, the city and ever-present surrounding prairie can be seen. The cheap cafeteria is open Monday to Friday from 7.30 am to 4 pm, but you don't need to buy anything to have a peek out the windows.

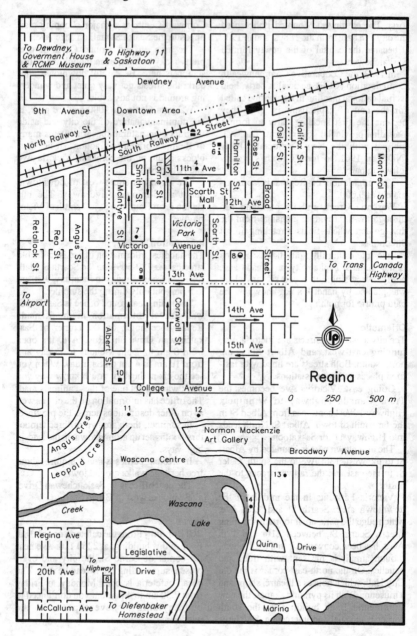

To Dewdney, Goverment House & RCMP Museum

To Highway 11 & Saskatoon

Dewdney Avenue

9th Avenue

Downtown Area

North Railway St

South Railway

2 Street

Smith St

Lorne St

McIntyre St

11th Ave

Hamilton St

Rose St

Osler St

Halifax St

Montreal St

Scarth St Mall

12th Ave

Broad St

Victoria Park

Scarth St

Victoria Avenue

Retallack St

Rea St

Angus St

13th Ave

Street

To Trans Canada Highway

To Airport

Albert St

Cornwall St

14th Ave

15th Ave

Regina

0   250   500 m

College Avenue

Angus Cres

Leopold Cres

Creek

Norman Mackenzie Art Gallery

Wascana Centre

Broadway Avenue

Regina Ave

20th Ave

Wascana Lake

Quinn Drive

To Highway 6

Legislative Drive

Marina

McCallum Ave

To Diefenbaker Homestead

1	Union Station
2	Post Office
3	Market Mall
4	Cornwall Centre Shopping Mall
5	Ramada Renaissance Hotel
6	Tourist Office
7	YWCA
8	Bus Station
9	YMCA
10	Youth Hostel
11	Museum of Natural History
12	University Campus
13	Science Centre
14	Wascana Place

Gallery on the Roof This art gallery (☎ 566-3174) for provincial artists has an observation deck offering great views of the city. It's on the 13th floor of the Power building, 2025 Victoria Ave, and is free.

Wascana Centre
Regina is blessed with many parks, nearly all of them adjoining Wascana Creek, which meanders diagonally through the southern portion of the city. Wascana Centre park is the largest of these, at around eight times the size of the city centre. The park begins five blocks south of 12th Ave. Take Hamilton, Lorne or Broad Sts south; the park extends to the south-east.

The predominant feature is artificial Wascana Lake. But as well as the lake, the picnic areas and sports fields, the green park contains many of the city's points of interest.

The headquarters of the park, Wascana Place, is on Wascana Drive, west of Broad St, east of Wascana Lake and north of the marina. There's not really much of interest, but there is an information office there and a good view from the 4th level of the building. From the centre, on weekends from mid-May until early September, inexpensive 50-minute guided tours of the park on London double-decker buses depart. You can also catch the bus from the landing by the flower garden, north of the Legislative building.

Guided half-hour boat tours leave from

the Wascana Marina, where there is also a good, low-cost restaurant. Another little ferry, which is very cheap, runs to Willow Island on the lake for picnics. Catch this boat off Wascana Drive by the north end of the lake. Bikes, boats and roller skates can be rented beside the Wascana Pool building off College Ave.

Free Sunday afternoon concerts are given at the Bandshell.

A waterfowl park off Lakeshore Drive, east of the Centre of the Arts, has 60 species of birds and helpful identification displays. A boardwalk leads into the marsh, and naturalists are on duty through the week.

The tourist office has a map of the Wascana Centre.

Saskatchewan Science Centre The newest edition to the park complex is the Science Centre with its series of exhibits, hands-on participatory displays and demonstrations, on the planet, its place in the solar system, physical laws and life.

The Science Centre is in the interesting, overhauled old Regina Power Plant (see the bank of old dials and meters in the lobby) on the north shore of the lake, east of Broad St near the corner of Wascana Drive and Winnipeg St. A bus up Broad St from downtown will get you within a two-block walk of the door. There is a restaurant and a nifty little store there also.

A large-format IMAX movie theatre and the Kalium Observatory are other features of the centre, and have their own programmes. Stargazing nights at the observatory are well worthwhile at $1.

Entry to the centre is $5, with lower senior and family rates. From June to Labour Day (early September) it's open from 10 am to 6 pm during the week, and from noon on the weekend. The rest of the year it closes at 5 pm. Except for holidays, it's always closed on Monday.

Provincial Legislature Just off Albert St, on the park's west side, is this beautiful building, done in 1919 in loose English Renaissance-style at a cost of $3,000,000.

Inside, 34 kinds of marble were used. The building is open all day and there are free tours given on the hour, except at lunch time.

Museum of Natural History Also in the park, the museum is south of College Ave at Albert St. Upstairs there are very realistic displays of North American wildlife, particularly animals native to Saskatchewan, with good explanations accompanying the exhibits. Downstairs the displays outline the biology of insects, birds, fish and animals and attempt to explain their behaviour. Space is given to palaeontology (fossils) and archaeology; another room depicts the Native Indian history of Saskatchewan.

There are often films on a variety of topics; a visit will take about one hour. Admission is free.

Norman Mackenzie Art Gallery Next door to the Museum of Natural History is the Norman Mackenzie Art Gallery which specialises in Canadian painting, much of it by local artists. Exhibits change and may be historical or contemporary. The collection also contains works from US and European artists and good touring shows are staged. The gallery is free and open daily in the afternoons.

Diefenbaker Homestead Although not in its original location, this house is the boyhood home of former Prime Minister John Diefenbaker and is furnished with pioneer articles, some from the politician's family. It's open daily and is free.

University Campus The University of Regina is on the east side of the park.

Plains Historical Museum
Yes, Virginia, there is life away from the park. The Plains Historical Museum is on the 4th floor of the old City Hall, on the corner of Scarth St and 11th Ave. There are several employees who will guide you around, lovingly telling stories about the various items from Saskatchewan's past. The museum deals with the various people in the province's life: the Native Indians, Métis and European settlers.

Through the summer the small museum is open Monday to Friday from 11.30 am to 5 pm, on the weekend from 1 pm. The rest of the year it's closed on Monday and Tuesday. Admission is $2, less for seniors.

Government House
Government House is the restored home of the lieutenant-governor of the Northwest Territories and Saskatchewan from 1891 to 1945. Indeed, Saskatchewan's lieutenant-governor continues to work in this house.

The Northwest territorial government was set up in 1870 to oversee the huge tract of land which was passing from control by the fur-trading companies. You can imagine what a sight this building must have been in the dusty western village of Regina in the 1890s.

Government House contains period furnishings from the turn of the century and interpreters are on hand to show visitors around.

Government House is north-west out of the centre a bit at 4607 Dewdney Ave, slightly west of Lewvan Drive. It's open Tuesday to Saturday from 1 to 4 pm, Sunday from 1 to 5 pm, and is closed on Monday. Admission is free.

Government House is also the venue for dramatic performances of *The Trial of Louis Riel*, which are held in summer; see the Entertainment section for details.

RCMP Centennial Museum & Depot
This museum (☎ 780-5838) details the history of the Royal Canadian Mounted Police, or Mounties, from 1874 when they first headed west to keep the peace. It was in this part of the country that their slogan 'we always get our man' became legend. On display are uniforms, articles, replicas and stories of some of the famous and/or notorious exploits of the force.

The training facilities and barracks, known as the depot, can also be seen. Mounties still police many of Canada's western and more remote towns and communities as well as having various federal responsibilities, such as being part of the national security forces. Tours run hourly until 3.30 pm, Monday to Friday. In addition, a daily drill takes place each weekday at 12.45 pm.

Open every day, the museum is on Dewdney Ave West, beyond Government House, not far from the corner of McCarthy Rd.

Also at the depot you can see the very popular RCMP Sunset Ceremony, a formal drill spectacle of drumming and marching surrounding the flag-lowering. It's a bit slow – call it a long hour – but the uniforms are colourfully impressive, and hey, the Mounties are one of Canada's symbols! The ceremony like everything here is free but is held only once a week in July and August at 6.45 pm. Ask the tourist office for details.

Sports Hall of Fame
In the former Land Titles building, a heritage site, this small provincial museum at 2205 Victoria Ave honours local athletes and teams. Gordie Howe, a local boy made good and arguably the greatest hockey player yet seen, is one of the features. The museum is open daily, but only during the afternoon on weekends, and is free.

Firefighters' Museum
You can see displays of old firefighting equipment here, at 1205 Ross Ave. The museum is open weekdays only and is free.

Wild Slides
Out of town, 1.6 km east on Highway 1, is this water-slide park with snack bars and a picnic area. It's open daily from June to September.

Activities
A pass can be bought at the YMCA for use of their courts, gym or pool.

The tourist office can tell you about swimming at public pools. There's one in Wascana Centre.

The Devonian Pathway is 11 km of paved bike routes through four city parks. Bicycle rentals are available in Wascana Centre park.

The office, which is open only in the afternoon, is at the Wascana Pool off College St. There are discounts for those with youth hostel cards.

The Regina Astronomical Society has a telescope set up on Broad St, opposite the CBC building by Wascana Centre, and is open on Wednesday nights in summer for public viewing. Also ask about the Kalium Observatory at the Science Centre.

Organised Tours There are 20-minute boat tours throughout the afternoon on Wascana Lake. They leave from the Wascana Marina on Wascana Drive. Tickets are not expensive.

Fifty-minute bus tours of Wascana Centre depart from Wascana Place and from the landing behind the Legislative building. Again trips are in the afternoon only, and there are five of them per day, run on the hour. The cost is just $2. An historical commentary is included.

The Saskatchewan Wheat Pool (☎ 569-4411) can help you plan a visit to a grain elevator or a livestock saleyard.

Festivals
The big annual event is Buffalo Days – a 12-day celebration held towards the end of July. Stores put up special decor and some workers wear pioneer garb. A talent stage is set up offering free entertainment and the days are filled with competitions, pancake breakfasts, a beard-growing contest and parades, peaking with a big concert/barbecue in Wascana park known as Pile o' Bones Sunday. Midway the exhibition features rides, music shows, a casino and various displays and exhibits. A fireworks display wraps up the festival.

Mosaic is a three-day multicultural event with ethnic foods, music and entertainment. It's held in early June.

The three-day folk festival, based in Victoria Park but with concerts elsewhere around town, is also usually held in early June. Through the summer there are free Sunday performances in the Bandshell in Wascana Centre.

Places to Stay

Camping As you approach Regina from the east on Highway 1, there are a few campsites which are geared mainly to trailers and RV's, not tenters. They might prove useful for a short stay but are definitely not rustic.

Hostels The youth hostel, called *Turgeon Hostel* (☎ 522-4200), is in a fine old house once belonging to an Acadian French person from eastern Canada. It's at 2310 McIntyre St, not right downtown but is quite central. McIntyre St is a residential street very near Wascana Centre. The rates are $10 for members, $13 for nonmembers. They have 50 beds, cooking facilities, a laundromat and canoe rentals. It's closed during the day but in summer remains open until midnight.

The *YMCA* (☎ 757-9622), at 2400 13th Ave, only rents rooms to men for $18. There is a cheap cafeteria and pool you can use (see Activities).

The *YWCA* (☎ 525-2141), at 1940 McIntyre St, is a little more expensive at $26.50 plus a $2 key deposit. They have a cafeteria, pool and kitchen.

For men in need there's the *Salvation Army* on Osler St between 11th and 12th Aves. As in many cities, they'll offer a free bed and breakfast. The place is not especially pleasant.

B&Bs There are quite a few of these places around the province – mostly in small towns – and they are not expensive. In Regina there is *B & J's* (☎ 522-4575), at 2066 Ottawa St, only about three blocks from the downtown area, just south of Victoria Ave St near the General Hospital. In this two-storey house on a residential street there are four rooms at singles/doubles $15/25, with evening coffee and breakfast; it's good value.

Another choice is *Eileen's* (☎ 586-1408) at 2943 Grant St.

Hotels Nearly all the low-budget and bottom-end hotels have disappeared. The last of the basics that's half decent is the *Empire* (☎ 522-2544), 1718 McIntyre St, on the corner of Saskatchewan Drive. It is north-west of central downtown area but an easy walk. They have clean, simple rooms without a toilet or bath but with a sink. Singles/doubles are $16/23. Any other remaining cheap hotels around town are pretty grim.

Moving up-market is the large and good *Relax Inn* (☎ 565-0455), 1110 Victoria Ave East, with nearly 200 modern rooms. Rates are $33 to $44 for singles or doubles.

Other hotels in the downtown area are costlier, though the *Plains Motor Hotel* (☎ 757-8661) is an exception, with rooms from $32 to $45. The *Sheraton Centre* (☎ 569-1666), at 1818 Victoria Ave, costs $75 and up. The *Hotel Saskatchewan* (☎ 522-7691), on the corner of Scarth St and Victoria Ave, costs $69 to $150.

The *Ramada Renaissance* (☎ 525-5255) features a three-storey-high indoor water slide along with a swimming pool and whirlpools. Prices start at $75 for singles, but there are weekend specials. It's central at 1919 Saskatchewan Drive.

Motels Most of the motels are on Highway 1 east of town. Cheapest is the *Siesta* (☎ 522-0977), on the corner of Park St and Victoria Ave by the Pump Bar, with singles at $30 to $44.

The *North Star* (☎ 352-0723), a few km from town, is the last motel on the north side of the highway. It's pale blue and set back from the road. Rooms cost from $32 to $55 for singles/doubles with air-con.

The *Coachman Inn Motel* (☎ 522-8525) is closer to town. It's the orange place at 835 Victoria Ave. Rooms vary in price from $35 to $44.

The *Sunrise* (☎ 527-5447) is near the overpass on Highway 1 East, just out of town. Rooms with TV and air-con cost from $38 to $60.

The *Inntowner* (☎ 525-3737), 1015 Albert St, has rooms from $40 to $54.

Places to Eat

There's a pretty decent range of places to eat in town and a number of places offering international cuisine have recently added to the variety of restaurant fare. Most choices listed here are in the central area, so note that many of them are closed on Sunday. The Saturday newspaper is full of ads for Sunday brunch buffets around town. Most of the eateries around the outskirts remain open on Sunday too.

A basic friendly place for simple meals is the *Town & Country* at 1825 Rose St. Open from 7.30 am to 8 pm daily, it's a good place for breakfast. The *Sandwich Tree* at 1819 Hamilton St is an office worker's kind of lunch place that makes excellent sandwiches with some 'off-beat' ingredients such as avocado, shrimps and bean sprouts.

The 1928 Market Mall, a restored building on Lorne St near the corner of 11th Ave, has the *Emporium*, a cafeteria-style restaurant with fresh salads, soups and sandwiches. It's open every day for lunch and is inexpensive. On Sundays they run a brunch for $7. Downstairs is *Olga's Deli & Desserts* for bagels, blintzes and pastries.

For Chinese food, there's *Lang's Café* at 1745 Broad St. It's open for lunch and closes late. The decor includes red-and-white tablecloths with vinyl chairs (what else?). But the food is cheap and not bad. A Vietnamese place, the *Vien Dong*, at 1841 Broad St, has an inexpensive lunch buffet. Neither place is anything to write home about but they get the job done adequately.

At 2425 11th Ave, near Smith St, is *Café Ashani*, open for Indian dinners nightly. It's not cheap but it's a nice place and the well-rounded menu is prepared carefully.

The *Copper Kettle* at 1953 Scarth St opposite the park is open all day, seven days a week and offers pizzas, other Italian food as well as Greek dishes and cheap breakfasts.

The *Elephant & Castle*, a British-style pub, is found in the Cornwall Centre, which you enter on the corner of 11th Ave and Scarth St. Part of the restaurant façade is from the bank building built on the site in 1911. Also in the mall is a cheap food fair.

The restaurant at the Wascana Marina, in the park near Broad St, is recommended. It's a small place with some pleasant outdoor tables run as a teaching restaurant by a youth

organisation; it's good value. It's open every day but not for dinner on Sunday. Try a bison burger.

For a steak, try the *Diplomat* at 2032 Broad St, where they have been serving them up for over 10 years.

Away from the centre at 3926 Gordon Rd, the *Brown Derby* is a large, casual place where you can't go wrong picking from the good, extensive and moderately priced menu, which includes steaks, roast beef and Greek main courses. It's open every day too.

On the corner of Lindsay St on Victoria Ave is *Robin's Donuts*, open 24 hours. It's a handy place to go if you're cold, tired, or just need a break from the road.

Entertainment

The Trial of Louis Riel Held in the restored ballroom of Government House, the trial is a theatrical dramatisation of the 1885 court battle fought over this leader of the Métis (Canadians of French and Native Indian stock). One of Canada's most famous historical figures, Riel led two uprisings against the government. The re-creation of the trial highlights issues that are still important as well as demonstrating the animosity between the country's French and British settlers.

It's presented with authentic costumes and is worth catching if your timing is right. There are shows only three nights a week in July and August. Tickets, a little pricey at $9, are available at the tourist office or at the door.

Spectator Sports In summer and fall the Saskatchewan Roughriders play professional football as part of the Canadian Football League (CFL) at Taylor Field.

Curling is a major winter sport on the prairies and the Curlodrome at Exhibition Park holds major competitions known as bonspiels through the snowy months.

Other *Barthelby's*, on the corner of Broad St and 12th Ave, is a popular and nicely decorated restaurant-bar where the food prices are slightly more than low-budget, though it's also a good place for just a beer, a snack and chat. No live music is offered.

The *Copper Kettle* is a restaurant, though it's popular with students as a place for beer. No music is played here either.

In the Market Mall on the corner of 11th Ave and Lorne St, the *Post Time Lounge* is a small, quiet bar with a Happy Hour special and some tables outside.

The *Club* presents good pop, blues and rock bands from western Canada.

The better hotels have lounges: some quiet, some with live music. *Stage West* is a popular and successful dinner theatre which doesn't cost an arm and a leg.

The Saskatchewan Centre of the Arts in the Wascana Centre has performances of opera and musicals and by the symphony orchestra.

Getting There & Away

Air The airport is a 15-minute drive southwest of the downtown area.

Air Canada (☎ 525-4711), with an office at 2015 12th Ave, has flights east and west with standard one-way fares including to Vancouver for $239 and Thunder Bay for $216. Canadian Airlines also serves Regina.

Bus The station is downtown on Hamilton St, just south of Victoria Ave. There are lockers and a quick-lunch counter. Three bus companies operate out of the station.

The Saskatchewan Transportation Company covers the small towns in the province and runs to Saskatoon and Prince Albert. Moose Mountain Lines has one route into rural Saskatchewan. Greyhound (☎ 565-3340), for daily inter-provincial trips, runs west to Calgary and Vancouver, and east to Winnipeg and Toronto.

There are five trips a day to Saskatoon for $22. The trip takes three hours to cover the 240-odd km.

Train Fine old Union Station sits boarded up on Saskatchewan Drive, at the foot of Broad St in the northern portion of the downtown area. Train services in and out of the city have been cut completely.

Car & Motorbike Dollar Rent-A-Car (☎ 525-1377) is at 1975 Broad St. Other companies are Hertz and Avis.

Hitching For hitching east take the No 4 bus from downtown.

Getting Around

To/From the Airport The airport is about a 15-minute drive from downtown. The only way to and from the airport is by taxi, which costs about $6 to $7. There are half a dozen car rental agencies at the airport.

Bus Regina Transit (☎ 569-7810) operates the bus routes around the city and one of them will be likely to get you anywhere you need to go.

Bicycle Rentals are available in Wascana park, at the Wascana pool building off College Ave. Discounts are available to youth hostel members. The office opens at noon.

There is a system of 11 km of paved bike routes through four city parks, called the Devonian Pathway.

AROUND REGINA

North of Regina, **Lumsden** sits nestled and protected in a convoluted, lumpy, hilly little valley on the main road (Route 11) to Saskatoon. The Franciscan monks here run the St Michael's retreat.

The **Qu'Appelle Valley** runs east-west from the town of Fort Qu'Appelle, northeast of Regina. Following the Qu'Appelle River, and interspersed with lakes, this valley is one of the green and pretty 'playgrounds' of Saskatchewan.

There are several provincial parks and historic sites along the glacially formed valley, both east and west of Regina.

In **Fort Qu'Appelle** there is a **museum**, and in mid-August a large **Native Indian powwow** is held at the Standing Buffalo Reserve.

Moose Jaw

Moose Jaw is a small, typical farm-supply town, but with some industry as well. There are some heritage buildings along Main St. The tourist office has a self-guided walking tour brochure which details some of the points of historic interest.

One of four Western Development museums around the province is in Moose Jaw. Each museum specialises in an aspect of provincial history. This one concentrates on the development of transportation in the west and has old carts, cars and trains. Admission costs $2.50.

Also here is Wild Animal Park, with mainly indigenous animals including bison. Curiosity seekers might enjoy the **Sukanen Ship & Pioneer Village Museum**, 13 km out of town, with plenty of pioneer relics and remains and the ship built way out here for sailing on the sea.

The town also hosts an international band festival annually. There is an Armed Forces base in Moose Jaw and it is home to the famous Snowbirds, an aerial acrobatic squadron which performs at air shows across the continent.

There are half a dozen or so motels and a tourist office.

Lastly, Moose Jaw has long had a bad reputation as a place to get stuck hitchhiking. It ranks right up there with Ontario's Wawa and Nipigon.

East Saskatchewan

YORKTON

Yorkton, a major town in eastern Saskatchewan, reflects the area's Ukrainian heritage with its onion-domed churches. There's a branch of the provincial museum system here, which depicts the various immigrant groups of the province, particularly the Ukrainians.

St Mary's Church is worth seeing, particularly the painted dome.

Nearby are two provincial parks: **Good Spirit Provincial Park**, with good swimming, and the larger **Duck Mountain Provincial Park** on the border of Manitoba.

The *Corona Motor Inn* (☎ 783-6571), at 345 West Broadway Ave, has been recommended. It costs $48 for doubles and has very good service, quiet rooms, a restaurant and bar.

VEREGIN

Veregin is a small, essentially unknown town, more or less in the middle of nowhere, has a rather unexpected international and intriguing history. The town and its surrounding area were settled between 1898 and 1899 by the Doukhobours, a determined and somewhat extraordinary religious sect from Russia.

At the turn of the century, with help from writer Leo Tolstoy, a good many of these people left their homeland and the persecution there, and came to Saskatchewan seeking religious freedom and seclusion. Here, under the leadership of Peter Veregin, they created a small but successful community.

Bliss was not to last here either, however, and soon the Doukhobours were in trouble with their neighbours and government again. They resisted all mainstream authority, be it church or state.

Partially based in fact, but somewhat exaggerated, are the well-known tales of nude demonstrations and arson which, rightly or wrongly, have come to be closely associated with the group.

After about 20 years here, many of the group moved to British Columbia where there's still a community. In the 1950s some of them returned to Russia, or headed to new lands once again, this time settling in Paraguay.

In town is the **Doukhobour Heritage Village**, a series of mainly reconstructed buildings and homes which reveal aspects of the settlers' lives at the beginning of the 1900s.

Houses and the Prayer Home are decorated in typical traditional fashion and include some very attractive textiles. The museum contains many other artefacts as well as photographs. Bread baked in the old-style brick ovens can sometimes be purchased.

The village is open daily in summer, but only on weekdays through the winter. There is a small admission charge for visitors.

There is also a statue of author Leo Tolstoy, commemorated for his assistance in their emigration.

Veregin lies near the provincial border with Manitoba. It is north of Yorkton, 265 km north-east of Regina.

Southern Saskatchewan

Running across the southern section of the province is the Red Coat Trail, a highway route from Winnipeg to Lethbridge, Alberta, which is named after and roughly parallels the route the Mounties took in coming to tame the west. The tourist office has a pamphlet which points out the historical and geographical things of interest along the way.

Whitetail deer

ESTEVAN

Nearly down at the US border, Estevan with a population of 10,000 is one of the largest towns in southern Saskatchewan. It's a very dynamic town, and has the world's largest deposits of lignite coal, three electical generating stations, natural gas pockets and surrounding oilfields.

Local attractions include the sandstone rock formations at **La Roche Percée**, once a site of Native Indian religious observance, and the **Estevan Brick Wildlife Park**, which has samples of most local species including bison and antelope.

At the **Sanderson Buffalo Kill Site**, archaeologists are at work and visitors are welcome to watch or join in. The site is in the Souris River Valley about 10 km west-north-west of town.

Ask at the tourist office about rockhounding or visiting the dam and coal mines.

South of town in North Portal, Al Capone used to hang out in the Cadillac Hotel, in Prohibition days when this was a big booze-smuggling area.

WEYBURN

From Weyburn, a farming supply centre with 10,000 or so residents, the so-called CANAM International Highway leads northward to Regina and beyond and southward all the way through North and South Dakota and down through Wyoming. A promotional pamphlet lists the attractions of a trip along the designated route.

There isn't a lot in Weyburn, but there is a park with camping facilities, a tourist office and a small museum with some Native Indian artefacts.

BIG MUDDY BADLANDS

South of Regina and Moose Jaw, down near the US border off Highway 34, are these badlands: a vast, hot area of sandstone formations, hills and valleys once used by stagecoach robbers, cattle rustlers and all the other bad-guy types you see in Western movies. In fact, the outlaw Butch Cassidy used to ride here.

Food, accommodation and camping is

available in the town of Bengough. There is another campground in Big Beaver and guided tours of the badlands are available here.

ASSINIBOIA

South of this small centre are two historic parks which may be of interest. At St Victor's are prehistoric Native Indian petroglyphs, carvings in rock. **Woods Mountain Park** has more recent history with displays on the North West Mounted Police (RCMP) and the Sioux people. There are some reconstructed buildings and tours are given. Note that the park is closed Tuesday and Wednesday, and closes for the season at the beginning of September.

GRASSLANDS NATIONAL PARK

Not yet completed, this new park near Val Marie, south of Swift Current, will be the first on the continent to preserve a section of original shortgrass prairie land. Also protected in the park are a prairie dog town, badlands, some historic Native Indian sites and other geographical features. Ask for the latest details at the Park Service Office and visitor centre in Val Marie.

SWIFT CURRENT

Though a fairly large town, there is little here for the visitor but a bed or a meal can be found without difficulty.

GREAT SAND HILLS

Just west of Swift Current (or north of Gull Lake and Maple Creek) is a semi-desert area with dunes and near-arid vegetation. The best viewing area is near the little village of Sceptre, in the north-western section of the hills near the town of Leader. There are farm B&Bs in the area; ask in Swift Current.

CYPRESS HILLS

This is a small region on the border of southern Saskatchewan and Alberta, which offers geographical respite from the prairies. It's a pretty area of small lakes, streams, and green hills up to 1400 metres high. Much of the land is a park which stretches across the

provincial border. There's organised camping on the Alberta side around the lakes, where tenting costs $8, but it gets very crowded in summer.

A dirt road links this area to Fort Walsh, where there's a national historic park. The fort, built in the late 1870s as a North West Mounted Police base, is a remnant of the district's rich but sad history.

The hills, always a sanctuary for animals, were at one time a sanctuary for Plains Indians. Information at the old fort tells the story of the time when 'a man's life was worth a horse and a horse was worth a pint of whisky'.

Saskatoon

Saskatoon, a small quiet city, sits smack in the middle of the Canadian prairies. The clean, wide streets, low skyline and flat surroundings give the city a western flavour and with the South Saskatchewan River drifting through, makes for a peaceful, easy-paced community. The largest employer in town is the university and it has become pretty much the provincial cultural centre with an active arts community.

However, Saskatoon, as the second city of the province, is also a farm trading centre. It also acts as a transportation, communication and commercial centre. In addition, the city has a major agricultural research centre called Innovation Place.

In 1883, 35 members of the Temperance Colonisation Colony from Ontario founded a settlement on these Cree lands. The town stayed but the ban on alcohol didn't. In 1890 the railway hit town and growth began. The city has had its ups and downs but is now well established and sits confidently with both uranium mines and some of the world's largest potash deposits nearby.

There isn't a lot here for the visitor and after a short look-see you'll have a feel for the place. It's an attractive little city with a few things to see, and the new Wanuskewin Heritage Park will make it an even better and

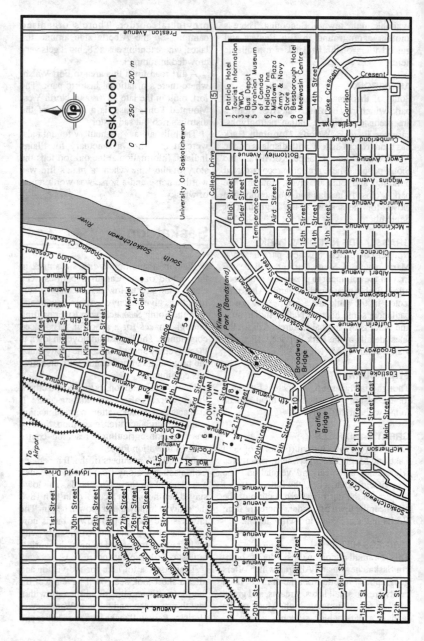

Saskatoon

0   250   500 m

1 Patricia Hotel
2 Tourist Information
3 YWCA
4 Bus Depot
5 Ukrainian Museum
6 Patricia
7 Midtown Plaza
8 Army & Navy Store
9 Bessborough Hotel
10 Meewasin Centre

more convenient crossroads for the traveller. Accommodation is reasonable and you can get a fair meal.

Just off the main thoroughfares, residential streets are lined with small neat, square houses – some old, some new. Six bridges link the city across the river.

Orientation

The South Saskatchewan River cuts through the city diagonally from north-east to south-west. The small main downtown area lies on the west bank; the university is on the opposite side.

Idylwyld Drive divides the city's streets into their east and west designations. Out of town in each direction Idylwyld Drive becomes Highway 16, the Yellowhead Highway. The city is split into north-south sections by 22nd St and the streets either side are marked accordingly.

The downtown core extends to the river to the south, 1st Ave to the west, 25th St to the north, and Spadina Crescent and the river again (which changes direction) to the east.

Streets run east-west, avenues north-south. The main street is 2nd Ave. Another important street is 21st St East, again with a blend of new and old architecture and with lots of stores. It's framed by the Bessborough Hotel at one end and the Midtown Plaza, the former site of the railway station, at the other end. At 23rd St East, between 3rd Ave North and 2nd Ave North, is the city bus depot, a block open only to bus traffic. Most bus routes can be picked up here.

Behind the Bessborough Hotel is one of the city's large parks, Kiwanis Memorial Park running beside the river. At each end of the park, Spadina Crescent continues on along the river.

Information

The Tourism Saskatoon office (☎ 242-1206) is quite central at 102-310 Idylwyld Drive North, on the corner of 24th St East, in a small strip complex about four blocks north-west of the Midtown Plaza. It's open at least from 9 am to 5 pm Monday to Friday; it's open longer hours and probably on Saturday in summer. During the summer months there are also smaller information booths set up along the main routes into town. These are open every day and also have information on other destinations around the province.

The lobby of the town's oldest and largest hotel, the Bessborough, has a desk for tour information and has maps and pamphlets on local attractions.

Old Commercial Area

Just west of Idylwyld Drive on 20th St West is an interesting old commercial area which is now in decay and has become the centre for the Native underclass. Formerly a largely Ukrainian area, there are remnants of this, along with quite a few other ethnic restaurants. Most of these are Chinese, but there are also a few cafés with Ukrainian food. In between are a couple of cheap hotels, many pawnshops, a second-hand bookshop and a Kentucky Fried Chicken shop.

Broadway Ave

Broadway Ave, another old shopping district and actually the town's oldest, has recently undergone some gentrification. A full range of stores can be found along this historic street, which is south of the river from downtown over the Broadway Bridge at the foot of 4th Ave South. The area of interest is around the corner of 8th St.

Western Development Museum

You open the door of this museum and voilà! you're looking down Main St, circa 1910. It looks like a movie set and contains stores, workshops, a hotel, a printing shop and other establishments. The general store is good. Don't miss the model of men playing chess. There are all manner of goods, tins, relics and supplies on display, as well as old wagons, cars and farm machinery.

The museum is at 2610 Lorne Ave, quite a way south from town. To get there, take a No 1 Exhibition bus from 2nd Ave downtown. When leaving the museum, get on the bus going the same way as when you arrived. It loops around then goes back a different way. It's open daily and admission costs $3, less for seniors and kids; it may be worth showing a youth hostel card too. There is a restaurant at the site.

Ukrainian Museum of Canada

This museum, at 910 Spadina Crescent East, preserves and presents articles from Ukrainian immigrants' heritage. The highlight is the collection of fantastic textiles used in formal and everyday dress as well as for other household purposes. In style, colour and design they rival South American textiles. Also interesting is the exhibit on symbolic, festival or special-occasion breads, eg wedding breads. Other items are the painted eggs and a brief history of the pioneers' arrival. A visit is worthwhile at only $2. The museum is near the downtown area, along the river. During the summer it's open Monday to Friday from 10 am to 4.30 pm, Saturday and holidays from 1 to 5 pm and Sunday from 1 to 8 pm. During the rest of the year, it's closed on Saturday and Monday.

Museum of Ukrainian Culture

A small museum at 202 Avenue M South, this one has examples of Ukrainian crafts and dress and through the exhibits portrays aspects of Ukrainian culture from prehistoric times to the mid-20th century. It's open daily in summer, on the weekend in winter and there is a small admission fee.

Meewasin Valley & Centre

The very pretty, green Meewasin Valley follows the South Saskatchewan River down the middle of the city. From behind the Bessborough Hotel, the valley park runs in both directions and on both sides of the river for a total of 15 km.

There are good views of the river, the Meewasin Valley Trail is good for walking and cycling and picnic tables are scattered among the trees, where black and white magpies flit. Bridges span the river at several places and the trail follows the banks on both sides. Many of the city's attractions and

events are located along the river. The university lies along the east shore.

The **Meewasin Centre**, really a museum about the river and the city's history, has some good displays and is free. Meewasin is a Cree word meaning 'beautiful valley'. It's at the bottom of 3rd Ave South on the corner of 19th St East. Although it's hard to imagine, the river is melted glacier ice from the Rockies far to the west near Lethbridge, Alberta. It flows north from Saskatoon joining the Assiniboine River on its way to Winnipeg. The Meewasin Centre is open daily and has good maps of the trail with its various parks.

Wannuskewin Heritage Park

Three km north of the city along the Saskatchewan River beyond Meewasin Park, Wannuskewin has the potential to be the prime attraction of the province and should not be missed. Still under development, this huge cultural, historical and geographical centre in a scenic valley setting is due to open in 1992.

The 100-hectare site is to present and interpret the area's archaeology, prehistory and the culture of the Northern Plains Indians.

At the time of writing, 19 prehistoric archaeological sites have been unearthed, attracting attention from researchers internationally. It's known that hunters and gatherers lived in the area at least 5000 years ago. Aside from the visitor information exhibits, research will continue to be carried out at the park.

The visitor centre, developed in conjunction with provincial Native Indian groups, is to tell the story of the regional Native peoples and their way of life on the once buffalo-filled prairies. Another section details the Native life now. Trails will range over the site and outdoor demonstrations and events are planned.

It's hoped the site will gain international recognition. Check at the Saskatoon tourist office for the latest information on construction and opening times.

Native Canadian woman

Beaver Creek

Going the other direction, about 13 km south of the Meewasin Valley (from the Freeway Bridge), is the Beaver Creek Conservation Area, a large park protecting some of the river valley and its wildlife. Walking trails run through the area and the information centre provides geographical and historical background. It's open daily and is free.

Mendel Art Gallery & Conservatory

These are at 950 Spadina Crescent East, a short walk from the downtown area along the river. The gallery has three rooms of changing exhibits usually featuring Canadian works. One of the three galleries shows historical works, the other two display contemporary art. The conservatory is small and has a few palms amongst other plants. Admission is free and they're open daily from 10 am to 10 pm. There is a coffee shop and gift store on the premises.

Forestry Farm Park

This park is north-east of the downtown area

across the river. Inside the park is a zoo with 300 animals, mostly those found in Saskatchewan and other parts of Canada: wolves, lynx, caribou and bison. There are also some gardens and picnic sites. In winter the park has a ski trail. There is also a restaurant. The park is over University Bridge; for details of how to get there, ask at the tourist office. It's open every day, all year.

University of Saskatchewan

There are a few things to look at on this campus, which is on a huge tract of land along the river. There's a small biology museum, an observatory for stargazing, an art gallery and other small faculty museums. For information on free tours of the campus and many of the points of interest and opening hours, call ☎ 966-5788.

Also on campus is the Diefenbaker Centre, detailing aspects of this former prime minister's life. It has changing exhibits on Dief as well as other historical and craft exhibits; it's open daily. His grave site is next to the centre.

The Little Stone School dating from 1905, the oldest public building in the city, can be visited every day from May to October. A costumed interpreter provides information. It's free too, as are all the university sights. The Natural Sciences Museum has some life-sized replicas of dinosaurs.

If you're going to stroll around the campus, pick up a copy of the architectural pamphlet *Building the University*, which offers details of the various structures and their dates of construction.

Potash Mine

If you're able to plan ahead a month or so, you can tour a potash mine. A trip involves descending 1000 metres underground and then travelling through tunnels to where machines dig out the potash. You can also see the stuff refined and prepared for shipping. For details call ☎ 664-5543 or write to 'Tours', Public Affairs Department, Potash Corporation of Saskatchewan, 500-122 1st Ave South, Saskatoon, Saskatchewan.

Activities

Canoes may be for rent at the Kiwanis depot. In winter there is a skating rink on the parkland beside the Bessborough Hotel.

Organised Tours Northcote River Cruises offer one-hour boat tours leaving either from the lookout behind the Mendel Art Gallery or from the bandstand area in Kiwanis Park, behind the Bessborough Hotel. They run on the hour through June, July and August and cost $6, less for kids.

Festivals

Folkfest is a festival that takes place in late summer and early September. The fee of $10 or so gets you into 20 multicultural pavilions set up around the city, presenting food, crafts, music and dances.

The Exhibition is a five-day event in mid-July with concerts, rides, parades and exhibits.

Rocktoberfest is a big beer bash with rock and Bavarian music held in October.

Shakespeare on the Saskatchewan is a summer theatre programme, held in a tent along the river by the Mendal Art Gallery. Performances are in the evening and advance tickets are advised.

At the end of June or beginning of July is the now annual Saskatchewan Jazz Festival, held at various locations around town. Some of the concerts are free.

Louis Riel Day is a one-day event held in the first week of July, with various activities taking place by the Bessborough Hotel.

Places to Stay

Camping Quite close to the centre is the *Gordon Howe Campsite* (☎ 975-3331) on Ave P, south of 11th St, which is operated by the City Parks Department. It's quite green, with trees, and there is a small store for basic supplies. It's open from April to October.

Hostels A year-round *Youth Hostel* (☎ 242-8861) is set up in the good and central Patricia Hotel, on 2nd Ave North near 25th St East and the bus station. Some of the many rooms have been converted to dorms with bunk beds. A bed costs $9 with a card or $10 without a membership, plus taxes.

The rooms are above the bar but there isn't live music every night. The bar is quite inexpensive, as is the restaurant in the basement which offers lots to look at while you eat the good, cheap food. The hotel lobby has a TV lounge area.

The *YWCA* (☎ 244-0944), on the northwest side of 25th Ave East at 5th Ave North, rents rooms all year round to women at $30 for singles. Look for the blue sign near 3rd Ave. They have a pool and a small kitchen.

Males, if they're in need, can stay at the institutional *Salvation Army* (☎ 244-6260), on the corner of 19th St and Ave C in south Saskatoon. If you arrive after 10.30 pm you'll need a slip from the police station before they'll let you in. A bed and meals are free, but you can only stay a few days.

B&Bs If you don't mind going out of town a bit, *Aspen Hills* (☎ 668-4463) is a rural B&B about 30 km south-west of Saskatoon.

It's not far from Highway 60 and Highway 7, but call for detailed directions.

Hotels – middle The *Patricia Hotel*, 345 2nd Ave North near 25th St East, is the best and cleanest of the low-budget places. It's good value at singles/doubles $26/34 and up; the price depends on facilities. The sports bar and restaurant on the premises are both good, friendly and inexpensive.

The *Senator* (☎ 244-6141), right in the centre of town on the corner of 3rd Ave South and 21st St East, is old but was recently renovated. The rooms are good and cost $37 for singles including breakfast. It has a beautiful pub-style bar although some of the patrons look as though they've enjoyed it a few too many times.

There are a couple of cheapies on 2nd Ave at 20th St, but neither is really recommended. And I'd stay away from the ones on 20th St West.

Moving up the scale, there are several moderately priced places. The *Westgate Inn* (☎ 382-3722) is at 2501 22nd St West with rooms from $40 to $49.

At the corner of 2nd Ave and 20th St is the *Capri Motor Hotel* (☎ 244-6104). They have 64 rooms with rates that vary a lot – prices range from $42.

The *King George* (☎ 244-6133), at 157 2nd Ave North, is large and central, and costs around the same price.

Hotels – top end There are quite a few expensive hotels out around the airport as well as these two more central ones.

Firstly, the *Holiday Inn* (☎ 244-2311), at 90 22nd St East, has rooms from $60 to $100.

The classic *Hotel Bessborough* (☎ 244-5521), a city landmark at 601 Spadina Crescent East, is a better choice at the same price of $60 to $100. It's a large chateau-like place and sits at the bottom of 21st St by the river. Built in 1932, it was run by Canadian National but is now operated by Delta Hotels.

Motels The *Travelodge Motel* (☎ 242-8881), near the airport, is like the others in the chain.

It's pale yellow with an orange name sign. The motel section has rooms from $60 to $99. You'll find it at 106 Circle Drive West, on the corner of Idylwyld Drive.

The following motels are all quite close to town.

The *Colonial Square Motel* (☎ 373-1676) is at 1301 8th St East, near the university. Rooms cost from $40 to $45.

Journeys End (☎ 934-1122) at 2155 Northridge Drive near the airport offers good value with rooms from $40 to $47.

The *Relax Inn Motel* (☎ 665-8121), 102 Cardinal Crescent, has singles/doubles at $40/50 and is very good and clean.

Places to Eat

The *Adonis*, on 3rd Ave on the corner of 22nd St, is recommended for lunch. It serves excellent soups, salads, sandwiches, vegetarian offerings and some Middle-Eastern items, which are all fresh and inexpensive. There are outside tables too. It's very busy at lunch time, and open from 9 am to 5 pm every day but Sunday.

The *Cage*, at 120 2nd Ave North, is a basic all-purpose restaurant with a varied menu, and decor and furniture a cut above the usual. They offer good-value breakfasts that will hold you long past lunch and the homefries are excellent. The dinner special, available Monday to Wednesday from 5 pm, consists of a large sirloin steak, potato, dessert, salad and coffee, all for $7.95. A lasagne costs $5.95. The Cage stays open daily until late, on Sunday from noon.

Next door is a quick *deli* with tasty vegetarian sandwiches.

Maxim's, at 156 2nd Ave right downtown, is rather nondescript but offers good-value buffets, dinner specials, and cheap steaks.

Johnny's Inn, on 3rd Ave just north of the corner of 22nd St East, is a small cafeteria popular with workers and has good hamburgers. They also serve homemade chilli dishes and large sandwiches. On 21st St East, between 2nd and 3rd Aves, is the very unassuming cafeteria in *Woolworth's* (a five-and-dime store). A simple three-course meal costs $5, a lighter soup-and-sandwich lunch costs $4. The food is decent and quick, if plain.

The *Artful Dodger*, at 119 4th Ave South, is an English-style pub with typically British meals. Similar, but perhaps a bit pricier, is the *Elephant & Castle* in the Midtown Plaza, an enclosed mall on the corner of 21st St East and 1st Ave South, flanked by Eaton's department store at one end and Sears at the other. Or you can eat cheaply at the Food Court on the 1st floor. The *Satay House* here has pretty good combination plates with vegetables.

Even Saskatoon has a modern Canadian-style trendy spot. It's called *Saint Tropez Café*, 243 3rd Ave South, and serves the standard quiche or crêpes for around $7 at lunch. Open-face sandwiches with salad are $5.50, and continental breakfasts consisting of a croissant, bun, cheese and fruit are offered. Dinners of pastas, stir fries, souffles, etc can be quite a bit more expensive, but the fondue for two is a nice deal. The surroundings are pleasant as is the recorded music and the food is well prepared. The café is open from 9 am to 11 pm.

Lucci's on 3rd Ave offers good but pricey Italian food. For Greek food, *Cousin Nik's* is recommended; it's a little out of the centre at 1100 Grosvenor Ave, about half a block from 8th St East, south of the downtown area. It's open every day for dinner with various daily specials and a full range of Greek dishes. The food is very good, the atmosphere congenial, and the prices in the middle-range.

For a splurge on a steak try *John's Prime Rib* at 401 21st St East.

There are a number of restaurants along 20th St West, an area once mainly Ukrainian but now with a small Chinatown among the hard-luck Native population. There are still several meat and sausage shops and a couple of Ukrainian eateries.

The pleasant *Dniepro*, at 343 20th St, serves all the standards at dinner time. The *Trio Café*, at 509 20th St, is very ordinary and standards are slipping, but it still serves three or four Ukrainian dishes, cabbage rolls and *varenyky* (stuffed savoury pastry) along with its basically Canadian menu. All along

20th St Chinese places can be found, but most of the better ones are on or near the cross street Ave C, a few blocks from Idylwyld Drive. The large *Golden Dragon* , at 334 Ave C South, has been around for years.

The *Gee Gong* at 617 20th St West is good for Cantonese and Mandarin food. They have a Sunday smorgasbord and dim sum daily.

There is also a large, cheap Chinese buffet which is offered for lunch or dinner in the *Capri Motor Hotel* in the downtown area.

Around the outskirts, and for those with wheels, 80th St East and 22nd St West both offer abundant choices. *Saskatoon Brewing Co* is a pub with its own beer at 32 2105 8th St East.

Out of town, *Tante Maria's Mennonite Kitchen* (☎ 931-3212), on the corner of Faithful Ave (coincidence?) and 51st St, offers basic, healthy farm food for any meal of the day.

Entertainment

Bud's at 817 Broadway Ave has live rhythm & blues nightly and a Saturday afternoon jam. *Amigo's* at 632 10th St East has fairly well-known local and regional bands.

The *Artful Dodger*, a pub at 119 4th Ave South, has entertainment and the *North 40 Inn*, on the corner of 20th Ave West and 6th St, has live country music. Admission is a few dollars.

At the Capri Motor Hotel, in *Club Soda* there's rock and blues music. It's on the corner of 2nd Ave South and 20th St East.

For jazz, check out the *Bassment* at 245 3rd Ave South. They bring in some pretty good acts and it's not expensive.

Things to Buy

A store that might be worth checking out is the large old Army & Navy on the corner of 21st St East and 3rd Ave South. This is one of Canada's oldest discount department stores and is a real classic, with three floors of cheap goods including clothes and some camping supplies. The elevator to get you up and down is still operated by a woman who shuts the metal gate and calls out the floors – one of the very few such operators in the country still with a job.

Another place to have a peek at is the Trading Post, 226 2nd Ave South. They specialise in Canadian crafts and souvenirs with an emphasis on Native Indian goods. There is some junk but also some good stuff including fine, wool Cowichan-style sweaters, Inuit prints and sculptures (ranging in price up to $1000, but it's interesting to see and compare the various styles), some jewellery, woodcarvings and BC jade. Some other eye-catching articles are moccasins, mukluks (Inuit boots), teas, spices and wild rice.

The Trading Post can also be found in other locations around the province.

Getting There & Away
Air The airport is in the north-east of the city off Idylwyld Drive. Air Canada and Canadian Airlines both fly in and out of Saskatoon. It's about a two-hour flight to either Winnipeg, Calgary, or Edmonton.

Bus The big, new bus station (☎ 933-8000), for destinations all over Saskatchewan, is the corner of 23rd St East and Ontario Ave. The latter is only a small street; the main corner of the bus station is 23rd St and 1st Ave North, up a short block from Ontario Ave. The station has a cafeteria and small store. The washrooms even have showers, which people with tickets can use.

Services include to Regina (daily at 8 am, 1.30 pm, 5.30 pm and 8 pm for $22), Winnipeg (three a day, including one at night, for $65) and Edmonton (four a day, including one late at night, for $47). There are also two buses a day to Prince Albert.

Train You won't be too happy with this station's location – it's way out, a long way west from downtown on Chappell Drive. The taxi fare is about $12; but a city bus runs from the curling rink across from the station to town at a quarter to and quarter past each hour. It doesn't run at night, however. For

train information, ring ☎ 800-561-8630, a toll-free number.

Trains run to Edmonton for $63, and to Jasper and Vancouver three times a week on Monday, Tuesday and Saturday (late in the evening).

To Winnipeg ($91) and Toronto, trains also run three times a week, but on Monday, Wednesday and Saturday (early in the morning). There is no more service to Regina.

Car & Motorbike For car rentals, Budget is at 234 1st Ave South (☎ 244-7925).

There are other local and well-known companies around town and at the airport.

Getting Around
Bus For city bus information, call ☎ 975-3100. Most things are within walking distance of the centre of town. Many of the bus routes begin at the Transit Terminal, a section of 23rd St East between 3rd Ave North an 2nd Ave North blocked off to all traffic but the buses. The depot area here is sometimes referred to as Transit Mall. There are signs here for all the bus routes, benches to sit on and lots of people milling about waiting. One of the drivers will be able to help you with any destination questions. For the railway station, which bus you catch will depend on the time of day, so ask. None go right into the station but you'll get within two blocks or so.

Bicycle Joe's Cycle & Sports (☎ 244-7332), at 221 20th St West, rents bicycles and does repairs.

AROUND SASKATOON
Manitou Springs
Near the town of **Watrous** on Lake Manitou, about 120 km south-east of Saskatoon, is the **Manitou Springs Mineral Spa**, one of the oldest spa areas on the prairies. It's open all year for bathing or swimming in the waters.

Batouche National Historic Site
North-east of Saskatoon, 80 km up Highway 11 and then along Route 225 off Highway

312 from the town of Rosthern is the site of the 1885 Battle of Batouche (more of an encounter really, although with tragic results) fought between the government and the rebellious Métis led by Louis Riel. The visitor centre tells the story of the battle and includes an audio-visual display on the Métis from the 1860s to the present. Also here are the few remains of the village of Batouche which include the church and some of the trenches dug for military purposes. The site is open every day from mid-May to mid-October.

Batouche was the centre of a Métis settlement and its provisional government in the late 1800s, after many of these people had left Manitoba due to running into difficulties over land there.

Northern Saskatchewan

The area north of Saskatoon seems like the northern portion of the province and I refer to it that way, but really this is central Saskatchewan. Geographically, Prince Albert National Park isn't even halfway to the northern border, so technically north begins somewhere beyond that point.

From Saskatoon the Yellowhead Highway, which comes from Winnipeg, runs north-west through North Battleford on its way to Edmonton and British Columbia. Pick up a copy of the Yellowhead map and pamphlet, which has some historical background, from the tourist office.

Between Saskatoon and Prince Albert there is a farm belt which runs the width of the province. At Prince Albert the land begins to change and the big national park just north marks the beginning of the vast Boreal forest which takes up the northern half of Saskatchewan.

Prince Albert seems a long way north, and indeed, the growing season is short even if this is the middle of the province. There are several good parks in the area which mark as far as most visitors (or residents) get.

PRINCE ALBERT

Prince Albert is the most northerly town of any size in the province. It also sits dead in the middle between Alberta and Manitoba. Known as PA, it acts as the jumping-off point for trips into the huge **Prince Albert National Park**. The area north of town is known as the lake district, a relatively undeveloped area of woods, bush, lakes and cottages. Aside from those found within the national park, other mega-lakes of the region are **Candle Lake** and **Montreal Lake.**

Still further north are three other immense parks: **Nipawin** to the north-east, **Meadow Lake** to the north-west and **Lac la Ronge** straight up north. The latter provincial park completely surrounds enormous, island-filled Lac la Ronge, which has the reputation of being one of the most attractive lakes in the province. Beyond these areas is pretty much untouched wilderness.

In Prince Albert itself, with a population of 34,000, there are a couple of minor attractions. A tourist information office is situated south of town on Highway 2. The **Historical Museum** in the old firehall has displays on the city's past. A tea room overlooks the North Saskatchewan River which flows through town. This river is joined not far east of town by the South Saskatchewan River.

Walking tours of the town begin at the museum for those interested in more historical detail.

Prince Albert is the location of a major maximum security prison. The **Rotary Museum of Police & Corrections** at the tourist office outlines related history.

East of town, 18 km out on Highway 55, the **Weyhaeuser pulp and paper mill** can be visited. On the other side of Prince Albert, 12 km out on Highway 3, the **Satellite Communications Station** can be toured; phone ☎ 764-3636 for details.

In 1988, De Beers, the diamond company from South Africa, staked a claim on some land 40 km or so from Prince Albert. Since then, with obvious respect for De Beers' expertise, millions of hectares nearby have been staked for diamond searching and processing of ore has begun at some of the sites.

Most of the town's accommodation is in motels and there is a campground less than two km north of town beside Highway 2.

PRINCE ALBERT NATIONAL PARK

The National Park is a huge primarily wilderness tract of softly rolling terrain where the prairie of the south turns to the woodland of the north. Among the geographic features are huge cool lakes, spruce bog and forested uplands. Trails of greatly varying lengths and good canoeing routes provide access to much of the park. The system of interconnected rivers and lakes is a good one. There's fishing, a range of camping possibilities and cross-country ski trails in winter.

Other highlights are **Lavallee Lake**, with the second-largest white pelican colony in the country, the herd of wild bison in the south-western grassland portion of the park, and the cabin controversial conservationist Grey Owl occupied for seven years.

Information

The park's service centre (where you'll find lodgings, groceries, petrol, canoe rentals and swimming) is the village of Wakesiu on the huge lake of the same name.

Places to Stay

The *Waskesiu International Hostel* (☎ 663-5450) is on the accessible eastern side of the park, directly north of Prince Albert. Members pay $10, nonmembers $13 and there is a family rate available. Meals can be provided with advance notice but there are cooking facilities. The hostel also has a laundry and accommodates up to 60 people.

The hostel is open from the beginning of May to the mid-October and is within walking distance of the park facilities. As is normal, it is closed through the day.

There are many campgrounds in the park but it is a popular place and fills up on the weekend, especially on holiday weekends. It's best to arrive as early as possible on a Friday.

One campground is geared to trailers, the rest for tenters. The smaller campgrounds are simple and quiet; or there is backcountry camping for canoeists and hikers.

Grey Owl

Once again read and quoted, naturalist Grey Owl was somewhat of a legend through the 1930s for his writings and lectures on conservation and love of the wilderness. He toured widely across North America and the United Kingdom encouraging preservation and appreciation of the environment.

His first book, *The Men of the Last Frontier*, was published in 1931. *Tales of an Empty Cabin* published in 1936 is possibly the best known work but in between there were several others.

When, upon his death in 1938 in Prince Albert, it was discovered that his identity and lifestyle as a Canadian Indian had been assumed and that in fact he was Archibald Stansfield Belaney of Hastings, England, the legend surrounding him was only further enhanced. He had emigrated to Canada, become a trapper and guide, married an Iroquois woman and been adopted as a brother by the Ojibwa tribe.

His wife, Anahereo, who died in 1986, was awarded the Order of Canada for her work in conservation. Her ashes are buried by the graves of Grey Owl and their only daughter, beside the cabin where they lived and worked in Prince Albert National Park. Much of his research was done in the park.

The small, simple one-room cabin on Ajawaan Lake has become a pilgrimage site of sorts. From the cabin known as Beaver Lodge, the couple worked to bring back the nearly obliterated beaver population. It sits right on a beaver lodge by the lake's edge.

It is still a fairly inaccessible spot which can be reached by one of two ways. First is the Grey Owl Trail, a 20-km hike along Kingsmere Lake. Alternatively, you can canoe from the end of the road on Kingsmere River upstream to Kingsmere Lake. From there, paddle across the lake to the north end where there is a choice of either a three-km walking trail or a one-km portage to Ajawaan Lake, from where the cabin can reached by paddling. ■

LAC LA RONGE PROVINCIAL PARK

Some of the 55 provincial canoe routes are here; you can hire canoes and other gear.

FLIN FLON

Just over the border in Manitoba, Flin Flon has several canoe outfitters for canoeing the northern lakes.

MEADOW LAKE PROVINCIAL PARK

Similar to Prince Albert National Park, this one runs along a chain of lakes by the Alberta border. There are nature trails and a series of longer hiking trails which allow for wildlife viewing. There is a lot of wildlife in the park, and good beaches on many of the lakes. Aside from campgrounds, visitors can stay in simple, privately operated rental cabins.

The park is north of Meadow Lake off Highway 55, and is part of the Northern Woods & Water Route, a road system that begins in Manitoba and ends in British Columbia.

West Saskatchewan

REDBERRY LAKE

Redberry Lake, about an hour's drive heading north-west from Saskatoon, is a prime bird-watching location. The lake and its islands are all protected as a bird sanctuary. Of most interest are the large, white pelicans and the small scarcer, piping plover but there are many others. Bird-watching tours can be taken and boats and canoes or windsurfers can be rented. The town of Hafford has all the conveniences.

FORT BATTLEFORD NATIONAL HISTORIC PARK

This historic site is five km from the town of North Battleford about 140 km north-west of Saskatoon off the Yellowhead Highway. The Northwest Mounted Police built the fort in 1876 to help settle the area and police the Native Indians, traders and White settlers. Inside the walls are five buildings you can visit which contain police and Native Indian artefacts, tools and memorabilia. The barracks contain an information display and there are guides in costume around the park. The Fort Battleford National Historic Park is open daily from 1 May to 10 October and entry is free.

In North Battleford across the river, the Western Development Museum deals with agricultural history.

There is some interesting landscape around the Battlefords; there's a little more topographic variety than you'll find in much of this region of Saskatchewan.

Alberta

Entered Confederation: 1 September 1905
Area: 661,188 sq km
Population: 2,250,000 fourth largest

Not so long ago Alberta was a vast, sparsely inhabited wilderness. Today it has two of the largest cities in Canada – Edmonton and Calgary. Its huge wheat farms, cattle ranches and rich deposits of minerals and fossil fuels are the basis of its wealth. For the visitor Alberta's main attractions are its wildlife, diverse scenery and the wide range of recreational pursuits it offers.

Alberta, the most westerly of the prairie provinces, is bordered in the north by the Northwest Territories; in the east by Saskatchewan; in the south by Montana; and in the west by British Columbia.

Although Edmonton is the most northerly of Alberta's major cities it is still in the southern half of the province. It's connected with Calgary by Highway 2; south from Calgary the highway goes to Montana in the USA. North-west from Edmonton Highway 2 heads through Peace River to Dawson Creek in British Columbia, where the Alaska Highway begins. North from Peace River Highway 35 takes you to the Northwest Territories.

The Yellowhead Highway goes east from Lloydminster on the Saskatchewan border, through Edmonton to Jasper in the Rockies and on to Prince George in British Columbia. The Trans Canada Highway goes north-west from Medicine Hat through Calgary to Banff and Lake Louise in the Rockies and on to Revelstoke.

Also from Medicine Hat the Crowsnest Highway (Highway 3) heads south-west to Lethbridge, Alberta's third largest city.

HISTORY

Beginning around 9500 to 5500 BC, Alberta – particularly the southern portion – was occupied by the Plains Indians. For millen-

nia they lived a nomadic life walking great distances hunting the vast herds of bison which they used for food, clothing and shelter.

From our cinema and TV screens many of us have an image of these people pursuing the herds on horseback. This period in fact only lasted from about 1750 when the horse was introduced, to the end of the 19th century when most of the bison had been destroyed – and therefore so had the Plains Indians traditional way of life.

The Plains Indians included the Blackfoot, Blood, Peigan, Atsina (also called Gros Ventre), Cree, Ojibwa, Sarcee and Assiniboine. The Sioux came from the south in the late 1800s.

The first Europeans in Alberta were fur traders who arrived around the middle of the 17th century. They were followed in the 18th century by the Hudson's Bay Company and its main rival the Northwest Company, both set up trading posts through the region. The two companies amalgamated in 1821 and the Hudson's Bay Company administered the area until 1870 when the territory became part of the Dominion of Canada. Settlers were then encouraged to migrate by the government's offers of cheap land.

The 1870s saw the establishment of the Northwest Mounted Police as a response to the lawlessness caused by the whisky trade in which the Plains Indians had been given cheap alcohol in exchange for bison hides. The police force were soon able to put a stop to the trade.

The coming of the railway in the 1880s made access to the west quicker and easier and led to a rapid expansion of the population. Wheat and cattle farming formed the basis of the economy but coal mining and

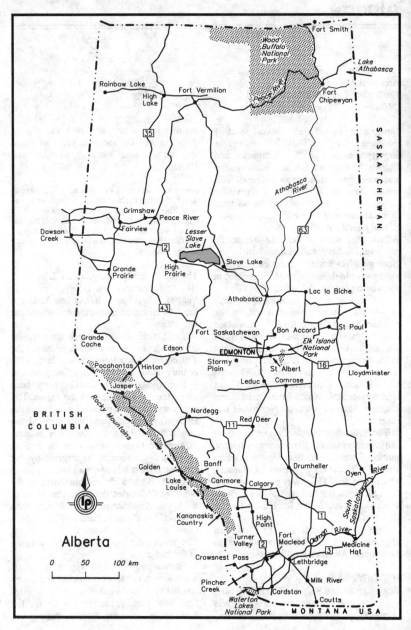

Alberta

0   50   100 km

timber were also important. The discovery of natural gas and oil in the early part of this century added to Alberta's actual and potential wealth.

In 1905 Alberta became a fully fledged province of Canada with Edmonton as its capital.

Between the World War I and II the economy and immigration slowed down. However, from 1947 further deposits of oil and natural gas were discovered. Then, with the oil crisis of the early '70s things began to change rapidly. For over a decade, people and money poured in from all parts of the country. Edmonton and Calgary became booming, modern cities – the fifth and sixth largest in the country.

In the mid '80s things took a new turn. With the fall in the price of oil and grains the boom ended and hard times came quickly to many people. Some Albertans left the province but most of those departing went back east to the homes they'd left in the middle of the Alberta boom. Still, there is a lot of wealth and potential and the province now has more political clout .

Development continues, although at a much reduced rate and, of course, things can change quickly depending on the world oil markets, especially with political instability and uncertainty in the Middle East.

Alberta's strongly independent, individualistic rancher mentality remains intact.

GEOGRAPHY & CLIMATE

Alberta has the most varied topography of any province. The east is a continuation of the Canadian prairies. The northern area is filled with rivers, lakes and forests; it's a rugged and largely inaccessible region especially in the north-east. The south-western edge of the province rises from foothills into the Rocky Mountains; while much of the rest of the south is dry and flat with badlands (barren, arid land) in some areas.

Alberta has about 2000 hours of sunshine per year – more than any other province. In winter the weather is dry, sunny and cold. However, in the south the harshness of the cold is reduced by the chinooks: warm, dry winds from the west which can quickly raise temperatures by as much as 20°C. Alberta's summers are warm. The average annual rainfall is about 450 mm, a good part of which falls between June and early August. In the mountains summers are short and it's always cool at night.

The weather in August and September makes it a particularly good time for travelling.

FLORA & FAUNA

On the prairies the vegetation consists mainly of grasses interspersed with cactuses and sagebrush, while in the Rockies and the north of the province varieties of coniferous forest predominate. A common sight is the wild rose, Alberta's official symbol.

In the rivers and lakes the numerous varieties of fish include pike, whitefish and trout. Birds are represented by the bald eagle, golden eagle, ptarmigan, raven, magpie, chickadee, nuthatch, gray jay and loon. Alberta is home to many mammals including the black and grizzly bear, wolf, coyote, lynx, fox, bison, moose, caribou, mountain goat, bighorn sheep and deer.

Chinook
The chinook is a warm, dry, south-westerly, winter wind which blows off the eastern slopes of the Rocky Mountains. The name is derived from the Chinook Indians who lived along the north-west Pacific coast, mainly in what is now Washington state. In the days of the fur trade a language developed which mixed Chinook and other Native Indian words with French and English and was known as Chinook jargon.

In British Columbia (as well as Oregon and Washington states) chinook is also the name given to a Pacific salmon (elsewhere called spring, quinnat, king or tyee salmon). ∎

Dall ram

National & Provincial Parks

Alberta has five national parks three of which are in the Rocky Mountains: Banff, Jasper and Waterton Lakes. Wood Buffalo National Park, the largest and least accessible, is in the far north-east while Elk Island National Park, the smallest, is just east of Edmonton.

Camping in the parks operates on a first come, first served basis and sites cost between $6 and $16 depending on the facilities available.

For more information contact Information Services (☎ (403) 292-4511), Canadian Parks Service, PO Box 2989, Station M, Calgary T2P 3H8. There are also information centres in the main townsite in each park.

There are over 100 parks and recreation areas throughout Alberta run by the provincial government and offering camping and a range of outdoor activities. For information get in touch with Visitors Services Branch (☎

(403) 427-9429), Alberta Recreation & Parks, 10405 Jasper Ave, Edmonton T5J 3N4.

Alberta Forest Service has set aside recreation areas and campgrounds within the government forest land (covering nearly 390,000 sq km) that it administers. For details contact Forest Land Use Branch (☎ (403) 427-3582), Alberta Forest Service, Recreation Section, 9920 108th St, Edmonton T5K 2C9.

ECONOMY

As well as oil and natural gas Alberta makes money by mining minerals especially coal, and by harvesting its widespread forests for timber and pulp. The processing of these products forms the basis of its manufacturing industries. Alberta also has a strong agricultural sector resting on wheat, barley, rye and beef. Tourism is the third most important source of revenue.

TOURIST OFFICES
Local Tourist Offices

Tourism Alberta is the provincial government body that oversees Alberta's tourism industry and operates a network of tourist offices called Visitor Information Centres. Its two main offices are in Edmonton and Calgary with another one in Ottawa, Ontario; their addresses are:

Main Level, City Centre Building, 10155 102nd St, Edmonton T5J 4L6 (☎ 427-4321)
Government Centre South, McDougall School, 455 6th St SW, Calgary T2P 4E8 (☎ 297-6574)Suite 1110, 90 Sparks St, Ottawa K1P 5B4 (☎ 237-2615)

Overseas Representatives

Tourism Alberta also has five offices abroad:

Hong Kong
    Room 1003-4, Admiralty Centre, Tower 2, Harcourt Rd, Central Hong Kong (☎ 284-729)
Japan
    Alberta Office, 17th Floor, New Aoyama Building (West), 1-1 1-chome, Minamiaoyama, Minato-Ku, Tokyo 107 (☎ 475-1171)

UK
1 Mount St, Berkeley Square, London W1Y 5AA
(☎ 491-3430)

USA
3535 333 South Grand Ave, Los Angeles, California 90071 (☎ 625-1256)
27th Floor, General Motors Building, 267 5th Ave, New York City, New York 10153 (☎ 759-2222)

INFORMATION
Money
Visitors can take advantage of the lowest gasoline prices in Canada and the lack of any provincial consumer sales tax. There is, however, a 5% tax on accommodation.

Time
Alberta is on Mountain Standard Time, one hour behind Saskatchewan and Manitoba.

Telephone
The telephone area code for Alberta is 403; in an emergency call ☎ 911.

ACTIVITIES
With its mountains, rivers, lakes and forested wilderness areas Alberta provides plenty of opportunities for outdoor recreational activities. Tourism Alberta's free brochure, *Alberta Adventure Guide*, has a list of companies offering fishing, horse riding, cycling, white-water rafting, rock climbing and mountaineering. It's available from any Visitor Information Centre.

There are lots of hiking and cycling trails in the national and provincial parks and in other recreation areas such as Kananaskis Country. One of the more spectacular cycling routes is the Icefields Parkway between Banff and Jasper. The leaflet *Trail Bicycling in National Parks in Alberta & British Columbia* lists trails where cycling is allowed. Edmonton and Calgary have also set aside trails within their city boundaries for hiking and cycling.

Tourism Alberta has produced a map showing canoe routes in the province. Some of the more popular places are the lakes and rivers in Banff, Jasper, Waterton Lakes and Wood Buffalo national parks and Writing-on-Stone Provincial Park. In Jasper National Park there is white-water rafting on the Athabasca, Maligne and Sunwapta rivers.

The best downhill skiing areas are Nakiska in Kananaskis Country, Mt Norquay and Sunshine Village in Banff National Park and Marmot Basin in Jasper National Park. Many of the hiking trails in the national and provincial parks become cross-country ski trails in winter.

The Rocky Mountains provide plenty of challenges for the climber.

ACCOMMODATION
Campers should get a copy of the *Alberta Campground Guide*, a free brochure available at Visitor Information Centres. It gives an alphabetical listing of places and the campgrounds, both government and private, in those locations. Also available is the *Alberta Accommodation Guide* which lists hotels and motels in the province. Both are published annually.

The Canadian Hostelling Association (CHA) has 16 hostels in Alberta. For information about CHA hostels in southern Alberta contact Southern Alberta Hostelling Association (☎ 283-5551), 203 1414 Kensington Rd NW, Calgary T2N 3P9. For northern Alberta contact Northern Alberta Hostelling Association (☎ 439-3089), 10926 88th Ave, Edmonton T6E 0Z1.

A number of B&B agencies operate a booking service in the province. These are:

B&B – Alberta's Gem
Mrs Betty Mitchell, 11216 48th Ave, Edmonton T6H 0C7 (☎ 434-6098) – has B&Bs throughout the province
Big Country B&B
Jim & Marj Patterson, PO Box 1027, Drumheller T0J 0Y0 (☎ 533-2203) – has places in the Drumheller region
Edmonton B&B
Pat & Dave Yearwood, 13824 110A Ave, Edmonton T5M 2M9 (☎ 445-2297) – offers accommodation in Banff, Calgary, Edmonton, Hinton and Jasper
High Country B&B Bureau
Doug Lyon, PO Box 611, Turner Valley T0L 2A0 (☎ 933-4714) – offers accommodation in the south-west of the province

Trails West B&B Agency
  Bruce Haig, 1115 8th Ave South, Lethbridge (☎ 328-9011) – covers the Lethbridge area

One agency operates out of Vancouver: Alberta B&B (☎ (604) 682-4610), c/o Mrs June Brown, PO Box 15477, Vancouver, British Columbia V6B 5B2. For the agencies that deal specifically with Edmonton and Calgary see Places to Stay in those cities.

Edmonton

Edmonton, like Calgary and the west in general, is in a period of reassessment after a series of fluctuating fortunes. Once known as 'The Gateway to the North' its title changed to 'Oil Capital of Canada' in the 1970s when the entire province boomed. Calgary had the head offices and oil management but Edmonton had the technicians, the scientists and the wells – some 7000 of them within a 160-km radius.

They were heady days. Edmonton, Alberta's largest city, experienced explosive growth; the downtown area was totally transformed and modernised. Towards the end of the 1980s there was a dramatic downturn in the oil business and the two main cities consequently eased up on development and began to forge new identities in a less hectic atmosphere.

The city averages over six hours of sun per day. Summers are short, generally dry and warm with daytime temperatures averaging 22°C. In January, the coldest month, the average daytime high is -11°C.

History
Until the arrival of White explorers and fur traders in the late 18th century the area had been populated by the Cree and Blackfoot nations for over 5000 years.

In 1795 the Hudson's Bay Company built Fort Edmonton, which grew as a fur-trading centre until about 1870, when the Canadian government bought the land from the company and opened up the area for pio-

neers. By 1891 the railway had arrived from Calgary and in 1892 Edmonton was officially incorporated as a town, then in 1904 as a city. In 1905, with the creation of Alberta, Edmonton – then with 8000 residents – became the capital. With the discovery of gold in the Yukon in 1897, Edmonton was the last outpost of civilisation for many gold seekers coming overland on their way north to the Klondike. In 1938, North America's first mosque was built here by 34 Muslims. WW II brought a large influx of people, mainly to work on the Alaska Highway.

It was in the late 1940s and '50s that real development in Edmonton began, when wells started hitting oil with great regularity. The rise in oil prices in the early '70s gave a further boost to development and brought a dramatic change in the city skyline.

The rapid changes to the city caused some problems that still continue. Many of the city's 25,000 Native Indians have little education or job training and the changes made life harder for them in particular. However, the establishment of educational programmes has meant more of these people are completing high school and going on to trade school or college. Despite the lack of much physical evidence around town, the city does have a fairly long history and the indigenous people played a major part in it.

Greater Edmonton now has a population of nearly 800,000 and many of the newcomers, from many different cultures, consider themselves Edmontonians. The steep prices of the '70s and early '80s have levelled off and the cultural life of the city has grown noticeably.

Orientation
From Edmonton the Rocky Mountains are about 300 km to the west, the lake country and Alaska Highway are to the north, Lloydminster in Saskatchewan is to the east and Calgary to the south. The North Saskatchewan River, which starts in the Columbia Icefield in the Rocky Mountains, drifts through the centre of town.

All avenues go east-west; streets run north-south.

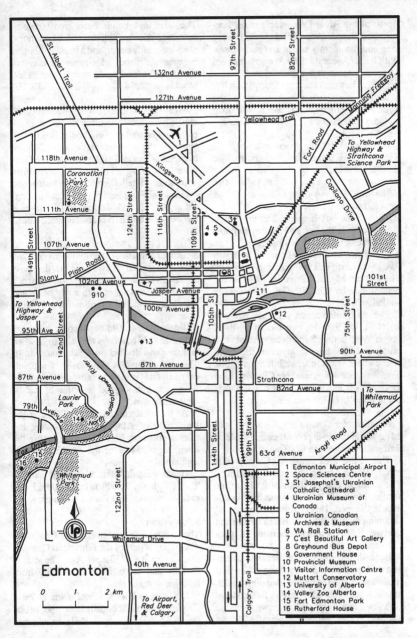

Edmonton

0   1   2 km

To Airport,
Red Deer
& Calgary

1 Edmonton Municipal Airport
2 Space Sciences Centre
3 St Josephat's Ukrainian
   Catholic Cathedral
4 Ukrainian Museum of
   Canada
5 Ukrainian Canadian
   Archives & Museum
6 VIA Rail Station
7 C'est Beautiful Art Gallery
8 Greyhound Bus Depot
9 Government House
10 Provincial Museum
11 Visitor Information Centre
12 Muttart Conservatory
13 University of Alberta
14 Valley Zoo Alberta
15 Fort Edmonton Park
16 Rutherford House

North of the River Edmonton's main thoroughfare, Jasper Ave (101st Ave), is very long and has mainly stores and restaurants. Both Jasper Ave and 102nd Ave go west from downtown through a middle-class residential area. They then lead into Stony Plain Rd, a commercial strip which becomes the Yellowhead Highway to Jasper. The strip includes motels and lots of fast-food restaurants.

North-west of the downtown area off Kingsway Ave is the municipal airport. The northern boundary of the airport is the Yellowhead Trail, which joins the Yellowhead Highway east to Saskatoon and west to Jasper.

Though the city is spread out, the downtown core with the bus and railway stations, restaurants and hotels is quite small. The central downtown area is bounded by 104th Ave to the north and 100th Ave to the south. The western edge is marked by 109th St, the eastern side by 95th St. The area is easily walkable.

The main intersection is Jasper Ave and 101st St. On 99th St, two blocks north of Jasper Ave, is the civic centre with several municipal buildings. Opposite the civic centre is Sir Winston Churchill Square, one block north of which is where City Hall used to stand – it has been pulled down and is being rebuilt. To the east are the art gallery and law courts.

Another block north to 104th Ave will bring you to the main post office and the VIA Rail station below the CN Tower.

This entire area consists of many mirrored, 1970s-design, high-rise buildings. The southern end of 100th St is the office section. Many of Canada's banks have buildings in the area. This is also the theatre and shopping district, with the Eaton Centre and the large Edmonton Centre housing all types of stores.

Beneath the downtown area are underground pedestrian walkways called 'pedways' which connect shopping malls, hotels, restaurants and the VIA Rail station.

A few blocks east of downtown there are a couple of sleazy streets, especially 96th St.

The bars and hotels here aren't recommended. Along 97th St are pawnshops, cash-for-goods stores, and a number of other inexpensive places which may or may not prove useful for the odd item or two. A few blocks further will take you to the CHA Hostel.

West a few blocks from Sir Winston Churchill Square are a number of hotels in all price ranges, and the Greyhound Bus Depot. West of the downtown centre, 124th St between 102nd and 109th Aves is an expensive shopping district, with fashion boutiques, art galleries and a few bistros and restaurants. From behind the Hotel Macdonald at 100th St and McDougall Hill, there is a good view of the river and southern side of Edmonton.

South of the River Across the river, 82nd Ave, also called Whyte Ave, is the main street. On 82nd Ave around 104th St there's a mini-downtown area with many stores and restaurants, including numerous Chinese ones.

To the east is Old Strathcona, a district with many old buildings that date from when this area was distinct from Edmonton itself. The area underwent some low-key redevelopment and is a very agreeable part of Edmonton with a good selection of restaurants and shops.

At the western end of 82nd Ave is the University of Alberta, and following the river south-west, Fort Edmonton, where the town began. Most of the southern side is residential.

Heading south, 104th St joins the Calgary Trail (Highway 2) which leads to the international airport, Red Deer, and Calgary.

Information

The central Visitor Information Centre (☎ 422-5505) is part of the Edmonton Convention Centre at 9797 Jasper Ave. The staff is friendly and the office is open daily from 8.30 am to 4.30 pm.

In Gateway Park south of town, at 2404 Calgary Trail northbound, is another office (☎ 988-5455). It's open daily in summer from 8 am to 9 pm; in winter Monday to Friday from 8.30 am to 4.30 pm and weekends from 9.30 am to 5 pm. Offices are also open in summer only, on the Yellowhead Highway east and west of town.

For information on other parts of Alberta, contact Alberta Tourism (☎ 427-4321; 800-222-6501 when you are in Alberta; 800-661-8888 from continental USA) Main Level, City Centre Building, 10155 102nd St.

The main post office (☎ 495-3100), 9808 103A Ave on the corner of 99th St, is open Monday to Friday from 8 am to 5.45 pm. Edmonton General Hospital (☎ 482-8111) is at 11111 Jasper Ave. The major banks have branches on Jasper Ave.

Parking is a problem in downtown Edmonton but you can get a map from the Visitor Information Centres giving the location of parking lots.

If you're looking for temporary work there are lots of personnel agencies listed in the yellow pages. One you could try is Northern Alberta Personnel (☎ 471-5197), 11109 95th St.

Note that on Sunday, many places are closed in Edmonton.

Consulates Some countries with diplomatic representation in Edmonton are:

Germany
  2500 CN Tower, 10004 104 Ave (☎ 422-6175/76/77)
Italy
  1240 Standard Life Centre, 10405 Jasper Ave (☎ 423-5153)
Japan
  2480 Manulife Place, 10180 101st St (☎ 422-3752)
Netherlands
  Suite 930, Phipps McKinnon Bldg, 10020 101A Ave (☎ 428-7513)

Walking Tours

If you'd like to explore the city on foot get a copy of the free booklet *Historical Walking Tours of Downtown Edmonton* from the Visitor Information Centre. It has four walking tours of the downtown area with maps and descriptions of the buildings you pass en route.

Parks

On each side of the North Saskatchewan River, which flows in a north-easterly direction through the centre of the city, is parkland. This appears to be one long park, though it's actually a series of small parks joined together. You can walk, jog or cycle all day along the system using the many trails and bridges. In **Whitemud Park**, south-west of downtown, and **Strathcona Science Park** north-east of town, are nature paths which become cross-country ski trails in winter. Whitemud Park also has a hang-gliding area. Throughout the parkland are dozens of picnic spots. One of the easiest ways to get there from town is to head south on 75th street and then turn right (west) along Whitemud Drive.

Many of the city's other sights are in this green belt area.

Provincial Museum

This excellent museum (☎ 427-1730), 12845 102nd Ave west of downtown, is well laid out with exhibits artistically displayed. The natural history section describes the natural forces which have shaped Alberta and the life forms, such as dinosaurs, that lived in the region millions of years ago. It has a large display of fossils and minerals. The habitat section shows animals and birds living in Alberta today in incredibly realistic settings.

The anthropology section covers the Native Indians of Alberta, their way of life and relationship with nature. There are drawings, photos and examples of various plants and how they used them for medicine, spice, tea and smoking; and of how feathers, animal hide and bark were used to decorate clothing and dwellings. Other displays include amulets incorporating the wearer's umbilical cord and many artefacts and crafts.

The history area covers the pioneer days and settlement of Alberta.

The museum also has frequent cultural shows and dancing, and free film pro-

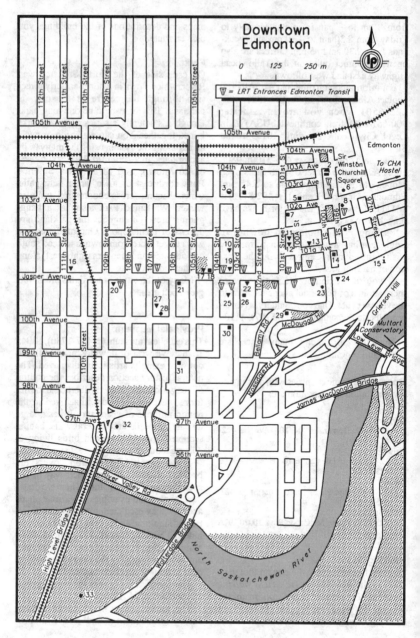

Downtown Edmonton

0   125   250 m

▽ = LRT Entrances Edmonton Transit

■ PLACES TO STAY

4	Grand Hotel
5	YMCA
7	Hilton International
14	Westin Hotel
18	Hotel Cecil
21	Best Western Ambassador Motor Inn
26	Alberta Place Hotel
29	Chateau Lacombe
30	YWCA
31	Royal Park Hotel

▼ PLACES TO EAT

10	Boardwalk Market
11	Bistro Praha
12	Mongolian Food Experience
13	Sherlock Holmes
16	Michael's Deli & Bar
17	Tivoli Gardens
19	Russian Tea Room
20	Mayfair Hotel
22	Silk Hat
24	Hotel Macdonald
25	Schnitzelhouse
27	Inn on 7th

OTHER

1	VIA Rail Station
2	Main Post Office
3	Greyhound Bus Depot
6	Edmonton Art Gallery
8	Chancery Hall Civic Centre
9	Citadel Theatre
15	Visitor Information Centre
23	AGT Tower
28	David Copperfield Pub
32	Alberta Legislature
33	John Walter Historic Site

grammes. To get there, take bus Nos 1 or 2 west along Jasper Ave. In summer it's open daily from 9 am to 8 pm; in winter it's open Tuesday to Sunday (except Wednesday) from 9 am to 5 pm, Wednesday from 9 am to 8 pm and is closed on Monday. Admission is free.

Government House
This is the large and impressive structure beside the museum, used for government conferences. It can be visited on Sundays. For information call ☎ 427-7362.

Alberta Legislature
The Alberta Legislature (☎ 427-7362), on the corner of 97th Ave and 109th St, is built on the site of the original Fort Edmonton. A beautiful Edwardian building from 1912, it is surrounded by fountains and manicured lawns overlooking the river. Its dome has remained one of the permanent landmarks of Edmonton. Free tours are given daily, offering interesting details about the building and the government. The tours start from a very Italianate lobby with marble walls and columns and last about half an hour. They begin at noon on weekends, 9 am weekdays. To get there catch bus No 43 west along 100th Ave.

Fort Edmonton Park
On the southern side of the river over the Quesnell Bridge off Fox Drive, in Fort Edmonton Park (☎ 435-0755), is a reconstruction of the **old Hudson's Bay Company fort** and the surrounding town, circa 1885. The fort contains the entire post of 1846 which was built to promote the fur trade (not as a military fort), and was presided over by Chief Factor John Rowland, head of Saskatchewan District from 1828 to 1854. It lacks some authentic feel but the carpentry, meant to re-create the times through furniture, tools and constructions, is excellent.

Outside the fort is a street re-creating downtown Edmonton between 1871 and 1891, when the railway arrived. It's quite interesting, with good explanations of the buildings, though hard to visualise as the early Jasper Ave. Along the wooden sidewalks are examples of the various merchants and their goods. A newspaper office and a schoolhouse are represented. Check all the cabinets, bottles and vials in the chemist's. Rides on the train and horse-trailer are included in tickets, which cost $5 and $2.50 for children.

From the middle of May to the end of June Fort Edmonton is open Monday to Friday from 9.30 am to 4.30 pm, weekends from 10 am to 6 pm; July to early September it's open daily from 10 am to 6 pm; till early October on Sundays and holidays it's open from 11 am to 5 pm. It's closed in winter.

To get there take bus Nos 32 or 132 west along 102A Ave or south on 101st St.

On the grounds beside the fort is the **John Janzen Nature Centre** (☎ 428-7900) where you'll find a few examples of both living and dead local animals, insects and reptiles. You'll see educational exhibits in simulated natural environments – best is the live bee display. In summer the centre's open daily from 10 am to 6 pm. Admission is free.

Valley Zoo

North-east of Fort Edmonton Park, this zoo (☎ 483-5511) in Laurier Park at the southern end of Buena Vista Rd has about 500 animals and birds, but it's mainly a children's zoo with models of storybook characters. It's open daily in summer from 10 am to 6 pm and admission is $3.50, children $1.75.

Vista 33

This is the name of the observation deck (☎ 493-3333), on the 33rd floor of the AGT Tower at 10020 100th St, which is the head office of Alberta General Telephones. On clear days you can peer out over 6475 sq km of the flat land surrounding Edmonton. Nearly a third of the population of Alberta lives in the area viewed. You also get a good view of the downtown area and the river valley. It's open every day from 10 am to 8 pm and entry is only 50 cents. Included in the price, and on the same floor, is a small but interesting museum of telecommunication equipment, including old telephones and switchboards. Some of the exhibits are meant to be played with, in an attempt to expose the magic of the hardware.

Muttart Conservatory

South of the river off James Macdonald Bridge, the Muttart Conservatory (☎ 428-5226), 9626 96A St, is comprised of four glass pyramids, three large and one small. Each contains a different climate and the plants that go with it; one is desert, one temperate, one tropical while the fourth has regularly changing exhibitions to mark the changing seasons. If you walk up the hills you can look without going in, but you miss the best part – the feel and smell. The conservatory is open from 11 am to 9 pm daily and costs $3. It's on bus routes Nos 45 and 51.

There are some interesting photos to be taken of the conservatory and it offers good views of the city.

Police Museum

This small museum (☎ 421-2274) is on the 3rd floor of the police headquarters building at 9620 103A St, downtown. Using artefacts, historical notes, uniforms and photographs, it tells something of the history of the Royal Canadian Mounted Police (RCMP) which formed in 1873, as well as that of the local city police department. Included in the displays are firearms, handcuffs, an old jail cell and even a preserved rat which became an early RCMP mascot. It's open Tuesday to Saturday from 10 am to 3 pm and admission is free.

Aviation Hall of Fame

This is a an extensive collection of models, photos, displays, films and biographies of important figures in Canadian aviation. On display is the country's first commercial flight simulator, an exact duplicate of a Douglas DC-6B cockpit. It's in the Edmonton Convention Centre, 9797 Jasper Ave. Admission is free and it's open daily. Call ☎ 424-2458 for information.

Space Sciences Centre

The Space Sciences Centre (☎ 452-9100) is west of town at 11211 142nd St in Coronation Park.

The city **planetarium** presents multimedia programmes on the solar system and universe. The shows are entertaining, educational and life-like. IMAX (large-format cinema) has a film theatre here as well, with changing films. Rock music laser shows are offered frequently in the **Margaret Ziedler Star Theatre**.

The centre also has galleries using photographs, video, film and hands-on exhibits to explain or show various aspects of the planets, the history of astronomy and stargazing equipment. Don't miss seeing the Bruderheim meteorite which fell near Edmonton in 1960. It's 4.6 billion years old – older than any rock on earth; as old as the solar system itself. There's a small science shop with some fun little items and a cafeteria.

The galleries are free but there are admission charges for the rest; the IMAX theatre is $4.50, laser shows cost $5.50 and a combination ticket costs $7.

Outside, an **observatory** permits sun and star observation when the sky is clear, and is free. Next door to the Space Sciences Centre the indoor **Coronation Swimming Pool**, is open to the public in the afternoons. There are also picnic tables in the grounds.

Catch bus No 22 to Westmount west on Jasper Ave near the corner of 103rd St; it takes you to within a block or so of Coronation Park.

Art Galleries
At 2 Sir Winston Churchill Square, the **Edmonton Art Gallery** (☎ 422-6223), is part of the civic centre and has changing exhibits which are well spaced and lit. Mainly modern Canadian painting is displayed, with some works from the USA. One room shows a few samples of Canadian work from the late 1800s to the present. Photography exhibitions are also presented. It's open Monday to Wednesday from 10.30 am to 5 pm, Thursday and Friday until 8 pm and weekends and holidays from 11 am to 5 pm. Admission is $2 or $1 for students; it's free on Thursday after 4 pm.

At 10116 124th St on the corner of Jasper Ave **C'est Beautiful** (☎ 482-6757), is one of a number of smaller galleries in Edmonton. It shows the work of Alberta artists and is open Tuesday to Saturday from 11 am to 5.30 pm. Admission is free.

John Walter Historic Site
This site (☎ 428-3033), 10627 93rd Ave, comprises four historic buildings, including the first home south of the river and Edmonton's first telegraph station. It's open daily in summer from 12 noon to 5 pm and admission is free.

Rutherford House
This house (☎ 427-3993), 11153 Saskatchewan Drive was built by Alexander Rutherford, the first premier of Alberta. Completed in 1911, the mansion is said to symbolise the end of the pioneer architectural style. The building has been restored and contains many antiques. Admission is free and it's open daily in summer from 10 am to 6 pm, in winter from 12 noon to 5 pm. Several buses service the campus including Nos 32 and 35.

St Josephat's Ukrainian Catholic Cathedral
This church – one of a number of Ukrainian churches in the Edmonton area – on 97th St on the corner of 108th Ave is worth a visit. With its rounded domes outside, it'll remind you of Turkey, whether you've been there or not. Inside the Byzantine structure, pastel paintings cover the walls. Check the figure on the ceiling in front of the altar. There's a lot of gilt-work here, including the large screen in front of the altar.

Ukrainian Museums
The **Ukrainian Museum of Canada** (☎ 483-5932), 10611 110th Ave, has a small collection of costumes, Easter eggs, dolls and very fine tapestries. In summer it's open Monday to Friday from 9 am to 4 pm, on Sunday from 2 to 5 pm and admission is free. Catch bus Nos 41 or 42 north on 101st St.

Close by, the **Ukrainian Canadian Archives & Museum** (☎ 424-7580), 9543 110th Ave, has a library, archives and artefacts of Ukrainian culture. It's open Monday to Saturday from 1 to 5 pm. Admission is free.

West Edmonton Mall
If you thought a shopping centre as a sight to visit had no place in this guidebook, think again. The West Edmonton Mall (☎ 444-5200), 8770 170th St on the corner of 87th Ave, is really something else; it's so overwhelming it's worth taking a look. More than just the world's largest shopping mall and largest indoor water park, it's a self-contained city complete with roof. You could live inside for years.

There are over 800 stores, a hotel, an amusement park, a water park with beach, an ice rink, a mini-golf course, cinemas, submarines in simulated oceans, restaurants galore and lots more, plus thousands of people. A few highlights are the Drop of Doom, a ride in Fantasyland guaranteed to put your stomach in your mouth (and that's just watching!), the pool complex with slides and waves, the ice rink with skate rentals and the ersatz New Orleans Bourbon St, complete with statues of prostitutes.

If you get too tired to make it around everything you can rent yourself a little powered scooter.

City buses, such as Nos 10 and 12 and an express run, do the trip from downtown in about 25 minutes.

Wild Waters Aquatic Park
This water-slide complex (☎ 447-4476) is at 21512 103rd Ave (Yellowhead Highway west). It's open daily in summer from 10 am to 7 pm. Admission is $9, children $7.

Farmers' Market
This city food market is in downtown Edmonton on the corner of 102nd Ave and 97th St. It's best on Saturday.

Strathcona
The area south of the river, by 82nd Ave and 106th St, was once the town of Strathcona. It amalgamated with Edmonton in 1912. Though now absorbed into the city, this area is rich in historical buildings dating from 1891. There are about 75 houses built prior to 1926 in the residential district and about

40 buildings of note in what was the commercial core.

You can pick up a walking-tour map of the district at the Visitor Information Centre or the Old Strathcona Foundation Office (☎ 433-5866) at 8520 104th St. The tour will take you past the old railway station, a hotel, movie theatre, church and many other gems. Along 82nd Ave from 103rd St to 105th St has been spruced up with brick sidewalks, old-style lampposts, etc. It's an area with numerous cafés, restaurants, buskers, street vendors and several bookshops and is a pleasant change from the high-rise buildings of the downtown area.

Activities
For information on park and recreation facilities like swimming pools, skating and skiing areas or bicycle paths, call Edmonton Parks & Recreation (☎ 428-3559).

The Kinsmen Sports Centre (☎ 428-4195), 9100 Walterdale Hill, has public swimming and other programmes. Admission is $3.

Mill Woods Recreation Centre (☎ 428-2888), 7207 28th Ave, has saunas, ball courts and other facilities. It's open daily in the summer from 1 to 5 pm and from 6 to 9 pm. Admission is $4.

You can go hot-air ballooning up to 300 metres – every day if the weather is fine – with Windship Aviation (☎ 438-0111), at 5615 103A St.

Edmonton has an extensive network of bicycle routes and the best area to cycle is on the paths by the river. A map showing these routes is available from the Visitor Information Centre.

Organised Tours Royal Tours (☎ 424-8687), Suite 600, 1 Thornton Court on the corner of Jasper Ave and 99th St, offers three tours of Edmonton. The 2½-hour tour of the city visits the Alberta Legislature, the university and Old Strathcona and costs $13. The 3½-hour tour goes out to the Provincial Museum and Fort Edmonton and costs $18. The day tour combines the two and costs $27.

On summer Sundays and holiday afternoons Edmonton Transit operates the Discovery Run, on bus No 123, for the basic fare. This route takes a circular tour of Edmonton, passing many of the city's sights, including the Provincial Museum, Fort Edmonton and the university.

Huckleberry Tours (☎ 441-1740) offers trips along the river for $12.

The Edmonton CHA Hostel (☎ 429-0140) organises group outings on an ad hoc basis.

Festivals
The Klondike Days This is Edmonton's biggest festival and is held towards the end of July. The event celebrates a less than honourable period in Edmonton's history when, in the gold rush days of 1898, unscrupulous entrepreneurs lured gold seekers to the city with tales of a trail, the Klondike Trail, from Edmonton to Dawson City in the Yukon, which didn't really exist. Many people didn't make it through and some returned to settle in Edmonton.

During the festival, locals dress up the streets, the stores and themselves in period style; stages dot the road and are alive with singers and dancers; parades run through the streets; the Northlands Coliseum presents nightly entertainment of rock, pop or country & western music; a Klondike village, with old-time stores and a gambling saloon, is set up in Northlands Park; and the Citadel Theatre puts on 'heroes & villains' melodramas. The street festivities last five days; the Northlands Park exhibition goes on for another five. Contact the Edmonton Klondike Days Association (☎ 426-40555), 10020 101A Ave, for information.

Folk Music Festival In early August the city holds a Folk Music Festival in Gallagher Park with blues, jazz, country & western and bluegrass as well as traditional folk music. Ask at the Visitor Information Centre.

Fringe Theatre Event Well worth catching is the Fringe Theatre Event, a nine-day programme that brings all kinds of live alternative theatre to the public with over 800 performances of 150 productions in 14 theatres, in the parks and on the streets. Many of the performances are free and theatre tickets cost only around $7; there's no booking, you choose a theatre and stand in line. The festival takes place in Old Strathcona around the middle of August. For information contact Chinook Theatre (☎ 448-9000), 10329 83rd Ave, or ask at the Visitor Information Centre.

Places to Stay
Camping There are several camping areas close to town. Some of them, run by the Alberta government, are free.

Ardrossan Campground, 18 km east of Edmonton on the Yellowhead Highway, has 24 free campsites. There are firepits but nothing else, and no water. Similar is *Bretona Campground*, 18 km south-east of Edmonton on Highway 14 at the junction of Highway 21; it has 28 free campsites with no facilities other than picnic tables and fireplaces.

The privately owned *Half Moon Lake Resort* (☎ 922-3045) 21524 Twp Rd, Sherwood Park, charges $10 for a site but has every convenience including showers and laundry. The resort is very large and there is swimming on the lake. It's 29 km south-east of Edmonton; follow 82nd Ave east to Wye Rd, then head south.

Hostels *Edmonton CHA Hostel* (☎ 429-0140), 10422 91st St, is within walking distance of downtown. It has a well-equipped kitchen, a view across the river to the southern side of Edmonton and a pub across the road. It sells a few basic staples and issues transit daily passes on Edmonton's public transport system for $3.25. There is a midnight curfew, but it's not strictly enforced especially when the Folk Music Festival and Fringe Theatre Event are on. The phone is open 24 hours but only ring after midnight if you're stranded. You can pit your wits at Trivial Pursuit with the staff! They might even be able to tell you where to find work. A dorm bed costs $9 for members,

$13 for nonmembers. Check in before 10 am and after 5 pm.

To get there from downtown, walk east on Jasper Ave or 103rd Ave (which eventually turns into Jasper Ave anyway) to 91st St. The hostel is down a few doors on the left. Between the downtown area and the hostel are a couple of run-down blocks which are not great at night, especially for women alone.

The central *YMCA* (☎ 421-9622), 10030 102A Ave opposite the Edmonton Centre, is close to the Greyhound Bus Depot and VIA Rail station and takes in men and women. Singles/doubles cost from $24/$32 with a $10 key deposit. There's also dormitory accommodation, a TV room, swimming pool and a very cheap cafeteria which is open from 6 am.

The *YWCA* (☎ 423-4922), 10305 100th Ave on the corner of 103rd St, is also central. It takes women only and charges from $7 in a dorm, $20 for a single or, with a private bath, $28. Sheets are supplied in all the rooms. There's a good, cheap cafeteria that anyone can use.

The *University of Alberta*, in south-west Edmonton, rents out rooms in the summer in Lister Hall opposite the Jubilee Auditorium. It has good facilities and cheap cafeterias. The rates are $25/34, cheaper if you're a student and weekly/monthly rates are available. Contact the Conference Coordinator (☎ 492-7200), 44 Lister Hall on the corner of 87th Ave and 116th St. On the university campus *St Joseph's College* (☎ 492-7681), on the corner of 89th Ave and 114th St, also rents out rooms.

B&Bs Two B&B agencies which keep a changing list of participants in and around Edmonton are:

Agency Holiday Home Accommodation
     10808 54th Ave (☎ 436-0649/4796)
Edmonton Holiday Home Association
     58 6220 172nd St (☎ 487-8371), rooms cost around $30/40.

Hotels – bottom end Edmonton is not blessed with a great selection of cheap central hotels. There are a few basic, torn-around-the-edges places which may fill your bill.

The *Grand Hotel* (☎ 422-6365), 10266 103rd St on the corner of 103rd Ave, is very central, right beside the bus depot. For singles/doubles with bath you'll pay $25.20/28.35. The hotel is very clean and all rooms have colour TV. There's a bar downstairs with snacks and a TV. The rooms are mainly used permanently rather than for overnighters.

Hotel Cecil (☎ 428-7001), 10406 Jasper Ave, is a little rougher, especially in the bar. It's old and worn but clean, and the rooms are fine. Some have a bath; all have sinks and are comfortable. Singles/doubles start from $21/24; rooms with shower cost $24/27. Downstairs there's a friendly, cheap restaurant.

West of town at the *Klondiker Hotel* (☎ 489-1906), 15326 Stony Plain Rd on the corner of 153rd St, the lobby has a gold rush feel and a mural symbolising that period. Rooms cost $25, plus $10 key deposit, and are alright. There are three bars downstairs so you won't go thirsty. The hotel is pretty popular and features live music at night.

In South Edmonton a cheapie to try is the *Strathcona Hotel* (☎ 439-1992), 10302 82nd Ave on the corner of 103rd St, which has rooms for $17.85 or $23.10 with a bath. Rooms have no TV or telephone. It's a great old timbered building dating from 1891 and is registered as an Alberta Historic Resource. A pretty good deal nearby is the *Park Hotel* (☎ 433-6441) at 8004 104th St, just south of 82nd Ave. It's in a good location and singles/doubles are $16/22 or $19/26 with a bath. The *Commercial Hotel* (☎ 439-3981), 10329 82nd Ave, has live music in the bar downstairs and costs singles/doubles $22/27.

Hotels – middle There are several apartment hotels in this price bracket. The friendly *Royal Park Hotel* (☎ 420-0209), 9835 106th St, is excellent value with singles/doubles (including kitchenette, bath, TV and phone) from $35. A grocery store is opposite and a small post office nearby. *Adventure Inn Hotel* (☎ 428-7133), 9710 105th St, has full facilities plus a gym. Singles/doubles are $49/66. More expensive is *Alberta Place Hotel* (☎ 423-1565), 10049 103rd St, but a small breakfast is thrown in and it has indoor parking. Rooms cost singles/doubles $69/77.

Weekly and monthly rates are also available at these hotels.

Hotels – top end *Chateau Lacombe* (☎ 428-6611), 10111 Bellamy Hill on the corner of 101st St, has singles/doubles for $105/120, and is close to the downtown core and has a revolving restaurant. A couple of blocks north-east next to the Citadel Theatre is the *Westin Hotel* (☎ 426-3636), 10135 100th St on the corner of 101A Ave, with singles/doubles $150/160. *Hilton International* (☎ 428-7111), 10235 101st St near the corner of 102A Ave, has singles from $139 to $185 and doubles from $159 to $200. Pedways connect the hotel with the Edmonton Centre and Eaton Centre.

Motels The bulk of the city's mid-price range accommodation is in motels. Most motels have plug-ins (electric sockets for engine heaters) for your car – a good thing for Edmonton winter mornings. There are two areas near town where most motels are located.

One area is on Stony Plain Rd and the Yellowhead Highway, west of downtown. To get to this area head out along Jasper Ave or 104th Ave which turns into Stony Plain Rd; further west, Stony Plain Rd becomes the Yellowhead Highway.

The other area is along the Calgary Trail south of the city with most of the motels there reasonably priced.

Royal Scot Motel (☎ 447-3088) is on the Yellowhead Highway, about 1½ km from Edmonton. It has singles/doubles for $32/45 or $5 extra for a kitchen. *Parkland Motel* (☎ 447-4455) is a little over three km from town on the Yellowhead Highway. It has 40 units with colour TV, priced at singles/doubles

$35/39. Closer to town *West Edmonton Motor Inn* (☎ 484-1136), 18245 Stony Plain Rd, has singles/doubles from $38/45 to $45/60. Weekly rates are available, as is a laundrette.

South of town try the *Derrick Motel* (☎ 434-1402), 3925 Calgary Trail, which has singles/doubles for $30/35. Kitchenette and waterbeds are available. *Chateau Motel* (☎ 988-6661), 1414 Calgary Trail, has 40 units with colour TV and telephone; a kitchenette is extra. Singles/doubles cost $35/45.

There are a couple of other motels worth mentioning. *Beverly Motel* (☎ 479-3923), 4403 118th Ave, is small with just 12 rooms but cheap at singles/doubles $28/32. *Best Western Ambassador Motor Inn* (☎ 423-1925), 10041 106th St, on the other hand, is more up-market with full facilities including cable TV, air-con, restaurant, cocktail lounge and pub. Singles/doubles cost $47/49.

There are many other motels besides these.

Places to Eat – bottom end
The *cafeteria* in the Alberta Legislature serves plain, decent food at the best prices in town. It's open Monday to Friday from 7 am to 4 pm, with lunches from 11.30 am to 1.30 pm. *Sarah Golden Cafeteria* in the YWCA is open daily to both men and women, resident or not. There's not a lot of choice but prices are good: breakfast of egg, toast, bacon and hash browns costs $2.50. The *YMCA cafeteria*, open Monday to Friday from 7 am to 6.30 pm, is similar.

The *Silk Hat*, 10251 Jasper Ave, opened in 1940 and was one of Edmonton's first restaurants. It still has the old, small wall-jukeboxes at the booths and is a hang-out for a lot of local characters. It has good prices: breakfast specials such as eggs, toast and fries cost $2.70, sandwiches cost from $2 to $6 and pancakes from $4.30. It's open Monday to Friday from 6.30 am to 7.30 pm, Saturday from 8 am to 7.30 pm and Sunday from 11 am to 7 pm.

Tivoli Gardens, 10432 Jasper Ave, does simple food well. A cafeteria-style office-worker lunch spot, it specialises in soup and sandwich-type lunches for $3.50; breakfasts are $2. It's open Monday to Friday from 7.30 am to 5.30 pm, Saturday from 8.30 am to 3.30 pm.

Michael's Deli & Bar, on the corner of 111st St and Jasper Ave, has outdoor tables and umbrellas and is busy at lunch serving sandwiches and burgers. Scrambled eggs and ham on toast costs $3.25 and its delicious cakes are $4. It's open Monday to Friday from 7 am to 9 pm, Saturday from 9 am to 11 pm and Sunday from 9 am to 9 pm.

Across the river in Old Strathcona on the corner of 104th St and 82nd Ave, *Uncle Albert's* is popular. It has pancakes for $2, burgers for $4 to $7 and fish & chips for $6. In Strathcona Market Square along 82nd Ave at 105th St, the basement is a food mart with a bakery and various other food shops.

Places to Eat – middle

The *Russian Tea Room*, 10312 Jasper Ave, is ideal for a late afternoon pick-me-up, especially for teas, coffees, sandwiches, cakes and pastries. Bagels cost from $6, salads from $2.50 to $6, pasta dishes around $7 and cakes $3.75. It's open daily.

Where 101A Ave and 100A St meet, right in the centre of the downtown area, a small restaurant district and people-place sanctuary sits amidst all the office towers. Trees have been planted and there are benches for lingering. Most of the restaurants have outdoor sections. The *Mongolian Food Experience* is pretty good and is open daily; it has seafood dishes from $9 to $12 and vegetarian meals for around $7. Close by, the *Bistro Praha*, 10168 100A St, is a European-style spot good for coffees, cakes and pastries. Meals are about $12, salads between $3 and $4. It also serves wine by the glass. During non-meal hours it's pleasant for a coffee and a flip through a newspaper.

Nearby at 10012 101A Ave and dwarfed by the tower blocks around it, is the *Sherlock Holmes*, a British-model pub good for both food and British and locally brewed beers. A ploughman's lunch is $4.75 and steak & kidney pie $6.50. It's open daily.

Another collection of eateries can be found in the Boardwalk Market on the corner of 103rd St and 102nd Ave, a renovated old building also containing offices and stores. The *Old Spaghetti Factory* is a combined bar and restaurant with decent food at moderate prices in an interesting environment: lots of plants, Tiffany lamps and a kitchen housed in an old streetcar (tram). Spaghettis cost from $7 to $9, steak $11.50. It's open Sunday to Thursday from 4 to 10 pm, Friday and Saturday from 4 pm to midnight. Next door is *Bones* for ribs (from $8 to $13), open Monday to Friday from 11.30 am to 4 pm; and a few doors down, *La Crêperie* which offers a range of crepes for $10. There are other places here both more and less expensive. Walk through the building and have a look.

For moderately priced dinners, *Mother Tucker's*, 10184 104th St, is open daily. Dishes like baked chicken, fish or steak include vegetables, bread and a trip to the huge salad bar; prices range from $10 to $18. *Schnitzelhouse*, opposite the Alberta Place Hotel on 103rd St south of Jasper Ave, is an Austrian restaurant offering a dozen types of schnitzel. Starters cost from $3 and main courses are between $8 and $10.

In Old Strathcona there are quite a few good eating places on and around 82nd Ave. The *New York Bagel Café*, 8209 104th St next to Uncle Albert's, is recommended. This is a small, comfortable little spot serving espresso coffee, possibly the best cappuccinos in Canada and light foods, with tables on the sidewalk. About 30 metres along from there on 104th St is another busy place, the *Old Strathcona Diner*, serving sauerkraut, bratwurst and a variety of vegetarian dishes from $4 to $7. *Veggies*, 10331 82nd Ave, is a vegetarian restaurant good for lunch and dinner. Felafels are $7.50, pizzas $7.75, vegetarian shepherd's pie $8.75 and sandwiches $4.75.

One of the best eating buys in Edmonton is at one of the places with a lunch buffet or Sunday brunch. Some of the larger hotels put on big spreads at reasonable prices. Check the weekend newspapers for places and times. The *Inn on 7th* (☎ 429-2861), 10001

107th St, and *Mayfair Hotel* (☎ 423-1650), 1018 Jasper Ave, have lunch buffets every weekday. A good feed at one of these could last you till the next day's breakfast. For about $8 you can eat from a choice of hot and cold buffets. Lunch is from 11 am to 2 pm.

One traveller has recommended the *Steak & Ale Restaurant*, 14203 Stony Plain Rd, for its good food and choice of 90 Canadian and imported beers.

Places to Eat – top end

For a great view while you eat try *La Ronde*, the revolving restaurant at the top of Château Lacombe. A three-course meal here costs about $35. In Old Strathcona at 9602 82nd Ave, *Unheardof*, which serves steak, chicken and seafood is similarly priced.

Entertainment

The *Bullet* is a local entertainment paper free around town. *Nightlife*, also free, is a broadsheet listing the latest in drama, comedy and concerts.

Theatre & Nightlife Edmonton offers a wide selection of live theatre. The *Citadel Theatre* (☎ 425-1820), 9828 101A Ave, Edmonton's foremost playhouse, is actually a complex of theatres showing mainstream drama, comedy, experimental productions, concerts, lectures and films. Depending on the production, theatre tickets cost from around $7 to $25, film tickets $4. The *Chinook Theatre* (☎ 448-9000), 10329 83rd Ave, puts on experimental plays and organises the annual Fringe Theatre Event.

The *Pickwick Theatre Restaurant* in the David Copperfield Pub (☎ 424-7016), 10610 100th Ave, puts on farces and musicals at weekends. While there you could try one or more of the 14 beers on tap. The *Mayfair Hotel* also has a theatre restaurant.

Northlands Coliseum (☎ 471-2791), 7428 118th Ave on the corner of 73rd St, and *Jubilee Auditorium* (☎ 427-2760), 8700 114th St, show name acts on a regular basis. Tickets cost from around $5 to $20 for performances that range from rock music to ballet. The Jubilee Auditorium is the venue

for the Edmonton Opera and the Edmonton Symphony Orchestra (one of Canada's best).

Yuk Yuk's Komedy Kabaret (☎ 466-2131), 7103 78th Ave, has off-beat stand-up comedy from Wednesday to Saturday.

Andante, 8230 103rd St, brings in rhythm & blues and funk bands. There's a $5 cover charge. In Old Strathcona the *Commercial Hotel* (☎ 439-3981), 10329 82nd Ave, features live blues music as does the *Sidetrack*. The *Yardbird Suite* (☎ 432-1077), 10203 86th Ave, is the jazz bar in town. Admission is $4 to $8, less for students.

Laser-light concerts are held at the *Space Sciences Centre* (see earlier for details).

Cinema The *Princess Repertory Theatre* (☎ 433-5785/0979), 10337 82nd Ave near 104th St, is Edmonton's main outlet for good, varying films at below-normal cost. It shows two different films per night and charges nonmembers $4.50 for each one. On Saturdays it shows matinees but the films are mostly for kids; tickets are $1.50 for both adults and children. The cinema itself is a historic site – it was the first marble-fronted building west of Winnipeg and at one time showed first-runs of Mary Pickford films.

The *Edmonton Film Society* (☎ 488-4335 after 4 pm), 6243 112A St, regularly shows classic films in the Provincial Museum auditorium (☎ 453-9100). Tickets are $4. The *National Film Theatre* shows commercial and classic films in the Edmonton Art Gallery for the same price.

Spectator Sports If you're here during the ice hockey season, from October to April, try to see a home game of the Edmonton Oilers at Northlands Coliseum (☎ 471-2791), 7428 118th Ave on the corner of 73rd St. Tickets are $6.50 to $27.

Alternatively you could see the Edmonton Eskimos play football, from July to October, at the Commonwealth Stadium (☎ 429-2881), 11000 Stadium Rd. Tickets are $15 to $22.

Getting There & Away

Air Edmonton International Airport is

around 30 km south of the city along the Calgary Trail, about a 45-minute drive from downtown. This airport handles most flights. Edmonton Municipal Airport, three km north of downtown off 97th St near 118th Ave, is generally used for smaller planes and therefore shorter flights, particularly within Alberta. City buses run between here and town.

Edmonton is well served by airlines. Canadian Airlines (☎ 428-8525) and Air Canada (☎ 421-5487) fly to the Yukon, Vancouver, and major cities in eastern Canada. Time Air (☎ 421-1414), in partnership with Canadian Airlines, is Alberta's commuter airline. It has daily services to Grand Prairie, Calgary, Lethbridge, Medicine Hat, and Red Deer and other destinations in western Canada. Delta Air Lines (☎ 426-5990) connects Edmonton with Alaska and many points in mainland USA. Northwest Airlines (☎ 800-225-2525 toll free) flies to Winnipeg and destinations in mainland USA.

Canadian Airlines/Time Air operates the 40-minute commuter service to Calgary with flights all day long. If you're not on business you'll probably find the one-way fare a bit pricey at $102; on weekends, however, there's a special fare of $93 return. One-way pre-tax fares to other cities are to: Inuvik $350, Vancouver $227, Yellowknife $293, Toronto $510, Winnipeg $283, and Ottawa $538.

Bus The large, modern Greyhound Bus Depot (☎ 421-4211), 10324 103rd St on the corner of 103rd Ave close to the VIA Rail station, is very central. Bus fares are usually cheaper than taking the train. Greyhound goes east to Winnipeg several times a day; the one-way fare is $96. Greyhound also goes to: Jasper $32.20, Banff $35.90, Calgary $24, Vancouver $84, Yellowknife $136.25, and Whitehorse $173.05. From Whitehorse you can catch a bus with Gray Line of Alaska to Fairbanks, Alaska.

Another bus line serving Calgary is Red Arrow (☎ 425-0820), CN Tower, 10004 104th Ave. It has four buses a day leaving from the CN Tower; the one-way fare is $24. You travel on deluxe buses with kitchenette.

Train Entry to the VIA Rail station (☎ 422-6032 and, for fares and reservations, 800-665-8630 toll-free) at 10004 104th Ave on the corner of 100th St is through the CN Tower. The station is open on Monday, Wednesday, Thursday and Saturday from 9 am to 4.30 pm; Sunday, Tuesday and Friday from 6.30 am to 2 pm and from 5 pm to 12.30 am. There's a coffee shop and newsstand.

Trains regularly depart eastward to Saskatoon, Winnipeg, Toronto, Ottawa and Montreal and westward to Jasper, Prince George and Prince Rupert. At Prince George you can connect with BC Rail to Vancouver. The one-way fare to Jasper is $57, to Prince George $92, to Vancouver $136.

Car Some of the car rental companies operating in Edmonton are:

Avis
    Main Floor, Chateau Lacombe Hotel, 10111 Bellamy Hill Rd (☎ 448-0066)
Budget
    10016 106th St (☎ 428-6155)
Rent-A-Wreck
    10140 109th St (☎ 423-1755)
Thrifty
    10036 102nd St (☎ 428-8555)

Rent-A-Wreck is the cheapest charging $25 a day plus 10 cents a km after the first 100 km. Avis charges $38 a day and 12 cents a km after the first 100 km. Budget and Thrifty both charge $40 a day plus 12 cents a km after the first 100 km. These are all weekday rates; it's cheaper to rent at weekends.

Getting Around
To/From the Airport City buses don't go as far south as the international airport, but you can take the Grey Goose Airporter Bus (☎ 463-7520). It leaves from the Hotel Macdonald every half hour from 5.15 am to 12.15 am for a one-way fare of $8.50 or $13 return. It also picks up and drops off at other top hotels and the Greyhound Bus Depot. A taxi from downtown costs about $30.

City buses run to and from the municipal airport. Take bus Nos 41 or 42 north along 101st St to Kingsway then change to bus No 23.

A shuttle bus connects the two airports.

Bus & LRT Edmonton Transit (☎ 421-4636 for information about fares, routes and schedules) operates city buses and Canada's smallest subway system, the Light Rail Transit (LRT). The LRT has nine stops running east-west along Jasper Ave, north along 99th St then north-west all the way to 139th Ave in Clareview. Another stop is planned for the university. Between Clareview Station and Stadium Station the LRT travels overground, from Churchill Station to Grandin Station it runs beneath the surface.

A single one-way fare is $1.25 on the LRT or buses. You can transfer from one to the other but you must get a transfer receipt when you pay your fare and use it within 90 minutes of it being issued. You can also buy a day pass for $3.50. From 9 am to 3 pm Monday to Friday and from 9 am to 6 pm Saturday, the five subway LRT stations, Churchill to Grandin, form a free zone.

There is an information centre at Central Station on the corner of Jasper Ave and 100A St. Churchill Station, on the corner of 102nd Ave and 99th St, also has an information centre and you can buy passes and ticket books there.

Buses cover all parts of the city but not all routes operate on Sundays and holidays. Bus No 46 goes from downtown to the university and back. Bus No 50 goes from downtown south-west to the Valley Zoo in Laurier Park.

Taxi There are several cab companies in Edmonton. Two of them are Yellow Cab (☎ 462-3456), 10135 31st Ave, and Alberta Co-Op Taxi (☎ 425-8310), 105440 110st St. The fare with Alberta Co-Op Taxi from downtown to the West Edmonton Mall is about $12.

Bicycle River Valley Cycle & Sports (☎ 465-3863), 9124 82nd Ave, rents out bikes

for $7 an hour or $21 per day. It also does guided history tours by bike. Sports Rent (☎ 438-7368), 6430 104th St, charges $5 per hour and $20 per day.

AROUND EDMONTON
Strathcona Archaeological Centre
This centre (☎ 427-2022) offers visitors a glimpse of an archaeological dig, with explanations at the interpretive centre. The site is a stone-age industrial plant where people living around 3000 BC worked making tools and weapons. It's a project of the Provincial Museum and makes an interesting and cheap (free) look at historical discovery. The site, open daily in summer from 10 am to 6 pm, is at the southern end of Strathcona Science Park west of town, near the Yellowhead Highway and 17th St.

Alberta Pioneer Railway Museum
This museum (☎ 472-6229) has a collection of steam and diesel locomotives and rolling stock depicting the railways from 1877 to 1950. There is also an artefact exhibit. Admission is $3 and it's open in summer Thursday to Monday from 10 am to 6 pm. To get there, drive north on 97th St (Highway 28) to Namao then turn east onto Highway 37 for seven km, then south onto 34th St for about two km.

Alberta Wildlife Park
This park (☎ 921-3918), north of Edmonton, is open daily year-round from 10 am to dark. Admission is $4. The 400-hectare park holds over 100 species of wild animals from around the world. How do they stand the winters? To get there travel 22 km north on Highway 28 to Bon Accord, turn east for about half a km, then north on Lily Lake Rd for 13 km.

Polar Park
Polar Park (☎ 922-3401), 22 km south-east of town on Highway 14, is run by the same man who started the Alberta Wildlife Park. This park specialises in animals of the north: snow leopards, polar bears and caribou are some of the 100 species. There are good

walking and cross-country ski trails. It's open daily all year from 8 am till dark and admission is $4.

Elk Island National Park
Thirty-five km east of Edmonton on the Yellowhead Highway is this 194-sq-km reserve of original forest that is actually a wildlife sanctuary. There are free-roaming herds of elk and plains bison and a small herd of endangered wood bison. About 35 other mammals inhabit the park. It's a popular weekend spot with camping, hiking and swimming in summer and cross-country skiing in winter. For information contact the Superintendent (☎ 992-6392), Elk Island National Park, RR 1, Site 4, Fort Saskatchewan T8L 2N7.

Ukrainian Cultural Heritage Village
This village (☎ 662-3640/1), 50 km east of Edmonton on the Yellowhead Highway, pays homage to Ukrainian immigrants. There is a replica pioneer home and other exhibitions of the first settlers in the area. From mid-May to the end of August it's open daily from 10 am to 6 pm. Admission is free.

Lac Sainte Anne
For about 100 years, since prayers at the lake by the Roman Catholic Mission to end a drought were answered, it has been believed these waters have God-given curative powers. Here, 50 km west of Edmonton, an annual pilgrimage takes place in July drawing about 10,000 people from around the province and across North America. It's a five-day event.

Vegreville
The Ukrainian community in this town (120 km east of Edmonton on the Yellowhead Highway) has constructed the world's biggest *pysanka* or painted Easter egg. Built of aluminium, the egg sits, over seven metres tall and 5½ metres wide, just off the highway on the eastern side of town. The Ukrainian Pysanka Festival takes place in early July.

Red Deer
Halfway to Calgary, this large town is in the centre of grain and cattle country. An international folk festival is held here every July and an international air show every August.

Travellers to either Calgary or Edmontom may find Red Deer a useful stopping-off point. During either Calgary's stampede or Edmonton's Klondike Days it might be worth considering Red Deer as a base. Accommodation will not be as tight and is not likely to be expensive either. By road either city is about an hour and a half away.

Northern Alberta

The land north of Edmonton is a vast, sparsely populated region of farms, forests, wilderness areas, lakes, open prairies and oilfields. The north-east has virtually no roads and is dominated by Wood Buffalo National Park. From the British Columbia border the mighty Peace River makes its way north-eastward to Lake Athabasca. West of Edmonton, Highway 43 heads north-westward to connect with Highway 34 and Highway 2 to Dawson Creek, the official starting point of the Alaska Highway. From near the town of Peace River the Mackenzie Highway (Highway 35) heads north to the Northwest Territories.

LAKE DISTRICT
From St Paul, 200 km north-east of Edmonton, to the Northwest Territories border lies Alberta's lake district. Fishing is very popular but many of the lakes, especially further north, have no road access and you have to fly in.

St Paul
St Paul, gateway to the lake district, is a trading centre. In the town is the only flying-saucer landing pad in the world. It's still waiting for its first customer.

WOOD BUFFALO NATIONAL PARK
Nearly 28,000 sq km in size, Wood Buffalo

(☎ 872-2349) is Canada's largest national park and one of the world's largest parks. Bigger than Switzerland, it lies two-thirds in Alberta and one-third in the Northwest Territories.

Vegetation in the park ranges from forest to plains to bogs and marshes.

This wilderness park has the world's largest free-roaming bison herd – about 6000 – and is the only nesting ground of the diminishing, rare whooping crane. Moose, caribou, bears and wolves abound as well as many smaller animals, and over a million ducks, geese and swans pass by in autumn and spring on their migratory routes. Also out of Fort Smith are the Slave River rapids where white pelicans nest.

On the shore of Lake Athabasca, **Fort Chipewyan** is the oldest settlement in Alberta.

Most of the scenic areas in the park are not visible from the roads and the roads themselves are not always open. For travel information contact the Park Superintendent (☎ 872-2349), Box 750, Fort Smith, Northwest Territories XOE 0P0.

If you want to get a glimpse of what the early fur traders overcame, this is a good place to look.

Activities
You can go swimming at **Pine Lake**, hike on the marked trails, or explore the deltas of the **Athabasca** and **Peace rivers** by canoe. The park staff run field trips and overnight camping trips or buffalo-observing hikes. In winter there are cross-country ski trails.

Northern Visions (☎ 872-3430), PO Box 1086, Fort Smith, NWT X0E 0P0, offers tours into the park.

Places to Stay
There are few comforts in Wood Buffalo National Park. There is one small campground in the park at Pine Lake, but in addition there are a couple just outside the park's border: one near Fort Chipewyan and the other near Fort Smith (see also Fort Smith & Wood Buffalo National Park in the Northwest Territories chapter). Within the park there are numerous designated basic campsites for individual campers which offer some primitive facilities such as an outhouse and sometimes a firepit. The more adventurous may set off on their own and camp anywhere they find agreeable.

Getting There & Away
Air Northwestern Air Lease (☎ 872-2216 in Fort Smith) has a scheduled air service between Fort Smith, Fort Chipewyan and Edmonton.

Car Wood Buffalo National Park is not easily accessible by road. To get there, you go up the Mackenzie Highway north-west of Edmonton to the Northwest Territories where Highway 1 then Highway 2 lead to Hay River on the southern shore of Great Slave Lake. South of Hay River, Highway 5 heads east to Fort Smith. From Fort Smith roads head south into the park as far as Fort Chipewyan.

Calgary

The name Calgary, meaning 'clear, running water' in Gaelic, comes from Calgary Bay on the Isle of Mull in Scotland.

The area was initially home to the Blackfoot but they were joined in the 18th century by the Sarcee and the Stoney. In the 1800s there was war between them and trouble with White trappers and traders, so the Northwest Mounted Police were sent to cool things down. They established Fort Calgary in 1875. The Canadian Pacific railway was built this far in 1883. Settlers were offered free land and the population jumped to 4000 by 1891. Soon, cattle herders from the USA were pushing north looking for better grazing. Calgary became a major meat-packing centre and cowboy metropolis. It's now a major transportation-distribution point and is still the leading cattle centre.

During the last three decades the city has had to deal with some dramatic ups and downs, exploding from a fair-sized cow town to a brand-new city of steel and glass in under 20 years.

The reason for Calgary's changeable fortunes is simple: oil. Oil had originally been discovered as far back as 1914, but it wasn't until the late 1960s that the black gold was found in vast quantities across the province. Coupled with the energy crisis of the 1970s which bumped prices up sharply, the industry boomed. The city took off, becoming one of the fastest growing cities in the country. It became the headquarters of 450 oil companies and home to more Americans than any place outside of the USA.

The population mushroomed to 640,000 and the city centre was transformed. For years it looked like a construction site as buildings seemed to rise with the morning sun.

After a brief breath-catching period, the cultural side of the city began to develop as well. However, during the 1980s things became tough. With the bottom falling out of the oil market and 70% of the workforce relying on it, things turned sour quickly. Just when the city was struggling, attempting to maintain what it had become, Calgary's fortunes and reputation got a big boost when it hosted the Winter Olympics in 1988.

Calgary has been labelled everything from a rootless boom town to a major new urban centre to a depressed area. But through it all, it continues to develop and remains quite a phenomenon.

The city's climate is dry and very sunny. It gets hot in summer but remains amazingly cool in the shade. In winter the warm chinook wind blows off the mountains, raising temperatures – at least temporarily.

One of Alberta's greatest assets, Banff National Park, is just 120 km to the west. Edmonton is 294 km to the north.

Orientation

Calgary, like the plains around it, lies on flat ground. It began at the confluence of the Bow and Elbow rivers and has spread equally in all directions, but the downtown area is still bounded by the Bow River to the

north. The Elbow River cuts through the southern portions of the city.

The person who originated the street-numbering system must have thought it great, but it's a jumbled mess and will take you a few days to get a grip of. The city is divided into four geographical segments: north-west (NW), north-east (NE), south-west (SW) and south-east (SE). These abbreviations are important as they're marked on street signs and included in addresses.

The Bow River and Memorial Drive divide the city between north and south, approximately. Centre St divides the northern part of the city and downtown between east and west; Macleod Trail divides the southern part of the city between east and west.

All city streets run north and south, all avenues run east and west. The downtown streets are all one-way except for 7th Ave. Here all cars go west to east but there's one bus and taxi lane which goes the opposite way. The Light Rail Transit (LRT – known as the C-Train) also runs along 7th Ave.

Downtown Around the downtown centre the 'Plus 15 Walking System' refers to pedestrian bridges and over-the-street walkways (enclosed sidewalks) which are at least five metres above the ground. Various buildings and shops are connected in this way.

The Calgary Tower, right downtown on 9th Ave at Centre St, is a good orientation point. If you look across the street up Centre St, you're looking north towards the downtown area.

Ninth Ave is lined with modern offices, expensive hotels, banks and parking lots as well as the railway station, Calgary Convention Centre and Glenbow Museum & Art Gallery complex.

Eighth Ave between 3rd St SW and 1st St SE is a very long pedestrian mall – Stephens Ave Mall also called 8th Ave Mall. It's lined with trees, benches, shops including the large department stores, restaurants and fast-food places. There are also a lot of vendors selling crafts, odds & ends and souvenirs. At

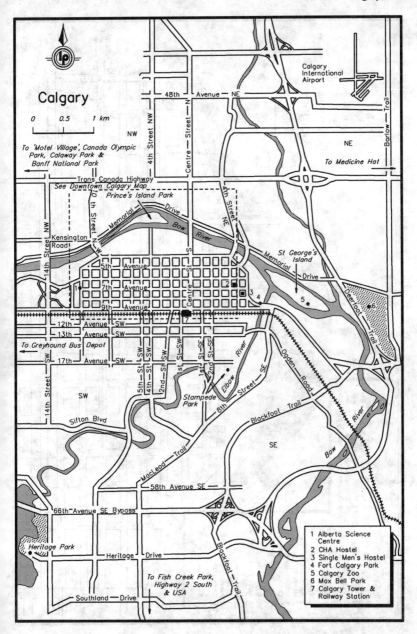

Calgary

0   0.5   1 km

To 'Motel Village', Canada Olympic Park, Calaway Park & Banff National Park

NW

NE

48th Avenue NE

Calgary International Airport

To Medicine Hat

Trans Canada Highway
See Downtown Calgary Map

Prince's Island Park

14th Street NW

10th Street NW

4th Street NW

Centre Street N

4th Street NE

Barlow Trail

Memorial Drive

Kensington Road

Bow River

Memorial Drive

St George's Island

5th Avenue

7th Avenue

9th Avenue

Deerfoot Trail

12th Avenue SW
13th Avenue SW

To Greyhound Bus Depot

17th Avenue SW

14th Street

5th St SW
4th St SW
2nd St SW
1st St SW
1st St SE
2nd St SE

Elbow River

8th Street SE

Ogden Road

SW

Sifton Blvd

Stampede Park

Blackfoot Trail

Bow River

SE

MacLeod Trail

58th Avenue SE

66th Avenue SE Bypass

Heritage Park

Heritage Drive

To Fish Creek Park, Highway 2 South & USA

Blackfoot Trail

Southland Drive

1 Alberta Science Centre
2 CHA Hostel
3 Single Men's Hostel
4 Fort Calgary Park
5 Calgary Zoo
6 Max Bell Park
7 Calgary Tower & Railway Station

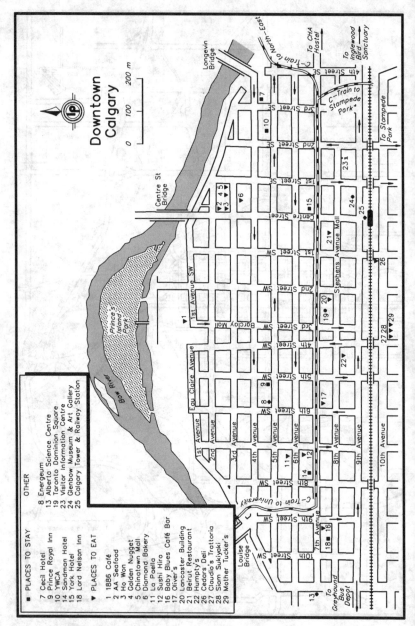

Downtown Calgary

■ PLACES TO STAY
7 Cecil Hotel
9 Prince Royal Inn
10 YWCA
14 Sandman Hotel
15 York Hotel
18 Lord Nelson Inn

▼ PLACES TO EAT
1 1886 Café
2 AA Seafood
3 Ho Won
4 Golden Nugget
5 Chinatown Mall
6 Diamond Bakery
11 La Paella
12 Sushi Hiro
16 Baby Blues Café Bar
17 Oliver's
20 Lancaster Building
21 Beirut Restaurant
22 Humpty's
26 Cedars Deli
27 Claudio's Trattoria
28 Siam Sukiyoki
29 Mother Tucker's

OTHER
8 Energeum
13 Alberta Science Centre
19 Toronto Dominion Square
23 Visitor Information Centre
24 Glenbow Museum & Art Gallery
25 Calgary Tower & Railway Station

its western end Stephens Ave Mall connects with Barclay Mall (3rd St SW) which heads north towards Prince's Island Park.

Around Centre St before it heads north over the river, between 1st St SW and 1st St SE, is the small Chinatown looking like it's desperately hanging on despite downtown redevelopment. It's still vibrant and has grocery stores and video shops as well as restaurants.

The western downtown area is mainly offices and businesses. The eastern section was the last to undergo redevelopment. It used to be the saviour of the impecunious with its cheap bars and tatty hotels of which a few vestiges remain but generally it's pretty cleaned up. The Single Men's Hostel and a couple of old hotels remain; the CHA Hostel is down this way as well. Among the older buildings, a couple of fine ones are the City Council building dating from 1907 on 7th Ave SE and the Anglican church dating from 1904 on 7th Ave SE at 1st St SE. The latter replaced a temporary cathedral built in 1884. One of the newer complexes is the large Centre for the Performing Arts on the corner of 9th Ave and 1st St SE with the park nearby.

Stone lions on each side mark the Centre St Bridge over the Bow River, which has the greyish-green colour of Rocky Mountain waters. The river marks the northern edge of the downtown area. To the west of the bridge is Prince's Island, a park. Over the bridge, on the northern side, are stairs on both sides leading up to the cliff. There's a footpath along the cliff and good views of the city, especially if you take the stairs on the western side. If you're driving, turn left on 8th Ave NW, then head back towards the river.

North The city north of the river is primarily residential. The Trans Canada Highway cuts east-west across here along 16th Ave NE and 16th Ave NW. In the north-west the University of Calgary is off Crowchild Trail (Highway 1A). To the north-east, off Barlow Trail is the international airport.

South South of Calgary Tower, over the railway tracks, is another section of the city – a sort of mini-downtown. It's centred on 11th Ave SW and 12th Ave SW and on 4th St SW running north-south. There are quite a few restaurants along 4th St SW. Central Park is in this area and to the south-east, Stampede Park.

Heading west from Stampede Park is 17th Ave SW. It's lined with a wide range of restaurants as well as a variety of other businesses including many antique shops. Fourth St SW, south of 17th Ave SW, has boutiques, a few galleries and yet more eating places and night spots.

Further south is Macleod Trail (Highway 2) which eventually heads to the USA. The best section of Calgary is east of Macleod Trail around the Bow River.

Information

The Visitor Information Centre (☎ 263-8510), 237 8th Ave SE, is run by the Calgary Tourist & Convention Bureau. It has maps of the city and pamphlets on things to do. It also operates a visitor accommodation service (☎ 800-661-1678 toll free) so you can ring ahead and book a place to stay. It's open Monday to Friday from 8 am to 6 pm, weekends from 8 am to 5 pm.

Another office, open year round, is northeast, at 6220 16th Ave NE (the Trans Canada Highway). Seasonal offices are north-west in Canada Olympic Park at the junction of the Trans Canada Highway and Bowfort Rd NW; the arrivals level of the international airport; and to the south, along the Macleod Trail.

Alberta Tourism (☎ 297-6574), Government Centre South, McDougall School, 455 6th St SW, has information and maps on all parts of the province.

The main post office (☎ 292-5512), 220 4th Ave SE, is open Monday to Friday from 8 am to 5.45 pm. Calgary General Hospital (☎ 268-9111) is north-east of the downtown area over the river in the Bow Valley Centre, at 841 Centre Ave NE; take bus No 3.

The USA consulate in Calgary (☎ 266-8962) is in Room 1050, 615 Macleod Trail SE.

Calgary Tower

This building (☎ 266-7171), 101 9th Ave SW, at the foot of Centre St downtown, acts as a landmark and symbol of the city. It may not dominate the skyline but it's always in there and can be seen from far away. The 191-metre tower houses a revolving restaurant, an observation gallery and, at the very top, a cocktail lounge. While the elevator (for $3.50) takes just 63 seconds, walking the 762 emergency steps takes a bit longer.

The observation gallery is open from 7.30 am to 11.30 pm daily except Sunday, when it closes at 10.30 pm.

Glenbow Museum & Art Gallery

The Glenbow Museum & Art Gallery (☎ 264-8300, 237-8988), 130 9th Ave SE, is excellent and well worth a visit. The collections are varied and interesting, the displays effectively laid out. Opened in 1966, the complex shows part of human history through artefacts and art.

The 2nd floor contains frequently changing exhibitions of international, national and local art; there is always some Inuit art and a painter's work on show.

The 3rd floor has historical displays, mainly to do with the Canadian west. There is a superb collection of Native Indian dress and jewellery. Woodcarving from coast to coast is also represented. There's a section with Inuit tools and a kayak, the traditional one-person boat. There is also a huge collection on pioneer days that includes old wagons, tractors, CP railway relics, saddles and cowboy tools and implements. Another area presents an interesting collection of stuff from the 1920s and '30s. Articles include old washing machines, a car, slot machines, bathing suits and a 1930 brassiere.

On the 4th floor is the military and arms collection. There are figures dressed in Japanese samurai armour and armoured knights of Britain's Middle Ages. The WW I and WW II posters are interesting and the newspaper headlines make it all come alive.

The museum is open daily from 10 am to 6 pm and costs just $2, students $1.

Heritage Park

This is an area of 26 hectares portraying life in a town of the Canadian west prior to 1914 and on a good day offers views of the Rockies. The park (☎ 255-1182/1858), 1900 Heritage Drive at the junction of 14 St SW south-west of downtown, sits on a peninsula jutting into the Glenmore Reservoir formed out of the Elbow River.

The reconstructed frontier village includes a Hudson's Bay Company fort, a working grain mill, a 1896 church and many stores full of artefacts and antiques. The well-laid out grounds have a ranch house, a teepee, a trapper's cabin and other housing. The old schoolhouse with its desks and slates is interesting. There is an excellent collection of horse-drawn buggies in section E, which includes stagecoaches, traps and surreys, and the chemist's and general store are particularly good. Also be sure to see the two-storey outhouse.

The park actually covers more than just pioneer days, encompassing development into the early 1920s. There are old cars, a railway exhibit of old coaches and a working steam engine.

Around the site are several eating places and you can buy fresh bread from the bakery. The park is open on weekdays until 4 pm, on weekends till 6 pm and admission is $5. To get there, take bus No 53 south from downtown.

Devonian Gardens

The Devonian Gardens (☎ 268-5207) are 15 metres above street level on the 4th floor of Toronto Dominion Square, which is a complex on Stephens Ave Mall, between 2nd and 3rd Sts SW.

This place makes a pleasant sanctuary from the concrete of downtown Calgary. Built entirely indoors, it's a one-hectare park with more than 20,000 plants and the smell and freshness of a greenhouse. There's over a km of pathways skirting fountains, pools, benches and a sculpture court. There's a small stage for regular entertainment, often during weekday lunch hours, and a special display area for art exhibitions. They're open daily from 9 am to 9 pm and admission is free. Outside regular business hours, elevators must be used to reach the gardens.

Fort Calgary

This is not really a fort but a 16-hectare park (☎ 269-7747), 750 9th Ave SE, east of downtown, where Calgary's original settlement began. In the park is an interpretive centre (☎ 232-1875), the remains of the fort and two of Calgary's earliest houses. The interpretive centre tells the story of Calgary's development; there are displays and a slide show on the Northwest Mounted Police every 30 minutes in the theatre.

Here in 1875, where the Bow River meets the Elbow River, the first detachment of the Northwest Mounted Police arrived. They built a fort and called the developing settlement the 'Elbow'. Later it became Fort Calgary and remained a police post until 1914, when it was sold to the Grand Trunk Railway. Of the fort itself all that remains are a few foundations. Plaques give some of the history.

The fort site is pleasant and has good views; you can follow paths down to the river and walk across the footbridge to St Patrick's Island and on to Calgary Zoo.

To the east, across the Elbow River, is Hunt House, probably the oldest building in the Calgary area. It was believed to be built by the Hudson's Bay Company for one of its employees. Next door is the larger Deane House, built in 1906 for the commanding officer and partially renovated.

The park is open every day and is free.

Energeum

The Energeum (☎ 297-4293), on the main floor of the Energy Resources Building at 640 5th Ave SW, outlines the development and uses of Alberta's energy resources. Models and charts depict the formation, discovery and exploitation of coal and oil, and include a good explanation of the province's valuable yet problematic oil sands. Some interactive computers supply further details, as does a film. A gorgeous 1958 Buick is on display. The Energeum is open from 10.30 am to 4.30 pm Monday to Friday and on Sunday during the summer. Admission is free.

Telecommunications Hall of Fame

This is a small telephone museum on the 2nd floor of the AGT Tower, 411 1st St SE, with exhibits on Alexander Graham Bell and other inventors. Also on view are various phones and systems and a couple of audio-visual displays.

Natural Gas, Light, Heat & Power Museum

That's quite a mouthful (and it's not even the complete title); it's a lot of name for a fairly superficial display in the Natural Gas Company's lobby on the corner of 11th Ave SW and 8th St SW. The gas stove from 1912 is quite a sight but beyond that, the few home appliances and old photographs don't amount to much. Admission is free.

Prince's Island Park

This is a pretty park on an island in the Bow River north of the downtown area, connected to both sides of the river by pedestrian bridges. It's a cool, quiet spot with lots of trees and flowers, picnic tables and jogging and cycling paths. This is a good antidote to a hot summer's day in Calgary. As the signs say, the water in the Bow River is dangerous for swimming: it moves fast and is cold. The bridge to the island from downtown is at the top (northern end) of 3rd St SW.

Alberta Science Centre

The Alberta Science Centre (☎ 221-3700/07), just west of downtown in Mewata Park at the junction of 7th Ave SW and 11th St SW, is an entertaining and educational complex.

The main attraction is the **Centennial Planetarium** (☎ 264-4060) with its ever changing one-hour show about different phenomena in our universe. Weekend nights are given over to laser rock-music shows.

Also on the premises is a small observatory with telescopes focused on the moon, the planets and star clusters. This is open on clear nights. In the display area, exhibits vary from scientific presentations to models of parts of our galaxy. The **Pleiades Theatre** (☎ 262-7548) puts on holiday variety shows and mystery plays four times a year.

The centre is open Wednesday to Sunday from 1 to 9 pm. Admission to the science centre is $2, to the planetarium $2.50, but a combined ticket is $4.

Calgary Zoo

The zoo (☎ 233-7838, 265-9310), one of Canada's largest and best, is north-east of downtown on St George's Island and the northern bank of the Bow River. It brings together 300 species of mammals, birds and reptiles, many in enclosures simulating the animals' natural habitats. Underwater viewing areas allow you to see polar bears, seals and other creatures as they behave beneath the water. Special blacked-out rooms enable you to see nocturnal animals. There is a section on Australian animals and pens for large, exotic mammals like tigers, giraffes and Himalayan cats. Hundreds of tropical birds are kept in greenhouses full of plants and flowers of warmer climes. Picnic areas dot the zoo and island and there is a restaurant at the site.

On St George's Island is a **Prehistoric Dinosaur Park**, an extension of the zoo. This three-hectare park contains fossil displays and life-size replicas of dinosaurs in natural settings.

The zoo is open year-round and charges $5.50, $2 for children under 12. In summer it's open from 9 am to 7 pm, in winter 9 am to 5 pm. Catch the C-Train east along 7th Ave to Zoo Station.

Inglewood Bird Sanctuary

This sanctuary (☎ 269-6688) is south-east of downtown at the end of 9th Ave, on a forested section of the Bow River flats. The area is home to many birds and a resting spot for those on the migratory trail. Trails lead through the sanctuary which is open daily from 7 am to 9 pm. Bus No 14 goes within a few blocks of the sanctuary.

Calgary Stockyards

The stockyards (☎ 234-7429), 100 2635 Portland St SE, are one of the centres for western livestock dealing. If you want to see what's going-on, there are cattle auctions on weekdays. Take bus No 24 from downtown.

Museum of the Regiments

The Museum of the Regiments (☎ 240-7694) is at the Canadian Forces base, Currie Barracks, 4520 Crowchild Trail SW between 33rd Ave SW and 50th Ave SW.

It pays homage to Calgary's home regiments: Lord Strathcona's Horse, Princess Patricia's Light Infantry, the Calgary High-

Mountain lion

landers and the King's Own Calgary regiment.

There are collections of uniforms, weapons, badges, toys and memorabilia from both the 19th and 20th centuries. It's free to get into and is open daily from 8 am to 4 pm. As it's on the base, you may be asked for identification – calling ahead is a good idea. To get there take bus Nos 18, 108, 111 or 112 from downtown.

Fish Creek Park

On the south-western edge of Calgary, quite a way from downtown, is this huge tract of land more than eight sq km in size, running along Fish Creek, which flows into the Bow River. It acts as a shelter for many animals and birds as well as people on weekends. Park interpreters present slide shows and walking tours to explain some of the local ecology. For details drop into the administration office or call ☎ 297-5293. To get there from downtown head south on the Macleod Trail.

Calaway Park

This large amusement park (☎ 240-3822), about 10 km west of town on the Trans Canada Highway, features over 20 rides, a cinema with a 180° screen, restaurants and entertainment events. It costs $8 to get in and see the shows, or $12 including rides.

Winter Olympics Site

Calgary hosted the 15th Winter Olympics in 1988, a first for Canada. Some of the locations and facilities were already in place, others were specially built for the Olympics, but they all remain in use.

A 15-minute drive west of town on the Trans Canada Highway, **Canada Olympic Park** (☎ 247-5404) is interesting to visit. There you can see the 70 and 90-metre ski jumps – from the top you realise how crazy those guys were – and the bobsled and luge runs built of concrete. Guided tours of the park cost $6.

There's an **Olympic Hall of Fame** (☎ 268-2632), open daily and admission is $3, and a Visitor's Information Centre, as well

as the facilities now used as an Olympic training centre. The adjacent downhill ski area is open to the public in winter. But the real alpine skiing took place 55 km west of town in **Kananaskis Country** at Nakiska on Mt Allan (☎ 591-7777), off Highway 40. The slopes were newly constructed for the games and skiers today can use the slopes there.

Bow River

The Bow River begins as clean, clear barely melted ice in Bow Lake in the Rockies not far from Banff, and flows swiftly through Calgary. From Calgary it slows and warms and eventually reaches Medicine Hat near the Saskatchewan border. Here it melds with other meandering rivers, changes name and eventually slips into Hudson Bay.

The Bow River in its middle section – the 60 km from Calgary east to Carseland – is considered one of the best trout-fishing rivers in North America and the best dry fly fishing river in the world. The fish, mainly brown and rainbow trout, are numerous and big, too. And the river will just float you along with no effort required. It sounds good even for those who don't fish. Swimming is out, though – the water here is still far too cool.

A good access point is just at the southern edge of Calgary's city limits under the Highway 22X bridge. There are numerous fishing guide services in town as well as sporting goods stores for fishing tackle and information. One place to try that combines the two is Country Pleasures (☎ 278-1815), 570 10816 Macleod Trail South.

Activities

Calgary has 180 km of bicycle and hiking trails, many in the parks and nature areas. Maps and information are available from Parks & Recreation (☎ 269-2531). See the Getting Around section later for information on where to rent bikes.

Two leisure centres run by Parks & Recreation have giant wave pools, year-round skating, racquet courts and hot tubs. They are: Family Leisure Centre (☎ 278-7542), 11150 Bonaventure Drive SE and Southland

Leisure Centre (☎ 251-3505), 2000 Southland Drive SW. Downtown the YMCA (☎ 269-6701, 262-9695), 101 3rd St SW, has keep-fit facilities.

If you're keen on hang gliding then the Alberta Hang Gliding Association (☎ 286-7599) can provide you with information.

Organised Tours The cheapest bus tour of town is to take the No 10 bus from along 6th Ave. For $1.25 this city bus goes on its 2½-hour circular route past old and new areas, the highest point of the city with views to the foothills, the university and some wealthy districts in the north-west.

Brewster Gray Line (☎ 221-8242), 808 Centre St SE, runs tours of Calgary and various Rocky Mountain locations from Calgary. The tour of Calgary takes four hours, covers about 50 km and costs $25. It includes Fort Calgary, Canada Olympic Park and the downtown area, with admissions included in the ticket. A history of the city is given. There are daily trips leaving from the Greyhound Bus Depot. White Stetson Tours (☎ 274-2281), 6312 Travois Crescent NW, does a similar city tour for $24.

Other tours offered by Brewster Gray Line and White Stetson go to the Columbia Icefield, Banff, or some of the mountain lakes. The Brewster Gray Line tour to Banff takes 9 hours and costs $39 including a ride on the gondola up Sulphur Mountain. White Stetson does a similar tour, taking in Lake Louise as well, for $38.

Pacific Western Transportation (☎ 243-4990) also runs bus tours.

Festivals
Calgary Stampede The Calgary Stampede, which originally began in 1912, is a wild 10-day festival that starts with a huge parade in the second week of July each year. Most organised events take place in Stampede Park south-east of the downtown area, but many of the streets are full of activity too. Stampede Park comes alive with concerts, shows, exhibitions, dancing and eating. There is also an amusement area with rides, a gambling hall and lots of contests.

Highlights are the chuck wagon race and the rodeo, which is said to be the biggest and roughest in North America. Events include rides on bucking broncos and bulls, and calf-roping and branding. At night the Stampede Stage Show takes over, with singers, bands, clowns and dancing girls.

Tickets for the main events go early and range in price from about $10 to $35. Prices all over town go up, so beware. And the town and nearby countryside are packed for the duration of the celebrations, so if you plan to be here at this time, it's a good idea to book ahead for somewhere to stay or arrive early.

For more information or tickets call or write to Calgary Exhibition & Stampede (☎ 261-0101; 800-661-1260 toll free), Box 1060, Station M, Calgary T2P 2K8.

Places to Stay
Camping There are several campgrounds near the city for both RVs and tents. They all have good facilities and are cheaper than other accommodation but are very developed and organised.

Closest to town is the *Max Bell Park* (☎ 248-4868), three km east of the zoo, in the triangle between Deerfoot Trail, Memorial Drive and Barlow Trail. The entrance is on Barlow Trail. It has 60 sites and showers; a tent for two people is $12. The C-Train station is nearby and the park is open from mid-June to the end of August.

Bow Bend Trailer Park (☎ 288-2161), 5227 13th Ave NW, is in north-west Calgary beside Shouldice Park and Bow River. A tent site for two is $12 and there are showers and a laundrette. The park is open from mid-May to the end of September. To get there, turn south off the Trans Canada Highway at Home Rd, then west (right) on 13th Ave. If it's full there are two others further west along the Trans Canada Highway.

Whispering Spruce Campground (☎ 226-0097) is in Balzac along Highway 2 about 15 minutes north of the city. It has complete facilities, including a small grocery shop and is open from mid-May to the end of October. South of Calgary, five km east of Okotoks on Railway St, is *Okotoks Wilderness Camp-*

ground (☎ 938-6036). Sites cost \$10 and there are showers and hiking trails. To get there go south on Highway 2 take the Okotoks turn off, then turn left at the lights and travel for about a km; the campground is just past the car wash.

Hostels The *Calgary CHA Hostel* (☎ 269-8239), at 520 7th Ave SE just east of downtown not far from Fort Calgary, is closed between 10 am and 5 pm and has a midnight curfew. It is a large hostel complete with laundry, kitchen and snack bar. It can get very crowded in summer; take care with valuables. The rates are \$10 for members, \$15 for nonmembers.

A little further east on the opposite side of the street from the CHA Hostel is the Salvation Army-run hostel for the needy, the *Single Men's Hostel* (☎ 262-6188), 631 7th Ave SE on the corner of 6th St SE. You can stay here and get a breakfast, too, for nothing, but the atmosphere can be quite grim. The *Salvation Army Hostel* (☎ 262-2756), 515 1st St SE, is much the same thing.

The *YMCA* no longer offers accommodation.

The central *YWCA* (☎ 263-1550), 320 5th Ave SE, is for women only. The single rooms are \$22/29.50 without/with bath, doubles are \$30/39.50. A dormitory bed is \$15. The rooms are clean, you can use the pool and there's a cafeteria which is open every day.

The *University of Calgary*, 3330 24th Ave NW, rents rooms in the residential blocks from mid-May to mid-August. For details and information call the Special Events Office (☎ 220-7101). The normal rate is singles/doubles \$29/42, but it's much less for students. All prices include breakfast. There are good facilities on campus, including a gym and a cheap cafeteria. The university is serviced by the C-Train.

B&Bs The Visitor Information Centre keeps a list of places offering B&B and will make a booking for you. An association which checks and lists houses offering B&B in the city is the B&B Bureau (☎ 242-5555), PO Box 7094, Station E, Calgary. The rates generally are singles/doubles \$30/50.

Hotels Central Calgary doesn't have an abundance of lodgings in any price range and many of the hotels are around the edges of the city. Downtown, the south-east section, once a rough and tumble area, was the centre for cheap hotels but as the area was cleaned up most of the small, older places disappeared. There are still a few blues hanging on though.

The *Cecil Hotel* (☎ 266-2982), on the corner of 4th Ave SE and 3rd St SE, is better maintained than most of the low-budget spots. Rooms are \$20 for singles/doubles with no TV, no phone and no bath, but a sink in each room. There's one room with a bath which costs \$32. At the bar downstairs you can get simple food. The *St Louis Hotel* (☎ 262-6341), 430 8th Ave SE, is basic, but shoestringers will find it cheap at \$22/30 for singles/doubles with bath and TV, or \$16 for singles with no bath. There's a busy blues bar and simple restaurant downstairs. Neither of these places is recommended for women.

Much better, but costlier, is the clean, safe and very central *York Hotel* (☎ 262-5581), 636 Centre St SE on the corner of 7th Ave SE. Rooms are \$50 for singles/doubles with all comforts. Also good is the *Lord Nelson Inn* (☎ 269-8262), 1020 8th Ave SW, where singles/doubles go for \$56/59. It has full facilities, including a fridge in each room.

Prince Royal Inn (☎ 263-0520), 618 5th Ave SW, is a modern all-suite hotel. There's a laundry service and rooms have a kitchenette, fridge, telephones and cable TV. Rates are \$65 for a single or \$75 to \$95 for a double but includes breakfast, and at weekends you can get special rates of singles/doubles \$45. You can also rent by the week or month. The *Sandman Hotel* (☎ 237-8626), 888 7th Ave SE, is similar with rooms at singles/doubles \$73/77. It has full facilities including gym, swimming pool, licensed restaurant and bar.

Westward Inn (☎ 266-4611), 119 12 Ave SW, is within walking distance of Stampede Park. Its normal rate is singles/doubles

$79/86 but has special weekend rates of $48 for either.

Motels Much of the cheaper and more moderate accommodation is found outside the central core. Calgary has dozens of motels in all parts of the city, but there are some areas of very heavy concentration, making it easy to shop around. One of these is along Macleod Trail south of the city. Macleod Trail is a commercial strip with service stations, fast-food restaurants, motels and furniture shops.

Cedar Ridge Motel (☎ 258-1064), 9030 Macleod Trail South, is reasonably priced at singles/doubles $45/49. *Flamingo Motor Hotel* (☎ 252-4401), 7505 Macleod Trail South near the corner of 75th Ave SW, is marked by – you guessed it – a large pink flamingo. Rooms are $52/54 for singles/doubles with a TV in each room, a laundrette, pool and a sauna. The surrounding grounds are pleasant and have lots of trees and there are also restaurants nearby. *Relax Inn* (☎ 253-7070), 9206 Macleod Trail South near 90th Ave SE, is a two-storey building containing a pool, whirlpool and sauna. Rooms have air-con, cable TV and telephones. Singles/doubles cost $46/54. The *Travelodge* (☎ 253-1111), 7012 Macleod Trail South, with a pool, sauna and free coffee is good value at singles/doubles $57/62.

Another motel area is in the north-western section of the city on and just off 16th Ave, which is also the Trans Canada Highway. South-east of the University of Calgary, 16th Ave meets Crowchild Trail; linking the two on a diagonal, forming a triangle, is Banff Trail (also called Highway 1A). Because of the many motels in and around this triangle, the area is called 'Motel Village'. It's a fair way from downtown but it is linked by the C-Train and city buses.

One of the cheapest motels is *Circle Inn Motel* (☎ 289-0295), 2373 Banff Trail NW. It has 30 rooms most of them at singles/doubles $36/38; those with kitchenettes cost $5 extra. There's a restaurant and a pub. The *Avondale Motel* (☎ 289-1921),

2231 Banff Trail NW, has a licensed restaurant, swimming pool and laundry. Rooms are $48/55 for a single/double. *Budget Motor Inn* (☎ 288-7115), 4420 16th Ave NW, is simple but fine and has free coffee. Singles/doubles are $56/63. *Panama Motor Inn* (☎ 289-2561), 2440 16th Ave NW, has a Latin American look about it. Some of its 55 rooms have kitchenettes but there's no extra charge. Singles/doubles are $58/65.

Places to Eat
Three reliable, cheap places are the cafeteria in *Woolworth's*, in Stephens Ave Mall, *Mr Submarine* on the corner of 6th Ave SW and Centre St, and the restaurants in the Bay department store, on the corner of 1st St SW and Stephens Ave Mall. For lunch or dinner, check out the 2nd floor of the Lancaster Building at 304 Stephens Ave Mall on the corner of 2nd St SW. There are 17 food kiosks serving cheap Chinese, Mexican, Indian deli and other foods. Curry dishes or tacos are around $4. You get street views, too.

Also in the Lancaster Building but downstairs, is the very agreeable *Unicorn Pub* with an Anglo-Irish flavour. It's a busy, friendly place which serves inexpensive food like ploughman's lunch for $5.25, fish & chips for $6.50 and steak & kidney pie for $4.25. It's open Monday to Saturday from 11 am to 1 am.

Stephens Ave Mall has numerous other places, most of the quick variety and some that set up tables in the mall in fair weather. *Beirut Restaurant*, 112 Stephens Ave Mall, offers the usual sandwiches but also quite a few Lebanese dishes with dips for $2 to $4 and felafel for $5.

Humpty's, 509 8th Ave SW, is somewhat plastic, but is open every day for standard breakfasts and meals from $3 to $7. There's good pizza for around $6 to $10 at the *Baby Blues Café Bar*, 937 7th Ave SW. Try the one with the spinach. The café has live music at night.

1886 Café, on the corner of 3rd St SW and 1st Ave SW, is an interesting little place in the old Calgary Water Power Company building, established in 1886. It's a worn, white wooden building away from the downtown area, by the river near the walking bridge for Prince's Island. It's open for breakfast and lunch daily from 7 am to 3 pm and serves mainly omelettes for $4.50; for something different try the breakfast sundae, for $5.25, consisting of muesli, yoghurt and three types of fruit. All the Colombian coffee you can drink is $1.50. The café is fast, efficient, friendly and very popular.

For dinners downtown, *Three Greenhorns*, on the corner of 4th Ave SW and 4th St SW, offers decent seafood and steaks. Soup costs from $2 to $4, various main prawn dishes are $11 to $14, while lobster costs $30. It has dancing in the evening. *Sushi Hiro*, on 7th St SW near the corner of 6th Ave SW, is a Japanese restaurant serving sushi appetisers for $4 to $6 and main dishes from $7 to $13. It's open in the evening Monday to Saturday from 5 to 11 pm, but is also open for lunch from 11.30 am to 2 pm. *La Paella*, on the corner of 6th Ave SW and 7th St SW, serves Spanish food; soups are $4, starters $6 and main dishes around $10. It's open Monday to Friday from 11.30 am to 11.30 pm, Saturday from 5 to 11 pm.

Oliver's, 609 7th Ave SW, serves traditional British-style food like roast beef & Yorkshire pudding for $12.75. It also serves seafood. To wash your meal down you could try an ale at the *Old Bailey* pub also on the premises.

There is a small Chinatown on 2nd and 3rd Aves at Centre St; the cheaper places are on Centre St while restaurants in the moderate range are concentrated in 3rd Ave SE. *Ho Won* and *A A Seafood* on Centre St offer dim sum lunches for around $5 or $6. *Chinatown Mall* on the corner of 3rd Ave SE and 1st St SE is fun on a Sunday around noon when the whole area is packed and lots of fresh pastries are offered. *Diamond Bakery*, 111A 3rd Ave SE, is a tiny place offering tasty Chinese treats and sweets from around 60 cents. The *Golden Nugget*, upstairs at 130 3rd Ave SE, is huge and can hold up to 600 people. Starters cost about $4 and main meals such as lemon chicken cost between $7 to $12. It's

open daily from 10 am to 3 am and has live entertainment every night after 10.30 pm.

South across the train tracks below 9th Ave there are also a couple of good areas for food searching. *Cedars Deli* on the right side, just after the underpass on 1st Ave SW, is worth the short walk for good, cheap Lebanese food in a green and white setting. It has good dips for around $3 to $4 and a felafel plate for $5. The coffee is good too.

Siam Sukyaki, 351 10th Ave SW, is a good Thai restaurant with lunch-time all-you-can-eat buffets for $7. It's open Monday to Saturday for lunch and dinner. Next door to Siam Sukyaki is the up-market *Claudio's Trattoria*, which serves Italian food in elegant surroundings at a reasonable price. Main dishes are $8 to $10. Nearby at *Mother Tucker's*, 347 10th Ave SW, you can get huge sandwiches and salads for $6 to $8 and seafood dishes for $6 to $10. It's a very popular place and has music at night. It's open Monday to Friday from 11.30 am to 2 pm and from 5 to 9.30 pm, Saturday from 4.30 to 10.30 pm and Sunday from 4.30 to 9 pm.

Further south, the *Soup Kitchen*, 738 17th Ave SW near 7th St SW, is a small, pleasant café with good sandwiches for about $3 to $4. *Bagels & Buns* across the street at 807 17th Ave SW, is also good for informal breakfasts and lunches and is very popular. Salami or cheese and tomato sandwiches cost $4. There's a variety of places around the corner of 17th Ave SW and 4th St SW – Indian, Greek, French, delis, etc.

North of the river, Kensington, a district based on Kensington Rd and 10th St NW, is an old city neighbourhood with plenty of restaurants. Outside the central area, the commercial strips along Macleod Trail south and the Trans Canada Highway east-west across the north of the city have many familiar food chains.

The Saturday edition of the *Calgary Herald* has lots of ads for Sunday brunch bargains.

Entertainment

For complete entertainment guides pick up a

copy of *Key to Calgary* in one of the good hotels and read the local newspapers the *Calgary Sun* and the *Calgary Herald*, especially on Friday or Saturday. *City Lites*, a broadsheet available from the Visitor Information Office, lists Calgary's entertainment.

Theatre The city has several live theatre venues. The *Lunchbox Theatre* (☎ 265-4292), in the Bow Valley Square on the corner of 6th Ave and 1st St SW, is a professional performing arts stage catering to downtown shoppers, workers and passers-by at lunch hours during the week. Shows vary from comedy to drama to musicals, and change regularly. They start around noon, usually with an additional afternoon programme each week. Admission is $4.

The *Calgary Centre for the Performing Arts* (☎ 294-7444), known as The Centre, is on Stephens Ave Mall on the corner of 1st St SE. It has performances by Alberta Theatre Projects (☎ 294-7495); it also has ballet, the Calgary Philharmonic Orchestra and more. *Pumphouse Theatre* (☎ 263-0079), 2140 9th Ave SW, puts on experimental plays. The *Alberta Science Centre* has laser shows and the Pleiades Theatre there puts on variety shows and mystery plays (see Alberta Science Centre section earlier). *Stage West*, 727 42 Ave SE, is a theatre restaurant that showcases well-known stars from south of the border.

Music In summer the Calgary Philharmonic Orchestra has a series of free community concerts at various locations around the city. There are also free concerts by various musicians in McDougall Centre Park, 455 6th Ave SE. Big-name concerts are held in the Olympic Saddledome in Stampede Park and in the Jubilee Auditorium, 1415 14 Ave SW; tickets cost around $30.

Downtown, the *Old Scotch* (☎ 269-7440), 820 10th St SW on the corner of 9th Ave SW, brings in good country, folk and jazz bands. There are jam sessions on Sunday nights. For rock, there's the *Cecil Hotel* on the corner of 4th Ave SE and 3rd Ave SE, *T Jay's* on 7th Ave SW, and north of downtown *Frankie &*

Johnny's in the North Centre Inn, 1621 Centre St N on the corner of 16th Ave. The *King Edward Hotel*, on the corner of 9th Ave SE and 4th St SE, has live blues bands and the *Unicorn Pub* has Irish music.

Marty's Café, on 17th Ave SW near 4th St SW, is an excellent little spot for blues, jazz and a varied assortment of music. There are other places along the street, some with dancing. South of town the *Inn on Lake Bonavista*, 747 Bonavista Drive SE, with views of the lake and mountains, is a more up-market place for a drink.

North over the river *Kensington's Delicafé*, 1414 Kensington Rd NW, is a good restaurant and nightspot. It has cheap food, a relaxed atmosphere, live music and an outdoor patio. It's open daily.

Cinema Calgary has many commercial cinemas all over town; see the local papers for listings.

The *National Film Board Theatre* (☎ 292-5338), 222 1st St SE, sometimes screens free films. The *Plaza Theatre* (☎ 283-3636), 1113 Kensington Rd NW, has two different shows a night plus midnight performances on Friday and Saturday. It presents off-beat US and foreign films. Tickets are $5.

The *University of Calgary* often has films in either the 148 Science Theatre or the Boris Roubakine Recital Hall. The films are mainly foreign.

Spectator Sports The Calgary Flames (☎ 261-0475), arch rivals of the Edmonton Oilers, play ice hockey from October to April in the Olympic Saddledome. Tickets cost from $8 to $28. The Calgary 88's who play in the World Basketball League also use the Olympic Saddledome as a home base. The Calgary Stampeders (☎ 289-0205) play Canadian-style professional football from July to September in McMahon Stadium in north-west Calgary off Crowchild Trail. Tickets range from $13 to $25.

Getting There & Away

Air Calgary International Airport is about 15

km north-east of the centre of town off Barlow Trail which is a 25-minute drive.

Air Canada (☎ 265-3090) and Canadian Airlines (☎ 235-1161) fly to many Canadian and US cities. Alaska Airlines (☎ 800-426-0333 toll free) and Delta Airlines (☎ 265-7610) connect Calgary with points in Alaska and mainland USA. Northwest Airlines (☎ 800-225-2525 toll free) flies to Winnipeg and destinations in mainland USA. United Airlines (☎ 800-241-6522) has an office at the airport.

Canadian Airlines operates a 40-minute commuter service to Edmonton with flights all day long. The one-way fare is a bit pricey at $102, but on weekends there's a special fare of $93 return. One-way fares to some other cities are to: Toronto $339, Victoria $209, Winnipeg $232, Whitehorse $381, and Los Angeles $258.

Bus The Greyhound Bus Depot (☎ 265-9111), 850 16th St SW at the junction with 9th Ave SW, is a bit away from the centre. It's walkable but most people opt for the free city shuttle bus which goes to the door.

There are frequent Greyhound buses to Edmonton ($24), Vancouver via the Okanagan or Fraser Canyon for $73; Banff, $11.90; Drumheller, $12.75; Lethbridge, $19.45; Winnipeg, $96; and Toronto, $198.

Red Arrow Express (☎ 531-0350) offers four luxury buses a day to Edmonton from its Calgary depot at Westward Inn, 119 12th Ave SW. The fare is $26 one way or $50 return.

Train Despite the closure of VIA Rail's southern route it is still possible to travel by train from Calgary to Vancouver via Banff and Jasper on the privately owned 'Rocky Mountaineer'. But it isn't cheap: one way direct to Vancouver costs $425 (which includes food and an overnight stop in a hotel in Kamloops). The service runs between the end of May and early October. For information contact a travel agent or the Great Canadian Railtour Company (☎ 643-3841; 800-665-7245 toll free), Suite 345, 625 Howe St, Vancouver, British Columbia V6C 2T6.

The railway station is conveniently located in the Calgary Tower.

Getting Around
To/From Airport The best way to and from the airport is the Airporter Bus, which runs from 5.30 am to 11.30 pm between all major downtown hotels and the airport and costs $6.50. One departs every 20 minutes from the Westin Hotel at 320 4th Ave SW. Alternatively you could take the C-Train north-east to Whitehorn then catch bus No 57 to the airport.

A taxi to the airport costs about $15 to $20.

Bus & LRT Calgary Transit (☎ 276-7801), at 216 7th Ave SW opposite the Bay department store, operates the bus and Light Rapid Transit (LRT) rail system. The office has route maps, information and tickets and is open Monday to Friday from 8.30 am to 5 pm. The Calgary LRT train is known as the C-Train.

One fare entitles you to transfer to other buses or the C-Train. The C-Train, is free in the downtown area along 7th Ave between 10th St SW and 3rd St SE. If you're going further or need a transfer, buy your ticket from a machine on the C-Train platform. A single one-way ticket costs $1.25 but you can get a day pass for $3.50.

The C-Train goes north-west to the university, north-east to the airport and south to Macleod Trail. Bus Nos 3, 17 and 53 go north-south along Centre St between the northern areas of the city and downtown. Bus No 19 runs east-west along 16th Ave (the Trans Canada Highway). Bus No 10 goes south along the Macleod Trail.

Note that most places in the downtown area are within walking distance of each other.

Car Various rental outlets can be found around town. Rent-A-Wreck (☎ 237-7093) with the lowest overall rates, requires reservations for small cars. It charges $37.95 per day plus 11 cents for every km over 150 km.

Thrifty Car Rental (☎ 262-4400), at 117 5th Ave SE, requires $48.95 a day plus 14 cents per km after the first 150 km. On weekdays Budget (☎ 263-0505), at 140 6th Ave SE, charges a flat $49.99; on weekends it's $31 per day plus 12 cents per km after the first 130 km.

Hitching Thumbing within the Calgary city limits is illegal and subject to very heavy fines. The law's enforced, so forget hitching here. If you're heading west to Banff take bus No 105 from downtown and ask the driver if there's a connecting bus going further. If not, walk to the city boundary before attempting to hitch.

Southern Alberta

Southern Alberta is cattle-ranching country, although wheat is very important, too. Here you can visit the badlands with their unusual rock formations and vestiges of prehistoric beasts around Drumheller and Dinosaur Provincial Park, or see Head-Smashed-In Buffalo Jump where the Blackfoot used to kill the herds for food, etc. Waterton Lakes National Park, Kananaskis Country and the provincial parks provide opportunities to see wildlife and beautiful scenery.

LETHBRIDGE
Lethbridge, on the Crowsnest Highway, is the largest town in southern Alberta, the third largest in the province, and a centre for the local agricultural communities. When you walk around town you'll see some people dressed in early 19th-century clothing. These are Hutterites, members of a Protestant sect who live on collective farms and eschew most aspects of modern society.

The Visitor Information Centre (☎ 320-1222) is on Brewery Hill at the western end of 1st Ave South. For information about the south-western region of Alberta visit the Chinook Country Tourist Association (☎ 329-6777) at 2805 Scenic Drive.

Nikka Yuko Japanese Gardens
Nikka Yuko Japanese Gardens (☎ 328-3511), on the corner of 7th Ave South and Mayor Magrath Drive, were built to symbolise Japanese-Canadian friendship. These authentic gardens consist of ponds, rocks and shrubs but no flowers. The buildings and bridges were built in Japan and reassembled here. 'Geisha' girls recite their oft-repeated explanations to you. The gardens are open from mid-May to early October and admission is $2.50, students $1.25.

Indian Battle Park
On the western side of the city beside Oldman River is Indian Battle Park, so named after a battle between the Blackfoot and the Cree. Within the park is Fort Whoop-Up (☎ 329-0444), a replica of a notorious whisky trading post; it's open daily in the summer from 10 am to 6 pm and admission is free.

Sir Alexander Galt Museum
This small museum (☎ 320-3898), at the western end of 5th Ave South, displays artefacts from Lethbridge history.

FORT MACLEOD
On Oldman River about 50 km west of Lethbridge, two hours south of Calgary, is the town of Fort Macleod. Fort Macleod Museum (☎ 553-4703), 219 25th St, is a replica of the Northwest Mounted Police fort of 1874, the first in the region. The fort is patrolled by Mounties wearing traditional red uniforms, four times daily in July and August. Inside there is a small local history collection. Admission is $3.

For trivia enthusiasts Fort Macleod is Joni Mitchell's home town.

HEAD-SMASHED-IN BUFFALO JUMP
About 20 km west of Fort Macleod, Head-Smashed-In Buffalo Jump (☎ 553-2731), on Spring Point Rd off Highway 2, is a UN World Heritage Site. It's the oldest, biggest and best preserved bison jump site in North America. For thousands of years Blackfoot used it to run buffalo, their 'living depart-

ment stores', over the edge of the cliff. They then used the meat, hide, bone, horns and nearly everything else for their supplies and materials.

The interpretive centre, opened in 1987 by the Duke and Duchess of York, provides explanations of the site and how the Blackfoot's work was achieved. There are nearly two km of outdoor trails. A 10-minute film, a dramatised re-enactment of the buffalo hunt, is shown regularly during the day. Admission to the centre is by donation.

KANANASKIS COUNTRY

Adjacent to the south-western corner of Banff National Park and 90 km west of Calgary, Kananaskis Country has been set aside as an outdoor recreational area. The 4000 sq km region offers facilities for skiing, cycling, hiking, horse riding, boating, camping and picnicking. Kananaskis Country is most notable for the downhill skiing at Nakiska, where the alpine events of the 1988 Olympic Winter Games were held.

CARDSTON

Cardston, south-west of Lethbridge at the junction of highways 5 and 2, is a centre for the Mormons. The town gets its name from Charles Ora Card who founded it. The huge, renovated, box-shaped Mormon Temple (☎ 653-4142), 348 3rd St, offers tours of its visitor centre in summer.

WATERTON LAKES NATIONAL PARK

This national park in the far south-western corner of Alberta was opened in 1895 and is joined with the Glacier National Park of Montana to form the Waterton Glacier International Peace Park. The land here rises from the prairie into rugged, beautiful alpine scenery with many lakes, waterfalls and valleys. The whole park has fewer visitors than its two more northerly sisters, Banff and Jasper. Partly because of this, spotting wildlife here is more common. The town of Waterton is smaller and much more low-key than Banff.

The park has over 180 km of trails – good for hiking or riding. Waterton Inter-Nation

Shoreline Cruises (☎ 859-2362) operates cruises on Upper Waterton Lake with boats holding up to 200 passengers. A limited operation begins in May with no stops in the USA; the full schedule operates between mid-June and the first weekend in September with most cruises stopping at Goat Haunt in Montana. The fare is $11, children $5.

In the north-east of the park you can visit **Buffalo Paddock** containing a small herd of bison.

Accommodation in the park consists of three government campgrounds and several lodges and motels. There are also a couple of privately owned campgrounds just outside the park.

DRUMHELLER

A small city in a strange setting, Drumheller is about 150 km north-east of Calgary in the Red Deer River Valley, dinosaur country. Thousands of years of wind and water erosion have generated the captivating surrounding badlands which reveal millions of years of the earth's animal and geological history. The area is renowned for its fossils of dinosaurs, petrified wood and weird land formations. More complete dinosaur skeletons of the Cretaceous Age (from 64 to 140 million years ago) have been found in the region than anywhere else on the planet.

Drumheller sits 122 metres below prairie level in a valley carved out by glaciers. As you come into town you'll see heavy farm machinery lined up for sale, looking like the work of a mad sculptor.

At 61 Bridge St the Fossil Shop is worth visiting for a look around and perhaps a purchase of a 75-million-year-old souvenir. There are all kinds of bones and dinosaur fragments to examine and the staff are very knowledgeable. Perhaps unexpectedly, some of the findings offered for sale are not at all expensive.

There are privately owned campgrounds in the area.

Drumheller Dinosaur & Fossil Museum

This museum (☎ 823-2593), 335 1st St East, gives a good introduction to the prehistoric life and geology of the badlands and has remains and fossils on display. One display is a pieced-together Edmontosaurus, a four to five-tonne, nine-metre-long beast found in 1923. The museum is open daily in May and June from 10 am to 5 pm, in July and August from 10 am to 6 pm.

Dinosaur Trail

Drumheller is at the beginning of Dinosaur Trail, a 48-km loop around the area taking in all the attractions – you'll need a car to cover it. The scenery along the trail is really good, as is the view from **Horsethief Canyon**

Point. There are trails here leading down into the valley where you can poke around in the petrified oyster beds. The **Hoodoos**, about 18 km south-east of Drumheller on Highway 10, are the best example of these weird, mushroom-like columns of rock.

Tyrell Museum of Palaeontology

Along the North Dinosaur Trail (Highway 838) north-west of town is the Tyrell Museum of Palaeontology (☎ 823-7707). This modern museum uses displays, videos, films, computers, etc to outline the study of early life on earth. Fossils trace the story of

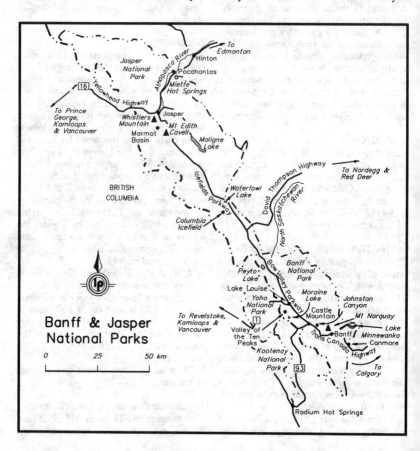

evolution and best of all is the extensive display of dinosaurs. It's open daily from 9 am to 9 pm in summer while the rest of the year it's open Tuesday to Sunday from 10 am to 5 pm. Admission is free.

In **Midland Provincial Park** south-west of Drumheller, there are tours of old mines at 10 am and 3 pm daily, except Wednesday and Thursday. There's no camping in the park.

DINOSAUR PROVINCIAL PARK

This six-sq-km park is a 70-million-year-old dinosaur graveyard and is a must if you're passing by. It's 78 km north of Brooks, roughly halfway between Calgary and Medicine Hat, off Highway 544. Entry to the park is free.

The badlands of the park are a dry, convoluted lunar landscape, but they weren't always like this: at one time the area was a jungle-like swamp and dinosaurs loved it. Their remains and fossils lie buried all over the valley. The **Tyrell Museum of Palaeontology** (☎ 378-4342), in Drumheller (118 km north-west of the park) has a field station here with four display areas where nearly complete skeletons have been uncovered, dusted off and encased in glass, just the way they were found. Close to 120 skeletons have been found, and many have been sent to museums around the world.

There are guided walks through the strange, eroded landscape, or in summer you can go on a bus tour for $1.50.

Good photographs are easy here; the Hoodoos make a good subject. Take plenty of water along in summer: walking in the valley can be as hot as hell.

There is a pretty good campground in the park, by a river, making a small, green oasis in this stark place. A site costs $5.

KINBROOK ISLAND PROVINCIAL PARK

This is a good camping spot on the way to or from Calgary. It's 19 km south-west of Brooks by Lake Newell, an artificial lake. You can swim and fish, or simply escape the very flat, totally treeless stretch of highway between here and Medicine Hat.

WRITING-ON-STONE PROVINCIAL PARK

This park is south-east of Lethbridge close to the US border, off Highway 501. It gets its name from the carvings and paintings made by the Plains Indians on the cliffs along the banks of **Milk River**. The river is used for canoeing and in winter there's cross-country skiing in the park. Camping is available too.

MEDICINE HAT

This city, on the banks of the South Saskatchewan River, was formed in 1883 when the Canadian Pacific railway, drilling for water, hit natural gas. Enough of it was subsequently found to prompt Rudyard Kipling to label it 'the city with all hell for a basement'. Today Medicine Hat still has very cheap heat, light and hot water.

The Visitor Information Centre (☎ 527-6422), 8 Gehring Rd south of downtown off the Trans Canada Highway, is open daily throughout the year.

If you miss Calgary's Stampede, there's one here during the third week of July at the Exhibition & Stampede Grounds (☎ 526-3979), five km south-east of downtown off 21st Ave SE. The **Altaglass Plant** (☎ 527-2339), 613 16th St SW, has free tours showing artisans blowing glass in the traditional manner.

CYPRESS HILLS PROVINCIAL PARK

This park straddling the Saskatchewan border is described in the Saskatchewan chapter.

Banff & Jasper National Parks

Much of the Rocky Mountain area of Alberta, running along the British Columbia border, is contained and protected within two huge, adjacent national parks – Banff to the south and Jasper to the north. The Icefields Parkway links the two, though there is no real boundary. The entire area is one of spectacular beauty with some of the best scenery, hiking and skiing to be found anywhere in the world.

The two national parks offer jagged, snow-capped mountains, peaceful valleys, rushing rivers, natural hot springs and alpine forests. The colour of many Rocky Mountain lakes will have you doubting your eyes. Both parks also have modern conveniences or backcountry trails to choose from. Wildlife abounds, particularly in Jasper National Park.

Banff National Park was Canada's first national park and is the best known and most popular, attracting three million visitors annually. It covers an area of 6641 sq km and contains 25 mountains of 3000 metres or more in height. The skiing and climbing are world famous. Jasper National Park is larger, wilder and less explored but, like Banff National Park, offers excellent hiking trails.

In order to preserve the region the Canada Parks Service controls visitors impact by designating specific park areas as campgrounds, picnic sites, fireplaces, service centres and townsites. Please stick to these areas and read the section in the *Backcountry Visitors' Guide* on how to minimise your effect on the parks' environment.

The small towns of Banff and Jasper act as focal points for orientation, supplies and information.

Precautions

When in the backcountry it's recommended that water be boiled for at least 10 minutes before drinking it, due to the risk of catching 'beaver fever' or giardiasis. This is caused by an intestinal parasite *(Giardia lamblia)* which is spread by animal waste.

If you're heading into wilderness regions, read the pamphlet *You are in Bear Country* which gives advice on how to steer clear of dangerous encounters with bears and what to do if this becomes unavoidable. You can get a copy from Visitor Information Centres.

The trails heavily used by horse trips are a real mess; long-distance hikers will want to avoid them. Ask at the park warden offices or the Visitor Information Centres which trails are used most by the horses.

Tenters should note that pretty well all the campgrounds in and around the Rockies are covered in pebbles or stones – rather lumpy for sleeping on the ground! A sleeping pad or foam mattress of some description is more or less essential. Also bending or snapping a few tent pegs can be expected.

BANFF & AROUND

Banff, 138 km west of Calgary, is Canada's No 1 resort town in both winter and summer, and as such is really the centre of the Rockies. Despite that, it's very small, consisting of one main street, and so can get crowded. The heaviest months are July and August. Although this can cause problems, the many vacationers generally create a relaxed and festive atmosphere. Many of the workers in and around town are newcomers, 'gorbies' (tourists) or long-term visitors themselves.

The town is clean and pleasant, the surroundings unbeatable. It makes a good R&R spot after travelling awhile, or hiking.

There are stores selling and renting skiing, hiking and camping equipment and supplies. Many good day trips and hikes can be done from Banff.

Orientation

Banff Ave, the main street, runs north-south through the whole length of town. It heads off north to meet the Trans Canada Highway. The street is lined with hotels, stores, restaurants and souvenir shops many of which cater to the heavy Japanese trade. Over the bridge at Banff Ave's southern end is the Parks Administration building. This is a good place for a view and a photo of the town. Behind the building are flower gardens with a stream, ponds and a few benches.

To the left over the bridge Mountain Ave leads to Sulphur Mountain and the hot springs, Spray Ave leads to the Banff Springs Hotel, the town's most famous landmark. To the right, Cave Ave goes to the Cave & Basin Hot Springs; these were the first springs found in the area and led to the creation of the national park.

The side streets in town are mainly residential but the central ones also have eating spots and a few shops.

Information

The Park Information Office and the Chamber of Commerce both have counters in the Visitor Information Centre (☎ 762-4256), 224 Banff Ave near the corner of Wolf St in the centre of town. Before doing any hiking, check in here: there are detailed maps and the staff will tell you about specific trail conditions and hazards. Anybody hiking overnight must sign in. The office also has the leaflet, *Your are in Bear Country*. There are posters around detailing the naturalist programmes and guided hikes which are free and happen regularly. The centre is open daily from 8 am to 10 pm in summer.

The main post office (☎ 762-2586), at the southern end of the downtown area on the corner of Buffalo and Bear Sts, is open Monday to Friday from 9 am to 5.30 pm. The public library (☎ 762-2661) is at 101 Bear St opposite the post office. Mineral Springs Hospital (☎ 762-4333) is on Bow Ave near the corner of Wolf St. In emergencies call the Banff Warden Office (☎ 762-4506).

If you need to change money the Foreign Currency Exchange (☎ 762-4698) in the Clock Tower Village Mall is open daily from 9 am to 11 pm. The Bank of Montreal opens on Saturdays from 10 am to 4 pm.

Bookshops The Book & Art Den (☎ 762-3919), 110 Banff Ave, is an excellent bookshop with all manner of guides and books on the mountains, hiking, canoeing and the history of the area.

Jobs Work is usually easy to come by in and around Banff in the hotels, bars, restaurants and ski areas. Some places offer accommodation, but don't expect great pay. Look for signs in the windows.

Warning Police are very strict in Banff and

after 1 am, cars are often checked for drunk drivers and drugs. The fines are heavy.

Hitchhikers should be aware they may often be thoroughly checked out.

Lastly, cars are frequently broken into so don't leave valuables in them, especially at night.

Banff Park Museum

The park museum (☎ 762-3324), 93 Banff Ave by the Bow River Bridge at the southern end of town, has a collection of mammals, birds, plants and animals found in Banff National Park. Included are two small stuffed grizzlies and a black bear so you can study the difference. There's also an 1841 tree graffiti carving. The old wooden building which houses the museum dates from 1903. It's open daily from 10 am to 6 pm and admission is free.

Natural History Museum

This museum (☎ 762-4747), on the 2nd floor of the Clock Tower Village Mall at 112 Banff Ave, has displays on early life forms, including Canadian dinosaurs. It has video and slide presentations and features a model of the notorious Sasquatch, the abominable snowman of the Rockies. The Loch Ness monster of Western Canada, the Sasquatch is said to be about three metres tall and to have been spotted over 500 times. You can also read descriptions of Castleguard Cave, one of Canada's biggest at 12 km long, which is in the north of Banff National Park. The museum is open daily in summer from 10 am to 10 pm and admission is $2.

Luxton Museum

Luxton Museum (☎ 762-2388), 1 Birch Ave, is in the fort-like wooden building to the right as you head south over the bridge. It deals mainly with the Plains Indians but also covers indigenous groups from all over Alberta. The museum has displays, models and re-creations depicting aspects of their traditional culture including clothing, weapons and crafts. Note the woven porcupine quills, the old photographs and the human scalp as well as the stuffed animals.

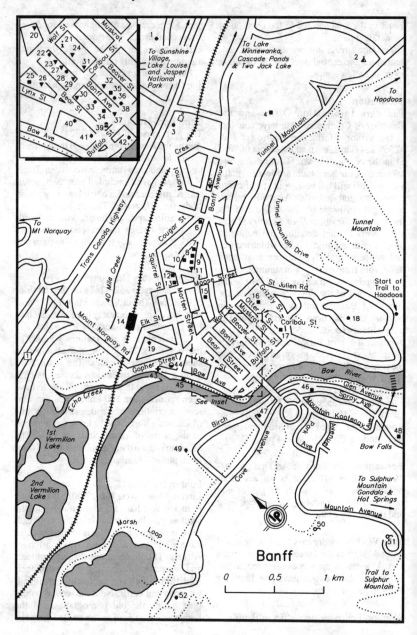

Banff

0   0.5   1 km

■ PLACES TO STAY

2   Tunnel Mountain Village Campground
4   CHA Hostel
6   Spruce Grove Motel
7   Irwin's Motor Inn
8   Red Carpet Inn
9   High Country Inn
10 Mrs McHardy B&B
12 Mrs Riva B&B
13 Holiday Inn Lodge
15 Mr Harnack B&B
16 Mrs Florence Wray B&B
17 Mrs J Cowan B&B
25 Banff Park Lodge
36 Cascade Inn
46 YWCA
48 Banff Springs Hotel

▼ PLACES TO EAT

5   Bumper's Beef House
11 Gus's Family Restaurant
20 Rundle Restaurant
23 Smitty's Family Restaurant
24 Fast Freddies
26 Melissa's Missteak
27 Joe Btfsplk's Diner
29 Grizzly House
30 Magpie & Stump
31 Rose & Crown

32 The Balkan Restaurant
37 Le Beaujolais

OTHER

1   Buffalo Paddock
3   Banff Warden Office
14 Railway Station
18 Banff Centre
19 RCMP
21 Visitor Information Centre
22 Banff Avenue Mall
28 Sundance Mall
33 Bank of Montreal
34 Barbary Coast
35 Silver City
38 Clock Tower Village Mall
39 Main Post Office
40 Whyte Museum
41 Public Library
42 Banff Park Museum
43 Mineral Springs Hospital
44 Bus Depot
45 Canoe Dock
47 Luxton Museum
49 Martin Stables
50 Middle Springs
51 Upper Hot Springs
52 Cave & Basin Centennial Centre

It's worth a visit. Admission is $2 and the museum is open from 10 am to 6 pm daily in summer, from 10 am to 5 pm the rest of the year.

Harmony Drugs
In this drugstore at 111 Banff Ave take a look at the old photos dating from about 1915 all around the ceiling. Some were taken by Byron Harmon, who once owned the drugstore and ran a photography business. Many of that business's early photos are for sale around town, and reproduced in books or as postcards.

Whyte Museum
The Whyte Museum complex (☎ 762-2291), 111 Bear St between Buffalo and Caribou Sts, contains an art gallery and a vast collec-

tion of photographs telling the history of the area. The archives also contain manuscripts, oral history tapes and maps. On the property are four log cabins and two Banff heritage homes, one dating from 1907 and one from 1931. There are guided tours of the heritage homes on weekend afternoons. The foundation presents films, lectures and concerts regularly. It's open daily in summer from 10 am to 6 pm and costs $2, seniors and students $1.

Banff Centre
The centre (☎ 762-6300), on St Julien Rd east of the downtown area, contains one of Canada's best known art schools with facilities for dance, theatre, music and the visual arts. Exhibits, concerts and various other events often take place there. Throughout the

summer, during the Festival of the Arts, students, together with internationally recognised artists, present their works in workshops and performances. There is something almost every day, usually free. The Visitor Information Office has a complete schedule.

Buffalo Paddock

Just north-west of Banff on the Trans Canada Highway (you can only enter from the westbound lane), this 40-hectare enclosure contains a small herd of bison like the ones which once roamed the prairies. Admission is free and you're not supposed to leave your car as you drive through. Evening or early morning is the best time to visit – during the middle of the day the beasts tend to keep a low and docile profile, out of view.

Sulphur Mountain & Gondola

Sulphur Mountain offers the closest gondola (☎ 762-3324/2523) to Banff. It runs to the summit and provides spectacular views of the surrounding mountains, Bow River and Banff townsite from an altitude of 2285 metres. You can walk up in about 1¼ hours if you don't fool around, and are rewarded with a free lift down: tickets are only needed going up.

The lower terminal is just over three km south of Banff on Mountain Ave, near the Upper Hot Springs. To get there, you can hitch fairly easily or take the Brewster Gray Line bus from town. The walking path starts under the gondola cables. The gondola runs from 9 am to 8 pm in the summer, with shorter hours in the winter. Tickets are $7.50.

Mt Norquay

Mt Norquay, also with a gondola, is about 10 minutes north of Banff by car along Mt Norquay Rd. The gondola ride here is shorter than at Sulphur Mountain and the overall height about 200 metres lower. Still the view is great. Tickets are $6. In summer the gondola is open from 9.30 am to 5.30 pm and there is a restaurant at the top.

Sunshine Village

Another gondola ride is found in Sunshine Village, 22 km north-west of Banff. At five km the gondola ride is the longest of the three. The gondola is open daily from 9 am to 8 pm and the round trip costs $12, children $5. There's a hotel at the top which isn't too badly priced, and a restaurant.

Upper Hot Springs

There is a soothing hot pool and steam room at the Upper Hot Springs spa (☎ 762-2056), three km south of town near Sulphur Mountain. Admission to the pool is $2 and you can rent bathing suits ($1) and towels (75 cents). In summer the hot springs are open daily from 8.30 am to 11 pm; in winter Monday to Thursday from 2.30 to 9 pm, Friday to Sunday from 8.30 am to 11 pm. Ahhhhhh.

Cave & Basin Centennial Centre

South-west of town at the end of Cave Ave is the Cave & Basin Centennial Centre (☎ 762-4900) with a swimming pool and complex rebuilt to the original style of 1914. It was the discovery of the hot sulphur springs in a cave here that led to the creation of Banff National Park. The water is not as hot as that of the Upper Hot Springs but it's still comfortably warm, with swimming daily from 10 am to 8 pm, mid- June to early September. The rented bathing suits ($1) are fun – they're 1914-style. Admission is $2 and the hire of a towel 75 cents. There are a couple of pleasant short walks here, the cave, exhibits in the centre (open year round) and a coffee shop.

Lake Minnewanka

Lake Minnewanka, 11 km east of Banff, is a scenic recreational area surrounded by forests and mountains with swimming, sailing, boating and fishing available. Lake Minnewanka Boat Tours (☎ 762-3473) has a 1½-hour cruise on the lake to Devil's Gap for $13.

Hiking

There are many good short hikes and day walks around the Banff area. From the

Visitor Information Centre get a copy of *Drives & Walks* which describes trails in and around Banff. For longer, more remote hiking, the leaflet *Backcountry Visitors' Guide* has a map showing trails in the whole park. Some good walks begin more or less right in town, like the ones to Tunnel Mountain and the Hoodoos; others begin a little further out.

You can take a pleasant, quiet stroll by **Bow River** just three blocks west of Banff Ave beside Bow Ave. The trail runs from the corner of Wolf St, along the river under the Bow River Bridge and ends shortly thereafter on Buffalo St. If you cross the bridge, you can continue left through the woods along a trail to **Bow Falls** – it's not far.

For a good short climb – to break in the legs and to view the town and area – walk up stubby **Tunnel Mountain** east of the downtown area. There's a trail leading up from St Julien Rd; you can drive here, but it's not a long walk from downtown to the start of the path.

From the southern end of Buffalo St a trail between Bow River and Tunnel Mountain heads north to the **Hoodoos**.

If you follow Banff Ave north from town towards Lake Minnewanka for about five km you come to **Cascade Ponds**, just past the Trans Canada Highway. You can climb up beside the waterfall for good views.

One good hike, that's not difficult, begins at **Johnston Canyon**. This is west of Banff on the Bow Valley Parkway (Highway 1A), that branches off, then later rejoins, the Trans Canada Highway en route to Lake Louise. The 12-km trail goes by many waterfalls, including two large ones, to some underground-fed crystal-clear pools known as 'inkpots'. Here in the meadow is an ideal picnic spot. Along the **Bow Valley Parkway** watch for impressive **Castle Mountain**, also called Eisenhower Mountain: it's a huge piece of rock that catches the late afternoon light.

At **Sunshine Village** you'll find long and short trails. On one of the trails you can walk across the boundary into British Columbia. A popular trail is the overnight trip to nearby

Egypt Lakes. From Sunshine Village it's a long, steady climb with great scenery over **Healy Pass**, including views to **Mt Assiniboine**, the highest in the park at 3618 metres. You'll see lots of butterflies and flowers in the alpine meadows. You can take hikes to the higher lakes and fish for cutthroat trout. At the lakes is a basic hut that sleeps about 10 people, but you should reg-

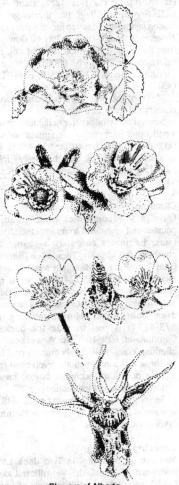

Flowers of Alberta

ister in Banff before you go – it may be booked out. There's tenting around the hut so a place inside is not essential.

Skiing

Two of the finest ski centres in Canada are Mt Norquay and Sunshine Village. At Mt Norquay the ski season is from November to April. For information contact Mt Norquay (☎ 762-4421), PO Box 1258, Banff T0L 0C0. Sunshine Village has the longer ski season lasting about seven months from mid-November to mid-June. It has 62 downhill runs the longest of which is eight km. For information call (☎ 762-6500), or write to Sunshine Village PO Box 1510, Banff T0L 0C0.

Many of the hiking trails become cross-country ski trails in winter.

Several companies offer heliskiing, where a helicopter flies you to a mountain and you ski out. Banff Helisports (☎ 678-4888), PO Box 2326, Banff T0L 0C0, has daily flights including guide and equipment for around $125.

Climbing

Quite a few companies offer climbing courses and organised tours into the mountains. Beginners can start by using the climbing wall Monday, Tuesday or Thursday from 7 to 9 pm at Mountain Magic Equipment (☎ 762-2591), 224 Bear St. It has classes each evening from Monday to Friday but will also give private lessons. The Canadian School of Mountaineering (☎ 678-4134) is just outside the park in Canmore at 629 10th St. A weekend of climbing costs $140 for beginners or $180 for those at the intermediate level; most fees include dormitory accommodation, breakfast, equipment and instruction.

The Alpine Club of Canada (☎ 762-4481), upstairs at 105 Banff Ave, can provide information and/or a guide.

Canoeing & Rafting

You can go canoeing on **Two Jack Lake** north-east of Banff, the **Vermilion Lakes** (which have lots of wildlife) west of town,

Echo Creek, 40 Mile Creek and **Bow River**. Western River Runners (☎ 762-3632) rents canoes from Canoe Dock by the river on the corner of Bow Ave and Wolf St. It also offers a one-hour rafting tour on the Bow River from Bow Falls to the Hoodoos for $16. For white-water rafting Kootenay River Runners (☎ 762-5385), on the corner of Banff Ave and Caribou St, has half-day and full-day trips.

Cycling

You can cycle on the highways and on some of the trails in the park. Get a copy of the leaflet *Trail Bicycling in National Parks in Alberta & British Columbia* which lists trails on which cycling is permitted. Excursions for a few hours, a day or several days with overnight stops at campgrounds, hostels or lodges are all possible. No cycling is allowed off the trails.

Two good, short cycling routes close to Banff are along **Vermilion Lakes Drive** and **Tunnel Mountain Drive**. For a longer trip the scenic **Bow Valley Parkway** connecting Banff and Lake Louise is very popular.

Rocky Mountain Cycle Tours (☎ 678-6770) operates out of Canmore and runs bicycle trips through the Rockies.

For bicycle rentals see the Getting Around section later.

Horse Riding

In Banff the most popular routes are south of Bow River on the trail beside **Spray River**, the **Marsh Loop**, the **Sundance Trail**, the trail alongside **Cave Ave** and the one to **Middle Springs**. Warner & Mackenzie Guiding & Outfitting (☎ 762-4551), 132 Banff Ave, offers horse-riding trips from one hour to one week in length. Martin Stables (☎ 762-2832), on Birch Ave, and Banff Springs Hotel (☎ 762-2848) offer one to three-hour trips. Rates start at $10 per hour.

Organised Tours

Brewster Gray Line does a tour of Banff which takes three hours and costs $23. The bus goes to the Hoodoos, Bow Falls, Tunnel

Mountain Drive, Buffalo Paddock and Sulphur Mountain.

Brewster Gray Line also runs tours to Lake Louise, the Columbia Icefield and Jasper. The tour to Lake Louise goes via the Vermilion Lakes and Bow Valley Parkway stopping at Johnston Canyon and Castle Mountain. The round trip takes four hours and costs $28. The tour to the Columbia Icefield in Jasper National Park takes approximately 9½ hours and costs $49 return.

The return trip to Jasper takes two days and requires an overnight stay there; you travel to Lake Louise along the Icefields Parkway stopping at the Columbia Icefield and Athabasca Falls. Time is allowed for rafting on the Athabasca River but that's not included in the price. The tour takes 9½ hours one way and the return fare is $68.

Tours in a helicopter are also available but they're not cheap. As an example, Assiniboine Heli Tours (☎ 678-5459), PO Box, Canmore, has flights to Mt Assiniboine for $644 for three people; the price, however, does include a guide and food.

If you're driving, you can hire self-guiding auto cassette tapes that describe the journey between Banff and Jasper via Lake Louise and the Columbia Icefield. These can be rented for $16.95 from Rocky Mountain Auto Tours in the Banff Ave Mall.

Places to Stay
Generally, accommodation here is fairly costly. The numerous motels are usually moderately priced, the hotels expensive. Private tourist homes are less expensive and in many cases are more interesting places to stay in.

As an alternative to finding accommodation in Banff, some people watching their wallets stay in the town of Canmore just outside the park, where the rates are lower and then enter the park on a day basis.

Camping
There are many campgrounds in the area around Banff. Note that they are all busy in July and August, so book in by 12 noon or you may well be turned away.

Tunnel Mountain Village is not bad. Tunnel Mountain is close to town and has three sites – two for RVs only and one for tents at $9.50 per site plus shower. At night you may hear coyotes yelping and howling. At Two Jack Lake there are a couple of campgrounds. *Two Jack Lakeside*, 12 km north-east of Banff on Lake Minnewanka Rd, is open from July to early September and costs $9 per site. One km north *Two Jack Lake Main* has 381 sites at $7 each. Both campgrounds have running water but no showers.

Along the Bow Valley Parkway there is a campground at Johnston Canyon, about 25 km west of Banff, and at Castle Mountain two km north of Castle Junction.

Alternatively there are those who unfold sleeping bags anywhere in the woods surrounding Banff, including just up the road towards Sulphur Mountain. If doing this do not ever light a fire and don't use the food bag for a pillow. Who knows what animal is on the prowl?

Hostels *Banff CHA Hostel* (☎ 762-4122), on Tunnel Mountain Rd three km from the downtown area, has 154 beds in small rooms, a cafeteria, laundry facilities and a common room with a fireplace. Members pay $12, nonmembers $17.

The good *YWCA* (☎ 762-3560), 102 Spray Ave, takes men and women, can hold up to 60 people and is very popular. Dorm beds are $14, singles/doubles $40/48. There's a cafeteria but no cooking facilities.

Castle Mountain CHA Hostel on the Bow Valley Parkway, holds up to 36 people, has pit toilets, hot showers and volleyball courts. For members a dorm bed is $9, for nonmembers $14. It's closed on Wednesday nights.

B&Bs & Tourist Homes The Chamber of Commerce desk in the Visitor Information Centre gives a short list of people offering B&B and tourist-home accommodation. Banff B&B Bureau (☎ 762-5070), PO Box 369, Banff T0L 0C0, is a reservation agency. Some places rent out rooms in their houses, others in small separate cabins.

The prices for B&Bs and tourist homes vary, depending on their size and facilities, your duration of stay and the season, but are generally in the $20 to $60 range for a single or double. Most are about $35 to $50. Banff has quite a few but you should telephone around first. Some prefer at least a week's stay, some prefer not to take young people or may ask if you're married. They get busy on weekends, so calling saves legwork.

Mrs J Cowan (☎ 762-3696), 118 Otter St, has nine rooms which she rents all year. Rooms without/with bathroom cost $20/50 with a continental breakfast. *Mrs Florence Wray* (☎ 762-3612), 206 Otter St, has two singles at $25 and two double rooms which are $30.

Marten St has several tourist homes. *Holiday Lodge* (☎ 762-3648), 311 Marten St, run by George Baptist, is one of the nicest in town. George is a good source of information about Banff and cooks a great breakfast. He rents singles/doubles for $25/35, or $40/65 with breakfast. Out the back, George also has two cabins with cooking facilities which hold four people and go for $80. *Mrs Riva* (☎ 762-2471), 345 Marten St, has one room with twin beds and shared bathroom for $35 and a cabin with private bath, cooking facilities and TV for $45. Both prices include a breakfast of coffee/tea and toast. *Mrs McHardy* (☎ 762-2176), 412 Marten St, offers cabins with hot plates for $35 a double.

Mr Harnack (☎ 762-3619), 338 Banff Ave, has 10 double rooms at $26.25 each. He also has some larger self-contained cabins out the back which must be rented for a minimum of two nights: one for four people is $94.50.

Hotels Banff has no cheap hotels anymore. Downtown, *Rundle Manor Apartment Hotel* (☎ 762-5544), 348 Marten St, has rooms with kitchens for $100 a single or double. Children under 17 years of age can stay in their parents' room for free. *Cascade Inn* (☎ 762-3311), 124 Banff Ave, has been totally refurbished and charges $120/125 for singles/doubles with all mod cons. The his-

torical *Banff Springs Hotel* (☎ 762-2211), on Spray Ave south of downtown, has everything including golf course, tennis courts, riding stables, bars and restaurants. Rooms cost singles/doubles $225/270.

Motels Most accommodation here is in motels many of which are on Banff Ave north of Elk St. They are not cheap either but are not as costly as the hotels.

Spruce Grove Motel (☎ 762-2112), 545 Banff Ave, has standard rooms with colour TV and charges singles/doubles $45/55. *Red Carpet Inn* (☎ 762-4184) at 425 Banff Ave is close to town and charges singles/doubles $60/70. It has a licensed restaurant and spa and is usually full in summer. Close by, *Irwin's Motor Inn*, 429 Banff Ave, has covered parking and charges singles/doubles $70/72. *High Country Inn* (☎ 762-2236), 419 Banff Ave, has air-con and heated parking and charges singles/doubles $70/85.

If you don't want to stay in town *Johnston Canyon Resort* (☎ 762-2971) is one of the cheaper motels but it's 26 km west on the Bow Valley Parkway. Singles/doubles cost $42/68; rooms with a kitchen cost extra. Groceries are available. The resort is open from 15 May to 20 September.

There are many places geared for skiers, which offer kitchens and can be good value if there are four of you or more. Of course, there are also many deluxe places around too if you're looking to really splurge.

Places to Eat

Like any resort town, Banff has plenty of restaurants. It's a good place to catch up on a meal or two if you've been in the backcountry. There are plenty of places to choose from but prices tend to be a bit high.

Places to Eat – bottom end For reasonably priced meals try the *cafeterias* in the *Banff CHA Hostel* and the *YWCA*. Their breakfast specials cost $3 or $4. If you make an early start you can have the breakfast special in the *Summit Restaurant* atop Sulphur Mountain for $3.45 before 9.30 am.

There are several places opposite the

Visitor Information Centre. *Coriander Nature Food*, upstairs in the Sundance Mall, is mainly a health-food shop but also has tables for serving food. It has fresh daily soups, lots of sandwiches and salads, which cost from $4 to $6. It's open Monday to Saturday from 10 am to 6 pm, Sunday from 11.30 am to 5.30 pm. *Joe Btfsplk's Diner* (pronounced 'bi-tif-splik'), 221 Banff Ave, is a busy US-style diner open daily from 8 am to 10 pm. It has breakfast specials of two eggs, bacon and toast for $3.50; it also serves sandwiches and omelettes from $4.50 and burgers from $5.

Smitty's Family Restaurant, 227 Banff Ave, is always reliable if not great. It's open daily from 6.30 am to 10 pm. The best value is the five pancakes with syrup for $4.

North along the street, *Rundle Restaurant*, 319 Banff Ave, is one of the few steady long-term places that doesn't even try to be trendy. It's straightforward, reasonable and a good spot for breakfast. Pancakes are $3.75 and omelettes start from $4. It also serves Chinese food. Nearby, *Piccadilly Fare*, 321 Banff Ave, is a small sandwich bar/deli with espresso coffee. It also has burgers for around $5 and spaghetti from $6 to $8.

For those of you who would rather be eating chocolate, go to *The Fudgery* or *Mountain Chocolates* in the Sundance Mall on Banff Ave. It's great for on the trails, and besides, you're burning calories off, right?

Places to Eat – middle For something a bit tastier try the popular *Magpie & Stump*, 203 Caribou St on the corner of Bear St. Built like an old-style saloon with cosy brown colours inside, it serves mainly Mexican food like tacos, enchiladas and burritos from $9 to $11. Guacamole salad is $6. It also serves steaks and is open from 12 noon till midnight.

Also up the ladder a rung is *Melissa's Missteak*, 218 Lynx St near the corner of Caribou St, looking sort of like a wood cabin inside and sort of like an English cottage outside. It specialises in deluxe heavy-duty hamburgers that make a meal, not a snack. There are 10 varieties from $5 to $7. The blue

cheese one is yummy. The rest of the menu includes pizza, and steaks for $15.

The *Balkan Restaurant*, 120 Banff Ave, is a moderately priced Greek-style restaurant with a very good reputation, open daily from 11 am to 11 pm. It offers moussaka for $10 and burgers from $5.50 to $7. It also serves a couple of vegetarian dishes: fettucini primavera is $9. *Cosy Corner Deli & Eatery* in the Banff Ave Mall has German food; bratwürst with sauerkraut is $10 and other main dishes are between $6 and $13.

Gus's Family Restaurant, 415 Banff Ave next to High Country Inn, is good for sandwiches including salad or fries for $7 and pizzas from $7. Main meals are between $9 and $11.

Places to Eat – top end For a splurge, *Grizzly House*, 207 Banff Ave, is recommended. It's basically a fondue place with prices for main courses starting from $15. It serves a variety of food including beef, seafood and escargots. Appetisers like French onion soup are $4.50 while rattlesnake fondue, at the top of the price list, is $56! The restaurant is open daily from 11.30 am to midnight.

There are several other places for splurges – serving steaks, seafood, Italian or French food. *Le Beaujolais*, 212 Buffalo St on the corner of Banff Ave, is expensive but highly rated. Starters cost between $7 and $10, while main dishes of steak, fish or poultry cost between $19 and $35. The restaurant is open daily from 5 to 11 pm. *Bumper's Beef House*, 603 Banff Ave north of downtown behind a service station, has good beef for around $15, a salad bar and a casual atmosphere.

The *Terrace Dining Room*, in the Banff Park Lodge at 222 Lynx St, serves mainly seafood. Main meals cost between $10 and $18. Also in the Banff Park Lodge, the *Chinook Restaurant* serves a good-value Sunday brunch. The excellent desserts and pastries are made here fresh daily.

Entertainment

Banff is the social and cultural focus of the

Rockies. The *Banff Centre* presents movies, theatre and concerts throughout the year, but especially from June to September during the Festival of the Arts, when it puts on over 130 performances.

On the corner of Bear and Wolf Sts, *Lux Cinema Centre* (☎ 762-8595) is a four-screen commercial cinema.

The *Rose & Crown*, 202 Banff Ave on the corner of Caribou St, is a British-style pub and restaurant which has live rock music and one room where you can play darts. Close by *Fast Freddies*, 212 Banff Ave, plays disco music till the wee small hours. At *Grizzly House* there's live jazz and recorded music nightly from 9 pm to 1 am. *Bumpers Beef House* has live music till 1 am. *Cascade Inn* has kept its piano bar and is more sedate than it used to be. *Silver City*, 110 Banff Ave, is a bar with live music at weekends; it's open from 9 pm to 2 am.

Many of the larger hotels and motels provide their own live entertainment.

Getting There & Away

Bus Greyhound (☎ 762-6767) buses run from the Brewster Transportation Depot, 100 Gopher St, near the police station. Greyhound no longer goes to Jasper. There are six buses daily to Calgary for $11.90 and nine to Vancouver for $67.35. All Vancouver buses stop at Lake Louise, some also stop in Kelowna or Kamloops. One bus makes the journey via Radium. You can stop off at Lake Louise for free with a ticket on to Vancouver – provided you let the company know beforehand; otherwise to go to Lake Louise is $7.

Note that some buses to Calgary go downtown, others go straight to the international airport.

Brewster Transportation (☎ 762-6767) has one bus a day to Jasper; it takes about 4½ hours and the one-way fare is $29.

Pacific Western (☎ 762-4558) runs three buses a day to Calgary's international airport; the one-way fare is $19.

Train VIA Rail no longer goes through Banff. However, the privately owned 'Rocky Mountaineer' travels via Banff between Calgary and Vancouver. The one-way fare from Banff to Vancouver is $395 which includes meals and an overnight stop in a hotel in Kamloops. The service runs between the end of May and early October, and leaves Banff every Thursday morning for Vancouver at 9.20 am. For information contact a travel agent or the Great Canadian Railtour Company (☎ 643-3841; ☎ 800-665-7245 toll free), Suite 345, 625 Howe St, Vancouver BC, V6C 2T6.

The railway station is the ochre building at the northern end of Lynx St past the police station, close to the downtown area.

Car Banff Used Car Rentals (☎ 762-3352), 230 Lynx St, has cars for about $34 per day plus 10 cents for every km over 100 km. Tilden (☎ 762-2688), on the corner of Lynx and Caribou Sts, charges $25 plus 17 cents per km for the smallest cars; by the week it's $150 plus the km charge. Avis (☎ 762-3222), 209 Bear St, charges $43.95 per day plus 19 cents per km after the first 100 km; by the week it's $284 with the first 1400 km free then it's 12 cents per km.

Getting Around

Bus Pacific Western operates the local Happy Bus along Banff Ave for $1 one way. It picks up and drops off from various hotels, including the Banff Springs Hotel but can also be waved down in the street.

Brewster Transportation has a bus departing the Banff Springs Hotel for Sulphur Mountain hourly between 9.40 am and 4.40 pm. It only goes as far as the Upper Hot Springs; if you're going to the gondola it's a short walk from there to the lower terminal. The one-way fare is $1.

Bicycle & Moped Park 'n' Pedal (☎ 762-3191), 229 Wolf St around the corner from Banff Ave rents bicycles and is open from 9 am to 9 pm. Most bikes cost $5 an hour, $20 a day or $25 for 24 hours. Spoke 'n' Edge (☎ 762-2854) at 202 Wolf St and Sports Rent (☎ 762-8222) at 208 Bear St rent mountain bikes for $4 an hour, $16 a day. Bactrax Bike Rental (☎ 762-8177) at the Ptarmigan Inn, 339 Banff Ave, charges $3.50 an hour and $15 a day; it's open from 8 am to 8 pm.

You can rent a moped or scooter at Mountain Moped (☎ 762-5611) at 451 Banff Ave for $8.50 an hour, $30 for four hours, or $45 a day. There's a deposit of $100.

Hitching Hitchhiking is common in and around town.

LAKE LOUISE

About 57 km north-west of Banff is Lake Louise, the jewel of the Rockies. There isn't much in the village of Lake Louise but don't let that put you off; carry on to the lake itself five km away. It's a much-visited but gorgeous lake sitting in a small glacial valley, surrounded by green, snow-capped mountains. A visit to the lake is best early in the morning – it's less crowded, and there are better reflections in the water.

There are some good nearby walks and hikes.

Information

The Visitor Information Centre (☎ 522-3833) in the village is open daily during the summer from 8 am to 10 pm. It has an exhibition on the geological and natural history of the Rocky Mountains. In the shopping mall area you can buy basic grocery supplies and hire camping equipment.

Things to See & Do

Mt Whitehorn East of the village along Lake Louise Drive is Mt Whitehorn. A gondola (☎ 522-3555) takes you to the top from which there are hiking trails and views of Lake Louise and Victoria Glacier. The gondola ride costs $7 for the round trip, $5 one-way. Mt Whitehorn is an important ski centre in winter.

Hiking For a short stroll, there's a path on the southern banks of Lake Louise beginning by the boathouse which goes through spruce forest and offers excellent views of the lake and the Chateau Lake Louise Hotel.

One trail follows the northern banks of the lake westward to the **Plain of Six Glaciers**. On the way, between the lake and the lookout at the end of the trail, is a teahouse. For a more rigorous venture take the switchbacks up to **Mirror Lake**. There's another teahouse here and good views from **Little Beehive** or **Big Beehive** (not real beehives, but mountains shaped like them). From here you can climb still higher to **Lake Agnes**, then around the long way to join the Plain of Six Glaciers trail and back along Lake Louise to the hotel. These are both a good day's walk.

Another option is to drive from Lake Louise 15 km south to **Moraine Lake** (this is the lake featured on the $20 bill). From there the roughly 20-km return hike through the **Valley of the 10 Peaks** is highly recommended. Take a quick detour to **Larch Valley** where there's a stream and superb scenery. Before Larch Valley a trail heads west past **Eiffel Lake** into Yoho National Park.

Better still, hike to Moraine Lake from Lake Louise via **Paradise Creek** and **Sentinel Pass**. This is a full day's hike with some steep parts but is an excellent route, with great scenery. You can do it the other way round but that's doing it the easy way! Getting up through Sentinel Pass is a long, scree-filled trek but well worth it. At the top, 2600 metres high, it's cool and breezy. Once at Moraine Lake you can hitch back to Lake Louise along Moraine Lake Rd.

There are other trails in the area as well: the brochure *Drives & Walks* lists and describes them.

It is common to see pikas (also called conies) – plump, furry animals – and the larger, more timid marmot along these trails. You often hear ice rumbling on the slopes, too.

After your hikes, back at the Chateau Lake Louise Hotel, the cafeteria in the basement has reasonably priced snacks.

Places to Stay

The two campgrounds in Lake Louise are run by the Canadian Parks Service and are

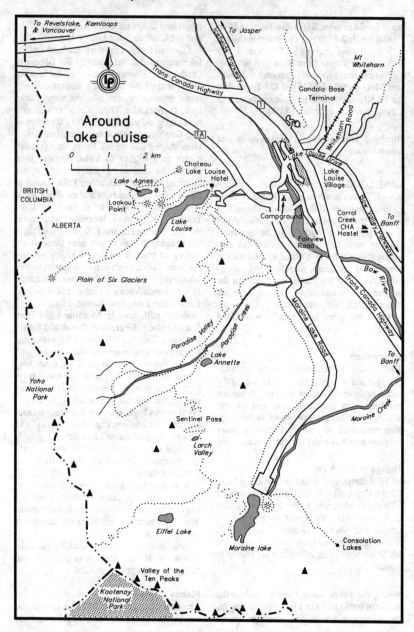

Around Lake Louise

0   1   2 km

To Revelstoke, Kamloops & Vancouver

To Jasper

Trans Canada Highway

Icefields Parkway

Mt Whitehorn

Gondola Base Terminal

Whitehorn Road

Lake Louise Drive

Lake Louise Village

Chateau Lake Louise Hotel

Lake Agnes

Lookout Point

BRITISH COLUMBIA

ALBERTA

Lake Louise

Campground

Fairview Road

Corral Creek CHA Hostel

To Banff

Bow Valley Parkway

Bow River

Plain of Six Glaciers

Paradise Valley

Paradise Creek

Moraine Lake Road

Trans Canada Highway

To Banff

Yoho National Park

Lake Annette

Sentinel Pass

Moraine Creek

Larch Valley

Eiffel Lake

Moraine lake

Consolation Lakes

Valley of the Ten Peaks

Kootenay National Park

both on the Trans Canada Highway. One is open all year round the other from mid-May to mid-September. A site costs $8.50.

At the time of writing a hostel is being built in Lake Louise village and may be open when you get there. In the meantime there is a hostel close by. *Corral Creek CHA Hostel*, five km east of Lake Louise on the Bow Valley Parkway, has a kitchen and pit toilets and charges $8 for members, $13 for non-members.

Getting There & Around

The bus to Jasper leaves from Lake Louise Inn and costs $25. No buses run from the village to the lake but hitching is fairly easy; taxis do the trip for about $15.

ICEFIELDS PARKWAY

This is the 230-km road (Highway 93) opened in 1940 which links Lake Louise with Jasper. The highway follows a lake-lined valley between two chains of the Eastern Main Ranges which make up the Continental Divide – the watershed from which rivers flow either eastward towards the Atlantic Ocean or westward towards the Pacific Ocean. The mountains here are the highest, most rugged and maybe the most scenic in all the Rockies.

The highway is good but slow, as animals such as goats, bighorn sheep and elk are often beside or on it. You can drive the route in a couple of hours but stopping at the many viewpoints, picnic spots and sights or hiking on one of the many trails can easily make it a full day or longer. Visitor Information Centres will have trail details.

Cycling the Icefields Parkway is very popular, but because of the terrain it's much easier going from Banff to Jasper than vice versa.

On the way see **Peyto Lake**, one of the world's most beautiful glacial lakes; again, early in the morning is the best viewing time. Further north, around **Waterfowl Lake**, moose are plentiful.

About halfway between Lake Louise and Jasper is the **Athabasca Glacier**, a tongue of the vast Columbia Icefield. The icefield

itself covers an area of 325 sq km and parts of it are nearly 900 metres thick. Brewster Snowmobile Tours (☎ 762-6735), PO Box 1140, Banff T0L 0C0, can take you on a 1¼-hour ride out on the ice for $15. Athabasca Glacier Walks (☎ 762-5385; or ☎ 852-5665 in Jasper), 304 Caribou St, Banff, has a three-hour walk of the glacier for $15 and a five-hour one for $20. The Visitor Information Centre across the road from the glacier has a display and film on glaciers for free. It also organises free walking tours daily (except Wednesday) at 1.30 pm, but you must have good boots. Ask about other walks. In summer the centre is open daily from 9 am to 7 pm

Other points of interest are **Sunwapta Falls** and **Athabasca Falls**, closer to Jasper.

Places to Stay

The route is lined with a good batch of rustic CHA hostels charging $8 for members, $12 for nonmembers. Most are quite close to the highway in scenic locations, small and without showers but usually there's a 'refreshing' stream nearby. *Mosquito Creek CHA Hostel*, on the Icefields Parkway about 27 km north of Lake Louise, is excellent, with a sauna, cooking facilities and friendly wardens. *Athabasca Falls CHA Hostel* (☎ 439-3089) is about 30 km south of Jasper and has 40 beds.

You can also find campgrounds and moderately priced motels along the way.

JASPER & AROUND

Jasper, 369 km west of Edmonton, is Banff's northern counterpart. It's smaller with fewer things to see and do and its setting is less grand, but some people prefer its quieter streets and less full-scale pandering to tourists. It's a good connecting point with the Yellowhead Highway and VIA Rail running east to Edmonton, west to Prince George; and the Icefields Parkway going south to Lake Louise.

The town is a good supply centre for trips around Jasper National Park, which is teeming with wildlife and has excellent backcountry trails of various lengths.

Orientation

The main street, Connaught Drive, has virtually everything including the bus depot, railway station, banks, restaurants and souvenir shops. Outside the toy-like train station is a 21-metre totem pole carved by a Haida artisan from British Columbia's Queen Charlotte Islands. Nearby is an old CN steam engine.

Off the main street, the town is made up of small wooden houses, many with flowered gardens befitting this alpine setting.

Information

Right in the centre of town at 500 Connaught Drive is Jasper's Visitor Information Centre (☎ 852-6176), easily one of Canada's most eye pleasing tourist offices. It's a stone place covered in flowers and plants and with a large lawn out the front. The lawn is a popular meeting place and often has people and backpacks lying all over the place.

The centre has information on trails in the park and will offer suggestions to fit your specifications. It has two good publications on hiking in the area – *Day Hikes in Jasper National Park* and *Backcountry Users' Guide* – and a list of tourist homes in town. In summer it's open daily from 8 am to 8 pm, in winter from 9 am to 5 pm.

South at 632 Connaught Drive, the Chamber of Commerce (☎ 852-3858) gives information on Jasper townsite. It's open Monday to Friday from 9 am to 5 pm. In the same building Alberta Tourism has maps and information on other parts of the province.

The main post office (☎ 852-3041) is at 502 Patricia St near Elm Ave.

Next to the post office is a laundrette where you can wash clothes and sleeping bags; it's open from 8 am to 10 pm. At another laundrette, further south on Patricia St opposite the Toronto Dominion Bank, you can have a shower for $1.50 as well as wash your clothes; it's open from 7 am to 10 pm.

Jasper Tramway

About six km south of Jasper off the Icefields Parkway, this gondola (☎ 852-3093) goes up Whistlers Mountain in seven minutes and offers views 75 km south to the Columbia Icefield and 100 km west to Mt Robson in British Columbia. The upper terminal is at 2285 metres. There's a restaurant and hiking trails around the top. The tramway is open every day in July and August from 7.30 am to 9 pm and costs $8.

Patricia & Pyramid Lakes

These lakes, about seven km north-west of town along Pyramid Lake Rd, are small and relatively quiet. They have hiking and horse-riding trails, picnic sites, fishing and beaches; you can rent canoes, kayaks, sailing boats and windsurfers. In winter there's cross-country skiing and ice skating.

It's not uncommon to see deer, coyotes or bears in the vicinity.

Lakes Annette & Edith

Off the Yellowhead Highway three km north-east of town along Lodge Rd, Lake Annette and Lake Edith, at about 1000 metres, and can be warm enough for a quick swim. There are hiking and bike trails, picnic areas and boat rentals in the wooded parks around the lakes.

Maligne Lake

The scenic Maligne Lake, 48 km south-east of Jasper at the end of Maligne Lake Rd, is the largest of the glacier-fed lakes in the Rockies and the second largest in the world. You can hike or go horse riding near it for a good view, or hire a canoe for $6 an hour from Maligne Tours (☎ 852-3370). Alternatively take the 40-km 1½-hour boat tour to Spirit Island with Maligne Tours: you can make a reservation in Jasper at Maligne Lake Office, 626 Connaught Drive.

There's excellent cross-country skiing in the highlands around the lake in winter (the season lasts from November to May).

About 11 km east of Jasper on the way to Maligne Lake you pass **Maligne Canyon**, a limestone gorge about 50 metres deep, with waterfalls and interesting rock formations. You can walk from the teahouse down to the floor of the canyon. A further 21 km brings you to **Medicine Lake** whose level rises and

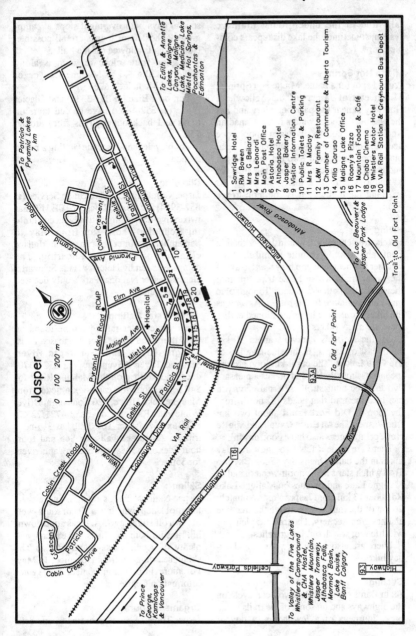

Jasper

0   100   200 m

To Patricia &
Pyramid Lakes
7 km

To Edith & Annette
Lakes, Maligne
Conyon, Maligne
Lake, Medicine Lake,
Miette Hot Springs,
Pocahontas &
Edmonton

To Patricia &
Pyramid Lakes

Pyramid Lake Road

Pyramid Ave

Colin Crescent

Geikie St

Patricia Ave

Connaught Drive

Elm Ave

RCMP

Hospital

Maligne Ave

Miette Ave

Pyramid Lake Road

Cabin Creek Road

Geikie St

Patricia St

Willow Ave

Connaught Drive

VIA Rail

Crescent

Patricia

Cabin Creek Drive

Yellowhead Highway

Yellowhead Highway

Icefields Parkway

To Prince
George,
Kamloops,
& Vancouver

To Valley of the Five Lakes
Whistlers Campground
& CHA Hostel,
Whistlers Mountain,
Jasper Tramway,
Athabasca Falls,
Marmot Basin,
Lake Louise,
Banff Calgary

Athabasca River

Miette River

Highway

93A

93

16

To Lac Beauvert &
Jasper Park Lodge

To Old Fort Point

Trail to Old Fort Point

1   Sawridge Hotel
2   RM Bowen
3   Mrs G Bellard
4   Mrs Leonardi
5   Main Post Office
6   Astoria Hotel
7   Athabasca Hotel
8   Jasper Bakery
9   Visitor Information Centre
10 Public Toilets & Parking
11 Mrs R Macloy
12 L&W Family Restaurant
13 Chamber of Commerce & Alberta Tourism
14 Villa Caruso
15 Maligne Lake Office
16 Roony's Pizza
17 Mountain Foods & Café
18 Chaba Cinema
19 Whistlers Motor Hotel
20 VIA Rail Station & Greyhound Bus Depot

falls due to the underground drainage system; sometimes the lake disappears completely.

Miette Hot Springs

A good spot for a bathe, Miette Hot Springs, 61 km east of Jasper off the Yellowhead Highway is near the park boundary and has the warmest mineral waters in the Canadian Rockies. The modern spa has two pools, one deep and one suitable for children. It's open in summer daily from 8.30 am to 10.30 pm and costs $2; you can hire bathing suits for $1 and towels for 75 cents.

Along the highway it is common to see goats.

Hiking

Hikers are generally fewer in Jasper than in Banff and wildlife is more plentiful. If the weather has been wet you may want to avoid the lower trails where horse trips are run; they make the path a mud bath. Topographic maps are available for all routes. As well as the hikes around the lakes mentioned earlier there are many others.

Off the Icefields Parkway, about 10 km south-east of Jasper, is the small **Valley of the Five Lakes**. The eight-km loop around the lakes is mostly flat and makes a pleasant two to three-hour stroll. Alternatively, you can take the trail that heads off north from the loop to **Old Fort Point** about two km from Jasper. The **Mt Edith Cavell** and **Miette Hot Springs** areas also have good day hikes.

There are quite a few two and three-day hikes in the park. One is the 45-km **Skyline Trail** which starts at the north-western end of Maligne Lake and finishes on Maligne Lake Rd about 13 km from Jasper. Approximately 26 km of the trail is at or above the tree line and has great scenery. The trail has plenty of wildlife too; watch out for grizzlies.

There are also a few four, seven and 10-day hikes.

Cycling

As in Banff National Park you can cycle on the highways and on some of the trails in the park. Journeys of a few hours, a day or several days with overnight stops at campgrounds, hostels or lodges are all possible. No cycling is allowed off the trails.

A good route close to town is along **Maligne Lake Rd** to Maligne Canyon or further to Medicine Lake.

Fun on a Bike (☎ 852-3338) and Glacier Cycle (☎ 852-4809) have guided tours on roads and backcountry trails from around $30.

For bicycle rentals see the Getting Around section.

Climbing

Jasper Climbing School & Guide Service (☎ 852-3964) PO Box 452, Jasper T0E 1E0, has two to five-day, beginner to advanced climbing schools. These run from May to September; in winter you can go waterfall ice climbing or ski mountaineering. The company is run by Helen & Hans Schwartz; Hans is Jasper National Park's only licensed climbing guide.

White-Water Rafting

Great white-water rafting can be found on the **Athabasca River** near Athabasca Falls, **Maligne River** and **Sunwapta River**. Maligne River Adventures (☎ 852-3370) does a 13-km trip on the Maligne River for $40 per person; you can book a ticket from Maligne Lake Office, 626 Connaught Drive. Whitewater Rafting Ltd (☎ 852-4721/7238), PO Box 362, Jasper T0E 1E0, has 3½-hour trips to Athabasca Falls for $45 and four-hour rides on the Maligne or Sunwapta rivers for $50.

Skiing

Jasper National Park's main skiing area is **Marmot Basin** which lies 19 km south-west of town off Highway 93A. It has good downhill runs for both beginners and experts, and plenty of scenic cross-country trails. The skiing season goes from December to May. For more information contact the Visitor Information Centre.

Organised Tours

Jasper Travel Agency coordinates and sells

tickets for various tours, river trips, sight-seeing tours and adventures.

Brewster Gray Line has a three-hour drive to some of the local sights including Jasper Tramway, Whistlers Mountain, Pyramid and Patricia lakes and Maligne Canyon. The trip costs $23. Its Maligne Lake tour takes five hours and costs $39. It also has tours along the Icefields Parkway to Lake Louise for $42 one way, taking 7½ hours.

Jasper Raft Tours (☎ 852-3613) runs trips along the Athabasca River for $25. The cost includes the bus trip and three hours on the river.

If you're driving, there are self-guiding auto cassette tapes that describe the journey between Jasper and Banff via the Columbia Icefield and Lake Louise. These can be rented for $16.95 from Rocky Mountain Auto Tours at 612 Connaught Drive.

Places to Stay
In general, prices here are better than those in Banff, but hotel and motel prices are still fairly steep. The B&Bs and tourist homes are the best bet after the campgrounds or hostels.

Camping Jasper National Park has 10 camp-grounds all operated by the Canadian Parks Service. Closest to town is *Whistlers Camp-ground* three km south off the Icefields Parkway on Whistlers Rd. It's quite good, with electricity, showers and flush toilets but, though large (it has 781 sites), it does get crowded. In summer, films and talks are presented nightly. Sites cost from $11 to $16.

A herd of wapiti (American elk) lives in the camp-ground at certain times of the year. In the autumn a male looks after a large number of females – the harem – and his bawling instructions are heard far and wide.

Two km further south on the Icefields Parkway *Wapiti Campground* is open from June to September and has sites for $11 to $13. Two other campgrounds reasonably close to town are *Wabasso Campground* 17 km south on Highway 93A, with sites for $9, and *Snaring River Campground*, 17 km

north on the Yellowhead Highway, with sites for $6.

Hostels *Whistlers CHA Hostel* (☎ 852-3215) is about five km south of Jasper on Skytram Rd towards the Jasper Tramway; the last two km are uphill. The hostel is one of the few big modern ones in the Rockies and has showers, laundry and a large kitchen. It opens at 5 pm and closes at midnight and you're woken up at 7 am. Members pay $12, nonmembers $16.

Maligne Canyon CHA Hostel (☎ 852-3584), 11 km north-east of town on Maligne Canyon Rd, is small but good with members paying $8, nonmembers $12.

Mt Edith Cavell CHA Hostel (☎ 439-3089) is south of Jasper on Mt Edith Cavell Rd, 11 km from the junction with Highway 93A. It's open from mid-June to early September and charges $8 for members, $12 for nonmembers.

B&Bs & Tourist Homes The Visitor Infor-mation Centre has a list of over 50 tourist homes, all clean, most in or close to town, most charging similar prices and some offer-ing B&B. In July and August many of these places fill up, so it's a good idea to book ahead. Most places charge from $30/40 for a single/double, but offer lower rates in the off season.

The cheapest of the lot is *RM Bowen* (☎ 852-4532), at 228 Colin Crescent, with a couple of rooms for singles/doubles $15/20; it's $5 for an additional person.

Mrs R Maclay (☎ 852-4543), 719 Patricia St, is open all year and has a double room for $30; each extra person costs $7. *Mrs Leonardi*, 315 Patricia St, has singles for $30 with shared bathroom, kitchen and TV; it's a friendly place. *Mrs G Beilard* (☎ 852-4338), 114 Patricia St, offers three rooms at $30/40 a double/triple.

Angus Lodging (☎ 852-5444), 1140 Cabin Creek Drive, has singles/doubles starting from $35. The price includes breakfast.

Hotels, Motels & Bungalows In town the *Athabasca Hotel* (☎ 852-3386), 510 Patricia

St, has basic singles/doubles for $33/35 and more deluxe rooms for $51/53. The *Astoria Hotel* (☎ 852-4955), 404 Connaught Drive, has singles/doubles with telephone and TV from $72/78. Both hotels have a pub and restaurant and provide entertainment.

Jasper Park Lodge (☎ 852-3301), beside Lac Beauvert north-east of town, is Jasper's answer to the Banff Springs Hotel. It has everything including a world-class golf course. Normally singles/doubles start from $250/290, but if you reserve and check in on the same day a single or double costs $125.

In Jasper many of the motels are north along Connaught Drive. Out of town some places offer motel-type rooms and bungalows (usually wooden cabins).

Patricia Lake Bungalows (☎ 852-3560), on Patricia Lake Rd about five km north of town, is reasonable with singles/doubles from $45. A little further north along the road *Pyramid Lake Bungalows* (☎ 852-3526) has singles/doubles for $40/90. It's beside the lake and has a licensed dining room.

Tekkara Lodge (☎ 852-3058) is one km south of Jasper off Highway 93A at the confluence of the Miette and Athabasca rivers. You can either stay in the lodge or in one of the bungalows. Singles/doubles are $45/108. It has a licensed restaurant and is open mid-May to mid-September.

Places to Eat

Mountain Foods & Café, on Connaught Drive opposite the railway station, is a good health-food café and shop. It serves soups, salads and sandwiches from $2 to $4.50, main meals such as lasagne for around $10 and has good desserts: try the carrot cake for $1.95. The shop also sells granola, nuts and other foods for hiking. It's open daily from 8 am to 10 pm.

Jasper Bakery, on the corner of Patricia St and Miette Ave, is very good.

L&W Family Restaurant, on the corner of Patricia St and Hazel Ave, is plastic-looking but serves decent pizza, spaghetti or lasagne for about $8 to $12. *Villa Caruso*, 628 Connaught Drive, is a popular up-market restaurant serving seafood, pasta, pizza and

steaks – the latter you can see being cooked in the window. It's open daily from 11 am and main meals average around $10 to $15.

Roony's Pizza, 618 Connaught Drive, has pizzas from $5 to $15, fish & chips for $6 and Middle Eastern food for around $6.

Many of the hotels have restaurants. *Whistler's Motor Hotel*, 105 Miette Ave on the corner of Connaught Drive, is a basic place ideal for breakfasts. Omelettes and burgers cost $4, pancakes cost from $4.35 to $5.50. *Sunrise Coffee Shop* in the Sawridge Hotel, 82 Connaught Drive, is also good for breakfast which costs about $5. It's open 24 hours daily from May to the end of September. *Papa George's* in the Astoria Hotel has good-value breakfast specials for $4.25; it also has sandwich lunch specials for $7.25 (small) or $10.25 (large) from 11.30 am to 3 pm.

There's also an *A&W*, 624 Connaught Drive; a *Kentucky Fried Chicken*, 608 Patricia St; and a *Smitty's Family Restaurant*, 109 Miette Ave.

Entertainment

Chaba Cinema (☎ 852-4749), 604 Connaught Drive opposite the VIA Rail station, shows the movie *Challenge* at 4 pm daily in summer. It lasts one hour and is narrated by Peter Ustinov. It chronicles kayaking, skiing, climbing and other activities in the Rockies well enough to have been shown at the Cannes Film Festival. The cinema also shows commercial movies. Admission costs $6.

The *Atha-B Bar* in the Athabasca Hotel regularly has live rock bands. Admission is $4 or $5. For disco music head to *Champs* in the Sawridge Hotel; it's open nightly. The *Astoria Bar* in the Astoria Hotel is famous for its imported draught beers.

Getting There & Away

Bus The Greyhound Bus Depot (☎ 852-3962) is situated in the VIA Rail station on Connaught Drive.

Four buses go to Kamloops, Vancouver and Edmonton daily. The one-way fares are: Kamloops $34.50, Vancouver $63.20 and

Edmonton $32.20. Greyhound no longer runs services between Jasper and Banff.

Brewster Transportation (☎ 852-3332), in the VIA Rail station, has one bus a day to Banff; it takes about 4½ hours and costs $29 one-way. It also goes to Calgary for $38 one way.

Train The VIA Rail station (☎ 852-4102) is open from 6.30 am to 8 pm daily. From here trains go west to Prince George and Prince Rupert, south-west through Kamloops to Vancouver and east through Edmonton to Saskatoon, Winnipeg and beyond. The train to Kamloops leaves Tuesday, Friday and Sunday at 3.05 pm arriving at 10.15 pm the same day. To Edmonton it leaves on the same days at 5.45 pm arriving at 11.20 pm the same day.

Examples of one-way fares are: Kamloops $60, Edmonton $57, Vancouver $98, Winnipeg $166.

Rocky Mountaineer takes you via Jasper (or Banff) between Calgary and Vancouver. The one-way fare from Jasper to Vancouver is $395. See the Banff Getting There & Away section for further details.

Car Budget (☎ 852-3222), 638 Connaught Drive, rents cars for $40 a day with 100 km free, plus 10 cents for each extra km. Jasper Rent-A-Car (☎ 852-3373), 626 Connaught Drive, has the same daily rate but only allows 50 km free before charging 22 cents for each km thereafter. Tilden (☎ 852-4972) has its office in the VIA Rail station; its rates are $43 a day with 100 km free, plus 20 cents for each extra km.

Getting Around

Bus Although Jasper doesn't have a public transport system, small 14-seater buses do go from outside the Maligne Lake Office, 626 Connaught Drive, to various destinations around Jasper. Some destinations and fares are: Jasper Tramway $4, Maligne Canyon $5, Whistlers Mountain $2, Maligne Lake $10 and Skyline Trail (southern trailhead) $10.

Bicycle Bikes can be rented at Sports Shop (☎ 852-3654), 416 Connaught Drive beside the CIBC Bank. They cost $4 an hour or $20 a day. Freewheel Cycle (☎ 852-5380), 600 Patricia St, rents mountain bikes for $4 an hour, $15 for five hours or $17 a day. Shovel Pass Hardware (☎ 852-5555), 625 Patricia St, rents bikes for $4 an hour or $12 a day.

Rentals are also available at Jasper Park Lodge and Sawridge Hotel.

British Columbia

Entered Confederation: 20 July 1871
Area: 948,600 sq km
Population: 2,950,000

British Columbia, known simply as BC, is probably the most beautiful province in the country and contains some of the most spectacular scenery in the world. The Rocky Mountains are in the east, the northern interior is full of mountains, hills, forests and lakes. The southern interior has a small desert – Canada's only one – while the lush Pacific coastal area has many inlets and islands. In short, there is the widest variety of landscapes in the country and they provide a range of habitats for wildlife and opportunities for outdoor activities to suit every taste.

The general atmosphere in BC, particularly on the south-west coast, is slightly different from that found in the rest of Canada. The culture, more permissive and lifestyle-conscious than that found in the east, partially reflects the influence of California.

These factors combine to make tourism – in a province with many lucrative industries – the second largest money-maker.

As in California, much of the early settlement was due to gold fever here around the 1850s. More than half the population lives in the south-west around Vancouver and Victoria so there is a lot of sparsely populated space, particularly to the north. Inaccessible areas of the province, however, continue to be developed. The bulk of the population is of British ancestry, although Vancouver has a large Chinese community.

ORIENTATION

BC is Canada's most westerly province bordered in the north by the Yukon and the Northwest Territories; in the east by Alberta; in the south by the three US states of Montana, Idaho and Washington; in the north-west by Alaska; and in the west by the Pacific Ocean.

Victoria, the province's capital, is at the southern tip of Vancouver Island, which lies south-west of the mainland. The city of Vancouver, the province's business centre and by far BC's largest city, is in the south-western corner of the province near the mouth of the Fraser River.

The Trans Canada Highway (Highway 1) is the major route connecting Vancouver and southern BC with the rest of southern Canada. The busiest section is between Hope and Vancouver, where the road follows the Fraser River. The Yellowhead Highway (mainly Highway 16, but also including part of highways 37 and 5) links Prince Rupert in BC's north-west with Prince George in the east, Jasper and Edmonton in Alberta, then Saskatoon and Winnipeg.

The Cassiar Highway (Highway 37; also called the Stewart-Cassiar Highway) links the north-west of the province with the Yukon, meeting the Alaska Highway near Upper Liard, just north of the BC/Yukon border.

Highway 97 from Washington State in the USA connects south-central BC with the north via Kamloops, Prince George and Dawson Creek. From Dawson Creek, Highway 97 is also known as the Alaska (or Alcan) Highway; it connects northern BC with Fairbanks in Alaska via Whitehorse in the Yukon.

HISTORY

The earliest known inhabitants of BC are believed to have arrived from Asia between 12,000 and 10,000 years ago, after the end of the last ice age. Some settled along the

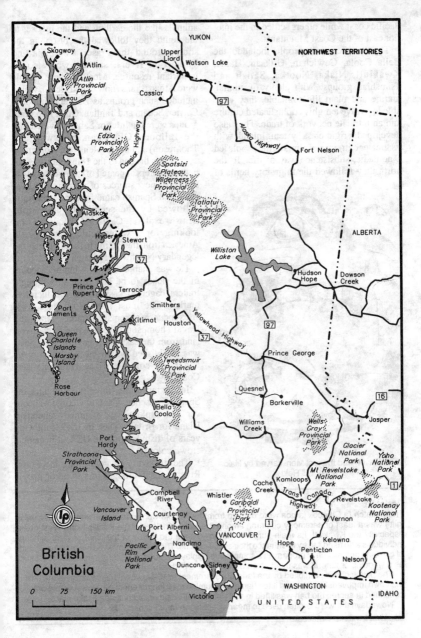

British Columbia

Pacific coast while others settled in the interior east of the Coast Mountains.

The Pacific coast people included the Bella Coola, Cowichan, Gitksan, Haida, Kwakiutl, Niska, Nootka, Salish and Tsimshian groups. With plenty of animal, marine and plant life available, they were able to evolve a highly sophisticated culture and an intricate network of trade. They also developed a rigid class system. Inland, with its greater extremes of climate, the people led a nomadic, subsistence way of life. To the north they followed the migratory herds of

'The Raven and the first Men' carved by Haida artist, Bill Reid

animals like the caribou and the moose; to the south they followed the bison. In the south, around the Fraser, Columbia and Thompson rivers, salmon was also an important resource. Most of these people were Athapaskans (now called Dene), which included such groups as Beaver, Chilcotin, Carrier, Sekani and Tahltan. Other important groups were the Interior Salish (divided into the Lillooet, Okanagan, Shuswap and Thompson) and the Kootenay (or Kootenai).

Towards the end of the 18th century European explorers appeared off the west coast in search of new sources of wealth. The Russians and Spanish came first and were soon followed by the seemingly ubiquitous British explorer Captain Cook, who was looking for a water route across North America from the Pacific to the Atlantic – the legendary Northwest Passage.

He was unable to find it, but his account of the riches to be had from furs brought traders eager to cash in on the lucrative market. The most famous of these were Alexander Mackenzie, Simon Fraser and David Thompson, who explored routes overland from the east. A series of trading posts was established which by the 1820s came under the control of the Hudson's Bay Company.

In the meantime, initially to counter the Spanish presence, Captain George Vancouver had explored and claimed Vancouver Island for Britain. Then in 1849, following years of dispute with the USA, it became a crown colony.

The discovery of gold along the Fraser River in 1858 brought in a flood of people

Potlatch

The potlatch (a Chinook jargon word derived from the Nootka word *patschmatl* meaning 'to give' or 'gift') was a feast or ceremony common among the Native Indians of the Pacific North-West coast, especially the Kwakiutl. Its main purpose was to validate the status of the chief or clan, although individuals also used it to try to enhance their social ranking. The potlatch involved the public exchange of gifts and destruction of property in a competitive display of affluence. A significant social event such as a wedding or funeral was used as an occasion for a potlatch.

The potlatch was prohibited by the federal government in 1884, when the Kwakiutl, at the cost of their own impoverishment, used it to shame and humble their former enemies. However, the practice continued in secret; the ban was lifted in 1951 and small-scale potlatches again take place.

Nowadays the word is often used to mean a 'spree' or 'raucous party'. ■

seeking their fortune and led to mainland BC also being declared a crown colony. A second wave of fortune hunters came when gold was discovered further north in the Cariboo region.

Although the gold rush only lasted a few years, many of those who came in the wake of the miners remained behind to form more permanent settlements. In 1866 the two colonies were united and, after much discussion, joined the Canadian Confederation in 1871 as the province of British Columbia.

The arrival of the trans-continental railway in 1885 opened up BC to the east; and the settlement of the prairies around this time created demand for the province's resources, particularly timber. The building of the Panama Canal, which was completed in 1914, meant easier access to markets in Europe and along North America's east coast. This brought about a boom for the BC economy. Following WW I, however, there was an economic downturn which led to industrial unrest and unemployment. After a brief recovery, the Wall St crash of 1929 brought severe depression and hardship.

Prosperity only returned with the advent of WW II and was sustained after the war with the discovery of new resources and the development of a manufacturing base.

The two major Canadian political parties, the Liberals and the Conservatives, have made little headway in this province. The Social Credit Party, ostensibly the party of small business, has been in power for much of the last two decades. Its main opposition is the New Democrat Party, which advocates a form of limited socialism. BC politics are the most volatile in the country, the unions are strong and active and the electorate very opinionated.

GEOGRAPHY

The north-eastern corner of British Columbia occupies part of the geographical region known as the Interior Plains. The bulk of the province, however, lies inside the Western Cordillera, which runs roughly north-west/south-east.

Within the cordillera there are three major mountain ranges – the Rocky Mountains to the east, the Cassiar (north) and Columbia

Steller's jay

Common loon

(south) Mountains in the centre and the Coast Mountains to the west.

The province contains scores of freshwater lakes and fast-flowing rivers and streams plus several plateaus, the largest of which is the Fraser Plateau in the south-west. The coastline is rugged, with numerous fjords and islands, including Vancouver Island. In the south of the Okanagan Valley is Canada's only desert.

CLIMATE & WHEN TO GO

BC's climate is very varied. On the coast it is mild with warm, mostly dry summers and cool, very wet winters.

The interior is much drier, particularly in the south along the Okanagan Valley; summers are hot and the winters cold. In the mountains summers are short, nights cool. Winter snowfalls are heavy.

Unless you're coming for the winter activities like skiing, the best time to visit is from around mid-June to mid-September. During this period there is little rain, temperatures are warm, daylight hours are long and the transport routes are open.

FLORA & FAUNA
Flora

Estimates vary, but somewhere around 60% of BC is covered by forest, consisting mainly of varieties of coniferous trees – spruce, fir, pine, hemlock and cedar. Other important types of trees are maple, birch, poplar and willow. Grasslands are found in drier areas of low elevation, while in the higher, tundra regions only the hardiest of plants, such as the saxifrage and phlox, can survive.

Wildflowers abound in BC; some have interesting names like old man's whiskers and nodding onion. One of the most common flowers is fireweed, which can be seen along roadsides and in fields.

Fauna

In the straits off the west coast are sea lions, seals, porpoises and different kinds of whales (killer, gray, sperm, humpback, minke and blue). The waters are rich in fish, particularly salmon, which lives most of its life in the ocean, but then heads upstream far inland to spawn and die. The waters off

Vancouver Island are home to the world's largest octopuses, as well as thousands of other species.

On land the most common animals are varieties of deer (moose, white-tail, black-tail, mule and caribou), black, brown and grizzly bears, cougars, wolves, marmots, squirrels, mountain goats and bighorn sheep.

BC also has a diverse birdlife. The bald eagle is widespread and can usually be seen near rivers and lakes; the golden eagle, on the other hand, is an endangered species but can still be seen along the coast and in the Rocky Mountains. There are waterbirds such as herons, swans, geese, ducks, grebes and loons. Other common varieties of birds are sparrow, swallow, thrush, warbler, owl, grouse, hawk, flycatcher and jay. The steller's jay is an official symbol for BC.

With so many lakes and rivers the warmer weather brings out dozens of insects. Some of these, like mosquitoes, horse flies, and no-see-ums, will become very familiar to you if you're camping or hiking. (See the Dangers & Annoyances section in the Facts for the Visitor chapter.)

National & Provincial Parks

BC has six national parks and more than 330 provincial parks. The *Road Map & Parks Guide*, produced by Tourism BC and available free at Travel Infocentres, lists them all with their location and facilities. There are also publications and maps on individual parks which you can get by visiting or writing to the following:

Ministry of Parks
    Visitor Services, 4000 Seymour Place, Victoria, BC V8V 1X5
Ministry of Environment
    780 Blanshard St, Victoria, BC V8V 1X5 (☎ 387-1161; in Vancouver 584-8822)
Outdoor Recreation Council of BC
    Suite 334, 1367 West Broadway, Vancouver, BC V6H 4A9 (☎ 737-3000/58; fax 738-7175)
Parks Canada Information Services
    Western Regional Office, PO Box 2989, Station M, Calgary, Alberta T2P 3H8
    Room 520, 220 4th Ave SE, Calgary, Alberta T2P 3H8

Four of the national parks are close to each other in the south-east – Yoho, Kootenay, Glacier and Mt Revelstoke. Yoho and Kootenay adjoin Alberta's Banff National Park in the Rocky Mountains while Glacier and Mt Revelstoke are to the east in the Columbia Mountains. The Trans Canada Highway passes through all four.

Pacific Rim National Park stretches along Vancouver Island's west coast and is divided in two by Barkley Sound. Highway 4 gives you access to the northern half, while the southern section can be reached either by gravel road from Port Alberni or along Highway 14 from Victoria. The park also includes the Broken Group Islands. South Moresby National Park is on Moresby Island in the Queen Charlotte Islands and is only accessible by boat or by hiking from Moresby Camp.

Provincial parks occur throughout BC. They vary enormously in size from, for example, the 6568 sq km of Spatsizi Plateau Wilderness Park in the north-west to the one hectare of Ballingall Islets between southern Vancouver Island and the mainland. Most of them can be reached on sealed or gravel roads in conventional vehicles, while for some you will need a 4WD. Some parks have no road access at all and you'll have to hike in. To a few you can take a ferry.

Some of the national and provincial parks are open all year, but the majority are closed during winter and only open from April or May to September or October. Many have vehicle (RV) and tent campsites, picnic areas and toilets and offer activities such as hiking, swimming, boating and fishing. At most of them a camping fee, between $5 and $13, is charged during the peak visiting season. Near the more popular parks there are motels and privately run campgrounds.

Some places considered historically significant have also been set aside as parks. Examples of these are Barkerville east of Quesnel and Fort Rodd Hill near Victoria.

The Ministry of Forests (☎ 387-6656; in Vancouver 660-7500), Integrated Resource Branch – Recreation Section, 1450 Government St, Victoria, V8V 1X4, has also allocated areas for camping and recreation. You can get information about these areas from the above address or from offices around the province.

ECONOMY

BC enjoys a high standard of living based on its major industries of forestry, mining, tourism, fishing and fruit-growing. Casual work is often available in these industries. However, with a downturn in resource-based businesses and labour troubles in the late 1980s, the province was weakened economically. More recently, as in the rest of the country, high interest rates which have kept the Canadian dollar strong against other currencies, rising inflation and uncertainty over the effects of the free trade agreement with the USA have led to fears of recession. Unemployment continues to be high in this, Canada's most unionised workforce.

BC has some serious problems with environmental degradation and pollution to which it has begun to seek solutions. Canada has become one of the countries at the forefront of world concern about the environment and early in 1990 Vancouver hosted Globe 90, the largest ever international conference on industrial and environmental issues.

POPULATION & PEOPLE

With nearly three million people BC is Canada's third most populous province, 11% of the total. Vancouver is Canada's third largest city with a population just under 1½ million. The overwhelming majority of people live in the south of the province, the north is virtually empty in comparison.

Britain and Ireland are the ancestral homelands of most British Columbians. However, successive waves of migrants, especially since WW II, have produced a multiracial society. There are large groups whose background is Ukrainian, German, Scandinavian, Dutch, Italian, Chinese, Japanese or Indochinese, and many other smaller groups.

The decline in the number of indigenous people has been reversed by the introduction of better health provisions, but there continue to be problems of poverty, unemployment and alcoholism.

TOURIST OFFICES
Local Tourist Offices

Tourism BC (☎ 387-1642), 1117 Wharf St, Victoria, V8W 2Z2, is the name of the body which operates the province's comprehensive tourism infrastructure. For further information on travel in BC contact the Ministry of Tourism (☎ 800-663-6000 toll free in North America), Parliament Buildings, Victoria, BC V8V 1X4.

There is a broad network of tourist offices – called Travel Infocentres – throughout BC, many of which operate as an arm of or in conjunction with the local chamber of commerce. Some are open year-round (mainly those in towns) but the majority are seasonal, only opening their doors between April or May and the first weekend in September.

Overseas Reps

Tourism BC has several offices in the USA and one in the UK. The addresses are:

Tourism BC
    March & McLennan Building, 720 Olive Way, Seattle, Washington 98101, USA (☎ (206) 623-5937)
Tourism BC
    400 100 Bush St, San Francisco, California 94104, USA (☎ (415) 981-4780)
Tourism BC
    1050 2600 Michelson Drive, Irvine, Los Angeles, California 92715, USA (☎ (714) 852-1054)
Tourism BC
    1 Regent St, London SW1Y 4NS, UK (☎ (71) 930-6857)

Tourism Regions

BC is divided into nine tourism regions. For information on individual regions you can contact:

BC Rocky Mountain Visitors Association
    495 Wallinger Ave, PO Box 10, Kimberley, V1A 2Y5 (☎ 427-4838)
Cariboo Chilcotin Tourist Association
    190 Yorkston Ave, PO Box 4900, Williams Lake, V2G 2V8 (☎ 392-2226)

High Country Tourism Association
    403 186 Victoria St, PO Box 962, Kamloops, V2C 5N4 (☎ 372-7770)
Kootenay Country Tourist Association
    610 Railway St, Nelson, V1L 1H4 (☎ 352-6033)
North by North-West Tourism Association of BC
    2840 Alfred Ave, PO Box 1030, Smithers, V0J 2N0 (☎ 847-5227)
    This region includes the Queen Charlotte Islands.
Okanagan Similkameen Tourist Association
    104 515 Highway 97 South, Kelowna, V1Z 3J2 (☎ 769-5959)
Peace River Alaska Highway Tourist Association
    10631 100th St, PO Box 6850, Fort St John, V1J 4J3 (☎ 785-2544)
Tourism Association of South-Western BC
    304 828 West 8th Ave, Vancouver, V5Z 1E2 (☎ 876-3088)
Tourism Association of Vancouver Island
    302 45 Bastion Square, Victoria, V8W 1J1 (☎ 382-3551)
    This region includes part of the mainland from Bute Inlet to just north of Rivers Inlet.

MONEY

The major credit cards are accepted in BC but Visa and MasterCard are more widely accepted than American Express.

There is a general provincial sales tax of 6%. Beer, wine and spirits have a tax of 10% while accommodation tax varies between 8% and 10%. There is no provincial tax on food bought in restaurants, or books.

TIME

Most of BC is on Pacific Standard Time, three hours behind Eastern Standard Time. Two areas bordering Alberta, however, are on Mountain Standard Time: one is in the north-east around Peace River; the other, in the south-east, covers the Rocky Mountains north from the Montana border to Vermount.

TELEPHONE

The area code for BC is 604; the fire/ambulance/police emergency number is 911. If, in your travels, you notice a forest fire, telephone the operator (☎ 0) and ask for Zenith 5555, the province-wide number for information on such emergencies.

ACTIVITIES
Skiing

BC's climate and terrain provide great conditions for downhill and nordic skiing. Pick up a copy of Tourism BC's brochure *Ski With Us!* (free from any Travel Infocentre), which lists all the major downhill and nordic skiing centres in the province. Most of these are in the south from Vancouver Island eastward to the Rocky Mountains.

Near Vancouver to the north are Blackcomb, Whistler and Grouse mountains and the Cypress Bowl and Seymour Ski Country resorts; Hemlock Valley and Manning Provincial Park resorts are to the east. On Vancouver Island you can ski on Cain, Washington and Arrowsmith mountains and Forbidden Plateau. In the Okanagan Valley region the ski resorts include Apex Alpine, Silver Star, Big White Mountain and Baldy Mountain. In the Rocky Mountains area there are ski resorts at Fernie Snow Valley, Kimberley, Panorama, Fairmont Hot Springs and Whitetooth.

In the centre of BC along the Yellowhead Highway between Prince Rupert and the Alberta border there is access to a number of ski areas, including Hudson Bay Mountain near Smithers, and Tabor and Purden mountains near Prince George.

Hiking

Almost any kind of hiking experience is possible in BC: from short walks of a few hours along well-marked, easily accessible trails to treks of one or two weeks in remote terrain where you have to take your own food and equipment and be flown in by helicopter.

Close to Vancouver there are many good walks: in the Coast Mountains, Garibaldi Provincial Park and around Whistler to the north; and in the Cascade Mountains to the east. From Manning Provincial Park the Pacific Crest Trail goes all the way to Mexico! On Vancouver Island the trails in the Pacific Rim National Park and Strathcona Provincial Park offer opportunities to see both marine and land wildlife, as do those in South Moresby National Park Reserve in the Queen Charlotte Islands.

In the south-east of the province there is a host of walks, ranging in degree of difficulty, in the provincial and national parks in and around the Rocky, Columbia and Cariboo mountains. Finally, to the north, for the adventurous, there is Tweedsmuir Provincial Park and in the far north Spatsizi Plateau and Kwadachi wilderness parks.

Many of these areas are also very good for rock-climbing or mountaineering.

Canoeing

With the Pacific Ocean to the west and so many inlets, lakes and rivers there are plenty of opportunities to go canoeing in BC. Some of the more popular spots are Bowron, Wells Gray, Slocan and Okanagan lakes inland; and around Vancouver, Gulf and Queen Charlotte islands. Write to the Recreational Canoeing Association of BC, 1200 Hornby St, Vancouver, V6Z 2E2 for details of canoe routes, etc.

White-Water Rafting

BC's topography means that there are many rivers throughout the province suitable for this increasingly popular sport. Check with the local Travel Infocentre for details of where to go and which companies to use. You don't need to be experienced, either, as many of these companies will teach you how to pitch in. Trips can last from three hours up to a couple of weeks.

The more favoured rivers are the Fraser, Thompson and Chilliwack close to Vancouver; to the east in the High Country near Kamloops the Adams and Clearwater rivers; in the Rockies the Kootenay, Kicking Horse and Illecillewaet rivers; the Chilko and Chilcotin rivers in the Cariboo region west of Williams Lake; and in the north the Skeena, Stikine, Alsek and Tatshenshini rivers.

Cycling

You can either go cycling on your own or in organised group tours. Many places in BC have bicycles for rent. The leaflet *Trail Bicycling in National Parks in Alberta & British Columbia* lists trails where cycling is allowed.

In Vancouver one of the most popular spots for cycling is along the 10-km road in Stanley Park. Around BC other favourite areas are the Rocky and Kootenay mountains for mountain-biking; the Fraser River Valley; the Gulf Islands; and along Vancouver Island's east coast. For information and maps contact the Bicycling Association of BC (☎ 737-3034), 1367 West Broadway, Vancouver V6H 4H9.

Fishing

Fishing, both saltwater and freshwater, is one of BC's major tourist attractions. Particularly popular are the waters around Vancouver Island (where several places claim the title 'salmon capital of the world') and Queen Charlotte Islands; the Fraser, Thompson, Nass, Skeena, Kettle, Peace and Liard rivers; and the lakes of the High Country, Cariboo, Chilcotin and Okanagan Similkameen regions.

Fishing is controlled by law and you will have to obtain a licence. For further information write to the tourism associations listed earlier under Tourism Regions or to:

Department of Fisheries & Oceans
    Communications Branch, 1090 West Pender St, Vancouver, V6E 2P1 (☎ 666-2074/0383)
Ministry of Environment
    Fish & Wildlife Branch, Parliament Buildings, Victoria, V8V 1X5

Scuba Diving

The rich and varied marine life in the waters along BC's 27,000 km Pacific coast make scuba diving a very rewarding activity. The best time to go is winter when the plankton has decreased and visibility often exceeds 20 metres. At depths of more than 15 metres, though, visibility is good throughout the year and temperatures vary little.

The best places to dive are in the waters off the Pacific Rim National Park on Vancouver Island's west coast; in Georgia Strait between Vancouver Island's east coast and the mainland's Sunshine Coast north of Vancouver; and in Queen Charlotte Strait off Vancouver Island's north-east coast.

Sailing
Sailing is another popular form of recreation and, though the best time is from mid-April to mid-October, in the sheltered waters of BC's Pacific coast it's possible almost year-round. Inland some of the more favoured places include Harrison, Okanagan, Arrow and Kootenay lakes in the south and Williston Lake in the north.

Surfing
In Pacific Rim National Park on Vancouver Island, Long Beach reputedly has the best surfing in BC.

Caving
For those who like to go cave exploring, Gold River and Horne Lake Provincial Park on Vancouver Island offer good opportunities.

Bungy Jumping
Bungy Jumping has finally come to North America. See the Nanaimo section for details.

ACCOMMODATION
Super Camping is a free guide available at Travel Infocentres. It gives region by region lists of private and government-owned campgrounds and their facilities, opening periods and prices.

The Canadian Hostelling Association has three hostels in BC – in Vancouver, Victoria and Whistler. For information contact the Canadian Hostelling Association BC Region (☎ 224-7177; fax 224-4852), 1515 Discovery St, Vancouver, V6R 4K5.

Also available from Travel Infocentres is the free brochure *Accommodations*, published annually, which lists places to stay approved by Tourism BC. Most of the hotels and motels listed begin in the moderate price range. It also includes YM-YWCAs, some campgrounds and some B&Bs. Near the back of the brochure is a listing of regional B&B agencies to contact.

For further information on B&Bs throughout the province get in touch with British Columbia B&B Association (☎ 276-8616), PO Box 593, 810 West Broadway, Vancouver, V5Z 4E2. You might also want to buy a copy of *Town & Country B&B in BC Canada*, now in its seventh edition (1990), which is written and published by Helen Burich in Vancouver. She also offers a reservation service (see the Places to Stay section in Vancouver).

Vancouver

Vancouver lies nestled between sea and mountains in the extreme south-western corner of British Columbia. Its physical setting and features make it easily one of the most attractive cities in Canada. The hilly terrain it's built on and the many bridges offer beautiful views of the ocean, sheltered bays and of the city itself. The parks are numerous and large. One – Stanley Park – is the size of the downtown business area. Sandy beaches dot the shoreline and, like the towering mountains just out of the city, can be used for sports and recreation. Few cities can match Vancouver for its number and variety of interesting sights.

The port, the busiest on North America's west coast, operates all year round in the beautiful and practical natural harbour. It handles nearly all of Canada's trade with Japan and the East.

HISTORY
The Vancouver area was first inhabited by Salish Indians. The first European to see the region was the Spanish explorer Don José María Narvaez in 1791. There wasn't a real settlement until 1865, when Hastings Timber Mill was built. In 1867 a town sprang up around 'Gassy' Jack Deighton's bar. Gastown, as it became known, was the centre around which Vancouver grew.

In 1884 the Canadian Pacific railway (CPR) chose Vancouver for the western terminal of the newly built national railway.

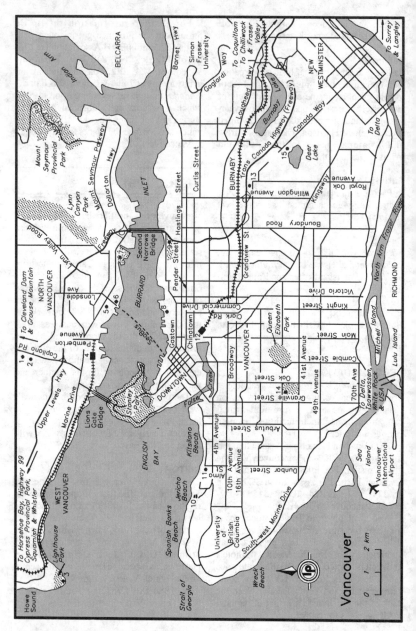

Vancouver

0   1   2 km

1	Capilano Salmon Hatchery
2	Capilano Suspension Bridge
3	Atkinson Lighthouse
4	BC Rail Station & Royal Hudson Steam Train
5	North Shore Museum & Archives
6	Lonsdale Quay Market
7	Park & Tilford Gardens
8	Vanterm
9	Exhibition Park
10	Vancouver CHA Hostel
11	Old Hastings Mill Store
12	VIA Rail Station
13	Vancouver International Centre
14	Van Dusen Botanical Gardens
15	Burnaby Village Museum

Soon after the town became incorporated, taking its name from Captain George Vancouver, a British explorer, who had sailed right into Burrard Inlet in 1792. By 1889, with the CPR's work done, the population jumped to 8000. The city became the port for trade to the Orient, and the population rose to 42,000 by 1901. In the next 10 years, the city boomed with the development of the fishing and wood-processing industries. Immigrants poured in. The completion of the Panama Canal increased Vancouver's significance as a port. WW II catapulted the city into the modern era, and from then on it changed rapidly. The western end became the high-rise apartment centre it now is. In 1974 Granville St became a mall. Redevelopment included housing as well as office buildings and this set the basis for the modern, liveable city Vancouver is today.

In 1986 the city hosted a very successful World's Fair (Expo 86); a few prominent structures remain, while the rest of the area

where it took place is now being redeveloped.

POPULATION & PEOPLE

With a population of around 1.4 million, the city is the third largest in Canada. Nearly half the people of British Columbia live in the Vancouver metropolitan area and the city continues to grow, stretching out to meet the confining mountains.

Vancouverites, once nearly all of British descent, now come from dozens of ethnic backgrounds. Two of the larger non-European communities in the city are the Chinese and East Indian.

The US border is just 40 km to the south. Aside from the city's physical resemblance to San Francisco, the attitudes and lifestyles of Vancouverites are more Californian than anywhere else in the country.

CLIMATE

The climate further extends the comparison with California, and attracts many eastern Canadians. The average January temperature is 2°C, the July average 17°C. It rarely snows and is not often oppressively hot. The only drawback is the rain – particularly in winter, when it rarely stops. Even in summer a rainy spell can last for weeks. But when the sun shines and the mountains reappear, most people here seem to forget all the soakings they've had.

ORIENTATION

Vancouver proper is built on a strip of land bounded on the north by Burrard Inlet and on the south by the Fraser River. The city,

Greenpeace
Originally called the Don't Make a Wave Committee, Greenpeace was founded in Vancouver in the early 1970s. Stressing the need for a balance between economic development and environmental conservation, it first drew attention when members hired a fishing boat to go to Amchitka Island in Alaska to protest against a hydrogen bomb test. More recently, in the mid-1980s, it became the focus of world attention when its ship the *Rainbow Warrior* was blown up in New Zealand by French agents attempting to end Greenpeace's activities against nuclear testing in the South Pacific. ■

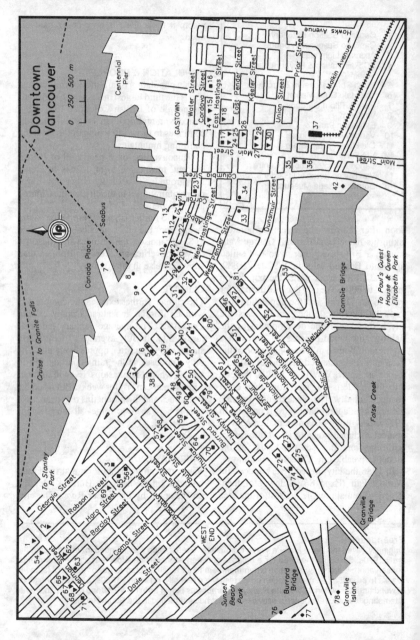

Downtown Vancouver

■ PLACES TO STAY

3	Riviera Motor Inn
5	YWCA
16	Patricia Hotel
17	Hazelwood Hotel
22	Dominion Hotel
23	Spinning Wheel Inn
31	Marble Arch Hotel
32	Niagara Hotel
36	Vincent's Backpackers Hostel
38	Royal Centre & Hyatt Regency
39	Delta Place Hotel
41	St Regis Hotel
43	Hotel Georgia
45	Pacific Centre
48	Hotel Vancouver
51	Hotel Kingston
52	Georgian Court Hotel
55	Robsonstrasse City Motor Inn
56	Barclay Hotel
64	YMCA
65	Dufferin Hotel
70	Century Plaza Hotel
71	English Bay Hotel
72	Austin Motor Hotel
73	Ambassador Hotel
74	Travelodge
75	Cecil Hotel
80	Salvation Army House for Men

▼ PLACES TO EAT

1	El Mariachi
2	Mushashi Japanese Restaurant
6	Jolly Taxpayer Hotel & Pub
11	Maharajah
12	Old Spaghetti Factory
13	Brother's Restaurant
14	Bodhi Vegetarian Restaurant
15	Buddhist Vegetarian Restaurant
18	The Only Café
19	Kilimanjaro
20	India Village
21	Water St Café
24	Mui Loong Chan
25	Max King Bakery & Restaurant

26	Maxim's Bakery & Café
27	On On Tea Garden
28	Hon's Wun Tun House
30	Punjab Restaurant
35	Mom's Kitchen
40	Elephant & Castle
54	Café Slavia
57	Pepita's
58	Heidelberg House
59	White Spot
61	India Gate
62	Dover Seafood Restaurant
63	Madeline's
66	Crumble Pie
67	Budd's
68	Ciao!
69	Saigon

OTHER

4	Travel Infocentre
7	Canada Place
8	Granville Square
9	Seabus & Skytrain Terminal
10	Steam Clock
29	Harbour Centre
33	World's Thinnest Office Building
34	Dr Sun Yat Sen Chinese Classical Garden
37	VIA Rail Station
42	Science World
44	Pendulum
46	Main Post Office
47	Queen Elizabeth Theatre & Vancouver Playhouse
49	Vancouver Public Library
50	Art Gallery
53	BC Place Stadium
60	Duthie Books
76	HR MacMillan Planetarium & Vancouver Museum
77	Vancouver Maritime Museum
78	Granville Island Market
79	Robson Square
81	Greyhound Bus Terminal

however, spreads south and east to include suburbs like Richmond, Burnaby, New Westminster, Surrey, Coquitlam and Langley. To the north of Burrard Inlet lie West Vancouver and North Vancouver. The many bays, inlets and river branches, as well as the Pacific coastline, are a major feature of the city.

Generally, the avenues in Greater Vancouver run east-west; the streets go north and south. Some of the streets in the downtown area and many of the avenues in the Greater Vancouver area are given east or west designations depending on which side of Main St they are. So Hastings St, for example, is divided into West Hastings St and East Hastings St.

Downtown

The real downtown area, in the north-western section of the city, is actually a peninsula, cut off from the southern portion of the city by False Creek. Robson Square, a three-block complex of offices, restaurants, shops and theatres, is pretty well the centre of downtown. It lies on the corner of Robson and Howe Sts. Robson St and, a block or so north, Georgia St, are the two principal north-west/south-east streets.

Both run into Stanley Park, Georgia St continuing through the park to Lions Gate Bridge which spans Burrard Inlet, joining it to the separate municipality of North Vancouver.

The main north-east/south-west streets are, from west to east: Burrard, Howe, Granville and Seymour. North of Georgia St, bordered by Howe and Burrard Sts, is the office, banking and financial district. Robson St is an interesting area with a blend of many ethnic shops and restaurants.

The area south of Robson St and west of Howe St all the way to Sunset Beach on English Bay is primarily residential in the form of rather expensive high-rise apartments.

This high-density area to the west of the downtown shopping area is known as the West End – *not* to be confused with West Vancouver on the North Shore, or the West Side, which is that part of Vancouver south of False Creek and west of Main St. Davie St, between Robson St and the beach, is a secondary commercial and shopping street.

On and around Granville and Seymour Sts, which run north-east from False Creek all the way to West Hastings St, are some of the cheaper hotels.

Much of Granville St, from Nelson St north to West Hastings St, is closed to cars. It's not a true mall as trucks and buses are still permitted and it has never worked very well as a central showcase. Many of the shops are boarded up and it's pretty drab and quiet during the day.

At night, however, it's a very lively focal point for some of the city's street scene. Musicians and various buskers line the street, teenagers by the dozen parade, and various eccentrics and misfits appear. The southern end towards the bridge is something of a red-light area, with sex shops and bars advertising 'exotic' dancers. A couple of large legitimate cinemas also draw crowds to the area, so it's quite a mix.

Also on Granville St are the two main department stores, Eaton's and the Bay. Below these, towards Burrard Inlet, is the modern underground shopping mall called the Pacific Centre.

Georgia St near Granville St is the area with some of the city's top hotels. At the northern end of Granville and Seymour Sts is West Hastings St – the east designations begin at Main St.

Further north, at the bottom of Granville St near Burrard Inlet, is Granville Place and Harbour Centre. Here you'll find modern shopping complexes with views of the harbour. At the water's edge at the foot of Howe St is Canada Place, an impressive Expo 86 leftover with jagged white 'sails'.

Hastings St in the downtown area is skid row, with many down-and-outs. It's especially bad between Cambie St and Dunlevy Ave. There are lots of cheap hotels, restaurants and bars.

By day it's safe and has a few places you may want to look at, including pawnshops and army surplus-type stores. At night it's a good area to stay out of.

Gastown is north of West Hastings St between Columbia and Richards Sts. This is the interesting, tourist-oriented, restored area of old Vancouver.

Chinatown is very close by to the south, in the area around Pender, Gore and Carrall Sts. The Pacific National Exhibition (PNE) stadium and exhibition grounds are further east on East Hastings St, near the Second Narrows Bridge.

Greater Vancouver

To the south of the West End and downtown, over False Creek, lies most of Vancouver – this vast area is primarily residential.

West Heading west after crossing Burrard Bridge or Granville Bridge is the area of Kitsilano, no longer a cheap area but still very popular with young people, students as well as professionals. When a kid from BC's interior moves to the city, this is where he or she wants to be. The main artery through the area is West 4th Ave. It's lined with shops, restaurants and cafés, few of which are pricey. The other important thoroughfare is West Broadway, south of West 4th Ave.

There are beaches all along English Bay, from Kitsilano past Jericho Beach and Spanish Banks Beach to the University of British Columbia (UBC) campus. Just before the campus is one of the expensive areas of town, with good views of the city. UBC is at the far western end of the 'hump' sticking out into the Strait of Georgia. You can walk around the coast all the way to Wreck Beach, south of the university (but wait until the tide is out).

South Between Kitsilano and Sea Island – where Vancouver International Airport is – are some of the city's most exclusive areas, such as Shaughnessy Heights. Estates line South-West Marine Drive, facing out to Sea Island.

Further south is the rapidly growing municipality of Richmond, built on a portion of the Fraser River Delta. On the southern side of Fraser River is Burns Bog; this is used for peat extraction so very little building goes on.

Still further south is the port of Tsawwassen, where you can catch a ferry to Vancouver Island, the Gulf Islands or Seattle.

East East of downtown running south from Powell St, Commercial Drive is Vancouver's main Italian street.

Burnaby, east of Vancouver proper, is another residential area and contains Simon Fraser University. The Trans Canada Highway runs through the centre of Burnaby on its way from Vancouver east to Chilliwack and north-west to Horseshoe Bay.

South-east of Burnaby is the city of New Westminster, BC's original capital, an area along the Fraser River with many old wooden houses and lots of industry. On the southern side of the river from New Westminster is Surrey.

North Over Lions Gate Bridge and Second Narrows Bridge lie West Vancouver and North Vancouver, both essentially middle-class residential areas, although parts of the western area are very exclusive. The shore of Burrard Inlet in North Vancouver is lined with commercial docks. In North Vancouver the principal north-south street is Lonsdale Ave. To the east is Lynn Canyon Park, and beyond is Mt Seymour Provincial Park. To the north along Capilano Rd are Capilano Canyon, the Lions Peaks, Grouse Mountain and the edges of the Coast Mountains. Further west and north lie Cypress Provincial Park, Horseshoe Bay (from where you can take a ferry to Vancouver Island) and the Sunshine Coast.

INFORMATION

The Travel Infocentre (☎ 683-2000) is at 1055 Dunsmuir St and is open daily from 8 am to 6 pm. It's usually very busy, but the staff is friendly and helpful; get a ticket from the dispenser and wait till your number is called. There is a public telephone and you can buy bus tickets here as well.

On the corner of Georgia and Granville Sts is a booth giving visitor information on Vancouver.

Travel information is available at the ferry dock for Victoria in Tsawwassen. There are information booths at either end of the George Massey Tunnel under the Fraser River on the way to Tsawwassen. If you're coming from the east along the Trans Canada Highway you'll see the signs as you get closer to town. There are a couple on the route.

The Vancouver CHA Hostel has a notice board that lists rides, plane tickets, goods for sale and sometimes job offers.

Vancouver Public Library is at 750 Burrard St, next to Hotel Vancouver, at the junction with Robson St. It's open Monday to Thursday from 9.30 am to 9.30 pm, Friday and Saturday from 9.30 am to 6 pm; in winter (October to March) it's open on Sundays from 1 to 5 pm.

The Western Canada Wilderness Committee (☎ 687-8224), at 20 Water St in Gastown, has information and maps on hiking trails in wilderness areas and books on environmental awareness issues relating mainly to Western Canada.

Vancouver General Hospital (☎ 875-4000) is at 855 West 12th Ave. The British Columbia Automobile Association (BCAA) (☎ 732-3911) is at 999 West Broadway.

Post
The main post office is on West Georgia St between Homer and Hamilton Sts and is open Monday to Friday from 8.30 am to 5.30 pm. It has no separate poste restante counter: you just join the queue, show some identification and the person behind the counter will look for your mail.

It has a good philatelic desk and a photocopier.

Foreign Embassies
The following countries have diplomatic representation in Vancouver:

Australia
    Suite 602, World Trade Centre, 999 Canada Place, V6C 3E1 (☎ 684-2191)
Austria
    716 525 Seymour St, V6B 3H9 (☎ 683-7571)
Barbados
    401 2020 Haro St, V6G 1J3 (☎ 872-4444)
Belgium
    Suite 1560, Pacific Centre, 1250 701 West Georgia St, PO Box 10119, V7Y 1C6 (☎ 682-1878)

Brazil
    Suite 1700, Royal Centre, 1035 West Georgia St, PO Box 11152, V6E 3TE (☎ 687-4589)
China (People's Republic of)
    3338 Granville St, V6H 3K3 (☎ 736-6784/5)
Denmark
    Suite 102, 475 Howe St, V6C 2B3 (☎ 684-5171)
Fiji
    1437 West 64th Ave (☎ 251-4124)
Finland
    Suite 120, 1100 1176 West Georgia St, V6E 4A2 (☎ 688-4483)
France
    Suite 1201, 736 Granville St, V6Z 1H9 (☎ 681-2301; telex 0453227)
Germany
    501 325 Howe St, V6C 2AZ (☎ 684-8377)
Greece
    Suite 501, 1200 Burrard St, V6Z 2C7 (☎ 681-1381)
India
    2nd Floor, 325 Howe St, V6C 1Z7 (☎ 681-0644)
Italy
    Suite 505, 1200 Burrard St, V6Z 2C7 (☎ 684-7288)
Japan
    900 Board of Trade Tower, 1177 West Hastings St, V6E 2K9 (☎ 684-5868)
Netherlands
    Suite 721, Crown Trust Building, 475 Howe St, V6C 2B3 (☎ 684-6448)
New Zealand
    PO Box 10071, Pacific Centre, IBM Tower, V7Y 1B6 (☎ 684-7388)
Sweden
    Suite 1109, 1177 West Hastings St, V6E 2K3 (☎ 683-5838)
Switzerland
    Suite 790, World Trade Centre, 999 Canada Place V6C 3E1 (☎ 684-2231)
UK
    Suite 800, 1111 Melville St, V6E 3V6 (☎ 683-4421; fax 581-0693)
USA
    1075 West Georgia St, V6E 4E9 (☎ 685-4311)

Bookshops
Vancouver has a number of very good bookshops. Duthie Books (☎ 684-4496), at 919 Robson St, on the corner of Hornby St, has a range of books including a travel and Canadiana section. It has several other branches including one at UBC. Book Warehouse (☎ 685-5711), 1150 Robson St, has good-quality books, many at bargain prices. It's open seven days a week from 10 am to 10 pm. Madeline's (☎ 688-7334) at 986

Gassy Jack

In the mid-19th century the men working in the sawmills along the shores of Burrard Inlet weren't allowed to drink alcohol on mill property. They had to travel a long way into town, New Westminster, to find somewhere to imbibe. An enterprising former riverboat captain, John Deighton, saw his opportunity and landed in his canoe close to the mill area with his wife, a few animals and a small barrel of whisky. He began selling the whisky almost immediately and soon became a huge success. He was called 'Gassy Jack' because he talked so much; the community that developed around his saloon, became known as Gassy's Town then Gastown. ∎

Denman St has international newspapers and magazines; it's open daily from 10 am to 11 pm. World Wide Books & Maps (☎ 687-3320), 736A Granville St, down a flight of stairs, has a variety of travel guides, atlases and maps for Canada and abroad.

Cole's and WH Smith's are general chain-store bookshops: they both have a branch downtown in the Pacific Centre.

DOWNTOWN
Gastown

The name is taken from 'Gassy' Jack Deighton, an English sailor who forsook the sea to open a bar servicing the developing timber mills. When a village sprang up around his establishment it was called Gassy's Town. The name stuck and Vancouver was on its way. The Gastown area today is bounded by Columbia and Richards Sts, with Water St the main thoroughfare. Burrard Inlet is just to the north. A statue of Gassy Jack has been erected in Maple St Square, where Cordova and Water Sts meet.

The whole Gastown area gradually became a skid row, but in the 1970s it was restored and renovated. The old Victorian buildings now house restaurants, bars, boutiques and galleries. The brick streets have been lined with old lamps. Street vendors and buskers add to the holiday feel of the area. The historic flavour is only a little marred by the parking lot several storeys high in Water St.

At the western end of Water St is the world's first clock run by steam. You can see it work through the side glass panels and will hear it toot every 15 minutes.

In the mall at 131 Water St is Perry's Old Time Portraits, a photography studio that will dress you in 1890s style, or as a 1920s gangster if you prefer, and have your picture ready in five minutes. They make good-quality souvenirs. Also worth looking at is the Inuit Gallery of Vancouver, one of just three galleries in Canada devoted exclusively to Inuit art. It's in Water St opposite Le Magasin and is open Monday to Saturday from 10 am to 6 pm, Sunday from noon to 5 pm. The art is free to look at, big bucks to buy.

Chinatown

About 35,000 people of Chinese descent live in the area around West Pender St, roughly bordered by Abbott and Gore Sts. For the most part it's genuine, serving the locals. Even some of the young people don't speak English. The streets are full of people going in and out of stores of hanging ducks and chickens: there are scores of restaurants and little grocery shops. The colours, signs and occasional old Chinese-style balcony can make you believe for a second that you're in the East, especially when you see the Chinese characters on signs for banks and Hertz Rent-a-Car. There are tourist and souvenir shops interspersed with the community businesses.

Warning Chinatown is not a good area at night, particularly towards the corner of Hastings and Main Sts. After dark it's advisable to stay out of the side streets.

World's Thinnest Office Building Called the Sam Kee, this building at 8 West Pender St, near the corner of Carrall St, has made it into Ripley's *Believe It Or Not* and the *Guinness Book of Records*. It's easy to miss because it looks like the front of the larger building behind, to which it is attached.

Dr Sun Yat-Sen Classical Chinese Garden This is the only full-scale classical Chinese garden (☎ 689-7133) found outside China. Its design is very subtle but exquisite in execution and effect. Modelled after the Ming Dynasty gardens best represented in the city of Suzhou, it makes a real sanctuary in the centre of the city. The Taoist principles of Yin and Yang are incorporated in numerous ways throughout the garden.

The guided tours are included in the admission and are well worthwhile. If possible, go during the week when it won't be too busy. It's at 578 Carrall St behind the Chinese Cultural Centre in Chinatown. It opens daily from 10 am to 8 pm and admission is $3.50, concession $2.50. The adjacent park, built by local artisans using Chinese materials, is similar in design and has free entry.

Robsonstrasse

Robsonstrasse is the local name given to the section of Robson St between Howe and Broughton Sts. At one time mainly German,

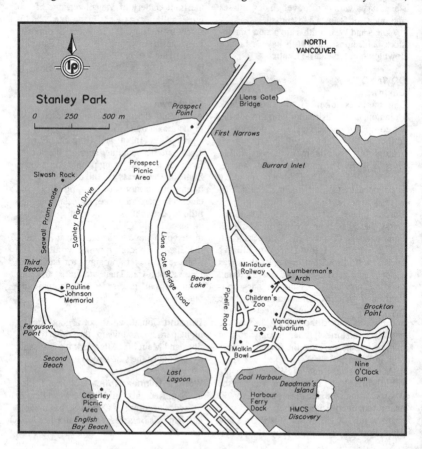

Killer whale

Vancouver Aquarium Within the park is the Vancouver Aquarium (☎ 682-1118), Canada's largest, with 9000 sea creatures. Most popular are the dolphins and killer whales that put on shows several times a day. There is also a special tank for beluga whales. Other exhibits include octopuses, crocodiles, eels, piranhas and a wide variety of local sea life and freshwater fish. The aquarium is also used for research. It's open every day from 10 am to 5.30 pm and admission is $7.

the area is now known for its many ethnic restaurants and shops. There are Italian, French, Japanese, Vietnamese and Danish places among them. For detailed information on restaurants, see the Places to Eat section. The bottom of the street, down towards Stanley Park, has some of the newer, better restaurants.

Stanley Park

The city's main green area, a 400-hectare park, is one of the best in the country. With its wooded hills, parkland, trails, sports fields, swimming pools and beaches, there's something for everyone. The 10-km sea wall that encircles the park makes a good walk or bicycle ride even if you don't go all the way round. From various points there are good views of downtown Vancouver, the North Shore, and out to sea towards the islands.

Along the western side are several sandy beaches; Lions Gate Bridge extends from the northern tip. Just to the west of Lions Gate Bridge is Prospect Point, a popular point for views of the Narrows and passing ships. There's a restaurant here as well: it's a nice spot for a coffee on the terrace.

Near Brockton Point there is a good collection of totem poles. There is a small, free zoo near Brockton Oval. Off the southern side, near the yacht club, is Deadman's Island, once used, it's said, by a northern Native Indian tribe as a camp for women captured in raids. Later it became a burial ground for Chinese people and Native Indians.

Vancouver Art Gallery

The city's art gallery (☎ 682-5621) is right at the centre of things, at 750 Hornby St. It has a large collection of work by Emily Carr, a one-time resident of the area and one of Canada's best known painters. There's also a survey collection of other Canadians and some US and British paintings. The gallery is open from 10 am to 5 pm Monday to Saturday (except Thursday), from 10 am to 9 pm on Thursday and from 12 noon to 5 pm on Sunday. Admission costs $3, $2 for students and unemployed, or if you go on Thursdays between 5 and 9 pm, it's free.

Pendulum

Worth a look (duck your head) is the swaying 26-metre sculptural piece called Pendulum in the Hong Kong Bank of Canada. It's on West Georgia St opposite the Vancouver Art Gallery.

Canada Place

Canada Place, one of the few prominent buildings remaining from Expo 86, juts into the harbour at the foot of Howe St. It resembles an ocean liner with tent-like sails and has become a major city landmark. At the northern end are the promenade shops and restaurants, and outside, good views across Burrard Inlet. The complex now contains the World Trade Centre, BC Convention Centre and Pan Pacific Hotel, and is a terminal for cruise ships. Also here is the CN IMAX Theatre (☎ 682-4629/6422) with a five-storey-high screen showing films made exclusively for such theatres. Canada Place is very close to Waterfront Station.

BC Place

This name refers to both a large tract of city land being totally redeveloped and the stadium which kicked off the entire project. The land runs along the waterfront at False Creek at the southern end of Robson St, near Cambie Bridge. Formerly an area of disused railway lines and warehouses, it will contain apartments, parks, a theatre and museums as part of a 25-year plan.

BC Place Stadium (☎ 661-3403), 777 Pacific Blvd South, was opened in 1983, and is a large sports arena covered by a translucent dome-shaped roof. The roof is 'air-supported', which means it is inflated by huge fans and kept in place by criss-crossed steel wires, hence its quilted appearance. Concerts, trade shows, sports events and other large-scale gatherings are held during the year in this 60,000-capacity stadium which is also the home ground of the BC Lions football team.

During the summer on Monday, Thursday and Saturday there are 45-minute tours at 12 noon, 1.15 and 2.30 pm which leave from Gate H and cost $3.50. To get to the stadium catch either bus No 15 or No 17, or take the SkyTrain to Stadium Station.

Science World

Another structure that remains from Expo 86 is the geodesic dome just off Quebec St near Main St Station. It now houses Science World (☎ 687-7832), a museum where you can get involved through touching and testing the displays. Aimed primarily at children, hands-on exhibits and experiments help explain scientific and physical phenomena. One of the main features is the Omnimax film theatre (☎ 875-6664). Science World is open every day from 10 am to 5 pm except Saturday when it's open till 9 pm; the admission fee is $6 for adults, $3.50 concession.

Vancouver Discovery Show

This is a half-hour film telling the city's story in a rah-rah style. It's in the Harbour Centre, a shopping and restaurant complex at 555 West Hastings St.

Port

The commercial harbour area stretches along Burrard Inlet from Stanley Park to the Second Narrows Bridge. The plaza at Granville Square beside the SeaBus terminal, or Canada Place's observation deck, offer a view where you watch the many types of vessels moving in and out of the harbour. For a closer look visit Vanterm (☎ 666-1629), the Vancouver Container Terminal. There you can see the inner workings of a port facility – the warehouse, cranes, containers and the guys lugging freight. The port viewing area is at 1300 Stewart St at the foot of Clark Drive. It's free and there is an audiovisual show included. It's open Monday to Friday from 9 am to 12 noon and from 1 to 3 pm.

Views

One of the best views of the city and surroundings is from the top of the Sheraton Landmark Hotel in the revolving restaurant. The elevator up is free and the view makes the $4 beer worthwhile. The hotel, one of the city's highest buildings, is at 1400 Robson St.

A second spot is the more-advertised observation deck (☎ 689-0421) and restaurant atop the Harbour Centre at 555 West Hastings St. The deck is open from 8.30 am to 10.30 pm (summer) and is reached by an external glass-walled lift (elevator), which takes 50 seconds. The cost is $5. Take a SkyTrain to Waterfront St or bus Nos 10, 14, 16, 20 heading towards the harbour on Granville Mall.

WEST SIDE
Granville Island

On the southern side of False Creek, under the Granville Bridge, this formerly industrial little island has been redeveloped into a busy blend of businesses, restaurants, arts and entertainment. Major attractions include two important performing-arts centres, numerous theatre companies, and, on the north-western tip, the popular Public Market with fresh fruit, vegetables and fish. A few prepared food counters sell small meals and snacks. There are several shops where local painters, jewellery makers and weavers make and display their crafts. Prices are fairly reasonable. You can also view the art galleries in the Emily Carr College of Art & Design. The Granville Island Brewing Co (☎ 688-9927) is worth visiting. It's a small company producing naturally brewed beer (ie without chemicals), and gives free tours at 1 and 3 pm with a sample at the end. On the north-eastern edge of the island it's interesting to have a look at the attractive, pricey, floating houses. Note that much of the island's activity is shut down on Monday.

To get to the island from either Water St in Gastown or Granville St downtown, catch the No 50 False Creek bus. There's an information centre where the bus stops. Alternatively, you can take the False Creek mini-ferry (see Getting Around).

Vancouver Museum

This museum (☎ 736-4431) is at 1100 Chestnut St, just west of Burrard Bridge in Vanier Park on English Bay. Also called the Vancouver Centennial Museum, it specialises in local history. On display are old photos of BC and sections on the archaeology of the area, concentrating on the Salish Indians and ethnology. There are a few examples of most Native Indian crafts. The basketry is impressive, especially the baskets made of cedar and pine roots. The part of the museum showing the European exploration and settlement of Vancouver is interesting. The last of the Hudson's Bay Company forts was here – Fort Victoria.

The museum is open September to May from 10 am to 5 pm Tuesday to Sunday; in June, July and August from 10 am to 9 pm Monday to Friday, from 10 am to 5 pm Saturday and Sunday. Admission costs $5, or $2.50 concession. Or you can buy a combination ticket for $7 which gives access to the Vancouver Maritime Museum as well. To get

there (and to the Vancouver Maritime Museum close by) take bus No 22 from Burrard St downtown.

HR Macmillan Planetarium

This planetarium (☎ 736-3656), part of the Vancouver Museum complex, has regularly changing entertaining and educational shows which are projected onto a 20-metre dome. The shows, at 2.30 and 7 pm during the week and 1, 2.30, 4 and 7 pm on the weekend, are very popular, so make reservations early. Admission is $4.25, or cheaper with a youth hostel card. There are also laser displays for $5.25 at 8.30 pm Sunday to Thursday and at 9.30 pm Friday and Saturday. The planetarium is closed on Monday during the winter, but open daily in the summer months. On Friday, Saturday and Sunday when the sky is clear the Gordon Southam Observatory (☎ 738-2855) is also open to the public and is free.

Vancouver Maritime Museum

The Maritime Museum (☎ 737-2211/2), is 1905 Ogden Ave at the foot of Cypress St, is a five-minute walk from the Vancouver Centennial Museum. It is divided into two sections. The museum itself is strictly for boat buffs – lots of wooden models and some old rowboats on display. It's open daily from 10 am to 5 pm and admission is $3, $1.50 concession.

The other section, designated a national historic site (☎ 666-3201), is good, and free. On display is the *St Roch*, a 1928 RCMP Arctic patrol sailing ship which was the first to navigate the legendary Northwest Passage in both an easterly and westerly direction. There are interesting free guided tours on the ship every half-hour or so. From the museum wharf you can take a ferry to Granville Island.

Old Hastings Mill Store

Built in 1865, this was the first store on Burrard Inlet. It survived the Great Fire of 1886 and was moved in 1930 to where it stands today on the corner of Point Grey Rd and Alma St at the eastern end of Jericho Beach. It's the large, off-white, barn-like building with brown trim. It houses a small collection of Native Indian artefacts and some local memorabilia and is open from 10 am to 4 pm. Admission is free.

University of British Columbia
The University of British Columbia (☎ 228-3131), often just called UBC, is at the most westerly point of Vancouver, on the spit jutting out into Georgia Strait. The huge campus serving 30,000 students is spread over 400 wooded hectares. Bus Nos 4, 10 and 14 heading south on Granville St run up to the university every 10 minutes or so; the journey takes about 30 minutes.

As well as the attractive grounds, there are several points of interest.

UBC Museum of Anthropology This museum (☎ 228-5087) is excellent. The exhibits include art and artefacts from cultures around the world. Asia, Africa and the Pacific are all well represented but the emphasis is on the work of BC's Coastal Indians, which includes a terrific totem pole collection – both indoors and out. The collection has some fine sculptures and carvings. All the items are stored in glass filing cabinets. Everything is numbered and catalogued, so you can look up details and cross-references yourself. The museum is open from 11 am to 9 pm Tuesday, 11 am to 5 pm Wednesday to Sunday and is closed Monday. The admission charge of $3 is waived on Tuesday.

Nitobe Memorial Gardens These beautiful Japanese-style gardens (☎ 228-4208) are near the museum. Designed by a leading Japanese landscape architect, they're a perfect display of this symbolic Eastern art form. Get a guide at the gate when you buy a ticket. The gardens are open from 10 am to 8 pm in summer, until 3 pm in winter. Admission is $1.50, students 50 cents.

Near the gardens, **Totem Park** has carvings and buildings representing part of a Haida Indian village. Admission is free.

Wreck Beach Along South-West Marine Drive, heading south past the Rose Garden and the Museum of Anthropology, are markers for trails into the woods. Follow trail No 3 or 4 down the steep steps to Wreck Beach, a pleasant and quiet – if notorious – nude beach.

Aquatic Centre If you don't fancy that, try the UBC Aquatic Centre (☎ 228-4521) back on the campus, off University Blvd, which has pools, saunas and exercise areas, and is open to the public.

Queen Elizabeth Park
This 52-hectare park, between Cambie and Ontario Sts and near 33rd Ave, is the city's second largest park. Up the hill to the Bloedel Conservatory there are great views of the city in nearly every direction. There's a well-designed sunken garden surrounded by small cliffs which has some fantastic plants, one with leaves a metre across. Next to the parking lot is an unusual, Oriental-looking garden consisting of many pools and fountains. The garden is mostly cement, but is dotted with wooden frames holding plants and flowers. There is a restaurant and a cheaper coffee shop for snacks or tea. Catch bus No 15 heading south-east on Robson St to get there. ·

Bloedel Conservatory The conservatory (☎ 872-5513) has tropical plants beneath its plastic dome, but for the admission prices of $2.40 or $1.20 for students you may consider it's not really worth it with all the flowers and gardens around for free.

It's open in summer from 10 am to 9 pm and in winter from 10 am to 5 pm.

Van Dusen Botanical Gardens
These 22-hectare gardens (☎ 266-7194), at 5251 Oak St between 33rd and 37th Aves, are not far from Queen Elizabeth Park. The gardens contain a small lake and a large collection of ornamental plants from around the world. They're open daily from 10 am to 8 pm in summer. The admission price is $4, students $2. Take bus No 17 south on Burrard St from downtown.

NORTH SHORE
Lonsdale Quay Market
Major redevelopment has transformed the area by the SeaBus terminal on the North Shore. Foremost among the changes, which include a water's edge park, offices and residential complexes, is the Lonsdale Quay Market (☎ 985-6261). The 1st floor is devoted to fresh and cooked food; the 2nd floor is mainly speciality shops but has a restaurant with good views. As you leave the ferry, there's an information booth to offer guidance on the North Shore's attractions. The local bus depot is here as well.

The market is open Saturday to Wednesday from 9.30 am to 6.30 pm and till 9 pm on Thursday and Friday. To get there catch the SeaBus from the downtown terminal at Waterfront Station.

North Shore Museum & Archives
The small museum (☎ 987-5618) at 209 West 4th St offers rather good changing exhibits on a wide range of subjects such as transport, antiques and Native Indian crafts. Admission is free and it's open Wednesday to Sunday from 1 to 4 pm. The archives section is open Wednesday to Friday from 9.30 am to 12.30 pm and from 1.30 to 4.30 pm.

Capilano Suspension Bridge
This bridge (☎ 985-7474), at 3735 Capilano Rd on the left-hand side going north, spans the Capilano River for almost 140 metres at a height of 70 metres. Open daily in summer from 8 am till dusk, it's very tourist oriented and, with little else in the small park, is really not worth the $5 (students $3.50) admission.

To get there from downtown take bus No 246, marked 'Highlands', going west on West Georgia St or bus No 236 from Lonsdale Quay to Edgemont Village; you then change to bus No 232. (This bus also goes to Capilano Salmon Hatchery and Cleveland Dam; in summer No 236 also goes all the way to Grouse Mountain.) If you're driving, head north over Lions Gate Bridge to Marine Drive then turn left (north) at Capilano Rd.

Capilano Salmon Hatchery
The hatchery is a fish farm (☎ 987-7474) run by the government to help stop the depletion of valuable salmon stocks. Although you can't see the holding pools, there are exhibits with good explanations of the whole process. Salmon in various stages of growth are on display in tanks, and you can see how they are channelled from the river into the hatchery when they head upstream to spawn. Admission is free. It's in Capilano Park, off Capilano Rd not far north of the suspension bridge.

Cleveland Dam
The dam (☎ 987-1411) blocks Capilano Lake, which supplies much of Vancouver's drinking water. You'll get good views of the Lions, two peaks of the Coast Mountains. There are picnic areas and trails and it's free. The dam is slightly further north of the salmon hatchery, up Capilano Rd which becomes Nancy Greene Way.

Grouse Mountain
Grouse Mountain (☎ 984-0661), off Nancy Greene Way (the northern extension of Capilano Rd), is famous for its Swiss-built Superskyride cable car which operates daily from 9 am to 10 pm. From the top – 1110 metres – you can see all of Vancouver, the coast, part of Vancouver Island and northward over the mountains. It's an expensive ride at $11 or $7.50 for students. An open chair lift goes from the upper plateau to the peak but this is a further few bucks. There are restaurants at the top and bottom of the mountain.

If you take the Superskyride, make sure it's a clear day. If it's raining, foggy or at all hazy with low clouds, forget it: by the time you reach the top you won't see a thing. Go in late afternoon; then you can see the city by day and night. (See Capilano Suspension Bridge earlier for details on how to get there.)

Lynn Canyon Park
Set in thick woods, this park gives a good glimpse of the rainforest vegetation so dif-

ferent from that found in eastern Canada. There are many hiking trails, and you can find your own picnic and swimming spots. Over Lynn Canyon is a suspension bridge; although not as big as Capilano, it's much the same and is free. The **Ecology Centre** here has displays, films and slide shows about the biology of the area. It's open daily from 10 am to 5 pm.

To get to the park take bus Nos 228 or 229 from Lonsdale Quay. If you're driving go over Second Narrows Bridge, take Lynn Valley Rd then go right (east) on Peters Rd, where you'll see signs that lead you into the park.

Park & Tilford Gardens

These 1.2 hectares of flower gardens, at 1200 Cotton Drive south-west of Lynn Canyon Park, were developed by the distillery of the same name. There are some unusual tree specimens, tropical birds and lots of flowers. Although free, these gardens are not highly recommended; they're used mainly by wedding photographers. They're open daily from 9.30 am till dusk.

To get there take bus No 239 from Lonsdale Quay to Phibbs Exchange, then change to No 232 heading east to Brooksbank, where the gardens are.

Royal Hudson Steam Train

This 1930s steam engine pulls restored coaches on a 5½-hour return excursion to Squamish. The route follows the coast northward through some beautiful scenery. The cost is $24 return. The train leaves from BC Rail's station, 1311 West 1st St at the southern end of Pemberton Ave, North Vancouver. For details of the rather complicated schedule contact 1st Tours (☎ 688-7246), 1810 Alberni St. A variation is to take the train one way and cruise back on the MV *Britannia*; the fare is $42 return. (See Organised Tours in the Vancouver Activities section later.)

Lighthouse Park

Here in a stand of original forest are some of the largest trees in the Vancouver area. Trails lead to the lighthouse and bluffs, with views

of the Georgia Strait. The park is at Point Atkinson in West Vancouver, eight km to the left (west) on Marine Drive after going over Lions Gate Bridge. Catch bus No 250 going west on West Georgia St.

EAST VANCOUVER
Simon Fraser University

The university sits atop Burnaby Mountain in Burnaby, about 20 km east of downtown. Its intriguing modern architecture and excellent vistas make it a worthwhile place to visit. The design, incorporating unusual use of space and perspective, was – and remains – controversial. There are huge courtyard-like quadrants and many fountains, including one on a roof. Some areas of the complex are reminiscent of Mayan ruin sites in Mexico. For information on tours around the university, call ☎ 291-3111. To get there, catch bus Nos 10 or 14 on East Hastings St then change near Boundary Rd to bus No 135, which will take you to the university.

Museum of Archaeology & Ethnology

On the campus, this museum (☎ 291-3325) features a collection of Pacific Coast Indian artefacts and has a cheap cafeteria.

Burnaby Village Museum

Located at 6501 Deer Lake Village Road, beside Deer Lake, this museum (☎ 294-1231) is in Burnaby's Century Park, close to the Trans Canada Highway. It's a replica of a village community which attempts to preserve both the artefacts and atmosphere of a south-western BC town in the years 1890 to 1925. There's an old schoolhouse, printing shop, drugstore and other establishments; a large, working steam train model is next to the village. Friendly, informed workers are in period dress. The restaurant is quite good and inexpensive for a soup and sandwich lunch. It's open daily from 11 am to 4.30 pm during summer. Admission is $4, $3 for students. Catch bus No 120 on East Hastings St.

Teleglobe Canada

The displays and exhibits here focus on

videos, satellite and undersea international communications, telecommunications artefacts and related electronic equipment. Free guided tours are offered Monday to Friday from mid-June to Labour Day. It's in the Vancouver International Centre, 3033 Beta Ave, Burnaby, off Canada Way, 13 km from downtown. To get there, go south of the Trans Canada Highway on Willingdon Ave and turn left onto Canada Way; Beta Ave is the second turning on the left. Alternatively, take the SkyTrain to Nanaimo Station then catch bus No 25.

ACTIVITIES
Swimming & Water Sports
You can swim at a number of city beaches, for example Second and Third beaches in Stanley Park, English Bay and Sunset beaches downtown, or at Kitsilano and Jericho beaches on the southern side of English Bay. Call ☎ 738-8535 for information.

Kitsilano Beach is the largest and most popular and where the beach culture scene is at its peak. On a hot summer day as many as 10,000 hit the sands. The prime spot to see and be seen is apparently around the lifeguard section; other areas attract those who prefer a little more material used in the construction of their bathing suits. For swimming, the saltwater Kitsilano Pool is generally busier than the waters of English Bay. (At one portion of the beach you might catch one of the semi-pro or professional volleyball tournaments which occur regularly through the summer months.)

The Vancouver Aquatic Centre (☎ 665-3424), at 1050 Beach Ave near Sunset Beach, has an indoor heated swimming pool, whirlpool, diving tank, gym and sauna. Admission is $2.50. There's another aquatic centre at UBC (see earlier) and in West Vancouver at 776 22nd St. Kitsilano Beach has an outdoor heated saltwater pool (☎ 731-0011). It's open in summer Monday to Friday from 8.45 am to 8.45 pm, on Saturday and Sunday from 10.00 am to 8.45 pm. Admission is $1.50.

If you've got the energy for canoeing or kayaking you can rent equipment at Sports Rent (☎ 733-1605), 2560 Arbutus St in Kitsilano: the daily rate starts at $25 and there's a 10% discount for CHA hostellers. It has several other offices around town. In North Vancouver, on Indian Arm, Deep Cove Canoe & Kayak (☎ 929-2268), 2156 Banbury Rd, has rentals and will teach you how to use a canoe. Granville Island is another area where you can hire canoes: try Vancouver Canoe & Kayak (☎ 688-6010) at 1666 Duranleau St, or next door at 1668 Duranleau St, Ecomarine Ocean Kayak Centre (☎ 689-7575), which also gives a 10% discount to CHA hostellers.

For the yachting enthusiast this street has a few places where you can hire boats: there's Corcovado Yacht Charters (☎ 669-7907) at 104 1676 Duranleau St, and Blue Ocean Yacht Services (☎ 682-8354) at 106A 1650 Duranleau St. The West Coast School of Seamanship (☎ 684-9440), at 1620 Duranleau St, offers three-hour sailing trips with a qualified instructor for $25 per person.

Windsure Windsurfing School (☎ 734-7245) gives lessons and rents boards. Its offices are at English Bay Beach, Kitsilano Beach and Jericho Sailing Centre. Sports Rent (see earlier) hires out windsurfing equipment.

English Bay is a popular area for salmon fishing, for which the west coast is famous. Boats and equipment are for hire and there are expensive guided charters. Corcovado Yacht Charters and Blue Ocean Yacht Services are two companies offering these facilities. For information on good fishing locations call the Department of Fisheries & Oceans (☎ 666-2074/0383).

Divers World, at 1523 West 3rd Ave, has equipment and scuba trips.

Skiing
Vancouver has some great downhill and nordic skiing a short distance away. Just north of the city there are major resorts at Grouse, Whistler and Blackcomb mountains; the latter two, further from town, are very close to each other but are operated separately.

Grouse Mountain (☎ 984-0661) is the nearest to the city and is notable for its night-time skiing, when most of the downhill runs are illuminated and open till 10.30 pm. The day pass for an adult is $25. For a snow report call ☎ 986-6262.

For information on Whistler and Black-comb mountains see the Around Vancouver section later.

Other nearby ski resorts include Cypress Bowl and Hollyburn (☎ 926-5612 for either resort) both in Cypress Provincial Park on Vancouver's North Shore; Mt Seymour (☎ 986-2261) in Mt Seymour Provincial Park in North Vancouver; Hemlock Valley (☎ 797-4411), a two-hour drive east along the Fraser Valley on Highway 7; and Manning Park (☎ 840-8822) in Manning Provincial Park, a 2½-hour drive east on the Trans Canada Highway to Hope, then Highway 3 into the park. Garibaldi Provincial Park (☎ 929-1291) has cross-country skiing only (see entry under Around Vancouver later).

Hiking
Hiking is available in many of the provincial parks around Vancouver.

Cypress Provincial Park is the closest, just eight km north of West Vancouver off Highway 99. It has eight hiking trails including the Baden-Powell, Yew Lake and Howe Sound Crest trails. Mt Seymour Provincial Park, 15 km north-east of downtown, has 10 trails varying in difficulty and length. On clear days both parks offer magnificent views. At both parks you should be prepared for continually changing mountain weather conditions.

There's hiking in Garibaldi Provincial Park (see Around Vancouver later).

Golden Ears Provincial Park is 48 km east of Vancouver. Take Highway 7 as far as Haney, then turn left (north) and follow the 13-km road to Alouette Lake. The park has eleven hiking trails, and camping and picnic areas.

Cycling
A good way to get around town and Vancouver's numerous parks and beach

areas is by bicycle (see the Getting Around section later).

Strolling
In the heart of the city, Sunset Beach at sunset is beautiful and busy and there are cafés on the corner of Denman St. A stroll is highly recommended. The sea-wall promenade in Stanley Park is also worth a leisurely walk.

Organised Tours
The Gray Line Bus Company (☎ 681-8687) offers a wide selection of tours, ranging from ones of Vancouver or its immediate sur-roundings, to a 10-day tour of the Rockies. Most tours begin at the Hotel Vancouver. All major hotels sell tickets. The most complete tour of Vancouver is called the Grand City Tour: it costs $29.50, lasts 3½ hours, will acquaint you with varying districts within Vancouver and stops at a few attractions. A shorter introduction to the city costs $20.

There are other tours, some cheaper, some more costly, that include visits to Granville Island and UBC. Another takes you to the sights of North Vancouver and includes a ride up Grouse Mountain. This one lasts four hours and costs $38.50.

Another company with local area tours is Town Tours (☎ 879-5852). A tour of Vancouver including Stanley Park and Gastown costs $24 and lasts for 3½ hours; of similar duration is the tour to the North Shore sights and Grouse Mountain for $35. Town Tours also does a full-day tour to Victoria for $70.

Pacific Coach Lines (☎ 662-3222) oper-ates a number of one-day excursions for about the same price as a normal bus ticket. It's at the Greyhound Bus Depot, 150 Dunsmuir St. Some destinations are Vancou-ver Island, the Sunshine Coast and Fort Langley.

Landsea Tours (☎ 687-5640) and Vance Tours (☎ 222-1966) use minibuses for their tours. A 2½-hour tour of the city costs $20.

Harbour Ferries' subsidiary, 1st Tours (☎ 688-7246; 800-663-1500 toll free), 1810 Alberni St, offers a sight-seeing tour by boat and train. The 6½-hour trip past good scenery goes up Howe Sound to Squamish.

You can travel to Squamish on the MV *Britannia* and return by the Royal Hudson Steam Train, or vice versa. The cost is $42, $38 for students. You can go both ways by train for $24 return. There are also shorter, narrated harbour tours by paddleboat ($18). All these tours are available between the end of May and the end of September.

On Granville Island several places offer cruises of False Creek, English Bay and Burrard Inlet. One is Malecite Marine Charters (☎ 687-6838) at 1656 Duranleau St.

If you have the cash a number of companies provide helicopter tours. Vancouver Helicopters (☎ 683-4354) will show you Greater Vancouver for $75 per person or take you up to Grouse Mountain and back for $25 per person. Bel-Aire Helicopters have a half-hour of the city and Burrard Inlet for $175.

Wine Tours Wine tours are held at the Jordan Sainte Michelle Cellars (☎ 576-6741) in Surrey, 30 minutes from town and 12 km from the US border. A free tasting is included.

FESTIVALS
Following is a list of some of the major events in Vancouver during the year. For more details phone or get a copy of the leaflet *Calendar of Events* from the Travel Infocentre.

Polar Bear Swim
This popular, chilly affair has been taking place on English Bay Beach annually on 1 January since 1819. If you can't handle the water, watching is allowed.

Chinese New Year
In mid-February Chinatown provides the setting for one of Vancouver's most colourful events, with dancers, music, fireworks and food.

International Dragon Boat Festival
Originally staged as part of Expo 86, this annual event takes place in False Creek over three days in late June. It attracts nearly 2000 competitors from around the world and

about 150,000 spectators. As well as the boat races there's music, theatre and international cuisine.

Vancouver Folk Festival
Held on 1 July, this is the province's largest multicultural festival. The main events take place in Gastown, Robson Square and the Orpheum Theatre – all free. There is music, dance, performances and, of course, traditional costumes and foods. For information call ☎ 879-2931.

Vancouver Sea Festival
During this festival in mid-July there are concerts, parades, fireworks and salmon barbecues, which take place on the shores of English Bay. For details and times call ☎ 669-4091.

Vancouver Folk Music Festival
Also in mid-July, the Folk Music Festival is three days of music, including concerts and workshops, from some of the best North American folk musicians. Most of the action takes place at Jericho Beach Park near the CHA Hostel and UBC. For information about tickets call ☎ 879-2931.

Carnival
From 1 to 3 August Carnival celebrates various ethnic cultures with pavilions scattered around town offering music, dance, foods, etc.

Abbotsford International Air Show
Known as Canada's National Air Show, the Abbotsford has been voted the world's best. The three-day event, held in early August, celebrated its 30th anniversary in 1991. It has everything that flies, from fighters to the Concorde. It's held 56 km south-east of Vancouver in Abbotsford near the US border.

Festival of the Written Arts
Held in early to mid-August in Sechelt, north up the Sunshine Coast beyond Horseshoe Bay, this event, which has been held annually since 1982, features writers from across

Canada speaking to and meeting those attending.

Pacific National Exhibition

Known as the PNE (☎ 253-2311), this big fair, the second largest in Canada (Toronto's CNE is the biggest) features a little bit of everything – sports, competitions, international exhibits, concerts and shows, as well as amusement park rides. It starts off each year with a two-hour parade. The exhibition lasts about two weeks, from late August to Labour Day. The PNE takes place in Exhibition Park on East Hastings St near the Second Narrows Bridge. Catch bus Nos 14 or 16 from downtown.

Vancouver Fringe Festival

This is an increasingly popular theatre event with offerings in drama, musical theatre, comedy and dance from around the world. It takes place over two weeks from early to mid-September in various theatres around Main St, between East 6th and East 17th avenues in the Mount Pleasant area. Call ☎ 873-3646 for information.

Oktoberfest

The German-based Oktoberfest takes place in the Commodore Ballroom over three weekends from early to mid-October. There's the usual oompah and Tyrolean music, Bavarian dancers, beer and more beer. It usually lasts until 2 am.

PLACES TO STAY
Camping

There are no government-run campgrounds in the Vancouver area and the trailer (RV) parks right in Vancouver do not allow tenting. The closest camping areas that do are south of the city, on or near Highway 99, which runs to the US border. There are also a couple near the ferry terminal for Vancouver Island in Tsawwassen.

Timberland Motel & Campground (☎ 531-1033) at 3418 King George Highway (Highway 99a), Surrey, has sites for tents and trailers. A site costs $14 and there's a laundr-

ette and showers. The campground is half an hour's drive from Vancouver, six km from the US border. *Parklander Motor & Trailer Court* (☎ 531-3711) at 16311 8th Ave, Surrey, has campsites for $14. Showers are available and the campground is surrounded by trees.

South of the middle arm of Fraser River, *Richmond RV Park* (☎ 270-7878) at 6200 River Rd, Richmond, near Hollybridge Way is one of the closest to town. It's open from April to October and has sites for $14 for two people; it's $2 per extra person.

ParkCanada RV Inns (☎ 943-5811), 4799 Highway 17, Delta, is north-east of the Tsawwassen ferry terminal. It has free showers and sites from $12.

There are several places to camp along Beach Rd, White Rock. One is *Oddfellows & Rebeka Campsite* (☎ 531-5600) at 16249 Beach Rd, 40 km from Vancouver. It has hot, coin-operated showers, and a beach. Tenting is just $7.

On the eastern side of town is the *Four Acres Trailer Court* (☎ 936-3273) at 675 Lougheed Highway, Coquitlam, which has some places for tents at $12. It's about 25 km from the city centre. The Lougheed Highway is also called Highway 7.

Hostels

Although the *Vancouver CHA Hostel* (☎ 224-3208; fax 224-4852), at 1515 Discovery St, Kitsilano, is away from the centre of town, its location is great. It's close to the beach in Jericho Beach Park on English Bay, about 20 minutes from downtown by bus. The hostel is open from 7.30 am to 12 pm and has well over 300 beds, making it the largest in Canada; other facilities include kitchens, cafeteria, laundry room, notice board, TV lounge and parking. The rates are $10 for members, $15 for nonmembers. Ask about the places in town where the hostel card will get you reductions, eg Sports Rent, CN IMAX Theatre and the Vancouver Museum.

From downtown take bus No 4 south on Granville St, it continues south over False Creek then west along West 4th Ave to

Marine Drive. Turn right (north) onto Discovery St and you'll come to it – it's the big white building on the left. This is one of the country's more stable hostels, so it's likely to stay in the same place.

Vincent's Backpackers Hostel (☎ 688-2441/0112) at 927 Main St, next to the Cobalt Motor Hotel, is not in the best of areas but it's popular and is within walking distance of downtown and not too far from the Main St Station, Science World and the VIA Rail station. There's no curfew and the rates are $8/16/20 a dormitory/single/double for IYHF members, $10/20/24 for nonmembers. Weekly rates are offered. The entrance is under the sign which says 'The Source'.

Globetrotter's Inn (☎ 988-5141) at 170 West Esplanade in North Vancouver is near the Lonsdale Quay SeaBus terminal. It's a friendly place with shared rooms at $12 per person, $25/30 for a single/double and $35 for a double with own bath.

The *Salvation Army House for Men*, on Dunsmuir St between Seymour and Richards Sts, is for men on skid row. Male travellers who are low on cash can get a single room there for $12, or $15 with a bath.

The *YMCA* (☎ 681-0221) is right downtown at 955 Burrard St. Depending on whether you'd like a TV or not, singles are $27 or $29, doubles are $46 or $48. Single rooms can also be rented by the week for $136. Women and couples are allowed and quite a few travellers stay here. There are gym and pool facilities and a small inexpensive restaurant serving good-value breakfasts and sandwiches.

The *YWCA* (☎ 662-8188) is at 580 Burrard St, further down towards Canada Place and not far from the Travel Infocentre. It's really like a hotel, with full facilities including gym, pool and child care. Singles are $34 to $39, twins $44 to $49, doubles $49 to $53 and rooms for four $59 to $63. Single men are not allowed. It's scheduled to move, but not before 1993.

The *University of British Columbia* rents rooms in the Walter Gage Residence (☎ 228-2963) from about the first week in May to the end of August. Singles are from $28 to

$45 and doubles $60. Contact the Conference Centre manager at Gage Towers, 5961 Student Union Blvd, UBC Campus, Vancouver. Self-contained apartments are also available. The pleasant campus has a cafeteria, some cafés, laundrette, pub and sports facilities.

Simon Fraser University (☎ 291-4201/4503), Room 239, Shell House, Burnaby, V5A 1S6, also rents out rooms from May to August. They're all fully furnished and bathrooms are shared; singles cost from $18 to $30, doubles $40.

B&Bs

B&B accommodation has really mushroomed across the country, perhaps more so in BC than anywhere. The Travel Infocentre has information on agencies who select, inspect and book individual houses. The *Accommodations* guide also has a list of agencies operating in Vancouver.

A couple to try are Born Free B&B (☎ 298-8815) at 4390 Frances St, Burnaby, and Old English B&B Registry (☎ 986-5069) at 1226 Silverwood Crescent, North Vancouver. Another is Vancouver B&B (☎ 291-6147) at 4390, Frances St, Burnaby, V5C 4L8. Town & Country B&B in BC Canada (☎ 731-5942), PO Box 46544, Station G, Vancouver, V6R 4G6, offers a reservation service for the Vancouver area as well as publishing its home accommodation guide. B&Bs in Vancouver cost from around $30 to $60 for singles, $45 to $90 for doubles.

Other operators run independently and many have advertisements at the Travel Infocentre. Some are very central but nearly all have only two or three rooms, so you may have to call several to get a room.

One place which is recommended is *Paul's Guest House* (☎ 872-4753), south of the downtown area at 345 West 14th Ave between Cambie and Yukon Sts. It's very popular with travellers and is in a quiet residential area. Paul himself speaks 11 languages and will pick you up from the airport and cook your breakfast. The rooms are clean, and there's a laundry service, TV lounge and free coffee or tea during the day. Singles/doubles are $30/40. He operates another house close by, the *Cambie Lodge*, at similar rates.

Hotels – bottom end

Many people find the CHA Hostel or universities too far from the centre and prefer one of the older, cheap central hotels. Vancouver, despite its rapid growth, has a great number of them, right in the downtown core. Many are well kept and offer good value, but Vancouver is one of Canada's biggest tourist towns so rooms in summer may be rather scarce. In winter you may get places a little cheaper, and if you're staying a week it's worth asking for a reduction any time of the year.

There are also numerous hotels serving the downtrodden and the fringe – Vancouver has more than any other Canadian city.

There are more cheapies than you can shake a stick at in Gastown, Chinatown and Hastings St; Cordova and Abbot Sts have several too; a few of these are all right for shoestringers. Rooms are rented by the day, week or month. Nightly rates are from as low as $16; weekly rates range from $60.

In central Gastown with a great location is the *Spinning Wheel Inn* (☎ 681-1627/2814), 210 Carrall St. Unfortunately, things have slipped quite a bit here and it's also not the bargain it was. It's still cheap enough, however, at singles/doubles $25/30 and housekeeping rooms at $40, or $170 a week.

The old *Dominion Hotel* (☎ 681-6666), dating from 1899, at 210 Abbot St is also in Gastown, on the corner of Water St. The rooms go for $40/50 singles/doubles, including breakfast. There are many others in the area but most are bottom-of-the-line.

Hastings St for a couple of blocks either side of Main St is a less-than-wholesome part of town (especially at night), but there are a couple of reasonable places to stay. *Hazelwood Hotel* (☎ 687-9126) at 344 East Hastings St costs $20 for a single room without bath, $30 with. Weekly rates are available. You might have to wait a while for the desk clerk to appear. *Patricia Hotel* (☎

255-4301), 403 East Hastings St, is much better. It's large, clean, well kept and good value at $36 for singles and $49 to $59 for doubles, all with a bath or shower.

The downtown area has a better selection of hotels, ranging from basic ones through moderate to expensive.

At 435 West Pender St on the corner of Richards St is the *Niagara Hotel* (☎ 688-7574) with a sign depicting Niagara Falls tumbling four floors. It's old but good, with singles/doubles at $30/40. All rooms have colour TV. Nearby, the central *Piccadilly Hotel* (☎ 669-1556), 620 West Pender St, has 45 small simple rooms. Singles/doubles cost $30/40.

The *St Regis Hotel* (☎ 681-1135), 602 Dunsmuir St on the corner of Seymour St, is a little more costly. All rooms come with bath and there is a bar and restaurant. Singles/doubles are $45/50. The *Marble Arch* (☎ 681-5435), 518 Richards St near the corner of West Pender St, offers bathless singles for $30 including breakfast.

Also in the area is the recommended *Hotel Kingston* (☎ 684-9024) at 757 Richards St. It was the city's first B&B hotel and still offers the morning meal. Prices depend on your room and facilities: singles cost from $30 to $45, doubles from $50 to $65. It's a good, older hotel with a sauna and guests' laundry.

There are several hotels in Granville St, south past Nelson St towards the bridge. It's a seedy area and one that streetwalkers use; a few hotels are OK but are not recommended for female travellers.

The *Austin Motor Hotel* (☎ 685-7235) at 1221 Granville St, is fine and big with singles/doubles for $36/48. Rooms include bath, telephone and TV and there's free parking. For budgeters, the *Ambassador Hotel* (☎ 685-4781) at 1212 Granville St has rooms from $35 with TV and laundry service. The *Cecil Hotel* (☎ 683-8505), at 1336 Granville St near the bridge, has simple rooms which aren't bad at $35/40 for singles/doubles. There's a popular bar downstairs with 'exotic' dancers working to loud rock music.

Hotels – middle

The *Abbotsford Hotel* (☎ 681-4335), 921 West Pender St, is central and has a pub as well as a dining room. All rooms are self-contained and some have kitchens. Singles range from $55 to $65, doubles from $65 to $75.

The *Dufferin Hotel* (☎ 683-4251), 900 Seymour St, has rooms similar to those at the Abbotsford Hotel. Rooms are $35 to $40 for singles, $35 to $55 for doubles. There's a good dining room and free parking, which is a plus. There's also a *Travelodge* (☎ 682-2767) at 1304 Howe St near Granville Bridge and not far from Sunset Beach. It has a dining room and heated outdoor pool. Singles cost $50 to $80, doubles $50 to $90.

Down Robson St towards Stanley Park are several good, moderately priced hotels. The *Barclay Hotel* (☎ 688-8850), 1348 Robson St, has air-con, TVs and a licensed lounge. Singles/doubles cost $50/65. The *Robsonstrasse City Motor Inn* (☎ 687-1674), 1394 Robson St, has rooms from $60 a night and offers weekly and monthly rates as well. Across the street at 1431 Robson St, the *Riviera Motor Inn* (☎ 685-1301) has apartments with fully equipped kitchens. From some of the apartments you get a good view of the North Shore. Singles cost $60 to $68, doubles $78 to $98.

Two other apartment hotels worth considering staying at are the *English Bay Hotel* (☎ 685-2231) at 1150 Denman St and the *Shato Inn Hotel* (☎ 681-8920), a couple of blocks from Stanley Park and English Bay Beach, at 1825 Comox St off Denman St. The English Bay Hotel has good views over the bay and charges $65 for apartments with a kitchen. You can also rent by the week or month. At the Shato Inn Hotel, you can only rent apartments by the day at a cost of $70.

Hotels – top end

One of the older, more elegant hotels with its wooden panelling and chandeliers is the *Hotel Georgia* (☎ 682-5566), 801 West Georgia St. It has air-con rooms with TV, movies and a minibar. Singles cost from $111 to $131 and doubles from $126 to $146.

Just downhill (north) from the Hotel Georgia is the modern *Delta Place Hotel* (☎ 687-1122) at 654 Howe St. It offers full facilities including racquet ball courts, a library and business centre. Room prices start from $120 a single or a double.

The *Four Seasons Hotel* (☎ 689-9333), 791 West Georgia St, is in the Pacific Centre building. To get to reception you take the escalator left of the statue of the Buddha. Prices depend on the size of the bed as well as the number of people! Singles/doubles start from $129/159.

The largest hotel in Vancouver is the *Hyatt Regency* (☎ 687-6543), 655 Burrard St, where singles/doubles cost from $155/180. At the *Century Plaza* (☎ 687-0575), 1015 Burrard St, the rooms include a kitchen and satellite TV. Singles cost from $95 to $145 and doubles from $110 to $160.

Despite the rising skyline the *Hotel Vancouver* (☎ 684-3131), 900 West Georgia St, remains a city landmark recognisable by its green copper roof. It's one of the largest hotels in Vancouver and has just about everything including a pool, saunas and three restaurants. Its rates are $125/145/165 for ordinary/business/deluxe.

Not far from BC Place is the elegantly furnished *Georgian Court Hotel* (☎ 682-5555; 800-663-1155 toll free) at 773 Beatty St. Singles/doubles here cost $130/150.

Motels

There are three distinct areas where you'll find motels around Vancouver. They're all outside the downtown area but not a great distance away, and with a car they're very accessible. Some of the cheaper ones follow.

The closest strip to downtown is along East Hastings St around Exhibition Park and east into Burnaby. This is a convenient area, close to Second Narrows Bridge over to North Vancouver. *Rainbow Auto Lodge* (☎ 298-1828) at 5958 East Hastings St is also a trailer camp and has a laundrette. Basic singles/doubles are $32/39. Some units have a kitchen, which is well worth the $5 extra. The refurbished *Exhibition Park Travelodge* (☎ 294-4751) is at 3475 East Hastings St on the corner of Cassiar St. Singles are from $60 to $80, doubles from $65 to $85.

The second motel area is along Kingsway, a major road which branches off Main St south of 7th Ave. It is the former highway and runs south-east out of downtown through Burnaby, New Westminster and across the Fraser River. It's also called Highway 1A and is south of the Trans Canada Highway. One of the closest motels to town is the *Biltmore Motor Hotel* (☎ 872-5252) at 395 Kingsway. It has air-con, TV, licensed restaurant and coffee shop. Singles are $44/69 in the low/high season, doubles are $44/79.

The other motel area is on the North Shore, over Lions Gate Bridge. Look along Marine Drive and north up Capilano Rd. There are also a couple of spots on the Esplanade, which runs east-west along the North Shore, past the SeaBus terminal. *Avalon Motor Hotel* (☎ 985-4181) is at 1025 Marine Drive, North Vancouver, about five minutes' drive east of the bridge. Singles cost from $40 to $65, doubles from $65 to $90.

The good-value *Canyon Court Motel* (☎ 988-3181) is at 1748 Capilano Rd, North Vancouver. Singles range from $40 to $65, doubles from $55 to $80 and use of a TV or kitchen is $5 extra. All rooms are cheaper after 1 October. There's a laundrette, free coffee and a swimming pool. The motel is close to Lions Gate, Stanley Park and Grouse Mountain.

One of the more central motels is *City Centre Motel* at 2111 Main St, a short walk south of Main St Station. It has singles/doubles for $50/60 and offers free coffee.

PLACES TO EAT

With its continuing increase in population and sophistication Vancouver's reputation as a good town for eats is true now more than ever. As in many places known for good restaurants, the quality and variety filters down through all budget levels. The following is a sample of what you can expect to find.

Downtown

We should start with the *White Spot*, a BC chain begun in 1928. These are family restaurants serving good food at reasonable prices, and open every day. The chocolate milkshakes and sandwiches are excellent. There are numerous White Spots in Vancouver. In the central area there's one at 1616 West Georgia St on the corner of Cardero St, one at 580 West Georgia St on the corner of Seymour St, and another on the corner of Burrard and Robson Sts. A sandwich with fries or salad is a meal in itself and costs from $5.

For lunch you could try one of the eateries in the Royal Centre Mall on the corner of Burrard and Dunsmuir Sts. *Manny's Deli* has sandwiches from $2 to $4 and delicious, freshly squeezed orange juice for $1.50. Also in the Royal Centre Mall is the up-market *Royal Mandarin Restaurant*; it serves soups for $8 and main dishes of seafood, poultry or beef for around $15.

A couple of places with great names are the *Jolly Taxpayer Hotel & Pub* at 828 West Hastings St near Howe St, and the *Elephant & Castle*, 700 Dunsmuir St, on the corner of Granville St. The Jolly Taxpayer is a British-style pub selling burgers for $4 or $5, nachos for $4.25 and vegetarian club sandwiches for $6.

The Elephant & Castle is a restaurant open from 11 am to 9 pm serving different sorts of chicken burgers for $6.50. It has a bar and the decor is made to resemble a British pub. The name of the restaurant is derived from a district of London, UK.

The *Bodhi Vegetarian Restaurant*, 337 East Hastings St, and the *Buddhist Vegetarian Restaurant* close by, both serve lots of appetising, filling soups and dishes, some of which include simulated meat. A bowl of chilli bean curd with sesame seed oil costs $6.20, and diced mushroom with cashew nuts $6.50. You can also get lunch specials from $3.

A few doors from Vincent's Backpackers Hostel in Main St is the friendly *Mom's Kitchen* which is open 24 hours a day, seven days a week. Breakfasts with coffee cost around $4; burgers are $4 too. It's popular with travellers.

For a minor splurge try the *Punjab Restaurant*, at 796 Main St on the corner of Union St a few blocks south of Chinatown. It serves good Indian food at reasonable rates: starters are around $3, vegetarian main meals around $7, non-vegetarian around $10. It's small, quiet and popular and has long opening hours: 11.30 am to 11 pm daily.

Another minor splurge can be had at the *Ferguson Point Tea House* in Stanley Park. With its wicker furniture, hanging plants, large windows and a view over the ocean, the atmosphere is right out of *The Great Gatsby*. The best prices are at lunch time, which is from 11.30 am to 2 pm Monday to Friday. Dinner is served from 5.30 to 10 pm seven days a week. The mostly seafood main meals cost between $8 and $14; fisherman's soup at $5 is nearly a meal in itself; the salads are good and wine is served.

Also in Stanley Park, near Lions Gate Bridge, *Prospect Point Café* has a varied menu, again mostly seafood. Main meals cost between $8 and $13; fish & chips at $8.25, sandwiches are $8.50. You can choose from one of 20 flavours of ice cream ($2). The food's a little overpriced, but the cafe is in a great spot with an outdoor patio and views across the inlet.

On Granville Island a good restaurant to try for snacks, reasonably priced lunches or full meals is *Isadora's Co-operative Restaurant* at 1540 Old Bridge Rd. It has a play area for children and some of the money you spend on food goes to help community organisations. Fish burgers cost around $6.50, sandwiches $7 and main dishes $10. It's open Monday to Thursday from 7 am to 10 pm, Friday from 7 am to 11 pm, Saturday from 9 am to 11 pm and Sunday from 9 am to 10 pm.

Robson St This is one of the main eating areas of Vancouver and has a cosmopolitan collection of restaurants including Mexican, Indian, French, Greek, German, Chinese and Thai.

There's a good food fair with cafeteria-style eateries in Robson Square, down a level on the corner of Robson and Howe Sts. Robson Public Market, 1610 Robson St, has a bakery, cheese shop, fruit stalls, etc.

Pepita's, at 1170 Robson St, offers very good Mexican and Spanish meals. Starters are from $5 to $7, eg nachos $6, enchiladas $5; and main dishes like chicken with cream are around $13. You also get complimentary corn chips and salsa.

For a good, inexpensive dinner, the *Saigon*, 1500 Robson St on the corner of Nicola St, is a very popular Vietnamese place. Its menu includes curries and seafood, and meals cost around $6 to $12.

Heidelberg House at 1164 Robson St has been serving various German specialities for years. The reasonably priced menu includes goulashes, schnitzels and a variety of sandwiches. For lunch there is an all-you-can-eat smorgasbord for $6.25.

A long-time favourite is the *India Gate* at 616 Robson St, between Granville and Seymour Sts. It has an extensive menu of Indian vegetarian and meat dishes. Starters and vegetarian main meals are between $5 and $7, lamb or chicken dishes cost around $8 and a vegetarian thali costs $12.

Denman St Denman St, near Stanley Park, is a very lively, pleasant street to visit around evening meal time. There's a good selection of eateries, particularly towards the Georgia St end, and lots of people strolling and menu-reading. The choice includes Mexican, French and Greek food, as well as the selections which follow.

Musashi Japanese Restaurant, 780 Denman St between Robson and Alberni Sts, is cosy, casual and cheap. Diagonally opposite is *El Mariachi*, a busy Mexican restaurant with starters for $4.50 and main meals from $10. *Café Slavia*, 815 Denman St, is a small, friendly, inexpensive place with a Slavic slant; it serves food like goulash and perogies (dumplings) for $5 to $7.

Dover Seafood Restaurant (with the old-fashioned British phone booth outside), 945 Denman St on the corner of Barclay St, serves mostly seafood including fish & chips, but you can also get meat pies. Main meals are around $10 and it's open daily till 10 pm. Another place for fish & chips, and a bit cheaper, is *Budd's* at 1007 Denman St. Here you can get a plate of oysters, prawns and chips for $6.70 or cod and chips for $4.25. It's open daily from 11.30 am to 9 pm and is often packed.

Close to Budd's, on the corner of Denman and Nelson Sts, *Crumble Pie* sells freshly baked bread ($1.50) and an assortment of pastries ($1.75) and cakes ($2.75 a slice). It's definitely worth a try. *Ciao!* at No 1074 is a small Italian-style café with freshly baked croissants from $1.50 and a variety of coffees including espresso ($1.25) and cappuccino ($1.65).

Gastown Area The *Only Café* at 20 East Hastings St is a Vancouver institution and a must – it's been going since 1912 and has hardly changed. There's no toilet, no liquor licence and seating for only 25, mostly on stools. And there's always a queue: about 500 people eat here daily and over 200 litres of chowder are served every day. The people create the atmosphere: there are all types, including tourists on every kind of budget, and no shortage of drunks.

The fare consists of large portions of seafood fresh from the docks which is served quickly by the Chinese waitresses. A bowl of clam chowder with one piece of warm fresh French bread and two pieces of fresh brown bread is $3.50. A full meal of clams, oysters, or various fish is between $5 and $9. The café will also boil, steam or fry whatever fish you choose. The Only Café is open Monday to Thursday from 11.30 am to 9.30 pm, Friday and Saturday from 11 am to 10 pm; it's closed on Sundays. If it's too busy, the nearby *Coney Island* serves good fish & chips.

For soup and sandwich lunches, try the *Cottage Deli* at 131 Water St, which has views of the inlet; or the corner of Carrall St near the statue of Gassy Jack, where there are several good-value cafés. *Orlando's Fresh*

Pasta Bar, at 238 Abbot St near Water St, serves very cheap pastas for around $6 or $7; it has some outdoor tables, and serves breakfasts, too.

At *Brother's Restaurant*, 1 Water St, the decor has a monastic theme and the waiting staff is dressed in monks' habits. It serves seafood, pasta and poultry and includes items like 'Monastery burger'; starters are $3 to $4 and main meals $7 to $10. It's open daily from 11.30 am to 11 pm.

The *Old Spaghetti Factory* at 53 Water St is good value. This is a branch of the popular Canada-wide chain. The decor is interesting; it's lined with all types of old machinery, stained-glass Tiffany lamps and even a 1910 Vancouver streetcar (tram). Starters cost between $2 and $4 and main meals go for $7 to $12. It's open Monday to Saturday from 11.30 am to 10 pm, on Sunday until 9 pm.

Water St Café, 300 Water St opposite the steam clock, is very busy and has a large sidewalk seating area. This was once the Regina Hotel, built in 1875 and the only major building to escape the Great Fire of 1886. The food's good and reasonably priced with lunches at $6 to $7 and dinners for $10 to $14.

If you like Indian food, Water St offers several choices. *Kilimanjaro*, at 332 Water St in the Le Magasin shopping complex, serves African dishes based on Indian cuisine. There's a restaurant upstairs and a bistro downstairs. It's a very attractive place with quality food; main meals cost around $12. *Maharajah*, at 137A Water St, has tables outside and is a good spot to do some people-watching. It offers good, mild to hot curries such as malai kofta; starters cost from $3 to $4, main meals from $9 to $14. *India Village*, next to the Water St Café, is a little cheaper, with main dishes from $7 to $10.

Chinatown For good-value, simple Chinese food you can't beat *Mui Loong Chan* at 207A East Pender St. It has daily lunch specials priced at $4.50, or you could have 10 dim sums with soup for $4. An à la carte menu is available too; it's more expensive but still reasonably priced. *Ming's* at 147 East Pender

Left: Sentinel Pass, Banff National Park, Alberta (JL)
Right: Jasper National Park, Alberta (JL)
Bottom: Chuck wagon race, Calgary, Alberta (JL)

Top Left: Flora in the Valley of the 10 Peaks, The Rockies (ML)
Top Right: Sunset over Igloolik, NWT (JL)
Bottom Left: The Athabasca Glacier, off the Icefields Parkway, Alberta (ML)
Bottom Right: Flora in the Valley of the 10 Peaks, The Rockies (ML)

St has excellent dim sum between 11 am and 2 pm daily. A wide variety of dishes, each priced at about $2, are served from a cart whirled around by the waiting staff. Arrive early for the best selection.

On On Tea Garden at 214 East Keefer St is small, inconspicuous and cheap, and has good Cantonese food. It's open from 11 am to 9 pm Tuesday to Sunday, closed Monday. Close by is *Hon's Wun Tun House*, a Chinese fast-food place selling bowls of noodles from $2; it's also famous for its 'pot-stickers' – quick-fried dumplings. It's very popular and is open Monday to Saturday from 8.30 am to 1 am, Sunday from 8.30 am to 8 pm. *Maxim's Bakery & Café* at 257 East Keefer St and *Max King Bakery & Restaurant* in East Pender St a few doors from Mui Loong Chan, both have tasty pastries and cakes starting from 70 cents. Try the walnut sponge cake.

Kitsilano

This is an area of students, alternative lifestylers, cafés and second-hand stores. In recent years, it's also become very desirable real estate, attracting more professionals. Between Burrard and Alma Sts, West 4th Ave has a large, varying selection of eating spots with many nationalities represented. West Broadway also has numerous spots for stomach satisfaction.

At 1754 West 4th Ave is the *Heaven & Earth Curry House*. It serves meat or vegetarian dishes, priced at about $8 to $10. It looks a little run down on the outside but the place is established and good. At No 1938, *Pistachio's* is a nice little café for breakfast, snacks and light meals. *Dar Lebanon*, 1961 West 4th Ave, is a small, pleasant and reasonably priced Middle-Eastern restaurant. Pita sandwiches cost between $3 and $5 and main courses such as spinach pie are from $5 to $8. It has three other outlets in Vancouver (including one at 678 West Broadway) and is open every day.

Sophie's Cosmic Café, 2095 West 4th Ave on the corner of Arbutus St, gets very busy at meal times with queues out on the street.

It sells a range of burgers from $5, vegetarian felafel burgers for $6, or steak meals from $8.

Ristorante Simpatico at 2222 West 4th Ave is a very attractive, Greek-style taverna, also offering – as its name suggests – Italian food. It has great pizzas for around $8. Further west is the open-fronted *Maria's Taverna* at 2324 West 4th Ave. There you can have spinach pie or hummus with bread for $3; or as a main course trout cooked in lemon juice for $9.

Naam Restaurant at 2724 West 4th Ave is a good, inexpensive 'new age' vegetarian and health-food restaurant. It's very casual, has live folk music every night and is open 24 hours. Main meals are around $7 to $9, or you could have a tofu burger for $4.50.

Topanga Café at 2904 West 4th Ave is a good place offering the standard Westernised Mexican fare. Nachos cost $4.15 and enchiladas with rice, beans and corn chips cost $7.30; other main meals go up to $12. It's open from 11.30 am to 10 pm Monday to Saturday, closed Sunday.

Nyala Café, 2930 West 4th Ave, provides Ethiopian food to be eaten without the use of knife, fork or spoon: instead you use bread to get it from plate to mouth. Starters like lentils cost $2; main dishes of lamb, poultry, beef and seafood are $10 to $11, vegetarian main meals are $7 to $8. It gives a 15% discount to Vancouver CHA hostellers. Every Saturday night between 10 pm and 2 am there's African or Caribbean music and dancing.

Over on West Broadway in the 3000 block the ethnic mix includes *Da Tandoor* at No 3135, serving good tandoori Indian food. Starters such as vegetable pakoras are around $3, chicken vindaloo is $8 and main tandoori dishes start from $8. It's open Monday to Saturday from 4.30 to 11 pm, Sunday from 4.30 to 10 pm.

The inexpensive *Dos Amigos*, 3189 West Broadway on the corner of Trutch St, serves a wide variety of tapas from $2 to $5. It's open Friday and Saturday from 11.30 am to 11 pm, Tuesday to Thursday from 11.30 am to 10 pm, closed Sunday. For a caffeine fix try *Yoka's* at No 3171, which sells 20 varieties of home-roasted coffee.

Greens & Gourmet, 2681 West Broadway, is a cheap vegetarian and health-food restaurant. Its appetisers start from $1, salads from $1.50 and main courses from $3. For lunch there's *Glen's Fabulous Sandwiches*, giving the office workers a break from brown baggin' it. It's at 601 West Broadway. The *Sitar*, 564 West Broadway, is another good Indian tandoori restaurant. Starters are around $3 and main dishes from $7 to $10 and it has a good selection of beers. It's open Monday to Friday from 11 am to 2.30 pm and 5 to 10 pm; Saturday from 11 am to 10 pm and Sunday from 12 noon to 10 pm.

Little India
The Vancouver area has the largest Indian community in the country and the majority are Sikhs from the Punjab. (In North America people from the subcontinent are usually called East Indians to distinguish them from the indigenous peoples.)

The focal point of the population is south on Main St between 48th and 51st Aves. Here you'll find Indian groceries, and shops selling saris, spices and Indian records and tapes.

Bombay Sweets, 6556 Main St, is a simple place offering very cheap lunch and dinner buffets, including half a dozen or so curries, lentil dishes and various breads. Lunch-time buffets are $4, dinner ones are $6. Samosas are $1 each and you can buy a bag of mixed Indian sweets from $4.50. Next door and along the street are other places specialising in Indian sweets.

Zeenaz Restaurant, 6460 Main St, offers East African-style Indian food – the spices used are more delicate. The friendly proprietor claims to have the best samosas ($2.70) in town. The chicken curry is $9 as is the vegetarian thali. Meals are cheaper at lunch time. It's open every day from 11 am to 10 pm.

Pabla's Trade Centre, 6587 Main St opposite Bombay Sweets, is a new Indian market with restaurants and shops.

Commercial Drive
There are several interesting neighbourhood restaurants and cafés along a portion of Commercial Drive popular with the mix of artists, professionals and various alternative types who live in the area. *Joe's Cappuccino Bar*, 1120 Commercial Drive, long popular for snacks and conversation with an array of characters from punks to media personalities, is one with a measure of notoriety.

The owner recently got himself some unwanted national publicity by allegedly making some comment about two women customers kissing. Whether the ensuing tempest in a demitasse has changed the clientele or charm remains to be seen.

There are several other nearby inexpensive eateries and coffee houses including the *Restaurant Fettucini* at 1210 Commercial Drive; and *La Quena* at No 1100, which presents an array of political, social and musical evenings.

North Vancouver
Lonsdale Quay Market has lots of places to munch at or buy food to take away. The British-style *Cheshire Cheese Inn* on level 2, sells traditional British food like steak and kidney pudding and shepherd's pie, both for $7.

Several restaurants are concentrated near the corner of Lonsdale Ave and Esplanade. *Corsi Trattoria*, 1 Lonsdale Ave, is an Italian place where everything is made on the premises, including the pasta and bread. Starters are between $3.50 and $7, and main meals like spinach fettucini are around $9. It's open Monday to Friday for lunch from 12 noon to 2 pm, and every day for dinner from 5 pm to 12 midnight.

Frankie's Inn, 59 Lonsdale Ave, is a basic eatery with the usual Western food, but there's a Vancouver twist: Japanese dishes like sukiyaki, tempura and teriyaki are available, served with chopsticks. Meal prices average $4 to $5. This spot is popular with workers from the nearby docks. It's open Monday to Friday from 9 am to 8 pm, Saturday from 9 am to 3.30 pm.

At 69 Lonsdale Ave, the *Jägerhof* specialises in schnitzels and also serves deer and moose meat. On the walls it has old framed photographs and prints and mounted animals' heads. Reindeer steak with soup and salad costs $15.

North up the hill at 1344 Lonsdale Ave, near the corner of East 14th St, *Cafe Nairobi* is a rather posh Indian restaurant with an East African slant. All the items on the menu are given special names so, for example, a dish called 'Nairobi: the first glimpse' is really chicken curry ($14). Samosas cost $2.25 and main meals are between $10 and $15.

Two doors up, at 1352 Lonsdale Ave, *Cazba* is a cheaper, more casual Greek-Persian place. Kebabs cost $4 and souvlaki costs $6. *Khayyam* on the corner of Lonsdale Ave and East 13th St is similar.

ENTERTAINMENT

The best source of information on entertainment in Vancouver is the *Georgia Straight*, which comes out every Friday. The twice-monthly *Vancouver Boulevard* gives dates of events in the visual and performing arts. The daily newspapers also have complete entertainment listings, including theatre, dance and concerts. The Travel Infocentre will also be able to help you or you could call the Vancouver Arts Hotline ☎ 437-2787.

Theatre

The theatre, from mainstream to fringe, is flourishing in Vancouver. Next to the main post office, in Hamilton St, the *Queen Elizabeth Theatre* (☎ 665-3050) puts on major international productions; the *Vancouver Playhouse* (☎ 665-3050) is part of the same complex. The *Metro Theatre* (☎ 266-7191), 1370 South-West Marine Drive, and *Firehall Arts Centre* (☎ 689-0926), 280 East Cordova St, put on plays by Canadian and foreign playwrights. The *Arts Club* (☎ 687-1644) has more experimental productions with three locations in town – two in Johnston St on Granville Island, and the other at 1181 Seymour St on the corner of Smithe St. The *Waterfront Theatre* (☎ 685-6217), at 1405

Anderson St on Granville Island, is the venue for a number of local theatre companies.

For spontaneous comedy visit the *Back Alley Theatre* (☎ 688-7013), 751 Thurlow St, to see the competitors in the Vancouver TheatreSports League perform. Tickets are from $8. If you fancy your chances the *Punchlines Comedy Theatre* (☎ 684-3015), 15 Water St, has an amateur night on Monday ($2), or you can see stand-up comedy shows on Friday and Saturday ($8). Another place offering off-beat comedy is *Yuk Yuk's Comedy Club* (☎ 683-8687) at 750 Pacific Blvd near Cambie Bridge. It has one show on Wednesday ($3) and Thursday ($5) at 9 pm; two on Friday and Saturday at 9 pm and 11.30 pm ($7.50 for each performance).

Several fringe theatres worth checking out are the *Underground* (☎ 873-3646) on the corner of Kingsway and Broadway, *Vancouver Little Theatre* (☎ 876-4165), 3102 Main St, and *Station St Arts Centre* (☎ 688-3312), 930 Station St.

The two universities have theatrical events during the year which give drama students the chance to practise their craft. The universities also put on professional productions. Call Simon Fraser University (☎ 291-3514) and UBC (☎ 228-2678) for details.

For theatre tickets check the little booth on ground level in Robson Galleria, 1025 Robson St. It sells tickets for local shows at half price, usually close to showtime. It's open from 12 noon to 1 pm and from 4.30 to 6 pm Monday to Saturday. Otherwise you can call the Vancouver Ticket Centre (☎ 280-4411) for normal-priced tickets.

Cinema

At 919 Granville St the *Paradise* cinema shows commercial films at half price ($2.50) every day.

The following repertory theatres show a mix of North American and overseas films. *Hollywood Theatre* (☎ 738-3211) is at 3123 West Broadway; tickets are $3 from Wednesday to Sunday, $2 on Monday, $2.50 on Tuesday. *Ridge Theatre* (☎ 738-6311), 3131 Arbutus St on the corner of 16th Ave, normally charges $6 but it's $3 on Tuesday nights. At the *Pacific Cinémathèque* (☎ 688-3456), 1131 Howe St, tickets are $4, or $5 for a double bill; and at the *Starlight* (☎ 689-0096), 935 Denman St on the corner of Barclay St, it's $4 for a single feature, $6 for a double bill.

Music
In summer, every Friday at 12 noon, there are concerts at the *Orpheum Theatre* (☎ 665-3050) at 884 Granville St. The programme varies each day but you might hear folk, blues, jazz or classical music. The Vancouver Symphony Orchestra often performs here.

There is a fair bit of nightlife in the Gastown area. The inexpensive *Savoy*, 6 Powell St, is a long-standing casual bar with live rock and reggae. The *Spinning Wheel*, 212 Carrall St, is small but comfortable with mainly rhythm & blues bands. Nearby the *Town Pump*, 66 Water St, has rock, jazz or reggae bands. Two clubs playing current pop music as well as golden oldies are *Amnesia*, 99 Powell St, and *Notorious* at 354 Water St. The cover charge for both is around $5. The *Lamplighter's Pub*, in the Dominion Hotel on the corner of Water and Abbott Sts, has live blues music all week.

The *Railway Club*, at 579 Dunsmuir St on the corner of Seymour St, is a pub-like place with live music seven nights a week and good-quality, often original jazz sessions on Saturday afternoons between 3 and 7 pm. Nearby, Granville St is interesting after dark with lots of street activity. The *Commodore Ballroom*, 870 Granville St, has had a face-lift, can accommodate over 1000 people and plays everything from punk to Lambada. At 1300 Granville St, on the corner of Drake St, the *Yale* is one of the best blues bars in the country. It's open with live music seven nights a week from 9.30 pm to 1.30 am.

Richard's on Richards, 1036 Richards St, is a popular, dressy singles bar. The entry charge is about $7 or $8. In the same street at No 818 is the *Shaggy Horse*, a gay club. At the southern end of Hamilton St near Pacific Blvd, the *Gandydancer* is another gay club, which is open daily till 2 am.

Lovers of hard rock could try *Club Soda*, 1055 Homer St, which has live bands on Sunday, Monday and Wednesday.

There's live, mostly traditional jazz at the *Hot Jazz Club*, 2120 Main St. Admission is $4 to $6, less for students. The *Landmark Jazz Bar* in the Sheraton Landmark Hotel, 1400 Robson St on the corner of Nicola St, has shows that range from standards and bebop to New Orleans, but the emphasis is moving more to rhythm & blues.

Most clubs close at around 2 am, and pubs around 12 midnight or 1 am.

THINGS TO BUY
Several shops in Vancouver sell Native Indian wares, but most have fairly poor-quality stuff. One store that has only good quality is Hill's Indian Crafts at 165 Water St. It's open seven days a week from 9 am to 9 pm and has a good selection of carvings, prints, masks and the excellent Cowichan sweaters for about $180. These sweaters are hand-knitted and 100% wool. Originally from the Lake Cowichan area on Vancouver Island, they are now made in many places.

The Inuit Gallery, opposite Le Magasin in Water St, sells Inuit paintings and woodcraft. It's open Monday to Saturday from 10 am to 6 pm, Sunday from 12 noon to 5 pm. With the same opening hours, Images for a Canadian Heritage, 779 Burrard St opposite the Vancouver Public Library, sells Inuit and Indian craft. Marik Arctic in Alexander Ave in Gastown sells antiques as well as Inuit art.

There are a number of good places selling camping and outdoor equipment, guide-books and maps. Downtown there's Gulliver's at 757 West Hastings St and Wanderlust at 1244 Davie St. In the Kitsilano area are the Travel Bug at 2667 West Broadway and Coast Mountains Sports at 1828 West 4th Ave. All these shops give a discount to people staying at the Vancouver CHA Hostel. If you don't want (or can't afford) to buy your equipment, two stores rent stuff out: Rudy's Sporting Goods, 3279 West Broadway; and Sports Rent, 2560 Arbutus St (and several other locations around town), which is open seven days a week.

For general shopping Vancouver has a number of large indoor malls. Downtown these are in the Pacific Centre, 700 West Georgia St which connects with the Vancouver Centre Mall and Eaton's and the Bay department stores; the Royal Centre in the same building as the Hyatt Regency Hotel, at 665 Burrard St; and the Harbour Centre, 555 West Hastings St. Granville Mall, Robsonstrasse and Denman St have lots of shops.

In North Vancouver the Lonsdale Quay Market has a shop or stall for just about everything.

As well as art galleries and restaurants Granville Island has many speciality shops.

GETTING THERE & AWAY
Air

Vancouver International Airport is about 10 km south of the city on Sea Island – between Vancouver and the municipality of Richmond. Major Canadian airlines fly to Vancouver, as do many US and Asian airlines. Some Canadian and foreign airlines with offices in Vancouver are:

Air BC
    4740 Agar Drive, Richmond (☎ 278-3800/5100; toll free 800-663-0522)
Air Canada
    1040 West Georgia St (☎ 688-5155)
Air China
    1040 West Georgia St
Air India
    601 West Broadway (☎ 879-0271, 873-9923)
British Airways
    1176 West Georgia St (☎ 222-2508, 270-8131; toll free 800-668-1080)
Canadian Airlines International
    1004 West Georgia St (☎ 279-6611)
    1301 West Cordova St (☎ 279-6611)
    999 Canada Place (☎ 279-6611)
Cathay Pacific
    1018 West Georgia St (☎ 682-9747, 661-2907)
Delta Air Lines
    1030 West Georgia St (☎ 682-5933)
Garuda
    1040 West Georgia St (☎ 681-3699)
KLM Royal Dutch Airlines
    305 1030 West Georgia St (☎ 682-4606)
Korean Air
    1010 1030 West Georgia St (☎ 689-2000)

Lufthansa
    1401 1030 West Georgia St (☎ 683-1313, 270-3611; toll free 800-387-9210)
Qantas
    4 Bentall Centre, 1714 1055 Dunsmuir St (☎ 684-8231, 279-6688)
Singapore Airlines
    1111 1030 West Georgia St (☎ 689-1730/1233)
Thai Airways
    666 Burrard St (☎ 687-1412; toll free 800-426-5204)

Fares can be cheaper if notice is given and may vary with the day of the week. Those given in this section are all full economy fares. Some one-way fares (before tax) with Canadian Airlines are:

Destination	Fare
Toronto	$647
Edmonton	$241
Seattle	$97
Yellowknife	$517
Whitehorse	$394

Air Canada prices are virtually the same as those for Canadian Airlines. Air BC is a local airline run by Air Canada, serving Vancouver Island, some points in the interior and Seattle. The pre-tax fare from Vancouver to Victoria is $73 one way.

On United Airlines (☎ 683-7111), to Seattle one way is $93.10 including tax. The flight time is about 45 minutes. Some flights carry on to San Francisco or various US connections from either point.

Many people going across the continent find it cheaper to go, say, Seattle to Buffalo rather than Vancouver to Toronto. You may want to do this to get a flight to New York – it's likely to be cheaper from Seattle than from a Canadian point.

Bus connections can be made between the Canadian and US airports at either end. Flights to Asia also may be cheaper from US west coast cities than from Vancouver.

Northwest Airlines (☎ 800-225-2525 toll free) and Alaska Airlines (☎ 800-426-0333 toll free) fly to Alaska.

American Airlines (☎ 800-433-7300 toll free) and Horizon Air (☎ 800-547-9308 toll free) fly to many destinations in the western states of the USA.

See the Introductory Getting There & Away chapter for information about flights from Australia, New Zealand and Asia into Vancouver.

Bus

The Greyhound Bus Depot, 150 Dunsmuir St between Cambie and Beatty Sts, is the main terminal for Vancouver. It has a left-luggage area open from 6.30 am to 12 midnight and a coffee shop. Maverick Coach Lines (☎ 662-8051, 255-1171), Pacific Coach Lines (☎ 662-8074) and Cascade Coach Lines (☎ 795-7443) also stop here. For information about Greyhound buses call ☎ 662-3222 or 624-3456 between 7 am and 11.30 pm. Some examples of one-way fares with Greyhound are: Banff (six daily) – $72.20; Kelowna (two daily) – $33.50; Calgary (eight daily) – $73.

Maverick Coach Lines operates eight buses daily to Nanaimo for $14 one way (including ferry); the trip takes 3½ hours. It also has buses to Powell River, Squamish, Whistler and Pemberton. Pacific Coach Lines has eight buses daily to Victoria, leaving the Greyhound Bus Depot every two hours at 10 minutes to the hour from 5.50 am to 7.50 pm. The one-way fare is $17.50 including ferry and the journey takes about three hours. If you're only going as far as Swartz Bay it costs $11.25.

Cascade Coach Lines goes to destinations along the Fraser Valley such as Abbotsford, Chilliwack, Harrison and Agassiz.

Quick Coach Lines (☎ 591-3571) operates a daily bus shuttle to Seattle for $25 and to Seattle's Sea Tac Airport for $32. Buses leave downtown Vancouver from outside the Sandman Inn, 180 West Georgia St, but also pick up from other major hotels.

If you're heading for the USA you can also catch a city bus to White Rock close to the US border. Catch bus Nos 351, 352, or 354 south on Granville St.

Train

VIA Rail Vancouver is the western terminal for VIA Rail. The station is off Main St at 1150 Station St between National and Terminal Aves. The closest main intersection is the corner of Main and Prior Sts. The station is marked 'Canadian National' and has a park in front of it. It's a magnificent building inside, having been renovated in 1985, but is now under-utilised because of budget cutbacks. There are few passenger facilities: if you want anything to eat or drink while you're waiting for a train, bring it with you. For 24-hour information on fares and reservations call the toll-free number ☎ 800-561-8630. The ticket office is only open restricted hours: Monday and Saturday from 7.30 am to 9.30 pm; Tuesday, Wednesday and Sunday from 7.30 am to 3 pm; Thursday from 3 to 9.30 pm; and Friday from 10 am to 5.30 pm.

The southern leg of VIA Rail's trans-Canada route between Vancouver, Banff, Calgary (see the Rocky Mountaineer section later), Regina and Winnipeg is no longer operating.

The existing route goes through Kamloops, Jasper, Edmonton and Saskatoon to Winnipeg. Trains leave Monday, Thursday and Saturday at 9.30 pm. The one-way fares are: Jasper $98, Edmonton $136, Saskatoon $174 and Winnipeg $228. Stopovers are permitted but you must re-reserve.

VIA Rail does provide a bus service between the towns of the southern and former northern routes: Kamloops to Penticton, Edmonton to Calgary and Saskatoon to Regina.

There is no rail connection with Seattle, only buses.

BC Rail British Columbia has its own railway system which heads north from Vancouver to Whistler, Lillooet, Williams Lake and Prince George, where it connects with VIA Rail (from Prince George you can go west to Prince Rupert or east to Jasper). Some examples of one-way fares are: Whistler $11, Lillooet $25 and Prince George $61. Call ☎ 631-3500 for information. The train leaves daily at 7.30 am from BC Rail's station, 1311 West 1st St at the southern end of Pemberton Ave, North Vancouver. To get to the station take bus No 239 west from the SeaBus terminal at Lonsdale Quay.

Rocky Mountaineer Despite the closure of VIA Rail's southern route it is still possible to travel by train from Vancouver to Calgary and Banff (and Jasper) on the privately owned 'Rocky Mountaineer'. But it isn't cheap: one way direct to Calgary costs $425, to Banff or Jasper is $395 (both fares include food and an overnight stop in a hotel in Kamloops). The service runs between the end of May and early October; the train leaves VIA Rail's terminal every Sunday at 7.30 am. For information contact a travel agent or the Great Canadian Railtour Company (☎ 643-3841; 800-665-7245 toll free), Suite 345, 625 Howe St.

Also see the train section in the introductory chapter for another privately run train with a route through the Rockies. This one is based in Toronto.

Car
If you're coming from the USA (Washington state), you'll be on Highway 5 until the border town of Blaine. At the border is the Peace Arch Provincial and State Park. The first town in British Columbia is White Rock. Highway 99 veers west, then north to Vancouver. Close to the city, it passes over two arms of the Fraser River and eventually turns into Granville St, one of the main thoroughfares of downtown Vancouver. In the centre of town Granville St becomes a pedestrian mall, and ordinary traffic is forbidden. Remember there is a network of one-way streets around here too.

If you're coming from the east, you'll almost certainly be on the Trans Canada Highway, which takes the Port Mann Bridge over the Fraser River and snakes through the eastern end of the city, eventually meeting with Hastings St before going over the Second Narrows Bridge to North Vancouver. If you want to go downtown, turn left when you reach Hastings St.

From Horseshoe Bay the Trans Canada Highway heads through West Vancouver and

North Vancouver before going over the Second Narrows Bridge into Burnaby. If you're heading downtown leave the highway at the Taylor Way exit; from there Highway 99 takes you over Lions Gate Bridge into Stanley Park.

Car Rentals There are many car rental companies in Vancouver; the larger ones have several offices around town and some also have offices at the international airport. Check the yellow pages for a thorough listing of car rental companies and their agencies' addresses. Following is a list of a few companies and their central address:

Avis
  757 Hornby St (☎ 682-1621)
Budget
  450 West Georgia St (☎ 685-0536)
Lo-Cost
  1105 Granville St (☎ 689-9664)
Rent-A-Wreck
  1085 Kingsway (☎ 876-7155)
Thrifty
  1400 Robson St (☎ 688-2207)

Rent-A-Wreck is one of the cheapest. It charges from $24.95 a day, plus 15 cents a km over 150 km and $12.99 for insurance. Lo-Cost charges $27.95 a day, plus 12 cents a km over 150 km and $9.95 for insurance. Budget charges from $39.95 a day, plus 15 cents a km over 100 km and $15 for insurance. Rates vary depending on the size and type of car and how long you intend to rent for.

Car Sharing Check the newspaper classifieds or the yellow pages for car drive-aways. Also check the notice boards at the hostels for opportunities to share car rides.

BC Ferries
The two main routes between Vancouver and Vancouver Island are from Tsawwassen to Swartz Bay and from Horseshoe Bay to Nanaimo. The one-way fare on both routes is $5.25 per adult, $24.50 per car. There are about 15 ferries in each direction daily in

summer leaving every hour on the hour between 7 am and 10 pm. If you have a car there is often a one or two-ferry wait, particularly on weekends and public holidays.

A new ferry between Tsawwassen and Nanaimo, called the Mid-Island Express, goes four times a day in each direction. The fares are the same.

To get to Tsawwassen by city bus catch the southbound bus No 601 from the corner of Granville St and West 4th Ave to the Ladner Exchange. From the exchange take bus No 640 to the ferry terminal. The fare is $1.25, or $2.75 if you travel in peak traffic time. From Swartz Bay you can take bus No 70 into Victoria.

Hitching

For hitching east take bus No 9 along East Broadway to Boundary Rd. Walk south to Grandview Highway (which connects with the Trans Canada Highway) and stick your thumb out. A reader has suggested that hitching on the Trans Canada Highway is illegal until 40 km out past city limits and recommends going on the smaller highway to Langley and then getting onto the main route.

GETTING AROUND
To/From the Airport

There are two ways of getting to the airport by bus, but the quickest is to take the Airport Express from the Greyhound Bus Depot for $7.25 ($12 return). It also goes to top hotels. The bus leaves every 30 minutes starting at 6.15 am and takes about 45 minutes. Buses leave the airport from level 2, the last one departing about 12.15 am. For information about the fare and schedules contact Perimeter Transportation (☎ 273-0071).

To get to the airport by city bus, take No 20 south on Granville St to 70th Ave. From there transfer to bus No 100 which will take you to the airport. The total travel time is one hour and the fare is $1.25 ($1.75 during peak traffic time). Call ☎ 261-5100 for information.

A taxi between downtown Vancouver and

the airport takes about 25 minutes and costs around $20.

Bus, SkyTrain & SeaBus

Vancouver doesn't have a subway, but does have an integrated bus network, light-rapid-transit (LRT) system using the SkyTrain, and ferry links using the SeaBus. For local transit information call ☎ 261-5100 or get a copy of the *Transit Guide* ($1.25) from the Travel Infocentre. Try to avoid buses at rush hour as the traffic jams are unbelievable.

The transport system is divided into three zones: the inner zone covers central Vancouver; the next zone includes the suburbs of Richmond, Burnaby, New Westminster, North Vancouver, West Vancouver and Sea Island; the outer zone covers Ladner, Tsawwassen, Delta, Surrey, White Rock, Langley, Port Moody and Coquitlam.

During off-peak times (between 9.30 am and 3 pm and after 6.30 pm Monday to Friday, and weekends and public holidays) you pay a flat $1.35 for a single journey good for bus, SkyTrain or SeaBus. In peak times it depends on how many zones you travel across: $1.35 for one zone, $2 for two, $2.75 for three. All-day transit passes are $4 (good for unlimited rides on the bus/Sky-Train/SeaBus after 9.30 am. Buy passes at the SeaBus or SkyTrain stations or from shops displaying the 'FareDealer' sign.

SkyTrain The SkyTrain was introduced for Expo 86 and connects downtown Vancouver with Burnaby, New Westminster and Whalley in Surrey. The trains are fully computerised (ie there's no driver!) and travel mostly above ground along a specially designed track. From downtown they operate between 5.50 am and 1.15 am during the week, between 6.50 am and 1.15 am on Saturday, and 8.50 and 12.15 am on Sunday. The trains are scheduled to connect with buses. They leave from Waterfront Station.

SeaBus These super-modern catamarans zip back and forth across Burrard Inlet between Waterfront Station downtown and Lonsdale Quay in North Vancouver. They leave every 15 minutes on weekdays, every half hour at other times. The trip lasts only 12 minutes but gives good views of the harbour and city skyline. Try to avoid rush hours when many commuters go aboard. Waterfront Station, originally the western terminal for the Canadian Pacific railway, is a beautiful building that has been tastefully renovated.

Car
If you're driving, you'll notice the city doesn't have any expressways: everyone must travel through the city. Congestion is a big problem, especially around the bridges and right downtown. On a wet or snowy day it's worse: try to avoid rush hours. It's also costly to park and/or very difficult to find a parking spot in the inner city. You're better off parking the car out a bit and catching a bus or SkyTrain into the centre; it'll probably be quicker too.

Mini-Ferry
The False Creek mini-ferry shuttles between the Vancouver Aquatic Centre on Sunset Beach at English Bay, Granville Island and the Vancouver Maritime Museum on Kitsilano Point. Other stops are at the eastern end of False Creek, including one by BC Place Stadium. From the aquatic centre to the maritime museum costs $1.25 one way.

Taxi
Unless you're staying at a big hotel, if you want to take a taxi somewhere your best bet is to phone for one; trying to hail one in the streets is likely to prove unsuccessful. Three of the companies are Black Top (☎ 681-2181, 683-4567), MacLure's (☎ 731-9211, 683-6666) and Yellow Cab (☎ 681-3311/1111). For a complete list check the yellow pages. From downtown to the Vancouver CHA Hostel costs approximately $10.

Bicycle
Cycling is a good way to get around town. Get a copy of the Bicycling Association of BC's cycling map of the city (see the Activ-

ities section at the start of the chapter). One of the most popular routes is along the 10-km road in Stanley Park which has a number of rental places close by, including:

A-1 Kitzco
    1168 Denman St (☎ 684-6269)
Bayshore Bicycles
    745 Denman St (☎ 688-2453, 689-5071)
Franco's Bike Rental
    560 Cardero St (☎ 681-2453)
Stanley Park Rentals
    676 Chilco St (☎ 681-5581)

Rates are around $6 an hour or $20 a day.

AROUND VANCOUVER
North of Vancouver
Mt Seymour Provincial Park This park, 15 km north-east from downtown, is a quick, close escape from the city. There is a road up most of the way and a chair lift goes to the peak. The views of Vancouver's surroundings are beautiful. There's skiing here in winter.

There are parking lots for trailers but no real tent campground; you can pitch a tent along the many alpine trails. Some areas are very rugged, so visitors going on overnight trips should register. From Lonsdale Quay take bus Nos 229 or 239 to Phibbs Exchange then No 215.

Sunshine Coast The name refers to the coastal area north of Vancouver from Horseshoe Bay to Lund, 23 km north of Powell River. The scenery is excellent: hills, mountains, forests, inlets, harbours and beaches. Highway 101 along the coast is broken at two separate points and ferries are necessary. The highway ends completely at Lund. At Powell River there is a ferry over to Comox on Vancouver Island; the ferry to Nanaimo leaves from Horseshoe Bay. The ferries are all rather expensive if you take your car. For detailed information about the ferries, call BC Ferries (☎ 685-1021).

Horseshoe Bay is a pretty spot, but commercial and expensive. To head further north up the Sunshine Coast you catch the ferry from here to Langdale. Highway 99 north-east from Horseshoe Bay leads to Squamish, Garibaldi Provincial Park and Whistler.

In Powell River is the Beach Gardens Resort Hotel (☎ 485-6267) at 7074 Westminster St. It rents boats and diving equipment and runs charters out to diving spots. There's a Travel Infocentre (☎ 485-4701) at 6807 Wharf St. Around Egmont near Earl's Cove, south of Powell River, there are good diving spots and wrecks off the coast.

Shannon Falls Squamish is the main town in this resort area. South of Squamish, the Shannon Falls tumble over a 120-metre cliff just off the road in a park. There's hiking, rock climbing and camping in summer, skiing in winter.

Garibaldi Provincial Park This park is a 195-sq-km mountain wilderness, 64 km north of Vancouver. Most of the park is undeveloped and it's a full day's hike from the parking lot off Highway 99 to the campground. There's some good hiking and cross-country ski trails. For more information and a map of the park, stop at one of the Travel Infocentres in Squamish or Whistler.

Garibaldi Provincial Park has five hiking areas – Diamond Head, Garibaldi Lake, Cheakamus Lake, Singing Pass and Wedgemount Lake – covered by more than 60 km of developed trails. Garibaldi is a wilderness park so you should take your own supplies and equipment, especially if you intend to go far from developed areas.

Brandy Wine Waterfall Just south of Whistler (perhaps 10 km, look for the sign) is a waterfall with some interesting pioneer lore. Evidently, they threw bottles of brandy into the falls – mesmerised by the fine view? It is quite a scenic little place.

Whistler Mountain Just outside the northern end of Garibaldi Provincial Park is this major resort area geared mainly for skiing, an activity available there all year round. In summer you can go hiking, cycling, canoeing, take the cable car up the mountain or visit an aquatic park. Ask about the 'singing

tunnels', an old mine site, which can be visited. Whistler Village offers hotels, lodges, restaurants and bars.

The Whistler ski district has three centres, Whistler Village, Blackcomb and Whistler's South Side. The latter is the least expensive while the village has the most action and socialising – with the larger hotels it is also more costly. Together the three areas make up Canada's largest ski resort. Blackcomb Mountain (☎ 932-3141; in Vancouver ☎ 687-1032) has the largest downhill ski area in North America, from novice slopes to glacier skiing. The latter is available pretty well all year, providing the country's only summer skiing. The day pass for an adult is $40. For a snow report call ☎ 932-4211. On Whistler Mountain (☎ 932-3434; in Vancouver ☎ 685-1007) the skiing and facilities (including the new base station at Whistler Village and the 10-passenger, high-speed, enclosed cable car) make it one of the best resorts in the world. The day pass for an adult is $40. For a snow report call ☎ 932-4191; in Vancouver call ☎ 687-6761.

Whistler CHA Hostel (☎ or fax 932-5492) is in a beautiful setting on Alta Lake (West) Rd about five km from Highway 99 and about 12 km from Whistler Village. It's open all year from 8 to 10 am and from 4 to 10 pm, with room for 35 people. During the ski season it's a good idea to book ahead. Facilities include kitchen, wood stove and ski waxing. The BC Rail train will stop at the hostel upon request.

Whistler Backpackers Guest House (☎ 932-1177), 2124 Lake Placid Rd in Whistler, is close to the centre of things. Private and shared rooms start from $15 a day in winter, $12 in summer.

Maverick Coach Lines (☎ 255-1171) has four buses daily to Whistler from the Greyhound Bus Depot in Vancouver. It's about a two-hour drive from Vancouver. Once there you don't need transport to get about.

South of Vancouver
Reifel Bird Sanctuary The 340-hectare bird sanctuary is on Westham Island, 10 km west of Ladner, south of Richmond. Each year,

over 240 bird species pass through, including herons, eagles, falcons and swans. There are about three km of pathways and an observation tower. The sanctuary is open daily from 9 am to 6 pm in summer, to 4.00 pm in winter. Admission is $3.

Buddhist Temple More than simply a temple, this Chinese Buddhist centre (☎ 274-2822), in Richmond at 9160 Steveston Highway, consists of a temple, garden, small museum and library. You may also catch an art show or tea ceremony. The temple is ornate and has some fine work, but compared to the temples of the East it may seem a little clean, modern and sterile. The centre is free and open daily from 10 am to 5 pm. It's accessible by bus from the city: No 403 on Howe St.

Steveston This little town, on the coast near the Buddhist Temple, is heavily promoted as a quaint fishing village, but that's rather a promotion writer's notion. There's certainly nothing overly wrong with the place and you can get some alright fish & chips, but a quaint fishing village it ain't. There's a wharf where some of the fishing fleet moors and a place to buy fresh seafood. The local museum (☎ 271-6868) is open Monday to Saturday from 9.30 am to 5 pm and is free. To get to Steveston catch bus Nos 401, 402, 406 or 407.

White Rock Still further south, on Semiahmoo Bay south of Surrey and about two km from the US border, is White Rock. All summer long the beach strip, with expanses of sand and warm waters, is quite a scene; strut your stuff if you've done your sit-ups. Unfortunately the annual summer sand castle competition has been cancelled: apparently participants got a little too rowdy.

Take the SkyTrain to 22nd St Station then catch bus No 353 to the beach, or catch bus No 354 heading south on Granville St.

Fort Langley Historic Park The 19th-century fort (☎ 888-4424) is at 23433 Mavis St, Fort Langley, 48 km east of Vancouver

along the Trans Canada Highway. It was erected in 1827 and served as a Hudson's Bay Company post until 1858, long before Victoria or Vancouver were established. It was here in 1858 that BC was proclaimed a crown colony. Most of the buildings were restored in 1956 and you can see the old palisades, furnishings and utensils. The park is open in summer from 10 am to 6 pm and admission is $2.

Take the SkyTrain to Scott Rd Station, catch bus No 501 to the Exhibition Centre in Fort Langley, then bus No 507 to the park.

Vancouver Game Farm The 48-hectare site (☎ 856-6825), off 264 St in Aldergrove about 12 km south-east of the fort, has 60 different kinds of animals in large, open pens, including tigers, lions, elephants and buffalo. It's open daily from 8 am till dusk and admission is $7.

Vancouver Island

The attractions of Vancouver Island, the largest island off the west coast of the Americas, range from its rugged wilderness to the grand rooms of its provincial legislature.

The island is 450 km long and has a population of over 500,000 people, most of whom live along the south-eastern coast.

The geography is scenically varied. A mountain range runs down the centre of the island, its snow-capped peaks setting off the woods and many lakes and streams. The coast can be either rocky and tempestuous or sandy and calm.

South of the island, across the Juan de Fuca Strait, the sea is backed by the substantial Olympic Mountains of Washington state, the most evident being snowy Mt Baker. Across Georgia Strait, which runs along the island's eastern shore, the mainland's Coast Mountains form the skyline. The open west coast is fully exposed to the Pacific. The waters around the island are filled with marine life, much of which is commonly seen and some, like the salmon, eaten.

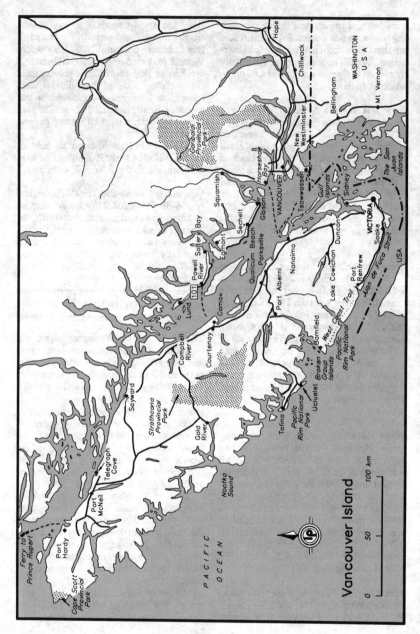

Vancouver Island

The central north-south mountain chain divides the island into two distinct halves. The sparsely populated west coast is rugged, hilly, forested and cut by deep inlets. The more gentle eastern side is suitable for farming. The island's industries – forestry, mining and fishing – and nearly all of the principal towns are found along this side of the ridge. However, don't imagine the entire coast to be urban sprawl. It's still quite undeveloped in places, especially north of the Campbell River.

The island has the mildest climate in the country. It's particularly moderate at the southern end, where the northerly arm of Washington state protects it from the ocean. There is substantially less rain in Victoria than in Vancouver, and August and September, when the sky is usually blue, are excellent months during which to visit.

Obviously, this is a popular tourist destination. Victoria can get especially crowded in mid-summer. For those seeking quieter spots, a little effort should be sufficient to be rewarded.

VICTORIA

Victoria, the second largest city in the province, lies at the south-eastern end of Vancouver Island, 90 km south-west of Vancouver. Although bounded on three sides by water, it is sheltered from the Pacific Ocean by the Olympic Peninsula across the Juan de Fuca Strait in Washington state. It is a gentle and genteel town-like city. Both visitors and residents alike seem to indulge the British and resort flavour that has arisen. With the mildest climate in the country, its neat, clean streets, the interesting – and in many cases, visible – history, and its flowers to attract people, it's not surprising that two million tourists visit Victoria annually. This quiet, easy-paced traditional seat of – dare we say it – civilisation was once described by Rudyard Kipling as 'Brighton Pavilion with the Himalayas for a backdrop'.

Although it is the provincial capital and home to an important university and naval base, Victoria is not an industrial city. About 30% of its 275,000 or so residents work in

tourist and service-oriented businesses, while another 20% work in the public sector. The island is also a major retirement centre, with retirees making up around 20% of the population.

The first residents were the Salish Indians. Although Captain Cook landed on Nootka Island on the west coast in 1778, it was not until 1843 that the Hudson's Bay Company founded Victoria in the name of the queen as a fur-trading post. The town boomed as a drop-off point when gold was discovered in the Cariboo area in the late 1850s. Soon Victoria was full of merchants and brothels, and home to one 'Gassy Jack' Deighton, who later played an important role in Vancouver's development.

The gold rush ended, however, and the Canadian Pacific railway never fulfilled its promise of a railway link. But it did build the fabulous Empress Hotel, and when the hotel opened in 1908, the tourist trade began in earnest. Without the railway connection, industry was forgotten. As the seat of emerging political power and with an increasing reputation as a graceful social centre, Victoria blossomed in its own way.

Today there are still more British-born residents here than anywhere else in Canada, and they have entrenched their style rather than forgotten it.

Orientation

The city lies at the south-eastern tip of Vancouver Island, actually closer to the USA than to the Canadian mainland. The downtown area is simply laid out and really not very large. Bounded on two sides by water, the central area of the city is easy and pleasant to explore on foot, so you'll have little trouble getting your bearings. The city has very few high-rise buildings, so you can see a long way.

The focal point is the Inner Harbour, a section of Victoria Harbour that fronts several of the most important structures. The Empress Hotel faces out across its lawns to the Inner Harbour.

Across the way are the enormous provincial Parliament Buildings. In between the

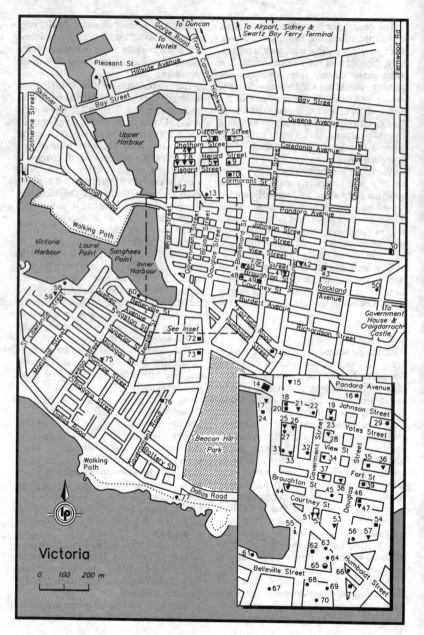

Victoria

0   100   200 m

■ PLACES TO STAY

2	Imperial Inn
3	Paul's Motor Inn
10	Fairfield Hotel
16	Hotel Douglas
18	Salvation Army Centre
20	Victoria CHA Hostel
24	Victoria Regent Hotel
29	Dominion Hotel
30	Backpackers Hostel
35	Ritz Hotel
39	Sussex Apartment Hotel
46	Strathcona Hotel
49	YM-YWCA
54	Courtyard Inn Hotel
62	Empress Hotel
71	Crystal Court Motel
72	Helm's Inn & T-Bird Motel
73	Shamrock Motel
74	Beaconsfield Inn
76	James Bay Inn

▼ PLACES TO EAT

4	Herald St Café
5	Taj Mahal
6	Don Mee
7	Wong's
8	Foo Hong
12	Swan's Pub & Café
15	Market Square
17	Chandler's Seafood Restaurant
19	Old Victoria Café
21	Las Flores
23	Day & Night
25	Flying Rhino
26	Periklis
28	Eugene's Restaurant & Snack Bar
33	Koto Japanese Restaurant
34	Murchie's
36	Dion's Restaurant
37	La Petite Colombe
38	Pagliacci's

40	Fanny's Cultured Cow
41	Victoria Restaurant
42	Da Tandoor
44	Portts
47	Sticky Wicket Pub
51	Sam's Deli
52	Chauney's Restaurant
53	Smitty's Family Restaurant
57	Millos Restaurant
59	Barb's Place
75	French Connection

OTHER

1	Point Ellice House
9	The Bay
11	Spinnaker's
13	McPherson Playhouse
14	E&N Railiner Station
22	Crown Publications
27	Bastion Square
31	Emily Carr Gallery
32	Munro's Books
43	BC Ferries
45	Victoria Eaton Centre
48	Royal Theatre
50	Art Gallery of Greater Victoria
55	Tourist Office
56	Classic Car Museum
58	Fisherman's Wharf
60	Ferry Terminals
61	Royal London Wax Museum
63	Miniature World
64	Victoria Conference Centre
65	Greyhound Bus Depot
66	Crystal Garden
67	Parliament Buildings
68	Royal BC Museum
69	Thunderbird Park
70	Helmcken House & St Anne's Pioneer Schoolhouse
77	'Mile O' Trans Canada Highway

two, on the corner beside the Netherlands Carillon bell tower, is the Royal BC Museum. To the east of the museum is Thunderbird Park, with its totem poles, and south of this is Beacon Hill Park, the city's largest. Surrounding the park and extending down to the ocean are well-kept residential houses, many with attractive lawns and gardens.

Along Wharf St, north of the Empress Hotel, is the central Travel Infocentre, on the corner of the Inner Harbour. Following Wharf St along the water will take you through the Old Town, the original area of Victoria that has now been restored.

Meeting Wharf St at right angles are Fort, Yates and Johnson Sts. Just up a few steps from Wharf St is Bastion Square, the Old Town's square, lined with historic buildings.

Parallel to Wharf St and a couple of blocks east is Government St, one of the major downtown thoroughfares.

In it are numerous government buildings, including the large main post office between Yates St and Bastion Square. Diagonally opposite the main post office is Trounce Alley, once the tiny byway where miners sold their gold. It has been renovated and has many boutiques – some selling gold.

One block east is Douglas St, the main commercial street of Victoria. The area around Douglas St, Government St and Bastion Square is the centre of the business area, with banks, offices and department stores.

City Hall is on the corner of Douglas and Cormorant Sts. The brownish-purple building with the mansard roof, built in 1890, is worth noting. With the clock tower and flowers, it looks like a very accessible municipal office.

East again is Blanshard St, running near the edge of the downtown area. Going further leads you into residential areas. Marine Drive, along the waterfront east of town, is a wealthy district with parks and beaches.

The northern boundary of the downtown area is marked by Fisgard St. Its Chinese style buildings, including one that houses the Chinese Public School, are interesting. This building has a roof that will remind you of a pagoda.

Fisgard St between Government and Wharf Sts is a small Chinatown, with Oriental-style street lamps, Chinese characters on the street signs and, of course, restaurants. The area is remarkably neat and clean but very colourful due mainly to the colour schemes of the buildings.

Fan Tan Alley, halfway along, has a few small shops and connects Fisgard St with Pandora Ave; the alley is locked at night. About 130 years ago, when this, Canada's first Chinatown, was in its heyday and much bigger, the alley was lined with opium dens and gambling houses – it's a lot quieter now.

Both Douglas and Blanshard Sts lead north out of the city: the former to the Trans Canada Highway and Nanaimo, the latter to Highway 17 (Patricia Bay Highway), Sidney and the Swartz Bay ferry terminal. To the north-west is Gorge Rd, an area of heavy motel concentration.

It forms part of Island Highway 1A, which cuts across both Douglas and Blanshard Sts, runs along the northern side of the gorge and meets up further west with Craigflower Rd and the Trans Canada Highway.

Victoria International Airport is in Sidney, about 20 km north of Victoria on Highway 17. The Greyhound Bus Depot is at 710 Douglas St, on the corner of Belleville St and opposite Crystal Garden.

Information

The Travel Infocentre (☎ 382-2127), at 812 Wharf St, is by the water at the Inner Harbour, across the road from the Empress Hotel. It has dozens of pamphlets, maps and information on shopping, sight-seeing, transport, where to stay and where to eat. There is also an office two km from the Swartz Bay ferry terminal.

Two countries with diplomatic representation in Victoria are France, 3946 Emerald Place, V8P 4T6; and Italy, Suite 207, Park Blvd V8V 2T4 (☎ 386-3277).

The main post office is at 1230 Government St, on the corner of Yates St; it's open Monday to Friday from 8.30 am to 5 pm.

The Royal Jubilee Hospital (☎ 595-9200; 595-9212 in an emergency) is at 1900 Fort St. Victoria General Hospital (☎ 727-4212; 727-4181 in an emergency) is at 35 Helmcken Rd, north-west of the downtown area, off the Trans Canada Highway.

The Royal Bank is on the corner of Douglas and Fort Sts; the Toronto Dominion Bank is at 1070-1080 Douglas St. You can change money at Money Mart, at 1720 Douglas St, opposite the Bay department store, and at Currency Exchange (open seven days a week from 7 am to 10 pm), in Douglas St, opposite the Avis office.

Crown Publications, at 546 Yates St, is a

government bookshop selling maps and federal and provincial publications on Canadiana, Native Indian culture, flora & fauna. It's open Monday to Friday from 8.30 am to 5 pm and Saturday from 9.30 to 5 pm. Earth Quest Books, at 1286 Broad St, has a good selection of travel books, guides and maps.

Munro's Books, at 1108 Government St, is in a beautiful old building originally built for the Royal Bank and restored in 1984. It is now classified as a heritage building; the atmosphere inside is almost ecclesiastical. It sells a whole range of books and has a good Canadiana section. In summer it's open Monday to Friday from 9 am to 9 pm, Saturday from 9 am to 5 pm and Sunday from 11 am to 5 pm.

The National Film Board of Canada has an office at 1412 Douglas St. It sells videos for $31 including tax, but most have to be ordered from Montreal and take three to four weeks to arrive. You can also rent videos there.

There are a lot of commercial attractions in Victoria, especially around the Inner Harbour, designed to separate tourists from their money. Many are overpriced and would only be worth a visit if you were particularly interested.

Walking Tours

Ask about walking tours at the Travel Infocentre or buy a copy of the booklet *Victoria on Foot* (Terrapin, Victoria, 1989), by Barrie Lee, which gives details of walking tours around the Old Town.

Inner Harbour

Royal BC Museum This excellent museum (☎ 387-3701), at 675 Belleville St, is a must, even for people who normally avoid such places. The wide variety of displays is artistically arranged, beautifully lit and accompanied by informative, succinct explanations. There are sections on geology, vegetation, wildlife and ethnology. Many of the models and exhibits are incredibly realistic.

In the areas devoted to the BC Native Indians, see the detailed models of villages, the documentary 1914 film *In the Land of the War Canoes* on the Kwakiutl people, and the rock on which a man fell from the sky. Also look at the Haida craftwork in argillate, a dense black carbon shale. The pipes represent some of the best Native Indian art anywhere.

There's a town made up of 19th century and early 20th-century buildings and goods, including a Model T Ford. Chaplin movies are shown in the old movie theatre. The museum also has an interesting collection of artefacts from the 1920s through to the 1970s.

Admission is $5, or $3 for students; it's worth calling to check whether the policy allowing free entry on Monday is in effect. The museum provides free tours and is open daily from 9.30 am to 7 pm in summer and from 10 am to 5.30 pm in winter.

Helmcken House Right beside the Royal BC Museum, this house is the oldest in BC to have remained unchanged. The rooms are shown much the way they would have appeared in the early 1850s.

John Helmcken, a doctor and politician, was very active in the local community. The house contains much period furniture and examples of decorations and implements. Staff members are friendly and helpful, and a visit is free. Helmcken House is in Eliot Square and is open daily from 10 am to 5 pm.

St Anne's Pioneer Schoolhouse Also in Eliot Square, this schoolhouse, operated as part of the Royal BC Museum, is one of the oldest buildings in Victoria still in use. Built sometime between 1840 and 1860, it was moved to its present site in 1974 from the grounds of St Anne's Academy.

Thunderbird Park This is a small but interesting strip of grass beside the Royal BC Museum. It has a collection of both plain and painted wooden totem poles. Some of them are labelled.

Parliament Buildings The multi-turreted Parliament Buildings (☎ 387-6121), at 501

Belleville St, facing the Inner Harbour, were designed by Francis Rattenbury and finished in 1898. On top of the main dome is a figure of Captain George Vancouver, the first British navigator to circle Vancouver Island. Rattenbury also designed the Empress Hotel and the Parthenon-like Royal London Wax Museum, which was once a CP ticket office.

There are regular free tours of the building Monday to Friday from 9 am to 5 pm. They last about 30 minutes and are worthwhile. The paintings in the lower rotunda depict scenes from Canadian history. Around the upper rotunda are paintings of four of BC's main industries. The Legislative Chamber is where all the laws of BC are made (there is no Senate in the provincial parliament). You can view the debates from the public gallery when the session is in.

In the Legislative Library is the dagger used to kill Captain Cook, while on the lawn are a statue of Queen Victoria and a sequoia tree from California planted in the 1860s. The buildings are spectacularly lit at night.

Royal London Wax Museum
This museum (☎ 388-4461), at 470 Belleville St, in front of the Parliament Buildings, contains more than 200 wax models of historical and contemporary figures. It's open daily from 8.30 am to 10.30 pm and admission is $5.25.

Miniature World
At Miniature World (☎ 385-9731), at 649 Humboldt St, beside the Empress Hotel, you'll find numerous layouts depicting in exact detail various themes, such as the world of Dickens. The highlight is a large model train representing the development of the Canadian Pacific railway from 1885 to 1915. The model is very realistic. Miniature World is open daily from 9 am to 8 pm and admission is $6.

Douglas St Beacon Hill Park
Just southeast of the downtown area, along Douglas St, this 62-hectare park is Victoria's largest. Bus No 5 will take you there. The park is a very well-cared-for oasis of trees, flowers, ponds and pathways. Trees of this size you don't see anywhere but on the west coast. Also in

the park is the 'world's tallest totem'; and a cricket pitch (told you it was British here). The southern edge overlooks the ocean and offers good views of the coastline. At the lookout above Dallas Rd is a marker indicating the direction of places such as Seattle, and noting the elevations of mountains. At the south-western corner of the park, the path along the water meets the 'Mile 0' marker, the Pacific terminal of the Trans Canada Highway.

Crystal Garden
This seems to be one of the more popular commercial attractions, but at $5 for admission, it's not really cheap. Designed by (who else?) Francis Rattenbury, it was fashioned after London's Crystal Palace and built in 1925. Once a focal point for the social elite, it was restored in 1977 as a visitor attraction, but remains a venue for splashy events. The principal draw is the indoor tea room overlooking a tropical-like garden complete with wildlife. It's at 713 Douglas St and is open daily from 9 am to 9 pm.

Victoria Conference Centre
The centre (☎ 361-1000), at 720 Douglas St, near Crystal Garden, was opened in 1989. It has the capacity to hold 1500 people and has an indoor waterfall and totem pole. A covered walkway connects it with the rear of the Empress Hotel.

Classic Car Museum
This museum (☎ 382-7118), at 813 Douglas St, has over 40 beauties on display for auto lovers, ranging from the 1904 Olds to the 1967 Lincoln Limo. It's open daily from 9 am to 6 pm and admission is $5.

Old Town
The original Victoria was centred along Wharf St and Bastion Square. This was where the first fur-trading ships moored. Wharf St was once busy with miners, merchants and all those heading for the Klondike.

Bastion Square was where Fort Victoria

was situated and held the courthouse, jail, gallows and brothel.

The whole area has been restored and redeveloped. The square is pleasant for strolling around or sitting in and people-watching. Many of the old buildings are now restaurants, boutiques, galleries or offices. The same is true of those in Wharf St.

Further north along Wharf St you'll come to Market Square, on the corner of Johnson St. This is a quadrangle of buildings dating from between 1894 and 1900. Renovated in 1975, this compact, attractive area now has over 45 shops and restaurants.

Emily Carr Gallery At 1107 Wharf St, this gallery (☎ 387-3080) pays homage to one of Canada's best known and liked painters, a native of Victoria. Many of her paintings incorporated subject matter drawn from the culture of the west coast Native Indians, particularly the totems poles. The gallery shows changing exhibits and daily free films about the life and career of Emily Carr. It's open Monday to Saturday from 10 am to 4.30 pm and admission is free. Prints from originals are sold.

Maritime Museum This collection of arte-facts, models, photographs and naval memorabilia is for nautical buffs only. They'll find it at 28 Bastion Square, near Government St, at the big anchor. It's open daily from 9.30 am to 6.30 pm and admission is $4, or $1 for students.

Victoria Eaton Centre Although this is a shopping centre, it's worth a visit just to wander round. The whole complex has been modernised incorporating the facades of original buildings. As well as shops and eateries, it has fountains, pools and a rooftop garden. It occupies two blocks between Government and Douglas Sts.

Rockland Area
Art Gallery of Greater Victoria The gallery (☎ 384-4101), in a Victorian mansion at 1040 Moss St, 1½ km east of the downtown area, just off Fort St, is best known for its

excellent Asian art, including the Japanese and Chinese collections. It also has artworks from other parts of the world and from widely varying periods of history including pre-Columbian Latin American objects through to contemporary Canadian paint-ings. There are some good Inuit pieces. Take bus Nos 11 or 14 from the downtown area. It's open Monday to Saturday from 10 am to 5 pm, Thursday from 10 am to 9 pm and Sunday from 1 to 5 pm. Admission is $2, or $1 for students. It has a restaurant too.

Government House This is the official res-idence of the province's lieutenant-governor. The impressive grounds are open to the public except when British royalty is in res-idence. The building is not far from the Art Gallery of Greater Victoria, away from the downtown area, on Rockland Ave.

Craigdarroch Castle Near Government House, but off Fort St, at 1050 Joan Crescent, this rather impressive home (☎ 592-5323) was built in the mid-1880s by Robert Dunsmuir, a coal millionaire, for himself and his wife. The interior remains decorated in the manner of that time. Admission is $3 and it's open daily from 9 am to 7.30 pm. To get there take bus Nos 10 or 11.

Butchart Gardens
If you're coming from the east, you'll prob-ably notice the signs for this attraction beginning in Banff. They are without a doubt the most publicised of all Victoria's sights. No doubt the gardens are beautiful and extensive, but admission is costly at $8.50. Whether it's worth it depends on you and your budget.

Parts of the gardens are sectioned into specialities like the English Rose Garden and the Japanese Garden. There are hundreds of species of trees, bushes and flowers. You can walk through in about 1½ hours, but linger as long as you wish.

In the evenings from June to September the gardens are illuminated, giving a very different effect from daylight.

There are also concerts and puppet shows

around dusk. On Saturday night in July and August there is a spectacular fireworks display set to music – there's no extra charge to watch it.

Open daily year round from 9 am till dusk, the gardens (☎ 652-4422/5256) are about 21 km north-west of the downtown area, on Saanich Inlet, at the foot of Keating Cross Rd. City bus Nos 74 and 75 go within one km during the week and three km on Sunday.

Dominion Astrophysical Observatory

On the way to the Butchart Gardens you could visit this observatory (☎ 388-0001), where you can peer out to space through a 183-cm telescope. There is a museum and equipment used to record earthquakes. The observatory is open Monday to Friday from 9.30 am to 4.30 pm and admission is free. It's north-west of the centre, at 5071 West Saanich Rd, on Little Saanich Mountain.

English Village

This gimmicky but effective re-creation of some English Tudor-style buildings is in Lampson St, across Victoria Harbour from the Empress Hotel. The highlights are the replicas of Shakespeare's birthplace and the thatched cottage of his wife, Anne Hathaway. The cottage (☎ 388-4353), at 429 Lampson St, and the rest of the 'village' are furnished with authentic 16th-century antiques. It is open daily from 9 am to 10 pm in summer, and from 9 am to 5 pm in winter. Admission is $5. Take bus No 24 from the downtown area.

Point Ellice House

This beautifully kept house (☎ 385-5923), built in 1861, was sold in 1868 for $2500. The buyer, Peter O'Reilly, was a member of government and a successful businessman. Many of the house's immaculate furnishings now on display belonged to him and his wife. Admission is free and it's open daily from 10 am to 5 pm. It's north of the downtown area, at 2616 Pleasant St, off Bay St, at Point Ellice Bridge.

Craigflower Farmhouse

The farmhouse (☎ 387-4697) was built by Kenneth McKenzie in 1856. It was the central home in the first farming community on Vancouver Island and its construction heralded Victoria's change from a fur-trading settlement to a permanent one. Built to remind McKenzie of Scotland, the house was decorated with the many furnishings he had brought from his homeland. Because the family entertained frequently, the house became a social centre for Fort Victoria and the Esquimalt Naval Base.

The farmhouse is open Thursday to Monday from 10 am to 5 pm and admission is by donation. It's a little north-west of town, on the corner of Craigflower and Admiral's Rds, near Gorge Water. To get there catch bus No 14 from town.

Regents Park House

At 1501 Fort St is a large award-winning restored Victorian Italianate house from 1855. It has a collection of antiques and Victorian furnishings as well as eight sizeable fireplaces. You'll notice the smell of age as soon as you enter. Admission is $3, and it's open from 1 to 6 pm daily. It's a fair walk from the downtown area, but a short bus ride.

Fort Rodd Hill National Historic Park

This scenic 18-hectare park (☎ 388-1601) overlooking Esquimalt Harbour contains some historical points of interest. There are the remnants of three turn-of-the-century gun batteries. These artillery installations were built to protect the naval base in the bay and, until 1956, when such a defence system was deemed obsolete, were regularly upgraded. There are information signs around the park, as well as guides. The park is open daily from 9 am to sunset and admission is free.

Also in the park is **Fisgard Lighthouse**, which still works and has been in continuous use since 1860. It was the first lighthouse to shine its beam across the water in western Canada.

The park is at 603 Fort Rodd Hill Rd, off Ocean Blvd, about 12 km north-west of downtown, on the western side of Esquimalt Harbour. To get there catch bus No 50 or 61 to Western Exchange and change to a No 60.

Sealand of the Pacific

Sealand of the Pacific (☎ 598-3373) is at 1327 Beach Drive, at Oak Bay Marina. This is Canada's largest oceanarium and includes octopuses, seals, sea lions, sharks and many other creatures.

The main feature is a show put on by 5000-kg killer whales. Tickets are $6. Double-decker buses run from the Inner Harbour to Sealand every 15 minutes.

Fisherman's Wharf

The wharf area is on Victoria Harbour, west around the bay from the Inner Harbour, along Belleville St past Laurel Point, and is worth a look. It's a busy spot, with fishing boats and pleasure craft coming and going. You can sometimes buy fresh seafood from the boats or the little shed and there's a place selling fish & chips (see under Places to Eat). At one end of the dock houseboats are moored – there are a few that wouldn't be bad to call home.

Scenic Marine Drive

Starting either from Fisherman's Wharf or Beacon Hill Park, the Scenic Marine Drive, with great views out over the sea, skirts the coast along Dallas Rd and Beach Drive.

The road continues to Sealand then heads north past some of Victoria's wealthiest neighbourhoods and Oak Bay, a retirement community.

You'll see many parks and several beaches along the way. The double-decker buses include Marine Drive in their tours.

Lookouts

At the northern end of Shelbourne St, **Mt Douglas Park Lookout** provides views of the Saanich Peninsula, the Georgia Strait and the islands in it and Washington state of the USA.

There are good views at **Mt Tolmie Park Lookout**, off Cedar Hill Cross Rd; it is near the University of Victoria.

Fishing & Diving

The waters around Victoria are renowned as a place for deep-sea fishing (with salmon being the top prize) and diving. The Travel Infocentre can supply you with information.

There are freshwater lakes and streams within an hour or two of Victoria as well as up-island that are good for trout and/or salmon fishing. Saanich Inlet has one of the highest concentrations of salmon in the world.

Scores of charter companies offer deep-sea fishing trips of varying lengths. Check the yellow pages for information. Most supply all equipment, bait and even coffee. Let's Go Fishing (☎ 598-3366), at 1327 Beach Drive, charges $6 per hour. Other companies go out for a minimum of three or four hours and charge around $25 or $30.

The Georgia Strait provides opportunities for world-class diving. The undersea life is tremendously varied and has been featured in *National Geographic*. Visibility is best in late winter and early spring, when the plankton has decreased, although, of course, the weather is cool at that time of year.

There are diving charters and equipment shops around the island. In Victoria Harbour, west of the downtown area, there's an underwater park by the pier at Ogden Point that has kelp 'forests' and quite a bit of sea life.

Swimming

One of the best swimming places is the **Sooke Potholes**, about an hour's drive west of Victoria on Highway 14, by the town of Sooke, on the southern shore. Watch for signs at Milne's Landing. You can find your own swimming hole but the water ain't balmy. There's good picnicking and some walking trails too. Don't get caught drinking alcohol: the fines are heavy.

Also popular is **Thetis Lake Municipal Park**, not too far north-west of town (about 20 minutes), off the Trans Canada Highway. It's very busy at the main beach but if you hike around the lake you'll find a quiet spot.

Organised Tours

Some companies offer a variety of tours,

from bus rides around downtown Victoria to quick trips around the island. Other companies only do one kind of tour, such as day and evening harbour boat trips, tours by horse-drawn carriage, self-drive tours using recorded tapes or tours up-island to view wildlife. It's best to find out what's available, decide what you want then shop around a little; again, the Travel Infocentre is a good place to start.

A couple of companies operate in Wharf St, right in front of the Empress Hotel. One is Marguerite Tours Ltd (☎ 388-9383/4352). It has six different tours; its basic sight-seeing trip around Victoria in a British double-decker bus takes 1½ hours and costs $10.50.

Gray Line (☎ 388-5248), at 700 Douglas St, offers a variety of tours here, as they do in so many North American cities. Its city bus tour costs $10.50 for 1½ hours and takes in some of the major historical and scenic sights. Many of its bus tours include admission to attractions like Sealand or Butchart Gardens. It also does cruises of the harbour: 1½ hours costs $12.

Heritage Tours (☎ 474-4332), at 713 Bexhill St, offers more personalised city tours in London-style taxis for $45 an hour, or $55 for 1½ hours.

Tallyho Sightseeing (☎ 479-1113) gives you a one-hour tour of the city in a horse-drawn carriage for $8 per person. It leaves from the corner of Belleville and Menzies Sts.

Victoria Harbour Cruises runs an enjoy-able, albeit short, ferry trip of about half an hour return from the Inner Harbour out to Westbay Terrace. The boat takes just a dozen people per trip.

Other
Windsurfing is popular, especially in Cadboro Bay near the university, and at Willow's Beach in Oak Bay. Rentals are available at both for around $12; some places offer lessons too.

A few people offer horseback trips in the nearby highlands. Some include overnight camping. Ask at the Travel Infocentre.

The Crystal Pool Recreation Centre (☎ 383-2522), at 2275 Quadra St, on the corner of Wark St – an easy walk from the downtown area – has a pool, a sauna, a whirlpool and locker rooms. Entry to the pool is $2.

Ocean River Sports (☎ 381-4233), at 1437 Store St, rents kayaks and runs courses.

Scenic Marine Drive makes a good bike trip.

Festivals
The Victoria Day Festival, held during the fourth week of May, features a parade, performances by the town's ethnic groups, stage shows and many sporting events. Many of the townspeople dress in 19th century-style clothes, and some shopkeepers dress their windows in period manner. Call ☎ 382-3111 for information.

The Swiftsure Lightship Classic, a sailing race, ends the event. Call ☎ 592-2441 for information. The last weekend can get pretty wild – a real street party.

The start of the annual Yacht Race from Victoria to Maui is another cause for celebration.

The Victoria International Festival offers classical music performed by Canadian and foreign musicians. It lasts through the summer till the middle of August. For information and schedules contact the McPherson Playhouse (☎ 386-6121), on the corner of Pandora Ave and Government St.

In late June the Victoria Jazz Society (☎ 381-4042) puts on its annual jazz festival at various locations around town.

At the end of June and beginning of July is the annual Folkfest, which celebrates Canada's cultural diversity. Dance and musical performances take place in front of the Royal BC Museum.

During the Classic Boat Festival, held during the first weekend in September each year, vintage wooden boats powered by sail or engine compete in various categories. The competition is held on the Inner Harbour. On the quayside free entertainment is provided for the spectators. For information you can call ☎ 385-7766.

Places to Stay

Camping Closest to town is *Fort Victoria Trailer & Camp Park* (☎ 479-8112), at 127 Burnett Rd, off Island Highway 1A, 6½ km from the city centre. Take bus No 14 or 15 from the downtown area; there's a bus stop at the gate. The site has 150 sites and full facilities, including free showers. It charges $12.50 for a site.

Thetis Lake Campground (☎ 478-3845), at 1938 Trans Canada Highway, on Rural Route 6, is about a 15-minute drive northwest of the city centre. All facilities are available, including laundrette and shower. There's a store, and you can swim in the nearby lake. A site for two people is $10; electricity is $2 extra. The campground is open all year.

There's a government-run campground in *Goldstream Provincial Park* (☎ 387-4363), on the Trans Canada Highway, about 20 km north-west of Victoria. A tent site costs $12 and you can go swimming, fishing or hiking. Take bus No 50 from Douglas St. South of Goldstream Provincial Park, about 3½ km off the Trans Canada Highway, at 2960 Irwin Rd, on Rural Route 6, is *Humpback Valley Campground* (☎ 478-6960). It's open from early June to the end of September, has full facilities and kayak rentals, and charges $12 for a tent site.

The Travel Infocentre can tell you of other campgrounds not too far from town.

Hostels The *Victoria CHA Hostel* (☎ 385-4511) is in the old part of town, at 516 Yates St, just up from Wharf St. It has room for over 100 people. It has been fully renovated and now has more family rooms, a larger common area, kitchen, laundry and good notice board. Memberships are available.

A bed costs $10 for members and $15 for nonmembers. The hostel is open Sunday to Thursday from 7.30 am to midnight, and until 2 am on Friday and Saturday nights. During the busy summer months it's advisable to book in before 4 pm. In the peak season preference is given to IYHF members, and nonmembers may be asked to wait till 8 pm to check in. If the hostel is full

there is a list of alternative accommodation on the notice board. You can find out, too, about the good mini-hostels around the island, some of which are in relatively remote places while others are more conveniently located.

The *Backpackers Hostel* (☎ 386-4471), at 1418 Fernwood Rd, has doubles for $30 or dormitory beds for $10. Breakfast is $5 extra. It has weekly and monthly rates too. The hostel has no curfew, is close to shops and restaurants and is served by bus Nos 1, 10, 11, 14, 27 and 28 from the downtown area.

The *YM-YWCA* (☎ 386-7511) are both in the same building at 880 Courtney St, but the residence is only for women. There are 31 beds in single and double rooms with shared bathrooms. Singles/doubles are $26/43. It has a cafeteria that anyone can use and a heated swimming pool.

The *University of Victoria* rents rooms from the start of May to the end of August. Singles/doubles are $22/36.10, including breakfast and free parking. You can make use of the facilities and several licensed cafeterias on campus. Contact Housing & Conference Services (☎ 721-8395) at the University of Victoria, PO Box 1700, Victoria V8W 2Y2. Catch bus No 14 on Douglas St to the campus: it takes about 20 minutes.

The *Cool Aid Hostel* (☎ 383-1951), at 1900 Fernwood Rd, on the corner of Gladstone Ave, is actually a kind of halfway house for outpatients or for those on the skids or out of work.

The place is not great and is not really for travellers but will take them in. The rate is $7. It's a bit of a way north-east of the downtown area; take bus No 10 from outside Marks & Spencers in Douglas St.

The *Salvation Army Centre* (☎ 384-3396) is in a modern building at 525 Johnston St, on the corner of Wharf St, and is for men only. A bed in a dormitory costs $6, while a private room is $10. Meals are extra.

B&Bs This form of accommodation is very big in town and makes a good alternative to standard hotels. There are several B&B associations that approve members, list them and make reservations at one central office. Check the listings of B&B agencies in the *Accommodations* brochure. Prices are between $30 and $50 for singles and between $40 and $95 for most doubles, though some go up to as much as $150.

Several associations to try are VIP B&B (☎ 477-5604), at 1786 Teakwood Rd; All Season B&B Agency (☎ 595-2337), PO Box 5511, Station B, Victoria; and Heritage Homes B&B (☎ 384-4014), at 829 Fort St. The latter has turn-of-the-century homes at good prices within three km of the downtown area.

Many other B&Bs advertise independently: see the pamphlets at the Travel Infocentre. A few are listed here.

Battery St Guest House (☎ 385-4632) is south of the centre, near Beacon Hill Park, at 670 Battery St. It's an old house dating from 1898 which now is run by a Dutch woman. Singles/doubles are $30/55.

Craigmyle Guest House (☎ 595-5411), at 1037 Craigdarroch Rd, about 1½ km from the downtown area, is next to Craigdarroch Castle. Singles/doubles are $45/70.

Laird House (☎ 384-3177), at 134 St Andrews St, is a 15-minute walk from the downtown area. The building dates from 1912. Someone will pick you up from the ferry terminal or bus depot, and free coffee and tea are available all day. It's for non-smokers only. Singles/doubles are $45/65.

Bryn Gwyn Guest House (☎ 383-1878), the blue house at 7-809 Burdett Ave, is very close to the centre of things and has singles/doubles for $40/60.

Hotels – bottom end There are a good many reasonable places right in the downtown area. The city really fills up in summer and room prices rise; after 1 October many are lower.

The *Fairfield Hotel* (☎ 386-1621) is basic and not really geared to short-term visitors, but it's cheap, clean, friendly and perfectly located at 710 Cormorant St, on the corner of Douglas St. It's an old place; many of the rooms have cooking facilities, though bathrooms are communal. Singles/doubles are $33.

A similar place is the *Ritz Hotel* (☎ 383-1021), at 710 Fort St. It's mainly rented long term to local people but short-term visitors are accepted. Singles/doubles with a shared bathroom are $30/33.

Better, and good value, is the *James Bay Inn* (☎ 384-7151). It's the big old place with bay windows at 270 Government Rd, a few blocks south of the downtown area, in a residential area of small, attractive houses. Rooms with a shared bathroom are $44, while those with a private bathroom are $55. It has a TV room, bar, restaurant and food machines downstairs.

First opened in 1897, *Cherry Bank Hotel* (☎ 385-5380), at 825 Burdett Ave, is east of the downtown area, up the hill a few blocks, opposite the law courts. It's simple but reasonable value and has singles/doubles for $38/45.10 with a shared bathroom, or $65/73 with a private bathroom. Prices include breakfast but rooms have no TV or telephone. A bar and restaurant are on the premises.

At the *Sussex Apartment Hotel* (☎ 386-3441), at 1001 Douglas St, all rooms come with private bath, TV and telephone. Singles/doubles are $45/50. Apartment units with kitchen and small dining area are available too: singles/doubles are $50/60. They are clean, good and suitable for families.

Hotel Douglas (☎ 383-4157), centrally located at 1450 Douglas St, on the corner of Pandora Ave, has singles/doubles for $50/55. It shares its lobby with an art gallery and has a restaurant and bar downstairs.

Hotels – middle At the *Strathcona Hotel* (☎ 383-7137), at 919 Douglas St, a couple of blocks north of the Inner Harbour, you can get singles/doubles from $45/50 to $50/75. All the rooms have private bathroom, telephone and TV. It has free parking, several bars and a restaurant. At the *Dominion Hotel* (☎ 384-4136), situated at 759 Yates St, singles/doubles start from $80/90. It has free parking and a restaurant. The *Courtyard Inn*

Hotel (☎ 385-6787), at 850 Blanshard St, is close to the Inner Harbour and has an indoor pool, as well as a sauna and a restaurant. Singles/doubles are $85/95.

Hotels – top end *Beaconsfield Inn* (☎ 384-4044), at 998 Humboldt St, is a few blocks east of the downtown area and a couple north of Beacon Hill Park. It's in an Edwardian mansion and the rates include breakfast. Singles/doubles are $90/100.

The *Empress Hotel* (☎ 348-8111), at 721 Government St, looks out over the Inner Harbour and is the focal point of Victoria. As you face the building, the reception area is to the left of the main entrance. Even if you're not staying here, the Empress Hotel is worth a visit. Singles/doubles are priced from $130/155 to $175/200.

Victoria Regent Hotel (☎ 386-2211), at 1234 Wharf St, near the corner of Yates St, specialises in suites. Single/double rooms are $125, while single/double suites cost $175/285 (more if they're overlooking the harbour). There's underground parking and the staff is friendly and helpful.

Oak Bay Beach Hotel (☎ 598-4556), at 1175 Beach Drive, is a seaside hotel east of the downtown area, overlooking Oak Bay. It provides a shuttle service into the centre and lunch-time cruises. All rooms range from $75 to $400. *Laurel Point Inn* (☎ 386-8721), at 680 Montreal St, west of the downtown area, near Laurel Point, is generally considered the best of all and is one of the most expensive. Singles/doubles start from $125/135 and go up to $450.

Motels Douglas St, being one of the main roads into Victoria, has a lot of motels, many of them just to the north of town.

The *Doric Motel* (☎ 386-2481), at 3025 Douglas St, is a five-minute drive north of the downtown area. It has TV, laundrette and free coffee. Singles/doubles are $44/55; a kitchen is $5 extra. *Paul's Motor Inn* (☎ 382-9231), at 1900 Douglas St, has a 24-hour restaurant. Singles/doubles are priced from $72/77.

The *Imperial Inn* (☎ 382-2111), at 1961 Douglas St, costs $59/65 for singles/doubles and has a restaurant and bar.

Crystal Court Motel (☎ 384-0551) is at 701 Belleville St, on the corner of Douglas St, across the road from the Greyhound Bus Depot and Crystal Garden. Singles/doubles are $48/52, and a kitchen costs just $2 more. It's clean and the rooms have a TV, radio and telephone. The staff is friendly and helpful but note that you have to pay with cash or travellers' cheques. The motel is white, blue and gold.

Although the *T-Bird Motel* (☎ 385-5767), at 600 Douglas St, and *Helm's Inn* (☎ 385-5767), at 668 Superior St, have separate addresses, they adjoin each other and share the same reception area and phone number. Singles/doubles at the T-Bird Motel are $70, while at Helm's Inn they are $80/90. All rooms at both places have a kitchen. Opposite is the *Shamrock Motel* (☎ 385-8768), at 675 Superior St, where singles/doubles are $75.

A good area for motels not far north-west of the downtown area is along Gorge Rd, which forms a section of Island Highway 1A. From Gorge Rd it's about a five-minute drive to town.

At the *Capri Motel* (☎ 384-0521), at 21 Gorge Rd East, singles/doubles are $42/50. *Friendship Inn* (☎ 386-8335) is at 39 Gorge Rd East. Singles are priced from $30 to $35, doubles from $55 to $60; rooms with a kitchen cost $8 extra. *Budget Host Maple Leaf Inn* (☎ 388-9901), at 120 Gorge Rd East, has a sauna, heated pool and laundrette. Singles are priced from $32 to $44, doubles from $34 to $44. Rooms with a kitchen are $10 extra.

The *Royal Victorian Inn* (☎ 385-5771), at 230 Gorge Rd East, charges $45 to $49 for singles and $56 to $60 for doubles. There's a heated outdoor pool, laundrette and complimentary coffee or tea.

Places to Eat
Though a small city, Victoria has a varied array of restaurants, due in part to its many visitors, and prices are generally good. As befits a tourist town, especially one with

British roots, there are numerous cafés and tea shops. Some dining rooms offer good lunch specials but are fairly pricey in the evenings. The pubs in town are also good for reasonably priced meals.

Places to Eat – bottom end *Smitty's Family Restaurant*, at 850 Douglas St, is an old standby and best for cheap pancake breakfasts for around $6 or $7 including coffee. It's open from 6 am to 1 am. The modest and casual *Day & Night*, at 622 Yates St, is good for any meal, with good-value plain food, including one of the cheapest breakfasts in town. Sandwiches are $4, French toast $3.25 and pasta dishes, such as fettucini primavera, around $6.

Scott's Restaurant, at 605 Yates St, is open 24 hours a day and is clean and friendly. It offers the standard burgers and sandwiches for $4, grilled meats for $6 and desserts such as cheesecake for a little over $2. *Dion's Restaurant*, on Fort St, between Douglas and Blanshard Sts, is open between 8.30 am and 10 pm. It has breakfast specials for $2.75 and omelettes with fries, toast and a slice of melon for $5.

The *Flying Rhino*, at 1219 Wharf St, opposite the Victoria Regent Hotel, serves good, inexpensive vegetarian and health food. A vegetable, potato and parmesan casserole served with soup and salad costs $6.75. The café sells batik shirts and has a notice board listing various natural therapies, meditation courses, etc.

The fish & chips are excellent in Victoria and there are several outlets for them. Try the *Old Victoria Café* at 1316 Broad St. A $6 order comes with chowder and bread. Beer from around the world is also offered. It's open Monday to Saturday from 11 am to 2 pm and from 4 to 7.30 pm, but closed on Sunday. At Fisherman's Wharf try *Barb's Place*, at 310 St Lawrence St. The *Sticky Wicket Pub*, on the corner of Douglas and Courtney Sts, has fish & chips for $4.50 as well as other dishes such as nachos ($5.45) and pizza (from $5.65) and a variety of Canadian, US and UK beers. It's open from 11.30 am to 11 pm.

Another cheap but good place is the busy *Eugene's Restaurant & Snack Bar*, at 1280 Broad St. Simple, basic Greek foods at about $3 to $6 are served cafeteria style. It's open Monday to Friday from 8 am to 10 pm and Saturday from 10 am to 9 pm, but closed on Sunday. *Fanny's Cultured Cow*, at 801 Fort St, on the corner of Blanshard St, specialises in burgers for around $6, but also does sandwiches for $3 to $4. The waiter/manager has a great sense of humour.

In Bastion Square near the Maritime Museum, is *C'est Bon*, a small French-style café with continental breakfasts for $3.50, cakes for $1.30 and coffee for 65 cents. Mel Gibson once ate here when shooting a film close by.

Market Square, at 560 Johnson St, has several places to munch at: try *Annabell's Coffee Shop* for sandwiches ($3 to $4), and the *Bavarian Bakery* for good bread ($1.50). *Burrito Express* has quick Mexican items such as tacos for under $6; it's a pleasant little place and is licensed.

The friendly *Las Flores*, at 536 Yates St, just up from the hostel, is another inexpensive, but more authentic Mexican place with an outdoor courtyard. Main meals are about $7 and some nights of the week a guitar player dressed in a Mexican outfit will serenade you at your table. Canadian breakfast is served too.

Places to Eat – middle For dinners the *Spare Rib House*, in the Cherry Bank Hotel, at 825 Burdett Ave, is good. It serves rib dinners, steaks and seafood. Main dishes cost around $7 to $16. There's a children's menu and the restaurant features live sing-along entertainment.

Pagliacci's, at 1011 Broad St, between Fort and Broughton Sts, is mainly Italian. It costs $5 to $7 for lunch or a little more than twice that for dinner, and the food is good. It's one of the 'in' spots in town, so it's best to book for the evenings, as there are often queues outside then.

Taj Mahal is an Indian restaurant at 679 Herald St, just north-east of Chinatown. It has a good selection, including vegetarian, and food is spiced as hot as you like, but it's not cheap: dinner will cost you around $10 to $15. It's open for lunch Monday to Friday from 11.30 am to 2 pm and Saturday from 12 noon to 2 pm, and for dinner every day from 5 pm. Also with a good selection and similarly priced is *Da Tandoor*, at 1010 Fort St. It's open for lunch Thursday and Friday from 11.30 am to 2 pm and for dinner daily from 5 to 10.30 pm.

Periklis, at 531 Yates St, is a Greek place opposite the CHA Hostel. Dips are $3 and main courses between $5 and $8. It's open for lunch Monday to Friday from 11.30 am to 2 pm, and daily in the evenings from 5.30 pm till late. *Millos Restaurant*, at 716 Burdett Ave, east off Douglas St, behind the Classic Car Museum, is housed in a blue and white windmill. It has dips from $4 to $7 and main meals, like rack of lamb, between $15 and $21.

Chinatown, marked by the Gate of Harmonious Interest over Fisgard St, has its share of eating spots. *Foo Hong*, at 564 Fisgard St, is small and basic yet has good, simple Cantonese food. Starters cost around $5 and main dishes $8. *Don Mee*, at 538 Fisgard St, in Chinatown, serves Cantonese food. Combination plates are good value at lunch time. Spring rolls cost $2.50 and other starters cost up to $5; seafood, beef, pork or vegetable main courses cost from $5 to $12. *Wong's*, at 548 Fisgard St, opposite Fan Tan Alley, serves Cantonese and Sichuan food but is a little pricier than the Don Mee: starters cost from $3 to $9, main dishes from $7 to $15.

For afternoon tea try the *Victoria Restaurant*, at 919 Fort St, which is away from the crowds and somewhat formal in style and decor. It serves a variety of salads priced from $4 to $8 and sandwiches priced from $7 to $8. It's open Monday to Wednesday from 10 am to 5 pm, Thursday to Saturday from 10 am to 9 pm and Sunday for lunch. *Murchie's*, at 1110 Government St, between View and Fort Sts, is a west coast tea and coffee merchant with some of the best teas and coffees available and a decadent assortment of pastries and chocolates. Scones with strawberry jam and Devonshire cream cost $2.50.

The most popular place with the locals is the *Blethering Place*, at 2250 Oak Bay Ave, away from the centre of town. It has Devonshire teas for around $6 or $7 and is open every day from 8 am to 10 pm.

Sam's Deli, under the maroon awnings at 805 Government St, on the corner of Wharf St and diagonally opposite the main Travel Infocentre, is a perfect spot to have an espresso and write a postcard. There are about 10 tables outside on the sidewalk and more inside, where the walls are covered in 1920s and 1930s posters. This is a popular place with a European flavour. It serves good-value soups, salads and sandwiches. The *Causeway Restaurant & Club Café*, at 812 Wharf St, right on the harbour, below the Travel Infocentre, has a few tables outside and is also a good spot for an afternoon brew and view.

Herald St Caffé, at 546 Herald St, is a small Italian restaurant serving delicious pastas for around $7 to $10. It has a wine bar and gets busy after 10 pm.

Places to Eat – top end The *Empress Room* in the Empress Hotel has very good starters, including soups from $7, salads from $5 to $7, meat and seafood main courses from $22 to $28, and an array of desserts. The *Bengal Lounge*, also in the hotel, is a real treat. It serves seafood and poultry and every day a different curry for $10.50 (other daily specials are cheaper). The service and the style make it well worth the price. There is a tiger skin on the wall and it's all very colonially British. The *Crystal Room* has similar fare and prices, while downstairs in the *Garden Café* lunch is cheaper. Finally, the tradition of afternoon tea is upheld in the lobby of the hotel, but you have to be suitably attired – a 'dress code is in effect'. There are regular sittings between 11 am and 5 pm.

La Petite Colombe, at 604 Broughton St, near the corner of Government St, serves good crêpes, but the main fare is French-style seafood. With a starter, lunch costs from about $16 to $20, dinner from $21 to

$30. The restaurant is small and quiet and has a good reputation. Or try *Portts* upstairs in the Inner Harbour Square Mall. It offers fresh seafood, steaks and a view of the harbour. Soup costs about $8, steamed halibut $17.95 and the vegetarian platter $13.25.

The best seafood house in town is *Chauney's Restaurant*, at 614 Humboldt St, opposite the Empress Hotel. A three-course meal could cost you somewhere between $25 and $40, unless you have the lobster special, which is $75. The restaurant also serves steak and poultry dishes.

In Bastion Square opposite C'est Bon, on the corner of Wharf St, is the elegant *Rebecca's*. It serves mainly seafood with, starters from $3 to $9 and main meals between $12 and $18. *Chandler's Seafood Restaurant* near the Victorian Regent Hotel and the corner of Yates and Wharf Sts has starters from $5 to $7 and main dishes between $12 and $16. It also has a bar.

Koto Japanese Restaurant, at 510 Fort St, just up from Wharf St, serves mainly seafood and has a sushi and salad bar. Sushi starts at $3 for six pieces and main courses cost from $14 to $24. There's a detailed, colourful display in the window of the kinds of dishes available in the restaurant. It's open for lunch Monday to Saturday from 11.30 am to 2 pm and for dinner daily from 5 pm.

You can get a good meal at the *French Connection*, at 512 Simcoe St, a couple of blocks south of the Parliament Buildings. A full table d'hôte costs about $18.

Entertainment

Night Moves is a good free monthly entertainment paper. The weekly *Monday Magazine* is similar but more extensive. You can pick up a copy of either around town. The Travel Infocentre will also have information on what's currently happening in town.

Theatre Victoria has a number of live theatres that provide venues for plays, concerts, comedies, ballets and operas. The *MacPherson Playhouse* (☎ 386-6121), at 3 Centennial Square, on the corner of Pandora Ave and Government St, regularly puts on plays and comedies. The box office is open Monday to Saturday from 9.30 am to 5.30 pm. The *Royal Theatre*, at 805 Broughton St, between Blanshard and Quadra Sts, hosts a range of performances, from ballet to Ziggy Marley. You can get tickets and information for the Royal Theatre from the MacPherson Playhouse. Other theatres worth checking out are the *Belfry* (☎ 385-6815), at 1291 Gladstone Ave, north-east of the downtown area, and the *Phoenix Theatre* (☎ 721-8000), on the University of Victoria campus.

Open Space Gallery, at 510 Fort St, presents young poets, dancers and musicians.

Music One of the most popular nightclubs is *Harpo's* (☎ 385-5333), at 15 Bastion Square on the corner of Wharf St, above Rebecca's. It has live bands playing a variety of music, including rock, celtic rock, ska, reggae and blues. The cover charge may be up to $6 on occasions but is generally about $4. It's open Monday to Saturday from 9 pm to 2 am.

In the same building as the Strathcona Hotel there are several clubs where music is played – including the *Forge* and *Big Bad John's* – charging about $4 or $5 admission and open until 2 am. The Forge is a long-standing nightclub and plays mostly live rock and blues music. Big Bad John's is more for country & western fans.

Merlin's Nightclub (☎ 381-2331), at 1208 Wharf St, features rock music. It's on the Inner Harbour, down the stone staircase, opposite Bastion Square; the cover charge is around $4. Amateur comedy nights are held on Thursdays. Merlin's is open Monday to Wednesday from 8 pm to 2 am and Thursday to Saturday from 7 pm to 2 am.

Pagliacci's is popular not only for its food but also for the entertainment it provides. It's the centre for jazz in Victoria but varies this with comedy sessions. For information about jazz around town call ☎ 658-5255.

Pubs If you like a beer then Victoria's pub scene should please you. The Campaign for Real Ale (CAMRA), so successful in the UK in the 1970s in getting big brewers to produce naturally brewed beers and in encouraging some pubs to make their own, had an influence across the Atlantic.

In Victoria there are now a number of 'brew pubs' – pubs that brew their own beer. Admittedly they're a bit trendy but the beer is good.

Spinnaker's, opened in 1984, was Canada's first brew pub. It's at 308 Catherine St, right on the water of Victoria Harbour, off Esquimalt Rd, west of the downtown area. It has a variety of excellent beers made in-house. A pint of Spinnaker's Ale costs $3.30. To get there cross Johnson Bridge into Esquimalt Rd, then turn left into a pathway that follows the shoreline round to the pub. There are good views back towards town. *Swan's Pub-Café*, opposite Johnson Bridge, on the corner of Pandora Ave and Store St, has a variety of homemade beers served in glasses of five different sizes: a taster, the smallest, is $1.20. Two other brew pubs are the *Garrick's Head*, at 69 Bastion Square, and the *Sticky Wicket Pub*.

Casinos If you like to gamble you could try *Casino Victoria* (☎ 380-3998), at 716 Courtney St, or *Red Lion Inn* (☎ 384-2614), at 3366 Douglas St. At both places some of the money you'll probably lose goes to help local charities.

Things to Buy

There are a number of craft shops along Douglas and Government Sts selling Native Indian art and craftwork such as sweaters, moccasins, carvings and prints. Be careful: the good stuff is expensive. There are lots of imitations and lots of junk.

For the best in Native Indian art or crafts, go to Arts of the Raven Gallery, at 1015 Douglas St. Canadian Impressions, at 811 Douglas St, specialises in Native Indian crafts and has some quality items.

Check the prints upstairs, which cost from $25 to around $170. The greeting cards – replicas of the prints, but signed by the artist – make good presents or souvenirs at $4. Canadian Impressions has another shop at the airport.

Sasquatch Trading, at 1233 Government St, opposite the main post office, has a good selection of Cowichan sweaters. These hand-spun, hand-knitted sweaters average about $180 but are warm and should last a decade or more. No dyes are used. The store is open daily from 8.30 am to 9 pm.

Other stores selling quality sweaters are Cowichan Trading, at 1328 Government St, and Indian Craft Shoppe, at 905 Government St.

Gallery of the Arctic, at 611 Fort St, sells and exhibits Inuit craftwork from Cape Dorset, Pangnirtung and other areas of the Arctic. The Art of Man Gallery in the lobby of the Empress Hotel specialises in jade sculptures.

In Fort St, between Blanshard and Quadra Sts, there are numerous antique and bric-a-brac shops.

For chocolate lovers, Roger's Chocolates, at 913 Government St, dating from 1855, offers a treat to both nose and tongue. Try one (or more) of the Victoria creams – chocolate-covered discs in 15 flavours at $1.50. Everything on sale here is made on the premises.

It's open Monday to Friday from 9.30 am to 8 pm, Saturday from 9.30 am to 5.30 pm and Sunday from 11 am to 5 pm.

For general shopping try the Victoria Eaton Centre. It has been expanded, now covers two blocks and has over 140 shops and eateries on four levels. It's open seven days a week and the main entrance is on the corner of Government and Fort Sts.

Market Square, near the harbour, on the corner of Johnson and Wharf Sts, has two storeys of shops and restaurants built around a courtyard shaded by trees. The wooden stairs and balconies make the place seem like part of a pioneer museum.

You will find the Bay department store at 1701 Douglas St. It is open on Monday, Tuesday and Saturday between 9.30 am and 5.30 pm, and from Wednesday to Friday between 9.30 am and 9 pm and on Sunday between noon and 5 pm.

Getting There & Away

Air Some airlines with offices in Victoria are:

Air BC
    1000 Wharf St, Inner Harbour (☎ 388-4521)
Air Canada
    20 Centennial Square (☎ 382-9242)
Canadian Airlines
    615 Broughton St (☎ 382-6111)

If you're flying to Vancouver and beyond, the cost of a ticket from Victoria is just a few dollars more than one from Vancouver itself, so it's not worth paying the ferry price to catch a flight directly from Vancouver.

Air Canada and Canadian Airlines connect the airports of Vancouver and Victoria. However, if you're not taking an onward flight it may be easier to travel with Air BC, which lands in the centres of these cities. The one-way pre-tax fare on Air BC is $73.

Burrard Air (☎ 656-0055/5521) flies to Vancouver for $41 one way; Skylink Airlines (☎ 384-2331) flies to Boundary Bay Airport in Delta, south of Vancouver, for around $26.

Horizon Air (☎ 762-3646 in Seattle; 800-547-9308 toll free), in conjunction with Alaska Airlines (☎ 800-426-0333 toll free), has regular flights to destinations in Alaska and mainland USA.

Lake Union Air (☎ 800-826-1890 toll free) connects Victoria with Tofino, Nootka Sound and Campbell River in central Vancouver Island, the San Juan Islands and Seattle.

Bus The Greyhound Travel Bureau (☎ 385-5248), at the bus depot at 710 Douglas St, is open Monday to Saturday from 8.30 am to 4 pm. The one-way fares on Greyhound to the following destinations are: Calgary ($90.50), Edmonton ($101.50), Kamloops ($48.85), and Winnipeg ($144.50). There are reductions on some of these fares if you book in advance.

Pacific Coach Lines (PCL) (☎ 385-4411) and Island Coach Lines (☎ 385-4411) operate out of the same depot that Greyhound uses. Pacific Coach Lines covers Vancouver Island and some of the southern BC mainland and also runs to Seattle. There's a bus to Vancouver every two hours between 6 am and 8 pm; the one-way fare, which includes the cost of the ferry, is $17.50 It's the same price to Vancouver Airport. To Tsawwassen the fare is $11.25. The bus to Seattle leaves at 11 am and gets there at 5.45 pm. The one-way fare, including the cost of the ferry, is $27.50.

Island Coach Lines covers Vancouver Island. From Monday to Friday there are seven buses a day to Duncan and Nanaimo between 6.15 am and 7 pm. On Saturday and Sunday there's an extra bus at 9.15 pm. From Nanaimo there are three buses to Port Alberni and two to Port Hardy. The fares are to Duncan $7, Nanaimo $12.25, Port Alberni $21, and Port Hardy $62.65.

Train The Esquimalt & Nanaimo Railiner (or E&N Railiner), operated by VIA Rail (☎ 383-4324; 800-561-8630 toll free), connects Victoria with Nanaimo, Parksville and Courtenay. There is one train in each direction per day – northbound from Victoria at 8.15 am, southbound from Courtenay at 1.15 pm. The journey, through some beautiful scenery, takes about 3½ hours.

Some one-way fares are to Nanaimo $14, Parksville $18, and Courtenay $26.

For the full schedule, get a copy of the E&N Railiner pamphlet from the station, a travel agency or the Travel Infocentre. The station, at 405 Pandora Ave, is close to town, right at Johnson Bridge, near the corner of Johnson and Wharf Sts. It's open from 7.30 am to 12 noon and from 1 to 3.30 pm. The name of the train is *Malahat* and reservations are often required.

Ferry BC Ferries (☎ 386-3431, 24 hours), at 1112 Fort St, on the corner of Cook St, runs frequent trips from Swartz Bay to Tsawwassen, on the mainland. The 38-km crossing takes about one hour 40 minutes. There are between 10 and 15 sailings per day: the schedule varies according to the season. The walk-on fare is $5.25, while for driver and car it's $24.50. Bus No 70 from the downtown area to the ferry terminal costs $1.25.

BC Ferries also operates between Swartz Bay and five of the southern Gulf Islands: Galiano, Mayne, Saturna, Salt Spring and Pender. There are about three or four services a day. The fare to the southern Gulf Islands is $1.75 per person, $1.25 for a bicycle and $6.50 for a car.

BC Ferries also links other more northerly islands in the Georgia Strait to towns along the coast up-island. For ferries north to Prince Rupert see Port Hardy at the end of the Vancouver Island section.

For Washington state, there are several alternatives. Firstly, BC Stena Line (☎ 388-7397), at 390 Belleville St, has two ships, the *Princess Marguerite* and the *Vancouver Island Princess*. They ply between Seattle and Victoria's Inner Harbour for US$30 per person one way or US$40 return. Each boat goes once daily and takes 4½ hours. There are slot machines on board.

Faster, at just 2½ hours, are the *Victoria Clipper* and *Victoria Clipper II*, run by Clipper Navigation (☎ 382-8100), at 1000 Wharf St. They sail between Seattle and Ogden Point, not far from downtown Victoria. The clippers are water jet-propelled catamarans and don't take cars. The fare one way is US$43.

The ferry MV *Coho*, operated by Black Ball Transport (☎ 386-2202), at 430 Belleville St, is much cheaper. It sails between the Inner Harbour and Port Angeles just across the Juan de Fuca Strait. It costs US$5.75 per person or US$23 with a car. It's a 1½-hour trip, and there are four a day in each direction during the summer months. From Victoria the ferry leaves at 6.20 and 10.30 am and 3 and 7.30 pm.

Lastly, Washington State Ferries (☎ 656-1531; ☎ 381-1551 in Victoria), at 2499 Ocean Ave in Sidney, has a ferry service from Swartz Bay through the San Juan Islands to Anacortes on the Washington mainland, costing US$7.50 or US$35 with a car. It's a very scenic trip and you can have stopovers on the islands (see San Juan Islands later for more details).

The Travel Infocentre has information on all these possible trips.

Getting Around
To/From the Airport Skyways Airport Service (☎ 384-5604) runs a bus service to Victoria International Airport. It picks up from Harbour Towers, in Quebec St, near the Parliament Buildings; the Courtyard Inn, at 850 Blanshard St; and the Empress Hotel. The 25 km or so trip takes a while and the fare is $10.

City bus No 70 passes within 1½ km of the airport, while a taxi to the airport from the downtown area costs about $25 to $30.

Hustle Bus Airport Service (☎ 388-9916) runs buses to and from Vancouver Airport to meet all scheduled flights. Departures are from the Courtyard Inn Hotel.

Bus For local transit information call Victoria Regional Transit (☎ 382-6161) or get a copy of its guide listing bus routes and fares from the Travel Infocentre. The city buses cover a wide area and run quite frequently: every 10 to 30 minutes. The normal one-way fare is $1.25; it's $1.75 if you wish to travel out to suburbs such as Callwood or Sidney. You can get an all-day pass for $4 for as many rides as you want, starting as early as you like. Bus drivers sell them.

Bus No 70 goes to the ferry terminal in Swartz Bay. Bus No 2 goes to Oak Bay. Also, the circular Explorer Shuttle route takes you around the central core and out to Ogden Point west of the downtown area.

Car For rentals, it's best to shop around before parting with your money. One of the cheapest places is ADA Rent A Used Car (☎ 388-6230), at 892 Goldstream Ave, which rents used cars by the day for $16.95 plus 10 cents per km and $7 insurance.

Another is Rent-A-Wreck (☎ 384-5343), at 2634 Douglas St, where you can rent a car from $19.95 a day plus 10 cents per km and $7.95 insurance.

All the major companies and more are represented in and around the downtown area.

Three of these companies are:

Avis
   843 Douglas St (☎ 386-8468)
Budget
   727 Courtney St (☎ 388-7874)
Hertz
   755 Douglas St (☎ 388-4411)

At Avis the daily rental for a car is $31, with the first 200 km free and 12 cents for every km after that. Budget offers a weekly rate of $119 plus 10 cents per km and Hertz $210 with the first 1400 km free and 12 cents per km after that.

Taxi There are several taxi companies in town. Two to try are Victoria Taxi (☎ 383-7111) and Blue Bird Cabs (☎ 382-4235).

You can also hire three-wheeled bicycle taxis called pedicabs – a more leisurely way of getting around.

Bicycle Downtown you can hire bikes from Harbour Scooters (☎ 384-2133), at 843 Douglas St, adjacent to the Avis car rental office. Cruise bikes are $5 per hour or $10 per day, while mountain bikes are $6 per hour or $18 per day; you must also pay $2 insurance. You could try Explore Victoria (☎ 381-2453), at 1007 Langley St, which has similar prices. Oak Bay Bicycle (☎ 598-4111), at 1968 Oak Bay Ave, has a good selection of bikes. A bike costs $5 an hour or $15 per day.

AROUND VICTORIA
Western Shore
From Metchosin, 25 km west of Victoria, Highway 14 runs through Sooke along the coast to Port Renfrew at the southern end of the West Coast Trail (see Pacific Rim National Park later). There are parks and beaches along the way for walking, beachcombing, picnicking, etc.

At Port Renfrew, often the destination for a day trip from town, the main attraction is Botanical Beach, a sandstone shelf, which at low tide is dotted with tidal pools containing all manner of small marine life: starfish,

anemones, etc. To return to Victoria without retracing your tracks, take the logging road across the island to Lake Cowichan, from where better roads connect with Duncan and Highway 19.

San Juan Islands (USA)
Lying north-west off the coast of Victoria are the San Juan Islands, just beyond the US border, making them a part of Washington state. The big three of the grouping, San Juan Island, Orcas Island and Lopez Island, form a rough circle about halfway between Vancouver Island and the US mainland.

Washington State Ferries connects Swartz Bay in Sidney with Anacortes on the Washington mainland via the islands, making it a very scenic route between these ports. Stops are made at Orcas, Shaw, Lopez and San Juan. Cars, bicycles and kayaks are taken and buses connect Anacortes with Seattle. For information about buses contact Evergreen Trailways (☎ (206) 624-5077) in Seattle.

The islands are very good for cycling around and bicycles can usuallly be accommodated. The ferries sell a very good road map with the topography indicated, and there are numerous campgrounds and guesthouses on the principal islands. Note that you must pass through customs. Also, foot passengers may travel free between the main islands in either direction.

Southern Gulf Islands
Lying north-east of Victoria, off Sidney really, at the top of the Saanich Peninsula, this string of nearly 200 islands is squeezed between the mainland and southern Vancouver Island. The ferry from Tsawwassen edges between a handful of them on its route into Sidney.

With a few important exceptions, most are very small and nearly all of them virtually uninhabited, but this island-littered channel is a boater's dream. Vessels of all descriptions cruise in and out of bays, harbours and marinas much of the year. The fishing is varied and excellent: several species of the prized salmon can be caught in season. BC

Top: Saw logs in Lake Kamloops, British Columbia (RB)
Left: Cascade Lakes, Yoho National Park, British Columbia (JL)
Right: Vancouver Harbour, British Columbia (ML)

Top: Crow Glacier south of Columbia Icefield, Jasper National Park (TS)
Bottom: Icebound fishing boats (CG)

Ferries connects with some of the larger islands, so you don't need your own boat to visit them. The fare from Tsawwassen is $4.25; from Swartz Bay it's $1.75 and between the islands it's $1.75. Before heading to the islands check at the Travel Infocentre in Victoria about activities, accommodation and transport.

Due to the mild climate, abundant flora & fauna, relative isolation and natural beauty, the islands are one of Canada's escapist-dream destinations. Indeed, many of the inhabitants are retired people, artists or counterculture types of one sort or another.

There are cycling routes on the islands: contact the Bicycling Association of BC for details.

Salt Spring Island Salt Spring Island is the largest island in both size and population; its usual population of over 7000 swells to three times that size in summer.

The island has a long, interesting Native Indian history followed by settlement not by White people but by pioneering US Blacks. Seeking escape from prejudice and social tensions, a small group of settlers formed a community at **Vesuvius Bay**. Unfortunately the Native Indians didn't care for them any more than they cared for the British in the area. Still, the Blacks stuck it out, began farms and set up schools. Later immigrants came from Ireland, Scotland and England.

There are three ferry terminals: Long Harbour serves Vancouver and the US mainland; Fulford Harbour and Vesuvius Bay are for ferries plying back and forth to Vancouver Island.

Ganges, not far from the Long Harbour landing, is the principal village and has a summer arts and crafts fair, a few tourist-oriented shops and a Saturday morning market. Artists welcome visitors to their studios – the Travel Infocentre (☎ 537-5252) in Ganges has a list. **Mouat Provincial Park** is here and has 15 campsites.

Mt Maxwell Provincial Park offers excellent views, fishing and picnic areas, while hiking, fishing and wilderness camping can be enjoyed at **Ruckle Provincial Park**, a former homestead. You can also camp at Mouat Provincial Park near Ganges. There is no public transport on the island other than taxi. Bicycles are good but this is a fair-sized island.

There are quite a few B&B places, some of which will have someone pick you up at the ferry terminal. Scattered around the island are resorts – usually with cottages for rent and maybe with some camping, a beach, boat rentals, etc. The cottages range in price from around $40 a night for doubles to $140 for those with fireplaces, hot tubs and other creature comforts. Around the ferry terminals there are also a few motels with singles/doubles for about $50/60.

North & South Pender Islands Together these two islands have a little over 1100 people. Again there are art and craft studios to visit and the ever-present golf course. For beaches, try **Hamilton** on North Pender and **Mortimer Spit** on South Pender (just after crossing the bridge). You might well see some of the more-or-less tame deer around the islands. You can hike and camp at **Prior Centennial Provincial Park** on North Pender, close to **Medicine Beach** at Bedwell Harbour.

Accommodation is mainly in B&Bs and cottages. If you want to splurge you can try the heritage farmhouse *Corbett House* (☎ 629-6205), in Corbett Rd, one km from the ferry terminal. It has singles/doubles for $45/70 including breakfast.

Saturna Island At Saturna Point by the ferry terminal there's a store and pub. There's a good sandy beach at **Winter Cove Marine Park** where you can go swimming, fishing, boating and hiking. At the top of Mt Warburton Pike is a wildlife reserve with wild goats and fine views. There are also good views of the Washington Mountains from the road on the island's leeward side. Just north of Saturna Island is **Cabbage Island Marine Park**, with swimming, fishing and wilderness camping.

Boot Cove Lodge (☎ 539-2254), less than two km from the ferry terminal, has singles/doubles for $40/55 including breakfast. It offers boat and bicycle rentals as well as other meals.

Mayne Island On the ferry to Victoria from the Canadian mainland you squeeze through Active Pass, between Mayne and Galiano islands. Village Bay, on the southern side of Mayne Island, is the ferry terminal, although there are docking facilities for boaters at other points. There are some 100-year-old buildings at Miners Bay, including the museum, which was formerly the jail. There are only a few places to stay, so it's best to book ahead.

Galiano Island Galiano is a good island to visit. Despite its relatively large size, it has only a little under 800 residents stretched along its long, narrow land mass. About 75% of the island is forest and bush.

You can hike almost the length of the east coast and climb either Mt Sutil (323 metres) or Mt Galiano (342 metres), from both of which you can see the Olympic Mountains about 90 km away. If you're willing to tackle the hills, you can go cycling, while Porlia Pass and Active Pass are popular places for diving and fishing.

The coast is lined with cliffs and small bays, and canoeing along the western shoreline is possible in the calmer waters. There's a place that rents canoes and mountain bikes and also offers evening and one or two-day kayak trips along the coast.

There's a Travel Infocentre (☎ 539-2233) at the ferry terminal in Sturdies Bay. Again, local artists and artisans invite visitors to their studios.

There are B&Bs, several places with cottage rentals, and camping at Montague Harbour Marine Park. *Sutil Lodge* (☎ 539-2930) dates from the 1920s and is on the beach at Montague Harbour. It has singles/doubles from $34/45 and offers free use of canoes.

From Tsawwassen there are two ferries daily to Sturdies Bay; from Swartz Bay, there are two a day to Montague Harbour.

DUNCAN & COWICHAN VALLEY

About 60 km north of Victoria along the Trans Canada Highway is the small town of Duncan. It marks the beginning of the Cowichan Valley running westward and containing the large Lake Cowichan. This is the land of the Cowichan people, who comprise BC's largest Native Indian group. They arrived here before White people and, despite some problems, still maintain aspects of their unique culture.

The Travel Infocentre (☎ 746-4421) in Duncan, on the corner of the Trans Canada Highway and Coronation St, is open seven days a week from 9 am to 7 pm. In Lake Cowichan the Travel Infocentre (☎ 749-4141) is open Sunday to Thursday from 9 am to 5 pm and Friday and Saturday from 8.30 am to 8 pm. It has lots of information on the area and Pacific Rim National Park. There really isn't much in Duncan (although the old part of town is worth a look round) or the town of Lake Cowichan but the valley and lake are good for camping, hiking, swimming, fishing and canoeing in. The turn-off for Lake Cowichan is about four km north of Duncan.

Since 1986, Duncan has developed a project with the Cowichans to have totem poles carved and displayed in the town area. There are now more than 20 examples of this west coast art form. The railway station houses the locally oriented **Cowichan Valley Museum**; it's open in summer Monday to Saturday from 11 am to 4 pm. At the **old stone church** near the **Cowichan Native Arts & Craft Shop**, the excellent locally hand-knitted sweaters are available.

Native Heritage Centre

Coming to Duncan from the south along the highway take the first turn left after crossing the bridge, into Cowichan Way. The centre (☎ 746-8119), at 200 Cowichan Way, is 150 metres along on the left. It has exhibits of Cowichan craftwork and carvings which you can see being made. There's a gift shop and the admission price of $5.50 includes a 20-minute movie about the centre. It's open daily from 9 am to 10 pm.

Sawmill Tours
The valley is a logging centre, worked by
several companies. Some of them offer free
tours of their mills. They are: MacMillan
Bloedel (☎ 746-1611), at Chemainus Mill (☎
246-3221); Doman Industries (☎ 748-3711);
and Fletcher Challenge (☎ 246-3241). The
tours run Monday to Friday in summer. At
Youbou, west of Lake Cowichan township,
there's a working sawmill.

BC Forest Museum
This is about three km north of Duncan,
offering on its 40 hectares both indoor and
outdoor features. The museum (☎ 748-9389)
is open daily in summer from 9.30 am to 6
pm and admission is $4.50. There's a stand
of original forest of Douglas firs, 55 metres
tall, that were present before Captain Cook
arrived in 1778. Included in the price is a ride
around the site in a small steam train. You
can visit a bird sanctuary or view a replica of
an old logging camp and logging equipment.
There are also indoor displays and movies of
logging that took place years ago.

Activities
There are many hiking trails around Cowichan River and Lake Cowichan. One is the
Cowichan River Footpath. It's about 18 km
long and there is a good variety of scenery
along the way. You can do it in a day or camp
on the way. The path goes to Skutz Falls;
from there you can head back to Duncan or
keep going up the river. Maps of the trail are
available at sporting stores. The lake gets
warm enough to swim in. You can go fishing
and canoeing in the lake and river.

A good day trip from Victoria is to head
up to Chemainus, back to Duncan, then over
to Lake Cowichan, across to Port Renfrew
and down the west coast back to town. It's a
lot of driving but if you're in no hurry and
can stop a lot it makes an interesting, full day.

Places to Stay & Eat
There are plenty of hotels and motels, especially along the Trans Canada Highway in
Duncan and in the small townships along the
river and lake. One of the cheapest is *Duncan

Motel* (☎ 748-2177), at 2552 Alexander St,
Duncan; it has singles/doubles from $30/35.

Camping is best, however, and there is a
wide variety offered. *Lakeview Park Municipal Campground* (☎ 749-3350) is on the
southern shore of Lake Cowichan about
three km west of the town. It has showers,
toilets and free firewood. A tent site costs
$10. Further west along the lake there is a
government-operated campground at
Gordon Bay Provincial Park with 130 sites
for trailers and tents. The fee is $12. For more
remote camping, some of the forestry companies have set up unsupervised sites mainly
between Lake Cowichan and the west coast
of Vancouver Island. The Travel Infocentres
or the logging companies have more information on these.

In Duncan most of the eating places are
along the Trans Canada Highway but there
are a few small places in the old part of town.
Totem Restaurant, on the corner of Government and Jubilee Sts, serves nothing over $5
and is good for breakfasts.

Getting There & Away
Buses go to Duncan from Victoria for $7.
The 70-minute train trip on the E&N Railiner
costs $8. There is one a day in each direction.

Getting Around
Hitching here and all over the island is
common and accepted.

The area around Lake Cowichan is full of
logging roads, some of which you can use,
though they're often rough; for some advice
and rules, ask at the Travel Infocentres. The
well-used logging road from Lake Cowichan
to Port Renfrew has been gravelled and is in
good shape; with a basic map, you shouldn't
have any difficulty. The detailed maps
showing all the logging roads look like a
dog's breakfast so are more difficult to
follow.

DUNCAN TO NANAIMO
Crofton
About 16 km north of Duncan on Highway
1A is the small town of Crofton, from where
you can catch ferries to Vesuvius in the north

of Salt Spring Island (see Southern Gulf Islands earlier).

Chemainus

Chemainus, 10 km north of Crofton, had a novel and interesting way of putting itself on the tourist map. In 1983 the town sawmill shut down, and to counter the inevitable slow death, a tremendously successful concept was nursed to fruition: murals. An artist was commissioned to paint a large outdoor mural relating to the town's history. People took notice and another mural was painted. Now with over 20 murals and more being added, a bustling and prosperous community has developed, and the sawmill has re-opened. Craft shops have sprung up as well as several new restaurants, all making a short visit a worthwhile proposition.

The Travel Infocentre (☎ 246-3944) is in an old railway carriage on Mill St.

Off the coast at Chemainus are **Thetis** and **Kuper islands**. The ferries leave from Oak St and the ticket office is opposite the Harborside Café; the fare is $2.25, or $6.75 for a car. The ferry to each island takes about 30 minutes from Chemainus. Thetis Island is primarily geared to boaters and has two marinas. There is a pub, however, at Quinn's Marina: turn left when you get off the ferry then left again into Harbour Drive where you see the anchor sign. There's one restaurant, the Pump House, which you can see to the left as the ferry pulls in. At Pilkey Point there are sandstone formations along the beach. Kuper Island is a Native Indian reserve.

Ladysmith

Ladysmith sits on the 49th Parallel which on the mainland divides Canada from the USA. This is a small town about 26 km north of Duncan, on the Trans Canada Highway. The Travel Infocentre (☎ 245-2112) and the Black Nugget Museum, in Gateacre Ave, are in the same building, constructed in 1896 as

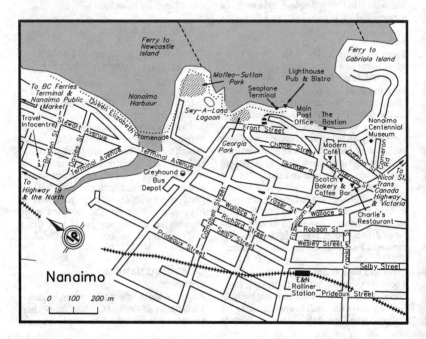

Nanaimo

a hotel. Many of the turn-of-the-century buildings have been or are being restored.

The warmest sea waters north of San Francisco are said to flow at Transfer Beach Park; it's right in town and you can camp there.

About 13 km north of town, off the highway, on Yellow Point Rd, pub aficionados will find the Crow & Gate, the oldest British-style brew dispensary in the province.

Petroglyph Provincial Park

About three km south of Nanaimo on the Trans Canada Highway, this park features some ancient Native Indian carvings in sandstone. As well as the original petroglyphs there are castings from which you can make rubbings.

You can tour a pulp mill and a local cannery in summer. Ask the Travel Infocentre in Nanaimo for details. These tours are interesting and free.

NANAIMO

Nanaimo is Vancouver Island's second major city, with a population of 51,000. Its small-town character is continuing to change into that of a modern city.

A number of Native Indian bands once shared the area, which was called Sne-Ny-Mos, a Salish word meaning 'meeting place'. Coal was discovered here in 1852 and for the next 100 years coal mining was the main industry in the town. Coal has declined in importance, but the city is now the centre of a forest-products industry as well as being a major deep-sea fishing port and a terminal for BC Ferries.

There are a few points of interest in town as well as some in the immediate vicinity.

Information & Orientation

Nanaimo, about 120 km north of Victoria, is a convenient stopover and a departure point to Vancouver and the islands just off Nanaimo Harbour. Behind the harbour is the central core. Most of the restaurants and shops are in Commercial and Chapel Sts and Terminal Ave, which run more or less parallel to the harbour. To the south, Nicol St, the southern extension of Terminal Ave, leads to the Trans Canada Highway. To the north, Terminal Ave forks: the right fork becomes Stewart Ave and leads to the BC Ferries terminal in Departure Bay; the left fork becomes Highway 19, which heads north up-island to Courtney, Campbell River and Port Hardy.

The Travel Infocentre (☎ 754-8474), at 266 Bryden St, just north of the downtown area, has a walking guide of the town's historic area around the harbour. Many of the original buildings have been destroyed and are now marked only by plaques. If you're interested in seeing the ones that are left, get a copy of *Step Into History*, a booklet giving a walking tour of Nanaimo's historic buildings.

The main post office, at 66 Front St, is open Monday to Friday from 8.30 am to 5 pm. Nanaimo Regional General Hospital (☎ 754-2121) is at 1200 Dufferin Crescent, north-west of the downtown area. Hill's Indian Crafts, at 34 Nicol St, sells the famous Cowichan sweaters.

Nanaimo Centennial Museum

The small museum (☎ 753-1821) on 100 Cameron Rd has been renovated and displays things of significance in the growth of Nanaimo. Included are Native Indian, Hudson's Bay Company and coal mining artefacts. It's open Monday to Friday from 9 am to 6 pm and Saturday and Sunday from 10 am to 6 pm. Admission is by donation.

Down the steps is Fisherman's Wharf.

The Bastion

The Bastion, in Front St, on the corner of Bastion St, is the highlight of Nanaimo's old buildings. Built by the Hudson's Bay Company in 1853 for protection from Native Indians, it was never used. It's now a museum and is open daily from 9 to 11.30 am and from 12 noon to 5 pm. Admission is free. From Monday to Saturday at 12 noon and on Friday at 8.30 pm, the cannons are fired over the water.

Parks

There are many parks in and around Nanaimo. The promenade, which takes in a number of them, begins at the seaplane terminal and heads north to Georgia Park, where there are a few totem poles, a fine view of Nanaimo Harbour and a display of Native Indian canoes, including a large war canoe. It then continues to Swy-A-Lana Lagoon (good for children to splash in) and Maffeo-Sutton Park, from where ferries leave to Newcastle Island.

Three nearby spots where you can go hiking or canoeing are Nanaimo Lakes, Nanaimo River and Green Mountain. Hikes from Colliery Dam Park lead to Harewood and Overton lakes. Buttertubs Marine Bird Sanctuary isn't far from the centre of town.

Newcastle Island Marine Park

Just offshore of the downtown area is Newcastle Island, which offers cycling, hiking and beaches. It's also a good place for a picnic or overnight camping. Cars are not allowed. The island was once dotted with mine shafts and sandstone quarries but later became a quiet resort. In summer a small ferry travels between the island and the mainland every hour.

Gabriola Island

Further out into the strait is Gabriola Island, the most northerly of the Southern Gulf Islands. It has three provincial parks offering swimming, fishing and hiking. At Malaspina Galleries are some unusual sandstone caves carved out by the wind and tides. There is a ferry from Nanaimo (see Getting There & Away later).

Bungy Jumping

In August 1990 Nanaimo became the first place in North America where people went bungy jumping. If you fancy diving 42 metres off a bridge into the Nanaimo River secured only by a rubber band then call ☎ 753-5867 for details. It's $95 a jump.

Festivals

The top annual event is the Nanaimo Bathtub Race to Vancouver, held each mid-July as part of the Marine Festival. Hundreds of fibreglass tubs start out, about 100 sinking in the first five minutes.

Through June and July the Nanaimo Festival, which used to be called Shakespeare Plus, presents both classic and modern plays at the Malaspina College south of town. For information call ☎ 754-7587.

Places to Stay

Camping The best places to stay are not in Nanaimo itself but on the islands just off the coast. At *Newcastle Island Marine Park* there are 18 tent sites. Further out is the much larger *Gabriola Island*; there's no camping in the provincial parks but there are private campsites.

North of town are several campgrounds. *Jingle Pot Campsite & RV Park* (☎ 758-1614), at 4012 Jingle Pot Rd, is eight km north of Nanaimo off Highway 19. It has showers and laundry and sites for $10. The closest to town is *Beban Park Campground* (☎ 758-1177), at 2300 Bowen Rd, about 1½ km west of Highway 19, which has sites for $7. *Brannen Lake Campsites* (☎ 756-0404), at 4228 Briggs Rd, is on a working farm; sites are $10.

Hostels Nanaimo has two mini-hostels affiliated with the CHA. The closest is *Nicol St Mini-Hostel* (☎ 753-1188), at 65 Nicol St, several km south of the downtown area. Beds are $10 for members or $12 for nonmembers. *Thomson Hostel* (☎ 722-2251), at 1660 Cedar Highway, is about 10 km south of town. Bus No 11 stops right outside. It offers use of the kitchen and canoes. It's $10 for members or $12 for nonmembers. You can camp on the lawn for $5 per person. The congenial owner will often pick up travellers at the bus station.

B&Bs There are quite a few of these in town: ask at the Travel Infocentre. Rates drop by about $5 per person outside June-September; otherwise singles/doubles are roughly $35/$45.

Motels Many of the motels are on the highway north and south of the city. Four blocks south of the downtown area, is the *Diplomat Motel* (☎ 753-3261), at 333 Nicol St. Singles/doubles cost from $30/35. Two blocks further south is *Big 7 Motel* (☎ 754-2328), at 736 Nicol St, which offers singles/doubles for $30/40. There is a restaurant.

In northern Nanaimo, at 950 North Terminal Ave, is the *Colonial Motel* (☎ 754-4415). It's near the ferry terminal and has free coffee. Singles/doubles cost $33/38; those with a kitchen cost an extra $4. Similar and close by, is the *Bluebird Motel* (☎ 753-4151) at 955 North Terminal Ave. Singles/doubles cost $40/44, and there's a 24-hour restaurant next door.

Places to Eat

Next to the ferry terminal in Stewart Ave, the *Nanaimo Public Market* has many food stalls. Downtown, near the seaplane terminal, is the *Lighthouse Pub & Bistro*, which has good views of the harbour and serves sandwiches, burgers and salads priced from $5 to $7.

In Commercial St, *Modern Cafe* has 'special' sandwiches (ie with a choice of side orders) for $4. *Scotch Bakery & Coffee Bar*, at 87 Commercial St, has great cakes priced from around 70 cents and bread. On the same side and up the hill is *Charlie's Restaurant*, a large spacious restaurant with sandwiches priced from $4 to $6, including fries or potato salad, and burgers for $7.

Getting There & Around

Burrard Air flies to Vancouver for $45 one way. Island Coach Lines (☎ 753-4371) connects Nanaimo with points north and south; the one-way fare to Victoria is $12.25. The E&N Railiner passes through once a day in each direction; the one-way fare to Victoria is $14.

The 39-km ferry trip to Horseshoe Bay take about 1½ hours. There are about 12 to 15 services in each direction daily, depending on the season. Tickets are $5 per person, or $22.50 for a vehicle. The new ferry between Nanaimo and Tsawwassen, the *Mid-Island Express*, goes four times a day in each direction and takes two hours. The terminal is in Departure Bay, at the northern end of Stewart Ave.

Ferries to Newcastle Island leave from Mafeo-Sutton Park and cost $2.50 return. The ferry to Gabriola Island leaves from near the Harbour Square Mall and takes cars for $6.75, but only charges $2.25 if you're walking. After 2 pm you're stuck on the island until the next morning when the ferry returns. The ferry trip takes about 20 minutes.

For information about local buses call ☎ 390-4531.

NANAIMO TO CAMPBELL RIVER
Parksville & Qualicum Beach

These towns and the coast towards Comox are known for long stretches of sandy beach. You can stop by the road, tone up the tan and have a quick swim in the nippy water. There is camping at **Rathtrevor Beach Provincial Park**, three km south-east of Parksville. Mt Arrowsmith, west of town, has skiing in winter, hiking trails in summer.

South of Parksville is Highway 4, the road to Port Alberni and the west coast. You can also connect with Highway 4 from Qualicum Beach via Highway 4A. At Coombs check out the goats grazing on the roof of the general store! Between Parksville and Port Alberni is some very fine scenery with several good places and provincial parks where you can stop a while.

Englishman River Falls Park

This impressive provincial park 13 km south-west of Parksville, at the end of Errington Rd, has waterfalls, hiking, swimming and camping.

Little Qualicum Falls Park

Little Qualicum is another good provincial park a little east of Cameron Lake, with hiking, fishing and camping. Both areas are forested and scenic.

Stamp Falls

At Stamp Falls, nine km north of Port Alberni, salmon can sometimes be seen jumping on their way up the river.

MacMillan Provincial Park

At the western end of Cameron Lake is Mac-Millan Provincial Park. Right by the road is **Cathedral Grove** – a grove of virgin forest with huge Douglas firs and red cedars dating back hundreds of years. This half-hour stop is a must.

There is a campsite on Cameron Lake and petroglyphs at nearby Sproat Lake. Both lakes are in fine settings.

Port Alberni

Halfway across the island is this town built on forestry and fishing. Over 300 commercial fishing boats work out of the area, most catching salmon. At Harbour Quay, at the bottom of Argyle St, there's an observation tower. Also here is the Forestry Visitor Centre, open daily from 10 am to 8 pm. Visitors can tour both the paper mill and the sawmill: for information call ☎ 724-7888.

Hikers can reach Dalla Falls (see Strathcona Provincial Park later) by an alternative route: canoeing the length of Great Central Lake from Port Alberni and taking the trail up from there.

Perhaps the most noteworthy feature of Port Alberni is the MV *Lady Rose*, which sails out of Harbour Quay to the west coast of the island. It's operated by Alberni Marine Transportation (☎ 723-8313). The freighter, which takes mail and cargo as well as passengers, plies between Kildonan on Alberni Inlet, Bamfield at the end of the West Coast Trail, the Broken Islands and Ucluelet. Those planning to canoe or kayak around the Broken Islands can take their boats on board. The ferry company is one place that rents canoes and kayaks.

Fares to Bamfield are $13 one way or $25 return. Fares to Ucluelet are $16 or $32 return. One-day return trips allow passengers some free time at Bamfield and Ucluelet for exploring. On summer Sundays a longer stay in Bamfield is possible.

The freighter departs Port Alberni for Bamfield Tuesday, Thursday and Saturday all year, and for Ucluelet and the Broken Islands Monday, Wednesday and Friday from 1 June to 30 September. In midsummer there are Sunday cruises to Bamfield only. Regardless of the weather, take a sweater and/or raincoat.

Pacific Rim National Park

Of the many parks in the area, this is the granddaddy! A rough, rugged, inhospitable yet beautiful coastal area, the park is a long, thin strip of land divided into three distinct sections. Each is separated by land and water and is reached by a different route.

Whale-watching trips can be a highlight of a visit to the west coast. From mid-February to June Pacific grey whales migrate up the coast from Mexico to the Arctic Ocean; the peak time to catch them heading north is mid-April. In late fall they head back south. At these times you have a good chance of seeing one.

Long Beach The most northerly third of the park is Long Beach. It is the easiest to get to and the most developed. Highway 4, the scenic road from Port Alberni, leads into this park section.

Long Beach is exactly that – about 20 km of wide, log-strewn sandy beach. At other parts, the waves pound into a craggy, rocky shoreline. At each end of Long Beach is a small fishing and tourist village – Tofino in the north, Ucluelet in the south. In summer there are interpretive programmes and guided walks.

There are several short hiking trails in the park; the Park Information Office (☎ 726-4212) will have a description of them. The South Beach Trail leads to an area good for watching and hearing the huge waves roar in. Half Moon Bay Trail leads to a calm, sandy bay. Radar Hill is good for views and has trails leading down to some small, secluded beaches.

Another activity is looking for and maybe watching some of the local marine life. Seals, sea lions and porpoises are common, killer and grey whales a possibility depending on the time of year. Good viewing spots are Schooner Cove, Quistis Point, Radar Hill with its telescope, and Combers Beach near Sea Lion Rocks.

Hundreds of thousands of geese and ducks fly overhead in spring and fall. Also, the pools left behind by the tides are often filled with interesting life forms: starfish, anemones, sponges, fish, snails and many other small creatures.

Long Beach reputedly has the best surfing in BC. Note that the weather is generally poor here. Most days are cold, windy and rainy. A warm, sunny day about a km or so from the coast can disappear into mist and fog at Long Beach. A sweater or raincoat is protection not only against the weather but also against the mosquitoes. The water, too, is cold – those doing any water sports should use wetsuits or drysuits.

In Long Beach there are two campgrounds. The more primitive one is *Schooner Campground*, at the northern end; camping costs about $5. *Green Point Campground* (☎ 726-4245) has showers and flush toilets and costs $11. Both grounds are often full in summer: arrive in the morning to get a place. Around the villages are private campgrounds and some motels.

Tofino At the northern end of Long Beach, just outside the park boundary, is the picturesque fishing village of Tofino, with a winter population of a little over 900 and a summer population of nearly twice that. The Travel Infocentre (☎ 725-3414) is at 351 Campbell St.

There are charters of several types in town. For fishing, check at the MV *Sea Joy* on the Lower Government Dock (Whiskey Dock). It'll cost $35. For sight-seeing charters, try Sea Forth Charter at the Mackenzie Beach Resort (☎ 725-3439), two km south of Tofino. The tours last between two and five hours. For around $30 several boat companies offer boat trips to see Pacific grey whales which frequent the area in spring and summer.

At the dock near Grice Rd you can find

out about seaplane tours. These cost around $30 per person. A good trip is to get the plane to take you to **Hot Springs Cove** where a 20-minute hike will lead you to the hot springs (the only ones on Vancouver Island) overlooking the ocean. There are several pools, which become progressively cooler down the hillside to the sea. You can also get a boat to the cove: contact Coastal Adventures (☎ 725-3777). Overnight camping is possible.

Highly recommended is a trip to **Meares Island**, a 15-minute cruise past the Harbour Islands. This is a magical place of virgin rainforest with trees of mind-boggling age and stature: one is over 1000 years old and nearly 19 metres in diameter. Many are large enough to accommodate a tunnel that cars can pass through. Species include cedar, yew and varieties of spruce. You can arrange trips out to the island at Weigh West Marine Resort (☎ 725-3277), at 634 Campbell St, for $12. One dollar of that goes towards fighting logging plans for Meares. There are several rugged but well-marked trails on the island; the basic loop takes about 2½ hours.

Places to Stay & Eat As well as the campgrounds in Long Beach there are several private campgrounds around Tofino. On MacKenzie Beach *Bella Pacifica Resort & Campground* (☎ 725-3400) has full facilities and sites for $16. *Crystal Cove Beach Resort* (☎ 725-4213) has sites from $12. It also has housekeeping log cottages from $65/80 for singles/doubles. There are several other places offering housekeeping cottages for rent.

Tin Wis Guest House (☎ 725-3402), at 1119 Pacific Rim Highway, two km south of Tofino, on MacKenzie Beach within easy walking distance of everything, has hostel-type accommodation with bunks for $10. Camping is available for $12 to $15. *Dolphin Motel* (☎ 725-3377), three km south of Tofino, is one of the cheapest, with singles/doubles at $35/58.

There are several places to eat at, and the *Common Loaf Bake Shop*, at 131 1st St, is recommended. It has just a few tables but a large selection of excellent, delicious home-made muffins, cookies, breads and cakes from around 70 cents. In the morning try the bran muffins or the still-warm cinnamon buns. The latter are ready at about 11.30 am. The shop's open Monday to Saturday from 8 am to 8 pm and Sunday from 8 am to 7 pm.

Ucluelet Ucluelet (the name is a Nootka word meaning 'people with a safe landing place'), with a population of just over 1500, is more tourist oriented than Tofino and not as attractive. You might like to walk to the lighthouse at **Amphitrite Point**, at the foot of Peninsula Rd, or take one of the trails at **Terrace Beach**.

Subtidal Adventures in Ucluelet is an outfit offering whale-watching trips, at $30 for three hours, in March and April only. It also runs tours around the Broken Group Islands and will drop off people wishing to camp on an island. Scuba-diving cruises and full-day trips to Bamfield are also offered.

Places to Stay Ucluelet Campground (☎ 726-4355) overlooking the harbour, with hot showers and flush toilets, has sites for $14. There are several motels and a couple of simple cheaper hotels. *Ucluelet Lodge* (☎ 726-4324), in Main St, has singles/doubles for $25/30; *Burley's* (☎ 726-4444), at 1078 Helen Rd, has singles/doubles priced from $30/35, including continental breakfast. It has shared baths.

Broken Group Islands The middle section of Pacific Rim National Park, called the Broken Group Islands, is made up of about 100 islands at the entrance to Barkley Sound. The only way to reach this section is by boat from Bamfield, Ucluelet or Port Alberni. There are some primitive campsites on the islands.

This area is popular with canoeists, is good for wildlife and offers some of the best scuba diving in Canada. You can view wrecks in shallow waters and the abundant sea life found around all the islands.

West Coast Trail The third section of the park is called the West Coast Trail. It's a 72-km stretch between Port Renfrew and Bamfield. Either end can be reached by road, but to reach one from the other you've got to walk – and that's a challenge along this rugged, often rain-soaked path.

The trail is clogged with trees, and the camping areas are wherever you can find them. Passing cliffs, beaches and rainforests, the trail takes between five and eight days to travel. You've got to take all your food. The southernmost part is the most rough and difficult. For your trouble you get some spectacular scenery and a test of stamina. The trail has historically been used as a life-saving route for shipwreck survivors. The trail is open between May and October, with July and August being the driest and best months. This is one only for the very experienced hiker.

Bamfield, the village at the northern head of the West Coast Trail, has a Marine Biological Station, a life-saving station and not much else. The West Coast Trail Information Centre (☎ 728-3234) is five km south-east of the village on **Panchena Bay**. Bamfield can be reached by boat from Ucluelet and Port Alberni; the one-way fare on the MV *Lady Rose* from Port Alberni is $13. There is also 100 km of gravel road from Port Alberni. Western Bus Lines (☎ 728-3491; 723-3341 in Port Alberni) operates the Panchena Bay Express, which connects Bamfield with Port Alberni on Monday, Wednesday and Friday; the fare is $13 one way.

There are only a few places to stay. There are two campgrounds. The nearest is eight km east of town and is run by the Ohiaht people. The other is 20 km north of town. *Sea Beam Hostel* (☎ 728-3286) has beds for $15 a night and camping for $10. *Bamfield Trails Motel* (☎ 728-3231) has singles/doubles from $52/55. Most northbound hikers should try to get to town in time to catch a boat to Ucluelet or Port Alberni.

At the southern end of the trail is **Port Renfrew**, which can be reached by dirt road from Lake Cowichan or by a mainly paved road – Highway 14 – along the coast from Victoria. There is a trail information booth

(☎ 647-5434). To reach the start of the trail you must get one of the locals take you across the narrow San Juan River in a boat. Because of the difficult terrain, getting out of the bay here is, well, let's say, one of the less enjoyable segments of the trail northbound. You can camp along the beach in Port Renfrew or there is a hotel with a pub and one B&B. There is also a small store, but supplies are very limited. Botanical Beach, not far from town, is pleasant to pick over at low tide, when you can peer into tidal pools and watch the waves.

Horne Lake Provincial Park

North of Qualicum Beach, off Highway 19, spelunking enthusiasts can explore limestone caves at Horne Lake Provincial Park. From July to early September cave tours of varying lengths and difficulty are given by knowledgeable guides. An admission fee is charged; bring a sweater.

Denman & Hornby Islands

Further up the east coast are two lesser known Gulf Islands – Denman and Hornby. There's good bird-watching on Hornby Island. The ferry for Denman Island leaves from Buckley Bay, about 20 km south of Courtenay, and takes 10 minutes. For Hornby Island you take another ferry from Denman Island. The fare for each is $2 per person, or $5.75 with a car.

Each island has provincial parks, hiking, swimming, fishing and beaches, but only **Fillongley Provincial Park** on Denman Island allows camping. There are several private campgrounds and quite a few guesthouses and B&Bs.

Courtenay & Comox

Basically commercial centres for the local farming, logging and fishing industries, these two towns are also important as supply hubs for Mt Washington 32 km west of Courtenay, and Forbidden Plateau in Strathcona Provincial Park, two major summer and winter recreation areas. Courtenay is the larger of these two essentially adjacent towns. The Travel Infocentre

(☎ 334-3234) at 2040 Cliffe Ave in Courtenay serves both towns.

In Courtenay there is a small museum (☎ 334-3234) at 360 Cliffe Ave, and not far out is the Pantledge River Salmon Hatchery. At the Canadian Air Force base in Comox an annual international air show takes place each August.

There is very good hiking in the area, from afternoon walks to overnight climbs. Miracle Beach Provincial Park (☎ 755-2483), north of Comox, has hiking trails, a campground and a long, sandy beach.

Comox Glacier is a good two-day hike, as is Mt Albert Edward, which offers an excellent view. Ask at the Travel Infocentre for more information. You must register if you're going on an overnighter.

A good circular tour is to take the ferry from Tsawwassen to Victoria on Vancouver Island, travel up the island to Courtenay, go back across to the mainland by ferry from Little River near Comox to Powell River and then down to Vancouver along the Sunshine Coast.

Places to Stay Six km out of Courtenay, at 4787 Lake Trail Rd is the *North Comox Lake Mini-Hostel* (☎ 338-1914), which charges $12.

Meals are available and someone can pick you up at the bus or railway station. It's open all year and in summer there is extra sleeping space in a teepee.

In both towns you'll find numerous motels, and near Comox are several places renting cottages by the beach.

The *Economy Inn* (☎ 334-4491), at 2605 Cliffe Ave, is the cheapest of the lot, with singles/doubles for $28/30. It has a pool.

If you prefer to stay in a B&B, contact Courtenay North B&B Homes (☎ 338-1328), 825 Nikoliasen Rd, Courtenay V9N 6C9.

It offers a reservation service and covers Courtenay, Comox, Campbell River and Quadra Island. Prices average from $30 to $45 for singles and from $40 to $60 for doubles.

NORTH VANCOUVER ISLAND
Campbell River

Campbell River, a major centre for salmon fishing, marks the beginning of the northern part of the island – a less populated, less visited rugged area with lots of opportunities for outdoor activities. Campbell River is also the departure point for Strathcona Provincial Park. The Travel Infocentre (☎ 286-0764), at 1235 Shoppers Row, is open daily from 8 am to 8 pm. In the same building is the Campbell River Museum, open daily from 10 am to 4 pm. Outside is a wooden sculpture of a logger, 'Mike', climbing a cedar tree. The main post office is in Beech St but there's another one in Tyee Plaza.

As well as fishing, activities in the parks and lakes around the town include hiking, swimming, canoeing, sailing and cycling. On Quadra Island just offshore you can see marine and birdlife or the ancient petroglyphs of the Kwakiutl people at Cape Mudge in the south. Cortes Island, east of Quadra Island, has plenty of deserted beaches and lots of wildlife.

Places to Stay West of Campbell River there are government-run campgrounds in *Elk Falls Provincial Park*, on Highway 28, and in *Loveland Bay Recreation Area*, at Campbell Lake. Sites are $8 and $5 respectively. There are also several private campgrounds. RV parks and numerous motels line the highway south of the downtown area. For B&Bs contact Courtenay North B&B Homes (see earlier) or get a copy of the leaflet listing places and prices from the Travel Infocentre.

Getting There & Around Island Coach Lines (☎ 287-7151), on the corner of 13th Ave and Cedar St, runs one bus north daily to Port Hardy and four south to Victoria. Ferries leave regularly from Discovery Crescent across from Tyee Plaza for Quathiaski Cove on Quadra Island. Another ferry departs Heriot Bay on Quadra Island for Whaletown on Cortes Island. For information about local buses call ☎ 287-RIDE.

Strathcona Provincial Park

This is the largest park on the island and is basically a wilderness area – with a few unfortunate exceptions. Campbell River is the main access point. However Mt Washington, just out of the park, and Forbidden Plateau are reached from Courtenay. Highway 28 between Campbell River and Gold River cuts across the park and provides access to campgrounds and some developed trails.

At Forbidden Plateau, in the east of the park, the ski lift runs in summer and there's a restaurant at the top. There are lots of hiking trails, as well as trout fishing in the lakes on the plateau. In winter it's a major ski area.

Two well-known hikes are the Elk River Trail and the Flower Ridge Trail. Both lead to very fine alpine scenery. Like other developed trails, these two are suitable for all age groups. Other less-developed trails demand more preparation and lead to remote areas.

There are many excellent backcountry hiking trails within the park. The Dalla Falls Trail, for example, is a tough two or three-day walk but is great for scenery and ends at the highest falls in North America. You need a good map. Other good walks are those in the Beauty Lake area and one crossing the Big Interior Massif up to Nine Peaks. Camel Ridge apparently has some still unknown species of lichen and alpine plants.

From the highest peaks, such as Golden Hinde (at 2200 metres the highest on the island), Colonel Foster and others in the 650-metre range, you can see both the ocean to the west and Georgia Strait to the east. One thing you won't have to look at is a grizzly bear: there aren't any on Vancouver Island.

Places to Stay *Strathcona Park Lodge* (☎ 286-2008), a resort outside the park on Upper Campbell Lake, has a range of accommodation.

You can camp near the beach for $15 with the use of facilities. Camping equipment can also be rented. Alternatively, you can bed down in a CHA-affiliated hostel (☎ 286-2008) for $12 with use of a communal kitchen. There are also lakefront cottages and apartments, with singles priced from $40 to $85 and doubles or triples priced from $50 to $100. Meals are offered but are not cheap: breakfast is about $7. You can rent canoes, kayaks and bicycles, or go rock climbing, windsurfing, hiking, sailing and swimming. Or you can take organised day trips if you wish. The lodge has an education centre which offers courses in the various outdoor activities. To phone, try the number listed here or call the operator and ask for Campbell River Radio, Strathcona One, H688568.

You can also go wilderness camping within the park along Butte Lake. Sites are $8.

Gold River

In the centre of the island, west of Strathcona Provincial Park, Gold River is the last stop on surfaced roads. The little town is a caving capital and is the headquarters of BC's Speleological Association. Visitors can join spelunking trips to Upana Caves and also to Quatsino Cave, the deepest vertical cave in North America. For more information, ask at the Travel Infocentre (☎ 283-7123) in Village Square Plaza. Summer cruises go to Friendly Cove, where Captain Cook first met the west coast Indians in 1778, and to Nootka Sound. A smaller freighter makes year-round trips to villages in the area.

Valley of 1000 Faces

Along this woodland trail near Sayward, north of Campbell River, are over 1400 figures painted on slabs of cedar. The natural wood grain is used as a base for the image. The slabs are then nailed to trees. Facial portraits, with their wide variety, are best. These paintings are the work of a Dutch-born artist, Hetty Frederickson. Unfortunately the trail is currently closed but may open again. However, there is a gallery which is open; $1.50 is asked for to help maintain the place. It's worth a visit.

Telegraph Cove

East off Highway 19, about eight km south of Port McNeill, this small community is one of the best of the west coast's so-called boardwalk villages – villages in which most of the buildings are built over the water on wooden pilings. It's a good place to go fishing, but its main attraction is the killer whale boat tour to Robson Bight, in Johnstone Strait, which is offered from June to October. It's run by Stubbs Island Charters (☎ 928-3185/17) and is a bit pricey at $55, but you're out for five hours and it includes lunch. Take warm clothing and a camera.

Port McNeill

Three major logging companies have regional offices in this town of 2500 people. You can book fishing charters or go on killer whale tours from here. Port McNeill is the departure point for Cormorant and Malcolm islands and there are several campgrounds, including one near the ferry terminal, and hotels.

Ferries run to **Alert Bay** on Cormorant Island where the Alert Bay Museum and U'Mista Cultural Centre show examples of

Totem Poles

Totem is an Ojibwa word meaning 'guardian spirit' or 'mark of my family'. The word refers to an object, plant, animal or natural occurrence – or its representation – believed to have some connection with a tribe, clan or family group. Originally, totem poles were house corner posts and beams with designs of these totems carved on them. Eventually the totem poles came to signify the chief's prestige which was emphasised by the poles' height and detail. Totem pole carving reached its peak in the second half of the 19th century when Native Indians were able to use the metal tools bartered from Europeans.

The practice was most common among Native Indian peoples along the north-west Pacific coast. Anthony Island in the Queen Charlotte Islands has the largest, original group of totem poles in the world. In Alert Bay on Cormorant Island off Vancouver Island's north-east coast, stands the world's tallest totem pole at almost 52 metres. ■

Kwakiutl art. There are also a few minor historical sites and the world's tallest standing totem pole.

Port Hardy

There's not much in this small town at the northern end of the island, but about 60 km west over gravel road is **Cape Scott Provincial Park**, with swimming off the pristine beaches in San Josef Bay, hiking trails and wilderness camping. Note that the west coast of this northern tip of the island is known for strong winds, strong tides and heavy rain.

Take all supplies and equipment if you're going on camping trips.

The area around Port Hardy has good salmon fishing.

In and around town there are campgrounds, motels and about 20 B&Bs. Check the *Accommodations* guide or ask at the Travel Infocentre (☎ 949-7622), at 7250 Market St, which is open daily from 9 am to 6 pm. Remember the town fills up the night before a ferry is due to depart.

Getting There & Away Island Coach Lines (☎ 949-7532), on the corner of Market and Hastings Sts, has one bus a day to Victoria for $62.65.

Port Hardy is best known as the departure point for ferries through the famed Inside Passage to Prince Rupert. The terminal is three km south of town, at Bear Creek. BC Ferries run the 15-hour 440-km trip along the coast, around islands and past some of the province's best scenery. The ferry leaves every second day at 7.30 am and arrives in Prince Rupert at 10.30 pm. There's a stop at Bella Bella, about a third of the way up. The one-way fare is $80, going up to $245 for a car and $330 for RVs. Please note that to take a vehicle in summer you should reserve well in advance. Binoculars may be useful as you're often close to land. Wildlife viewing is good: possibilities include porpoises, seals, whales and bald eagles.

Once in Prince Rupert you can continue on Alaska State Ferries further north to Juneau and Skagway; catch BC Ferries to the Queen Charlotte Islands; or go by land into the BC interior and up to the Yukon and Alaska.

South-Western British Columbia

At the small town of Hope, 150 km from Vancouver, the road east splits. The Trans Canada Highway goes north up the Fraser River Valley towards Cache Creek. This was the route the old wagon trail took up to the Cariboo gold rush. The road follows the river, which winds and twists through the canyon it has made. As the river is just at the edge of the road, there are many points of interest and viewing areas. The further north you go, the drier the land becomes and the fewer trees there are, until at the Cache Creek area the landscape resembles that of a cowboy movie.

North-east of Hope the Coquihalla Highway heads to Kamloops. It's a wide, straight express route with a $10 toll. Service stations are few, so leave with a full tank. The scenery along the way is pleasant and there are plenty of places to stop. Further west, between Chilliwack and Vancouver, the road is uninterestingly flat and straight. It's more or less an expressway right into the city. There's no point trying to hitch along this stretch, as it's illegal for cars to stop for you.

The Crowsnest Highway (Highway 3) east of Hope heads first southward and then into the Okanagan Valley – the dry, beautiful fruit-growing region of BC. The green hills of the Hope area fade to brown as the road heads towards Osoyoos.

HOPE & AREA

There's not much in Hope itself but it's a good access point for the Fraser River Canyon and southern BC. The Travel Infocentre (☎ 869-7322), at 919 Water Ave, near the river, is a good place from which to collect information. The Greyhound Bus Depot is on the corner of Fort and 3rd Sts; the one-way fare to Vancouver is $11.95. There are several provincial parks close by.

South-east of town, on the Crowsnest Highway, are the remains of the infamous 'Hope slide': in 1965 four people were killed when a small earthquake caused part of a mountain to crumble.

Fraser River Canyon

Fraser River connects Vancouver with central BC; Thompson River is a major tributary. A trip along the steep-sided canyon offers some of the most spectacular scenery in the province.

White-water rafting is a very popular activity down the Fraser and its tributaries' fast-flowing rapids, and a number of companies offer raft trips. Fraser Rafting Expeditions (☎ 863-2336), in Yale, 32 km north of Hope, has river trips of from one ($75) to 10 days ($1640) duration; food is provided. Kumsheen (☎ 455-2296), in Lytton, north of Yale, does trips of from three hours ($62) to three days ($298) duration.

About 25 km north of Yale is the Hell's Gate Airtram, a widely advertised cable-car system that goes down to the rushing Fraser River. Look it over before buying the hype and a ticket.

There are several provincial parks along the canyon. Emory Creek Provincial Park, just north of Hope, has camping, fishing and hiking. You can also camp at Skihist and Goldpan provincial parks north of Lytton.

Manning Provincial Park

This 714-sq-km park in the Cascade Mountains, close to the border with the USA, offers year-round outdoor activities. In the summer there's swimming, fishing, sailing, hiking and wilderness camping; in the winter there's downhill and cross-country skiing, and snowmobiling. The park also has fully serviced campgrounds with sites for $8 or $13. The Crowsnest Highway goes through the park.

The Pacific Crest Hiking Trail begins in this park and goes south all the way to Mexico. See you, good luck!

KAMLOOPS

Sitting at the point where the North Thompson, South Thompson and Thompson rivers meet, Kamloops has always been a service and transport crossroads. In fact the town was once called 'Kahmoloops', a Shuswap word meaning 'meeting of waters'. Today, the Trans Canada Highway cuts east-west through town; the Yellowhead Highway (Highway 5) heads north, Highway 5A heads south and the Coquihalla Highway heads south-west to Vancouver. With this strategic location, the city has grown rapidly since the

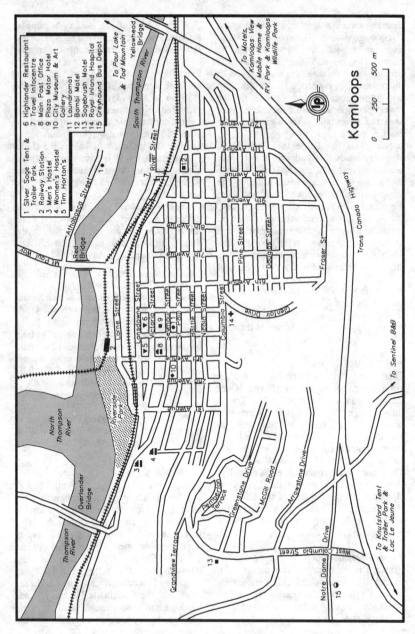

1 Silver Sage Tent &
   Trailer Park
2 Railway Station
3 Men's Hostel
4 Women's Hostel
5 Tim Horton's
6 Highlander Restaurant
7 Travel Infocentre
8 Main Post Office
9 Plaza Motor Hotel
10 City Museum & Art
   Gallery
11 Laundromat
12 Bambi Motel
13 Sagebrush Motel
14 Royal Inland Hospital
15 Greyhound Bus Depot

Kamloops

0   250   500 m

late 1960s and is the major service and industrial centre in the district.

The city is not all business, though. It is surrounded by some 200 lakes, making it a good fishing area. The dry, rolling hills make interesting scenery and excellent ranching territory. This can be a very hot spot in the summer.

Kamloops, with a population of just 65,000, is spread over a very wide area. There are many motels, restaurants and other services in both directions along the Trans Canada Highway. The core itself is quiet, clean and pleasant. Because it sits at a transport crossroads, accommodation is more expensive than might be expected.

Vancouver lies 356 km to the south-west, Calgary 619 km to the east.

Orientation & Information

Train tracks separate the Thompson River's edge from the downtown area. Next to the tracks, running east-west, is Lansdowne St, one of the main streets. The other principal streets are Victoria and Seymour, both parallel to and south of Lansdowne. The Trans Canada Highway is a few blocks further south. On the north-western corner of the city, along Lorne St, is Riverside Park, a pleasant spot for picnicking and swimming. The North Thompson meets the Thompson across from the park's shoreline. Some great sunsets can be seen over the Overlander Bridge from this point.

The Travel Infocentre (☎ 374-3377) is at 10 10th Ave; it's open daily from 8 am to 8 pm. The main post office (☎ 374-2444) is at 301 Seymour St near the corner of 3rd Ave. The Royal Inland Hospital (☎ 374-5111) is at 311 Columbia St. There's a laundrette on Seymour St, between 4th and 5th Aves.

City Museum & Art Gallery

These are in the same building, at 207 Seymour St, on the corner of 2nd Ave. On display are pioneer implements and Salish tools and ornaments. Admission is free. Call ☎ 828-3576 for information.

Kamloops Wildlife Park

This park (☎ 573-3242) is 18 km east on the Trans Canada Highway. Open year round, it has many animals found in Canada's west as well as camels, jaguars, monkeys and other animals from foreign lands. Admission is $4.50.

Activities

You can fish for salmon, trout and steelhead; as a general rule, the bigger the lake, the bigger the trout. **Adams River** is said to have very large sockeye salmon. There is even a Kamloops trout. The lakes and rivers also provide plenty of opportunities for swimming, canoeing, sailing, windsurfing, water skiing and scuba diving.

In winter there's downhill and cross-country skiing. **Tod Mountain**, north-east of Kamloops, off the Yellowhead Highway, is the best spot for downhill, with long, powder-snow runs. Cross-country skiing can be found at **Lac Le Jeune**, 25 km south of town.

Places to Stay

Camping *Silver Sage Tent & Trailer Park* (☎ 828-2077), north-east over the river, is the closest to town and has a laundrette and showers. *Knutsford Tent & Trailer Park* (☎ 372-5380) is south of town, on Highway 5A, about six km from the Trans Canada Highway. All facilities are available, including showers and a laundrette; a site for two people costs $10.

Kamloops View Mobile Home & RV Park (☎ 573-3255) is about 10 km east of town, on the Trans Canada Highway. It has all facilities plus a swimming pool and fishing. A tent site for two people is $10.

You can also camp in two nearby provincial parks. *Paul Lake Provincial Park*, 24 km north-east of Kamloops, has sites for $8, as does *Lac Le Jeune Provincial Park*, 37 km south-west of town.

Hostels The *Men's Hostel*, in West Victoria St, past 1st Ave, offers free accommodation. It's not great and essentially a community service, but it's free and OK for a night or two. The *Women's Hostel*, a block south on Seymour St, charges $10. The YM-YWCA has no rooms.

B&Bs The Travel Infocentre has a folder listing B&Bs in and around Kamloops. You could also try the Okanagan High Country B&B (☎ 542-5493) based in Vernon which provides a reservation service for B&Bs in the region. Some of the cheaper B&Bs are: the *Sentinel* (☎ 374-0841), at 492 Sentinel Court, with rooms for $25 in summer; *Mr & Mrs McKay* (☎ 372-0533), at 2034 High Country Blvd, south-east of the downtown area, with singles/doubles for $25/30; and *Will & Noreen Mather* (☎ 376-3801), at 81 Schubert Drive, north-west of the downtown area, who have singles/doubles for $25/35.

Motels There are two main areas for motels: in Columbia St, west of the downtown area, and on the Trans Canada Highway, east of town. *Monte Vista* (☎ 372-3033), at 2349 Trans Canada Highway, is an old motel with singles/doubles for $32/35. It serves free coffee. *Thrift Inn* (☎ 374-2488), at 2459 Trans Canada Highway, has a heated swimming pool and singles/doubles for $35/37. Rooms have air-con and colour TV. Motels in Columbia St are pricier. One of the cheapest is the *Sagebrush Motel* (☎ 372-3151), at 660 West Columbia St. It has singles/doubles for $38/48, or $51/65 with private bath.

Bambi Motel (☎ 372-7626) is at 1084 Battle St, which runs east-west just south of the downtown core. Single/doubles cost from $32/38. The central *Plaza Motor Hotel* (☎ 372-7121), at 405 Victoria St, has singles for $27 or singles/doubles with bath for $47/52. It has a café and bar downstairs.

Places to Eat
Along and around Victoria St there are several places in which to eat. *Tim Horton's*, at 336 Victoria St, is a fast-food place serving quiche ($3.69 a slice), sandwiches (from $2.55) and cakes (65 cents each). It's open 24 hours a day. The *Plaza Café* in the Plaza Motor Hotel serves breakfasts from $3 to $7 and is open from 6 am to 8 pm. *Highlander*

Restaurant, at 444 Victoria St, has specials like fish & chips and soup for $5, breakfast specials of eggs, bacon, hash browns and toast for $3.80 and salads for around $4.

Getting There & Away
Bus The Greyhound Bus Depot (☎ 374-1212) is south-west of the downtown area, at 725 Notre Dame Drive, off West Columbia St. There are regular buses to Vancouver, Calgary, Jasper, Edmonton, Prince George, Prince Rupert and Penticton. Some sample fares are:

Jasper – $34.15
Edmonton – $66.35
Calgary – $52.05
Vancouver – $31.85
Prince George – $44.30

Train VIA Rail no longer operates a passenger service through Kamloops, but you can take a tour on the privately operated Rocky Mountaineer (see Getting There & Away in Vancouver for details).

Getting Around
For information about local bus routes call Kamloops Transit Service (☎ 376-1216). A one-way fare is $1 and a day pass costs $3.

Okanagan Valley

The Okanagan, a beautiful and unique area of Canada, is a series of valleys running about 180 km north-south in south-central BC. To the east are the Monashee Mountains, to the west the Cascade Mountains. The valleys were carved out by glaciers and are linked by a series of lakes, the largest of which is Okanagan Lake. The varied and interesting landscape makes the entire region very scenic.

The northern end is gentle green farmland that climbs to woods of evergreens. The further south you get, the drier the terrain becomes. Near Osoyoos, close to the US border, cactuses grow on desert slopes that

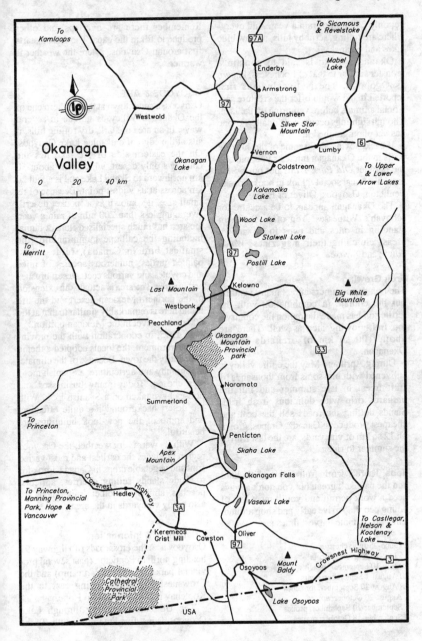

Okanagan Valley

0   20   40 km

To Kamloops

To Sicamous & Revelstoke

97A

Enderby

Armstrong

Mabel Lake

Westwold

97

Spallumsheen

Silver Star Mountain

Okanagan Lake

Vernon

Lumby

6

Coldstream

To Upper & Lower Arrow Lakes

Kalamalka Lake

To Merritt

Wood Lake

Stalwell Lake

Postill Lake

97

Last Mountain

Kelowna

Big White Mountain

Westbank

Peachland

Okanagan Mountain Provincial park

33

Naramata

Summerland

To Princeton

Penticton

Skaha Lake

Apex Mountain

Okanagan Falls

Crowsnest Highway

To Princeton, Manning Provincial Park, Hope & Vancouver

Hedley

3A

Vaseux Lake

Keremeos Grist Mill

Cawston

Oliver

97

To Castlegar, Nelson & Kootenay Lake

Cathedral Provincial Park

Mount Baldy

Osoyoos

Crowsnest Highway

3

Lake Osoyoos

USA

get only 250 mm of rain a year. And everywhere are rolling, scrubby hills, narrow blue lakes and clear sky.

Okanagan Lake is said to contain a monster similar to that of Loch Ness, known as Ogopogo. The Native Indians first reported it and would offer the creature sacrificial animals before venturing on the lake. Though sightings occur occasionally, no-one has yet photographed it.

If backpacking along some of the historic trails in the Okanagan interests you, pick up the booklet *Old Park Trails* put out by the local historical society; look in bookshops in Penticton, Osoyoos, Oliver or Hope.

The Okanagan appears to be a centre for Jehovah's Witnesses. You often see them standing in ones and twos in downtown areas, clutching their magazines, *Watch Tower* and *Awake*.

Fruit Growing

The hot, dry summers attract many visitors, but the climate in combination with the fertile soil has made the region the country's top fruit-growing area as well. There are about 100 sq km of orchards in the Okanagan.

During April and May the entire valley is enlivened with blossoms from thousands of fruit trees. In late summer and fall the orchards drip with delicious fresh fruit. Stands dotting the roads sell the best and cheapest produce in Canada. Grapes, grown on 12 sq km of vineyards, are the last fruit of the summer to ripen.

Jobs There's work fruit-picking; it's hard and the pay isn't great, but you don't always need a work permit and you'll meet lots of young people. Arrive early and shop around. The approximate harvest times are:

25 June-25 July: cherries
15 July-10 August: apricots
20 July-10 September: peaches
20 August-1 September: pears
28 August-30 September: tomatoes
1 August-20 October: apples
1 September-20 September: prunes
9 September-18 October: grapes

Remember there are overlaps and other produce to fill in the gaps. The season starts first around Osoyoos, where the weather is warmer.

OSOYOOS & AREA

Osoyoos, a small town at the southern end of the Okanagan Valley, is unique in several ways. In an area of stark, dry rolling hills, it sits at the edge of dark-blue Lake Osoyoos. On the eastern side of the lake lies the country's only desert, which runs about 50 km northward to Skaha Lake and is about 20 km across at its widest point. Because of its small size, it's known as a 'pocket desert'. Averaging less than 200 mm of rain a year, the area has much specialised flora & fauna, including the calliope hummingbird (the smallest bird in Canada), rattlesnakes, painted turtles, numerous species of mice and coyotes and various cacti, desert brushes and grasses. The area is actually an extension of the northern Mexican desert and the life found here is remarkably similar to that at the 600 metres level in the Mexican portion.

In 1975, in cooperation with the provincial government, the locals adopted a theme to beautify the town. Because of the climate, topography and agriculture, a Spanish motif was chosen. Today many businesses and houses have taken on a Spanish look. With the desert background it's quite effective, and some of the new-look buildings are beautiful.

With its warm, dry weather, the Osoyoos region produces the earliest and most varied fruit and vegetable crops in Canada. Look for roadside stands selling cherries, apricots, peaches, apples and other fruit. There are also many vineyards in the area.

Orientation & Information

Osoyoos is at the crossroads of Highway 97 heading north to Penticton (past several provincial parks where you can camp) and the Crowsnest Highway running east to the Kootenay region and west to Hope.

The US border, cutting through Lake Osoyoos, is just five km to the south. To the west of Osoyoos is Cathedral Provincial Park.

The Travel Infocentre (☎ 495-6052) is slightly north-west of town, on the corner where the Crowsnest Highway branches off westward from Highway 97. The office of the Agricultural Employment Services is at 8523 Main St; it's open Monday to Friday from 7 am to 3.30 pm.

Things to See & Do

The small **museum** (☎ 495-6723) on Main St has displays on natural history, the Inkameeo people, orchards and irrigation. Admission is $1. At 700 metres, just east of town, on the Crowsnest Highway, the **Anarchist Mountain Lookout** offers a superb view of the town, valley, desert, lake and US border. You need a car or a ride to get there.

Less than a km east of town, over the bridge, is **Dutch Windmill** (☎ 495-7318), a replica of one built in Holland in 1816. You can tour the windmill, see grain being ground and buy the delicious bread baked there. The warm water and sandy beaches of **Lake Osoyoos** make it the warmest lake in the country, and good for swimming. **Haynes Point Provincial Park** sits on the lake, two km south of town.

West of Osoyoos is **Cathedral Provincial Park**, a 33-sq-km mountain wilderness area characterised by unusual rock formations. It's accessed by a gravel road off the Crowsnest Highway west of Keremeos.

Places to Stay

Haynes Point Provincial Park (☎ 494-0321) has showers; a tent site costs $12. At *Cathedral Provincial Park* (☎ 494-0321) there's no charge for camping.

The area is chock full of private campgrounds. Though often crowded and not very natural, they are the most economical places to stay. *Cabana Beach Campground* (☎ 495-7705), in East Lakeshore Drive, on Rural Route 1, three km south-east of town, has small cabanas priced from $15 to $30 for doubles, as well as tent and trailer space. Two people tenting costs $12. *Brook Vale Camp-*

site (☎ 495-7514), along the same road, offers the same thing for the same price.

The good-value *Rialto Hotel* (☎ 495-6922) is downtown near the lake. It has colour TV, air-con, restaurant and a pub downstairs. Singles/doubles cost $18/35. *Boundary Motel* (☎ 495-6050) is on Rural Route 2, close to the border with the USA. Singles/doubles cost $26/28. There are many more motels along 83rd St (Crowsnest Highway) east of the downtown area, over the bridge.

PENTICTON

Penticton, the southernmost of the three Okanagan sister cities, sits between Okanagan Lake and Skaha Lake which are connected by Okanagan River. The sun shines for an average of 600 hours in July and August – about 10 hours a day – and that's more than it shines in Honolulu! It's not surprising, then, that the number-one industry is tourism.

To the Salish, Pen-Tak-Tin means 'place to stay forever', an idea that many White people took to heart. Between 1975 and 1985 the population rose from 13,000 to 25,000 but has remained steady since then. Penticton became a townsite in 1892, when several nearby mine claims were being developed. The Canadian Pacific railway made it a freight terminal and fruit companies started buying up land in early 1900. The industries grew and by the 1930s Penticton's location and climate was gaining a reputation. It soon became a vacation destination.

There is not a lot to do here, but this land of peaches and beaches is a good spot in which to cool your heels for a day or two.

Orientation

The downtown area lies just south of Okanagan Lake. Most of the land along the lake is park. Lakeshore Drive runs west through this land from the downtown area to Riverside Drive and Highway 97. The main street is Main St, running north-south; at the southern end it forks: to the left (east) it becomes South Main St, to the right (west) it becomes Skaha Lake Rd, which then turns into Highway 97.

The downtown area extends for about 10 blocks southward from the lake. Martin St to the west and parallel to Main St is also important. Running west-east, Westminster, Nanaimo and Wade Aves are the principal thoroughfares. Most of the restaurants and bars are in this area. This central area is small and easy to get around.

Information
The Travel Infocentre (☎ 492-4103) is in the Jubilee Pavilion of the Chamber of Commerce, at 185 Lakeshore Drive. There's another on the corner of Westminster and Eckhardt Aves and one on Highway 97 south of town. The main post office (☎ 492-5717) is on the corner of Nanaimo Ave and Winnipeg St. Penticton Regional Hospital (☎ 492-4000) is south of the downtown area, at 550 Carmi Ave.

For fruit-picking information contact Agricultural Employment Services (☎ 493-3727) 212 Main St.

Beaches
Close to the downtown area, **Okanagan Beach** is about 1300 metres long. It's sandy and the water temperature is about 22°C. Near the Travel Infocentre you can rent windsurfers from Roli's (☎ 493-0244) for $11 an hour (lessons are available as well). This end of the Okanagan Lake has some of the best windsurfing conditions in the Okanagan Valley. You can also go parasailing: you start on the beach and a speedboat pulls you up 50 metres into the air. People say the feeling and the view are worth the money. Contact H & H Parasailing (☎ 492-6068).

At the southern end of town **Skaha Beach** is about 1½ km long and has sand, trees and picnic areas. At the marina you can hire boats from $20 an hour from Skaha Lake Rentals (☎ 492-0600).

Casabello Wines
This winery (☎ 492-0621), at 2210 Main St, offers free tours that include taste samples.

It's near the turn-off for Skaha Lake Rd. It's closed on Sunday.

Dominion Radio Astrophysical Observatory
Seen many of these lately? The observatory contains radio telescopes that receive radio waves from outer space. The waves are then amplified and analysed to provide information that conventional equipment cannot. Tours are given on Sunday between 2 and 5 pm in July and August. At other times you can see the equipment and hear a recorded explanation. It's on White Lake Rd, about a 15-minute drive from the first turn south of Kaleden Junction on Highway 97.

Agricultural Research Station
This centre was designed for the study of fruit trees, their growth, diseases and production. There is an ornamental garden displaying a variety of plants and trees, as well as picnic grounds. It's 11 km north of town, on Highway 97.

Summerland Trout Hatchery
You can tour the Summerland Trout Hatchery (☎ 494-3346), at 13405 Lakeshore Drive, from 8.30 to 11.30 am and from 1.30 to 4.30 pm all year for free. Summerland is one of three BC hatcheries used to stock lakes. Here they concentrate on rainbow, eastern brook and kokanee trout.

Okanagan Game Farm
On 2¼ sq km of semidesert overlooking Skaha Lake, this game farm (☎ 497-5405) has about 650 animals of 130 species, including Canadian and more exotic animals. It's eight km south of Penticton, on Highway 97, and is open all year from 8 am to dusk. Admission is $7, or $5 for students.

Wonderful Waterworld
North of Skaha Lake you'll find adults' and children's waterslides at Wonderful Waterworld (☎ 493-8121), at 225 Yorkton Ave. Full-day tickets cost $9. It's open in summer from 10 am to 10 pm daily.

Skiing

For skiing enthusiasts, Apex Alpine Ski Resort (☎ 492-2880), a 30-minute drive west of Penticton, off Green Mountain Rd, has cross-country trails and more than 36 downhill runs.

Festivals

The city's premier event is the Peach Festival, a week-long event that has taken place around the beginning of August since 1948. There are sports activities, novelty events, music and dance, nightly entertainment, and a major parade held on Saturday.

The week following the festival is the Annual British Columbia Square Dance Jamboree. It goes on for six nights from 8 to 11 pm, and about 3500 dancers take part. There's an enormous dance floor in Kings Park. There are also street dances, dances held at both lakes – in the water! – pancake breakfasts and other activities.

At the end of August athletes are put through their paces in the Ironman Ultradistance Triathlon.

Places to Stay

The beach closes at midnight and stays that way until 6 am. If you try to sleep on it you'll probably be rudely awakened by the police. There is no hostel or YMCA, so budget travellers are stuck with the usual alternatives.

Camping There are many tent and trailer parks, especially south of town, around Lake Skaha. Many are just off Highway 97. Most are about $12 to $16 for two people in a tent. This is in no way wilderness camping, but is a cheap place to stay. The Travel Infocentre has a complete list.

B&Bs The Travel Infocentre also has a list of local B&Bs. One that's been going a long time is *Apex Ranch* (☎ 492-2454) in Green Mountain Rd, 22 km west of Penticton. Singles/doubles cost $30/35. It's close to the ski resort and offers horseback riding and hiking.

Hotels There aren't many hotels in Penticton and they're not cheap. *Three Gables Hotel* (☎ 492-3933), at 353 Main St, is the most reasonable one, with singles/doubles for $45/50. It's right in the centre of town, three blocks south of Okanagan Lake, and has a good pub downstairs. Right on the shore of Okanagan Lake, at 21 Lakeshore Drive West, is *Lakeside Resort* (☎ 493-8221), one of the top places in town. It's expensive, however, with singles/doubles costing $110/170.

Motels Penticton is chock full of motels with Lakeshore Drive/Riverside Drive and South Main St/Skaha Lake Rd being the two main areas. *Kozy Guest House* (☎ 493-8400), at 1000 Lakeshore Drive, is a motel fronting Okanagan Lake. It has free coffee and air-con and singles/doubles cost $26/50. Also fronting the lake but closer to the downtown area is the more expensive *Slumber Lodge Motel* (☎ 492-4008), at 274 Lakeshore Drive, where singles/doubles cost $60/65.

At *Holiday House Motel* (☎ 492-8422), at 3355 Skaha Lake Rd, singles/doubles cost $38/46. *Paradise Valley Motel* (☎ 492-2756), at 3118 Skaha Lake Rd, has singles/doubles from $32/49. Both have air-con and are close to Skaha Lake Beach.

Places to Eat

Nearly all the downtown restaurants are on Main St, but there isn't a lot of choice. Many of the chain-store restaurants are also on Main St, south of Duncan Ave.

The *Elite*, at 340 Main St (the restaurant with the 1950s Las Vegas-type sign outside) serves standard fare. Eggs with hash browns and toast cost $5, while omelettes cost from $4.50; it has three-course specials for $7. It's open daily from 6 am to 12 midnight. At *Taco Grande*, at 452 Main St, the food isn't great but its cheap and filling. Tacos, burritos, enchiladas are priced from $3 to $4 each. It also serves taco burgers, salads and Mexican-style pizzas. *Grandma Lee's* is a cheap, cafeteria-style café diagonally opposite the Three Gables Hotel. It offers soup and salad for $3, or soup and a sandwich for $4.

Pepperoni's, in Main St, near the corner of Nanaimo Ave, has pizzas priced from $5 to $15, salads priced from $2 to $6 and pasta dishes for $7.

Edible Dried Goods, at 407 Main St, sells fruit leather, which is a blend of fruit purees dried into thin sheets and pressed together. It's great for backpacking and hiking. The store also sells spices, nuts and grains and is open every day.

Entertainment
Tiffany's, at 535 Main St, is the rock-music place in town, bringing in bands from Vancouver. There's usually a cover charge of $3 or $4. Nearby is *Down Under Nite Club*, which has rock & roll and opens at 8.30 pm. *Nite Moves* is a disco next to the Three Gables Hotel. A quieter spot at night or during the day is the large pub-like bar open from 10.30 am in the *Three Gables Hotel*.

Getting There & Around
There is no railway station. The Greyhound Bus Depot (☎ 493-4101) is at 307 Ellis St, on the corner of Nanaimo Ave, one block east of Main St. Buses depart regularly for Vancouver, Banff, Calgary, Prince George, Kelowna and Vernon. Some sample fares are to Banff $47.30, Prince George $63.35, Vancouver $31.95, and Vernon $9.85.

For local bus information contact Penticton Transit (☎ 492-5602), or visit the Travel Infocentre and pick up a copy of the leaflet *Penticton Rider's Guide*, which lists routes and fares. The one-way fare is 65 cents and a day pass is $1.75. City buses go from town to both beaches. Bus No 202 from the corner of Wade Ave and Martin St goes down South Main St to Skaha Lake. There are no buses on Sundays or holidays, except for the summer lake-to-lake shuttle.

KELOWNA
Kelowna is one of the most pleasant small cities in the country. It sits halfway down Okanagan Lake, midway between Vernon and Penticton. All around are the rounded,

scrubby hills typical of the valley. Closer to town they become greener, with terraced orchards lining their slopes and, unusually, the greenest area is the town itself, with its many parks and gardens. Beneath skies that are almost always clear, sandy beaches rim the dark blue water of the lake.

There are nearly 2000 hours of sunshine here each year. Summer days are usually hot but the nights are pleasantly cool. Winters are not harsh either. The combination of excellent weather and a good water supply makes Kelowna an ideal fruit and wine-producing area as well as a popular tourist destination. The dry, mild climate attracts both young and retired people.

Kelowna is the largest city in the Okanagan, with 70,000 people. As the hub of the fruit-growing area, and with an important lumber and wine industry, it is a valuable economic centre. Tourism is important too and the town has a distinct resort feel.

The city's name is a Salish word meaning 'grizzly bear'. A number of Oblate missionaries arrived in 1858. One of them – Father Pandosy – established a mission and planted the area's first apple trees. He has become Canada's lesser known equivalent of the USA's Johnny Appleseed. It was the success of his work that led to the first full-scale planting of apples, which was done in 1890. In 1892 the townsite of Kelowna was drawn up and today it is in the centre of Canada's largest fruit-growing district.

Orientation
The large City Park on the lake's edge forms the western boundary of town. Starting from the big white modern sculpture 'Sails' and the model of Ogopogo at the edge of City Park, Bernard Ave runs east and is the city's main drag. Other important thoroughfares are Water, Pandosy and Ellis Sts, all running north-south. South of town Pandosy St becomes Lakeshore Rd. Highway 97, called Harvey Ave in town, is the southern edge of the downtown area; it heads westward over the bridge towards Penticton.

At the northern end of Pandosy St, where

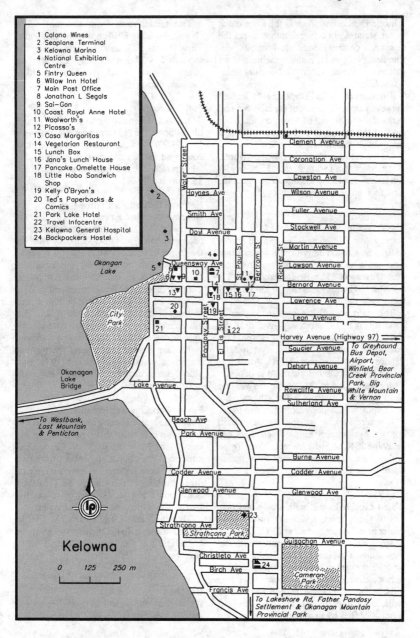

1 Calona Wines
2 Seaplane Terminal
3 Kelowna Marina
4 National Exhibition
  Centre
5 Fintry Queen
6 Willow Inn Hotel
7 Main Post Office
8 Jonathan L Segals
9 Sai–Gon
10 Coast Royal Anne Hotel
11 Woolworth's
12 Picasso's
13 Casa Margaritas
14 Vegetarian Restaurant
15 Lunch Box
16 Jana's Lunch House
17 Pancake Omelette House
18 Little Hobo Sandwich
   Shop
19 Kelly O'Bryan's
20 Ted's Paperbacks &
   Comics
21 Park Lake Hotel
22 Travel Infocentre
23 Kelowna General Hospital
24 Backpackers Hostel

Clement Avenue
Coronation Ave
Cawston Ave
Wilson Avenue
Fuller Avenue
Stockwell Ave
Martin Avenue
Lawson Avenue
Bernard Avenue
Lawrence Ave
Leon Avenue
Harvey Avenue (Highway 97)

Haynes Ave
Smith Ave
Doyl Avenue
Queensway Ave

Water Street
St Paul St
Bertram St
Richter St
Pandosy Street
Ellis Street

Okangan Lake

City Park

Okanagan Lake Bridge

To Westbank,
Last Mountain
& Penticton

To Greyhound
Bus Depot,
Airport,
Winfield, Bear
Creek Provincial
Park, Big
White Mountain
& Vernon

Saucier Avenue
Dehart Avenue
Rowcliffe Avenue
Sutherland Ave

Lake Avenue
Beach Ave
Park Avenue
Burne Avenue
Cadder Avenue
Cadder Avenue
Glenwood Avenue
Glenwood Ave
Strathcona Ave
Strathcona Park
Guisachan Avenue
Christleto Ave
Birch Ave
Cameron Park
Francis Ave

To Lakeshore Rd, Father Pandosy
Settlement & Okanagan Mountain
Provincial Park

Kelowna

0   125   250 m

it meets Queensway Ave, is the town clock tower, standing in a fountain that marks the new civic centre. Beside the fountain, surrounded by flowers, is the museum and art gallery contained within the National Exhibition Centre.

There are 65 parks in the city area, including seven along the shore of the lake. Several parks are south-west of town, on the other side of the bridge. The beach continues a long way in this direction.

On the eastern side of the downtown area, along roughly a 15-km stretch, Highway 97 is a commercial strip lined with gas stations, junk food spots and motels.

Information

The Travel Infocentre (☎ 861-1515), at 544 Harvey Ave (Highway 97), near the corner of Ellis St, is open daily from 8 am to 8 pm. Another is on the western side of the lake, near Okanagan Lake Bridge, and there's a third on Highway 97, about 10 km north of town, near the airport.

The main post office is on the corner of Pandosy St and Queensway Ave, near the clock tower. Kelowna General Hospital (☎ 762-4000) is south of Harvey Ave, at 2268 Pandosy St, on the corner of Royal Ave. Most of the banks are on Bernard Ave, between Water and Ellis Sts. At 269 Leon Ave, one block up from City Park, is Ted's Paperbacks & Comics, a used-book store that will trade.

If you're looking for fruit-picking work, contact Agricultural Employment Services (☎ 860-8384), at 591 Lawrence Ave. There is also some information posted on the notice board at the Greyhound Bus Depot.

City Park

It's an excellent park, with sandy beaches, lots of shady trees, and water just slightly cooler than the summer air at 23°C. There are flower gardens and tennis courts; with the view across the lake, it's no wonder would-be fruit pickers are sitting around picking only guitars. Frisbees fill the air, boys toss girls in the lake, some people strut, some work overtime on the tan and the odd waterskier flies by in a foamy wake.

The beach runs from the marina to **Okanagan Lake Bridge** west of City Park. This is Canada's longest floating bridge; it's supported by 12 pontoons and has a lift span in the middle so boats up to 18 metres high can pass through.

Fintry Queen

At the foot of Bernard Ave, behind the model of Ogopogo, the old ferry boat *Fintry Queen* (☎ 763-2780) is moored in the lake. Now converted into a restaurant, it also provides lake cruises. The two-hour cruise alone costs $8. Lunch only is $7.

National Exhibition Centre

Housing the museum (☎ 763-2417) and art gallery (☎ 762-2226), this is part of the civic centre complex, at 470 Queensway Ave, on the corner of Pandosy St. It features a reconstructed Salish underground winter home. Other exhibits in the National Exhibition Centre include an old stagecoach and models of some of the town's first buildings and stores, stocked with goods and relics. The museum is open from 10 am to 5 pm Monday to Saturday and from 2 to 5 pm on Sunday.

The art gallery has a small permanent collection, mainly of the works of BC artists, plus regularly changing displays. Admission to both is free.

Father Pandosy Settlement

This is the major historic site in the area. On the spot where this Oblate priest set up his mission in 1859 are some of the original buildings. The church and school from that time have been restored, as have a couple of other buildings: the barn, one furnished house and a few sheds from what was the first White settlement in the Okanagan.

The site is small, and there's not a lot to see, but it's free. To get there, go south along Lakeshore Rd, then east on Casorso Rd to Benvoulin Rd. It's open from 8 am to sundown.

Beaches

As well as the beach in town, there are several beaches south of Okanagan Lake

Bridge along Lakeshore Rd. You could walk this far. Some of the campgrounds along the lake also have beaches.

Activities
Fishing is possible on Okanagan Lake and many of the 200 lakes near Kelowna. Windsurfers leave from the old seaplane terminal near the corner of Water St and Cawston Ave. From Kelowna Marina you can take cruises or fishing trips.

About 8½ km north-west of Kelowna, **Bear Creek Provincial Park** also has windsurfing as well as fishing, swimming, hiking and wilderness camping. The 10½-sq-km **Okanagan Mountain Provincial Park**, south of Kelowna off Lakeshore Rd, is a popular spot for hikers and horse riders. Many of the trails date from the days of the fur trade. Okanagan Canoe Holidays (☎ 762-8156), at 2910 Glenmore Rd, has one-day and one-week trips, white-water rafting and teaching clinics.

For skiers there's **Big White Mountain**, west of Kelowna, off Highway 33; or south-east of town, in Westbank, off Highway 97, there's **Last Mountain**, which has night skiing.

Wine & Whisky Tours Wine tours are one attraction you might not want to miss. There are seven wineries in BC and five of them are in the Okanagan. From Kelowna southwards, there are 12 sq km of vineyards. Several companies are near Kelowna. They offer tours and free samples.

Calona Wines (☎ 762-9144), at 1125 Richter St, right in Kelowna, is BC's largest producer and was the first in the Okanagan: it started in 1932. In Westbank, about 13 km south-west of Kelowna, is Mission Hill Winery (☎ 768-7166). It's on Rural Route 1, in Mission Hill Rd, off Boucherie Rd, and has tours, tastings and sales. Cedar Creek Wineries (☎ 764-8866), at 5445 Lakeshore Rd, has won international awards for its wine.

Hiram Walker Okanagan Distillery (☎ 763-4922), in Jim Bailey Rd, Winfield, north of Kelowna, is the home of Canadian Club

whisky and has free tours and tastings Monday to Friday.

Places to Stay
Camping is the cheapest way to stay in the area, though you'll be a fair way from town. Most of the motels are along Highway 97, north of the downtown area. There aren't many hotels so staying right in the city can be a problem in summer. It's a good idea to book in early as places fill up fast. There is a hostel now, though, which should make things a bit easier for budget travellers.

Camping The best place to camp is *Bear Creek Provincial Park* (☎ 494-0321), which has full facilities including showers and laundry. A site is $12.

There are numerous privately owned places around Kelowna, especially in Westbank and south along Lakeshore Rd. The grounds are usually crowded and the sites close together.

To get to Westbank, head west along Highway 97 over Okanagan Lake Bridge then turn off at Boucherie Rd. Follow this for quite a while and you'll hit the so-called resort area. This area is quite far from town – you'll need a car. Sites here cost between $10 and $13.

About six km south of the city, at 3327 Lakeshore Rd, is *Tiny Town Tent & Trailer Park* (☎ 762-6302). It's on the beach and has showers and bike rentals; sites are $12. Also on the beach, a littler further south, is *Shady Lane Campground* (☎ 764-4032), at 4576 Fuller Rd, west off Lakeshore Rd. It's open from mid-May to mid-September and has sites for two people at $12.

Hostel The *Gospel Mission*, in Leon Ave, is a good, clean and free hostel. It's not really set up for travellers but rather offers a helping hand for those in need.

The *Backpackers Hostel* (☎ 763-6024) is just south of the general hospital, at 2343 Pandosy St – a short walk from the beach. It costs $10 for a dormitory bed here. Breakfast costs extra and they serve free coffee, there are showers, and there's no curfew.

B&Bs Contact Okanagan B&B (☎ 768-4469), PO Box 5135, Kelowna, V1Y 8T9, for information about staying in B&Bs, or ask at the Travel Infocentre. Most places have singles/doubles for around $35/40.

Hotels There are no cheap hotels in Kelowna. Downtown, the *Willow Inn Hotel* (☎ 762-2122), at 235 Queensway Ave, on the corner of Abbott St, is right by City Park and the lake. It has a restaurant and bar on the premises, but is not recommended for female travellers. Singles/doubles are priced from $42/50.

Close by and better is *Park Lake Hotel* (☎ 860-7900), at 1675 Abbott St, which has air-con singles/doubles with TV, free movies and minibars priced from $55/60. *Coast Royal Anne Hotel* (☎ 860-7200), at 348 Bernard Ave, is more up-market, with singles/doubles priced from $100/110.

Motels There are some good choices north along Highway 97, not far past the Highway 33 junction. *Western Budget Motel* (☎ 763-2484), at 2679 Highway 97 North, is the cheapest, with singles/doubles priced from $25/28.

The *Town & Country Motel* (☎ 860-7121), situated at 2620 Highway 97 North, has singles/doubles for $43/48 with air-conditioning and TV. It also has a pool and sauna. *Ponderosa Motel* (☎ 860-2218), at 1864 Highway 97 North, is reasonable, with singles/doubles including kitchen priced from $34/38.

Places to Eat

Many of the eateries are in Bernard Ave. *Woolworth's*, on the corner of Bernard Ave and St Paul St, has a standard very cheap cafeteria; sandwiches are $2. The *Pancake & Omelette House*, opposite Woolworth's, is open every day and has good breakfast specials of two eggs, toast and hash browns for $3. It has all types of pancakes and omelettes, priced between $3 and $5.

Next door is *Jana's Lunch House*, which sells German-style food; schnitzels are $4.50, and the delicious cakes are $1.

Between Pandosy and Ellis Sts, at 467 Bernard Ave, is the *Vegetarian Restaurant*, which serves good food at reasonable rates. Freshly made soup costs $1.70, while salads are priced from $1.70 to $4, sandwiches from $2.70 and freshly squeezed juices from $1.50 to $2. At the *Lunch Box*, in Bernard Ave, near the corner of Ellis St, you can sit outside and take your choice of sandwiches for $4 and pies such as chicken and asparagus for $2.50.

Between Water and Mills Sts there's a cluster of restaurants in the middle-range price bracket. *Casa Margaritas* serves Mexican food; tacos cost $5 and main dishes are priced from $10 to $14. The Vietnamese *Sai-Gon* has spring rolls for $5, shrimp for $4.50 and beef and shrimp for $20.

Jonathan L Segals has specials of spare rib or seafood with soup and salad for $8. You can eat on the roof, from where you get a good view of the lake.

East along Bernard Ave, on the corner of Bertram St, is *Picasso's*, which serves tapas for $2.50. Pasta dishes are priced from $6 to $9 and lamb curry is $10. The food is good and the restaurant offers a wide range of beers and local wines.

The *Little Hobo Sandwich Shop*, at 438 Lawrence Ave, specialises in sandwiches of all kinds and is very popular with office workers. It's open from 7.30 am to 2 pm every day except Sunday. There's another at 1626 Richter St.

Kelly O'Bryan's, in Lawrence Ave, opposite the Little Hobo Sandwich Shop, has pasta, seafood and beef dishes. Fettucini costs $8 as does a steak sandwich, and you eat to the strains of Irish music.

Entertainment

The Sunshine Theatre Company (☎ 763-4922/4302) puts on a range of productions during the summer at the *Kelowna Community Theatre*, on the corner of Water St and Doyle Ave. Every summer Sunday afternoon there are free music concerts in City Park.

The *Coast Royal Anne Hotel*, though an expensive place to stay at, contains a very popular bar downstairs. It's frequented by all types, mainly young, and has cheap beer, pool tables and pinball. The bar is busy during the day, too. Groups of French people from Quebec meet here as well as visitors, workers and locals. *Cave Nightclub* (☎ 763-1199), at 427 Leon Ave, has rock music nightly from 7 pm to 2 am. There's a $4 cover charge.

Getting There & Away

Air The airport is about 20 km north of town, on Highway 97. Air BC, Air Canada, Canadian Airlines, Shuswap Air and Time Air all fly into Kelowna. There are daily flights to and from Vancouver, Calgary and Edmonton; the pre-tax one-way fares with Canadian Airlines are $141, $181 and $217 respectively.

Bus The Greyhound Bus Depot (☎ 860-3835) is north of the downtown area, at 2366 Leckie Rd, off Highway 97. To get there, take city bus No 110 from the corner of Bernard Ave and Ellis St. It goes back and forth roughly every half hour from 6.30 am to 9.30 pm. The depot is open from 6.30 am to 10.30 pm daily.

There are five buses to Penticton and Vancouver daily, two to Osoyoos, two to Vernon and Kamloops, two to Prince George, Prince Rupert and Dawson Creek and two to Revelstoke and Calgary. Some sample one-way fares are to Calgary $53.80, Prince George $52.16, Prince Rupert $106.25, and Vancouver $30.15.

Hitching If you're hitching south, walk over Okanagan Lake Bridge and start; northbound on Highway 97, begin west of the commercial strip.

Getting Around

To/From the Airport The Airporter bus (☎ 764-8519) shuttles between town and the airport. The one-way fare is $5.50 and the bus stops at the larger hotels as well as at other places on request. The one-way fare in a taxi is about $18.

Bus For information about local buses call Kelowna Transit Systems (☎ 860-8121); there are three zones and the one-way fare in the central zone is 70 cents.

Car The Travel Infocentre sometimes has promotional coupons giving discounts on the cost of rental cars: those worth $5 apply to Budget (☎ 860-2464), at 1553 Harvey Ave, and Tilden Rent-A-Car (☎ 861-5242), at 1140 Harvey Ave; those worth $11 apply to Thrifty Car Rentals (862-9091), at 1980 Springfield Rd. Thrifty rents cars at $41.95 per day ($30.95 with the coupon); the first 100 km are free, and it's 17 cents per km after that. Budget is slightly dearer, at $43.95 per day. They all offer free pick-ups and drop-offs.

Taxi Most of the local taxi companies are on Kirschner Rd, west of the downtown area. You could try Kelowna Cabs (☎ 762-4444/2222/1433), at 1943 Kirschner Rd, or Checkmate Cabs (☎ 861-4445), at 1854 Kirschner Rd.

VERNON

Vernon, the most northerly of the Okanagan's 'Big Three', lies in a scenic valley encircled by three lakes: the Okanagan, Kalamalka and Swan. The town developed because of its location. First there were the fur traders, then the gold prospectors streaming up the valley to the Cariboo district. Later, cattle were brought in, and in 1891 the railway made it. But it was in 1908, with the introduction of large-scale irrigation, that the town took on an importance that was more than transitory. Soon the area was covered in the orchards and farms present today.

Vernon's population of 21,000 is surprisingly cosmopolitan, with good numbers of Germans, Chinese and Native Indians. The Native Indians have a reservation to the west of town.

Orientation

Surrounded by rolling hills, downtown Vernon is a clean, neat, quiet place. Main St, also called 30th Ave, is lined with trees and benches. To the north of 30th Ave, 32nd Ave is an important thoroughfare, as is 25th Ave to the south. The major north-south streets are 27th St and, a few blocks west, 32nd St. North out of town 27th St becomes Highway 97; but south out of town 32nd St becomes Highway 97.

On 27th St is the provincial courthouse, the city's most impressive structure. All the downtown sights are within easy walking distance of each other.

Information

There are three Travel Infocentres. The biggest one, with lots of maps, pamphlets and information, is in the Chamber of Commerce (☎ 545-0771), downtown at 3700 33rd St. Another is south of the downtown area, on Highway 97, towards Kelowna, near the army camp, and the third is north of town, also on Highway 97. The latter two are closed during the winter.

The main post office is on the corner of 32nd Ave and 31st St, opposite the civic centre. The Vernon Jubilee Hospital (☎ 545-2211) is at 2101 32nd St. Two banks are open on Saturdays.

The Bank of Montreal, on the corner of 30th Ave and 32nd St, is open from 9 am to 2 pm; the Bank of British Columbia, on the corner of 30th Ave and 34th St, is open from 10 am to 3 pm. Bookland, in 30th Ave, between 33rd and 34th Sts, has topographical maps of the region.

For fruit-picking work contact the Agricultural Employment Services (☎ 542-9565).

Polson Park

Polson Park, off 25th Ave, between 32nd and 30th Sts, is very pleasant, with lots of flowers and shade. If it's hot this is a good rest spot, especially if you're hitching or cycling.

The Japanese influence is obvious (as is the Chinese) in the open cabana-like structures dotting the park. At the end of the park is a floral clock.

Provincial Courthouse

Built entirely of local granite, the courthouse sits majestically at the eastern end of the downtown area, on the corner of 30th Ave and 27th St. In front is a rather bizarre garden with a waterfall over a log platform which is supported by concrete sculptures.

Vernon Museum & Archives

This museum (☎ 542-3142) is in the civic centre, on the corner of 32nd Ave and 31st St, behind the glockenspiel-like clock tower. On display are historical artefacts from the area, including old carriages and clothes.

It has a good antique telephone collection and lots of photographs of the area and of the local people.

It's open daily except Sunday from 10 am to 5 pm and admission is free. There's an art gallery here too.

O'Keefe Historic Ranch

Twelve km north of Vernon, this old ranch (☎ 542-7868), on Highway 97, was founded and lived on by the O'Keefe family from 1867 to 1977.

Most of the buildings and artefacts were the property of this family. See the original log cabin, a general store and the oldest Roman Catholic church in the province.

It's open daily spring to fall from 9 am to 5 pm. Admission is $4.

Beaches

Kalamalka Beach is on blue-green Kalamalka Lake, south of town, with campgrounds nearby.

There's also **Kin Beach** on Okanagan Lake, which is west of town, on Okanagan Landing Rd. It has a campground, too.

Provincial Parks

The 8.9-sq-km **Kalamalka Lake Provincial Park**, south of town and on the eastern side of Kalamalka Lake, provides swimming, fishing, hiking and picnic areas.

Ellison Provincial Park, 25 km southwest of Vernon on Okanagan Lake, is the only freshwater marine park in Western

Canada. Scuba diving is a popular activity here.

Silver Star Provincial Park is 22 km north-east of Vernon, on Highway 97. It offers good walking in summer, with views possible all the way west to the Coast Mountains. In winter it has 50 km of cross-country skiing on **Silver Star Mountain** and downhill ski runs. **Mable Lake Provincial Park**, 76 km north-east, off Highway 6, has beaches, swimming, sailing and fishing.

Places to Stay
Vernon has a wide range of campgrounds, B&Bs, hotels and, especially, motels.

Camping By far the best campground is *Ellison Provincial Park* (☎ 494-0321); it has only 54 campsites and is often full, so call ahead. A site costs $12. *Mable Lake Provincial Park* (☎ 494-0321) has more sites at $8.

There are lots of privately owned campgrounds, some close to town at Okanagan and Kalamalka lakes. These, too, get crowded. At *Seymour Marina* (☎ 542-6466) you can camp right next to Okanagan Lake; a site costs $12 for two people. One of the closest campgrounds to town is *Swan Lake RV Park* (☎ 545-2300), at 7255 Old Kamloops Rd, five km north of Vernon, which has tent sites for $10.

B&Bs For information on B&Bs, contact the Travel Infocentre or one of the following agencies in Vernon: Okanagan High Country B&B (☎ 542-4593), Rural Route 8, Site 10, Comp 12; or Top of the Okanagan B&B Network (☎ 549-2804), PO Box 402. The latter has singles/doubles priced from around $30/35. Within walking distance of the downtown area is *Pleasant Valley B&B* (☎ 545-9504), at 4008 Pleasant Valley Rd. It's clean and pleasant and doesn't allow smoking inside; singles/doubles are $30/40.

Hotels The *National Hotel* (☎ 545-0731), at 2922 30th Ave, on the corner of 30th St, is a reasonably kept downtown hotel with the usual working-class bar downstairs. Singles/doubles are $26/28. Rooms include

bath, TV and air-con; a sauna is available and there's an old-style barber shop downstairs. *Kalamalka Hotel* (☎ 549-1011) opposite is similar. Further north *Vernon Lodge & Courtyard Garden* (☎ 545-3385), at 3914 32nd St, on the corner of 39th Ave, is more expensive. Singles/doubles cost $53/56. The hotel has an indoor tropical garden, disco and nightclub.

Motels There are many, many motels in and around Vernon. Two of the more central ones are *Polson Park Motel* (☎ 549-2231), opposite the park, at 3201 24th Ave, and *Schell Motel* (☎ 545-1351), at 2810 35th St, on the corner of 30th Ave. Polson Park Motel is good value and offers free coffee, a heated pool, bath, air-con and TV movies. Singles/doubles are $29/36, and a kitchen is $5 extra. *Schell Motel* has a heated pool, sauna, TV, and air-con. Singles/doubles are $35/40, or $6 extra with a kitchen.

Places to Eat
For a small town, Vernon has lots of places in which to eat – particularly little coffee shops and sandwich places. It seems to keep the quality up and the prices reasonable.

At 3313 30th Ave, near the corner of 34th St, is *Jackie's Coffee Shop*, popular with the locals. The food is the usual, the prices normal and the decor plain, so who can tell why? Burgers and sandwiches cost between $2 and $4, bacon and eggs are $3.25 and salads $5. It's open Monday to Saturday from 7 am to 5 pm.

Sheila's Soup & Sandwich, at 2908 32nd St, between 29th and 30th Aves, does good-value breakfast specials such as scrambled eggs, hash browns, toast and coffee all for $2.50. It's open Monday to Friday from 7 am to 4.30 pm and Saturday from 8 am to 4.30 pm. The cafeteria in the *Greyhound Bus Depot* has good breakfasts for $3.35 and lunch specials for $3.50. It's basic but clean.

Opposite the bus depot is *Paddington Station*, at 2921 31st Ave, which has halibut and chips for $6.50 and salads for $3. It has an old-fashioned street lamppost in the dining room and is open Monday to Saturday from 11.30 am to 7.30 pm, except Friday, when it closes at 8 pm.

RJ's is now in part of what used to be the railway station, at 3131 29th St. It has chicken and rib dishes for around $10, chicken tacos for $2.75 and burgers priced from $2.25. It's open Monday to Saturday from 11 am and Sunday from 12 noon. *Tyrone's*, at 3210 30th Ave, serves beef, seafood and pasta; all-you-can-eat beef and pork belly ribs costs $10; the blackberry shortcake is $2.50.

The many Asian people here not only worked on the gardens in the park but have also set up several Chinese restaurants. There are a couple opposite each other in 33rd St, near 29th Ave: *Lotus Gardens* and *Hong Kong Village*. Starters are around $6 and most main dishes cost between $7 and $10, but sweet and sour Mongolian beef is $13.50.

For a splurge, try *Kelly O'Bryan's*, at 2905 29th St, near 30th Ave, which serves mainly seafood; starters are $4 and for main course the catch of the day costs around $14. The restaurant has subdued lighting, stained-glass windows and an Irish theme. It's open Monday to Saturday from 11 am to 12 midnight and Sunday from 12 noon to 12 midnight.

Entertainment

The *OK Corral* is on the corner of 30th Ave and 29th St, next to Kelly O'Bryan's. It features live country music or country rock nightly Wednesday to Saturday from 8 pm to 2 am. On Friday and Saturday there's a $3 cover charge. On the corner of 30th St and 30th Ave is *Julia's*, which puts on comedy shows at weekends.

Getting There & Around

The Greyhound Bus Depot (☎ 545-0527), on the corner of 31st Ave and 30th St, could be the cleanest bus depot in Canada – wipe your feet. The ticket office is open from 6.15 am to 9 pm. Buses depart regularly for Vancouver, Kelowna, Penticton, Calgary, Jasper and Prince George. Some sample fares are to Vancouver $35.65, Calgary $48, Prince George $54.15, and Jasper $44.

For information about local buses contact KIA Transit (☎ 545-7221), at 4210 24th Ave, or get a copy of the leaflet *Vernon Regional Rider's Guide*, which gives details of fares and routes, from the Travel Infocentre. The single one-way fare is 75 cents. For Kalamalka Lake catch bus No 1 south on 33rd St; for Okanagan Lake take bus No 7 west on 30th Ave.

For a taxi, try City Cabs (☎ 549-2227), at 2906 32nd St.

NORTH OF VERNON

At Sicamous there's a major highway junction where Highway 97A meets the Trans Canada Highway. From there the Trans Canada Highway heads east past Shuswap Lake to Salmon River and Kamloops; west the highway goes to Revelstoke then through Mt Revelstoke, Glacier and Yoho national parks to Lake Louise in Alberta.

The district around Mara and Shuswap lakes is picturesque, with its green wooded hills and farms. The grazing cattle and lush cultivated land make a nice change of scenery no matter where you're coming from. There are many provincial parks in the region, three of which you can camp at: Shuswap Lake, Herald and Yard Creek.

South-Eastern British Columbia

The south-eastern part of BC is dominated by the Rocky, Selkirk, Purcell, Monashee, Cariboo and Columbia mountain ranges. This is an area for outdoor activities: camping, hiking and climbing in summer, and some of North America's best skiing in winter. Nestled between the parallel mountain chains is a series of populated valleys. There are national and provincial parks throughout the area. Summers are short in the mountains: it's not unusual to have snow in the Rockies at the end of August.

WELLS GRAY PROVINCIAL PARK

About halfway between Kamloops and Jasper, off the Yellowhead Highway, is this huge, undeveloped and relatively little-visited wilderness park. You can go canoeing, mountain climbing or camping, or hike along any of 19 trails of various lengths. Only experienced, fully equipped mountaineers should attempt climbing or venture onto the snowfields and glaciers. Access to the park is by gravel road from Clearwater and Blue River and also off Highway 97 from 100 Mile House. Camping costs $6.

REVELSTOKE & AREA

This small town of 8500, on the Trans Canada Highway, 70 km east of Sicamous, is picturesque, with quiet residential streets lined with neat wooden houses and tidy gardens. It's surrounded by mountains at the western edge of Mt Revelstoke National Park and is about halfway between the Okanagan Valley and the Rocky Mountains. Revelstoke is also a busy railway centre.

The main street is 1st St. The downtown area was given a facelift in 1986, and Grizzly Plaza, between McKenzie and Orton Aves, is now a pedestrian precinct. The Travel Infocentre (☎ 837-3522) is in the Chamber of Commerce, on the corner of 1st St and Campbell Ave. The main post office (☎ 492-5717) is on 3rd St, near the corner of Rokey Ave. For information about Mount Revelstoke and National Glacier national parks contact Parks Canada (☎ 837-7500), at 301 Campbell Ave; it's open from 8 am to 4.30 pm.

Most of the things to see are not in the town itself but around the Revelstoke area, so you'll need transport.

Museum & Art Gallery

Revelstoke Museum (☎ 837-3067), in 1st St, on the corner of Boyle Ave, is open Monday to Saturday from 12 noon to 9 pm. Admission is free. It holds a permanent collection of furniture and odds and ends of historical interest from the area. There are also mining, logging and railway artefacts. It's worth a few minutes. The art gallery upstairs has changing exhibits.

Canyon Hot Springs

These springs (☎ 837-2420) are a great spot for a quick visit, 35 km east along the Trans Canada Highway. The site consists of a hot pool (40°C) and a larger, cooler swimming pool. The site opens from 8 am to 10 pm and early in the morning you can have the place to yourself – stay as long as you want. Admission is $5.50 and that includes a locker and shower.

Mount Revelstoke National Park

This is a relatively small national park, just east of Revelstoke, in the Selkirk Mountains. The Selkirks have jagged, rugged peaks and steep valleys. The view of these from Mount Revelstoke is excellent. Access is along the 26-km Summit Rd (1½ km east of Revelstoke, off the Trans Canada Highway) which leads to the peak through cedars, alpine meadows and near-tundra at the top. There are some good hiking trails from the summit, with backcountry camping permitted. No other camping is allowed in the park. There's good skiing in the very long winters. Much of the summer is rainy.

Three Valley Gap

On the Trans Canada Highway, 19 km west of Revelstoke, is this re-creation of a pioneer community. It has more than 20 buildings and continues to grow; there's a saloon, an old hotel, a barber shop and a blacksmith's, amongst others. Nearby is the site of Three Valley, a mining town which blossomed and died in the late 1880s.

Dams

BC Hydro (☎ 837-6211) runs two free tours of the Mica Dam daily. One of the world's highest dams, it's 149 km north of Revelstoke, in a bend of the Columbia River, at the end of Highway 23. There are also free tours of the newly constructed Revelstoke Dam, four km north of town, off Highway 23 and adjacent to Columbia View Provincial Park.

Mt Mackenzie

Five km south of Revelstoke, this is a major downhill and cross-country skiing area. Call ☎ 837-5268 for information.

Places to Stay

South of Revelstoke, on Highway 23, you can camp at *Blanket Creek Provincial Park* (☎ 825-4421). It has running water but no showers and a site costs $6. There are many private campgrounds east and west of Revelstoke along the Trans Canada Highway. *Canyon Hot Springs* (☎ 837-2420) has full facilities including showers, toilets and a grocery store. Sites cost $12.

Vern Enyedy B&B (☎ 837-2120), at 815 MacKenzie Ave, has singles/doubles for around $35/45. Vern collects pianos from all over the world (he now has about 60) and keeps them all in working order.

King Edward Hotel (☎ 837-5104), on the corner of 2nd St and Orton Ave, is a good, low-budget place. Singles/doubles cost $25/30. *Peaks Motel* (☎ 837-2176), five km west of town, on the Trans Canada Highway, charges $28/36 for a single/double, with TV and free coffee. There are many other places – nearly all motels – which are better, newer and more expensive.

Getting There & Away

The Greyhound Bus Depot (☎ 837-5874) is west of town, at 1899 Fraser Drive, off the Trans Canada Highway. Greyhound makes four trips east and west daily. The fare to Vancouver is $44, to Calgary $35. The Rocky Mountaineer train comes through on Tuesday and Thursday (see Getting There & Away in Vancouver).

GLACIER NATIONAL PARK

About halfway between Revelstoke and Golden lies this 1350-sq-km park. There are more than 400 glaciers here and it snows nearly every day in winter. The annual snowfall can be as much as 23 metres. Because of the sheer mountain slopes, this is one of the world's most active avalanche areas. Around Rogers Pass you'll notice the many snowsheds protecting the highway. With the narrow road twisting at up to 1327 metres, this is a dangerous area, sometimes called Death Strip – an unexpected avalanche can wipe a car right off the road. Still, the area is controlled: often snows are brought tumbling down with artillery before they fall by themselves.

At Rogers Pass there's an information centre and park warden office (☎ 837-6274 for both); the latter is open 24 hours a day. There are three campgrounds in the park.

GOLDEN

As you travel along the Trans Canada Highway from Alberta, this town of 3800 people is the first of any size in BC. Golden is the town to which workers in the area come for something to eat and a booze-up. The *Mad Trapper*, in 9th St, beside the railway, is a pretty good pub-like bar. There's also a bakery and a laundrette in town.

The Travel Infocentre (☎ 344-7125) is in the Chamber of Commerce caboose (cabin) next to the theatre.

Heli-Skiing

South of Golden, in the Purcell Mountains, is the world's centre for helicopter skiing – in districts such as the Gothics, Caribous and, perhaps best known, the Bugaboos. The latter is a region of 1500 sq km of rugged, remote mountains accessible only by helicopter during the winter months. This dangerous, thrilling sport attracts rich visitors from around the world each winter and spring. The Bugaboos has been a favourite area for over a decade and a half.

The skiing is superb but a portion of the appeal is the danger. Avalanches are not uncommon, tumbling snows claim lives on a regular, though not frequent, basis – just often enough to give the run down that extra kick.

Canadian Mountain Holidays (CMH), based in Banff (PO Box 1660), is one of the oldest, most established operators providing visitors with transportation, comfortable lodges and helicopter lifts to pristine mountain tops of spectacular scenery and fine powder snows. A week-long ski holiday can cost $4000.

During the summer months some of the lodges can be visited and hiking enjoyed.

YOHO NATIONAL PARK
Yoho National Park is in the BC Rockies, adjacent to the Alberta border and Banff National Park to the east and Kootenay National Park to the south. The name is a Cree word expressing wonder. It's a park offering peaks and valleys, glacial lakes, beautiful meadows – a bit of everything. It's more accessible and the weather is better than at Glacier.

The town of **Field**, lying in the middle of the park, is the first town in BC along the highway. There's a grocery store – closed on Sunday – which is a good place to get supplies if you're going to stay in the park. It's cheaper than the store near Takakkaw Falls. Field also has a post office, a gas station, the park information centre and the warden office (☎ 343-6324 for the latter two). There is a Travel Infocentre 12 km from the Alberta border.

Near Field is the turn-off for **Takakkaw Falls** – at 380 metres, one of the highest falls in Canada. There is a campground nearby. Also near Field are the famous **spiral tunnels**, the feats of engineering that enable the Canadian Pacific trains to navigate the challenging Kicking Horse Pass.

The trail from Takakkaw Falls to **Twin Falls** makes a good day hike. The trail is mostly flat, with views of lots of rapids and waterfalls. There's camping on the way. The beautiful green **Emerald Lake** has a walking trail around it. It's small and warm enough for a quick swim in late summer. **O'Hara Lake** is another beauty spot with excellent hiking. You can hike the 13 km in, or take a bus, but it's a busy spot. The rushing Kicking Horse River flows through the park and has a natural stone bridge near Emerald Lake.

At **Burgess Shale**, a World Heritage Site, you can see the fossilised remains of over 120 marine animal species dating back more than 500 million years.

KOOTENAY NATIONAL PARK
Kootenay National Park is solely in BC but is adjacent to Banff National Park and runs south from Yoho National Park. It has a more moderate climate than the other Rocky Mountain parks have. In the southern regions especially, summers can be hot and dry. In fact it's the only national park to contain both glaciers and cacti. Highway 93 runs down the centre and is really the only road in the park. From the north to Radium Hot Springs at the park's southern end there are campgrounds, points of interest, hiking trails and views of the valley along the Kootenay River.

There is a short, easy trail into what are called **Paint Pots**, which are ochre beds. For years, first the Kootenay people and then European settlers collected this oddly coloured earth as a colouring agent. Now artificial dyes are used.

Stop at **Marble Canyon** for the walk here – it is a real adrenalin-maker. The trail follows a rushing river from side to side, crossing it frequently on small wooden bridges with longer and longer drops below. Nearby, across the road, the campground is good. It's a basic one with no electricity or showers. There's an information centre open between June and September.

As you travel along the highway you may see a park warden by the side of the road carrying the pelts of the many types of animals that have been hit by cars.

At the end of the park, **Radium Hot Springs** is a rather plain little town but the hot springs here are always worth a visit.

MT ASSINIBOINE PROVINCIAL PARK
Between Kootenay and Banff national parks is this lesser known 39-sq-km provincial park. There's no campground but it does have wilderness camping, fishing and hiking. Access is from Highway 93.

NAKUSP & AROUND
Nakusp is the main town in the valley south of Revelstoke, east of the Okanagan Valley. The dry, picturesque valley follows a chain of lakes between the Monashee and Selkirk

mountain ranges. This is a very attractive portion of the province which benefits from not having the high profile and hence major attention of some of the other famous districts.

Nakusp sits on Upper Arrow Lake. South-west of Nakusp, Highway 6 heads to Vernon, going over the 1189-metre Monashee Pass. Near Vernon, the road goes through beautiful country scenery of small farms and wooded hills. There are campgrounds and a few small provincial parks along this route. South-east of Nakusp, Highway 6 heads to Castlegar and Nelson, past Slocan Lake and Valhalla Provincial Park, which has hiking trails and wilderness camping.

About 13 km north of Nakusp, off Highway, is a pleasant hot-springs site with a busy campground.

CASTLEGAR

Castlegar, a town of just over 6000, sits at the southern end of Lower Arrow Lake, at the junction of the Crowsnest Highway and Highway 22. This is an area where many members of a Russian Christian pacifist sect – the Doukhobors – settled at the beginning of the century. There is a reconstructed **Doukhobor village** to visit and a museum with a restaurant next door serving Doukhobor specialities. North-west of Castlegar, on Lower Arrow Lake, is 2¼-sq-km **Syringa Creek Provincial Park**, open from April to October. It has hiking, fishing, swimming, sailing, beaches and campsites.

TRAIL

Trail is an industrial town 27 km south-west of Castlegar, at the junction of the Crowsnest Highway and Highway 3A. It's home to Cominco, the world's largest smelter of silver, zinc and lead; there are free tours. You can also visit the Italian Community Archives (☎ 368-3144) in Columbo Lodge, at 584 Rossland Ave, which records the history of Italian migrants who came here at the end of the last century to work in the mines. There are several provincial parks close by. Try **Beaver Creek Provincial Park**, south-west of town, on the eastern side

of the Columbia River close to the US border; or **Champion Lakes Provincial Park**, north-west of Trail, off Highway 23. Both have hiking, fishing and campsites.

NELSON

Nelson, 43 km north-west of Castlegar, at the junction of Highway 6 and Highway 3A, is very picturesque, with many carefully preserved and restored turn-of-the-century buildings. The town is beautifully situated on the shore of Kootenay Lake surrounded by the Selkirk Mountains. One of the main attractions of this area is skiing. You can go downhill skiing at **Morning Mountain**, north-west of town, off Highway 3A; or at **Whitewater Ski Area**, 19 km south-east, off Highway 6. The latter also has well-developed cross-country skiing; for wilderness skiing head for **Kokanee Glacier Provincial Park**, to the north-west, off Highway 31.

KIMBERLEY

At 1117 metres, this is the highest city in Canada. Before 1973, Kimberley looked like what it is – a small mountain mining town. But as one of BC's 'theme' towns, it was made to look like a Bavarian alpine village. Most of the downtown section was transformed and with enough detail to make it interesting. Kimberley is now home to the world's largest functioning cuckoo clock. The Julyfest is a week of dancing, parades and lots of beer. In winter the skiing on nearby **North Star Mountain** is excellent. To the north-west, **Purcell Wilderness Conservancy** has hiking trails, fishing and wilderness camping; access is by a gravel road off Highway 95A.

CRANBROOK

Sitting at the base of the Rocky Mountains, Cranbrook, with a population of over 15,000, is about 30 km south-east of Kimberley, on the Crowsnest Highway. There's not a lot to see in the town itself, but it is located where you can enjoy many outdoor activities. You can go hiking or horse riding along the mountain trails or go swimming, fishing, sailing, windsurfing, etc on any of the dozens of lakes. At **Jim Smith Lake** and **Moyie Lake** provincial parks you can camp; there's running water but no showers.

Northern British Columbia

PRINCE GEORGE

Prince George, 'The Gateway to the North', is not an interesting town but does serve as a useful crossroads point. BC Rail and VIA Rail meet here, as do the Fraser and Nechako rivers, the Yellowhead Highway and Highway 97.

The town of 68,000 sprawls over a large area. To serve the through traffic there are dozens of motels and several hotels. Pulp and paper is an important industry. The prices are high in this area – you'll notice it most in the restaurants.

Orientation & Information

Highway 97 from Cache Creek cuts through the centre of town on its way north to Dawson Creek and the Alaska Highway. Highway 97 between Cache Creek and Prince George is also known as the Cariboo Highway and is part of the Goldrush Trail, which begins north of Hope. The Yellowhead Highway (Highway 16) runs east-west through town: westward is the long, winding route to Prince Rupert on the coast; eastward, it goes through Jasper to Edmonton.

The downtown area is small, with little character. The main roads running east-west are 2nd, 3rd and 4th Aves, parallel to the train tracks. The main north-south thoroughfare is Victoria St, which forms part of the Yellowhead Highway; Patricia Blvd, which becomes 15th Ave, is also a main street.

The Travel Infocentre (☎ 562-3700) is at 1198 Victoria St on the corner of Patricia Blvd. It's open Monday to Friday from 8 am to 5 pm. There's another office (☎ 563-5493) south of the downtown area, on the corner of Highway 97 and the Yellowhead Highway.

It operates during summer, when it is open daily from 9 am to 8 pm. The main post office (☎ 561-5184), at 1323 5th Ave, on the corner of Quebec St, is open Monday to Friday from 8.30 am to 5 pm.

Things to See & Do

At **Fort George Regional Museum** (☎ 562-1612), in Fort George Park, south-east of the downtown area, on the corner of 20th Ave and Queensway, you can see a number of stuffed animals, some Carrier, Cree and Kwakiutl artefacts and a few pioneer leftovers. It's open daily from 10 am and charges $1.50. There are many parks in Prince George. One close to the downtown area is **Cottonwood Island Nature Park**, north between the railroad tracks and the river.

Around Prince George there are dozens of lakes and rivers with good fishing. Some have camping sites; most have boats for hire. There's good skiing at **Mt Tabor**, about 25 km east of town. Ask at the Travel Infocentres for more information.

Places to Stay

Camping *Prince George Municipal Campground* (☎ 563-8131), at 4188 18th Ave, opposite Exhibition Park, south-west of the downtown area, is open May to early September. It has hot showers, and a site for two people is $9. *Purden Lake Provincial Park* (☎ 565-6340), 50 km east on the Yellowhead Highway has sites for $8. There are a few private campgrounds. *Spruceland KOA* (☎ 964-7272) is about six km south-west of town, off the Yellowhead Highway. It has full facilities and sites for $13 for two people.

B&Bs The Travel Infocentres have lists of B&Bs. *Adrienne's B&B* (☎ 561-2086), at 1467 Fraser Crescent, off 15th Ave, is close to the downtown area. Singles/doubles are $35/45.

Hotels Many of the cheaper hotels are in or around George St. The *National Hotel* (☎ 564-7010), at 1201 1st Ave, on the corner of Dominion St, one block from the VIA Rail station, is alright for a low-budget place.

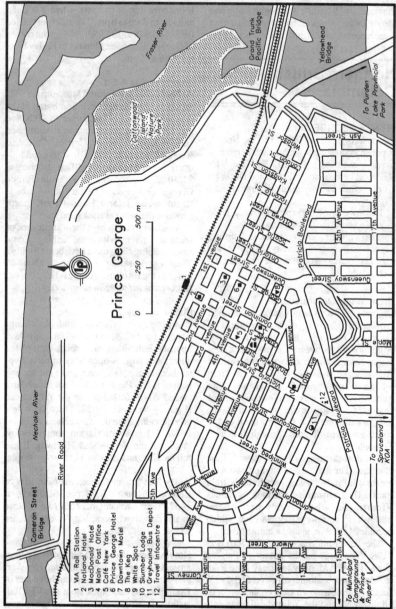

Prince George

0   250   500 m

1   VIA Rail Station
2   National Hotel
3   MacDonald Hotel
4   Main Post Office
5   Café New York
6   Prince George Hotel
7   Downtown Motel
8   The Keg
9   White Spot
10 Slumber Lodge
11 Greyhound Bus Depot
12 Travel Infocentre

Singles/doubles are $20/35. On the ground floor is a popular restaurant and a bar with live country music at night. The bar also serves food during the day. *MacDonald Hotel* (☎ 561-0134), at 1090 3rd Ave, on the corner of George St, has singles/doubles for $26/32. The bar presents rock bands. *Prince George Hotel* (☎ 564-7211), at 487 George St, is better. Singles/doubles cost $32/34; all rooms have a TV. There's music in the bar at night.

Motels There are plenty of motels to choose from. A good bet close to town is the *Bel Air Motel* (☎ 562-1191), at 1811 Victoria St. Singles/doubles are $36/42. Rooms have colour TV and free coffee. *Downtown Motel* (☎ 563-9241), at 650 Dominion St, has air-con and TV and singles/doubles for $34/40. *Slumber Lodge* (☎ 563-1267), at 910 Victoria St, looks a little run down but has all the usual features. Singles/doubles are $42/46.

Places to Eat
There aren't many places to eat at in the downtown area, though the older hotel bars usually serve a decent cheap meal that goes well with a draught beer. There are chainstore restaurants along Victoria St. The busy *White Spot*, at 820 Victoria St, has sandwiches with fries or salad for $4.50 to $6.25 and burgers for around $5. *Café New York*, at 1215 5th Ave, is a small bistro that sells sandwiches and burgers priced from around $5 to $7. For dinner you could try the *Keg*, at 582 George St, on the corner of 6th Ave, which serves steak dishes for $12 to $20. It also has seafood and poultry and is very popular.

Getting There & Away
From Prince George, it's 377 km to Jasper, 734 km to Prince Rupert and 781 km to Vancouver.

Bus The Greyhound Bus Depot (☎ 564-5454) is at 1566 12th Ave, near the junction of Victoria St and Patricia Blvd. The ticket office is open Monday to Saturday from 7 am to 6.15 pm and from 8.30 pm to 12.15 am; and Sunday from 7 to 10 am, 3.30 to 6.15 pm and 8.30 pm to 12.15 am. The depot has a cafeteria. Buses to Jasper and Edmonton leave at 12.15 am and 7.30 am; those to Vancouver leave at 8 am and 6.15 and 11 pm. Some sample one-way fares are to Vancouver $62.85, Jasper $29.90, Edmonton $62.10, Prince Rupert $60.10, and Kamloops $44.30.

Train The VIA Rail station (☎ 564-5233; 800-361-6180 toll free) is at 1300 1st Ave, near the top of Quebec St. The station is closed on Wednesday. There are three trains a week west to Prince Rupert and another three a week east to Jasper and Edmonton. The one-way fare to Prince Rupert is $59, to Jasper $46 and to Edmonton $92.

The BC Rail station (☎ 561-4033) is south-east of town, over the Fraser River, at Terminal Blvd, off Highway 97. The train goes south to Vancouver, following the historic Cariboo Trail through Quesnel, an old mining town, to Lillooet and North Vancouver. The one-way fare to Vancouver is $61.

Hitching Hitching is not allowed within the city limits. It's OK to hitch between Prince George and Prince Rupert, although the weather is unpredictable. There are plenty of places to camp at along the way, but many campgrounds close after Labour Day (the first weekend in September).

Getting Around
Contact Prince George Transit (☎ 563-0011), at 1039 Great St, for information about local buses; or get the leaflet *Prince George Rider's Guide* from the Travel Infocentre. A one-way fare in the central zone is 75 cents.

BARKERVILLE HISTORIC PARK
South of Prince George, 89 km east of Quesnel, is this restored town in the northern reaches of the gold rush district known as Cariboo country. Between 1858 and 1861 the Cariboo Trail, now Highway 97, was pushed north from Kamloops to Quesnel. It was lined with hastily built towns and gold

prospectors from around the world. In 1862, a Cornishman, Billy Barker, hit the jackpot, making $1000 in the first two days of his claim. Soon Barkerville sprang up, to become the largest city west of Chicago and north of San Francisco. The big boom was instrumental in British Columbia's becoming a crown colony in 1858.

Although Barkerville soon diminished in importance, today you can see it as it was, with its general store, hotel, shops and, of course, saloon. In the Theatre Royal, dancing shows are staged in the manner the miners once whistled at. There is also a museum that gives some of the background story and displays artefacts. It's open from 9 am to 4 pm daily. Try your luck panning for gold at the site and maybe you'll have a town named after you.

There's no bus to Barkerville so you'll have to hitch if you don't have a car. There are campsites in the park for $8 to $10 and hotels in Wells, eight km north-west. Admission to the park is $6.

BOWRON LAKE PROVINCIAL PARK
There is an excellent circular canoe route in Bowron Lake Provincial Park, near Barkerville. A number of lakes, separated by rapids and portages, form a connecting route around the perimeter of the park. The 116-km route takes an average of seven days to complete. Canoe rentals are available. Mountains in and around the park are about 2000 metres high. Access to the park is along a gravel road that leaves Highway 26 just before you get to Barkerville. There are tent sites for $8.

ALEXANDER MACKENZIE TRAIL
Heading north-west from Quesnel, this refurbished route follows ancient trails from the Fraser River west to Bella Coola, which is on the Pacific Ocean. Mackenzie made the first recorded crossing of continental North America on this route in 1793. His graffiti can still be seen carved in a rock near Bella Coola. This 250-km trail winds its way through forest and mountains and is a tough 16-day walk. At least one food drop is

required. You can do some of the more accessible segments for a few days: for example, the section in Tweedsmuir Provincial Park. For detailed trail guides contact Alexander Mackenzie Trail Association, PO Box 425, Kelowna, V1Y 7P1.

DAWSON CREEK
Dawson Creek, a city of 10,000 people 412 km north of Prince George, on Highway 97, is most notable as the starting point – 'Mile 0' – for the Alaska or Alcan (short for Alaska-Canada) Highway. The highway goes via Whitehorse in the Yukon all the way to Fairbanks in Alaska. At Mile 244 (393 km north-west of Dawson Creek), past Fort Nelson, Highway 77 heads north to the Northwest Territories.

The Dawson Creek Travel Infocentre (☎ 782-9595), at 900 Alaska Ave, can give you the details.

Pacific North-West

PRINCE RUPERT
After Vancouver, Rupert, as it's called, is the largest city on the BC coast. It's the fishing centre of the Pacific North-West, although it can no longer lay claim to being the world's halibut capital. It has adopted a new title – the 'City of Rainbows'.

Despite being one of the rainiest spots in Canada, the town's setting can look magnificent. If it's not misty, foggy or under heavy cloud you'll appreciate it. Surrounded by mountains, sitting at the mouth of the Skeena River, looking out at the fjord-like coastline, the area is ruggedly beautiful.

Prince Rupert is a good starting point for trips to Alaska and the Queen Charlotte Islands. Many people, mainly young, arrive here in summer looking for work; and this town with around 17,000 inhabitants fills its needs quickly. Remember, too, that with the influx of tourists, accommodation in July and August can be difficult to find in Prince Rupert.

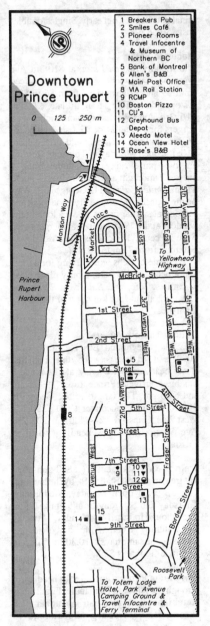

Downtown
Prince Rupert

0   125   250 m

1 Breakers Pub
2 Smiles Café
3 Pioneer Rooms
4 Travel Infocentre
   & Museum of
   Northern BC
5 Bank of Montreal
6 Allen's B&B
7 Main Post Office
8 VIA Rail Station
9 RCMP
10 Boston Pizza
11 CU's
12 Greyhound Bus
   Depot
13 Aleeda Motel
14 Ocean View Hotel
15 Rose's B&B

Prince
Rupert
Harbour

Monson Way

Market Place

3rd Avenue East
4th Avenue East
5th Avenue East

To
Yellowhead
Highway

McBride St

1st Street

2nd Street

3rd Street

3rd Avenue West
4th Avenue West
5th Avenue West

5th Street

6th Street

7th Street

8th Street

9th Street

2nd Avenue

Fraser Street

1st Avenue West

Borden Street

Roosevelt
Park

To Totem Lodge
Hotel, Park Avenue
Camping Ground &
Travel Infocentre &
Ferry Terminal

Orientation & Information

Prince Rupert is on Kaien Island and is connected to the mainland by a bridge. The Yellowhead Highway passes right through the downtown area, becoming McBride St then 2nd Ave which, along with 3rd Ave, forms the downtown core. McBride St divides the city between east and west. The ferry terminal is in Fairview Bay, two km south of town.

The Travel Infocentre (☎ 624-5637) is in the same building as the Museum of Northern BC, on the corner of 1st Ave and McBride St. There's another one at Park Avenue Camping Ground, which is south of town, about one km from the ferry terminal; it's open till midnight on nights when the ferry arrives/departs. The main post office (☎ 627-3085) is in 2nd Ave, on the corner of 3rd St. The general hospital (☎ 624-2171) is southwest of the downtown area, in Roosevelt Park.

The Bank of Montreal (☎ 624-9191), at 180-309 2nd Ave West, doesn't charge for cashing travellers' cheques.

Museum of Northern BC

This museum (☎ 624-3207) has a good collection of Tsimshian art and craftwork, including masks, carvings and beadwork. In summer it's open Monday to Saturday from 9 am to 9 pm and Sunday till 5 pm. Admission is free. Outside the museum are some fine totem poles.

Mt Hays

A gondola (☎ 627-6263) takes you up to 732-metre Mt Hays from where – on a clear day – you can see local islands, the Queen Charlotte Islands and even Alaska. The gondola is at the end of Wantage Rd, about three km from where the road turns off the Yellowhead Highway. In summer it's open daily from 12 noon to 9 pm; winter opening hours depend on the weather. The cost is $6.

There's skiing here in winter.

Oldfield Creek Hatchery

On the way to Mt Hays along Wantage Rd, stop off at this salmon hatchery (☎ 624-

6733). It's open daily in summer from 8 am to 4 pm and there are tours.

North Pacific Cannery

This restored cannery (☎ 628-3538), at 1889 Skeena Drive, Port Edward, 20 km south of Prince Rupert, gives a history of fishing and canning along the Skeena River. It's open in summer daily from 10 am to 5 pm and admission is $3. Try not to say 'something smells fishy around here'.

Provincial Parks

Diana Lake and Prudhomme Lake are two provincial parks about 16 km east of town. At both you can picnic, swim, fish, hike or take out a canoe.

Places to Stay

Camping You can camp at *Prudhomme Lake Provincial Park* (☎ 847-7320) for $8. It's open from April to November. *Park Ave Campground* (☎ 624-5861) has 87 sites, hot showers, laundry and flush toilets. A tent site for two people costs $9; in summer on ferry nights it's best to book ahead.

B&Bs There are several B&Bs in Prince Rupert: ask at the Travel Infocentre for an up-to-date list. The central *Rose's B&B* (☎ 624-5539), at 943 1st Ave West, has singles/doubles for $35/45. *Allen's B&B* (☎ 624-6100), at 4011 4th Ave West, has singles for $35 and doubles for $44 and $48. It also has beds for backpackers for $15.

Hotels One of the cheapest places is *Pioneer Rooms* (☎ 624-2334), at 167 3rd Ave East, which has singles/doubles with kitchenettes for $20/25. Bathrooms are shared and it has a small café. The basic but friendly *Ocean View Hotel* (☎ 624-6259/9950), at 950 1st Ave, has singles/doubles for $23/25.

Motels *Aleeda Motel* (☎ 627-1367), at 900 3rd Ave West, has singles/doubles for $42/55 with free parking underneath. *Totem Lodge Motel* (☎ 624-6761), at 1335 Park Ave, is good but because it's close to the ferry ter-

minal gets booked out early. Singles/doubles cost $50/56.

Places to Eat

The friendly *Boston Pizza*, at 810 3rd Ave West, has sandwiches for $6, pasta priced from $5 and pizzas priced from $6 to $20. It's open daily from 11 am till late. *CU's*, at 816 3rd Ave West, has sandwiches and burgers for around $4 or $5, fish & chips for $6 and seafood such as squid priced from $10. It's open Monday to Thursday from 11 am to 11 pm, Friday and Saturday from 11 am to 12 midnight and Sunday from 4 pm to 11 pm. *Smiles Café*, at 113 George Hills Way, on the waterfront, serves very good steak and seafood at similar prices. Have a look in the window at the 1945 menu: hamburgers then were 25 cents. The café is open Monday to Saturday from 7 am to 10 pm.

A couple of pubs worth trying for a meal and a beer are *Breakers*, a busy place close to Smiles Café, and *Solly's*, at 2209 Seal Cove Rd, about four km north of the downtown area.

Getting There & Away

Bus The Greyhound Bus Depot (☎ 624-5090) is in 3rd Ave, between 7th and 8th Sts. Buses head east twice a day, at 11 am and 8 pm, buses arrive in Prince Rupert at 9.25 am and 6.45 pm. The fare to Prince George is $60.10, while to Vancouver it's $122.90. Far West Bus Lines (☎ 624-6400), at 225 2nd Ave West, has buses heading north to Cassiar.

Train The VIA Rail station (☎ 800-665-8630 toll free) is at 1150 Station St, by the harbour. The office is open Monday, Wednesday, Thursday and Saturday from 9 am to 3 pm. The inbound train arrives Monday, Thursday and Saturday at 1 pm; the outbound one leaves on the same days at 10.30 am. The fare to Prince George is $59.

Ferry From Prince Rupert ferries head north through the Alaskan Panhandle. First stop is Ketchikan, but you can go north past Wrangell, Petersburg and Juneau to

Skagway, where the Klondike Highway comes south from Whitehorse in the Yukon. Various commercial cruise lines do the route as well, but all are costly. The ferry systems are much cheaper. Alaska State Ferries (☎ 624-1744), also called Alaska Marine Highway, has its office – open from 5 am to 12 noon – at the ferry terminal. The one-way fare to Juneau is $90, or $185 with a car.

The route between the Alaskan Panhandle and Washington state is known as the Inside Passage. It's a long, expensive trip but offers beautiful scenery past many bays, inlets, islands and small Native Indian settlements. It's not uncommon to see seals, herds of sea lions or pods of killer whales. You can take just part of the trip rather than the whole voyage.

BC Ferries (☎ 624-9627) runs the MV *Queen of the North* from Rupert to Vancouver Island. It stops only at Bella Bella and Ocean Falls, both of which have no roads, so for this part of the trip you must go all the way to Port Hardy. The one-way walk-on fare to Port Hardy is $80, or $245 with a car. An overnight cabin is $46 extra. The trip takes about 15 hours. Reservations are a good idea, especially if you're taking a vehicle.

BC Ferries also operates between Prince Rupert and Skidegate in the Queen Charlotte Islands; there are five ferries a week in each direction. The one-way fare is $16, or $77 with a car.

Getting Around

For information about local buses contact Coastal Bus Lines (☎ 624-3343), at 225 2nd Ave West. Catch the bus from here for the ferry terminal. The one-way fare on buses is 75 cents and a day pass costs $2.

AROUND PRINCE RUPERT

In **Kitimat**, south of Terrace, at the end of Highway 37, there are free tours of the Alcan Aluminium Smelter and Eurocan Pulp & Paper Mill. Just north of Hazelton, which is off the Yellowhead Highway, is **K'san**, a restored village of the Gitksan people who are known for their craftworks in gold, silver and hardwood. There are longhouses, totem poles and examples of their tools.

CASSIAR HIGHWAY

Between Terrace and New Hazelton, the Yellowhead Highway's northern tributary, Highway 37, goes to Meziadin Junction and Stewart. The part of Highway 37 extending north from Meziadin Junction is known as the Cassiar Highway (also called the Stewart-Cassiar Highway) and meets the Alaska Highway in the Yukon.

The Cassiar is mostly gravel road and passes through some beautiful countryside at places like **Spatsizi Plateau Wilderness Park** and **Dease Lake**. The highway is about 750 km long and there aren't many service stations along the way, so if you're driving, make sure the vehicle is in good working condition and take spare parts and extra gasoline. Flying gravel can crack the windscreen or headlights and dust can severely restrict your vision so treat approaching vehicles with caution especially logging trucks.

Stewart & Hyder

From Meziadin Junction it's 67 km west to Stewart on the Alaskan border. On the way you pass **Bear Glacier**, 49 km from Stewart; there's a rest area where you can view the glacier. From Stewart the road goes straight through to Hyder in Alaska: there are no immigration or customs and Hyder accepts Canadian money except in the post office. At **Fish Creek**, about three km past Hyder, between late July and September you can see salmon swimming upstream to spawn and bears coming to feed on them.

In Stewart *Rainey Creek Campground* (☎ 636-2537) has sites for $9. There are only two motels and one hotel, all with similar prices; book for all three at the *King Edward Hotel* (☎ 636-2244), situated on Main St. Singles/doubles cost around $45/52. In Hyder you can stay at the *Grizzly Bear Lodge*.

Seaport Limousine Service (☎ 636-2622), PO Box 217, Stewart, operates a bus to Terrace. There's one a day in each direction

Monday to Saturday; the trip takes four hours and costs $25.

QUEEN CHARLOTTE ISLANDS

The Queen Charlotte Islands, sometimes known as the Canadian Galapagos, are an archipelago of some 154 islands lying 80 km off the BC coast and about 50 km from the southern tip of Alaska. As the only part of Canada that escaped the last ice age, the islands are rich in flora & fauna markedly different from those of the mainland. Essentially still a wilderness area, the Queen Charlottes are warmed by an ocean current from Japan and hit with 127 cm of rain annually. All these factors combine to create a landscape of 1000-year-old spruce and cedar rainforests, abundant animal life and waters teeming with marine life.

The islands have been inhabited continuously for 10,000 years and are the traditional homeland of the Haida nation, generally acknowledged as the prime culture in the country at the time of the arrival of Europeans. The arts of the Haida people – notably their totem poles and carvings in argillate (a black, glass-like stone) – are world renowned. They were also fearsome warriors who dominated the west coast.

Today the Haida are still proud, defiant people. Some time ago they led an internationally publicised fight to preserve the islands from further logging. A bitter debate raged, but finally the federal government decided to save South Moresby and create a national park. Chalk up one for Mother Nature.

About 80% of the population lives on **Graham Island**, the only island with any real road system. On the eastern shore are the principal towns of **Skidegate**, which is at the southern end, and **Masset**, which is in the north. The north-eastern part of the island is taken up by **Naikoon Provincial Park**; most of the full 60 km of its east coast is sandy beach. Near Skidegate is a good museum on the area's history, including an excellent collection of Haida works. Skidegate and Masset both have a couple of motels and there is camping at several locations around the island.

Most of the region is inaccessible. Tiny **Anthony Island**, near the southern end of the chain, is a provincial park and UN World Heritage Site. It protects an old Haida village, Ninstints, called the most impressive coastal Indian site in the Pacific North-West. There are 32 totem poles and remains of 10 longhouses. The only trouble is that you can't get there! Tourism is increasing on the islands and operators may soon be offering trips to some of the more inaccessible areas.

Getting There & Away

The ferry from Prince Rupert to Skidegate, the MV *Queen of Prince Rupert*, makes five trips a week, each taking 6½ hours and costing $15, or $58 with a car. Some crossings are day trips and some overnight.

Another ferry goes between Skidegate and Alliford Bay on Moresby Island; the one-way fare is $1.75, or $5.50 with a car.

ATLIN

This small, remote town in the north-western corner of the province is reached by road via the Yukon. The scenery around it is good, with forests in Atlin Provincial Park and snow-capped mountains surrounding Atlin Lake.

The Yukon & Northwest Territories

Canada's northern territories make up a vast tract of land stretching from the northern boundaries of the provinces to within 800 km of the North Pole and from the Atlantic Ocean to the Pacific. A third ocean, the Arctic, links Alaska and Greenland across the many islands of the far north.

For the most part, this land of the midnight sun is as reputation has it: a barren, treeless tundra that's nearly always frozen. But it is definitely not all this way. There are mountains and forests, abundant wildlife and warm summer days with 20 hours of light.

In general, the development of the far north occurred where conditions were most hospitable and the land most varied and scenic. Fortunately, these places are still the most accessible; tourism increases each year.

The designation of the Yukon and Northwest as territories rather than provinces is a political one. Because they have relatively small populations, the territories have not been given full status in parliament, something the locals are moving to change.

Yukon Territory

Area: 483,450 sq km
Population: 27,000

The Yukon is a triangular slice of northern Canada wedged between the Northwest Territories and Alaska. To the south is British Columbia; the north is bounded by the Beaufort Sea in the Arctic Ocean. It's a sub-Arctic region about one-third the size of Alaska. Mountain ranges, including some that continue from the Rockies, almost entirely cover the Yukon. Forests, wooded hills, lakes and streams flow and grow amidst the mountains.

There are only about 27,000 people in the area of 483,450 sq km, and most of them live in towns. About two-thirds are in the Whitehorse region. The bulk of the rest live in and around mining camps. By far the majority of the people are White. The Dene, or Athapaskans, may have inhabited the region for up to 40,000 years, which would make them the oldest residents of North America. They number around 3000.

In the 1840s, Robert Campbell, a Hudson's Bay Company explorer, was the first White person to travel the district. In

Native Indians wearing goat wool blankets

685

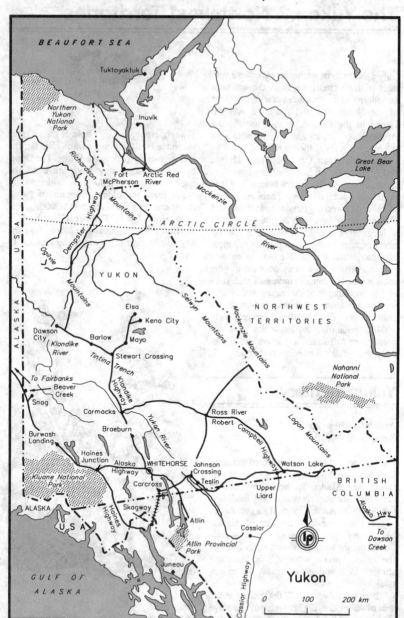

Yukon

0   100   200 km

1870 the area became part of the region known as the Northwest Territories. But it was in 1896 that the biggest changes began. Gold was found in a tributary of the Klondike River and all hell broke loose. The ensuing gold rush attracted hopefuls from around the world. The population boomed to over 35,000 – quite a bit higher than today's. Towns grew up overnight to support the rough-and-ready wealth-seekers. It was the suppliers and entertainers though, rather than the prospectors, who were raking in the money.

In 1898, the Yukon became a separate territory with Dawson City the capital, but the city declined as the gold ran out. In 1953 Whitehorse became the capital, for it had the railway and the Alaska Highway; it now acts as the main distribution and transport centre of the Yukon.

The most important industry in the Yukon is mining, and, despite fishing, forestry and furs, tourism is the second-biggest money-maker.

Poet Robert Service and writer Jack London both lived and worked in the Yukon. Their words are highly respected and oft-repeated throughout the territory.

To the visitor, the Yukon is for outdoor activities: camping, hiking, climbing and fishing amidst scenic wilderness.

INFORMATION
Money
Outside Whitehorse the most generally accepted credit card is Visa, then MasterCard. Whitehorse is the last town going north (at least in Canada) where the food is not too pricey. At Inuvik, for example, costs are nearly three times higher, so take supplies with you. Alaska, however, is cheaper than anywhere in the Yukon.

Tourist Offices
The Yukon has six tourist offices, called Visitor Reception Centres (VRCs): these are at Beaver Creek, Carcross, Dawson City, Haines Junction, Watson Lake and Whitehorse. They're all open mid-May to mid-September. Most have audiovisual dis-

plays and exhibits of some sort as well as the usual information. Tourism Yukon (☎ 667-5340), PO Box 2073, Whitehorse Y1A 2C6, sends out free information on the territory.

Time
The Yukon is on Pacific Standard Time and the telephone code for the territory is the same as Alberta's – 403.

Maps
Topographical maps of the territory are available in Whitehorse from:

Northern Affairs Program
   Geological Services, 200 Range Rd, Whitehorse Y1A 3V1 (☎ 667-3100)
Jim's Toy & Gift
   208 Main St, Whitehorse Y1A 2A9 (☎ 667-2606)
Yukon Gallery
   2093 2nd Ave, Whitehorse Y1A 2C6 (☎ 667-2391)
Tourism Industry Association of the Yukon
   Suite 102, 302 Steele St, Whitehorse Y1A 2C5 (☎ 668-3331)

You can also get them from Canada Map Office (☎ (613) 952-7000), 615 Booth St, Ottawa, Ontario K1A 3A9.

Dangers & Annoyances
If drinking water from lakes or streams boil it for at least 10 minutes. The lakes and streams may contain the intestinal parasite (Giardia lamblia) which causes giardiasis. If you're camping take some insect repellent with you.

Accommodation
If you rent or buy a recreational vehicle (RV), you've not only got a means of transport, but a place to stay as well. The Yukon government's series of campgrounds is good, with many along the highways; most have drinking water. There are also numerous private grounds which offer showers and laundry facilities; some of these campgrounds are geared strictly to the RV market.

ACTIVITIES
The Yukon Visitor Reception Centres can

supply you with general descriptions and specific information on hiking, canoeing, rockhounding, gold prospecting, climbing, skiing, fishing and various adventure tours. There are outfitters and tour companies to cover all these activities. Adventure trips range from white-water rafting to backpacking to do-it-yourselfers which provide no more than advice or drop-off and pick-up. There are places where you can rent canoes or boats in various parts of the territory. You don't need an organised trip and don't need to be wealthy to enjoy camping, hiking or canoeing in the Yukon.

For hiking, the most well-known trail is the Chilkoot Trail and there are other good ones in Kluane National Park.

GETTING AROUND
The major towns in the Yukon are connected by air and bus: see the Getting There & Away sections for Whitehorse and Dawson City for details.

Car
Driving your own vehicle is the best way to get around, and there are car and RV rental outlets in Whitehorse.

The road system in the Yukon is fairly extensive, if rough. Remember that most roads apart from the Alaska Highway are not sealed – most are gravel. The main highways in the Yukon are the Klondike, the Dempster and the Alaska. The Visitor Reception Centres have information on the highways and what there is to see from them. There are roads connecting most southern towns. To the north the Dempster Highway connects Dawson City with Inuvik in the Northwest Territories (see the Dempster Highway section later).

A good circular trip is to travel the Klondike Highway from Whitehorse to Dawson City, then take the Top of the World Highway and Taylor Highway south to Tetlin Junction in Alaska and from there follow the Alaska Highway north-west to Fairbanks. Coming back take the Alaska Highway south-east past Beaver Creek, Kluane National Park and Haines Junction to Whitehorse.

There are campgrounds along most of the highway routes.

Gasoline Gasoline prices along the highways are pretty outrageous any way you look at it, but you're stuck with them unless you take advantage of cheaper places and fill up even if you don't need to. It's a good idea always to have some spare. Generally, along the main routes, there's a service station every 50 km, but in some areas there may be no competition for 150 km. Prices are lower in the main towns than they are out on the stretches, but they can vary considerably for no apparent reason.

Three places where the gasoline is not so expensive are Dawson Creek in British Columbia, Whitehorse and Dawson City. Gasoline is very expensive in Inuvik; expect to pay, pay, pay. The good news is that prices are much lower all over Alaska than they are in Canada.

WHITEHORSE
Whitehorse, on the banks of the Yukon River, is by far the largest town in the territory. In fact its official city limits cover 421 sq km, making it one of the largest urban-designated area in Canada. Whitehorse is on the Alaska Highway about halfway between Dawson Creek in British Columbia, where the highway starts, and Fairbanks in Alaska. The city has a population of nearly 21,000 and the people are condescendingly known as 'southerners' by those living in the more northerly areas of the territory. Despite its growth Whitehorse still has something of a frontier feel about it.

Orientation & Information
The downtown core is between 1st and 6th Aves and Hanson and Strickland Sts. The main routes through town are 2nd and 4th Aves. The Visitor Reception Centre (☎ 667-2915) is housed in the T C Richards Building at 302 Steele St on the corner of 3rd Ave. It's open from 8 am to 8 pm. There's also a Parks Canada information office next to the SS *Klondike*, on the banks of the Yukon River south of downtown. The post office is on

Wood St, between 2nd and 3rd Aves, next to the Westmark Whitehorse Hotel. It's open Monday to Saturday from 7 am to 7 pm. There's also a postal counter in Books on Main at 203 Main St between 2nd and 3rd Aves.

Several banks are on the corner of Main St and 2nd Ave, but only the Bank of Montreal (☎ 668-4200) is open on a Saturday – from 10 am to 3 pm.

Whitehorse General Hospital (☎ 668-9333) is at the end of Hospital Rd on the eastern side of the river. To get there take Robert Campbell Bridge from the southern end of 2nd Ave, go over the river onto Lewes Blvd then turn left.

Mac's on Main, on Main St between 3rd and 4th Aves sells a good selection of books on the history, geography and wildlife of the Yukon.

Topographical maps of the Yukon are available at several places in Whitehorse (see the Information section at the start of this chapter).

Things to See & Do
In the town itself there isn't much to see but in the surrounding area you can go hiking and cycling, particularly at **Mt McIntyre Recreation Centre** and at **Grey Mountain** east of town and **Miles Canyon** south of town. The hiking trails become cross-country ski trails in winter.

'Log Skyscrapers' Look for these small two and three-storey wood cabins built with turf on their roofs to keep the heat in. There are a couple on Lambert St between 2nd and 3rd Aves.

SS *Klondike* The SS *Klondike* (☎ 667-4511) was one of the last and largest stern-wheel riverboats used on the Yukon River. Built in 1929, it made its last run upriver in 1955. Now restored as a museum and dry-docked near the junction of South Access Rd and 2nd Ave, it's open daily mid-May to mid-September from 9 am to 6 pm. Admission is free.

MacBride Museum This museum (☎ 667-

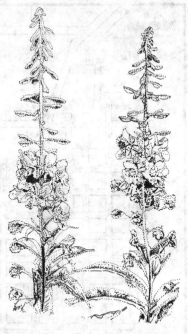

Fireweed

2709) on the corner of 1st Ave and Wood St is in a log cabin with a turf roof. It contains a collection of materials from the indigenous cultures, the fur trade, gold rush days and the construction of the Alaska Highway. It also has displays of Yukon wildlife. It's open daily mid-May to the end of September until 6 pm and admission is $3.

Old Log Church Museum The church (☎ 668-2555), on the corner of Elliot St and 3rd Ave, was built by the town's first priest in 1900. Known as the only wooden cathedral in the world, it is also the oldest building in town. Inside are artefacts from early churches around the territory. It's open early June to the end of August, Monday to Saturday from 9 am to 8 pm and Sunday from 12 noon to 4 pm. Admission is $2.50. Services

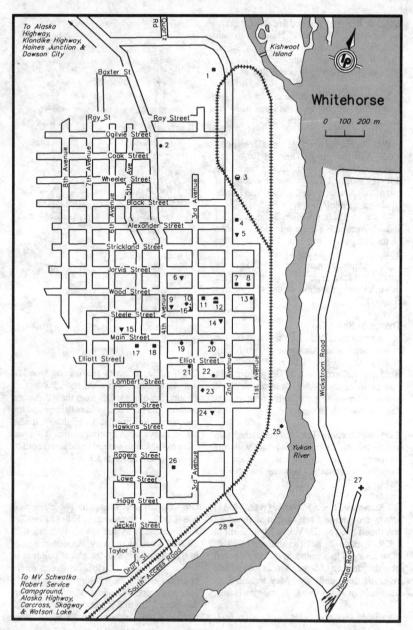

To Alaska
Highway,
Klondike Highway,
Haines Junction &
Dawson City

Quartz Rd

Baxter St

Ray St

Ray Street

Ogilvie Street

8th Avenue

7th Avenue

Cook Street

5th Ave

Wheeler Street

3rd Avenue

Black Street

6th Avenue

Alexander Street

Strickland Street

Jarvis Street

Wood Street

4th Avenue

Steele Street

Main Street

Elliott Street

Elliot Street

Lambert Street

2nd Avenue

1st Avenue

Hanson Street

Hawkins Street

Rogers Street

3rd Avenue

Lowe Street

Hoge Street

Jeckell Street

Taylor St

Drury St

South Access Road

To MV Schwatka
Robert Service
Campground,
Alaska Highway,
Carcross, Skagway
& Watson Lake

Kishwoot Island

Whitehorse

0   100   200 m

Wickstrom Road

Yukon River

Hospital Road

■ PLACES TO STAY

1	Sourdough City RV Park
4	Fort Yukon Hotel
7	98 Hotel
8	Regina Hotel
11	Westmark Whitehorse Hotel
17	Gold Rush Inn
18	Town & Mountain Hotel
26	Fourth Ave Residence

▼ PLACES TO EAT

2	Qwanlin Mall
5	Mom's Kitchen
6	China Gardens
9	No Pop Sandwich Shop
14	Talisman Café
15	Sam 'n' Andy's
24	The Deli

OTHER

3	Greyhound Bus Depot
10	Donnenworth House
12	Post Office
13	MacBride Museum
16	Visitor Reception Centre
19	Mac's on Main
20	Books on Main
21	Old Log Church Museum
22	Log Skyscraper
23	Klondyke Medical Building
25	MV Anna Maria
27	Whitehorse General Hospital
28	SS *Klondike*

are held on Sunday evening, mostly for the Native Indians in their own language.

Yukon Transportation Museum The transportation museum (☎ 668-4191), east of town at Whitehorse Airport, features the history of transport in the territory. It's open daily July to the end of August from 9 am to 5 pm. Entry is by donation.

Yukon Botanical Gardens The Yukon Botanical Gardens (☎ 668-7972) are on South Access Rd close to the Alaska Highway, about three km south-west of town. The gardens, covering almost nine

hectares, have large displays of wild plants and flowers that can only be found in the north, plus vegetables and fruit trees. The gardens are open daily mid-May to mid-September from 9 am to 9 pm and admission is $5.75.

Takhini Hot Springs These hot springs (☎ 633-2706) are about 27½ km north-west of town on the Klondike Highway. You can rent bathing suits and towels for 50 cents each. The springs are open daily all year, from 8 am to 10 pm. Admission is $3.

Organised Tours The Yukon Historical & Museums Association (☎ 667-4704) at Donnenworth House, 3126 3rd Ave between Wood and Steele Sts, conducts free guided walking tours daily of the downtown area.

The Yukon Conservation Society (☎ 668-5678), 302 Hawkins St, offers free nature walks in the area on weekdays during July and August.

From early June to mid-September there are two-hour boat trips on the MV *Schwatka* down through Miles Canyon from Schwatka Lake south of town. The fare, including bus transfer to the lake, is $20. Contact Atlas Tours (☎ 668-3161) in the Westmark Whitehorse Hotel for bookings.

Gray Line Yukon (☎ 668-3225), also in the Westmark Whitehorse Hotel, has several bus tours of the Whitehorse area. The two-hour city tour features the Yukon Botanical Gardens and Miles Canyon and costs $18.

Places to Stay
Camping *Robert Service Campground* (☎ 668-8325) is one km south of town on South Access Rd. It's open late May to early September and has toilets, showers and firepits. A tent site, of which there are 40, costs $5. *Sourdough City RV Park* (☎ 668-7938), at the northern end of 2nd Ave, past the Greyhound Bus Depot, has a laundry, free showers and sites for $16. *Pioneer RV Park* (☎ 668-5944), eight km south of Whitehorse on the Alaska Highway, has drinking water, laundry and showers and tent sites for $6.

South of Whitehorse there is a govern-

ment campground at Wolf Creek and one at
Marsh Lake; sites cost $5. You can camp at
Takhini Hot Springs for the same price.

B&Bs *Whitehorse B&B Agency* (☎ 633-
4609), 102 302 Steele St, is worth trying and
is open all year. It has homes in town and in
other parts of the Yukon, including Dawson
City.

Barb's B&B (☎ 667-4104), 64 Boswell
Crescent, south of downtown on the eastern
side of the river, has two rooms with private
bathroom. A single/double costs $45/55 and
includes a complimentary evening snack.
International House B&B (☎ 633-5490), 17
14th Ave in Porter Creek, north of downtown, has the same facilities and prices.

Hotels & Motels For a smallish town,
Whitehorse has plenty of hotels and motels
but most are not cheap. About $60 to $70 a
single is average. Generally speaking, the
smaller places cost less.

Fourth Ave Residence (☎667-4471), 4051
4th Ave, is a motel that offers hostel-type
accommodation and a 10% discount if
you're a member of the CHA or IYHF. A bed
in a shared room is $15 while a single/double
costs $32/40 without bath. You get free use
of the city swimming pool next door. *98
Hotel* (☎ 667-2641), 110 Wood St, is basic
but central and cheap, with singles/doubles
for $25/35. *Fort Yukon Hotel* (☎ 667-2595),
2163 2nd Ave, is another inexpensive place,
with singles/doubles for $35/40.

Close to 98 Hotel is the more up-market
Regina Hotel (☎ 667-4243), 102 Wood St,
with a licensed restaurant and heated underground parking. All rooms have private
baths, and singles/doubles cost from $58/72.

Town & Mountain Hotel, (☎ 668-7644),
situated at 401 Main St, has 30 rooms, with
singles/doubles at $80/85. There's a licensed
restaurant and a piano bar.

Places to Eat
Food is more costly here than it is further
south but not greatly so. There are several
fast-food outlets and Chinese restaurants and

most of the hotels have restaurants or dining
rooms.

Woolco Cafeteria, in the Qwanlin Mall on
the corner of 4th Ave and Ogilvie St, has
cheap meals. It's open Saturday and Monday
to Thursday from 9 am to 6 pm and Friday
from 9 am to 9 pm. *Mom's Kitchen,* in a log
cabin at 2157 2nd Ave near Fort Yukon
Hotel, is good for breakfast. Sandwiches and
omelettes with toast and hash browns cost
from $5; coffee is 95 cents. It's open daily
from 6.30 am. The exterior of *Talisman Café,*
2112 2nd Ave, between Steele and Main Sts,
is a little grubby but inside it's clean. Breakfast of eggs, hash browns, toast and jam costs
$4; sandwiches and burgers start from $5 and
coffee is $1. It also serves Middle Eastern
food and is open daily from 6 am to 11 pm.

The Deli, 203 Hanson St, is reasonably
priced at around $5 for light meals of soups,
salads or homemade sausages. It's open Saturday and Monday to Thursday from 9.30
am to 9.30 pm and Friday from 9 am to 7 pm.
The decor at the *No Pop Sandwich Shop,* 312
Steele St, is functional but the food is good.
The sandwiches have interesting names like
Beltch, Roman or Tel Aviv and cost around
$4. It also caters for vegetarians.

Sam 'n' Andy's, 506 Main St, is a licensed
restaurant serving good Mexican food, with
a garden in the front. Nachos cost $5 and
main dishes are around $7 to $12.

Twenty-four varieties of pizza are available at *G&P Pizza House* in the Kopper King
complex on the Alaska Highway; it has
another outlet at 95 Lewes Blvd in the southern suburb of Riverdale.

China Gardens, 309 Jarvis St, has chicken
and seafood dishes from $10, chow mein
from $8 and special lunch-time buffets.

Entertainment
The Frantic Follies is an 1890s-style revue
with comedy skits, dancing girls and the
poetry of Robert Service. The show is held
nightly in the *Westmark Whitehorse Hotel*
through the summer and tickets cost $15.
You book through Atlas Tours (☎668-3161),
which has an office in the hotel.

The Eldorado Musical Revue, held in the

Gold Rush Inn at 411 Main St, is a more dramatic depiction of the gold rush era. There are nightly performances at 8 pm from June to September and tickets cost $14. Call ☎ 668-6472 for details.

Robert Service Campground has regular poetry readings.

Getting There & Away
Air Whitehorse Airport is east of town off the Alaska Highway. Canadian Airlines (☎ 668-3535) has a daily service to Calgary, Edmonton and Vancouver. The one-way fare to Calgary is $381; to Vancouver it's $394.

Air North (☎ 668-2228) connects Whitehorse with Dawson City, Watson Lake and the Alaskan towns of Fairbanks and Juneau. Delta Air Lines (☎ 667-2700) connects Whitehorse with other parts of Western Canada, Alaska and many points in mainland USA. Alkan Air (☎ 668-6616) goes to places within the Yukon and to Inuvik in the Northwest Territories; the one-way fare to Dawson City is $250, to Inuvik $405.

Bus The Greyhound Bus Depot (☎ 667-2223), 2191 2nd Ave, is open Monday to Friday from 8 am to 12 noon and 1 to 5.30 pm, Saturday from 9 am till 12 noon and Sunday from 5.30 to 9 am. Greyhound has buses daily to Vancouver and Edmonton; the one-way fare to Edmonton is $173.05.

Norline Coaches (☎ 668-3355) runs buses three times a week to Dawson City from the Greyhound Bus Depot for $66 one way. Northwest Stage Lines (☎ 668-6975) has buses to Kluane National Park, Beaver Creek, Faro and Ross River. Gray Line of Alaska (☎ 667-2223) operates Alaskon Express buses to Skagway, Anchorage, Fairbanks and Haines in Alaska.

Train There is a privately owned 177-km narrow-gauge railway line called the White Pass & Yukon Route (WP&YR) that connects Whitehorse with Skagway, Alaska. The trip is an interesting one over rough terrain. It has a good historical angle, too: the line opened in 1900 to feed the gold rush.

The train relied heavily on fees raised from transporting ore from mines, but with the fall in world metal prices the line was closed from 1982 till 1988. Currently the line only operates between Skagway and Fraser in northern British Columbia, from where a connecting bus takes you to Whitehorse. The train departs daily from Skagway at 1 pm and arrives in Whitehorse at 6.30 pm; from Whitehorse the bus leaves at 8.30 am, and the train arrives in Skagway at 12.10 pm. The one-way fare is US$89.

For information and bookings contact Whitehorse Travel (☎ 668-5598) in the Klondyke Medical Building on the corner of 3rd Ave and Lambert St.

Car Whitehorse is connected with Watson Lake in the east and Haines Junction and Beaver Creek in the west by the Alaska Highway. The Klondike Highway (Highway 2) heads south to Carcross then to Skagway in Alaska; north of Whitehorse the Klondike Highway connects the city with Stewart Crossing and Dawson City.

Cars can be rented from:

Budget
    4178 4th Ave (☎ 667-6200)
Hertz
    4158 4th Ave (☎ 667-2505)
Tilden
    2089 2nd Ave (☎ 668-2521)
Thrifty
    9038 Quartz Rd (☎ 667-7936)

Boat The MV *Anna Maria* (☎ 667-4155) runs trips on the Yukon River between Whitehorse and Dawson City.

Getting Around
Bus Whitehorse Transit (☎ 668-2831), 110 Tlingit St, operates buses Monday to Saturday; there are no buses on Sundays or public holidays. The one-way fare is $1 but a day pass for $3 allows unlimited travel. For schedules and routes, get a copy of the city bus guide from the Visitor Reception Centre.

ALASKA HIGHWAY
The Alaska Highway (also called the Alcan Highway), the main road in the Yukon, is

2400 km long and starts in Dawson Creek, British Columbia. It enters the Yukon in the south-east and passes through Watson Lake, Whitehorse, Haines Junction and Beaver Creek en route to Fairbanks, Alaska. It was built in just nine months in 1942 as part of the war effort and was originally known as the Alaska-Canada Military Highway. Now, each summer, it's very busy (some even say clogged) with visitors, mainly driving RVs. At times there are 10 of these homes-on-wheels for every car or truck.

Improvements on the Alaska Highway continue and it is now nearly all sealed. Still, there are a few stretches of it which are not: make sure the floor of your car isn't about to rust through. Actually, the road is not that rough. The biggest problems are dust and flying stones from other vehicles on the unsealed stretches: slow down and keep well to the right. A bug and gravel screen is recommended, as are covers for your gasoline tank and lights, a spare tyre, fan belt and hose.

Hitching on the highway is good, especially in summer when there are more vehicles. However, you should be prepared for the occasional long wait so it's a good idea to carry a tent, some food, water and warm clothing.

WATSON LAKE

Billed as the 'Gateway to the Yukon', Watson Lake is the first town in the territory as you head north-west on the Alaska Highway from British Columbia. The Visitor Reception Centre (☎ 536-7469), at the junction of the Alaska and Robert Campbell highways, has an excellent slide show on the history of the Alaska Highway. The centre is open from 8 am to 8 pm.

The town is most famous for its **Signpost Forest** just outside the VRC. The original signpost of 'Danville, Illinois' was put up in 1942 by the homesick Carl Lindlay, a US soldier working on the construction of the Alaska Highway. Other people added their own signs and now there are well over 10,000.

KLUANE NATIONAL PARK

Kluane National Park is a rugged wilderness area covering 22,015 sq km that sits in the extreme south-western corner of the Yukon adjacent to Alaska's Wrangell-St Elias National Park. Kluane means 'many fish' and is pronounced 'klu-ah-nee'.

Haines Junction is just outside the park and is reached by the Alaska Highway from Whitehorse or by the Haines Highway (Highway 3, also called Haines Rd) from Haines in Alaska. The Visitor Reception Centre (☎ 634-2345) in Haines Junction has information about the park, including an audiovisual display. It's open daily from 9 am to 9 pm. There's also a park information office at Sheep Mountain north-west of Haines Junction.

The park is very mountainous: Mt Logan, part of the St Elias Range, is, at 5950 metres, Canada's highest mountain; Mt St Elias, at 5488 metres, is Canada's second highest. Within the park there are valleys, lakes, alpine forest and tundra plus the world's largest non-polar ice fields. Winters are long and harsh while summers are short; generally temperatures are comfortable from mid-June to mid-September, which makes that the best time to visit.

Fishing is good and wildlife abounds, including moose and Dall sheep which can be seen on Sheep Mountain even from the road. There are also grizzly bears, a small herd of caribou and 150 varieties of birds, among them the rare peregrine falcon and eagles.

The scenery makes for excellent hiking. There are several good trails, some following old mining roads, others, traditional Native Indian paths. There's a hiking trail leading to **Kaskawulsh Glacier** – one of the few that can be reached by foot. The leaflet *Hiking in Kluane National Park* has a map and lists the trails with distances and starting points. You can buy topographical maps at the Visitor Reception Centre. Hikers should take precautions to avoid attack from bears.

The St Elias Range provides excellent climbing and mountaineering.

The only campground within the park is

at Kathleen Lake, 24 km south of Haines Junction off the Haines Highway. It's open mid-June to mid-September and costs $7 for an unserviced site. There are several other campgrounds just outside the park. Of course, you can try backcountry tenting along overnight trails.

CARCROSS

Carcross, 74 km south-east of Whitehorse, is the first settlement you reach when coming to the Yukon from Skagway on the Klondike Highway. The town's name is an abbreviation of Caribou Crossing – so called because of the caribou herds which crossed the narrow strip of land between Lake Bennett and Lares Lake.

The Visitor Reception Centre (☎ 821-4431) is next to the old sternwheeler SS *Tutshi*.

SKAGWAY (ALASKA)

Skagway is at the southern end of the Klondike Highway, which heads north through Whitehorse to Dawson City. The drive between Skagway and Whitehorse takes about three hours, passing lakes, mountains and meadows. A narrow-gauge railway line over White Pass, which was completed in 1900, connects the towns. (For more information on the train, see the Whitehorse Getting There & Away section.)

Skagway is the northern terminal for ferries and cruise ships plying the continental west coast. Beginning in San Francisco, Bellingham (Washington state), Vancouver, Vancouver Island and Prince Rupert, these ships edge along the coastline to Skagway. For details of ferries going south contact Alaska State Ferries (☎ (907) 983-2229); (907) 465-3941 in Juneau). The Alaska State Ferries company is commonly referred to as the Alaska Marine Highway.

BC Ferries handles most of the traffic south of Prince Rupert along the Inside Passage (see the Getting There & Away section of Prince Rupert in the British Columbia chapter for more information).

Skagway was the landing point for many in the gold rush days. From here began the long, slow, sometimes deadly haul to the Klondike gold area near Dawson City. The old route, the Chilkoot Trail over the Chilkoot Pass, is used today by hikers.

CHILKOOT TRAIL

The trail begins near Dyea, 13 km north-west of Skagway, and heads north-eastwards following the Taiya River to Bennett in British Columbia. The trail takes three to four days and is 56 km long; you must be in good physical condition to attempt it. You must also be fully equipped and prepared for the unpredictable weather conditions: take a few layers of clothes and be ready constantly to peel them off then pile them back on again.

Along the trail you can see hardware, tools and supplies dumped by the gold seekers. At several places there are wooden shacks where you can put up for the night.

At the northern end you can either catch a boat from Lake Bennett to Carcross from where you can catch a bus to Whitehorse; or you can head to the Klondike Highway and hitch or take the bus to Whitehorse.

ATLIN (BRITISH COLUMBIA)

The small, remote town of Atlin, 182 km south-east of Whitehorse in British Columbia, is reached by road via the Yukon – take Highway 7 south off the Alaska Highway. The scenery is good, with forests in Atlin Provincial Park and snow-capped mountains around Atlin Lake.

BEAVER CREEK

Beaver Creek, on the Alaska Highway 457 km north-west of Whitehorse close to the Alaska border, is Canada's westernmost town. The Visitor Reception Centre (☎ 862-7321) has information on the Yukon and Alaska and the customs checkpoint is just north of the town.

STEWART CROSSING

Stewart Crossing is a supply centre between Dawson and Whitehorse and sits at the junction of the Klondike Highway and the Silver Trail (Highway 11). The Silver Trail heads north-eastward to three old, small mining

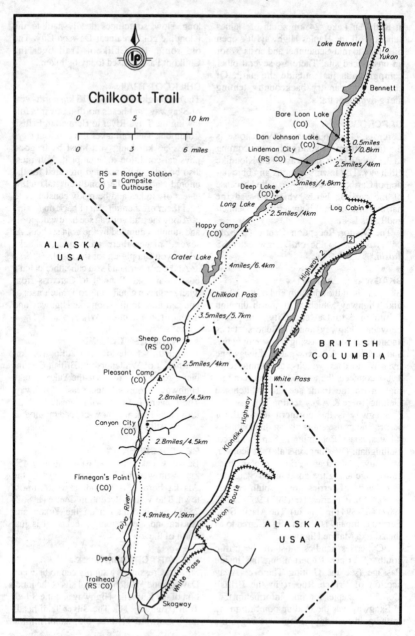

Chilkoot Trail

| 0 | 5 | 10 km |

| 0 | 3 | 6 miles |

RS = Ranger Station
C = Campsite
O = Outhouse

Lake Bennett

To Yukon

Bennett

Bare Loon Lake (CO)

Dan Johnson Lake (CO)

Lindeman City (RS CO)

0.5miles/0.8km

2.5miles/4km

3miles/4.8km

Deep Lake (CO)

Long Lake

Log Cabin

2.5miles/4km

Happy Camp (CO)

ALASKA USA

Crater Lake

4miles/6.4km

Chilkoot Pass

3.5miles/5.7km

Highway 2

2

BRITISH COLUMBIA

Sheep Camp (RS CO)

2.5miles/4km

Pleasant Camp (CO)

White Pass

2.8miles/4.5km

Canyon City (CO)

2.8miles/4.5km

Klondike Highway

Finnegan's Point (CO)

White Pass & Yukon Route

4.9miles/7.9km

Taiya River

ALASKA USA

Dyea

Trailhead (RS CO)

Skagway

and fur-trading towns: Mayo, Elsa and Keno City. Mayo is the starting point for a popular canoe trip to Dawson City via the Mayo, Stewart and Yukon rivers. Keno Hill in Keno City, with its signposts and distances to cities all over the world, offers good views.

DAWSON CITY

The Klondike Highway from Skagway in Alaska, through the north-western corner of British Columbia to Whitehorse and Dawson City, more or less traces the trail some 40,000 gold seekers took in 1898. Dawson City, at the confluence of the Yukon and Klondike rivers just 240 km south of the Arctic Circle, became the heart of the gold rush. Today it is the most interesting of the Yukon towns, with many attractions remaining from its fleeting but vibrant fling with world fame and infamy.

Once known as 'the Paris of the North', with deluxe hotels and restaurants, plush river steamers and stores stocking luxury items cherished by the world's wealthy, Dawson City is now a small town of about 1700 people. Many of the original buildings are still standing and Parks Canada has restored or preserved quite a few. Regulations ensure that new buildings are built in sympathy with the old.

As many as 300 companies are still mining for gold in the region around Dawson City. One entrepreneur once offered to pay compensation for the complete removal of the town and the inconvenience it would cause, mine the land beneath it, then replace the town just as it was. The residents refused.

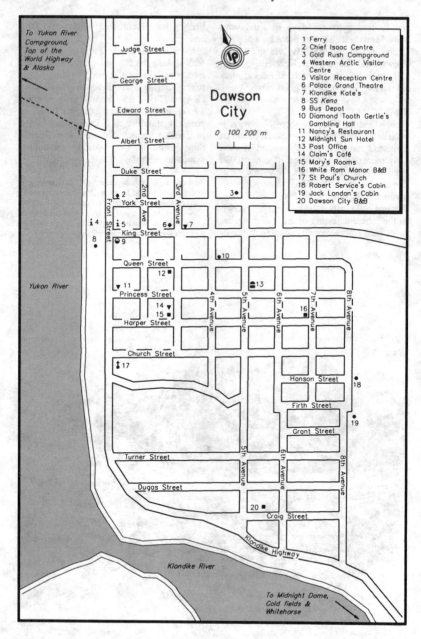

To Yukon River
Campground,
Top of the
World Highway
& Alaska

Judge Street

George Street

Edward Street

Albert Street

Duke Street

York Street

King Street

Queen Street

Princess Street

Harper Street

Church Street

Hanson Street

Firth Street

Grant Street

Turner Street

Dugas Street

Craig Street

Front Street

2nd Ave

3rd Avenue

4th Avenue

5th Avenue

6th Avenue

7th Avenue

8th Avenue

Dawson City

0   100 200 m

Yukon River

Klondike Highway

Klondike River

To Midnight Dome,
Gold fields &
Whitehorse

1 Ferry
2 Chief Isaac Centre
3 Gold Rush Campground
4 Western Arctic Visitor
   Centre
5 Visitor Reception Centre
6 Palace Grand Theatre
7 Klondike Kate's
8 SS Keno
9 Bus Depot
10 Diamond Tooth Gertie's
   Gambling Hall
11 Nancy's Restaurant
12 Midnight Sun Hotel
13 Post Office
14 Claim's Café
15 Mary's Rooms
16 White Ram Manor B&B
17 St Paul's Church
18 Robert Service's Cabin
19 Jack London's Cabin
20 Dawson City B&B

Orientation & Information

Dawson City is small enough to walk around in a few hours. The Klondike Highway leads into Front St (also called 1st Ave) beside the Yukon River. On the corner of Front and King Sts is the Visitor Reception Centre (☎ 993-5566), housed in a large wooden building. It's open each day from mid-May to mid-September between 9 am and 9 pm. Staff are dressed in turn-of-the-century costumes.

Opposite the VRC is the Western Arctic Visitor Centre (☎ 993-5175), open daily June to August from 9 am to 9 pm, which has maps and information on the Dempster Highway and Inuvik.

The post office (☎ 993-5342) is on the corner of Princess St and 5th Ave.

The Chief Isaac Centre, on the corner of Front and York Sts, has a laundrette and showers; it's open Monday to Friday from 9 am to 7 pm and at weekends from 10 am to 6 pm.

Things to See & Do

Diamond Tooth Gertie's Gambling Hall

This hall, on the corner of Queen St and 4th Ave, is a re-creation of an 1898 saloon, complete with gambling, honky-tonk piano and dancing girls. It's open May to September daily except Sundays from 8 pm to 2 am and admission is $4.50.

Palace Grand Theatre

The large, flamboyant opera house/dance hall, on the corner of 3rd Ave and King St, was built in 1899 by 'Arizona Charlie' Meadows. Like other restored buildings in town, it has a western movie-type front. There are free guided tours of the theatre.

In the theatre the Gaslight Follies presents stage shows – musicals or melodramas with villains in black and Mounties to the rescue. The shows are on every night (except Tuesday) at 8 pm from the end of May to early September and cost $11.

Dawson City Museum

The museum (☎ 993-5291) on 5th Ave houses a collection of 25,000 gold rush artefacts and displays on the district's people. Admission is $3 and it's open daily June to early September from 10 am to 6 pm.

SS Keno

The SS *Keno*, one of the area's last riverboats, is on display as a national historic site beside the Yukon River. Admission is free.

Midnight Dome

To the north the quarried face of this hill overlooks the town, but to get to the top you have to travel eight km outside Dawson City off the Klondike Highway. The Midnight Dome, at 880 metres above sea level, offers good views of the Ogilvie Mountains, Klondike Valley and Yukon River. The hill gets its name because on 21 June the midnight sun barely sinks below the Ogilvie Mountains to the north before rising again.

Gold Panning

You can try panning for gold in nearby creeks. There are tours, or you can go by car, to one of the historic mining sites. Many other claims in the area are private, so pick your spot carefully. People have been killed for less! Contact the Klondike Visitors Association (☎ 993-5575), in the same building as the Visitor Reception Centre, or Gold City Tours (☎ 993-5175) on Front St opposite the SS *Keno* for information.

Worth a look are the Klondike-era films on mining, the gold rush and other subjects shown daily in summer at 9 am and 5 pm in St Paul's Church. The church, which opens from 1 June to 1 September, is on the corner of Front and Church Sts. Admission is by donation.

Readings

Of literary interest are professional poetry recitals at 10 am and 3 pm of poems by Robert Service in the log cabin on 8th Ave where he lived from 1909 to 1912. His poems sing the praises of and hardships associated with life in the developing wilderness. Parts of 'Songs of a Rolling Stone' were written here.

In 1898, Jack London lived in the Yukon and wrote many of his popular animal stories. He's best known for *Call of the Wild*.

In the cabin on 8th Ave you can hear recitals from and talks about his works daily at 1 pm. Admission is free.

Organised Tours The Visitor Reception Centre has walking tours of the city four times daily. Gold City Tours has tours of the city and gold fields and along the Dempster Highway.

Festivals
Events to look for include the Midnight Dome Race and the three-day Dawson City Music Festival in late July. In August, there's Discovery Days, a three-day event commemorating the discovery of gold in the Klondike in 1896. Featured are parades, music and dances. In early September is the three-km Great Klondike International Outhouse Race (on wheels) – four people propel the outhouse through town while one sits on the seat!

Places to Stay
Camping *Yukon River Campground* on the western side of the river has toilets, drinking water and sites for $5. In town *Gold Rush Campground* (☎ 993-5247), on the corner of York St and 5th Ave, is mainly for RVs and has sites for $10 or $15 with electricity.

B&Bs *Whitehorse B&B Agency* (☎ 633-4609), 102 302 Steele St, Whitehorse, has a list of homes in Dawson City.

White Ram Manor B&B (☎ 993-5772), on the corner of Harper St and 7th Ave, is a friendly, easy going place with a laundry and kitchen; they'll also pick you up from the airport. Singles/doubles cost $50/60 or $55/65 with private bath. *Dawson City B&B* (☎ 993-5849), 451 Craig St at the southern end of town, has singles/doubles for $49/59; lunch, dinner and transport to and from the airport are also provided.

Hotels & Motels One of the cheapest places to stay is *Mary's Rooms* (☎ 993-6013), on the corner of Harper St and 3rd Ave, which has singles/doubles with a communal bathroom for $39/45. It doesn't accept credit cards. Nor

does the *Gold Nugget Motel* (☎ 993-5445), on the corner of Dugas St and 5th Ave. It has singles/doubles with showers for $54/56. More up-market is the *Midnight Sun Hotel* (☎ 993-5495), on the corner of Queen St and 3rd Ave. It has a licensed restaurant, a bar and singles/doubles for $97/106.

Places to Eat
There isn't a lot of choice in town. Many of the hotels have their own dining rooms.

Nancy's Restaurant on Front St has outdoor tables and reasonably priced soups, salads, sandwiches and pastries from $4 to $7. It's open daily May to September from 6 am to 9 pm. *Klondike Kate's*, next to the motel of the same name on the corner of King St and 3rd Ave, does good breakfast specials for around $4. *Claims Café*, 833 3rd Ave, specialises in German-style food and has main meals starting from around $10. The cakes are delicious.

Getting There & Around
Air There is an airport 19 km from town, with regular flights to Whitehorse and to Inuvik in the Northwest Territories. The flight to Inuvik with Alkan Airways costs $270 one way or $460 return.

Bus From the bus depot on the corner of Front and King Sts Norline Coaches runs buses to Inuvik, Fairbanks and Whitehorse; the one-way fare to Whitehorse is $66. Gold City Tours has two buses a week to Inuvik for $180 one way.

Car At the northern end of Front St a free ferry crosses the river to the start of the scenic Top of the World Highway (Highway 9). It's a gravel road which extends 105 km to the Alaska border. From there Taylor Highway heads south through Alaska to meet the Alaska Highway at Tetlin Junction. The Klondike Highway connects Dawson City with Skagway via Stewart Crossing and Whitehorse. The road is open all year and the surface is now sealed almost all the way.

See the Dempster Highway section following for information on that road.

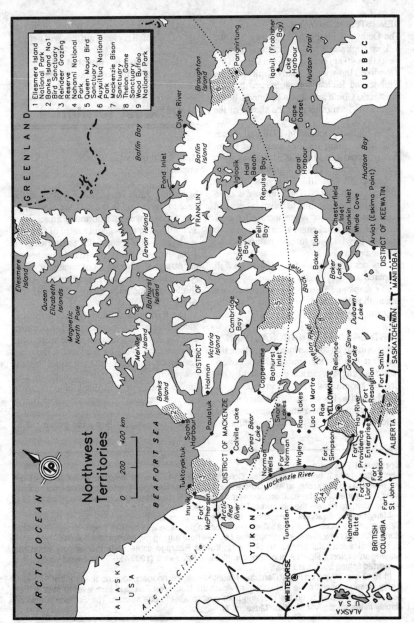

DEMPSTER HIGHWAY

The Dempster Highway (Highway 5 in the Yukon, Highway 8 in the Northwest Territories) starts 40 km east of Dawson City off the Klondike Highway. It heads north over the Ogilvie and Richardson mountains beyond the Arctic Circle and down to Inuvik in the Northwest Territories near the shores of the Beaufort Sea.

The highway opened in 1978 and makes road travel along the full length of North America possible. Inuvik is a long way from Dawson – along 741 km of gravel road – but the scenery is beautiful: hills, valleys, rivers and vast open spaces. The highway is open all year but the best time to travel is between June and September when the ferries over the Peel and Mackenzie rivers are able to operate. In winter ice forms a natural bridge over the rivers.

Services along the route are few so go well prepared and carry extra gasoline.

For maps and information on conditions ask at the Western Arctic Visitor Centre in Dawson City.

NORTHERN YUKON NATIONAL PARK

The Northern Yukon National Park along the Beaufort Sea and adjoining Alaska covers 10,170 sq km. The park is dominated by the British Mountains and its vegetation is mainly tundra. It's on the migration route of the Porcupine caribou and is also a major waterfowl habitat. Its facilities are minimal

and, though there's no road access, flights on one of the small regional airlines will get you there.

Off the coast is **Herschel Island**, the Yukon's first territorial park.

Northwest Territories

Area 3,380,000 sq km
Population 54,000

Stretching 3200 km from the Yukon in the west to Greenland in the east, the Northwest Territories cover an enormous area: over $3\frac{1}{4}$ million sq km – about a third of Canada. With just 54,000 people, the territories have a population density of around one person per 60 sq km. That's a lot of breathing room. Nearly half the region is north of the Arctic Circle and includes many islands in the Arctic Ocean.

The territories are divided into three districts: Mackenzie, Franklin and Keewatin. The District of Mackenzie in the west is the only one accessible by road and is the most developed, containing the territories' largest towns of Yellowknife, the capital, and Inuvik. The District of Franklin to the north and east includes the huge islands of Baffin and Ellesmere. The District of Keewatin is bordered in the south by the provinces of

---

Northwest Passage

Soon after 1492 it became clear that Columbus had landed on a 'new' continent and had not discovered a westerly route to Asia. Others then began the search for a waterway to the Orient sailing around the Americas. The southern route was successfully navigated by Ferdinand Magellan in 1521, but the northern route – the Northwest Passage – was to take a good deal longer.

Many famous explorers – including Sir Martin Frobisher, Sir Francis Drake, Henry Hudson and Captain James Cook – tried but failed. The most tragic failure was in 1845 when Sir John Franklin, along with 128 crew members, disappeared somewhere among the islands of the Arctic.

The first successful navigation of the Northwest Passage came early this century when the Norwegian explorer, Roald Amundsen, completed a three-year (1903-1906), east-west voyage in a converted fishing boat, the *Gjöa*.

In 1942, the *St Roch*, a Royal Canadian Mounted Police schooner under the command of Sargeant Henry Lawson, became the first ship to navigate the Northwest Passage from west to east. It then became the first ship to do the crossing from east to west in one season. The *St Roch* is now on display in the Vancouver Maritime Museum. ■

'Inukshuk' – the likeness of man

Manitoba and eastern Saskatchewan and in the east by Hudson Bay.

HISTORY

The earliest known inhabitants of the North-west Territories, the Dene, or Athapaskans, came to the region from Asia somewhere between 10,000 and 40,000 years ago. The Inuit are thought to have arrived between 4000 and 8000 years ago.

The Vikings were the first Europeans to see the Northwest Territories, arriving in about 1000 AD. Later the search began for the legendary Northwest Passage – a sea passage from the Atlantic to the Pacific Ocean and the shortest route to China and its riches. Canada was thought of as merely a stopping-off point on the way to Asia. From 1524, British, French and Dutch adventurers all joined the search for a waterway through the continent. Many died but the north was mapped out in the process.

The first successful navigation was made in 1906 by Roald Amundsen. Since then, several others have done it, mostly in military vessels. In 1960, the US submarine *Seadragon* was the first to do it under water. Today the route is used little except as a supply line during the very short summer thaw.

With the prospect of wealth being made from whaling and the fur trade, Europeans, like Alexander Mackenzie, began to appear and explore in greater numbers during the 18th and 19th centuries. In their wake came missionaries who built churches, schools and hospitals. Until 1870, when the Canadian government took over, administration of the territories was shared between the Hudson's Bay Company and the British government.

Following the discovery of oil in the 1920s near Fort Norman, a territorial government was set up. In the 1930s the discovery of radium around Great Bear Lake marked

Aurora Borealis

The Arctic aurora or Aurora Borealis can be seen from the Yukon, the Northwest Territories and in the far north of the provinces. The best time to see it is around March and April and from late August to late October. It appears in many forms – pillars, streaks, wisps, haloes of vibrating light and sometimes looks like the rippling folds of a curtain. Most often, the Arctic aurora glows faintly green or pale rose, but during periods of extreme activity it can flare into bright yellows and crimsons.

The Aurora Borealis is commonly known as the northern lights, while in the southern hemisphere the phenomenon is known as the Aurora Australis or southern lights.

The visible aurora is created by solar winds (streams of charged particles from the sun) flowing through the earth's magnetic field in the polar regions. These winds are drawn earthward where the particles collide with electrons and ions in the ionosphere about 160 km above the earth. This collision releases the energy which creates the visible aurora.

The Inuit and other groups attach a spiritual significance to the aurora. Some consider it to be a gift from the dead to light the long polar nights, while others believe it to be a storehouse of events past and future. ■

Timber Wolf

the beginning of more rapid change and 20th-century development. WW II brought airfields and weather stations. The discovery of gold in 1934 near Yellowknife swelled the town's numbers and in 1967 it became the capital.

In the 1950s the federal government began health, welfare and education programmes. The 1960s saw accessibility to the territories increase, with roads being built and more aeroplanes connecting more places.

An intriguing, thought-provoking aside is that the modernisation and development of the region has meant all but the disappearance of the last North Americans to have lived their entire lives out of doors.

The search for oil, gas and minerals changed some areas rapidly and still continues.

Given the ever fluctuating fortunes in natural resources, the territories are relying more each year on tourism as a money-earner. Increased accessibility, together with the lure of pristine wilderness, means a continuing rise in the number of visitors to the territories. Other sources of income include fish, fur and handicrafts.

Canada and the USA are currently debating sovereignty of the of the far north, with the Americans arguing that portions fall into the international realm so no one country can lay claim to them. The USA, of course, is interested in the area militarily. To the consternation of some Canadians, the US navy plies the waters of the far north at will – and without seeking what opponents view as Canada's rightful permission.

GEOGRAPHY & CLIMATE

The Northwest Territories can be separated into two geographical regions – the sub-Arctic and the Arctic. The dividing line runs more or less obliquely from the Yukon coast to the south-eastern corner of the District of Keewatin on the shores of Hudson Bay.

To the south of this line the land is characterised by short coniferous forests which spread westward to the Mackenzie Mountains straddling the Yukon border. To the north lie the flat, treeless plains of the tundra.

The glacial action of the last ice age left hundreds of lakes and rivers and a permanently frozen layer of subsoil called permafrost.

Winters are long and extremely cold, but summers in the south are surprisingly warm, with temperatures reaching 30°C, which, coupled with the long daylight hours, makes travelling very pleasant. The climate is dry, with the average annual rain/snowfall being less than 30 cm.

FAUNA

Whales, walruses and seals can be seen along the northern coastlines and in the waters around the northern islands in summer. In the rivers and lakes is a huge variety of fish, including char, pike, trout, pickerel (walleye), whitefish and inconnu (a relative of the whitefish whose name is French for 'unknown'). In the skies you'll see birds such as the raven, eagle, hawk, ptarmigan, gull, snowy owl and auk.

On land there are black, grizzly and polar bears. (The polar bear is the official symbol of the Northwest Territories and all car licence plates are shaped like one.) Other animals include the musk ox, fox, wolf, moose, caribou, beaver, porcupine and otter.

National & Territorial Parks

The Northwest Territories have four national parks. Auyuittuq National Park is on Baffin Island to the east. Ellesmere Island National Park is on the north of Ellesmere Island, just across Robeson Channel from north-western Greenland. Nahanni National Park is in the Mackenzie Mountains in the far south-west. Wood Buffalo National Park, south of Great Slave Lake, is the only one accessible by road.

There are three historic parks: Kekerten Island and Qaummaarviit, both off the east coast of Baffin Island; and Northwest Passage at Gjoa Haven on King William Island.

There are also more than 30 parks run by the territorial government for recreation, and a number of wildlife sanctuaries. Most parks and their campgrounds are open mid-May to mid-September.

PEOPLE

Around Mackenzie River and Great Slave Lake the people call themselves the Dene, or Athabaskans, and, together with the Inuit, are the original northern peoples. The word Inuit refers in general to an Eskimo in Canada, as opposed to the Eskimo of Asia or the Aleutian Islands (Alaska). The term Eskimo is not appreciated by the Inuit and is being used less and less. The term Inuit simply means 'people'.

The Inuit number about 16,000 and the Dene 11,000; the rest are mainly Métis (of mixed race) and Whites.

The following is the longest word in the language of the Inuvialuktun Inuit (are you read for it?): *Tuktusiuriagatigitqingnapinngitkyptinnga.*

It means, 'You'll never go caribou hunting with me again'. So there.

INFORMATION
Tourist Offices

For information on all parts of the territories contact Travel Arctic (☎ 873-7200), Dept 487, Yellowknife, NWT, X1A 2L9. A branch of the government, it also operates the toll free 800-661-0788 number for visitor information. The free brochure *Explorers' Guide* is published annually and contains useful information on travel and accommodation in the Northwest Territories.

The territories have been divided into eight different travel zones and the regional offices to contact are:

Arctic Coast Tourism Association
   PO Box 91, Cambridge Bay (☎ 983-2224)
Baffin Tourism Association
   PO Box 820, Iqaluit X0A 0H0 (☎ 979-6551)
Big River Tourism Association
   PO Box 185, Hay River X0E 0R0 (☎ 874-2422)
Delta-Beaufort Tourism Association
   PO Box 2759, Inuvik X0E 0T0 (☎ 979-4321)

Travel Keewatin
> Department EG, PO Box 328, Rankin Inlet X0C 0G0 (☎ 645-2618)

Nahanni-Ram Tourism Association
> PO Box 177, Fort Simpson X0E 0N0 (☎ 695-3182)

Northern Frontier Visitors Association
> PO Box 1107, Yellowknife X1A 2N8 (☎ 873-3131)

Sahtu Tourism Association
> PO Box 115, Norman Wells X0E 0V0 (☎ 587-2054)

As in Alberta, the tourist offices are called Visitor Information Centres. These can be found in Yellowknife, Inuvik, Fort Smith, Fort MacPherson, Rae-Edzo and Hay River. There's also one on Highway 1 at the Alberta border, open May to September.

Holidays
As well as the national holidays, the first Monday in August is a public holiday.

Telephone
The telephone code for places within the District of Mackenzie is the same as that for Alberta and the Yukon – 403. In Franklin and Keewatin it's 819.

Time
The Northwest Territories cover four time zones. From west to east these are Mountain, Central, Eastern and Atlantic standard time. So when it's 12 noon in Yellowknife it's 2 pm in Iqaluit at the eastern end of Baffin Island.

Maps
Detailed topographical maps are available in Yellowknife, from Energy, Mines & Resources (☎ 920-8299), 8th Floor, Bellanca Building, 50th St. The Canada Map Office (☎ (613) 952-7000), 615 Booth St, Ottawa, Ontario K1A 0E9, has all types of detailed maps of the territories, including small-scale topographical ones which are good for hikers. The office will send you an index and you'll have to pick the map numbers you need from that. Maps in Yellowknife are in short supply, so getting one beforehand is not a bad idea.

ACTIVITIES
For a lot of visitors, a trip to the Northwest Territories means hiking, climbing, canoeing and camping in the national and territorial parks during the short summer season. For others it's to observe the wildlife. These activities permit the visitor to see the area's uniqueness and rugged beauty. There is every manner of tour and guided trip for visitors to pursue these outdoor activities, but – in the District of Mackenzie at least – most things can also be done on your own, which is much cheaper.

Organised Tours
For many the best way to see the more inaccessible parts of the Northwest Territories, especially the districts of Franklin and Keewatin, is on an organised tour. These can be either general or highly specialised trips. They are, however, usually quite expensive. The *Explorers' Guide* has lists of companies, their addresses and the types of tours they offer. For further information contact Travel Arctic.

In 1988 a New York-based cruise ship became the first tourist vessel to navigate the legendary Northwest Passage, from Newfoundland to Alaska. The 40-day history-making trip cost each passenger a tidy $20,000. Sign here.

GETTING THERE & AROUND
Air
Canadian Airlines flies from Edmonton, Winnipeg, Montreal and Whitehorse to Yellowknife, Inuvik, Fort Simpson, Iqaluit and other places. Air Canada flies from Edmonton and Calgary to Yellowknife, with connecting flights on NWT Air to Inuvik, Cambridge Bay, Fort Simpson and Coppermine. NWT Air also flies between Winnipeg and Rankin Inlet, and between Yellowknife and Iqaluit.

From Whitehorse, Alkan Air has flights four times a week to Inuvik, while Delta Air

Charter has three flights a week to Yellowknife. First Air flies from Ottawa, Montreal and Nuuk (Greenland) to Yellowknife, Pangnirtung, Broughton Island, Rankin Inlet and other destinations.

Air Inuit connects northern Quebec with communities in the District of Keewatin.

About 10 small companies have scheduled flights between points within the territories. Many more operate on a charter basis, using floats (on lakes) or wheels to land in summer, skis in winter. The *Explorers' Guide* lists many of these companies. Charter fares can sometimes be figured by finding out the price per distance rate – say $1.50 per km as a rough guide.

Bus

Greyhound Bus Lines has a daily service from Edmonton, Alberta, to Hay River for $136.25 one way. Connections for points further north are available three times a week with Arctic Frontier (☎ 873-4892 in Yellowknife). If you're coming from Edmonton and you don't want to go to Hay River you can change buses in Enterprise and continue via Fort Providence and Edzo to Yellowknife. Fares and schedules are available through Greyhound Bus Lines.

North of 60 Bus Lines (☎ 872-2031 in Fort Smith) has a service Monday to Friday between Hay River and Fort Resolution. The one-way fare is $30.

Car

Only the District of Mackenzie in the west, north of Alberta, is accessible by car, and most of the highways are gravel. The highway north from Edmonton is almost completely paved as far as Enterprise. Gravel roads connect Hay River, Wood Buffalo National Park, Yellowknife and Fort Simpson. The Mackenzie Highway is the name for the section linking Alberta to Fort Simpson and Fort Smith.

The Liard Highway, which heads north off the Alaska Highway near Fort Nelson, is also gravel and links northern British Columbia to Fort Liard in the Northwest Territories. It then goes on to meet the Mackenzie

Highway (Highway 1) south of Fort Simpson. From there the Mackenzie Highway heads eastward to Enterprise.

The road from Fort Providence north to Yellowknife runs along the edge of the Mackenzie Bison Sanctuary and it's not uncommon to see bison on the road. Sandhill cranes and ptarmigans from the bird world are also fairly common. The ponds you'll notice by the side of the road are due to holes dug for sand and gravel needed for the road's construction.

In the northern part of the District of Mackenzie, the Dempster Highway connects the Yukon with Inuvik. This route passes through excellent mountain scenery much of the way to the Mackenzie River Delta, nipping into a portion of the huge Reindeer Grazing Reserve before ending up at Inuvik.

There are vehicle rental outlets in Hay River and Yellowknife.

For information about conditions on the Dempster Highway the numbers to call are ☎ 800-661-0752 toll free, ☎ 873-0158 (Yellowknife) or ☎ 979-2040 (Inuvik). For other highways call ☎ 800-661-0752 toll free or ☎ 873-0157 (Yellowknife).

For information about Dempster Highway ferries call ☎ 800-661-0750 or ☎ 873-0158 (Yellowknife). For other ferries call ☎ 800-661-0751 toll free or within Yellowknife ring ☎ 873-7799 .

Warning During a six-week period in the late fall and early spring, when river freeze-ups and ice break-ups occur, ferries cannot run over the rivers. Therefore there is no road access or bus service for this period. This includes to Yellowknife.

Precautions There can be long distances between service stations, so travellers should have some extra gasoline, spare parts, water and food with them. Because most of the roads in the Northwest Territories are not sealed it's a good idea to protect your gasoline tank, lights and windscreen with coverings.

DISTRICT OF MACKENZIE

The District of Mackenzie is the most accessible area, being the only district with any roads, and is where most visitors go.

It borders the Yukon in the west and Alberta in the south. This is the only area of the territories with a forestry business, and it has most of the fishing as well.

The Mackenzie Mountains, with peaks of 2700 metres, straddle the Yukon border. The Mackenzie River, the longest waterway in Canada, runs north-west along the Mackenzie Valley from Great Slave Lake to the Beaufort Sea in the Arctic Ocean. Most of the population lives around Great Slave Lake and Great Bear Lake, which has many mines. The two national parks in the District of Mackenzie are Nahanni in the south-west, and Wood Buffalo, which spreads across the Alberta border.

The District of Mackenzie has fairly warm summers with an average temperature of 13°C.

RV or tent camping is really the only way to see this part of the country at a reasonable price.

Longer-distance travelling with food and accommodation in towns is expensive with a capital E.

Both camping and canoeing are possible along the district's highway system. Several communities rent boats or canoes. From roadside campgrounds, trips can be taken around the lakes, and away from the roads you can pick your own camping spot. It is not hard to have a lake to yourself; inquire at one of the Visitor Information Centres for more information. Remember that the water is cold enough to kill you in 15 minutes, so keep close to shore in a canoe.

Along the highway system the fee for a site at a government campground is $5. Permits are required: get them from Visitor Information Centres, from park information offices or from officers when they visit the campground. Campgrounds have firewood and are open from 15 May to 15 September. Don't forget to bring insect repellent.

Yellowknife

Europeans were attracted to this area by the discovery of gold, first in 1934 and again in 1945.

Today Yellowknife has a population of

Husky puppies

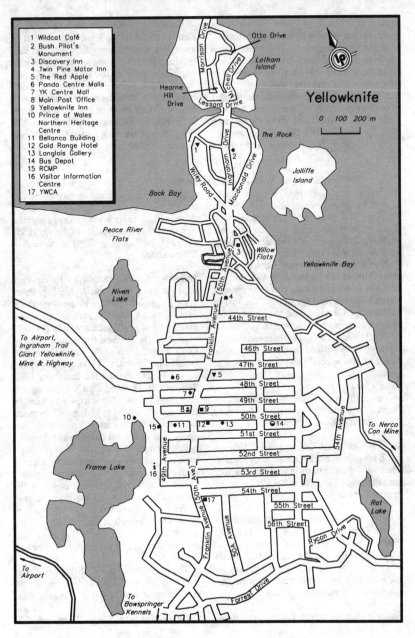

1 Wildcat Café
2 Bush Pilot's Monument
3 Discovery Inn
4 Twin Pine Motor Inn
5 The Red Apple
6 Panda Centre Malls
7 YK Centre Mall
8 Main Post Office
9 Yellowknife Inn
10 Prince of Wales Northern Heritage Centre
11 Bellanca Building
12 Gold Range Hotel
13 Langlois Gallery
14 Bus Depot
15 RCMP
16 Visitor Information Centre
17 YWCA

Yellowknife

0   100   200 m

Otto Drive
Morrison Drive
Mitchell Drive
Latham Island
Hearne Hill Drive
Lessord Drive
Ingraham Drive
The Rock
Macdonald Drive
Wiley Road
Back Bay
Jolliffe Island
Peace River Flats
Willow Flats
50th Avenue
Yellowknife Bay
Niven Lake
44th Street
To Airport, Ingraham Trail Giant Yellowknife Mine & Highway
46th Street
Franklin Avenue
47th Street
48th Street
49th Street
50th Street
54th Avenue
To Nerco Con Mine
Frame Lake
51st Street
52nd Street
49th Avenue (50th Ave)
53rd Street
54th Street
Franklin Avenue (50th Ave)
50A Avenue
55th Street
Rat Lake
56th Street
Rycon Drive
To Airport
To Bowspringer Kennels
Forrest Drive

around 15,000 and is by far the largest town in the territories, of which it is the capital.

A modern, fast-growing settlement on the northern shores of Great Slave Lake, 341 km from Fort Smith by road, Yellowknife is essentially a government town, but it also acts as the regional commercial centre and people from all over Canada now live and work there. Visitors use Yellowknife as a base for camping and fishing trips and for exploring the rocky landscape and nearby lakes.

Orientation & Information Yellowknife is divided into the new (south) and old (north) parts of town, which are connected by Franklin Ave (50th Ave), the main thoroughfare. Coming from the south into the city, the highway leads you past the airport, along 48th St and into Franklin Ave.

The Visitor Information Centre is currently housed in a log cabin on 49th Ave but is due to move to 48th St, near the Prince of Wales Northern Heritage Centre. The Visitor Information Centre is also the home of the Northern Frontier Visitors Association (☎ 873-3131). You can get maps, canoe routes and a guide to settlements across the territories, and also special fishing, canoeing and motoring guides. The centre is open daily from 9 am to 7 pm.

The main post office, on the corner of Franklin Ave and 49th St, is open Monday to Friday from 8.30 am to 5.30 pm.

Gold Mines Nerco Con and Giant Yellowknife are gold mines at either end of the city. They used to offer tours in summer and may start them again – check at the Visitor Information Centre.

Prince of Wales Northern Heritage Centre This is a good museum (☎ 873-7551) beside Frame Lake off 49th St with diorama displays on the lifestyles of the Dene and Inuit and natural sciences. It now has a gallery on the history of aviation in the Northwest Territories too. Admission is free.

Eskimo Dog Research Foundation Here,

at Bowspringer Kennels (☎ 873-4252) on Kam Lake Rd at the south-western end of town, you can see a project which has successfully preserved the *kingmik*, a rare Inuit dog. There are over 100 at the kennel.

Bush Pilot's Monument For a good view of the town, walk north up Franklin Ave to the Bush Pilot's Monument in Old Town. You can see over the lake and the town's odd assortment of housing.

Dettah This is a small Dogrib Dene village south-east of town across the bay where you can get a look at the traditional way of life of these people. There are no tourist facilities. You can either hire a boat or take the 11 km road off the Ingraham Trail north-east of Yellowknife.

Activities Starting from Fred Henne Park opposite the airport, the 72-km **Ingraham Trail** (Highway 4) leads to areas good for fishing, hiking, canoeing, camping and picnicking – but you'll need a vehicle.

In Fred Henne Park itself there is **Long Lake Beach**, reputedly one of the best beaches in Canada, and hiking trails. About 10 km further east on the Ingraham Trail, **Yellowknife River** is used for fishing and both short and long canoe trips. At **Madeline Lake** there is a 3.2-km hiking trail. **Prelude Lake Park**, 30 km east of Yellowknife, is a pretty spot with good fishing and hiking.

Further east at **Cameron River Bridge** there is a trail to a small waterfall where the local people swim, though these waters ain't Miami Beach. You can also canoe in the river. At **Reid Lake**, 60 km from Yellowknife, you can go canoeing or hike back to town. The road ends at **Tibbett Lake**, which is said to be excellent for fishing and is also the start of some charted canoe routes including one to

The Sportsman (☎ 873-2911) and Overlander Sports (☎ 873-2474), both on 50th St, rent canoes by the day and camping supplies.

Organised Tours Raven Tours (☎ 873-

4776) has its office in Yellowknife Inn and offers three-hour bus tours of the city and nearby gold mines for $25. You can combine this tour with a cruise on Great Slave Lake for $45; this cruise takes you to the village of Dettah. Raven Tours also arranges half-day excursions along the Ingraham Trail and fishing trips.

Latham Island Airways (☎ 920-2891) is one of a number of air charter companies offering flightseeing tours. A 25-minute flight costs $65.

Other outfitting and wilderness businesses offer longer-term, much more expensive specialised trips in the Yellowknife area. Great Slave Sledging Company (☎ 920-4542), to give an example, has dog-team expeditions for one week to two months. These would be great trips, travelling some traditional routes and seeing wildlife, but they're very, very costly.

Festivals There are various festivals and events held periodically through the year. The Visitor Information Centre will have an up-to-date list of activities planned.

The Caribou Carnival is an annual festival held in late March each year, with parades, concerts, skits and contests like igloo building.

There's also the Canadian Championship Dog Derby, a three-day dog-sled race about 240 km long. Folk on the Rocks is a folk concert with musicians from all over the country and the USA. It takes place at Long Lake on the second or third weekend in July.

Places to Stay & Eat Accommodation and food are costly in Yellowknife. The cheapest way to live is to buy food at the supermarket in the YK Centre Mall and stay at one of the campgrounds.

Several campgrounds exist along the Ingraham Trail. The closest to town is at *Fred Henne Park* (☎ 920-2472) which has full facilities including showers and toilets. A site costs $10. You can also camp at *Prelude Lake Park* or *Reid Lake Park* for $8; both have toilet and washing facilities.

The *YWCA* (☎ 920-2777), 5004 54th St on the corner of Franklin Ave, takes in both sexes and has 70 rooms that can be rented by the night, week or month. Singles/doubles with kitchenettes cost $80/90. There's dormitory accommodation but it's mainly for people down on their luck who stay on a long-term basis – and it's usually full.

If you want to stay at a B&B you can make a reservation through *Yellowknife B&B* (☎ 873-6238), 20 Hearne Hill Drive, which has a list of those in the Yellowknife area. Prices seem fairly standardised at $50/70 for singles/doubles.

Ones you could try are *Barb Bromley* (☎ 873-4786), 31 Morrison Drive; *Sharon Robinson* (☎ 873-5574), 123 Arden Ave; *Yetta Turner* (☎ 873-5219), 43 Otto Drive; or *Bernard Straker* (☎ 873-2893), 41 Calder Crescent. These places are open all year but they don't have a lot of space, so phone before going.

In the hotel category, *Gold Range Hotel* (☎ 873-4441), 5010 50th St, is one of the cheapest, with singles/doubles from $60/70. It has a bar downstairs which can get a bit noisy. *Yellowknife Inn* (☎ 873-2601), on Franklin Ave between 49th and 50th Sts, has rooms for $70 per person. *Twin Pine Motor Inn* (☎ 873-8511), 4115 Franklin Ave halfway between downtown and the old town, is a friendly place and charges $90/95 for singles/doubles. At the *Discovery Inn* (☎ 873-4151), 4701 Franklin Ave, rooms are $100/125 without/with a kitchenette.

The eateries in Yellowknife are also a bit pricey, but there are some fast-food places in the shopping malls. The *Lunch Box* in YK Centre Mall has burgers and fries for $7. *Smitty's Family Restaurant*, on the main floor of Panda II Mall, is always reliable and has pancakes or omelettes with hash browns for $7; coffee is $1. The *Red Apple*, on the corner of Franklin Ave and 47th St, serves Western and Chinese food and has a bar. Sandwiches cost from $3.25, fish & chips $7.25 and breakfasts (served all day) from $4.

For a treat head for the *Wildcat Café* on the corner of Wiley Rd and Doombos Lane in the old town. Set in a log cabin reminiscent of Yellowknife's early days, the Wildcat Café is acknowledged as one of Canada's top 100 restaurants. It serves salads for $4 or main dishes like caribou bourgignon for $18 and is open daily.

Things to Buy Yellowknife is the distribution centre and major retailer of craft items from around the territories. Of course, prices are lower in more remote areas but also higher in southern Canada. Whether artistic or purely functional, the goods are not cheap but are authentic and usually well made. Northern Images (☎ 873-5944) in YK Centre Mall has various Dene and Inuit works. The Langlois Gallery (☎ 873-4721), 5016 50th St, also displays and sells arts and crafts.

Getting Around Arctic Frontier runs a bus service from Rainbow Valley along Franklin Ave to Frame Lake. The one-way fare is $1.50.

Fort Providence
Fort Providence, a town of 700, lies on the banks of the Mackenzie River, 312 km south of Yellowknife. Nearby is the Mackenzie Bison Sanctuary, with the largest herd of free-ranging pure wood bison in the world. About two km before town is a campground by the river; it has pit toilets and drinking water. In town itself are a couple of motels. *Big River Motel* (☎ 699- 4301) has a service station, dining room, general store and singles/doubles for $55/65. *Snowshoe Inn* (☎ 699-3511) charges $70 for a single or a double.

Fort Smith & Wood Buffalo National Park
Fort Smith, a town of 2500, is on the Alberta border at Mile 0 of the Northwest Territories highway system. It was once a fur-trading post in the north-western network of depots. Nearby is the entrance to Wood Buffalo National Park, for which the town acts as a supply centre. Get your food in town: there is nowhere to buy it in the park. For details on the park see the Alberta chapter.

There is a campground at Queen Elizabeth Park on the banks of Slave River close to town. In Fort Smith the *Pinecrest Hotel* (☎ 872-2320) is quite reasonable, at $40/45 for single/doubles without bath. *Pelican Rapids Inn* (☎ 872-2789) has singles/doubles with kitchenettes for $65/70.

Hay River
The town of Hay River sits on the southern shore of Great Slave Lake, 38 km north of Enterprise. It's a major distribution centre where barges load up for trips to settlements on connecting waterways as far north as the Arctic coast. Fish packing is done here too. About 50 km south on the Hay River itself is Alexandra Falls, 32 metres high.

The Visitor Information Centre is on the corner of Mackenzie and McBryan Drives.

There is a campground on Vale Island and several hotels in town. *Cedar Rest Motel* (☎ 874-37632) is near the bus depot and has rooms from $37. *Migrator Motel* (☎ 874-6792) has furnished apartments with kitchenettes for $55.

As well as the bus (see Getting There & Around earlier) two airlines service Hay River: Canadian Airlines (☎ 874-2434), which flies to Inuvik, Yellowknife and points south, and Ptarmigan Airways (☎ 873-4461 in Yellowknife), to Yellowknife and Fort Simpson.

Nahanni National Park
This is a wilderness park in the south-western corner of the District of Mackenzie, close to the Yukon border. Nahanni National Park is designated as a World Heritage Site by UNESCO because of its spectacular, pristine nature. The park has plenty of wildlife, with good hiking, climbing and photographic opportunities. It is visited mainly by canoeists wishing to challenge the white waters (considered amongst the best on the continent) of the South Nahanni River. Canoeists should know that runs rushing through the three huge canyons are only for the experienced.

Also in the park are sulphur hot springs at **Rabbitkettle** and **Wildmint** and waterfalls such as **Virginia Falls**, which at 96 metres is about twice the height of Niagara Falls. For camping, there are seven primitive areas set aside with tables and fireplaces.

The main park access point is **Fort Simpson**, about 360 km west of Yellowknife at the confluence of the Liard and Mackenzie rivers. The town has a park information office, camping facilities and several hotels.

Organised Tours From Fort Simpson there are boat, raft and canoe trips into the park. The park information office can supply details. Simpson Air (☎ 695-2505) in Fort Simpson and Nahanni National Park Tours (☎ 703-4421) in Fort Liard are two companies offering tours of the park.

From Yellowknife, Canada North Expeditions (☎ 920-2196) has trips to Virginia Falls including a two-night stay in Fort Simpson for $579; Raven Tours (☎ 873-4776) does a similar trip for $675. Trail Head (☎ (613) 722-9717), 1341 Wellington St West, Ottawa, Ontario K1Y 3B8, runs canoe and hiking trips; a one-week rafting trip along the South Nahanni River costs $1695 while a three-week canoeing trip will set you back $3195. Whitewolf Adventures (☎ (604) 736-0664), 2565 West 2nd Ave, Vancouver, British Columbia V6K 1J7, also has rafting and canoe tours.

Getting There & Away The park is not easy – or cheap – to get to. From Fort Simpson or from Watson Lake in the Yukon, you can fly in by charter. There is no road access but the Liard Highway, which connects Fort Liard with Fort Simpson following the eastern side of the Liard River, may make Nahanni more accessible. As yet no bridge has been constructed, but when this is done, getting to the park will be a lot less hassle and considerably cheaper.

Norman Wells

On the northern shore of the Mackenzie River halfway between Fort Simpson and Inuvik, this town of 800 has long been (and remains) an oil town. There's a campground in town and several hotels. Air service is available from Edmonton, Yellowknife and Inuvik. Canadian Airlines (☎ 587-2361) has an office in town. North-Wright Air (☎ 587-2288) flies between here and Inuvik.

Of more interest is the **Canol Heritage Trail**, a hiking trail designated a national historic site which leads 372 km south-west to the Yukon border. From there, a road leads to Ross River and the Yukon highway system. Originally intended as an oil-supply route to Whitehorse during WW II, the trail has the remains of army camps and abandoned equipment, as well as peaks, canyons, barrens and lots of wildlife. There are no facilities along this trail.

Inuvik

Inuvik, with a population of 3500, is the territories' second largest town, although it was only founded as late as 1955 as a supply centre. It lies on the East Channel of the Mackenzie River about 90 km south of the Arctic coast. For nearly two months each year, from the end of May, it has 24 hours of daylight every day. The population is roughly one third Inuit, one third Dene and one third White.

The Visitor Information Centre is on Mackenzie Rd.

Note that the first snow falls sometime around the end of August.

The two main attractions in town are the igloo-shaped **Catholic church** and **Ingamo Hall**, a three-storey community centre built of logs. Crafts, including locally made parkas, are for sale.

Walking, bus and boat tours are available. Arctic Tour Company (☎ 979-4100) offers 1½-hour bus tours of the town and surrounding landscape for $20.

Festivals The Arctic Northern Games, the biggest northern games of their kind, are often held in Inuvik in July, but the location and dates change, so ask where and when somewhere further south. The games feature traditional Dene and Inuit sports, contests, dancing, music, crafts and the 'Good Woman' contest, during which women display various household skills such as animal skinning.

Delta Daze is a smaller celebration held on Thanksgiving weekend (October) before the long winter sets in.

Places to Stay *Chuk Park Campground*, about 3½ km before town on the Dempster Highway, is open from June to October and provides hot showers and firewood; the office is open 24 hours a day for the duration. The Dene band operates the campground, charges $8 a site and puts on various activities. The campground has a good view and the breeze keeps the mosquitoes down a bit. In town, *Happy Valley Campground* has similar facilities and also charges $8 a site.

There are four hotels in Inuvik, all charging about the same price. Cheapest is *Mackenzie Hotel* (☎ 979-2861), which has rooms from $100. *Finto Motel Inn* (☎ 979-2647), on the corner of Mackenzie Rd and Marine Bypass, has rooms from $115.

Places to Eat If you're driving, consider bringing in your food (especially from Alaska) and you'll save a few bucks. The *Roost*, a sandwich and burger takeout, has the lowest prices in town. The hotels all have restaurants but meals are not cheap. On the menu at *Mackenzie Hotel* is musk ox stew, something you won't see down south.

Getting There & Around A couple of local airlines fly to places within the region. Antler Aviation (☎ 979-2220) and Aklak Air (☎ 979-3555/777) fly to Tuktoyaktuk, Aklavik and Fort MacPherson. The regular return fare to Tuktoyaktuk is $196, to Aklavik $118 and to Fort MacPherson $198, but there are discounts available. Both airlines offer charter services. There are scheduled air services from Edmonton, Yellowknife and Whitehorse. (See also the introductory Getting There & Around section for the Northwest Territories.)

Several companies run buses along the Dempster Highway between Dawson City and Inuvik. Arctic Tour Company (☎ 979-4100) has three buses a week in each

direction; Gold City Tours (☎ 993-5175 in Dawson City) has two a week. Both charge $180 one way. Norline Coaches (☎ 668-3355 in Whitehorse) runs buses from Whitehorse.

Around Inuvik
About 100 km north-east of Inuvik on the Arctic coast is **Tuktoyaktuk**, commonly known as Tuk, a land base for some of the Beaufort Sea oil and gas explorations. Pods of beluga whales can sometimes be seen from there. In the land around Tuk are **pingos** – huge mounds made of earth and ice.

Inuvik lies in the **Mackenzie Delta** which, covering an area of over 12,000 sq km, is the largest river delta in Canada and one of the world's great wildlife regions. It's home to many fur-bearing animals and hundreds of species of bird use it for summer nesting.

The 1800-km **Mackenzie River** is the longest in Canada and the 13th longest in the world. It's an important transport route, linking Fort Providence on Great Slave Lake with Inuvik in the north but because of the extreme cold is only navigable for about four months of the year.

A number of companies offer a variety of trips on the river. With Midnight Express Tours (☎ 979-2104) you can do a three-hour midnight cruise for $60. Arctic Tour Company (☎ 979-4100) has cruises along the East Channel of the river. It also runs a seven to eight-day river boat/camping trip up the Mackenzie River from Inuvik to Fort Simpson. You can go either way. All food and gear is supplied. The 1300-km trip includes stops at villages, old trading posts and abandoned trappers' cabins. Mackenzie River Cruises (☎ 695-2506) in Fort Simpson does a similar trip.

DISTRICT OF FRANKLIN
The District of Franklin is the most northerly and has many islands, including Baffin Island, one of the world's largest. The island contains Auyuittuq National Park. Ellesmere Island National Park consists of the northern section of Ellesmere Island way up at the

peak of the Canadian Arctic, not far from Greenland's north-western edge. Not one tree grows in the entire District of Franklin but many flowers bloom during the short summer. The northern regions are almost completely uninhabited. There is the odd weather station, military installation or biological research centre.

Access to the district is by boat or plane.

Baffin Island

Iqaluit This town, formerly called Frobisher Bay, is on the east coast of Baffin Island in the eastern section of the territories. In 1984 the town voted to change the name back to Iqaluit (pronounced 'ee-KAL-oo-it'), its original Inuit name meaning 'salmon'. It was established in 1942 as a US Air Force base and is now a fairly large settlement of 2600. It's the first stop on the fly-in trip to Auyuittuq National Park. There is not much to see or do here but a variety of side trips is possible. Most people coming here stop off as part of a package tour en route to somewhere else.

Accommodation is expensive. *Mariner Lodge* (☎ 979-0344) is one of the cheapest places, with rooms starting at $48. *Kamotiq B&B* (☎ 979-5937) has singles/doubles for $75/95, while the *Bayshore Inn* (☎ 979-6733) has doubles for $95. There is a campground as well.

Once a week in the summer, First Air (☎ 979-5810) flies from here to Nuuk, the capital of Greenland.

Auyuittuq National Park Covering an area of 21,470 sq km, this is Canada's third largest national park and one of the world's few national parks north of the Arctic Circle. Pronounced 'ah-you-EE-tuk', the word means 'the land that never melts'. Actually, most of the park is a beautiful, pristine wilderness consisting of mountains, valleys, fjords and meadows. Most visitors go for the hiking along 96-km **Pangnirtung Pass** – between late June and early September when it's free of snow. Cross-country skiing in the spring and climbing are also good. Being north of the Arctic Circle the park has 24 hours of daylight each day from May to the end of July.

There are two primitive campgrounds in the park: at Overlord and Summit Lake. There are also seven emergency shelters along the Pangnirtung Pass. Hikers should be in good condition as the trail is considered fairly hard going. Most visitors spend four to seven days. For more info on the park, contact the Superintendent (☎ 473-8828), Auyuittuq National Park, Pangnirtung, NWT, X0A 0R0.

The problem with the place is getting there – it's expensive. First you must fly from one of the major cities to Iqaluit, which is nearly 300 km from the park. Canadian Airlines (☎ 979-5331) is one airline that flies there. From Iqaluit you have to catch another flight to Pangnirtung near the southern edge of the park or to Broughton Island, at the eastern edge. First Air flies from Iqaluit to both places and from either point you can walk or go by canoe into the park.

Many tour companies offer trips in the park – see the Northwest Territories *Explorers' Guide*.

Pangnirtung Pang, as it's often referred to, is a town with about 1100 residents, beautifully set alongside a fjord amidst mountains at the entrance to Auyuittuq National Park. It lies at the southern end of Pangnirtung Pass 40 km south of the Arctic Circle and acts as the jumping-off point for park visitors.

No alcohol is permitted in the town: this is one of several northern communities that have voted themselves 'dry' to help alleviate alcohol-related problems.

Accommodation, meals, boat tours and craftwork are available here.

Things to See & Do Two walking trails begin in town, one following the **Duval River** and taking about three hours and another, the **Ikuvik River**, climbing a mountain for a fine view of the fjord. The latter takes about six hours. Good boots are recommended for either one.

About 50 km south of town is the **Kekerton National Historic Park**, an old whaling station. A trail leads around parts of the island past the remains of the 19th-century houses, tools and graves. An interpretive centre provides background information.

The park is about two hours by boat from Pangnirtung. Getting a group of six or eight people together is really the only way to make the cost (over $400) of hiring a boat and guide reasonably acceptable. During the summer there are often enough tourists around to form the necessary small group.

Things to Buy The town has a reputation for its woven tapestries which can be seen and purchased at several shops or at the Inuit Co-op in town. Most of the tapestries are pictorial, depicting scenes from the traditional lifestyle of the region. Prices range from the high hundreds to several thousand dollars. Less costly items such as sweaters, scarves and the popular crocheted Pang hats are also available.

Cape Dorset Cape Dorset, on the south-east coast of Baffin Island, is most noted as a centre for contemporary Inuit art. It's also a good place from which to go hiking and bird-watching.

Ellesmere Island

Ellesmere Island National Park This national park, way up at the northern tip of Ellesmere Island at the top of the world, is for wealthy wilderness seekers only. It features **Cape Columbia**, the northernmost point of North America, **Mt Barbeau**, one of the highest peaks on the eastern side of the continent, and **Lake Hazen**. Around the park are thermal oases where plants and animals are able to survive despite the harsh climate.

DISTRICT OF KEEWATIN

To the west, the District of Keewatin consists of a vast, rocky, barren plateau, part of the Canadian Shield, with only 4000 people; to the east its official boundaries incorporate

much of Hudson Bay and James Bay. Most of the Inuit population lives in this district, in settlements along the western shores of Hudson Bay.

Farley Mowat's *Never Cry Wolf* tells of a man who lived among the wolves in Keewatin; another, *People of the Deer*, tells of the hardship inflicted on the Padlirmiut Inuit as a result of the change in migration patterns of the caribou in the 1940s and 1950s.

Rankin Inlet

Founded in 1955, Rankin Inlet, with a population of 1500, is Keewatin's largest community and the transport centre for the district. From here you can go fishing in the bay or in the many rivers and lakes. In Hudson Bay, about 50 km from Rankin Inlet, is **Marble Island**, a graveyard for James Knight and his crew who were seeking the Northwest Passage in the 18th century. Some 19th-century whaling ships are also there.

Arviat

Formerly called Eskimo Point, Arviat is Keewatin's most southerly settlement. From here you can arrange a trip to **McConnell River Bird Sanctuary** where about 400,000 snow geese nest, as do snowy owls and falcons.

Repulse Bay

Sitting on the Arctic Circle at the southern end of Melville Peninsula, Repulse Bay is a natural harbour. For centuries whaling ships set off from there. Today you can go fishing or take a boat out to catch sight of the beluga or the narwhal.

Baker Lake

Geographically, Baker Lake lies at the centre of Canada. It's good for fishing and is the departure point for canoe or raft trips on the Dubawnt, Kazan and Hanbury-Thelon rivers. You can also arrange a visit west to **Thelon Game Sanctuary** where many indigenous animals are protected.

Index

730

THANKS

Thanks to all the following travellers and others (apologies if we've misspelt your name) who took time to write to us about their experiences of Canada.

To those whose names have been omitted through oversight – apologies – your time and efforts are appreciated.

Doug Albert (USA), Lene Andersen (Dk), Mark Anderson (Aus), Gun Andreasson (Sw), Rob Atkins (UK) Thomas Barry (USA), Paul Beagley (UK), Craig Bennett (UK), Sally Bernstein (USA), James Blakemore, Lynn Bleiberg (USA), Sue & Kevin Bolton (Aus), Janet Borlass (C), Mr & Mrs R D Bratton (C), Paul Bridge (Aus), Paul Britton (Aus), Mark Brown (UK), Richard Bryant (UK), Rhona Buckingham (UK), Bjarte Bugstad (N), Helen Burich (C), Des Burke (Aus), JF Burke (C), Evelyn Burnham (C), Des Bushe (Aus), Anne Campbell (C), Kathryn Campbell (C), Bridget Carter (UK), Alison Castle (UK), Al Clarkson (C), Cynthia Cook (C), Marc & Nora Crauwels (B), Mrs L J Cull (UK), G W Davies (UK), Jim Dorrill, Patricia Doucette (C), Peter Duncan (C), Ron Egan (C), Ruth Ennals (UK), Peter Farrell (UK), Bob Finkelsteing (C), Mark Fisher (Aus), Vincent Foderg (C), M Ford (C), Leila Frances (UK), Claudia Gagnon (C), Sylvie Gentizon (CH), J P Glaisher (UK), Roseanne Greenfield (USA), Jan Griffiths (UK), Richard Haddon (UK), R J Haney (C), Catherine Hankey (UK), J Harkin (Nl), D Hart (Aus) Alistair Hay (Ken), Mats Heder (Sw), Laura Hill (C), James Hitselberger (USA), Philip A Humphrey (Aus), Yvonne Huntington (C), Tania James (Aus), Tony Jenkins (C), Jane Johnston (C), Lloyd Jones (C), Malka Kaufman (C), Adam Kerr (C), Bob Korzeniowski, Alex Kostopoulos (D), Elaine Landray (C), Eileen Larrigan (UK), Robert Le Riche (C), F Lewais (C), Jim Liston (USA), Ann Logan (UK), Monica Loow (Sw), Michael Lundy (C), Sarah Lynam (UK), Phyllis Lyon (C), Ruth MacLachlan (C), Margaret Magennis (UK), Zsalt Makray (Bra), Maikao Manzi (Fr), Susan Marshall (C), Captain D J Marshall (C), José A Martin (Sp), Rod Martin (UK), Marty Mascarin (C), Ev McEwen (C), Trish McPherson (USA), Rohinton Medhora (USA), Janet PC Meijlis (C), Jeff Mills, Richard Mitchell (C), Sean Mitchell (USA), Stephen Mortimer (UK), Heike Muller (D), Jennifer Munns (C), Maria Musso (It), Victor Norman (UK), Mary O'Brien (C), Barbara Off (CH), Lynn Owen (C), Andrew Pickles (Aus), Jan T Pollack (C), C A Price (C), Mark Prince (C), Richard Proctor (Aus), Yves Rault (F), H F Reichenfeld (C), Thomas Reiser (USA), David Reynolds (C), Bill Riccinto (C), Francis Rodio (USA), Olive Rogers (C), Betty Rose (C), Janice Ruhl (USA), Maure Rupp (USA), Anthony Saez (C), Josef Scenter (C), J Schiebelbeing (C), Laura Schisgall, Herbert Schulz (D), Molly Shelton (C), Aaron Shields (USA), Gary & Joan Silverman (USA), M Simmons (Aus), Nick Smedley (UK), Sherryn Smith (C), Elizabeth Smith (Aus), Rick Stenhouse (C), Marie Taylor (C), Marc Thibault (C), M L Thomson (UK), Mr V P Toni (USA), Jennifer Troll (UK), Heather van Doorninck (C), JJ van Harken (Nl), Audrey Walsh (Aus), Mrs S Walsh (C), Andy Walton (UK), Brian Waters (C), William Wang (USA), Ernest Weintraub (C), Charles Westrope (UK), Ken White (Aus), H H Wilson (NZ), Joanna Winternite (UK), Mario Witteman (C), Brent Wolf (NZ), Brian Wood (C) and Bronte Wuttke (Aus).

Aus - Australia, A - Austria, B - Belgium, Bra - Brazil, C - Canada, CH - Switzerland, D - Germany, Dk - Denmark, Fr - France, It - Italy, Ken - Kenya, N - Norway, Nl - Netherlands, NZ - New Zealand, Sp - Spain, Sw - Sweden, UK - United Kingdom, USA - United States of America.

Where Can You Find Out.........

HOW to get a Laotian visa in Bangkok?

WHERE to go birdwatching in PNG?

WHAT to expect from the police if you're robbed in Peru?

WHEN you can go to see cow races in Australia?

In the Lonely Planet Newsletter!

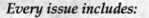

Every issue includes:

- *a letter from Lonely Planet founders Tony and Maureen Wheeler*
- *a letter from an author 'on the road'*
- *the most entertaining or informative reader's letter we've received*
- *the latest news on new and forthcoming releases from Lonely Planet*
- *and all the latest travel news from all over the world*

Guides to the Americas

Alaska - a travel survival kit
Jim DuFresne has travelled extensively through Alaska by foot, road, rail, barge and kayak, and tells how to make the most of one of the world's great wilderness areas.

Argentina - a travel survival kit
This guide gives independent travellers all the essential information on Argentina — a land of intriguing cultures, 'wild west' overtones and spectacular scenery.

Baja California - a travel survival kit
For centuries, Mexico's Baja peninsula — with its beautiful coastline, raucous border towns and crumbling Spanish missions — has been a land of escapes and escapades. This book describes how and where to escape in Baja.

Bolivia - a travel survival kit
From lonely villages in the Andes to ancient ruined cities and the spectacular city of La Paz, Bolivia is a magnificent blend of everything that inspires travellers. Discover safe and intriguing travel options in this comprehensive guide.

Brazil - a travel survival kit
From the mad passion of Carnival to the Amazon — home of the richest and most diverse ecosystem on earth — Brazil is a country of mythical proportions. This guide has all the essential travel information.

Central America on a shoestring
Practical information on travel in Belize, Guatemala, Costa Rica, Honduras, El Salvador, Nicaragua and Panama. A team of experienced Lonely Planet authors reveals the secrets of this culturally rich, geographically diverse and breathtakingly beautiful region.

Chile & Easter Island - a travel survival kit
Travel in Chile is easy and safe, with possibilities as varied as the countryside. This guide also gives detailed coverage of Chile's Pacific outpost, mysterious Easter Island.

Colombia - a travel survival kit
Colombia is a land of myths — from the ancient legends of El Dorado to the modern tales of Gabriel Garcia Marquez. The reality is beauty and violence, wealth and poverty, tradition and change. This guide shows how to travel independently and safely in this exotic country.

Costa Rica - a travel survival kit
This practical guide gives the low down on exceptional opportunities for fishing and water sports, and the best ways to experience Costa Rica's vivid natural beauty.

Ecuador & the Galápagos Islands - a travel survival kit
Ecuador offers a wide variety of travel experiences, from the high cordilleras to the Amazon plains — and 600 miles west, the fascinating Galápagos Islands. Everything you need to know about travelling around this enchanting country.

Hawaii - a travel survival kit
Share in the delights of this island paradise — and avoid its high prices — both on and off the beaten track. Full details on Hawaii's best-known attractions, plus plenty of uncrowded sights and activities.

La Ruta Maya: Yucatán, Guatemala & Belize - a travel survival kit
Invaluable background information on the cultural and environmental riches of La Ruta Maya (The Mayan Route), plus practical advice on how best to minimise the impact of travellers on this sensitive region.

Mexico - a travel survival kit
A unique blend of Indian and Spanish culture, fascinating history, and hospitable people, make Mexico a travellers' paradise.

Peru - a travel survival kit
The lost city of Machu Picchu, the Andean altiplano and the magnificent Amazon rainforests are just some of Peru's many attractions. All the travel facts you'll need can be found in this comprehensive guide.

South America on a shoestring
This practical guide provides concise information for budget travellers and covers South America from the Darien Gap to Tierra del Fuego. By the author the *New York Times* nominated 'the patron saint of travellers in the third world'.

Also available:
Brazilian phrasebook, *Latin American Spanish* phrasebook and *Quechua* phrasebook.

Lonely Planet Guidebooks

Lonely Planet guidebooks cover every accessible part of Asia as well as Australia, the Pacific, South America, Africa, the Middle East and parts of North America and Europe. There are four series: *travel survival kits*, covering a country for a range of budgets; *shoestring guides* with compact information for low-budget travel in a major region; *walking guides*; and *phrasebooks*.

Australia & the Pacific
Australia
Bushwalking in Australia
Islands of Australia's Great Barrier Reef
Fiji
Micronesia
New Caledonia
New Zealand
Tramping in New Zealand
Papua New Guinea
Papua New Guinea phrasebook
Rarotonga & the Cook Islands
Samoa
Solomon Islands
Sydney
Tahiti & French Polynesia
Tonga
Vanuatu

South-East Asia
Bali & Lombok
Burma
Burmese phrasebook
Indonesia
Indonesia phrasebook
Malaysia, Singapore & Brunei
Philippines
Pilipino phrasebook
Singapore
South-East Asia on a shoestring
Thailand
Thai phrasebook
Vietnam, Laos & Cambodia

North-East Asia
China
Mandarin Chinese phrasebook
Hong Kong, Macau & Canton
Japan
Japanese phrasebook
Korea
Korean phrasebook
North-East Asia on a shoestring
Taiwan
Tibet
Tibet phrasebook

West Asia
Trekking in Turkey
Turkey
Turkish phrasebook
West Asia on a shoestring

Indian Ocean
Madagascar & Comoros
Maldives & Islands of the East Indian Ocean
Mauritius, Réunion & Seychelles

Mail Order

Lonely Planet guidebooks are distributed worldwide and are sold by good bookshops everywhere. They are also available by mail order from Lonely Planet, so if you have difficulty finding a title please write to us. US and Canadian residents should write to Embarcadero West, 112 Linden St, Oakland CA 94607, USA and residents of other countries to PO Box 617, Hawthorn, Victoria 3122, Australia.

Europe
Eastern Europe on a shoestring
Iceland, Greenland & the Faroe Islands
Trekking in Spain
USSR
Russian phrasebook

Indian Subcontinent
Bangladesh
India
Hindi/Urdu phrasebook
Trekking in the Indian Himalaya
Karakoram Highway
Kashmir, Ladakh & Zanskar
Nepal
Trekking in the Nepal Himalaya
Nepal phrasebook
Pakistan
Sri Lanka
Sri Lanka phrasebook

Africa
Africa on a shoestring
Central Africa
East Africa
Kenya
Swahili phrasebook
Morocco, Algeria & Tunisia
Moroccan Arabic phrasebook
Zimbabwe, Botswana & Namibia
West Africa

North America
Alaska
Canada
Hawaii

Mexico
Baja California
Mexico

South America
Argentina
Bolivia
Brazil
Brazilian phrasebook
Chile & Easter Island
Colombia
Ecuador & the Galápagos Islands
Latin American Spanish phrasebook
Peru
Quechua phrasebook
South America on a shoestring

Central America
Central America on a shoestring
Costa Rica
La Ruta Maya

Middle East
Egypt & the Sudan
Egyptian Arabic phrasebook
Israel
Jordan & Syria
Yemen

The Lonely Planet Story

Lonely Planet published its first book in 1973 in response to the numerous 'How did you do it?' questions Maureen and Tony Wheeler were asked after driving, bussing, hitching, sailing and railing their way from England to Australia.

Written at a kitchen table and hand collated, trimmed and stapled, *Across Asia on the Cheap* became an instant local bestseller, inspiring thoughts of another book.

Eighteen months in South-East Asia resulted in their second guide, *South-East Asia on a shoestring*, which they put together in a backstreet Chinese hotel in Singapore in 1975. The 'yellow bible' as it quickly became known to backpackers around the world, soon became *the* guide to the region. It has sold well over half a million copies and is now in its 7th edition, still retaining its familiar yellow cover.

Today there are over 80 Lonely Planet titles – books that have that same adventurous approach to travel as those early guides; books that 'assume you know how to get your luggage off the carousel' as one reviewer put it.

Although Lonely Planet initially specialised in guides to Asia, they now cover most regions of the world, including the Pacific, South America, Africa, the Middle East and Eastern Europe. The list of *walking guides* and *phrasebooks* (for 'unusual' languages such as Quechua, Swahili, Nepalese and Egyptian Arabic) is also growing rapidly.

The emphasis continues to be on travel for independent travellers. Tony and Maureen still travel for several months of each year and play an active part in the writing, updating and quality control of Lonely Planet's guides.

They have been joined by over 50 authors, 40 staff – mainly editors, cartographers, & designers – at our office in Melbourne, Australia, and another 10 at our US office in Oakland, California. Travellers themselves also make a valuable contribution to the guides through the feedback we receive in thousands of letters each year.

The people at Lonely Planet strongly believe that travellers can make a positive contribution to the countries they visit, both through their appreciation of the countries' culture, wildlife and natural features, and through the money they spend. In addition, the company makes a direct contribution to the countries and regions it covers. Since 1986 a percentage of the income from each book has been donated to ventures such as famine relief in Africa; aid projects in India; agricultural projects in Central America; Greenpeace's efforts to halt French nuclear testing in the Pacific and Amnesty International. In 1991 $68,000 was donated to these causes.

Lonely Planet's basic travel philosophy is summed up in Tony Wheeler's comment, 'Don't worry about whether your trip will work out. Just go!'